HUMAN DEVELOPMENT

Academic Reviewers

For their reading of all or part of the manuscript in various stages of development, and for the helpful comments they offered, we thank the people listed below.

Diane E. Papalia
Sally Wendkos Olds

Ariel L. H. Anderson
Western Michigan University
Barbara L. Biales
College of St. Catherine
Patricia K. Bishop
Cleveland State Community College
Michael Brosnan
Indiana State University
Sally Carr
Lakeland Community College
Donna M. Chirico
York College
Dana H. Davidson
University of Hawaii-Manoa
R. Dale Dick
University of Wisconsin-Eau Claire
Donna K. Duffy
Middlesex Community College
David B. Fellows
St. Petersburg Junior College
Juanita L. Garcia
University of South Florida

Lynn Godat
Portland State University
Evelyn F. Hatfield
Mankato State University, Professor Emeritus
David W. Hebda
Mt. Vernon Hospital
Kathleen Hulbert
University of Lowell
Donald B. Irwin
Des Moines Area Community College
D. Lamar Jacks
Santa Fe Community College
Lee Kimmons
University of Nebraska—Lincoln
Timothy J. Lehmann
Valencia Community College
Dorothea Leonard
Miami-Dade Community College
Harriett Light
North Dakota State University
Joan N. McNeil
Kansas State University— Manhattan
Stephen M. Marson
Pembroke State University
Michele Y. Martel
Northeast Missouri State University
Robin K. Montvilo
Rhode Island College
Sandra Mott
Boston College School of Nursing

Jean A. O'Neil
Boston College School of Nursing
Sharyl B. Peterson
St. Norbert College
Patricia Petretic-Jackson
University of South Dakota— Vermillion
Richard W. Rogers
Daytona Beach Community College
Janet A. Simons
Des Moines Area Community College
Frank Sjursen
Shoreline Community College
Peggy Skinner
South Plains College
Nancy Snyder
Northeastern University
James R. Stuart
Iowa Central Community College
Jeanne L. Thomas
University of Wisconsin—Parkside
Shirlen Triplett
Olive-Harvey College
James Turcott
Kalamazoo Valley Community College
Patricia Weenolsen
Seattle University
Ursula White
El Paso Community College
Walter Zimmermann
New Hampshire College

FOURTH

EDITION

HUMAN DEVELOPMENT

DIANE E. PAPALIA
University of Pennsylvania

SALLY WENDKOS OLDS

with
RUTH DUSKIN FELDMAN

McGRAW-HILL BOOK COMPANY

New York   St. Louis   San Francisco   Auckland   Bogotá   Caracas
Colorado Springs   Hamburg   Lisbon   London   Madrid   Mexico
Milan   Montreal   New Delhi   Oklahoma City   Panama   Paris
San Juan   São Paulo   Singapore   Sydney   Tokyo   Toronto

HUMAN DEVELOPMENT

This book was set in Baskerville
by York Graphic Services, Inc.
The editors were Rhona Robbin,
James D. Anker, and Susan Gamer;
the designer was Joan O'Connor;
the production supervisor was
Diane Renda.
The photo editor was Inge King.
The permissions editor was
Elsa Peterson.
The cover photograph was taken
by DeMarco/Tomaccio.
Von Hoffman Press, Inc., was
printer and binder.

Acknowledgments appear on
pages 673–676,
and on this page by reference.

34567890 VNH VNH 93210

ISBN 0-07-048416-3

Library of Congress
Cataloging-in-Publication Data

Papalia, Diane E.
    Human development / Diane
E. Papalia, Sally Wendkos
Olds, with Ruth Duskin
Feldman. —4th ed.
    p.   cm.
    Bibliography: p.
    Includes indexes.
    ISBN 0-07-048416-3
    1. Developmental
psychology. 2. Developmental
psychobiology. I. Olds, Sally
Wendkos. II. Feldman, Ruth
Duskin. III. Title.
BF713.P35 1989   88-13207
155—dc19

ABOUT THE AUTHORS

DIANE E. PAPALIA is a professor who taught thousands of undergraduates at the University of Wisconsin. She received her bachelor's degree, majoring in psychology, from Vassar College, and both her master's degree in child development and family relations and her Ph.D. in life-span developmental psychology from West Virginia University. She has published numerous articles in such professional journals as *Human Development, International Journal of Aging and Human Development, Sex Roles, Journal of Experimental Child Psychology,* and *Journal of Gerontology.* Most of these papers have dealt with her major research focus, cognitive development from childhood through old age. She is especially interested in intelligence in old age and factors that contribute to the maintenance of intellectual functioning in late adulthood. She is a Fellow in the Gerontological Society of America. She is currently affiliated with the University of Pennsylvania.

SALLY WENDKOS OLDS is an award-winning professional writer who has written more than 200 articles in leading magazines and is the author or coauthor of six books addressed to general readers, in addition to the three textbooks she has coauthored with Dr. Papalia. Her book *The Complete Book of Breastfeeding,* a classic since its publication in 1972, has just been issued in a completely updated and expanded edition. She is also the author of *The Working Parents Survival Guide* and *The Eternal Garden: Seasons of Our Sexuality,* and the coauthor of *Raising a Hyperactive Child* (winner of The Family Service Association of America National Media Award) and *Helping Your Child Learn Right from Wrong.* She received her bachelor's degree from the University of Pennsylvania, where she majored in English literature and minored in psychology. She was elected to Phi Beta Kappa and was graduated summa cum laude.

DIANE E. PAPALIA and **SALLY WENDKOS OLDS** are coauthors of the extremely successful textbooks *A Child's World* (now in its fourth edition) and *Psychology* (second edition published in 1988).

RUTH DUSKIN FELDMAN is the award-winning author of two books, including *Whatever Happened to the Quiz Kids? Perils and Profits of Growing Up Gifted,* and hundreds of articles for newspapers and national magazines on education and other topics. She has also written educational materials for all levels from elementary school through college. She received her bachelor's degree from Northwestern University, where she was graduated with highest distinction and was elected to Phi Beta Kappa.

To our husbands,
Jonathan L. Finlay and David Mark Olds,
our loved and loving partners
in growth and development.
D. E. P. and S. W. O.

To my parents,
Boris and Rita Duskin;
my husband, Gilbert Feldman;
and my adult children, Steven, Laurie, and Heidi Feldman—
the most valued influences on my development.
R. D. F.

CONTENTS IN BRIEF

CONTENTS

LIST OF BOXES

PREFACE

In the prefaces to the previous three editions of *Human Development*, we spoke of change as a principle that governs our lives. We noted that people change, grow, and develop throughout life. This book has also continued to change and develop. The fourth edition retains much of the flavor of earlier editions, most notably in its emphasis on the interrelationships among the different stages of the life span and among the physical, intellectual, social, and personality influences on development. However, there are some differences. The changes in this revision represent growth and development in our own thinking about human development—from the moment of conception until that moment at the other end of the life span when death ends the developmental process.

THE FOURTH EDITION

Our Aims for This Edition

The goals of this fourth edition are the same as that of the first three editions: to emphasize the continuity of development throughout the life span; to show how experiences at one time of life affect future development; and to understand the influences of people's genes, their families, and the world they live in. As before, we look at the findings of scientific research and the theories of social scientists and apply these to our understanding of humankind. And we ask the same basic questions: What influences have made people living in the final decades of the twentieth century the way they are? What factors are likely to affect all of us in the future? How much control do people have over their lives? How are people like each other? How is each person unique? What is normal? What is cause for concern?

We also ask some new questions and come up with some new answers. This revision continues to update the literature, as we discuss new research and new theories, many of which have been published as recently as the mid-1980s. We continue to synthesize research findings and to help students interpret them and think critically about controversial issues. Our continued work on two other college textbooks, *A Child's World* (for courses in child development) and *Psychology* (for introductory courses), has helped us refine and sharpen our thinking about life-span development. The changes in this revision, then, (as we noted above) represent growth and development in our own ideas.

Organization

There are two major approaches to writing about and teaching human development: the *chronological approach* (looking at the functioning of all aspects of development at different stages of life, such as infancy or late adulthood) and the *topical approach* (tracing one aspect of development at a time). We have chosen the *chronological* approach, which provides a sense of the multifaceted nature of human development. Accordingly, we get to know first the infant and toddler, then the young child, the schoolchild, the adolescent, the young adult, the adult at midlife, and the person in late adulthood. As we discuss the ages and stages of human beings, we provide evenhanded treatment of *all* periods of the life span; we have taken special pains not to overemphasize some or slight others.

In line with this approach, we have divided the book into nine parts. Part One is an introduction. In Parts Two through Nine, we discuss physical, intellectual, and social and personality development at each stage of the life span. Readers who prefer a *topical* approach may read the book in this order: Chapters 1, 2, and 3 (general theories and issues, and prenatal and early physical development); the first sections of Chapters 6, 8, 10, 12, 14, and 16 (physical development); the second sections of these chapters, plus Chapter 4 (intellectual functioning); then Chapters 5, 7, 9, 11, 13, 15, and 17 (social and personality development); and finally Chapter 18 (death and bereavement).

Content

This new edition continues to provide comprehensive coverage of development from the prenatal period through late adulthood. Full descriptions of each age period draw on the most up-to-date information available about physical, intellectual, and social and personality development. The text integrates theoretical, research-related, and practical concerns about every stage of the life span, reflecting our belief that all stages of life are important, challenging, and full of opportunities for growth and change.

While we have retained the scope, emphasis, and level of previous editions of *Human Development,* we have made a number of significant

changes in this fourth edition. We have updated the text whenever new findings or interpretations have been available, reorganized some material to make it more effective, and added completely new sections. Among the important changes are the following:

■ *New sections.* There are new sections on early growth and development of the brain; development of self-control and self-regulation in infancy and toddlerhood; computers as teachers; psychological maltreatment of children; causes of and cures for underachievement; Robert Sternberg's triarchic theory of intelligence; Sandra Bem's gender schema theory; how work can enhance personality and intellectual growth; and the relationship between older adults and their pets.

■ *Important revisions.* There has been significant revision of several discussions: explanations of major theories; environmental hazards during pregnancy; how information processing in infancy is related to IQ in childhood; the effects of nonmaternal care of infants; kindergarten; coregulation in middle childhood; gifted, talented, and creative children; parent-child relationships; use and abuse of drugs; eating disorders; the high school experience; teenagers' sexual behavior and attitudes; how parenthood affects parents; marital satisfaction; women's development in adulthood; "Type A" behavior; memory functioning and intelligence in late life; Alzheimer's disease; grandparenthood; adult friendships; and suicide.

Special Features

This edition of *Human Development* includes three kinds of boxed material:

■ *"Window on the World"* boxes are new to this edition. Most give readers glimpses of human development in societies other than our own, showing that people grow up, live, and thrive in many different kinds of cultures, under many different influences. These discussions treat such issues as cross-cultural differences in acquiring physical, intellectual, and social skills; puberty rites; ages of marriage; and mourning customs.

- *"Practically Speaking"* boxes build bridges between academic study and everyday life by showing ways to apply research findings on various aspects of human development. They cover such topics as the risks in using infant walkers; talking with babies and dealing with them when they are fussy; helping children make friends, do well in school, and cope with being on their own without adult supervision; visiting people in nursing homes; preventing suicides; easing the lives of older adults; and evoking memories for "life reviews."
- *"Food for Thought"* boxes explore important research issues, many of which are quite controversial. These include discussions of the stress of being born, private speech in children, causes of obesity, avoiding gender stereotyping, psychological ramifications of the menstrual cycle, and origins of creativity.

Learning Aids

We also continue to provide a number of basic teaching and learning aids, including the following:

- *Part overviews.* At the beginning of each part, an overview provides the rationale for the chapters that follow.
- *Chapter-opening outlines.* At the beginning of each chapter, an outline clearly previews the major topics included in the chapter.
- *"Ask Yourself" questions.* At the beginning of each chapter, a few key questions identify the most important issues addressed in the chapter.
- *Highlighting of key terms.* Whenever an important new term is introduced in the text, it is highlighted in **boldface italic** and defined in the text.
- *End-of-chapter lists of key terms.* At the end of every chapter, key terms are listed, along with the pages on which they first appear.
- *End-of-book glossary.* The extensive glossary at the end of the book includes the definitions of key terms and indicates the pages on which they first appear.
- *Chapter summaries.* At the end of every chapter, brief statements—organized by major topics in the chapter—clearly summarize the most important points.

- *Bibliography.* A complete listing of references enables students to evaluate the sources of major statements of fact or theory.
- *Recommended readings.* Annotated lists of readings (classic works or lively contemporary studies) are provided for students who want to explore issues in greater depth than is possible within these covers.
- *Indexes.* Separate name and subject indexes appear at the end of the book.
- *Extensive illustrations.* Many points in the text are underscored pictorially through carefully selected drawings, graphs, and photographs. The expanded illustration program in this edition includes new diagrams and many full-color photographs.

SUPPLEMENTARY MATERIALS

An extensive package of supplementary materials will add to the value of this book as a teaching and learning tool.

The *Study Guide with Readings* includes articles from professional journals and popular sources, a section on how to study for and take tests, self-test and completion exercises, learning objectives, and chapter overviews. The *Test Bank* contains about 2000 questions keyed to the learning objectives stated in the Study Guide and Instructor's Manual. The Test Bank can be used with a microcomputer test-generating system for the Apple and IBM PC computers. The *Instructor's Manual* includes chapter outlines, overviews, objectives, teaching strategies, lecture topics, demonstrations and projects, essay questions, and an audiovisual guide. An *overhead transparency set* includes 50 transparencies of illustrations from the text.

ACKNOWLEDGMENTS

We would like to express our gratitude to the many friends and colleagues who, through their work and their interest, helped us clarify our thinking about human development. We are especially grateful for the valuable help given by those who reviewed the published third edition of *Human Development* and the manuscript drafts of this fourth edition; their evaluations and suggestions helped greatly in the preparation of the new edition. These reviewers, who are affiliated with both two- and four-year institutions, are listed on page ii.

We want to acknowledge the valuable assistance of Ruth Duskin Feldman. She drafted sections that were new to this edition, brought a fresh eye to the organization of some of the material, and implemented other helpful changes, many of which reflect her special interest and background in writing about educational issues and about gifted and talented children.

We appreciate the strong support we have had from our publisher and would like to express our special thanks to Rhona Robbin, who graciously and capably took over the editorship of this edition in midstream; to our meticulous and conscientious production editor, Susan Gamer, who helped steer the book through on schedule; and to Maria Molinari, who helped in innumerable ways. Inge King, who has been the photo editor for all four editions of *Human Development*, again used her sensitivity, her interest, and her good eye to find outstanding photographs. Joan O'Connor and the artists working with her produced a creative, unique cover and book design noteworthy for aesthetics, as well as for the rendering of concepts. Julie Jensen provided valuable help with research, and Steven J. Feldman and Suzanne Davis contributed their painstaking assistance in the preparation of the bibliography and glossary.

Diane E. Papalia   *Sally Wendkos Olds*

HUMAN
DEVELOPMENT

PART

INTRODUCTION

Life is change. From the moment of conception to the moment of death, human beings undergo many complex processes of development. Throughout life, people have the potential to grow, to change, to develop.

The study of human development will help you to understand yourself and the people you know. You will become aware of influences and choices that have made you the person you are, and of forces that may affect the person you will become. Our approach to the study of human development begins with an overview.

■ In **Chapter 1**, you will get to know how we, the authors, view and present many of the issues in human development. You will see how developmentalists divide the life span into periods and what major aspects of development they study in all these phases of life. You will learn how the study of human development has itself developed and changed as social scientists have learned more about infants, older children, and adults. You will be introduced to the most prominent theories relating to human development, which will come up again and again throughout this book. And you will learn how social scientists study people, what they learn from different research methods, and what ethical standards guide their work. Then you will be ready, in Part Two, to look at what happens as a human life begins.

CHAPTER 1

ABOUT HUMAN DEVELOPMENT

There is nothing permanent except change.

> Heraclitus, Fragment
> (sixth century B.C.)

- What can you gain from the study of human development, and how does this book approach the subject?

- What are the major changes that characterize the course of human life, and what common and individual influences affect people?

- How has the study of human development developed?

- What major theoretical perspectives attempt to explain human development, and what are their strengths and weaknesses?

- What methods do social scientists use to study people, and what are some ethical considerations about the use of these methods?

When you look through your family photo album, do you ever wonder about the lives of the people whose images are frozen there at a succession of moments in time? When you see that snapshot of your mother on her first bicycle, do you suppose that she had trouble learning to ride? Did she take a lot of spills? And why is she smiling shyly in that photo taken of her on her first day of school? Was she nervous about meeting her teacher? There she is holding you as a baby. How did she feel about becoming a parent? How did that little girl on a bike turn into the woman with an infant in her arms? How did *you* become the person you are today? How will you become the person you will be tomorrow?

Snapshots tell us little about the *process* of inward and outward change that makes up a human life. Even a series of home movies or videotapes, with the extra insight they give us, will not capture a progression of changes so subtle that we often cannot detect them until long after they have occurred. That process is the subject of this book.

HUMAN DEVELOPMENT: THE SUBJECT AND THE TEXT

What Is Human Development?

This book is about **human development,** the scientific study of the quantitative and qualitative ways in which people change over time. **Quantitative changes** are changes in the number or amount of something, such as height, weight, or size of vocabulary. **Qualitative changes** are changes in kind, structure, or organization, such as changes in the nature of a person's intelligence or in the way the mind works. We can see the distinction between quantitative and qualitative change in the area of memory development. When Jenny was 4 years old, she could recall only three objects out of a group she had seen a few minutes before; now, at 7, she can recall seven objects. Her memory has undergone a quantitative change, that is, an increase in how much she can remember. She has also experienced a qualitative change in memory, since she has now begun to use such strategies as putting objects she wants to remember into categories to help her recall them (P. H. Miller, 1983).

Human development is about all people, and it is also about each person. Students of development are interested in patterns that govern the development of all individuals of the species *Homo sapiens*. But since each member of the species is unique, developmentalists also want to know what factors make one person turn out different from another. What influences one person to become a mass murderer and another to become a humanitarian? What made you turn out different from your next-door neighbors—and even from your own brothers and sisters?

Because human personality is complex, developmentalists cannot fully answer such questions. But by examining how people develop throughout life, they have learned—and you can learn—much about human beings: what people's needs are, how they respond to the many influences upon and within them, and how they can best fulfill their potential as individuals and as a species.

How This Book Approaches the Study of Human Development

Before we introduce you to the study of human development, we will introduce some of the ideas that we—the authors—have on the subject. Like all human beings, we have our assumptions and beliefs. We want to present to you, our readers, the viewpoints from which this book was written, so that you may keep them in mind as you read.

We Celebrate the Human Being We recognize that people have much in common with other animals, but we are interested in what theory and research have to tell us specifically about human beings. Thus, whenever possible, we cite research that has been performed on people rather than animals. Sometimes, of course, we need to refer to studies of animals—classic studies and contemporary ones in which ethical standards prevent us from using humans in research (such as explorations of what harmful consequences a baby might experience when the mother takes drugs during pregnancy). When we do present conclusions based on animal research, we apply them with caution, since we cannot assume that they apply equally to humans.

More important, our interest is in uniquely human qualities. People are more adaptive than animals appear to be. They can imagine and pursue goals that animals cannot; they use symbols like words and drawings that animals do not use; they participate in culture in ways that animals do not. These powers make the study of human development more complex than it otherwise would be. We celebrate that complexity because it reflects the richness of humanity.

So that you can explore that rich diversity, every major subdivision of this book contains a box titled "Window on the World," which focuses on some aspect of a culture other than the dominant one in the United States (see Box 1-1 later in this chapter). We will also examine cross-cultural differences at appropriate points in the main body of the text.

We Believe That Knowledge Is Useful As people who live in the real world, we carefully examine research findings to see how they can be used to solve practical problems. *Basic research*, the kind undertaken in the spirit of intellectual curiosity with no immediate practical goal in mind, and *applied research*, which addresses an immediate problem, complement each other. Whenever possible, we extract from research findings and theories their practical implications for everyday life.

Each chapter contains many examples and guidelines for action, some of them highlighted in boxes titled "Practically Speaking." Another group of boxes, headed "Food for Thought," call attention to recent research or to controversial issues, many of them on the cutting edge of knowledge of human development.

We Respect All Periods of the Life Span We are convinced that people have the potential to change throughout their lives. The changes of early life are especially rapid and dramatic, as virtually helpless newborns transform themselves into competent, exploring children. Change during childhood normally involves increases in size and improvements in abilities. Change during adulthood occurs in more than one direction. Some powers, like vocabulary,

Development proceeds from the moment of conception throughout life. Although the changes of infancy and early childhood are the most rapid and dramatic, even very old people can show growth, particularly in translating knowledge and experience into wisdom.

continue to expand, while others, like strength and reaction time, diminish. Still other capacities seem to emerge for the first time, like the synthesis of knowledge and experience into wisdom. Even very old people can exhibit growth. In this book, we describe the experience of dying as a final attempt to come to terms with one's life—in short, to develop.

We Believe in Human Resilience There is strong evidence of what one psychologist has called "growth for health": the ability to bounce back from difficult early circumstances or traumatic experiences and make a good adaptation to life (Kagan, 1979). A traumatic incident or severely deprived childhood may well have grave emotional consequences. But the stories of countless people, some of whom have been followed by researchers from childhood far into adulthood, demonstrate that one experience is not likely to cause irreversible damage. A nurturing environment can often help a child overcome the effects of early deprivation.

We Recognize That People Help Shape Their Own Development People are not passive recipients of influences. They actively shape their own environment, and then they respond to the environmental forces that they have helped to bring about. You can see this bidirectional influence repeatedly. When infants babble and coo, they encourage adults to talk to them, and this talk in turn stimulates the babies' language development. Teenagers' burgeoning sexuality may stir their parents' fear of growing older and make them regret their lost youth; the parents' reactions, in turn, may affect the teenagers' attitudes toward the changes they are undergoing. Older adults also shape their own development; for example, by deciding when to retire from paid work, by taking up new activities, and by forming new relationships.

Now that you know something about how we approach the study of human development, we introduce that study itself, sketching its outlines and summarizing its history and the perspectives of its most influential thinkers. Finally, we discuss various methods of studying human development, their advantages, and their pitfalls.

HUMAN DEVELOPMENT: THE STUDY AND ITS HISTORY

The field of human development has itself developed as a scientific discipline. Originally, its focus was on describing behavior from which age norms for growth and development could be derived. Today, developmentalists try to *explain why* certain behaviors occur by looking at the factors that influence people's development. The next step, in keeping with scientific tradition, is to *predict* behavior—a challenging and complex task—and, in some cases, to try to *modify* or *optimize* development by offering some type of training or therapy.

The study of human development, then, has very practical implications. If Sue, at 9 months of age, seems slow in development, her parents may, with the proper knowledge, either be reassured that she is developing normally or be advised how to help her overcome her deficiencies. If educators understand how children of different ages learn best, they can plan better classroom programs.

Similarly, understanding adult development helps professionals and laypersons alike to be prepared for life's transitions: those experienced, for example, by the mother returning to work after her maternity leave, the 50-year-old man who realizes he will never be president, the person about to retire, the widow or widower, or the dying patient.

Students of human development draw on many disciplines, including psychology, sociology, anthropology, biology, education, and medicine. In selecting the materials for this book, we have combed the research literatures of all these disciplines.

Aspects of Development

One reason for the complexity of human development is that growth and change occur in different aspects of the self. We talk separately in this book about physical, intellectual, and personality and social development at each period of life. But in reality, these strands are intertwined—each aspect of development affects the others.

Physical Development Changes in the body, brain, sensory capacities, and motor skills are all part of physical development, and they exert a major influence on both intellect and personality. For example, much of an infant's knowledge of the world comes from the senses and from motor activity. In late adulthood, physical changes in the brain, as in Alzheimer's disease (which affects about 5 percent of people over the age of 65), can result in loss of memory for recent events and in personality deterioration.

Intellectual Development Changes in a wide variety of mental abilities, such as learning, memory, reasoning, thinking, and facility with language, are aspects of intellectual development. These changes are closely related to both the motor and the emotional aspects of development. A baby's growing memory ability, for example, stimulates the development of *separation anxiety*, the fear that the mother will not return once she has gone away. If children lacked the ability to remember the past and anticipate the future, they could not worry about the mother's absence. Memory also affects what babies do physically. For example, a 1-year-old boy who remembers being scolded for knocking down

his sister's block tower may (or may not!) refrain from doing the same thing again.

Personality and Social Development Personality—the unique way in which each person deals with the world, expresses emotions, and gets along with others—and social development affect both the physical and the cognitive aspects of functioning. For example, anxiety in taking a test can lead to a lower score than a student might make without it. And the social support that older people receive from their friends is an important antidote to the potentially negative effects of stress on their physical and mental health.

Periods of the Life Span

For purposes of our discussions, we divide the human life span into eight periods. These age divisions are approximate and somewhat arbitrary—especially in adulthood, in which there are no clear-cut social and physical criteria like those in childhood (such as entering school, and puberty) to signal the shift from one period to another.

Prenatal Stage (Conception to Birth) The period of greatest physical growth is before birth. In the prenatal stage, the human organism grows from a single cell to a being composed of billions of cells. The basic body structure and organs are formed, and so prenatal development is a time of extreme vulnerability, especially during the first 3 months.

Infancy and Toddlerhood (Birth to 3 Years) The first 1½ to 2 years of life make up the period of infancy. Although newborn babies (neonates) are dependent on adults, they are competent in many ways. Infants can use their senses from birth and are able to learn. They form attachments to their parents, their brothers and sisters, and other caregivers, who also become attached to them. During toddlerhood, which lasts from about 18 months to 3 years of age, children progress in language and motor skills, and they achieve considerable independence. Even though children this age usually spend most of their time with adults, they show a great deal of interest in other children.

Early Childhood (3 to 6 Years) During early childhood, other children become more important in youngsters' lives. So does language, which lets children communicate better with playmates, as well as with adults. They are better able to ask for and get what they want, to take care of themselves, and to exercise self-control. In their language, play, and drawing they display a broad imagination and inventiveness.

Middle Childhood (6 to 12 Years) The huge strides that school-age children make in the ability to think logically enable them to gain from formal education. The peer group assumes a central place in their lives, but the family remains important. Children absorb the many details of their particular cultures, and their everyday lives vary enormously from one culture to another (see Box 1-1).

Adolescence (12 to 20 Years) The main concern in adolescence is the search for identity, a theme that may recur throughout adulthood. Profound physical changes signal the onset of adolescence, and profound intellectual changes enable many teenagers to think abstractly. Adolescents may look and sometimes act like adults, but in some ways (particularly in their emotional reactions) they are still immature. Still, the desire to be independent impels them to become increasingly involved with their peers and to separate from the parental nest. In modern industrial societies, no one marker signals the end of adolescence.

Young Adulthood (20 to 40 Years) The main issues during the two decades of young adulthood are the basic ones of love and work. During these years, people usually form intimate relationships and make career choices. Although both kinds of choices are subject to later change, the options chosen now may set the tone for a person's future life.

Many young adults become parents. Some decide not to have children, and others who want to have children but are unable to do so must cope with infertility.

Middle Adulthood (40 to 65 Years) The search for meaning in life is an important theme in middle age. People in this age group are fre-quently caught between teenage children and aging parents, who may need their help. The stress created by this double pull and by the awareness of the passage of time sometimes—but not necessarily—brings on a "midlife crisis." During these years, people are often at the height of their earning powers and have achieved the peak of their success in their chosen fields. Pressed by the need to recognize the inevitability of their own eventual death, they begin to think of their lives in terms of the time they have left to live rather than the time they have already lived.

Late Adulthood (65 Years and Over) The last years of life still hold promise of growth. Most older people are mentally alert and active. They are typically free from the pressures of child rearing and, often, of full-time employment and have more time to be involved with family, friends, and community. They must also deal with the losses of aging, which may include the decline of some faculties (such as hearing, vision, and physical strength and stamina) and the loss of loved ones—spouses, siblings, and life-long friends.

Individual Differences in Development

Although people normally proceed through the same general sequence of development, there is a wide range of individual differences: differences in the timing and specific expression of developmental changes. Throughout this book, we talk about *average* ages for the occurrence of certain behaviors: the first smile, the first word, the first step. In all cases, these ages are *merely* averages. Only when deviation from these norms is extreme is there cause for considering a person's development to be exceptionally advanced or delayed.

Not only the rates but the results of development vary. People differ in their height, weight, and body build; in constitutional factors like health and energy level; in their ability to understand complex ideas; and in their emotional reactions. Their lifestyles differ too: the kinds of work they do, how well they do their work, and how much they like it; the kinds of homes and communities they live in, and how they feel about them; the people they see and the kinds

BOX 1-1   WINDOW ON THE WORLD

ACQUIRING CULTURAL SKILLS IN MIDDLE CHILDHOOD

A 10-year-old Masai boy in east Africa expertly leads a herd of cattle through the Great Rift Valley, prodding them with a long stick. If any of the cattle stumble and get hurt, the boy knows how to treat their injuries.

A child of the same age in an American city would be unlikely to know how to herd cattle or to administer first aid to them but would be more likely to be skilled at operating a home computer, while a child of that age in rural France would probably be learning how to drive a hard bargain in selling the family's produce at the town market.

Children in urban and pastoral cultures learn vastly different skills; but the acquisition of whatever skills a society considers socially important is typical of middle childhood around the world.

(© Paul Conklin/Monkmeyer)

Daily life in middle childhood varies around the world—for one reason, because children practice the skills needed in their own culture. This Masai boy in Tanzania herds cattle; an American boy or girl may learn to use a personal computer.

of relationships they have; and the ways they spend their leisure time.

Influences on Development

Development is subject to many influences: the characteristics that people are born with plus the effects of the experiences they have. Some experiences have more impact than others. Some are purely individual, while others are common to certain groups—age groups, generations, or people who live in or were raised in particular societies and cultures. People's own behavior and choice of lifestyle also influence their development.

Internal and External Influences   Internal influences originate with **heredity**—the inborn biological endowment that people inherit from their parents. External influences, or **environmental influences**, are the noninherited influences on development attributable to people's experiences with the world outside the self.

But this distinction blurs. We change the world around us even as it changes us. A baby girl with a cheerful disposition, for example, elicits positive responses from other people, which, in turn, strengthen her trust that her efforts will be rewarded. With this self-confidence, she is motivated to attempt to do more—and is likelier to succeed than a child who does not feel such trust.

The range of individual differences increases as people grow older. Normal children pass the same milestones in development and pass them at nearly the same ages, because so many of the changes in childhood are tied to basic maturational processes of body and brain. With the years, though, an individual's experiences and the world he or she lives in come to exert a greater influence, and since each of us undergoes different kinds of experiences, it's only logical that we should reflect these differences.

Normative and Nonnormative Influences
The effects of certain major events on large groups of people have led some researchers to distinguish between normative influences and nonnormative influences (Baltes, Reese, & Lipsitt, 1980).

When we say that something is normative, we mean that it occurs in a similar way for most people in a given group. *Normative age-graded influences* are biological and environmental influences that are highly similar for people in a particular age group, no matter when and where they live. These influences include such biological markers as puberty and menopause, as well as such cultural markers as entry into formal education (which occurs at about age 6 in most societies) and retirement from paid employment (which usually occurs sometime between the fifties and the seventies).

Normative history-graded influences are biological and environmental influences common to people of a particular generation, or *cohort* (those growing up at the same time in the same place). These influences include, for example, the worldwide economic depression of the 1930s, the political turmoil in the United States during the 1960s and 1970s caused by the Vietnamese war, and the massive famines in Africa during the 1980s. These influences also encompass such cultural factors as the changing roles of women, the use of anesthesia during childbirth, and the impact of the computer.

Nonnormative life events are unusual events that have a major impact on individual lives—events that either do not happen to most people or happen to a person at an atypical time in life. Such events may include the death of a parent when a child is young, a disaster, a life-threatening illness, or the birth of a child with a congenital defect. They can also, of course, include happy events like sudden wealth, the opportunity to live in a foreign country, or a particularly fortunate career opportunity. Whether such an event is positive or negative, it may cause more stress than a normative event, because the person does not expect it, is not prepared for it, and may need special help in adapting.

People often help to create their nonnormative life events, demonstrating their ability to be active participants in their own development.

Critical Periods A *critical period* is a specific time during development when a given event will have its greatest impact. For example, pregnant mice that receive x-rays 7 or 8 days after conception are likely to have pups with brain damage, whereas those irradiated 9½ days after conception are more likely to bear pups with

(© Peter Vadnai 1986/Stock Market)

Graduating from secondary school is an important life experience shared by most late adolescents. Other normative age-graded influences on development, which normally occur at particular ages, include such biological markers as puberty and menopause and such cultural events as entering school and retirement.

spina bifida, a disease of the nervous system (Russell & Russell, 1952). Similarly, if a woman receives x-rays, takes certain drugs, or contracts certain diseases at specific times during the first 3 months of pregnancy, her unborn baby may show specific effects. The amount and kind of damage to the fetus will vary according to the particular shock and its timing.

The event need not be physical; as we shall see, Freud maintained that certain early experiences can set people's personalities for life. And Erikson proposed eight "ages," each of which constitutes a critical period for social and emotional development.

Some of the supporting evidence for critical periods of *physical* development is undeniable, such as that involving fetal development. In other spheres of development, however, the concept of an irreversible critical period generally seems too limiting. Although the human organism may be particularly sensitive to certain experiences at various times of life, later events can often reverse the effects of early ones. (In Chapter 5, we discuss some of the arguments for and against the existence of a critical period for bonding between mother and baby.)

How the Study of Human Development Developed

Human development has, of course, been going on as long as human beings have existed; but ideas about it have changed drastically. Formal *scientific study* of human development is relatively new, and changes in the way adults look at children are particularly dramatic.

Studies of Children   Although people have long held differing ideas about how children should be raised, childhood as we understand it is apparently a very recent concept. For centuries children seem to have been considered nothing more than smaller, weaker, less intelligent versions of adults. Adults often did not see children as being qualitatively different from themselves, or as having any special needs, or as making any significant contributions to their own development (Aries, 1962).

Except for the ancient Greeks, early painters and sculptors in western civilization typically portrayed children as shrunken adults. Not until the thirteenth century did artists again

This seventeenth-century painting seems to reflect a view of children as miniature adults. The children have been rendered with adult-like body proportions, and they are wearing adult clothing. If this is the sort of clothing they wore all the time, it may be that they were not expected to run, jump, or engage in other activities that we now consider characteristic of childhood.

represent children who actually looked like children. And not until the seventeenth century did the concept of childhood itself become exalted in art as well as in life. At around this time, parents began to speak of the "sweet," "simple," and "amusing" nature of children. They began to dress children differently, instead of just putting them into adult-styled garments cut in small sizes, and they confessed to deriving joy from playing with their children.

The first books of advice for parents began to appear during the sixteenth century, most of them written by physicians. These books expressed little more than the pet theories of their authors. They told mothers not to nurse their babies right after feeling anger, lest their milk prove fatal; to begin toilet-training their infants at the age of 3 weeks; and to bind their babies' arms for several months after birth to prevent thumb-sucking (Ryerson, 1961).

By the nineteenth century, several important trends had prepared the way for the study of

(National Library of Medicine)

The psychologist G. Stanley Hall (1846–1924) was a pioneer in the studies of childhood, adolescence, and aging. He was a founder and the first president of the American Psychological Association, and he established the nation's first professional psychology journal and its first psychology laboratory. But his theories, while popular, had little scientific basis.

child development. Scientists had unlocked the mystery of conception and were beginning to argue about the relative importance of heredity and environment (which we discuss in Chapter 2). The discovery of germs and immunization made it possible for people to protect their children from the widespread plagues and fevers that had made growing up a highly uncertain prospect. Meanwhile, the rise of Protestantism, which emphasized self-reliance, made adults feel more responsible for the way children turned out instead of simply accepting misfortune or misbehavior as something brought by fate.

The passage of laws protecting children from long hours of labor meant that they could spend more time in school. The spirit of democracy filtered into both home and classroom; parents and teachers, rejecting the old, autocratic methods, became concerned about identifying and meeting children's needs. And the new science of psychology led people to believe that they could understand themselves by learning what influences had affected them during childhood.

Adolescence was not even considered a stage of development until the twentieth century. G. Stanley Hall, a pioneer in the child study movement, was the first psychologist to formulate a theory of adolescence. His two-volume work *Adolescence,* published in 1904, was very popular and provoked a great deal of thought and discussion; but it had very little scientific basis, serving mainly as a platform for Hall's ideas.

Studies of Adulthood and Aging   Hall was also one of the first psychologists to become interested in the study of the other end of the life span; in 1922, when he was 78, he published *Senescence: The Last Half of Life.* Six years later, Stanford University opened the first major scientific research unit devoted to the study of aging. It was not until a generation later, though, that this area of study blossomed. By 1946, the National Institutes of Health had established a large-scale research unit, and specialized organizations and journals were reporting the newest findings—at first primarily on such topics as intellectual ability and reaction time, and later on emotional aspects of aging.

Since the late 1930s, a number of long-term studies have focused on adults, beginning with the Grant Study of Adult Development, which followed 18-year-old students from Harvard University into middle age. In the mid-1950s, Bernice Neugarten and her associates at the University of Chicago began their studies of middle-aged people, and K. Warner Schaie launched his ongoing study of adult intelligence. During the past two decades, Daniel Levinson and his colleagues at Yale University and Grace Baruch and Rosalind Barnett of Wellesley College have examined the lives of men and women in their middle years to identify important factors in their development during adulthood. All these studies and others, which we will discuss at appropriate points in this book, add to our understanding of human development.

Life-Span Studies   Meanwhile, though, the continuity of the entire human life span was not widely recognized. Today many psychologists recognize that human development is a lifelong process. Each portion of a person's life span is influenced by what has already occurred, and each period affects the ones that follow.

Life-span studies in the United States grew

out of programs designed to follow children over a period of years. When the children grew up, the researchers continued to follow them through adulthood. The Stanford Studies of Gifted Children (begun in 1921 under the direction of Lewis Terman) continue to focus upon the development of people who were identified as unusually intelligent children. Other major studies that began around 1930—the Berkeley Growth Study, the Oakland Growth Study, and the Fels Research Institute Study—have yielded a great deal of information on long-term development.

HUMAN DEVELOPMENT: THEORETICAL PERSPECTIVES

Theories and Hypotheses

The way people explain development depends on how they view the fundamental nature of human beings. Different thinkers, looking through different lenses, have come up with different explanations, or theories, about why people behave as they do.

A *theory* is a set of related statements about *data*, the information obtained through research. Scientists use theories to help them integrate, or make sense of, their data and then to predict what data might be obtained under certain conditions. Theories are important, then, in helping scientists to *explain, interpret,* and *predict* behavior.

Both research and theory are essential. Painstaking research adds, bit by bit, to the body of knowledge. Theories help researchers to find a coherent structure in the data—to go beyond isolated observations and make generalizations.

Theories guide *future* research by suggesting hypotheses to be tested. A *hypothesis* is a possible explanation for a phenomenon and is used to predict the outcome of an experiment. Sometimes research confirms a hypothesis, providing added support for a theory. At other times, scientists must modify their theories to account for unexpected facts that emerge.

Some theories are not much more than simple hunches; others, like the major ones we discuss in this chapter and throughout this book, are elaborate structures that put together a great deal of information. No one theory is accepted by all developmentalists, nor does any one theory explain all facets of development.

The perspectives from which theorists look at development are important because they dictate the questions that researchers ask, the methods they use, and the way they interpret their results. Today human development is studied from at least four rival perspectives: psychoanalytic, mechanistic, organismic, and humanistic. Each has its dedicated supporters and its equally impassioned critics. All of them make some contribution to the understanding of human development.

In this book, we examine and evaluate some of the more influential theories that arise from these perspectives, and we call attention to the interplay between theory and research. In this chapter, we give a brief overview of each of the four perspectives, summarizing some of their strengths and weaknesses. We present and analyze age-related aspects of the theories more fully at pertinent places throughout the book.

Psychoanalytic Perspective

Do you ever try to analyze your dreams? Do you believe that unconscious feelings, of which people are unaware, often dictate their actions? If so, you are operating under the assumption of the *psychoanalytic perspective*, a view of humanity concerned with the unconscious forces motivating human behavior. This view was virtually unheard of before the beginning of the twentieth century. That was when a Viennese physician named Sigmund Freud originated psychoanalysis, a therapeutic approach that aims to give people insight into unconscious conflicts, originating in childhood, that affect their behavior and emotions.

Sigmund Freud: Psychosexual Theory Freud (1856–1939) was the oldest of eight children. He believed himself to be his mother's favorite, and he expected to accomplish great things (E. Jones, 1961). His initial goal was medical research; but limited financial resources and barriers to academic advancement for Jews forced him into the private practice of medicine.

One of his main interests was neurology, the study of the brain and treatment of disorders of

(Bettmann Archive)

The Viennese physician Sigmund Freud constructed an original, influential, and highly controversial theory of emotional development in childhood, based on recollections of his disturbed adult patients.

the nervous system—a branch of medicine then in its infancy. To relieve symptoms for which he could not find a physical cause, Freud began to ask questions designed to summon up his patients' long-buried memories. This led him to conclude that the source of emotional disturbances lay in traumatic experiences of early childhood.

Freud theorized that powerful unconscious biological drives, mostly sexual and also aggressive, motivate human behavior, and that these natural urges put people in conflict with the constraints of society, producing anxiety.

Freud's ideas were shocking to Victorian society, in which sexuality was something nice people did not discuss or even (supposedly) think about. Although his theory was at first rejected by the European medical establishment, it eventually achieved wide international attention. But it remained controversial, particularly in its overarching emphasis on sex and aggression as motivators of human behavior, and some of Freud's most prominent followers ultimately broke away or developed their own variations on psychoanalytic theory. His daughter Anna Freud, though, carried on her father's work and developed psychoanalytic methods for use with children.

ID, EGO, AND SUPEREGO   Freud conceptualized the human personality as being made up of three components: the id, the ego, and the superego.

The id, which is present at birth, is the unconscious source of motives and desires; it operates on the "pleasure principle," seeking to reduce tension through immediate gratification of the person's needs. Initially, infants are egocentric in that they do not differentiate themselves from the outside world. All is there for gratification, and only when it is delayed (as when they have to wait for food) do they develop their egos and begin to differentiate themselves from their surroundings.

The ego represents reason, or common sense; it develops sometime during the first year of life and operates on the "reality principle," seeking an acceptable way to obtain gratification. Eventually the ego mediates between the id and the superego, which does not develop until the age of 4 or 5.

The superego represents the values that parents and other agents of society (like teachers) communicate to the child. Largely through the child's identification with the parent of the same sex, the superego incorporates these socially approved "shoulds" and "should nots" into the child's own value system.

STAGES OF PSYCHOSEXUAL DEVELOPMENT   In Freudian thought, children and adolescents go through an unvarying sequence of stages of *psychosexual development*, in which gratification, or pleasure, shifts from one bodily zone to another—from the mouth to the anus and then to the genitals. At each stage, the behavior that is the chief source of gratification changes, from feeding to elimination and then to sexual activity. Although the order of these stages is always the same, a child's maturation level determines when the shifts will take place. (See Table 1-1 on the opposite page for a summary of Freud's stages. Each stage will be discussed in the appropriate chapter.)

Fixation, an arrest in development, may occur if children are gratified too little or too much at a given stage; they may then become emotionally fixated, or stuck, at that stage and may need help in order to move beyond it. For example, a baby who is weaned too early or is allowed to

TABLE 1·1 DEVELOPMENTAL STAGES ACCORDING TO VARIOUS THEORIES		
PSYCHOSEXUAL STAGE (FREUD)	PSYCHOSOCIAL STAGE (ERIKSON)	COGNITIVE STAGE (PIAGET)
Oral (birth to 12–18 months). Baby's chief source of pleasure is mouth-oriented activities like sucking and eating.	*Basic trust versus mistrust (birth to 12–18 months).* Baby develops sense of whether world can be trusted. Virtue: hope.	*Sensorimotor (birth to 2 years).* Infant changes from a being who responds primarily through reflexes to one who can organize activities in relation to the environment. Infant learns through the senses and motor activities.
Anal (12–18 months to 3 years). Child derives sensual gratification from withholding and expelling feces. Zone of gratification is anal region.	*Autonomy versus shame and doubt (12–18 months to 3 years).* Child develops a balance of independence over doubt and shame. Virtue: will.	*Preoperational (2 to 7 years).* Child develops a representational system and uses symbols such as words to represent people, places, and events.
Phallic (3 to 6 years). Time of the "family romance"; Oedipus complex in boys and Electra complex in girls. Zone of gratification shifts to genital region.	*Initiative versus guilt (3 to 6 years).* Child develops initiative when trying out new things and is not overwhelmed by failure. Virtue: purpose.	
Latency (6 years to puberty). Time of relative calm between more turbulent stages.	*Industry versus inferiority (6 years to puberty).* Child must learn skills of the culture or face feelings of inferiority. Virtue: skill.	*Concrete operations (7 to 12 years).* Child can solve problems logically if they are focused on the here and now.
Genital (puberty through adulthood). Time of mature adult sexuality.	*Identity versus identity confusion (puberty to young adulthood).* Adolescent must determine own sense of self. Virtue: fidelity.	*Formal operations (12 years to adulthood).* Person can think in abstract terms and deal with hypothetical situations.
	Intimacy versus isolation (young adulthood). Person seeks to make commitments to others; if unsuccessful, may suffer from sense of isolation and self-absorption. Virtue: love.	
	Generativity versus stagnation (middle adulthood). Mature adult is concerned with establishing and guiding the next generation or else feels personal impoverishment. Virtue: care.	
	Integrity versus despair (old age). Elderly person achieves a sense of acceptance of own life, allowing the acceptance of death, or else falls into despair. Virtue: wisdom.	

Note: All ages are approximate.

suck too much may become an excessively distrustful or dependent adult. (However, Freud was vague about what constituted "too early" or "too much.")

DEFENSE MECHANISMS   Freud described a number of **defense mechanisms**, ways in which people unconsciously combat anxiety by distorting reality. He believed that everyone uses defense mechanisms at times; only when these mechanisms interfere with healthy emotional development are they pathological. Among the most common defense mechanisms are the following:

- *Regression:* a return to behavior characteristic of an earlier age. During trying times, people often regress to try to recapture remembered security. For example, a girl who has just entered school may go back to sucking her thumb or wetting the bed. Or a young man in college may react to his parents' recent separation by asking them to make decisions for him as they did when he was a child. When the crisis is past, the inappropriate behavior usually disappears.
- *Repression:* blocking anxiety-producing urges and experiences from consciousness. Freud believed that people's inability to remember much about their early years is due to repression of disturbing sexual feelings toward their parents. (See the discussion of the Oedipus and Electra complexes in Chapter 7.)
- *Sublimation:* channeling uncomfortable sexual or aggressive impulses into socially acceptable activities, such as study, work, sports, and hobbies.
- *Projection:* attribution of a person's own unacceptable thoughts and feelings to another. For example, a little girl who is jealous of the new baby talks about how jealous the baby is. Or a husband who entertains fantasies of having an affair accuses his wife of being unfaithful.
- *Reaction formation:* replacement of an anxiety-producing feeling with its opposite. People may say the opposite of what they really feel: Buddy says, "I don't want to play with Tony, because I don't like him," when the truth is that Buddy likes Tony a lot but is afraid that Tony doesn't want to play with *him*.

(UPI/Bettmann Newsphotos)

The psychoanalyst Erik H. Erikson departs from Freudian thought in emphasizing societal, rather than chiefly biological, influences on personality. Erikson sees development as proceeding through eight crises, or significant turning points, at different times throughout life.

Erik Erikson: Psychosocial Theory   Erik Erikson (b. 1902), a German-born psychoanalyst who was trained under Anna Freud in Vienna, fled from the threat of Nazism (which eventually forced the breakup of Sigmund Freud's entire circle) and came to the United States in 1933. His personal and professional experience—far broader than Freud's—led him to modify and extend Freudian theory.

ERIKSON'S APPROACH   Erikson's mixed parentage (Danish and Jewish), the dissolution of his parents' marriage and his total lack of contact with his father, his youthful vocational floundering, and his need to redefine his identity as an immigrant found echoes in the "identity crises" he observed among disturbed adolescents, World War II combat soldiers, and members of minority groups (Erikson, 1968, 1973; R. I. Evans, 1967). He concluded that the quest for identity is a major theme in life.

An important area of Erikson's experience was with children. Before becoming a psychoanalyst, he taught art in a small progressive school in Vienna. He was also trained in the Montessori method, which stresses the way young children learn through play. His later studies ranged from child-rearing practices of the Sioux Indians and the Yurok Indians of northern California to social customs in India.

Erikson became convinced that Freudian theory gave too little weight to the influence of society on the developing personality. A girl growing up on a Sioux reservation, where females are trained to serve their hunter husbands (P. H. Miller, 1983), will develop different personality patterns and different skills from a girl growing up in a wealthy Jewish family in turn-of-the-century Vienna, like most of Freud's patients. Erikson also felt that Freud's view of society was too negative. Whereas Freud saw civilization as a source of discontent—an impediment to biological drives—Erikson sees society as a potentially positive force, shaping the development of the ego, or self.

ERIKSON'S EIGHT CRISES   Erikson's *psychosocial-development theory* traces personality development across the life span, stressing societal and cultural influences on the ego at each of eight "ages" (1950). Each stage of psychosocial development revolves around a turning point, a crisis in personality, involving a different major conflict—one that is particularly critical at the time, though it remains an issue to some degree throughout life. Erikson believes that the crises emerge according to a maturationally determined timetable for ego development. Healthy ego development involves making appropriate adjustments to the demands of a particular crisis at a particular stage in the life span. If the conflict is not satisfactorily resolved, the person will continue to struggle with it and healthy ego development will be impeded.

Successful resolution of each of the eight crises (listed in Table 1-1 and discussed in appropriate chapters) requires the balancing of a positive and a corresponding negative trait, such as (in the first crisis) trust and mistrust. Although the positive quality should predominate, some element of the negative is needed, too. Healthy people, for example, basically trust their world, but they need to learn some mistrust to be prepared for dangerous or uncomfortable situations. The successful outcome of each crisis includes the development of a particular "virtue"—in this case, the "virtue of hope."

Critique of Psychoanalytic Theory   Freud's original and creative thinking has made immense contributions to our understanding of children and has had a major impact on the child-rearing practices of the western world. He made us aware of infantile sexuality, the nature of our unconscious thoughts and emotions, our defense mechanisms, the significance of dreams, the importance of parent-child relationships in the early years and the ambivalence in those relationships, and many other aspects of emotional functioning. He also founded the psychoanalytic method of treatment, which inspired much of the psychotherapy being practiced today.

Yet in many ways Freud's theory grew out of his own place in history and in society. For example, much of his theory seems patronizing or demeaning toward women, no doubt because of its roots in the social system of a European culture convinced of the superiority of the male. Also, the source of the data on which Freud based his theories about normal development was not a population of average children but a highly selective clientele of upper-middle-class adults in therapy. His concentration on the resolution of psychosexual conflict as the key to healthy development seems too narrow, and the subjective way in which he enunciated his theories has made them difficult to test by research.

Recent criticism suggests that Freud suppressed his original belief that his patients' parents had maltreated and sexually abused them, claiming instead that children are naturally aggressive and seductive toward their parents (Masson, 1984; Tribich & Klein, 1981). Freud's apparent misinterpretation of his patients' childhood memories aggravated tendencies in society to "blame the victim" and to overlook the existence and extent of child abuse. One reason advanced for Freud's change of heart is that he may have suspected but repressed the possibility that his own father was sexually seductive; another might be that Freud was unable to own up to sexual fantasies about his daughters (D. Tribich, personal communication to the authors, 1982).

A strength of Erikson's theory is that it goes beyond Freud's focus on biological and maturational factors, recognizing social and cultural influences on development. Another strength is that it covers the entire life span, while Freud's stops at adolescence. Erikson, however, has also been criticized for an antifemale bias, one that emerges from his failure to take into account the social and cultural factors that influence the attitudes and behaviors of the sexes. Furthermore, some of his concepts are difficult to assess objectively as a basis for follow-up research.

Mechanistic Perspective

The *mechanistic perspective* views human development primarily as a response to external events; it discounts purpose, will, and intelligence, as well as the unconscious fantasies that occupy Freudian analysts. According to the classical mechanistic outlook, people are like machines, reacting automatically to external stimuli. Thus, *if* we can identify all the significant influences in a person's environment, we can predict that person's behavior.

Mechanistic theorists see change as quantitative (change in amount rather than kind) and development as continuous (allowing prediction of later behaviors from earlier ones). Psychological research spurred by this viewpoint attempts to identify and isolate the factors in the environment that make certain people behave in certain ways. It focuses on how experiences affect later behavior. It tries to understand the effects of experience by breaking down complex stimuli and complex behaviors into simpler elements.

The mechanistic model governs two related schools of psychological thought: behaviorism and social-learning theory.

Behaviorism It would be hard to imagine two perspectives more at odds than those of psychoanalysis and behaviorism. Whereas psychoanalytic thinkers consider unconscious motives and desires to be the foundation of human behavior, followers of *behaviorism* study behaviors that can be seen, measured, and recorded. They try to identify immediate, readily observable factors that determine whether a particular behavior will continue to occur; they generally do *not* concern themselves with underlying, unobservable factors. Although behaviorists recognize that biology sets limits on what people do, they stress the role of the environment.

Behaviorism (also called *traditional learning*

theory) holds that *learning* is what changes behavior and thus causes development. Behaviorists believe that human beings of all ages learn about the world in the same way that other animals do, by reacting to features of their environments that they find pleasing, painful, or threatening.

Behaviorists are interested only in quantitative, not qualitative, change and, therefore, do not describe stages of development. They hold that learning occurs primarily through conditioning and that development is simply the sum of a person's conditioned responses. There are two kinds of conditioning: classical (also known as *respondent*) and operant (also called *instrumental*).

CLASSICAL CONDITIONING Ivan Pavlov (1849–1936), a Russian physiologist, taught dogs to salivate upon hearing a bell by repeatedly offering them food immediately after the bell sounded. Because the dogs had learned to associate the sound of the bell with the food, the bell eventually induced salivation even when no food appeared. Pavlov's famous experiment demonstrated *classical conditioning*—a kind of learning in which a person or animal learns a response to a stimulus that did not originally elicit that response, after the stimulus is repeat-

Ivan Pavlov, a Russian physiologist, established the principles of classical conditioning by teaching dogs to salivate upon hearing a bell.

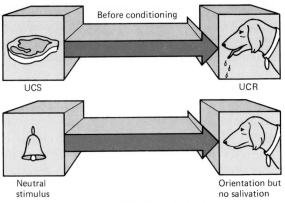

UCS automatically produces UCR. Neutral stimulus
does not produce salivation.

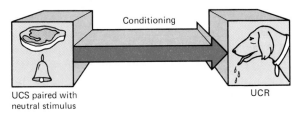

UCS is paired with neutral stimulus. UCS produces UCR.

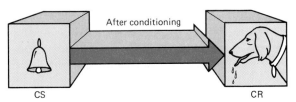

Neutral stimulus is now the conditioned stimulus. It produces
CR, salivation, which is similar to the UCR produced by the meat.

Figure 1-1 Classical conditioning. Classical
conditioning occurs in three stages. The neutral
stimulus, after repeated pairings with the
unconditioned stimulus, eventually produces a
conditioned response.

edly associated with another stimulus that *does*
ordinarily evoke the response.

We trace the three steps in classical conditioning in Figure 1-1. In the first step, before conditioning, the dog does not salivate at the sound of
the bell but salivates only when the food appears. The food is an ***unconditioned stimulus
(UCS)***, a stimulus that automatically elicits an
unlearned (unconditioned) response (in this
case, salivation). The salivation is the ***unconditioned response (unconditioned reflex) (UCR)***, an
automatic, unlearned response to a particular
stimulus (food). The sound of the bell is a ***neu-***

tral stimulus, one that does not ordinarily elicit a
reflex response.

In the second step, during conditioning, the
experimenter repeatedly pairs the neutral stimulus (the bell) with the unconditioned stimulus
(food). Every time the bell rings, food appears
and the dog salivates in response to the food.

In the third step, after conditioning has occurred, the dog salivates at the sound of the bell.
The dog has learned to associate the bell with
food and to respond in essentially the same way
to both stimuli. The bell has become a ***conditioned stimulus (CS)***, an originally neutral stimulus that, after repeated pairings with an unconditioned stimulus (food), elicits a response (salivation) similar to that elicited by the unconditioned stimulus. The salivation has become a
conditioned response (CR), a response elicited by
a conditioned stimulus (the bell).

John B. Watson (1878–1958) was the first
behaviorist to apply stimulus-response theories
of learning to the study of child development.
We will see in Chapter 4 how he conditioned a
child known as "Little Albert" to fear furry objects.

OPERANT CONDITIONING   B. F. Skinner (b.
1904), an American who is currently the leading
behaviorist, was the primary person responsible
for developing a type of conditioning that parents, teachers, animal trainers, and others often
use to shape desired behavior. Skinner (1938)
taught pigeons to respond to different-colored
bars by rewarding them with food when they
happened to press the right bar. He then
showed how the principle underlying the animals' responses could also be used to control
human behavior. The principle is that an organism will tend to repeat behavior followed by a
satisfying experience and not to repeat behavior
followed by an unsatisfying experience—to seek
reward and avoid punishment.

This principle is the basis of ***operant (instrumental) conditioning***, a kind of learning in which
an animal or person continues to make a response because the response has been reinforced (strengthened) or stops making the
response because it has been punished. A ***reinforcement*** is a stimulus that follows a behavior
and *increases* the likelihood that the behavior will
be repeated. ***Punishment*** is a stimulus that fol-

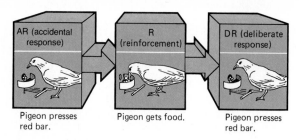

| AR (accidental response) | R (reinforcement) | DR (deliberate response) |
| Pigeon presses red bar. | Pigeon gets food. | Pigeon presses red bar. |

Figure 1-2 Operant, or instrumental, conditioning.

lows a behavior and *decreases* the likelihood that the behavior will be repeated. This kind of learning is also called *instrumental conditioning*, because the learner is instrumental in changing the environment in some way—that is, in bringing about either reinforcement or punishment.

Figure 1-2 shows how operant conditioning occurs. A pigeon happens to press a red bar. This random or accidental response (AR) is reinforced (R) by a grain of food. The reinforcement strengthens the response, and the pigeon keeps pressing the red bar. The originally accidental response has now become a deliberate response (DR).

Reinforcement is most effective when it is immediate. If a response is no longer reinforced—that is, if the pigeon presses the red bar several times and gets no food—then the bird will eventually give up the response or at least will be no more likely to show it than in the first place. This cessation of a response that is no longer reinforced (or its return to its original, or baseline, level) is called **extinction**.

Reinforcement can be either *positive* or *negative*. *Positive reinforcement* consists of giving a reward like food, gold stars, money, or praise. *Negative reinforcement* consists of taking away something that the individual does not like (known as an *aversive event*), such as a bright light, a loud noise, or a dirty diaper.

Negative reinforcement is sometimes confused with punishment, but they are two different things. Negative reinforcement *takes away* an aversive event to encourage an individual to repeat a behavior, whereas punishment *brings on* an aversive event (like spanking a child or giving an electric shock to an animal) to try to keep a behavior from being repeated.

Intermittent reinforcement, in which a given response is sometimes reinforced and some-

times not reinforced, produces more durable behaviors than reinforcing a response on every occasion. This is because it takes longer for the individual to realize that intermittent reinforcement has ended, and so the behavior tends to persist.

Operant conditioning is a powerful tool that has been used in programmed learning and other efforts to train or alter adults' or children's behavior. Desired actions are encouraged by reinforcement; undesired ones are punished or ignored. The choice of an effective stimulus depends on the individual being trained: one person's reinforcement may be another's punishment.

What can be done if there *is* no "desired behavior" to be encouraged (for example, if a child consistently refuses to talk)? **Shaping** is a way to bring about *new* responses by reinforcing responses that are progressively more like the desired one. When the person does something that is "on the right track" (is similar to the response being sought), a reinforcement is given. When that reinforcement has taken hold, the shaper continues to reward responses that are closer and closer to the desired behavior. For example, the parent of a little boy who refuses to talk might first give him candy after he makes any sound at all. Then the parent would give the candy only after the child says a word, and then only after a sentence.

Shaping is often used in *behavioral modification*, a form of operant conditioning that is used to eliminate undesirable behavior or to teach desirable behavior, as in toilet training. It is most often used for children with special needs, such as retarded or emotionally disturbed youngsters, but its techniques are also used effectively in the day-to-day management of normal children (see Chapters 7 and 9).

Social-Learning Theory *Social-learning theory*, a modern offshoot of traditional learning theory which has become more influential than the parent theory, holds that children, in particular, learn by observing and imitating models (like their parents). The theory—of which Albert Bandura (b. 1925), a professor at Stanford University, is the most prominent advocate—is mechanistic in that it stresses responses to the environment. But it sees the learner as more active than behaviorism does, acknowledging the role of cognitive factors that affect people's ability to acquire and use knowledge about their world.

Like behaviorists, social-learning theorists emphasize rigorous laboratory experimentation. Unlike behaviorists, they contend that theories developed through experiments with animals cannot adequately explain the learned behavior of human beings, which occurs in a social context, and that human learning cannot be reduced to simple principles of conditioning.

According to social-learning theory, children's identification with their parents, who shape their behavior through a system of reinforcements and punishments, is the most important element in the way they learn a language, deal with aggression, develop a sense of morality, and learn the socially expected behavior for their gender. (A boy may be praised for acting "like Daddy," a girl, "like Mommy.")

Children take an active part in their own learning, according to this theory. In addition to imitating their parents, they choose other models, usually people who seem powerful and respected. The child's own characteristics influence the choice of models. For example, a child with strongly aggressive tendencies will be more likely to imitate an aggressive model than a child whose usual behavior is conciliatory. Boys are more likely to copy aggressive models than girls are.

What sort of behavior a person imitates depends, of course, on what kinds of behavior exist and are valued in a particular culture. In a tropical climate, where there are no deer, children will not learn to hunt deer. Thus "there is no one universal goal or endpoint to development. . . . What is universally developed is a skilled ability to learn by observing . . . " (P. H. Miller, 1983, p. 232).

Whereas behaviorists view the environment as molding the child, social-learning theorists believe that the child also acts upon the environment—in fact, *creates* the environment to some extent. For example, a child who spends a great amount of time watching television rather than playing with other children is likely to take his or her models from those on the screen.

Social-learning theory makes another important departure from a purely mechanistic out-

According to social-learning theory, children who spend many hours watching television tend to imitate the dress, speech, and other behavior of models they see on the screen.

look in recognizing the influence of cognitive processes, which (as we shall see) are the main concern of the organismic perspective. According to social-learning theorists, people learn specific "chunks" of behavior by observing models and then mentally combine what they have observed into complex new behavior patterns. For example, a woman learning tennis may try to model her backhand stroke after Chris Evert's and her serve after Martina Navratilova's. Such cognitive factors as a person's ability to pay attention and to mentally organize sensory information determine what effect, if any, the observed behavior has on the person's own. Children's developing ability to use mental symbols to represent a model's behavior enables them to form standards for judging their own behavior.

Critique of Learning Theory Both behaviorism and social-learning theory have contributed much to the respectability of the science of human development by their insistence on rigorous laboratory experimentation and on clear definitions of terms. On the other hand, by concentrating on laboratory experimentation, they have neglected the study of human behavior in its natural settings. The emphasis that the theories place on environmental influences is valuable, but they tend to underestimate the role of biological influences and fail to acknowledge the importance of unconscious factors in behavior, of internal motivation, and of free choice. Furthermore, these theories are not truly developmental: they pay little attention to what children and adults are like at different periods of their development.

Behaviorism has made its greatest contribution through programs or therapies that can effect rapid changes in behavior (like giving up smoking) or bring about the learning of new behaviors (as in toilet training) without going through a long search for deep-seated emotional conflicts. But psychoanalysts charge that a major weakness of learning theory is its lack of concern with the underlying causes of symptoms. They argue that eliminating one undesirable behavior (like stealing) through punishment may merely result in the substitution of some other negative behavior (like bed-wetting), leaving the basic problem unresolved. Another serious objection is to the ethics of experts' "playing God" and controlling other people's behavior.

The distinguishing features of social-learning theory—its focus on the social context of learning, its recognition that people actively influence their own development, and its acknowledgment of cognitive influences on behavior—are improvements on traditional learning theory.

Organismic Perspective

The third major theoretical perspective views people not as machines but as organisms—living, growing beings with their own internal impulses and patterns for development. In contrast with traditional learning theory, the **organismic perspective** sees people as active agents in their own development and sees development as occurring in qualitative stages. Let's examine each of these two points:

1   *People are active organisms.* According to this view, people set their own development in motion. They initiate acts. Although internal and external forces interact, the *source* of

change is internal. Organicists see life experiences not as the cause of development but as factors that can speed it up or slow it down. These theorists do not try to determine, as mechanists do, how external reinforcements shape a person's responses. Nor do they focus, as psychoanalysts do, on underlying motivational forces of which a person is unaware. Instead, they look at human beings as doers who actively construct their worlds.

2   *Development occurs in qualitative stages.* Organicists focus on qualitative change. Like some other "stage" theorists,* they describe development as occurring in a set sequence of qualitatively different stages. At each stage, people develop different kinds of abilities and cope with different kinds of problems. Each stage builds on the previous one and lays the foundation for the next. Because thought and behavior at each stage are qualitatively different from before, it is only through knowledge of the common course of human development that we can anticipate (in broad outlines) what a person will be like in a later stage of life. Although all people go through the same stages in the same order, the actual timing varies, making any age demarcation only approximate.

Piaget's Cognitive-Stage Theory   The Swiss theoretician Jean Piaget (1896–1980) was the most prominent advocate of the organismic world view. Much of what we know about the way children think is due to his creative inquiry.

When he was a boy, Piaget's wide-ranging curiosity led him to observe and write about such diverse topics as mechanics, mollusks, and an albino sparrow he saw in a park. As an adult, he applied his broad knowledge of biology, philosophy, and psychology to meticulous observations of children. In line with his early interests in physical organization, structure, and logic, he constructed complex theories about *cognitive development:* changes in children's thought processes that result in a growing ability to acquire and use knowledge about their world.

---

*Although Freud and Erikson describe qualitative stages, they do not, to the extent that true organismic theories do, view human beings as active initiators of development.

By the time of his death in 1980, Piaget had written more than 40 books and more than 100 articles on child psychology as well as works on philosophy and education, much of this material produced with his long-time collaborator, Barbel Inhelder. Piaget's theory influenced other organicists like Lawrence Kohlberg, whose theory of moral development is discussed later in this book.

Let's look at some of the principal features of Piaget's theory.

COGNITIVE STRUCTURES   Piaget believed that people have an innate tendency to adapt to the demands of their environment, a tendency he saw as the essence of intelligent behavior. Building on the foundation of their sensory, motor, and reflex capacities, children actively construct their knowledge of the world—from feeling a pebble, for example, or exploring the boundaries of a living room. The mental structures become more complex as children gain experience and progress through a series of stages of cognitive development. (Piaget's four stages, summarized in Table 1-1, are discussed in the appropriate chapters.)

The cognitive structures of infants are called schemes. A *scheme* is an organized pattern of behavior that a baby uses to interact with the environment in a certain way. An infant has, for example, a scheme for sucking, a scheme for seeing, and a scheme for grasping. Schemes gradually become differentiated; for example, babies develop different ways to suck at the breast, a bottle, or a pacifier. Schemes also become coordinated; for example, infants learn to grasp what they see. As they develop the ability to think, their schemes become organized patterns of thought that correspond to particular behaviors.

The cognitive structures of older children enable them to perform different kinds of mental operations—first in concrete situations involving things that they can see, hear, smell, taste, or feel, and later through abstract thought.

PRINCIPLES OF COGNITIVE DEVELOPMENT   How do people's cognitive structures advance from simple behavioral schemes to formal logic?

Piaget's answer lies in three interrelated prin-

The influential Swiss psychologist Jean Piaget studied children's cognitive development by observing and talking with his own youngsters and others.

ciples of development, which he believed to be innate, inherited tendencies. They are called *functional invariants*, because they operate at all stages of cognitive growth. These three principles are organization, adaptation, and equilibration.

Cognitive *organization* is the tendency to create systems that bring together all of a person's knowledge of the environment. At all stages of development, people try to make sense of their world. They do this by systematically organizing their knowledge, at whatever level of complexity they are capable of. Development progresses from simple organizational structures to more complex ones. At first, for example, infants' schemes of looking and grasping operate independently. Later the infants integrate these separate schemes into a single, higher-order scheme that allows them to look at an object while holding it—to coordinate eye and hand—and thus to better understand that particular part of their environment.

More complex organization goes hand in hand with the acquisition of more information. *Adaptation*, or effective interaction with the environment (the second functional invariant), occurs through the dual processes of assimilating this new information and accommodating to it.

Assimilation is the attempt to fit new information into an existing cognitive structure. When breast-fed babies begin to suck on a rubber nipple, they are showing assimilation; that is, they are using an old scheme to deal with a new object or situation. *Accommodation* is a change in an existing cognitive structure to cope with new information. For example, when babies discover that sucking on a bottle requires somewhat different tongue and mouth movements from those used to suck on a breast, they modify the old scheme. Thus the complementary processes of assimilation and accommodation work together to produce cognitive growth—advancements in the way a child understands and acts upon the environment.

Equilibration, the third functional invariant, refers to the tendency to strive for a state of balance (equilibrium), both between the organism and the outside world and among the cognitive elements within the organism. Equilibration leads a child to shift, for example, from assimilation to accommodation. When children's existing structures cannot handle new experiences, they seek a new state of equilibrium by organizing new mental patterns that *can* meet the environmental demands.

Critique of Piaget's Theory Although American psychologists were slow to accept the ideas of this European pioneer, Piaget has inspired more research on children's cognitive development than any other theorist. One of his most important contributions was to shift attention from overt behaviors (as in learning theory) to internal cognitive processes.

Critics fault Piaget on several counts. He speaks primarily of the "average" child and takes little notice of the influences of education and culture upon performance. He says little about emotional and personality development, except as they relate to cognitive growth. He has been criticized because so many of his ideas emerged from his highly personal observations of his own three children and from his idiosyncratic way of interviewing children, rather than

from established, standardized experimental procedures. He also appears to have underestimated the abilities of young children in certain ways.

Still, Piaget's careful observations have provided a wealth of information about cognitive development, including some surprising insights. For example, it was he who first noticed that to a young infant, an object or person no longer exists when out of sight. He also discovered that preschool children believe that changing the shape of an object (such as a ball of clay) can change its weight, or that rearranging a group of objects can change their number. Piaget pointed out unique elements of children's thought processes and made us aware that a child's mind is very different from an adult's. Furthermore, by describing what children can do and what they can understand at various stages of cognitive development, Piaget gave valuable guidance to educators and to others who deal with children.

Humanistic Perspective

In 1962, a group of psychologists founded the Association of Humanistic Psychology. Protesting against what they considered to be the essentially negative beliefs underlying behaviorist and psychoanalytic theories, they maintained that human nature is either neutral or good and that any bad characteristics are the result of damage that has been inflicted on the developing self.

Like organicism, the *humanistic perspective* views people as able to take charge of their lives and foster their own development. Humanistic theorists emphasize people's potential for positive, healthy development through exercise of the distinctively human capacities for choice, creativity, and self-realization.

The humanistic approach is less developmental than the organismic and psychoanalytic views, since its proponents generally do not distinguish stages of the life span but make a broad distinction only between the periods before and after adolescence. However, two leaders in humanistic psychology, Abraham Maslow and Charlotte Bühler, do talk about sequential stages or phases in development.

Maslow's Hierarchy of Needs Maslow (1908–1970) identified a hierarchy of needs that motivate human behavior (see Figure 1-3). According to Maslow (1954), only when people have satisfied elemental needs do they strive to meet higher needs. The first priority is physiological survival. Starving persons will take great risks to get food; only when they have obtained it can they worry about the next level of needs, those concerning personal safety and security. These needs, in turn, must be met (at least in part) before people can seek love and acceptance, esteem and achievement, and, finally, self-actualization, or the full realization of potential.

A self-actualized person shows high levels of all the following characteristics (Maslow, 1968): perception of reality; acceptance of self, of others, and of nature; spontaneity; problem-solving ability; self-direction; detachment and the desire for privacy; freshness of appreciation and richness of emotional reaction; frequency of peak experiences; identification with other human beings; satisfying and changing relationships with other people; democratic character structure; creativity; and a sense of values. It is estimated that only about 1 person in 100 attains this lofty ideal (R. Thomas, 1979). Furthermore, no one is ever completely self-actualized; the healthy person is always moving up to levels that are even more self-fulfilling.

On first impression, Maslow's hierarchy of needs seems grounded in human experience. But the priorities he outlined do not invariably hold true. For example, history is full of accounts of self-sacrifice, in which people give up what they need for survival so that someone else (a loved one or even a stranger) can live.

Bühler's Five Phases of Goal-Orientation Bühler (1893–1974), who was the first president of the Association of Humanistic Psychology, analyzed more than 200 biographical studies and conducted intensive interviews over a period of years to come up with her five-phase theory of human development, which focused on setting and attaining personal goals.

Bühler maintained that self-fulfillment is the key to healthy development and that unhappy or maladjusted people are unfulfilled in some way. She emphasized the intentionality of

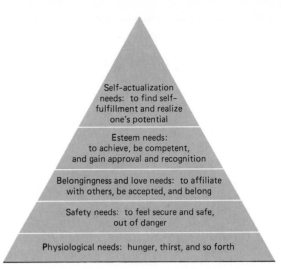

Figure 1-3 Maslow's hierarchy of needs. According to Maslow (1954), human needs have different priorities. First comes survival, represented by the physiological needs shown at the base of this pyramid. As each succeeding layer of needs is addressed, the person is motivated to address the needs at the next higher step.

human nature, with special attention to those activities that people do on their own initiative. She contended that people who lead fulfilling lives have a lifelong orientation toward goals, even though in the early years they may not be conscious of these goals. Sometimes only in looking back over their lives can people see them as a total unit, recognize expectations that they held throughout the years, and evaluate the degree to which those expectations have been met.

Bühler (1933, 1968) described five phases of goal setting and goal attainment:

1 *Childhood* (till age 15): People have not yet determined life goals; they think about the future in vague ways.
2 *Adolescence and young adulthood* (15 to 25): People first grasp the idea that their lives are their own, analyze their experiences so far, and think about their needs and their potential.
3 *Young and middle adulthood* (25 to 45–50): People adopt more specific, definite goals.
4 *Mature adulthood* (45 to 65): People take stock of their past and revise their planning for the future.

5 *Old age* (after 65 or 70): People rest from their concentration on achieving goals.

Critique of the Humanistic Perspective   The humanistic outlook offers a positive, optimistic model of humankind and its potential for development, as opposed to the negative Freudian viewpoint; and it goes deeper than learning theory in its consideration of internal factors, such as feelings, values, and hopes. Humanistic theories have made a valuable contribution by promoting child-rearing approaches that respect the child's uniqueness.

The limitations of humanistic psychology as a scientific theory rest largely on its subjectiveness. Since concepts are not clearly defined, they are difficult to communicate and to use as the basis for research designs. Furthermore, humanistic theories are incomplete in their attempt to show how human beings develop in different parts of the life span. For this reason, we cannot readily discuss humanistic theories in connection with specific periods of life.

HUMAN DEVELOPMENT: RESEARCH METHODS

Ultimately, theories must be tested by research if they are to merit the name of science. The results of the research are then used to adjust the theories; this, in turn, stimulates further research.

Researchers in different branches of the physical and social sciences use different methods. But the term *scientific method* refers to certain underlying principles that characterize *scientific* inquiry in any field: careful observation and recording of data; testing of alternative hypotheses, or different explanations for the data; and widespread public dissemination of findings and conclusions so that other observers can learn from, analyze, repeat, and build on the results. Only when developmentalists stick to these principles can they produce soundly based conclusions that satisfactorily explain and predict human behavior.

Developmentalists use a variety of nonexperimental and experimental research methods and designs for data collection when they observe people, either going about their daily lives or in special, planned situations.

Nonexperimental Methods

Nonexperimental techniques fall into five categories: case studies, naturalistic observations, clinical studies, interviews, and correlational studies.

Case Studies   *Case studies* are studies of a single case, or individual life. Much of the support for Freudian theory consists of case studies: careful notes and interpretations kept by Freud and his followers on the disclosures that their patients made under psychoanalysis. Other researchers have used published biographic materials as sources of data for case studies.

Our earliest information about infants' development comes from baby biographies, journals kept by parents to record changes in the development of their children. The first known baby biography was begun in 1601, and countless parents since then have kept such records. Charles Darwin published notes about his son, and Piaget based much of his theory about how children learn on observations of his own offspring.

Baby biographies offer useful, in-depth information, allowing developmentalists to glimpse individual personalities as they could in no other way. But baby biographies and other case studies have several shortcomings from a scientific point of view. Often they only record behavior; they do not explain it, and if they do, there is no way to test the validity of the explanations. Also, they may suffer from "observer bias," in which the recorder emphasizes some aspects of a person's development and gives short shrift to others. And, while isolated biographies may tell a great deal about individuals, it is questionable how such information applies to people in general.

Naturalistic Observation   In *naturalistic observation*, researchers observe and record people's behavior in their real-life settings (such as preschools or nursing homes), making no effort to manipulate the environment or to alter behavior. One use of such studies is to gain normative information about the occurrence of certain behaviors. To do this, researchers have observed people and recorded information about their development at various ages to derive average

Clinical studies, unlike naturalistic observation, take place away from the subject's natural setting, and the researcher may become involved in the study situation—as the psychologist Howard Gardner does in his studies of intelligence and creativity in children.

ages, or norms, for the appearance of various skills, behaviors, or growth measures.

One type of naturalistic observation is *time sampling,* a technique used to observe the occurrence of a particular type of behavior (such as aggression, babbling, or crying) at intervals throughout a given period of time. One researcher used this method to study the ways infants and their parents act with each other. He went into the homes of forty 15-month-old babies and looked around during two typical 2-hour periods on separate days. He refrained from giving the parents any guidance or instructions and just watched what went on. He had drawn up a checklist of 15 behaviors to observe in parents and 8 to observe in infants, and he recorded the presence or absence of these behaviors during alternating 15-second observe-record periods. From his observations, he concluded that mothers and fathers were more alike than different in the ways they treated their babies, that parents showed a slight preference for paying attention to a child of their own sex, that parents did more with their babies when they were alone with them than when both parents were together with them, and that the babies were more sociable when alone with one parent (Belsky, 1979).

Naturalistic studies like this one do not attempt to explain behavior or to determine its causes and effects. The study does not tell us, for example, *why* parents prefer to be with their children of their own sex, or whether a baby's being alone with one parent *causes* the baby to be more sociable. It is also important to realize that the very presence of an observer can alter the behavior being observed. To get around this problem, observers sometimes station themselves behind one-way mirrors or try to "blend in" unobtrusively with the background.

Clinical Studies The *clinical method* combines observation with flexible, individualized questioning. It differs from naturalistic observation in that the subject is not necessarily in a natural setting, and in that the researcher participates in the study situation.

Piaget developed this method to find out how children think. He explored individual children's responses to his questions by asking them follow-up questions to gain insight into the ways their minds worked. By this technique he discovered, for example, that a typical 4-year-old believed that pennies or flowers were more numerous when arranged in a line than when heaped or piled up.

This open-ended method is quite different from standardized testing techniques, which are intended to make the testing situation as similar as possible for all subjects. The clinical method is tailor-made for each person; no two people are questioned in exactly the same way. With the clinical method, an experimenter can probe further into responses that seem to be especially interesting, can use language that a particular individual understands, and can even change to the language that a child is using spontaneously.

The main drawback of the clinical method is that it depends upon the interviewer's ability to ask the right questions and to draw the right conclusions. The only check on the method is to provide it to a great number of investigators who have varying points of view and then see whether their results corroborate one another's.

Interview Method In the *interview method*, instead of being *observed*, people are asked directly to state their attitudes or opinions or to relate aspects of their life histories. By interviewing large numbers of people, investigators get a broad picture of what the people being interviewed *say* they believe or do or did. Studies using this method have focused on parent-child relationships, on sexual activities, on occupational aspirations, and on life in general.

A problem with relying on interviews alone for information is that the memory and accuracy of interviewees are often faulty. Some subjects forget when and how certain events actually took place, and others distort their replies to make them more acceptable to the interviewers or to themselves.

Correlational Studies Suppose that we want to measure the relationship between two factors: for example, between the number of hours students study for a test and the grades they get. By carefully measuring both factors—which are called variables, because they vary among members of a group or can be varied for purposes of an experiment—on a number of occasions, we might find that the more hours students spend studying, the higher the grades they get. If so, we have found a positive correlation between hours of study and grades.

Correlational studies show the direction and magnitude of a relationship between variables. That is, they can tell us whether two variables are related *positively* (that is, whether both increase or decrease together) or *negatively* (whether as one increases, the other decreases), and to what degree. Correlations are reported as numbers ranging from −1.0 (a perfect negative, or inverse, relationship) to +1.0 (a perfect positive, or direct, relationship). The higher the number (whether + or −), the stronger the rela-

tionship (either positive or negative). (A correlation of zero indicates that there is no relationship between the variables.)

A positive correlation does not tell us that increased studying *caused* better grades. In fact, the higher grades might have resulted from a third factor: a *negative* correlation between the hours of study and anxiety before taking the test. (That is, they might indicate that the more people study, the less anxious they feel and the better they do.) Correlational studies, then, do not give us information about cause and effect; only controlled experiments can do that.

Experimental Methods

An *experiment* is a rigorously controlled procedure in which the investigator, called the *experimenter*, manipulates variables to determine how one affects another. Scientific experiments must be conducted and reported in such a way that another investigator can replicate (repeat) them to verify the results and conclusions.

Suppose that we want to examine the influence of television viewing on the development of prosocial behavior (helping behavior, such as sharing). We might design an experiment comparing two groups of children: 5-year-olds who were exposed to a prosocial program, *Mr. Rogers' Neighborhood*, and a similar group of 5-year-olds who were not. We would assess both groups on measures of prosocial behavior (such as how much sharing the child does at home or school), and we could then draw conclusions about the impact that watching prosocial shows has on altruistic behaviors.

Variables and Groups In the experiment just described, we would call the viewing of *Mr. Rogers' Neighborhood* the *independent variable* and the prosocial behavior the *dependent variable*. The **independent variable**, then, is the one over which the experimenter has direct control. The **dependent variable** is the characteristic that may or may not change as a result of changes in the independent variable (in other words, it *depends* upon the independent variable). In an experiment, we manipulate the independent variable to see the effect that changes in it have on the dependent variable.

To conduct an experiment, we need two types

of groups of subjects: one or more experimental groups and one or more control groups. The **experimental group** is composed of people who will be exposed to the experimental manipulation or *treatment* (such as being shown prosocial television programs). Following exposure, the effect of the treatment on the dependent variable is measured one or more times. The **control group** is composed of people who are similar to the experimental group but who do not receive the treatment whose effects we want to measure.

Sampling and Assignment   If our experimental results do show a causal relationship between two variables, how do we know that this relationship is true *generally*, and not just for the people who are subjects of the experiment? And how can we be sure that the relationship is not due to some third factor? The answers hinge on careful selection of subjects and on how we assign them to experimental and control groups.

First of all, we must make sure that our **sample** (the group of subjects chosen for the experiment) is representative of the entire population under study (that is, of all the members of the larger group from which the sample is taken). Since we generally can't study the entire population, usually because this would be too costly and time-consuming, we want a sample that is representative of this larger group. Only if the sample is representative can we generalize the results of the experiment to the population as a whole.

Experimenters ensure representativeness by random sampling. A sample is a **random sample** if each member of the population has an equal chance of being selected. For example, if we want a sample of all the students in a human development class, we might put all their names into a hat, shake it, and then draw out the number of names we want.

Next, we should randomly *assign* these subjects to experimental and control groups. If the sample is large enough, differences in such factors as age, sex, race, IQ, and socioeconomic status will be evenly distributed so that the groups are as nearly alike as possible in every respect except for the independent variable, the one to be tested. Random assignment *controls* for all other variables (that is, prevents them from affecting the results) so that the results of our ex-

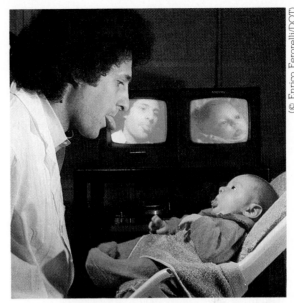

(© Enrico Ferorelli/DOT)

Experiments must be done under rigorously controlled conditions so that other researchers can replicate them and confirm or challenge the findings. K. Moore and A. N. Meltzoff videotaped infants as young as 2 weeks old apparently imitating adults by sticking their tongues out. Other researchers, however, found this to occur only in the youngest infants, suggesting that the tongue movement may be a primitive reflex rather than true imitation.

periment will reflect only the impact of the independent variable and not some other factor.

We could, of course, try to control for all the other factors we can think of that might have an effect, by deliberately matching the experimental and control groups. But no matter how carefully we match groups for certain characteristics, we will probably miss others that may turn out to be just as important. The best way to control for these unforeseen factors is to randomly assign subjects to the experimental and control groups, so that each subject has an equal chance of being assigned to either group.

Types of Experiments   There are three principal types of experiments: those conducted in the laboratory; those conducted in the field, a setting that is part of the subject's everyday life; and those that make use of naturally occurring experiences.

Currently, much research in development depends upon laboratory experiments, in which the subject is brought into a laboratory setting and is subjected to conditions that are under the experimenter's control. The subject's reaction to these conditions is recorded. It may be contrasted with the same person's behavior under different conditions or with the behavior of people who are brought into the laboratory and subjected to a different set of conditions. An example of the first type of laboratory experiment is one in which parents and children are brought into the laboratory together so that researchers can measure the strength of parent-child attachment. They look to see what happens when the mother leaves the child, when the father leaves the child, or when a stranger leaves the child. An example of the second type of laboratory experiment is one in which some children see a person behaving aggressively while other children do not; then both groups of children are measured on the degree to which they act aggressively themselves.

Laboratory experiments permit the greatest control over the situation and are the easiest studies to replicate (that is, they are the easiest for other researchers to carry out in exactly the same way). But because of the artificiality of the situation, the subjects may not always act as they would outside the laboratory.

In field experiments, experimenters introduce a change in a setting familiar to the subject, like the school or the home. For example, researchers conducting a field experiment might provide some preschool children with a special cognitive enrichment program and then compare these children's progress with that of children not included in the program.

A natural experiment compares people who have been accidentally divided into separate groups by circumstances of life—one group who were exposed to some naturally occurring event and another group who were not. Natural experiments are not true experiments, because they do not attempt to manipulate behavior; but they provide a way of studying events that cannot be created artificially. For example, it would be unethical to separate identical twins at birth merely to do an interesting experiment; but if we discover identical twins who *did* happen to be separated at birth and raised in different circumstances, we can compare the effects of different environments on people with the same heredity.

Comparing Experimentation with Other Methods Experiments have several advantages over clinical and naturalistic studies. Although clinical studies are more flexible than both experiments and naturalistic studies in the way they permit an investigator to pursue a specific topic, they are merely descriptive in nature. Only experiments can tell us about cause-and-effect relationships. In addition, the rigor of the experimental method allows studies to be replicated with different groups of subjects, so that other researchers can check the reliability of results.

By the same token, however, experiments may be designed so narrowly that they focus on one or two aspects of development and miss the overall picture. A second problem arises from the differences in the three types of experiments. Laboratory experiments, which offer the greatest possibilities for control and thus for reliability, typically have the *least* generalizability. That is, we cannot be sure that conclusions drawn from the laboratory apply to real life. Experimental manipulation shows what *can* happen if certain conditions are present: for example, that children who watch violent television shows in the laboratory *can* become more aggressive in that setting. It does not tell us what actually *does* happen in the real world: *do* children who watch a lot of "shoot-'em-ups" hit their little brothers or sisters more than children who watch a different kind of show?

Some developmentalists criticize the great emphasis in recent years on the use of laboratory experiments and the relative lack of contemporary interest in naturalistic description. Bronfenbrenner (1974) charges that developmental psychology has become "the science of the influence of one strange environmental factor or one strange person on one isolated behavior of a single child placed in a largely artificial context." He contends, therefore, that "the process of development as it naturally transpires in children growing up in actual life circumstances has been largely ignored" (in R. McCall, 1977, p. 5).

Greater understanding of human development may well result only from combining the naturalistic and experimental approaches. Researchers can observe people as they go about their everyday lives, determine what correlations exist, and then design experimental studies of the apparent relationships to assess cause and effect.

Methods of Data Collection

Information about development can be obtained by *cross-sectional*, *longitudinal*, or *sequential* studies.

Cross-Sectional Studies In a ***cross-sectional study***, people of different ages are assessed on one occasion. This kind of study provides information about differences in behavior among different age groups, rather than changes with age in the same person (which longitudinal studies show).

In one cross-sectional study, people in six age groups across the life span took a battery of cognitive tests. Middle-aged subjects scored the highest, and young children and older people scored the lowest of all the groups (Papalia, 1972). It could not be concluded from these findings, however, that when the middle-aged subjects in this study became older themselves, their scores would drop to the lower levels of the older people in the original sample. It is possible that the older cohort had poorer education or had other experiences that affected their performance. The only way to see whether or not change occurs over time is to conduct a longitudinal study.

Longitudinal Studies In a ***longitudinal study***, researchers follow the same people over a period of time, measuring them more than once to see the changes, with age, in development. The researchers may measure one specific characteristic, such as vocabulary size, IQ, height, or aggressiveness. Or they may look at several aspects of development, with an eye to assessing interrelationships among various factors. This design provides a picture of the *process* of development, rather than of its status at any given time. One classic longitudinal study was initiated by Terman on gifted children. Researchers followed the original group of young schoolchildren into late adulthood, drawing conclusions about development throughout life.

Comparing Longitudinal and Cross-Sectional Studies Longitudinal studies, then, assess *changes* undergone by one or more persons, while cross-sectional studies look at *differences* among groups of people. Each design has certain weaknesses.

One methodological shortcoming of longitudinal studies is a probable bias in the sample. People who volunteer for them tend to be of higher-than-average socioeconomic status and intelligence. Also, those who stay with a longitudinal project over a period of time tend to be more competent than those who drop out. Then there is the effect of repeated testing. People tend to do better upon subsequent administration of certain tests simply because of the "practice effect."

The cross-sectional method has its drawbacks, too. It masks differences among individuals by yielding average measures for various age groups. Its major disadvantage is that it cannot eliminate cohort, or generational, influences on subjects born at different times.

Cross-sectional studies are sometimes misinterpreted to yield information about developmental changes in groups or individuals; when this happens, such information is often misleading and may contradict that provided by longitudinal studies. For example, someone might incorrectly conclude from research like the study by Papalia discussed above that intellectual functioning declines in later years. In reality, longitudinal data would be required to determine whether the age *differences* that were found constituted actual age *changes*.

Sequential Studies The ***cross-sequential study*** is one of a number of sequential strategies that have been designed to overcome the drawbacks of longitudinal and cross-sectional studies. This method is a combination of the other two: people in a cross-sectional sample are tested more than once, and the results are analyzed to determine the differences that show up over time for the different groups of subjects. Some important research on intellectual functioning in adulthood employs sequential techniques. As we will see in Chapter 16, these techniques seem to provide a more realistic assessment than either the cross-sectional method, which tends to overestimate a drop in intellectual functioning in the later years, or the longitudinal method, which tends to underestimate it because of selective dropout and the practice effect.

Ethical Issues in Human Research

A few years ago, a doctor recommended giving psychological tests to young underprivileged children in hopes of finding signs that might predict which youngsters might someday become delinquent. These children could then be watched and given social support to forestall their criminal tendencies. Many people—justifiably, we believe—attacked the doctor's proposal, pointing out that through the principle of self-fulfilling prophecy, the children who were labeled as potential delinquents and treated differently might actually *become* delinquent as a result.

Should research that might harm the subjects ever be undertaken? What if the risk of harm is small and the opportunity to gain valuable knowledge is great? How do we balance the possible benefits to humanity against the chance of intellectual, emotional, or physical injury to individuals? Researchers confront many such ethical questions, among them questions that relate to the following principles.

Right of Privacy   Is it ethical to use one-way mirrors and hidden cameras to observe people without their knowledge? How can we protect the confidentiality of personal information (for example, about income or family relationships or even about illegal activities, like smoking marijuana or shoplifting) that subjects may reveal in interviews or questionnaires?

Right of Informed Consent   When parents or guardians consent to a child's participation, can we assume that they have acted in the child's best interests? According to one ethics panel, children aged 7 or more should be asked for their consent and should be overruled only if the research promises direct benefit to the child, such as the use of an experimental drug (National Commission for the Protection of Human Subjects of Biomedical and Behavioral Research, 1978). Similarly, when research is done on institutionalized older people, we need to make sure that the subjects are competent to give consent and are not being exploited. And what guidelines should govern research on fetuses, which, of course, cannot consent? How do we weigh the "rights" of a fetus that is about to be aborted against the possibility of learning something that may save the lives of many babies?

Avoidance of Deception   How much do subjects need to know about an experiment before their consent can be considered informed? What if children are told that they are testing a new game when they are actually being tested on their reactions to success or failure? Suppose that adults are told that they are participating in a study on learning when they are really being tested on their willingness to inflict pain on another person. Experiments like these, which cannot be done without deception, have added significantly to our knowledge—but at the expense of the subjects' right to know what they are getting involved in. And what if a subject is troubled by his or her own behavior in such an experiment? That brings us to the next point: a subject's right to self-esteem.

Right of Self-Esteem   Studies that seek to determine the limits of children's capabilities have a built-in failure factor: the investigator continues to pose problems until the child is unable to answer. How seriously might the resulting feelings of failure affect subjects' self-confidence? As another example, when researchers publish findings that middle-class youngsters are academically superior to poor children, there can be unintentional harm to the latter's self-esteem. Furthermore, such studies may become self-fulfilling prophecies, affecting teachers' expectations and students' performance.

Ethical Standards   Since the 1970s, federally mandated committees have been established at colleges, universities, and other institutions to review proposed research from an ethical standpoint. In 1982, the American Psychological Association adopted guidelines covering such points as protection of subjects from harm and loss of dignity, guarantees of privacy and confidentiality, informed consent, avoidance of deception wherever possible, the right of subjects to decline or withdraw from an experiment at any time, and the responsibility of investigators for correcting any undesirable short-term or long-term effects of participation. Nevertheless, specific situations often call for difficult judgments. Everyone in the field of human development must accept the responsibility to try to do good when possible and, at the very least, to do no harm.

A WORD TO STUDENTS

Our final word in this introductory chapter is that this entire book is far from the final word. Developmentalists are still learning about people. As you read this book, many questions will no doubt come to your mind. By pursuing your questions through thought and eventually through research, it may be that you yourself, now just embarking upon the study of human development, will someday advance this study for the benefit of all.

Human Development: The Subject and the Text

■ Human development is the scientific study of the quantitative and qualitative ways people change over time. *Quantitative change* refers to changes in *number* or *amount*, such as those in height, weight, and vocabulary. *Qualitative change* refers to changes in *kind*, such as those in the nature of a person's intelligence or memory.

■ The perspectives taken in this book include: an emphasis on human research, a practical orientation, an appreciation of the lifelong capacity for change, an acknowledgment of the resilience of human beings, and a recognition that people influence their own development.

Human Development: The Study and Its History

■ Although we can look separately at various aspects of development (for example, physical development, intellectual development, and personality and social development), we must remember that these do not occur in isolation. Each affects the other.

■ Although we have divided the human life span into eight distinct periods, the age ranges are often subjective. Individual differences must be taken into account.

■ Influences on development include both the internal (hereditary) and the external (environmental). Influences that affect large groups of people are either normative age-graded or normative history-graded influences. Nonnormative life events are those that are unusual in their occurrence or timing and often have a major impact on people's lives.

■ The concept of a critical period, or time when an event will have its greatest impact, seems more applicable to physical and especially prenatal development than to psychological development.

■ Attitudes about children were quite different in the past, and they affected how children were studied. As researchers became interested in following children's development over a longer period, into adulthood, life-span development expanded as a subject for study.

Human Development: Theoretical Perspectives

■ A theory is a set of interrelated statements about a phenomenon. In this book we consider four different groups of theories about development: psychoanalytic, mechanistic, organismic, and humanistic.

■ Theorists who take the psychoanalytic perspective are interested in the underlying forces that motivate behavior. Although they differ markedly in some of the specifics of their theories, Sigmund Freud and Erik Erikson both reflect this approach.

■ The mechanistic position holds that human beings are reactors rather than initiators, and views change as quantitative. The focus is on observable behaviors. Behaviorists and social-learning theorists reflect the mechanistic perspective. Behaviorists are interested in shaping behavior through conditioning. Social-learning theory, which stresses imitation of models, incorporates some elements of the organismic perspective.

■ The organismic position sees people as active contributors to their own development. Organismic theorists view development as occurring in a series of qualitatively different stages. Jean Piaget and Lawrence Kohlberg represent this position.

■ The humanistic perspective, represented by Abraham Maslow and Charlotte Bühler, views the individual as having the ability to foster his or her own development and to do this in a positive way through the human characteristics of choice, creativity, and self-realization.

Human Development: Research Methods

■ There are five major nonexperimental methods for studying people: case studies, naturalistic observation, the clinical method, interviews, and correlational studies. Each approach has strengths and weaknesses.

■ Controlled experiments are the only method of discovering cause-and-effect relationships. The three principal types of experiments are laboratory experiments, field experiments, and natural experiments.

■ The two major techniques of data collection are the longitudinal and the cross-sectional designs. Each has advantages and disadvantages. Sequential strategies have been developed to overcome the drawbacks of the other two designs.

■ The study of people must reflect certain ethical considerations. In a carefully designed study, the researcher considers its effect on the participants, as well as its potential benefit to the field of human development.

KEY TERMS

accommodation (page 24)
adaptation (23)
assimilation (24)
behaviorism (18)
case studies (26)
classical conditioning (18)
clinical method (27)
cognitive development (22)
conditioned response (CR) (19)
conditioned stimulus (CS) (19)
control group (29)
correlational studies (28)
critical period (10)
cross-sectional study (31)
cross-sequential study (31)
data (13)
defense mechanisms (16)
dependent variable (28)
environmental influences (9)
equilibration (24)

experiment (28)
experimental group (29)
extinction (20)
fixation (14)
heredity (9)
human development (4)
humanistic perspective (24)
hypothesis (13)
independent variable (28)
interview method (28)
longitudinal study (31)
mechanistic perspective (18)
naturalistic observation (26)
neutral stimulus (19)
operant (instrumental)
   conditioning (19)
organismic perspective (22)
organization (23)
psychoanalytic perspective (13)

psychosexual development (14)
psychosocial-development theory
   (17)
punishment (19)
qualitative changes (4)
quantitative changes (4)
random sample (29)
reinforcement (19)
sample (29)
scheme (23)
scientific method (26)
shaping (20)
social-learning theory (20)
theory (13)
unconditioned response
   (unconditioned reflex) (UCR)
   (19)
unconditioned stimulus (UCS)
   (19)

American Psychological Association. (1982). *Ethical principles in the conduct of research with human participants.* Washington, DC: American Psychological Association. A guidebook by the APA to the ethics of psychological experimentation.

Bringuier, J. (1980). *Conversations with Jean Piaget.* Chicago: University of Chicago Press. Fourteen conversations with Piaget that give insight into the man as well as his theory of cognitive development.

Erikson, E. H. (1963). *Childhood and society.* New York: Norton. A collection of Erikson's writings that includes the classic "Eight Ages of Man," in which he outlines his theory of psychosocial development from infancy through old age.

Kagan, J. (1984). *The nature of the child.* New York: Basic Books. A beautifully written and compelling argument against the idea of the irreversibility of early experience. Kagan believes that people have the ability to change throughout life and that later events transform early childhood experiences.

Masson, J. M. (1984). *The assault on truth.* New York: Farrar, Straus & Giroux. (Paperback edition, 1985, Penguin.) A controversial book which proposes that Freud suppressed evidence that some of his patients may have been sexually mistreated as children.

Mead, M., & Heyman, K. (1971). *Family.* New York: Collier-Macmillan. A warm pictorial essay by the anthropologist Margaret Mead and her colleague, the photographer Ken Heyman, that sketches the lives of mothers, fathers, brothers and sisters, grandparents, friends, and the child alone, from a cross-cultural perspective. Many expressive black-and-white photographs.

Pryor, K. (1985). *Don't shoot the dog: The new art of teaching and training.* New York: Bantam. A fascinating and practical explanation of the way principles of operant conditioning can be used to change the behavior of children, adults, and animals. The author, a trainer of dolphins, uses humor and a wealth of anecdotes to make her points.

Secunda, V. (1984). *By youth possessed: The denial of age in America.* New York: Bobbs-Merrill. A very readable, thought-provoking book by a self-admitted late bloomer which challenges the current tendency to judge people more by their chronological age than by personal characteristics, questions age norms and stages, and discusses the segregation by age that is common in American society.

2

PART

BEGINNINGS

Human development is most dramatic during its earliest stages: prenatal development, infancy, and toddlerhood. In a mere 9 months in the womb and 3 years after birth, you—like every other human being—went through a succession of changes broader in scope and more rapid in pace than any you have experienced since then or will experience throughout the rest of your life.

■ In **Chapter 2,** we see what unfolds as a new human being prepares to come into the world. We examine how conception takes place and which of the forces that will guide development are already present; how the new life grows in the womb and what influences affect it during gestation; and how some revolutionary tech-niques are being used to inter-vene in the natural process of prenatal development. Finally, we focus on the climax, birth it-self, which is not a simple event but a complex process.

After that introduction, you will learn some fascinating things about the newborn baby, who emerges into the world with impressive capabili-ties and even more impressive potential for growth. In the rest of Part Two, you will follow human development through infancy (the first 1½ or 2 years after birth); and then through toddlerhood, which is marked by the wobbling gait that gives the stage its name. As you will see, we now know more than ever before about the capabili-ties of such young children, thanks to new techniques for studying people too young to tell us what they know or think but who do, in fact, know and think a great deal.

■ In **Chapter 3,** we first look at how newborn infants make the transition from the womb to the world outside. We then explore the physical changes they un-dergo during their first 3 years and some important health con-cerns during this period.

■ In **Chapter 4,** we cover their intellectual growth, with special attention to language skills and ways in which psychologists describe and measure the intel-lectual functioning of the very young child.

■ In **Chapter 5,** we examine how babies show their emo-tions, how prominent theorists believe their personalities form, and how family life helps to shape their personal and social development.

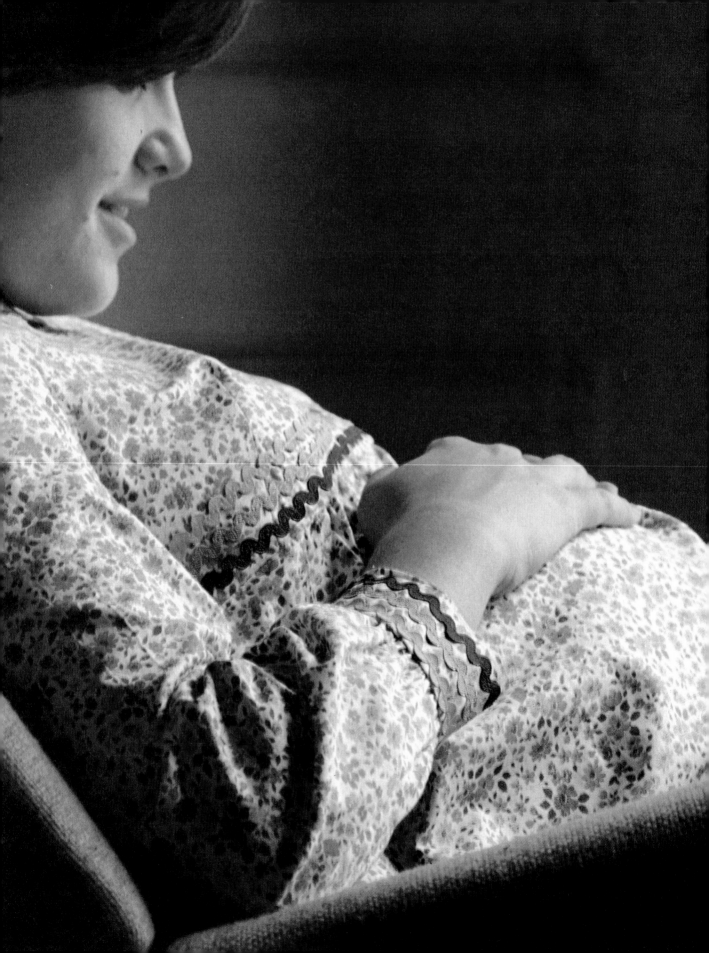

CHAPTER 2

CONCEPTION THROUGH BIRTH

If I could have watched you grow
as a magical mother might,
if I could have seen through my magical
transparent belly,
there would have been such ripening
within . . .

                              Anne Sexton, 1966

ASK YOURSELF

- How does human life begin?

- How do heredity and environment affect the new human being's sex, appearance, health, and personality?

- How do babies develop inside their mothers' bodies, and how does the prenatal environment influence their development?

- What causes birth defects and other abnormalities in newborns, and how can they be anticipated or minimized?

- What happens during birth, and how can medical intervention affect that natural process?

The beginning of human life has inspired wonder and curiosity in scientists and laypersons alike. Some of the notions that people used to hold about it seem surprising today. Between the seventeenth and nineteenth centuries, debate raged between two schools of biological thought. The homunculists believed that fully formed "little people" were contained in the heads of sperm (the male's reproductive cells), ready to grow when deposited in the nurturing environment of the womb (see Figure 2-1). The ovists held an opposed but equally incorrect view: that a female's ovaries, or reproductive glands, contained tiny, already formed humans whose growth was activated by the male's sperm. These mistaken ideas arose from misunderstandings of discoveries made by scientists who examined animal embryos and peered through rudimentary microscopes at live sperm and egg cells. During the late 1700s, the German-born anatomist Kaspar Friedrich Wolff demonstrated that embryos are not preformed in either parent and theorized that par-

ticles in both egg and sperm contribute to the formation of a new being—an idea that came to be accepted by the mid-nineteenth century.

Even today, when we know much more about the origin of life, an element of awe remains. The beginning for you, as for each of us, came long before you gave your first yell after leaving your mother's womb. Your true beginning was a split-second event when a single spermatozoon, one of millions of sperm cells from your father, joined an ovum, or egg cell, one of the hundreds of thousands of ova produced and stored in your mother's body during her lifetime.

Which sperm meets which ovum has tremendous implications for the new person: what sex it will be, what it will look like, what diseases it will be susceptible to, and even what kind of personality it may possess. For the sperm and the ovum are partial microcosms of two human beings, man and woman, whose relationship brings the new life into existence. There are also environmental influences, of course. Who the mother and father are, how they look, what tal-

Figure 2-1 Homunculus. A human sperm as imagined by a seventeenth-century scientist, who believed that the preformed embryo was contained in the head of the sperm and was enabled to grow in the nurturing environment of the womb. (*Source:* National Library of Medicine.)

ents they have, where and how they live, how they feel about each other and about parenthood—these and many other factors profoundly affect their child's development, both within and beyond the womb. Let us see how this important union takes place and what then occurs during the 9 months the new life grows inside the womb until birth.

FERTILIZATION

Fertilization, the process by which sperm cell and ovum fuse to form a single new cell, is most likely to occur about 14 days after the beginning of a woman's menstrual period. The new cell formed by the two *gametes,* or sex cells—the ovum and the sperm—is called a *zygote.* Once conceived, this single cell duplicates itself again and again by cell division.

How does fertilization take place? When a human female is born, she already has about 400,000 immature ova in her two ovaries—each ovum in its own small sac, or follicle. Although the ovum is only about one-fourth the size of the period that ends this sentence, it is the largest cell in the human body. After a female matures sexually, and until menopause, *ovulation* occurs about once every 28 days, when a mature follicle in one of her ovaries ruptures and expels its ovum. The ovum travels through the fallopian tube toward the uterus, or womb. It is in the fallopian tube that, if the ovum meets a sperm cell, fertilization normally occurs. (See Figure 2-2 on page 42 for a diagram of the female and male reproductive systems.)

In contrast to the ovum, the sperm, which is tadpole-like and only 1/600 inch from head to tail, is one of the smallest cells in the body. Furthermore, sperm are much more numerous and more active than ova; a mature male's testicles (testes), or reproductive glands, normally produce several hundred million spermatozoa each day, which are ejaculated in the semen at sexual climax.

The sperm enter the vagina and try to swim through the cervix and into the fallopian tube. Only a few of the sperm cells get that far;

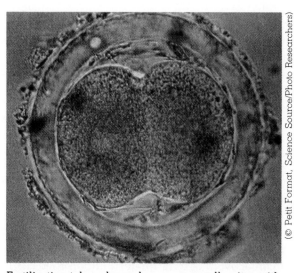

(© Petit Format, Science Source/Photo Researchers)

Fertilization takes place when a sperm cell unites with an ovum to form a single new cell. The fertilized ovum shown here has begun to grow by cell division. It will eventually differentiate into 800 billion or more cells with specialized functions.

Female

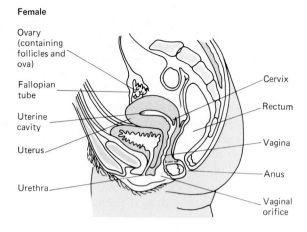

Ovary (containing follicles and ova)

Fallopian tube

Uterine cavity

Uterus

Urethra

Cervix

Rectum

Vagina

Anus

Vaginal orifice

Male

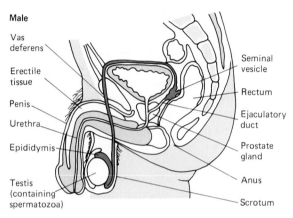

Vas deferens

Erectile tissue

Penis

Urethra

Epididymis

Testis (containing spermatozoa)

Seminal vesicle

Rectum

Ejaculatory duct

Prostate gland

Anus

Scrotum

Figure 2-2 Human reproductive systems.

any that do must penetrate a protective barrier to reach the ovum. An estimated 20 million sperm cells must enter a woman's body at one time to make fertilization likely, but only one can fertilize the ovum to conceive a new human being.

Because spermatozoa remain active (able to fertilize an ovum) for up to 48 hours and ova can be fertilized for about 24 hours, there is a "window" of at least 48 hours during each menstrual cycle—24 hours before and after the release of the ovum—when sexual relations can result in conception. (Theoretically, the window "opens" 48 hours before release of the ovum, but it is unlikely that enough sperm would remain active that long for fertilization to occur.)

If conception does not take place, the sperm cells are devoured by white blood cells in the woman's body and the ovum passes through the

uterus and exits through the vagina. (For a discussion of infertility and alternative ways to conceive, see Chapter 13.) If, however, fertilization occurs, that union of egg and sperm sets in motion powerful forces that affect the future of the new human being.

HEREDITY AND ENVIRONMENT

The Hereditary Endowment

Do you ever read your horoscope? Those popular but unreliable predictions are based on the ancient pseudo science of astrology. Astrologers claim that a new life is influenced or controlled by the positions of heavenly bodies at the moment of birth.

If we want to understand the true sources of our physical, intellectual, and emotional makeup, however, the best place to look is, as Shakespeare put it, "not in our stars, but in ourselves." The science of *genetics* is the study of *heredity*—the inborn factors, inherited from our parents, that affect our development. Genetics tells us that it is the meeting of ovum and sperm, not the crossing of heavenly orbits, which determines much of our future course. When two gametes unite to form a zygote, they endow the new life with a unique legacy.

Mechanisms of Heredity GENES AND CHROMOSOMES The basic unit of heredity is the *gene,* a bit of *DNA (deoxyribonucleic acid);* genes determine inherited characteristics. DNA carries the "program" that tells each cell in the body what specific functions it will perform and how it will perform them, in a way unique to the particular person. Human beings have as many as 150,000 genes distributed among 46 *chromosomes,* larger segments of DNA that carry the genes. Each gene appears to be located according to its function in a definite position on a particular chromosome. Half the chromosomes come from each parent, 23 from the ovum and 23 from the sperm. At the moment of conception, then, the zygote has all the biological information needed to guide its development into a complete human being.

As this single cell develops into a complex

Body cells of women and men contain 23 pairs of chromosomes.

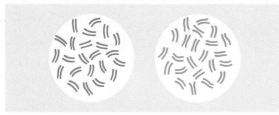

At maturity, each sex cell has only 23 single chromosomes. Through meiosis, a member is taken randomly from each original pair of chromosomes.

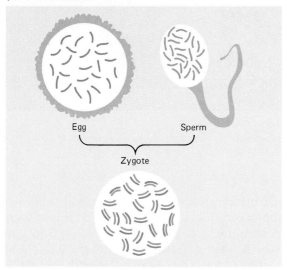

Egg

Sperm

Zygote

At fertilization, the chromosomes from each parent pair up so that the zygote contains 23 pairs of chromosomes—half from the mother and half from the father.

Figure 2-3 Hereditary composition of the zygote.

organism, with billions of cells specializing in different functions, each cell except the sex cells—through a process of cell division called *mitosis*—will have 46 chromosomes identical to those in the original zygote. Thus each has the same genetic information, which remains stable throughout life. Mature gametes, as we have seen, contain only 23 chromosomes each—the result of *meiosis*, a form of cell division in which the number of chromosomes is reduced by half (see Figure 2-3). This special type of division, which implies an almost unlimited variety of combinations of chromosomes and genes in ova and sperm, accounts for the differences in genetic makeup of children of the same parents.

WHAT CAUSES MULTIPLE BIRTHS? "Just close the windows and leave everything dark when

you go to bed," said Maria Goncalves Moreira, a mother in Brazil, citing the formula that she claims worked for her 10 times—producing 10 sets of twins ("Saturday News Quiz," 1984). The actual mechanisms responsible for multiple births are somewhat more complicated.

One mechanism involves the fertilization of two eggs. Occasionally, a woman's body releases two ova within a short time of each other. If both are fertilized, two babies will be conceived. These two infants will be known as *dizygotic* (fraternal, or two-egg) *twins.* Since they are created by different ova and different sperm cells, they are no more alike in their genetic makeup than any other siblings. They may be of the same or different sexes.

The other mechanism for producing twins is the division in two of a single ovum after it has been fertilized. The babies that result from this cell division are *monozygotic* (identical, or one-egg) *twins.* They have exactly the same genetic heritage, and any differences they will later exhibit must be due to the influences of environment. They are, of course, always of the same sex.

Other multiple births—triplets, quadruplets, quintuplets, and so forth—result from either one of these processes or a combination of both.

Identical twins seem to be born through an accident of prenatal life, with no relationship to either genetic or environmental influences. They account for one-fourth to one-third of all twins in all ethnic groups.

Fraternal twins are becoming more common because of the increased use of fertility drugs that spur ovulation and often cause the release of more than one ovum. These drugs have also caused a surge in the births of three or more babies at a time. In addition, fraternal twins are more likely to be born in third and later pregnancies, to older women, in families with a history of fraternal twins, and in various ethnic groups (Vaughan, McKay, & Behrman, 1979). Twin births are most common among black Americans (1 in 70 births), East Indians, and northern Europeans, and least common among Asians other than East Indians (1 in 150 births among Japanese and 1 in 300 among Chinese); these differences are probably due to hormonal differences in women.

Multiple births are more common today than they used to be because of the increased use of fertility drugs, and the chances of survival are better because of advances in caring for small babies. These Belgian sextuplets are celebrating their first birthday.

WHAT DETERMINES SEX?   Henry VIII of England divorced Catherine of Aragon because (among other reasons) she had borne him a daughter rather than the son he desperately wanted. It is ironic that this basis for divorce has been recognized in so many societies, since we now know that the father determines a child's sex.

To understand why, we must first realize that at conception, the 23 chromosomes received from the sperm and the 23 from the ovum align themselves in pairs. One pair are **sex chromosomes,** which determine whether the new human being will be a boy or a girl. The other 22 pairs are **autosomes,** or nonsex chromosomes.

In a female, both sex chromosomes are called *X chromosomes;* in a male, an X chromosome is paired with a smaller-sized chromosome called a Y chromosome. As a result, when meiosis occurs, an ovum can carry only an X chromosome, whereas sperm can carry either an X or a Y. When an ovum (which must carry an X) joins an X-carrying sperm, the resulting zygote contains the pair XX, which makes it female. When an ovum is fertilized by a Y-carrying sperm, the zygote has the pair XY and so is male (see Figure 2-4). Therefore, the sex of the child depends entirely on whether the sex chromosome carried by the sperm cell that fertilized the ovum was X or Y.

Until recently, geneticists did not know *how* the presence or absence of the Y chromosome determines sex. But late in 1987, a research team headed by David C. Page at the Whitehead Institute for Biomedical Research in Cambridge, Massachusetts, discovered the gene that appears to be responsible. This gene, located on the Y chromosome, apparently instructs cells to produce a chemical that—if present in large enough amounts—causes the fetus to develop as a male rather than a female.

Some differences between the sexes begin to appear at conception. About 120 to 170 males are conceived for every 100 females, but since males are more likely to be spontaneously aborted or stillborn, only 106 are born for every 100 females (U.S. Department of Health and Human Services, USDHHS, 1982). More males die during the first years, and males are more susceptible to many disorders throughout life, so that there are only 95 males for every 100 females in the United States.

A variety of hypotheses have been proposed to explain males' greater vulnerability: that the X chromosome contains genes that protect females against life stresses, that the Y chromosome contains harmful genes, or that there are different mechanisms in the sexes for providing immunity to various infections and diseases.

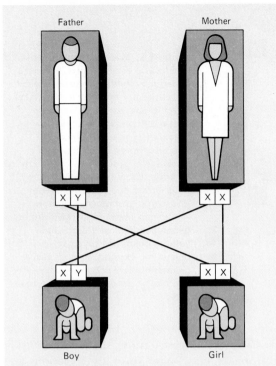

Father has an X chromosome and a Y chromosome. Mother has
two X chromosomes. Male baby receives an X chromosome from
the mother and a Y chromosome from the father. Female baby
receives X chromosomes from both mother and father.

Figure 2-4 Determination of sex. All babies receive an
X chromosome from the mother; therefore, sex is
determined by whether an X or a Y chromosome is
received from the father.

Furthermore, the male develops more slowly
from early fetal life into adulthood. At 20 weeks
after conception, he is 2 weeks behind the female; at 40 weeks he is 4 weeks behind; and he
continues to lag behind till maturity (Hutt,
1972).

Patterns of Genetic Transmission   Why does
one person have blue eyes and another brown?
Why is one person tall and another short? What
causes such defects as color blindness? To answer questions like these, we need to look more
closely at how hereditary characteristics are
transmitted through the genes.

MENDEL'S LAWS   Gregor Mendel, an Austrian
monk, conducted a series of experiments with
plants during the 1860s—before anything was
known about genes and chromosomes—that

laid the foundation for our understanding of
inheritance in all living things.

Mendel cross-pollinated purebred pea plants
that produced only yellow seeds with pea plants
that produced only green seeds. All the resulting plants produced yellow seeds. But when he
bred these hybrids, 75 percent of their offspring
had yellow seeds, while the other 25 percent had
green seeds. Mendel got the same proportions
of types when he experimented with tall and
short plants or plants with smooth and wrinkled
seeds. Mendel believed—incorrectly, as it
turned out—that this 3 to 1 ratio held true
throughout nature.

Mendel's explanation was what he called the
law of **dominant inheritance,** which holds that
when an organism inherits competing traits
(such as green and yellow coloring), only one of
the traits will be expressed. That trait is called
the *dominant* one, and the nondominant trait is
said to be *recessive*.

Mendel also tried breeding for two traits at
once. Mating plants that produced round yellow
pea seeds with plants that produced wrinkled
green ones, he found that color and shape were
transmitted independently of each other. In the
first generation, all the seeds were round and
yellow, those traits being dominant. But when
the hybrid plants self-fertilized, most of the offspring produced seeds that were yellow and
round; less than half were either yellow and
wrinkled or green and round; and the smallest
number were green and wrinkled. Thus Mendel
proved that hereditary traits are transmitted as
separate units. He called this principle the law
of **independent segregation.**

DOMINANT AND RECESSIVE INHERITANCE   With
our knowledge of genes, we can explain how
dominant inheritance and recessive inheritance
work. Genes that govern alternative expressions
of a particular characteristic (such as the color of
seeds) are called **alleles.** A plant or animal receives a pair of alleles for a given characteristic,
one from each parent. When both alleles are the
same, the organism is **homozygous** for the characteristic; when they are different, the organism
is **heterozygous.** In a heterozygous situation, the
dominant allele is expressed. **Recessive inheritance** occurs only when a homozygous organism
has received the same recessive allele from each

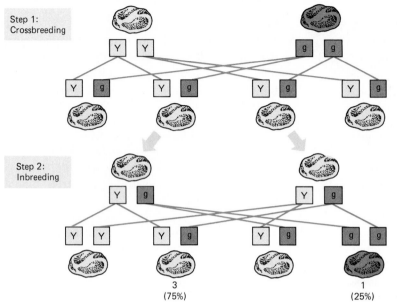

Step 1:
Crossbreeding

Step 2:
Inbreeding

3
(75%)

1
(25%)

Figure 2-5 Mendel's experiments with colors of pea seeds. Mendel's experiments with peas established the pattern of dominant inheritance. When plants are crossbred, the dominant characteristic (yellow seeds) is expressed. When the offspring breed, dominant and recessive characteristics show up in 3:1 ratio. Because of dominant inheritance, the same observable phenotype (in this case, yellow seeds) can result from two different genotypes (yellow-yellow and yellow-green). However, a phenotype expressing a recessive characteristic (such as green seeds) can have only one genotype (green-green).

parent; it is then that the recessive trait shows up.

Mendel's original purebred plants were homozygous—each had two alleles for either yellow or green. The crossbred plants were heterozygous, having inherited alleles for both colors. Since yellow is dominant and green recessive, the crossbred plants all had yellow seeds. When those hybrids reproduced, one-fourth of the offspring had two yellow alleles, half had yellow and green, and one-fourth had two green alleles. Because of the law of dominance, three out of four plants in the third generation bore yellow seeds and one bore green seeds (see Figure 2-5).

An observable trait (like the color of seeds) is called a *phenotype,* while the underlying, invisible genetic pattern that causes certain traits to be expressed is called a *genotype.* Organisms with identical phenotypes may have different genotypes, since (because of the principle of dominant inheritance) the same observable trait (like yellow seeds) can result from different genetic patterns.

The difference in genotypes explains why Mendel's first generation of homozygous yellow-seeded plants could have only yellow-seeded offspring, while the heterozygous second generation—just as consistently bearing yellow seeds—could produce some green-seeded offspring when mated with other hybrids of their generation. This difference also explains why recessive traits, such as albino skin in humans, may "skip" several generations and then suddenly show up when two people carrying the recessive gene happen to mate. (Another difficulty in detecting genotypes is that phenotypes may be modified by experience. For example, illness or malnutrition can "shrink" a person whose genetic "blueprint" calls for tallness.)

SEX-LINKED INHERITANCE AND OTHER FORMS
Dominance and recessiveness are not always absolute. We see evidence of incomplete dominance when red and white snapdragons are crossbred and pink flowers result; and in people with blood type AB, who have alleles for types A and B.

In *sex-linked inheritance,* certain recessive genes, carried on the sex chromosomes—usually the X chromosome—are transmitted differently to males and females. Red-green color blindness, for example, is a recessive trait that usually shows up only in males.

Indeed, the genetic picture in humans is far more complex than Mendel imagined. It is hard to find a single normal trait that people inherit through simple dominant transmission—unless we count the ability to curl the tongue lengthwise! Some genes, such as those for blood types A, B, and O, exist in three or more alternative forms known as **multiple alleles.** And most normal characteristics, from height and weight to intelligence, are probably affected by many genes as well as environmental factors, through a pattern called **multifactorial inheritance.**

It is in the inheritance of genetic defects and diseases that we see most clearly the operation of dominant, recessive, and sex-linked transmission in humans.

Genetic and Chromosomal Abnormalities

"Is my baby normal?" is a parent's first question, spoken or unspoken. Over 90 percent of all babies born in the United States are healthy and normal; nevertheless, each year more than 250,000 are born with physical or mental handicaps of varying degrees of severity (March of Dimes Birth Defects Foundation, 1983b). These babies account for nearly 7 percent of total births (which amounted to 3.75 million in 1985) and 20 percent of infant deaths (National Institutes of Health, NIH, 1979; Wegman, 1986). Nearly half the serious malformations involve the central nervous system.

Not all inborn conditions are exhibited at birth. Symptoms of cystic fibrosis, for example, may appear as late as 4 years of age; those of Tay-Sachs disease and sickle-cell anemia show up at 6 months or later; and glaucoma and Huntington's disease are manifested in the late thirties or later (March of Dimes Birth Defects Foundation, 1983b).

Some abnormalities or defects are transmitted genetically; some are of chromosomal origin. Some are due to mutations—alterations in genes or chromosomes. Some may be attributed to hazards in the prenatal environment or, as we'll see in Chapter 3, to traumatic events during birth. Some abnormal conditions appear to arise through the interaction of genetic predispositions and environmental factors, either before or after birth. Spina bifida (a defect in the closure of the vertebral canal) and cleft palate (incomplete fusion of the roof of the mouth or upper lip) are among the abnormalities thought to be passed on through interaction of factors. Schizophrenia, discussed later in this chapter, and hyperactivity, a behavior disorder discussed in Chapter 9, may also be transmitted multifactorially.

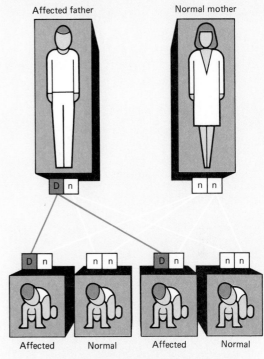

One affected parent has a single faulty gene (**D**) which *dominates* its normal counterpart (**n**).

Affected father   Normal mother

Affected   Normal   Affected   Normal

Each child's chance of inheriting either the **D** or the **n** from the affected parent is 50 percent.

Figure 2-6 Dominant inheritance.

DEFECTS TRANSMITTED BY DOMINANT INHERITANCE Usually, normal genes are dominant over those carrying abnormal traits. But sometimes this situation is reversed and an abnormal trait is carried by a dominant gene. When one parent, say the mother, has one normal gene that is recessive and one abnormal gene that is dominant and the other parent, the father, has two normal genes, each of their children will have a 50-50 chance of inheriting the abnormal gene from the mother and of having the same defect she has. (See Figure 2-6.) Every offspring who has this abnormal gene will have the defect. The defect cannot be one that kills a person before the age of reproduction: if it did, the defect could not be passed on to the next generation. Among the disorders known to be passed on this way are achondroplasia (a type of dwarfism) and Huntington's disease (a progressive degeneration of the nervous system) (March of Dimes Birth Defects Foundation, 1983b).

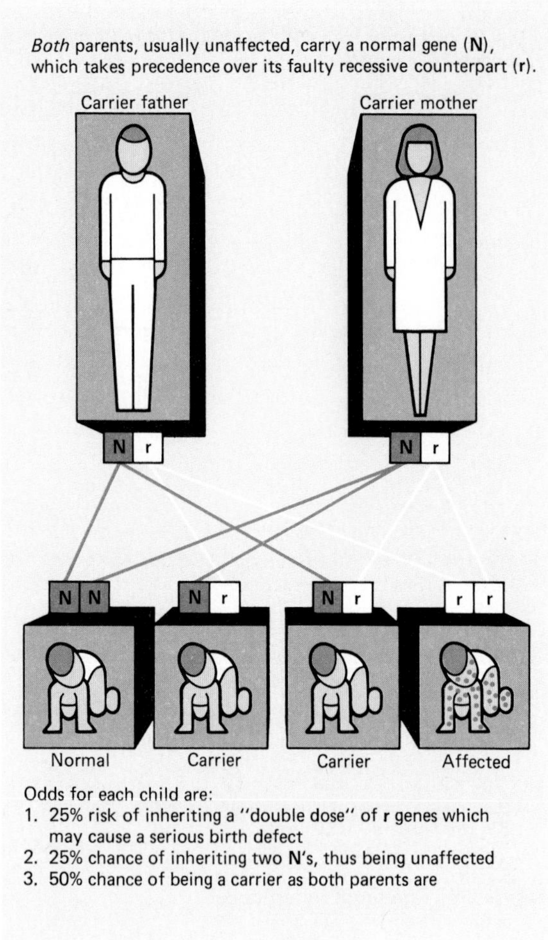

Both parents, usually unaffected, carry a normal gene (N), which takes precedence over its faulty recessive counterpart (r).

Carrier father   Carrier mother

N r   N r

N N   N r   N r   r r

Normal   Carrier   Carrier   Affected

Odds for each child are:
1. 25% risk of inheriting a "double dose" of r genes which may cause a serious birth defect
2. 25% chance of inheriting two N's, thus being unaffected
3. 50% chance of being a carrier as both parents are

Figure 2-7 Recessive inheritance.

DEFECTS TRANSMITTED BY RECESSIVE INHERITANCE Diseases transmitted by recessive genes are often killers in infancy. An example is Tay-Sachs disease, a deteriorative disease of the central nervous system that occurs mainly among Jews of eastern European ancestry.

Some apparently healthy people act as carriers of diseases and defects transmitted by recessive genes. Recessive traits show up only if a child has received the same recessive gene from each parent. When only one parent—for instance, the father—has the faulty recessive gene, none of the children will show the defect. Each child, though, will have a 50–50 chance of being a carrier like the father and of passing the recessive gene on to his or her own children. Sometimes both parents carry the faulty gene, and though both may be unaffected, they never-

theless are capable of passing it on to their children. In such cases, a child has a 25 percent chance of a birth defect and a 50 percent chance of being a carrier, like the parents (see Figure 2-7).

Inbreeding—mating of relatives—used to be common among the European upper classes, concerned about preserving their pedigrees. But these days, family members are usually discouraged from marrying. The reason for this advice is to diminish the chance of children's inheriting a disease passed on through recessive genes that both parents may have inherited from a common ancestor.

DEFECTS TRANSMITTED BY SEX-LINKED INHERITANCE Hemophilia, a blood-clotting disorder, used to be called the "royal disease," because it was prevalent among the highly inbred ruling families of Europe. Hemophilia is a sex-linked condition transmitted by a recessive gene; red-green color blindness, as we have seen, is another. Because they are carried on one of the X chromosomes of an unaffected mother, these sex-linked recessive traits almost always show up only in male children, who have no countermanding dominant trait on the Y chromosome.

The sons of a normal man and a woman with one abnormal gene will have a 50 percent chance of inheriting the abnormal X chromosome and the disorder, and a 50 percent chance of inheriting the mother's normal X chromosome and being unaffected. Daughters will have a 50 percent chance of being carriers. (See Figure 2-8.) An affected father can never pass on such a gene to his sons, since he contributes a Y chromosome to them; but he can pass the gene on to his daughters, who then become carriers.

ABNORMAL CHROMOSOMES Most of the time, chromosomal development proceeds normally, but in those exceptional cases when something does go wrong, serious abnormalities may develop. Some chromosomal defects are inherited; others result from accidents that occur during the development of an individual organism. Accidental abnormalities are not likely to recur in the same family.

Certain relatively rare chromosomal disorders of varying degrees of severity are caused

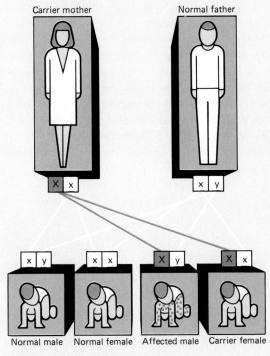

In the most common form, the female sex chromosomes of an unaffected mother carry one faulty gene (**X**) and one normal one (**x**). The father has normal male x and y chromosome complement.

Carrier mother   Normal father

| X | x | | x | y |

Normal male   Normal female   Affected male   Carrier female

| x | y | | x | x | | X | y | | X | x |

Odds for each *male* child are:
1. 50% risk of inheriting the faulty **X** and the disorder
2. 50% chance of inheriting normal x and y chromosomes

Odds for each *female* child are:
1. 50% risk of inheriting one faulty **X**, to be a carrier like mother
2. 50% chance of inheriting no faulty gene

Figure 2-8 Sex-linked inheritance.

by either a missing (O) or an extra sex chromosome (either X or Y). Examples are Klinefelter's syndrome (with the pattern XXY), Turner's syndrome (with the pattern XO, and thus missing a second sex chromosome), and the XYY and XXX syndromes. The most obvious effects are sexually related characteristics (underdevelopment, sterility, or the appearance of secondary sex characteristics of the other sex). In addition, children with these disorders, while not usually seriously retarded, often have reading problems and general learning disabilities ("Long-Term Outlook," 1982).

Down syndrome is the most common of many chromosomal disorders that are not sex-related.

The most obvious sign of this disorder is a downward-sloping skin fold at the inner corners of the eyes. Other signs are a small head; a flat nose; a protruding tongue; defective heart, eyes, and ears; and mental and motor retardation.

About 1 in every 800 babies born alive has Down syndrome. Older parents are at increased risk for bearing children with this disorder. Among 25-year-old mothers, the chances are 1 in 2000; for 40-year-olds, 1 in 100; and for mothers 45 and older, 1 in 40. The risk also rises with the age of the father: slowly up to age 49, sharply among men 55 and over (Abroms & Bennett, 1981).

The disorder—usually caused by an extra twenty-first chromosome—is hereditary only about 3 percent of the time, more likely when the affected child is born to younger parents; when the parents are older, the defect is more often a chromosomal accident. The mistake in chromosome distribution may occur during development of the ovum, the sperm, or the zygote (D. W. Smith & Wilson, 1973).

So far, almost all research into the causes of the syndrome has concentrated on the mother's role. Researchers have suggested that the ova of some women deteriorate with advancing age, that younger mothers of babies with Down syndrome may be characterized by acceleration of biological aging, and that seasonal variations in the births of these babies may be related to seasonal fluctuation in women's hormonal levels (Emanuel, Sever, Milham, & Thuline, 1972; L. Holmes, 1978; Janerick & Jacobson, 1977; M. J. Robinson et al., 1974). More recent research, however, has shown that more than 1 case in 4 may be traceable to the father (Abroms & Bennett, 1981). Now that newer techniques for identifying parental chromosomes have shown a greater paternal involvement, more attention will no doubt be paid to finding the mechanism behind the father's contribution.

People with Down syndrome are usually mildly or moderately retarded. Many children with Down syndrome can be taught skills that will allow them to support themselves as adults, and these children's progress has caused educators to revise their expectations upward (Hayden & Haring, 1976). Because of improvements in medical treatment, more than 70 percent of

(© Tony Mendoza/Picture Cube)

Children with Down syndrome—about 1 in every 800 born—often have greater intellectual potential than was recognized in the past. With loving care and patient teaching, many of these children have made considerable progress.

people with the syndrome live at least until age 30 (Baird & Sadovnick, 1987). Support groups have helped parents learn about and deal with the condition (Abroms & Bennett, 1981).

The Influence of Heredity and Environment

From what you have read so far, you might have the impression that almost everything about human beings—the way they look, the way their minds work, and the way they feel—is determined at the moment of conception. Actually, of course, heredity is only part of the story. Environment also plays a critical role in making people what they are and what they will become.

Nature versus Nurture Which makes more difference—nature or nurture, heredity or environment? That issue has been debated for decades. The answer differs for different traits.

Certain physical characteristics, like eye color and blood type, are clearly inherited. But more complex traits affecting health, intelligence, and personality are subject to an interplay of forces. How much is inherited? How much is environmentally influenced?

These questions matter very much because they may affect the way parents and caregivers behave. If we discover that a baby's intelligence can be enhanced by environmental factors, we can try to make the environment as favorable as possible. On the other hand, if we find that a child's activity level is determined mainly by heredity, we can be realistic in our expectations for children. And if we find that a certain birth defect is hereditary, we can better counsel prospective parents. (See Box 2-1, pages 52–53.)

HOW HEREDITY AND ENVIRONMENT INTERACT
The answer to the question "Nature or nurture?" is rarely "either-or." Which of the two makes the greater difference may depend on many factors. For example, the different-shaded bands in Figure 2-9 illustrate how these two forces, in varying degrees, can cause or contribute to mental retardation.

Figure 2-9 How nature and nurture can contribute to intellectual retardation. As colors can be mixed to different shades and intensities, so heredity and environment interact to varying degrees to shape a trait such as intellectual retardation. (*Source:* Adapted from Anastasi, 1958.)

NATURE
Hereditary defect causes mental retardation. Superior environment has no salutary effect.
Hereditary defect or disease (deafness, long-term illness) interferes with normal life and may contribute to retarded development.
Inherited factors that have social implications (color, sex, body build) may affect environment and limit opportunities for personal development.
Lower social class, poor education, or emotional deprivation may stunt intellectual development.
Birth injury or prenatal insult causes physical problem that interferes with regular schooling and retards development.
Birth injury or prenatal insult is so massive that it causes mental retardation despite normal, healthy genetic endowment.
NURTURE

In considering the nature-nurture controversy, it is helpful to think in terms of a **reaction range**—the potential variability in the expression of a hereditary trait, depending on environmental conditions. Even if heredity controls a particular trait, the genetic instructions may allow some latitude. For example, body size is genetically regulated, but a range of body sizes is possible depending on the nutrition of the growing child. In societies where there is a sudden improvement in dietary standards, it is common to see an entire generation of people tower over their parents. The better-fed children share their parents' genes; but within the range those genes allow, the youngsters have responded to their healthier world. Conversely, as we saw in discussing phenotypes, growth may be stunted as a result of illness or malnutrition; in that case, environmental factors hold the response near the lower end of the genetic range.

MATURATION One reason it is so difficult to untangle the relative effects of heredity and environment is that human beings change from the moment of birth. Whereas some changes seem to be affected by environmental influences, others are very clearly programmed by the genes. We know, for example, that such motor behaviors as crawling, walking, and running develop in that order at certain approximate ages. *Maturation* is the unfolding of such a biologically determined, age-related sequence of behavior patterns. Behaviors that depend largely on maturation generally appear when the organism is ready—not before, and rarely afterward.

Yet environmental forces can affect this hereditary timetable, particularly when they take extreme forms, such as long-term deprivation. This effect was seen in infants in Iranian orphanages, who received little attention and no exercise. These babies sat up and walked quite late, compared with Iranian children who were well cared for (Dennis, 1960). Yet even under these extreme conditions, maturation did occur, though at a slowed pace.

It is in the development of intellect and personality that the balance between nature and nurture appears most delicate. Consider language, for example. Maturation dictates that

(© Michael Nichols/Magnum)

Identical twins are more concordant (similar) than fraternal twins in many personality characteristics, suggesting a hereditary basis for such traits. The "Jim" twins (one shown here with his wife, the other with his fiancée) were reared apart by adoptive parents, who named them both James. Before they were reunited, each drank the same brand of beer, each had a carpentry workshop, and each had built a bench around a tree in his yard. Coincidentally, both married and later divorced women named Linda.

before children can talk, they have to reach a certain level of neurological and muscular development. No matter how enriched their home life might be, at the age of 6 months they cannot speak the sentence you are reading. Yet environment does play a large part in language development. If parents encourage children's first unintelligible sounds by talking back to them, children start to speak earlier than if their early vocalizing is ignored. Heredity, then, draws the blueprint for development, but environment affects the pace at which "construction" proceeds and even the specific form of the structure.

How the Relative Effects of Heredity and Environment Are Studied Researchers use a number of methods to discover the relative influences of heredity and environment on various traits. These include:

■ *Studies of twins.* If a trait is basically hereditary, identical twins, who have the exact same genetic legacy, should be more *concordant* (simi-

BOX 2-1 PRACTICALLY SPEAKING

GENETIC COUNSELING

When Bill and Mary Brown decided to have a baby, Mary had no trouble becoming pregnant. The couple turned their study into a nursery and eagerly looked forward to bringing its occupant home. But the baby never entered that brightly decorated nursery. She was born dead, a victim of a fatal birth defect.

The young couple were heartbroken. Furthermore, they were afraid to try again. They were afraid that they might not be able to conceive a normal child, and they felt that they could not go through another crushing disappointment.

Genetic counseling was developed to help couples— like Mary and Bill—who have some reason to believe that they may be at high risk of bearing a child with a birth

Through genetic counseling, a couple can learn about the risk of bearing a child with a birth defect. Besides performing laboratory tests, the counselor takes a family history.

defect. People who have already borne one handicapped child, who have family histories of hereditary illness, or who suffer from conditions known or suspected to be inherited can get information through genetic

counseling that will help them determine their chances of producing afflicted children in the future. A great deal of progress has been made in developing tests to identify carriers of genetic defects.

The genetic counselor may

---

lar) in regard to that trait than fraternal twins, who are no more alike genetically than any brother and sister. Identical twins who have been raised in different homes are sought as subjects for such studies, to single out the factor of heredity from that of environment. But such people are hard to find, and often their environments turn out to be culturally similar.

■ *Consanguinity studies.* By examining as many blood relatives as possible in a particular family, we can discover the degree to which they share certain characteristics and whether the closeness of the relation affects the degree of similarity. This is also called the *pedigree* method.

■ *Adoption studies.* When adopted children are

more like their biological parents and siblings, we see the influence of heredity; when they resemble their adoptive families more, we see the influence of environment.

■ *Prenatal studies.* By investigating relationships between various conditions in offspring and their mothers' experiences during pregnancy, we can often pinpoint a specific cause for a specific condition.

■ *Comparisons of actual histories.* By interviewing parents about their child-rearing practices (remembering to discount the effects of faulty and distorted memories!) and by comparing other life-history factors, researchers can sometimes isolate specific environmental influences on specific characteristics.

■ *Manipulating the environment.* By making

be a pediatrician, an obstetrician, a family doctor, or a genetic specialist. He or she takes a thorough family history. Then both parents and any children in the family receive physical examinations, since a person's physical appearance often gives a clue to the presence of certain genetic abnormalities.

Sophisticated laboratory investigations of a patient's blood, skin, urine, or fingerprints may also be indicated. Chromosomes prepared from a patient's tissue are analyzed, then photographed. Enlarged photographs of the chromosomes will then be cut out and arranged according to size and structure on a chart called a *karyotype* to demonstrate any chromosomal abnormalities that may exist.

On the basis of all these tests, the counselor determines the mathematical odds for this couple's having an afflicted child. If a couple feel that the risks are too high, the husband or wife sometimes chooses to be sterilized or the couple may consider adoption or artificial insemination by donor (see Chapter 13).

A genetic counselor should not give a couple advice on whether to take the risks indicated for the condition in question. Rather, the counselor should help a couple understand the mathematical risks and the implications of particular diseases and defects and make them aware of possible alternative courses of action.

Some people think that a 25 percent risk of inheriting a recessive disease, for example, means that if the first child is affected, then the next three children will not be similarly affected. But the saying "Chance has no memory" applies here. A 25 percent risk means that the odds are 1 out of 4 for *every* child born of the union to inherit the disease. If a disorder is not extremely disabling or is amenable to treatment, a couple may choose to take a chance. In other cases, counseling will enable a couple to realize that the risk they fear so much is actually quite slight or even nonexistent. In the future, geneticists hope that they will be able to do much more to help parents; they even hope to be able to modify abnormal genetic structure in order to cure inherited genetic defects.

The National Clearinghouse for Human Genetic Diseases, Department of Health and Human Services, can answer questions relating to genetics and genetic diseases. It has a library on the topic and makes available a directory of places that offer genetic counseling. The address of the clearinghouse is 805 15th Street, Suite 500, P.O. Box 28612, Washington, DC 20050. Other information and services are available from the March of Dimes Birth Defects Foundation, 1275 Mamaroneck Avenue, White Plains, NY 10605, or from local chapters of the March of Dimes.

changes in diet, opportunities for exercise, intellectual enrichment, and sensory stimulation in one group of animals or people and then comparing this group with a control group, we can draw conclusions about the effects of such environmental differences.

■ *Selective breeding of animals.* If animals can be bred for certain characteristics (such as the ability to run mazes or the tendency to become obese), we conclude that the trait is at least partly hereditary. In some cases, we can generalize the findings to human beings.

Our ability to manipulate either the heredity or the environment of human beings is, of course, limited by both ethical and practical considerations. We cannot, for example, mate human beings for selective characteristics, and we would not separate identical twins, make adoption placements, institutionalize children, or prescribe questionable drugs to pregnant women for experimental purposes. Therefore we often have to rely on animal studies or after-the-fact observations of events that have occurred naturally.

Some Characteristics Influenced by Heredity and Environment In September 1980, Robert Shafran, who was 19 years old, enrolled as a first-year student in a college in New York. For two days, students he had never met before greeted him like an old friend and called him "Eddy." Finally one showed him a snapshot of Eddy Galland, who had attended the same school the year before. Bobby Shafran said later, "What I saw was a photograph of myself." The story became even more startling when a third look-alike, named David Kellman, turned up, and the three youths learned that they were identical triplets who had been separated at birth and adopted by different families (Battelle, 1981).

PHYSICAL AND PHYSIOLOGICAL TRAITS The many instances of mistaken identity among identical twins attest to their carbon-copy physical appearance. Identical twins also have a number of other physiological traits in common, supporting a belief that these characteristics are genetically determined. For example, identical twins are more concordant (similar) than fraternal twins in their rates of breathing, perspiration, and pulse and in their blood pressure (Jost & Sontag, 1944). When both identical and fraternal twins were measured with respect to galvanic skin response (GSR), which records the rate of electrical changes in the skin, identical twins showed greater concordance than did fraternal twins (Lehtovaara, Saarinen, & Jarvinen, 1965).

Height and weight can both be environmentally influenced, but they seem to be determined primarily by heredity, since identical twins reared together or apart are more similar in both these measures than are fraternal twins reared together. The correlation is not quite so strong for weight as it is for height (Mittler, 1969; H. H. Newman, Freeman, & Holzinger, 1937). However, when weight is measured against height, it appears that the tendency to obesity is 80 percent genetic, and that tendency continues throughout adult life. A recent study of 4000 pairs of male twins over a 25-year span found that identical twins were twice as concordant for being overweight as were fraternal twins, both at age 25 and at age 40 (Stunkard, Foch, & Hrubec, 1986). This does not mean that environment has no influence; what it means is that people genetically "at risk" of obesity must work harder not to get fat.

Identical twin girls are likely to begin to menstruate within a couple of months of each other, but fraternal twin sisters show a mean difference of a year for the age of menarche, or first menstruation (Petri, 1934). Even our days on earth may be numbered by our genes, since se-

nescence (the process of growing old) and death occur at more similar ages for identical twins than for fraternal twins (Jarvik, Kallmann, & Klaber, 1957). And a recent adoption study revealed that adopted children (born between 1924 and 1926) whose *biological* parents died before age 50 had twice the risk of dying prematurely than adopted children whose biological parents were alive at age 50 (Sorensen, Nielsen, Andersen, & Teasdale, 1988).

INTELLIGENCE Researchers have probably studied intelligence more extensively than all other characteristics combined (Plomin, 1983). The evidence, mostly from twin studies or adoption studies, points to the great importance of genetic influences on intelligence, which appear to become more manifest with age.

In the Texas Adoption Project, Horn (1983) studied the IQs of adopted children, aged 3 to 10 and over, their adoptive parents, and their biological mothers. The resemblance between the children and their birth mothers, from whom they had been separated since they were under 1 week old, was *twice* that found between the children and the adoptive parents, who had raised them from birth.

In the Minnesota Adoption Study, Scarr and Weinberg (1983) compared IQ scores of adopted children with those of their adoptive siblings and parents, and related them to the educational levels of their biological mothers (whose IQs were not known). Young siblings scored similarly, whether related by blood or adoption, but adolescents' scores had zero correlation with those of their adoptive siblings. Furthermore, the adolescents' IQs correlated more highly with their biological mothers' levels of schooling than with their adoptive parents' IQs. The researchers concluded that family environments are more important for younger children, but that older adolescents find their own niches in life on the basis of innate abilities and interests.

The Louisville Twin Study followed 500 pairs of twins, both identical and fraternal, and their siblings from infancy to adolescence (R. S. Wilson, 1983). For these youngsters, genetic influences became more important with age. Identical twins became increasingly similar in IQ, while fraternal twins regressed to lower levels of concordance, comparable to those between any two siblings. This study also found that individual children followed their own distinct patterns of "spurts and lags" in mental development. The home environment had some impact, but not to the same degree as hereditary factors.

PERSONALITY If we define *personality* as "the pattern of collective character, behavioral, temperamental, emotional and mental traits of an individual" (*American Heritage Dictionary*, 1971), we realize that we are talking about something so complicated that it would be impossible to ascribe it all to one major influence, either hereditary or environmental. But specific aspects of personality appear to be inherited, at least in part (Tellegren, Lykken, Bouchard, Wilcox, Segal, & Rich, in press).

In 1956, two psychiatrists and a pediatrician (A. Thomas, Chess, & Birch, 1968; A. Thomas & Chess, 1984) launched the New York Longitudinal Study. By closely following 133 children from infancy into early adulthood, the researchers concluded that *temperament*, or a person's basic style of approaching and reacting to situations, appears to be inborn.

They looked at such characteristics as a baby's activity level; regularity in biological functioning (for hunger, sleep, and bowel movements); readiness to accept new people and new situations; adaptability to changes in routine; sensitivity to noise, bright lights, and other sensory stimuli; tendency toward cheerfulness or unhappiness; intensity of responses; distractibility; and degree of persistence.

They found that babies vary enormously in all these characteristics, almost from birth, and that these variances tend to continue, as we'll see in Chapter 5. However, many children show changes in behavioral style, apparently reacting to special experiences or parental handling.

Using twin-study and adoption methods, other researchers have established evidence for genetic influences for such wide-ranging personality characteristics as extroversion and introversion, emotionality, and activity (Vandenberg, 1967); depression, psychopathic behaviors, and social introversion (Gottesman, 1963, 1965); anxiety and obsession (Gottesman, 1962; Inouye, 1965); neuroticism (Eysenck & Prell, 1951; Slater, 1953); shyness (Daniels & Plomin, 1985); some fears (R. Rose & Ditto, 1983); and leadership ability (Tellegren et al., in

press). Identical twins show more similar responses than fraternal twins to the Rorschach test, an inkblot test used to assess personality. Hyperactivity (see Chapter 8), sleepwalking (see Chapter 5), bed-wetting (see Chapter 7), nail biting, and car sickness (Bakwin, 1970, 1971a, 1971b, 1971c, 1971d) also seem to have a genetic base.

Some Disorders Influenced by Heredity and Environment ALCOHOLISM Alcoholics may be largely born, not made. Studies, done in the past decade, suggest that alcoholism runs in families and that a heightened risk results from the interaction of genetic factors with environmental ones. The studies show that there is significantly higher concordance for alcoholism in identical than in fraternal twins. Also, sons of alcoholics are 4 times as likely as sons of nonalcoholics to become alcoholics themselves, even when they are adopted at birth, and regardless of whether the adoptive parents are alcoholics. Children whose adoptive parents are alcoholics but whose biological parents are nonalcoholics do not appear to be unusually at risk (Schuckit, 1985, 1987). Thus, although "no one is predestined to become an alcoholic, . . . genetic factors increase or decrease the level of vulnerability" (p. 2616).

Just what mechanisms are involved is a question that needs further study. Tests of preteen boys and young men from families of alcoholics indicate a lowered reaction to ethanol in the blood, which may interfere with the ability to learn when to stop drinking. The implication is that alcoholism should be regarded as a biologically influenced problem, not a moral weakness, and alcoholics as people who need help. Children of alcoholics should be warned that they may not be able to handle liquor as their peers do.

SCHIZOPHRENIA *Schizophrenia* is a blanket term for a complex of mental disorders marked by a loss of contact with reality and characterized by such symptoms as hallucinations, delusions, and other types of thought disorder. From many studies seeking to determine its causes, evidence has emerged for a strong hereditary element. The biological children of schizophrenic mothers are more likely to suffer from the disorder themselves than are people in the general population; identical twins are more likely to be concordant for it than are fraternal twins; and the closer a biological relation one is to a person with schizophrenia, the more likely a person is to develop it (Gottesman & Shields, 1966; Heston, 1966; Kallman, 1953; Mittler, 1971).

Although there is, then, strong evidence of biological transmission of schizophrenia, we have to ask why not all identical twins are concordant for this trait. One answer may be that it is not the illness itself that is transmitted, but a predisposition toward it. If certain environmental stresses occur in the life of someone who is so genetically predisposed, that person may respond to these stresses by developing schizophrenia. At this time, we do not know either the actual genetic mechanisms involved in transmitting such a predisposition or the precise stresses that act as its trigger.

INFANTILE AUTISM **Infantile autism** is a developmental disorder characterized by a lack of responsiveness to other people. It develops within the first 2½ years of life, sometimes as early as the fourth month, when a baby may lie in the crib, apathetic and oblivious to other people. Boys are 3 times more likely than girls to be afflicted with autism. An autistic baby does not cuddle, does not make eye contact with caregivers, and either treats adults as interchangeable or clings mechanically to one person. Such a child may never learn to speak but may be able to sing a wide repertory of songs.

Parents often think that autistic children are deaf, brain-damaged, or mentally retarded. Many, in fact, *are* retarded; only 30 percent have IQs of 70 or more. They often, however, perform well on tasks requiring manipulative or visual-spatial skill, and may display unusual feats of memory (like being able to memorize entire train schedules). Their behavior is often bizarre: they may scream when their place at the table is changed, insist on always carrying a particular rubber band, clap their hands constantly or engage in other repetitive behavior, or show a fascination with moving objects, staring for hours, for example, at an electric fan.

One in six autistic children make an adequate adjustment and can do some kind of work as adults. One in six make a fair adjustment. The other two-thirds remain severely incapacitated. Certain drugs sometimes help these children, when given along with intensive education and behavior therapy (Geller, Ritvo, Freeman, & Yuwiler, 1982).

Fortunately, autism is very rare (about 3 cases per 10,000 people). Although a number of environmental causes (such as cold, unresponsive parents) have been hypothesized, autism is now recognized as a neurobiological disorder (DSM III, 1980), sometimes associated with epilepsy and mental retardation and with rubella during the mother's pregnancy.

Autism tends to affect siblings: one study found a concordance of about 96 percent among identical twins and 23 percent among fraternal twins. This pattern suggests that autism is inherited, that it may be associated with a recessive gene, and that the contribution of the environment to the condition is minimal (Ritvo, Freeman, Mason-Brothers, Mo, & Ritvo, 1985).

DEPRESSION **Depression** is an emotional disorder characterized by feeble responses to stimuli, low initiative, and sullenness or despondency. Depressed people are sad and have difficulty eating, sleeping, and concentrating. In any 6-month period, 6 percent of American adults will experience depression at some time, and the condition is more prevalent among women than among men (J. K. Myers et al., 1984). Children, too, may become depressed (see Chapter 9) and, although the extent of childhood depression is difficult to determine, it has been reported even in infants.

Although the condition has often been regarded as an overreaction to life's sorrows, a physical basis for depression has now been demonstrated. Laboratory experiments show that the use of a chemical inhibitor to increase levels of acetylcholine in the brain can temporarily induce or increase depression. (Acetylcholine is a neurotransmitter, one of several chemicals in the brain that help transmit messages between nerve cells and also control emotions.) Depressive episodes also seem to be an occupational hazard for agricultural workers who are exposed for prolonged periods to insecticides containing similar chemical inhibitors. Apparently, the cells of depressed patients and their similarly disturbed relatives are more sensitive to acetylcholine than the cells of people without such a history (Nadi, Nurnberger, & Gershon, 1984). Some depressed people have been helped by medications that restore their chemical balance.

This evidence of a selective chemical influence suggests the probability of a reaction range, a genetically varied response to the same chemical stimulus. Studies of twins also offer strong support for the hypothesis of a genetic basis of depression. Identical twins have a 70 percent concordance rate; fraternal twins, other siblings, and parents and their children have about a 15 percent concordance rate (USDHHS, 1981b).

Although much work remains to be done before the sources of depression are fully understood, we can see many of the classic elements of a nature-nurture interaction emerging. Nature establishes a biochemical sensitivity in certain people; the environment affects the probability of encountering a particular chemical. Because of hereditary factors, different people respond to the same environment in different ways.

PRENATAL DEVELOPMENT

Many overlapping influences, then—both hereditary and environmental—affect each person from the moment of conception on. Some of the most far-reaching of these come to bear during the prenatal period, long before an infant enters the world beyond the womb.

Stages of Prenatal Development

Prenatal development proceeds according to a genetic blueprint that directs the construction of an extremely complex being from what starts out as only a single cell. This development before birth, called gestation, takes place in three stages: germinal, embryonic, and fetal. A month-by-month description is given in Table 2-1 (pages 58–59). Let's look at some of the highlights of each stage.

Germinal Stage (Fertilization to 2 Weeks)

During the *germinal stage*, the organism divides, becomes more complex, and is implanted in the wall of the uterus.

Within 36 hours after fertilization, the single-celled zygote enters a period of rapid cell division. Seventy-two hours after fertilization, it has divided into 32 cells; a day later it has divided into 70 cells. Cell division continues until the original cell has given way to an estimated 800 billion or more cells that make up the adult human body.

While the fertilized ovum is dividing, it also is making its way down the fallopian tube to the uterus, a journey that takes 3 or 4 days. By the time it gets there, its form has changed into a fluid-filled sphere, a blastocyst, which then floats freely in the uterus for a day or two. Some cells around the edge of the blastocyst cluster on one side to form the embryonic disk, a thickened cell mass from which the baby will develop. This mass is already differentiating into two layers. The upper layer, the ectoderm, will eventually become the outer layer of skin, the nails, the hair, the teeth, the sensory organs, and the nervous system, including the brain and spinal cord. The lower layer, the endoderm, will develop into the digestive system, liver, pancreas, salivary glands, and respiratory system. Later, a middle layer, the mesoderm, will develop and differentiate into the inner layer of skin, muscles, skeleton, and excretory and circulatory systems.

During the germinal stage, other parts of the blastocyst develop into the nurturing and protective organs: the placenta, the umbilical cord, and the amniotic sac. The placenta, an organ with several important functions, is connected to the embryo by the umbilical cord, through which it delivers oxygen and nourishment to the fetus and removes its body wastes. The placenta also helps to combat internal infection and protects the unborn child from various diseases. It produces the hormones that support pregnancy, prepare the mother's breasts for lactation, and eventually stimulate the uterine contractions that will expel the baby from her body. The amniotic sac, a fluid-filled membrane, encases the developing baby, protecting it and giving it room to move.

The trophoblast, the outer cell layer of the blastocyst, produces tiny threadlike structures that penetrate the lining of the uterine wall. In this way, the blastocyst burrows in until it is implanted in a nesting place where it will receive

TABLE 2·1 DEVELOPMENT OF EMBRYO AND FETUS

APPROXIMATE DATE	DESCRIPTION
1 month	During the first month, the new life has grown more quickly than it will at any other time during its lifetime, achieving a size 10,000 times greater than the zygote. It now measures from ¼ to ½ inch in length.
	Blood is flowing through its tiny veins and arteries. Its minuscule heart beats 65 times a minute. It already has the beginnings of a brain, kidneys, a liver, and a digestive tract. The umbilical cord, its lifeline to its mother, is working. By looking very closely through a microscope, it is possible to see the swellings on the head that will eventually become its eyes, ears, mouth, and nose. Its sex cannot yet be distinguished.
2 months	The embryo now looks like a well-proportioned, small-scale baby. It is less than 1 inch long and weighs only $\frac{1}{13}$ ounce. Its head is one-half its total body length. Facial parts are clearly developed, with tongue and teeth buds. The arms have hands, fingers, and thumbs, and the legs have knees, ankles, and toes. It has a thin covering of skin and can even make hand and foot prints.
	The embryo's brain impulses coordinate the function of its organ systems. Sex organs are developing; the heartbeat is steady. The stomach produces digestive juices; the liver, blood cells. The kidneys remove uric acid from the blood. The skin is now sensitive enough to react to tactile stimulation. If an aborted 8-week-old embryo is stroked, it reacts by flexing its trunk, extending its head, and moving back its arms.
3 months	The developing person, now a fetus, weights 1 ounce and measures about 3 inches in length. It has fingernails, toenails, eyelids (still closed), vocal cords, lips, and a prominent nose. Its head is still large—about one-third its total length—and its forehead is high. Its sex can easily be determined.
	The organ systems are functioning, so that the fetus may now breathe, swallow amniotic fluid in and out of the lungs, and occasionally urinate. Its ribs and vertebrae have turned to cartilage, and its internal reproductive organs have primitive egg or sperm cells.
	The fetus can now make a variety of specialized responses: it can move its legs, feet, thumbs, and head; its mouth can open and close and swallow. If its eyelids are touched, it squints; if its palm is touched, it makes a partial fist; if its lip is touched, it will suck; and if the sole of the foot is stroked, the toes will fan out. These reflex behaviors will be present at birth but will disappear during the first months of life.
4 months	The body is catching up to the head, which is now only one-fourth the total body length, the same proportion it will be at birth. The fetus now measures 6 to 10 inches and weighs about 7 ounces. The umbilical cord is as long as the fetus and will continue to grow with it. The placenta is now fully developed, and all organs are formed.
	The mother may be able to feel the fetus kicking, a movement known as *quickening*, which some societies and religious groups consider the beginning of human life. The reflex activities that appeared in the third month are now brisker, because of increased muscular development.

TABLE 2·1 CONTINUED

APPROXIMATE DATE	DESCRIPTION
5 months	The fetus, now weighing about 12 ounces to 1 pound and measuring about 1 foot, begins to show signs of an individual personality. It has definite sleep-wake patterns, has a favorite position in the uterus (called its *lie*), and becomes more active—kicking, stretching, squirming, and even hiccuping. By putting an ear to the mother's abdomen, it is possible to hear the fetal heartbeat. The sweat and sebaceous glands are functioning. The respiratory system is not yet adequate to sustain life outside the womb; a baby born at this time is not expected to survive. Coarse hair has begun to grow on the eyebrows and eyelashes, fine hair is on the head, and a woolly hair called *lanugo* covers the body.
6 months	The rate of fetal growth has slowed down a little—the fetus is now about 14 inches long and 1¼ pounds. It is getting fat pads under the skin; the eyes are complete, opening and closing and looking in all directions. It can maintain regular breathing for 24 hours; it cries; and it can make a fist with a strong grip. If the fetus were to be born now, it would have an extremely slim chance of survival because its breathing apparatus is still very immature. There have been instances, however, when a fetus of this age has survived outside the womb, and these are becoming more common.
7 months	The fetus, 16 inches long and weighing 3 to 5 pounds, now has fully developed reflex patterns. It cries, breathes, swallows, and may suck its thumb. The lanugo may disappear at about this time, or it may remain until shortly after birth. Head hair may continue to grow. Survival chances for a fetus weighing at least 3½ pounds are fairly good, provided it receives intensive medical attention. It will probably have to live in an incubator until a weight of 5 pounds is attained.
8 months	The fetus is now 18 to 20 inches long, weighs between 5 and 7½ pounds, and is fast outgrowing its living quarters. Its movements are curtailed because of cramped conditions. During this month and the next, a layer of fat is developing over the fetus's entire body, to enable it to adjust to varying temperatures outside the womb.
9 months	About a week before birth, the baby stops growing, having reached an average weight of about 7½ pounds and a length of about 20 inches, with boys tending to be a little longer and heavier than girls. Fat pads continue to form, the organ system is operating more efficiently, the heart rate increases, and more wastes are expelled. The reddish color of the skin is fading. On its birth day, the fetus will have been in the womb for approximately 266 days, although gestation age is usually estimated at 280 days, since doctors date the pregnancy from the mother's last menstrual period.

Note: Even in these early stages, individuals differ. The figures and descriptions given here represent averages.

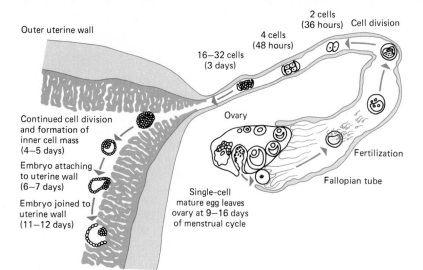

Continued cell division and formation of inner cell mass (4–5 days)

Embryo attaching to uterine wall (6–7 days)

Embryo joined to uterine wall (11–12 days)

Outer uterine wall

Single-cell mature egg leaves ovary at 9–16 days of menstrual cycle

Ovary

16–32 cells (3 days)

4 cells (48 hours)

2 cells (36 hours)   Cell division

Fertilization

Fallopian tube

Figure 2-10 How an ovum becomes an embryo.

nourishment. Upon implantation, the blastocyst has about 150 cells; when this cell mass is fully implanted in the uterus, it is an embryo (see Figure 2-10).

Embryonic Stage (2 to 8–12 Weeks) During the *embryonic stage,* or second stage of gestation, the major body systems (respiratory, alimentary, nervous) and organs develop. Because of rapid growth and development in this stage, the embryo is most vulnerable to prenatal environmental influences. Almost all developmental birth defects (cleft palate, incomplete or missing limbs, blindness, deafness) occur during the critical first trimester (3-month period) of pregnancy. The most severely defective embryos usually do not survive beyond this time and are aborted spontaneously (Garn, 1966).

A *spontaneous abortion,* commonly called a *miscarriage,* is the expulsion from the uterus of a conceptus (prenatal organism) that could not have survived outside the womb. Three out of four miscarriages occur within the first trimester, affecting an estimated 30 to 50 percent of all pregnancies (Garn, 1966; J. Gordon, 1975; J.F. Miller, Williamson, Glue, Gordon, Grudzinskas, & Sykes, 1980). The risk that a mother will die from a spontaneous abortion, while quite small, is greater for women who abort after the first trimester (S.M. Berman, MacKay, Grimes, & Binkin, 1985).

In ancient times, people believed that miscarriage could be brought on by fear of a sudden, loud thunderclap or by jostling when a woman's chariot hit a rut in the street. Today we realize that the normal conceptus is well protected from almost all jolts and is as unlikely to be shaken loose as an unripe apple on a tree (Guttmacher, 1973).

Chromosomal abnormalities may be present

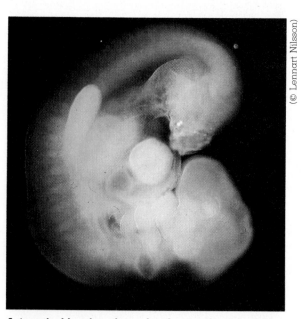

(© Lennart Nilsson)

A 4-week-old embryo has a head, a trunk, and a tail. In this photo, taken with a microscope, you can see the beginnings of an arm and a leg on the side of the trunk.

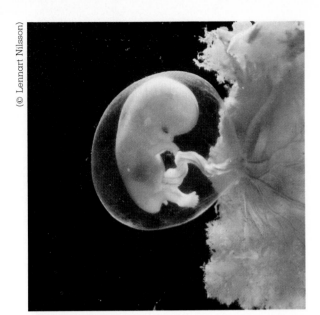

A 3-month-old fetus has fully developed fingers and toes, and even eyelids.

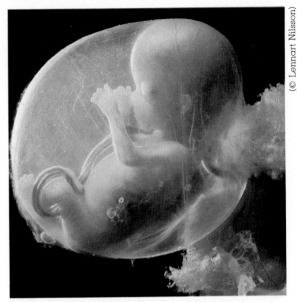

When this 4-month-old male fetus puts his feet against the amniotic sac, his mother can feel him kicking.

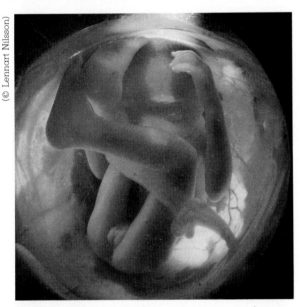

This 5-month-old female fetus is beginning to show signs of a distinct personality, including a favorite position in the uterus and her own pattern of sleeping and waking.

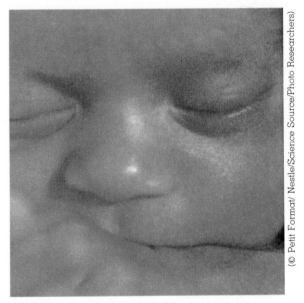

A baby born at the seventh month of gestation has fully formed features.

in about half of all spontaneous abortions (Ash, Vennart, & Carter, 1977). Other miscarriages may result from a defective ovum or sperm, an unfavorable location for implantation, a breakdown in supplies of oxygen or nourishment caused by abnormal development of the umbilical cord, or some physiological abnormality of the mother.

Women who have already borne babies with neural-tube defects, such as spina bifida or anencephaly (a rare defect in which all or part of the brain is missing), are more likely to have spontaneous abortions. Transferrin C3, a gene which occurs in about 17 percent of white couples, appears to be linked to recurrent spontaneous abortions and also may have something to do with the development of neural-tube defects (Weitkamp & Schacter, 1985). About 30 percent of spontaneous abortions may be caused by a symptomless herpes virus present in the uterus (Goldsmith, 1985). Although the mother is apparently healthy, the virus seems to be able to cross the placenta and harm the embryo.

Fetal Stage (8–12 Weeks to Birth) With the appearance of the first bone cells at about 8 weeks, the embryo begins to become a fetus, and by 12 weeks it is fully in the *fetal stage,* the final stage of gestation. During the long period until birth, the finishing touches are put on the various body parts, and the body changes in form and grows about 20 times in length.

The fetus is far from a passive passenger in its mother's womb. It kicks, turns, flexes its body, somersaults, squints, swallows, makes a fist, hiccups, and sucks its thumb. It responds to both sound and vibrations, indicating that it can hear and feel.

Even within the womb, each of us is unique. Fetuses vary in the amount and kind of their activity and in the regularity and speed of their heart rates. Some of these patterns seem to persist into adulthood, supporting the notion of inborn temperament.

The Prenatal Environment

Only recently have we become aware of some of the myriad environmental influences that can affect the developing fetus. The role of the father, for example, used to be virtually ignored. Today we know that various environmental factors can affect a man's sperm and thus the children he conceives. While the mother's role has been recognized far longer, we are still discovering many elements that affect the life she is carrying inside her body.

Maternal Factors Most of our knowledge about prenatal hazards has been gleaned from animal research or from studies in which moth-

ers reported on such factors as what they had eaten while pregnant, what drugs they had taken, how much radiation they had been exposed to, and what illnesses they had contracted. Both these methods have limitations: it is not always accurate to apply findings from animals to human beings, and mothers do not always remember what they did in the past.

Particular influences in the prenatal environment affect different fetuses differently. Some environmental factors that are **teratogenic** (birth-defect-producing) in some cases have little or no effect in others. We still do not know why this should be so, but research seems to indicate that the timing of an environmental blow, its intensity, and its interaction with other factors are all relevant. (Box 2-2 summarizes ways that prospective mothers can reduce the risks of pregnancy.)

PRENATAL NOURISHMENT   *Why prenatal nutrition is important* Babies develop best when their mothers eat well. Indeed, many studies have found that a woman's diet *before* as well as during pregnancy is crucial to the future health of her child. Mothers who eat nutritiously have fewer complications of pregnancy and childbirth and bear healthier babies, while mothers with inadequate diets are more likely to bear premature or low-birth-weight infants or babies who are stillborn (born dead) or die soon after birth (J.L. Brown, 1987; Burke, Beal, Kirkwood, & Stuart, 1943; Read, Habicht, Lechtig, & Klein, 1973). As we'll see in Chapter 3, low-birth-weight babies (babies who weigh less than 5½ pounds at birth) are likelier than other babies to die in infancy or to have health problems. This is a special concern for low-income families, in which other kinds of environmental deprivation may aggravate the effects of poor nutrition.

When malnourished women are given dietary supplements during pregnancy, their babies weigh more at birth than babies whose mothers do not receive supplements; are healthier, more active, and more visually alert; are less likely to be born prematurely; and are less likely to die during the late fetal period or during infancy (J.L. Brown, 1987; Read et al., 1973; Vuori, Christiansen, Clement, Mora, Wagner, & Herrera, 1979). In addition, better-nourished moth-

BOX 2-2 ■ PRACTICALLY SPEAKING

REDUCING RISKS DURING PREGNANCY

Following are some guidelines for reducing risks during pregnancy:

■ *Eat properly.* A well-balanced diet gives every pregnant woman the best odds of having a successful pregnancy and a healthy baby. It may also help to prevent various disorders of pregnancy.

■ *Gain weight sensibly.* A gradual, steady, moderate weight gain (26 to 35 pounds for a woman of average weight) may help prevent a variety of complications, including diabetes, hypertension, varicose veins, hemorrhoids, and a difficult delivery due to an overly large fetus.

■ *Keep fit.* It's best to begin pregnancy with a well-toned, exercised body, but it's never too late to start deriving the benefits of fitness. Regular exercise prevents constipation and improves respiration, circulation, muscle tone, and skin elasticity, all of which contribute to a more comfortable pregnancy and an easier, safer delivery.

■ *Don't smoke.* Quitting as early in pregnancy as possible reduces the many risks to mother and baby, including prematurity and low birth weight.

■ *Don't drink alcohol.* Drinking very rarely or not at all will reduce the risk of birth defects, particularly of fetal alcohol syndrome, which results from high alcohol intake.

■ *Avoid drugs.* It is best to avoid taking any drugs during pregnancy that are not absolutely essential and prescribed by your doctor.

■ *Get good medical care.* Even a low-risk pregnancy is put at high risk if prenatal care is absent or poor. Seeing a qualified practitioner regularly, beginning as soon as pregnancy is suspected, is vital for all expectant mothers. Use an obstetrician experienced with your particular condition if you are in a high-risk category. But just as important as having a good doctor is being a good patient. Be an active participant in your medical care—ask questions, report symptoms—but don't try to be your own doctor.

■ *Prevent or promptly treat infections.* All infections—from common flu to urinary tract and vaginal infections to the increasingly common venereal diseases—should be prevented whenever possible. When contracted, however, infection should be treated promptly by a physician who knows you are pregnant.

■ *Beware the "superwoman syndrome."* Today's mothers, often well-established in their careers and highly motivated in everything they do, tend to be overachievers and overdoers. Getting enough rest during pregnancy is far more important than getting everything done, especially in high-risk pregnancies. Don't wait until your body starts pleading for relief before you slow down. If your doctor recommends that you begin your maternity leave earlier than you had planned, take the advice. Some studies have suggested a higher incidence of premature delivery among women who work until term, particularly if their jobs entail physical labor or long periods of standing.

Source: Adapted from A. Eisenberg, Murkoff, & Hathaway, 1984, p. 56.

ers tend to breast-feed longer, a practice that confers an advantage on infants, as we'll see in Chapter 3 (Read et al., 1973).

Malnutrition also affects the developing brain—as researchers demonstrated in a study of fetuses obtained from therapeutic abortions on malnourished women, as well as infants who died accidentally or of severe malnutrition. The brains of the malnourished infants contained as few as 60 percent of the normal number of cells, suggesting that they had suffered malnutrition in utero (Winick, Brasel, & Rosso, 1972).

It may be possible to counteract the damaging effects of fetal malnutrition by a favorable environment after birth. In one study of mothers and babies from very difficult socioeconomic circumstances, researchers randomly assigned some infants who showed poor signs of development to an intellectually enriching program at a day care center before 3 months of age, while others remained at home with their mothers. Three years later the children took intelligence tests, and the babies who had been part of the enrichment program tested higher (Zeskind & Ramey, 1981).

Proper prenatal nourishment, though, is a far easier, surer, and more effective way than postnatal intervention to safeguard a child's development.

What expectant mothers should eat   A well-balanced daily diet for pregnant women (or anyone else) should include foods from each of the seven basic groups: protein (meat and meat alternatives), dairy products, bread and cereals, fruits and vegetables rich in vitamin C, dark-green vegetables, other fruits and vegetables (including yellow ones rich in vitamin A), and fats and oils.

Of course, women need to eat larger amounts than usual when pregnant: typically, 300 to 500 more calories a day, including an additional 30 grams of protein (Winick, 1981). Teenagers, women who are ill or undernourished or under considerable stress, and those who have taken birth control pills until shortly before pregnancy need extra nutrients (J.E. Brown, 1983).

About one-third of the weight a pregnant woman gains goes to the fetus; the rest is distributed among parts of the mother's body that sustain and nourish the new life (including the breasts, blood, and uterus) and the placenta and amniotic fluid.

Most pregnant women do not gain enough weight, in part because of the influence of former obstetric guidelines that recommended a gain of no more than 22 to 27 pounds. The latest recommendation is 26 to 35 pounds, and a smaller gain apparently is riskier than a bigger one (National Center for Health Statistics, 1986). A study of 16,000 pregnancies showed that women who gain in the prescribed range have significantly less chance of stillbirths or late miscarriages or of low-birth-weight babies, regardless of the mother's weight before pregnancy. Unfortunately, women who are already at high risk (who smoke; are underweight or overweight before pregnancy; are poor, black, unwed, teenagers, or over 35; have only a grade-school education; or have three or more children) are likeliest to gain too little.

Since fetal nutrition affects both the long-term physical and the long-term intellectual development of the child, proper care of the fetus is important both to individual parents and to society as a whole.

MATERNAL DRUG INTAKE   At one time it was believed that the placenta protected the developing baby from injurious elements in the mother's body. We now know that virtually everything the mother takes in makes its way to the new life in her uterus. Drugs may cross the placenta, just as oxygen, carbon dioxide, and water do. They have the strongest effects if taken early in pregnancy. As we have seen, the fetus develops most rapidly in its first few months and is especially vulnerable then.

Medical drugs   Drugs known to be harmful include the antibiotics streptomycin and tetracycline; the sulfanomides; excessive amounts of vitamins A, B_6, C, D, and K; certain barbiturates, opiates, and other central nervous system depressants; and several hormones, including progestin, diethylstilbestrol (DES), androgen, and synthetic estrogen. In recent years, Accutane, a drug which has frequently been prescribed for severe acne, has been implicated in a variety of birth defects (Lott, Bocian, Pribram, & Leitner, 1984).

Even ordinary aspirin can cause trouble.

When a woman takes aspirin within 5 days preceding delivery, there is an increased tendency toward bleeding in both mother and infant (Stuart, Gross, Elrad, & Graeber, 1982). Although this bleeding is not serious for normal full-term babies, it could be harmful for low-birth-weight infants. For safety's sake, aspirin should be added to the list of drugs to be avoided throughout pregnancy. In fact, the Committee on Drugs of the American Academy of Pediatrics (1982) recommends that *no* medication be prescribed for the pregnant or breast-feeding woman unless it is absolutely essential for her health or for that of her child.

Studies indicate, for example, that the children of women who take oral contraceptives early in pregnancy may suffer birth defects. The most likely potential problem is a slightly elevated incidence of certain cardiovascular defects. Women who smoke more than a pack of cigarettes a day and also take "the pill" are more apt to have babies with birth defects (Bracken, Holford, White, & Kelsey, 1978).

The effects of taking a drug during pregnancy do not always show up immediately. In the late 1940s and early 1950s, the synthetic hormone diethylstilbestrol (DES) was widely prescribed (ineffectually, as it turned out) to prevent miscarriage. Years later, when the daughters of women who had taken DES during pregnancy reached puberty, some of them developed a rare form of vaginal or cervical cancer. At first, doctors were afraid that as many as 1 in 250 of "DES daughters" would develop this cancer (Herbst, Kurman, Scully, & Poskanzer, 1971) or show microscopic abnormalities of the vaginal tract (A. Sherman et al., 1974). However, it is now estimated that only 1 out of every 1000 DES daughters will contract genital cancer by their mid-thirties (Melnick, Cole, Anderson, & Herbst, 1987).

A number of other problems linked to DES have emerged. DES daughters have more trouble bearing their own children, with higher risks of miscarriage or premature delivery (A. Barnes et al., 1980), and DES sons seem to show a higher rate of infertility and reproductive abnormalities (Stenchever et al., 1981). In light of all these problems, it is advisable for all children of women who took DES during pregnancy to get regular medical checkups.

Let's look at the effects of some other drugs in wide use today.

Alcohol Each year in the United States, more than 40,000 babies are born with alcohol-related birth defects. About 1 infant in 750, according to American and European studies, suffers from ***fetal alcohol syndrome (FAS)***, a combination of slowed prenatal and postnatal growth, facial and bodily malformations, and disorders of the central nervous system. The latter can take the form of alcohol withdrawal symptoms, at birth; of poor sucking response, brain-wave abnormalities, and sleep disturbances, during infancy; and, throughout childhood, of a short attention span, restlessness, irritability, hyperactivity, learning disabilities, and motor impairments. For every child with this full cluster of alcohol-related characteristics, as many as 10 others may be born with one or more of them. Fetal alcohol syndrome is one of the three leading causes of mental retardation (along with Down syndrome and neural-tube defects) and the only one of the three that is preventable (Ioffe, Childiaeva, & Chernick, 1984; National Institute on Alcohol Abuse and Alcoholism, NIAAA, 1986; Shaywitz, Cohen, & Shaywitz, 1980; Spiegler, Malin, Kaelber, & Warren, 1984; Streissguth, Martin, Barr, Sandman, Kirchner, & Darby, 1984).

Although alcoholic women are likeliest to bear babies with FAS, even moderate social drinking may harm the developing fetus—though studies have mixed results. A large study of nearly 32,000 pregnancies found that consuming at least one or two drinks a day can substantially heighten the risk of growth retardation. The effect increased sharply with heavier alcohol intake. Taking less than one drink a day had a minimal effect (Mills, Graubard, Harley, Rhoads, & Berendes, 1984). A recent study, however, found that drinking up to *two* drinks a day was no more strongly associated with malformations than *not* drinking (Mills & Graubard, 1987). It is important to remember, of course, that the same amount of alcohol may affect different women differently (NIAAA, 1986).

Because of the risks of alcohol and the lack of any clearly safe level of drinking, women are advised to avoid alcoholic drinks completely during pregnancy—better yet, from the time

As preschoolers, children whose mothers abused drugs during pregnancy may show deficiencies in perception, learning, and social adjustment—long-range effects of addiction developed while in the womb. Shown here is "Mother" Clara Hale, who has cared for many such children in New York City's Harlem.

they begin *thinking* about becoming pregnant until they stop breast-feeding (March of Dimes Birth Defects Foundation, 1983a; NIAAA, 1986).

Marijuana Animal research shows that marijuana can produce fetal malformations, and there is mounting evidence from research on humans of an association between birth defects and a general lifestyle that includes heavy marijuana use. One study found that pregnant marijuana users were 5 times more likely than nonusers to deliver infants with features compatible with FAS, but it was hard to isolate the role of marijuana from other lifestyle factors (Hingson et al., 1982). A Canadian study that *did* isolate that factor found that newborn babies of regular marijuana smokers showed transient neurological disturbances, such as tremors and startles and a marked decrease in visual response. Heavy users delivered their babies an average of a week early. In that sense, marijuana seems to have a minor effect, except that when it is combined with other factors such as drinking and tobacco smoking, the result can be a premature, low-birth-weight baby (Fried, Watkinson, & Willan, 1984). The most prudent advice, since the potential that marijuana has for producing birth defects is unknown, is for women of childbearing age to avoid its use, as the National Institute of Mental Health recommended in 1972.

Opiates Women addicted to such drugs as morphine, heroin, and codeine are likely to bear premature babies who have become addicted to the drugs while in the womb. Even after infants are cured of the addiction (by being given substitute drugs), effects may linger until at least the age of 6.

At birth, addicted infants are restless and irritable and often suffer tremors, convulsions, fever, vomiting, and breathing difficulties; they are twice as likely to die soon after birth as nonaddicted babies (Cobrinick, Hood, & Chused, 1959; Henly & Fitch, 1966; Ostrea & Chavez, 1979). As older babies, they cry often and are less alert and less responsive to stimuli (Strauss, Lessen-Firestone, Starr, & Ostrea, 1975). And in early childhood—from age 3 to age 6—they weigh less, are shorter, are less well adjusted, and score lower on perceptual and learning tests (G. Wilson, McCreary, Kean, & Baxter, 1979). In the study by Wilson and others, the children exposed to heroin also had less contact with their natural mothers than other children did, a factor that may have influenced their development, either alone or in combination with prenatal exposure to the drug.

Although long-term follow-up studies on children of narcotics-addicted mothers have been few and inconclusive, researchers have found educational deficits, excessive anxiety in social situations, and poor socialization in later childhood (Householder, Hatcher, Burns, & Chasnoff, 1982).

Nicotine The clearest finding related to smoking is the tendency of pregnant smokers to bear small babies (Landesman-Dwyer & Emanuel, 1979; Sexton & Hebel, 1984). Indeed, smoking during pregnancy is "the single most powerful determinant of poor fetal growth in the developed world," according to doctors at the Centers for Disease Control in Atlanta. These physicians have identified a **fetal tobacco syndrome**—growth retardation attributable to mothers' smoking five or more cigarettes a day (Nieburg, Marks, McLaren, & Remington, 1985).

Maternal smoking has also been linked to complications ranging from bleeding during pregnancy to death of the fetus or newborn. A recent Swedish study demonstrated that children whose mothers smoke 10 or more cigarettes a day during pregnancy run a 50 percent greater risk than other children of contracting cancer during childhood (Stjernfeldt, Berglund, Lindsten, & Ludvigsson, 1986). Future studies may detect a greater impact, since "the first sizable cohort of individuals exposed to maternal smoking is only beginning to reach the age at which most cancer commonly occurs" (D.H. Rubin, Krasilnikoff, Leventhal, Weile, & Berget, 1986).

Mothers who both smoke and drink during pregnancy have an increased chance of bearing low-birth-weight babies who will show early learning deficits (J. Martin, Martin, Lund, & Streissguth, 1977; Wright et al., 1983). In fact, smoking in pregnancy appears to have some long-term effects on school-age children similar to those of drinking in pregnancy: poor attention span, hyperactivity, learning problems, perceptual-motor and linguistic losses, social maladjustment, poor performance on IQ tests, low grade placement, and minimal brain dysfunction (Landesman-Dwyer & Emanuel, 1979; Naeye & Peters, 1984; Streissguth et al., 1984). Of course, since mothers who smoke during pregnancy also tend to smoke after the birth, it is hard to separate the effects of fetal and postnatal exposure.

Other stimulants When pregnant rats were force-fed huge doses of caffeine, their offspring developed birth defects. Can the caffeine that a pregnant woman swallows in coffee, cola, chocolate, or tea cause trouble for her fetus? We are not certain. Because questions do remain, however, the U.S. Food and Drug Administration recommends that pregnant women avoid or use sparingly any food, beverages, or drugs that contain caffeine.

Recently the effects of cocaine use have begun to be studied, and the first indications are that cocaine can influence both the outcome of a pregnancy and the health of the baby. Women who use cocaine appear to have a significantly

(American Cancer Society)

The nicotine in tobacco can move from the mother's lungs to the blood of the fetus and may impede normal development. Smokers typically bear smaller babies than nonsmokers do.

higher rate of spontaneous abortions and their babies have a greater risk of developing neurological problems—they do not interact as well as other babies and they do not respond as appropriately to environmental stimuli (Chasnoff, Burns, Schnoll, & Burns, 1985). Use of cocaine during pregnancy has also been related to sudden infant death syndrome (Chasnoff, Hunt, Kletter, & Kaplan, 1986).

In addition, babies born to mothers who used cocaine during pregnancy were found to be shorter, to weigh less, and to have smaller heads than children of drug-free mothers. Cocaine abuse also appeared to result in stillbirths due to bursting of the placenta, or in the birth of malformed babies (Bingol, Fuchs, Diaz, Stone, & Gromisch, 1987). The indications seem clear, then, that pregnant women should avoid cocaine.

OTHER MATERNAL FACTORS   *Illness* A number of illnesses contracted during pregnancy can have serious effects on the developing fetus, depending partly on *when* the mother gets sick. Rubella (German measles) before the eleventh week of pregnancy is almost certain to cause deafness and heart defects in the baby, but chances of such consequences are about 1 in 3 between 13 and 16 weeks of pregnancy, and almost nil after 16 weeks (E. Miller, Cradock-Watson, & Pollock, 1982). Diabetes, tuberculosis, and syphilis have also been implicated in problems in fetal development, and both gonorrhea and genital herpes can have harmful effects on the baby at the time of delivery.

AIDS (acquired immune deficiency syndrome) may be contracted by a fetus if the mother has the disease or even has the virus in her blood. Apparently this danger arises from the intimacy of the placenta, in which the contents of the mother's blood are shared with the fetus. Recent studies detected abnormalities in infants and young children infected with the AIDS virus while in the uterus. These included small heads; prominent, boxlike foreheads; flat nasal bridges; short, flattened noses; "scooped-out" profiles; slanting eyes; fat lips; and growth failure (Iosub, Bamji, Stone, Gromisch, & Wasserman, 1987; Marion, Wiznia, Hutcheon, & Rubinstein, 1986). So far, AIDS has *not* been transmitted by close postnatal contact between mother and baby, including breast-feeding (M.F. Rogers, 1985).

Incompatibility of blood types A problem resulting from the interaction of heredity with the prenatal environment is incompatibility of blood type between mother and baby. When a fetus's blood contains the **Rh factor,** a protein substance, but the mother's blood does not, antibodies in the mother's blood may attack the fetus and possibly bring about spontaneous abortion, stillbirth, jaundice, anemia, heart defects, mental retardation, or death. Usually the first Rh-positive baby is not affected, but with each succeeding pregnancy the risk becomes greater. A vaccine can now be given to an Rh-negative mother which, when administered within 3 days after childbirth or abortion, will prevent her body from making antibodies. Babies already affected with Rh disease can be treated by repeated blood transfusions, sometimes even before birth.

Medical x-rays We have known for about 60 years that radiation can cause gene mutations, minute changes that alter a gene to produce some new, often harmful, characteristic (D.P. Murphy, 1929). Although we don't know the exact dosage of x-rays that can harm the fetus, it does appear that the greatest potential occurs early in pregnancy. Therefore it is best to avoid radiation exposure, especially during the first 3 months (Kleinman, Cooke, Machlin, & Kessel, 1983). With the availability of ultrasound (discussed later) medical x-rays are less necessary and less prevalent than in the past.

External environmental hazards Anything that affects a pregnant woman can affect the fetus. We have become more conscious of dangers posed to the developing fetus by chemicals, radiation, extremes of heat and humidity, and other hazards of modern life. For example, babies whose mothers ate fish contaminated with PCBs (polychlorinated biphenyls, chemicals widely used in industry before they were banned in 1976) weighed less at birth, had smaller heads, and showed weaker reflexes and more jerky movements than infants whose mothers did not eat the fish (J.L. Jacobson, Jacobson, Fein, Schwartz, & Dowler, 1984). More recently, genetics researchers found a fivefold increase in the average number of West German babies born with Down syndrome 9 months after the spill-out of nuclear radiation at the power plant at Chernobyl in the Soviet Union. Laboratory reports began to detect prenatal chromosomal malformations 4 months after the reactor failed (West Berlin Human Genetic Institute, 1987). Other research has found that infants exposed to high levels of lead prenatally scored lower on intelligence tests than infants exposed prenatally to low or moderate levels (Bellinger, Leviton, Watermaux, Needleman, & Rabinowitz, 1987).

Paternal Factors: Environmental Influences Transmitted by the Father

Researchers have begun to devote more attention to the male's role in transmitting environmentally caused defects. Sperm samples from alcoholic men have been found to be highly abnormal (R. Lester & Van Theil, 1977). Exposure to lead, marijuana and tobacco smoke, large amounts of radiation, DES, and certain pesticides may result in the production of sperm abnormal in number, shape, and motility and may also produce genetic abnormalities in the sperm cells (J. Brody, 1981).

Recent research has focused on passive exposure to smoking by the father. In a Danish study, smoking by the father had two-thirds as much effect in reducing birth weight as did maternal smoking (D.H. Rubin et al., 1986). And retrospective questionnaires completed by cancer patients at the hospital of the University of North Carolina found a twofold increased risk of developing cancer in adulthood among offspring of men who smoked. Again, however, it was difficult to distinguish between prebirth and childhood exposure to smoke (Sandler, Everson, Wilcox, & Browder, 1985).

Advanced paternal age is associated with increases in several rare conditions, including achondroplastic dwarfism, Marfan's syndrome (deformities of the head and limbs), and fibrodysplasia ossificans progressiva (bone malformations). In studies on each of these conditions, the mean paternal age was in the late thirties (G. Evans, 1976). Advanced age of the father also seems to be a factor, as we have seen, in about 1 out of 4 cases of Down syndrome (Abroms & Bennett, 1979).

Prenatal Assessment

Not long ago, almost the only decision parents had to make about their babies before birth was the decision to conceive; most of what happened in the intervening 9 months was beyond their control. We now have an array of altogether new tools to assess fetal development and well-being during gestation and birth.

Prenatal Diagnosis of Birth Defects

New techniques for diagnosing birth defects prenatally, coupled with the legalization of induced abortion, have encouraged many couples with troubling medical histories to take a chance on conception. Without such techniques, these couples might not have dared risk a pregnancy. For example, a couple who know through genetic counseling (refer back to Box 2-1) that they both carry a recessive gene for a disorder may conceive and then take tests to determine whether the fetus does indeed have the condition. As a result, many couples have been reassured by prenatal examinations that their babies would be normal, while other expectant parents have terminated problem pregnancies. Parents who choose to bear a child that they know will be handicapped have more time to adjust to and plan for the child's special needs.

AMNIOCENTESIS In the medical procedure called *amniocentesis,* a sample of the amniotic fluid in which a fetus floats while in the uterus (and which therefore contains fetal cells) is withdrawn and analyzed to detect whether any of a variety of genetic defects are present. The procedure can be done around the fifteenth or sixteenth week of pregnancy (see Figure 2-11, page 70). Amniocentesis can also reveal the sex of the fetus, which may be crucial in the case of a sex-linked disorder such as hemophilia.

Amniocentesis is generally recommended for pregnant women if they are at least 35 years old; if they and their partners are both known carriers of Tay-Sachs disease or sickle-cell disease; or if they and their partners have a family history of such conditions as Down syndrome, spina bifida, Rh disease, and muscular dystrophy. An analysis of 3000 women who had the procedure indicated that it was "safe, highly reliable and

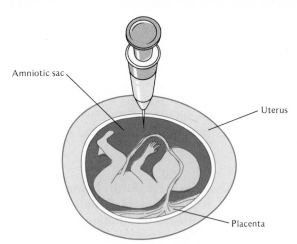

Amniotic sac

Uterus

Placenta

Figure 2-11 Amniocentesis. A sample of amniotic fluid can be withdrawn and analyzed for the presence of a variety of birth defects. A needle is inserted through the mother's abdominal wall to remove the fluid. Analysis of the sampled fluid generally takes 2 to 4 weeks. (*Source:* F. Fuchs, 1980.)

extremely accurate" (Golbus, Loughman, Epstein, Halbasch, Stephens, & Hall, 1979, p. 157). However, a recent random controlled study of 4600 Danish women found a slightly elevated risk of spontaneous abortion in women who had amniocentesis (Tabor, Philip, Madsen, Bang, Obel, & Norgaard-Pedersen, 1986).

CHORIONIC VILLUS SAMPLING **Chorionic villus sampling** consists of taking tissue from the end of one or more villi, hairlike projections of the membrane around the embryo that are made up of rapidly developing fetal cells, and then testing these cells for the presence of various conditions. This new method for obtaining fetal cells is becoming an important alternative to amniocentesis. It can be performed earlier than amniocentesis can (during the first trimester), and it yields results faster (within about a week). A recent study found spontaneous abortions to be "acceptably low (3.8 percent) *when the procedure is performed from the ninth through the eleventh menstrual week*" (Hogge, Schonberg, & Golbus, 1986, p. 1249; emphasis added). This rate is said to be equivalent to miscarriage rates in normal pregnancies of the same gestational length and maternal age. While the technique appears to be "acceptably safe and reliable" (p. 1252), with a 1.7 percent diagnostic error rate, the authors say that such side effects as infection and

membrane damage need further investigation before it receives widespread use.

MATERNAL BLOOD TESTS   Blood taken from the mother between the fourteenth and twentieth weeks of pregnancy can be tested for the amount of alpha fetoprotein (AFP) it contains. This **maternal blood test,** one of several diagnostic tests of maternal blood samples to detect fetal abnormalities, is indicated for women considered to be at risk for bearing children with defects in the formation of the brain or spinal cord (such as spina bifida or anencephaly). If the test reveals an unduly high AFP level, ultrasound and amniocentesis may then be performed. Alpha fetoprotein levels have recently been found to be lowered in women carrying fetuses with Down syndrome, and so the blood test, when followed up with amniocentesis or chorionic villus sampling, may also serve as a screening device for that condition (Cuckle, Wald, & Lindenbaum, 1984; DiMaio, Baumgarten, Greenstein, Saal, & Mahoney, 1987). In addition, blood tests can identify carriers of sickle-cell disease (blood disorders that are seen mostly in black people), Tay-Sachs disease, and thalassemia (a blood disorder that affects people of Mediterranean origin).

ULTRASOUND   High-frequency sound waves directed into the woman's abdomen can be made to yield a sonogram, a picture of the uterus, fetus, and placenta. The technique, called **ultrasound,** allows a physician to "look"

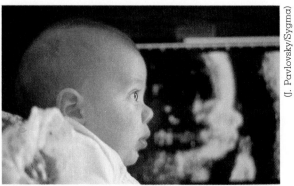

(J. Pavlovsky/Sygma)

This 6-month-old baby is posing with an ultrasound picture of him taken during the fourth month of gestation. Ultrasound is a popular diagnostic tool that presents an immediate image of the fetus within the womb.

inside the womb with little or no discomfort to the woman. Ultrasound is used to measure the baby's head size, to judge gestational age, to detect multiple pregnancies, to evaluate uterine abnormalities, to detect gross structural abnormalities in the fetus, and to determine whether a fetus has died, as well as to guide other procedures, such as amniocentesis. Although some obstetricians administer ultrasound routinely, it has been in use for a relatively short time, and so long-term effects are as yet unknown (Kleinman et al., 1983). Because animal studies have suggested possible harmful effects, the National Institutes of Health (1984b) recommend ultrasound only when there is a specific medical reason.

Electronic Fetal Monitoring The most widely used of all fetal assessment technologies is *electronic fetal monitoring* (Kleinman et al., 1983), in which machines monitor the fetal heartbeat throughout labor and delivery. Although the procedure provides valuable information during high-risk births, including premature deliveries and births where there is some indication of fetal distress, it is often used in low-risk deliveries. However, in a recent study, routine monitoring was shown to result in twice as many deliveries by the riskier cesarean method (discussed on page 74), without corresponding improvements in the outcome (Leveno et al., 1986). For that reason, it is best *not* to do continuous, routine monitoring when a pregnancy appears to be uncomplicated.

BIRTH

Birth is a beginning but also an end: the climax of all that has happened from the moment of fertilization through 9 months of growth in the mother's womb. One of the mysteries of human life is the precise mechanism that triggers the contractions of the uterus that expel the fetus, normally after 266 days of gestation. One possibility is suggested by the discovery that fetal urine, placed in a laboratory dish, stimulates the action of prostaglandins, hormones that carry out a number of functions in the body and may initiate birth. Perhaps, then, a specific substance

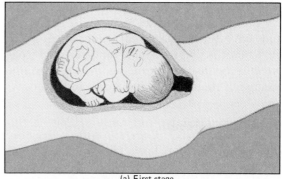

(a) First stage

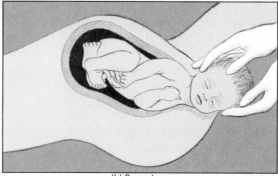

(b) Second stage

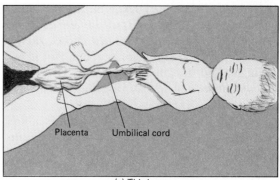

Placenta   Umbilical cord

(c) Third stage

Figure 2-12 Birth of a baby. (a) During the first stage of labor, a series of stronger and stronger contractions dilates the cervix, the opening to the mother's womb. (b) During the second stage, the baby's head moves down the birth canal and emerges from the vagina. (c) During the brief third stage, the placenta and umbilical cord are expelled from the womb. Then, the cord is cut. (*Source:* Adapted from Lagercrantz & Slotkin, 1986.)

released into the urine of the fetus and from there into the amniotic fluid may cause labor to begin (Strickland, Saeed, Casey, & Mitchell, 1983).

The contractions begin as a mild tightening of the uterus, lasting 15 to 25 seconds. A woman may have felt similar contractions during the final months of pregnancy, but she can recognize the birth contractions as the "real thing" because of their greater regularity and intensity.

Stages of Childbirth

Childbirth, or labor, takes place in three overlapping stages (see Figure 2-12). The *first stage*, the longest, lasts an average of 12 to 24 hours for a woman having her first child. During this stage, uterine contractions cause the cervix, the opening of the uterus, to widen until it becomes large enough for the baby's head to pass through. At the beginning of this stage, the contractions tend to be fairly mild. Toward the end of this stage, they become more severe and more uncomfortable. Women who have been prepared for childbirth through special classes learn breathing techniques that help them overcome the discomfort of these stronger contractions.

Much of the pain of labor is caused by the stretching of the lower part of the uterus, especially the cervix. If a woman's cervix dilates quickly, she will feel little or no pain. But if her cervix is rigid and must be forcibly dilated by the contractions of her uterus, the contractions will be painful (Timiras, 1972).

The *second stage*, which typically lasts about 1½ hours, begins when the baby's head begins to move through the cervix and the vaginal canal, and it ends when the baby emerges completely from the mother's body. During the second stage, the prepared mother bears down hard with her abdominal muscles at each contraction, helping the baby in its efforts to leave her body. At the end of this stage, the baby is born but is still attached by the umbilical cord to the placenta, which is still inside the mother's body.

During the *third stage*, which lasts only a few minutes, the umbilical cord and the placenta are expelled.

Methods of Childbirth

Babies are delivered in a variety of ways. Historically, two concerns have been primary: safety for the baby and comfort for the mother. Another concern, growing sensitivity to the emotional needs of family members, has resulted in efforts to bring the father and sometimes the other children into the experience.

Medicated Delivery According to the Bible, God told Eve, "In travail thou shalt bring forth children." (*Travail* can mean either "hard work" or "sorrow.") Still, most societies have evolved techniques to hasten delivery, make the mother's work easier, and lessen her discomfort. Some type of pain relief during labor and delivery is taken for granted among most western middle-class women. A **medicated delivery**, or delivery involving anesthesia, is normally used.

Some women receive general anesthesia, which renders them completely unconscious; others get a regional anesthetic (such as a spinal or caudal block), which blocks the nerve pathways that would carry the sensation of pain to the brain; still others receive analgesics, which relax the mother.

All these drugs pass through the placenta and enter the fetal blood supply and tissues. Critics attribute the relatively high rate of infant mortality in the United States to the routine use here of obstetric medication.

Regional, or local, anesthetics seem to have fewer harmful effects for babies. Still, in one study, infants whose mothers received one particular drug (bupivacaine) by spinal block did not seem to do as well as those whose mothers received little or no medication. When the two groups were compared, the effects of the drugs were strongest on the first day, when the medicated babies showed poorer motor and physiological responses. By the fifth day, the differences were less dramatic but still present, favoring the babies of undrugged mothers (A.D. Murray, Dolby, Nation, & Thomas, 1981).

By 1 month, the babies in the two groups were not acting differently—but their mothers felt differently about them. The medicated mothers seemed to view their infants less favorably and to find them harder to care for. This may well be because there is no such thing in human beings as "maternal instinct." Much of a woman's motherly feeling comes about because of the positive responses she receives from her baby. An infant who nurses eagerly and who acts alert

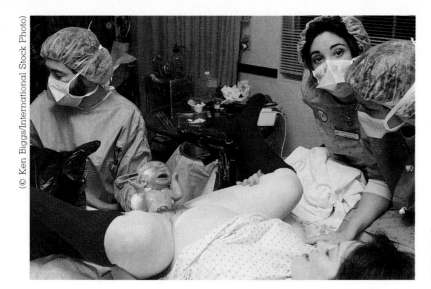

Women who choose natural rather than medicated childbirth can remain alert enough to participate fully in the birth process.

sets up positive feelings in the mother. If the first encounters between mother and baby do not elicit a strong reaction from the baby, then even after the effects of the drug wear off, the effects of the mother's early impressions of her baby may well remain. (It is also possible that mothers who choose unmedicated deliveries have more positive attitudes toward parenting than those who do not and that these attitudes affect the way they act with their babies.)

Other research suggests that the actual physical effects of childbirth medication may persist through the first year of life—and possibly longer. In a study of 3500 healthy full-term babies, Brackbill and Broman (1979) found that children whose mothers had received no obstetric medication showed the most progress in sitting, standing, and moving around. Those whose mothers had received regional anesthesia showed less progress, and those whose mothers had received general anesthesia did the most poorly.

Because of possible negative consequences for the infant of drugs given during labor and delivery, doctors should give a woman the minimum dose for reasonable relief of pain (American Academy of Pediatrics Committee on Drugs, 1978). Because the woman is the only person who can gauge the degree of her pain and is most personally concerned about the well-being of her child, she should have a strong voice in decisions about obstetric medication.

During the twentieth century, alternative methods of childbirth have emerged that seek to minimize the use of harmful medications while maximizing the parents' satisfaction as participants.

Natural and Prepared Childbirth In 1914 a British physician, Dr. Grantly Dick-Read, questioned the inevitability of pain in childbirth and put forth the theory of *natural childbirth,* according to which fear is the cause of most pain during childbirth. To eliminate fear, Dick-Read educated women in the physiology of reproduction and delivery and trained them in breathing, relaxation, and physical fitness. By midcentury, Dr. Fernand Lamaze was using the psychoprophylactic, or *prepared childbirth,* method of obstetrics. This method substituted new breathing and muscular responses to the sensations of uterine contractions for the old responses of fear and pain.

The Lamaze method of prepared childbirth has become popular in the United States. It includes instruction in anatomy and physiology to remove fear of the unknown; training in respiration techniques (such as rapid breathing and panting) to ease pain at each stage of labor; and cognitive restructuring through focusing the eyes on something or sucking on ice, to help the woman concentrate on sensations other than her contractions. The mother learns to relax her muscles as a conditioned response to the voice of her "coach" (usually the father or a friend). The method also provides social support: the coach—by attending classes with the expectant mother, participating in the delivery, and helping with the exercises—enhances her sense of self-worth and reduces her fear of loneliness (Wideman & Singer, 1984).

Gentle Birth A controversial method called *gentle birth* involves delivering babies in quiet, dimly lit delivery rooms, without forceps and with only a local anesthetic, if any. The umbilical cord is not clamped immediately, nor is the newborn slapped to initiate breathing. Instead, the infant is bathed in warm water and placed on its mother's belly right after birth. Leboyer (1975) maintains that such gentle practices eliminate much of the trauma of birth and produce happier people. Critics object that the low lighting may cause doctors to miss vital signs of distress and that babies may be exposed to infections from the water or the mother's body (Cohn, 1975).

A study in 1986 to test Leboyer's claims found that infants delivered by gentle birth techniques were no "easier" temperamentally (or only slightly so) during the first year of life than those delivered by other methods (Maziade, Boudreault, Cote, & Thivierge, 1986). The authors suggested that mothers need not choose gentle delivery on the basis of its claimed effect on a child's personality development. On the other hand, if there is no danger to the mother's or baby's physical health, there is no harm in using the method. A previous study (N. Nelson, Enkin, Saigal, Bennett, Milner, & Sackett, 1980) suggested that the greatest advantage of the Leboyer method was a mother's perception that her baby had been positively influenced; this perception itself could benefit a child and might be one of the strongest reasons to choose gentle birth.

Cesarean Delivery A *cesarean section* (or "C-section") is a medical procedure in which the baby is removed surgically from the uterus. Over 1 out of every 5 babies are delivered in this way in the United States, a threefold increase in rate since 1970 (Placek, 1986).

The operation is commonly performed when labor is not progressing as quickly as it should, the baby appears to be in trouble, or the mother is bleeding through the vagina. Often a C-section is needed when the baby is in the breech position (head last) or in the transverse position (lying crosswise in the uterus), or when the baby's head is too big to pass through the mother's pelvis.

A frequent reason for resorting to a cesarean delivery is that the mother has had a previous cesarean delivery; only 8 percent of women who have a cesarean section have subsequent vaginal deliveries.

The undoubted benefits of a C-section in certain circumstances need to be weighed against its risks, not the least of which is depriving the infant of the experience of labor (see Box 2-3). And, although the cesarean has a superior safety record for delivery of breech babies, it does present several disadvantages to the mother, including greater risk of infection and a longer hospital stay and recovery period, not to speak of the physical and psychological impact that occurs with any surgery (Sachs, McCarthy, Rubin, Burton, Terry, & Tyler, 1983). Cesarean sections have saved the lives of mothers and babies who could not have managed traditional deliveries, but many critics assert that too many cesareans are now being performed in the United States when they are not strictly necessary (deRegt, Minkoff, Feldman, & Schwartz, 1986).

Alternative Settings for Childbirth

Ninety-nine percent of the 3.75 million babies born each year in the United States are delivered in hospitals (Wegman, 1986). A small but growing number of women with good medical histories and normal pregnancies are opting for more intimate, less impersonal settings. Some couples elect to have their babies in the comfort and familiarity of their homes or in small, homelike birth centers.

More than 96 percent of births, whether in hospitals or elsewhere, are attended by physicians—usually obstetricians, who specialize in delivering babies. However, in 1984 more than 93,000 births were attended by midwives, an increase of almost 7000 from the previous year, which occurred almost entirely among white couples (Wegman, 1986).

If a pregnancy is of low risk and the birth is uncomplicated, almost any of these arrange-

BOX 2-3 FOOD FOR THOUGHT

THE STRESS OF BEING BORN

Being born is quite an ordeal—for the baby as well as the mother. First the fetus must spend one or more hours squeezing (usually headfirst) through the narrow walls of the birth canal. The placenta and umbilical cord compress during contractions, causing pressure on the head as well as intermittent oxygen deprivation and the risk of asphyxiation. Then there is the shock to the neonate of emerging "from a warm, dark, sheltered environment into a cold, bright hospital room, where some large creature holds it upside down and in many cases slaps it on the buttocks" (Lagercrantz & Slotkin, 1986, p. 100). Yet photos taken for the Karolinska Institute of Stockholm show that most newborns look aroused and cheerful, not unhappy.

On the basis of studies of rats, sheep, and humans, researchers are now finding that the birth struggle may serve a useful purpose: aiding the transition to life outside the uterus. The stress of being born apparently stimulates the production of huge amounts of adrenaline and noradrenaline. These hormones—the same ones that prepare an animal or human being for fight or flight in the face of danger—may equip the fetus to survive the dangerous journey. The fetal glands produce these hormones (called *catecholamines*) throughout

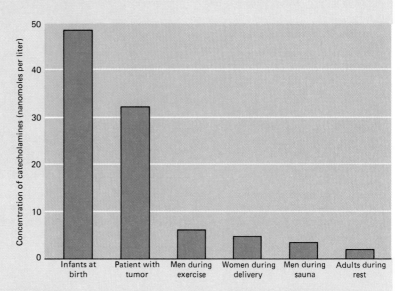

Figure 2-13 Stress hormones in newborn babies and adults. Umbilical samples from newborns show levels of stress hormones 20 times higher than those in resting adults. The surge of hormones during birth is also greater than is found in adults who are exercising or under great physical stress. (*Source:* Adapted from Lagercrantz & Slotkin, 1986.)

most of gestation, but during birth their concentration rises to levels higher than in an adult having a baby or a heart attack (Lagercrantz & Slotkin, 1986; see Figure 2-13).

This burst of catecholamines apparently prepares the newborn for life outside the womb. It clears the lungs for breathing, mobilizes stored fuel for cell nourishment, and sends blood to the heart and brain. By sharpening the newborn's alertness, it may even facilitate immediate bonding between mother and child.

These findings support the growing concern about overuse of cesarean

deliveries, since infants delivered by elective cesarean section, before the onset of labor, miss out on the normal hormonal surge, which seems to be triggered by uterine contractions. (Babies delivered by emergency cesarean, after labor has begun, show catecholamine levels almost as high as vaginally delivered infants.) The breathing problems that C-section babies often suffer may be traceable to the lack of catecholamines, which help absorb liquid in the lungs.

Ironically, catecholamine production may encourage the performance of C-sections by bringing on the irregular heartbeat often detected by electronic fetal monitoring. Unless the electronic data are supplemented by biochemical tests of scalp blood samples, the unsteady beat may be misinterpreted as a danger sign.

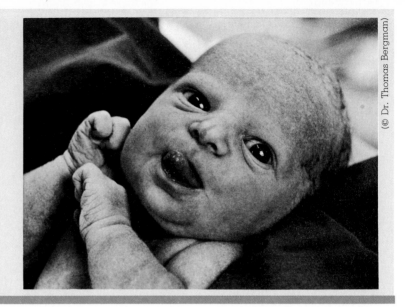

(© Dr. Thomas Bergman)

Only 5 or 6 minutes after birth, this Swedish infant is alert and wide-eyed. A surge of hormones— called *catecholamines*— apparently brought on by labor contractions helps prepare a baby for life outside the womb.

ments can work well. It is often impossible to predict a sudden emergency during childbirth, however, and so it is vital to have backup plans in case there is trouble. A good center will have a contract with an ambulance service, an agreement with a nearby hospital, and on-premises emergency equipment for resuscitation and for administration of oxygen. Provisions for a home birth should include making arrangements for emergency transportation to a hospital no more than 10 minutes away.

Many hospitals *are* big and impersonal, with rigid rules that often seem designed for the smooth functioning of the institution rather than for the benefit of patients. Others, though, are run more to the comfort of patients. In recent years, as hospitals have competed for maternity cases, they have become more responsive to the desires of patients. Many now have rooming-in policies, so that babies can stay in the mother's room for much or all of the day, and permit fathers or other birth coaches to remain with the mother during labor and delivery.

Freestanding maternity centers offer a happy compromise between the comfort of home and the security of a well-equipped medical facility. They are usually staffed principally by nurse-midwives, with one or more physicians and nurse-assistants; they are designed for low-risk, uncomplicated births; and they offer prenatal care, birth in a homelike setting, and discharge the same day.

What are the psychological implications of the new ways of giving birth? First, the techniques that minimize drugs provide a better start in life for the baby. Second, the active participation of both parents reinforces close family attachments between mother, father, and infant. Last, women's insistence on assuming a major role in the births of their children has helped spur a major movement in which people take more active responsibility for their own health rather than sitting back passively and relying on doctors. Of course, there are many ways to have a baby, and many healthy, well-adjusted adults have been born in traditional hospital settings. In view of what we have learned about the importance of feeling in control of one's life, the availability of alternative means of childbirth seems to be a healthy trend, but choice is the crucial element. Children born in a variety of ways can grow up physically and psychologically healthy. In the remainder of this book, we'll trace how that happens.

Fertilization

- Human life begins with the union of an ovum and a sperm cell, which form a one-celled zygote.

- The zygote duplicates itself by cell division.

Heredity and Environment

- At conception, each normal human being receives 23 chromosomes from the mother and 23 from the father. These align into 23 pairs of chromosomes—22 pairs of autosomes and 1 pair of sex chromosomes. Chromosomes carry the genes that determine inherited characteristics.

- Although conception usually results in single births, multiple births can occur. When two ova are fertilized, fraternal (dizygotic) twins will be born; these have different genetic makeups and may be of different sexes. When a single fertilized ovum divides in two, identical (monozygotic) twins will be born; these have the same genetic makeup and therefore are always of the same sex. Larger multiple births result from either one of these processes or a combination of the two.

- A child who receives an X chromosome from each parent will be a female. But if the child receives a Y chromosome from the father, a male will be born.

- The chief patterns of genetic transmission are dominant inheritance, recessive inheritance, sex-linked inheritance, and multifactorial inheritance. Various birth defects and diseases can be transmitted through each of these patterns of inheritance.

- Chromosomal abnormalities can also result in birth defects. The most common is Down syndrome.

- Through genetic counseling, expectant parents can receive information about the mathematical odds of having children who will be afflicted with certain birth defects.

- It is difficult to disentangle the relative contributions of heredity and environment to development. Today, developmentalists look at the *interaction* of heredity and environment rather than attributing development exclusively to one factor or the other.

- Certain aspects of development are influenced more heavily by heredity, and others are influenced more heavily by environment.

Prenatal Development

- Prenatal development occurs in three stages. The germinal stage is characterized by rapid cell division and increased complexity of the organism. The embryonic stage is characterized by rapid growth and differentiation of major body systems and organs. The fetal stage is characterized by rapid growth and changes in body form.

- Nearly all birth defects and three-quarters of all spontaneous abortions occur during the critical first trimester of pregnancy.

- The developing organism is affected greatly by its prenatal environment.

- Important dangers include improper maternal nutrition, drug intake by the mother, incompatibility of blood type with the mother's blood type, medical x-rays, and external environmental hazards. Hazards similar to some of these that affect the father's sperm can also result in harm to the offspring.

- Amniocentesis, chorionic villus sampling, maternal blood testing, and ultrasound are procedures used to determine whether a fetus is developing normally or is afflicted with certain abnormal conditions.

- Electronic fetal monitoring is widely used during labor and delivery, especially in high-risk births, to detect signs of distress in the fetus.

Birth

- Birth normally begins 266 days after conception and occurs in three stages: (1) dilation of the cervix, (2) descent and emergence of the baby, and (3) expulsion of the placenta and the umbilical cord.

- Excessive use of anesthesia in medicated deliveries can have harmful effects on the newborn.

- Natural and prepared childbirth can offer both physical and psychological benefits. "Gentle birth" is a childbirth technique designed to minimize the trauma of birth.

- In recent years, the rate of cesarean deliveries has risen to more than 20 percent in the United States.

- Delivery at home or in birth centers is a feasible alternative to hospital delivery for some women with normal, low-risk pregnancies.

alleles (page 45)
amniocentesis (69)
autosomes (44)
cesarean section (74)
chorionic villus sampling (70)
chromosomes (42)
concordant (51)
depression (56)
dizygotic twins (43)
DNA (deoxyribonucleic acid) (42)
dominant inheritance (45)
Down syndrome (49)
electronic fetal monitoring (71)
embryonic stage (60)
fertilization (41)
fetal alcohol syndrome (FAS) (65)
fetal stage (62)
fetal tobacco syndrome (67)

gametes (41)
genes (42)
genetic counseling (52)
genetics (42)
genotype (46)
germinal stage (57)
heredity (42)
heterozygous (45)
homozygous (45)
independent segregation (45)
infantile autism (56)
karyotype (53)
maternal blood test (70)
maturation (51)
medicated delivery (72)
monozygotic twins (43)
multifactorial inheritance (47)
multiple alleles (46)

natural childbirth (73)
ovulation (41)
personality (55)
phenotype (46)
prepared childbirth (73)
reaction range (51)
recessive inheritance (45)
Rh factor (68)
schizophrenia (55)
sex chromosomes (44)
sex-linked inheritance (46)
spontaneous abortion (60)
temperament (55)
teratogenic (62)
ultrasound (70)
zygote (41)

DeFrain, J., Montens, L., Stork, J., & Stork, W. (1986). *Stillborn: An invisible death.* Lexington, MA: Heath. A sensitive study of the effects of a stillbirth on a family, based on data from 300 questionnaires and 25 in-depth interviews, the book provides concrete information about the reactions of parents, family, and friends to this experience and gives suggestions for coping.

Eisenberg, A., Murkoff, H. E., & Hathaway, S. E. (1984). *What to expect when you're expecting.* New York: Workman. An excellent, comprehensive description of pregnancy, month to month, that incorporates research on care for both mother and baby.

Fried, P. A. (1983). *Pregnancy and life-style habits.* New York: Beaufort. An extensive discussion of the effects of alcohol, caffeine, nicotine, marijuana, and prescription and over-the-counter drugs on the developing fetus.

Leboyer, F. (1975). *Birth without violence.* New York: Knopf. Presents Leboyer's controversial techniques to minimize the trauma of birth; includes beautiful photographs.

Lesko, M., & Lesko, W. (1984). *The maternity sourcebook: 230 basic decisions for pregnancy, birth, and baby care.* New York: Warner. A comprehensive listing of facts, pros and cons, and rival viewpoints concerning every major decision that must be made about pregnancy and the first year of life. The book includes lists of helpful organizations and further readings.

Nilsson, L., Ingelman-Sundberg, A., & Wirsen, C. (1966). *A child is born: The drama of life before birth.* New York: Delacorte. A clearly told description of fetal development, especially notable for beautiful photographs of a live fetus taken inside the womb.

Orenberg, C. L. (1981). *DES: The complete story.* New York: St. Martin's. A thorough discussion of the physical and psychological effects of DES both on the women who have taken the drug and on their daughters and sons.

Singer, S. (1985). *Human genetics* (2d ed.). New York: Freeman. A solid account of genetic principles and how they apply to people. The book begins with Mendel's principles and considers genes, gene pools, genetic disorders, and genetic counseling.

3

CHAPTER

PHYSICAL DEVELOPMENT IN INFANCY AND TODDLERHOOD

The experiences of the first three years of life are almost entirely lost to us, and when we attempt to enter into a small child's world, we come as foreigners who have forgotten the landscape and no longer speak the native tongue.

Selma Fraiberg, *The Magic Years*, 1959

ASK YOURSELF

- How do newborn infants adjust to life outside the womb, and how can we tell whether they are healthy and are developing normally?

- What conditions can complicate newborn babies' adjustment and even endanger their lives?

- What can infants do at birth, and how do they acquire more sophisticated sensory and motor capabilities?

- What can be done to facilitate infants' physical growth and development?

Suppose that, after a rough voyage, you are cast ashore alone and without possessions in an unknown land. You are taken into the care of giants, whose behavior is strange, and whose speech is gibberish. What's more, you find yourself physically helpless and unable to communicate your wants or your needs.

Although you undoubtedly don't remember it, you have been through just such an experience—at the moment of your birth. A newborn baby is, in an extreme sense, an immigrant. After struggling through a difficult passage, the infant is faced with much more than the task of learning the language and the customs. A baby has to start to breathe, eat, adapt to the climate, and respond to confusing surroundings. This is a mighty challenge for beings who weigh but a few pounds and whose organ systems are still not fully mature. But as we'll see, infants normally come into the world with body systems and senses all working to some extent and ready to meet that challenge.

THE NEONATE

The first 4 weeks of life constitute the *neonatal period*, a time of transition from intrauterine life—when a fetus is supported entirely by its mother's body—to an independent existence. Who are these newcomers to the world? What do they look like? What can they do?

Physical Characteristics

An average newborn, or **neonate,** is about 20 inches long and weighs about 7½ pounds. At birth, 95 percent of full-term babies weigh between 5½ and 10 pounds and measure between 18 and 22 inches in length (Behrman & Vaughan, 1983). Size at birth is related to such factors as race, sex, parents' size, maternal nutrition, and maternal health. Males tend to be a little longer and heavier than females, and a firstborn child is likely to weigh less at birth than later-borns. Size at birth is related to size during childhood (Behrman & Vaughan, 1983).

In their first few days, neonates lose as much as 10 percent of body weight, primarily because of a loss of fluids. On about the fifth day, they begin to gain, and they are generally back to birth weight by the tenth day to the fourteenth. Light full-term infants lose less weight than heavy ones, and firstborns lose less than laterborns (Behrman & Vaughan, 1983).

The neonate's head may be long and misshapen because of the "molding" that eased its passage through the mother's pelvis. This temporary molding was possible because the baby's skull bones are not yet fused; they will not be completely joined for 18 months. The places on the head where the bones have not yet grown together—the soft spots, or fontanels—are covered by a tough membrane. Since the cartilage in the baby's nose is also malleable, the trip through the birth canal leaves it looking squashed for a few days.

Newborns are quite pale—even black babies who will later be very dark. They have a pinkish cast because of the thinness of their skin, which barely covers the blood flowing through tiny capillaries. The *vernix caseosa* ("cheesy varnish"), an oily covering that protects new babies against infection, dries in a few days' time. Some neonates are very hairy, but within a few days, the *lanugo*, the fuzzy prenatal hair, drops off.

"Witch's milk," a secretion that sometimes issues from the swollen breasts of newborn boys and girls, was believed during the Middle Ages to have special healing powers. Like the blood-tinged vaginal discharge of some baby girls, this fluid emission results from high levels of the hormone estrogen, which is secreted by the placenta just before birth.

Body Systems

Before birth, the fetus's blood circulation, respiration, nourishment, elimination, and temperature regulation are all accomplished through its connection with the mother's body. After birth, infants must perform these functions on their own. The transition from intrauterine life to life on the outside makes major demands on all body systems (see Table 3-1, page 84). In almost all cases, the body systems are equal to these demands.

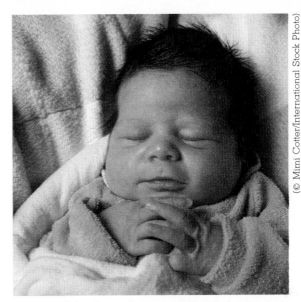

A neonate's head may be temporarily misshapen as a result of the passage through the birth canal. The skin of newborns is thin, pale, and pinkish; and they may have a great deal of hair, which drops out within a few days. Neonates spend most of their time sleeping, but they awaken, hungry, every 2 to 3 hours.

Circulatory System Before birth, mother and baby have independent circulatory systems and separate heartbeats; but the fetus's blood is cleansed through the umbilical cord, which carries blood to and from the placenta. Upon birth, the baby's own system must take over to circulate blood through the body. The neonate's heartbeat is still accelerated and irregular, and blood pressure does not stabilize until about the tenth day.

Respiratory System The umbilical cord brings oxygen to the fetus and carries back carbon dioxide. The newborn needs much more oxygen and must now get it all alone. Most infants start to breathe as soon as they emerge into the air. A baby who is not breathing within 2 minutes after birth is in trouble; if breathing has not begun within 5 minutes or so, some degree of brain injury from *anoxia*, lack of oxygen, may result. Infants have only one-tenth the number of air sacs that adults do and thus are vulnerable to respiratory problems.

Gastrointestinal System In the uterus, the fetus relies on the umbilical cord to bring food

TABLE 3-1 A COMPARISON OF PRENATAL AND POSTNATAL LIFE

CHARACTERISTIC	PRENATAL LIFE	POSTNATAL LIFE
Environment	Amniotic fluid	Air
Temperature	Relatively constant	Fluctuates with atmosphere
Stimulation	Minimal	All senses stimulated by various stimuli
Nutrition	Dependent on mother's blood	Dependent on external food and functioning of digestive system
Oxygen supply	Passed from maternal bloodstream via placenta	Passed from neonate's lungs to pulmonary blood vessels
Metabolic elimination	Passed into maternal bloodstream via placenta	Discharged by skin, kidneys, lungs, and gastrointestinal tract

Source: Timiras, 1972, p. 174.

from the mother and to carry body wastes away. Upon birth, the infant has a strong sucking reflex to take in milk, as well as the gastrointestinal secretions to digest it. *Meconium* (stringy, greenish-black waste matter formed in the fetal intestinal tract) is excreted during the first 2 days or so after birth. When the neonate's bowels and bladder are full, the sphincter muscles open automatically. Many months will pass before the baby can control these muscles.

Three or four days after birth, about half of all babies, particularly those who were born prematurely, develop *physiological jaundice:* their skin and eyeballs look yellow. This kind of jaundice is caused by the immaturity of the liver; it is usually not serious and has no long-term effects. It is generally treated by putting the baby under fluorescent lights.

Temperature Regulation The layers of fat that develop during the last months of fetal life enable healthy full-term infants to keep their body temperature constant despite changes in air temperature. Newborn babies also maintain body temperature by increasing their activity in response to a drop in air temperature.

The Brain and Reflex Behaviors

What makes newborns respond to the touch of a nipple? What tells them to start the sucking movements that allow them to control their own intake of nourishment?

These are functions of the nervous system, which consists of the brain, the spinal cord (a bundle of nerves running down the backbone), and a growing network of nerves, which eventually reaches every part of the body. Through this network, sensory messages travel to the brain, and motor commands travel back. This complex communication system governs what a baby—or an adult—can do both physically and mentally. Because the brain controls human behavior, its normal growth before and after birth is fundamental to future development.

Growth of the Brain The human brain grows most rapidly during gestation and early postnatal life. Developmental neurobiologists estimate that the developing fetus forms 250,000 brain cells per minute through cell division (mitosis), and most of the 100 billion cells in a mature brain are already formed at birth (Cowan, 1979; see Figure 3-1).

A spurt in the growth of brain cells comes just before birth and shortly afterward. The newly formed cells sort themselves out by function, migrating to their proper positions either in the *cerebral cortex,* the upper layer of the brain, or in the subcortical levels (below the cortex). In a newborn infant, the subcortical structures, which regulate basic biological functioning (such as breathing and digestion), are the most fully developed; cells in the cortex, which is responsible for thinking and problem solving, are

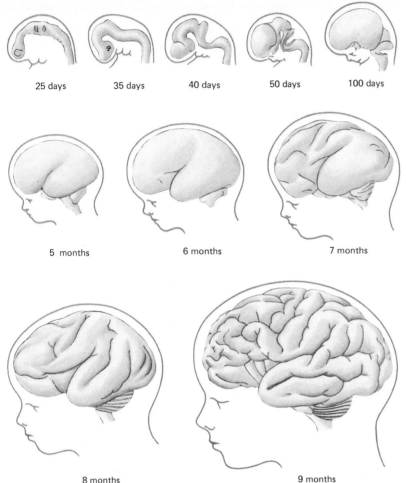

25 days   35 days   40 days   50 days   100 days

5 months   6 months   7 months

8 months   9 months

Figure 3-1 Fetal brain development from 25 days of gestation through birth. As the brain develops, the front part expands greatly to form the cerebrum (the large, convoluted upper mass). Specific areas of the cerebral cortex, the gray outer covering of the brain, are devoted to particular functions, such as sensory and motor activities; but large areas are "uncommitted" and thus are free for higher intellectual activities, such as thinking, remembering, and problem solving. The subcortex, which consists of the brain stem and other structures below the cortical layer, handles reflex behavior and other lower-level functions. The newborn's brain contains most of the cells it will eventually have, but it weighs only about 25 percent of its adult weight. A rapid increase in cortical connections during the first two years of life results in a dramatic gain in the brain's weight (to four-fifths of adult weight) and in the capacity for thought. (Source: Restak, 1984.)

not yet well connected. Connections between cells in the cortex increase astronomically as the child matures, allowing more flexible, higher-level motor and intellectual functioning.

Within 2 months after birth, the formation of new cells diminishes greatly (Lipsitt, 1986), though the existing cells continue to grow. Cells that do not function as well as others or that have migrated to the wrong part of the brain die out. Pruning of excess cells helps to create an efficient nervous system. In addition, the nerve fibers become encased in a white, fatty substance called *myelin*, which speeds the transmission of neural messages.

The brain, which is only 25 percent of its adult weight at birth, reaches about two-thirds of its eventual weight during the first year and four-fifths by the end of the second year. It continues to grow more slowly until, by age 12, it is virtually adult size (Behrman & Vaughan, 1983).*

An infant's neurological growth, then, permits a corresponding growth in motor and intellectual activities. Reflex behaviors—or their absence—are early signs of this growth.

A Newborn's Reflexes When babies (or adults) blink at a bright light, they are acting involuntarily. Such automatic responses to external stimulation are called *reflex behaviors.*

Human beings have an array of reflexes, many of which are present before birth, at birth,

*In late life, brain development reverses itself to some extent. The brains of 75-year-olds weigh 10 percent less, have 20 percent less blood flow and 33 percent fewer fibers, and are 10 percent slower in conducting messages than those of 30-year-olds, so that a small but significant degree of memory loss and other changes in intellectual functioning result.

TABLE 3-2 HUMAN PRIMITIVE REFLEXES

REFLEX	STIMULATION	BEHAVIOR	APPROXIMATE AGE OF DROPPING OUT
Rooting	Baby's cheek is stroked with finger or nipple.	Baby's head turns; mouth opens; sucking movements begin.	9 months
Moro (startle)	Baby is dropped or hears loud noise.	Baby extends legs, arms, and fingers; arches back; draws back head.	3 months
Darwinian (grasping)	Palm of baby's hand is stroked.	Baby makes strong fist; can be raised to standing position if both fists are closed around a stick.	2 months
Swimming	Baby is put into water face down.	Baby makes well-coordinated swimming movements.	6 months
Tonic neck	Baby is laid down on back.	Baby turns head to one side, assumes "fencer" position, extends arms and legs on preferred side, flexes opposite limbs.	2 months
Babinski	Sole of baby's foot is stroked.	Baby's toes fan out; foot twists in.	6–9 months
Walking	Baby is held under arm, with bare foot touching flat surface.	Baby makes steplike motions that look like well-coordinated walking.	2 months
Placing	Backs of baby's feet are drawn against edge of flat surface.	Baby withdraws foot.	1 month

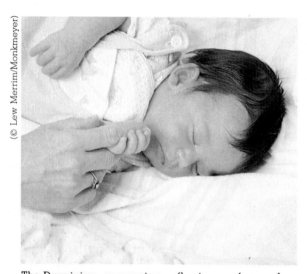

(© Lew Merrim/Monkmeyer)

The Darwinian, or grasping, reflex is one of several primitive reflexes that newborn babies show. These primitive reflexes drop out within the first year, as voluntary behavior controlled by the developing cortex takes over.

or slightly after birth (see Table 3-2). Some of them appear to promote survival or to offer protection. In the normal course of neurological development, the primitive reflexes disappear during the first year or so; for example, the Moro, or startle, reflex drops out at 2 to 3 months, and rooting for the nipple at about 9 months. Such protective reflexes as blinking, yawning, coughing, gagging, sneezing, and the pupillary reflex (dilation of the pupils in the dark) remain. (Reflexes vary somewhat, however, according to culture; see Box 3-1, pages 88–89.)

Because the subcortex controls the primitive reflexes, their disappearance is a sign of the development of the cortex and the shift to voluntary control of behavior. Since there is a timetable for shedding these reflexes, their presence or absence in the first few months of life is a guide to evaluating neurological development.

One of the first things a doctor does upon delivering a baby is to test for normal reflexes.

Environmental Influences on Development of the Brain Until the middle of the twentieth century, the established scientific view was that brain growth followed an unchangeable pattern. Now it is known that, especially during its period of rapid growth, the brain is—figuratively speaking—plastic: it can be easily molded. The experiences of early life may have lasting effects, for better or worse, on the capacity of the central nervous system to learn and to store information (Wittrock, 1980).

As we saw in Chapter 2, chronic malnutrition during the prenatal period can result in brain damage. So can undernourishment in the critical period shortly after birth.

By the same token, an enriched environment can enhance brain growth and structure. In a series of experiments starting in the late 1950s, rats and other animals raised in "enriched" cages with a variety of stimulating apparatus were found to have heavier brains with thicker cortical layers, more connective cells, and higher levels of neurochemical activity (which facilitates the formation of connections between brain cells) than littermates raised in "standard" cages or in isolation (Rosenzweig, 1984; Rosenzweig & Bennett, 1976). Furthermore, the brain's plasticity apparently continues, though to a lesser degree, throughout most of the life span; the researchers found similar neural differences when older animals were exposed to differing environments.

These findings have sparked successful efforts to stimulate the development of children with Down syndrome, to keep aging people mentally fit, and to help victims of brain damage recover functioning. The findings also help explain why infants with birth complications sometimes develop normally, as we'll see in the next section.

IS THE BABY HEALTHY?

How can we tell whether a neonate's systems are functioning normally? What can be done to help babies who suffer from complications of birth, who are born prematurely, or whose birth weight is dangerously low? In short, how can we ensure that babies will live, grow, and develop as they should?

Medical and Behavioral Screening

Because those first few weeks, days, and even minutes after birth are crucial for future development, it is important to know as soon as possible whether a baby has any problem that requires special care. To find out, doctors and psychologists use a variety of scales that measure physical and psychological development, including the Apgar scale (Table 3-3), neonatal screening, and the Brazelton scale.

TABLE 3-3 APGAR SCALE			
SIGN*	0	1	2
Appearance (color)	Blue, pale	Body pink, extremities blue	Entirely pink
Pulse (heart rate)	Absent	Slow (below 100)	Rapid (over 100)
Grimace (reflex irritability)	No response	Grimace	Coughing, sneezing, crying
Activity (muscle tone)	Limp	Weak, inactive	Strong, active
Respiration (breathing)	Absent	Irregular, slow	Good, crying

*Each sign is rated in terms of absence or presence from 0 to 2; highest overall score is 10.
Source: Adapted from Apgar, 1953.

BOX 3-1 WINDOW ON THE WORLD

HOW UNIVERSAL IS "NORMAL" DEVELOPMENT?

Are behaviors universal? We might expect so, but research suggests that they are not (D.G. Freedman, 1979). For example, western children's normal response to having the nose briefly pressed with a cloth is the "defensive reaction," an immediate turning away of the head or swiping at the cloth. Among Chinese babies, however, the usual reaction is a prompt opening of the mouth to restore breathing, without a fight.

Another typical behavior among western newborns is the Moro reflex. To test for this reflex, the baby's body is lifted, and the head supported. The head support is then released, and the head is allowed to drop. Typical newborn white children reflexively extend both arms and legs, cry persistently, and move about in an agitated manner. Navajo babies, however, typically respond with a reduced reflex extension of the limbs. Crying

is rare, and agitated motion ceases almost immediately.

If reflex behaviors may not be universal, are motor skills? When the Denver Developmental Screening Test was given to southeast Asian children (V. Miller, Onotera, & Deinard, 1984), the youngsters failed on three standard measures of normal development: they did not play pat-a-cake, they did not pick up raisins, and they did not dress themselves at the usual ages. Before we jump to the conclusion that these youngsters were backward in their development, we should recognize that in their culture, pat-a-cake is not played; that raisins look like a medicine they are taught to avoid; and that they are not expected to dress themselves until a later age than western children. Because the test was devised for American children, it may be skewed, or biased, against children in cultures with different customs.

Even when we look at behaviors common to human

beings everywhere, such as sitting and walking, what is normal and typical for children in one culture may not be so in another. Black African babies appear to be more precocious in gross motor skills, and Asian infants less so, than infants of European origin. These differences may be related to cultural differences in temperament. Asian infants, for example, are typically more docile and thus may tend to stay closer to their parents (Kaplan & Dove, 1987).

Although short-term experiments suggest that it is difficult (and not necessarily desirable) to accelerate or modify a child's motor development, certain child-rearing practices that are widespread in a culture may advance or retard it. The anthropologist Margaret Mead observed that Arapesh infants in New Guinea could stand while holding on to something before they could sit alone. The apparent reason was that

Immediate Medical Asessment: The Apgar Scale One minute after delivery, and then again 5 minutes after delivery, infants are checked using the *Apgar scale* (see Table 3-3). The name of this scale commemorates its developer, Dr. Virginia Apgar (1953), and also helps us remember its five subtests: *a*ppearance (color), *p*ulse (heart rate), *g*rimace (reflex irritability), *a*ctivity (muscle tone), and *r*espiration (breathing).

The infant receives a rating of 0, 1, or 2 on each measure, for a maximum of 10. Ninety

percent of normal infants score 7 or better. A score below 7 generally means that the baby needs help to establish breathing. A score below 4 means that the baby is in danger and needs immediate life-saving treatment. In that case, the test is repeated at 5-minute intervals to check on the effectiveness of resuscitation. If the effort is successful and the score rises to at least 4, there usually are no serious long-term consequences. A score of 0 to 3 at 10, 15, and 20 minutes suggests a greater risk of neurological damage, particularly cerebral palsy (American

these infants were often held in a standing position, "so that [Mead reported] they can push with their feet against the arms or legs of the person who holds them" (1935, p. 57).

At 3 months of age, babies from the Yucatan peninsula in Mexico are ahead of American babies in motor skills; yet by 11 months the Yucatecan babies are far behind—so much so that the same pattern in an American child might be taken as an indication of neurological disease (Solomons, 1978). The Yucatecan babies' manipulative precocity may result from their having no toys and thus discovering and playing with their fingers sooner. Their delayed skills in moving about may have to do with their being swaddled as infants and restrained in various ways as they get older. However, Navajo babies—who are also swaddled for most of the day—begin to walk at approximately the same time as other American babies (Chisholm, 1983).

Some cultural differences in motor development may reflect genetic differences among peoples, which have arisen through the process of natural selection. This evolutionary process occurs as individuals who adapt successfully to their environment survive and reproduce, passing on their hereditary traits to their descendants. This is one possible reason why Ache children in eastern Paraguay show delays in gross motor skills, learning to walk about 9 months later than American babies (Kaplan & Dove, 1987). Until the mid-1970s, the Ache economy was based entirely on hunting and foraging. It is possible, then, that natural selection favored the more cautious, less exploratory members of this society.

An environmental explanation for the later motor development among the Ache may lie in child-rearing practices. Ache mothers traditionally inhibit their children from exploring the forest by pulling the babies back to their laps when they begin to crawl away. This intense supervision, a response to the hazards of nomadic life, also reflects women's primary responsibility for child rearing and their lack of involvement in subsistence labor. It is possible that when mothers spend less time in direct child care, children become independent sooner because their caretakers are less vigilant—an observation that may apply to American babies at a time when day care is prevalent and certain aspects of development appear to be typically occurring at earlier ages than they did previously.

Children in the Ache and other cultures who exhibit early developmental lags compared with American children often catch up later on. Ache 8- to 10-year-olds climb tall trees, chop branches, and engage in complicated play that enhances their motor skills. The researchers suggest that development may be viewed "as a series of immediate adjustments to current conditions as well as a cumulative process in which succeeding stages build upon earlier ones" (Kaplan & Dove, 1987, p. 197).

It is clear that differences in development exist among various cultures; the reasons for those differences bear further study.

Academy of Pediatrics Committee on Fetus and Newborn, 1986).

Low Apgar scores do not always indicate that the baby is suffocating. An infant's tone and responsiveness may be affected by the amount of sedation or pain-killing medication the mother was given. Neurological and cardiorespiratory conditions may interfere with one or more of the vital signs. And premature infants may score low purely because of their physiological immaturity.

Neonatal Screening for Medical Conditions
Children who inherit the enzyme disorder phenylketonuria (PKU) become mentally retarded unless they are fed a special diet beginning in the first 3 to 6 weeks of life. To discover the presence of PKU and certain other correctable defects, researchers have developed screening tests that can be administered immediately after birth.

Routine screening of all newborn babies for such rare conditions as PKU (1 case in 14,000 births), hypothyroidism (1 in 4250), galactosemia (1 in 62,000), or other, even rarer disorders is, of course, expensive. Yet the cost of detecting one case of a rare disease is often less than the cost of caring for a mentally retarded child for a lifetime. Almost all states require routine screening for PKU, and about half of them require screening for one or more other conditions.

Assessing Responses: The Brazelton Scale

The *Brazelton Neonatal Behavioral Assessment Scale* is a neurological and behavioral test used to measure the way neonates respond to their environment (Brazelton, 1973). The Brazelton scale assesses four dimensions of infants' behavior:

- *Interactive behaviors,* such as alertness and cuddliness
- *Motor behaviors* (reflexes, muscle tone, and hand-mouth coordination)
- *Physiological control,* such as ability to quiet down after being upset
- *Response to stress* (the startle reaction)

The test takes about 30 minutes, and scores are based on a baby's best performance, rather than an average. The testers try to get babies to do their best, sometimes repeating an item and sometimes asking the mother to alert her baby. The Brazelton scale may be a better predictor of a baby's future development than the Apgar scale or standard neurological testing (Behrman & Vaughan, 1983).

Effects of Birth Trauma

For a small minority of babies, the passage through the birth canal is a most harrowing journey. A study of more than 15,000 births over a period of 6 years at an outstanding medical school (A. Rubin, 1977) found that fewer than 1 percent of the infants suffered **birth trauma** (injury sustained at the time of birth) but that injury at birth was the second most common cause of neonatal death (after suffocation because of failure of the lungs to expand). Birth trauma may be caused by **anoxia** (oxygen deprivation at birth), neonatal diseases or infections, or mechanical injury; some infants who experi-

ence it are left with permanent brain damage, causing mental retardation or behavior problems.

Often, however, the effects of birth injuries can be counteracted by a favorable environment. In a longitudinal study of almost 900 children born on the island of Kauai, Hawaii, those whose births had been difficult, whose birth weight had been low, or who had been sick when born were examined at the ages of 10 and 18. The findings were clear: "Perinatal complications were consistently related to later impaired physical and psychological development *only* when combined with persistently poor environmental circumstances" (E. E. Werner, 1985, p. 341). Unless the damage was so severe as to require institutionalization, these children—when their environment was stable and enriching—did better in school and had fewer language, perceptual, and emotional problems than children who had not experienced unusual stress at birth but who had suffered "environmental trauma" in poor homes where they received little intellectual stimulation or emotional support (E. E. Werner et al., 1968).

These studies have done much to demonstrate the resilience of children and to establish the fact that even very alarming transitory events can be less important than day-to-day experience.

Low Birth Weight and Infant Mortality

We have made great strides in protecting the lives of new babies. Today in the United States, the **infant mortality** rate—the proportion of babies who die within the first year of life—is the lowest in our history. In 1984, there were fewer than 11 deaths in the first year for every 1000 live births, a 59 percent improvement since 1960.

Even so, the nearly 40,000 infants who died before their first birthday represented the largest number of deaths in any single year of life up to age 65; and 70 percent of those babies died in their first 4 weeks. Of that group, two-thirds were **low-birth-weight babies,** babies who weighed less than 5½ pounds at birth (S. S. Brown, 1985; C. A. Miller, 1985; Morbidity and Mortality Weekly Report, MMWR, 1987a). Thus low birth weight is the major factor in infant

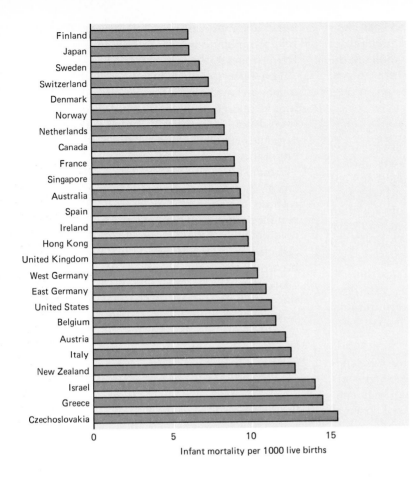

Figure 3-2 Infant mortality rates in industrialized countries. A nation's infant mortality rate is one indicator of its health status. The United States is only eighteenth among 25 industrialized nations with populations of 2.5 million or more. (*Source:* J. L. Brown, 1987.)

deaths and in the poorer chances American babies have for survival than babies in 17 other industrialized countries (J. L. Brown, 1987; see Figure 3-2).

Nearly 7 percent of all babies born in the United States—about 1 in 14—have low birth weights. These infants are 40 times more likely to die during the critical neonatal period than are babies of normal weight; when a baby weighs 3½ pounds or less, the risk jumps to 200 to 1 (Behrman, 1985; S. S. Brown, 1985).

Furthermore, birth weight is the key to racial and socioeconomic differences in mortality rates. About twice as many black babies die as white babies; and while prospects for survival of black infants have improved, they have not kept pace with the dramatic overall decline in infant deaths (MMWR, 1987a).

This overall improvement—which, unfortunately, seems to be slowing, possibly because of a rise in deaths *after* the neonatal period—has been attributed to such factors as centers for prenatal and postnatal care, early identification of high-risk pregnancies, and spacing of pregnancies to reduce the danger of high-risk births (American Academy of Pediatrics Task Force on Infant Mortality, 1986; C. A. Miller, 1985). Why have these factors had less effect within the black community?

The main difference is in black and white babies' birth weights. Black newborns are twice as likely as white newborns to have low birth weights and 3 times as likely to have very low birth weights (MMWR, 1987a).

The average baby from a socioeconomically disadvantaged group weighs half a pound less at birth than the average middle-class baby (Winick, 1981). Yet, as Winick (who is a pediatric nutritionist) points out, "Pound for pound, the poor baby does as well as the rich baby; black babies do as well as white babies" (p. 80). Therefore, a major contribution to saving the lives of babies would be to raise the average birth weight by even half a pound.

Types of Low-Birth-Weight Babies All very small infants used to be considered premature; that is, they were said not to have completed the full term of a normal gestation. Doctors now assign very small babies to one or both of two categories:

■ *Preterm (premature) babies,* who are born before the thirty-seventh gestational week, dated from the first day of the mother's last menstrual period (40 weeks is normal gestation). These babies typically weigh less than 5½ pounds and, according to estimates by the U.S. Public Health Service, account for 60 percent of low-birth-weight babies.
■ *Small-for-date babies,* who weigh less than 90 percent of all babies of the same gestational age and may or may not be preterm infants. These babies suffer from slowed fetal growth.

Because the distinction between the two types of low-birth-weight babies has evolved only within the past decade or so, it has not been considered in most studies of the effects of "prematurity." Therefore we don't actually know whether most studies of low-birth-weight babies yield information about babies who were born early or about those who were small for their gestational age or both.

The risks to both types of babies are similar, but premature babies are more likely to die in infancy than small-for-date babies (Behrman, 1985; March of Dimes Birth Defects Foundation, undated). The shorter the gestation period (if it is less than 36 weeks), the more problems the baby is likely to have. The neonatal transition takes longer for preterm babies because they enter the world with less fully developed body systems.

Consequences of Low Birth Weight Very small babies suffer from many potentially fatal complications. Because they have less fat to insulate them and to generate heat, they have more trouble maintaining normal body temperature, and so it is especially important to keep them warm. Because their immune systems are not fully developed, they are more vulnerable to infection. Their reflexes are not mature enough

to perform functions basic to survival; they may, for example, be unable to suck and have to be fed intravenously.

Low-birth-weight babies have a higher incidence of low blood sugar, jaundice, and bleeding in the brain than babies of normal size (March of Dimes Birth Defects Foundation, undated). Their lungs may not be strong enough to sustain breathing.

About 10 percent of all infant deaths occur from respiratory distress syndrome, also called hyaline membrane disease, a condition most common among premature babies, whose bodies sometimes do not produce enough of a crucial lung-coating substance and who, as a result, breathe irregularly or stop breathing altogether (Wegman, 1983). Such deaths have declined since 1970 as a result of the improved medical care offered to premature infants.

In the past, studies indicated that even when low-birth-weight babies survived the dangerous early days, they were left with various disabling conditions. More recent research, however, gives greater cause for optimism. One study found that 80 percent of babies who weighed less than 2 pounds at birth died, but that 13 out of 16 survivors were developing well when followed up at ages 6 months to 3 years. They showed no major handicaps of the central nervous system and no major problems with vision or hearing, and only 1 out of the 16 was of subnormal intelligence (Bennett, Robinson, & Sells, 1983).

A later study tested eighty 5-year-olds who had weighed less than 3 pounds at birth and found them doing "remarkably well" (N. Klein, Hack, Gallagher, & Fanaroff, 1985, p. 536). Their IQs were normal, and their central nervous systems were functioning well. The researchers did detect lacks in spatial perception and eye-hand coordination but suggested that with early identification, such problems could be reduced.

Who Is Likely to Have a Low-Birth-Weight Baby? Women in certain categories are statistically more likely than others to give birth to underweight infants (see Table 3-4). These predictions can be made on the basis of the following factors:

TABLE 3.4 PRINCIPAL MATERNAL RISK FACTORS FOR DELIVERING UNDERWEIGHT INFANTS

CATEGORY	RISKS
Demographic risks	Age (under 17 or over 34) Race (black) Low socioeconomic status Unmarried Low level of education
Medical risks predating current pregnancy	No children or more than four Low weight for height Genital or urinary abnormalities or past surgery Diseases such as diabetes or chronic hypertension Lack of immunity to certain infections, such as rubella Poor obstetric history, including previous low-birth-weight infant and multiple spontaneous abortions Genetic factors in the mother (such as low weight at her own birth)
Medical risks in current pregnancy	Multiple pregnancy Poor weight gain (less than 14 pounds) Less than 6 months since previous pregnancy Low blood pressure Hypertension or toxemia Certain infections, such as rubella and urinary infections Bleeding in the first or second trimester Placental problems Anemia or abnormal hemoglobin Fetal abnormalities Incompetent cervix Spontaneous premature rupture of membranes
Behavioral and environmental risks	Smoking Poor nutritional status Abuse of alcohol and other substances Exposure to DES and other toxins, including those in the workplace High altitude
Risks involving health care	Absent or inadequate prenatal care Premature delivery by cesarean section or induced labor

Source: Adapted from S.S. Brown, 1985.

- *Demographic factors,* such as race, age, education, and marital status
- *Medical factors predating the pregnancy,* such as previous abortions, stillbirths, or medical conditions
- *Medical factors associated with the current pregnancy,* such as bleeding or too little weight gain
- *Prenatal behavioral and environmental factors,* such as inadequate nutrition, smoking, use of alcohol and drugs, and exposure to toxic substances (see Chapter 2)

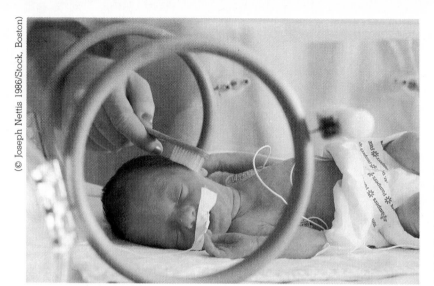

To improve their chances for survival, low-birth-weight babies are typically placed in germ-free isolettes in which they are fed through tubes and have no human contact except for basic care. To avoid sensory impoverishment, however, personal attention and stimulation are important.

These factors interact with socioeconomic ones. For example, teenagers' propensity to bear underweight infants may result from poor nutrition and prenatal care rather than from age. And the fact that black women bear more low-birth-weight babies than white women has to do with a number of factors, including poverty, low educational levels, and the greater likelihood that black women will become teenage mothers (S.S. Brown, 1985).

Preventing Low Birth Weight The surgeon general of the United States has set a goal of cutting the incidence of low birth weight to 5 percent by 1990. Toward that end, women can reduce their risk factors before pregnancy. They can stop smoking, improve their diets, cut down or eliminate alcohol use, and get treatment for chronic illnesses. Public information programs and prepregnancy counseling for women who have previously lost low-birth-weight infants can also help.

Once a pregnancy is in progress, early and regular prenatal care lessens the likelihood of low birth weight. In the 1970s more women than before received prenatal care in the first trimester (U.S. Department of Health and Human Services, USDHHS, 1982). Unfortunately, that was not the case in the 1980s for the most vulnerable groups—teenagers, women with little education, and black women—though it continued to be true for whites and for col-

lege-educated women (S.S. Brown, 1985; Ingram, Makuc, & Kleinman, 1986).

Treatment of Low-Birth-Weight Babies Much of the rise in neonatal survival is attributable to improved care of low-birth-weight babies. The standard procedure is to place the baby in an isolette (formerly called an incubator), an antiseptic, temperature-controlled crib intended to simulate the womb. Feeding is done through tubes. Babies who have jaundice are placed under special lights, anemic babies get iron supplements, and those with low blood sugar are fed glucose through the veins.

Until recently, most hospitals maintained a "hands off" policy in the belief that these delicate creatures were best left undisturbed except for having their basic needs met. But life in the womb, where sounds and motion reach the fetus, is not as dull as life in an isolette. Researchers now believe that isolation and the resulting sensory impoverishment may be a source of difficulties for both infant and parents.

Parents tend to view a low-birth-weight baby negatively, to be anxious about the baby's health and reluctant to become too attached for fear that the baby may die (Jeffcoate, Humphrey, & Lloyd, 1979). Frequent visits can give parents a more realistic idea of how the baby is doing and, perhaps, a more optimistic prognosis. In addition, regularly visited babies seem to recover more quickly and to leave the hospital sooner

(Zeskind & Iacino, 1984). Parents who get extra counseling tend to care for their babies better afterward (Minde, Shosenberg, Marton, Thompson, Ripley, & Burns, 1980), unless the mothers are so overwhelmed by other life stresses that they can barely get through each day (J. Brown, LaRossa, Aylward, Davis, Rutherford, & Bakeman, 1980). In such cases, intervention and support from professional agencies are especially important.

Other efforts are being made to overcome the physiological and psychological problems of low-birth-weight babies, with promising results. One recent study found that infants who were given pacifiers to suck during their tubal feedings developed the sucking reflex faster than those who were not given pacifiers. The babies given pacifiers also gained weight more quickly and were able to switch to oral feedings and as a result were able to go home earlier (Bernbaum, Pereira, Watkins, & Peckham, 1983). Low-birth-weight babies who got more sensory stimulation (for example, mobiles hung in their isolettes) and more attention in the hospital (from nurses who rubbed or rocked them and talked and sang during feedings) did markedly better than other low-birth-weight babies on tests of infant intelligence (Leib, Benfield, & Guidubaldi, 1980). More recent research demonstrated that touch stimulation (including body massage) facilitates growth, behavioral organization, weight gain, motor activity, and alertness (T.M. Field, 1986; Schanberg & Field, 1987).

Through prevention of low birth weight and through wise intervention when it occurs, the number of babies who survive the neonatal period and the first year of life may be further increased.

Sudden Infant Death Syndrome (SIDS)

One kind of infant death follows a particularly tragic scenario: a baby goes peacefully to sleep at the usual time, but when the parents come in later to check, they find their baby dead. *Sudden infant death syndrome (SIDS),* the sudden and unexpected death of an apparently healthy infant, takes the lives of some 7000 babies a year, or 2 out of every 1000 born. It is the leading cause of infant deaths after the neonatal period and occurs most frequently between 2 and 4 months of age (Arnon, Midura, Damus, Wood, & Chin, 1978).

We know little about SIDS. The death is not caused by suffocation, vomiting, or choking, and there is no known way to predict or prevent it. It is most common in winter, and it is not contagious.

A number of risk factors are related to SIDS. Babies who succumb are more likely to be of low birth weight, black, and male. Their mothers are more likely to be young, unmarried, and poor; to have received little or no prenatal care; to have been ill during the pregnancy; to smoke or abuse drugs or both; and to have had another baby less than a year before the one they have lost. Their fathers are also more likely to be young (Babson & Clark, 1983; C.E. Hunt & Brouillette, 1987; Kleinberg, 1984; D.C. Shannon & Kelly, 1982a, 1982b; Valdes-Dapena, 1980). It seems clear that whatever these babies' problems are, they are worsened by living in low socioeconomic circumstances. This is not the only answer, however, since many infants in advantaged families also succumb.

The babies themselves are more likely to have abnormal breathing patterns, to have some respiratory tract infection, and to have experienced *apnea* (a temporary stoppage of breathing) for either short or long periods of time (D.H. Kelly, Golub, Carley, & Shannon, 1986; D.C. Shannon & Kelly, 1982a, 1982b). New theories about the cause of SIDS are constantly being proposed, including such possibilities as a respiratory dysfunction, a neurological dysfunction, and an abnormality in brain chemistry. A recent review concluded that the most compelling hypothesis about SIDS relates it to a brain abnormality involving the regulation of respiratory control (C.E. Hunt & Brouillette, 1987).

So far, none of the research has shown us how to prevent SIDS. Monitoring machines have been developed that sound an alarm during a period of apnea, but they are expensive and hard to operate. Furthermore, they can cause the parents considerable anxiety and stress (Wasserman, 1984).

The bereaved families suffer greatly. In studies of SIDS families, all the parents contacted rated SIDS as the most severe family crisis they had ever experienced (DeFrain & Ernst, 1978;

DeFrain, Taylor, & Ernst, 1982). The parents felt guilty and under criticism from society, the siblings reacted with such emotional problems as nightmares and school problems, and it usually took almost a year for the families to recover.

One recent and controversial study questions the attribution of some infant deaths to SIDS. By examining the circumstances surrounding 26 consecutive deaths reported at a Brooklyn hospital in a low-income neighborhood, the researchers concluded that all but two of the victims may have died from accidental causes: they may have been smothered by pillows, blankets, or other objects or by someone sleeping in the same bed; been shaken or bundled too closely; or slept in defective beds, near a radiator or furnace, or in a room with a hazardous heating system. Poverty, overcrowding, and inattention or poor judgment on the part of caretakers was implicated in many of the cases (Bass, Kravath, & Glass, 1986).

Fortunately, 989 out of 1000 children do *not* die in infancy but go on with the development typical of the first 3 years.

THE DEVELOPING BABY

Because human beings live and behave only as whole persons, all aspects of their development are intimately connected. When we try to separate these aspects (as in a textbook), we find ourselves making arbitrary divisions, cutting the person into jigsaw pieces.

For example, although we usually think of learning as a mental function, infants learn a great deal by action. Newborns cannot tell themselves apart from their surroundings until they begin to explore their environment and learn from their own movements where their bodies end and the rest of the world begins. As they drop toys, splash water, and hurl sand, they learn how their bodies can alter their world. Physical gestures also accompany a baby's first attempts to speak. As Judy says "Bye-bye," she opens and closes her hand. When Doug says "Up," he raises his arms, showing Grandpa where he wants to go. Even more to the point, if both babies had not developed the motor coor-

dination to form certain sounds, they would not be able to speak at all. Because the brain itself, the center of intellectual as well as much of emotional functioning, is a physical organ, such topics as intelligence, learning, and personality are inextricably linked with the physical aspects of growth and development.

Thus, as we look in this chapter at early physical growth and sensory and motor development, then in Chapter 4 at the intellectual development of infants and toddlers, and in Chapter 5 at their personality and social development, we should bear in mind that these categories are arbitrary.

Principles of Development

As we observe how growth and development progress both before and after birth, three guiding principles appear to be at work.

Top-to-Bottom Development Babies develop head first: the *cephalocaudal principle* ("head to tail," from Greek and Latin roots) dictates that development proceeds from the head to the lower parts of the body. As we saw in Table 2-1, an embryo's head, brain, and eyes develop earliest; the head of a 2-month-old embryo is half the length of the entire body. By the time of birth, the head is only one-fourth the body size but still disproportionately large; it becomes less so as the child grows (see Figure 3-3).

(© Bob Krist 1986/Black Star)

In keeping with the cephalocaudal principle, infants can make good use of their hands before they can do much with their legs. This baby, not yet walking, can reach for the mother's nose.

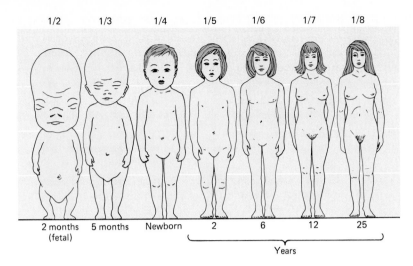

| 1/2 | 1/3 | 1/4 | 1/5 | 1/6 | 1/7 | 1/8 |

2 months   5 months   Newborn   2   6   12   25
(fetal)

Years

Figure 3-3 Changes in proportions of the human body during growth. The most striking change is that the head becomes smaller in proportion to the rest of the body; the trunk (shoulders to crotch) remains relatively stable. The proportionate increase in the leg is almost exactly the reverse of the proportionate decrease in the head. Proportional head size at different ages is expressed in fractions.

Furthermore, infants learn to *use* the upper parts of their bodies before their lower ones. Babies can see objects before they can control their trunks, and they can use their hands to grasp long before they can walk.

Inner-to-Outer Development Before infants can use their hands purposefully, they are quite adept at moving their arms—evidence of a second principle of development that is at work beginning in the womb.

According to the *proximodistal principle* (from Latin roots: "near to far"), development proceeds from the central part of the body to the outer parts. Thus, the embryonic head and trunk develop before the limbs, and the arms and legs before the fingers and toes. Babies first develop the ability to use their upper arms and upper legs (which are closest to the central axis), then their forearms and forelegs, then their hands and feet, and finally their fingers and toes.

Simple-to-Complex Development Dorri was able to sit up at 6 months, Mark not until 11 months, but both could sit with support before they could sit alone. The third rule of development is obvious yet profound: in acquiring practically all skills, physical or otherwise, we progress from the simple to the complex.

As we saw in Chapter 2, maturation follows an apparently preordained course. Even though the times when individual babies reach specific milestones vary widely—there is no "right" age

when a child should be able to stand or speak—almost all children progress in a definite order from simpler movements and activities to more complicated ones. (Only with specific kinds of stimulation, like those sometimes found in mother-child interactions in certain nonwestern cultures, is the sequence altered noticeably; refer back to Box 3-1.)

Development, then, is not haphazard or idiosyncratic. Rather, it progresses along logical lines that are similar for all human beings.

As we look at the physical development that proceeds during the first 3 years of life, let's first see how babies spend their time—the increasing wakefulness that allows them to develop in response to environmental stimulation. We'll note their dramatic physical growth, and then we'll examine their increasing sensory and motor capabilities.

An Infant's States

The human body has an inner "clock" that regulates cycles of eating, sleeping, elimination, and maybe even mood. These patterns of timing, which appear to be inborn, govern the various *states* that infants go through, the periodic variations in their daily cycles of wakefulness, sleep, and activity (see Table 3-5, page 98).

Sleep dominates the neonatal period. Friends who come to see a new baby are almost certain to be greeted with "She's asleep," or "Shhh! Don't wake him up."

	TABLE 3-5 STATES IN INFANCY			
STATE	EYES	BREATHING	MOVEMENTS	RESPONSIVENESS
Regular sleep	Closed	Regular	None, except for sudden, generalized startles	Unable to be aroused by mild stimuli.
Irregular sleep	Closed	Irregular	Muscles twitch, but no major movements	Sounds or light bring smiles or grimaces in sleep.
Drowsiness	Open or closed	Irregular	Somewhat active	May smile, startle, suck, or have erections in response to stimuli.
Alert inactivity	Open		Quiet; may move head, limbs, and trunk while looking around	An interesting environment (with people or things to watch) may initiate or maintain this state.
Waking activity and crying	Open		Much activity	External stimuli (such as hunger, cold, pain, being restrained, or being put down) bring about more activity, perhaps starting with soft whimpering and gentle movements and turning into a rhythmic crescendo of crying or kicking, or perhaps beginning and enduring as uncoordinated thrashing and spasmodic screeching.

Source: Adapted from information in Wolff, 1966, and Prechtl & Beintema, 1964.

Each baby's sleep pattern is different. The average is about 16 hours of sleep a day, yet one healthy baby may sleep only 11 hours, while another sleeps 21 (Parmelee, Wenner, & Schulz, 1964). This sleep, of course, is not continuous. The next time you say "I slept like a baby," remember that new babies usually wake up every 2 to 3 hours, around the clock.

To the relief of parents, this pattern soon changes. At around 3 months, babies grow more wakeful in the late afternoon and early evening and start to sleep through the night. By that age, most babies "sleep through" without eating or crying, and by 6 months, babies do more than half their sleeping at night. Their increasing daytime wakefulness, alertness, and activity are accompanied by rapid physical, intellectual, and emotional development.

Sleep patterns themselves change, too. Newborns have about six to eight sleep periods, which alternate between quiet and active sleep. Active sleep—probably the equivalent of rapid eye movement (REM) sleep, which in adults is associated with dreaming—appears rhythmically in cycles of about 1 hour and accounts for 50 to 80 percent of a newborn's total sleep time. During the first 6 months, the amount of this active sleep diminishes until it accounts for only 30 percent of sleep time, and the lengths of the cycles become more consistent (Coons & Guilleminault, 1982).

Babies' states give us clues to how their bodies work and how they are responding to their environment. A baby in a state of deep sleep responds to stimulation quite differently from an alert baby or a drowsy one. Parents, for their part, react differently to a baby who is frequently awake and crying from the way they react to one who is almost always sleepy or who spends a great deal of time in a state of interested, quiet wakefulness. Thus infants' states influence the way their parents treat them, which in turn influences the kinds of people they will turn out to be.

Parents try to change a baby's state when they pick up or feed a crying infant or ease a fussy one to sleep. In most cases, crying is more distressing than serious, but it is important to find ways to calm low-birth-weight babies, because quiet babies maintain their weight better. Steady stimulation is the age-old way to soothe crying babies—letting them hear rhythmic sounds or suck on pacifiers, rocking or walking them, or wrapping them snugly.

A baby's behavior during wakeful periods is unique from birth. Jenny sticks her tongue in and out; Davey makes rhythmic sucking movements. Some infants smile frequently; others do not. Some boys have frequent erections; others rarely do.

Neonatal activity and responsiveness can give us important clues to the way a child will develop. One recent study followed up children at ages 4 and 8 whose movements had been electronically monitored during the first 3 days of life. The most vigorous neonates tended to become highly active children who welcomed new experiences, while the least vigorous neonates tended to be the least active when they got older (Korner, Zeanah, Linden, Berkowitz, Kraemer, & Agras, 1985).

Growth and Nourishment

Children grow faster during the first 3 years—and especially during the first few months—than they ever will again (see Figure 3-4). Their early physical growth and muscular development make possible the rapid motor advancements of this period.

At 5 months, the average baby's weight has doubled from the birth weight to about 15 pounds. By 1 year, babies weigh 3 times their birth weight, or about 22 pounds. During the second year, this rapid growth tapers off; the baby gains 5 or 6 pounds to weigh about 4 times the birth weight by the second birthday. During the third year, the gain is even less, about 4 to 5 pounds.

The same pattern holds true for height, which increases by about 10 to 12 inches during the first year, making the typical 1-year-old about 30 inches tall. The average 2-year-old has grown about 6 inches to be 3 feet tall and will add another 3 to 4 inches in the third year.

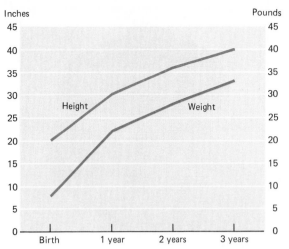

Figure 3-4 Growth in height and weight during infancy and toddlerhood. Babies grow most rapidly in both height and weight during the first few months of life, then taper off somewhat by the third birthday.

As young children grow in size, their shapes change, too. The rest of the body catches up with the head, which becomes proportionately smaller until full adult height is reached, as shown graphically in Figure 3-3. Most children become leaner in these years; the 3-year-old is slender, compared with the chubby, pot-bellied 1-year-old.

Teething usually begins around 3 or 4 months (when infants begin grabbing almost everything in sight to put into their mouths), but the first tooth may not arrive until sometime between 5 and 9 months of age or even later. By the first birthday, babies generally have 6 to 8 teeth, and by age 2½, a mouthful of 20 (Behrman & Vaughan, 1983).

Influences on Growth The genes that babies inherit have the biggest say in molding their bodies: whether they will be tall and thin, short and stocky, or in between. Certain gender and racial differences exist: Boys are slightly longer and heavier than girls at birth and remain larger through adulthood, except for a brief time during puberty when the girls' growth spurts make them overtake the boys. The bones of black children harden earlier than those of white children, and their permanent teeth appear sooner; they mature earlier than white children, and they tend to be larger (American Academy of Pediatrics, AAP, 1973).

Breast-feeding brings many benefits beyond the milk itself. The close, warm contact helps to establish bonding between mother and baby. More than 60 percent of contemporary American mothers choose this natural method of feeding.

Height and weight are also affected by health and by such environmental factors as nutrition, living conditions, and medical care. Well-fed, well-cared-for children grow taller and heavier than children who are fed and cared for inadequately; they mature sexually and attain maximum height earlier, and their teeth erupt sooner. Differences in growth usually show up by the first year and remain consistent throughout life (AAP, 1973).

Certain illnesses can have grave effects on growth. Children who are ill for a long time may never achieve their genetically programmed normal stature, because they may never be able to make up for the growth time lost while they were sick.

Thus, in the fundamental process of physical growth, we see the interaction of heredity and environment. Because of the importance of proper nourishment to this process, let's look at feeding practices that can influence babies' healthy growth.

Breast-Feeding After a 50-year decline in the popularity of breast-feeding, this natural means of nutrition has made a strong comeback, especially among better-educated, higher-income women. In 1971, only 25 percent of new mothers breast-fed their babies; today, more than 60 percent do (Eiger & Olds, 1987). In addition, at least 5 times as many mothers now continue to nurse their babies until at least the fifth or sixth month.

These increases are occurring across socioeconomic and educational levels (Martinez & Kreiger, 1985), but even so, breast-feeding is still less popular than bottle-feeding among younger, poorer, and minority women. White women are more inclined to nurse their babies than are Mexican-American or black mothers (Fetterly & Graubard, 1984; Rassin et al., 1984).

Even though technological advances have provided excellent infant formulas that approximate human milk, breast milk is the best food for newborn infants unless mother or child has some physical condition that makes nursing impossible or undesirable (AAP, 1978). Indeed, breast milk has been termed "the ultimate health food," because it offers so many benefits to babies (Eiger & Olds, 1987, p. 26).

Breast milk is a complete source of nutrients for young infants, more digestible than cow's milk and less likely to produce allergic reactions. Sucking at the breast is good for teeth and jaws, because babies have to suck harder than on a bottle; as a result, they are less likely to suck their thumbs. Breast-fed children get varying degrees of protection against such illnesses as diarrhea and respiratory infections including pneumonia and bronchitis (Fallot, Boyd, & Oski, 1980; Forman, Graubard, Hoffman, Beren, Harley, & Bennett, 1984; Jelliffe & Jelliffe, 1983). Low-birth-weight infants digest and absorb the fat in breast milk better than that in cow's milk formula (Alemi, Hamosh, Scanlon, Salzman-Mann, & Hamosh, 1981), and the milk of the mothers of premature babies has a different composition from that of the mothers of full-term infants, which may be "nature's way" of meeting these infants' special needs.

Breast-feeding is an emotional as well as a

physical act. The warm contact with the mother's body facilitates bonding, or emotional linkage, between mother and baby (see Chapter 5). A mother's health, her emotional state, her lifestyle, and her attitude toward breast-feeding affect her ability to nurse her child. A small proportion of women are physically unable to nurse; and some women have strong feelings against it or are prevented by work or travel. To give more mothers success in breast-feeding, the American Academy of Pediatrics (AAP, 1978) has called for better education about nutrition and lactation both in schools and for doctors, nurses, and expectant parents; "demand" feeding in hospitals and at home, rather than rigid 3- or 4-hour schedules; and day nurseries adjoining workplaces, so that working women may nurse their infants.

Bottle-Feeding Breast-feeding is not the only way, of course, to nourish an infant. Babies fed with formula and raised with love also grow up healthy and well adjusted. Most bottle-fed babies receive a commercially prepared formula based on either cow's milk or soy protein. Formulas are manufactured to resemble mother's milk as closely as possible (although they will never be *exactly* identical), with the exception that they contain supplements of vitamins and minerals that breast milk does not have. Like breast milk, formula feedings, when used, are the only food most babies need till about 4 to 6 months of age.

Long-term studies that have compared breast-fed and bottle-fed children have found no significant differences (M. H. Schmitt, 1970). The quality of the relationship between mother and child is probably more important than the feeding method.

Mothers and fathers who bottle-feed their babies can achieve a closeness akin to that of breast-feeding by holding their children close during feedings. Babies who take a bottle of milk, juice, or sweetened liquid to bed miss out on that important emotional nutrient. This common practice has another drawback: the sugar in the drink causes teeth to decay in the area where the liquid comes out of the bottle. To avoid "nursing-bottle mouth," dentists recommend that children who nurse for a long time between meals or while sleeping get only water

in their bottles. Other suggestions: Teach a baby to drink from a cup before the first birthday, always offer juice from a cup, and don't use a bottle of milk to help a baby fall asleep (AAP, 1978).

Cow's Milk and Solid Foods Because infants who were fed plain cow's milk in the early months of life were found to suffer from iron deficiency (Sadowitz & Oski, 1983), the AAP Committee on Nutrition (1986) recommends that babies receive breast milk or formula until they are at least 6 months old. Then they can switch to cow's milk if they are getting a balanced diet of supplementary solid foods consisting of one-third of their caloric intake. The cow's milk they drink should be homogenized whole milk fortified with vitamin D, not skim milk—babies need the calories in whole milk for proper growth (Fomon, Filer, Anderson, & Ziegler, 1979).

Although the AAP recommends waiting to start solid foods until 4 to 6 months of age, many infants in the United States begin getting solids—usually cereal or strained fruits—by the age of 2 months. This practice seems to be due mainly to aggressive marketing by the baby food industry, to parents' competitiveness in raising their babies, and to the belief that the solid food will help the baby sleep through the night. Some pediatric nutritionists condemn early feeding of solids as a form of "forced feeding" (Fomon et al., 1979, p. 54), since babies who cannot sit without support or control their heads and necks cannot effectively communicate when they have had enough. (See Box 3-2, page 102, for a discussion of obesity in infants, a possible consequence of overfeeding.)

Of course, good nutrition should continue beyond infancy. After 1 year, children should have a varied diet drawn from all the major food groups. Children from families with histories of high cholesterol should be screened after age 2 to see whether they need special diets or medicine. Current trends toward less consumption of saturated fats, cholesterol, and salt should be followed in moderation: "Diets that avoid extremes are safe for children for whom there is no evidence of special vulnerability" (American Academy of Pediatrics Committee on Nutrition, 1986, p. 524).

BOX 3-2   FOOD FOR THOUGHT

DOES OBESITY BEGIN IN INFANCY?

Obesity is a major problem among American children today. Studies suggest that the tendency to get fat is predominantly genetic (see Chapter 2); overweight youngsters may have inherited more subcutaneous fat or a more sluggish metabolism. But it also seems that most fat people, young or old, eat too much food for the energy they expend.

Some nutritionists have suggested that people may become obese in later life from being overfed in infancy (Jelliffe & Jelliffe, 1974; Mayer,

1973). This belief rests on research in rats, which has shown that feeding rat pups too many calories makes them develop too many fat cells, which persist through life (Hirsch, 1972). Recent research has cast doubt, however, on the long-term effects of fatness in human infants. Roche (1981), for example, found almost no correlation between obesity before age 6 and at age 16. After age 6, however, there was an increasingly strong correlation: children who were fat at age 6 or later were more likely to be fat adults. Roche concludes (p. 38),

"The medical significance of infantile obesity may have been exaggerated." Because we have no evidence that fatness hurts babies, and because children have critical growth needs, the American Academy of Pediatrics Committee on Nutrition (AAP, 1981) warns against putting young children on any kind of weight-loss diet.

As usual, moderation appears to be the safest course. Babies should be fed as much as they reasonably seem to need—neither more nor less.

As the saying goes, we are what we eat. Children who are fed well, with loving care, have the best possible start toward becoming the persons they have the potential to be.

Early Sensory Capacities

"The baby, assailed by eyes, ears, nose, skin, and entrails at once, feels that all is one great blooming, buzzing confusion," wrote the psychologist William James in 1890. We now know that this is far from true. From birth, the normal infant's senses all operate to some degree, and these sensory capacities develop rapidly.

Touch   Although the sense of touch has not been studied extensively in infants, it appears to be the earliest sense to develop. If you stroke a hungry newborn's cheek near the mouth, the infant will respond by rooting for the nipple. Early signs of this rooting reflex have been noted in fetuses as early as 2 months after conception, and all body parts are sensitive to touch before 32 weeks of gestation. Infants' sensitivity to touch, and particularly their sensitivity to

pain, increases during the first 5 days of life (Haith, 1986).

Taste   Newborns can discriminate between different tastes. They reject bad-tasting food, and they seem to prefer sweet tastes to sour or bitter ones. The sweeter the fluid, the harder they suck and the more they drink (Haith, 1986). When pure water or a sweet glucose solution is placed on newborns' tongues, the babies move their tongues to the side; the higher the concentration of glucose, the greater the response (Weiffenback & Thach, 1975).

Smell   Newborns are sensitive to smell, and they seem to show by their facial expressions that they like the smell of vanilla and strawberries and do not like to smell rotten eggs or fish odors (Steiner, 1979). They can also tell where smells are coming from. When the noses of babies from 16 hours to 5 days old are dabbed on one side with an ammonium compound, the babies turn their noses to the other side (Rieser, Yonas, & Wilkner, 1976).

Very young infants can make subtle discriminations based on smell; like touch, this sensitivity increases during the first few days of life. Six-day-old breast-fed infants showed a definite preference for their mother's breast pad over that of another nursing mother, but 2-day-old infants did not, suggesting that they needed a few days' experience to recognize their mother's odor (Macfarlane, 1975).

Hearing The inner and middle ears reach nearly adult size and shape in the womb (Aslin, Pisoni, & Jusczyk, 1983; Haith, 1986). Newborns turn their heads toward sounds (Haith, 1986); even premature infants appear to respond to auditory stimulation (A. Starr, Amlie, Martin, & Sanders, 1977).

Infants' hearing abilities are often studied through the phenomenon of *habituation,* a simple type of learning in which a baby becomes used to a stimulus and stops responding to it. When a new stimulus is presented, the response (such as hard sucking on a pacifier) resumes, indicating that the infant has perceived a difference between the two stimuli. From habituation experiments, researchers learned that as early as 3 days after birth, infants can already distinguish between new speech sounds and those they have already heard (L. R. Brody, Zelazo, & Chaika, 1984). The babies stopped responding to familiar words, but when they heard new ones, they became more attentive.

In another study of habituation, 1-month-old babies showed that they could discriminate between two sounds as close as "bah" and "pah" (Eimas, Siqueland, Jusczyk, & Vigorito, 1971). The babies were provided with special nipples, which, when sucked, could turn on a recording. At first the infants sucked vigorously to hear the "bah" sound, but after they got used to that, their sucking slowed down. When the "pah" sound replaced the "bah" sound, they started to suck strongly again, showing that they could tell this minor difference in sound. (We will discuss habituation further in Chapter 4.)

In another study based on a method called *discriminative sucking,* infants less than 3 days old showed that they could tell the mother's voice from that of a stranger. By sucking on a nipple, the babies (at different times) were able to turn on recordings of the mother or another woman reading a story. As young as they were, the ba-

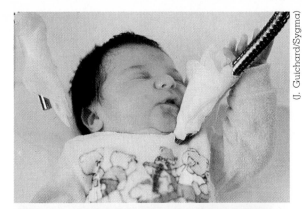
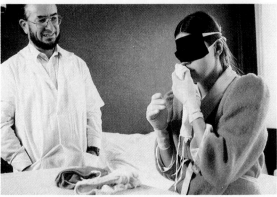

The sense of smell becomes more acute during the first few days of life. In laboratory experiments, neonates in the first week of life showed more peaceful behavior when they smelled pieces of gauze that had been worn by their mothers than when they smelled gauze worn by other women. At the same time, blindfolded mothers began to distinguish by odor the shirts worn by their own babies from those worn by other babies.

bies sucked about 24 percent more when it was the mother's voice on the recording. Apparently, knowing this voice, they had more interest in producing it. This early preference for the mother's voice may be an important mechanism for initiating bonding between mother and child.

Sight The eyes of neonates are smaller than those of adults, the retinal structures are incomplete, and the optic nerve is underdeveloped. Still, newborn babies blink at bright lights and shift their gaze to follow a moving light or target (Behrman & Vaughan, 1983).

Infants appear to have relatively mature color perception within the first few months of life. The cones, or receptors, in the retina that per-

Babies perceive depth from a very early age. Even this baby's mother cannot induce the infant to crawl across what looks like a cliff.

ceive red and green are functioning by about 2 months of age, and by about 3 months the cones for blue are working (Haith, 1986). By 4 months, infants (like adults) show a preference for red and blue (Teller & Bornstein, 1987).

Peripheral vision, which is very narrow at birth, more than doubles between 2 and 10 weeks of age (Tronick, 1972). The baby's eyesight becomes more acute, approaching adult visual acuity by age 3 (Behrman & Vaughan, 1983).

Very young babies seem to have some depth perception, which may be innate or learned during the first couple of months. E. J. Gibson and Walk (1960) constructed a *visual cliff* consisting of a clear glass tabletop with a checkered cloth draped underneath to give the illusion of a ledge ending in a sudden drop-off. In an experiment based on differences in heart rate, 2- to 3-month-old babies placed on their stomachs on the "deep" side had slower heart rates than in-

fants placed on the "shallow" side. The slower heart rate probably showed that the infants on the "deep" side were responding to the illusion of depth (Campos, Langer, & Krowitz, 1970).*

The amounts of time that babies spend looking at different sights tell us about their *visual preferences,* which depend on the ability to differentiate between sights. Research shows that this ability to view things selectively is present from birth.

Using an apparatus that enables an observer to watch an infant's eyes and time the fixations on a visual stimulus, researchers have found that infants less than 2 days old show definite preferences. Babies prefer curved lines to straight, complex patterns to simple, three-dimensional objects to two-dimensional objects, pictures of faces to pictures of other things, and new sights to familiar ones (Fantz, 1963, 1964, 1965; Fantz, Fagan, & Miranda, 1975; Fantz & Nevis, 1967).

In one experiment, 1- and 2-month-old babies saw three expressionless faces: the mother's, a strange woman's, and a strange man's (Maurer & Salapatek, 1976). The 1-month-olds tended to look away from the faces, perhaps because the lack of expression was disturbing to them, while the 2-month-olds looked longer, possibly because they had become more familiar with a variety of expressions. The 1-month-olds turned away particularly from the faces of their own mothers, indicating that they could already recognize their mothers and apparently did not like to see them showing no expression. The babies' eyes focused on the borders of the faces, indicating that their recognition was probably based on distinctiveness of the mother's chin or hairline. This observation is consistent with findings that infants less than 6 weeks old tend to fix on a small part of a visual stimulus rather than on the whole (Leahy, 1976; Salapatek & Kessen, 1966). The 2-month-olds gazed especially at the eyes; other studies have shown that by this age, babies look longer at a face if the eyes are open and that they smile at it only if both eyes are shown.

*Babies of this age are not likely to exhibit *fear* of the drop-off. Fear would most likely have resulted in an *accelerated* heart rate.

Early Motor Development

Newborn babies are busy. They turn their heads, kick their legs, flail their arms, and display an array of reflex behaviors. Even fetuses move around a great deal in the womb; they turn somersaults, kick, and even suck their thumbs. But as we've seen, neither fetuses nor neonates have much conscious control over their own movements.

By about the fourth month, voluntary, cortex-directed movements largely take over. Motor control, the ability to move deliberately and accurately, develops rapidly and continuously during the first 3 years after birth, as babies begin to consciously use specific body parts. The order in which they acquire this control follows the three principles of development outlined earlier: head to toe, inner to outer, and simple to complex.

Two of the most distinctively human motor capacities are the precision grip, in which the thumb and index finger meet at their tips to form a circle; and the ability to walk on two legs. Neither of these capacities is present at birth, and both develop gradually. First, for example, Sharon picks things up with her whole hand. Then she begins to use neat little pincer motions with her thumb and forefinger to pick up tiny objects. After Sharon has gained control of separate movements of her arms, legs, and feet, she will be ready to put these movements together to manage walking.

Milestones of Motor Development Babies do not have to be taught the basic motor skills; they just need freedom from interference. As soon as their central nervous systems, muscles, and bones are mature enough, they need only room and freedom to move in order to keep showing surprising new abilities. They are persistent, too—as soon as they acquire a new skill, they keep practicing and improving it. Parents may become irritated when the baby keeps letting go of a small object from the high chair and then crying for it, only to drop it again once it is retrieved; but this repetition is an important part of mastery. Each newly mastered skill prepares a child to tackle the next one in the preordained sequence. And the proliferation of motor skills gives the infant increasing opportunity to ex-plore and manipulate the environment, and thus to experience sensory and cognitive stimulation.

Motor development is marked by a series of milestones: achievements that indicate how far development has come. The ***Denver Developmental Screening Test*** was designed to spot children who are not developing normally (Frankenburg, Dodds, Fandal, Kazuk, & Cohrs, 1975), but it may also be used as a benchmark for *normal* development between the ages of 1 month and 6 years. The test covers such gross motor skills as rolling over and catching a ball and such fine motor skills as grasping a rattle and copying a circle. It also covers language development (for example, knowing the definition of words) and personal and social development (for example, smiling spontaneously and dressing).

The test provides norms for the ages at which 25 percent, 50 percent, 75 percent, and 90 percent of children pass in each skill (see Table 3-6, page 106, for selected milestones). A child who fails to exhibit a skill at an age when 90 percent of children ordinarily pass is considered developmentally delayed. A child with two or more delays in two or more sectors is thought to need special attention.

In the following discussion, when we talk about what the "average" baby can do, we'll be referring for convenience to the 50 percent Denver norms. It's important to remember, however, that there is no "average" baby. Normality covers a wide range; about half of all babies master these skills before the ages given and about half afterward.

HEAD CONTROL At birth, most newborns can turn their heads from side to side while lying on their backs. While lying chest down, many can lift their heads enough to turn them. Within the first 2 to 3 months, they lift their heads higher and higher. By 4 months of age, almost all infants can keep their heads erect while being held or supported in a sitting position.

HAND CONTROL At about 3½ months, most infants can grasp an object of moderate size, like a rattle, but have trouble holding a small one. Next they begin to grasp objects with one hand

TABLE 3-6 MILESTONES OF MOTOR DEVELOPMENT

SKILL	25 PERCENT	50 PERCENT	90 PERCENT
Rolling over	2 months	3 months	5 months
Grasping rattle	2½ months	3½ months	4½ months
Sitting without support	5 months	5½ months	8 months
Standing while holding on	5 months	6 months	10 months
Grasping with thumb and finger	7½ months	8½ months	10½ months
Standing alone well	10 months	11½ months	14 months
Walking well	11 months	12 months	14½ months
Building tower of two cubes	12 months	14 months	20 months
Walking up steps	14 months	17 months	22 months
Jumping in place	20½ months	22 months	36 months
Copying circle	26 months	33 months	39 months

Note: This table shows the approximate ages when 25 percent, 50 percent, and 90 percent of children can perform each skill.
Source: Adapted from Frankenburg, 1978.

and transfer them to the other, and then to hold (but not pick up) small objects. Sometime between 7 and 11 months, their hands become coordinated enough to pick up a tiny object like a pea with a pincer-like motion. After that, hand control becomes increasingly precise. At 14 months, the average baby can build a tower of two cubes. About 3 months before his or her third birthday, the average toddler can copy a circle fairly well.

LOCOMOTION   After 3 months, the average infant begins to roll over purposefully, first from front to back and then from back to front. Before this time, however, babies sometimes roll over accidentally, and so even the youngest ones should never be left alone on a surface from which they might roll off.

Babies sit either by raising themselves from a prone position or by plopping down from a standing position. The average baby can sit

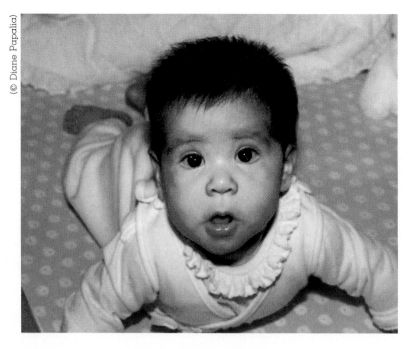

(© Diane Papalia)

Although the age when infants develop head control varies, within the first 2 to 3 months of life most babies can lift their heads high while lying on their chests.

(G and J Images/Image Bank)

The "bear walk" is one of several methods of locomotion that babies use before they are ready to walk. This baby can get around with considerable speed with hands and feet touching the ground.

without support between the ages of 5 and 6 months and can assume a sitting position without help 2 months later.

At about 6 months, most babies—rather than always having to be carried from place to place—begin to get around under their own power, in several primitive ways. They crawl by wriggling on their bellies and pulling their bodies along with their arms, dragging their feet behind. They hitch or scoot by moving along in a sitting position, pushing forward with their arms and legs. They bear-walk, with hands and feet touching the ground. And they creep on hands and knees with their trunks raised, parallel to the floor. By 9 or 10 months, babies get around quite well by such means, and so parents have to keep a close eye on them.

By holding on to a helping hand or a piece of furniture, the average baby can stand at a little less than 6 months of age, but an erect posture is only occasionally achieved. About 4 months later, after dogged practice in pulling themselves up to an upright posture, babies can at last let go and stand alone. The average baby can stand well about two weeks or so before the first birthday.

All these developments are milestones along the way to the main motor achievement of infancy: walking. For some months before they can stand without support, babies practice walking while holding on to furniture—sitting down

abruptly when they reach table's end, and crawling or lurching from chair to sofa. Shortly after most infants can stand alone well, they take their first unaided steps, tumble, go back to creeping, and then try again. Within a few days, the average baby is walking regularly, if shakily, and within a few weeks—soon after the first birthday—is walking well and can now be described as a toddler.

During the second year, youngsters begin to climb stairs one at a time. (They can crawl upstairs before that—and fall down long before; therefore vigilance and baby gates are required.) At first they put one foot after the other on the same step before going on to the next higher one; later they alternate feet. Going down comes later. In their second year, toddlers are running and jumping; their parents become exhausted trying to keep up with them. At the age of 3, most children can balance briefly on one foot, and some begin to hop.

Environmental Influences on Motor Development Human beings, then, appear to be genetically programmed to perform such activities as sitting, standing, and walking. These skills unfold in a regular, largely preordained pattern. Children must reach a certain level of physiological maturation before they are ready to exercise each ability.

The role of the environment in this timetable

is usually quite limited, though recent studies indicate that early experience can affect maturation rates in certain spheres, such as vision (Lipsitt, 1986). In general, when children receive good nutrition and good health care, have physical freedom, and are given the opportunity to practice motor skills, their motor development will be normal (Clarke-Stewart, 1977; refer back to Box 3-1 for a discussion of cultural differences in normal development). When the environment is grossly deficient in any of these areas, development can suffer—as in the following classic study of orphanages in Iran.

The overworked attendants in two orphanages hardly ever handled the children. The younger babies spent practically all their time on their backs in cribs. They sucked from propped bottles. They were never put in a sitting position or placed on their stomachs. They had no toys and were not taken out of bed until they could sit without help (often not till 2 years of age, as compared with 5½ months for the average American child). And once a sitting child did reach the floor, there was no child-sized furniture or play equipment. These children were retarded in their motor development because of the deficient environment, which kept them from moving around initially and provided little stimulation.

The children in a third home were fed in the arms of trained attendants, were placed on their stomachs and propped up sitting, and had many toys. These children showed normal levels of motor development.

When the children in the first two orphanages did start to get about, they scooted (moved around in a sitting position, pushing their bodies forward with their arms and feet), rather than creeping on their hands and knees. Since they had never been placed on their stomachs, they had had no opportunity to practice raising their heads or pulling their arms and legs beneath their bodies—the movements needed for creeping. Also, since they had never been propped in a sitting position, they had not practiced raising their heads and shoulders to learn how to sit at the usual age. Surprisingly, this retardation appeared to be temporary. Older children in one of the poor institutions, who presumably had also been retarded as toddlers, worked and played normally (Dennis, 1960).

Such severe environmental deprivation is fortunately rare. But it is clear that the environment can play a part in motor development, and the more abnormal a child's environment, the greater its effect will be.

"Precocious" Motor Development Normally, as children become older, they become better at all sorts of tasks. Bower (1976), however, has pointed out a few specific abilities that children may display at a very early age and then seem to lose until later; he calls them repetitive processes.

From the age of 4 to 8 weeks, Billy exhibited a definite walking reflex: when held under the arms, with his bare feet touching a flat surface, he would make steplike motions that looked like walking. Yet after 8 weeks, he stopped doing that and did not walk at all for about a year. Beth, in her first few weeks of life, reached for objects. But when she was about 4 weeks old, her eye-hand coordination disappeared, not to reappear till the age of 20 weeks; and her ear-hand coordination—the ability to reach out and grasp objects she could hear but not see—left her temporarily when she was about 6 months old.

Bower believed that the early appearance of some abilities is important to a child's use of them later on and that such abilities disappear because they are not exercised. When he tested this hypothesis, however, the results were mixed. Babies who were given practice in eye-hand coordination in their first 4 weeks showed an earlier reappearance of the ability later on, and indeed some of the babies never lost their reaching abilities. However, ear-hand coordination seemed to disappear more quickly with practice, and its reappearance was retarded (T. G. R. Bower, 1976).

Experiments like these raise ethical questions about providing artificial types of practice, especially since normal development seems to be retarded in some cases. Furthermore, we don't know what the long-term effects of artificially induced precocious development might be. Will other areas of development that are not practiced suffer? What is the value of trying to accelerate behaviors that are going to develop anyway, in the normal course of events—even if it can be done?

BOX 3-3 PRACTICALLY SPEAKING

ARE "WALKERS" WORTH THE RISK?

A 6-month-old baby died in a Toronto hospital of a head injury suffered after falling down 14 steps onto a concrete floor. The infant had been sitting in a "walker"—a seat in a collapsible frame on wheels. In 1984, in that one hospital alone, 139 children were treated for walker-related injuries, most of them resulting from falls (Rieder, Schwartz, & Newman, 1986).

During the past decade, walkers for infants have become popular items. Studies report that anywhere from 55 to 86 percent of babies are placed in them at some time before they begin to walk. About 1 million walkers were distributed in the United States in 1980, a year in which nearly 24,000 walker-related injuries are estimated to have occurred.

Most of the injuries in the Toronto study took place in the home and were caused by falls down stairs; in one-third of the cases, stair gates had been in place but were improperly attached or left unlatched. In 10 of the cases,

the baby fell from the walker itself. In 21 cases, no one was in the room with the baby.

Surprisingly, 2 months after the accidents, nearly one-third of the babies were still being placed in their walkers; another one-third had stopped only after learning to walk. The parents' most frequently stated reasons for using the walkers were that they made the babies happier by helping them get around, that they served as passive baby-sitters, and that they encouraged early walking.

Ironically, a study of twins found that infant walkers do not speed up independent walking (Ridenour, 1982). One twin in each pair was placed in a walker for an hour a day from 4 months of age until walking began; the other twin was not. Twins in the two groups walked at approximately the same average age.

These findings reinforce others, cited in this chapter, that motor control and coordination generally develop at a natural pace, and that attempts to hurry the

Despite a high risk of injury, many babies spend part of their time in infant walkers designed to give them greater mobility. Studies show that walkers do not help babies learn to walk any faster than they would on their own.

process are likely to be useless or even harmful (Gesell, 1929; McGraw, 1940). At the very least, walkers should be used only when a parent or caretaker is within arm's reach—and never near open stairs.

Can Motor Development Be Speeded Up? A number of researchers have tried to see whether it is possible to train children to walk, climb stairs, and control their bladder and bowels earlier than usual.

In a classic experiment, Gesell (1929) examined one set of identical twins to study the effects of training babies to perform a number of motor activities. He trained twin T, but not twin C, in climbing stairs, building with blocks, and

hand coordination. Since, with age, twin C became just as expert as twin T, Gesell concluded that "the powerful influence of maturation of infant behavior pattern is made clear." Even though this study was conducted more than 50 years ago on only two infants, its conclusion still seems to stand. Children perform certain activities only when they are ready to, despite the efforts of parents and psychologists.

Toilet training, for example, is often begun

long before a baby can control his or her sphincter muscles. When a child is successful at a very early age, it is because the *parent* is trained to recognize the child's readiness and can get the child to the potty-chair in time. Before children can control elimination, they have much to learn. Initially, elimination is involuntary: when an infant's bladder or bowels are full, the appropriate sphincter muscles open automatically. To control these muscles, children have to know that there is a proper time and place to allow them to open. They have to become familiar with the feelings that indicate the need to eliminate, and they have to learn to tighten the sphincter muscles until seated on the potty-chair, and then to loosen them.

In another classic study, McGraw (1940) measured the effects of very early training. She put one twin on the toilet every hour of every day from 2 months of age; the other twin was not put on the toilet until 23 months. The first twin began to show some control at 20 months, and by about 23 months he had achieved almost perfect success. The other twin quickly caught up. Again, we see that maturation must occur before training can be effective.

While it is usually not advisable to attempt to hurry motor development for an individual child (see Box 3-3), developmental ages for certain skills do, as we've seen, appear to vary significantly from one culture to another (refer back to Box 3-1). What these observations tell us about the relative roles of heredity, maturation, and environment awaits further research.

How Different Are Boys and Girls?

As we saw in Chapter 2, males are physically more vulnerable than females from conception throughout life. And as we saw earlier in this chapter, boy babies are a bit bigger than girl babies. But aside from these physical differences, infant boys and infant girls seem to be much alike, despite a considerable amount of research that has looked for dissimilarities.

Although some research has found baby boys more active than baby girls (Maccoby & Jacklin, 1974), other research has found the two sexes equally active during the first 2 years of life (Maccoby, 1980). There also do not appear to be gender differences in sensitivity to touch, and very little difference shows up in strength (although males may be a little bit stronger). Girls and boys show more similarities than differences in reaching maturational milestones (such as sitting up, tooth eruption, walking, and so forth). Recently a surge of interest in possible differences between male and female brains has led to attempts to explain girls' earlier language acquisition (see Chapter 4) and boys' greater problems in learning how to read (see Chapter 8). Close analysis of the brains of babies who died at birth or soon afterward, however, has yielded no evidence that indicates any marked gender difference in the readiness of the newborn's brain for language acquisition (Maccoby, 1980).

Gender differences in personality and social development are more pronounced and will be discussed in Chapter 5.

Whether they are male or female, by the time small children can run, jump, and play with a variety of toys requiring fairly sophisticated coordination, they are quite different from the neonates who were described at the beginning of this chapter. The changes that have taken place in their intellectual activity while this physical development has gone on are equally dramatic, as we'll see in Chapter 4.

The Neonate

■ The neonatal period, the first 4 weeks of life, is a time of transition from intrauterine to extrauterine life. At birth, the neonate's circulatory, respiratory, gastrointestinal, and temperature-regulation systems become independent from the mother's.

■ The newborn baby's brain is one-fourth the weight of an adult brain and grows to 80 percent of that weight by the end of the second year. Primitive reflexes drop out as involuntary (subcortical) control of behavior gives way to voluntary (cortical) control. The brain can be molded by experience.

Is the Baby Healthy?

■ At 1 minute and 5 minutes after birth, the neonate is assessed medically by the Apgar scale, which measures five factors (appearance, pulse, grimace, activity, and respiration) that indicate how well the newborn is adjusting to extrauterine life. The neonate may also be screened for one or more medical conditions.

■ The Brazelton Neonatal Behavioral Assessment Scale may be given to assess the way a newborn baby is responding to the environment and to predict future development.

■ Birth trauma and low birth weight can influence a child's early adjustment to life outside the womb and may even exert an influence on later development. A supportive postnatal environment can often improve the outcome.

■ Low birth weight is the major factor in infant mortality. Although the infant mortality rate in the United States has improved, it is still disturbingly high, especially for black babies.

■ Sudden infant death syndrome (SIDS) is the leading cause of death in infants between 1 month and 1 year of age, affecting some 7000 infants each year in the United States. There are many theories about the cause of SIDS, and no one theory is universally accepted.

The Developing Baby

■ Normal physical growth and motor development proceed in a largely preordained sequence, according to three principles:

1 According to the cephalocaudal principle, development proceeds from the head to lower body parts.

2 The proximodistal principle dictates that development proceeds from the center of the body to the outer parts.

3 Development usually proceeds from simple to complex behavior.

■ Newborn babies alternate between states of sleep, wakefulness, and activity, with sleep taking up the major (but a diminishing) amount of their time. State patterns are indicators of how an infant is responding to the environment.

■ A child's body grows most dramatically during the first year of life; growth proceeds at a rapid but diminishing rate throughout the child's first 3 years.

■ Breast-feeding seems to offer physiological benefits to the infant and facilitates the formation of the mother-infant bond. However, the quality of the relationship between parents and the infant is more important than the feeding method in promoting healthy development.

■ Sensory capacities, which are present from birth, develop rapidly in the first few months of life. Very young infants show pronounced abilities to discriminate between stimuli.

■ During the first 3 months of life, infants gain control over their body movements. Motor skills normally develop when an infant is maturationally ready. Certain abilities, however, seem to appear at an early age and then to disappear and reappear later.

■ The Denver Developmental Screening Test is widely used to assess motor, linguistic, and personal and social development.

■ Environmental factors may retard motor development if deprivation is extreme. Environmental factors that are pervasive in a given culture may affect the timetable of motor development, but short-term experiments aimed at accelerating specific types of motor development—such as stair climbing or toilet training—have generally had little effect.

■ Although infant boys are somewhat larger and more vulnerable than girls, researchers have found few other significant physical or maturational differences between the sexes in infancy.

anoxia (page 90)
Apgar scale (88)
apnea (95)
birth trauma (90)
Brazelton Neonatal Behavioral
   Assessment Scale (90)
cephalocaudal principle (96)
cerebral cortex (84)
Denver Developmental Screening
   Test (105)

habituation (103)
infant mortality (90)
lanugo (83)
low-birth-weight babies (90)
meconium (84)
neonatal period (82)
neonate (82)
physiological jaundice (84)
preterm (premature) babies (92)

proximodistal principle (97)
reflex behaviors (85)
small-for-date babies (92)
states (97)
sudden infant death syndrome
   (SIDS) (95)
vernix caseosa (83)
visual cliff (104)
visual preferences (104)

SUGGESTED READINGS

Adebonojo, F., & Sherman, W., with Jones, L. C. (1985). *How baby grows: A parent's guide to nutrition.* New York: Arbor. An up-to-date study of infant feeding during the first year. The book includes clear discussions of topics like breast-feeding and obesity in infancy.

Bower, T. G. R. (1977). *The perceptual world of the child.* Cambridge, MA: Harvard University Press. A fascinating discussion of the sensory and perceptual abilities of infants.

DeFrain, J., Taylor, J., & Ernst, L. (1982). *Coping with sudden infant death.* Lexington, MA: Heath. An investigation of the experiences and special problems of families who have lost a child to sudden infant death syndrome.

Eiger, M. S., & Olds, S. W. (1987). *The complete book of breastfeeding.* New York: Workman. A newly revised edition of a classic guidebook for nursing mothers that draws on findings from recent research on the benefits and techniques of breast-feeding and incorporates many suggestions appropriate to the lifestyles of contemporary families.

Gansberg, J. M., & Mostel, A. P. (1984). *The second nine months.* New York: Pocket Books. A reassuring and compassionate guide for new mothers, based on interviews with mothers of young babies. The book covers common physical and emotional concerns, including typical experiences in the hospital and such at-home postpartum issues as coping with fatigue, the husband-wife relationship, going back to work, and the impact of a second child.

Goldberg, S., & Divitto, B. A. (1983). *Born too soon: Preterm birth and early development.* San Francisco: Freeman. A sympathetic book about the problems and unique experiences of a preterm infant, focusing on the first 3 years of life.

Klaus, M. H., & Klaus, P. H. (1985). *The amazing newborn: Making the most of the first weeks of life.* Reading, MA: Addison-Wesley. Over 125 photos of newborns, some just minutes old, show some of their capabilities. The authors, a researcher and a psychotherapist, report the latest scientific findings on newborns, and give practical suggestions for parents.

Leach, P. (1983). *Babyhood* (2d ed). New York: Knopf. A comprehensive look at the period of infancy, covering everything about a newborn baby. Although written for the layperson, the text covers the whole field of study about babies.

Restak, R. M. (1986). *The infant mind.* Garden City, NY: Doubleday. A readable examination of early brain development by a neurologist who presents facts, speculation, and the most up-to-date experimental research about the capabilities of the baby's brain.

Samuels, M., & Samuels, N. (1979). *The well baby book.* New York: Summit. A thorough treatment of caring for a child's health during the first 4 years.

Spock, B., & Rothenberg, M. (1985). *Dr. Spock's baby and child care* (40th anniversary ed.). New York: Pocket Books. An extensively revised version of the classic work on child care, which covers such issues as the role of the father in childbirth and child rearing, vegetarian diets, day care, children's fear of nuclear war, and other current topics.

So runs my dream; but what am I?
An infant crying in the night;
An infant crying for the light,
And with no language but a cry.

Alfred, Lord Tennyson,
In Memoriam, canto 54

ASK YOURSELF

■ What can infants learn, and how can they learn it?

■ What can the psychometric, Piagetian, and information-processing approaches tell us about infants' and toddlers' intellectual development?

■ Can we measure or predict a baby's intelligence?

■ How does language ability develop in the early years?

■ How do babies begin to develop a sense of competence?

If newborn infants could speak, they would have protested years ago that their intelligence was underestimated. Until recently, parents were told that their babies were blind at birth, could not taste, smell, or feel pain, and—because their brains were not fully developed—could not learn or remember (Lipsitt, 1986).

That view was perpetuated in part by the effects of sedatives during childbirth and in part by attempts to study infants by methods used for older children, adults, or animals. Today, the estimate of infants' abilities has changed radically. In the past few decades more direct research has been done on infants' capabilities than in all previous history (Lipsitt, 1982, 1986; Rovee-Collier & Lipsitt, 1982). We now know that the normal, healthy human baby is quite competent intellectually. As we saw in Chapter 3, normal infants enter the world with all their senses working. They are able to learn, and they actively change their environment as well as react to it.

HOW INFANTS LEARN

Do babies learn to suck on a nipple? They probably do not; sucking is a reflex they are born with. But sucking quickly becomes a learned behavior when it leads to a comfortably full stomach. Similarly, a baby's first cry is not learned behavior; but babies soon learn to *use* crying to get what they need or want.

Learning is a relatively permanent change in behavior that results from experience. Human beings are born with the *ability* to learn; learning itself takes place only with experience, which may include study, instruction, observation, exploration, experimentation, or practice.

Babies learn from what they see, hear, smell, taste, and touch. Newborns begin sizing up what their senses tell them. They use their intellect to distinguish between sensory experiences (such as the sounds of different voices) and to build on their small inborn repertoire of behaviors (such as sucking).

It may be that learning begins in the womb. One study based on sucking patterns showed that newborns preferred hearing a story that their mother had read aloud frequently during pregnancy to one she had never read before (DeCasper & Fifer, 1980). DeCasper also found differences in fetal heart rates when familiar and unfamiliar stories were read (M. Roberts, 1987).

Learning, then, is a form of adaptation to the environment. Before we examine some of the ways in which learning takes place, we need to clarify the relationship between learning and maturation.

Learning and Maturation

People often say things like "Jonathan has learned to walk" and "Jennifer is learning to talk." Such expressions ignore the role of *maturation,* or biologically determined readiness to master new abilities. Learning based on experience undoubtedly played a part in Jonathan's walking, but that ability could not develop until he was ready, no matter how much his parents "danced" him on the floor. Nor will Jennifer be able to learn a spoken language until her mouth and vocal cords have developed enough to form verbal sounds and her brain and nervous system are mature enough to assign meanings to sounds and remember them. Certain neurological, sensory, and motor capacities must be present before related learning can take place.

A connection between maturation and learning is seen in some interesting experiments with the visual cliff. Very young infants, when placed on a clear surface with an illusion of a sudden drop-off, give evidence of depth perception; their slowed heart rate indicates that they are aware of the apparent difference between the "edge" and the "cliff." But *fear* of the "deep" side seems to be a learned response that does not come until about 9 months of age, with the onset of locomotion. Babies who can crawl are more likely to have accelerated heart rates (an index of fear) when placed near the "edge" than infants who are not yet capable of self-locomotion or whose crawling is delayed because of orthopedic problems (Bertenthal & Campos, 1987). Thus an older infant's own activity (the ability to get around), which depends on maturation, apparently has a significant impact on learning about and interpreting the environment.

On the other hand, as we saw in Chapter 3, environmental conditions may affect maturation rates (though apparently to a limited extent) and thus may enhance or inhibit learning.

Simple Learning

Now we are ready to look at three simple ways in which infants learn: habituation, classical conditioning, and operant conditioning.

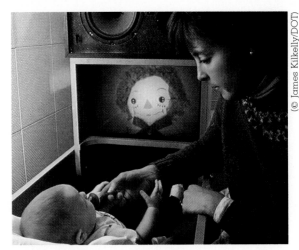

Researchers can measure a baby's interest in a picture projected on a screen, or in sounds coming out of the speaker above it, by the vigor with which the baby sucks on a special nipple that keeps the image in place or the recording playing. In one such experiment, 4-month-old babies sucked more rapidly when they first heard a new sound but more slowly when they got used to it. The speed with which an infant becomes habituated, or accustomed, to a sight or sound may be a sign of intelligence.

Habituation *Habituation* is the process of getting used to a sound, a sight, or some other stimulus, which results in loss of interest and a reduced response. Since habituation involves an alteration of behavior based on experience, it is a simple form of learning.

Habituation allows people to conserve energy by remaining alert to things and events in the environment only as long as they appear to merit attention, because they seem either desirable or threatening. Habituation is not responsible for *all* lowered responses: for example, those that occur when you no longer feel a watch after it has been on your wrist for a while, or when your eyes become accustomed to the dark at night. Other nonhabituative factors that can decrease response include maturation, illness, aging, and drug use (Lipsitt, 1986).

Researchers study habituation in newborns by repeatedly presenting a stimulus (a sound or pattern). Typically, a baby will stop sucking when the stimulus is first presented and will not start again until after the stimulation has ended. After the same sound or sight has been presented again and again, it loses its novelty and does not influence the baby's sucking, showing that the infant has habituated to it. A new sight or sound, however, will get the baby's attention and again interrupt sucking.

As we have seen, studies based on habituation have found that newborns can distinguish between sounds they have already heard and those they have not. In the first week of life, neonates can also distinguish between visual patterns (J. S. Werner & Siqueland, 1978), and their discriminatory ability becomes more refined by 5 months of age (Fantz et al., 1975). The greater the difference between the patterns, the less time a baby needs to tell them apart (Fagan, 1982; see Figure 4-1).

The capacity for habituation increases during the first 10 weeks of life (Lipsitt, 1986). Because it is associated with normal development, its presence or absence, as well as the speed with which it occurs, can tell us a great deal about a baby's present and future development. Habituation studies show us how well babies can see and hear, how much they can remember, and what their neurological status is. Babies with low Apgar scores and those with brain damage, distress at the time of birth, or Down syndrome show impaired habituation (Lipsitt, 1986). Infants whose mothers had high doses of medication during childbirth do not habituate well at 2 and 5 days after birth, or even as late as 1 month of age (Bowes, Brackbill, Conway, & Steinschneider, 1970).

Figure 4-1 Visual recognition in infancy. The more two pictures differ, the less time a baby needs to look at them. A 5-month-old baby may need only 4 seconds to distinguish two very different patterns, but 17 seconds are needed for less varied patterns, and 20 to 30 seconds for faces. (*Source:* Fagan, 1982.)

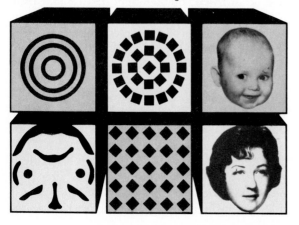

As we shall see in our discussion of information processing, speed of habituation shows promise as a predictor of intelligence, especially verbal abilities. Poor habituation during the neonatal period often foreshadows slow development; when habituation is lacking altogether, the child is likely to have future learning problems (Lipsitt, 1986).

Classical Conditioning   Anna's proud father often took pictures of her: Anna crawling, Anna waving bye-bye, Anna "dancing." Whenever a flashbulb went off, Anna blinked. One evening when Anna was about 11 months old, as her father was about to snap her picture, she blinked *before* the flash. Anna had learned to associate the camera with the blinding light and no longer needed the flash itself to call forth the reflex of blinking.

Anna's behavior is an example of ***classical conditioning,*** which was introduced in Chapter 1 in connection with Pavlov's experiments on dogs. In this basic kind of learning, a person or animal learns to respond automatically to a stimulus that originally was neutral (did not bring forth the response).

Let's analyze what happened in Anna's case. The flash was an ***unconditioned stimulus:*** it naturally caused her to blink. The blinking after the flash was an ***unconditioned response:*** it came of its own accord. The sight of the camera was originally a ***neutral stimulus:*** it would not, by itself (without the flash), provoke the blinking response. After the two stimuli—camera and flash—were paired repeatedly, the camera became a ***conditioned stimulus:*** one that was neutral before the conditioning but now elicited the response of blinking. Anna's blinking at the camera was a ***conditioned response:*** it came only after repeated association of the camera with the flash.

A famous example of classical conditioning is that of a baby known in the psychological literature as "Little Albert" (J.B. Watson & Rayner, 1920). When "Little Albert" was 9 months old, he showed no fear of any animal. Two months later, as he reached toward a white rat, laboratory experimenters sounded a loud noise, and he began to cry. This happened again and again. Eventually, Albert would whimper in fear as soon as he saw the rat.

An Indian snake charmer's baby eagerly plays with a snake the father has trained, showing that fear of snakes is a learned response. Children can be conditioned to fear animals that are associated with unpleasant or frightening experiences, as "Little Albert" was in a classic study by John B. Watson and Rosalie Rayner.

How would we describe "Little Albert's" experience in psychological terms? The noise (a hammer struck against a steel bar just behind his head) was the unconditioned stimulus; the crying automatically produced by the noise was the unconditioned response. The rat was originally a neutral stimulus. But after repeated pairing of the white rat with the loud noise, the rat became a conditioned stimulus. "Little Albert" would cry as soon as he saw the rat; he no longer needed the noise. The crying response that "Little Albert" now made to the rat (and later to other furry white things, including a rabbit and a Santa Claus mask) was a conditioned response: it arose only after repeated association of the rat with the loud noise.

Watson and Rayner's conditioning of "Little Albert" raises controversial issues. The first, of course, is the moral one. This experiment would not be permitted today, under contemporary ethical standards, as explained in Chapter 1. On top of this, there is serious criticism of the conclusions; it is charged (among other things) that this experiment was not pure classical conditioning, since the punishing aspects of the frighteningly loud noise resembled operant conditioning (B. Harris, 1979) as defined in Chapter 1. Yet this study is considered a classic and does suggest that fears can be learned through association.

How early can conditioning occur? Some critics maintain that newborn infants cannot be conditioned classically and that studies purporting to show that they can be are flawed methodologically (Sameroff, 1971; Stamps, 1977). The most recent research, however, seems to indicate that there *are* ways to classically condition newborn infants. Newborns have learned to suck when they hear a buzzer or a tone; to exhibit the Babkin reflex (turning the head and opening the mouth) when their arms are moved (instead of the traditional stimulus, pressure on the palm of the hand); to dilate and constrict the pupils of the eye; to blink; and to exhibit a change in heart rate (Rovee-Collier & Lipsitt, 1982).

Operant Conditioning As early as 3 days after birth, infants will suck more on a nipple that activates a tape of the mother's voice than on a nipple that produces the voice of a strange woman (DeCasper & Fifer, 1980). They have learned two separate things: they can distinguish between the mother's voice and somebody else's, and they have discovered an action that brings a pleasing sound. The latter is an example of **operant** (or **instrumental**) **conditioning;** the child learns to make a certain response in order to produce a desired effect.

When Timmy's sucking results in hearing his mother's voice, he is being rewarded, or reinforced, for the effort of sucking; and this **rein-**

forcement encourages repetition of the behavior. As we saw in Chapter 1, operant conditioning differs from classical conditioning in that the learner acts on the environment.

Neonates' ability to learn through operant conditioning allows things to be learned about *them*. In one study, 2-day-old infants were rewarded by hearing music as long as they sucked on a dry nipple. The babies would prolong their sucking when the music continued, but not when the sucking turned the music off (Butterfield & Siperstein, 1972). The researchers concluded that babies like music and that they can learn to do certain things in order to keep music playing. Such studies, which change babies' behavior by rewarding them in various ways, show that operant conditioning works in the neonatal period—if the conditioning is based on a preexisting, biologically important behavior such as sucking, rather than a type of action that the baby would not ordinarily perform.

Complex Learning

The two kinds of conditioning can be combined to produce increasingly complex learning. In one series of studies, researchers first taught infants as young as 1 week, through operant conditioning, to turn their heads left at the sound of a bell to receive milk. The babies who failed to learn in this way were given classical conditioning through stroking of the left corner of the mouth when the bell sounded; these babies would then turn their heads and get the milk. By the age of 4 to 6 weeks, the babies had learned to turn their heads when they heard the bell. After that, the infants were trained to differentiate the bell from a buzzer. They were fed on the left when the bell rang and on the right when the buzzer sounded. At about 3 months of age, the babies had learned to turn to the appropriate side. Four-month-olds even learned to reverse the response to bell and buzzer, demonstrating the remarkable complexity of babies' learning capacities (Papousek, 1959, 1960a, 1960b, 1961).

Habituation and conditioning are not the only ways in which infants learn. Social learning, based on observation and imitation of models, is discussed later in this chapter, as well as in

Chapters 1 and 6. Complex skills are often acquired through a mixture of several kinds of learning. Toilet training, for example, requires a mix of maturation with different kinds of learning (for practical suggestions about toilet training, see Box 4-1).

Infants' Memory

Can you remember anything that happened when you were less than a year old? Chances are that you can't. We're not sure why this is the case. Perhaps, as Freud believed, our early memories are repressed; or perhaps they are simply replaced in our consciousness by later, more complex ones.

One thing is clear: if infants did not possess at least a short-term ability to remember, they would not be able to learn (Lipsitt, 1986). Anna learned to blink at the camera because she remembered that its appearance was associated with a bright flash. Timmy would not suck on a nipple to hear his mother's voice unless he had some memory that his sucking had produced that voice. Similarly, infants who become habituated to a familiar stimulus must be aware of having been exposed to that stimulus before; otherwise, it would seem fresh and novel to them.

Research has revealed that very young infants have surprising capacities to remember. In a series of experiments, brightly colored mobiles were hung over the cribs of 6-week-old babies and attached to the infants' legs so that when they kicked, they set the mobiles in motion. When the mobiles were put in place again 2 weeks to a month later, the babies showed by kicking that they remembered how they had activated the mobiles (Rovee-Collier & Fagen, 1976, 1981; M.W. Sullivan, 1982). Two- to four-week-old infants have even been taught to recognize words. Mothers repeated a single word 60 times a day for 13 days. Fifteen to forty-two hours later, the babies responded more (with eye movements) to that word than to other words, including their own names (Ungerer, Brody, & Zelazo, 1978).

Aspects of infants' memory appear to be tied in with how intelligence develops and how we may predict it.

BOX 4·1 PRACTICALLY SPEAKING

USING LEARNING PRINCIPLES IN TOILET TRAINING

One of the most frustrating jobs of modern American parents is teaching a child how to use the toilet. Toilet training days, however, do not have to be full of tears, shouting, and unhappiness for parent or child. Two psychologists who devised a program using a combination of learning principles to teach retarded people how to use the toilet then applied the same principles to a program for normal children (Azrin & Foxx, 1981). If you use Azrin and Foxx's method to toilet-train little Jimmy, here are the basic steps to take:

1 Wait till Jimmy is about 20 months of age and then test him for bladder control (does he stay dry for 2 or 3 hours at a time?), physical readiness (can he dress and undress himself?), and readiness to take instructions. If he doesn't seem ready, wait a few weeks and test him again. Maturation is essential.

2 Before you begin training, encourage Jimmy to take part in dressing himself, allow him to watch family members using the toilet, teach him toilet vocabulary, and teach him to follow instructions. Imitation (learning based on observing models) is important. This kind of learning was described in Chapter 1 when social-learning theory was introduced.

3 Accumulate a variety of small snack items and drinks to use as reinforcers. You'll also be using praise, hugging, stroking, smiling, and clapping. Knowing your child, you'll know which reinforcers will be most effective.

4 Get a potty-chair that's easy for Jimmy to empty. The more responsibility he takes, the more quickly he'll learn.

5 Buy a doll that wets, drinks from a bottle, and can wear "training pants." This is another form of learning by imitation, as well as learning by teaching.

6 Dress Jimmy in training pants and show him how to put them on and take them off. Part of his being a "big boy" is dressing and undressing himself.

7 Teach Jimmy to teach his doll to use the potty. Encourage him to praise it enthusiastically when it does and to offer it a treat (which Jimmy will get to eat once he agrees that he intends to do the same). This is the beginning of "shaping" Jimmy's behavior. (See Chapter 1.)

8 Teach Jimmy to check his pants for dryness and reward him by treat and praise when he tells you he's dry. This is another step in shaping.

9 Teach him to walk to the potty chair, lower his pants, sit down, stay quietly for several minutes, and then stand up and raise his pants. This is a further step in shaping.

10 Praise and reassure him to encourage him to relax while on the potty. Anxiety and tension often interfere with learning; feeling relaxed enhances it.

11 Develop a way to detect urination as soon as it starts and praise Jimmy immediately. This emphasizes the pairing of the biological mechanism of relaxing the sphincter muscles with being on the potty, an important element of classical conditioning. It also strengthens the association between the action and the rewards, an important element of operant conditioning.

12 Deal with accidents by encouraging him to use the potty right afterward, making him aware of his wet pants, and having him take them off and put them into the laundry hamper himself. The major emphasis throughout this program is on reward and encouragement.

(Bettmann Archive)

The French psychologist Alfred Binet (1857–1911) devised a test that was the first attempt to measure intelligence psychometrically, with numerical ratings.

STUDYING INTELLECTUAL DEVELOPMENT: THREE APPROACHES

Rebecca, at 1 year, loved Cheerios—and loved to play games with her father. One day he put some Cheerios into his hand, closed it, and put his fist on the tray of her high chair. She immediately pulled his fingers open and reached for the Cheerios. As soon as she released her father's fingers, however, they snapped closed. After two tries, she discovered that she could hold his fingers open with one hand while she picked up Cheerios with the other. One day when one hand held a toy that she did not want to drop, she came up with another solution. She opened her father's fingers with the other hand and then held them open with her chin, freeing her hand to retrieve the prized Cheerios.

Rebecca's problem solving demonstrates the intelligent behavior that many normal babies of her age are capable of—behavior involving far more complex and self-initiated learning than conditioning or habituation. How did her intelligence develop? Why do some children appear to be more intelligent than others of the same age? Can we measure a baby's intelligence, and

can we predict how smart that baby will be as an older child or as an adult?

There is much argument over such questions, which have implications for how children are raised and schooled and the fairness of the opportunities that are made available to them. The questions are difficult ones because intelligence is an extremely complicated subject: hard to analyze, difficult to describe and to account for fully.

First, what do we mean by intelligence? Although there are many definitions, *intelligent behavior* is generally considered to have two aspects: it is goal-oriented, meaning that it is conscious and deliberate rather than accidental; and it is adaptive, meaning that human beings use it to identify and solve problems. Intelligence is affected by both inherited ability and environmental experience. Intelligence results in a person's being able to acquire, remember, and use knowledge; to understand concepts and relationships among objects, ideas, and events; and to apply knowledge and understanding to everyday problems.

Most investigators of intelligence have taken one of three approaches:

■ *Psychometric approach.* This approach attempts to measure intelligence in terms of quantity, or *how much* intelligence a person has. It measures intelligence by using *intelligence tests;* the higher the test score, the more intelligent the person is assumed to be.
■ *Piagetian approach.* This approach looks at the quality of intellectual functioning, or *what* people can do. The very nature of a person's intelligence is believed to develop in stages.
■ *Information-processing approach.* This approach analyzes the processes underlying intelligent behavior, or *how* people use their intelligence.

All three approaches help us to understand intelligence. No single approach gives us a full picture, but a combination of approaches opens several windows to let us examine what is intelligent, effective behavior.

Let us see what each of the three approaches to studying intelligence can tell us—particularly about the intellectual development of infants and toddlers.

Psychometric Approach: Intelligence Tests

At the beginning of the twentieth century, the schools in Paris were crowded with youngsters who seemed unable to handle academic learning; administrators therefore asked the psychologist Alfred Binet to devise a test to identify children who should be removed from regular classes and given more suitable programs. The test that Binet and his colleague Théodore Simon developed was the forerunner of a variety of psychometric tests that attempt to score intelligence numerically. One of these tests is the Stanford-Binet Intelligence Scale, an American version of the original Binet-Simon tests (see Chapter 6). Binet's original purpose was to find out which children were the least educable; today, however, psychometric testing is also used to discover unusually able youngsters, who may benefit from enriched or accelerated learning.

What Do Intelligence Tests Measure? Proponents of the *psychometric approach* seek to determine and measure quantitatively the factors that make up intelligence. Using *IQ tests,* they assess *how much* a person has of certain abilities, such as comprehension and reasoning abilities. Psychometric tests consist of certain questions or tasks (usually verbal and mathematical) that appear to be indicators of intellectual functioning in these areas. The test scores show how well, relative to other persons, someone can perform the tasks. Children's performance in such tests can predict future school performance fairly accurately.

Because children normally grow in their ability to solve tasks, a child's performance is evaluated on the basis of age. Each child's score is compared with **standardized norms,** standards obtained from the scores of a large, representative sample of children who took the test while it was in the process of preparation. The result is the child's **mental age,** which corresponds to the average age of normal children in the sample group who received a like score. For example, a mental age of 3 would indicate that a child's score is close to that of the average 3-year-old in the original sample—regardless of the test-taker's actual, chronological age. Mental age, then, tells us how a child's intellectual develop-

ment compares with that of a "normal" child the same age.

To compare intelligence in children of *different* ages, or to detect changes in a particular child's intelligence over time, we need a number that can be used for all age groups. The **intelligence quotient (IQ)** shows the relationship between mental age and chronological age. The IQ is obtained by dividing mental age (MA) by chronological age (CA) and multiplying by 100:

$$IQ = \frac{MA}{CA} \times 100$$

Thus a child whose mental age is the same as his or her chronological age has an IQ of 100, which is average or normal. A 10-year-old with a mental age of 12 has an IQ of 120, showing more advanced development than the norm; a 10-year-old with a mental age of 8 has an IQ of 80, indicating less than normal development.

This traditional calculation does not take into account, however, the *range* of scores that go into calculating the mean, or average. A 10-year-old with an IQ of 110 might be superior to 84 percent of his or her age group, while a 14-year-old with the same IQ might have a higher score than 90 percent of youngsters the same age. To take this variability into account, IQ scores are now reported using the *deviation IQ,* which standardizes comparative scores for all ages. In this way, an IQ of 110 means the same thing at all ages. The distribution of IQ scores in the general population takes the form of a bell-shaped curve, with the great majority of scores clustered around the middle (between 85 and 115) and fewer and fewer approaching the upper and lower ends. Test developers have also devised techniques to try to ensure that the tests are **valid** (that they measure the abilities they claim to measure) and **reliable** (that the results are reasonably consistent from one time to another).

Unfortunately, many people have the misconception that the IQ represents a fixed quantity of intelligence that people are born with, rather than simply an indicator of relative intellectual development. While intelligence tests are often presumed to measure innate intellectual ability, what they actually measure is achievement and performance, which are affected by factors be-

It is difficult to measure infants' intelligence. Since they cannot speak or write, the main evidence of their intelligence is often observable motor behavior, which may not be a good indication of intellectual potential.

yond "pure" intelligence. Although IQ scores of school-age children and of adults tend to be fairly stable, some people show marked changes, perhaps reflecting environmental circumstances (Kopp & McCall, 1982). Binet himself recognized the effects of nurturance when he urged that students who did poorly on his test be given "mental orthopedics" (special training) to increase their intelligence (Kamin, 1981).

Indeed, test-takers on the whole have been doing better on the Stanford-Binet test in recent years (Anastasi, 1976), forcing test developers to raise previously established norms. A person who scores 100 today has passed more test items than one who got 100 in 1937. This broad improvement probably reflects exposure to educational television programs, preschools, more educated parents, and a wider variety of experiences—as well as to the tests themselves—rather than genetic changes in the population.

Intelligence is difficult to define, much less to measure—especially in terms of a single number. Yet, as one researcher said (in effect), we know it when we see it (Sternberg, 1982). There undoubtedly are real differences in intellectual ability among children, but there is considerable disagreement over how accurately psychometric testing assesses those differences. We will con-

tinue our general discussion of issues regarding intelligence testing in Chapter 8, when we examine the intellectual development of school-age children. Right now, let's see why it's especially hard to gauge a baby's intelligence.

Difficulties in Measuring Infants' and Toddlers' Intelligence Faced with the striking differences in intelligence scores between infants and older children, one researcher concluded 40 years ago that "attempting to measure infantile intelligence may be like trying to measure a boy's beard at the age of three" (Goodenough, 1949, p. 310).

Though we now know that infants are intelligent from birth, measuring their intelligence is another matter. For one thing, babies can't talk. You can't ask them questions and get answers. They can't tell you what they know and how they think. The most obvious way to gauge their intelligence is by what they can do, but very young infants don't do very much. Experimenters try to catch their attention and coax them into a particular behavior; but if they don't grasp a rattle, for example, it's hard to tell whether they don't know how, don't feel like doing it, or don't realize what's expected of them.

124   PART 2 ■ BEGINNINGS

Not surprisingly, an infant's test scores are not very **reliable;** that is, they tend to vary widely from one time to another. Their value in sizing up a baby's current abilities is questionable enough; they are virtually useless for predicting future functioning. It is almost impossible to predict the adult or even childhood IQ from psychometric scores of normal children before the age of 2. A more reliable predictor of childhood IQ is the parents' IQ or educational level (Kopp & McCall, 1982). Not until the third year of life do the child's own scores, when combined with these factors, add to the reliability of prediction.

Even for toddlers, predictions based on psychometric tests are highly unreliable. In one longitudinal study, individual IQs changed by an average of 28½ points between ages 2½ and 17, and the IQs of 1 in 7 children shifted by more than 40 points (R.B. McCall, Appelbaum, & Hogarty, 1973). As youngsters are tested closer to their fifth birthday, however, the relationship between their intelligence scores and those in later childhood becomes stronger (Bornstein & Sigman, 1986).

Why do early intelligence scores fail to predict later ones? One answer probably lies in the fact that the primarily sensory and motor nature of the tests traditionally used for babies and the heavily verbal nature of the tests used for older children imply that the tests measure different and largely unrelated kinds of intelligence (Bornstein & Sigman, 1986). Even when we look at motor skills alone, children who are good at the large-muscle activities tested at an early age may not be equally adept at fine motor, or manipulative, skills considered to be a sign of intelligence a little later on. A child who at 1 year, for example, could build towers with blocks may not, by the age of 7, be able to copy a design made from colored blocks.

It is a little easier to predict the future IQ of a handicapped infant, or one thought to be at risk of developing a handicap because of prematurity or for some other reason. Yet some children born with mental and motor handicaps make impressive strides in tested intelligence as they grow older. A supportive environment can help such a child learn special ways to cope (Kopp & McCall, 1982).

In addition, human beings seem to have what some observers have called a "strong self-righting tendency" (Kopp & McCall, 1982) and what others have called "growth for health" (Kagan, 1979). That is, given a favorable environment, infants will generally follow the developmental patterns for their species unless they have suffered severe damage. Sometime between the ages of 18 and 24 months, however, this self-righting tendency seems to diminish as children begin to acquire skills (such as verbal abilities) in which there will eventually be great variations in proficiency. As these sophisticated skills develop, individual differences become more pronounced and lasting.

Developmental Testing Despite the recognized difficulties in measuring infant intelligence, there are sometimes reasons to test babies, either for research purposes or to see how a particular child is developing. If parents are worried that their baby is not doing the same things as other children the same age, early testing may reassure them that the child's development is normal, though different. Or tests may alert them to abnormal development and to the need to make special arrangements for the child's upbringing.

Developmental tests are based on careful observations of large numbers of babies. After determining what most infants can do at particular ages, researchers plot the results on a standardized scale, assigning a developmental age to each specific activity.

The DQ (development quotient), often used to gauge an infant's developmental level, is computed similarly to the IQ. Tasks are set up in order of increasing difficulty. Each task is given a numerical value, and the total score determines the child's mental age.

One important test for this purpose is the **Bayley Scales of Infant Development** (Bayley, 1933; revised 1969). This instrument, which is used to assess the developmental status of children from 2 months to 2½ years of age, has three parts:

1 *Mental scale,* which measures such abilities as perception, memory, learning, and verbal communication. Test items include turning the head to follow an object and imitating simple actions and words.
2 *Motor scale,* which measures gross motor skills (such as standing and walking) and fine

motor skills (such as grasping a piece of paper or drinking from a cup).

3 *"Infant behavior record,"* which, as the name implies, is a behavioral history.

The separate scores calculated for each scale are useful to assess an infant's current abilities rather than to predict later intelligence; they "can be most helpful in the early detection of sensory and neurological deficits, emotional disturbances, and environmental deficits" (Anastasi, 1976, p. 273).

Can Infants' and Toddlers' Intelligence Be Increased? Improved parenting skills can apparently increase very young children's intelligence.

From 1970 to 1975, federally sponsored Parent Child Development Centers tested the notion that the school performance of low-income children can be improved by influencing parental attitudes and behavior during the children's first 3 years of life. Mothers of children placed in the centers' nursery school received comprehensive information and training in child development, child-rearing practices, home management, nutrition, health, and other topics, along with a wide range of support services. In recognition of cultural differences in parenting practices, the centers let parents decide what was best for their children and hired staff members of the same ethnic and cultural backgrounds as the parents.

The results were striking. "Trained" mothers gave their children more instruction, information, and praise; asked them more questions and encouraged them to think and talk; provided more appropriate play materials and more flexible routines; and were more emotionally responsive, sensitive, and accepting and less interfering and critical than mothers of children in control groups. Children of the mothers in the program did better on Stanford-Binet tests at the age of 3 than the other children, and they maintained their gains a year later (Andrews et al., 1982).

Unfortunately, the project was dropped because of funding problems, and so we don't know how those children did after they entered school. But the results do show that the kind of care babies get and the way their mothers handle them can have a definite effect on their intellectual development.

Piagetian Approach: Cognitive Stages

The Swiss psychologist Jean Piaget took a totally different approach from that of the psychometricians to the question of children's **cognitive development,** the growth in their thought processes that enables them to acquire and use knowledge about the world. Piaget, who initially worked in France to help standardize the early IQ tests, concluded that standardized tests miss much that is special and interesting about children's thought processes, and he set out to describe those processes.

To learn how children learn, Piaget posed unusual questions, such as "Is a rock alive?" or "Where do dreams come from?" Then, unlike the psychometricians, who looked for the *right* answers to their questions, Piaget paid more attention to the apparently *wrong* answers children gave. He drew out their reasons for those answers, thus getting clues to the way they thought. Their thinking, he concluded, was not *quantitatively* different (different in amount) from adult thought, not merely less developed. Instead, he believed that children's thought processes are *qualitatively* different (different in kind) from those of adults, and that their thought evolves in a sequence of stages as they mature. Whereas psychometricians were interested in the *differences* among individuals, Piaget was more interested in sequences of intellectual development that seemed to him *universal* for normal children. The **Piagetian approach,** then, describes qualitatively different stages of cognitive development that typically characterize children from infancy through adolescence.

Piaget's theory traces cognitive development from infancy. Of course, his insights into infant cognition did not come from asking questions of babies (who would not have been able to answer). They emerged from his careful observations of his own three children. These meticulous observations provided the underpinnings for his theory of the first stage of development— the sensorimotor stage—and became the basis for much research on infant cognition and intelligence.

Sensorimotor Stage (Birth to about 2 Years)

Piaget's first cognitive stage is called the *sensorimotor stage:* a time when infants learn about their world through their own developing sensory and motor activity. During the first 2 years, babies change from creatures who respond primarily through reflexes and random behavior to goal-oriented toddlers who organize their activities in relation to their environment, coordinate the information they receive from their senses, and progress from trial-and-error learning to using rudimentary insights in solving simple problems.

COGNITIVE CONCEPTS OF THE SENSORIMOTOR STAGE During the years in the sensorimotor stage, children begin to develop several important cognitive concepts. One is *object permanence:* the realization that an object or person continues to exist even when out of sight. Object permanence is the basis for children's awareness that they exist apart from objects and other people. It allows a child whose parent has left the room to feel secure in the knowledge that the parent continues to exist and will return. It is essential to understanding time, space, and the multiplicity of objects in the outside world.

Another important concept that emerges during this stage is *causality,* the Piagetian term for the recognition that certain events cause other events. In one study, babies saw films that showed physically impossible events, such as a ball moving toward a second ball which then moved before the first ball touched it. Infants under 10 months of age showed no surprise, but older babies did. Evidently the older infants realized that something necessary for movement of the second ball was missing (Michotte, 1962, cited in Siegler & Richards, 1982).

It is not surprising that the awareness of causality develops at about 10 months. That is the time when many babies begin making their own experiments. They play with light switches and delight in making the lights go on and off. Their favorite toys are those that they can do something with—roll, make noise with, or drop. By their actions, infants of this age show an understanding that *they* can cause things to happen.

While the roots of such important concepts as causality are taking hold in the sensorimotor period, infants cannot fully grasp them. The reason, said Piaget, is that children at this age have limited *representational ability:* the capacity to mentally represent objects and actions in memory. This ability to remember and imagine things and actions—largely through the use of symbols such as words, numbers, and mental pictures—blossoms as children are about to enter the next cognitive stage, the preoperational stage, which we discuss in Chapter 6.

SUBSTAGES OF THE SENSORIMOTOR STAGE Let's look more closely at the way development progresses during the sensorimotor stage. In doing so, we will see the enormous cognitive growth that occurs before most babies can even talk—growth that helps them form bonds with the important people in their world.

Much of this growth occurs through what Piaget called *circular reactions,* in which the child learns how to reproduce pleasurable or interesting occurrences originally discovered by chance. The process has elements of operant conditioning. Initially, an activity produces a sensation so welcome that the child is motivated to repeat the activity. The repetition then feeds on itself in a continuous cycle in which cause and effect become virtually indistinguishable (see Figure 4-2, page 128).

The sensorimotor stage consists of six substages (see Table 4-1, page 129), which flow from one to another as a baby's *schemes,* or organized patterns of behavior (discussed in Chapter 1), become more elaborate. As we examine each substage, we will pay particular attention to what Piaget regarded as the single most important cognitive acquisition of the sensorimotor period: the development of object permanence.

Substage 1: Use of reflexes (birth to 1 month) As neonates exercise their few innate reflexes, they gain some control over them. They begin to engage in a behavior even when the stimulus that elicits it as an automatic reflex is not present. For example, newborn babies suck reflexively when their lips are touched. During the first month, infants learn to find the nipple even when they are not touched, and they begin to practice sucking at times when they are not hungry. Thus infants become energetic initiators of activity, not just passive responders. Their in-born schemes for sucking are modified and extended by experience.

Object permanence is completely lacking—the presence or absence of any object appears random and unpredictable.

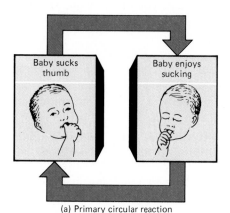

(a) Primary circular reaction

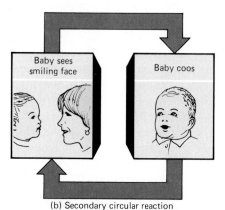

(b) Secondary circular reaction

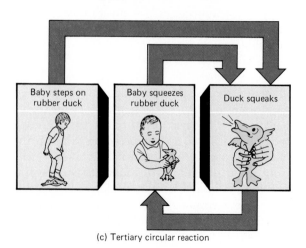

(c) Tertiary circular reaction

Substage 2: Primary circular reactions and acquired adaptations (1 to 4 months) The baby lying in a crib blissfully sucking a thumb exemplifies what Piaget called a ***primary circular reaction:*** a simple, repetitive act, centered on the baby's own body, to reproduce a pleasant sensation first achieved by chance. One day Max exercises his sucking scheme while his thumb happens to be in his mouth. He likes the feeling and attempts to recapture it through trial and error. Once successful, he makes deliberate efforts to put his thumb into his mouth, keep it there, and keep sucking. In so doing, he also makes his first ***acquired adaptations:*** he learns to adjust or accommodate his actions by sucking on his thumb differently from the way he must suck on a nipple. The result of this learning is a reorganized scheme for sucking.

At this time a baby also starts to coordinate and organize different kinds of sensory information—for example, vision and hearing. When Linda hears her mother's voice, she turns toward the sound and eventually discovers that it comes from her mother's mouth. Her world is beginning to make sense.

Object permanence is still absent. Linda can now follow a moving object with her eyes; but when something disappears, she does not look for it. However, she will continue to stare briefly at the spot where the object was last seen, as if passively watching for it.

Figure 4-2 Primary, secondary, and tertiary circular reactions. according to Piaget, infants learn to reproduce pleasing events they accidentally discover. (a) In a primary circular reaction, a baby happens to suck a thumb, enjoys sucking, and puts the thumb back in the mouth (or keeps it there). The stimulus of the thumb elicits the sucking response, and the pleasure of sucking, in turn, stimulates the baby to put the thumb in the mouth or keep it there. (b) A secondary circular reaction involves something outside the baby's body. The baby may coo upon seeing a smiling face, and because the coo causes the face to continue smiling, the baby coos again. (c) In a tertiary circular reaction, the baby tries different ways of reproducing a discovered response. When the baby steps on a rubber duck, for example, the duck squeaks. The baby then tries to reproduce the squeak—not by stepping on the duck again, but by squeezing it.

use information processing as the basis for testing the intelligence of developmentally disabled infants (Kearsley, 1981; Zelazo, 1981).

Information-processing tests can be used for children from 3 months to 3 years of age. In one, a baby sits, usually on the mother's lap, in a room set up like a puppet theater. Through wires attached to the chest (which do not cause any discomfort), the child is hooked up to an instrument that records changes in heartbeat, while hidden observers watch and record facial and physical changes. The child sees or hears five episodes that are designed to set up expectations and then to surprise the child by changing the expected pattern. In one of the little dramas, a toy car rolls down a ramp and knocks over a doll. A hand stands the doll back up and rolls the car back up the ramp. The same action occurs six times. The seventh time, the doll does not fall down when it is hit by the car. This happens twice more, and then the original sequence is repeated a few more times.

Children react to these events in a number of ways. A child may stare at the stage, point or clap, wave, twist, or turn to the mother. At two points—the first time the doll does not fall down and the first time it falls down again—the child's heart is likely to speed up; the child may frown the first time the doll does not fall and smile the next time it does. These reactions reveal whether a child has learned to expect the doll to fall; how the child adjusts when the doll does not fall; and whether he or she recognizes the restoration of the original pattern when the doll again falls. Thus the child's reactions indicate the extent to which a memory of the event has been formed.

Although each child's reactions are, of course, somewhat different, the researchers have charted the ways children typically react and have developed standards for different age levels, paying special attention to the speed with which a child reacts to the episodes. At 5½ months, infants are likely to make sounds when they recognize the familiar pattern in which the doll falls. One-year-olds tend to stare and search. A typical 20-month-old smiles, vocalizes, and points. Not until about 30 months of age do most children respond to the change when the doll does not fall; but 3-year-olds react almost immediately to both situations. Zelazo (1981)

concludes that the test measures the child's "increasing speed of information processing over the first three years of life" (p. 244).

This approach has advantages for testing normal children, as well, since it does not matter whether the child understands, likes, or is willing to cooperate with the examiner. The test itself is so interesting that the child pays attention to what is going on.

The information-processing approach itself is still in its infancy. With further research, we may learn more about the precise mechanisms that enable very young children to move from one developmental stage to the next. And as techniques to measure and predict individual differences in cognition are further refined, we may yet better understand intelligence.

DEVELOPMENT OF LANGUAGE

At 4½ months Steven chuckles out loud. He also says "Ngoo-ooo" and "Ngaaah." At 7 months he makes more sounds, mostly sounding like "da" or "ga." At 11 months he says "Dada," and at 14 months he points to everything, asking "What zis?" or saying "Da" for "I want that." At 17 months he points to the right places when asked "Where is your nose? Tongue? Belly button?" and so forth. By 21 months he says, or tries to say, at least 50 words, and understands many more. He can now tell you exactly what he does or does not want, in his own language. When asked "Do you want to go to bed?" he answers "Eh-eh-eh," accompanied by vigorous arm waving. In other words, "No!" He has also said his first three-word sentence: "Choo-choo bye-bye da-da." (His mother translates, "The train went away and now it's all gone.")

Aside from being a source of amusement, delight, and pride to his parents, Steven's language ability is a crucial element in his cognitive growth. Once he knows the words for things, he can use a system of symbols to stand for the objects around him; he can reflect on people, places, and things in his world; and he can communicate his needs, feelings, and ideas in order to exert control over his life. (See Table 4-2, page 136, for a list of language milestones during the first 3 years of life.)

TABLE 4-2 LANGUAGE MILESTONES FROM 6 MONTHS TO 3 YEARS

AGE IN MONTHS	LANGUAGE DEVELOPMENT
6	Cooing changes to babbling with introduction of consonants.
12	Imitation of sounds begins. Child understands some words. Child applies some sounds regularly to signify persons or objects (that is, uses the first words).
18	Child has repertoire of 3 to 50 words. Patterns of sound and intonation resemble discourse. Child has made good progress in understanding.
24	Vocabulary is over 50 words. Two-word phrases are most common. Child is more interested in verbal communication. Babbling ceases.
30	New words are learned almost every day. Utterances consist of three or more words. Comprehension is excellent. Child makes many mistakes in grammar.
36	Vocabulary reaches some 1000 words; about 80 percent are intelligible. Grammar is close to colloquial adult speech. Syntactic mistakes are fewer.

Source: Adapted from Lenneberg, 1969.

Prelinguistic Speech

Before babies say their first words—which usually come between the ages of 12 and 18 months—they make a variety of sounds that progress in a fairly set sequence from crying to cooing and babbling, accidental imitation, and then deliberate imitation. These sounds are known as *prelinguistic speech.*

Babies can distinguish between sounds long before they can utter anything but a cry. Throughout infancy, they understand more than they can express, since verbalization is limited by physical maturation.

Crying is the newborn's first and only means of communication. To a stranger, a baby's cries may sound alike; but to the baby's parents, the cry for food is different from the cry of pain. Different pitches, patterns, and intensities signal hunger, sleepiness, or anger.

At about 6 weeks, babies coo when they are happy (making squeals, gurgles, and vowel sounds such as "ahhh"), and at about 6 months they babble, repeating a number of simple sounds (usually consonant and vowel combinations like "ma-ma-ma-ma"). During their second 6 months, they accidentally imitate sounds they hear, and then they imitate themselves making these sounds. At about 9 to 10 months they deliberately imitate other sounds, although they do not understand them. Once they have this basic repertoire of sounds, they string them together in patterns that sound like language but seem to have no meaning (Eisenson, Auer, & Irwin, 1963; Lenneberg, 1967).

Although this prelinguistic speech lacks any semantic content, it can be rich in emotional expression. Starting at about 2 months, when infants' cooing begins to express contentment, there is a steady increase in the range of emotional intonation. Long before children can express any ideas in words, parents find themselves attuned to their infants' emotions through the sounds they make (Tonkova-Yompol'skaya, 1973).

Linguistic Speech

The First Word The average baby says his or her first word at about 1 year of age (give or take a few months), thus initiating *linguistic speech*—the use of spoken language to convey meaning. Before long, the baby will use *many* words, and will show some understanding of grammar, pronunciation, intonation, and rhythm as well. At this point, though, the sum total of an infant's linguistic repertoire is likely to be "mama" or "dada." Or it may be a simple syllable that has a variety of meanings, depending on what is on the baby's mind at the moment. As with Steven, "Da" may mean "I want that," "I want to go out," "Where's Daddy?" and so forth. A word like this is called a *holophrase,* because it expresses a complete thought in a single word.

When K. Nelson (1973; 1981) studied the first 50 words spoken by a group of 1- and 2-year-olds, she found that the most common were *names* of things, either in the general sense ("oof-oof" for dog) or the specific ("Bo" for one particular dog). Others were *action* words ("bye-bye"), modifiers ("hot"), words that express *feelings or relationships* (the ever-popular "no"), and a few *grammatical* words ("for").

Typically, by 15 months of age a child of either sex has spoken 10 different words or names (K. Nelson, 1973), and that vocabulary continues to grow throughout the single-word stage (which tends to last until the age of about 18 months). There is also an increasing reliance on words. More and more occasions inspire the child to speak a word or a name. The sounds and rhythms of speech grow more elaborate, and even if much of the child's speech is still babbling (and many children over the age of 1 year babble steadily), it does seem quite expressive.

The First Sentence At 18 months, Adam first spoke two words to express one idea. "Shoe fall," he said, looking up from his stroller at his father, who was pushing him along. His father paused, saw the shoe on the sidewalk, and picked it up. Adam had spoken his first sentence, putting two words together to express a single thought—and a practical one, at that.

The age at which children begin combining words varies. Generally they do this before the second birthday. Whereas prelinguistic speech is fairly closely tied to chronological age, linguistic speech is not. Roger Brown (1973a, 1973b),

of Harvard University, who has done a great deal of work on this phase of language acquisition, maintains that knowing a child's age tells us very little about his or her language development.

Stages of Linguistic Development According to Brown, language development goes through five stages, in which a child's speech becomes increasingly complex as the child combines *morphemes,* or the smallest elements of speech that have meaning. (A word such as *skate* is a single morpheme; so are the endings *-s* and *-ed,* which indicate plural and past tense. The words *skates* and *skated* each consist of two morphemes.) As children move from stage 1 to stage 5, their *mean length of utterance (MLU)*—the average number of morphemes in a single utterance—increases.

In stage 1, primitive speech, a child begins to combine morphemes occasionally (as in Adam's first sentence, "Shoe fall"), raising the MLU over 1.0. Tense and case endings, articles, and prepositions are missing, and, frequently, so are subjects or verbs (as in "That ball" and "Mommy sock").

Next the child may string two basic relationships together ("Adam hit" and "Hit ball") to get a more complicated relationship ("Adam hit ball"). Although that more advanced sentence combines three morphemes, Adam is still using single morphemes so frequently that his MLU has risen only to 1.5.

In stage 2, the MLU is 2.0, although the child may utter as many as seven morphemes at a time. In this stage, children acquire functional morphemes, including articles (*a, the*), prepositions (*in, on*), plurals, verb endings, and forms of the verb *to be* (*am, are, is*). Children start to use these forms gradually. In his intensive study of three children, Brown (1973a) noted that the variation in *rate* of development even among such a small sample is great, but that the *order* in which the children acquired the different constructions was almost constant.

As children leave stage 2, their speech becomes longer and more complex, and they advance to a new stage with each increase of 0.5 in MLU. Speech in stage 3 is called *telegraphic;* it omits many parts of speech but still conveys meaning (as in "Mommy put dolly table").

The next two stages develop later in childhood: in stage 4, grammar is close to that of adults, although children often cannot use the subjunctive ("If I were a bird, I could fly") or make up tag questions ("That's a horse, isn't it?"). By stage 5, which occurs by late childhood, children are fully competent in grammar, although they continue to enlarge their vocabulary and improve their style.

Characteristics of Early Speech When Eddie was 14 months old, he jumped in excitement at the sight of a gray-haired man on the television screen and shouted, "Gampa!" When Jennifer was 15 months old, she saw a cow and squealed, "Oof-woof!" Both these toddlers were doing something common in early speech: *overgeneralizing concepts.* Eddie thought that because his grandfather had gray hair, all gray-haired men could be called "Grandpa." Jennifer thought that because a dog has four legs and a tail, all animals with these characteristics are "oof-woofs."

Children's speech is not just an immature version of adult speech. It has a character all its own. This is true whether the child is speaking German, Russian, Finnish, Samoan, or English (Slobin, 1971).

These are some other characteristics of early speech:

- Children *simplify.* They utter just enough to get their meaning across ("No drink milk!").
- Children *overregularize rules,* applying them rigidly, without exception. Having learned grammatical rules for plurals and past tense, they will say "mouses" and "goed" instead of "mice" and "went."
- Children *understand grammatical relationships that they cannot yet express.* A child in stage 1 may understand that a dog is chasing a cat, but children at this stage cannot string together enough words to express the complete action. The sentence comes out as "Puppy chase" rather than "Puppy chase kitty."

Theories of Language Acquisition

Although both maturation and environment are important in the development of language, different linguists assign major importance to one or the other of these factors. *Learning theory* (which we introduced in Chapter 1) holds that learning (including language learning) is based on experience, while *nativism* holds that there is an inborn capacity for learning language.

Learning Theory According to learning theory, children learn language in the same way they learn other kinds of behavior—through reinforcement. Parents reinforce children for making sounds that resemble adult speech, and so children make more of these sounds, generalizing and abstracting as they go along. Behaviorists hold that children utter sounds at random, and that those which sound like adult speech are then reinforced. Social-learning theorists maintain that children imitate the sounds they hear adults making and then are reinforced for doing so; thus children in English-speaking countries learn English rather than another language. Imitation may explain why children generally outgrow incorrect usages even when their parents do not correct their grammar (R. Brown, Cazden, & Bellugi, 1969).

Learning theorists point to the fact that children reared at home, who presumably have more exposure to adult speech as well as more attention and more reinforcement than those who grow up in institutions, do babble more (Brodbeck & Irwin, 1946). However, learning theory does not account for the ability to produce novel utterances, like one little girl's description of walking on her heels as "tip-heeling."

Nativism According to the nativist view, human beings have an inborn capacity for acquiring language and learn to talk as naturally as they learn to walk. Evidence for this viewpoint comes from several facts. All normal children learn their native language, no matter how complex, mastering the basics in the same age-related sequence without formal teaching. Human beings, the only animals to master a spoken language, are the only species whose brain is larger on one side than the other, and who seem to have an innate mechanism for language localized in the larger hemisphere (the left). And, as we have seen, newborns respond to language in surprisingly sophisticated ways.

How does a baby learn what to call a ball? Learning theorists maintain that parents reinforce sounds the baby makes that approximate *ball*. Nativists, on the other hand, believe that a child has an inborn ability to discern the structure of language and picks up words naturally, from hearing them.

They move their bodies in the rhythm of the adult speech they hear (Condon & Sander, 1974); they can tell their mothers' voices from those of strangers (DeCasper & Fifer, 1980); and they can, in the first month of life, tell apart such similar sounds as "bah" and "pah" (Eimas et al., 1971).

One researcher suggests that neonates can put sounds into categories because all human beings are "born with perceptual mechanisms that are tuned to the properties of speech" (Eimas, 1985, p. 49). Contact with the sounds of a particular language leads children to "tune in" the corresponding preset "channels" and "tune out" unused ones. These perceptual mechanisms, along with the vocal cords and the specialized speech centers of the brain, allow a child to "join the community of language" as quickly as possible (p. 52).

How, starting with simple sound recognition, do babies go on to create complex utterances that follow the specific rules of language in their society? Noam Chomsky (1972) proposes that an inborn ***language acquisition device (LAD)*** programs children's brains to analyze the language they hear and to extract from it the rules of grammar. Using these rules, they can then create original sentences.

Deaf children make up their own sign language when they do not have models to follow—evidence that internal mechanisms play a large role in a young child's growing capacity for linguistic expression (H. Feldman, Goldin-Meadow, & Gleitman, 1979; Hoff-Ginsberg & Shatz, 1982). Still, the nativist approach does not explain why children differ considerably in grammatical skill and fluency, how they come to understand the meanings of words, or why (as we will see) speech development is dependent on having someone to communicate with.

Most developmentalists today adopt a combination of nativism and learning theory; they believe that children enter the world with an inborn capacity to acquire a language, which is then activated and enhanced by learning through experience.

Influences on Language Acquisition

What determines how quickly and how well a baby learns to speak? Again, the issue is nature versus nurture.

Recent studies found a moderate relationship between parents' intelligence and the rate at which their biological children developed communication skills during the first year of life. Since a similar relationship was found for adopted children and their biological mothers but not their adoptive parents, a genetic influence appeared to be at work. The authors of these studies added, however, that environmental factors, such as parents' imitation of the sounds infants made, might also affect the pace of linguistic learning (Hardy-Brown & Plomin, 1985; Hardy-Brown, Plomin, & DeFries, 1981).

Another study placed more emphasis on environmental influences, finding that many, if not most, of the marked differences in language abilities that surface by the end of a child's second year can be attributed to differences in children's surroundings (K. Nelson, 1981). One important environmental influence, of course, is how much and what kind of speech babies

BOX 4-2   PRACTICALLY SPEAKING

TALKING WITH BABIES

Most parents talk to their babies. It's natural to coo at an infant while changing a diaper, or to make a game of imitating sounds. Though the conversations may seem one-sided at first, babies are great imitators and soon begin responding.

Talking and reading to babies can enhance not only their language development but their self-esteem and their social growth—the ability to interact with people around them. Verbal as well as nonverbal communication with caring adults tells babies that they are valued individuals and encourages them to try to communicate their own feelings.

Here are some suggestions for talking with a baby at different stages of language development (E.B. Bolles, 1982):

1   *Babbling.* When a baby babbles, repeat the syllables. Make a game of it, and soon the baby will be repeating syllables back to *you.* While "dee, dee, doo, doo" may not be scintillating conversation, it gives a baby practice in the art of vocal interaction.

2   *First words.* Around 1 year of age, when babies say their first words, many adults only mimic their sounds of "ma-ma" or "da-da," missing an opportunity for helpful feedback. Instead, repeat the word, pronouncing it correctly, or, if you can't understand what the baby is trying to say, smile and compliment the effort. Babies can understand many more words than they can say. Help them build associations by naming things around them. For example, point to Cindy's doll, saying, "Please give me Kermit." If Cindy doesn't respond, reach over and take the doll, pleasantly repeating "Kermit." By engaging in such games, children can discover through language what is on another person's mind.

3   *Multiword speech.* Toddlers begin to make sentences by stringing first two and then three or more words together. Help them expand their telegraphic utterances. When Billy says "Mommy sock," his mother can reply, "Yes, that is Mommy's sock."

Let the babies decide when they have had enough. While adults may take speech for granted, forming sounds that approximate English is at least as hard work for a baby as it is for an American to learn to speak Chinese. And don't expect a baby to talk in fully formed sentences right away. Normal children begin to speak at different ages and advance linguistically at their own pace.

---

hear. Three-month-olds whose mothers talk to them while breast-feeding make more sounds than those whose mothers are silent (M. K. Rosenthal, 1982). And a study made in Bermuda found that 2-year-olds in day care centers where caregivers frequently speak to them (especially to give or ask for information rather than to control their behavior) do better on tests of language development than children who do not have such conversations with adults (McCartney, 1984). Conversely, when children with normal hearing grow up in homes with deaf parents who communicate only through sign language, the children's speech development is slowed (Moskowitz, 1978).

To learn how to speak, then, children need practice and interaction. Hearing speech on television is not enough; for example, Dutch children who watch German television every day do not learn German (C. E. Snow, Arlman-Rupp, Hassing, Jobse, Joosten, & Verster, 1976). Language is a social act. By talking to babies, parents or other caregivers demonstrate how to use new words, structure phrases, and express ideas in

BOX 4-3 FOOD FOR THOUGHT

MOTHERESE

You do not have to be a mother to speak "motherese." If you pitch your voice high, use short words and sentences, speak slowly, ask questions, and repeat your words when you speak to a baby or toddler, you are speaking motherese. Most adults—and even slightly older children—do it intuitively. And until recently, the idea that motherese enables children to learn their native language, or at least to pick it up faster, was generally accepted.

Advocates of the importance of motherese say that by speaking simply to a child, adults show acceptance of childlike speech and encourage a baby to verbalize. Because motherese is confined to simple, down-to-earth topics, youngsters can draw on their own knowledge to help them work out the meaning of what they hear (C.E. Snow, 1977). Of course, parents may not consciously have such purposes in mind when they tell a baby to "wave bye-bye"; that kind of talk just seems to come naturally in talking to a child too young to talk back.

Parents usually do not start speaking motherese until babies are able to show by their expressions, actions, and vocalizations that they have some understanding of what is being said to them. In one study, women used motherese less when asked to make tapes addressed to unseen children (C.E. Snow, 1972). This finding suggests that interaction with an infant encourages the use of motherese.

Recently some researchers have questioned the value of motherese, arguing that complex rather than restricted parental speech leads to fast, accurate language development. These investigators contend that it is what *children* select from what they hear, rather than what adults preselect *for* them, that makes the biggest difference in language learning (Gleitman, Newport, & Gleitman, 1984).

Other recent research, however, found positive correlations between use of motherese and the rate of 2-year-olds' language growth (Hoff-Ginsberg, 1985, 1986). In one particularly interesting study, twins showed slower language development than nontwins at 15 and 21 months of age, the period when language normally flowers. The apparent reason was that, because of the need to divide their mothers' time, the twins had less speech directed specifically to each of them, received less maternal attention, and had fewer and shorter conversations with their mothers. The two groups also differed in the *quality* of their language experience. The mothers of twins spoke more directly, imitated their children's utterances more, and were less likely to continue or elaborate on a topic a child brought up than the mothers of single children—who were not so busy (Tomasello, Mannle, & Kruger, 1986).

Although the jury is still out on the issue of motherese, it is clear that language development depends on babies' hearing *some* sort of live speech directed at them—not just listening to television or to parents conversing with each other. As a review of the literature concluded, "No child has been observed to speak a human language without having had a communicative partner from whom to learn" (Hoff-Ginsberg & Shatz, 1982, p. 22).

speech; and they give children a rudimentary sense of how to carry on a conversation—how to introduce a topic, comment on and add to it, and take turns talking.

Unquestionably, conversation with babies is important. The question is, What sort of conversation? Box 4-2 gives practical suggestions for talking with babies, and Box 4-3 discusses "motherese," a particular kind of speech often directed at infants.

DEVELOPMENT OF COMPETENCE

Why do some children persevere in finding a way around an obstacle (as Rebecca did when she went after the Cheerios) while others burst into tears and give up?

Burton L. White and his colleagues at the Harvard Preschool Project wanted to discover why some children function better than others. In 1965, they began testing and observing some 400 preschoolers and rating them on their competence in both cognitive and social skills (B. L. White, 1971; B. L. White, Kaban, & Attanucci, 1979).

The most competent children (who were termed "A's") displayed a wide range of intellectual abilities: they planned and carried out complicated activities, they could pay attention to one task while remaining aware of what else was going on, and they used language well. They were socially adept, too: they knew how to get positive attention and help from adults, and they got along well with other children. In the emotional realm, they showed both affection and hostility. They were proud of their accomplishments and wanted to act in grown-up ways. The "B" children were less developed in these areas, and the "C's" were very deficient. Follow-up studies 2 years later found little movement from one group to another.

What Influences Competence?

To find out how the children became the way they were, the researchers looked for differences in the home environments of the A and C children. Socioeconomic level proved to be unimportant: some welfare mothers had A children, while some middle-class women had C children.

The important difference had to do with mothering styles after the children were about 8 months old. (The researchers limited their study to mothers because they felt that few fathers spent enough time with babies at this age to have much influence—a situation that is now changing.)

Eight months is the age when children start to understand language, and so the way parents talk to them at this time is important. This is also about the time when they begin to crawl; some parents react with pleasure, some with annoyance. And at this age infants become attached to the person they spend the most time with, and so that individual's personality becomes more important.

The A and C mothers differed greatly in three important aspects of child-rearing style. The A mothers showed more ability to "design" a child's world, to serve as a "consultant" for a child, and to exert appropriate control (set reasonable limits while giving a child plenty of opportunity to explore).

The A mothers designed safe physical environments full of interesting things to see and touch, often common household objects rather than expensive toys. These mothers were generally "on call" to their babies, but they did not devote their entire lives to them. A number had jobs, and those who did stay home generally spent less than 10 percent of their time interacting with their infants. They went about their daily routines but made themselves available for a few seconds or minutes when needed to answer a question, label some object, help the toddler climb stairs, or share in an exciting discovery. These women generally had positive attitudes toward life, enjoyed being with young children, and generously gave of themselves. They were energetic, patient, tolerant of mess, and relatively casual about minor risks. They were firm and consistent; they set reasonable limits while showing love and respect. When they wanted to change their babies' behavior, they usually used distraction; for toddlers, they combined distraction with physically separating the child from a forbidden object and speaking firmly.

The C mothers were a diverse group. Some were overwhelmed by life, ran chaotic homes, and were too absorbed by daily struggles to spend time with their children. Others spent too much time: hovering, being overprotective, pushing their babies to learn, making them dependent. Some were physically present but rarely made real contact, apparently because they did not really enjoy the company of babies and toddlers. These mothers provided for their children materially but confined them in cribs or playpens.

How Can Parents Enhance Children's Competence?

Here are the project's major findings:

1 The best time for enhancing a child's development of competence is from the age of 6 or 8 months up until about 2 years.
2 The most competent children have close relationships with important people in their lives (parents or others), especially in the first few months after their first birthday.
3 Full-time parenting is not crucial: quality, rather than quantity, of time spent with the child is more important, and parent substitutes can provide rich experience.
4 Children who know that they will get help from an interested adult when they need it develop better than those who either are not attended to regularly or are seen as burdens to be dealt with as quickly as possible.
5 It is good for children to learn how to gain attention. To do this, they need the fairly close presence of a responsive adult—but *not* someone who hovers over them. Constant attention will discourage them from developing their attention-seeking skills.
6 Children develop best when adults talk to them about whatever they are interested in at the moment (as opposed to trying to redirect their attention to something else).
7 Live language directed to the child helps children develop language, social, and intellectual abilities better than television, radio, or overheard adult conversations.
8 Physical freedom is important. Children who are not regularly confined in a playpen, crib, seat, or small room develop better.

Once the Harvard team had identified guidelines for successful parenting, they undertook a pilot training study with 11 carefully chosen families in which the parents were considered to have "average child-rearing ability." The goal was to help the parents adopt practices that seemed to enhance children's competence and to avoid unhelpful practices.

Surprisingly, while the children's progress more closely resembled that of the original A children than that of the C children, they did not, by and large, do as well as the A's. It may be that naturally effective parenting styles are hard to duplicate by training, or that personalities of both parents and children play a significant role. Thus, while we can learn from research on successful parenting (as in the Parent Child Development Centers discussed earlier in this chapter), no one has yet found the perfect recipe for raising children.

One important element, for example, which the researchers did not investigate in depth, was the children's own contributions to their mothers' child-rearing styles. It is possible that the children of the A mothers had personality characteristics that made their mothers *want* to respond as they did. Perhaps these children showed more curiosity, more independence, and more interest than the C children in what their mothers said and did.

Interaction is a key to much of childhood development—intellectual, social, and emotional. Children call forth responses from the people around them and then, in turn, react to those responses. In the next chapter, we'll look more closely at these bidirectional influences as we explore early personality and social development.

How Infants Learn

■ Learning is a relatively permanent change in behavior that occurs as a result of experience. Learning and maturation interact to produce changes in cognitive abilities.

■ Very young infants are capable of several kinds of simple learning, including habituation and classical and operant conditioning. Complex learning consists of combinations of several types.

■ Infants exhibit some memory ability virtually from birth.

Studying Intellectual Development: Three Approaches

■ Intelligence involves both adaptive and goal-oriented behavior.

■ Three major approaches for studying intelligence are the psychometric, Piagetian, and information-processing approaches.

1 The psychometric approach seeks to determine and measure quantitatively the factors that make up intelligence. Psychometric testing for infants emphasizes motor skills, which may not measure the same thing as verbal tests do. Psychometric tests of infant intelligence are generally poor predictors of intelligence in later childhood and adulthood.

2 The Piagetian approach is concerned with qualitative stages of cognitive development, or the way people develop the ability to acquire and use knowledge about the world. During the sensorimotor stage, infants develop from primarily reflexive creatures to persons capable of symbolic thought. A major development during the sensorimotor stage is object permanence, the realization that an object or person continues to exist even when out of sight.

3 The information-processing approach is concerned with the processes underlying intelligent behavior, that is, how people manipulate symbols and what they do with the information they perceive. An important way to assess infants' ability to process information is by measuring their visual-recognition memory, which is related to attention and habituation. Such assessments show promise of predicting later intelligence.

Development of Language

■ The development of language is a crucial aspect of cognitive growth.

1 Prelinguistic speech, which precedes the first words, includes crying, cooing, babbling, and imitation. During the second year of life, the typical toddler begins to speak the language; that year seems to be particularly important for understanding language.

2 Early speech is characterized by overgeneralizing concepts, simplicity, and overregularizing rules. The child can understand grammatical relationships before being able to express them in speech.

■ The major theories of language acquisition are learning theory (which emphasizes the role of reinforcement and imitation) and nativism (which maintains that people have an inborn capacity to acquire language). Today, most psychologists hold that children have an inborn language capacity that is activated and enhanced by certain environmental experiences, especially the way adults talk to them.

■ At least some communication between caregivers and children is important for children's linguistic growth. It is not clear whether hearing simple, direct language ("motherese") is crucial to infants' language development.

Development of Competence

■ Parents' child-rearing styles (especially during the first 2 years) affect children's intellectual, social, and emotional competence.

■ Parents of the most competent children are those who are skilled at "designing" a child's environment, are available as "consultants" to a child, and use appropriate controls.

acquired adaptations (page 127)
Bayley Scales of Infant
  Development (125)
causality (127)
circular reactions (127)
classical conditioning (118)
cognitive development (126)
conditioned response (118)
conditioned stimulus (118)
habituation (117)
holophrase (137)
information-processing approach
  (122, 132)
intelligence quotient (IQ) (123)
intelligent behavior (122)
invisible imitation (132)
language acquisition device
  (LAD) (139)

learning (116)
learning theory (138)
linguistic speech (137)
maturation (117)
mean length of utterance (MLU)
  (137)
mental age (123)
morphemes (137)
nativism (138)
neutral stimulus (118)
object permanence (127)
operant (instrumental)
  conditioning (119)
Piagetian approach (122, 126)
prelinguistic speech (136)
primary circular reactions (127)
psychometric approach (122, 123)

reinforcement (119)
reliable (123, 125)
representational ability (127)
schemes (127)
secondary circular reactions (129)
sensorimotor stage (127)
standardized norms (123)
telegraphic (137)
tertiary circular reactions (130)
unconditioned response (118)
unconditioned stimulus (118)
valid (123)
visible imitation (132)
visual-recognition memory (133)

SUGGESTED READINGS

Bolles, E. B. (1982). *So much to say*. New York: St. Martin's. A detailed description of children's speech from birth to 5 years of age, written for parents. The book presents the child as a poet discovering new things to say and new ways to say them.

Brown, R. (1973). *A first language: The early stages*. Cambridge, MA: Harvard University Press. A classic book that describes the language development of three young children: Adam, Eve, and Sarah.

deVilliers, P. A., & deVilliers, J. (1979). *Early language*. Cambridge, MA: Harvard University Press. An engaging discussion of early linguistic development, containing many examples of child language.

Ginsburg, H., & Opper, S. (1979). *Piaget's theory of intellectual development.* (2d ed.). Englewood Cliffs, NJ: Prentice-Hall. A clear, readable discussion of Piaget's concepts. It includes outlines of Piaget's basic ideas, his early research and theory, his use of logic as a model for adolescents' thinking, and a discussion of the implications of his work.

Piaget, J. (1952). *The origins of intelligence in children*. New York: International Universities Press. Piaget's now classic presentation of the six substages of sensorimotor development. Based on abundant observations of his three children.

White, B. L. (1985). *The first three years of life* (rev. ed.). Englewood Cliffs, NJ: Prentice-Hall. A presentation for lay readers of White's findings on children's competence. It is a thorough treatment of cognitive changes during infancy and toddlerhood.

White, B. L., Kaban, B. T., & Attanucci, J. S. (1979). *The origins of human competence*. Lexington, MA: Heath. The final report of the Harvard Preschool Project focusing on the interrelationship between child-rearing practices and children's development of competence during the first few years of life.

5

CHAPTER

PERSONALITY AND SOCIAL DEVELOPMENT IN INFANCY AND TODDLERHOOD

I'm like a child
trying to do everything
say everything
and be everything
all at once

        John Hartford, "Life Prayer"

ASK YOURSELF

■ What are some common influences on personality and social development, and how do individual babies develop distinct personalities?

■ What do Freud and Erikson say about a baby's personality and social development?

■ What emotions do babies have, and how do they show them?

■ What are the effects of differences in temperament and gender?

■ How do family relationships contribute to personality and social development?

■ How do separations from the parents affect personality and social development?

■ What causes child abuse and neglect, and what can be done to combat these problems?

■ How do babies develop self-awareness and self-control?

Talk about the "terrible twos" often sends new parents into tremors of fear—and brings sighs of relief from parents of older children. This period in a child's life—often ushered in before the second birthday and lasting well beyond it—dramatizes one of the most important aspects of early psychosocial development. When we look beyond the tears and the tantrums, the "no's" and the noise, we can appreciate that a toddler's emphatic expressions of what he or she wants to do, as opposed to what *we* want him or her to do, signal the all-important shift from the dependency of infancy to the independence of childhood. Tracing the course of this shift is one of the major themes of this chapter.

The parent-child relationship is another theme. This chapter will explore the ways in which parents influence their children in infancy and toddlerhood—and how children influence their parents. It will also examine the development and measurement of emotions in infancy—the ways in which babies are like each other and the many ways they differ, because of temperament, sex, birth order, or early experiences.

These issues underlie two important theories of early personality development, those proposed by Sigmund Freud and Erik Erikson. They have also inspired research into the relationships between babies and their mothers and fathers, as well as their other caretakers, their siblings, and other babies. And they have spurred study of those situations when parent-

APPROXIMATE AGE IN MONTHS	CHARACTERISTICS
0–1	Infants are relatively unresponsive, rarely reacting to outside stimulation.
1–3	Infants are open to stimulation. They begin to show interest and curiosity, and they smile readily at people.
3–6	Babies can anticipate what is to happen and experience disappointment when it does not. They show this by becoming angry or acting wary. They smile, coo, and laugh often. This is a time of social awakening and early reciprocal exchanges between the baby and the caregiver.
7–9	Babies play "social games" and try to get responses from people. They "talk" to, touch, and cajole other babies to get them to respond. They express more differentiated emotions, showing joy, fear, anger, and surprise.
9–12	Babies are intensely preoccupied with their principal caregiver, may become afraid of strangers, and act subdued in new situations. By 1 year, they communicate emotions more clearly, showing moods, ambivalence, and gradations of feeling.
12–18	Babies explore their environment, using the people they are most attached to as a secure base. As they master the environment, they become more confident and more eager to assert themselves.
18–36	Toddlers sometimes become anxious because they now realize how much they are separating from their caregiver. They work out their awareness of their limitations in fantasy, in play, and by identifying with adults.

Source: Adapted from Sroufe, 1979.

child relationships are disrupted by separation—or when they go tragically wrong, resulting in child abuse and neglect. All these issues will raise some basic questions about the roots of personality. (See Table 5-1 for the highlights of infants' and toddlers' personality and social development that will be discussed in this chapter.)

EARLY PERSONALITY DEVELOPMENT: TWO THEORIES

Among the most important theories of early personality development are those proposed by the psychoanalytic thinkers Sigmund Freud and Erik H. Erikson (both of whom were introduced in Chapter 1). Although parts of these theories have not held up under scrutiny, as will be shown later in this chapter, the theories' impact on the field of child development and child rearing has been significant.

Sigmund Freud: Psychosexual Theory

Freud believed that personality is decisively formed in the first few years of life, as children deal with conflicts between their biological, sexually related urges and the requirements of society. As Table 1-1 shows, Freud believed that these conflicts occur in a series of stages, each of which centers on a particular part of the body and its needs. Two of these stages fall during the first 3 years.

Oral Stage (Birth to 12–18 Months)* Babies in the *oral stage* are "all mouth." Feeding is the main source of their sensual gratification, or pleasure, which is achieved by stimulation of the mouth, lips, and tongue. They also enjoy nipples, bottles, fingers, pacifiers, and anything else they can put into their mouths. At first they suck

*All ages are approximate.

According to Sigmund Freud, infancy is the oral stage, when pleasure comes primarily from putting things into the mouth.

and swallow; when their teeth begin to erupt, biting and chewing become important.

According to Freud, newborns are governed by the *id,* the instinctual part of the personality, which is present at birth and operates under the *pleasure principle,* striving for immediate gratification. The *ego,* which operates under the *reality principle*—striving to find acceptable and realistic ways to obtain gratification—develops later to help the baby deal with the real world, in which gratification sometimes must be delayed.

Freud maintained that babies whose oral needs are not met may become fixated, or stuck, in the oral stage and continue trying to meet those needs throughout life. They may become nail-biters, perhaps, or develop "bitingly" critical personalities. Babies who receive so *much* gratification at the oral stage that they do not want to abandon this pleasure may also become fixated. They may become compulsive eaters or smokers or perhaps gullible "swallowers" of whatever they are told.

Freudian theory maintains that because the oral stage begins at a time of almost total dependence on the mother, some people who are neglected by their mothers during infancy or are kept dependent too long become fixated in this stage and develop dependent personalities. At times when they feel anxious and insecure, they may unconsciously long to return to infancy, when they were taken care of—or even to the womb.

Anal Stage (12–18 Months to 3 Years) During the *anal stage,* the chief source of gratification shifts from the mouth to the anus and rectum. Toddlers get a great sense of relief and pleasure from moving their bowels.

Toilet training is the decisive event of this stage, because it forces the child to delay this gratification. The developing ego must come to terms with a major externally imposed curb on the id's instinctual impulses.

The outcome of this stage, according to Freud, depends upon methods of toilet training and attitudes toward it. If these are too strict and threatening, the child may retaliate by holding back the feces (resulting in constipation) or by releasing them at inappropriate times. A person fixated in the anal stage may develop a "constipated" personality, becoming obsessively clean and neat, obsessively precise, or rigidly tied to schedules and routines. Or the person may become defiantly messy. Some anal personalities become fixated on the idea that their feces are a gift to their parents. They may hoard their possessions (as they once withheld their feces) or may identify love with the bestowal of material objects.

Erik H. Erikson: Psychosocial Theory

At each stage in Erikson's theory of psychosocial development (see Table 1-1), a crisis occurs that must be resolved with a satisfactory balancing of opposites if there is to be healthy progress through the next stage. Two of those crises come during the first 3 years, at times corresponding roughly to Freud's oral and anal stages.

Crisis 1: Basic Trust versus Basic Mistrust (Birth to 12–18 Months) The first critical pair of opposites is *basic trust versus basic mistrust.* The infant must decide whether the world is or is not a place where people and things can be relied upon.

To come out of this stage in good psychological health, a baby must achieve a proper balance of trust (which allows intimacy) over mistrust (which permits self-protection). If trust predominates, as it should, children develop what Erikson calls the *virtue of hope*: the belief that their needs will be met and their wishes can be attained. If mistrust predominates, children will view the world as unfriendly and unpredictable. They may become overwhelmed by disappointment and will have trouble developing close relationships.

The feeding situation is the crucible for this mixture; and the mother, according to Erikson, plays a principal role. Unlike Freud, whose theory treats feeding as a source of essential oral gratification, Erikson regards feeding principally as an opportunity for interaction between mother and infant. Does the mother respond quickly enough? Can the baby count on being fed when he or she is hungry and, therefore, trust the mother as the representative of the world?

Trust enables an infant to let the mother out of sight, "because she has become an inner certainty as well as an outer predictability" (Erikson, 1950, p. 247). The mother's "sensitive care of the baby's individual needs" lays the groundwork for the child's sense of self: "a sense of being 'all right,' of being oneself, and of becoming what other people trust one will become" (p. 249).

Crisis 2: Autonomy versus Shame and Doubt (12–18 Months to 3 Years) The next crisis is *autonomy versus shame and doubt,* or self-control versus external control. The push toward *autonomy* (independence, or self-determination) is related to maturation. Toddlers try to use their

developing muscles to do everything themselves—to walk, to feed and dress themselves, and to expand the boundaries of their world. During this stage, the *virtue of will* emerges: the growing power to make one's own decisions, to apply oneself to tasks, and to use self-restraint. Having come through stage 1 with a sense of basic trust in the world and an awakening sense of self, toddlers (says Erikson) begin to trust their *own* judgment and to substitute it for the mother's.

Total license, of course, is neither safe nor healthy. A sense of shame helps children learn to live by reasonable rules. And a certain amount of self-doubt is needed for toddlers to recognize what they are not yet ready to do.

To strike the proper balance, children need the right amount of control from adults—neither too much control nor too little. Otherwise they may rebel against all rules or be thrown back on themselves, and the fear of los-

During Erik Erikson's second developmental crisis (autonomy versus shame and doubt), children strive for independence. They often insist on feeding themselves—even if half of the food ends up on the table instead of in the mouth.

ing control may fill them with inhibitions, doubt, and shame.

Toilet training, which Freud sees as the imposition of social control on a child's natural function, is for Erikson an important step toward self-control and autonomy. So is language; as babies are more able to make their wishes understood, they become more powerful and independent.

The "terrible twos" are a normal manifestation of this need for autonomy. Dependent, docile infants who trustingly accepted what their parents wanted them to do are transformed into strong-willed, sometimes ill-tempered creatures with minds of their own. Toddlers have to test the new notion that they are individuals, that they have a measure of control over their world, and that they have new, hitherto undreamed-of powers. They are no longer content to let someone else decide what they should do but are driven to try out their own ideas and find their own preferences. Because their favorite way of testing seems to be to shout "No!" at every opportunity, this behavior is called *negativism*. "Me do" becomes the watchword in the relentless quest to do everything without guidance or help. Parents need to provide a safe harbor, with safe limits, from which children can set out and discover the world—and to which they can come back for support. (See Box 5-2 for suggestions for dealing with negativism.)

Evaluating the Theories

These theories of personality development have contributed useful insights to our understanding of the way children develop. Erikson's theory is especially helpful in its description of the shift from the dependency of infancy to the autonomy of toddlerhood. But both theories have serious shortcomings. Both assign the major responsibility for the way a child turns out to the mother. Little attention is paid to the child's own contribution or to the impact of other people and of circumstances in the child's life. Most research psychiatrists and developmental psychologists today recognize that although the mother is an important influence, these other factors are also important (Chess & Thomas, 1982).

Furthermore, the theories of Freud and Erik-son are difficult to test objectively. It is hard to define such concepts as *oral personality* and *basic trust* for rigorous scientific testing. Thus, although there have been many attempts to prove (or disprove) each theory, the evidence that exists for them is far from conclusive. Nevertheless, these theories have raised important developmental issues for exploration—such questions as how babies develop a sense of self and what kinds of attachments they form with adults. We'll consider these and other issues as we examine the findings of research on how babies' personalities and relationships develop.

EMOTIONS: THE FOUNDATION OF PERSONALITY

Have you ever cried in the movies only to hear someone behind you snicker? Have you ever screamed on a roller coaster while the person next to you looked totally at ease?

All human beings have the same basic *emotions*—such subjective feelings as sadness, joy, and fear, which arise in response to situations and experiences. But people differ in the frequency with which they feel a particular emotion, in the kinds of stimuli that call it forth, and in the ways they act as a result. Emotional reactions to events and people, which are intimately tied in with cognitive perceptions, form a fundamental element of personality.

How Babies' Emotions Are Studied

When you hear babies cry, you know that they are unhappy. But it is hard to know whether they are angry, frightened, lonely, or uncomfortable. It is hard to tell what babies are feeling, or how their feelings first develop. It is no wonder, then, that the study of infants' emotions has long been a source of controversy. Early researchers believed that infants were born with only one emotion, an undifferentiated excitement later called *distress* (Bridges, 1932), or perhaps no more than three emotions: love, rage, and fear (J.B. Watson, 1919). Recently, however, researchers have developed innovative ways of studying the infant's psyche and have made several discoveries.

Studies conducted by Carroll Izard and his

This baby's face shows interest in a crib mobile. Interest is one of the earliest emotions seen in infants; very young babies have also been observed to exhibit joy, sadness, and fear.

colleagues suggest that babies in the first few months of life express a fairly wide range of emotions. In one study, the researchers videotaped the facial expressions of 5-, 7-, and 9-month-olds as the babies played games with their mothers, were surprised by a jack-in-the-box, were given shots by a doctor, and were approached by a stranger. When college students and health professionals were asked to characterize the babies' expressions just from the tapes, they believed that they were able to recognize joy, sadness, interest, and fear, and to a lesser degree anger, surprise, and disgust (Izard, Huebner, Resser, McGinness, & Dougherty, 1980). When observers were trained with Izard's Facial Expression Scoring Manual, which is based on patterns of facial movements, they felt even more confident about their identifications (Izard, 1971, 1977). Of course, we do not know that these babies actually had the feel-

ings they were credited with, but they did show a range of expressions that were very similar to adults' expressions of these emotions, and so it is at least likely that these expressions reflected similar feelings.

How Babies' Emotions Develop: The Sense of Self

Babies' emotions, like everything else about them, are products of a dynamic process of development. An infant cries at birth and smiles a few weeks later but does not laugh until about 4 months of age.

What internal mechanisms produce emotional activity? As with motor development, the emergence of various emotions (see Table 5-2) seems to be governed by the biological "clock" of the brain's maturation. This timetable can be altered somewhat by environmental influences.

TABLE 5-2 ARRIVAL TIMES OF INFANTS' EMOTIONAL EXPRESSIONS	
EXPRESSION OF FUNDAMENTAL EMOTIONS	APPROXIMATE TIME OF EMERGENCE
Interest Neonatal smile (a "half smile" that appears spontaneously for no apparent reason) Startle response Distress (in response to pain) Disgust (in response to unpleasant taste or smell)	Present at birth
Social smile	4–6 weeks
Anger Surprise Sadness	3–4 months
Fear	5–7 months
Shame, shyness, self-awareness	6–8 months
Contempt Guilt	2d year of life

Note: The most recent research suggests that infants have a wide range of emotions, even in the early months of life, and that specific feelings appear in a typical sequence.
Source: Adapted from Trotter, 1983.

For example, abused infants show fear several months earlier than other babies do, very likely having learned the feeling through their unhappy experiences (Gaensbauer & Hiatt, 1984).

Very soon after birth, babies show signs of interest, distress, and disgust; and within the next few months, these primary emotions differentiate into joy, anger, surprise, sadness, shyness, and fear. But "self-conscious" emotions such as empathy, jealousy, shame, guilt, and pride come later—some of them not until the second year. Not until then do babies typically develop *self-awareness*—the understanding that they are separate from other people and things—which enables them to reflect on their actions and measure them against social standards (Kopp, 1982; Lewis, cited in Trotter, 1983).

The psychologist Michael Lewis noticed that his 8-month-old daughter failed to show fear of strangers (which, as we'll see, is characteristic of that age) when the stranger was another child. Apparently, she realized that the child was "like" her. In other words, her emotional reaction reflected a glimmer of self-awareness (Trotter, 1987).

When does self-awareness emerge? Lewis and his colleagues have found it to be present by the age of 18 months, about the time when Piaget said object permanence is fully developed (see Chapter 4). This is also the age when *self-recognition*—babies' ability to recognize their own images—arrives. To test for self-recognition, mothers of 6- to 24-month-old babies dabbed rouge on their babies' noses and then sat them in front of a mirror. By counting the number of times babies of different ages touched their red noses while looking at the mirror, compared with how often the babies had touched their noses before, the researchers could tell when the babies recognized themselves (M. Lewis & Brooks, 1974).

How Babies Show Their Emotions

It is easy to tell when newborns are unhappy. They let out piercing yells, flail their arms and legs, and stiffen their bodies. It is not always so obvious when newborns are happy. During the first month, they quiet at the sound of a human voice or upon being picked up, and they smile when their hands are moved together to play pat-a-cake. With every passing day, infants respond more to people—smiling, cooing, reaching out, and eventually going to them. These signals, if we become adept at reading them, give us fairly reliable clues to a baby's emotional state.

By expressing their feelings, babies gain a growing amount of control over their world. When they want or need something, they cry; when they feel sociable, they break into a smile or laugh. When these early messages get a response, babies' sense of connection with other people is strengthened. Their sense of personal power is enhanced as they see that their cries bring help and comfort and that their smiles and laughter elicit smiles and laughter in return.

The meaning of this emotional language changes as babies develop. At first, crying is a signal of physical discomfort; later it more often expresses psychological distress. The early smile comes spontaneously as an expression of internal well-being; later smiles express pleasure in other people.

Crying Crying is the most powerful way—and sometimes the only way—in which newborn babies can communicate their vital needs. Babies have four patterns of crying (Wolff, 1969):

1 Basic *hunger cry*: a rhythmic cry, which, despite its name, is not always associated with hunger
2 *Angry cry*: a variation of the rhythmic cry in which excess air is forced through the vocal cords
3 *Cry of pain*: a sudden onset of loud crying without preliminary moaning (an initial long cry may be followed by an extended period of holding the breath)
4 *Cry of frustration*: a cry that begins with two or three long drawn-out cries and involves no prolonged holding of the breath

Babies in distress cry louder, longer, and more irregularly than hungry babies and are more apt to gag and to interrupt their crying (Oswald & Peltzman, 1974).

Parents often wonder how best to respond to crying. If they come whenever a baby cries, do they risk creating a spoiled child who whines

HOW TO DEAL WITH A FUSSY BABY

Normal crying is a distress signal: a sign that the baby is hungry, unhappy, or uncomfortable. If you find and correct the problem, the crying will usually stop. But some babies cry longer, louder, and more piercingly, even to the point of screaming, and seem to be inconsolable no matter what their parents do.

In some infants, colic—unexplained intermittent crying—may begin during the first week or month of life. The crying usually comes at the same time of day (often late afternoon or early evening) and may last anywhere from 30 minutes to 2 hours. The puzzling thing is that colicky babies are well fed, healthy, and happy between crying spells, and so the crying isn't due to hunger or physical pain.

Colic seems to run in families and probably has something to do with temperament—some babies seem to have more trouble getting used to the assault of sound, light, and other stimuli in the world outside the womb. Household discord may also play a part. Since colic is more common among firstborns, parents' inexperience or anxiety may contribute to their inability to comfort the baby. Fortunately, colic usually goes away by 3 months of age.

Here are some suggestions for calming fussy or colicky babies and preventing excessive crying (B.D. Schmitt, 1986):

■ *Hold the baby*. Gentle motion and close physical contact, accompanied by soothing words, are helpful. Carry the newborn for at least 3 hours a day when the baby is *not* crying. A flexible front pouch that leaves the parent's hands free is better than a backpack—it lets the baby see you and feel your heartbeat. A baby carried by the mother in a front pouch can also feel the mother's breasts.

■ To deal with night crying, *rock the baby* by hand or in a cradle or other device. A pacifier often helps.

■ *Discourage daytime sleeping* for more than 3 consecutive hours in order to shift the colicky period from night to daytime. Keep the infant awake and busy during the day and in the evening.

■ *Don't overfeed* the baby. Try to keep feedings at least 2 hours apart. Bloating can cause discomfort. Also, the baby's crying may be unrelated to hunger.

■ *Get enough rest and relaxation*. Daily naps and warm baths are good for parents as well as the baby. An exhausted, edgy parent may lack the confidence to deal with a distressed baby.

■ *Don't try to do everything alone*. Get baby-sitting or household help from relatives or friends. Use household shortcuts. Take a complete break from child care once in a while.

---

and fusses whenever frustrated? If they ignore too frequent crying, will the child feel abandoned?

Babies whose cries bring relief apparently gain a measure of confidence that their actions will evoke a response. By the end of the first year, babies whose mothers have regularly responded to their crying with tender, soothing care cry less (Ainsworth & Bell, 1977; S. Bell & Ainsworth, 1972). By now they are communicating more in other ways—with babbling, ges-tures, and facial expressions—than the babies of more punitive or ignoring mothers, who cry more. Thus, although parents do not need to leap to a baby's side at every whimper, it seems safe to err in the direction of responding more rather than less—and not to worry about spoiling the baby. (See Box 5-1 for suggestions for managing a "fussy" baby.)

Smiling   Somehow, a baby's smile seems irresistible. When adults see a smiling baby, they will almost always smile back (Gewirtz & Gewirtz, 1968).

A baby's first smile is usually met with great excitement. But the earliest smile, the faint smile that appears shortly after birth, is only a reflex. Once it was thought to be due to gas, but now we know that it occurs spontaneously as a result of central nervous system activity, generally without external stimulation, and often at a time when the infant is falling asleep (Sroufe & Waters, 1976).

In their second week, babies often smile after a feeding, when they are drowsy and may be responding to sounds made by the caregiver. After the second week, smiles are more likely to occur when babies are alert but inactive. At about 1 month, the smiles become more frequent and more social, directed toward people. The early reflex smile uses only the lower facial muscles; the social smile also involves the eye muscles. Babies smile at this age when their hands are clapped together or when they hear a familiar voice (Kreutzer & Charlesworth, 1973; Wolff, 1963). During the second month, as visual recognition develops, babies respond more selectively, smiling more at people they know than at those they do not know.

Some infants smile considerably more than others (Tautermannova, 1973). A baby who rewards parents' caretaking with smiles and gurgles is likely to form more positive relationships with them than a baby who smiles less readily.

Laughing   At about the fourth month of life, babies start to laugh out loud. They chortle at all sorts of things—being kissed on the stomach, hearing various sounds, and seeing their parents do unusual things. In addition, some researchers propose that a baby's laughter is related to fear. Babies sometimes show reactions of both fear and laughter to the same stimulus, such as an object looming toward them (Sroufe & Wunsch, 1972).

As babies grow older, they laugh more frequently and at more stimuli. A boy 4 to 6 months old may respond to sounds and touch; a 7- to 9-month-old girl may delight in peekaboo games or howl with glee when she sees her mother wearing a Halloween mask. This shift reflects cognitive development: the older baby

has learned to recognize what is expected and to perceive an incongruity when it appears. Thus laughter is a response to the environment, which helps babies discharge tension in situations that otherwise might be upsetting, and represents "an important tie between cognitive development and emotional growth and expression" (Sroufe & Wunsch, p. 1341).

DIFFERENCES IN PERSONALITY DEVELOPMENT

Even in the womb each person begins to show a unique personality. As was pointed out in Chapter 2, before babies emerge into the world some differences, such as personal activity levels and favorite positions in utero, already exist. After birth, individual differences become even more apparent. We'll look now at differences in emotional makeup and temperament, which seem to be largely inborn, though also influenced by the environment; and at those between the sexes, which again seem to arise as the result of both biological and social influences.

Emotional Differences

Some babies seem to be born cheerful. They smile and laugh often, from an early age. Other babies cry often and seem to take less joy in living.

In some instances, environmental influences may be at work. An infant whose mother is depressed and unresponsive may become sad, withdrawn, fussy, or drowsy, or may show signs of emotional disturbance (T.M. Field, Sandberg, Garcia, Vega-Lahr, Goldstein, & Guy, 1985; Tronick & Field, 1986; B.S. Zuckerman & Beardslee, 1987). Likewise, babies who are rejected or neglected by their parents may become emotionally troubled (Rutter, 1974; L. Yarrow, 1961). Sometimes more positive experiences later overcome the effects of such early emotional deprivation.

More often, though, very young infants' normal emotional responses seem to reflect patterns or traits that persist as they get older, suggesting a biological component of an infant's personality. A 2-month-old who screams in outrage when given a shot is likely to become

Individual differences in temperament appear soon after birth. Some babies are more active and responsive than others. Some have regular cycles of hunger, sleep, and wakefulness; some are highly irregular. Some are cheerful most of the time; others cry often.

equally enraged at 19 months when a playmate takes away a toy, whereas a 2-month-old who takes the shot more calmly will probably put up with later indignities without much fuss. In other words, babies no more than 8 weeks old already show signs of emotional differences that form an important part of their personalities (Izard, cited in Trotter, 1987).

Such characteristic emotional reactions may stem from differences in temperament. Let's see what some of those differences are.

Temperamental Differences

The eldest of three sisters was a cheerful, calm baby who ate, slept, and eliminated at regular times. She greeted each day and most people with a smile, and the only sign that she was awake during the night was the tinkle of the musical toy in her crib. The second sister opened her mouth to cry upon waking before she even opened her eyes. She slept and ate little and irregularly; she laughed and cried loudly, often bursting into tantrums; and she had to be convinced that new people and new experiences were not threatening before she would have anything to do with them. The youngest sister was mild in her responses, both positive and negative. She did not like most new situations, but if allowed to proceed at her own slow pace, she would eventually become interested and involved.

Each of these infants was showing her own *temperament*—her characteristic style of approaching and reacting to people and situations. Temperament has been defined as the *how* of behavior: not *what* people do, or *why*, but how they go about doing it. Two toddlers, for example, may be equally able to dress themselves and equally motivated to do it, but the ways they approach the task may be different (A. Thomas & Chess, 1984).

Components of Temperament The New York Longitudinal Study (NYLS), which we introduced in Chapter 2, followed 133 people from early infancy into early adulthood. The researchers identified nine aspects or components of temperament that showed up soon after birth. In many cases, these aspects remained relatively stable, though some people did show considerable change (A. Thomas, Chess, & Birch, 1968; A. Thomas & Chess, 1984). These nine components of temperament are:

1 *Activity level*: how and how much a person moves
2 *Rhythmicity, or regularity*: the predictability of biological cycles such as hunger, sleep, and elimination
3 *Approach or withdrawal*: how a person initially responds to a new stimulus, such as a new toy, food, or person
4 *Adaptability*: how easily an initial response is modified in a desired direction
5 *Threshold of responsiveness*: how much stimulation is needed to evoke a response

6 *Intensity of reaction*: how energetically a person responds
7 *Quality of mood*: whether a person's behavior is predominantly pleasant, joyful, and friendly; or unpleasant, unhappy, and unfriendly
8 *Distractibility*: how easily an irrelevant stimulus can alter or interfere with a person's behavior
9 *Attention span and persistence*: how long a person pursues an activity and continues in the face of obstacles

Three Patterns of Temperament On the basis of temperamental patterns, many children fall into one of three categories identified by these researchers and confirmed by many other studies (see Table 5-3). The eldest sister described above is an ***easy child*** (like 40 percent in the NYLS sample): a child with a generally happy temperament, regular biological rhythms, and a readiness to accept new experiences. The middle sister is a ***difficult child*** (like 10 percent in the study sample): a child with an irritable temperament, irregular biological rhythms, and intense responses to situations. The youngest sister is considered a ***slow-to-warm-up child*** (like 15 percent in the sample): a child whose temperament is generally mild and who is hesitant about

TABLE 5-3 THREE TEMPERAMENTAL PATTERNS

EASY CHILD	DIFFICULT CHILD	SLOW-TO-WARM-UP CHILD
Responds well to novelty and change	Responds poorly to novelty and change	Responds slowly to novelty and change
Quickly develops regular sleep and feeding schedules	Has irregular sleep and feeding schedules	Sleeps and feeds more regularly than difficult child; less regularly than easy child
Takes to new foods easily	Accepts new foods slowly	
Smiles at strangers	Is suspicious of strangers	Shows mildly negative initial response to new stimuli (e.g., a first encounter with a bath; a new food, person, or place; entering school or another new situation)
Adapts easily to new situations	Adapts slowly to new situations	
Accepts most frustrations with minimal fuss	Reacts to frustration with tantrums	
Adapts quickly to new routines and rules of new games	Adjusts slowly to new routines	Gradually develops liking for new stimuli after repeated, unpressured exposures
Has moods of mild to moderate intensity, usually positive	Has frequent periods of loud crying; also laughs loudly	Has mildly intense reactions, both positive and negative
	Displays intense and frequently negative moods	

Source: Adapted from A. Thomas & Chess, 1984.

accepting new experiences (A. Thomas & Chess, 1977, 1984).

Many children, of course, do not fit neatly into one of these three groups. A child may have some difficult and some easy traits; for example, a baby may have regular eating and sleeping schedules, yet be fearful of strangers. A child may be extremely easy or relatively easy most of the time but not always. A child may warm up slowly to new foods but adapt quickly to new babysitters. All of these variations are normal (A. Thomas & Chess, 1984).

Influences on Temperament Temperament appears to be inborn and largely (though not exclusively) genetic (A. Thomas & Chess, 1977, 1984). Temperamental differences, which crystallize in the first few months of life, may also be influenced by both the prenatal and postnatal environments.

Whether these differences are shaped in part by prenatal chemical or physiological influences on the brain has yet to be tested. Newborns with lower levels of the enzyme monoamine oxidase (MAO) are more active, more excitable, and crankier than neonates with higher MAO levels (Sostek & Wyatt, 1981). Temperament does *not* seem to be decisively determined by parental attitudes and practices (A. Thomas & Chess, 1984) or by gender, birth order, or social class (Persson-Blennow & McNeil, 1981).

A child's basic temperament seems, then, to be largely innate, but *changes* in temperamental style may be triggered by unusual events, such as the death of a parent, the sudden emergence of a talent, or peer-induced use of drugs (A. Thomas & Chess, 1984). Women's degree of satisfaction with their roles may indirectly affect a child's temperament. Among the subjects in the NYLS study, mothers who were dissatisfied either with their jobs or with their status as homemakers were more likely to show intolerance, disapproval, or rejection of their 3-year-olds' behavior, and the rejected children were more likely to become "difficult" (J. V. Lerner & Galambos, 1985).

How Temperament Can Affect Children's Adjustment About one-third of the subjects in the NYLS sample developed behavior disorders

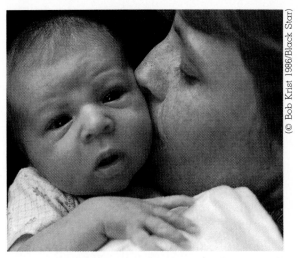

While parents have little influence on a baby's natural temperamental style, "goodness of fit" between children's temperament and parents' expectations is important. If a mother recognizes that fussiness reflects an inborn tendency, she will be better able to accept a "difficult" child, and the child will probably be better adjusted.

at one time or another during childhood. The majority were mild disturbances that appeared between the ages of 3 and 5 years and cleared up by adolescence. However, a significant number did not improve or even grew worse by adulthood.

We might assume that the difficult children had a harder time while the easy children coasted along. Actually, the effect of temperament on a child's adjustment, or ability to cope with the environment in a healthy way, is more complicated. Although the study showed that difficult children *are* more likely to develop behavior problems, even an easy child may do so under excessive stress. Excessive stress occurs when children are frequently expected to behave in ways inconsistent with their basic temperament: for example, when a highly distractible child is expected to concentrate on tasks for a long time, when a persistent child is constantly interrupted while absorbed in solving puzzles and problems, or when a highly active child is regularly confined in a cramped apartment. Thus the key to adjustment is the "goodness" or "poorness" of fit between temperament and the environment within which people find themselves (A. Thomas & Chess, 1984).

Parents, of course, are an important factor in that equation. The fit between parent and child—the degree to which parents feel comfortable with the child they have—affects their feelings toward that child. Thus, energetic, active parents may become impatient with a slow-moving, docile child, while more easygoing parents might welcome such a personality (A. Thomas & Chess, 1977).

Although socioeconomic factors do not appear to influence the formation of temperament, they may well influence the fit between child and parent. Upper-middle-class white parents in the NYLS sample preferred easy temperament; but among lower-middle-class Puerto Ricans, children with some of the "difficult" attributes fitted parental demands, and these children showed no adjustment problems (Korn, 1978, cited in J.V. Lerner & Galambos, 1985).

Implications for Parenting To deal with behavior problems, then, parents may need to identify the poorness of fit that is responsible for the problem and develop a strategy to improve the fit, by revising their expectations and imposing appropriate new demands. One of the most important things parents can do is to ride with a child's basic temperament instead of trying to cast the child into a mold of their own design. The parents of a girl who is more rhythmic, for example, can use a "demand" feeding schedule, letting her set the pace, while the parents of a boy who is irregular will help him by setting a flexible schedule based on the needs of both baby and parents. The parents of a slow-to-warm-up child need to learn to give the child time to adjust to new situations and need to feel comfortable about asking other people, like relatives and nursery school teachers, to do the same.

When parents can recognize that a child behaves in a certain way not out of willfulness, hostility, laziness, or stupidity but because of inborn temperament, they are less likely to respond with guilty, anxious, and hostile feelings and with impatient, inconsistent, or rigid behavior. Children do respond to the way their parents treat them, and some difficult children learn to temper their traits in ways that help them function better. In any case, recognition of children's

basic temperament relieves parents of a feeling of omnipotence—that they, and they alone, are responsible for turning children out from a certain mold.

Gender Differences

As we saw in Chapter 3, there are few physiological differences between baby boys and baby girls. Are there differences in personality?

Research has been done on infants' activity levels, their responses to things they see as opposed to those they hear, how irritable they are, and how interested they are in exploring their surroundings as opposed to staying close to a parent. A number of studies have found some differences between the sexes, but these findings have rarely held up when the studies were repeated by the same investigators or other investigators. After a review of the literature, Birns (1976) concluded that gender differences cannot be described clearly until after age 2.

Other studies have focused on the ways adults act toward infants. The findings of these studies are much clearer. A baby, even a newborn, who is identified as a female will be treated differently from one who is identified as a male. When strangers think that a crying baby is a male, they are likely to assume that "he" is crying from anger; when they think that the baby is female, they think that "she" is afraid (J. C. Condry & Condry, 1974).

In one study, twenty-four 14-month-old children, 12 boys and 12 girls, were introduced to adults who did not know them. Sometimes the babies were identified according to the sex to which they actually belonged, and sometimes they were said to belong to the other sex. When the adults were asked to play with the children, they were more likely to encourage the "boys" in active play and more likely to choose a ball rather than a doll for the two of them to play with. The adults tended to talk more to the "girls" and to pick a doll or a bottle to play with. Interestingly, though, these children did not show gender differences themselves; the boys and girls played in very similar ways, even though they were treated differently by the adults (H. Frisch, 1977).

Parents' behavior toward their babies is affected by the parent's own sex, the age of the

(© Michal Heron 1981/Woodfin Camp)

The family may well be the largest single influence on children's development, and children also influence other family members in many important ways. Research now focuses on relationships between children and their fathers and siblings, as well as their mothers.

infant, and the personality of the infant, but there do seem to be some consistent findings. Baby boys get more attention in infancy, but the attention baby girls get is designed to make them smile more and be more social creatures (Birns, 1976). Mothers' facial expressions show a wider range of emotion to their baby daughters than to their sons—which may explain why girls are better than boys at interpreting emotional expression (Malatesta, cited in Trotter, 1983).

Thus, although differences may not be present at birth, environmental shaping of boys' and girls' personalities does begin very early in life. As we look more closely at the extremely important influence of the family in which a child grows up, we will see other differences between boys and girls.

THE FAMILY AND PERSONALITY DEVELOPMENT

Was your birth planned and welcomed? How old were your parents? Were they physically and emotionally healthy? Were they wealthy, comfortable, or poor? How did your personality

mesh with theirs? How many people lived in your home?

Such early social factors undoubtedly had a major influence on the infant you were and the child you became. Furthermore, you yourself influenced your family in ways you may never have imagined. Your parents' feelings and actions toward you were undoubtedly influenced by your sex, your temperament, your health, and your place in the birth order—whether you were the oldest child, the youngest, or somewhere in between.

The kind of family you grew up in was probably quite different from what it would have been a century earlier, and family life will probably change even more in the future. A baby born today is likely to have only one sibling, a mother who works outside the home, and a father who is more involved in his children's lives than his own father was. An infant has a 40 percent chance of spending part of his or her childhood with only one parent, probably the mother and probably because of divorce (Masnick & Bane, 1980).

These changes in family life are revolutionizing the ways in which researchers study *socialization*—how children learn the behaviors their culture deems appropriate. The relationships formed in infancy set the pattern for much of a child's early socialization. In the past, most research focused on the relationship between mothers and babies. Now we also recognize the importance of the relationships infants have with their fathers, brothers and sisters, grandparents, and other caregivers.

Another new trend in family research is to focus on the way the entire family system operates. How does the marital relationship affect the relationship each spouse has with the baby? Do Johnny's parents act differently with the baby when either one is alone with him and when they are all together? Questions like these have produced provocative answers. It has been found, for example, that when both parents are present and talking to each other, they pay less attention to their child. In some families the spouses' closeness to each other may detract from their ability to be close to their children, while in others parenting itself strengthens or adds stress to the marriage (Belsky, 1979). By looking at the family as a unit, we get a fuller picture of the web of relationships among all family members.

The ability to form intimate relationships throughout life is widely believed to hinge on the quality of the relationships formed in infancy. Let us see how babies influence and are influenced by the people close to them.

The Mother's Role

The Mother-Infant Bond The early literature suggests that most developmentalists once agreed with Napoleon that "the future good or bad conduct of a child depends entirely on the mother." Psychoanalytic theory, as we have seen, also concentrates on the mother's influence. Although it is now recognized that the relationship with the mother is not babies' only significant relationship, it certainly plays a central role in their development.

How and when is this special intimacy established? What causes mothers to lavish on their babies the care and attention that babies so urgently need?

To answer such questions, some researchers have looked at what happens among other animals. For example, newly hatched chicks follow the first moving thing they see—usually, but not

always, the mother hen. Lorenz (1957) called this behavior ***imprinting,*** an instinctive form of learning in which, after a single encounter, the animal learns to recognize and trust a particular individual. Imprinting, according to Lorenz, takes place automatically and irreversibly during a very brief critical period in the animal's early life.

Among goats and cows, certain standardized rituals occur immediately after birth. If these rituals are prevented or interrupted, neither mother nor baby will recognize the other. The results for the baby can be devastating: abnormal development, or physical withering and death (Blauvelt, 1955; A.U. Moore, 1960; Scott, 1958).

IS THERE A CRITICAL PERIOD FOR MOTHER-INFANT BONDING? Do these findings tell us anything about human beings? Is there a critical period after a baby's birth in which a healthy mother-child relationship must be established?

At least two researchers have said yes. Klaus and Kennell (1976) contend that if mother and baby are separated during the first hours after birth, the ***mother-infant bond***—the mother's feeling of close, caring connection with her newborn—may not develop normally. Her mothering urge may be weakened, and the baby's future development may be jeopardized.

Klaus and Kennell reached this controversial conclusion by comparing mothers and babies who had extended contact immediately after birth with those who followed the usual hospital routine in which newborn babies and their mothers were separated for much of the day. The researchers reported differences in bonding that persisted during the first few years of life.

This research inspired many hospitals to establish rooming-in policies, which allow mothers and babies to remain together from birth throughout the hospital stay. Although developmentalists have generally welcomed these humane changes, follow-up research has not confirmed the notion of a critical time for bonding (Chess & Thomas, 1982; Lamb, 1982a, 1982b; Rutter, 1979b). Although some mothers in some circumstances seemed to achieve closer bonding with their babies after early extended contact, no long-term effects were demonstrated. In

1982, Klaus and Kennell modified their original position, and in 1983 the psychiatrist Stella Chess wrote, "By now the whole 'critical period concept' has been generally discredited in human development theory" (p. 975).

This finding relieved adoptive parents and parents who had to be separated from their infants immediately after birth from much unnecessary worry and guilt over their babies' future emotional development. Unlike chickens, goats, and cows, which act primarily from instinct, human beings are remarkably resilient. Concern with bonding is still a vital issue, however, and some developmentalists urge research on groups at risk of weak bonding (such as poor, young single mothers and fathers) to find out what factors other than early contact affect parent-child bonds (Lamb, Campos, Hwang, Leiderman, Sagi, & Svejda, 1983).

WHAT DO BABIES NEED FROM THEIR MOTHERS? Can animal studies tell us anything about the relationship between mother and baby?

In one famous study, rhesus monkeys were separated from their mothers 6 to 12 hours after birth and were raised in a laboratory. The infant monkeys were put into cages with one of two kinds of surrogate "mothers"—either a plain cylindrical wire-mesh form or a form covered with terry cloth. Some monkeys were fed from bottles connected to the wire "mothers"; others were "nursed" by the warm, cuddly cloth ones.

When the monkeys were allowed to spend time with either kind of "mother," they all spent more time clinging to the cloth surrogates—even if they were being fed only by wire ones. In an unfamiliar room, the babies "raised" by cloth surrogates showed more natural interest in exploring than those "raised" by wire surrogates—even when the appropriate "mothers" were there. The monkeys remembered the cloth surrogates better too. After a year's separation, the "cloth-raised" monkeys eagerly ran to embrace the terry-cloth forms, whereas the "wire-raised" monkeys showed no interest in the wire forms (Harlow & Zimmerman, 1959). None of the monkeys in either group grew up normally, however (Harlow & Harlow, 1962), and none of them were able to mother their own offspring (Suomi & Harlow, 1972).

(Harry Harlow Primate Laboratory/University of Wisconsin)

Given a choice between a wire "mother" with a nipple that gives milk (shown in background) and a terry-cloth "mother" without the nipple, infant rhesus monkeys spend more time clinging to the soft, warm cloth form —suggesting that food is not the main path to a baby's heart.

It is hardly surprising that a dummy mother would not provide the same kind of stimulation and opportunities for development as a living mother. The experiment illustrates the importance of mothering, and it shows that (contrary to the Freudian emphasis on satisfaction of biological needs) the essential feature of the mother-infant relationship is not just the giving of food; it includes the comfort provided by close bodily contact and, in monkeys, the satisfaction of an innate need to cling. Surely, human infants also have needs that must be satisfied, or at least acted upon, if they are to grow up normally. A major task of contemporary psychology is to find out what those needs are and what promotes normal emotional development.

In contrast to such one-way concepts as imprinting (a newborn animal's instinctive adherence to a mother object) and the mother-infant bond (a mother's early emotional tie to her newborn), research since the 1970s has shifted to focus on a two-way process called *attachment*—a process that becomes more evident during the second 6 months of infancy and is based on the ways mothers and babies behave toward each other.

Patterns of Attachment   When Andrew's mother is in the room, he looks at her, smiles at her, talks to her, and crawls after her. When she leaves, he cries; when she comes back, he squeals with joy. When he is frightened or unhappy, he clings to her. Andrew has formed his first attachment to another person.

ATTACHMENT: A RECIPROCAL CONNECTION
Attachment is an active, affectionate reciprocal relationship specifically between two individuals, as distinguished from all other persons. The interaction between the two parties continues to reinforce and strengthen their closeness. It may be, as Ainsworth (1979) has said, "an essential part of the ground plan of the human species for an infant to become attached to a mother figure" (p. 932)—who does not have to be the infant's biological mother but may be anyone who acts as the child's primary caregiver.

TYPES OF ATTACHMENT   To study attachment, Ainsworth devised a "strange situation" to call forth behavior that would reveal feelings of closeness between parent and child (Ainsworth, Blehar, Waters, & Wall, 1978). In a series of eight 3-minute staged episodes, researchers watch what a baby does when faced with a strange room and an unfamiliar adult, both when the mother is in the room and when she is not. Usually they also observe the baby at home. When Ainsworth and her colleagues put 1-year-olds into this strange situation, they found three main patterns of attachment: *secure attachment* (the most common category, into which 66 percent of the babies fell) and two forms of anxious attachment—*avoidant* (20 percent of the babies) and *ambivalent* (12 percent).

Securely attached babies use their mothers as a secure base from which to explore. They are able to separate readily from their mothers to go off and investigate their surroundings, so long as they can return from time to time for reassurance. They are usually cooperative and relatively free of anger.

Securely attached 18-month-olds are better able to negotiate their environment than those who lack a secure base (Cassidy, 1986). The securely attached babies maneuver around furniture, cross open spaces, assume appropriate positions for playing with their toys, and reach for objects without stumbling and falling. A possible explanation is that babies who view their mothers as available when needed are free to pay more attention to learning about their surroundings than babies who feel that they must keep an anxious eye on their mothers.

Avoidant babies rarely cry when the mother leaves, but they avoid her upon her return. These babies fail to reach out in time of need and tend to be very angry. They dislike being held, but they like even less being put down.

Ambivalent (resistant) babies become anxious even before the mother leaves. They are extremely upset when she does go out, and when she comes back they show their ambivalence by seeking contact with her while at the same time resisting it by kicking or squirming. Resistant babies do little exploration and are harder to comfort than other babies (Egeland & Farber, 1984).

HOW IS ATTACHMENT ESTABLISHED?   According to Ainsworth, the baby builds up a "working model" of what he or she can expect from the mother. As long as the mother continues to act in basically the same ways, the model holds up. If the mother substantially changes her behavior toward the baby—consistently, not just on one or two occasions—the baby can revise the model, and the nature of the attachment may well change.

Babies' own characteristics—such as their tendency to cuddle or cry and their way of adapting to new situations—exert an influence too. The quality of attachment is affected not by the mother's actions alone but by what both mother and baby do and how they respond to each other.

What the mother does   Secure attachment thrives when the mother is affectionate, attentive, and responsive to the baby's signals. The mother's caretaking skills and the amount of time she spends taking care of the infant are less important than the amount of positive interaction between them (Clarke-Stewart, 1977).

In the study by Ainsworth et al. (1978), several sharp differences in the quality of mothering appeared. During the first year after birth, the mothers of the securely attached babies were the most sensitive to their infants. For example, these mothers truly observed "demand" feeding. Not only did they take their cues from their babies about when to feed them, but they were also very responsive to the babies' signals regarding when to stop feeding, how quickly or slowly the feeding should go, and how best to introduce new foods (Ainsworth, 1979). These mothers tended to hold their babies closer to their bodies than did the mothers of the babies in the other two groups.

The mothers of the avoidant babies were the angriest of all three groups of mothers. But they had difficulty expressing their feelings and shied away from close physical contact with their babies. Babies who were subjected to such physical distancing and rebuffs became angry in turn.

In a study of low-income, mostly single mothers (Egeland & Farber, 1984), the mothers of avoidant babies seemed tense, irritable, lacking in confidence, and uninterested in caring for their babies. By contrast, mothers of resistant babies were well-meaning but less capable; they tended to have lower intelligence and less understanding of how to meet their babies' needs. The mothers of securely attached infants, in addition to being more responsive and skilled in caretaking, had more positive feelings about themselves "and, consequently, had more to give their infants" (p. 768).

"Mother love" apparently is not automatic, nor is love necessarily enough to guarantee nurturing care and a sound mother-child attachment. Many factors may affect the way a woman acts toward her baby: for example, her reasons for having the baby, her experience and competence in child care, her emotional state and view of her life, her relationship with the baby's father, her interest in job achievement and other outside activities, her living circumstances, and the presence of other relatives in the home, such as a supportive or intrusive grandmother (Egeland & Farber, 1984).

What the baby does   Far from considering infants to be passive recipients of child rearing, we now realize that they influence the people who take care of them. Virtually any activity on a baby's part that leads to a response from an adult is an attachment behavior: sucking, crying, smiling, clinging, choking, hiccupping, moving the body, changing the rhythm of breathing, sneezing, burping, and looking into the caregiver's eyes (Bowlby, 1958; Richards, 1971; Robson, 1967).

As early as the eighth week, babies initiate some of these behaviors more toward their mothers than toward anyone else. Their overtures are successful when their mothers respond warmly, expressing delight and giving the babies frequent physical contact along with freedom to explore (Ainsworth, 1969). The babies gain a sense of the consequence of their own actions—a feeling of power and confidence in their ability to bring about results.

An infant's early characteristics may be a strong predictor of whether the baby is likely to become securely or anxiously attached. Many resistant babies, for example, have had problems as neonates—about 50 percent in one study (Ainsworth et al., 1978). Many showed developmental lags which continued into later infancy and which may have made them harder to care for (Egeland & Farber, 1984). However, no infant is "predestined to be anxiously attached; as in any relationship, the partner's responses [are] critical" (Egeland & Farber, 1984, p. 769). It is the interaction between mother and infant, then, that determines the quality of attachment.

CHANGES IN ATTACHMENT   Although attachment patterns, once established, normally remain set, they may be altered by significant events (Ainsworth, 1982). In one study, almost half of a group of 43 middle-class babies changed their attachment patterns between the ages of 1 year and 19 months (R.A. Thompson, Lamb, & Estes, 1982). The changes were associated with changes in family and caregiving circumstances, including mothers' taking jobs outside the home and providing other kinds of care for their children. Changes that affected the babies' everyday lives "forced a renegotiation, so to speak, of the mother-infant relationship" (p. 148). The changes were not all in one direction: some of the babies became less securely attached, but most of the babies who changed in attachment status became more securely attached.

What makes the difference? Although a mother's caretaking skills are important in forming the initial attachment, her underlying affective behavior—how much joy she shows in feeding her baby, for example—may influence whether secure attachment patterns are maintained or changed, especially during the second year of life. Some initially resistant infants of young, immature mothers become more secure as their mothers gain experience, skill, and more positive attitudes (Egeland & Farber, 1984).

LONG-TERM EFFECTS OF ATTACHMENT   Common sense might suggest that infants who are very closely attached to their mothers grow into children who are very dependent on adults. But research says that this is not so. Paradoxically, the stronger a child's attachment to a nurturing adult, the easier it is to leave that adult. Children who have a secure base, as we have seen, do not need to stay close to their mothers. Their freedom to explore enables them to try new things, to attack problems in new ways, and to have more positive attitudes toward the unfamiliar.

These effects may persist for at least 5 years after birth. When securely attached 18-month-olds were followed up at the age of 2, they turned out to be more enthusiastic, persistent, cooperative, and, in general, effective than children who had been insecurely attached babies (Matas, Arend, & Sroufe, 1978). At 3, securely attached children get more positive responses from their playmates than anxiously attached children (Jacobson & Wille, 1986). At 3½, securely attached children are described as "peer leaders, socially involved, attracting the attention of others, curious, and actively engaged in their surroundings" (Waters, Wippman, & Sroufe, 1979, cited in Sroufe, 1979, p. 839). At the age of 4 or 5 years, they are more curious and more competent (Arend, Gove, & Sroufe, 1979).

One study of 4- and 5-year-olds found that the ones who had been securely attached at 12 and 18 months were most likely to be independent, seeking help from their nursery school teachers only when they needed it. The children who had been anxiously attached earlier, however, were now more likely to be so dependent on their teachers that their needs for contact, approval, and attention interfered with their ability to form relationships with other children and to learn how to do things appropriate for their age (Sroufe, Fox, & Pancake, 1983).

EFFECTS OF MOTHERS' EMPLOYMENT AND NON-MATERNAL CARE   All mothers are, of course, "working mothers," since rearing children and caring for a family are a valuable—though unpaid—form of work. Here, however, we'll define the working mother as one who works for pay, usually outside the home.

The traditional family with a breadwinner father and homemaker mother is becoming a rarity. Since 1980, the number of children with working mothers has grown by 2½ million, and babies and children under the age of 6 have accounted for 90 percent of this upsurge, according to the U.S. Bureau of Labor Statistics (American Academy of Pediatrics, AAP, 1986a). The number of working wives with infants 1 year old or less has doubled since 1970. As of 1985, nearly half of new mothers entered or reentered the work force soon after giving birth (Hayghe, 1986). The statistics reflect societal changes that include a growing number of single-parent families, more employment opportunities for women, and an economy that often requires two incomes to maintain a desired standard of living.

A decade ago, most babies whose mothers went to work were taken care of in their own homes (Hofferth, 1979). Today, about 55 percent of these infants (including some as young as 3 weeks) receive care outside the home. In fact, day care for infants is the fastest-growing type of supplemental care in the United States. Babies are placed in various settings, including licensed and unlicensed day care centers and family or group day care homes; but it is most common (and usually least costly) for an infant to spend the day in the home of a relative or friend (Gamble & Zigler, 1986; U.S. Bureau of the Census, 1987; Young & Zigler, 1986). (We will discuss the effects of mothers' employment on children of various ages in Chapter 9, and we'll look at the quality of day care in Chapter 6.)

Particular concern has recently been raised about the effects of nonmaternal care on babies' attachments. The effects may depend upon a number of factors, including the mother's satisfaction with her marriage; whether (and why) she works full time or part time; the age, sex, and temperament of the child; and the kind and quality of care the infant receives.

The first year of life—when attachments are formed and consolidated—appears to be critical. Several studies have found that when infants experience unstable or poor-quality community-based day care during their first 12 months, they are more likely to avoid their mothers and to have emotional and social problems later on. The personalities of mother and child, the amount of stress present in the family, and the mother's responsiveness to her baby also seem to make a difference. Studies that have found no striking ill effects have been mostly of stable middle-class families using high-quality university-based centers, and these studies have not followed children long enough to support firm long-term conclusions (Gamble & Zigler, 1986; Young & Zigler, 1986).

Recent research (Belsky, 1987) suggests that some infants under 1 year old who spend more than 20 hours a week away from their mothers tend to be insecurely attached to the mother—*unless* the caregiver is the father. (This relationship between paternal care and maternal attachment bears out the findings of Easterbrooks and Goldberg, 1984, which we discuss later in connection with the father's role.) Boys are more vulnerable than girls; in fact, sons who are given full-time care by someone other than the mother (more than 35 hours a week) are likely to be insecurely attached to their fathers as well. Also especially vulnerable to extensive workday separation from their mothers are infants who are temperamentally difficult and those whose mothers are relatively unsatisfied with their marriages, show little sensitivity in dealing with people, or have strong motivation toward careers.

Interestingly, another study found that 18-month-old boys whose mothers started work in the *second half* of their first year of life were more likely to be insecurely attached than those whose mothers went to work when the boys were younger and presumably had not yet formed firm attachments. This suggests that the second half of a child's (particularly a boy's) first year may not be the best time for a mother to return to work and that mothers who must or who choose to go back to work by that time should try to do so before the baby is 6 months old (Benn, 1986). One proposed alternative is a paid leave for working parents, allowing them to stay home with their infants (as is done in other western industrial nations).

While the mother-child attachment has far-reaching impact on personality, it is not the only significant tie that babies form. Infants who have the chance to interact with other adults become attached to them too. A mother may be the only one who can suckle her young, but, contrary to Freud's and Erikson's emphasis on feeding, suckling is not the only source of attachment. Fathers, particularly, but also grandparents, siblings, friends, and babysitters can meet babies' physical needs, comfort them, play with them, and give them a sense of security that will help them face the world. Let's now examine the father's role.

The Father's Role

Television commercials show fathers diapering and bathing their infants. Stores offer strollers with longer, man-sized handles and diaper bags with fewer frills. Psychologists have noticed the increasing presence of fathers in the nursery and are devoting more research to the father's role in his children's lives, a role that has generally been ignored or minimized in the past.

The findings from such research underscore the importance of sensitive, responsive fathering to optimum child development. Bonds and attachments form between fathers and babies during the first year of life, and fathers go on to exert a strong influence on their children's social, emotional, and cognitive development.

Bonds and Attachments between Fathers and Babies Like mothers, many fathers form close bonds with their babies soon after birth. Proud new fathers admire their babies and feel drawn to pick them up. M. Greenberg and Morris (1974) describe this initial paternal reaction as *engrossment*: a father's absorption in, preoccupa-

Fathers, as well as mothers, form close, caring bonds with newborns. Attachment, a mutual connection in which parent and child respond to each other's behavioral signals, develops around the second half of the baby's first year. The ability to form intimate relationships later in life may well be affected by the quality of these early bonds and attachments.

tion with, and interest in his baby. The babies contribute to the bond simply by doing the things all normal babies do: opening their eyes, grasping their fathers' fingers, or moving in their fathers' arms.

Infants develop attachments to their fathers and to their mothers at about the same time. In one study, babies aged 12 months and older protested against separation from both their mothers and their fathers about equally, while babies 9 months or younger did not protest against either parent's departure. When both parents were present, a little more than half of the babies were more likely to go to their mothers, but almost half showed as much or more attachment to their fathers (Kotelchuck, 1973).

Another study found that although babies prefer either the mother or the father to a stranger, they usually prefer their mothers to their fathers, especially when upset (Lamb, 1981). This may be because babies are more often cared for by their mothers than by their fathers. It will be interesting to see whether the nature of the father-infant attachment changes in families in which fathers assume an equal or larger caregiving role.

How Do Fathers Act with Young Babies? The earliest studies on father-infant interaction examined how much time fathers spent with their babies, but more recent research has emphasized what fathers *do* with them. Despite long-held beliefs that women are biologically predisposed to respond more sensitively to babies' cues, such research suggests that there may be "no biologically based sex differences in responsiveness to infants" (Lamb, 1981, p. 463). Fathers talk "motherese" (see Chapter 4); during feedings, they adjust the pace to what the baby appears to want; and when they see crying or smiling infants on a television monitor, their physiological responses (changes in heart rate, blood pressure, and skin conductance) are similar to mothers'.

Still, fathers typically are not as responsive as mothers. Societal expectations lead them to take a less active role in child rearing. Apparently the crucial factor in determining how sensitive an adult is to a baby's cues is the amount of care that the adult gives the baby (Zelazo, Kotelchuck, Barber, & David, 1977).

In our culture, fathers *care for* their babies less than they *play with* them (Clarke-Stewart, 1978; Easterbrooks & Goldberg, 1984; Kotelchuck, 1975; Rendina & Dickerscheid, 1976). And whatever they do, they tend to do differently. Fathers videotaped face to face with 2- to 25-week-old infants typically provide a series of short, intense bursts of stimulation, whereas mothers tend to be more gentle and rhythmic. Fathers pat the babies; mothers softly talk to them (Yogman, Dixon, Tronick, Als, & Brazelton, 1977). Fathers toss infants up in the air and wrestle with toddlers; mothers typically play gentler games and sing and read to their children (Lamb, 1977; Parke & Tinsley, 1981).

Interestingly, the picture changes when we look at families in which the mother works full time. Working mothers stimulate their babies more than mothers who stay at home full time, and they play with their babies more than their husbands do. They still spend more time taking care of their babies, however, than the babies' fathers do (Pedersen, Cain, & Zaslow, 1982). Another study, of fathers who were their babies' primary caretakers, found that these fathers behaved more like mothers than did fathers who were secondary caretakers (T.M. Field, 1978).

It seems likely, then, that differing roles and differing societal expectations of what fathers and mothers are supposed to do influence their styles of interacting with their babies.

What Is the Significance of the Father-Infant Relationship? The differences between men and women, both biological and social, make each parent's role in the family unique—and each one's contribution special. For example, the physical way in which fathers typically play with babies offers excitement and a challenge to conquer fears. During the first 2 years, babies often smile and "talk" more to their fathers, probably because the male parent is more of a novelty (Lamb, 1981).

In a recent study, a group of toddlers of whom two-thirds had mothers who were employed outside the home tended to develop more secure attachment patterns with their mothers and more effective problem-solving abilities when their fathers were highly involved in their care and in playing with them— especially when the father showed sensitive and positive attitudes toward the child. Fathers' behavior had a particularly strong influence on competence in problem solving; and although it was the mothers' behavior that had more impact on attachment, fathers' involvement had a surprisingly significant effect in making boys' attachment to their mothers more secure (Easterbrooks & Goldberg, 1984).

As we noted earlier, adults behave differently toward babies depending on whether the baby is perceived to be a girl or a boy. Fathers behave more differently toward girls and boys than mothers do, even during their babies' first year (M.E. Snow, Jacklin, & Maccoby, 1983). By the second year, this difference intensifies; fathers talk more and spend more time with their sons than with their daughters (Lamb, 1981). For these reasons, fathers, more than mothers, seem to affect the development of gender identity and gender-typing—the process by which children learn behavior that their culture considers appropriate for members of their sex.

Some research also suggests that fathers may influence their sons' cognitive development more than mothers do. The more attention a father pays to his baby son, the brighter, more alert, more inquisitive, and happier that baby is likely to be at 5 or 6 months (Pedersen, Rubenstein, & Yarrow, 1973). Baby boys raised without fathers tend to lag cognitively behind those raised in two-parent families, even when the mothers do not seem to behave differently (Pedersen, Rubenstein, & Yarrow, 1979). This finding may be further evidence of the father's importance in cognitive development; or it may simply reflect the value of having two parents and the possible economic, social, or other disadvantages of growing up in a single-parent family.

The very fact that a child's two parents have two different personalities—no matter what those personalities are—influences development in unknown ways. We don't know what effects stem from babies' learning that a similar action will bring different results, depending on whether they are with their mothers or their fathers. It seems clear, though, that anyone who plays a large part in a baby's day-to-day life will have an important influence.

Stranger Anxiety and Separation Anxiety

Robin used to be a friendly baby, smiling at strangers and going to them, continuing to coo happily as long as someone—anyone—was around. Now, at 8 months, she seems like a different child. She howls when a new person approaches her or when her parents try to leave her with a sitter. Robin is experiencing both *stranger anxiety,* wariness of a person she does not know; and *separation anxiety,* distress when a familiar caregiver leaves her.

Separation anxiety and stranger anxiety, both of which often occur during the second half of a child's first year, are thought to be signs that attachment has taken place; indeed, as we have seen, researchers identify attachment patterns by what babies do when faced with strangers or when briefly separated from their mothers.

Cognitive Effects Kagan (1979) suggests that it is the cognitive ability to recall stored information which enables these emotional events to take place. In other words, Robin becomes attached to her father because—even in his absence—she remembers the warmth and good feelings she experiences when he is with her. She cries when he leaves the room because she remembers what it was like when he was there—but she cannot yet predict what it will be like when he is *not* there.

This cognitive interpretation of separation anxiety helps to explain why it is rare for babies in many different cultures studied to show distress upon being left with an unfamiliar person or in an unfamiliar place before the age of 7 months; why the likelihood of their being disturbed rises to a peak at 13 to 15 months; and why it declines after that until it becomes quite rare by the age of 3.

The period when attachment occurs and separation anxiety emerges—sometime between 8 and 12 months of age—is just about the time when babies develop the concept of the permanent object (see Chapter 4). Thus circumstances that threaten a baby's confidence that the mother still exists seem to increase the degree of separation anxiety. Researchers have found that babies who are playing happily will begin to cry if the mother leaves the room and shuts the door (Ainsworth & Bell, 1970), but not if she leaves without shutting a door (J.N. Anderson, 1972; Corter, 1976; Corter, Rheingold, & Eckerman, 1972). When it is the baby who wanders away from the mother, he or she usually does so cheerfully (Rheingold & Eckerman, 1970). Ten-month-old babies leave their mothers' side to play with appealing toys much sooner than they leave the toys to go to their mothers—especially if they can see their mothers sitting in another room (Corter, 1976).

Effects of Attachment Patterns The more securely attached babies are, the less separation anxiety they show; perhaps, on the basis of experience, they learn more readily to trust their parents to return (Ainsworth, 1982; Jacobson & Wille, 1984). But when separation from the mother *does* cause them distress, securely attached infants are more likely than other babies to be wary of strangers. This is not as paradoxical as it may seem. Given enough time to get used to a new person, secure infants will play with a stranger in the mother's presence as they might explore any new experience. But those same babies may stiffen and scream if a stranger tries to pick them up while the mother is out of the room or before they have had a chance to settle down upon her return. This kind of behavior is perfectly reasonable from the baby's point of view; it is the less healthily attached infant who will readily go to a stranger after the distress of being left alone (Sroufe, 1977). Indeed, many avoidant babies would rather be picked up by a stranger than by their mothers (Harmon, Suwalsky, & Klein, 1979).

Other Factors A variety of other factors can influence the degree of stranger anxiety. Babies raised around many adults show less stranger anxiety than those who know just a few (Schaeffer & Emerson, 1964; Spiro, 1958). Temperamentally easy babies are usually only mildly ruffled by strangers, if at all, and calm down quickly, whereas difficult and slow-to-warm-up infants become more upset and remain upset longer (A. Thomas & Chess, 1977).

The situation makes a difference. Sometimes babies do not want anyone to pick them up, even their mothers (R.P. Klein & Durfee, 1975); they may wish not to be disturbed. They react negatively when taken by surprise. They are more likely to welcome a strange child or small adult, such as a midget, than a taller adult stranger (Brooks & Lewis, 1976; M. Lewis & Brooks, 1974).

The Role of Siblings—or Their Absence

If you have one or more brothers or sisters, your relationships with them are likely to be the longest-lasting you'll ever have. You and your siblings may have fought continually as chil-

(Cliff Speakman)

An older sibling's normal rivalry with a new baby is usually mixed with genuine caring and affection. Older children may deal with their jealousy by occasionally acting like babies themselves. This older brother seems content lying in the baby's crib and "reading" the newcomer a story.

dren, or you may have been each other's best friends. Either way, these are the people who share your roots, who "knew you when," who accepted or rejected the same parental values, and who probably deal with you more candidly than almost anyone you'll ever know.

The lack of siblings, too, affects a person's life. An only child has a very different childhood from a child with brothers or sisters.

The Arrival of a New Baby Ruth, who was 2½, came into the nursery, where her mother was breast-feeding the new baby. Ruth stood for a few minutes, quiet and staring, and then burst out, "Baby sister, I want my Mommy!"

Children react in a variety of ways to the arrival of a new baby. Some regress to earlier behaviors—sucking their thumbs, wetting their pants, asking to suck from the breast or a bottle, or using baby talk. Others withdraw by becoming silent and refusing to talk or play. Some openly suggest taking the baby back to the hospital, giving it away, or flushing it down the toilet. And some take pride in their being the "big ones," who can dress themselves, use the potty-chair, take their meals at the table with the grown-ups, and help take care of the new baby. Fortunately, most behavioral problems of older siblings disappear by the time the younger one reaches 8 months of age (Dunn, 1985).

Sibling rivalry is an old, old story—as old as

Cain and Abel. Alfred Adler (1928), one of Freud's early disciples, gave it a psychological interpretation: the theory that the "dethroning" of the first child was bound to produce feelings of competition.

The birth of a younger sibling does change the way in which a mother acts toward her first child. She is likely to play less with the older child, to be less sensitive to the older one's interests, to give more orders, to have more confrontations, and to initiate fewer conversations and games (Dunn, 1985; Dunn & Kendrick, 1982). Some children respond by taking the initiative themselves—coming up to the mother to start a conversation or asking her to play a game. Other children respond by withdrawing. The "initiators" may have less of a problem with sibling rivalry, because they have found a way to salvage their close relationships with their mothers; the withdrawers, losing more, have more resentment toward the usurping baby.

The more confrontational the relationship between the mother and the firstborn was *before* the birth of the sibling, the more upset the older child is likely to be. Also, if the mother becomes fatigued or depressed after giving birth, the firstborn is more likely to become withdrawn (Dunn, 1985).

Is it better for siblings to be close in age, or farther apart? Psychologists disagree. One author argues that the hostility received from a sibling only 1 year older will be harmful to an infant's development (B.L. White, 1975), while another contends that close spacing in age will encourage intimacy and companionship and help children learn how to deal with peer competition from a very early age (R. Gardner, 1973). A third points out that children under 5 years old are more likely to be upset by a sibling's birth than older children are (Dunn, 1985).

There is little research on how to help children adjust to a new sibling. Popular wisdom—influenced by the writings of the pediatrician Benjamin Spock (1976; Spock & Rothenberg, 1985) and others—advises parents to prepare the older child ahead of time for the birth of a new baby and to make any changes in the child's life (such as moving into another bedroom, giving up the crib for a big bed, or starting nursery school) well beforehand to minimize any feeling of being displaced. Parents should accept anxious and jealous feelings as normal but should protect the new baby from the expression of those feelings while encouraging the older child to become involved in playing and helping with the baby. In talking to the older child about the new baby, they can emphasize that each child is a valued person.

Finally, children adjust better to the birth of a new baby if their fathers devote extra time and attention to them to make up for the mother's sudden involvement with the new baby (Lamb, 1978).

How Siblings Interact Interaction with older siblings becomes more common after the first 6 months of a baby's life. In many societies around the world, including our own, older siblings assume some responsibility for taking care of babies (Dunn, 1985). One-year-olds spend almost as much time with their older siblings as with their mothers and far more time than with their fathers (Dunn & Kendrick, 1982; Lawson & Ingleby, 1974).

How do brothers and sisters get along? In one study, researchers observed 34 pairs of same-sex middle-class siblings at home. The younger ones averaged 20 months of age; their brothers and sisters were 1 to 4 years older. The older ones more often initiated both positive and negative behaviors, while the younger ones imitated more. Older boys were more aggressive; older girls, more likely to share, cooperate, and hug. The researchers found sibling interaction to be "rich and varied, clearly not based predominantly on rivalry" (Abramovitch, Corter, & Lando, 1979, p. 1003). Thus, although sibling rivalry is often present, so is genuine affection.

Children under the age of 3 hug and kiss their little sisters and brothers and try to help and comfort them. They also tease and annoy them, and by the second year, the younger siblings are teasing and annoying back. Often, though, the relationship is out of balance, one sibling (usually the younger) being friendly while the other (usually the older) is more aggressive (Dunn & Kendrick, 1982; Pepler, Corter, & Abramovitch, 1982).

Young children commonly develop feelings of attachment to their older brothers and sisters, as one 1-year-old showed by referring to her 4- and 6-year-old sisters as "my choo-jun" ("my children"). Infants become upset when their siblings go away, greet them when they come back, prefer them as playmates, and go to them for security when a stranger enters the room. Younger siblings take great joy in imitating older ones (Dunn, 1983; R.B. Stewart, 1983).

The environment that siblings create for each other affects not only their future relationship but each one's personality development as well (Dunn, 1983). For example, when little girls imitate their big brothers, they may take on some characteristics commonly thought of as masculine.

The Only Child Since the 1970s, more couples have been having fewer babies; about 1 in 10 couples today choose to have children who never will have any siblings. Although people often think of only children as spoiled, selfish, lonely, or maladjusted, research does not bear out this negative view. In fact, according to a recent statistical analysis of 115 studies comparing only children of various ages and backgrounds and children with siblings (Falbo & Polit, 1986), only children do quite well. In occupational and educational achievement, intelligence, and character (or personality), the "onlies" surpassed children with siblings, especially those with many siblings or older siblings. In these three categories, as well as in adjustment and sociability, only children were similar to firstborns and people with only one sibling.

The authors explain these results by pointing out that only children, like firstborns and offspring of two-child families, have parents who can spend more time and focus more attention on them. Perhaps these children do better because their parents talk to them more, do more with them, and expect more of them.

Disturbances in Family Relationships

As we have seen, the attachments that infants form with their parents exert a major influence on the children's physical, intellectual, personality, and social development. When these attachments are interfered with, because a child is separated from the parents or has a painful relationship with them, the consequences can be grave.

Parental Deprivation What happens to infants who are deprived of their parents very early in life, either permanently or temporarily? The answer may depend on a number of factors, including the reason for the separation, the kind of care the child receives, and the quality of the child's relationships before and after the separation.

DEATH AND DIVORCE We know little about the effects of parents' death and divorce on infants' personality development, since most of the research in these areas pertains to older children (see Chapters 9 and 18). We do know that toddlers show signs of great stress—whining, crying, clinging, disturbed sleep, and bed-wetting—when their parents divorce. On the other hand, children of this age do not really understand death and tend to regard it as a temporary separation.

INSTITUTIONALIZATION When orphanages were the most common way of taking care of children whose parents were dead or unable to care for them, many of the babies placed in these institutions died during the first year (Spitz, 1945). Children who remained institutionalized for a long time often declined in intellectual functioning and developed major psychological problems. This devastating effect of long-term insti-

tutionalization on healthy children is called **hospitalism** (not to be confused with *hospitalization*, the temporary hospital care of an ill child, which we will discuss in a moment).

A classic study (Spitz, 1945, 1946) compared 134 children reared in two institutions (called "Nursery" and "Foundling Home") with 34 children reared in their own homes. At the end of a year, the "Nursery"-reared and home-reared children were healthy and normal. But those in "Foundling Home" were significantly below average in height and weight, and their developmental quotients had deteriorated (from 124 at the outset to 75, and then to 45 in the second year). They were also highly susceptible to disease, often fatal disease. This was true even though the babies in "Nursery" had been born to delinquent girls, many of whom were emotionally disturbed or retarded, while many of the babies in "Foundling Home" had favorable backgrounds.

The most important difference between the two institutions turned out to be the amount of personal attention the babies got. In "Nursery" they all received full-time care from their own mothers or from individual full-time substitutes; in "Foundling Home," eight children shared one nurse—a situation more typical of institutional care.

By demonstrating the need for care similar to good mothering, Spitz's work hastened the trend toward placement in foster homes and much earlier adoption (Stone, Smith, & Murphy, 1973). True, the Spitz study showed (and other studies confirm) that children in well-run institutions, which provide plenty of conversation and active, meaningful experiences, suffer no impairment of intelligence. But even where such conditions exist, children remain at risk of social deprivation. Children admitted to institutions—even good ones—during the first 2 years of life are likely to have trouble forming close relationships; those placed in foster homes are not (Rutter, 1979b). The damaging factor apparently is not separation from the natural parents or the presence of more than one caregiver, but frequent changes in caregivers, a situation that prevents the formation of "early emotional bonds to particular individuals" (p. 151).

As the above studies suggest, the drop in intellectual and emotional responsiveness that an

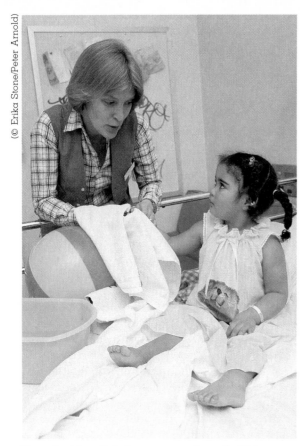

(© Erika Stone/Peter Arnold)

Even short hospital stays can upset small children. Stress can be reduced if parents are allowed to stay with the child overnight, if other family members can visit often, and if the child is prepared ahead of time for the experience.

infant typically shows when placed in an institution may be overcome by a great deal of attention and stimulation from a person to whom the baby becomes attached as a "substitute mother" (Clarke-Stewart, 1977). Dramatic gains, especially in verbalization, have been demonstrated (Rheingold, 1956).

In a classic study that yielded striking long-term results, 13 apparently retarded 2-year-olds were moved from an orphanage to an institution for mentally retarded young adults. The young men and women doted on the babies and spent much time playing with, talking to, and training "their" children. When the children were followed up as adults, all 13 were found to be functioning in the community. All were married and had normal children. Four had attended college. By contrast, a control group of 12 youngsters who had stayed in the orphanage longer awaiting placement were much lower in average IQ, and four were still in institutions (Skeels, 1966; Skeels & Dye, 1939). Thus individual attention from a warm, affectionate person can compensate considerably for the absence of relationships with parents.

HOSPITALIZATION   Even short hospital stays can be disturbing to infants and toddlers. As in institutionalization, their intellectual responsiveness tends to decline until they return home unless they get a great deal of attention from substitute caregivers.

Hospitalized babies 15 to 30 months old have been observed to go through three stages of separation anxiety (Bowlby, 1960):

1   *Protest:* Babies actively try to get their mothers back by shaking the crib and throwing themselves about.
2   *Despair:* Babies become withdrawn and inactive, crying monotonously or intermittently. Because they are so quiet, it is often assumed that they have accepted the situation.
3   *Detachment:* Babies accept care from a succession of nurses and are willing to eat, play with toys, smile, and be sociable; but when their mothers visit, the babies remain apathetic and even turn away.

When a baby or young child needs to be hospitalized, steps can be taken to reduce stress and fear. Many hospitals allow a parent to stay with the child, even to sleep overnight. Daily visits from other family members, limits on the number of caregivers, and familiar routines can alleviate the strangeness of the situation (Rutter, 1979b).

Providing occasional happy separations ahead of time can take some of the sting out of an impending hospital visit. Children who are used to being left with grandparents or sitters or who have stayed overnight at friends' houses are less likely to be upset by having to go to a hospital (Rutter, 1971; Stacey, Dearden, Pill, & Robinson, 1970).

OTHER TEMPORARY SEPARATIONS   Other studies have looked at children who have experienced various types and lengths of separation from their parents. Children who are separated from *one* parent for at least 4 consecutive weeks are no more likely to develop any kind of psychiatric or behavioral disorder than are those who have never been separated (Rutter, 1971). It does not matter how old a child is when the separation occurs or which parent is absent. Children who are separated from *both* parents are more likely to be disturbed, but it is not only the *fact* of separation that is important but the *reason* behind it. When the separation results from family discord, children are 4 times as likely to show antisocial behavior as when the separation results from vacation or physical illness. Children separated from both parents are more likely to become disturbed when the parents' marriage is rated very poor than when it is rated good or fair (Rutter, 1971).

Child Abuse and Neglect Who would deliberately hurt a child? You might find it hard to believe that the child's own parents could do such a thing. But in 1962, the **battered child syndrome,** a pattern of child abuse and neglect, was identified by Kempe.

Today, the tragic results of child abuse (deliberate injury of helpless children) and neglect (deliberate withholding of adequate care) are less likely to be "mistaken" for accidents. In 1986, nearly 2.2 million children were reported to be victims of abuse and neglect (see Figure 5-1). One out of seven of these cases involved sexual abuse—more than 16 times the number of cases reported in 1976, when the rate was less than 1 case in 10,000 children.

Although reported child abuse has increased greatly, we don't know whether abuse is actually on the rise or whether we are simply more aware of it now. This is particularly true of sexual abuse (heterosexual or homosexual activity between a boy or girl and an older person), which used to be a terrible secret that children rarely spoke of and adults seldom believed.

EFFECTS OF ABUSE AND NEGLECT To understand what child abuse means, we have to see what the statistics are measuring. Abused youngsters are kicked, beaten, burned, or even killed. Infants are choked to stop their crying or slapped when they soil their clothes. Impres-

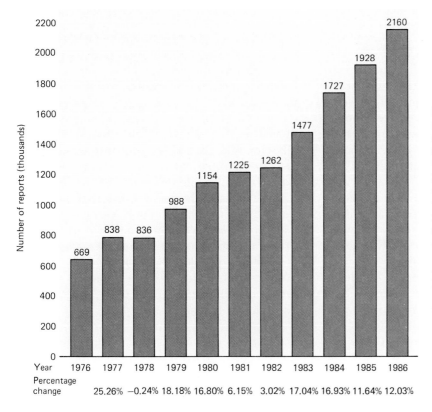

Figure 5-1 Reports of child abuse and neglect, national estimates, 1976–1986. Nearly 2.2 million children in the 50 states, the District of Columbia, Puerto Rico, the U.S. Virgin Islands, Guam, and the Marianas were victims of child abuse and neglect in 1986, according to reports from child-protection agencies. This represents about a 12 percent increase from 1985 and a 223 percent increase from 1976. More such cases are being reported now than in past years, but the official reports are still believed to represent only a small proportion of all children suffering from abuse and neglect. (*Source:* American Association for Protecting Children, 1987a, 1987b.)

sionable youngsters are terrorized, insulted, and shamed (see our discussion of psychological abuse in Chapter 9). Children—even very young ones—are used repeatedly to satisfy a parent's or another adult's sexual needs, and when they are warned not to tell, they often comply because they feel that what has happened is somehow their fault.

Neglect is harder to pin down than abuse, because there is no widely agreed-upon definition of adequate care. Neglect may mean failure to provide for a child's safety and physical or emotional needs: food, medical treatment, supervision, affection, and comfort. Neglected children may freeze, starve, or die in fires when left alone in unsafe buildings. They may languish unattended in sickbeds, wander alone on dangerous city streets, or withdraw into an inner world because they receive no love.

A syndrome that apparently results from emotional neglect is called *failure to thrive.* A baby who is well-fed and apparently healthy mysteriously fails to grow or to gain weight yet improves rapidly when removed to a hospital and given the emotional support that is lacking at home. In one longitudinal study, when such babies reached their teens they were found to have physical, intellectual, and emotional deficits, apparently due to persistent emotional neglect (Oates, Peacock, & Forrest, 1985).

Sexual abuse is likely to be most traumatic if the abuser is the father or stepfather, if the parents are unsupportive when the abuse is disclosed, or if the victim is removed from home (Browne & Finkelhor, 1986). Victims of sexual abuse are likely to grow up fearful, anxious, depressed, angry, hostile, or aggressive. They often have persistent feelings of isolation and stigma, have low self-esteem, and have difficulty trusting others. They tend to be sexually maladjusted and to engage in self-destructive behavior and substance abuse, and they are likely to again be victims of rape or sexual assault.

Although both abuse and neglect can have serious long-range consequences, many babies show amazing resilience, forming secure attachments with supportive grandmothers or other family members (Egeland & Sroufe, 1981).

FACTORS PRODUCING ABUSE AND NEGLECT
Why do adults hurt or neglect children? Re-

search has identified some associated or contributing factors at several levels, including characteristics of the abuser or neglecter, the victim, the family, the community, and the culture (Belsky, 1980).

Abusers and neglecters Most parents, of course, do the best they can to provide loving care. Yet (despite highly publicized reports of sexual abuse in day care centers) more than 90 percent of all child abuse occurs at home (Child Welfare League of America, 1986).

Except in sexual abuse, in which the perpetrator is usually a male (Browne & Finkelhor, 1986), the abusive parent is typically the mother. More than 90 percent of abusers are not psychotic and do not have criminal personalities. Many are simply lonely, unhappy, angry, depressed, and under great stress; or they have health problems that impair their ability to handle their children. Abuse may be a displaced attempt to gain control over their *own* lives by demonstrating their power over the child (B.D. Schmitt & Kempe, 1983; Wolfe, 1985).

Abusers often hate themselves for what they do, yet feel powerless to stop. They are likely to have been mistreated in their own childhood and to have felt rejected by their own parents.

Deprived of good parenting themselves, they do not know how to be good parents to their own children. They do not know how to make a baby stop crying, for example, and will sometimes lose all control when they cannot get their children to do what they want them to do. Furthermore, they often look to their children to take care of them and become furious when this does not happen. They are often grossly ignorant of normal child development and hold unrealistic ideas of the age at which their children can be toilet-trained or stay clean and neat. They have more confrontations with their children than most parents do and are less effective in resolving problems (J.R. Reid, Patterson, & Loeber, 1982; Wolfe, 1985). Abusive parents use more punitive discipline than other parents do (Trickett & Kuczynski, 1986).

The neglectful parent, on the other hand, is likely to be personally irresponsible and apathetic and to ignore rather than fight with the child (Wolfe, 1985). Mothers whose infants fail to thrive tend to have been poorly nurtured themselves and to have had stressful relationships with the babies' fathers. Many of these mothers gain less weight during pregnancy than other mothers, have more complications, deliver earlier, have smaller babies, and have trouble feeding their infants (Altemeir, O'Connor, Sherrod, & Vietze, 1985). They neither hug nor talk to their babies, they tend to resent the infants' presence, and they fail to organize a safe, warm home environment (P.H. Casey, Bradley, & Wortham, 1984).

Victims Children who require an unusual degree of care and attention because of a mental or physical problem are more likely to be abused than those who do not. Abused children tend to have had low birth weights; to be hyperactive, mentally retarded, or physically handicapped; or to exhibit behavioral abnormalities (J.R. Reid et al., 1982; Wolfe, 1985). They cry more and show more negative behavior than other children—almost 50 percent more, in one study (Tsai & Wagner, 1979). Similarly, babies who fail to thrive because of apparent emotional neglect have often had medical problems during their first few days of life (Altemeir et al., 1985). It is sad that the very children who most need concerned, loving care may be the ones who do not get it.

Family climate Abusive parents are likely to have more marital problems than other couples do and to fight physically with each other. They have more children and have them closer together, and their households are more disorganized. They experience more stressful events than other families do (J.R. Reid et al., 1982; Wolfe, 1985). The presence of a new man in the home—a stepfather or the mother's boyfriend—often triggers child abuse.

Neglectful parents tend to be emotionally withdrawn from their spouses and children (Wolfe, 1985). Abusive parents, on the other hand, tend to cut themselves off from outsiders—neighbors, relatives, and friends—and so there is no one for them to turn to in times of stress and no one to see what is happening within the family.

Community and culture Conditions in the community in which a family lives—for example,

widespread or chronic unemployment and financial hardship—affect parents' attitudes and their ability to care for their children (Wolfe, 1985). Men who are unemployed or unhappy in their jobs are more likely than other men to maltreat their wives and children (Gil, 1971; McKinley, 1964). Prevailing cultural attitudes may set the stage for violence within the family. In countries where violent crime is infrequent and parents seldom spank children, child abuse is rare.

COMBATING ABUSE AND NEGLECT To *prevent* abuse and neglect, help must be offered to parents who feel overwhelmed by the demands and strains of parenting, particularly of caring for children with special needs. Suggestions include community support and training programs, subsidized day care, volunteer homemakers, and temporary "respite homes" or "relief parents" to take over when child care becomes too burdensome (Wolfe, 1985). Within the past 10 years, programs to help families head off trouble have emerged in many American communities.* One effective program teaches child-management skills while offering therapy to help parents deal with stress.

To *stop* abuse or neglect, the child may have to be separated from the parent. However, this step must be taken only with extreme care, especially when the victim is a baby or a very young child. A direct way to stop abuse is to treat abusers as criminal offenders; people who are arrested for family violence are less likely to continue mistreating their families (L.W. Sherman & Berk, 1984).

Combating sexual abuse must begin with being able to recognize it. Telltale signs that a baby or very young child may have been sexually abused include loss of appetite or other extreme change in behavior; recurrent nightmares, disturbed sleep, and fear of the dark; bed-wetting, thumb-sucking, or excessive crying; torn or stained underclothes; vaginal or rectal bleeding; vaginal discharge or infection; painful, itching, or swollen genitals; unusual interest in or knowledge of sexual matters; inap-

*For information on any of 2000 free or low-cost local programs offering child development classes, hot lines, and support groups, contact The Family Resource Coalition, 230 North Michigan Avenue, Suite 1625, Chicago, IL 60601.

propriate expressions of affection; and fear or dislike of being left somewhere or with someone (U.S. Department of Health and Human Services, USDHHS, 1984).

To combat sexual abuse, very young children need to be told that their bodies belong to them and that they can say "no" to anyone who might try to touch them in an uncomfortable way, even if it is someone they love and trust. They need to know that they are not to blame for what an adult does. And they need to be reassured that the vast majority of adults do not wish to harm children.

DEVELOPMENT OF SOCIABILITY

Changes in Sociability

Although the family is the center of a baby's social world, infants and (more so) toddlers do show interest in people outside the home, particularly people their own size. Since more babies now spend time in day care settings where they come into contact with other babies, psychologists have become more interested in studying the way in which infants and toddlers react to each other.

From the first days of life in a hospital nursery, infants who have been lying quietly in their cribs will start to cry when they hear the cries of another baby (G.B. Martin & Clark, 1982; Sagi & Hoffman, 1976; Simner, 1971). This "inborn empathic distress response" shows up as early as 18 hours after birth. The babies cry only in response to the cries of other infants, either live or tape-recorded—not to the tape-recorded sound of their own crying and not to the cries of chimpanzees or older children (G.B. Martin & Clark, 1982).

Babies' interest in other children rises and falls, depending on their developmental priorities. During the first few months of life, they are very interested in other babies and respond to them in about the same way they respond to their mothers: they look, they smile, they coo (T.M. Field, 1978). From the age of 6 months till about the end of the first year, they increasingly smile at, touch, and babble to another baby, especially when they are not distracted by the presence of either adults or toys (Hay, Peder-

sen, & Nash, 1982). At about 1 year, however, when the biggest items on their agenda seem to be learning to walk and to manipulate objects, they pay more attention to toys and less to other people (T.M. Field & Roopnarine, 1982).

In the second year, babies become more sociable again, and now they have a deeper understanding of their relationships. A 10-month-old who holds out a toy to another baby pays no attention to whether the other's back is turned. A child in the second year of life knows when such an offer has the best chance of being accepted and how to respond to another child's overtures (Eckerman & Stein, 1982).

Individual Differences in Sociability

Some people, of course, are more sociable than others, starting from a very early age. Among a group of five 8- to 10-month-old babies in a day care center, Lee (1973) was able to identify a most popular child and a least popular child. The baby whom the others approached most consistently was nonassertive but reciprocated the attention that the other babies gave her. The baby whom the others avoided most consistently was described as "almost asocial." He acted very differently toward the other children, depending on whether or not he had initiated the contacts with them.

What makes some babies friendlier than others? Some aspects of sociability, such as the readiness to accept new people, the ability to adapt to change, and a baby's usual mood, appear to be inherited traits of temperament (A. Thomas, Chess, & Birch, 1968) that remain fairly stable over time. Children who at the age of 2½ are friendly, involved with other children, and able to cope with aggression remain sociable at the age of 7½ (Waldrop & Halverson, 1975).

Babies are influenced by the attitudes of those around them. Sociable infants tend to have sociable mothers, according to a study of 40 middle-class 1-year-olds and their mothers. The sociable babies also scored higher on intelligence tests, suggesting that babies who feel comfortable with a strange tester may perform better than babies who are uncomfortable with new people (M. Stevenson & Lamb, 1979).

Children who spend time from infancy onward with other babies seem to become sociable at earlier ages than those who spend all their time at home. Babies in day care interact more with other children—both positively and negatively—and are, in general, more socially competent. As children grow older, they enter more and more into the world beyond their own home, and their social skills become increasingly important.

DEVELOPMENT OF SELF-CONTROL AND SELF-REGULATION

At the beginning of this chapter, we described the "terrible twos," when toddlers often seem intent on doing everything but what their parents want them to do. As we pointed out, Freud explains such negative behavior in terms of a struggle over delayed gratification, and Erikson explains it in terms of the development of autonomy. How do children begin to make the transition from negativism to socially acceptable behavior?

As Erica, who is 12 months old, toddles toward an electric outlet and pokes her finger at it, her mother yells, "No!" Erica pulls back her finger. She has obeyed a command. The next time she approaches an outlet, Erica hesitates, shakes her head, and says, "No." She has now stopped herself from doing something she recalls being told not to do. Though she certainly does not realize it, Erica has now taken definite steps on the road to *self-regulation:* the independent control of her own behavior to conform with understood social expectations.

The growth of self-regulation parallels that of cognitive awareness. As Erica complies or does not comply with adults' requests, she absorbs a great deal of information about what sorts of behavior are socially approved. As she processes, stores, and acts upon this information, a gradual shift from external to internal control takes place. Let's consider the phases that are characteristic of this shift.

Phases Leading to Self-Regulation

Starting from birth, children appear to go through four phases on the way to self-regulation (Kopp, 1982).

Phase 1: Neurophysiological Modulation (Birth to 2–3 Months) In the early weeks, infants begin to soothe themselves when overstimulated, by using such originally reflexive behaviors as sucking. But because they have limited control over their arousal, they need help (in varying degrees) to quiet them or to divert their attention from whatever is exciting them.

Phase 2: Sensorimotor Modulation (2–3 to 9–12 Months) Once babies reach the age when they are awake more in the daytime, they become more aware that their actions can affect their world. However, they will exert their influence on their environment only when something or someone captures their attention—not from any conscious intent.

Phase 3: Control (9–12 to 18 Months and Over) Walking gives babies the ability and incentive to plan their movements, and they pay more attention to the effects of what they do. They also begin to recognize the demands of the caregiver and to respond to them either negatively or positively. Whether or not they comply with orders, they are now exercising control over their actions.

Control is linked with the development of what Piaget described as intentional, or goal-directed, behavior, but it is limited to a specific situation. Children in the third phase do not yet have the cognitive ability to generalize, and their memory is limited. Also, their delight in what they *can* do may suppress the knowledge of what they are *supposed* to do. And because self-awareness is only beginning to develop, they do not really understand what it means to control *themselves*. Erica may stay away from electric outlets only for a short while, and only when her parents are around, and she may poke her finger into another, equally dangerous place—like a hot stove—unless someone stops her.

Phase 4: Self-Control and the Progression to Self-Regulation (18 to 24 Months and Over) In the fourth phase, children are developing the ability to form symbolic mental images and to recall past events. They are also developing the ability to reflect on their own actions, and so they can mentally connect what they do with what their caregivers have told them to do. To-

Physical punishment—the traditional method of disciplining young children—is not very effective with toddlers who have not yet developed control of their impulses. Instead, parents and caregivers can remind the child of what is "off limits" and suggest safe, permissible areas to explore.

Self-control, then, means that, on the basis of remembered information, children will alter or delay an action to fit their knowledge of what is socially acceptable even when the caregiver is absent. However, children's adaptability to new situations is still quite limited, and under pressure of a strong stimulus or desire, they easily forget the rules. If a ball rolls into the street, they run after it. They also have trouble accepting long or unexpected delays; waiting to go outside until father gets off the phone is almost unbearable.

The subtle shift to self-regulation, which may develop around the age of 3 or later, involves much greater flexibility, conscious thought, and willingness to wait. Self-regulation may help to explain the greater ability of children over 3 to adapt to dislocations, such as hospitalization or institutionalization, which can be devastating to younger children.

Helping Babies Develop Self-Control and Self-Regulation

There is wide variation in the rate at which babies advance through the phases leading to self-regulation. Their progress may depend on their energy level and their urge to explore, as well as on other temperamental factors; on their maturation, language ability, and experiences; and on the way their caregivers act toward them. Caregivers need to be sensitive to such individual differences.

During the control phase, babies may benefit from repeated reminders of what is expected of them, as well as suggestions for alternative activities. According to one study of 14-month-olds, physical punishment (such as slapping Timmy's hand when he breaks a vase) does not work; if children have not yet developed control of their impulses, they are likely to ignore commands and may even do more damage. "Baby-proofing" the home by removing everything in sight is one solution; but valuable objects should be replaced with plenty of safe, unbreakable objects that the baby *can* explore—otherwise the child is likely to be hampered in learning to solve problems involving physical manipulation (Power & Chapieski, 1986).

gether, these cognitive abilities allow children to monitor their own behavior: to form an idea of what their caregivers have approved of in the past and to recognize what is called for in the present situation. Most 2-year-olds, for example, know the rules concerning what to eat and how to eat, and how to dress for sleep or play; and they know what they are expected to do when playing alone, so that they may sometimes put away their toys without being reminded.

BOX 5-2 **PRACTICALLY SPEAKING**

MINIMIZING NEGATIVISM

The "terrible twos"—a period in which children seem to express their urge for autonomy by resisting almost everything they are told to do—is a perfectly normal stage that often continues through the preschool years. But not all children in this stage are equally negative. Indeed, many seem to wish to tease or "play with" their parents, not to be taken seriously.

Flexible parents who view a child's expressions of self-will as a striving for independence, not as stubbornness, are more likely to have compliant preschoolers. A certain amount of opposition is undoubtedly healthy. Parents can avoid excessive conflict and contribute to a child's sense of competence by following these suggestions (Haswell, Hock, & Wenar, 1981):

■ *Don't interrupt an activity* unless the interruption is necessary; try to wait until the child's attention has shifted to something else.

■ If an activity must be interrupted, *give advance warning:* "In 10 minutes, it will be time to put your toys away and come to dinner." This gives the child time to adjust and perhaps to finish what he or she is doing.

■ *Suggest; don't command.*

Accompany requests with smiles or hugs, not criticism, threats, or physical control.

■ *Wait a few moments* before repeating a request when a child doesn't immediately comply.

■ *Give the child a choice*— even a limited one. That way, the child feels in control. ("Would you like to have your bath now, or in 5 minutes?")

■ *Be consistent* in discipline.

■ When you and the child get into a power struggle, *take time out.* Leave the child alone for a few minutes; the resistance may diminish or even disappear.

Two-year-olds' self-control appears to reflect the way in which their parents or caregivers treat them and talk to them. It may be effective to link a command with something pleasurable: "It's time to stop playing so that you can go to the store with me."

When children are under extra stress (such as that caused by divorce), there may be some backsliding, and parents should be wary of expecting too much self-control (Kopp, 1982). (See Box 5-2, above, for more suggestions for increasing compliance and minimizing negativism.)

Research—particularly in the past 2 decades— has told us much about the way infants and toddlers develop physically, intellectually, emotionally, and socially (see Box 5-3 on page 182 for ways to apply some of the findings discussed in Chapters 3, 4, and 5). In Part Three, we'll see how young children build on the foundation laid during their first 3 years.

BOX 5-3 PRACTICALLY SPEAKING

PUTTING RESEARCH FINDINGS TO WORK

If you are a parent, or are about to become a parent, or if you have occasion to care for infants or toddlers, you can put into practice some of the most important findings to emerge from recent research in child development. The following four recommendations are just a sampling, based on theories and findings discussed in Chapters 3 to 5:

1 *Respond to babies' signals.* This is probably the single most important thing that caregivers can do. Meeting the needs of an infant—whether for food, cuddling, or comforting—establishes a sense of trust that the world is a friendly place. Answering cries or requests for help gives a baby a sense of having a measure of control over his or her life, an important awareness for emotional and intellectual development. Adults often worry about spoiling children by reacting too quickly to meet their needs, but the children who have the most problems in life are those whose needs go unmet.

2 *Provide interesting things for babies to look at and do.* By first watching a mobile hanging over a crib and then handling brightly colored toys and simple household objects, babies will learn about shapes, sizes, and textures. Playing helps them develop their senses and motor skills. And handling objects helps them realize the difference between themselves and things that are separate from them.

3 *Be patient.* When a baby keeps throwing toys or other objects out of the crib or high chair, remember that the purpose is not to annoy you but to learn. By throwing things, babies learn such concepts as space and distance, what hands can do, and the fact that objects remain the same even when they are moved to a different place. It may be easier on your back and disposition if you tie one or two items to a string and attach it so that it can be pulled up each time. Of course, you should not leave the string near an unattended baby—or leave a baby alone in a high chair.

4 *Give babies freedom to explore.* It's better to baby-proof a room than to confine the baby in a playpen. Take away breakables, small things that can be swallowed, and sharp objects that can injure. Jam books into a bookcase so tight that a baby can't pull them out. But leave plenty of unbreakable objects around to explore. Babies need opportunities to crawl and eventually to walk, to exercise their large muscles. They need to learn about their environment, to feel a sense of mastery over it. And they also need freedom to go off on their own (under a parent's or a caregiver's watchful eye) and develop a sense of independence.

Early Personality Development: Two Theories

■ Two major theories of personality development are the psychosexual theory of Sigmund Freud, which stresses biological and maturational factors, and the psychosocial theory of Erik Erikson, which emphasizes cultural influences in addition to maturational factors. Both theories emphasize the critical importance of the mother in the earliest stages.

■ According to Freud, certain events that occur during the first 3 years are among those having the greatest influence on adult personality.

1 In the oral stage (birth to 12–18 months), an infant receives pleasure through oral stimulation.

2 In the anal stage (12–18 months to 3 years), a toddler receives pleasurable stimulation from moving the bowels.

3 A baby's id operates under the pleasure principle, striving for immediate gratification. When gratification is delayed, the ego develops and operates under the reality principle, striving to find socially acceptable ways to obtain gratification.

■ According to Erikson, infants and toddlers experience the first two crises in a series of eight that influence personality development throughout life.

1 The first critical task, which an infant faces in the first 12 to 18 months, is to find a balance between basic trust and basic mistrust of the world. Like that of the Freudian oral stage, the resolution of this crisis is influenced greatly by events surrounding feeding and by the quality of the mother-infant relationship.

2 The second crisis, which a toddler faces from 12–18 months to 3 years, is that of autonomy versus shame and doubt. As it is in the Freudian anal stage, toilet training is a key event in the resolution of this crisis, which is greatly affected by the help the child receives from parents.

Emotions: The Foundation of Personality

■ Recent research suggests that the expressions of different emotions are tied to brain maturation, although experiences and the development of self-awareness also affect the timing of their arrival.

■ Babies communicate their feelings through their tears, smiles, and laughter, as well as through a variety of facial expressions.

Differences in Personality Development

■ Early differences in emotional expression, which may stem from temperament, are indicative of future personality development.

■ The New York Longitudinal Study identified nine fairly stable components of temperament, or a person's individual style of approaching people and situations.

1 These traits appear to be largely inborn but may be affected by significant environmental changes.

2 On the basis of these temperamental patterns, most children can be classified as easy, difficult, or slow to warm up. These classifications determine the "fit" between a child's temperament and that of the parents and thus have implications for child rearing.

■ Significant physiological and behavioral differences between the sexes typically do not appear until after infancy. However, parents treat their sons and daughters differently from birth, and so some personality differences result.

The Family and Personality Development

■ Social changes—more mothers working outside the home, more divorces, more single-parent families, and a trend toward smaller families—have had important effects on children's development.

- Although the mother's role continues to be significant, recent research on socialization has focused on fathers and other caregivers, as well as on siblings. Researchers also examine the interrelationships among several family members.

- Some research has suggested that the first few hours or days of life constitute a critical period for forming the mother-infant bond, but follow-up research has failed to support this conclusion. However, infants do have strong needs for closeness and warmth as well as physical care from one caregiver or a few caregivers.

- Mother-infant attachment, a reciprocal connection that forms and consolidates later in infancy, is receiving considerable attention in research. Patterns of attachment (secure, avoidant, or ambivalent) appear to have long-term implications for the child's development.

- When mothers work outside the home, babies' (especially boys') attachment patterns may be affected. Significant factors include the amount of time the baby spends away from the mother (unless the caregiver is the father), the child's age and temperament, the mother's attitudes, and the quality of substitute care.

- Fathers and babies also become attached early in a baby's life. The nature of infants' and toddlers' experiences with their mothers and with their fathers appears to differ, and the variety is valuable.

- Separation anxiety and stranger anxiety are normal phenomena that usually arise during the second half of the first year and appear to be related to attachment. Separation anxiety is a child's distress upon the departure of the caregiver. Stranger anxiety is wariness of strangers. There is considerable individual difference in the expression of both separation anxiety and stranger anxiety.

- Siblings influence each other both positively and negatively from an early age. Parents' actions and attitudes can help reduce sibling rivalry.

- Contrary to a widespread impression, children without siblings generally do as well as or better than other children. Their intellectual and personality characteristics are similar to those of firstborns and children with one sibling.

- Studies of parental deprivation—generally conducted among orphans in institutions in which considerable sensory deprivation is common—point to the need for consistent parenting or caregiving in a stimulating environment. Attempts at enriching institutional environments have dramatically benefited children's emotional and intellectual development.

- Effects of short-term separations, such as for hospitalization, depend on particular circumstances.

- Child abuse, including sexual abuse, and neglect, which can result in failure to thrive, have received widespread attention and medical documentation. Particular characteristics of victim, abusers or neglecters, families, the community, and the larger culture either are associated with or contribute to child abuse and neglect.

Development of Sociability

- Researchers are becoming interested in how babies react to their peers, especially in day care settings.

- Although infants' interest in each other fluctuates with their developmental priorities, individual differences in babies' sociability tend to remain stable over time.

Development of Self-Control and Self-Regulation

- The "terrible twos" is a period in which children tend to display resistant or negative behavior. This stage is normal and may begin well before the second birthday and last through the early childhood years.

- Children during the first 3 years and beyond move gradually toward self-control and self-regulation (self-initiated socially accepted behavior). This development is largely dependent on cognitive self-awareness, awareness of social standards, and the ability to apply this knowledge in new situations.

- By understanding individual variations in this process, parents can help children develop more positive behavior.

KEY TERMS

ambivalent (resistant) (page 164)
anal stage (150)
attachment (164)
autonomy (151)
autonomy versus shame and
    doubt (151)
avoidant (164)
basic trust versus basic mistrust
    (151)
battered child syndrome (175)
difficult child (158)

easy child (158)
ego (150)
emotions (152)
failure to thrive (176)
hospitalism (173)
id (150)
imprinting (162)
mother-infant bond (162)
oral stage (149)
pleasure principle (150)
reality principle (150)

securely attached (164)
self-awareness (154)
self-control (180)
self-recognition (154)
self-regulation (179)
separation anxiety (170)
slow-to-warm-up child (158)
socialization (161)
stranger anxiety (169)
temperament (157)

SUGGESTED READINGS

Caplan, T., & Caplan, F. (1983). *The early child-hood years.* New York: Bantam. A liberally illustrated guide to overall development from age 2 through age 6.

Chess, S., Thomas, A., & Birch, H. G. (1965). *Your child is a person: Psychological approach to parenthood without guilt.* New York: Viking. A very readable book that translates the findings of the New York Longitudinal Study into practical words of wisdom and reassurance for parents. The major premise is that children differ temperamentally from birth and that parents will be most successful if they take the differences into account.

Dunn, J. (1985). *Sisters and brothers.* Cambridge, MA: Harvard University Press. A beautiful volume summarizing what is known about sibling relationships.

Evans, J., & Ilfeld, E. (1982). *Good beginnings: Parenting in the early years.* Ypsilanti, MI: High/Scope. An informal guide, with charming photographs, that takes into account the individual styles of parents and other caregivers.

Greenberg, M. (1985). *The birth of a father.* New York: Continuum. A first-person account of becoming a father, written by the psychiatrist who coined the term *engrossment* for a father's absorption in and preoccupation with his baby. It is written with sensitivity and humor, and the chapter "Who Changes the Diapers?" is a gem.

Hollingsworth, J. (1986). *Unspeakable acts.* New York: Congdon & Weed. A horrifying account of the sadistic sexual abuse of dozens of small children by the operator of a Florida day care center—acts that went on for months because the children

were too frightened to talk about them. The effects of the abuse and its aftermath (including the children's encounter with the legal system and its pitfalls for young victims) vividly illustrate small children's cognitive development and emotional defenses.

Kempe, C. H., & Helfer, R. E. (Eds.). (1987). *The battered child* (4th ed.). Chicago: University of Chicago Press. A collection of articles emphasizing assessment, intervention, treatment, and prevention of child abuse.

Klaus, M., & Kennell, J. H. (1982). *Parent-infant bonding* (2d ed.). St. Louis: Mosby. A discussion emphasizing the role of early experience in the formation of the parent-infant bond.

Lamb, M. E. (Ed.). (1981). *The role of the father in child development* (2d ed.). New York: Wiley. A collection of writings on the impact of the father on the developing child, by leading researchers on paternal influences.

Sanford, L. T. (1982). *The silent children: A parent's guide to the prevention of child sexual abuse.* New York: McGraw-Hill. This straightforward book, by a therapist who works with victims of sexual abuse, stresses that a child's self-esteem is the best defense against giving in to an abuser. The book calmly presents the facts about child sexual abuse and tells parents how to make children aware of the dangers without being unduly fearful.

Stern, D. (1977). *The first relationship: Infant and mother.* Cambridge, MA: Harvard University Press. A look at how mothers' interactions with infants influence socialization.

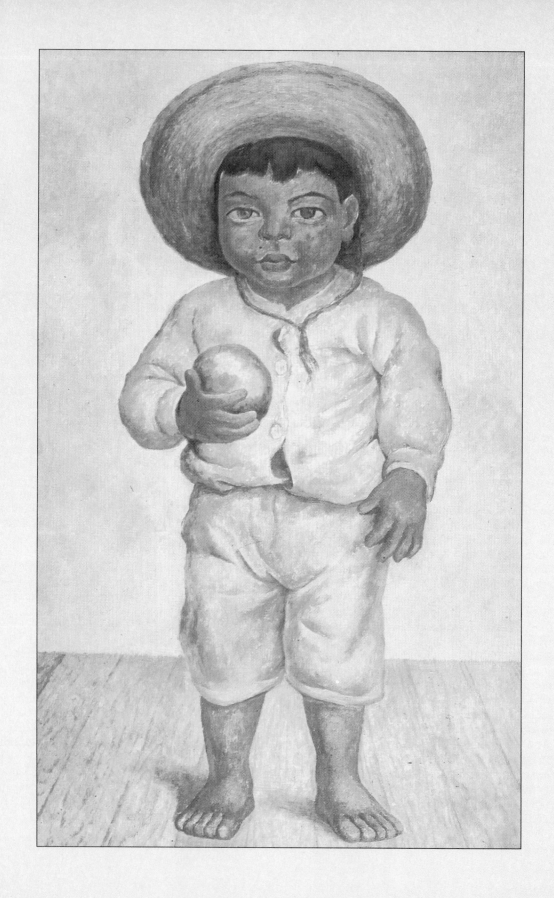

3

EARLY CHILDHOOD

In the days when most children did not go to school until kindergarten or first grade, the years from 3 to 6 were called *the preschool years*. Today, when most children attend some kind of school from the age of 3 and many go to day care centers even earlier, *preschool* no longer carries the same meaning. *Early childhood* is a more accurate description of this stage, just over the threshold from babyhood.

■ As you will see in **Chapter 6**, where we discuss physical and intellectual development, children look different in early childhood as they lose their babyish roundness. They act differently, too. They become better at a variety of fine motor tasks that include tying shoelaces (in bows instead of knots), mastering crayons (on paper rather than on walls), and pouring cereal (into the bowl, not onto the floor). They improve in large motor abilities like running, hopping, skipping, jumping, and throwing balls. They also think differently, as they leap forward in their ability to handle a wide range of intellectual concepts and to express their thoughts and feelings in the language of their culture.

■ These are critical years for personality development, as well, as we show in **Chapter 7**. Children's conceptions of themselves grow stronger. They know what sex they are—and they want everyone else to affirm their sense of maleness or femaleness. Their behavior becomes more socially directed—sometimes helping other people, sometimes hurting them. The number of important people in their lives expands, and friends and playmates become more important.

All aspects of development—physical, intellectual, emotional, and social—continue to intertwine to make each person unique.

6

CHAPTER

PHYSICAL AND INTELLECTUAL DEVELOPMENT IN EARLY CHILDHOOD

Children live in a world of imagination and feeling. . . . They invest the most insignificant object with any form they please, and see in it whatever they wish to see.

Adam G. Oehlenschlager

■ ASK YOURSELF

■ How do children's bodies and their motor skills grow and develop during early childhood?

■ How can young children be kept healthy?

■ What sleep patterns and problems develop during early childhood, and how can they be handled?

■ How do young children think and remember, and what does research tell us about their cognitive competence?

■ How does language ability flower in early childhood?

■ How can we assess intelligence in early childhood, and how do parents influence intellectual performance?

■ What options are available for young children's care and schooling, and what purposes do they serve?

It is the day before Amy's third birthday. "Pretty soon," she tells her mother, "I'll be big enough to sleep without sucking my thumb. And maybe tomorrow I'll be big enough to wear pajamas like Daddy's."

The big day dawns. Amy leaps out of bed at her usual early hour and runs to the mirror. As she stands there, first on one foot and then on the other, she examines her mirror image closely, then runs to her parents' room. "Mommy, Daddy!" she squeals into sleepy ears. "I'm 3!" But then a note of disappointment creeps into her voice as she acknowledges sadly, "But I don't look different."

Amy's change from the day before may be infinitesimal, but in terms of what she was a year earlier, she is very different indeed. Her next 3 years of life will show still greater changes.

Children who have celebrated their third birthday are no longer babies. They are capable of bigger and better things, both physically and intellectually. The 3-year-old is a sturdy adventurer, very much at home in the world and eager to explore its possibilities, as well as the developing capabilities of his or her own body. A child of this age has come through the most dangerous phase of life—the infant and toddler years—to enter a healthier, less threatening time.

Youngsters grow more slowly in early childhood, between the ages of 3 and 6, than during the preceding 3 years; but they make so much progress in coordination and muscle development that they can do much more. Intellectual development, too, continues at a staggering pace. Children in this age group can remember more, reason better, and speak proficiently, and their thinking takes huge leaps forward.

In this chapter, we'll trace all these developing capabilities and concerns. We'll also describe the profound effects of young children's expanding environment: at day care centers, preschool, and kindergarten.

PHYSICAL GROWTH AND CHANGE

Physical changes may be less obvious during early childhood than during the first 3 years of life, but they are, nonetheless, important ones that make possible dramatic advancements in motor skills and intellectual development.

Height, Weight, and Appearance

During early childhood, boys and girls lose their chubbiness and begin to take on the slender, athletic appearance of childhood. The potbellies typical of 3-year-olds slim down as abdominal muscles develop. The trunk grows longer, and so do the arms and legs. Children's heads are still relatively large, but (in keeping with the cephalocaudal principle, described in Chapter 3) the other parts of their bodies continue catching up as children's proportions steadily become more adult.

Within that overall pattern, though, children show a wide range of individual and sex-based differences. Boys tend to have more muscle per pound of body weight than girls, while girls have more fatty tissue.

Although Amy's growth has slowed now that she is 3, she is 4 inches taller than she was a year ago; she now measures almost 38 inches and weighs almost 32 pounds. Her friend Gary, whose birthday is within a week of hers, is slightly taller and heavier. Each year for the next 3 years, both will grow about 2 to 3 inches and gain 4 to 6 pounds. Boys' slight edge in height and weight normally continues until puberty, when girls suddenly surpass them—only to be overtaken and passed by their male age-mates a year or two later.

Structural and Systemic Changes

The changes in young children's appearance reflect some of the important developments inside. Muscular and skeletal growth progresses, making children stronger. Cartilage turns to bone at a faster rate than before, and bones become harder, giving the child a firmer shape and protecting the internal organs. These changes, coordinated by the maturing brain and nervous system, permit a proliferation of both large-muscle and small-muscle motor skills. In addition, the increased capacities of the respiratory and circulatory systems increase physical stamina and, together with the developing immune system, keep children healthier.

By the age of 3, all the primary, or deciduous, teeth are in place, and so children can chew anything they want to. The permanent teeth, which will begin to appear at about age 6, are developing; therefore, if thumb-sucking persists past the age of 5, it can affect how evenly they come in.

Nutrition

For young children, as for infants and toddlers, proper growth and health depend on good nutrition. As children's growth rate slows down, so does their appetite, and parents often worry that their children are not eating enough. Because their caloric requirements per pound of body weight decline, it is normal for children between 3 and 6 to eat less in proportion to their size than infants do. A child who is energetic, with good muscle tone, bright eyes, glossy hair, and the ability to recover readily from fatigue, is unlikely to be suffering from inadequate nutrition, no matter how traumatic mealtimes are.

Actually, the nutritional demands of early

Early childhood, before permanent teeth come in, is the best time to develop good habits of oral hygiene.

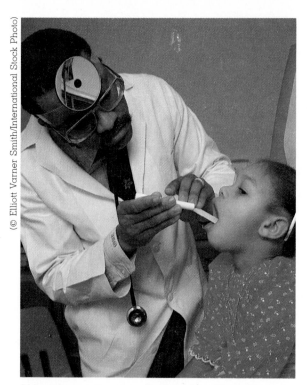

(© Elliott Varner Smith/International Stock Photo)

Although sore throats and other minor illnesses are common among 3- to 6-year-olds, they are usually not serious enough to require visits to the doctor. This 5-year-old will probably have fewer colds and sore throats in the next few years, as her respiratory and immune systems mature.

HEALTH

The early childhood years are basically healthy ones. There are, of course, the usual colds and other minor illnesses, which may have some cognitive and emotional as well as physical benefits (see Box 6-1). But major diseases that used to strike young children are now relatively rare, because of widespread vaccinations. Frequent scrapes, cuts, and bruises are the price for practicing new motor skills.

Health Problems

Minor Illnesses Coughs, sniffles, stomachaches, and runny noses are part of early childhood. These minor illnesses typically last from 2 to 14 days but seldom are serious enough to require a doctor's attention.

Because the lungs are not fully developed, respiratory problems are common during these years, though not quite as common as in infancy. Three- to five-year-olds average about seven to eight colds and other respiratory illnesses per year, but children average fewer than six during middle childhood (Denny & Clyde, 1983), because of the gradual development of the respiratory system and of natural immunity, or resistance to disease.

Major Illnesses Vaccinations of children have become routine in the United States. Immunization has largely banished the specter of such contagious diseases as measles, rubella (German measles), mumps, whooping cough, diphtheria, and poliomyelitis—illnesses that until the middle of the twentieth century frequently reached epidemic proportions and caused many untimely deaths. Vaccines discovered since then have reduced the incidence of all these diseases dramatically since 1950. More than 90 percent of children in kindergarten and first grade are immunized against major childhood illnesses (U.S. Department of Health and Human Services, USDHHS, 1982).

These diseases, though now preventable by vaccines, do still exist, however, and can be dangerous if parents become complacent and neglect to take children for their shots or if society fails to provide vaccines for children whose families cannot afford them. Between 1968 and

childhood are satisfied quite easily. For example, a small child's protein needs can be met with two glasses of milk and one serving of meat or an alternative (like fish, cheese, or eggs) every day. Vitamin A requirements can be met with modest amounts of carrots, spinach, egg yolk, or whole milk (among other foods); and vitamin C can be obtained from citrus fruits, tomatoes, and leafy dark-green vegetables (E. R. Williams & Caliendo, 1984).

If children do not get these and other essential nutrients, there is cause for concern. That commonly happens when children and their families succumb to seductive television commercials for foods heavy in sugar and fat. If children's diet includes a lot of sugared cereals, chocolate cake, other snacks low in nutrients, and fast foods, their small appetites will not allow them room to eat the foods they really need. Therefore the snacks they eat should have nutritional value.

BOX 6-1 FOOD FOR THOUGHT

IS ILLNESS GOOD FOR CHILDREN?

Nobody likes to be sick. But the frequent minor illnesses of early childhood may be blessings in disguise. Besides their acknowledged physical benefits in building up immunity, one researcher has identified some possible cognitive and emotional benefits of common childhood illnesses (Parmelee, 1986).

When children feel ill, they may experience aches and pains, a feeling of muscular weakness, a drop in energy level, and a depressed mood. When they get well, their usual sense of physical well-being is restored. Repeated experiences with illness call children's attention to their sensations and states and give them greater awareness of their physical selves. Illness gives children an opportunity to learn how to cope with physical distress, and such coping is an experience that enhances their sense of competence.

When contagious illnesses spread, children see their brothers, sisters, playmates, and parents going through experiences similar to their own. As a result of Adam's bouts with the flu, he learns empathy—the ability to put himself in someone else's place. He can understand how his little sister Jenny feels when *she* catches the flu and can help give her the comfort and care he gets when *he* is ill.

At this age, Adam may also show some confusion between "feeling bad" when his throat hurts and "feeling bad" when he has hurt Jenny. His confusion is natural, since the same expression is used for both physical and emotional upsets and both are regarded as unwanted states. Children are often convinced that they feel bad (are sick) because of something bad they did (like disobeying their parents). Illness gives parents a chance to deal with children's confusion and guilt and to reassure the child: "I know you feel bad because you're sick, but you'll soon be well."

1971, for example, when the measles vaccination rate temporarily declined, the number of cases more than tripled.

The disorders that are most likely to be fatal in childhood, besides birth defects, are cancer and heart disease. Fortunately, however, death rates from illness have come down in recent years. Since 1950, deaths from influenza and pneumonia have dropped by 84 percent and deaths from cancer have dropped by 48 percent, primarily because of advances in the treatment of leukemia, lymphoma, and Hodgkin's disease, forms of cancer that often strike children (USDHHS, 1982). The federal government also credits improved access to health care and improved living conditions in low-income and minority groups.

Accidental Injuries Now that preventable diseases are largely under control, accidents have become the leading cause of death in childhood. Of these, deaths due to automobile accidents are most common. Today, all 50 states and the District of Columbia have laws requiring young children to be restrained in cars, either in specially designed seats or by standard seat belts. The restraints themselves are effective: children *not* in restraints are 11 times more likely to die in an automobile accident than children who are restrained (Decker, Dewey, Hutcheson, & Schaffner, 1984). Unfortunately, however, the laws are not always effective. Young children love to be active and often rebel against the discomfort of wearing seat belts, and parents—to avoid argument—frequently give in. A recent Australian study on ways to overcome resistance to the use of restraints (Bowman, Sanson-Fisher, & Webb, 1987) found that educating children in preschools about the importance of wearing restraints was more effective than threatening parents with police checks and fines.

Most fatal accidents that do not take place in automobiles occur in and around the home: children drown in bathtubs and pools (they may also drown in lakes, rivers, and oceans); are fatally burned in fires and explosions; drink or eat poisonous substances; fall from heights; get caught in mechanical contrivances; and suffocate in unexpected traps, such as abandoned refrigerators.

Children are naturally venturesome and are naively ignorant of the dangers that surround them. Their innocence puts a large burden on parents and other adult caretakers, who must tread a delicate line between supervising children adequately and smothering them with oversolicitousness. Federal laws help by requiring, for example, "childproof" caps on medicine bottles. However, parents and other caregivers must be ever alert to hazards.

Influences on Health

Young children do become sick fairly often, and they are bound to have occasional accidents. But why do some children have more illnesses or injuries than others?

Regarding illness, there may be hereditary reasons: certain children seem to be predisposed toward particular medical conditions. Environmental factors such as nutrition and physical care also make a difference. So does frequency of contact with other children, who may be harboring bacteria or viruses. In addition to purely physical factors, family situations involving stress and economic hardship may make some children more prone to illness or injury than others.

Exposure   Children in large families are sick oftener than children in small families (Loda, 1980). Likewise, children in day care centers seem to pick up more colds, influenza, and other infections than children raised at home (Wald, Dashevsky, Byers, Guerra, & Taylor, 1988), and to have a higher risk as well of contracting more serious gastrointestinal diseases, hepatitis A, and meningitis, which is often fatal (*Pediatrics*, 1986, cited in American Academy of Pediatrics, AAP, 1986c).

Contributing to the risk are the close physical contact and the sharing of meals, snacks, and paint materials among babies in diapers and toddlers, all of whom have imperfect hygiene habits and immature immune systems. The spread of bacteria can be minimized if caregivers teach children how to wash their hands properly after using the toilet and if they follow basic health precautions themselves, such as washing their hands after changing diapers. Caregivers should also separate children in diapers from those who are toilet-trained, and toilets should not be near food preparation areas. Such practices can cut the rate of illness by more than half, and safe playground equipment and supervision can help prevent falls and other injuries.

In fact, children in *high-quality* day care (see Box 6-3), where nutrition is well planned and illnesses may be detected and treated early, tend to be healthier than children who are not in day care programs (AAP, 1986c).

Stress   Stressful events in the family—moves, job changes, divorce, and death—seem to increase the frequency of minor illnesses and home accidents. In one study, children whose families had experienced 12 or more such events were more than twice as likely to see a doctor and 6 times as likely to have to go into the hospital as children from families that had experienced fewer than 4 such events (Beautrais, Fergusson, & Shannon, 1982).

Of course, such events also affect the adults upon whom small children are dependent. Anything that reduces a parent's or caregiver's ability to cope may result in neglect of basic safety and sanitary precautions. A distraught adult is more likely than one who is not under stress to forget to put away a kitchen knife, fasten a gate, or make sure that a child washes before eating.

Poverty and Hunger   Poverty is unhealthy. In fact, studies have shown that income is the *chief* factor associated with ill health (J. L. Brown, 1987). Poor children often do not eat properly, do not grow properly, and do not get required immunizations or adequate medical care. (Figure 6-1 shows the relationship between poverty and stunted growth.) Poor families often live in crowded, unsanitary housing, and the parents may be too busy trying to feed and clothe their children to supervise them adequately.

In 1987, according to the World Food Council, as many as 730 million men, women, and children were hungry—that is, were chronically deprived of the nutrients needed for an active,

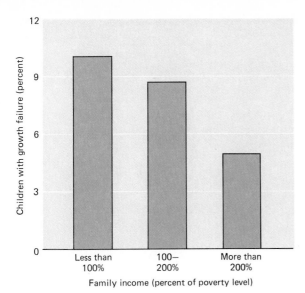

Figure 6-1 Poverty and stunted growth. The bars show percentages of children who were short for their age in the Massachusetts Nutrition Survey of 1983, in relation to their family income. Insufficient growth was approximately twice as prevalent among children whose families earned less than the poverty level as among children whose family income was double that amount. (*Source*: J. L. Brown, 1987.)

healthy life—and the number was growing by 8 million a year. Even in the relatively affluent United States, more than 33 million people were living in poverty (had less than $11,000 annual income for a family of four) in 1985. Nine percent of the population—12 million children and 8 million adults—suffered from hunger, and the problem appears to be growing worse (J. L. Brown, 1987). Minorities are especially at risk: according to the House Select Committee on Children, Youth, and Families, about 43 percent of black children and 40 percent of Hispanic children are poor, compared with fewer than 16 percent of white children.

The problems of poor children begin before birth. Poor mothers often do not eat well or receive adequate prenatal care, and their babies are likely to have low birth weight, to be stillborn, or to die soon after birth (see Chapters 2 and 3). Poor children are likely to be malnourished, and malnourished children—and their mothers—tend to be weak, lethargic, and susceptible to disease. They are apt to have such diverse maladies as lead poisoning, hearing and vision loss, and iron-deficiency anemia, as well

as such possibly stress-related conditions as asthma, headaches, insomnia, and irritable bowels. They also tend to have behavior problems, psychological disturbances, and learning disabilities (J. L. Brown, 1987; Egbuono & Starfield, 1982).

In view of the far-reaching effects of poverty and hunger on the bodies and minds of growing children, it is essential to make sure that every child has an adequate diet and adequate health care. All of society suffers when hunger and disease flourish.

MOTOR SKILLS

Children between ages 3 and 6 make important advances in motor development. When we see what 3-year-olds can do, we have to remind ourselves that they were babes in arms just 3 years earlier and have been walking for only about 2 years. One minute, Alicia puts on her older sister's tutu, stretches on tiptoe, and balances shakily on one foot; the next, she's back in overalls, riding her tricycle. With her stronger bones and muscles, greater lung power, and improved coordination between senses, limbs, and central nervous system, she can do more and more of the things she wants to do.

Large-Muscle Coordination

At 3, Greg could walk a straight line and stand on one foot—but only for a second. At 4, he could hop on one foot and could catch a ball his father bounced to him, with hardly any misses. On his fifth birthday, he could jump nearly 3 feet and was learning to roller-skate.

Such motor skills—advanced far beyond the reflexes of infancy—are prerequisites for sports, dancing, and other activities that begin during middle childhood and may last a lifetime. (See Table 6-1 on page 197 for a sampling of large-muscle skills that develop in early childhood.)

Small-Muscle and Eye-Hand Coordination

A few months ago, given a crayon and a large piece of paper, Bobbie, who is now 3, would cover the sheet with scribbles decipherable only

(© B. Mitchell 1985/Image Bank)

(© Bob Daemmrich)

(© Miro Vintoniv/Stock, Boston)

(© Tom McCarthy/Image Bank)

Children make significant advances in motor skills during the preschool years. As they develop physically, they are better able to make their bodies do what they want. Large-muscle development allows them to run, jump, and hop, while increasing eye-hand coordination helps them to use scissors or chopsticks.

TABLE 6·1 LARGE-MUSCLE MOTOR SKILLS IN EARLY CHILDHOOD		
3-YEAR-OLDS	4-YEAR-OLDS	5-YEAR-OLDS
Cannot turn or stop suddenly or quickly	Have more effective control of stopping, starting, and turning	Start, turn, and stop effectively in games
Jump a distance of 15 to 24 inches	Jump a distance of 24 to 33 inches	Can make a running jump of 28 to 36 inches
Ascend a stairway unaided, alternating the feet	Descend a long stairway alternating the feet, if supported	Descend a long stairway unaided, alternating the feet
Can hop, using largely an irregular series of jumps with some variations added	Hop 4 to 6 steps on one foot	Easily hop a distance of 16 feet

Source: Corbin, 1973.

to her. Now she can draw a nearly straight line or a recognizable circle. At 4, Chris can cut on a line with scissors, draw a person, make designs and crude letters, and fold paper into a double triangle. At 5, Ellen can string beads and copy a square.

With their small muscles under control, children are able to tend to more of their own personal needs and so have a sense of competence and independence. Bobbie, at 3, can eat with a spoon and pour milk into her cereal bowl. She can button and unbutton her clothes well enough to dress herself without much help. Therefore she can use the toilet alone and can wash her hands afterward (with some reminding). By the time she starts kindergarten, she will be able to dress without supervision. By age 2 or 3, she will have shown a preference for using one hand, probably her right; only about 1 child in 10 is left-handed.

SLEEP: PATTERNS AND PROBLEMS

The baby who sleeps virtually around the clock, waking up every 3 hours for feedings, grows into a toddler who sleeps 12 hours at night plus an hour or two in the morning and afternoon and then cuts down to one nap after lunch. At the age of 3, a youngster lies awake at nap time but, if allowed to skip the nap altogether, is quite grouchy by evening.

Sleep patterns change throughout life, and early childhood has its own distinct rhythms.

Young children generally sleep deeply through the night—more so than they will later in life (Webb & Bonnet, 1979)—and they need a daytime nap (or at least a quiet rest) until around the age of 5.

Normal Patterns

The closer children are to age 5, the more they try to prolong going to bed. They find it harder to part with a stimulating world full of people to be by themselves in their beds. Also, it takes them longer to fall asleep, and so they often try to find ways to avoid it. Parents may not like an elaborate bedtime routine, but they can reassure themselves that such behavior reflects their child's increased mastery over the environment.

Children under the age of 2 will play quietly by themselves or with a sibling before falling asleep. Slightly older children are more likely to want a light left on in their rooms or to sleep with a favorite stuffed animal or blanket (Beltramini & Hertzig, 1983). Psychologists call these objects *transitional objects,* because they help a child make the transition from the dependence of infancy to the independence of later childhood.

Kathy's parents smile at the sight of their 3-year-old peacefully clutching her teddy bear, but they also worry that she is too dependent on a *thing* to help her fall asleep. Such fears are unfounded, according to one longitudinal study, which found that 4-year-olds who insisted on taking cuddly objects to bed were outgoing, self-confident, and self-sufficient at the age of 11. They enjoyed playing by themselves and were not likely to be worriers; and at 16, they were no worse- (or better-) adjusted than boys and girls who had not needed transitional objects (Newson, Newson, & Mahalski, 1982).

Sleep Disturbances

Sometimes more serious sleep problems come on during early or middle childhood. Such problems, if they persist for a long time, may be signs of emotional difficulties.

The child who demands a light on at night may simply be trying to put off going to sleep. But if this kind of behavior continues, it may mean that the child is afraid of being left alone in the dark. Bedtime fears can be successfully treated. In one program, children who had had severe and chronic fears for an average of 5 years starting between the ages of 1 and 8 learned how to relax, how to substitute pleasant thoughts for frightening ones, and how to give themselves verbal instructions to cope with stressful situations (Graziano & Mooney, 1982).

Many children—from 20 to 30 percent of those in their first 4 years of life—engage in prolonged bedtime struggles (lasting more than an hour) and wake their parents frequently at night. The problem tends to reach its height when the children are between the ages of 2 and 4. These children are likely to have experienced such stressful phenomena as an accident or illness in the family, a depressed or ambivalent mother, or the sudden onset of a mother's regular absence during the day. In addition, they often sleep in the same bed with their parents—though this may be a reaction to, rather than a cause of, disturbed sleep (Lozoff, Wolf, & Davis, 1985).

About 1 in 4 children between the ages of 3 and 8 (most of them under 6) suffer from night-mares or night terrors (Hartmann, 1981). Nightmares are frightening dreams, often triggered by staying up too long, eating heavy meals late in the evening, or overexcitement just before going to bed. Upon awakening from nightmares, a child (or an adult) can often recall them vividly. An occasional bad dream is no cause for alarm, but frequent nightmares, especially if they produce fear or anxiety during waking hours, may signal excessive stress.

Night terrors are not connected with dreams; they apparently result from awakening suddenly from a deep sleep. Children who experience night terrors wake in an unexplained state of panic. They may scream and sit up in bed, breathing rapidly and staring ahead unseeing, yet they are not aware of any frightening dreams or thoughts. They go back to sleep quickly, and in the morning they do not remember the occurrence. These episodes, which alarm parents more than they do children, are rarely serious and usually stop by themselves.

Sleepwalking—literally, walking while asleep—is a fairly common and usually harmless disorder. About 15 percent of all children between the ages of 5 and 12 sleepwalk at least once, and some 1 to 6 percent do it regularly (T. Anders, Caraskadon, & Dement, 1980). Children who sleepwalk will typically sit up abruptly, with their eyes open; get out of bed; and move about so clumsily that they need to be protected from hurting themselves. Their surroundings should be "sleepwalk-proofed," with gates at the top of stairs and in front of windows, but nothing else needs to be done, since they will probably outgrow this tendency.

Sleeptalking—talking while asleep—is also purposeless and does not require any corrective action. It is usually difficult, if not impossible, to understand what children talking in their sleep are saying, and contrary to popular belief, it is next to impossible to engage them in conversation.

INTELLECTUAL DEVELOPMENT

At the breakfast table, Terry, aged 3½, overhears his grandparents discussing the number of square feet of tile in their kitchen. In his small voice he pipes, "But then you'd need to have square shoes!" Later that morning he takes the P from his set of magnetic letters and puts it under his doll's mattress to find out whether the doll is a real princess. He defines spareribs as

"Remember the giraffe we saw at the zoo?" Young children's ability to recognize things they have seen before is better than their ability to recall information from memory without a visual cue.

"sideways rectangle things with a bone in the middle."

Terry's growing facility with speech and with ideas is helping him form his own individual view of the world—often in ways that surprise the adults around him. During the years from age 3 to age 6, Terry becomes more competent in cognition, intelligence, language, and learning. He is developing the ability to use symbols in thought and action, and he is able to handle more efficiently such concepts as age, time, and space.

ASPECTS OF INTELLECTUAL DEVELOPMENT

Development of Memory: The Child as a Processor of Information

Until the mid-1960s, research afforded little knowledge about the workings of memory in children younger than 5. Since then, particularly as a result of the information-processing approach to the study of intellectual development, interest in the development of memory has surged.

We are beginning to have a picture of the "remembering child." From infancy on, children are processors of information, who base their actions on the information they receive and remember. They are limited, however, by their relatively small knowledge base (N. Myers &

Perlmutter, 1978). They also have a limited memory span—that is, the ability to transfer information into long-term memory or to bring it back to the "surface" of the mind, where it becomes usable. And they have an extremely limited metamemory, or understanding of their own memory processes. All these abilities flower in middle childhood (as we'll see in Chapter 8).

Recognition and Recall In a typical memory experiment, children are shown a series of small toys or pictures and then the objects are put away. The experimenter later shows the same objects again, along with new items. To test for *recognition* (the ability to identify correctly something encountered before), the children are asked to point to the items they have previously been shown. Young children do very well on this type of task; 2-year-olds identify about 80 percent of the items, and 4-year-olds recognize more than 90 percent. However, when experimenters test for *recall* (the ability to reproduce knowledge from memory) by asking the children to name the objects without seeing them again, 2-year-olds can recall only 23 percent of the items and 4-year-olds only 35 percent. The younger children tend to recall only the last object they have seen, while the older children are more likely to remember the other objects too (N. Myers & Perlmutter, 1978).

In early childhood, then, recognition ability is considerably better than in infancy, but recall is still relatively poor. Both abilities improve dramatically by the age of 5, more so than at any later time of life (N. Myers & Perlmutter, 1978; Paris & Weissberg-Benchell, cited in Chance & Fischman, 1987).

Influences on Young Children's Memory
At any age, dredging material from memory is harder than recognizing something familiar. But recall is particularly hard for young children. For one thing, their vocabulary is smaller than that of older children, and so even if they recall an item, they may not be able to name it readily. Second, they have not yet acquired much general knowledge and so in a memory test will be familiar with fewer of the items they are expected to recall. We know that general knowledge is important because young children recall material better when items bear a relation to each other which the children can understand. When 3-year-olds and 4-year-olds were shown pairs of pictures, they did much better recalling pairs that were related in some way than pairs of unrelated pictures (Staub, 1973).

Because of their limited metamemory, young children tend not to have found strategies for remembering information, or to use special methods to remember (N. Myers & Perlmutter, 1978). For example, 3-year-olds are less likely than 6-year-olds to rehearse (repeat) a list of groceries they want to buy, to help them recall the items. Interestingly, though, those 3-year-olds who *do* use this strategy can remember the items as well as the 6-year-olds do (Paris & Weissberg-Benchell, cited in Chance & Fischman, 1987).

**Cognitive Development:
Piaget's Preoperational Stage**

Although Piaget made his observations of children's intellectual development long before the recent research on memory, the growth of recall is fundamental to his description of the development of thought processes during early childhood. When children can recall events and objects, they can begin to form and use concepts—representations of things not in their present environment. And communication improves as they become able to share their representational systems with others.

Children between age 3 and age 6 are in Piaget's second major stage of cognitive development, the preoperational stage. In the United States and other western cultures, children enter this stage at about the age of 2, as they come out of the sensorimotor stage; and they move on to the third stage, concrete operations, at about age 6 or 7. (The ages at which individual children move from one stage to another may vary.)

As we saw in Chapter 4, thought begins in the sixth and last substage of the sensorimotor period, when toddlers begin to generate ideas and solve problems through mental representations. But those representations are limited to things that are physically present. The *preoperational stage* lays the groundwork for logical thinking: children can now think about objects, people, or events in their absence, by using mental representations of them, though they cannot yet manipulate those representations through logic. As we will see in Chapter 8, the latter ability is what distinguishes the stage of concrete operations.

The preoperational stage is a significant step beyond the sensorimotor period because children can learn not only by sensing and doing, but by thinking as well; not only by acting but by reflecting on their actions.

The Symbolic Function "Can I have an ice cream cone?" Nell, aged 4, begs her mother. The two of them are not in the supermarket, where a display case of frozen foods might have caught the girl's eye. Nor are they in the kitchen, where an open freezer door might have given her the suggestion. Nell is playing in the yard, it is hot, and her throat is dry. With no prompting from her sensory environment, she remembers the taste and coolness of ice cream and seeks out her mother to ask for it. This absence of sensory signals or cues is what distinguishes the *symbolic function:* the ability to learn through the use of mental representations to which, consciously or unconsciously, the child has attached meaning.

SYMBOLS AND SIGNS If there are no sensory cues, Piaget reasoned, there must be mental ones. These mental representations can be either symbols or signs. A *symbol* is an idiosyncratic (personal) mental representation of a sensory experience. Nell's symbol of an ice cream cone, for example, includes her own remembered sensations of its coldness, flavor, texture, and appearance. A *sign,* such as a word or a numeral, is more abstract; it need not have any sensory connotations. Signs are conventional rather than idiosyncratic; that is, they are socially agreed-upon representations. Not surprisingly, children at first think almost entirely in symbols. As they mature, they use signs more, and these enhance their ability to communicate with others.

In Piaget's terminology, both symbols and signs are called *signifiers,* and *significates* are what they represent to a particular child. The child's understanding of the real objects and events that symbols and signs represent is what gives these signifiers their meanings. For example, an ice cream cone may signify one thing to Nell and a different thing to Peter, who has never tasted one.

USES OF THE SYMBOLIC FUNCTION   Three ways in which children display the symbolic function are deferred imitation, symbolic play, and language. *Deferred imitation* is the imitation of an observed action after time has passed. David, aged 3, sees his father shaving. When he goes to preschool, he heads for the housekeeping corner and begins to "shave." According to Piaget, David saw the shaving, formed and stored a mental symbol of it (probably a visual image), and later—when he could no longer see it—reproduced the behavior by calling up the stored symbol.

In *symbolic play,* children make an object stand for something else. For example, in playing house, they use a doll as a symbol of a real child. Piaget's daughter Jacqueline exhibited symbolic play when she lay down on a piece of cloth that reminded her of her pillow, sucking her thumb and blinking as if closing her eyes in sleep, but laughing all the while.

It is in language that the symbolic function is most impressive. Preoperational children use language to stand for absent things and for events that are not taking place at the time. By using the words *ice cream cone* to stand for something that was not there, Nell invested her utterance with symbolic character. Language will be further discussed later in this chapter.

A child in Jean Piaget's preoperational stage can understand that a brother or sister is still the same person when wearing a Halloween costume.

Achievements of Preoperational Thought
Through the use of symbols based on recall, then, preoperational children think in new and creative ways. Although their thinking is not yet fully logical, it does show what Flavell (1977) calls a "partial logic or semilogic" (p. 72). Let us see how a child at this semilogical level of cognitive development thinks.

UNDERSTANDING OF FUNCTIONS   The preoperational child understands, in a general way, basic functional relationships between things and events in the environment. For example, Heidi knows that when she pulls the cord of a curtain, the curtain opens, and when she flicks the wall switch up, the ceiling light goes on. Although she does not yet understand that one action causes the other, she does perceive a connection between the two.

UNDERSTANDING OF IDENTITIES   Philip, aged 5, now understands certain things stay the same even though they may change in form, size, or appearance. For example, the day Pumpkin, his cat, was nowhere to be found, Philip suggested, "Maybe Pumpkin put on a bear suit and went to someone else's house to be their pet bear." When his baby-sitter questioned him about this possible turn of events, however, Philip showed that he still believed that Pumpkin would, even underneath her disguise, continue to be his beloved cat.

Philip also knows that even though he has grown and changed since he was a baby, he is still Philip. This belief is not unshakable, however, especially in the early part of the preoperational stage. At times, he may believe that if he does "girlish" things, such as wearing girls' clothes, and that if he *wants* to turn into a girl, he will be able to (DeVries, 1969). At other times he may be confused by changes in physical appearance. For example, when Philip saw his mother wearing a new pair of huge sunglasses that practically covered the top half of her face, he asked, "Who are you? " When his mother took off the glasses, he said, "Now you're Mommy."

In most instances, though, a preoperational child seems to understand that the basic nature of a thing remains the same even if it changes in some ways. For example, in a replication of one of Piaget's most famous experiments, Philip is shown two identical clear glasses, each one short and wide and each one holding the same amount of water. When the water in one of the short, wide glasses is poured into a tall, thin one, Philip, when asked, says that it is still the same water, even though its shape has changed to fit the taller glass. (However, as we'll see, he does *not* recognize that the *amount* of water is still the same.)

The preoperational child's grasp of functions and identities is an important achievement of early childhood, one that is too easily taken for granted. Heidi's and Philip's knowledge that certain events are followed by other events and that things remain what they are (even though they change in certain ways) makes the world more predictable and orderly and lets them make sense of it (Flavell, 1977).

Limitations of Preoperational Thought In some ways, of course, preoperational thinking is still rudimentary compared with what children will be able to do when they reach the stage of concrete operations in middle childhood. For example, preoperational children do not yet clearly differentiate reality from fantasy; such a child thinks and learns "by running off reality sequences in his head just as he might do in overt action" (Flavell, 1963, p. 158). Let us look at some other ways in which children in this stage are intellectually immature, according to Piaget.

CENTRATION Preoperational children tend to *centrate:* they focus on one aspect of a situation and neglect others, often coming to illogical conclusions. They cannot **decenter,** or think simultaneously about several aspects of a situation.

A classic example is the experiment with the water glass mentioned above. Piaget designed this experiment to test children's development of **conservation**—the awareness that two things that are equal in size remain so if their shape is altered so long as nothing is added or taken away. He found that children do not fully understand this principle (which builds on the idea of object permanence) until the stage of concrete operations, normally in middle childhood (see Chapter 8).

When shown the two identical short, wide glasses containing equal amounts of water, Philip is asked whether one of them has more water. He correctly answers, "They're both the same." However, after Philip watches the experimenter pour the water out of one of the short, fat glasses into a tall, thin glass, he then says that the taller glass contains more water. When asked why, he says, "This one is bigger this way," stretching his arms to show the height. Some young children, when asked the same question, will say that the wide glass contains more water. Children in this stage cannot consider height and width at the same time. They center on one or the other and so cannot solve the problem. In addition, their logic is flawed because their thinking is tied to their perceptions: if one glass *looks* bigger, they think it must *be* bigger.

IRREVERSIBILITY Preoperational children's logic is also limited by *irreversibility:* failure to understand that an operation can go both ways. If

Philip could conceptualize restoring the original state of the water by pouring it back into the other glass, he would realize that the amount of water in both glasses is the same.

Irreversibility of thought is also apparent when we ask Ellie, aged 5, whether she has a brother. She says, "Yes," but when we ask her whether her brother has a sister, she says, "No." By the age of 7 years, 60 percent of children can handle this question correctly; by the age of 9 years, 75 percent can (Piaget, 1928).

FOCUS ON STATES RATHER THAN ON TRANS-FORMATIONS   Preoperational children think as if they were watching a filmstrip with a series of static frames. They focus on successive states and are not able to understand the meaning of the transformation from one state to another. We saw this in the experiment with conservation. We also see it when we ask children to identify the successive movements of a bar that falls from an upright position to a horizontal position, as when a pencil drops after one has tried to balance it on end (Flavell, 1963). Preoperational children find it very difficult to reconstruct the various positions occupied by the quickly falling bar; they focus on the initial and final states and not on the transformations in between. This failure to understand the implications of transformations prevents them from thinking logically.

TRANSDUCTIVE REASONING   Logical reasoning is of two basic types: deduction and induction. **Deduction** goes from the general to the particular: "Eating a lot of candy can make people sick. I ate a lot of candy today, and so I may get sick." **Induction** goes from the particular to the general: "Yesterday I ate a lot of candy and felt sick. Last week I ate a lot of candy and felt sick. The same thing happened to Jeremy and Freddie. Therefore it looks as if eating a lot of candy can make people sick."

Preoperational children, according to Piaget, do not think along either of these lines. Instead, they reason by **transduction:** they move from one particular to another particular without taking the general into account. This kind of reasoning leads Adam to see a causal relationship where none actually exists: "I had bad thoughts about my sister. My sister got sick. Therefore, I made my sister sick." Because the bad thoughts and the sister's sickness occurred around the same time, Adam assumes illogically that one caused the other (compare Adam's thinking here with his confusion in Box 6-1).

EGOCENTRISM   At the age of 4, Lisa sees the ocean for the first time. Awed by the constant thundering of the waves, she turns to her father and asks, "But when does it stop?" "It doesn't," he replies. "Not even when we're *asleep*?" asks Lisa incredulously. Her thinking is so egocentric, so focused on herself as the center of her universe, that she cannot consider anything—even the mighty ocean—as having a life of its own when she is not there to see it.

Egocentrism is inability to see things from another's point of view. A classic Piagetian experiment known as the *mountain task* illustrates this kind of thinking. A child sat on a chair that faced a table holding three large mounds. The experimenter placed a doll on another chair, on the opposite side of the table, and asked the child to tell or show how the "mountains" would look to the doll. Young children could not answer the question; instead, they persistently described the mountains from their own perspective. Piaget took this as proof that they could not imagine the reality of a different point of view (Piaget & Inhelder, 1967; see Figure 6-2).

Egocentrism, to Piaget, is not selfishness, but self-centered understanding, and it is fundamental to the limited thinking of young children. Egocentrism is a form of centration: these children are so centered on their own points of view that they cannot take in another's view at the same time. Three-year-olds are not as ego-

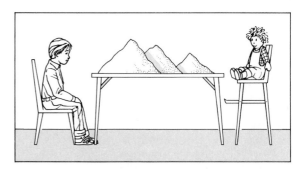

Figure 6-2   Piaget's "mountain task." A preoperational child is unable to describe the "mountain" from the doll's point of view—an indication of egocentrism.

centric as newborn babies, who cannot distinguish between the universe and their own bodies; but they still think that the universe centers on them. This inability to decenter helps explain why they have trouble separating reality from what goes on inside their own heads and why they show confusion about what causes what. When Adam believes that his "bad thoughts" have made his sister sick, he is thinking egocentrically. Egocentrism for Piaget explains why young children often talk to themselves or seem to "talk past" other people.

Egocentrism is not only an intellectual limitation but a moral limitation. Children in this stage tend to have their own sets of rules for games or behavior, which they insist are the correct ones; yet they may not follow these rules if it does not suit them. (We will further discuss moral development in Chapter 8.)

Assessing Piaget's Theory Did Piaget underestimate children's abilities? No thinker about cognitive development during early childhood has been more influential than Piaget. Yet recent research suggests that the mental powers of children he would categorize as "preoperational" may be considerably greater than he supposed.

One problem seems to have been his tendency to *over*estimate young children's comprehension of language. He assumed that wrong answers revealed faults in thinking, when the errors may actually have arisen because of the way he phrased the problems. In many of Piaget's experiments, children apparently misinterpreted tasks they were asked to do and answered questions that may not have been the ones the experimenter was asking (Donaldson, 1979).

DO YOUNG CHILDREN UNDERSTAND CAUSE AND EFFECT? Young children apparently have more understanding of cause and effect than Piaget thought. One psychologist, who looked up some of the stories that Piaget had asked children to retell, found that she had trouble remembering them herself. When she simplified them to clarify cause-and-effect connections, first-graders had no trouble retelling them correctly (Mandler, cited in Pines, 1983).

To eliminate the complicating factor of language, other researchers asked 3- and 4-year-

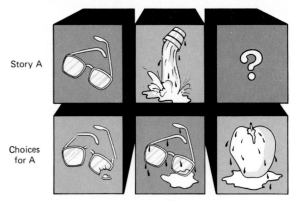

Figure 6-3 Examples of sequences to test understanding of causality. A child is asked to look at pictures like those in the top row, to pick the one in the bottom row that would show what happened, and to tell a story about what happened. (*Source:* Gelman, Bullock, & Meck, 1980.)

olds to look at pictures like those on the top in Figure 6-3, and then to choose the picture on the bottom that would tell "what happened" (Gelman, Bullock, & Meck, 1980). These children showed an understanding of causality, telling stories like: "First you have dry glasses, and then water gets on the glasses, and you end up with wet glasses."

When we listen to children talk, we hear them spontaneously using such words as *because* and *so*. "He's crying because he doesn't want to put his pajamas on—he wants to be naked," says Marie, 27 months old, watching her twin brother's bedtime struggle. Even at this early age, children seem to understand some causal relationships, long before they can answer adults' "why" questions.

HOW ANIMISTIC IS THE YOUNG CHILD? *Animism* is the tendency to attribute life to objects that are not alive. When Piaget asked children about the sun, the wind, and clouds, he received answers that led him to think that young children are confused about what is alive and what is not. Piaget attributed this to egocentrism; one child, for example, expressed the belief that the moon is alive "because we are."

However, when a later researcher questioned 3- and 4-year-olds about differences between a rock, a person, and a doll, they showed that they understood that people are alive and that rocks are not (Gelman, Spelke, & Meck, in press). They did not attribute thoughts or emotions to rocks, and they talked about the fact that dolls cannot move on their own as evidence that dolls are not alive. The confusion Piaget observed may have been due to the fact that the objects he asked about are all capable of movement and, in addition, are very far away. Since children know so little about sun, wind, and clouds, they are less certain about the nature of these phenomena than about the nature of more familiar objects like rocks and dolls.

HOW EGOCENTRIC IS THE YOUNG CHILD? Let's consider this variation on the mountain task. A child is seated in front of a square board, with dividers that separate it into four equal sectors. A figure of a police officer is put at the edge of the board. Then a doll is put into one after another of the sectors, and each time, the child is asked whether the police officer can see the doll. Another police officer is then brought into the action, and the child is told to hide the doll from both police officers. When 30 children between the ages of 3½ and 5 were given this task, they gave the correct answer or did the right thing 90 percent of the time (Hughes, 1975).

Why were these children able to take another person's point of view—in this case the police officer's—if children doing Piaget's classic mountain task were not? The difference is probably that this task involves thinking in ways that are more familiar and less abstract. Most children do not look at mountains and do not think about what other people might see when looking at a mountain. But even 3-year-olds know about dolls and police officers and hiding.

Another example—from real life rather than from the laboratory—shows a similar lack of egocentrism. When Pam opened the present Stuart gave her for her fourth birthday, she found a bag of marbles. "I already have some marbles," she said, and then added quickly, "but it's OK; I need some more." This additional remark of Pam's came because she could imagine how Stuart might feel if he thought that she did not like his gift. When children are in situations that are familiar and important to them, they are likely to show empathy—the ability to put themselves into another's place (see Box 6-1). Even 10- to 12-month-old babies often cry when they see another child crying; by 13 or 14 months, they pat or hug a crying child; by 18

months, they may hold out a new toy to replace a broken one or give a bandage to someone with a cut finger (M.R. Yarrow, 1978).

HOW WELL CAN THE YOUNG CHILD CLASSIFY? Researchers today differ with Piaget on yet another question. Piaget maintained that young children are not capable of true *classification*— the ability to sort objects according to characteristics such as size and shape. (See Figure 6-4 for the stages of classification that Piaget proposed.)

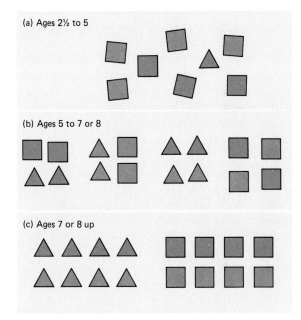

(a) Ages 2½ to 5

(b) Ages 5 to 7 or 8

(c) Ages 7 or 8 up

Figure 6-4 *Stages of classification. According to Inhelder and Piaget's research with Swiss children (1964), preoperational children do not consistently classify objects according to two characteristics, like color and shape. The studies found that children go through three stages. (a) Between 2½ and 5 years of age, they may group items to form a design such as a house; or they may group them according to changing criteria—a child may put blue and red squares in the same pile and then add a red triangle because it is the same color as the red square. (b) From age 5 to age 7 or 8, children group items according to similarity but may use inconsistent criteria, sorting some groups by color and others by shape or size. Preoperational children may subclassify—for example, they may put all the triangles together and then divide them into red triangles and blue triangles. (But children of this age are likely to say that there are just as many triangles in all as there are red triangles.) (c) Finally, at the stage of concrete operations, children are able to classify according to an overall plan and to understand the relationships between classes and subclasses.*

Other research indicates that many 4-year-olds can classify things according to either one or two criteria (Denney, 1972).

In her studies of American children, Denney (1972) showed pieces of cardboard of different shapes, colors, and sizes to 2-, 3-, and 4-year-olds and asked them to put the things that were alike or the things that went together in groups. On the basis of their responses, she proposed a series of stages different from Piaget's: first, *inability to group according to similarity;* second, *partial grouping by similarity;* and third, *complete grouping by similarity.* She found that almost two out of three 4-year-olds (23 out of 36) sorted on the basis of complete similarity.

In explaining the difference between her findings and Piaget's, Denney suggests that American children today may be able to classify at an earlier age because they learn about color, shape, and size from television and in preschools.

CAN COGNITIVE ABILITIES BE ACCELERATED? The results of efforts to teach specific cognitive abilities show that such programs do seem to work—when the child is already on the verge of acquiring the concept being taught—and that certain kinds of training are more effective than others.

In one attempt to teach conservation (D. Field, 1981), 3- and 4-year-olds were shown various arrangements of items such as checkers, candies, jacks, sticks, and rods. The child was asked to pick the two rows that had the same number of items or to show which two objects were the same length. Then the objects were moved or changed in some way, and the child was asked whether they were the same as before (see Figure 6-5).

The child was then given one of three verbal rules to explain why items that did not appear the same might *be* the same:

- *Identity,* or sameness of the materials: "No matter where you put them, they're still the same candies."
- *Reversibility,* or the possibility of returning the items to their original arrangement: "Look, we just have to put the sticks back together to see that they are the same length."
- *Compensation,* or showing that a change in one

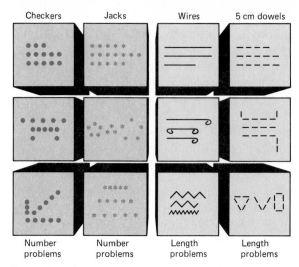

Figure 6-5 Sample of conservation training problems. In these experiments, the child was shown arrangements of items like those in the top row, then shown rearrangements of the same objects (as in the second or third row) and asked whether they were the same. The child was then told why they were the same on the basis of identity, reversibility, or compensation. Identity was the strongest concept for teaching conservation. (*Source:* D. Field, 1977.)

dimension was balanced by a change in the other: "Yes, this stick does go farther in this direction, but at the other end the other stick is going farther, and so they balance each other."

The children who were given the identity rule made the most progress in learning the principle of conservation. Those who learned reversibility also advanced, but those who were taught compensation benefited little from the training.

The importance of cognitive readiness is demonstrated by the fact that the 4-year-olds were more apt than the 3-year-olds to learn the concept and to retain it up to 5 months later. The 3-year-olds were not as able to conserve as many quantities and tended to lose whatever abilities they did gain, as evidenced by follow-up testing. The researcher suggested, therefore, that this kind of training benefits children only when their intellectual structures are well enough developed to handle the principle of conservation; the training then gives them a strategy for integrating it into their thought processes. The strategy also appears to work because it is useful in everyday life (D. Field, 1981).

Such experiments suggest that children of the ages corresponding to the preoperational stage are more competent than Piaget believed. They do, of course, have more cognitive limitations than children in the next higher phase of development, which Piaget identified as the concrete operations stage. However, when faced with tasks compatible with what they are familiar with and explained in language they understand, they show more competence than they do on traditional Piagetian tasks. Our estimation of young children's intellectual abilities has changed for the better as a result of new, more appropriate research techniques.

Development of Language

"Why is the sky?" "When is tomorrow?" "Where do clouds go?" Young children are interested in the whole wide world, and they ask questions about everything—partly because they are hungry for knowledge and partly because they quickly learn that "why" questions will always keep a conversation going. They can give and follow simple commands—when they want to—and they can name familiar things, such as pets, body parts, and people.

Command of Words, Sentences, and Grammar
Speech becomes more adult once children pass the age of 3. Children over 3 use plurals and past tense, and they know the difference between *I, you,* and *we.*

Between the ages of 4 and 5, children's sentences average four to five words. They can now deal with prepositions like *over, under, in, on,* and *behind.* They use verbs more than nouns.

Between the ages of 5 and 6, children begin to use sentences of six to eight words. They can define simple words, and they know some opposites. They use more conjunctions, prepositions, and articles.

Between 6 and 7 years of age, children's speech becomes quite sophisticated. They now speak in grammatically correct compound and complex sentences, and they use all parts of speech.

Although young children speak fluently, understandably, and fairly grammatically, they often make errors by failing to note exceptions to rules. A mistake like saying "holded" instead of "held" or "hurted" instead of "hurt" is a normal sign of progress in learning a language. Younger children correctly say, "I held the baby" or "I hurt myself," but at that point they are merely repeating expressions they have heard. When children begin to discover rules (such as adding *-ed* for past tense), they tend to overregularize—to use the rule on all occasions. That works perfectly well most of the time, but not with irregular verbs, such as *to hold* and *to hurt.*

Parents smile at the cuteness of such expressions as "holded" and rarely bother to correct them. Eventually, as children hear people talking and take part in conversations themselves, they notice that *-ed* is not always used to form the past tense of a verb. Thus we might think of such "mistakes" as a case of taking one step backward in order to take two steps forward.

Speaking to Communicate
The form and function of speech are linked. As children master words, sentences, and grammar, they communicate more effectively.

Social speech is intended to be understood by someone other than the speaker. It takes into account the needs of other people and is used to establish and maintain communication with them. It must be adapted, then, to the other

Children in a sandbox may avoid fights over toys or territory by claiming their own possessions in no uncertain terms. Even very young children use social speech to communicate their feelings and thoughts to others.

TABLE 6-2 DEVELOPMENT OF SOCIAL SPEECH

AGE	CHARACTERISTICS OF SPEECH
2½	Beginnings of conversation: Speech is increasingly relevant to others' remarks. Need for clarity is being recognized.
3	Breakthrough in attention to communication: Child seeks ways to clarify and correct misunderstandings. Pronunciation and grammar sharply improve. Speech with children the same age expands dramatically. Use of language as instrument of control increases.
4	Knowledge of fundamentals of conversation: Child is able to shift speech according to listener's knowledge. Literal definitions are no longer a sure guide to meaning. Collaborative suggestions have become common. Disputes can be resolved with words.
5	Good control of elements of conversation.

Source: E.B. Bolles, 1982, p. 93.

person's speech patterns and behavior (Garvey & Hogan, 1973). It may take the form of questions and answers or other means of exchanging information, or it may involve criticism, commands, requests, or threats (Piaget, 1955).

Piaget characterized most of young children's speech as egocentric (not adapted to the listener), but recent research suggests that children's speech is quite social from an early age (see Table 6-2). Indeed, it may make sense to regard children as *sociocentric* right from birth (Garvey & Hogan, 1973). When 3- to 5-year-olds were asked to communicate their choice of a toy, they behaved very differently with a person who could see and with one who could not. They were likely to point to the toy for a sighted listener, but to describe it to a blindfolded listener (Maratsos, 1973). Four-year-olds speak "motherese" (see Chapter 4) to 2-year-olds (Shatz & Gelman, 1973). Even 2-year-olds use a great deal of social speech as they point out or show objects to each other or to adults. Most of the time (almost 80 percent in one study), the feedback they get shows that they have captured their listeners' attention (Wellman & Lempers, 1977).

Children's general knowledge affects their ability to communicate. Asked to describe a variety of pictures, 4½-year-olds did very well on simple, familiar subjects like monkeys and people but not on abstract designs (Dickson, 1979).

Even youngsters as old as 14 were unable to describe unusual designs clearly enough for others of their age to understand (Krauss & Glucksberg, 1977).

Research suggests, however, that when children do not communicate with others, it is usually not because they are unable but because they do not intend to. Indeed, it is becoming clear that children's speech can serve different but equally important functions—as we see in Box 6-2, on *private speech.*

Development of Intelligence

Measurement of Intelligence: The Stanford-Binet and Wechsler Scales Because the child of 3, 4, or 5 has become quite proficient with language, intelligence tests can now include verbal items. As a result, tests taken from this age on produce more stable results than the largely nonverbal tests used in infancy (see Chapter 4). As children approach their fifth birthday, there is a growing correlation between their intelligence scores and those they will achieve later on (Bornstein & Sigman, 1986; Honzik, Macfarlane, & Allen, 1948).

Children of this age are easier to deal with in a testing situation than infants and toddlers, but they still need to be tested individually rather than with the group tests used for older children (see Chapter 8).

BOX 6-2 FOOD FOR THOUGHT

PRIVATE SPEECH

As Sergei, who is 4 years old, picks up his friend Dorri's art book, he says quietly to himself, "Now I can use this—I washed my hands so now they're clean and I can hold this book." As he jumps on Dorri's bed, he says—also to himself—"I have to take my shoes off to do this. I took them off, so now I can jump."

Private speech—talking aloud to oneself with no intent to communicate with others—is normal and common in early and middle childhood. Twenty to sixty percent of what children say at these ages consists of private utterances, which may range from playful rhythmic repetition (similar to babies' babbling) to the kind of "thinking out loud" Sergei does or barely audible muttering.

Psychological theorists have disagreed on the function of private speech. The behaviorist John Watson saw it as inappropriate behavior that parents, through socialization, eventually get their children to stop. Piaget defined it as egocentric speech reflecting inability to recognize another person's viewpoint and therefore inability to communicate. Piaget believed that young children talk while they do things because they do not yet fully differentiate between words, or signs, and what the words represent.

Rather than regarding private speech as irrelevant to communication (as Watson did) or as indicating unreadiness for communication (as Piaget did), Vygotsky (1962) saw it as a special *form* of communication: communication with oneself. Like Piaget, he believed that private speech helps children integrate language with thought. But unlike Piaget, he believed that private speech *increases* through the early school years, as children use it to guide and master their actions, and then fades away as they establish internal control through silent thought.

A number of studies support that observation. Kohlberg and his colleagues, observing nearly 150 children 4 to 10 years old, found that not only did private speech rise and fall with age, but the most sociable children used private speech the most—apparently confirming Vygotsky's view that private speech is stimulated by social experience (Berk, 1986; Kohlberg, Yaeger, & Hjertholm, 1968). Its use peaked earliest—around age 4—for the brightest children and between ages 5 and 7 for the average child; it was virtually nonexistent by age 9.

Kohlberg's sample was middle-class. A recent study (Berk & Garvin, 1984) of low-income 5- to 10-year-olds in the Appalachian mountains of Kentucky found a similar but slower pattern; 25 percent of the children (especially boys) in this stern, largely nonverbal culture still used private speech at the age of 10. The Appalachian youngsters talked to themselves the most when they were trying to solve difficult problems and no adults were around.

If private speech guides behavior and helps children think, then children who talk out loud in school are not necessarily "naughty" or weak in self-control, and forbidding such behavior may slow their learning (Berk, 1986).

Egocentric speech (that is, socially directed speech which fails to get its message across) made up less than 1 percent of the Appalachian children's language. In another study, Berk found almost no egocentric speech among 3- to 5-year-old lower- and middle-class children in a small midwestern city (Berk, 1986). That is, when young children tried to communicate with other people, they were almost always able to make themselves understood.

(© Gregory K. Scott 1986/Photo Researchers)

A home full of books and toys is a key factor in this boy's intellectual growth. Parents who provide an enriched environment for learning are most likely to have children with high IQs.

Two important individual tests for measuring intelligence in early childhood are the **Stanford-Binet Intelligence Scale** and the **Wechsler Preschool and Primary Scale of Intelligence (WPPSI).**

The Stanford-Binet test takes 30 to 40 minutes. The child is asked to give the meanings of words, to string beads, to build with blocks, to identify the missing parts of a picture, to trace mazes, and to show an understanding of numbers. The intelligence quotient, or IQ (see Chapter 4), yielded by the Stanford-Binet test is supposed to measure practical judgment in real-life situations, memory, and spatial orientation.

The WPPSI, an hour-long test used with children aged 4 to 6½, yields separate scores for verbal and performance IQs as well as a combined score called the *Full Scale IQ*. Eleven subtests are grouped into the two separate scales; they are similar to those in the Wechsler Intelligence Scale for Children (see Chapter 8). Because children of this age tire quickly and are easily distracted, the test is sometimes given in two separate sessions.

How Parents Influence Children's Intellectual Achievement How well children do on intelligence tests may be influenced by many factors, including their temperament, the match between their cognitive style and the tasks they are asked to do, their social and emotional maturity, their ease in the testing situation, and their socioeconomic status and ethnic background. (We'll examine the latter two factors in Chapter 8.) One of the most important influences of all is a child's parents.

PROVIDING AN ENVIRONMENT FOR LEARNING Is there something special that parents who raise bright children do? On the basis of the results of many studies (Clarke-Stewart, 1977), we can draw a picture of the parents of young children who score high on intelligence tests and whose IQs *increase* during the early childhood years. Although much of this research focuses on mother-child interaction, it suggests that there are a number of ways in which either parent can help children grow intellectually.

Parents of children with higher IQs are sensitive, warm, and loving. They are very accepting of their children's behavior, letting them express themselves and explore. When they do want to change certain aspects of their children's behavior, they use reasoning or appeals to feelings rather than enforcing rigid rules. They use relatively sophisticated language and teaching strategies, and they encourage their children's independence, creativity, and growth by reading to them, teaching them to do things, and playing with them. The children respond by expressing curiosity, being creative, exploring new situations, and doing well in school.

A test has been devised to measure how a child's home environment encourages intellectual growth. It is called the *Home Observation for Measurement of the Environment* (appropriately, HOME), and it is remarkably accurate in predicting children's IQs on the basis of specific aspects of the surroundings in which they spend their infancy and early childhood.

A statistical analysis compared HOME scores

for low-income 2-year-olds with the same children's Stanford-Binet scores at the age of 4 (Stevens & Bakeman, 1985). The researchers found that the single most important factor in predicting which children would have the highest intelligence scores was the mother's skill in creating and structuring an environment for learning. (This same factor was identified by the Harvard Preschool Project, discussed in Chapter 4, as a major influence on children's competence.) Mothers whose children later had high IQs were likely to be those who provided books and toys that encouraged conceptual thinking and language development. These mothers read to their children regularly, paid attention to their play, and got involved in it. The mothers of children with higher IQs also talked with their children more and punished them less than did the other mothers. Mothers who had a high educational level *and* provided an enriched environment were even more likely to have children with high IQs.

Although the study did not consider the father's role (in fact, there was no father present in three-fourths of the households), it seems safe to conclude that a parent—either mother or father—who draws on his or her own background and interests to provide challenging, pleasurable learning opportunities for the child can lay a foundation for optimum intellectual growth.

THE FATHER'S ROLE Although most studies of parents' influence on children's intellectual development have concentrated on the mother's role, some research does reflect the increasing awareness of the father's impact. Radin (1981) has reviewed this literature; unless otherwise noted, all material in this section is drawn from that source.

The father influences his children not only through the genes he furnishes, but also through the way he feels and acts toward the children, the kind of relationship he has with their mother, and his position in the family structure. Probably because of sons' identification with their fathers (which we'll discuss in Chapter 7), fathers seem to exert more influence on their sons than on their daughters. As young boys take on their fathers' attitudes, values, roles, gestures, and emotional reactions, they also pick up their fathers' styles of thinking, their problem-solving strategies—even the very words they use. Boys are especially likely to imitate fathers who are nurturant and approving and who are seen as strong but do not dominate or intimidate.

A father's influence on his daughter is more complex, but girls whose fathers show interest in their intellect and allow them some autonomy seem to do best. Neither boys nor girls develop as well intellectually when their fathers are strict, dogmatic, and authoritarian.

Given the importance of the father, what happens when there is no father in the home? Each family's situation is different, of course, but a father's absence does seem to inhibit children's cognitive development. Boys who lose their fathers before the age of 5 do less well in mathematics than boys who have fathers (Shinn, 1978); so do girls who lose their fathers before the age of 9 (Radin, 1981).

The mother's reaction to a father's death or to a separation or divorce is likely to affect her child's response. So will any resulting changes in the family's financial situation. Economic hardship—often a direct result of the loss of a father—can handicap children's intellectual as well as physical and emotional development.

Much of the research on the father's absence was done at a time when single-parent families were rarer than they are today. Now that this lifestyle is becoming more common, some of its disadvantages, such as social stigma and the lack of male models and other support systems, may be diminishing. Sometimes a supportive stepfather, an older brother, a grandfather, or an uncle helps to make up for the lack of a father.

THE MOTHER'S ROLE: WHEN MOTHERS ARE EMPLOYED What if the mother works outside the home—as 60 percent of mothers now do by the time their youngest child is 4 years old (Hayghe, 1986)? Overall, the cognitive as well as social and emotional development of preschool children seems to be at least as good when mothers are employed as when they are not (Hoffman, 1979; Zimmerman & Bernstein, 1983). But when we look at boys and girls separately, the picture changes.

Some research suggests that mothers' employment tends to have a negative effect on their sons. Middle-class boys—but not girls, and not boys in lower-income families—seem to have poorer academic achievement when their mothers work. This is especially true when mothers work full time during their sons' preschool years. Daughters of working mothers tend to be more independent and to have a more positive attitude toward being female (Bronfenbrenner, Alvarez, & Henderson, 1984).

What accounts for these differences? Recent interviews with 152 parents of 3-year-olds suggest a possible explanation: that children's intellectual development may be affected by the way their parents view them. And working parents—when the mother is well educated and works full time—are likely to regard young boys less positively than young girls. Both the women and their husbands praised girls as competent and self-reliant but described boys as disobedient and aggressive. The parents' attitudes may reflect professional women's aspirations for their daughters, as well as boys' tendency to be more active and to require more parental supervision and control (Bronfenbrenner et al., 1984).

A follow-up analysis indicated that the parents' view of the child—and thus, arguably, the child's intellectual advancement—may be influenced by the mother's attitude toward her roles. Both husbands and wives described their 3-year-olds (of both sexes) less favorably when the mothers worked out of necessity rather than out of choice and felt conflict between the demands of work and home. This was particularly true for women of limited education who worked full time. Part-time working mothers' more positive attitudes toward both their sons and their daughters may have derived from their greater ease in balancing work and child care (Alvarez, 1985).

We must be careful in interpreting such results, however. Although the attitudes the parents expressed toward their sons and daughters seem to mesh with the earlier findings about differences in boys' and girls' development when mothers work, the studies did not actually demonstrate a link; further investigation is needed. (We will discuss gender-role differences more fully in Chapter 7, and the effects of parents' working in Chapter 9.)

THE WIDENING ENVIRONMENT

As important as parents are in a child's life, they are by no means the only environmental influence on intellectual development during early childhood. Today more young children than ever spend part or most of the day in day care, preschool, or kindergarten.

Trends in Early Childhood Care and Schooling

The difference between preschool and day care lies in their primary purpose. Preschool, which has existed since early in the twentieth century, is designed to provide educational experiences for young children and emphasizes their developmental needs; typically, a session lasts only two hours or so. Day care meets the need for a safe place where children can be cared for, usually all day, while their parents are at work or school.

Today the distinction between day care and preschool is blurring. Good day care centers seek to meet children's intellectual and emotional needs, while many preschools have extended their day to meet the needs of the growing number of families with working mothers.

Kindergarten is the traditional introduction to formal schooling for 5-year-olds, an optional year of transition between the relative freedom of home or preschool and the structure of the primary grades. But during the past 20 years, the kindergarten curriculum has changed in response to demands in society for accelerated academic achievement, and some communities are experimenting with all-day kindergarten.

On the basis of the success of compensatory early education for disadvantaged children, some educators advocate compulsory public schooling for 5-year-olds and even for 4-year-olds. But some experts on early childhood worry about the effects of hurrying young children's intellectual growth.

Let's look at these trends in more detail.

Day Care

The need for good day care is reaching crisis proportions. More than half of all American children under 6 years old have employed

TABLE 6-3 PRIMARY CHILD CARE ARRANGEMENTS USED BY EMPLOYED MOTHERS FOR CHILDREN UNDER 5

FORM OF CARE	PERCENT OF MOTHERS MAKING ARRANGEMENT
Care in child's home:	31.0
By father	15.7
By grandparent	5.7
By other relative	3.7
By nonrelative	5.9
Care in another home:	37.0
By grandparent	10.2
By other relative	4.5
By nonrelative	22.3
Organized child care facilities	23.1
Day or group care center	14.0
Nursery school or preschool	9.1
Kindergarten or grade school	0.7
Parent caring for child*	8.1

*Includes mothers working at home or away from home.
Source: U.S. Bureau of the Census, 1987.

mothers, and this figure is expected to reach two-thirds by 1995, according to the National Institutes of Health (AAP, 1986a). About 60 percent of working mothers with children under the age of 5 use some form of day care outside the home, either in someone else's home or at group care centers (see Table 6-3). The demand for day care is so great that parents who cannot afford private care often have to wait up to 2 years to get their children into sub-sidized programs (AAP, 1986c).

What Is Good Day Care? Good day care is, as much as possible, like good parenting. It is char-acterized by small groups; a high adult-to-child ratio; and a stable, competent, highly involved staff trained in child development and sensitive to the needs of very young children. It requires caregivers who are sensitive to children's needs; authoritative but not overly restrictive; stimulat-ing; and affectionate (Belsky, 1984). In such a setting, children may not only thrive physically but become more capable intellectually and more secure emotionally. (See Box 6-3, page 214, for suggestions on how to find a good day care progam.)

What Are the Benefits of Good Day Care? Al-though the literature on the effects of day care is growing rapidly, much of what we know about day care comes from studies of high-quality, well-funded university-based centers. Consider-able research shows that children in these good day care programs do at least as well, both phys-ically and cognitively, as those who are raised at home. Studies suggest that high-quality day care can enhance emotional development, too, and may even improve relationships with the par-ents. Parents may feel less stress because their child is well cared for while they earn needed income and because they get some relief from the demands of parenting.

Day care centers in which children have plenty of opportunities to interact with adults and other children can enhance linguistic skills. In Bermuda—where, by the age of 2, eighty-four percent of children spend most of the work week in day care—166 children from nine cen-ters were tested for language development. The children did better on the tests in centers where caregivers spoke to them frequently and en-couraged them to initiate conversations (Mc-Cartney, 1984).

Children from low-income families or stress-ful home environments are the ones most likely to benefit from good day care. Although the average child in a good program is not much affected for better or for worse, disadvantaged

BOX 6-3 PRACTICALLY SPEAKING

HOW TO CHOOSE A GOOD DAY CARE CENTER

The quality of day care varies enormously. A licensed center meets minimum state standards for health, fire, and safety, but many centers and home care facilities are not licensed or regulated. Furthermore, licensing does not tell anything about the program's quality (American Academy of Pediatrics, AAP, 1986c).

What makes a day care center good? Children get the best care when they interact in small numbers with small numbers of adults. When groups are too large, adding more adults to the staff does not help. It does not seem to matter how many years of formal education adult caregivers have had. What does matter is how much they have specialized in a child-related field, such as developmental psychology, early childhood education, or special education. Adults with such special training give better care, and children in their care do better on tests of school readiness skills (Abt Associates, 1978).

Here are some things to look for in deciding whether to use a particular day care facility (AAP, 1986c).

DOES THE CENTER . . .

■ Provide a safe, clean setting?

■ Use trained personnel who are warm and responsive to all children?

■ Promote good health habits?

■ Offer a stimulating environment to help children master cognitive and communicative skills?

■ Encourage children to develop at their own rate?

■ Nurture children's self-confidence, curiosity, creativity, and self-discipline?

■ Stimulate children to ask questions, solve problems, make decisions, and engage in a variety of activities?

■ Foster children's social skills, self-esteem, and respect for others?

■ Help parents improve their skills in raising children?

■ Promote cooperation between parents, personnel, public and private schools, and the community?

BE WARY IF THE PROGRAM . . .

■ Is not licensed or registered with the state

■ Refuses to let parents visit unannounced

■ Employs staff members who are not educated, trained, or experienced

■ Is overcrowded, unclean, or inadequately supervised

■ Does not have enough heat, light, or ventilation

■ Has no written plans for meals or emergencies

■ Has no smoke alarms, fire extinguishers, or first aid kit

■ Does not designate separate areas for playing, feeding, resting, and diapering

■ Has no policy on managing injuries, infections, or children who are sick

■ Does not have a medical consultant

children in good programs tend not to show the declines in IQ often experienced by such children when they reach school age. Children in day care may be more motivated to learn (AAP, 1986c; Belsky, 1984; Bronfenbrenner, Belsky, & Steinberg, 1977).

These findings need to be qualified, however, by an understanding of their limitations. First, some of the studies had serious flaws in methodology and did not follow children long enough to determine long-range effects. Second, most children in the United States are cared for in their own homes or other people's homes by relatives, neighbors, or paid caretakers, but almost all the research has been about group care in day care centers. More important, as we've pointed out, almost all this research was carried out in centers of exceptionally high quality, although most of the care that children actually receive is run-of-the-mill at best.

(© Michael Salas 1986/Image Bank)

Children in day care centers where they have much opportunity to interact with caring adults develop stronger linguistic skills than those in centers that do not provide such opportunities.

Preschool

One of the reasons for the rapid growth of day care has been the scarcity of affordable preschools. Preschools have flourished in the United States since 1919, when the first public nursery schools were established. Many preschools are privately run and serve mainly well-educated, affluent families. More and more public schools, however, are moving into preschool education. As a result, preschool enrollment has grown dramatically since 1970, even in the face of a sharp decline in the birthrate (see Table 6-4). According to the U.S. Bureau of the Census, one-third of preschool programs—which altogether now enroll approximately 2.5 million children—are run by public schools.

How Good Preschools Foster Development

Jenny, 4 years old, scoots around in a wheelchair, 3 weeks after breaking her leg in a sled-

ding accident. She is already back at school making paper placemats, finger-painting, and building block towers. Like many other children at good preschools, Jenny wants to be sure not to miss anything. For her, a day without school is incomplete.

A good preschool gives children a new world to explore outside their homes and many choices of activities, which enhance their sense of autonomy and help them learn about themselves. Because these activities are tailored to their interests and abilities, children experience many successes that build their confidence and self-image.

Preschool is particularly valuable for only children and children who—like many children today—have just one sibling. By playing with other children, they learn to cooperate and become less egocentric. And when cooperation turns into conflict, they learn to deal with frustration, anger, and hurt feelings.

Some preschools stress social and emotional growth. Those based on the theories of Piaget or the Italian educator Maria Montessori have a strong cognitive emphasis. Whether or not these preschools teach the alphabet and numbers (some early childhood educators believe that the alphabet and numbers should wait at least until kindergarten), they provide experiences that enable children to learn by doing. They stimulate children's senses through art, music, and

TABLE 6·4 SCHOOL ENROLLMENT AS A PERCENTAGE OF ALL CHILDREN IN EACH AGE GROUP		
	3 AND 4 YEARS OLD (%)	5 AND 6 YEARS OLD (%)
1970	20.5	89.5
1980	36.7	95.7
1984	36.3	94.5

Source: National Center for Education Statistics, 1986.

tactile materials such as clay, water, and wood. They encourage children to observe, to talk, to create, and to solve problems—activities that lay the foundation for more advanced intellectual functioning.

Above all, children in good preschools find that school is fun, that learning is satisfying, and that they themselves are competent.

The Montessori Method The remarkably successful system that Dr. Maria Montessori designed to teach poor and retarded Italian children has spread rapidly in the United States, where Montessori schools are often attended by normal children of the affluent.

The Montessori curriculum is child-centered, based on respect for the child's natural abilities. It focuses on motor, sensory, and language education. To help children realize their full potential, they enter a "prepared environment," a carefully planned arrangement of surroundings, equipment, and materials in which they advance in a graduated sequence from the simple to the complex. Children learn from their own experiences, with the guidance of skilled teachers who provide support and help and who observe when children are ready to move on to the next phase. Students select their own materials, which are designed so that they themselves can tell whether they are using them correctly. The method fosters moral development by emphasizing order, patience, self-control, responsibility, and cooperation.

Compensatory Preschool Programs for Disadvantaged Children Children from deprived socioeconomic backgrounds often enter school with a considerable handicap. Their parents—caught up in the daily struggle for survival—may not have spent much time talking with them, answering their questions, or telling them stories. These children, unlike their more fortunate age-mates, may never have seen a book and rarely a crayon or toy. They may never have been outside their own neighborhoods. During the past 3 decades, large-scale programs have been developed to help such children compensate for the experiences they have missed and to prepare them for the challenge of school.

PROJECT HEAD START The best known compensatory preschool program in the United States is *Project Head Start,* which was launched in 1965 as a major weapon in the federal government's war against poverty. Its founders felt that providing health care, intellectual enrichment, and a supportive environment to the children of low-income families could improve their social competence, their everyday effectiveness in dealing with the present and in preparing for the future. Now, more than 20 years later, the program has provided services to well over 8 million children and their families. Still, it reaches fewer than one-fourth of the nation's poor 3- and 4-year-olds.

A comprehensive review (R.C. Collins & Deloria, 1983) showed that Head Start has lived up to its name. Head Start children have shown substantial intellectual and language gains, with the neediest children benefiting the most. Still, Head Start children have not equaled the average middle-class child in performance either in school or on standardized tests.

One reason why Head Start children do better in school than they might otherwise have done is that they are absent less. They are healthier than other youngsters from impoverished homes, are more likely to be of average height and weight, and do better on tests of motor control and physical development.

The most successful Head Start programs have been the ones with the most participation by parents, as well as the best teachers, the smallest groups, and the most extensive services. In many cases the positive effects have gone beyond the children themselves; families report educational and financial gains and an increased sense of satisfaction with and control over their lives.

LONG-TERM BENEFITS OF COMPENSATORY PRESCHOOL EDUCATION Research shows that compensatory preschool education can have a number of long-term benefits—and that the kind of program matters. Children enrolled in good programs show long-lasting gains that repay society's initial investment in their future.

Increases in IQ were short-lived, but some of the positive effects of Head Start have held up through high school. Head Start students are less likely to be held back and more likely to stay in school and to be in regular rather than special

(© Bob Daemmrich)

Kindergarten today has become much like first grade. Children may spend more time working on skills like word recognition than in creative activities and free play.

classes than are needy children who have not participated in Head Start programs (L.B. Miller & Bizzel, 1983).

An influential study followed two groups of poor black children from early childhood through age 19. One group attended intensive preschool classes for 2½ hours a day when they were 3 and 4 years old. The other group had no formal schooling until kindergarten or first grade. Those who had had preschool education were less likely to require special education for slow learners; and they were much more likely at age 19 to have finished high school, to have enrolled in college or vocational training, and to have jobs. They did better on tests of competence and were less likely to have been arrested, and the young women were less likely to have become pregnant (Clement, Schweinhart, Barnett, Epstein, & Weikart, 1984).

The study inspired a number of states and school districts to inaugurate programs for early childhood education. But a warning against too strong an academic emphasis in preschool came from a more recent longitudinal study by the same research group (Schweinhart, Weikart, & Larner, 1986).

This time, the researchers compared low-income youngsters who had been placed in three different types of preschool programs. One stressed social and emotional development and activities initiated by the child; one was a highly structured, teacher-directed program where children were taught to recognize numbers, letters, and words; and the third took a middle ground. All three groups did better in elementary school than children with no preschool experience. The children who had been in the academic program outperformed the others by narrow margins, but they had more behavior problems. And by the time they were 15 years old, they tended to have lost interest in school and to have developed serious social and emotional problems, including vandalism and delinquency.

Thus, although early childhood education can help to compensate for deprivation, we need to keep in mind the developmental needs of young children for play, exploration, and freedom from undue demands. Today, similar questions are being raised about the benefits of different kinds of education for 5-year-olds.

Kindergarten

In many ways, kindergarten is an extension of preschool, but there are differences. Kindergarten is usually held in a neighborhood public school and thus marks the beginning of "real" school. During the past 2 decades, kindergarten has become more like first grade. Many kindergartners today spend less time on freely chosen activities that stretch their muscles and imaginations, and more time on worksheets and learning to read (Egertson, 1987).

The push for more academic content comes partly as a result of findings about previously unsuspected learning capacities of young children and partly in response to parents' anxiety about their children's future. At a time of growing concern about illiteracy and the quality of the educational system, schools have bowed to pressures from parents and society for children to learn more and learn earlier.

To cover its expanded curriculum, kindergarten in some communities has been extended from a morning or an afternoon program to a full elementary school day (Ames, 1984). Studies on the effects of all-day kindergarten are mixed (Robertson, 1984; Rust, cited in Connecticut Early Childhood Education Council, CECEC, 1983). Advocates claim that a full-day program carefully designed around the needs of young children can provide ample time to sharpen skills at a child's own pace, without sacrificing play, movement, stories, music, and art (CECEC, 1983). But 5-year-olds often tire by the middle of a long day, and they need time to run around outside and to play with friends.

Some 5-year-olds have not yet developed the physical coordination or cognitive readiness to form numbers or to identify beginning and ending sounds. Although tests of readiness identify children who would be better off entering kindergarten or first grade a year later, some par-

ents whose children "fail" these tests feel that there is something wrong with their child, and the children's sense of competence may suffer. On the other hand, some parents, to avoid pressure on their children, opt to keep them out of kindergarten until the age of 6. This "graying" of kindergarten reinforces the tendency to raise the level of the curriculum (Egertson, 1987).

Some psychologists, worried about the short-term and long-term effects of accelerated formal schooling, cite evidence that "hurrying" young children is stressful (Elkind, 1981, 1987a). And educators who maintain that young children learn differently from older children warn that pencil-and-paper tasks are not as nurturing to the young intellect as creative, open-ended activities (CECEC, 1983; Egertson, 1987).

We know that many 5-year-olds—and even some younger children—can be taught that 2 times 2 equals 4, just as we know that 9-month-old infants can be taught to recognize words printed on flash cards. But unless the motivation comes from *them,* or the learning arises naturally from their experience, their time might be better spent on the business of early childhood: on the concrete sensory activities that help young children make sense of their world and on the widening network of social interactions that, as we'll see in Chapter 7, help children to define their emerging identities.

SUMMARY

Physical Growth and Change

■ Physical growth increases during the years from 3 to 6, but more slowly than during infancy and toddlerhood. Boys are on average slightly taller and heavier than girls.

■ The muscular, skeletal, nervous, respiratory, circulatory, and immune systems are maturing, and all primary teeth are present.

■ Proper growth and health depend on nutrition. Children eat less than before; a balanced diet of essential nutrients is important.

Health

■ Minor illnesses help build immunity to disease

and may also have cognitive and emotional benefits.

■ Major contagious illnesses are rare when children receive vaccinations.

■ Accidents are the leading cause of death in childhood and most commonly occur in automobiles or at home.

■ Factors such as exposure to other children, stress in the home, and poverty and hunger increase children's risk of illness or injury.

Motor Skills

■ Motor development advances rapidly during early childhood. Children progress in large- and small-muscle and eye-hand coordination.

- By the time they are 6, children can tend to many of their own personal needs.

Sleep: Patterns and Problems

- Sleep patterns change during early childhood, as they do throughout life. Young children tend to sleep through the night, take one daytime nap, and sleep more deeply than later in life.
- It is normal for children close to age 5 to develop bedtime rituals that delay going to sleep. However, prolonged bedtime struggles and nighttime fears may indicate emotional disturbances that need attention.
- Night terrors, nightmares, sleepwalking, and sleeptalking may appear in early childhood.

Aspects of Intellectual Development

- Studies of memory development indicate that recognition ability is better than recall ability in early childhood, but both abilities increase during this period. Recall is required for the processing and use of information.
- According to Piaget, the child is in the preoperational stage of cognitive development approximately from 2 years of age to 7 years. Because of the development of recall, thought is not limited to events in the immediate environment as in the sensorimotor stage. But the child cannot yet think logically as in the next stage, concrete operations.
- The symbolic function—as shown in deferred imitation, symbolic play, and language— enables children to mentally represent and reflect upon people, objects, and events through symbols and signs.
- Preoperational children can understand basic functional relationships and the concept of identity. However, they confuse reality and fantasy, they are unable to decenter, they reason transductively, and they do not understand reversibility and the implications of transformations. They are unable to conserve.
- Research shows that in some ways, Piaget may have underestimated abilities of the children he described as "preoperational." They seem better able to understand causal relationships and classification than he thought, and they appear to be less animistic and egocentric. Researchers

have been able to teach conservation when children are mature enough to grasp it.
- During early childhood, speech and grammar become fairly sophisticated. Speech is of two main types: social and private.

  1 Social speech is intended to communicate with others. Piaget characterized much of early speech as egocentric, but recent research indicates that young children engage in social speech more than was previously thought.

  2 Private speech—children's talking aloud to themselves—is not intended to communicate to the listener but appears to help children gain control over their actions. Private speech usually disappears by age 9 or 10.

- Since psychometric intelligence tests for young children (such as the Stanford-Binet Intelligence Scale and the Wechsler Preschool and Primary Scale of Intelligence) include verbal items, they are better predictors of later IQ than tests of infants are.
- Intelligence test scores are influenced by factors such as social and emotional development and parent-child interaction.

The Widening Environment

- Many children between 3 and 6 years of age attend day care centers, preschool, and kindergarten. Some of these programs are changing to meet the needs of working parents, as well as children's intellectual and other developmental needs.
- Little is known yet about the effects of most day care. Studies of the highest-quality day care suggest that good day care enhances children's social and emotional development.
- Preschool and kindergarten prepare children for formal schooling. Some programs focus more on structured cognitive tasks, and others, on activities of the children's initiating. In the past 20 years, the academic content of the kindergarten curriculum has increased.
- Evaluations of compensatory preschool programs demonstrate that they can have long-term positive outcomes. However, it is important not to put too much academic pressure on children 3 and 4 years old.

KEY TERMS

animism (page 204)
centrate (202)
classification (205)
conservation (202)
decenter (202)
deduction (203)
deferred imitation (201)
egocentrism (203)
induction (203)
irreversibility (202)

preoperational stage (200)
private speech (209)
Project Head Start (216)
recall (199)
recognition (199)
sign (201)
social speech (207)
Stanford-Binet Intelligence Scale (210)

symbol (200)
symbolic function (200)
symbolic play (201)
transduction (203)
transitional objects (197)
Wechsler Preschool and Primary Scale of Intelligence (WPPSI) (210)

SUGGESTED READINGS

Hechinger, F. M. (Ed.). (1986). *A better start: New choices for early learning.* Ypsilanti, MI: High/Scope. A useful guide for teachers, parents, and administrators to the many alternatives now available for giving all young children a better start.

Iwamura, S. G. (1980). *The verbal games of preschool children.* New York: St. Martin's. A study of two children's speech as they traveled to and from nursery school. It is an unusually good source for getting a sense of what preschool children actually say.

Pomeranz, V. E., with Schultz, D. (1984). *The first five years: The relaxed approach to child care.* New York: St. Martin's. A sensible, reassuring book addressed to parents by a pediatrician and a medical writer.

Piaget, J., & Inhelder, B. (1969). *The psychology of the child.* New York: Basic Books. Piaget's own summary of his theory of cognitive development. Piaget and his longtime collaborator Barbel Inhelder trace the stages of cognitive development from infancy through adolescence.

Scarr, S. (1984). *Mother care/other care.* New York: Basic Books. An optimistic report of child-care alternatives that reflects Professor Scarr's belief that children can thrive under a variety of arrangements. This book is designed to assist parents in making appropriate child-care decisions and is of particular value for mothers who work outside their homes.

Schickedanz, J. A. (1986). *More than the ABCs: The early stages of reading and writing.* Washington, DC: National Association for the Education of Young Children. A thoughtful, easy-to-read illustrated manual to help parents and caregivers lay the foundation for literacy in the early childhood years—not through formal lessons but by giving language "a playful, interesting, useful, and joyous place in all children's lives, both at home and at school."

Wood, D., McMahon, L., & Cranstoun, Y. (1980). *Working with under fives.* Ypsilanti, MI: High/Scope. Analysis of tape-recorded conversations, with extensive quotations, of 24 British nursery teachers and play-group workers and the children in their charge. The workers show their individual working styles, and the analysis points up behavior patterns effective in stimulating children's competence. The book is one of six in the Oxford Preschool Series, a landmark study of the care of British children under the age of 5 conducted under the direction of the American psychologist Jerome Bruner.

7

CHAPTER

PERSONALITY AND SOCIAL DEVELOPMENT IN EARLY CHILDHOOD

Children's playings are not sports and should be deemed as their most serious actions.

Montaigne, *Essays*

- How do various theories explain important personality developments of early childhood?

- How do boys and girls identify their sex, and how does their identification affect their personalities and standards of behavior?

- What kinds of play do children engage in?

- What accounts for common fears in early childhood, and what can be done about them?

- What influences lead to aggressive or to altruistic behavior among young children?

- How do parents' child-rearing practices influence young children's personality development?

- How do young children get along with their siblings, and how do they begin to form friendships?

At the age of 1 year, Steven loved to bang on the tiny red piano that he got for his birthday. At 2, he was climbing onto the bench at the big piano in the living room and enjoying the wider range of sounds he could produce on its keys. And by his third birthday, he was able to pick out nursery tunes with an unerring ear while sitting on a phone book, his feet dangling above the pedals.

Usually Steven gets along very well with his friend Kevin, as the boys build with wooden blocks or turn old boxes into carriers. They do fight sometimes, though, as they did when Kevin unloaded sand from his dump truck into the tunnel Steven was digging and Steven retaliated by throwing sand in Kevin's face. Kevin is an important presence in Steven's life. After the boys buried Kevin's dead goldfish, for example, Steven refused to eat fish for months. At about the time of his fourth birthday, though, his parents took him to New Orleans, where he tasted shrimp bisque for the first time and loved it.

"He's becoming a real person," his father says.

What does it mean to become a real person? It means that Steven is developing a sense of himself as someone different from Kevin or anyone else, with his own traits, his own likes and dislikes, and his own ideas about what he wants to do and believes he ought to do. This sense did not come to Steven overnight on his third or fourth birthday; his basic temperament, for example, showed up quite clearly soon after birth. Nor is the process anywhere near complete; there are some important issues about his identity that Steven will not focus on until adolescence and beyond. But now, in early childhood, he has left behind the days of passive infantile dependence, he is coming out of the "no"-for-its-own-sake stage, and he has begun to show definite signs of his unique personality. He is also becoming a more social being, defining himself through his relationships with others.

We'll begin this chapter by examining several theoretical views of these developments of early

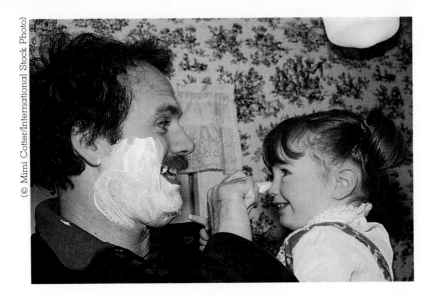

(© Mimi Cotter/International Stock Photo)

This young girl playfully interacting with her father is learning that males shave their faces but females do not. Awareness of what it means to be a girl or a boy shapes personality and behavior in many subtle and not-so-subtle ways.

childhood. Then we'll look at various aspects and issues of personality development during this period of the life span. Differences between the sexes begin to surface at this age, as children identify themselves and others as male or female; and so we'll first consider how gender affects personality. Next we'll consider play. Young children express their budding personalities and social skills, as well as their cognitive abilities, in play—and in fact play is what they spend most of their time doing. We'll also examine fearfulness, aggression, and altruism in young children; how parenting affects children's competence and moral development; and how children get along with their brothers and sisters and form their first friendships.

PERSONALITY IN EARLY CHILDHOOD: THEORETICAL VIEWS

Timmy sometimes goes to the library with his grandfather. One afternoon the librarian teasingly asks, "Can you read?" and hands him an open volume of Shakespeare. Timmy is momentarily taken aback by this book without pictures, but then in perfect imitation of his grandfather he pats all his pockets and says, "I must have left my glasses at home."

Timmy's action illustrates an important personality development: *identification,* the adoption by a child of the characteristics, beliefs, atti-

tudes, values, and behaviors of another person or of a group. Between the ages of 3 and 6, a boy normally forms a strong identification with his father or another male, while a girl normally identifies with her mother or another female. Some psychologists believe that this identification largely shapes children's moral codes as well as their understanding of what is expected of members of each sex.

The sex we are born with is a key element of our identity. It is usually one of the first things people want to know about us at birth and one of the first things others notice about us throughout our lives. It affects how we look, what we wear, and how we work and play. It influences what we think about ourselves and what others think of us. All those characteristics—and more—are included in what we refer to when we use the word *gender:* what it means to be male or female.

How do young children achieve *gender identity*—awareness of their maleness or femaleness? How do they develop standards of socially and morally correct behavior? And how do other important aspects of personality development take place? Let's see what insights several theoretical perspectives can give us: the psychoanalytic theories of Sigmund Freud and Erik Erikson; the social-learning theories of Albert Bandura, Jerome Kagan, and others; and the cognitive theories of Lawrence Kohlberg and Sandra Bem.

Freud's Psychosexual Theory: The Phallic Stage

Anatomic differences between girls and boys and between adults and children fascinate 3- to 6-year-olds. They want to find out how adults "make" babies. "Dirty" jokes fill their conversation (though more of these still seem to be centered on the bathroom than on the bedroom).

Why do children of this age behave this way? The Freudian explanation is that they have entered the **phallic stage,** when the chief source of biological gratification—which previously centered on the mouth and then on moving the bowels—shifts to the genital area. The phallic stage is named for the phallus, or penis. (The fact that Freud gave the name of the male organ to a stage that applies to girls as well as boys shows his male orientation.)

Because of the sexual focus of children's feelings at this time, the nature of their attachments changes. Freud attributed the change to the Oedipus and Electra complexes, which he believed to be the central forces in male and female personality development, underlying the anxieties and fears that commonly arise at this age. An important result of the resolution of these forces is the emergence of the superego, the part of the personality that monitors the child's behavior.

Oedipus Complex Freud's concept of the **Oedipus complex**—a young boy's sexual attachment to his mother and rivalry with his father—is named after an ancient Greek myth in which Oedipus kills his father and marries his mother. Freud believed that a boy in the phallic stage has sexual fantasies about his mother and murderous thoughts about his father, whom he sees as a competitor for her love and affection. Unconsciously, the little boy wants to take his father's place, but he recognizes his father's power. The child is caught up in conflicting feelings—genuine affection for his father, tempered by hostility, rivalry, and fear. Noticing that little girls do not have a penis, he wonders whether something has happened to it; and his guilt over his feelings for his mother and father makes him worry that his father will castrate him. This tangle of overwhelming fear and guilt is called the **castration complex.** Because of it, the boy represses his sexual strivings toward his mother, stops trying to rival his father, and begins to identify with him. This *identification with the aggressor* relieves the boy's anxiety: the powerful enemy is now an ally.

Electra Complex The **Electra complex**—the female's counterpart of the Oedipus complex—involves sexual attachment to the father and rivalry with the mother. It is named after a Greek legend in which Electra, a king's daughter, helps her brother kill their mother to avenge the murder of their father.

According to Freud, little girls' desire for their fathers stems from **penis envy,** the desire for a penis, which they notice on their brothers or male playmates and recognize as larger and therefore superior to their own anatomic equipment.

Whereas a little boy fears the loss of his penis, a little girl assumes that she has already had one and lost it. She blames her mother for this imagined castration and envies her father because he has the organ she wants. But eventually the girl, realizing that she cannot have a penis, wishes instead for a child, and with this aim, she now sees her father as a love object and becomes jealous of her mother. Freud viewed the very desire for motherhood, then, as the result of penis envy. He claimed that a woman's procreative urge is most fully satisfied by the birth of a son, who brings the penis she longs for.

According to Freud, a little girl cannot be satisfied. If she succumbs to penis envy, she hopes to get a penis for herself and become a man. If she denies her envy, she is likely to have emotional problems in adulthood. Either way, she feels inferior.

Realism eventually forces a girl to give up the idea of replacing her mother. Instead, she identifies with her and thus vicariously achieves the coveted relationship with her father. Her attachment to her father and jealousy of her mother tend to persist, though—at least until she has a man and a man-child of her own.

In Freud's scenario, then, identification results from repression or abandonment of the wish to possess the parent of the opposite sex; and the achievement of identification puts the child into the next stage, latency.

Development of the Superego The identification with the aggressor that occurs at the end of the phallic stage, around the age of 5 or 6, permits the creation of the *superego,* the aspect of the personality that represents the values communicated by the parents and other agents of society. The process by which these values are incorporated is called **introjection.** Operating unconsciously, for the most part in response to fear, the superego internalizes parental rules of right and wrong. Freud believed that girls' moral development is incomplete—they cannot develop as strong a superego as boys because they do not fear castration.

The superego, then, is the last part of the personality to develop, after the id and the ego (discussed in Chapter 5). The superego tries to prevent the id from acting on its impulses. The ego acts as a mediator. It tries to find ways to gratify the id while accommodating the demands of the superego.

The superego consists of positive and negative parts:

■ *Ego-ideal* defines the "shoulds": behavior we aspire to, receive approval for, and feel proud of.
■ *Conscience* defines the "should-nots": behavior we are punished for and feel guilty or ashamed about.

In early childhood, the superego is rigid. The daughter of parents who value cleanliness may become so compulsive that she will want to change her clothes six times a day. A little boy may be tormented with guilt because he has fought with a friend, even though his parents do not disapprove of harmless tussling. With maturity, the superego becomes more realistic and flexible, allowing people to consider their self-interest.

Evaluating Psychosexual Theory After taking a bath with her male cousin and noticing his penis, a little girl said to her mother at bedtime, "Isn't it a blessing he doesn't have it on his face?" (Tavris & Offer, 1977). Freudian thinkers would dismiss the girl's remark as a defense against her true feelings of penis envy.

But a critic recently claimed on the basis of Freud's unpublished correspondence that Freud himself may have fallen prey to an elaborate defense mechanism. The letters suggest that Freud had doubts about having discarded an earlier theory that his patients were actually victims of their parents' sexual advances (Masson, 1984). The resistance and disbelief that Freud's initial "seduction" theory met apparently led him to look into his patients' psyches for an explanation of the traumatic events they described. The Oedipus and Electra theories were the result.

Although there are many moments in children's development in which their parents can detect what might be considered Oedipal feelings, there is little scientific evidence for Freud's concept of penis envy (Matlin, 1987). Women who are proud of their sexuality reject the *phallocentric* idea that the penis is the ideal for both sexes. Karen Horney, a psychoanalyst who began as a disciple of Freud, contended that the male's social status is more enviable than his reproductive organ and that boys are as likely to experience "womb envy"—envy of a woman's ability to conceive and bear children—as girls are to experience penis envy.

Thus, bold and imaginative as Freud's ideas were, many psychologists today consider them to be of limited value in explaining the personality issues of childhood.

Psychosocial Theory: Erikson's Approach

Though Erikson accepts Freud's concept of the superego and its Oedipal origins, he sees the central issues of early childhood as social rather than sexual. The child's fantasies of mastery and guilt—enacted largely through play—are not limited to the genital area.

Crisis 3: Initiative versus Guilt In Chapter 5, we discussed Erikson's view of how babies deal with issues of trust and how toddlers deal with issues of autonomy. Erikson's third crisis—*initiative versus guilt*—is a conflict between children's urge to form and carry out goals and their moral judgments of what they want to do.

Like Freud, Erikson sees a moral faculty emerging in early childhood as a result of identification with the powerful parents. A split occurs between the part of the personality that remains an exuberant child, eager to try new things and test new powers, and the part that is becoming an adult, constantly examining the propriety of the child's motives and actions and punishing the child for sexual fantasies and "bad" behavior. Thus, in playing house, a child may play the roles of both a "naughty" child and an admonishing father.

If the crisis is resolved well, children acquire the *virtue of purpose:* "the courage to envisage and pursue valued goals, uninhibited by the defeat of infantile fantasies, by guilt and by the foiling fear of punishment" (1964, p. 122). They can then develop into adults who combine spontaneous enjoyment of life with a sense of responsibility. If the crisis is not resolved well, children may become guilt-ridden and repressed—they may turn into adults who inhibit their own impulses and are self-righteously intolerant of others'. In extreme cases, they may suffer from psychosomatic illness, impotence, or paralysis. On the other hand, if initiative is overemphasized, they may feel that they must be constantly achieving.

Erikson calls on parents to help children strike a healthy balance: to let them do things on their own but to provide guidance and set firm limits. (This is the goal of the authoritative child-rearing style, described later in this chapter.)

Evaluating Psychosocial Theory As we pointed out in Chapters 1 and 5, Erikson's theory (like Freud's) is based not on scientifically controlled research but on his psychoanalytic training and on his personal and clinical experience. He has been criticized for failing to take into account the differing effects of social and cultural influences on males and females. Nevertheless, his broad view of the issues of human development provides a helpful structure for interpreting behavior at different stages throughout life.

Social-Learning Theory: Observing and Imitating Models

Freud stresses biology, and Erikson, society and culture, but both agree that parents have a vital impact on a child's psyche. Social-learning theorists also stress the parents' role, but in a different way. These theorists hold that children *learn,* from watching their parents and other adults, what it means to be male or female and what kinds of behavior are right and proper.

How Identification Takes Place Whereas Freud viewed identification as the resolution of the Oedipal conflict, social-learning theory sees identification as the consequence of observing and imitating a model. Most typically, one's model is a parent, but children can also model themselves after a grandparent, an older brother or sister, a teacher, a baby-sitter, a baseball player, or a television personality. Children usually pick up characteristics from several different models, whom they choose on the basis of how much power a person seems to have and how nurturant, or caring, the person is (Bandura & Huston, 1961).

According to Jerome Kagan (1958, 1971), four interrelated processes establish and strengthen identification:

1 *Wanting to be like the model.* For example, children may want to be like a sports hero whose strength and agility they wish to have.
2 *Acting like the model.* In play and in conversation, children often adopt the mannerisms, voice inflections, and phrasing of the model. Many parents are startled to hear their own words and tone of voice come out of the mouth of a small child.
3 *Feeling what the model feels.* Children often experience emotions like those the model exhibits. For example, when a little girl sees her mother cry after an out-of-town relative's death, the girl cries too, not for someone she barely knew, but because her mother's sadness makes her feel sad.
4 *Believing that they are the model.* Children believe that they look like the model, tell jokes like the model, walk like the model. Identification with a parent is often reinforced by other people's comments ("You certainly have your father's eyes!").

Through identification, then, children come to believe that they have the same characteristics as a model. Thus, when they identify with a nurturant and competent model, children are pleased and proud. When the model is inadequate, the child may feel unhappy and insecure.

Effects of Identification According to social-learning theory, young children generally identify with the parent of the same sex; and when they imitate that parent, they are reinforced. A little boy sees that he is physically more like his father than like his mother. He imitates his father (especially when he sees him as nurturant, competent, and powerful) and is rewarded for acting "like a boy." Morally acceptable behavior is learned in the same way, by imitation and reinforcement. By the end of early childhood, these lessons are largely internalized; the child no longer needs frequent praise or punishment or the presence of a model to sustain socially appropriate behavior.

Evaluating Social-Learning Theory Although social-learning theory seems to make sense, it has been hard to prove. Children do imitate adults, but not always adults of their own sex (Maccoby & Jacklin, 1974; Raskin & Israel, 1981)—as you may have noticed if you've ever seen a little girl put on her father's hat or a little boy, his mother's shoes. Often children do not imitate a parent at all. When children are tested for similarity to their parents, they are found to be no more like them than like other parents chosen from a random group; and those who do score as similar to their own parents score no closer to the parent of the same sex than to the other parent (Hetherington, 1965; Mussen & Rutherford, 1963).

Furthermore, studies cast doubt on the reinforcement aspect of social-learning theory, at least as it applies to gender. Although, as we will see later in this chapter, parents do treat their sons and daughters somewhat differently, in some respects the differences in treatment are not great; indeed, many parents feel that it is quite appropriate for boys to play with dolls and for girls to play with trains. Parents of young children punish fighting and reward helpfulness in both boys and girls (Maccoby & Jacklin, 1974), though fathers are more likely to encourage "masculine" or "feminine" behavior (J. H. Block, 1978).

Social learning may have something to do with children's acquisition of gender identity and behavioral standards. But simple imitation and reinforcement seem to be inadequate explanations for how this comes about.

According to social-learning theory, children often choose models they see as powerful, and they adopt the characteristics of their models, particularly those of the same sex. This boy wants to be strong and muscular like a firefighter.

Cognitive-Developmental Theory: Mental Processes

Marcy figures out that she is something called a "girl" because people call her a girl. She figures out the kinds of things girls are supposed to do, and she does them—just as she figures out how light switches and drapery cords work. In other words, she learns her gender in the same way she learns about everything else in her world—by actively thinking about her experience. This is the cognitive-developmental theory proposed by Lawrence Kohlberg (1966).

Moral development, too, depends on cognition, according to cognitive-developmental theory. Young children's moral judgment is limited by their inability to shift perspective (a sign of their egocentrism) and so their morality must be based on external constraints and rigid rules. (We will discuss this view of moral development in more depth in Chapter 8.)

Gender Identity and Gender Conservation

To learn their gender, according to Kohlberg, children do not depend on adults as models or dispensers of rewards and punishments; instead, they actively classify themselves and others as male or female and then organize their lives around their gender.

Gender identity—awareness of being male or female—may begin at about age 2 (the end of Piaget's sensorimotor stage); by 3 years of age, according to Kohlberg, most children have a firm idea of which sex they belong to. A 3-year-old boy, for example, will object strenuously if someone teases him by telling him, "You're a girl."

Gender conservation—children's realization that their sex will *always* stay the same—usually arrives sometime between the ages of 5 and 7. At age 3, this awareness may not be present—as was clear in the case of Eric, who told his mother, "When I grow up, I want to be a mommy just like you so I can play tennis and drive a car."

According to Kohlberg, differences in behavior follow the establishment of gender identity; thus the reason behind Marcy's preference for dolls and dresses is not the approval she gets for those preferences (as social-learning theory claims) but her cognitive awareness that such things are consistent with her thinking of herself as a girl.

Evaluating Cognitive-Developmental Theory

Research supports the theory that gender concepts and cognitive development are linked, though the timing has been found not to coincide fully with Kohlberg's. Children as young as 2 years old can classify pictures as "boys" or "girls," or "mommies" or "daddies." By the age of 2½, children can tell which pictures they themselves resemble, and they know whether they will be fathers or mothers when they grow up (S. K. Thompson, 1975).

Studies using anatomically correct dolls, or flip pictures dressed in different ways, show that young children tend to rely on externals such as clothing and hairstyles rather than on genitals and body build to recognize gender. They are likely to believe that a boy doll can become a girl doll by putting on a skirt, or that a girl can become a boy by cutting her hair (Emmerich, Goldman, Kirsch, & Sharabany, 1976). The understanding that a person's gender remains constant even though physical appearance may change (this is similar to Piaget's conservation principle, discussed in Chapters 6 and 8) develops as children get older (Emmerich, Goldman, Kirsch, & Sharabany, 1977).

Cognitive-developmental theory has a few weaknesses. If gender-related behavior does not occur until a firm sense of gender identity is established around the age of 3, why do children younger than that age often choose "gender-appropriate" activities? More important, why—of all the differences among people—do children pay attention to sex in establishing the classifications by which they make sense of their world? Gender-schema theory attempts to answer that question.

Cognitive-Social Theory: Gender Schema

What Is a Schema? Gender-schema theory, proposed by Sandra Bem (1983, 1985), is a variation on cognitive-developmental theory that also draws from the social-learning approach. In Bem's theory, a *schema* (which is similar to what Piaget called a *scheme*) is a mentally organized pattern of behavior that helps a child sort out perceived information. Bem believes that children organize information around the principle of gender because they notice that their society defines and classifies people that way. Girls get tea sets for their birthdays; boys get wagons. In school, the girls line up first for the water fountain. At recess, the boys head for the ball field.

Thus, as children observe what boys and girls are supposed to be and do—the society's gender schema—they construct a self-concept which fits that schema. In other words, they adopt for themselves the social definitions of male and female. Out of the full range of human attributes, children learn which ones are relevant to their sex and which are not. In the United States, for example, boys learn that it is important to be strong and aggressive, while girls learn that it is important to be sympathetic. Children learn to judge their own behavior and to measure their self-esteem by those social standards.

Changing the Schema Since the gender schema is culturally determined, Bem believes that it is possible to help children substitute other schemata. One is the *cultural-relativism schema,* the understanding that people in different cultures have different beliefs and customs. Another is the *sexism schema,* which holds that "the view of women and men conveyed by fairy tales, by the mass media—and by the next-door neighbors—is not only different, but wrong" (Bem, 1983, p. 615; see Box 7-1).

Evaluating Cognitive-Social Theory When it comes to gender, cultural relativism has little effect. Although it is true that in a few cultures women are expected to be strong and aggressive, in almost all cultures men are more aggressive than women (Maccoby, 1980).

The idea that a culture's gender schema can be deliberately changed has been tested in Israel, with mixed results (see Box 7-3 later in the chapter). And although the past 20 years have brought major changes in the way men and women—and boys and girls—in the United States think, feel, and act about gender, in many respects the customary patterns persist. In the next section, we will look at those patterns and see how they have been changing.

ASPECTS AND ISSUES OF PERSONALITY DEVELOPMENT

How Gender Affects Personality

Two 4-year-olds, Wendy and Michael, are neighbors. When they were infants, their mothers wheeled them together in the park. They learned to ride tricycles at about the same time and pedaled up and down the sidewalk, often colliding with each other. They go to preschool together.

Wendy and Michael have followed very similar paths. But there is a definite difference between them: their sex. They are anatomically distinct, with unlike internal and external sexual organs. How much difference does being a girl or a boy make in a child's development?

How Different Are Girls and Boys? Anatomy is not all that distinguishes Wendy and Michael.

They are different in size, strength, appearance, physical and intellectual abilities, and personality. Which of their differences are due to the fact that Wendy is a girl and Michael is a boy, and which are simply differences between them as two individual human beings? As we discuss this question, we need to distinguish between *sex differences,* which we define as the physical differences between males and females; and *gender differences,* which may or may not be based on biology.

We saw in Chapters 2 and 3 that physical differences between baby boys and girls are slight (boys are slightly larger and more vulnerable), and other differences are virtually nonexistent before the age of 3, except for some evidence that boys are more active. Differences become more pronounced after that; but boys and girls, on the average, are "more alike than they are different" (Maccoby, 1980). Knowing a child's sex will not let us predict whether that individual boy or girl will be faster, stronger, smarter, more confident, or more of a leader than another child.

A review of more than 2000 studies (Maccoby & Jacklin, 1974) found only a few marked gender differences. The cognitive differences that are well established—girls' superior verbal ability and boys' superior mathematical and spatial abilities—are very small, according to statistical analysis (Hyde, 1981) and do not begin to show up until after the age of 10 or 11.

Personality differences, too, are few. Both boys and girls, for example, become attached to their parents.

The clearest gender difference, which shows up in early childhood, is that males tend to be more aggressive. Boys play more boisterously; they roughhouse more, they fight more, and they are more apt to try to dominate other children and challenge their parents. Girls are more likely to cooperate with their parents and to set up rules (such as taking turns) to avoid clashes with playmates (Maccoby, 1980). Boys become involved in conflict more often and are more apt to use force or threats of force to get their way, while girls tend to try to defuse conflicts by persuasion rather than confrontation (P.M. Miller, Danaher, & Forbes, 1986).

Girls are more likely to be empathic, that is, to identify with other people's feelings (M. Hoff-

TABLE 7-1 GENDER DIFFERENCES

CATEGORY	BOYS	GIRLS
Physical differences	Are slightly larger and heavier. Are more physically vulnerable.	Mature more quickly.
Cognitive differences	Show slight mathematical and spatial superiority after age 10 or 11.	Show slight verbal superiority after age 10 or 11.
Personality differences	Are more aggressive. Play boisterously. Dominate other children. Challenge parents. Threaten or use force.	Are more cooperative. Set up rules to avoid conflict. Use persuasion, not confrontation. Are more empathic. Are more responsive and helpful to younger children.

Sources: Adapted from Maccoby, 1980; Maccoby & Jacklin, 1974; P.M. Miller, Danaher, & Forbes, 1986.

man, 1977). And girls are more apt to respond to and help babies and younger children (Maccoby, 1980). (We will further discuss aggressive and helping behavior later in this chapter.)

We need to be careful not to overemphasize such differences; they are statistically small and are valid for large groups of boys and girls but not necessarily for individuals. Some girls love rough play, and some boys hate it. But despite the rarity of observable differences between the sexes (see Table 7-1 for a summary), both males and females *believe* that they are more different than they actually are (Matlin, 1987). Where does that belief come from, and what are its effects?

Attitudes toward Gender Differences When Wendy and Michael play house, she, as the "mommy," is likely to play at cooking and taking care of the baby while Michael puts on a hat and "goes to work." When he comes home, sits at the table, and says "I'm hungry," Wendy drops what she is doing to wait on him. This scenario would be less surprising if both Wendy's and Michael's mothers did not work outside the home and if both their fathers did not do a fair amount of the housework. These children have absorbed the gender roles of their culture.

GENDER ROLES AND GENDER TYPING *Gender roles* are the behaviors, interests, attitudes, and skills that a culture considers appropriate for males and females and expects them to fulfill. By tradition, American women are expected to devote most of their time to their roles as wives and mothers, while men are supposed to devote most of their time to being breadwinners. Those roles include certain personality expectations: for example, that women are compliant and nurturant while men are active and competitive.

Gender-typing is a child's learning of the appropriate gender role. Children acquire gender-typing early, through the socialization process; the brighter they are, the faster they learn it. Bright children are the first to notice the physical differences between the sexes and the expectations of their society for each sex and to attempt to live up to those expectations (S.B. Greenberg & L. Peck, personal communication, 1974).

Children become increasingly gender-typed between the ages of 3 and 6. In preschools, little girls are likely to be found in the housekeeping corner while boys play with toy bulldozers and cranes.

It may be that strong gender-typing in early

childhood helps children develop gender identity. Ultimately, individuals vary in the degree to which they take on the customary gender roles. Perhaps children can be more flexible in their thinking about gender differences only after they know for sure that they are male or female and will always remain so.

GENDER STEREOTYPES   Unfortunately, gender-typing frequently leads to *gender stereotypes:* exaggerated generalizations about male or female behavior. These myths about differences between the sexes result in false assumptions that individuals will conform to gender roles: for example, that a male is bound to be aggressive and independent while a female is passive and dependent.

Stereotyped attitudes are found in children as young as age 3. The children in one study described babies in different ways, depending on whether the baby was identified to them as a girl or a boy. They were more likely to call a "boy" big, a "girl" little; a "boy" mad, a "girl" scared; a "boy" strong, a "girl" weak (Haugh, Hoffman, & Cowan, 1980).

Gender stereotypes restrict children's views of themselves and their future. As recently as 1975, boys and girls between the ages of 3 and 6 had quite different expectations for their adult lives. The boys looked forward to a wide range of active careers, while the girls saw themselves mainly as mothers, nurses, or teachers (Papalia & Tennent, 1975).

Gender stereotypes restrict people in their simplest, most everyday endeavors as well as in far-reaching life decisions. Children who absorb these stereotypes may become men who will not prepare a baby's bottle or wind yarn, or women who "can't" nail boards together or bait a fish hook (Bem, 1976). Because they view certain activities as unmasculine or unfeminine, people often deny their natural inclinations and abilities and force themselves into ill-fitting academic, vocational, or social molds.

ANDROGYNY: A NEW VIEW OF GENDER   Convinced that the wholesale acceptance of gender stereotypes prevents both men and women from achieving their potential, Bem (1974, 1976) maintains that the healthiest personalities have a balance of positive characteristics from among those thought appropriate for males and those thought appropriate for females. A person having such a balance—whom Bem would describe as *androgynous*—might well be assertive, dominant, and self-reliant ("masculine" traits), as well as compassionate, sympathetic, and understanding ("feminine" traits). Androgynous men and women are free to judge a particular situation on its merits and to act on the basis of what seems most effective rather than of what is considered appropriate for their gender.

(© Carol Palmer/Picture Cube)

Is it "sissyish" for a boy to embroider? Such gender stereotypes are harmful because they prevent people from following their natural inclinations and abilities.

BOX 7-1 FOOD FOR THOUGHT

INOCULATING CHILDREN AGAINST GENDER STEREOTYPES

In the United States today, women carry briefcases as well as babies, men push strollers as well as wheelbarrows, and many social institutions are trying to overcome gender stereotypes that restrict children's view of their capabilities. For example, preschools recruit male teachers to show children that men, too, can be nurturers. The doll corner is now the family corner, and it is stocked with tools as well as dishes. The emphasis in school, in the media, and in the family is less on what *boys* or *girls* can do than on what *children* can do.

Nevertheless, children do absorb subtle or blatant gender stereotypes still present in the culture. The following suggestions are adapted from those that Sandra Bem (1983, 1985) recommends for parents who want to "inoculate" their children against these harmful stereotypes. Although these suggestions have not been experimentally tested for effectiveness, they seem to make good sense.

According to Bem, parents should:

- *Be models of nonstereotyped behavior.* Share or alternate tasks such as bathing the baby or keeping household accounts.

- *Give children nonstereotyped gifts.* Boys can get dolls; girls can get trucks.

- *Expose children to men and women in nontraditional occupations.* Children who know that Aunt Alice is a plumber and that Dad's friend Joe is a nurse are unlikely to think that plumbers have to be male and nurses female.

- *"Censor" young children's reading and television viewing.* Select books and programs that are not stereotyped.

- *Emphasize anatomy and reproduction as the main distinctions between males and females.* Divert children's attention from traditional gender-typed clothing and social behavior.

As we saw in discussing Bem's gender-schema theory, she believes children can be taught to substitute other schemata for the prevailing schema in the culture. Box 7-1 lists some of Bem's suggestions to parents for counteracting gender stereotypes and substituting androgynous ideals.

How Do Gender Differences Come About?
Are gender roles the result of natural differences, or are they merely customs? Some people insist that the root of gender differences is biological. But many psychologists besides Bem believe that the cultural environment, as interpreted to young children through their parents and the media, is at least as influential.

We have already looked at several theoretical explanations for how children acquire gender identity and gender-typing. Some of these theories emphasize nature; some emphasize nurture. Now let's see what research tells us. As usual, we'll find that the answer is not either-or.

BIOLOGICAL INFLUENCES   One physical difference between the sexes is hormonal balance. Although (as we saw in Chapter 2) there is a chromosomal difference between male and female zygotes, embryonic body structures are identical in appearance until about 5 or 6 weeks after conception. At that time, androgens (male sex hormones, including testosterone) flood the bodies of embryos destined to be males. These hormones trigger the formation of male body structures, including the sex organs. If little or no testosterone is present, female body structures begin to form about 11 or 12 weeks after conception (Hoyenga & Hoyenga, 1979; Money & Ehrhardt, 1972). The presence or absence of testosterone, then, is critical for sexual differentiation.

Do hormones produce gender differences? A number of experiments, mostly with animals, suggest that high levels of androgens circulating before or around the time of birth result in masculine characteristics and that low levels of male hormones result in feminine characteristics. Testosterone, for example, has been linked to aggressive behavior in mice, guinea pigs, rats, and primates; and prolactin can cause motherly behavior in virgin or male animals (Bronson & Desjardins, 1969; Gray, Lean, & Keynes, 1969; Levy, 1966; R.M. Rose, Gordon, & Bernstein, 1972). But because human beings are far less limited by their biological makeup than animals are, it is risky to apply conclusions drawn from animal studies to human beings.

One line of research on humans focuses on persons who have had unusual prenatal exposure to hormones or were born with sexual abnormalities. A classic study (Ehrhardt & Money, 1967) concerned 10 girls between the ages of 3 and 14 whose mothers had taken synthetic progestins (hormones that interfere with female fertility) during pregnancy. Nine of the girls were born with abnormal external sex organs; but after surgery, they looked normal and had normal female reproductive capability. Although raised as girls from birth, they behaved like "tomboys": they enjoyed playing with trucks and guns and competed with boys in sports.

However, another classic study (Money, Ehrhardt, & Masica, 1968) had quite different implications. The subjects were 10 people aged 13 to 30 who were chromosomally male and had testes instead of ovaries but who (perhaps because their bodies were unable to utilize androgens prenatally) looked like females and had been brought up as girls. All were "typically female" in behavior and outlook. They all considered marriage and raising a family to be very important, and all had had repeated dreams and fantasies about bringing up children. Eight had played primarily with dolls and other "girls'" toys, and the seven who reported having played house in childhood had always played the mother. In this case, biology—unsupported by environmental influences—fails to account for gender-typing.

Another line of research seeks to explain cognitive differences between males and females by pointing to differences in brain functioning or hormonal levels. Some studies suggest that the right and left hemispheres are more specialized in men's brains than in women's; but these differences are so small that only sophisticated statistical analyses can detect them.

A study of men with a hormonal deficiency disorder (Hier & Crowley, 1982) suggests that androgens may be responsible for normal males' superior spatial abilities. But this gender difference does not exist in all cultures; and in a culture where it does, such as ours, women (or men who do not feel fully masculine) may give up on a task that they feel is for "real men" (Kagan, 1982).

Both these lines of biological research, then, are as yet inconclusive. One reason is that the studies involve very small samples. And since variations among people of the same sex are larger than the average differences between the sexes, studies involving handfuls of people cannot come near to explaining gender differences.

CULTURAL INFLUENCES   In Pakistan, when an Afghan boy is born, the event is celebrated with feasts and rifle shots. A girl's birth goes unnoticed. In Afghan refugee camps there, where food supplies are short, women and girls must wait to eat until the men and boys have had their fill (Reeves, 1984). It is easy to see how, in such a society, individual personalities would be strongly influenced by gender. But even in the United States, males and females are treated and valued differently.

Do societal forces encourage and accentuate biological differences, or does the culture itself create gender differences? This question is hard to answer. We do know that in almost all societies, some roles are considered appropriate for males and others for females. These gender roles vary from one culture to another; nevertheless, in many cultures men are more aggressive, competitive, and powerful than women. And in one culture—that of the *kibbutzim*, or communal settlements of Israel—a determined attempt to break down traditional gender roles has been less than fully successful (see Box 7-3 later in this chapter).

Yet attitudes toward gender roles are changing. Today in the United States, women are moving into untraditional occupations and are gaining power in business, in government, and in the family. Egalitarian attitudes are becoming more prevalent, especially among younger and better-educated people and those with higher incomes (Deaux, 1985). And both men and women are exploring aspects of their personalities that were suppressed by the old gender stereotypes.

SOCIALIZATION *How parents treat sons and daughters* Even in the more "liberated" society that exists today, parents treat sons and daughters differently. The differential treatment begins in infancy and increases in early childhood, accentuating gender differences. Parents socialize boys and girls with deeply held, often unconscious attitudes that have originated in the parents' own childhood.

Parents pay more attention to boys than to girls—not only in Pakistan, but in the "enlightened" United States (Birns, 1976; Maccoby & Jacklin, 1974; Shepherd-Look, 1982). Boys tend to be punished more, but they are praised and encouraged more, too. Why does this happen? Are parents responding to actual differences in children's behavior? There are mixed reports on whether baby boys are more active than baby girls, but we do know that young boys show greater resistance to parental guidance (Maccoby, 1980; Maccoby & Jacklin, 1974). And working parents of 3-year-old boys tend to perceive them as needing more supervision and control than girls do (Bronfenbrenner et al., 1984). It is also likely that residual gender expectations cause parents to be more concerned about how boys will turn out and about their sons' ability to make something of themselves.

In many ways, of course, parents treat their sons and daughters about the same. They expect children of both sexes to take similar responsibilities for dressing and bathing themselves; and they impose similar limits on aggressive behavior and on how far from home children may go (Shepherd-Look, 1982).

The biggest difference in the ways boys and girls are socialized is in the stress placed on their respective gender roles. Boys are under more pressure to act like "real boys" than girls are to be "feminine." Girls have much more latitude in choosing clothes, games, activities, and the sex of their playmates (Maccoby & Jacklin, 1974).

The father's role Much of the pressure on boys comes from their fathers, who react strongly to any signs of "sissy" behavior in their sons. Fathers care much more about gender-typing than mothers do. Mothers tend to be more accepting when their daughters play with trucks and their sons with dolls, but such "cross-gender" play tends to upset men, especially when their sons do it (Maccoby, 1980).

In other ways, too, fathers (more than mothers) tend to act differently toward their sons and daughters and to reinforce gender stereotypes. Fathers generally play more with baby boys than with baby girls. They roughhouse with sons and cuddle daughters. They spank their sons more than their daughters, but they are also more accepting of a very active and temperamentally difficult son than of such a daughter (Biller, 1981). As children get older, fathers emphasize competence for a son, relationships for a daughter. They encourage their daughters to be dependent and their sons to be achievers (Shepherd-Look, 1982).

Fathers, however, can also help both sons and daughters to feel good about their gender without limiting their possibilities. Adults who function well at work and in heterosexual relationships are most likely to have had warm relationships with fathers who were competent, strong, secure in their own masculinity, and nurturant toward their children. The son of such a father is likely to identify with him, and his daughter will be able to carry over her good feelings from her relationship with him to relationships with other males in her life. Conversely, the children of a punitive, rejecting father or a passive, ineffectual one are less likely to function well (Biller, 1981).

In view of the father's influence on his children's gender development, what happens to children who grow up in homes headed by a single mother? Some of these children, especially if they were 5 years old or younger when their fathers left or died, become rigidly gender-typed or go to the other extreme, taking on inappropriate behaviors associated with the other sex. Others grow up normally—especially when the mother has compensated well for the father's absence (Hetherington, Cox, & Cox, 1975; see Chapter 6). So far, there has been very

(© Ruth Duskin Feldman)

Fathers often transmit cultural attitudes about gender roles because they care more about gender-typing than mothers do. A father who cuddles a girl while expecting a boy to "stand on his own feet" is sending a powerful message about what kinds of behavior are acceptable for males and females.

little research on single-parent homes headed by the father, though this family pattern appears to be growing in the United States.

MEDIA INFLUENCES It has been estimated that by the time the typical child has graduated from high school, he or she has watched more than 25,000 hours of television, including 356,000 commercials (Action for Children's Television, undated). What messages are conveyed in the "megaviewing"?

Children will have seen about twice as many males as females on the screen, and they will have observed that the sexes act quite differently—more so than in real life. Traditionally, males on television have been more aggressive, more active, and more competent than females, who have often been portrayed as submissive, inactive, and interested mainly in either keeping house or becoming more beautiful (Mamay & Simpson, 1981; Sternglanz & Serbin, 1974; D.M. Zuckerman & Zuckerman, 1985). Similar content-analysis studies have found highly gender-stereotyped behaviors and attitudes in children's books (Weitzman, Eifler, Hokada, & Ross, 1972).

Social-learning theory would predict that children who watch television a great deal would become more gender-typed (by imitation) than those who watch less; and research indicates

that this is so (Frueh & McGhee, 1975). Today, television producers and book publishers are becoming more sensitive to the damaging effects of stereotyped messages. Now women are more likely to be shown working outside the home, to be portrayed as smarter, and not to be cast in the role of family servant; while men are sometimes shown taking care of children and doing the shopping.

Can such images break down stereotypes? This appears to be so. For example, girls who were shown television commercials in which women were pharmacists or butchers became more interested in such nontraditional occupations (O'Bryant & Corder-Boltz, 1978). This research underlines the power of television to shape our picture of ourselves and offers a glimpse of what can be accomplished as portrayals in the media begin to catch up with reality.

We'll discuss another negative influence of television—the stimulation of violence and aggression—in a later section and in Box 7-2.

Children's Play

Play as the "Business" of Early Childhood

Tracy wakes up to see her clothes for the day laid out for her. She tries putting her overalls on backward, her shoes on opposite feet, her socks on her hands, and her shirt inside out. When she finally comes down to breakfast, she pretends that the little pieces of cereal in her bowl are "fishies" swimming around in the milk, and, spoonful by spoonful, she goes fishing.

Throughout the long, busy morning, she plays. She puts on an old hat of her mother's, picks up a discarded briefcase, and is the "mommy" going to work. Next she becomes the doctor, giving her doll a "shot." She runs outside to splash in the puddles with a friend, and then comes in for an imaginary telephone conversation.

An adult might be tempted to smile indulgently (or enviously) at Tracy and to dismiss her activities as a pleasant way to pass the time. Such a judgment would be grievously in error. For play is the work of the young.

Through play, children grow. They learn how to use their muscles; they coordinate what they see with what they do; and they gain mastery over their bodies. They find out what the world is like and what *they* are like. They stimulate their senses by playing with water, sand, and mud. They acquire new skills and learn when to use them. And they cope with complex and conflicting emotions by reenacting real life.

Types of Play Researchers have looked at children's play in two ways: as a social activity and as an aspect of cognition. The first approach examines the amount of children's *social play*—the extent to which they interact with other children when they play—as an indication of social competence. The second approach looks at *cognitive play,* or forms of play that reveal and enhance children's cognitive development.

SOCIAL AND NONSOCIAL PLAY Laura's preschool teacher notices that she spends most of her free time playing alone, perhaps pretending to be a frog or a firefighter. Her classmate Doug prefers to build block towers with his friends. What can we learn about children like Laura and Doug by observing how they play?

In the late 1920s, Mildred Parten observed forty-two 2- to 5-year-olds during free play periods at nursery school. In her report published in 1932, she distinguished six types of play, determined the proportion of time spent in each type, and charted the activities of the children.

Her work is a classic model of how social play develops.

Parten observed that between the ages of 2 and 3, children frequently engage in various types of nonsocial play: unoccupied behavior, onlooker behavior, solitary independent play, and parallel play (play alongside but not with other children). These forms of play diminish after the third birthday, and there is an increase in two forms of social play: associative play and cooperative play. (See Table 7-2 for a description of each type of play.)

A similar study of forty-four 3- and 4-year-olds, done 4 decades after Parten's study, found social play much less advanced than among the children in Parten's group (K.E. Barnes, 1971). The researcher speculated that the change might have reflected an altered environment: television encourages passive "onlooking," elaborate toys may encourage solitary play more than simple toys do, and children today grow up with fewer brothers and sisters. Another study found socioeconomic class to be a factor in the sociability of play. Preschoolers from lower socioeconomic groups engaged in more parallel play, while middle-class children engaged in more associative and cooperative play (K. Rubin, Maioni, & Hornung, 1976).

Is solitary play less mature than group play? Parten believed so, and some other observers have suggested that young children who play by themselves may be at risk of developing social, psychological, and educational problems. But recent research linking the *content* of play with its social aspect contradicts that assumption. Some of children's nonsocial play appears to contribute positively to their development.

In one analysis of children in six kindergartens, about one-third of the solitary play that took place consisted of such goal-directed activities as block construction and artwork; about one-fourth consisted of large-muscle play; about 15 percent was educational; and only about 10 percent involved just looking around at the other children (N. Moore, Everston, & Brophy, 1974). Such play, the researchers concluded, shows independence and maturity, not poor social adjustment.

Another study assessed various kinds of nonsocial play in relation to measures of the cognitive and social competence of 4-year-olds, such

TABLE 7-2 TYPES OF SOCIAL AND NONSOCIAL PLAY IN EARLY CHILDHOOD

CATEGORY	DESCRIPTION
Unoccupied behavior	The child apparently is not playing, but occupies himself with watching anything that happens to be of momentary interest. When there is nothing exciting taking place, he plays with his own body, gets on and off chairs, just stands around, follows the teacher, or sits in one spot glancing around the room (p. 249).
Onlooker behavior	The child spends most of his time watching the other children play. He often talks to the children whom he is observing, asks questions, or gives suggestions, but does not overtly enter into the play himself. This type differs from the unoccupied in that the onlooker is definitely observing particular groups of children rather than anything that happens to be exciting. The child stands or sits within speaking distance of the group so that he can see and hear everything that takes place (p. 249).
Solitary independent play	The child plays alone and independently with toys that are different from those used by the children within speaking distance and makes no effort to get close to other children. He pursues his own activity without reference to what others are doing (p. 250).
Parallel play	The child plays independently, but the activity he chooses naturally brings him among the other children. He plays with toys that are like those which the children around him are using, but he plays with the toy as he sees fit, and does not try to influence or modify the activity of the children near him. He plays *beside* rather than *with* the other children. There is no attempt to control the coming or going of children in the group (p. 250).
Associative play	The child plays with other children. The conversation concerns the common activity; there is a borrowing and lending of play material; following one another with trains or wagons; mild attempts to control which children may or may not play in the group. All the members engage in similar if not identical activity; there is no division of labor, and no organization of the activity of several individuals around any material goal or product. The children do not subordinate their individual interests to that of the group; instead each child acts as he wishes. By his conversation with the other children one can tell that his interest is primarily in his associations, not in his activity. Occasionally, two or three children engage in no activity of any duration, but are merely doing whatever happens to draw the attention of any of them (p. 251).
Cooperative or organized supplementary play	The child plays in a group that is organized for the purpose of making some material product, or of striving to attain some competitive goal, or of dramatizing situations of adult and group life, or of playing formal games. There is a marked sense of belonging or of not belonging to the group. The control of the group situation is in the hands of one or two of the members who direct the activity of the others. The goal as well as the method of attaining it necessitates a division of labor, taking of different roles by the various group members and the organization of activity so that the efforts of one child are supplemented by those of another (p. 251).

Source: Parten, 1932, pp. 249–251.

as role-taking and problem-solving tests, teachers' ratings of social competence, and other children's judgments about popularity. The study found that some kinds of nonsocial play are associated with a fairly high level of competence. For example, parallel constructive play (such typical preschool activities as playing with blocks or working with puzzles near another child) was most common among children who were good problem solvers, who were popular with other children, and whose teachers saw them as socially skilled (K. Rubin, 1982).

Not all nonsocial play, then, is immature. Children may need time alone to concentrate on tasks and problems; or they may simply enjoy nonsocial activities more than group activities. We need to look at what children *do* when they play, not just at whether they play alone or with someone else.

COGNITIVE PLAY According to Piaget (1951) and Smilansky (1968), children's cognitive development in early childhood allows them to progress from simple functional (repetitive) play (like rolling a ball) to constructive play (like building a block tower), pretend play (like playing doctor), and then formal games with rules (like hopscotch and marbles; see Table 7-3). These more complex forms of play, in turn, foster further cognitive development.

TABLE 7-3 TYPES OF COGNITIVE PLAY	
CATEGORY	DESCRIPTION
Functional play (sensorimotor play)	Any simple, repetitive muscle movement with or without objects, such as rolling a ball or pulling a pull toy.
Constructive play	Manipulation of objects to construct or to "create" something.
Dramatic play (pretend play)	Substitution of an imaginary situation to satisfy the child's personal wishes and needs. Pretending to be someone or something (doctor, nurse, Superman), beginning with fairly simple activities but going on to develop more elaborate plots.
Games with rules	Any activity with rules, structure, and a goal (such as winning), like tag, hopscotch, marbles. Acceptance of prearranged rules and adjustment to them.

Source: Piaget, 1951; Smilansky, 1968.

PRETEND PLAY A 13-month-old girl pushes an imaginary spoon holding imaginary food into the mouth of her very real father. A 2-year-old boy "talks" to a doll as if he were addressing a real person. A 3-year-old boy makes "vroom-vroom" noises as he runs around the room with a toy airplane. And a 5-year-old girl drapes a towel over her head as she walks in measured steps down an imaginary aisle as "the most beautiful bride in the world."

All these children are engaged in **pretend play**, play involving imaginary situations (also called *fantasy play, dramatic play,* or *imaginative play*). At one time the major professional interest in such play was its supposed role in helping children express their emotional concerns, but present psychological interest focuses more on the role of such play in cognitive and general personality development.

Pretend play—which emerges during the second year of life when functional or sensorimotor play is on the wane—is an important form of play in early childhood. Piaget (1962) maintained that children's ability to pretend to do or be something rests on their ability to use and remember symbols—to retain in their minds representations, or images, of things they have seen or heard. Thus the emergence of pretend play marks the beginning of the preoperational stage, which we discussed in Chapter 6. Pretend play increases during the next 3 to 4 years until children begin to become more interested in playing games with formal rules (see Chapter 9), around the time they advance to the stage of concrete operations.

About 10 to 17 percent of the play of preschoolers is pretend play, and the proportion rises to about 33 percent among kindergartners (K. Rubin et al., 1976; K. Rubin, Watson, & Jambor, 1978). The kind of play, as well as its amount, changes during these years from solitary pretending to *sociodramatic play* involving other children. A boy who at age 3 may climb inside a big box by himself and pretend to be a train conductor will, by age 6, want to have passengers on his train with whom he can enact minidramas (Iwanaga, 1973).

Through pretending, children learn how to understand another person's point of view, develop skills in solving social problems, and become more creative. Certain parental character-

(© Bill Stanton/International Stock Photo)

This preschooler pretending to feed her "baby" is demonstrating an important cognitive development of early childhood: the ability to use symbols to stand for people or things in the real world.

istics seem to be associated with a flowering of pretend play (Fein, 1981). The parents of children who are the most imaginative in their play get along well with each other, expose their children to interesting experiences, engage them in conversation, and do not punish by spanking. Children who watch a great deal of television tend not to play imaginatively, possibly because they get into the habit of passively absorbing images rather than generating their own.

Fearfulness in Young Children

When Kelly was 3 years old, she was frightened by a neighbor's large, barking dog. The next day, she refused to go out to play. When her mother asked why, she said she had a stomachache; but when dinnertime came, she cleaned her plate. The next day, Kelly again refused to go outside, even to play with her best friend. When her father insisted on taking her to the store, Kelly burst into tears and clung to his arm.

Kelly had developed a fear of dogs, one of the most common fears of this most fearful age. Yet by her sixth birthday, this fear had gone away; in fact, she had to be stopped from patting strange dogs in the park.

What Do Children Fear, and Why? Passing fears are characteristic of 2- to 4-year-olds, many of whom are afraid of animals, especially of dogs. By 6 years of age, children are more likely to be afraid of the dark. Other common fears are of thunderstorms and doctors (DuPont, 1983). Most of these fears evaporate as children grow older and lose their sense of powerlessness.

Girls tend to be more fearful than boys, possibly because girls are encouraged to be more dependent, because parents accept girls' fears and discourage those of boys, or because boys do not admit having fears (Bauer, 1976; Croake, 1973; Jersild & Holmes, 1935).

Why do children become so fearful at this age? The reasons may have to do with their intense fantasy life—their inability to clearly distinguish "pretend" from reality. In one study, 75 percent of kindergartners and 50 percent of second-graders expressed fear of ghosts and monsters, while only 5 percent of sixth graders did. Older children have different kinds of fears. Ten- to twelve-year-olds, who understand cause and effect, are more likely to fear bodily injury and physical danger, while 4- to 6-year-olds may fear a person who "looks ugly" (Bauer, 1976).

Various underlying anxieties (like the inner conflicts discussed at the beginning of this chapter) may cause some fears. Violent television shows and movies may then provide frightening images for these anxieties.

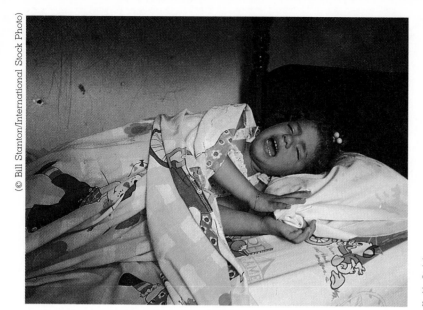

Many 6-year-olds develop fear of the dark. This and other characteristic fears of early childhood are usually short-lived.

Sometimes young children's imaginations are carried away, making them worry about being attacked by a lion or being abandoned. Often, however, their fears come from appraisals of real dangers—such as the likelihood of being bitten by a dog—or are triggered by actual events, as when a child who has been hit by a car becomes afraid to cross the street. Children of this age know more and have experienced more than before, and one thing they know is that there are many things to be afraid of.

Phobias Realistic fear is normal and healthy. *Phobias*—irrational, involuntary fears, inappropriate to the situation—are not (DuPont, 1983; all uncited material in this section is from that source). Kelly's initial fear of the barking dog was normal; her fear of going outdoors became a phobia. Specific fears are common among young children; phobias are rare.

Children's phobias may grow out of a specific event, as in Kelly's case; but they generally do not. However, they are not usually signs of mental illness. Worriers are not more subject to phobias than anyone else, but children whose mothers have phobias are. Childhood fears and phobias often disappear on their own, but sometimes they become severe and persistent. However, they rarely continue into adulthood; most adult phobias (except for animal phobias) are acquired between the ages of 17 and 40.

Preventing and Treating Fear We don't really know why some fears vanish and others develop into phobias. It appears, though, that adults' reactions play a part. Parents should accept fears as normal, offer reassurance, and encourage children to express their feelings freely without being subjected to ridicule or punishment. Children should not be allowed, however, to avoid what they fear; avoidance simply reinforces the fear.

Fears or phobias that linger can be treated before they become handicapping. Through conditioning and modeling, the phobia can be attacked head on rather than being treated as a symptom of a deeper problem.

An experiment involving gradual exposure to the feared object (a therapeutic technique known as *systematic desensitization)* was successful with 39 out of 45 first- through third-graders who had been afraid to touch snakes. After an average of two 15-minute desensitization sessions, these children held snakes in their laps for 15 seconds. By contrast, only 5 of 22 children in a control group did (C. M. Murphy & Bootzin, 1973).

Phobias may recur if exposure to the stimulus becomes infrequent; if they do, the "practice" sessions may need to be resumed. If home treatment under a pediatrician's supervision fails, a child may be referred to a phobia treatment program, a psychiatrist, or a psychologist.

Aggression in Young Children

Babies do not display truly *aggressive behavior*, hostile actions intended to hurt somebody or to establish dominance. Even a toddler who roughly grabs a toy from another child is interested only in the toy, not in hurting or dominating the other child. Anyone with much experience with children past the age of 2½ or 3, however, has seen enough hitting, punching, kicking, biting, and throwing to be satisfied that the age of aggression has arrived. But within the next 3 years or so, the expression of aggression normally shifts from physical to verbal means (Maccoby, 1980). Let's see how that happens—and why it sometimes doesn't happen.

The Rise and Decline of Aggression In the early stages of aggression, a child focuses on a desired object and makes threatening gestures against the person holding it. Between the ages of 2½ and 5, children's aggression centers on struggles over playthings and the control of space. Aggression surfaces mostly during social play, and the children who fight the most tend to be the most sociable and competent. This may mean that the ability to show aggression is a necessary step in the development of human beings as social animals.

The establishment of a dominance hierarchy—a recognized pecking order of leaders and followers—reduces the number of bloody noses; battles need not be fought, because everyone knows what the outcome would be. In addition, as children become physically stronger and more able to inflict actual harm, they turn to their growing language skills as a safer alternative. The tools of aggression shift from blows to insults, as the issues shift from struggles over objects to struggles over status.

Most children become less aggressive after the age of 6 or 7, as empathy begins to replace egocentrism. Children can now put themselves in someone else's place, can understand why another person is acting in a certain way, and can develop positive ways to deal with others.

(Drawing by Ross, © 1983 The New Yorker Magazine, Inc.)

"What have I read? I've read 'Tubby the Tugboat'! What have you read?"

Between the ages of 3 and 6, children begin to express aggression verbally rather than physically.

Not all children, however, learn to control aggression. Some become increasingly destructive. And even with an ordinary child who is progressing normally, aggression can get out of hand and can become dangerous. Because of these concerns, researchers have sought to discover what stimulates aggression. Let's look at some of their findings.

Triggers and Reducers of Aggression We have seen that boys tend to be more aggressive than girls; the male hormone testosterone has been implicated in this tendency. Other contributing factors (here the findings are consistent with social-learning theory) include *reinforcement* and a combination of *frustration* with *imitation of aggressive models*.

REINFORCEMENT, FRUSTRATION, AND MODELING The more successful children are in getting what they want by aggressive means, the more likely they are to continue to be aggressive. But sometimes (as we'll see when we discuss rewards and punishments) reinforcement is subtler— and unintended. Scolding or spanking can cause the unintended reinforcement, since some children seem to prefer negative attention to no attention at all.

Preschool teachers have successfully reduced boys' aggressive behavior by ignoring it and rewarding cooperation (P. Brown & Elliott, 1965). But aggression cannot always be safely ignored, and lack of interference may imply approval.

Effective ways to control children's behavior are reasoning with them, making them feel guilty, and withdrawing approval and affection when they act aggressively. When parents use these techniques, their children are more likely to develop strong consciences—and less likely to become aggressive—than children who are disciplined by spanking, threats, or the withdrawal of privileges. (Of course, it may be that parents are more likely to spank aggressive children.) In any case, parents' tendencies to use the former methods with girls and the latter with boys may accentuate girls' inclinations to feel guilty and boys' to be aggressive (R. R. Sears, Maccoby, & Levin, 1957).

One reason why punishment may backfire is that it produces frustration; and a frustrated child is more likely to act aggressively than a contented one (Bandura, Ross, & Ross, 1961). This is especially true when a parent hits a child. The child not only suffers frustration, pain, and humiliation but sees aggressive behavior in an adult with whom he or she identifies. Parents who spank provide a "living example of the use of aggression at the very moment they are trying to teach the child not to be aggressive" (R. R. Sears et al., 1957, p. 266).

A classic study (Bandura et al., 1961) shows the power of modeling. The researchers divided seventy-two 3- to 6-year-olds into three groups. One by one, each of the children in the first group went into a playroom for 10 minutes. An adult model (male for half the children, female for the other half) quietly played in a corner with some toys. The model for the second group began to assemble Tinker Toys for a minute but then spent the rest of the 10-minute session punching, throwing, and kicking a 5-foot inflated doll. The children in the third group saw no model.

After these modeling sessions, all the children were subjected to a situation involving mild frustration—they were shown attractive toys but were not allowed to play with them. Then they were taken into another playroom. The children who had seen the aggressive model were much more aggressive than those in the other groups. They said and did many of the same things they had seen the model do. Both boys and girls who had seen the aggressive male model were more strongly influenced than those who had seen the aggressive female model, apparently because they considered aggressive behavior appropriate only for males. The children who had been with the quiet models were less aggressive than those who had seen no model at all.

EFFECTS OF TELEVISED VIOLENCE Even if parents do not act aggressively, most children see aggressive models on television. Three- to five-year-olds have been found to spend an average of 2 hours a day watching television (Institute for Social Research, 1985), and children's programs are 6 times as violent as adults' programs (Signorielli, Gross, & Morgan, 1982). Is the effect of violence on the screen as strong as that of violence exhibited by live models? Research suggests that it is even stronger (Bandura, Ross, & Ross, 1963).

The overwhelming weight of evidence since the 1950s demonstrates that children who see violence on the screen behave more aggressively (National Institute of Mental Health, NIMH, 1982). This is true regardless of geographic location and socioeconomic level. It is true of both boys and girls and of normal children as well as those with emotional problems.

Aggressive children watch more television than nonaggressive children, identify more strongly with aggressive characters, and are more likely to believe that aggression on television reflects real life (Eron, 1982). The aggressive acts that children see make a more vivid impression than any punishment the "bad guy" receives (Liebert & Poulos, 1976, cited in Lickona, 1976). The report of the NIMH concludes that television encourages aggressive behavior in two ways: children imitate what they see on television, and they also absorb the values transmitted and come to accept aggression as appropriate behavior.

Children who see television characters—both heroes and villains—accomplishing their aims through violence and lawbreaking may fail to protect the victim of a bully. They are also more likely to break rules and less likely to cooperate to resolve differences.

In one study of 136 boys and girls aged 5 to 9, an experimental group watched a 3½-minute segment from a popular television series. In these 3½ minutes were a chase, two fistfights, two shootings, and a knifing. A control group watched 3½ minutes of athletic competition. Afterward, the children were asked to take part in a "game" that involved pushing either a "help" button (which would help an unseen child win a game) or a "hurt" button (which would make a handle touched by that child so hot that it would hurt). Of course, there was no such child; the only child in the experiment was the one pushing the buttons. Children who had watched the violent programming were more willing to hurt the unseen child and more willing to inflict more severe pain than were those who had watched the sports program (Liebert, 1972).

Several longitudinal studies demonstrate long-term effects of watching television (D. M.

Zuckerman & Zuckerman, 1985). For example, among 427 young adults whose viewing habits had been studied at the age of 8, the best predictor of aggressiveness at the age of 19 for both males and females was the degree of violence in the television shows they had watched as children (Eron, 1980, 1982).

The American Psychological Association (1985) has issued a policy resolution that calls for a joint effort by parents and broadcasters to reduce the number of aggressive models shown on television. Along with favoring parents' monitoring of children's watching of television, the resolution urges broadcasters to take more responsibility for limiting violence in children's programming, and it advocates research into ways to ameliorate the effects of televised violence.

Meanwhile, the amount of violent television entertainment continues to rise. In addition to action dramas, broadcasts of nationally televised war cartoons soared from 1½ hours a week in 1982 to 48 hours a week in 1987, and the average child in the United States saw 250 episodes of such cartoons in a year. Sales of war toys jumped 700 percent during that period. Some 40 studies covering more than 4500 children in the United States and six other countries show the effects of such cartoon violence and violent play: increases in fighting, kicking, choking, loss of temper, cruelty to animals, and disrespect for others, as well as decreases in sharing, imagination, and school performance (National Coalition on Television Violence, undated).

Viewing television, however, need not promote aggressive behavior; it can promote prosocial behavior instead (see Box 7-2, page 246).

Altruism: Prosocial Behavior

Anna, who was 4 years old, was picnicking with her family in the park when she noticed a man in rags, picking scraps of food out of a garbage can. Anna reached into the picnic basket for a tuna sandwich—her favorite food—and said, "Mommy, let's give this to him."

Anna was showing altruistic behavior, or **prosocial behavior**—acting out of concern for another person, with no expectation of reward. Prosocial acts like Anna's "often entail some cost, self-sacrifice, or risk" on the part of the

BOX 7-2 PRACTICALLY SPEAKING

BE YOUR CHILD'S TV GUIDE

Television can be a powerful force in children's lives. The average American child watches several hours of television every day; and by the time they graduate from high school, most children have spent more time in front of the television set than in the classroom. Television viewing can enhance a tendency toward obesity, promote an inclination toward violence, and convey unrealistic messages regarding drugs, alcohol, sexuality, and relationships (American Academy of Pediatrics, AAP, 1986b).

The following suggestions for parents, teachers, baby-sitters, and caregivers (Action for Children's Television, undated; AAP, 1986b) will help children gain the most benefit and suffer the least harm from television:

■ *Set limits*. Know the amount of television your children watch, and don't be afraid to reduce it. The AAP recommends that parents limit their children's viewing to 1 or 2 hours per day.

■ *Plan viewing in advance.* Help children learn to approach television like a movie rather than becoming indiscriminate "dial turners." Turn the set on for a particular program, and turn it off and discuss the program when it is over.

■ *Watch with your children.* Interpret and talk about the programs they see. Point out how much of what is shown on television is not real; discuss the differences between make-believe and real life.

■ *Talk about televised violence with your children.* Describe how violence hurts, and discuss how the characters on television could solve their problems without violence.

■ *Be a good role model.* Because children often follow their parents' example, examine your own television viewing habits and help your children form good habits early in life.

■ *Don't use television as a baby-sitter.* Provide alternatives for children in the form of both indoor and outdoor activities such as field trips, games, sports, hobbies, reading, chores, and special family activities.

■ *Resist commercials.* Help your children become smart consumers by teaching them to recognize a sales pitch. Talk about foods advertised on television that can cause cavities and toys that may break too soon.

■ *Complement television with new technologies.* Use a video recorder to tape worthwhile programs for convenient viewing or to show rented movies. Utilize educational tapes to enhance children's learning.

person who takes them (Mussen & Eisenberg-Berg, 1977).

Why do some children reach out to comfort a crying friend or stop to help an old man who falls while crossing the street? What makes these children generous, compassionate, and sensitive to other people's needs? From many studies within the past 20 years, we have learned about the origins of caring behavior. Socioeconomic status, for example, is *not* a factor: the amount of money the parents have or their social standing makes no difference in how a youngster will behave toward others.

In the majority of studies, no gender differences have turned up either, though some research has found more generosity, helpfulness, and considerateness in girls than in boys. This may be because nurturance is generally considered a more feminine trait, and so girls are encouraged more often to help others; it may also be related to the fact that girls are physically punished by their parents less than boys are, receive more affection from their parents, and are given more explanations of the consequences of their actions.

Age is a factor in altruism. Even 18-month-olds will show sympathy toward someone who is hurt or unhappy and may make efforts to help, although not until about the age of 4 do children display a significant amount of altruism. The level increases steadily until the age of 13, apparently in relation to children's growing empathy.

Altruistic children tend to be advanced in mental reasoning and able to take the role of others; they are also relatively active and self-confident. How do they become this way? The results of many studies point to the home. The family is important as a model, as a source of explicitly stated standards, and as a guide to outside models.

Parents of prosocial children typically set an example. In Anna's home, as far back as she can remember, an elderly neighbor who has no family of her own has been invited for Thanksgiving dinner. When Anna's parents clear the snow from their driveway, they clear this neighbor's driveway as well.

Parents of prosocial children encourage them to empathize with others and to reflect on the implications of their actions. When Anna took candy from a store, her father did not lecture her on what a bad girl she had been. Instead, he explained how the owner of the store would be harmed because she had not paid for the candy, and then he took her back to the store to return it. When incidents like this occur, Anna's parents ask, for example, "How do you think Mr. Jones feels?" or "How would you feel if you were Mary?"

The parents of prosocial children usually hold them to high standards. The children know explicitly that they are expected to be honest and helpful. They have some responsibility in the home and are expected to meet it.

Parents of prosocial children draw their attention to stories and television programs—such as *Mister Rogers' Neighborhood*—that depict cooperation, sharing, and empathy. Many studies have shown that children imitate the positive behavior modeled on such programs and that the programs encourage children to be more sympathetic, generous, and helpful (Mussen & Eisenberg-Berg, 1977; NIMH, 1982; D. M. Zuckerman & Zuckerman, 1985). And when the child's entire cultural environment is based on prosocial ideals, as it is in the Israeli kibbutzim,

prosocial behavior flourishes (see Box 7-3 on page 248).

Obviously, parents can have an enormous impact on children's personalities. Let's look more closely at how they use that influence.

How Child-Rearing Practices Affect Personality Development

"Just as the twig is bent, the tree's inclined," wrote Alexander Pope, an eighteenth-century English poet. Some parents, in exasperated moments, might wish that raising children were as straightforward as Pope's advice on moral training suggests. But children are not saplings to be bent to their parents' will. In early childhood, as children become their own persons, their upbringing can be a baffling, complex challenge.

How are parents raising their children today? Some parents, of course, repeat the child-rearing patterns they are most familiar with, those that their own parents followed in bringing them up. Others adopt practices that are very different from those their parents used.

Using Rewards and Punishment Billy's mother gives him a cookie when he is "good." Shari's mother spanks her when she is "bad." Parents often use rewards to get their children to do what they want them to do, and they use punishment to get the children to stop doing what they do *not* want them to do. Which way is better? Research has recently been shedding light on this age-old question. It appears that children learn more by being rewarded for good behavior than by being punished for bad.

REWARDS *Behavior modification,* or behavior therapy (a form of operant, or instrumental, learning, described in Chapter 1), is a relatively new name for the old practice of rewarding children to encourage desired behavior or punishing them to eliminate undesired behavior. *External* rewards may be social ones such as a smile, a word of praise, a hug, or a special privilege. Or they may take the more tangible form of candy, money, toys, or gold stars. Whatever the prize is, the child must see it as rewarding and must get it fairly consistently after showing the desired behavior. Eventually, the behavior should pro-

BOX 7-3 WINDOW ON THE WORLD

SOCIALIZATION ON THE KIBBUTZ

In the United States and other western countries, parents raise children and strongly influence their personalities, particularly their gender-typing. *Kibbutzim* (plural of *kibbutz*)—the communal farming or manufacturing settlements in Israel—have attempted to change this traditional child-rearing system; the results have been mixed.

Since the founding of the first kibbutz in 1910, these societies in miniature have sought to create a system of complete equality in which "people would be less selfish, more secure, and more generous" (Beit-Hallahmi & Rabin, 1977, p. 533). An important part of this socialist ideal was the elimination of special roles for men and women. To this end, the kibbutzim radically changed the family structure of their members.

Members of a kibbutz share equally in the work, decision making, and wealth of the settlement. They eat together in a common dining hall. In a classically organized kibbutz, children are raised more by nurses and teachers than by their parents. Almost from birth, they sleep, dress, play, and learn together in a larger communal housing unit. Group child rearing frees mothers for work and allows children to be socialized according to the supposedly gender-free values of the kibbutz. The children's nurses do not give little boys balls and little girls dolls but encourage all the children to play together. Because the children dress and often shower together, they become aware of their biological sex differences at an early age, in a natural way.

Critics' predictions that children would be emotionally damaged by separation from their parents have proved to be unfounded. But whereas the kibbutzim have been economic successes, the social vision of their founders has not been fully realized. The culture of the kibbutz has not succeeded in producing a new kind of personality (Beit-Hallahmi & Rabin, 1977). For one thing, a gender-based division of labor has resumed. Men tend to do skilled work, while women work in the laundries and kitchens. A second, related complication is a growing emphasis on the family.

Since the 1950s, there has been a push for more direct parental involvement in children's upbringing and a greater role for the family in the society of the kibbutz. This trend toward "familism" was instigated mainly by women. In the early 1960s, many mothers arranged their work schedules to permit more free time with their children, even taking the children out of school to be with them. The kibbutz response was to establish an "hour of love": one hour during each working and school day for mothers and children to spend together (Tiger & Shepher, 1975). Today, only the most classically oriented kibbutzim

---

vide its own *internal* reward to the child—for example, a sense of pleasure and accomplishment.

"REWARDING" WITH PUNISHMENT "What are we going to do with that child?" Erica's mother says. "The more we punish her, the more she misbehaves!"

There is little cause for wonder: Erica's parents ignore her most of the time when she behaves well but scold or spank her when she acts up. In effect, they are rewarding her with atten-tion when she does what they do *not* want her to do.

Most children, of course, prefer affection to disapproval. But children who are seldom given positive attention may consider disapproval bet-ter than no attention at all, and so they may de-liberately misbehave to get attention. Punish-ment becomes a "reward" that encourages the very behavior it is intended to stop.

WHEN DOES PUNISHMENT WORK? Although the carrot is usually a better motivator than the

Children on this kibbutz, an agricultural cooperative settlement in Israel, learn prosocial behavior—one of the ideals of their society. On a traditional kibbutz, infants and children live apart from their parents in groups supervised by nurses and teachers. Children raised in this way show more concern for the welfare of the community than many American children do.

place children under the age of 6 in sleeping facilities away from their parents'; some kibbutzim even wait until the children are 12.

In effect, a child on a kibbutz has two sets of parents—the natural parents and the kibbutz—and receives dual messages. Although the ideals behind the kibbutz deny traditional gender roles, the actual positions of mothers and fathers serve to maintain these roles—roles that, according to a major study of three generations of kibbutz women, they themselves prefer (Tiger & Shepher, 1975).

Still, gender-typing in the kibbutz family is relatively low, particularly with regard to child care; and by adolescence, kibbutz children "have a markedly lower level of polar gender classification than their . . . city peers." From this, the authors conclude that early socialization has "a considerable equalizing effect on the basic attitudes of children toward sexual division of labor" (p. 167).

Boys' academic performance, however, is "conspicuously superior" (p. 180).

Regarding prosocial behavior, on the other hand, kibbutz values have clearly prevailed. At every age and stage of development, kibbutz-reared children tend to think more about obligations to others than home-reared American children do; and as young adults, they are more concerned with preserving and maintaining social solidarity (Snarey, Reimer, & Kohlberg, 1985).

stick, there are times to consider punishment. For example, a slap on the backside may deter a child from running out into a busy street. Sometimes, too, a child is intractable and it is hard to find alternative, desirable behavior to reward.

A considerable body of laboratory and field research exists on the most effective ways to control children's behavior with punishment (Parke, 1977). The conclusions suggest that the following criteria are important:

■ *Timing.* The shorter the time that passes be-

tween behavior and its punishment, the more effective the punishment. When children are punished as they *begin* to engage in a forbidden act such as approaching an object they have been told to stay away from, they will go to it less often than if they are not punished until *after* they have actually touched it. In practical terms, of course, it is not always possible to punish children before they misbehave; however, parents and teachers may be able to move in quickly when a child is about to *repeat* misbehavior. And they can act immediately afterward rather than postponing punishment "until your father gets home" (a practice that seems to have diminished over the years anyway).

■ *Consistency.* The more consistently a child is punished, the more effective the punishment will be. When children are punished erratically, they persist in their undesirable behavior longer than if they had not been punished at all.

■ *The person who punishes.* The better the relationship between the punishing adult and the child, the more effective the punishment. Punishment is two-edged: as it presents something negative, it withholds something positive. Therefore, the more positive the element that is being withheld (acceptance by an affectionate, nurturing adult), the more effective the punishment.

■ *Explanation.* Punishment is more effective when accompanied by a short explanation (but not a long, involved one). Children are less likely to play with a fragile vase if, the last time they have broken one, they have been told, for example, "That vase belonged to Aunt Martha" than if they have been punished with no explanation.

Used with care, then, punishment can be effective, at least in the short run. However, it can be harmful when it is inconsistent and is administered in a hostile way, and it can have unwanted long-term effects. Children may learn to avoid a punitive parent, undermining the parent's ability to influence their behavior. Physical punishment (aside from the risk of injury) may encourage a child to imitate the aggression modeled by the parent. Children who are frequently punished may become passive because they feel helpless to escape punishment.

Some children are punished more often than others, and not necessarily because of the seriousness of their offenses. Parents tend to spare the rod if children express remorse and try to make up for their misdeeds, whereas children who are defiant or who ignore parents' rebukes are punished most severely.

Parents' Styles and Children's Competence

Why does Nicole hit and bite the nearest person when she is unable to finish a jigsaw puzzle?

What makes David sit with the puzzle for hours until he solves it? Why does Michele walk away from it after a minute's effort? In short, why are children so different in their responses to the same task? What makes them turn out the way they do? To answer these questions, we must look beyond such simple techniques as reward and punishment.

THREE KINDS OF PARENTS Diana Baumrind set out to discover relationships between different styles of child rearing and the social competence of children. Her research combined lengthy interviews, standardized testing, and home studies of 103 preschool children from 95 families. She identified three categories of child-rearing styles and described typical behavior patterns of the children raised according to each style (Baumrind, 1971; Baumrind & Black, 1967).

Authoritarian parents value control and unquestioning obedience. They try to make their children conform to a set standard of conduct, and they punish children forcefully for acting contrary to that standard. They are more detached and less warm than other parents, and their children are more discontented, withdrawn, and distrustful.

Permissive parents value self-expression and self-regulation. They make few demands, allowing their children to monitor their own activities as much as possible. They consider themselves resources, not standard-bearers or models. They explain to their children the reasons underlying the few family rules that do exist, consult with them about policy decisions, and hardly ever punish. They are noncontrolling, nondemanding, and relatively warm, and their children as preschoolers are immature—the least self-controlled and the least exploratory.

Authoritative parents respect a child's individuality, but they also consider it important to instill social values. They direct their children's activities rationally, with attention to the issues rather than to the children's fear of punishment or loss of love. They exert firm control when necessary, but they explain the reasoning behind their stands and encourage verbal give-and-take. While they have confidence in their ability to guide their children, they respect the children's interests, opinions, and unique personalities. They are loving, consistent, demand-

Parenting styles influence children's personality development. Children of authoritative parents, who balance firmness with love and respect, are often most self-reliant, self-controlled, and content.

(© Bill Stanton/International Stock Photo)

ing, and respectful of their children's independent decisions, but they are firm in maintaining standards and willing to impose limited punishment. They combine control with encouragement. Their children apparently feel secure in knowing that they are loved and knowing what is expected of them. As preschoolers, these children are most self-reliant, self-controlled, self-assertive, exploratory, and content.

WHY DOES AUTHORITATIVE CHILD REARING WORK? The essential factor in the success of authoritative child rearing appears to be the parents' reasonable expectations and realistic standards.

Children from authoritarian homes are so strictly controlled, by either punishment or guilt, that they often cannot make a conscious choice about the merit of a particular behavior because they are too concerned about what their parents will do. Children from permissive homes receive so little guidance that they often become uncertain and anxious about whether they are doing the right thing. But in authoritative homes, children know when they are meeting expectations, learn how to judge those expectations, and are able to decide when it is worth risking their parents' displeasure or other unpleasant consequences in the pursuit of some goal. These children are expected to perform well, to fulfill commitments, and to participate actively in family duties as well as in family fun. They experience the satisfaction of meeting responsibilities and achieving success.

Of course, no parent is authoritarian, permissive, or authoritative *all* of the time. Being human, parents are subject to different moods, and they react differently to different situations (Carter & Welch, 1981). And although it is easy to know the "right" way to act with children, it is not always easy to put it into action.

In evaluating Baumrind's work, we should note that she does not consider any innate differences between children, assuming that all differences in their social competence are related to what their parents do. Nor does she raise the question of a child's influence on the parents. It is possible, for example, that "easy" children will spur their parents to be authoritative while "difficult" children drive their parents to authoritarianism.

Love and Maturity In the long run, specific parenting practices during a child's first 5 years may be less important than how parents feel about their children and the ways they show their feelings. That is the conclusion of a major follow-up study (McClelland, Constantian, Regalado, & Stone, 1978) of young adults whose mothers had been interviewed about their child-rearing techniques 2 decades earlier (R. R. Sears et al., 1957).

The way these adults turned out seemed to bear little or no relation to the length of time they had been breast-fed, whether they had had early or late bedtimes, or a number of other factors. The most important influence in these people's lives—dwarfing all others—was how much their parents, especially their mothers, had loved them and had shown their affection for and enjoyment of them.

The most beloved children grew up to be the most prosocially mature as defined by Erikson and Kohlberg. They were the most tolerant of other people, the most understanding, and the most likely to show active concern for others. The least mature adults had grown up in homes where they were considered a nuisance and an interference with adult-centered standards. Their parents had tolerated no noise, mess, or roughhousing in the home and had reacted unkindly to the children's aggressiveness, sex play, or expressions of normal dependency.

Although the children of "easygoing, loving parents" had often behaved less acceptably when they were growing up than had the children of stricter parents, the authors emphasize that this is often a necessary step toward independence from the parents' values and adoption of one's own values (McClelland et al., 1978, p. 114).

Relationships with Other Children

Although babies are aware of other babies almost from birth, the *important* people in their world are those who care for them and provide for their needs. Relationships with peers begin to become important in early childhood. Virtually every characteristic activity and personality issue of this age—from play to gender identity and the exhibition of aggressive or prosocial behavior—involves a child's relationships with other children, both siblings and friends. Let's see how these relationships develop.

Brothers and Sisters Kathy at age 6 has enjoyed playing with her 2½-year-old brother Peter ever since he was old enough to be out of his crib. One time, their mother came into Kathy's room to find that she had arranged all of her biggest dolls in a row. One "doll" was Peter, who sat quietly sucking his thumb while

Kathy said, "*I'm* the mother here." Now that Peter is a toddler, he often gets to play the father. Kathy knows that her brother is still too young to follow the rules of games, and she happily makes allowances, often stopping during play to say to a parent or friend, "Isn't he cute?"

As we pointed out in Chapter 5, sibling rivalry is not the dominant pattern between brothers and sisters early in life. While a certain degree of rivalry does exist, so do affection, interest, companionship—and influence. Systematic observation in studies of young sibling pairs (same-sex and mixed-sex) has shown that siblings separated by as little as 1 year or as much as 4 years consistently interact a great deal, and do so in many different ways as they move through early childhood (Abramovitch, Corter, Pepler, & Stanhope, 1986; Abramovitch, Pepler, & Corter, 1982).

At the first observation by Abramovitch and her colleagues, the younger siblings were about 1½ years old, and the older ones ranged from 3 to 4½. It was clear that the children played important roles in each other's lives. Not surprisingly, the older siblings initiated more behavior, both friendly (sharing a toy, smiling, hugging, or starting a game) and unfriendly (hitting, fighting over a toy, teasing, or tattling). Also unsurprising was the tendency of the younger children to imitate their older siblings, whether in using scissors or blowing cake crumbs out of their mouths.

By the time of the first follow-up, when the younger children were 3 years old and the older ones were 4½ to 6, the siblings were more equal partners; but the same basic patterns remained, regardless of the age difference between them. Young siblings got along better when their mother was not with them, suggesting that a great deal of squabbling between siblings is a bid for the parents' attention.

The third observation took place when the younger siblings were 5 years old and the older ones were about 6½ to 8. The findings dovetail nicely with what we have seen in this chapter about personality development in early childhood. By this time, the balance of dominance had tipped back to the older siblings, who tended to be both more aggressive and more prosocial. The siblings were now less physical and more verbal with each other, both in expressing aggression (through commands, insults, threats, tattling, put-downs, bribes, and teasing) and showing care and affection (through compliments and comfort rather than hugs and kisses). The age difference between siblings apparently had only one effect: in closely spaced pairs, the older siblings initiated more prosocial behavior. Siblings of the same sex tended to be a bit closer and to play together more peaceably than boy-girl pairs.

Overall, the older siblings continued to be the initiators, the younger ones, the submitters. The older siblings initiated more play of all kinds and determined the rules for the play. Imitation was now infrequent, but when it did occur, it was still more likely to be the younger sibling who was the "copycat."

Abramovitch and her colleagues concluded that despite the undeniable existence of rivalry, "prosocial and play-oriented behaviors almost always constituted a majority of the interactions" and that "it is probably a mistake to think of siblings' relationships, at least during the preschool years, as primarily competitive or negative" (Abramovitch et al., 1986, p. 229).

The ties between siblings set the stage for other relationships in their lives. If children's relationships with their brothers and sisters are marked by an easy trust and companionship, they may carry this pattern over to their dealings with playmates, classmates, and eventually their friends and lovers in adulthood. If these early encounters have an aggressive cast, this, too, may influence later social relations.

First Friends Nancy and Janie, both 3 years old, have become fast friends. They have worn a path between their backyards, they ask for each other as soon as they wake up in the morning, and neither is so happy as when she is in the company of her friend.

Friendship develops as people develop. Although younger children may play alongside or near each other, it is only at about age 3 or so that they begin to have friends.

Through friendships and more casual interactions with other children, young children learn how to get along with others. They learn the importance of *being* a friend in order to *have* a friend. They learn how to solve problems centering on relationships, they learn how to put

Two sisters normally get along better than a sister and a brother do. The older sibling usually initiates activities, and the younger one follows.

themselves in another person's place, and they see models of other kinds of behavior. They learn values (including moral judgments and gender-role norms), and they get a chance to practice adult roles.

Young children define a friend as "someone you like." Because friendships are voluntary, they are more fragile than the more permanent ties with parents, siblings, and other relatives.

In choosing friends, preschoolers do not seem to care about mental age, IQ, height, outgoingness, laughter, or even attractiveness of personality. They usually become friendly with other children who like to do the same kinds of things, which generally means that friends usually have similar levels of energy and activity, and are of the same age and sex (Gamer, Thomas, & Kendall, 1975).

A recent investigation into the conceptions of friendship held by 4- to 7-year-olds confirms and adds to these findings (Furman & Bierman, 1983). The children were interviewed and were

Young children prefer playmates or friends who smile and laugh a lot, take turns, and are not overly shy or aggressive.

also shown pictures in which they were asked to recognize and rate activities that would make children friends. The most important features of friendships (which emerged most strongly from the picture tasks, probably because young children have difficulty putting such concepts into words) were *common activities* (doing things together), *affection* (liking and caring for each other), *support* (sharing and helping), and, to a lesser degree, *propinquity* (living nearby or going to the same school). The older children rated affection and support higher than the younger ones and rated *physical characteristics* (appearance and size) lower.

BEHAVIOR PATTERNS THAT AFFECT CHOICE OF PLAYMATES AND FRIENDS In any playground, preschool, or kindergarten, it is easy to pick out which children the others prefer to play with. Although playing with someone and being friends are not exactly the same, the characteristics that make young children desirable or undesirable seem to be quite similar for both purposes. Children who have friends are more verbal and take turns directing and submitting. Children who do not have friends tend to fight with those who do, or to stand on the sidelines and watch them (Roopnarine & Field, 1984). Children like to play with peers who smile and offer a toy or a hand. They tend to reject overtures from children who are disruptive or ag-

gressive and to ignore those who are shy or withdrawn (Roopnarine & Honig, 1985).

In one study, 65 kindergartners were shown pictures illustrating situations related to making and keeping friends and were asked what a child in the picture should do. The researchers found that the popular children's answers were more likely to promote positive relationships and to be effective. The unpopular children tended to give more aggressive responses (12 percent suggested that a child should "beat up" another child who grabs toys, compared with only 2 percent of the popular children). The unpopular children were also less resourceful; they tended to give vague strategies or to look for help from an authority rather than to cope with a situation themselves (Asher, Renshaw, Geraci, & Dor, 1979). Overall, however, the two groups were not greatly different; about two-thirds of the most common responses of popular children were also given by unpopular children.

PARENTING AND POPULARITY Not surprisingly, young children's relationships with their peers are influenced by the relationships they have had with their parents. One study found that preschoolers who had been securely attached as infants (see Chapter 5) had more friends and were ranked by their teachers as more socially competent than children who had been inse-

BOX 7-4　PRACTICALLY SPEAKING

HELPING YOUNG CHILDREN MAKE FRIENDS

Having friends is an important experience that helps children develop and contributes to good mental health; and children's ability to form friendships often reflects the relationships they have had with their parents. Research suggests that parents and other adults can help children who have trouble finding playmates or making friends by following these suggestions (Roopnarine & Honig, 1985):

■ Use positive disciplinary techniques. Give rewards, make rules and their reasons clear, and encourage cooperation in nonpunitive ways.

■ Be models of warm, nurturing, attentive behavior, and work to build children's self-esteem.

■ Demonstrate prosocial behavior, and praise signs of children's budding empathy and responsiveness.

■ Make a special effort to find a play group for children if they don't often have the opportunity to be with other children. Social skills grow through experience.

■ Encourage "loners" to play with small groups of two or three children at first.

■ Teach friendship skills indirectly through puppetry, role-playing, and books about animals and children who learn to make friends.

---

curely attached. The securely attached children were also more empathic: they responded to classmates who showed distress, whereas insecurely attached children did not (Sroufe, 1983).

Mothers of rejected or isolated children tend to lack confidence in their parenting. They seldom praise their children for good behavior, and they do not encourage independence. Fathers of such children often have very strong ideas about how children should behave, but they pay little attention to their children, dislike being disturbed by them, and regard child rearing as women's work (Peery, Jensen, & Adams, 1984, cited in Roopnarine & Honig, 1985).

Popular children generally have warm, positive relationships with their parents. When they need discipline, their parents reason with them rather than punishing them or taking away privileges (Roopnarine & Honig, 1985). As we have seen, children of authoritarian parents tend to be distrustful, withdrawn, and discontented; they are less popular than children who have learned (through authoritative parenting) to be both assertive and cooperative (Baumrind, 1977). See Box 7-4 for suggestions for putting findings such as these into practice to help young children make friends.

The connection between relationships with parents and relationships with peers seems to persist at least into the early part of the school years. One study of first-graders and their mothers suggests that children may pick up a repertoire of social behaviors which can affect their popularity (Putallaz, 1987). Friendship and popularity become more important in middle childhood—the years from about age 6 to age 12—which we'll examine in Chapter 8 and Chapter 9.

SUMMARY

Personality in Early Childhood: Theoretical Views

■ Several types of theories attempt to explain how young children acquire gender identity—awareness that they are male or female—moral standards, and other aspects of personality. These perspectives are the psychosexual, psychosocial, social-learning, cognitive-developmental, and cognitive-social approaches.

■ According to Freud, the preschool child is in the phallic stage of psychosexual development and receives pleasure from genital stimulation. The young child's sexuality is not like the mature adult's.

  1 Freud's concepts of the Oedipus complex in the male and the Electra complex in the female are meant to explain a child's feelings toward the parent of the other sex. Because of the conflict a child feels, he or she eventually represses sexual urges, identifies with the same-sex parent (undergoes *identification with the aggressor*), and enters latency.

  2 The superego (made up of the ego-ideal and the conscience) develops when the Oedipus or Electra complex is resolved.

■ Erikson maintains that the chief developmental crisis of early childhood is the development of a balance between initiative and guilt. The successful resolution of this conflict enables the child to undertake, plan, and carry out activities in pursuit of goals. The outcome of this stage is strongly influenced by how parents deal with their children.

■ The social-learning perspective holds that children acquire gender identity by identifying with models of the same sex and being rewarded for imitating them. Moral learning also takes place by imitation and reinforcement, according to this theory.

■ Identification is the adoption of the characteristics, beliefs, attitudes, values, and behaviors of another person or a group. It is an important personality development of early childhood.

  1 In Freudian terms, the child identifies with the same-sex parent at the resolution of the Oedipus or Electra complex.

  2 According to social-learning theory, identification occurs when the child observes and imitates one or more models.

■ The cognitive-developmental theory maintains that gender identity and moral development are related to cognitive development.

■ The gender-schema theory, a variation of cognitive-developmental theory that draws on aspects of social learning, holds that children fit their self-concept to the gender schema for their culture, a socially organized pattern of behavior for males and females. According to this theory, the gender schema of a culture or an individual can be changed.

Aspects and Issues of Personality Development

■ Sex differences are physical differences between males and females; gender differences are differences between the sexes that may or may not be based on biology.

■ Gender roles are the behaviors and attitudes a culture deems appropriate for males and for females. Gender-typing refers to the learning of culturally determined gender roles.

■ There are few actual behavioral differences between the sexes. After about age 10 or 11, girls do better in verbal abilities and boys in math and spatial abilities. Boys are more aggressive than girls from early childhood, and girls are more empathic.

■ Despite these relatively minor gender differences, our society holds strong ideas about appropriate behaviors for the two sexes, and children learn these expectations at an early age.

■ Gender stereotypes—exaggerated generalizations that may not be true of individuals—have the potential to restrict the development of both sexes. Androgynous child rearing, which encourages the expression of both "male" and "female" characteristics, is being fostered by many individuals and social institutions.

■ Explanations for gender differences have focused on both biological and environmental factors.

■ Play is both a social and a cognitive activity. Changes in the type of play children engage in reflect their development. Through play, children exercise their physical abilities, grow cognitively, and learn to interact with other children.

■ Preschool children show many fears of both real and imaginary objects and events. Sometimes these fears develop into phobias, which are irrational, involuntary, and inappropriate to the situation. Conditioning and modeling can help children overcome fears and phobias.

■ Whether children exhibit aggression or prosocial behavior is influenced by the way their parents treat them as well as by other factors, such as what they learn from the media and whether they observe aggressive or prosocial models.

■ Parents influence children's behavior partly through rewards and punishments. Rewards are generally more effective than punishments.

■ Punishments are most effective when they are immediate, consistent, accompanied by an ex-

8

CHAPTER

PHYSICAL AND INTELLECTUAL DEVELOPMENT IN MIDDLE CHILDHOOD

The child's growing need to take in the world soon becomes as acute as hunger or thirst. Stars in the night sky, the waxing and waning moon, the earth's relation to the sun, the meaning of seeds growing into plants, . . . the sound of nesting birds, the nuzzling movement of a day-old puppy . . . —all these must be assimilated if the child is to become a person, a perceiving person in a perceptible world.

Margaret Mead, *Family*, 1971

ASK YOURSELF

■ What gains in growth and motor development do children make in middle childhood, and what health hazards do they face?

■ How do schoolchildren think and remember, and what progress do they make in moral development and communicative abilities?

■ How can intelligence be measured, particularly in minority and disadvantaged children?

■ How can schools and parents enhance children's intellectual development?

■ What are the special needs of disabled and gifted children, and how can they be met?

■ What is creativity, and how can it be nurtured?

The words that best describe much of the physical and intellectual development of children between the ages of 6 and 12 might be "slow and steady." In middle childhood, as compared with early childhood, physical growth has slowed down considerably, and while motor abilities continue to improve, changes are not nearly so dramatic. Intellectual development, too, progresses at a more relaxed, even pace. Because the day-by-day changes are not so obvious, the differences between the 6-year-old and the 12-year-old can be startling. We realize that the first is a small child, the second a near-adult.

Normally, the years between 6 and 12 are among the healthiest in the life span. Children today, however, are not as healthy or as physically fit as their counterparts were in the 1960s.

Cognitive development proceeds largely within the framework of schooling. It is hardly coincidental that the usual age for starting school in the western world coincides with significant changes in children's mental abilities that are recognized by each of three major approaches to intellectual development.

As children enter what Jean Piaget described as the stage of *concrete operations*, their thinking becomes truly logical. They are now able to understand complex concepts and to solve more sophisticated problems. Logic allows them to make more mature moral judgments, as they grasp concepts of right and wrong and become less egocentric. (These changes also aid their social development, as we'll see in Chapter 9.)

The information-processing approach tells us that youngsters at this age are better able to use strategies to improve their memory and can better understand the processes involved in communication and cognition. And because children are now much more verbal, psychometric intelligence tests can more accurately predict academic performance.

We'll look at all these changes, and we'll also see how schools try to meet the special needs of children with physical or mental disabilities or exceptional gifts.

If we were to walk by a typical elementary school just after the last bell, we would see a virtual eruption of children of all shapes and sizes. Tall ones, short ones, chubby ones, and thin ones would be dashing helter-skelter through the school doors and into the freedom of the open air. A few of the children would be not just chubby but actually fat; and although it might not be obvious, many would not be as physically fit as they should be.

If we were to follow these children on their way home from school, we would be likely to see them leaping up onto narrow ledges and then walking along, balancing themselves, until they jumped off, trying to break distance records—but occasionally breaking bones instead. Some of these youngsters reach home (or, often, a baby-sitter's house) not to emerge for the rest of the day. They could be outdoors honing new skills in jumping, running, throwing, catching, balancing, cycling, or climbing—becoming stronger, faster, and better coordinated. Instead, many children stay indoors watching television or engaging in quiet play.

GROWTH AND FITNESS

Both boys and girls gain an average of 7 pounds and 2 to 3 inches a year until the adolescent growth spurt, which comes for girls at about age 10. Girls then outdistance boys physically until the boys have *their* spurt and overtake them at age 12 or 13.

These figures, of course, are averages. Individual children vary widely—so widely that "if a child who was of exactly average height at his seventh birthday grew not at all for two years,

School-age children are taller and thinner than they were as preschoolers. Although there is very little difference in height and weight between the sexes before puberty, girls generally retain more fatty tissue than boys do and will continue to do so throughout adulthood.

he would still be just within the normal limits of height attained at age nine" (Tanner, 1973, p. 35).

In addition, growth rates vary with race, national origin, and socioeconomic level. A study of 8-year-old children in different parts of the world yielded a range of about 9 inches between the mean heights of the shortest children (mostly from southeast Asia, Oceania, and South America) and the tallest ones (mostly from northern and central Europe, eastern Australia, and the United States) (Meredith, 1969). Although genetic differences probably account for some of this diversity, environmental influences also play a part. The tallest children come from parts of the world where malnutrition and infectious disease are not major problems. For similar reasons, children from affluent homes tend to be larger and more mature than children from poorer homes.

In view of the wide variance in size during middle childhood, we must be careful about basing judgments concerning children's health or possible abnormalities on their physical growth. Especially in the United States, with its racially and ethnically diverse population, we may need to develop separate growth standards for different groups (Goldstein & Tanner, 1980). But first we need to recognize the importance of nutrition to growth and health.

Nutrition

During these middle years, average body weight doubles, and children's play demands a lot of energy. To support steady growth and constant exertion, children need plenty of food. Children in this stage usually have good appetites and often eat rapidly. On average, they need 2400 calories per day, 34 grams of protein a day, and high levels of complex carbohydrates, such as those found in potatoes and cereal grains. Refined carbohydrates (sweeteners) should be kept to a minimum (E.R. Williams & Caliendo, 1984).

Poor nutrition causes slowed growth. It takes some energy and protein just to stay alive and some more energy and protein to grow. When meals cannot adequately support both these processes fully, growth must be sacrificed in order to maintain the body.

Nutrition also has social implications. Children cannot play and stay alert if they do not have enough food. The effects can be long-lasting; a longitudinal study in Guatemala, where malnutrition is a serious problem, found that a child's diet from birth to age 2 is a good predictor of social behavior in middle childhood. Researchers observed 138 children, aged 6 to 8, who had been given dietary supplements in infancy. All the children had received extra calories and vitamins, but only some had received proteins. Children who as infants had not received proteins tended to be passive, more dependent on adults, and more anxious, while the better-nourished children were happier, feistier, and more sociable with their peers (D.E. Barrett, Radke-Yarrow, & Klein, 1982).

Furthermore, poor nutrition may cause problems in family relationships. Mothers may respond less frequently and less sensitively to malnourished infants, who lack the energy to engage their mothers' attention. The infants, in turn, become unresponsive and develop poor interpersonal skills, further reducing their mothers' and other people's inclination or desire to interact with them (B.M. Lester, 1979). If the mother is malnourished too, the cycle worsens (Rosetti-Ferreira, 1978). Once more, we see how different domains of development—in this case, physical growth and personality—are related.

Obesity

Within the past 2 decades, obesity has become 54 percent more common among 6- to 11-year-olds and 39 percent more common among 12- to 17-year-olds in the United States. In one 6-year study of nearly 2600 mostly white middle-class children under the age of 12 who were enrolled in a prepaid health maintenance plan, about 4 percent (5½ percent of 8- to 11-year-olds) were diagnosed as obese (Starfield et al., 1984).

Extreme overeating is not necessarily the culprit. Obese children may begin by eating as little as 50 extra calories a day and putting on 5 extra pounds a year. Since these children tend to be less active, they do not burn up the excess calories. But we don't know whether they are less active because they are fat, or whether they become fat because they are less active (Kolata, 1986).

As was pointed out in Chapter 2, some people appear to have a genetic predisposition toward obesity; fat parents often have fat children, and not just because the children see their parents overeating (Stunkard et al., 1986). Environment also has a strong influence. Obesity is more common among lower socioeconomic groups, especially among women (Kolata, 1986).

There is a link between too much weight and too much television. A study of nearly 7000 children between the ages of 6 and 11 and a second study of 6500 adolescents found that every hour a day spent before a television set increases the prevalence of obesity by 2 percent. Children who watch more television eat more snacks (especially those advertised on commercials) and play less than other children (Dietz & Gortmaker, 1985).

Fat children do not usually "outgrow" being fat; they tend to become fat adults (Kolata, 1986), and obesity in adulthood puts them at a significant risk of serious health problems.

Improving Children's Fitness

Today's schoolchildren are less physically fit than children were during the mid-1960s. They are fatter, even though most are not actually obese, and their hearts and lungs are in worse shape than those of a typical middle-aged jogger.

One study found that 98 percent of the 7- to 12-year-olds in a typical midwestern working-class community had at least one major risk factor for developing heart disease later in life. Their levels of body fat averaged 2 to 5 percent above the national, unhealthily high average; 41 percent had high levels of cholesterol; and 28 percent had higher than normal blood pressure (C.T. Kuntzleman, personal communication, 1984).

Why are these children in such poor physical condition? Mainly, it is because they are not active enough. Only half of all elementary school children take physical education classes as often as twice a week, fewer than half stay active during cold weather, and most are not spending enough time learning such lifetime fitness skills as running, swimming, bicycling, and walking.

Many spend too much time watching television. Most physical activities, in and outside of school, are team and competitive sports and games. These do not promote fitness, will usually be dropped once the young person is no longer in school, and are generally engaged in by the fittest and most athletic youngsters, not by those who need more exercise.

Children can improve their health and fitness by changing their everyday behavior. One educational and behavior modification program has taught approximately 24,000 children in Michigan how to analyze the foods they eat; how to measure their own blood pressure, heart rate, and body fat; and how to withstand the influence of peers and advertising to smoke and to eat nutritionally unsound foods. The program also encourages children to take part in physically demanding games. When researchers looked at the effects of the program on 360 second-, fifth-, and seventh-graders, they found heartening results. The children in the program had significantly improved the time in which they could run a mile; they had lowered their cholesterol levels, their blood pressure, and their levels of body fat; and the number of children without any risk factors for developing coronary disease had risen by 55 percent (Fitness Finders, 1984).

This program is in line with recommendations by a prominent group of pediatricians that schools provide sound physical education programs with a variety of competitive and recreational sports for all children. The emphasis should be on activities that can be part of a lifetime fitness regimen, such as tennis, bowling, running, swimming, golf, and skating (American Academy of Pediatrics, Committee on Pediatric Aspects of Physical Fitness, Recreation, and Sports, 1981).

MOTOR DEVELOPMENT

Studies of 7- to 12-year-olds done nearly 30 years ago, when children seem to have been more physically active, suggested that motor abilities improve with age (see the examples in Table 8–1). These studies also found sex differences; boys tended to run faster, jump higher, throw farther, and show more strength than

TABLE 8-1 MOTOR DEVELOPMENT OF BOYS AND GIRLS IN MIDDLE CHILDHOOD

AGE	SELECTED BEHAVIORS
6	Girls are superior in accuracy of movement; boys are superior in forceful, less complex acts. Skipping is possible. Children can throw with proper weight shift and step.
7	Balancing on one foot without looking becomes possible. Children can walk 2-inch-wide balance beams. Children can hop and jump accurately into small squares. Children can execute accurate jumping-jack exercise.
8	Grip strength permits steady 12-pound pressure. Number of games participated in by both sexes is greatest at this age. Children can engage in alternate rhythmic hopping in a 2-2, 2-3, or 3-3 pattern. Girls can throw a small ball 40 feet.
9	Girls can jump vertically to a height of 8½ inches, and boys, 10 inches. Boys can run 16½ feet per second. Boys can throw a small ball 70 feet.
10	Children can judge and intercept pathways of small balls thrown from a distance. Girls can run 17 feet per second.
11	Standing broad jump of 5 feet is possible for boys; 6 inches less for girls.
12	Standing high jump of 3 feet is possible.

Source: Adapted from Cratty, 1979, p. 222.

girls did (Espenschade, 1960; Gavotos, 1959). After age 13, the gap between the sexes widened; boys improved, while girls stayed the same or declined (Espenschade, 1960).

Today, however, it seems clear that much of the difference between the sexes' motor abilities has been due to differences in expectations and participation. When researchers study prepubescent boys and girls who take part in similar activities, they find that their abilities are similar.

When third-, fourth-, and fifth-grade boys and girls who had been in excellent coeducational physical education classes for at least a year were compared on their scores on sit-ups, shuttle run, 50-yard dash, broad jump, and 600-yard walk-run, both sexes were found to improve with age, and the girls performed approximately as well as the boys on most measures. The girls who were tested in the third year of the program performed even better than the boys on a number of measures (E.G. Hall & Lee, 1984).

Such findings confirm statements by pediatricians that there is no reason to separate prepubertal boys and girls for physical activities. After puberty, however, girls should not play in heavy collision sports with boys, because their lighter, smaller frames make them too subject to injury (American Academy of Pediatrics, Committee on Pediatric Aspects of Physical Fitness, Recreation, and Sports, 1981).

HEALTH

Richard, aged 10, is home in bed with a cold, his second of the year. He sneezes, snoozes, watches a lot of television, pulls out his old books and toys, and in general, enjoys the rest from his usual routine. He is lucky. He has had no illnesses this year other than the two colds, while

(© George Ancona/International Stock Photo)

These enthusiastic soccer players are proving that girls are often much better athletes than they were given credit for being (or given the opportunity to be) in the past. Studies show that boys and girls who take part in similar activities show similar abilities.

some of his classmates have had six or seven respiratory infections. That number of respiratory infections is common during middle childhood, as germs pass freely among youngsters at school or at play (Behrman & Vaughan, 1983).

Even children who do get a lot of colds, however, are healthier than their counterparts early in this century. As we pointed out in Chapter 6, the development of vaccines for many childhood illnesses has made childhood an extremely safe time of life for most; the death rate in middle childhood is the lowest in the life span.

Because of their cognitive development, which we'll discuss in the next section, children in this age group are beginning to understand that health and illness have comprehensible causes and that people can do much to promote their own health (see Box 8-1, page 268).

Minor Medical Conditions

What kinds of health problems other than colds occur in middle childhood? The study (mentioned earlier) of mostly white middle-class children enrolled in a prepaid health maintenance organization found such varied conditions as allergies and warts (Starfield et al., 1984).

Almost all the youngsters became quite ill from time to time, but their ailments tended to be brief (though children who had a particular condition once were more likely to have

it again). During the 6 years of the study, more than 90 percent of the children had acute (short-term) medical conditions—usually upper-respiratory infections, viruses, or eczema—but only 1 in 9 had chronic (persistent) conditions such as migraine headaches or nearsightedness. Eighty percent of the children were treated for injuries. Upper-respiratory illnesses, sore throats, strep throats, ear infections, and bed-wetting decreased with age, whereas acne, headaches, and transitory emotional disturbances increased as youngsters approached puberty. The typical child had clusters of five to seven different types of problems over 6 years; more than 20 percent had eight types or more; about 15 percent had three types or fewer (Starfield et al., 1984).

Vision and Visual Problems

In middle childhood, most youngsters have much keener vision than they did before. Children under 6 years of age tend to be farsighted, because their eyes have not matured and are shaped differently from those of adults. After that age, the eyes not only are more mature but can focus better.

In a minority of children, however, vision does not develop properly. Ten percent of 6-year-olds have defective near vision, and 7 percent have defective distant vision; the latter

BOX 8-1 FOOD FOR THOUGHT

HOW CHILDREN LOOK AT ILLNESS

Being sick can be upsetting at any age. For young children, who understand little of what is happening to them, it can also be frightening and confusing. Karen, for example, overheard her doctor refer to *edema* (an accumulation of fluid) and thought that her problem was "a demon" (Perrin & Gerrity, 1981).

As children get older, their understanding of their own bodies and of what causes disease advances as cognitive development progresses.

At the beginning of middle childhood, children tend to believe that illness is magically produced by human actions, often their own. These magical explanations can last well into childhood. One 12-year-old girl with leukemia said, "I know that my doctor told me that my illness is caused by too many white cells, but I still wonder if it was caused by something I did" (Brewster, 1982, p. 361).

An adult might be tempted to reassure this child that her behavior did *not* bring on her illness, but such well-meaning intervention might actually be ill-advised. Egocentric explanations for illness may serve as an important defense against feelings of helplessness. Children may feel that if something they did has made them ill, then perhaps they can do something else to get better.

As children develop beyond the preoperational stage, their explanations for disease change. They now explain all disease in terms of germs, which—almost as magically as demons or guilt—automatically cause disease. "Watch out for germs" is their motto, and their only "prevention" is a variety of ineffectual behaviors designed to ward off these enemies.

As children approach adolescence, they enter a third stage, in which they see that there are many causes of disease. Contact with germs does not automatically lead to illness, nor can avoiding germs automatically prevent it—although they know that people can do much to keep themselves healthy.

---

number jumps to 17 percent by 11 years of age (U.S. Department of Health, Education, and Welfare, USDHEW, 1976).

Dental Health

Most of the teeth that must serve people for the rest of their lives appear near the outset of middle childhood. The primary teeth begin to fall out at about age 6, to be replaced by about four permanent teeth per year for the next 5 years. The first molars erupt at about age 6, followed by the second molars at about 13, and the third molars (that is, the wisdom teeth) usually during the early twenties (Behrman & Vaughan, 1983).

Approximately one-half of children aged 5 to 17 have no tooth decay, according to a recent government survey (U.S. Department of Health and Human Services, USDHHS, 1988). This study found that, in their permanent teeth, children have an average of 3 decayed or missing teeth or filled surfaces. American children today have 36 percent fewer dental cavities than were reported in similar surveys at the beginning of the 1980s, when they had an average of almost 5 decayed or missing teeth or filled surfaces (USDHHS, 1981a).

Even today, when many children go to preschool and most go to kindergarten, the first day of "real" school is a milestone, approached with a mixture of eagerness and anxiety. "What will the teacher be like?" Julie, aged 6, wonders as she walks up the steps to the big red-brick

schoolhouse, shiny new pencil case in hand. "What will we learn? Will I be able to do the work?"

Julie's ability to learn and to do schoolwork will expand greatly during the next 6 years, because of her growing capacities to think conceptually, to solve problems, to remember, and to use language—changes we'll examine in the remainder of this chapter. But the first day of school will always be a special day—a day of promise and anticipation.

ASPECTS OF INTELLECTUAL DEVELOPMENT IN MIDDLE CHILDHOOD

Cognitive Development: Piaget's Stage of Concrete Operations

Sometime between 5 and 7 years of age, according to Piaget, children enter the stage of *concrete operations,* when they can think logically about the here and now but not yet about abstractions. They generally remain in this stage until about the age of 11.

What Is Operational Thinking? Children in Piaget's third stage are capable of *operational thinking:* they can use symbols to carry out operations, or mental activities, as opposed to the physical activities that were the basis for most of their earlier thinking. For the first time, then, true logic becomes possible. Even though younger children, in the preoperational stage, have mastered the symbolic function (they can make mental representations of objects and events that are not immediately present), their learning is still closely tied to physical experience. Operational children are far more proficient at classifying, manipulating numbers, dealing with concepts of time and space, and distinguishing reality from fantasy.

Since they are considerably less egocentric by now, children in the stage of concrete operations can *decenter*—they can take all aspects of a situation into account when drawing conclusions, rather than focusing on only one aspect, as they did in the preoperational stage. They realize that most physical operations are reversible. Their increased ability to understand other people's viewpoints enables them to communi-

cate more effectively and to be more flexible in their moral thinking.

But while school-age children think more logically than younger children, their thinking is still anchored in the here and now. Not until the stage of formal operations, which usually comes with adolescence (see Chapter 10), will young people be able to think abstractly, test hypotheses, and understand probabilities, according to Piaget.

What Is Conservation? One important ability that develops during the stage of concrete operations is conservation. As we stated in Chapter 6, *conservation* is the ability to recognize that two equal quantities of matter remain equal—in substance, weight, or volume—so long as nothing is added or taken away.

ATTRIBUTES OF CONSERVATION In a typical conservation task, Stacy is shown two equal balls of clay. She agrees that they are equal. She is said to conserve *substance* if she recognizes that even after one of the balls has been rolled into the shape of a worm, both lumps of clay have equal amounts of matter. In *weight* conservation, she recognizes that the ball and the worm weigh the same. And in conservation of *volume,* she realizes that the ball and the worm displace equal amounts of liquid when they are placed in glasses of water.

Children develop different types of conservation at different times. At age 6 or 7, they typically are able to conserve substance; at 9 or 10, weight; and at 11 or 12, volume. *Horizontal décalage* is the term Piaget used to describe this phenomenon of children's inability to transfer what they have learned about one type of conservation to a different type, even though the underlying principle is identical for all three kinds of conservation. Thus, we see how concrete a child's reasoning is at this stage. It is tied so closely to particular situations that children cannot readily apply the same basic mental operation to a different situation.

STAGES IN DEVELOPING CONSERVATION Children go through three stages in mastering conservation. We can see how this works in relation to substance conservation. In the *first* stage, preoperational children fail to conserve. They center or focus on one aspect of the situation (for

According to Piaget, a child who has mastered the concept of conservation understands that even if liquid is poured into a differently shaped container, the amount will remain the same.

example, that the ball of clay becomes longer when it is rolled into a worm shape) and do not take notice of the fact that the worm is also narrower than the ball was. Thus they are fooled by appearances and decide that the worm contains more clay. Because preoperational children do not understand the concept of reversibility, they do not recognize that they could restore the original shape (and show that nothing has been added) by rolling the worm back into a ball.

The *second* stage is a transitional one. Children vacillate, sometimes conserving and sometimes not. They may notice more than one aspect of a situation—such as height, width, length, and thickness—but may fail to recognize how these dimensions are related.

In the *third* and final stage in conservation, children conserve and give logical justifications for their answers. These justifications may take the form of *reversibility* ("If the clay worm were shaped into a ball, it would be the same as the other ball"); *identity* ("It's the same clay; you haven't added any or taken any away"); or *compensation* ("The ball is shorter than the worm, but the worm is thinner than the ball, so they both have the same amount of clay"). Thus operational children in middle childhood show a qualitative cognitive advancement over preoperational preschoolers. Their thinking is revers-

ible, they decenter, and they are aware that transformations are only perceptual alterations.

FACTORS INFLUENCING THE DEVELOPMENT OF CONSERVATION Piaget stressed that children develop the ability to conserve when they are neurologically mature enough. He believed that this ability is only minimally affected by formal training. However, factors other than maturation do affect conservation. Children who learn conservation skills earliest have high grades, high IQs, high verbal ability, and nondominating mothers (Almy, Chittenden, & Miller, 1966; Goldschmid & Bentler, 1968). Black children of higher socioeconomic levels do better on conservation tasks (as well as on other Piagetian operations) than do black children of lower socioeconomic levels (Bardouille-Crema, Black, & Feldhusen, 1986). Also, children from different countries—Switzerland, the United States, Great Britain, and others—have been found to achieve conservation at different average ages. Therefore culture, and not maturation alone, apparently plays a role.

Moral Development: Three Theories

Why are we discussing morality in a chapter about intellectual development? Isn't moral thinking an outgrowth of personality, emotional attitudes, and cultural influences? Although all these factors do enter in, and although psychoanalytic and social-learning theories draw upon them to explain moral development (see Chapter 7), the most influential explanation these days is that the development of moral values is a rational process that coincides with cognitive growth.

The golden rule, "Do unto others as you would have them do unto you," points up that link. This widely accepted moral principle presumes an understanding that other people may react to your actions as you react to theirs. But we have seen that small children are egocentric. The golden rule is difficult for them to follow, not because they are evil, but because they have a hard time imagining how another person feels.

Jean Piaget and Lawrence Kohlberg, two of the most influential modern theorists on the development of moral reasoning, maintained

TABLE 8-2 PIAGET'S TWO STAGES OF MORAL DEVELOPMENT

ASPECT OF MORALITY	STAGE I	STAGE II
Moral concepts	Morality of constraint.	Morality of cooperation.
Point of view	Child views an act as either totally right or totally wrong, and thinks everyone sees it the same way. Children cannot put themselves in place of others.	Children can put themselves in place of others. They are not absolutist in judgments but see that more than one point of view is possible.
Intentionality	Child judges acts in terms of actual physical consequences, not the motivation behind them.	Child judges acts by intentions, not consequences.
Rules	Child obeys rules because they are sacred and unalterable.	Child recognizes that rules were made by people and can be changed by people. Children considers themselves just as capable of changing rules as anyone else.
Respect for authority	Unilateral respect leads to feeling of obligation to conform to adult standards and obey adult rules.	Mutual respect for authority and peers allows children to value their own opinions and abilities and to judge other people realistically.
Punishment	Child favors severe punishment. Child feels that punishment itself defines the wrongness of an act; an act is bad if it will elicit punishment.	Child favors milder punishment that compensates the victim and helps the culprit recognize why an act was wrong, thus leading to reform.
"Immanent justice"	Child confuses moral law with physical law and believes that any physical accident or misfortune that occurs after a misdeed is a punishment willed by God or some other supernatural force.	Child does not confuse natural misfortune with punishment.

Source: Adapted partly from M. Hoffman, 1970; Kohlberg, in M. Hoffman & Hoffman, 1964.

that children cannot make sound moral judgments until they shed egocentric thinking and achieve a certain level of cognitive maturity. Selman holds that moral development is closely linked to "role-taking" ability. Let's examine these three theories.

Piaget's Theory: Moral Stages According to Piaget, children's conception of morality develops in two major stages (summarized in Table 8-2), which coincide approximately with the preoperational and operational stages. People go through these moral stages at varying times, but the sequence is always the same.

The first stage, the *morality of constraint* (also called *heteronomous morality*), is characterized

by rigid, simplistic judgments. Young children see everything in black and white, not gray. Because they are egocentric, they cannot conceive of more than one way of looking at a moral question. They believe that rules are unalterable, behavior is either right or wrong, and any offense—no matter how minor—deserves severe punishment. (Of course, children often disobey the rules they insist upon for others.)

The second stage, the *morality of cooperation* (or *autonomous morality*), is characterized by moral flexibility. As children mature and interact more with other children and with adults, they think less egocentrically. They have ever-increasing contact with a wide range of viewpoints, many of which contradict what they have learned at home. Children conclude that there is not one unchangeable, absolute moral standard, but that rules are made by people and can be changed by people, including themselves. They look for the intent behind an act, and they believe that punishment should fit the "crime." They are on the way to formulating their own moral codes.

To illustrate one aspect of this change, Piaget (1932) told this story:

> Once upon a time there were two little boys, Augustus and Julian. Augustus noticed one day that his father's inkpot was empty, and he decided to help his father by filling it. But in opening the bottle, he spilled the ink and made a large stain on the tablecloth. Julian played with his father's inkpot and made a small stain on the tablecloth. Piaget then asked, "Which boy is naughtier and why?"

A child in the stage of constraint is likely to consider Augustus the greater offender, because he made the larger stain. But an older child will probably recognize that Augustus meant well, whereas the smaller stain Julian made was the result of doing something he should not have been doing. Immature moral judgments, being egocentric, center on one dimension: the magnitude of the offense. Mature judgments take intention into account.

Selman's Theory: Role-Taking Questions like the one about Augustus and Julian involve *role-taking:* putting oneself into another person's position and imagining how that person thinks and feels. Selman (1973) describes the development of role-taking in five stages (0 to 4), which are summarized in Table 8-3.

At *stage 0* (about age 4 to age 6), children think and judge egocentrically, and so they cannot assume other people's roles. Suppose that we tell Sara, who is 5 years old, a story about a little girl who has promised her father not to climb trees but then sees a kitten trapped on a high branch. At this stage, Sara sees no problem. Since she likes kittens herself, she assumes that her father or anyone else will automatically favor climbing the tree to save the kitten.

At *stage 1,* from about age 6 to age 8, children realize that other people may interpret a situation differently. Now Sara says, "If the father doesn't know why she climbed the tree, he will be angry. But if he knows why she did it, he will be glad." This answer shows that Sara now realizes the importance of intention.

TABLE 8-3 STAGES OF ROLE-TAKING

STAGE	APPROXIMATE AGES	DEVELOPMENT
0	4–6	Child thinks that his or her own point of view is the only one possible.
1	6–8	Child realizes others may interpret a situation in a way different from his or her own.
2	8–10	Child has reciprocal awareness, realizing that others have a different point of view and that others are aware that he or she has a particular point of view. Child understands the importance of letting others know that their requests have not been ignored or forgotten.
3	10–12	Child can imagine a third person's perspective, taking into account several different points of view.
4	Adolescence	Person realizes that communication and mutual role-taking do not always resolve disputes over rival values.

Source: Selman, 1973.

Reciprocal awareness marks *stage 2,* from 8 to 10 years of age. At this stage, not only can Sara put herself into someone else's place (as she could in stage 1), but now she knows that someone else can imagine *her* thoughts and feelings. Thus, she reasons, the little girl's father would realize that she believed that he would approve her breaking the promise under the circumstances, and so he would think that it was all right. But if he thought that she did not consider what his reaction might be, he would be angry.

In *stage 3,* from about age 10 to age 12, a child can step outside a relationship and view it from a third point of view—for example, that of an objective outsider like a judge.

Stage 4 arrives, usually during adolescence, when a person realizes that mutual role-taking does not always resolve disputes. There might be rival values that simply cannot be communicated away.

Selman's analysis of the development of role-taking was inspired by the ideas of Piaget and Kohlberg that moral development accompanies intellectual growth. Let's see how Kohlberg described children's moral reasoning.

Kohlberg's Theory: Moral Reasoning How would *you* respond to this moral dilemma? A woman is near death from cancer. A druggist has discovered a drug that doctors believe might save her. The druggist is charging $2000 for a small dose—10 times what it costs him to make the drug. The sick woman's husband, Heinz, borrows from everyone he knows but can scrape together only $1000. He begs the druggist to sell him the drug for less or let him pay later. The druggist refuses, saying, "I discovered the drug, and I'm going to make money from it." Heinz, desperate, breaks into the man's store and steals the drug. Should Heinz have done that? Why, or why not? (Kohlberg, 1969).

KOHLBERG'S MORAL DILEMMAS The problem of Heinz and the drug is the most famous example of Kohlberg's approach to moral development. For some 20 years, Kohlberg studied a group of 75 boys who varied in age from 10 to 16 years when he began working. Kohlberg told them stories that posed moral problems—dilemmas of the sort that Heinz faced—and he

The boy sliding into home plate and the boy trying to tag him out may or may not agree with the umpire's decision, but they understand that they are operating under the same rules. A child who has reached Kohlberg's fourth stage of moral reasoning, usually around the age of 10, respects authority and sees the need to obey rules so as to maintain order.

asked the boys how they would solve them. At the center of each dilemma was a question of how to act justly in consideration of any of 25 fundamental moral ideas, such as the value of human life, motives behind actions, individual rights, and the basis of respect for moral authority.

After telling the stories, Kohlberg and his colleagues asked the boys a number of questions designed to show how they arrived at their decisions. Kohlberg was less interested in the answers themselves than in the reasoning used to reach them; thus two youngsters who gave opposite answers to Heinz's dilemma could both be at the same moral level if their reasoning was based on similar factors.

KOHLBERG'S LEVELS OF MORAL REASONING From the responses he received, Kohlberg concluded that the level of moral reasoning is related to a person's cognitive level. The reasoning behind the boys' answers convinced Kohlberg that many people eventually arrive at moral judgments independently rather than merely "internalizing" the standards of parents,

TABLE 8·4 KOHLBERG'S SIX STAGES OF MORAL REASONING

LEVELS	STAGES OF REASONING	TYPICAL ANSWERS TO HEINZ'S DILEMMA
Level 1: Preconventional (ages 4 to 10) Emphasis in this level is on external control. The standards are those of others, and they are observed either to avoid punishment or to reap rewards.	**Stage 1** *Orientation to punishment and obedience.* "What will happen to me?" Children obey the rules of others to avoid punishment. They ignore the motives of an act and focus on its physical form (such as the size of a lie) or its consequences (for example, the amount of physical damage).	*Pro:* "He should steal the drug. It isn't really bad to take it. It isn't as if he hadn't asked to pay for it first. The drug he'd take is worth only $200: he's not really taking a $2000 drug." *Con:* "He shouldn't steal the drug. It's a big crime. He didn't get permission; he used force and broke and entered. He did a lot of damage, stealing a very expensive drug and breaking up the store, too."
	Stage 2 *Instrumental purpose and exchange.* "You scratch my back, I'll scratch yours." Children conform to rules out of self-interest and consideration for what others can do for them in return. They look at an act in terms of the human needs it meets and differentiate this value from the act's physical form and consequences.	*Pro:* "It's all right to steal the drug, because his wife needs it and he wants her to live. It isn't that he wants to steal, but that's what he has to do to get the drug to save her." *Con:* "He shouldn't steal it. The druggist isn't wrong or bad; he just wants to make a profit. That's what you're in business for— to make money."
Level II: Morality of conventional role conformity (ages 10 to 13) Children now want to please other people. They still observe the standards of others, but they have internalized these standards to some extent. Now they want to be considered "good" by those persons whose opinions are important to them. They are now able to take the roles of authority figures well enough to decide whether an action is good by their standards.	**Stage 3** *Maintaining mutual relations, approval of others, the golden rule.* "Am I a good boy or girl?" Children want to please and help others, can judge the intentions of others, and develop their own ideas of what a good person is. They evaluate an act according to the motive behind it or the person performing it, and they take circumstances into account.	*Pro:* "He should steal the drug. He is only doing something that is natural for a good husband to do. You can't blame him for doing something out of love for his wife. You'd blame him if he didn't love his wife enough to save her." *Con:* "He shouldn't steal. If his wife dies, he can't be blamed. It isn't because he's heartless or that he doesn't love her enough to do everything that he legally can. The druggist is the selfish or heartless one."
	Stage 4 *Social system and conscience.* "What if everybody did it?" People are concerned with doing their duty, showing respect for higher authority, and maintaining the social order. They consider an act always wrong, regardless of motive or circumstances, if it violates a rule and harms others.	*Pro:* "You should steal it. If you did nothing you'd be letting your wife die. It's your responsibility if she dies. You have to take it with the idea of paying the druggist." *Con:* "It is a natural thing for Heinz to want to save his wife, but it's still always wrong to steal. He still knows that he's stealing and taking a valuable drug from the man who made it."

TABLE 8-4 CONTINUED

LEVELS	STAGES OF REASONING	TYPICAL ANSWERS TO HEINZ'S DILEMMA
Level III: Morality of autonomous moral principles (age 13, or not until young adulthood, or never) This level marks the attainment of true morality. For the first time, the person acknowledges the possibility of conflict between two socially accepted standards and tries to decide between them. The control of conduct is now internal, both in the standards observed and in the reasoning about right and wrong. Stages 5 and 6 may be alternative methods of the highest level of moral reasoning.	**Stage 5** *Morality of contract, of individual rights, and of democratically accepted law.* People think in rational terms, valuing the will of the majority and the welfare of society. They generally see these values best supported by adherence to the law. While they recognize that there are times when human need and the law conflict, they believe that it is better for society in the long run if they obey the law.	*Pro:* "The law wasn't set up for these circumstances. Taking the drug in this situation isn't really right, but it's justified." *Con:* "You can't completely blame someone for stealing, but extreme circumstances don't really justify taking the law into your own hands. You can't have people stealing whenever they are desperate. The end may be good, but the ends don't justify the means."
	Stage 6 *Morality of universal ethical principles.* People do what they as individuals think right, regardless of legal restrictions or the opinions of others. They act in accordance with internalized standards, knowing that they would condemn themselves if they did not.	*Pro:* "This is a situation that forces him to choose between stealing and letting his wife die. In a situation where the choice must be made, it is morally right to steal. He has to act in terms of the principle of preserving and respecting life." *Con:* "Heinz is faced with the decision of whether to consider the other people who need the drug just as badly as his wife. Heinz ought to act not according to his particular feelings toward his wife, but considering the value of all the lives involved."

Source: Adapted from Kohlberg, 1969, 1976 (in Lickona, 1976).

teachers, or peers. On the basis of the different thought processes shown by the answers, Kohlberg described three levels of moral reasoning:

- *Level I: **preconventional morality** (ages 4 to 10 years).* Children, under external controls, obey rules to get rewards or avoid punishment.
- *Level II: **morality of conventional role conformity** (ages 10 to 13).* Children have internalized the standards of authority figures. They obey rules to please others or to maintain order.
- *Level III: **morality of autonomous moral principles** (age 13 or later, if ever).* Morality is fully

internal. People now recognize conflicts between moral standards and choose between them.

Each of the three levels is divided into two stages. Table 8-4 gives detailed descriptions of the six stages with illustrative answers to Heinz's dilemma.

Kohlberg's lower stages are similar to Piaget's, but his advanced stages go farther—into adulthood. Selman's stages also correspond to Kohlberg's. For example, the more advanced a person is in role-taking, the more complicated the dilemma of Heinz and the drug becomes. A child in Selman's stage 3 of role-taking development says that if Heinz were caught, a judge would listen to his explanation, see the validity of his argument, and let him go. But in Selman's stage 4, the child realizes that no matter how good the explanation seems to Heinz, the judge has sworn to uphold the law and will not excuse the theft.

EVALUATING KOHLBERG'S THEORY   Kohlberg's theory has generated considerable research, both by his own research team and by others. When Kohlberg and his colleagues followed 58 American boys (initially aged 10, 13, and 16 years) for 20 years, into adulthood, their study found that the boys progressed through Kohlberg's stages in sequence and none skipped a stage. Furthermore, moral judgments correlated positively with the boys' age, education, IQ, and socioeconomic status (Colby, Kohlberg, Gibbs, & Lieberman, 1983).

Cross-cultural studies confirm this sequence but only up to a point. Older subjects from countries other than the United States do tend to score at higher stages than younger ones, but people from nonwestern cultures rarely score above stage 4 (Edwards, 1977; Nisan & Kohlberg, 1982; Snarey, 1985). It is possible that these cultures do not foster higher development—but is also likely that Kohlberg's definition of morality as a system of justice is not as appropriate for nonwestern as for western societies. Thus Kohlberg's scheme may miss higher levels of reasoning in some cultural groups (Snarey, 1985).

Furthermore, some critics have questioned the appropriateness of Kohlberg's definition of morality for females in American society, on the ground that his theory stresses "masculine" values—justice and fairness—rather than "feminine" values, such as caring for others. In Chapter 12, we will examine an alternative, gender-based theory proposed by Carol Gilligan (1982), which is currently having considerable impact.

A fundamental challenge is directed at Kohlberg's belief that children are "moral philosophers," who work out their moral systems by independent discovery. Studies show, on the contrary, that moral judgments are strongly influenced by education—for example, by simply telling children the "right" answers to moral reasoning tasks (Carroll & Rest, 1982; Lickona, 1973).

Another problem with Kohlberg's system lies in the testing procedures themselves. Kohlberg's standard tasks (like the story of Heinz) need to be presented to each subject individually and then scored by trained judges—a cumbersome, time-consuming procedure. One alternative is the Defining Issues Test (DIT), which can be administered quickly to a group and can be scored objectively (Rest, 1975). The DIT asks 12 questions about each of 6 moral dilemmas. The results of the DIT correlate moderately well with scores on Kohlberg's traditional tasks.

Still another issue is the extent to which moral reasoning is translated into action. Studies suggest that people at postconventional levels of thought do not actually behave more morally than those at lower levels (Kupfersmid & Wonderly, 1980). This finding is not surprising in view of classic research on children's cheating (Hartshorne & May, 1928–1930). Studies found that almost all children cheat at times (though some are more inclined to do so than others, and the circumstances make a difference). Furthermore, children who cheat are just as likely to say that cheating is wrong as children who do not cheat.

While Kohlberg's stages do, then, seem to apply to American males, they are less applicable to women and to people in nonwestern cultures, and there are questions about the testing methods and about the link between moral judgment and moral behavior.

Finally, some critics fear that Kohlberg's stage 6, which elevates individual morality above law and other recognized external standards, could lead to moral chaos—allowing someone like Hitler, for example, to justify tyranny and mass murder by a "higher moral purpose."

Nevertheless, Kohlberg has had a major impact. His influential theory has enriched our thinking about the way moral development occurs, has furthered an association between cognitive maturity and moral maturity, and has stimulated both research and the elaboration of theories of moral development.

Development of Memory: Information Processing

When the police showed 12 photographs to a 3-year-old girl who had been kidnapped and sexually abused, she gasped at one and identified the man shown in the picture as her abductor. The man was arrested and confessed to the crime (Goodman, 1984). In this case, a very young child seemed to be an accurate witness, but in other instances children's testimony has turned out to be unreliable, mixing fact with imagination or being vague about details.

The accuracy of children's memory has been a controversial issue ever since the beginning of the twentieth century. Recent research shows that very young children can sometimes recall details better than adults can, but that at other times their memories are poorer. They have the most trouble remembering events they do not understand, apparently because they cannot organize such events in their minds. As cognitive development advances, so in most cases does memory.

The information-processing approach to cognitive development pays particular attention to memory. The ability to remember improves greatly by middle childhood. This happens in part because children's memory capacity—the amount of information they can remember—increases, and in part because they learn to use a variety of strategies, or deliberate plans, to help them remember. An important ability that develops at this time is *metamemory,* an understanding of how one's own memory processes work.

Memory Capacity According to information-processing theory, memory is much like a filing system. It operates through three basic steps: encoding, storage, and retrieval. After perceiving something, we need to decide where to file it. Thus the first step is to *encode,* or classify it— for example, under "people I know" or "places I've been." Second, we *store* the material so that it stays in memory. And finally, we need to be able to *retrieve* information, or get it out from storage. Forgetting can occur because of a problem with any of the three steps.

According to one theory, we have three different types of memory: *sensory, short-term,* and *long-term* (Atkinson & Shiffrin, 1968, 1971). *Sensory memory* is a fleeting awareness of images that lasts no longer than a second unless the awareness is transferred to short-term memory. *Short-term memory* is our working memory, the active repository of information we are currently using. Material in short-term memory disappears after about 20 seconds unless transferred to long-term memory. *Long-term memory* is a storehouse of memories. Our ability to retrieve information from long-term memory depends on how well it was organized and stored in the first place.

The capacity of short-term memory increases rapidly in middle childhood. One classic paper states that short-term memory is limited to seven pieces ("chunks") of information, plus or minus two. Thus, some people in some circumstances can hold only five items in short-term memory, whereas others or the same people at other times can hold up to nine (G.A. Miller, 1956). We can see how children develop the capacity for short-term memory by asking them to recall a series of digits in the reverse of the order in which they have heard them (to recite, for example, "8-3-7-5-1" if they have heard "1-5-7-3-8"). At ages 5 to 6, children can typically remember only two digits; by adolescence they can remember six.

Young children's relatively poor short-term memory can help to explain why they have trouble solving certain kinds of problems (such as conservation). They may not be able to hold all the relevant pieces of information in their working memory (Siegler & Richards, 1982).

Strategies for Remembering One reason why older children can usually remember a list of numbers better than younger children can is that by middle childhood they have discovered that they can take deliberate actions to help them remember things. Devices to aid memory are called *mnemonic strategies.* As children get older, they develop better strategies and tailor them to meet the need to remember specific things. These techniques need not be discovered haphazardly. Children can be taught to use them earlier than they would spontaneously. Let's take a look at some of the most common

(© Charles Gupton/Stock Boston)

Contestants in a spelling bee can make good use of mnemonic strategies—devices to aid memory. For example, they may remember the correct spelling of a word if they have mentally rehearsed it or if they have put it into a mental category with other words that contain similar elements.

strategies: rehearsal, organization, elaboration, and external aids.

REHEARSAL When you look up a telephone number, you may repeat it over and over in your mind on your way from the directory to the phone, much as actors rehearse their lines. Rehearsal (conscious repetition) is a commonly used mnemonic strategy.

A classic study (Flavell, Beach, & Chinsky, 1966) indicated that children do not begin using rehearsal techniques spontaneously until after the age of 6. In an initial study, first-graders who had been told that they would be asked to recall a sequence of pictures just sat and waited until they were asked for the information, but second- and fifth-graders moved their lips and muttered, suggesting that they were rehearsing the material. Not surprisingly, the older children remembered the material better than the

younger ones did. When the experimenters asked first-graders to name the pictures out loud when they first saw them (a form of rehearsal), the children recalled the order better. A later study showed that young children who were taught to rehearse applied the technique to the immediate situation but did not carry it over to new situations (Keeney, Canizzo, & Flavell, 1967).

More recent research, however, shows that some children between 3 and 6 years old do use rehearsal. And although 6-year-olds are more likely to rehearse than 3-year-olds, those 3-year-olds who do rehearse can remember a grocery list just as well as 6-year-olds can (Paris & Weissberg-Benchell, cited in Chance & Fischman, 1987).

Children older than 6 learn and use more sophisticated mnemonic techniques: organization, elaboration, and external aids.

ORGANIZATION It's much easier to remember material if we organize it in our minds by putting it into categories. Adults generally organize their memories automatically. Children younger than 10 or 11 do *not* normally organize things spontaneously, though they can be taught to do it or they may pick it up by imitating older children or adults (Chance & Fischman, 1987). If they are shown randomly arranged pictures of, say, animals, furniture, vehicles, and clothing, they do not mentally sort the items into categories. If shown how to do so, they recall the pictures as well as older children do; but they do not generalize and apply the learning to other situations.

ELABORATION The strategy of elaboration helps us remember items by linking them together in an imagined scene or story. To remember to buy lemons, ketchup, and napkins, for example, we might imagine a ketchup bottle balanced on a lemon, with a pile of napkins handy to wipe up spilled ketchup. Older children are more likely than younger ones to do this spontaneously; and they remember better when they make up the elaborations themselves, whereas younger children remember better when someone else makes up the elaborations for them (Paris & Lindauer, 1976; Reese, 1977).

EXTERNAL AIDS   The mnemonic strategies probably used most commonly by both children and adults involve prompting by something outside the person. You write down a telephone number, you make a list, you tie a string around your finger, you ask someone to remind you, you set a timer, or you put a library book by the front door where you can't miss it when you go out. Even kindergartners recognize the value of such external aids, and as children mature, they make increasing use of them (Kreutzer, Leonard, & Flavell, 1975).

Metamemory   One reason why older children are more likely to use mnemonic strategies than younger children is that they are more conscious of how memory works. *Metamemory*—knowledge of the processes of memory—develops in middle childhood.

From kindergarten through fifth grade, children advance steadily in their understanding of memory (Kreutzer et al., 1975). Kindergartners and first-graders know that people remember better if they study longer, that people forget things with time, that relearning something is easier than learning it for the first time, and that external aids can help them remember. Third- and fifth-graders know that some people remember more than others and that some things are easier to remember than other things. Older children can plan strategies better: they are more likely to think of putting their skates by their schoolbooks if they want to be sure to remember to take the skates to school the next day.

Development of Language

Language, too, develops rapidly in middle childhood. Children are more able to understand and interpret communications and to make themselves understood.

Grammar: The Structure of Language   Suppose that you are looking at a snow-covered driveway and you ask someone how you are going to get the family car out of the garage. You might get an answer like one of the following: "John promised Mary to shovel the driveway" or "John told Mary to shovel the driveway." Depending on which answer you received,

These girls sharing a secret demonstrate growing sophistication in the use of language to communicate. By the early school years, most children use complex grammar and have vocabularies of several thousand words. But because they still do not fully understand the processes of communication, they sometimes misinterpret what they hear.

you would know whether to expect John or Mary to appear with shovel in hand. But many children under 5 or 6 years of age do not understand the structural difference between these two sentences and think that *both* mean that Mary is to do the shoveling (C.S. Chomsky, 1969). Their confusion is understandable, since almost all English verbs that might replace *told* in the second sentence (such as *ordered, wanted, persuaded, advised, allowed,* and *expected*) would put the shovel in Mary's hand.

Most 6-year-olds have not yet learned how to deal with grammatical constructions in which a word is used as *promise* is used in the first sentence, even though they know what a promise is and are able to use and understand the word correctly in other sentences. By the age of 8, most children can interpret the first sentence correctly.

The above example shows us that even though 6-year-olds speak on a rather sophisticated level, using complex grammar and a vocabulary of several thousand words, they still have a way to go before they master the niceties of syntax—the way in which words are orga-

STRUCTURE	DIFFICULT CONCEPT	AGE OF ACQUISITION
TABLE 8-5 ACQUISITION OF COMPLEX SYNTACTIC STRUCTURES		
John is easy to see.	Who is doing the seeing?	5.6 to 9 years.*
John promised Bill to go.	Who is going?	5.6 to 9 years.*
John asked Bill what to do.	Who is doing it?	Some 10-year-olds have still not learned this.
He knew that John was going to win the race.	Does the "he" refer to John?	5.6 years.

*All children 9 and over know this.
Source: C.S. Chomsky, 1969.

nized in phrases and sentences. During the early school years, they rarely use the passive voice, verbs that include the form *have*, and conditional ("if . . . then") sentences.

Children develop an increasingly complex understanding of syntax up to and possibly after the age of 9 (C.S. Chomsky, 1969). When testing forty 5- to 10-year-old children's understanding of various syntactic structures, Chomsky found considerable variation in the ages of children who understood them and those who did not (see Table 8-5).

Metacommunication When Erin, aged 6, received a fluoride treatment from her dentist, she was told by the hygienist not to eat for half an hour. Erin interpreted the instructions to mean that she was not to swallow for half an hour. Soon after leaving the examining room, Erin started to drool and to look very upset. She was greatly relieved when the dentist saw her concern and convinced her that yes, she *could* swallow her saliva.

Despite the fact that Erin has a sophisticated level of linguistic ability, she still has problems with communication, as do many children her age. Of course, adults, too, often misinterpret what other people say. But children's failures in interpreting messages they receive often stem from difficulties in *metacommunication,* that is, in their knowledge of the processes of commu-

nication. This knowledge grows throughout middle childhood.

To study children's ability to transmit and to understand spoken information, researchers have designed a number of ingenious experiments. In one (Flavell, Speer, Green, & August, 1981), kindergartners and second-graders were asked to construct block buildings exactly like those built by another child and to do this on the basis of the first child's audiotaped instructions— without seeing the buildings themselves. The instructions were often incomplete, ambiguous, or contradictory. The "builders" were then asked whether they thought that their buildings looked like the ones they were supposed to be copies of and whether they thought that the instructions were good or bad.

The older children monitored their comprehension better. That is, they were more likely to notice when instructions were inadequate and to show this by pausing or looking puzzled. They were more likely to know when they did not understand something and to see the implications of unclear communication—that their buildings might not look exactly like the ones they were copying because they had inadequate instructions. The younger children sometimes knew that the instructions had been unclear, but they did not seem to realize that this would mean that they could not do their job well. Even the older children (who, after all, were only 8 years old or so) lacked a complete awareness of the communication process (Flavell, Speer, Green, & August, 1981).

Findings like these have important implications. Young children do not understand all of what they see, hear, or read, but they are often unaware of not understanding. They may be so used to not understanding things in the world around them that this does not seem unusual to them. Adults need to be aware that they cannot take children's understanding for granted. For the sake of children's safety, well-being, and academic advancement, we have to find out ways to tell whether children do, in fact, know what we want them to know.

Among other things, children's ability to understand and follow instructions makes a big difference in how accurately we can measure their intelligence—and their intelligence is measured quite frequently during middle childhood.

Development of Intelligence

Psychometrics: Measuring Schoolchildren's Intelligence

"I had a conference with Jared's teacher today," Jared's mother tells his father. "She said he's an underachiever—that he's not working up to his ability."

Jared is in the third grade. It is likely that when his teacher referred to his "ability," she meant his score on an IQ test. In many schools, all students receive group intelligence tests every few years, partly as a basis for judging each child's capabilities and partly to see how well the school is meeting its pupils' needs. Because individual tests are somewhat more precise, youngsters may be tested individually either for admission to a selective program or to discover any specific problems or strengths that the school should address.

A popular *group* test is the **Otis-Lennon Mental Ability Test,** which has several levels covering children from kindergarten up to the twelfth grade. Children are usually tested in small groups of 10 to 15 and are asked to classify items, to show an understanding of verbal and numerical concepts, to display general information, and to follow directions.

The most widely used *individual* test for schoolchildren is the **Wechsler Intelligence Scale for Children (WISC-R).** This test measures verbal and performance abilities, yielding separate scores for each, as well as a total score. Separating the subtest scores makes the diagnosis of specific deficits easier. For example, if a child does significantly better on the verbal tests (such as understanding a written passage and knowing vocabulary words) than on the performance tests (such as mastering mazes and copying a block design), this may signal problems with perceptual or motor development. If the child does much better on the performance tests than on the verbal tests, there may be a problem with language development.

NORMS, RELIABILITY, AND VALIDITY There are pros and cons to using the familiar IQ tests. On the positive side, they have been standardized,

and so we have extensive information about norms (standards of performance), *reliability* (consistency of results), and *validity* (whether the tests measure what they claim to measure).

Norms are established by giving a test to a representative group of test-takers; their average performance then becomes the standard against which later test-takers' performance is measured (see Chapter 4). Reliability can be determined by giving the same person the same test more than once, or (to eliminate such variables as differences in testing conditions and the tendency to do better the second time) by comparing a person's score on half the answers with the score on the other half. Validity depends on how well the results correlate with other measures.

IQ scores are good predictors of achievement in school, especially for highly verbal children, and they can identify youngsters who are especially bright or who need special help. On the other hand, we have already pointed out the poor predictive abilities of psychometric intelligence tests for infants and the likelihood that motor-oriented tests underestimate the abilities of disabled children. In this chapter, we'll examine how intelligence tests may underestimate the intellectual abilities of minority-group members. In Chapters 12, 14, and 16, we'll discuss the inadequacies of standardized IQ testing for adults, and particularly how it has contributed to an underestimation of intellectual ability in late life.

These problems with validity reflect fundamental criticisms of IQ tests: that they overlook some important aspects of intelligence and imperfectly measure others.

A CRITIQUE OF IQ TESTS When Robert Sternberg was a schoolboy, he did not do well on intelligence tests. Neither did some other people who later turned out to have brilliant minds. Sternberg—who is now a professor of psychology at Yale University—is among many who believe that intelligence is more than what IQ tests measure (Sternberg, 1985a, 1987). He and other critics point out that rather than assessing skills directly, psychometric tests infer them from children's knowledge, leading to problems of cultural bias, which we'll discuss in a moment.

And while the tests are fairly dependable predictors of academic performance starting in middle childhood, these critics say that they miss other aspects of intelligence which may be at least as important, especially outside of school.

Sternberg's triarchic, or three-part, theory of intelligence (which we'll discuss in detail in Chapter 12, because of its particular relevance to adults) suggests at least three important aspects of intelligence that psychometric tests tend to overlook. First, people best demonstrate an important dimension of their intelligence in dealing with novel tasks or situations; IQ test questions similar to questions that children have already met in school fail to measure creative insight. Second, people show intelligence by adapting to or shaping their environment; test questions that are divorced from the real world ignore this practical side of children's intelligence. Finally, although IQ tests are fairly accurate in measuring the skills that children actually use in thinking or solving problems, the tests—because their tasks are timed—wrongly equate efficiency with speed. Sternberg's new Multidimensional Abilities Test is an attempt to avoid these pitfalls.

RACE, CULTURE, AND IQ TESTS The failings of IQ tests become especially serious when the tests are misused to classify children (or adults) and to limit expectations and opportunities on the basis of test scores (Sternberg, 1987). The seriousness and sensitivity of these problems is most evident when we consider racial and cultural differences in test results.

Racial differences in test scores Black Americans tend to score about 15 points lower on IQ tests than white Americans do (E. B. Brody & Brody, 1976). Although there is considerable overlap in scores, so that some black people score higher than most white people, many educators are concerned about the difference in the *average* score between the two groups. The meaning of this difference is highly controversial.

One interpretation of these racial differences is that they reflect differences in the environments of the two groups—differences in education, in cultural traditions, and in other circumstances that affect self-esteem and motivation as well as academic performance itself (Kamin,

1974). Another viewpoint is that disparities in IQ reflect genetic differences and that black people are innately inferior in intellectual capability (Jensen, 1969).

This debate has important implications for social and educational policy. If the primary cause of racial differences in IQ is environmental, then we need to continue to help black children uncover and develop their intellectual potential. If the primary cause is genetic, then special help may be a waste of resources. We would, however, have to be very sure of our facts before writing off the intellectual potential of any individual or group—and, in fact, persuasive evidence exists that group differences can be attributed to environmental rather than hereditary factors.

A powerful argument against the viewpoint that racial differences are innate emerges when we compare people from different socioeconomic levels. The same pattern that holds between American white and black test-takers (an average difference of 15 points) also holds between American middle-class and deprived rural and mountain children, and between English middle-class and canal-boat and gypsy children (Pettigrew, 1964). Furthermore, black children who live in northern cities score higher than those in the rural south (Baughman, 1971), and middle-class black children score better than poor black children (Loehlin, Lindzey, & Spuhler, 1975). These results suggest that life experience, not race, accounts for the lower IQ performance of black children, who, as a group, have poorer socioeconomic backgrounds than white children.

Furthermore, differences favoring white children do not appear until about age 2 or 3 (Golden, Birns, & Bridger, 1973). Some research suggests, in fact, that black babies are precocious on infant intelligence tests, especially in motor abilities (Bayley, 1965; Geber, 1962; Geber & Dean, 1957).

The difference that shows up later may reflect the switch from predominantly motor tests to verbal tests. Verbal ability is highly responsive to environmental influences. Black children (especially those of lower socioeconomic levels) often grow up hearing a dialect quite different from the English spoken in middle-class white homes. And black parents tend to emphasize nonverbal rather than verbal communication (Sternberg, quoted in Quinby, 1985).

One argument, which is being made these days with increasing force, is that the apparent differences between black people's and white people's intelligence reflect culture-related defects in the construction of the tests. Let's examine that problem.

The problem of cultural bias In 1986, a 15-year lawsuit ended with the upholding of a federal court order that because IQ tests are "culturally biased," California schools may not use them to place black students in special classes. The court had found that a disproportionate number of black youngsters were being wrongly consigned to classes for the mentally retarded.

This controversial decision was unprecedented; but as far back as 1910, researchers had recognized the difficulty of devising tests to measure the intelligence of diverse cultural groups. Since then, test developers have tried in vain to devise tests that can measure innate intelligence without introducing cultural bias— the tendency to include test elements or procedures more familiar, significant, or comfortable for members of certain cultures. Language, of course, is one such factor. Another is the nature of the test questions themselves, which— because they do not adequately separate what children have already learned from their ability to acquire new knowledge—favor children from advantaged backgrounds (Sternberg, 1985a).

Culture-free versus culture-fair tests: It has been possible to design tests that do not require language: testers use gestures, pantomime, and demonstrations for tasks such as tracing mazes, finding absurdities in pictures, putting the right shapes in the right holes, and completing pictures. But it has not been possible to eliminate all cultural content. For example, if a test-taker is asked to find absurdities in a picture, customary artistic conventions in the person's culture may affect the way he or she views the picture. A group of Asian immigrant children in Israel, when asked to provide the missing detail for a picture of a face with no mouth, said that the *body* was missing. They were not accustomed to considering a drawing of a head as a complete picture and "regarded the absence of a body as

more important than the omission of a mere detail like the mouth" (Anastasi, 1968, p. 252).

Recognizing the impossibility of designing a **culture-free** test (one with no culture-linked content), test makers have tried to produce **culture-fair** tests that deal with experiences common to various cultures. But these tests are not really culture-fair, according to some observers. For one thing, they almost inevitably call for skills that are more familiar to some groups than to others. This may be why many studies have found that discrepancies between black and white children's scores on nonverbal tests, or performance tests, are even greater than on tests using language (Anastasi, 1968; Sternberg, 1985a).

Furthermore, it is almost impossible to screen for culturally determined values and attitudes. Different cultures define intelligent behavior differently. The ability to sort names of living things according to their biological classifications (for example, to put *bird* and *fish* under *animal*) is considered intelligent in western cultures. But among the Kpelle tribe of Nigeria, it is considered more intelligent to sort things according to what they do; for example, a Kpelle might put *animal* with *eat*. In the United States, parents at lower socioeconomic levels tend to value rote memory, while middle- and upper-class parents are more apt to encourage their children to reason (Sternberg, 1985a; Sternberg, 1986; Sternberg, quoted in Quinby, 1985). (See Box 8-2, pages 284–285, for a discussion of cultural factors affecting measurement of intelligence in Asian and American children.)

Nowhere are the effects of heredity and environment more closely interwoven than in the measurement of whatever it is that we mean by *intelligence.* To separate innate potential from the impact of life experience is a goal that, for the most part, has eluded test designers.

The test situation: Culture-laden attitudes may bias the testing situation as well as the test itself. Such factors as rapport with the test-giver, interest in the tasks, motivation to excel, and modes of problem solving may be culturally affected (Anastasi, 1968). A child in a society that stresses slow, deliberate, painstaking work is handicapped in a timed test. A child from a culture that stresses sociability and cooperation is handicapped in taking a test alone.

BOX 8-2   WINDOW ON THE WORLD

ARE ASIAN CHILDREN SMARTER THAN AMERICAN CHILDREN?

Japanese students consistently score high in international mathematics and science achievement tests; American students rarely do. Also, American students from Asian families tend to be high achievers. Researchers have therefore looked for differences in learning ability between American and Asian children.

One study (Lynn, 1982) found the average IQ of Japanese children (111) to be significantly higher than that of American children (about 100). But the study has been criticized because the Japanese children studied came from a much narrower socioeconomic and geographic group than the American children.

A comparative study of Japanese, Chinese, and American elementary school children's cognition (H.W. Stevenson, Stigler, Lee, Lucker, Kitamura, & Hsu, 1985) took a different approach. A research team designed a "culture-fair" test based on experiences common to the three cultures. Test items, which were constructed directly in the three languages, included both nonverbal tasks (learning a code, completing a square, matching shapes, and recalling rhythms) and verbal tasks (repeating lists of words and numbers, following spoken directions, answering questions about stories and everyday facts, and defining words). The tests were given to urban first- and fifth-graders in all three countries. The children also took specially designed reading and mathematics tests.

The results were surprising. Both the Japanese and the Chinese children surpassed American children in mathematical achievement, and the Chinese children had the highest scores in reading. Yet the American first-graders did best on many cognitive tasks—perhaps because they were more used to answering adults' questions and were exposed earlier to museums and cultural events, which Asian children do not experience until they start school. By fifth grade, the cognitive differences had largely disappeared.

The study suggests that we must look elsewhere than differences in intelligence or cognitive functioning to explain Asian children's superior school performance. A study of Japan's schools, sponsored by the United States government (McKinney, 1987), suggests that Japanese culture and family life have shaped an educational system based on hard work and competition:

- Japanese mothers are intensely involved with their children's learning, which is considered the chief measure of a woman's success.

- Japanese families celebrate a child's starting school with such gifts as a desk, a chair, and an expensive leather backpack.

- Japanese children spend more time studying arithmetic and are introduced to mathematical concepts earlier than American children.

- Japanese children must learn a great deal of new material quickly. If they fall behind, their families hire tutors or send them to *jukus*, private remedial and enrichment schools.

Research with hundreds of children in four American cities has shown that black and Hispanic students, as well as students who are disabled or who come from low socioeconomic backgrounds, often do better in familiar settings (like their own classrooms) with examiners they know (like their own teachers) than in strange testing rooms with unfamiliar examiners. These children also do better when tested more than once with standardized tests based on the curricula they have been studying (D. Fuchs & L. S. Fuchs, 1986; L. S. Fuchs & D. Fuchs, 1986).

Weighing environmental factors: Since it has proved to be extremely difficult to eliminate environmental factors from intelligence tests, another approach is to take such factors into

(© Peter Dublin/Stock, Boston)

Children from Asian families often do better in school than other American youngsters. Studies indicate that the reasons are cultural, not genetic.

■ Japanese children must either pass tough exams to get into public high schools or else go to expensive private schools.

■ Japanese teachers teach moral values, character, neatness, punctuality, and respect, along with the three R's, through ninth grade.

■ Japanese schools set curfews and dress codes, recommend study schedules, and ban visits to game parlors and other "undesirable" attractions. Smoking is grounds for expulsion, drinking is rare, and drugs are virtually unavailable.

■ Japanese students have spent about 180 more days in school than American students by the time they graduate from high school.

In addition, one study shows that Japanese children spend 2 to 3½ hours a day studying, whereas American children spend an average of only half an hour (Nakanishi, 1982).

Japanese education does have drawbacks. Many parents complain about lack of individuality and about pressure on the children, who get headaches, miss sleep, seldom play, and memorize facts but do not create ideas. And the showing is less

impressive at the college level. Although 90 percent of Japanese youngsters graduate from high school, compared with 76 percent in the United States, only 29 percent of Japanese high school graduates go on to college, compared with 58 percent here (Simons, 1987); and only 4 percent of college graduates seek advanced degrees (McKinney, 1987). Some educators say that a system that is effective in a society like Japan's, which is small and tightly knit and has a disciplined, military tradition, will not work in the United States.

account. For this purpose, some states now use the System of Multicultural Pluralistic Assessment (SOMPA). This is a battery of measures for 5- to 11-year-olds that includes a medical examination, a Wechsler IQ test, and an interview with the parents. The interview yields information about the environment (how many people live in the home, their levels of educa-tion, and so forth) and the child's level of social competence (how many classmates the child knows by name, whether the child prepares his or her own lunch, and so forth).

Thus, a 9-year-old girl (for instance) who scores only 68 on the Wechsler IQ test might be eligible for placement in a class for the mentally retarded. But if we find that she is living in a poor urban ghetto and compare her with other children from similar backgrounds, we may realize that her IQ score of 68 is only 9 points below the mean for her group. Her adaptive-behavior scores may show that she is unusually capable of taking care of herself and getting along in her community. She may have an estimated learning potential, or "adjusted IQ," of 89, which means that she belongs in a regular class that takes her background into account (Rice, 1979).

Training Intelligence Intelligence used to be regarded as an immutable quantity. Rises in test scores across whole populations have been explained as a result of wider early experience, exposure to television, and practice in taking tests, rather than as a growth of intelligence itself. (Practiced test-takers frequently know, for example, how to make educated guesses and how to allot their time most efficiently.)

Recent research, however, suggests that intelligence actually increases as children get older, more knowledgeable, and more skilled at using their mental processes. Furthermore, many researchers now agree that intelligence can be *trained* by teaching children how to plan and use effective thinking strategies (R. D. Feldman, 1986; Sternberg, 1984, 1985a, 1985b). (See Box 8-3.)

The function of intelligence tests, then, should be not just to measure intelligence but to find out how to improve it. The purpose of education is not served when we use numbers to circumscribe people's growth.

CHILDREN IN SCHOOL

Whether children love school or hate it, they spend a large proportion of their waking hours there. Because school is central in children's lives, it affects and is affected by every aspect of their development. But child-care professionals and educators often disagree on how school can best enhance children's development.

Conflicting views, in conjunction with historical events, have resulted in great swings in educational theory and practice during the twentieth century. The traditional curriculum, centered on the "three R's" (reading, 'riting, and 'rithmetic), gave way first to "child-centered" methods that focused on children's interests and then, during the late 1950s, to an emphasis on science and mathematics to overcome a Soviet lead in the space race. Rigorous studies, in turn, were supplanted during the turbulent 1960s by student-directed learning in "open classrooms," where children engaged in varied activities and teachers served as "facilitators." High school students took more electives and more courses initiated by students. Then, in the mid-1970s, a decline in high school students' scores on the Scholastic Aptitude Test (SAT) sent schools back to the "basics" (Ravitch, 1983).

It turned out, however, that while children were becoming better grounded in basic skills they were not learning to think (NAEP, 1981, 1985). Thus, a "fourth R"—reasoning—has now been added (R. D. Feldman, 1986; Mirga, 1984). Since research shows that intelligence can be trained, schools have adopted a variety of programs to teach thinking skills (see Box 8-3).

What do all these changes mean for children? They illustrate, for one thing, the underlying American faith that our future rests on the way our children turn out, and that an important way to affect children's development is through their education.

The Teacher's Influence

If you are fortunate, you may be able to recall a special teacher who had a major influence on you—who inspired a love of knowledge and spurred you to work and to learn. One study dramatically demonstrated the power of a teacher's influence, by linking the adult successes of a number of people who had grown up in a poor urban neighborhood and their having been in the first-grade classroom of a very special teacher.

Many more of "Miss A's" former pupils showed impressive increases in IQ over the years than did equally disadvantaged youngsters who had had other first-grade teachers. Even more remarkable, the alumni of Miss A's classroom scored higher on measures of occupational status, type of housing, and personal appearance (posture, dress, and grooming) than did other graduates of the same school (Pederson, Faucher, & Eaton, 1978).

BOX 8-3 PRACTICALLY SPEAKING

TEACHING CHILDREN TO THINK

National tests have found a serious lack in 9-, 13-, and 17-year-olds' ability to interpret, analyze, and defend their arguments (National Assessment of Educational Progress, NAEP, 1981, 1985). Research also shows a sharp falloff in creative thinking after the age of 7 (H. Gardner, cited in Chance & Fischman, 1987).

How can parents and teachers help children learn to think? Youngsters can exercise their thinking skills by performing ordinary tasks geared to their developmental level. For example, when children in Piaget's stage of concrete operations (who are becoming able to mentally organize their environment) arrange their shelves or plan how to spend their allowance, they lay the groundwork for more sophisticated classifying, categorizing, setting of priorities, and evaluating. As children near the stage of formal operations, they need to become more aware of how they think problems though.

Thinking skills should be integrated with regular studies, so that children have something to think *about*. Children learn best by solving open-ended problems from real life (preferably problems they think up themselves), rather than schoolbook problems with pat solutions (R.D. Feldman, 1986; Sternberg, 1985b).

The following additional tips have been gleaned from wide research (R.D. Feldman, 1986; Maxwell, 1987).

- Encourage children to *read with purpose*—to find answers to their questions or fill in gaps in their knowledge. After reading, they should decide whether their questions have been answered, whether their previous knowledge or opinions need revising, and whether they need to do further investigation.

- Have children *compare new words and information* with what they already know and let them try to resolve any discrepancies.

- Show children how to *pick out the important*, or *relevant, information* they need or want to remember. Then they can store and recall it more efficiently.

- When reading a story or watching a television program, *call attention to structure.* Ask, "What do you think will happen next?" or "How do you think the story ends?"

- Teach children to *evaluate statements* (like "The sky is green") by asking four questions: (1) Is it common knowledge? (2) Is it unusual? (3) If it's true, what's the proof? (4) If there's proof, is it reliable?

- *Use guided imagery*—imagining an event or experience. Ask a child who has never been near a desert to "see" its vast expanse, "touch" the sand, "hear" the wind, and "feel" hot and thirsty.

- Ask children to *make inferences* about details: How did the soldiers at Valley Forge feel? What were they wearing? What might they have written to their families?

- Ask children *"why" and "how" questions:* "Why do you think the boy in the picture is sad?" "How might the United States be different if the Pilgrims had landed on the west coast?"

- Teach children to *attack problems systematically:* identify and define the problem, select an appropriate strategy to solve it, carry out the strategy, and decide whether the strategy has worked. Children usually think best when they design their own strategies.

- Make sure that children know *how and when to use a procedure:* for example, whether to multiply or divide to figure a discounted price.

- *Encourage invention*—writing stories, drawing pictures, or devising gadgets to help with chores. Then suggest that children polish or revise their work. Writing is important because it forces children to organize their thoughts.

- Encourage children to *set goals* and a time frame for achieving them. It usually works best to set intermediate goals, or checkpoints, on the way to the final goals.

An exceptional teacher's influence can extend far into the future, and an interest he or she inspires may shape a child's whole life.

What did Miss A do that was so special? Apparently she showed her confidence in the children's ability and encouraged them to work hard to justify that confidence. She gave extra time to those who needed it, staying after school when necessary. And she cared about her students. She was affectionate, she shared her own lunch with children who had forgotten theirs, and she remembered pupils by name, even 20 years later. What miracles schools could accomplish with more Miss A's!

Self-Fulfilling Prophecies Miss A's belief in her pupils undoubtedly had much to do with how well they did. According to the principle of the *self-fulfilling prophecy,* students live up to or down to the expectations that other people have for them.

In the famous "Oak School" experiment, teachers were told at the beginning of the term that some of their students had shown unusual potential for intellectual growth. Actually, the children identified as potential "bloomers" had been chosen at random. Yet several months later, many of them—especially first- and second-graders—showed unusual gains in IQ. The teachers do not appear to have spent more time with these children than with the others or to have treated them differently in any obvious

ways. Subtler influences may have been at work—possibly the teachers' tone of voice, facial expressions, touch, and posture (R. Rosenthal & Jacobson, 1968).

Although this research has been criticized for methodological shortcomings, work by many other researchers using a variety of methods has established the basic principle—that teachers' expectations "can and do function as self-fulfilling prophecies, although not always or automatically" (Brophy & Good, 1974, p. 32). This principle of the self-fulfilling prophecy has important implications for minority-group and poor children. Since many middle-class teachers may be convinced (often subconsciously) that such students have intellectual limitations, they may somehow convey their limited expectations to the children, thus getting from them the little that they expect.

Why do teachers expect poor and minority children to do badly? The answer may be that there is little or no "fit" between a teacher's middle-class values and the values of the student's family and associates. This may make it hard for the teacher to understand or "get through" to the student and for the student to accept and conform to standards of behavior that the teacher takes for granted (like neatness, punctuality, and competitiveness).

Computers as Teachers Teachers may turn students on or off, but *students* can turn computers on or off. Therein lies both the advantage and the danger of computers. Computers do not doom students with negative self-fulfilling prophecies, and they give students a large measure of control over their own learning. But they cannot inspire students as Miss A did.

A recent survey pointed up several important questions about the use of computers (Lepper, 1985):

1 *Will technology increase the gap between advantaged and disadvantaged students?* It probably will, if the marketplace controls the distribution of equipment. Schools in poorer communities cannot afford to provide the experience with computers that a school in a more affluent area can give.

2 *Will computers help the best or the weakest students?* Low achievers who are more effectively motivated by working with computers than by traditional classroom instruction may benefit most. Private computer-based alternative learning centers claim excellent results with such students.

3 *Are boys and girls likely to be affected differently?* Studies repeatedly show that boys use computers more than girls do and that the difference increases with age.

4 *How will the computer affect social development?* Two rival hypotheses are (a) that computers will harm social development because they replace subtle human interaction with mechanical control and (b) that computers will nurture social development by promoting a degree of cooperation previously unknown in classrooms. Only longitudinal studies seem likely to answer the question.

5 *What kinds of activities will the computer replace?* Will students have less personal contact with their teachers? Will they read less? Will they write less? Will they answer fewer questions aloud? We don't know, but the introduction of computers seems certain to reduce the time devoted to other elements of the classroom schedule.

We appear to be on the verge of a revolution in schooling. We can only imagine the difference that will be created by the routine use of computers as teaching tools.

Parents' Influence

Teachers are not, of course, the only adults who make an important difference in how well children do in school. Parents are also very influential, and Box 8-4 (page 290) gives some practical suggestions about how they can help their children do better.

Children with Disabilities

Education for children with disabilities has come a long way since the 1880s, when Helen Keller, who was blind and deaf by the age of 2, was thought to be unteachable until her parents finally found a determined private tutor from a distant city. Keller became an internationally famous author and lecturer.

Today federal law requires that every disabled child be offered appropriate education at public expense and that parents be involved in deciding on the proper program for their child. Eight out of ten children covered by the Education for All Handicapped Children Act, passed in 1975, are mentally retarded or speech-impaired or have specific learning disabilities. (An amendment passed in 1986 requires states that have public preschool programs to serve handicapped 3- to 5-year-olds by 1990. States can also opt to participate in a program for handicapped and developmentally delayed infants.)

Mainstreaming Under the law, children must be placed in the "least restrictive" environment in which they can learn and thrive. This means that, as much as possible, children with disabilities must be **mainstreamed,** or integrated into regular classes, for all or part of the day, rather than segregated into special classes. A retarded child, for example, may be able to take regular physical education or shop while receiving academic instruction in a class with slow learners. A child with cerebral palsy may be in regular academic classes but receive special physical training while the rest of the class goes to gym. Sometimes a child who is initially placed in a special

BOX 8-4　PRACTICALLY SPEAKING

HOW PARENTS CAN HELP CHILDREN DO WELL IN SCHOOL

Parents' involvement in schools has traditionally consisted of activities like PTA bake sales. Parents often assume that education itself is best left to professionals. But some 50 recent studies covering preschool through high school show that direct or indirect involvement of parents improves children's grades and IQ and achievement test scores, as well as their behavior and attitude toward school. It also results in better schools (Henderson, 1987).

Parents can help at school as classroom aides or tutors, or by taking an active role in educational decision making. But the best place for parents to help their children is at home. When parents teach a skill, their child feels that they consider education important, and they develop greater confidence in helping their child (Stearns & Peterson, 1973).

One survey of nearly 1300 parents of elementary school children in Maryland found that most of them felt that they could help their children more if the teacher were to show them what to do (Epstein, 1983). Another study of almost 300 third- and fifth-graders found significant improvement in reading scores when teachers encouraged parents to help (Epstein, 1987).

The following suggestions are adapted from a report of the U.S. Department of Education (1986b).

WHAT PARENTS CAN DO

■ Create a "curriculum of the home." Read to your children, talk to them, and listen to them. Tell them stories, play games, and share hobbies. Discuss news, television programs, and current events.

■ Provide a place for study and for keeping reference books and supplies.

■ Set and insist on times for meals, sleep, and homework. Make sure that children meet school deadlines.

■ Monitor time spent watching television and on after-school jobs.

■ Be aware of children's lives at school. Talk about school events and about problems and successes.

WHAT TEACHERS CAN DO TO GET PARENTS INVOLVED

■ Ask parents to read aloud to children, to listen to children read, and to sign homework papers when they are done.

■ Encourage parents to drill students on math and spelling.

■ Encourage parents to discuss school activities with their children.

■ Suggest ways in which parents can teach children at home; for example, by alphabetizing books on a shelf.

■ Send home suggestions for schoolwork-related games and other activities that parents and children can do together.

■ Invite parents to visit the classroom to see how their children are being taught and to get ideas for what they can do at home.

The Home and School Institute, in cooperation with the National Education Association, has produced a series of quick everyday activities that teachers can send home for parents and children to do to reinforce (not duplicate) school learning. For example, a young child can get practice with numbers by dialing the telephone; an older child can figure out which can of soup is the best buy at the grocery store. Studies have shown significant short-term achievement gains after use of these home learning activities (Rich, 1985). The institute also publishes several paperback books of home learning activities. For information, write to the Home and School Institute, Special Projects Office, 1201 Sixteenth Street NW, Washington, DC 20036.

Mainstreaming in schools gives disabled and nondisabled children an opportunity to learn how to get along with and understand each other.

program because of a mild emotional or learning problem may improve enough to be moved to a regular classroom.

Proponents of mainstreaming emphasize the need for disabled children to learn to get along in a society where most people do not share their impediments, and they also point to the need for nondisabled people to learn to understand those who are disabled. Retarded children have been found to do as well academically in mainstreamed classes as in special classes, though not better (Gruen, Korte, & Baum, 1974). Unfortunately, mainstreaming does not seem to diminish the stigma experienced by children with disabilities.

Many classroom teachers (especially upper-grade teachers and those who do not have training in special education) resist mainstreaming. They doubt their ability to meet the needs of children of widely differing capabilities, and they worry that their other students may be disturbed by the behavior of disabled students and may be disadvantaged by the extra teaching time these students require. Nevertheless, many teachers have effectively integrated such children into their classes. Aides, tutors, and teaching machines, combined with careful placement and appropriate ratios of disabled to nondisabled students, may help to relieve teachers' burdens and concerns (D. Thomas, 1985).

Learning Disabilities "Mom, am I mentally retarded?" Terry asked her mother after being placed in a special class. Throughout elementary school, Terry could neither learn the alphabet nor write along a straight line. Her teachers thought that she was lazy, and a psychologist labeled her "emotionally deprived." Not until seventh grade, when her pediatrician sent her to a neurologist, was she diagnosed as learning-disabled (Merrow, 1983).

Learning disabilities are little understood disorders that interfere with specific aspects of achievement in school. Terry and other learning-disabled (LD) children are *not* mentally retarded. Their average IQ scores are only 5 to 10 points below the norm—within normal range (Feagans, 1983)—and some have high intelligence. They see and hear perfectly well, but they often have trouble processing sensory information. As one child said, "I know it in my head, but I can't get it into my hand."

Barbara, for example, has problems with auditory perception: she cannot grasp what the teacher is saying. Charles has difficulties with small-motor coordination: he cannot color inside the lines or write clearly. Derek is clumsy in his large-motor movements, a deficit that is painfully apparent in the school yard when he tries to run, climb, or play ball. Ellen began to talk quite late and still articulates so unclearly that she is embarrassed to speak out in class or to read aloud.

Dyslexia, an inability to learn to read or difficulty in doing so, is one of the most common learning disabilities (McGuinness, 1986). Dyslexic children often scramble or reverse letters and words; for example, they may read *was* instead of *saw*. Since success in school is important for self-esteem, such disabilities can have devastating effects on the psyche as well as on the report card.

Learning disabilities seem to be related to behavioral problems; LD children tend to be hyperactive and easily distracted (see Chapter 9). The cause may involve a failure of cognitive processing; LD children are less organized and less likely to use memory strategies than other children (Feagans, 1983). Or the difficulty may be physiologically based; some studies have uncovered differences in the brain structures of learning-disabled people (Blakeslee, 1984). Learning disabilities often run in families, and substantial research suggests that genetic transmission or chromosomal abnormalities may play a role (M. D. Levine, 1987). But it is also possible that many children classified as LD are youngsters whom schools have failed to teach and control effectively (McGuinness, 1986).

Learning disabilities tend to persist, but some people find ways to manage them—or get around them. For example, Nelson Rockefeller, who was governor of New York and vice president of the United States, had trouble reading, and so he ad-libbed his speeches rather than risk garbling written ones (Fiske, 1984).

Factors that may increase the risk of a poor outcome of childhood learning disabilities include extremely low birth weight or other birth trauma, "difficult" temperament, malnutrition, poverty, and family turmoil. Early screening and intervention can head off learning problems and increase a child's chances of leading a productive life (M. D. Levine, 1987). Highly structured day care or preschool programs, individualized instruction and tutorial help, behavior modification techniques to improve concentration, and training in cognitive strategies and organizational skills are among the approaches that have been tried with varying degrees of success.

Gifted, Talented, and Creative Children

The brightest and most promising children do not always do best in school or in later life. One national report found that more than half of gifted students achieve below their tested potential (National Commission on Excellence in Education, 1983). What accounts for this waste of ability?

Although it may not be as obvious as with disabled children, exceptionally able students have special needs for intellectual stimulation, which schools often do not meet. Of the estimated 3 to 5 percent of the school population—approximately 2.5 million children—who are gifted and talented according to the official definition of the U.S. Office of Education, only about 1 million get special attention (Henig, 1986).

One persistent set of issues focuses on what giftedness is, how to identify it, and its relationship to creativity. Other issues are how gifts can be nurtured and whether special resources should be devoted to an "elite" who (some people believe) "can fend for themselves" (Horowitz & O'Brien, 1986).

Definition and Identification of "Giftedness"

The official definition of *giftedness* is broad; it can mean superiority in general intellect, in specific academic aptitudes, in potential for leadership, in talent in the visual or performing arts, in creative thinking, or in psychomotor ability (Marland, 1972). But the criterion most often used to identify children eligible for special programs is narrow: an IQ of approximately 130 or more (Horowitz & O'Brien, 1986). This criterion often misses gifted minority or disadvantaged students and others with undeveloped potential, as well as exceptionally creative children and those with specific talents rather than general academic ability.

Underlying the difficulties with identification is uncertainty about the nature of giftedness (Horowitz & O'Brien, 1986). Do gifted youngsters think differently from others, or merely better and faster? Are there different kinds of giftedness? Why are some children extremely gifted in a specific realm of learning, such as mathematics or music, while others excel at almost everything they try?

A current theory, which has gained some acceptance, is that gifted children are highly efficient information processors, especially for novel tasks requiring insight (Davidson & Sternberg, 1984; Sternberg 1985a). Another theory is that people have not one kind of intelligence but many "intelligences," each of which develops at its own rate; some (such as musical intelligence) are not even measured by IQ tests (H. Gardner, 1983).

Academic Giftedness versus Creativity The use of IQ tests to identify gifted children goes back to Lewis M. Terman, the professor who brought the Binet test to the United States. Terman, in the 1920s, began a major longitudinal study of more than 1500 California children with IQs of 140 or more. Investigators at Stanford University have followed the progress of Terman's subjects up to the present. Over the years, their intellectual, scholastic, and vocational superiority has held up. They were 10 times more likely than an unselected group to have graduated from college and 3 times more likely to have been elected to honorary societies like Phi Beta Kappa. By midlife, they were highly represented in listings such as *Who's Who*. Almost 90 percent of the men were professional

or semiprofessional or were in high echelons of business (Terman & Oden, 1959).

Thus IQ tests (even in their early days) correctly spotted some children of unusual promise. Yet Terman's unusually bright group of subjects never produced a great musician, an exceptional painter, or a Nobel prize winner—evidence that IQ does not predict creative achievement.

Indeed, other classic studies found that the most academically able children are not necessarily the most creative thinkers—the innovators who solve problems in original ways or who find problems that others overlook (Getzels, 1964, 1984; Getzels & Jackson, 1962). By the same token, the most creative children, whose minds take twists that teachers do not expect, may not do especially well in school. In one study, one twin in each of 62 pairs had been identified as gifted, usually by a teacher's referral or through achievement tests. Questionnaires of the students, their parents, and their teachers revealed that the chosen twins tended to be conformists and approval seekers; the others, despite their lesser academic performance, were likely to be more creative, independent learners (Renzulli & McGreevy, 1984).

One line of research has attempted to identify

Questions	Common answer	Creative answer
How many things could these drawings be?		
	Table with things on top.	Foot and toes.
	Three people sitting around a table.	Three mice eating a piece of cheese.
	Flower.	Lollipop bursting into pieces.
	Two igloos.	Two haystacks on a flying carpet.
What do meat and milk have in common?	Both come from animals.	Both are government-inspected.
How many ways could you use a newspaper?	Make paper hats.	Rip it up if you're angry.

Figure 8-1 Tests of creativity. (*Source:* Adapted from Wallach & Kogan, 1967.)

creative children by analyzing the way they think. Guilford (1959) distinguished between two kinds of thought: *convergent thinking*, which seeks a single, "right" answer (usually the traditional one), and *divergent thinking*, which comes up with fresh, diverse possibilities.

Special tests have been devised to spot divergent thinkers (see Figure 8-1 on page 293). The Torrance Tests of Creative Thinking, for example, ask children to find ways of improving a toy, to list unusual uses for common objects, to draw pictures starting with a few given lines, and to write down what various sounds bring to mind. One problem with the tests is that scoring depends on speed, which is not a hallmark of creativity. Another important criticism is that although the tests are fairly reliable (they yield consistent results), there is little evidence that they are valid—that the children they identify are creative in real life (Anastasi, 1976; Mansfield & Busse, 1981). Much more research needs to be done before we can identify youngsters who promise the most significant creative contributions as adults (see Chapter 14).

Gifted Children: What Their Lives Are Like
When Terman's study began, the popular image of a bright child was that of a puny, pasty-faced bookworm. Terman debunked that stereotype. The children in his sample tended to be taller, healthier, and better coordinated than average, as well as better adjusted and more popular with other children (Wallach & Kogan, 1965).

Other studies, however, have found that gifted underachievers and extremely gifted children—those with IQs of 180 or more—do tend to have social and emotional problems, possibly caused in part by unchallenging school experiences (Janos & Robinson, 1985). Also, many exceptionally bright children hide their gifts in an attempt to fit in with their classmates (R. D. Feldman, 1982).

Nurturing Gifted Children Three elements essential to the flowering of gifts and talents seem to be an inborn ability, a drive to excel, and encouragement by adults (B. S. Bloom, 1985; H. Gardner, 1979; P. Sears, 1977; P. Sears & Barbee, 1978). Nurturing, especially, appears to be crucial (Horowitz & O'Brien, 1986). Gifted

(National Gallery, London)

Would Wolfgang Amadeus Mozart have composed some of the world's most beautiful music if his gifts had not been recognized and nurtured at an early age? His father, a fine musician and composer himself, taught Wolfgang, shown here with his sister, and encouraged him to perform.

children are likely to have well-educated, well-to-do, emotionally supportive, happily married parents who spend time with them, answer their questions, and encourage their curiosity (Janos & Robinson, 1985).

A review of 61 research reports on how the family influences creativity found, not surprisingly, that parents of creative children tend to be special themselves. They usually have occupations they consider meaningful or pursue intellectual or artistic hobbies. They are uninhibited and unconventional and do not worry about what "the Joneses" think. They expect their children to do well, and they give them a combination of freedom and responsibility. These parents are not rigidly controlling or authoritarian; they let their children be themselves (B. Miller & Gerard, 1979). However, a review of studies on the rearing of future scientists found a less clear-cut relationship between creativity and parental control (Mansfield & Busse, 1981).

Creativity often fades after children enter school, where they are rewarded for doing what adults want them to do. Those who remain creative tend to be the rebellious ones who annoy teachers with questions like "What would birds look like if they couldn't fly?" or are lost in their imagination when they should be doing their homework. When teachers accept unconventional questions, praise original ideas, and refrain from grading everything children do, schoolchildren show more creativity and are more likely to be free of the behavior problems that often accompany it (Torrance, cited in Chance & Fischman, 1987).

Educational Approaches for Gifted Children

What kind of education is best for gifted and talented students? One successful approach involves coaching by mentors, or experts in the child's field of talent or interest (B. S. Bloom, 1985). Another approach involves special schools or classes for the artistically talented or intellectually gifted.

Most programs concentrate on either enrichment (broadening and deepening children's studies through special activities like field trips and research projects) or acceleration (rapid movement through the curriculum), as exemplified by the "Talent Search" for mathematically and verbally precocious youth originated at Johns Hopkins University (Horowitz & O'Brien, 1986). A comprehensive national study concluded that a wide range of "able learners"— perhaps 25 percent of all students—should be served through a combination of enrichment and acceleration, geared to their individual needs (Cox, Daniel, & Boston, 1985; R. D. Feldman, 1985).

There is no firm line between being gifted and not being gifted. What we learn about fostering intelligence, creativity, and talent for the small, special population of the gifted and talented can help all children make the most of their potential.

SUMMARY

Growth and Fitness

- Physical development is less rapid in middle childhood than in the earlier years. Boys are slightly larger than girls at the beginning of this period, but girls undergo the growth spurt of adolescence at an earlier age and thus tend to be larger than boys at the end of the period. Wide differences in height and weight exist between individuals and between groups.

- Proper nutrition is essential for normal growth and health. Malnutrition can diminish activity and sociability.

- Obesity among children is an increasingly common problem.

- Although children today are healthier than children at the turn of the century, they are less healthy and less fit than children in the mid-1960s. This disturbing trend seems to be occurring because children are less physically active today.

Motor Development

- Because of improved motor development, boys and girls in middle childhood can engage in a wider range of motor activities than preschoolers. Studies done several decades ago suggest that boys excel in motor skills, but recent research indicates similar abilities for boys and girls.

Health

- Respiratory infections and other common health problems of middle childhood tend to be of short duration rather than persistent and tend to run in clusters.

- Vision becomes keener in middle childhood, but up to 17 percent of children have defective distance vision by the age of 11.

- Although about one-half of American children

aged 5 to 17 have no tooth decay, there are some dental problems in this group.

Aspects of Intellectual Development in Middle Childhood

- The child from age 7 to age 11 is in the Piagetian stage of concrete operations and can use symbols (mental representations) to carry out operations (mental activities).

- Children at this stage are less egocentric than before and are more proficient at tasks requiring logical reasoning, such as conservation. However, their reasoning is largely limited to the here and now.

- According to Piaget, Kohlberg, and Selman moral development coincides with cognitive development. Moral development is influenced by a child's maturational level, social role-taking skills, and interactions with adults and other children.

  1 According to Piaget, moral development occurs in two stages. The first, morality of constraint, is characterized by moral rigidity. The second, morality of cooperation, is characterized by moral flexibility.

  2 Selman has proposed a theory which links moral development to role-taking.

  3 Kohlberg, who defines morality as a sense of justice, extended Piaget's view to include six stages of moral reasoning organized on three levels: preconventional morality, morality of conventional role conformity, and morality of autonomous moral principles.

- Memory improves greatly during middle childhood because children's short-term capacity increases rapidly and because they become more adept at using memory strategies such as rehearsal, organization, elaboration, and external aids. Metamemory (the understanding of how memory works) also improves.

- Children's understanding of increasingly complex syntax develops up to and perhaps even after age 9. Although the ability to communicate improves, even older children may not have a complete awareness of the processes of communication.

- The intelligence of school-age children is assessed by group tests (such as the Otis-Lennon Mental Ability Test) and individual tests (such as the WISC-R).

- Critics claim that psychometric intelligence tests overlook practical intelligence and creative insight and falsely equate mental efficiency with speed. New methods are being devised to test and train intelligence.

- Black Americans tend to score lower on intelligence tests than white Americans. Numerous findings indicate that the difference in scores is more likely to reflect environmental than innate racial differences.

- Developers of intelligence tests have attempted to devise "culture-fair" tests, tests that focus on experiences common across cultures. None of the attempts has been completely successful.

Children in School

- Teachers influence children's success in school and thus their self-esteem. Self-fulfilling prophecies often limit the achievement of poor and minority children.

- Computers are becoming basic equipment in many classrooms. Their impact on the educational process has generated many unanswered questions.

- Parents' involvement enhances children's learning.

- Under the law in the United States, every handicapped child is entitled to an appropriate education at public expense, and parents must be consulted in planning the child's program. Children must be mainstreamed, or placed in regular classes, as much as possible.

- Learning disabilities interfere with learning to read and other school tasks. The causes of these disabilities are unclear. Many learning-disabled children can lead productive lives if they get individual attention early.

- An IQ of 130 is the most common standard for identifying gifted children for special programs, but this measure misses some children.

- Creativity is sometimes identified as divergent (rather than convergent) thinking. The validity of tests for creativity is questionable.

- Although Terman's study found that gifted children tend to be unusually successful as adults, some gifted children do not live up to their apparent potential, possibly because schools do not meet their needs.

- The development of gifts, talents, and creativity depends greatly on nurturance. The child's drive to excel is another crucial factor. Most special school programs for the gifted stress enrichment or acceleration. Each of these methods meets the needs of some students.

concrete operations (page 269)
conservation (269)
convergent thinking (294)
culture-fair (283)
culture-free (283)
decenter (269)
divergent thinking (294)
dyslexia (292)
giftedness (292)
horizontal décalage (269)
learning disabilities (291)
long-term memory (277)

mainstreaming (289)
metacommunication (280)
metamemory (277, 279)
mnemonic strategies (277)
morality of autonomous moral
  principles (275)
morality of constraint
  (heteronomous morality) (271)
morality of conventional role
  conformity (275)
morality of cooperation
  (autonomous morality) (271)

operational thinking (269)
Otis-Lennon Mental Ability Test
  (281)
preconventional morality (275)
reliability (281)
role-taking (272)
self-fulfilling prophecy (288)
sensory memory (277)
short-term memory (277)
validity (281)
Wechsler Intelligence Scale for
  Children (WISC-R) (281)

SUGGESTED READINGS

Adler, M. J. (Ed.). (1984). *The paideia program: An educational syllabus.* New York: Macmillan. A series of readable essays by eminent educators on an ambitious proposal to overhaul education in the United States in order to develop the intellectual potential of every child.

Bloom, B. S. (1985). *Developing talent in young people.* New York: Ballantine. An absorbing report of a project in which researchers interviewed 120 accomplished young pianists, sculptors, swimmers, tennis champions, mathematicians, and research neurologists, and their parents, teachers, and coaches. The book emphasizes the importance of parents' and teachers' active development of the young people's abilities.

Coles, R. (1986). *The moral life of children.* Boston: Atlantic Monthly. Coles, a prominent child psychiatrist, offers his rebuttal to Kohlberg's theory that moral development rests on cognitive development and that schoolchildren are too young to live moral lives. The book contains many moving quotations from children discussing morality in their own experience.

Cox, J., Daniel, N., & Boston, B. O. (1985). *Educating able learners: Programs and promising practices.* Austin: University of Texas Press. The comprehensive report of a 4-year nationwide study of programming for superior students. The book includes recommendations for discovering and nurturing talent and for building school programs.

Eysenck, H. J., & Kamin, L. (1981). *The intelligence controversy.* New York: Wiley. A debate on whether intelligence is the result of heredity or environment, by two prominent psychologists, each advocating one of the points of view; complete with attacks, counterattacks, and rebuttals.

Feldman, R. D. (1982). *Whatever happened to the quiz kids? Perils and profits of growing up gifted.* Chicago: Chicago Review Press. A highly readable series of profiles of precocious children who became celebrities while very young. The last chapter, "Reflections on Growing Up Gifted," treats questions such as the relationship between intelligence in childhood and success in adulthood, the difference between academic ability and creativity, and the effects of societal pressures and expectations on the psychological development of gifted children.

Greenfield, P. M. (1984). *Mind and media.* Cambridge, MA: Harvard University Press. A highly readable discussion of the positive and negative effects of television, video games, and computers on children and their development.

Silver, L. B. (1984). *The misunderstood child.* New York: McGraw-Hill. A thorough and easily readable discussion of the diagnosis and treatment of children's learning disabilities, geared to the needs of parents.

Simon, S. B., & Olds, S. W. (1977). *Helping your child learn right from wrong.* New York: McGraw-Hill. A self-help manual for parents to aid in establishing moral values and emotional self-awareness in children. The authors explain why values themselves cannot be taught but show how parents can teach children how to arrive at their own values.

9

CHAPTER

PERSONALITY AND SOCIAL DEVELOPMENT IN MIDDLE CHILDHOOD

The healthy human child will keep
Away from home, except to sleep.
Were it not for the common cold
Our young we never would behold.

Ogden Nash,
You Can't Get There from Here, 1956

ASK YOURSELF

■ How does children's self-concept develop, and how does it affect their behavior?

■ What do schoolchildren do with their time, and how do their daily lives today differ from those of children in previous generations?

■ How does the society of the peer group influence children?

■ Why do some children make friends more easily than others?

■ What changes occur in family relationships in middle childhood, and how do mothers' employment, divorce, and single-parent families affect children?

■ What are some emotional disturbances in childhood, and how are they treated?

■ How do school-age children handle stress?

At the age of 9, Laurie became a "published author" when her fourth-grade class put together a collection of its verse. Laurie's poem told how her mother cared for her when she was sick or hurt her knee or got a D or had a nightmare. Billy's poem extolled the pleasure of popping corn; Jeff's cheerfully ticked off his parents' complaints about his table manners; and Marcie's recalled how she had cried when her father and mother made her return her pet frog to the pond. Terry's confessed to an occasional urge to hit his pesty little brother, and Dina's revealed the "funny feeling" she got in her stomach right before a test.

The lives of school-age children are rich and varied, and their feelings about their broadening experiences are mixed. In this chapter, we trace the social and personality growth that ac-companies the cognitive changes of middle childhood.

From about age 6 to the onset of puberty at about age 12, youngsters develop more realistic concepts of themselves and of what is required for survival and success in their culture. They become more independent of their parents and more involved with other people, particularly the peer group. Through interaction with other children, they make discoveries about their own attitudes, values, and skills. But the family remains a vital influence. The lives of children of this age have been profoundly affected by new patterns of family life, as well as by other societal changes.

Although most children are healthy, both physically and emotionally, some succumb to emotional disorders of one sort or another, sometimes in response to stress, sometimes because of biological malfunction. Other, more resilient children face the stresses of childhood and emerge from them healthier and stronger.

THE SELF-CONCEPT

Developing a Self-Concept

"'Who in the world am I?' Ah, *that's* the great puzzle," said Alice in Wonderland, after her size had abruptly changed—again. Solving Alice's "puzzle" entails a lifelong process of getting to know our developing selves.

We may (like the psychologist William James) think of the self as having two sides: the "me" that is the object of our thoughts about ourselves and the "I" that does the thinking. The *content* of our *self-concept,* or sense of self, is our knowledge of what we have been and done; its *function* is to guide us in deciding what to be and do in the future. Self-concept, then, helps us to understand ourselves and also to control or regulate our behavior (Markus & Nurius, 1984). Let's see how these two complementary aspects of self-concept develop before and during middle childhood.

Beginnings: Self-Recognition and Self-Definition The sense of self grows slowly. It begins with *self-awareness:* the gradual realization (beginning in infancy) that we are beings separate from other people and things, with the ability to reflect on ourselves and our actions. Self-awareness crystallizes in the first moment of *self-recognition,* around 18 months of age, when toddlers recognize themselves in the mirror.

The next step is *self-definition:* identifying the inner and outer characteristics we consider significant in describing ourselves. At about the age of 3, children (like Alice) think of themselves mostly in terms of externals—what they look like, where they live, what they do. Some people never progress beyond this level, defining themselves even as adults by the image in the mirror, the work they do, and the neighborhood they live in.

Not until about age 6 or 7 do children begin to define themselves in psychological terms.

They now develop a concept of who they are (the *real self*) and also of who they would like to be (the *ideal self*). By the time they achieve this growth in self-understanding, young children (as we saw in Chapter 5) have made significant progress from parental control toward self-regulation.

The ideal self incorporates many of the "shoulds" and "oughts" children have learned and helps them control their impulses for the sake of being considered "good" boys or girls. Surprisingly, a large gap between a child's real and ideal selves is usually a sign of maturity and social adjustment (Maccoby, 1980). Apparently, children who set high standards for themselves are aware of the difference between what they are and what they would like to be, and working toward the goal of the ideal self helps children mature.

Coordination of Self-Regulation and Social Regulation It might seem that there is nothing more personal than the sense of self. But most theoreticians and researchers, according to a recent review, see self-concept as a *social* phenomenon, "the meeting ground of the individual and society" (Markus & Nurius, 1984, p. 147). Middle childhood seems to be the appointed time for that meeting. Children peer into the looking glass of their society and blend the image that they see reflected there with the picture they already have of themselves.

The expanding capabilities, activities, and social contacts of this period are accompanied by growing responsibilities: to do homework, to rake leaves, to wash dishes, to obey home and school rules, and perhaps to help care for younger brothers or sisters. Children begin to regulate their behavior not only to get what they need and want (as they did in infancy and early childhood), but also to meet the needs and wants of others.

As children internalize the behavioral standards and values of society, they coordinate personal and social demands. Now children voluntarily do things (like homework and sharing) that at an earlier age they would have needed prodding to do.

As they strive to become functioning members of society, children must complete several

(© Elliott Varner Smith/International Stock Photo)

This girl delivering newspapers is fulfilling several important self-concept tasks of middle childhood. In taking responsibility to match her growing capabilities, she learns something about how her society works, about her role in it, and about what it means to do a job well.

important tasks that contribute to the development of self-concept (Markus & Nurius, 1984). They must (among other things):

- *Expand their self-understanding* to reflect other people's perceptions, needs, and expectations. For example, they have to learn what it means to be a friend or a teammate.
- *Learn more about how society works*—about complex relationships, roles, and rules. Children come to realize, for example, that their own mother had a mother, and that the same person can be nice at one moment and mean at another.
- *Develop behavioral standards* that are personally satisfying and also incorporate accepted societal standards. (A complicating factor is that children belong to *two* societies—that of the peer group and that of adults—which sometimes have conflicting standards.)

- *Manage their own behavior.* As children take responsibility for their own actions, they must *believe* that they can behave according to both personal and social standards, and they must develop the skills and strategies to *do* it.

Self-Esteem   SELF-ESTEEM IN MIDDLE CHILD-HOOD   As Erikson (1950), among others, points out, middle childhood is an important time for the development of *self-esteem:* children's evaluation of themselves, or self-image. Children compare their real selves and their ideal selves. They judge themselves by how well they measure up to the social standards and expectations they have taken into their self-concept and by how competently they do their work.

Children's opinions of themselves have tremendous impact on their personality development. Indeed, a favorable self-image may be the most important key to success and happiness throughout life. Let's look at two typical examples:

Paul likes himself. He is confident of his own abilities and approaches life with an open attitude that unlocks many doors. He can take criticism well, and when he feels strongly about something he wants to say or do, he is willing to risk making other people angry. He challenges parents, teachers, and other people in authority. He feels that he can cope with obstacles; he is not burdened by self-doubt. He solves problems in original, innovative ways. Because he believes that he *can* succeed in the goals he sets for himself, he generally *does* succeed. His success renews his self-respect and makes it easy for him to respect and love others. They, in turn, admire, respect, and enjoy him.

Peter does not feel good about himself. He is hampered wherever he turns. Convinced that he cannot succeed, he does not try very hard. His lack of effort almost always ensures continued failure, resulting in a downward spiral of lack of confidence and lack of success. He worries a lot about whether he is doing the right thing. He breaks things and hurts people's feelings, and he is constantly plagued by one unexplained pain after another. He tries very hard to please others—often too hard, so that while he goes along with what other people want, he often strikes them as "wishy-washy." Because of his self-doubts, he is not much fun to be with, and so he has trouble making and keeping friends—which, of course, drives his opinion of himself even lower.

These two portraits are composites drawn from an important study on self-esteem in chilren, that of Stanley Coopersmith (1967). Coopersmith administered a questionnaire to hundreds of fifth- and sixth-graders, both male and female. The boys and girls in this initial sample did not differ, on the average; but for intensive interviewing and observation, Coopersmith chose 85 boys and no girls, to eliminate gender as a possible factor. Although it is important to remember that the final sample was limited to middle-class white boys within only a 2-year age span, the findings may apply to a wider group.

Coopersmith concluded that people base their self-image on four criteria: *significance* (the extent to which they feel loved and approved by those who are important to them); *competence* (in performing tasks they consider important); *virtue* (attainment of moral and ethical standards); and *power* (the extent to which they influence their own and others' lives). Although people may draw favorable pictures of themselves if they rate high on some of these dimensions and low on others, they are more likely to rate themselves high if they rate high on all four criteria.

Not surprisingly, the boys in the study who had high self-esteem were more popular and did better in school than those with low self-esteem, who were more likely to be loners, bedwetters, or poor students. No relationship showed up between self-esteem and height, weight, or physical attractiveness, and only a slim one between self-esteem and status. But family influences did make a difference. Boys who were firstborn or only children, those who had warm parents, and those with dominant mothers were likely to have high self-esteem.

PARENTING STYLES AND SELF-ESTEEM By and large, the parents of the boys with good self-images had authoritative parenting styles (see Chapter 7). These parents loved and accepted their sons and made strong demands for academic performance and good behavior. Within clearly defined and firmly enforced limits, they showed respect and allowed individual expression. In disciplining their sons, they relied more

A child's sense of competence—whether it derives from winning an athletic competition or from making the honor roll—contributes mightily to his or her self-esteem. A positive self-image can strongly influence a child's future success and happiness.

on rewards than on punishment. Furthermore, they themselves had high self-esteem and led active, rewarding lives.

Parents who are both democratic and strict help their children in several ways, according to Coopersmith. By establishing clear, consistent rules, they let children know what behavior is expected of them. Predictability of external control helps children gain internal control; as they function within rule systems, they learn to consider the demands of the outside world. And children of demanding parents know that their parents believe in their ability to meet demands—and care enough to insist that they do.

It makes sense that parents' treatment of their children affects the children's feelings about themselves, and yet there is another way to look at the relationship between parenting and children's self-esteem. Children with high self-esteem may have characteristics that encourage their parents to be loving, firm, and democratic.

Children who are self-confident, cooperative, and competent are easy to bring up. Thus it is probable that parents and children continually influence each other (Maccoby, 1980).

SEXISM AND SELF-ESTEEM Consider these statements by 8- to 11-year old boys who, in the 1950s, described what men need to know and be able to do:

> They need to be strong; they have to be ready to make decisions; they must be able to protect women and children in emergencies. . . . They are the ones to do the hard labor, the rough work, the dirty work, and the unpleasant work; they must be able to fix things; they must get money to support their families; they need "a good business head." . . . They also need to know how to take good care of children, how to get along with their wives, and how to teach their children right from wrong. (Hartley, 1959, p. 461)

And what did these boys say about women?

> They are indecisive; they are afraid of many things; they make a fuss over things; they get tired a lot; they very often need someone to help them; they stay home most of the time; they are not as strong as men; they don't like adventure; they are squeamish about seeing blood; they don't know what to do in an emergency; they cannot do dangerous things; they are more easily damaged than men; and they die more easily than men. . . .They are not very intelligent; they can only scream in an emergency when a man would take charge. . . . Women do things like cooking and washing and sewing because that's all they can do. (Hartley, 1959, p. 462)

These statements were clear examples of *sexism:* judging one sex (usually the male) as superior. Sexism can damage girls' self-esteem.

Fortunately, major changes have occurred in children's gender concepts since the 1950s. By the early 1970s, a survey of 1600 fourth-, sixth-, eighth-, and tenth-graders from various social classes revealed significant progress toward discarding stereotyped thinking. For example, 70 percent of the boys thought that a female doctor would be as good as a male, though only 33 percent thought that a trained female garage mechanic could fix a car as well as a male. Although 66 percent of the boys thought that "lady scien-

tists" are as smart as male scientists, only 35 percent thought that we should have female astronauts. The students' social class did not affect their answers. Girls were consistently more egalitarian than boys, and older students (after grade 4 for boys, 6 for girls) more so than younger students, possibly because they understood and had thought more about the social issues involved (S.B. Greenberg, 1972).

By the mid-1980s, when 283 kindergartners and fifth- and eleventh-graders were asked whether males, females, or either sex should do a number of specific jobs, the older children were much more equality-minded than children of the past had been, though the youngest ones (particularly the boys) still showed strong gender stereotyping (Archer, 1984). When asked about their own occupational goals, boys and girls thought that they might be able to do nearly equal numbers of jobs. But whereas a number of girls chose careers traditionally thought of as men's work, few males chose traditional "women's" occupations. Still, the extent of the change can be seen in the fact that not one fifth-grade girl saw her future career as "housewife" or "mother."

Theoretical Perspectives on the Self-Concept

Each of the major theoretical perspectives we discuss in this book has an explanation of why middle childhood is a favorable period for the development of a self-concept and how that development occurs.

Freud's Latency Period Freud—whose central concern was the development of the self—termed middle childhood the *latency period,* a period of relative sexual calm between the turbulence of early childhood and the storminess of adolescence. By this time, according to Freudian theory, youngsters have resolved their Oedipal conflicts, adopted their gender roles, and developed superegos, which keep their ids in check. Freed from the dominance of the id, children become socialized rapidly, develop skills, and learn about themselves and about society.

However, Freud's idea that latency is a period

of asexuality, or lack of interest in sex, has been largely discredited. Instead, many contemporary researchers believe that children in middle childhood hide their sexual interest because they have learned that adults disapprove of it, but that they still engage in sex play, masturbate, and ask questions about sex (Calderone & Johnson, 1981).

Erikson's Crisis 4: Industry versus Inferiority

Eriskon, too, sees middle childhood as a time of relative emotional calm, when children can attend to their schooling and learn the skills their culture requires. The characteristic crisis of this period is that of *industry versus inferiority,* and the issue to be resolved is a child's capacity for productive work. For example, the Arapesh boy in New Guinea, no longer content merely to play, learns to make bows and arrows and to lay traps for rats, and the Arapesh girl learns to weed and plant and harvest. The Alaskan Inuit learns to hunt and fish. Children in industrialized countries learn to count, read, and write numbers.

These fledgling efforts help children form positive self-concepts. The "virtue" that develops with successful resolution of this crisis is *competence,* a view of the self as able to master and complete tasks. As children compare their own abilities with those of their peers, they construct a sense of who they are. If they feel inadequate by comparison, Erikson believes, they may return to "the more isolated, less tool-conscious familial rivalry of the oedipal time" (1950, p. 260). If, on the other hand, they become *too* industrious, they may neglect their relationships with other people.

Social-Learning Theory   Social-learning theorists note that school-age children's keen self-awareness and observation make them more receptive to the influence of people they admire or of those who are perceived as powerful and rewarding. Whereas the young child responds mostly to material reinforcers, in middle childhood the approval or disapproval of parents, teachers, and peers becomes a powerful shaper of self-concept and of behavior.

Cognitive-Developmental Theory   Because (according to Piaget) school-age children are

less egocentric than younger children, they are better able to see themselves from other people's viewpoints and are more sensitive to what others think of them. Their increasing ability to decenter enables them to take more than one view of the self ("Today I'm being bad, but yesterday I was good."). This change permits growth in moral reasoning and the ability to consider social as well as personal needs.

The information-processing approach (one branch of cognitive theory) views the self-concept as a *self-schema,* or set of "knowledge structures," which organizes and guides the processing of information about the self (Markus & Nurius, 1984, p. 158). Children build, test, and modify their self-schemata (hypotheses about themselves) on the basis of their social experiences. Self-schemata help children use the results of their past behavior to make quick judgments about how to act in a given situation and help them define the possible self of the future. Strong and lasting self-schemata ("I am popular," "I am a good student," "I am a fast runner") may take shape during middle childhood as the many physical, intellectual, and social skills that children develop allow them to see themselves as valuable members of society (Markus, 1980).

ASPECTS OF PERSONALITY DEVELOPMENT IN MIDDLE CHILDHOOD

Everyday Life

"You're it!" "No, *you're* it!" For thousands of years, impromptu games of tag, catch, jacks, marbles, and "let's pretend" have served the time-honored mandate of childhood: to learn through play. Such games give children physical contact, confidence, and practice in using their imagination and getting along with others. They provide socially acceptable ways to compete, to discharge energy, and to act aggressively.

Today, however, new social patterns are replacing this traditional one, as technology changes the tools and habits of leisure. Television has seduced many children from active playing to passive watching. Computer games demand few social skills. Children are engaging in more organized sports, which replace childlike rules with adult rules, and in which adult referees settle disputes without children's having to find ways to resolve matters between themselves.

In other ways, too, the society of childhood mirrors changes in the larger society. Children of today's changing families act, think, and live differently from children born a generation or two ago. Many children live with only one parent. Some go to day care after school; others care for themselves and for younger brothers or sisters. Some children have a great deal of unsupervised time on their hands; some have heavily organized schedules of activities.

How Children Spend Their Time American children, according to one recent study, spend about two-thirds of their time on essentials— sleeping, eating, school, personal care, housework, and religious observance—leaving about 55 hours a week of leisure time (Institute for Social Research, 1985; see Table 9-1).

The two main things that children *choose* to do are playing (alone or with other children) and watching television. These two activities, by different accounts, take up anywhere from 50 to 70 percent of their free time. Younger children (aged 6 to 8) spend more time playing. But by the time children are 9 years old, the balance shifts in favor of television, which consumes an average of 2½ to 4 hours a day, according to various studies.

Children watch television more in middle childhood than during any other period of childhood, and 11- and 12-year-old boys watch the most, particularly action and adventure shows. Disadvantaged children are 3 times as likely to be heavy viewers as are other children (W.A. Collins, 1984; Institute for Social Research, 1985; Medrich, Roizen, Rubin, & Buckley, 1982). Children who read every day are, not surprisingly, likely to be less frequent viewers. Even children who read almost every day at age 9 are less likely to do so by age 13 (National Assessment of Educational Progress, NAEP, 1982).

Millions of school-age youngsters spend many hours on sports, clubs, religious groups, scouting, camps, private lessons, and other organized activities (W.A. Collins, 1984). One study (Institute for Social Research, 1985) found that the average child in this age group spends less than 45 minutes daily in sports (little more than 20 minutes on weekdays), but such averages can be misleading, because the amount of participation in athletics and other activities, as well as the type of activity, is strongly influenced by the ethnic and social group. For example, black boys are more likely to be involved in team games; white boys, in individual sports like swimming and tennis (Medrich et al., 1982).

A Child's Social Network When Andrea was 10, her parents drove 300 miles to visit her at summer camp. She waved, said, "Hi, Mom, hi, Dad," and then went back to playing softball.

School-age children spend relatively little

TABLE 9·1 HOW SCHOOL-AGE CHILDREN SPEND THEIR TIME: CHILDREN'S TOP 10 ACTIVITIES (AVERAGE HOURS AND MINUTES PER DAY)

ACTIVITY	WEEKDAY AGES 6–8	WEEKDAY AGES 9–11	WEEKEND AGES 6–8	WEEKEND AGES 9–11
Sleeping	9:55	9:08	10:41	9:56
School	4:52	5:15	—	—
Television	1:39	2:26	2:16	3:05
Playing	1:51	1:05	3:00	1:32
Eating	1:21	1:13	1:20	1:18
Personal care	0:49	0:40	0:45	0:44
Household work	0:15	0:18	0:27	0:51
Sports	0:24	0:21	0:30	0:42
Religious observance	0:09	0:09	0:56	0:53
Visiting someone	0:15	0:10	0:08	0:13

Source: Adapted from Institute for Social Research, 1985.

time with their parents (Medrich et al., 1982); the peer group becomes central. Time studies, however, can be deceptive. Relationships with parents continue to be the most important ones in children's lives.

In one recent study (Furman & Buhrmester, 1985), researchers gave questionnaires about relationships to 199 mostly middle-class fifth- and sixth-graders. The way the children rated the important people in their lives revealed that different relationships serve different purposes.

The children looked above all to their parents for affection, guidance, reliable alliance (a lasting, dependable bond), and enhancement of worth (affirmation of the child's competence or value as a person). Mothers got higher ratings for companionship than fathers, and children were generally more satisfied with their relationships with their mothers than those with their fathers. Although the children obtained guidance from their teachers, too, they were least satisfied with relationships with teachers. After parents, the most important people in the children's lives were their grandparents, who were often warm and supportive, offering affection and enhancement of worth.

Not surprisingly, the children felt more powerful among other children than among adults. Youngsters turned most often to their friends for companionship, and to their friends and their mothers for intimacy. Although the children also looked to siblings (especially those who were of the same sex and close in age) for companionship and intimacy and to older siblings for guidance, sibling relationships generally involved the most conflict and were relatively unsatisfying.

Some gender differences emerged. Girls had more intimate relationships with their mothers than with their fathers; for boys, there was no difference. Also, girls relied on their best friends more than boys did, and their friendships were more intimate, affectionate, and worth-enhancing. Since these three qualities seem to be more characteristic of older children's friendships, school-age girls' closest friendships may be more mature than boys'.

A school-age child's social world, then, is diverse and nurturing. Now, let's look more closely at the society of childhood: the peer group and the family.

Many children today spend more time in computer games and other solitary pursuits than in traditional group games like tag, catch, and marbles, which helped their parents and grandparents build social skills.

Life in the Peer Group

Babies are aware of one another, and preschoolers begin to make friends, but not until middle childhood does the peer group really come into its own. All societies throughout history have had childhood subcultures, but the peer group is particularly strong in our highly mobile, age-segregated society.

Functions and Influence of the Peer Group

The peer group can have both positive and negative effects. Let's look briefly at both.

POSITIVE EFFECTS OF THE PEER GROUP   The peer group is an important arena for the development of self-concept and the building of self-esteem. It helps children form opinions of themselves by seeing themselves as others see them. It gives them a basis of comparison—a realistic gauge of their own abilities and skills. Only within a large group of their peers can children get a sense of how smart, how athletic, and how personable they are.

The peer group helps children choose values to live by. Testing their opinions, feelings, and attitudes against those of other children helps them sift through the parental values they previously accepted unquestioningly and decide which to keep and which to discard.

The peer group offers emotional security. Sometimes another child can provide comfort that an adult cannot. It is reassuring to find out that a friend also harbors "wicked" thoughts that would offend an adult, and it can be emotionally healthy to enact forbidden fantasies in dramatic play with another child.

Finally, the peer group helps children learn how to get along in society. They learn how and when to adjust their needs and desires to those of others—when to yield and when to stand firm.

On the positive side, then, the peer group offers a counterweight to parents' influence, opens new perspectives, and frees children to make independent judgments.

NEGATIVE EFFECTS: CONFORMITY On the negative side, the peer group may impose values on the emerging individual, and children (especially if they have low status in the group) may be too weak to resist. In some countries, such as Israel, the Soviet Union, and China, as well as in some behavior modification programs in the United States, the peer group is used deliberately to mold behavior. Children are most susceptible to pressure to conform during middle childhood, and less so during adolescence (Costanzo & Shaw, 1966).

A classic study tested children's reactions to group pressures that contradicted the experience of their own eyes. Ninety 7- to 13-year-olds took a written test asking them to compare the lengths of lines on 12 cards, and to indicate which line was shorter or longer. They then repeated the test orally; this time the eight brightest children in each class sat in a room with a classmate. The eight had been told to give wrong answers to 7 of the 12 cards. The ninth child was caught unaware by the wrong answers and was torn between describing what he or she actually saw and going along with the group. When placed in that situation, only 43 percent of the 7- to 10-year-olds and 54 percent of the 10- to 13-year-olds answered the seven questions right, even though almost all of these youngsters had correctly answered the same questions on the written test (Berenda, 1950).

The effects of conformity can be more serious than giving wrong answers on a test. Peer influence is strongest when issues are ambiguous; since we live in a world with many ambiguous issues that require careful judgment, the consequences of peer-group influences can be severe. And although peer groups do many constructive things together—playing games, scouting, and the like—it is usually in the company of friends that children also shoplift, begin to smoke and drink, sneak into the movies, and perform other antisocial acts. Sixth-graders who are rated more "peer-oriented" report engaging in more of this latter kind of behavior than do "parent-oriented" children (J.C. Condry, Siman, & Bronfenbrenner, 1968). On the other hand, youngsters who are headed for real trouble with the law tend to be those who do *not* get along with their peers. These children are often immature and lack social skills (Hartup, 1984).

For children as well as for adults, some degree of conformity to group standards is a healthy mechanism of adaptation. It is unhealthy only when it becomes destructive or causes people to act against their own better judgment.

Who Is In the Peer Group? Peer groups form naturally among children who live in the same neighborhood or go to school together (Hartup, 1984). Children who play together are usually within a year or two of the same age, though an occasional neighborhood play group will form of a summer evening, including small children along with older ones. Too wide an age range brings problems with differences in size, interests, and ability levels.

In the elementary school years, peer groups are usually all girls or all boys. There seem to be at least two reasons for this: first, children of the same sex have common interests; and second, girls are generally more mature than boys.

Peer groups are usually of the same race and of the same or similar socioeconomic status, especially in segregated neighborhoods. Racial segregation in peer groups (as in adult society) often results from *prejudice*—negative attitudes toward certain groups, which can corrode the self-esteem of members of these groups. Studies conducted from the 1960s to the mid-1970s found bias against blacks among both white and black children in northern and southern American cities, from preschool through the early school years (Morland, 1966; J. Williams, Best, & Boswell, 1975).

Court-ordered school integration, which began in the mid-1950s, has brought more acceptance of racial differences, even though children still tend to choose friends of the same race. One study of midwestern third- and sixth-graders who had been in integrated classrooms from kindergarten on found that although the youngsters (particularly the older black children) preferred members of their own race, they rated classmates of the other race quite positively (Singleton & Asher, 1979). Some schools have worked to reduce prejudice by recruiting and training more minority-group teachers and by emphasizing the cultural contributions of minorities.

Friendship Jordan and his best friend play ball together and are in the same boy scout troop. Jane met her best friend at summer camp; now they write to each other every week and look forward to next summer, when they can be together.

Children may spend much of their free time in groups, but only as individuals do they form friendships. Children's ideas about friendship change enormously during the elementary school years. A school-age child is no longer so likely to define a friend as a younger child might, by saying, "She lives across the street and she has a lot of good toys." Instead, children of this age choose their friends from among a wide variety of children.

A friend in middle childhood is someone a child feels comfortable with, someone with whom he or she can share feelings and secrets. Friendship makes children more sensitive and loving, more able to give and receive respect. Children cannot be true friends or have true friends until they achieve the cognitive maturity to consider other people's viewpoints and needs, as well as their own.

Robert Selman has traced changing forms of friendship through five overlapping stages, on the basis of interviews with more than 250 people between the ages of 3 and 45 (Selman & Selman, 1979; see Table 9-2 on page 310). These stages have been validated by other research (Gurucharri & Selman, 1982; Smollar & Youniss, 1982; Youniss & Volpe, 1978).

(© Ida Wyman/International Stock Photo)

Members of a neighborhood peer group are usually of the same age, sex, race, and socioeconomic status, and they enjoy doing things together. While the peer group helps children build their self-concept and become independent from parents, it also exerts pressure to conform to group standards of dress, hair style, and behavior.

Most school-age children are in either stage 2 (fair-weather relationships based on reciprocal self-interest) or stage 3 (intimate, mutual relationships). In general, girls value *depth* of relationships, while boys value *number* of relationships (Furman, 1982).

Having a true friend is a milestone in development. Mutual affection enables children to express intimacy, to bask in a sense of self-worth, and to learn what being human is all about (Furman, 1982; H.S. Sullivan, 1953).

Popularity Most people want other people to like them. Indeed, the need to be liked and accepted is the source of the peer group's power. Popularity or unpopularity not only matters very much to children during their school years but may profoundly affect their later success and well-being.

TABLE 9-2 STAGES OF FRIENDSHIP

	STAGE	AGES*	CHARACTERISTICS
0	Momentary playmateship (undifferentiated)	3–7	Children are egocentric—they think only about what they want from a relationship. Children define friends by how close they live. ("She's my friend—she lives on my street.") Children value friends for material or physical attributes. ("He's my friend—he's got a giant Superman doll and a real swing set.")
1	One-way assistance (unilateral)	4–9	Children define a good friend as someone who does what they want the friend to do. ("He's my friend—he lets me borrow his eraser," or, "She's not my friend anymore—she wouldn't go skating with me.")
2	Two-way fair-weather cooperation (reciprocal)	6–12	Friendship involves give-and-take but still serves separate self-interests rather than common interests. ("We're friends—we do things for each other," or, "A friend is someone who plays with you when you don't have anybody else to play with.")
3	Intimate, shared relationships (mutual)	9–15	Children view a friendship as having a life of its own. Friendship is an ongoing, systematic, committed relationship involving more than doing things for each other. Children become possessive of their friends, demanding exclusivity. ("It takes a long time to make a close friend, and so you feel bad if she gets to be friends with someone else.") Girls develop one or two close friendships; boys have more, but less intimate, friends.
4	Autonomous interdependence (interdependent)	12 on	Children respect friends' needs for both dependency and autonomy. ("A good friendship is a real commitment, a risk you have to take. You have to be able to support and trust and give, but you have to be able to let go, too.")

*Ages of the various stages may overlap.
Source: Selman & Selman, 1979.

Why are some children sought out while others are ignored or rebuffed? Why do some children have many friends while others have none? What are popular and unpopular children like? To answer these questions, social scientists use **sociometric** techniques, which quantify the study of relationships. One such technique is a **sociogram,** a diagram of the social relationships that exist among members of a group.

In making a sociogram, a researcher observes children interacting, or asks them questions about their relationships with other children, and then plots the data on a "map" (see Figure 9-1). For example, children may be asked to name their three best friends or the three children they like the least; or they may be asked more specific questions, such as which three children they like to sit near, walk home with after school, or serve with on a committee. After plotting the data, the researcher can determine which children seek out others and which ones are sought out, which ones are chosen most often and which ones are chosen least often, and which ones are asked for help and advice. The researcher can then look at the characteristics of the children in the different categories to find personality patterns.

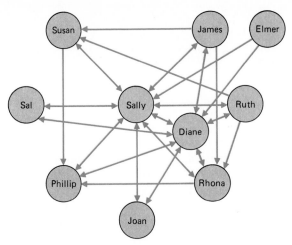

Figure 9-1 Sociogram. This hypothetical sociogram was plotted in response to asking members of the group whom they would most like to work with. Note the popularity of Diane and Sally and the social isolate status of Elmer. Note that neither Rhona nor Susan wants to work with James and Ruth—although James and Ruth want to work with them. In this sociogram most of the relationships are reciprocal. In real life there is usually more imbalance.

THE POPULAR CHILD Popular children tend to be healthy and vigorous, well poised, and capable of initiative; they are also adaptable and conforming. They are dependable, affectionate, and considerate, and are original thinkers (Bonney, 1947, cited in Grossmann & Wrighter, 1948). They think moderately well of themselves, rather than showing extremely high or low levels of self-esteem (Reese, 1961). They radiate self-confidence without being overbearing or seeming conceited.

Popular children show mature dependence on other children: they ask for help when they need it, and for approval when they think that they deserve it, but they do not cling or make infantile plays for affection (Hartup, 1970). They are not goodies-goodies, but they make other people feel good about being with them (Feinberg, Smith, & Schmidt, 1958; Tuddenham, 1951). Popular children also tend to be more physically attractive than unpopular ones (R. Lerner & Lerner, 1977).

THE UNPOPULAR CHILD One of the saddest figures among schoolchildren is the child who is chosen last for every team, is on the fringes of

every group, walks home alone after school, is not invited to birthday parties, and sobs in despair, "Nobody wants to play with me."

Why are some children unpopular? Children's unpopularity can result from many causes, some of which are in their power to change, while others are not. Unpopular youngsters may walk around with a chip on the shoulder, expressing unprovoked aggression and hostility. Or they may act silly and infantile, showing off in immature ways. Or they may be anxious and uncertain, exuding such a pathetic lack of confidence that they repel other children, who find them no fun to be with. Extremely fat or unattractive children, children who behave in any way that seems strange, and retarded or slow-learning youngsters also tend to be outcasts.

How unhappy are unpopular children? Unpopular children are not *always* miserable. One study found only a modest correlation between unpopularity and loneliness reported by children. The researchers administered a questionnaire to more than 500 third- through sixth-graders in a midwestern city, asking them how they felt about their social relationships, and then compared the results with sociometric ratings. More than 10 percent of the children reported feeling extremely lonely and dissatisfied with their relationships; these children tended—but only moderately so—to be the ones who were least popular according to the sociometric measures (Asher, Hymel, & Renshaw, 1984).

Why was the correlation so weak? Perhaps some unpopular children may not admit feeling lonely or may not be cognitively mature enough to know how their peers regard them. It is possible that some children who do not have friends among their classmates do have neighborhood friends or siblings to play with.

How can unpopular children be helped? Popularity in childhood is not a frivolous issue. Aside from the sadness, sense of rejection, and poor self-esteem that unpopular children feel, they are also deprived of a basic developmental experience: the positive interaction with other youngsters that helps them to grow as individuals.

Unpopularity during the preschool years is not necessarily cause for concern; but by middle childhood, peer relationships are strong predictors of later adjustment. Children who have trouble getting along with their peers are more likely to have psychological problems, to drop out of school, and to become delinquent (Hartup, 1984; Lamb, 1978). (It is not clear, though, whether unpopularity during middle childhood *causes* later disturbances or merely *reflects* developmental problems that show up in more serious form later on.)

Since relationships with other children are vital to children's happiness and healthy development, adults sometimes try to help unpopular children make friends. Children who are simply *neglected* or overlooked by their classmates or other peers may do better in a different class or a new school, or if they join a new club or go to a new camp. Those children, however, who are actively *rejected* by their peers—the ones who are most at risk of emotional and behavioral difficulties as adolescents and adults—usually cannot be rescued simply by being moved into a new group or situation. They need to learn how to make other children like them.

In one study, fifth- and sixth-graders who had problems with social skills received training in this area. They learned how to carry on a conversation: how to share information about themselves, how to show interest in others by asking questions about them, and how to give help, suggestions, invitations, and advice. When they had a chance to practice their new conversational skills in a group project with other children, they became better liked by the others and interacted more with them (Bierman & Furman, 1984).

The children who received the training showed more general and lasting improvement over a 6-week period (according to measures of conversational skills, rates of interaction, peer acceptance, and self-perception) than those who received no training, those who received the training but then did not participate in the peer-group project, and those who took part in the group project but were not taught any skills. This experiment showed that children not only need social skills but also have to be in situations in which they can use these skills and in which other children can see the changes in them.

Otherwise, other children may hold on to their former opinions about these youngsters and may not give them a chance to show their new skills.

The Child in the Family

School-age children spend more time away from home than they did when they were younger. School, friends, games, and movies all draw them away from the house and keep them apart from the family. Yet home is still the most important part of their world, and the people who live there are the most important to them (Furman & Buhrmester, 1985). Let's look at how relationships with parents and siblings develop during middle childhood and at how societal change is affecting family life.

Parent-Child Relationships Not surprisingly, children's outside obligations and interests increase at a time when youngsters are more self-sufficient and require less physical care and supervision than before. One study found that parents spend less than half as much time caring for 5- to 12-year-olds—teaching them, reading and talking to them, and playing with them—as they spend caring for preschoolers (C.R. Hill & Stafford, 1980). Still, the job of parenting is far from over.

ISSUES As children's lives change, the issues that arise between them and their parents change accordingly (Maccoby, 1984). One important new area of concern is school. Parents worry about how a child is doing with schoolwork and wonder how involved they should become. They may have to deal with a child who complains about his or her teacher, feigns illness to avoid going to school, or plays hooky. (Box 9-1 on page 314 discusses how to deal with an underachiever.)

Parents usually want to know where their children are and whom they are with when they are not in school. Some parents even tell children whom they may and may not play with. Parents and children often disagree over what household chores children should do, whether they should be paid for doing them, and how much allowance they should get. (Of course, many of these issues would not even come up in some nonwestern societies, where children over the age of 6 must often work to help the family survive.)

The profound changes of middle childhood in children's lives and in the kinds of issues that arise between them and their parents bring changes in the ways parents handle discipline and control. Yet, as we'll see, most parents' approach to their job remains fundamentally the same as their children mature.

DISCIPLINARY METHODS   When Jeremy was 18 months old and reached for the shaving cream, his father tried to distract him with a toy and, failing that, picked him up and moved him to another room. When Jeremy was 4 years old and made loud noises while his parents were trying to listen to a record, they first tried to ignore him and then threatened to send him to his room.

Now that Jeremy is in school, the nature of his transgressions has changed, and so have his parents' disciplinary methods. Instead of distraction, removal, isolation, threats, ignoring, or spanking, they use more subtle means (Maccoby, 1984; G.C. Roberts, Block, & Block, 1984). When he fails to do his homework, they deprive him of privileges, like watching his favorite television show. They rely more on praise for what he does right than on punishment for what he does wrong. They reason with him, appealing to his self-esteem ("What happened to the helpful boy who was here yesterday?"), sense of humor ("If you go one more day without a bath, we won't have to look to know when you're coming!"), sense of guilt ("A big, strong boy like you shouldn't sit on the train and let an old person stand"), or appreciation ("Aren't you glad that you have a father who cares enough to remind you to wear boots so that you won't catch a cold?"). Above all, Jeremy's parents let him know that he is responsible for what happens to him ("No wonder you missed the school bus today—you stayed up too late last night reading in bed!").

This evolution is typical as children gain cognitive awareness. Rather than responding to sheer power, children are now more likely to defer to their parents' authority because they recognize that the parents are fair, that they contribute to the whole family's well-being, and

Although school-age children spend less time with their parents than they did before, parents continue to be very important in children's lives, providing reassurance and guidance. Parents who enjoy being with their children are likely to raise children who feel good about themselves—and about their parents.

that they often "know better" because of their wider experience.

Yet, despite these changes, one longitudinal study found an underlying consistency in parents' child-rearing philosophies. Parents of 3-year-old boys and girls from a wide range of backgrounds filled out questionnaires consisting of 91 items in categories such as independence, control, suppression of aggression and sex, emphasis on health and achievement, expression of feelings, protectiveness, supervision, rational guidance, and punishment. The parents completed the questionnaires again when the children were 12 years old. Over the 9-year period, the researchers found significant correlations for the mothers on three-fourths of the items and for the fathers on more than half of the items. In general, the parents' basic values and approach to child rearing seemed to remain

BOX 9-1 FOOD FOR THOUGHT

UNDERACHIEVEMENT: CAUSES AND CURES

Paul yawns and daydreams in school. His desk is messy, he often loses assignments, and when his parents ask about homework, he assures them (falsely) that he has already done it or that he has none.

Rebecca's report cards are a mixture of A's and F's. She works only if she likes the teacher, she is rebellious and aggressive, and she reacts to her parents' scoldings by retreating to her bedroom and slamming the door.

Although Paul and Rebecca behave very differently, both children exhibit what the psychologist Sylvia Rimm (1985, 1986) calls "underachievement syndrome." Some *underachievers*—children who perform below their apparent potential—are perfectionists. Some are hyperactive. Some have trouble concentrating. Some are disorganized. Some are overaggressive, and some have no friends. Many are bright or even gifted.

These children start out doing well in school, but at some point their test scores and grades begin to slip—and keep on slipping. These youngsters begin to believe that they cannot succeed, and eventually they stop trying.

Underachievers often confuse ability, effort, and performance. In the early grades, because teachers reward effort, children often believe that working hard will make them smart. Then, when they come to see that ability counts, they may get the idea that a bright child does not have to work. If they fall into a habit of not working, later—

when the work gets harder and they begin to fail—they may think that they lack the ability to do better (U.S. Department of Education, 1986b).

The children themselves may claim that they are bored, that schoolwork is uninteresting or "irrelevant," and that the teacher is "no good." They may insist that they are not as smart as the tests say, or that they would rather be popular than make good grades.

Beneath these defenses, Rimm believes, underachieving behavior has psychological roots. As a way of getting attention and gaining or maintaining power in the family, these children learn to be either helplessly overdependent like Paul or overdominant like Rebecca, taking over and manipulating every situation. Such behavior begins and is reinforced long before school age.

The syndrome may be set in motion by overindulgent, overprotective parents. It may be fed by such early experiences as illness, extreme sibling rivalry, inconsistent discipline, opposition between parents, or divorce and a resulting overclose relationship with one parent. An unusually gifted or disabled child may get an unhealthy dose of parental attention.

A child with such a background may do well enough in school for a while. But the syndrome may surface when the child gets a poor teacher, when assignments become consistently too easy or too hard, or when there is

a dramatic change in family circumstances, like a move, a death, or divorce. A teacher may unwittingly make matters worse by giving extra help to a dependent child (thus increasing the child's dependence) or by getting into power struggles with a dominant child (and thus making the child even more hostile and negativistic).

The following suggestions for parents (adapted from Rimm, 1986) may help prevent or cure underachievement:

- Set clear, positive expectations.
- Offer models of achievement.
- Don't overreact to your child's success or failure.
- Help your children develop plans for doing their work—but don't help them do it. Children develop self-confidence through struggle.
- Give children power gradually as they show maturity and responsibility.
- Don't ally with a child against the other parent or the teacher—it makes the child too powerful.
- Avoid confrontations with children unless you can control the outcome.
- Help children learn to compete. If they constantly win, they don't learn to cope with defeat; if they constantly lose, they see no point in trying.
- Help children see the relationship between their efforts and the results they achieve.

constant, emphasizing rational guidance and praise; and shifts generally coincided with "developmentally appropriate areas for change" (G.C. Roberts, Block, & Block, 1984, p. 595).

CONTROL AND COREGULATION At some point, the power to control children's behavior shifts from the parents to the children themselves. The process begins during the preschool years, when a child's gradual acquisition of self-control and self-regulation reduces the need for constant parental scrutiny. But it is not until adolescence or even later that most young people can make their own decisions about how they should dress, how late they should stay out, with whom they should associate, and how they should spend their money.

Middle childhood is a transitional stage of *coregulation,* in which parent and child share power; "parents continue to exercise general supervisory control, while children begin to exercise moment-to-moment self-regulation" (Maccoby, 1984, p. 191). Parents tend to use their power more directly when children misbehave in their presence (for example, by making noise or throwing a ball in the living room) than when the misbehavior takes place away from the parent (for example, when children engage in shoplifting).

Coregulation reflects the self-concept development going on within the child. As children of this age begin to coordinate their own wishes with societal demands, they are more likely to anticipate how their parents or other people will react to what they do, or to accept a reminder from their parents that others will think better of them if they behave differently.

Coregulation is a cooperative process; if it is to be successful, parents and children must communicate clearly. If children do not keep parents informed of where they are, what they are doing, and what problems they are facing, or if parents become preoccupied with their own activities and fail to take an interest in their children's, the parents will not be able to judge when to step in.

To make this transitional phase work, parents have a threefold task: (1) influencing their children when they are together, (2) monitoring children when they are out of sight, and (3) teaching children to monitor their *own* behavior—to adopt acceptable standards, avoid undue risks, and recognize when they need their parents' support or guidance (Maccoby, 1984).

VARIATIONS IN PARENTING Of course, parents do not treat all their children the same, and the same parent may treat the same child differently from one day to the next. Different parents vary in what kinds of behavior they allow, in their goals for (and demands on) their children, in their disciplinary and motivational techniques, and in the degree of control they exercise.

Research shows some ethnic differences, which we must be careful in interpreting because they often turn out to be linked to educational level or to the relative prevalence of single-parent families. Black parents appear to be stricter and more punitive than white parents and to put more pressure on their children for achievement in school and on the athletic field. Hispanic families tend to stress traditional values, such as respect for authority (Maccoby, 1984).

Perhaps because they typically have more time available and are more free of financial worries, and perhaps because they have generally had more advanced education, middle-class parents are more likely than working-class parents to pay attention to children and spend time with them; to use complex language with them; to be permissive with them about their activities and about sexual issues; to tolerate anger; to value happiness, curiosity, and creativity above obedience and respect; to listen to a child's viewpoint and give the child a voice in family decisions; and to make greater demands for maturity, achievement, and independence. In regard to discipline, middle-class parents are likely to try to motivate a child rather than give direct orders, and to reason and explain rather than to punish (Maccoby, 1984).

Most parents, however (of whatever class or ethnic group), give their children warmth, love, and acceptance—the most important requirements for helping children make a successful transition to adolescence.

Sibling Relationships "I fight more with my little brother than I do with my friends," reports

(© Cary Wolinsky/Stock, Boston)

Relationships with siblings are important during middle childhood. Older sisters talk and explain more to their younger siblings than older brothers do.

Penny, who is a firstborn child; "but when I fight with Billy, we always make up."

Penny recognizes the special nature of her relationship with Billy, her nearest sibling in age. She can see that their tie is deeper and more lasting than ordinary friendships, which may founder on a quarrel or just fade away. She is also aware that her relationship with her brother is ambivalent, marked by a special affection as well as by intense competition and resentment.

How do siblings influence each other in middle childhood? For one thing, siblings help each other develop a self-concept. When Penny compares herself with Billy and sees how different they are despite all their shared bonds, she forms a stronger sense of herself as an individual.

Sibling relations are an arena for learning how to resolve conflicts. Although brothers and sisters often quarrel, the ties of blood and physical closeness impel them to make up, since they cannot avoid seeing each other every day. Thus they learn that the expression of anger does not mean the end of a relationship. Since siblings' quarrels often stem from uneven power bases, younger siblings in particular often become quite skillful at sensing other people's needs,

negotiating for what they want, and compromising. Eldest children like Penny tend to be bossy; they are more likely to attack, interfere with, ignore, or bribe their siblings, whereas second-borns like Billy plead, reason, and cajole—or sometimes take the older sibling's things (Cicirelli, 1976a).

Penny's relationship with Billy is helped by the fact that she is a girl and he is a boy. Children are more apt to squabble with same-sex siblings and to be conciliatory with siblings of the other sex; two brothers quarrel more than any other combination (Cicirelli, 1976a). When girls want their younger siblings to do something, they are more apt to reason with them or to make them feel obligated, whereas older brothers tend to attack (Cicirelli, 1976b).

Children who have siblings learn how to deal with dependency in relationships by experiencing their dependence on each other. Although siblings in our society do less active caretaking of their younger brothers and sisters than is common in many other countries, a good deal of it does take place. Working parents often depend on an older child to mind the younger children until the parents come home, and older children often help younger siblings with their homework. This help is most likely to be effective (and accepted) when it comes from a sibling—especially a sister—who is at least 4 years older.

Girls talk more to younger siblings than boys do: they give more explanations and feedback, and they are more likely to use the *deductive* method (explaining, describing, demonstrating, and illustrating), while boys more often use the *inductive* approach (giving examples and letting the learner abstract the concept) (Cicirelli, 1976a).

Some of the difference in the way boys and girls behave toward their siblings may be due to gender-typing—the fact that certain kinds of behavior are encouraged more for one sex than the other. It may also have roots in girls' tendency to identify more with their mothers. And it may relate to boys' greater emotional vulnerability, which may cause them to be more jealous and act more hostile when displaced by a younger "usurper."

Besides influencing each other *directly*, through interaction with each other, siblings also influence each other *indirectly,* through their impact on each other's relationship with the parents—particularly on the way parents divide their time among the children. For example, because girls seem to be more effective in handling younger siblings, mothers tend to talk more, explain more, and give more feedback to children with older brothers than to children with older sisters (Cicirelli, 1976a).

Children of Employed Mothers In 1969, for the first time in history, a majority of mothers of school-age children in the United States held paid jobs. Since then, that number has risen steadily (see Table 9-3), and so has researchers' interest in the impact of this major change on children. (Because fathers' employment is taken for granted, it has not received comparable research attention.)

In 1985, 61 percent of married women with children under 18 and nearly 68 percent of single mothers maintaining their families were in the work force—about two-thirds of the former and four-fifths of the latter working full time. All in all, about 25 million children had mothers who worked outside the home for at least part of the day (Hayghe, 1986). Indeed, with nearly half of all new mothers going to work soon after giving birth, substantial—and growing—numbers of children have never known a time when their mothers were *not* working.

How does a mother's outside employment affect her children? Because the phenomenon of widespread maternal employment is fairly recent, the research is in a state of flux. In the past, much of the literature concentrated on how working mothers could compensate for the smaller amounts of time and attention they could give their children; today many researchers emphasize the positive effects of the mother's employment on the entire family.

The mother's self-esteem often rises because she feels more competent, more economically secure, and more in charge of her life. In general, the more satisfied a woman is with her life, the more effective she is as a parent (L. Hoffman, 1979, 1986). The father can relax more, knowing that he is not the only adult responsible for the financial support of the family; and he is less likely to hold a second job. The father who becomes more active in taking care of his chil-

TABLE 9-3 PERCENT OF MOTHERS IN TWO-PARENT FAMILIES IN LABOR FORCE, 1975–1985

	1975	1985
With youngest child under 6	37	54
With youngest child 6–17	52	68
Total with children under 18	45	61

Note: Percentages are rounded to nearest whole number.
Source: Hayghe, 1986.

dren because of his wife's employment is more nurturing: he shows his love to his children, tries to help them with their worries and problems, can make them feel better when they are upset, and gives them continuing care and attention (Carlson, 1984). Thus he can display a side of the personality that has traditionally been less visible in men.

The children benefit from their exposure to new role models: employed women and child-rearing men. Daughters of working women and sons of fathers who participate in child care have fewer stereotypes about gender roles than children in "traditional" families (Carlson, 1984; L. Hoffman, 1979). One recent study, however, found this effect to be weak and to depend more on the mother's attitude toward the father's participation in home duties than on how much he actually does at home (Baruch & Barnett, 1986). In fact, it appears that fathers in two-earner families spend very little additional time on child care—only a few minutes a day, and usually only when the children are under age 3 (Maccoby, 1984).

The effects of a mother's employment may depend on many variables, including whether she is married or single, whether she works full time or part time, the family's economic circumstances, and the arrangements made for her children's care when they are not in school. For example, children whose mothers are poor, single, and not very well educated may benefit from the additional income as well as from the increased sense of self-worth the mothers derive from work.

Among the most significant factors are the age and sex of the child, which we'll now examine.

This mother, helping her children plan their day as she gets ready to leave for work, is typical of the majority of today's mothers, who have jobs outside the home. Mothers' employment may affect girls differently from boys and school-age children differently from younger ones.

EFFECTS ON INFANTS AND PRESCHOOLERS
Some research suggests that no ill effects on infants' or preschoolers' social, emotional, and cognitive development can be traced to their mothers' employment (Zimmerman & Bernstein, 1983). But the picture that emerges from some other studies is not quite so rosy. For example, middle-class boys have shown lower IQs and poorer academic achievement when their mothers worked full time during their preschool years (Bronfenbrenner, Alvarez, & Henderson, 1984; D. Gold & Andres, 1978b; D. Gold, Andres, & Glorieux, 1979).

During the critical first year of life, an infant's primary attachment is usually to the mother, whether she is working or not. When mothers work full time outside the home, babies (especially boys) may become insecurely attached to *both* parents unless the father is the one caring for the baby (Belsky, 1987). The risk of insecure attachment and later adjustment problems is greater when there is stress in the home, when the mother is emotionally distant, or when infants receive poor-quality day care (Gamble & Zigler, 1986; Young & Zigler, 1986).

Most babies receive care in their own homes or in the homes of relatives or baby-sitters; but more and more 3- and 4-year-olds are being placed in organized day care facilities (U.S. Bureau of the Census, 1987). We need more information about the effects of such care. *Highquality* day care (which, unfortunately, is rare) generally seems to be beneficial (Belsky, 1984; see Chapter 6).

Thus we need to know more than the simple fact that a mother is working. Why is she working, and how does her work make her feel? If she were at home full time, would she be resentful about not working and take out her resentment on the child? How effectively can she balance the demands of work and raising children? Does the mother find the child relatively easy to care for, or (as is often true with boys) does the child seem to need more supervision than the mother can comfortably give? What kind of care does the child get when the mother is away? Only when we have answers to questions like these can we evaluate the effects of a mother's employment on a young child.

EFFECTS ON SCHOOL-AGE CHILDREN   School-age children of employed mothers seem to benefit from two conditions of family life: they tend to live in more structured homes, with clear-cut rules, and they are usually encouraged to be more independent than the children of mothers who are at home (unless their mothers feel guilty about working).

On the other hand, both working mothers and their school-age children complain that they have too little time together. Children of working mothers are more likely than children of nonemployed mothers to associate with youngsters who skip school, run away from home, experiment with drugs, and get into trouble with the law (General Mills, 1977). Monitoring the whereabouts and activities of children—especially "latchkey children"—is difficult (see Box 9-2, page 320). Mothers who work part time or have flexible hours may be able to monitor their children more easily (Maccoby, 1984).

Research on the effect of mothers' employment on children's school achievement has yielded conflicting results, probably because of failure to control for such variables as marital status, socioeconomic background, parents' educational levels, home atmosphere, family size, whether the mother works full time or part time, how long she has been working, the children's age and sex, and the way the children spend their time (for example, how much is spent on homework and reading and how much on watching television). One large-scale study by the U.S. Department of Education, based on reading and mathematical achievement scores of more than 12,000 first- through sixth-graders in 1976–1977 and about 2700 high school students in 1980, did attempt to control for these variables (Milne, Myers, Rosenthal, & Ginsburg, 1986).

The study has been criticized on methodological grounds, including the failure of the government researchers to consider such additional factors as the parents' occupational status, the mother's age and work history, and her attitude toward her work (Heyns & Catsambis, 1986). But the key finding seems to have held up, at least for elementary school students: advantaged students, "whose mothers are potentially the most competent teachers" (Milne, Myers, & Ginsburg, 1986, p. 154), tend to have somewhat lower achievement when their mothers work.

Specifically, in white two-parent families (particularly large families), students did worse as their mothers worked more (Milne et al., 1986). This may be because working mothers spend less time teaching their children, reading to them, playing with them, and talking with them than full-time homemakers do and because fathers do not take up the slack (Foundation for Child Development, 1981).

By contrast, for black elementary school students living with both parents, any negative effect of mothers' working was offset by increased family income. And when the mother was single, black children (but not white children) tested better if their mothers worked—again, apparently because the added income in a poor family (most black one-parent families are in fact poor) outweighed the loss of the mother's time with the children (Milne et al., 1986).

Although the government study found that gender had no effect on achievement, other research suggests that, as in infancy, boys are more vulnerable than girls. Daughters of employed mothers achieve more than the daughters of homemakers and score higher on tests of self-esteem and other measures of adjustment. This may be due to a combination of such factors as both parents' encouragement of competency and independence in girls, daughters' closer relationship with their fathers, and the role model that mothers offer their daughters.

The findings for boys are less clear-cut, less uniformly positive, and more varied by social class. The sons of working mothers do have less stereotyped views of men and women, seeing women as more competent and men as warmer than do the sons of women who remain at home. This effect is less pronounced among boys in lower-class families. These boys are also more likely to have strained relations with their fathers, possibly because both fathers and sons may view the mother's going to work as an indication that the father is not able to fulfill his role as provider. This father-son tension does not show up in middle-class families, but (as we've seen) some middle-class boys score lower on intelligence tests and do less well in school than do their counterparts whose mothers do not work outside the home (L. Hoffman, 1979, 1986; Maccoby, 1984).

There are still unanswered questions about a working mother's influence on her son's academic achievement. Might the negative effects reflect a male view that a mother's employment is evidence of the father's inadequacy? If so, then perhaps as society adjusts to the fact that the *typical* mother now is a working mother, these feelings will abate and the adverse effects on sons will moderate.

EFFECTS ON ADOLESCENTS If all goes well, the needs of both adolescent and parent can be met by a mother's employment outside the home. In one study, 7 out of 10 teenagers said that their mothers' working at this time in the children's lives had either positive effects or no effects on them (General Mills, Inc., 1981). Teenagers

BOX 9-2 **PRACTICALLY SPEAKING**

WHEN SCHOOL-AGE CHILDREN CARE FOR THEMSELVES

When Benji, who is 11 years old, comes home from school, he unlocks the door to his house, enters, and fixes himself—and his cat—something to eat. Then he does his homework or goes outside or to a friend's house to play, being sure to call his mother to tell her where he'll be and whether he needs to have her pick him up at six o'clock on her way home from work.

Benji is among a growing number of *latchkey children,* children who regularly care for themselves at home without adult supervision because both their parents work outside the home or because a single custodial parent works outside the home. The number of latchkey children between the ages of 7 and 13 rose from about 1.8 million in 1974 to 2 million in 1984 (C. Cole & Rodman, 1987). Although most self-care takes place after school, some children spend time alone in the morning or evening.

It has been difficult to assess the impact of self-care on child development, because of the negative stereotypes associated with it. "The media give us the lonely latchkey child [and] equate latchkey children with delinquent and pre-delinquent activities, with idleness and fear, with abuse and abandonment" (Rodman, 1984, p. 93; cited in C. Cole & Rodman, 1987).

Although portrayals in the media have softened recently, we still have few objective research data. Some studies report no differences between children being cared for by adults and those caring for themselves for limited periods of time, while others suggest that self-care can result in developmental problems (C. Cole & Rodman, 1987; Rodman & Cole, 1987).

Children who are left alone, by choice or by necessity, need to be protected and to learn how to take care of themselves. To determine whether a child is ready for self-care, parents need to ask themselves whether the child meets the following criteria (adapted from C. Cole & Rodman, 1987, and Olds, 1986).

Children should:

■ Have enough control of their bodies that they are not likely to injure themselves when alone.

■ Be able to keep track of keys and to handle locks and doors well enough to avoid locking themselves in or out.

■ Be able to operate household equipment safely.

■ Tolerate separation from adults without being too fearful or lonely.

■ Not be withdrawn, hostile, or self-destructive.

■ Be flexible and resourceful enough to handle unexpected situations.

■ Be responsible enough to follow important rules without supervision.

■ Be able to understand and remember spoken and written instructions.

■ Read and write well enough to take telephone messages and other messages.

■ Know what to say to visitors and telephone callers.

■ Know how to request help from friends, neighbors, police, fire fighters, and other community resources when necessary. The child should, for example, know how to use a pay phone and know procedures to follow in case of emergency.

Parents or guardians considering self-care should:

■ Arrange to be in contact with and supervise their children even when they, the adults, are away from home.

■ Be available in emergencies or provide the names of adults who can be.

■ Train children in self-care.

Finally, the local community should be reasonably safe. *On My Own: The Kids' Self Care Book,* by Lynette Long (1984), is an attractive workbook with more than 125 activities to teach 8- to 12-year-olds how to care for themselves, plus a "Ready or Not" quiz to tell them whether they are ready to be on their own. The book is available from Acropolis Books, 2400 Seventeenth Street NW, Washington, DC 20009.

want to be independent—to make their own decisions. They like being on their own. They resent having to answer for the way they spend every minute. Mothers who are at home are more likely to continue to direct their adolescents' activities, and when their well-meaning advice or questions are rejected, they often feel personally rebuffed.

The employed mother avoids some of this conflict. In addition, she gains a sense of self-esteem in connection with her job as opposed to her mothering abilities, which are needed less at this stage of her children's lives. This is probably why working mothers of adolescents seem to feel better about themselves—their competence, their attractiveness, and their degree of self-fulfillment—than nonworking mothers of teenagers.

Adolescent children of employed women are better adjusted socially, feel better about themselves, have more of a sense of belonging, and get along better with their families and with their friends at school than other teenagers do (D. Gold & Andres, 1978a). Adolescent daughters of working women make a particularly strong showing. They "are more outgoing, independent, active, [and] highly motivated, score higher on a variety of indices of academic achievement, and appear better adjusted on social and personality measures" (L. Hoffman, 1979, p. 864).

On the negative side, latchkey arrangements for adolescents may have less-than-favorable outcomes, depending on how susceptible a teenager is to peer pressure (see Chapter 11).

The study by the U.S. Department of Education, discussed earlier, found a cumulative negative effect on the achievement of high school sophomores and seniors (particularly those in white two-parent families) when their mothers had worked at some time during their growing-up years, and the effect was stronger when mothers had worked full time over the child's lifetime (Milne et al., 1986). A possible reason is that students with working mothers tended to spend less time on homework and reading and more time watching television.

But when other researchers reanalyzed the data for a larger sample of sophomores, the negative effects of mothers' employment were insignificant. In fact, the sophomores—a more mixed group than the seniors, since some disadvantaged students and low achievers drop out before their senior year—did *better* when their mothers worked while the children were in high school. Furthermore, it appeared that high school students' achievement suffered only when their mothers had worked full time during the children's preschool years—at a time, historically, when most mothers were still staying home and child care options were severely limited (Heyns & Catsambis, 1986).

As Heyns and Catsambis concluded, "the effect of mother's employment on children's achievement is a complex phenomenon that we are only just beginning to untangle" (1986, p. 150). In general, though, older children appear at less risk than younger children—and may even be at an advantage—when mothers work.

Children of Divorce   Children suffer when their parents split up. The children, as much as or more than the parents, may feel pain, confusion, anger, hate, bitter disappointment, a sense of failure, and self-doubt. For many, this family disruption is the central event of childhood, with ramifications that follow them into adult life.

More than 1 million children under the age of 18 are involved in divorces each year. This figure, which has held fairly steady during the 1980s, is double what it was about 20 years ago (Wegman, 1986).

No matter how unhappy a marriage has been, its breakup usually comes as a shock to the children. During the process of adjustment, the children of divorcing parents often feel afraid of the future, guilty about their own (usually imaginary) role in causing the divorce, hurt at the rejection they feel from the parent who moves out, and angry at both parents. They may become depressed, hostile, disruptive, irritable, lonely, sad, accident-prone, or even suicidal; they may suffer from fatigue, insomnia, skin disorders, loss of appetite, or inability to concentrate; and they may lose interest in schoolwork and in social life.

AGE DIFFERENCES IN REACTIONS TO DIVORCE Although no two children react in exactly the same way, certain patterns emerge for children of different ages, largely as a result of their levels of cognitive and emotional development (Neal, 1983; Wallerstein & Kelly, 1980).

Preschoolers (2½ to 6 years) often show signs of great stress. Those from 2½ to 3½ whine, cry, cling, have sleep problems, and wet the bed. Four-year-olds whine and cry, hit other children, and blame themselves. Five- and six-year-olds are more anxious and more aggressive; they crave physical contact. Because young children are egocentric, they may feel that they have caused the divorce—that the parent who has left has done so because of something bad the child has done. These children are likely to have two kinds of fantasies: terrifying ones in which they are abandoned, and soothing ones in which their parents reunite. In one study of children of divorced parents, all the preschoolers who played house put the mother and father dolls in bed together, hugging each other (Wallerstein, 1983).

Children of elementary school age (6 to 12 years) also may be very frightened. When they first hear the news, they may run to a neighbor in a state of panic or be overcome by severe vomiting spells. They often become bitter toward, and angry with, one or both parents, especially the one they blame for causing the divorce. They may act out their anger by stealing or lying, or they may take it out on themselves with headaches and stomachaches.

Although they are often aware of conflicts between their parents, younger schoolchildren still feel responsible for having caused the divorce (perhaps thinking that they have done something that caused a fight between their parents), and they also feel responsible for making their parents feel better. Older schoolchildren have a better understanding of their parents' inner feelings and of the conflicts that arise when two people's attitudes and expectations conflict. These children often believe that their parents are separating because they have changed or because their relationship has changed, but the children believe that such changes can be reversed if the parents try hard enough.

Young adolescents (13 to 15 years) feel anger, depression, guilt, and despair. They may worry about money or become very active sexually. They may begin to compete with the parent of the same sex or buckle under the strain of being the "man" or "woman" of the household. They tend to believe that their parents have divorced because their relationship has gone bad on account of personality problems or irreconcilable differences.

Parents and counselors who want to help a child adjust to divorce need to be aware of what the child believes and what he or she is capable of grasping.

ADJUSTMENT TO DIVORCE The children of divorcing parents face a special set of challenges and burdens in addition to the usual tasks of emotional development during the growing-up years. In a longitudinal study of 60 divorcing families in California whose children ranged in age from 3 to 18 at the time of the separation, six special tasks emerged as crucial to such children's emotional development (Wallerstein, 1983; Wallerstein & Kelly, 1980):

1 *Acknowledging the reality of the marital rupture.* Small children often do not understand what has happened, and many children of various ages initially deny the separation. Others either are overwhelmed by fantasies of total abandonment or retreat into fantasies of reconciliation. Most children, however, do face the facts of the divorce by the end of the first year of separation.

2 *Disengaging from parental conflict and distress and resuming customary pursuits.* At first, children are often so preoccupied with worry that they cannot concentrate in school, play with other children, or take part in other usual activities. They need to put some distance between themselves and their distraught parents and to go back to living their own lives. Fortunately, most children are able to do this by the end of the first 1 to 1½ years after the separation.

3 *Resolving loss.* Absorbing the multiple losses caused by divorce may be the single most difficult task for children. They need to adjust to the loss of the parent they are not living with, the loss of the security of feeling loved and cared for by both parents, the loss of their familiar daily routines and family traditions, and often the loss of a whole way of life. Some children take years to deal with these losses, and some never do, carrying

their sense of being rejected, unworthy, and unlovable into adulthood.

4 *Resolving anger and self-blame.* "Children and adolescents do not believe in no-fault divorce. They may blame one or both parents or they may blame themselves" (Wallerstein, 1983, p. 239). Children realize that divorce, unlike death, is voluntary, and they often remain angry for years at the parent (or parents) who could do such a terrible thing to them. When and if they do reach the stage of forgiving both their parents and themselves, they feel more powerful and more in control of their lives.

5 *Accepting the permanence of the divorce.* Many children hold on for years to the fantasy that their parents will be reunited, even after both have remarried. Many youngsters accept the situation only after they achieve psychological separation from their parents in adolescence or early adulthood.

6 *Achieving realistic hope regarding relationships.* Many youngsters who have adjusted well in other ways come through a divorce feeling afraid to take a chance on intimate relationships themselves, for fear that they will fail as their parents did. They may become cynical, depressed, or simply doubtful of the possibility of finding lasting love.

Many children do, of course, succeed at all these tasks, more or less, and are able to come through the painful experience of divorce with their egos basically intact. Children's ability to do this seems to be related partly to their own resilience (see the discussion later in this chapter) and partly to the way their parents handle issues related to the separation (see Box 9-3 on pages 324–325) and the challenge of raising children alone.

The One-Parent Family An important consequence of a high divorce rate is that many children are raised by single parents. Single-parent families may be created when one parent dies or when the mother never marries, but they are most commonly the result of the breakup of the family after divorce, separation, or desertion. About 20 percent of American children (and about 46 percent of black American children) live in homes with only one parent, and in 90

percent of those homes the father is the absent partner. Still, the number of single fathers caring for children increased 180 percent between 1970 and 1984, when almost 600,000 divorced and separated men had custody of their children (U.S. Bureau of the Census, 1982, 1985). Children who do live with their fathers tend to be of school age or older (Espenshade, 1979). The number of single-parent families doubled between 1970 and 1982, but the rate of increase has slowed.

STRESSES ON CHILDREN   Children growing up in one-parent homes—whether these homes have resulted from divorce or some other factor—have special stresses to contend with. These homes do not have two adults to share child-rearing responsibilities, to take children to out-of-school activities, to serve as gender role models, and to demonstrate the interplay of personalities. What's more, the family's income is likely to be at or near the poverty level, with negative effects on children's health, well-being, and school achievement. The average income of families headed by women is less than half that of families with two parents (U.S. Bureau of the Census, 1984).

If the parent is divorced, the strains of the divorce often affect parenting. For several years following the separation, the parent may be preoccupied with personal concerns and less attentive to the child. Housekeeping and normal routines such as bedtime and bath time may be neglected. These effects often wear off in time, especially if the "live-in" parent forms a new relationship. But school-age children may continue to feel torn between two hostile parents and to reject a stepparent (Maccoby, 1984).

EFFECTS ON SCHOOLING   Not surprisingly, with all the stress they are under, children living with a single parent are at risk of having problems in school. A study of 18,000 elementary school and high school students in 14 states found that children with one parent at home achieved less in school and were more likely to require disciplinary action than students with two parents. The students with one parent were also more likely to live in low-income households and to move during the school year—factors that probably played a part in their

BOX 9-3 PRACTICALLY SPEAKING

HELPING CHILDREN ADJUST TO DIVORCE

Sensitive parents can help their children in making the difficult adjustment to divorce. The following guidelines are based on the advice of numerous experts on family relations:

■ *All the children should be told at the same time about the divorce, in language suited to their age.* Some 80 percent of preschoolers are given no explanation because their parents think they are too young to understand (Wallerstein & Kelly, 1980). Even very young children do understand, however, that a change is taking place, and they need to be told often, in different words, what's happening. Both parents should be present, in order to let the children see that both parents are still deeply involved with their lives and will continue to be available to them.

■ *Children should be told only as much as they need to know.* It may be tempting for parents to discuss openly what they see as causes for the divorce—an affair, alcoholism, compulsive gambling, sexual incompatibility. Yet this talk may confuse and wound children far more than it helps them. It puts a heavy burden on them to judge the parent "in the wrong." At a time when they need as much emotional support as possible, they may lose faith in at least one, and maybe both, parents.

■ *Children need to know that they have not caused the divorce.* Young children tend to see the whole world as revolving around themselves and often assume that something they have done or thought has driven their parents to

divorce. The ensuing guilt can torture a child.

■ *Parents must emphasize the finality of their decision.* The fantasy of reunion is almost universal. As long as children dream of this, they can't make progress in accepting reality. Once they give up believing that they have the power to reunite their parents, they can pay attention to lessening the pain of the rupture.

■ *Arrangements for the children's care should be carefully explained.* Although children may not express their fear of abandonment, they need reassurance that they will continue to be cared for. Parents need to explain custody arrangements in detail.

■ *Children should be reassured of both parents' continuing love.* They need

---

poorer school records. Indeed, a follow-up analysis and interviews with parents showed that family income (and the student's gender) affected achievement more strongly than the number of parents at home. But the data still confirmed the original finding that children living with a single parent tended to be lower achievers. Their grades were lower, they were absent more often, they were more defiant, and they were referred more often for special help. Children in two-parent households liked school better, had better relationships with teachers and peers, and thought better of themselves (Zakariya, 1982).

On the other hand, the large-scale study by

the U.S. Department of Education discussed earlier found that negative effects on achievement when elementary schoolchildren live with one parent are almost entirely dependent on other factors—particularly income, but also the parent's expectations for the child and the number of books in the home (Milne et al., 1986). (The negative effects on high school students were generally insignificant.)

Findings about the lesser achievement of students with one parent at home can lead to harmful stereotypes and self-fulfilling prophecies. Many teachers *expect* these students to do poorly or to have behavior problems, when, in reality, these children (like other children) do better if

to know that there is no such thing as divorce between parent and child and that the noncustodial parent will continue to love and care for them.

- *Children should be encouraged to express fear, sadness, and anger.* When they can express these emotions openly, they can begin to understand and deal with them. Parents can help by admitting their own sadness, anger, and confusion. They also can seek out a discussion group for children of divorced parents.

- *Limits should be set on children's behavior.* The single parent should maintain firm, friendly discipline. Children need to know that someone stronger loves them enough to stop them from losing control.

- *Parents should enlist the help of other adults— teachers, scout leaders, or relatives and friends.* A

person outside the immediate family often can demonstrate a caring concern that helps a child through the crisis.

- *Battling parents should declare a truce when they are with the children.* Divorced parents don't have to be friends, but it's a great help to their children if they can cooperate on child-rearing issues.

- *Children should not be used as weapons.* Children suffer when they are forced to transmit angry messages or relay information, when they are asked to choose sides, or when family visits turn into battles. Parents who use children this way are sacrificing their children's welfare for their own immediate satisfaction.

- *Parents must recognize that there is a real conflict between their needs and their children's needs.* Parents need to be out with other adults, but children need their parents'

company. Adults have to be sensitive to this problem and work out solutions that will meet the needs of both generations.

- *Children's lives should be changed as little as possible.* Any change is stressful; the fewer minor adjustments children have to make, the more energy they have to cope with the major one. If possible, the parent who has custody should postpone taking a job for the first time or moving to a new house. If changes must be made, parents should realize that children need extra understanding.

- *Parents should use whatever resources they can find for themselves and their children.* These include helpful books, discussion groups, and community programs.

Source: Adapted from Olds, 1986.

teachers take the lead in getting their parents involved—for example, by sending home learning activities. A survey of 82 first-, third-, and fifth-grade teachers and nearly 1300 parents in 11 school districts in Maryland found that when teachers made systematic efforts to get single parents as well as couples to help their children at home, the single parents helped as much and as effectively as the married ones (Epstein, 1984).

Schools have begun to look at other ways to cooperate with single parents (most of whom are working mothers), including evening, breakfast, or weekend meetings, conferences, and programs; baby-sitters for younger children during school events; late-afternoon transportation for students after football or band

practice; and sending notices and report cards to the noncustodial parent (who may also want to be involved).

LONG-TERM EFFECTS Do youngsters with only one parent get into more trouble than those with two parents? Some recent studies say that they do (see Chapter 11). Research also suggests that these children may be at greater risk of marital and parenting problems, themselves (Rutter, 1979a).

These findings support the commonsense view that the richer the family relationships, the more the children benefit. They also support the common idea that as children grow older and more independent, single parents need more help in guiding them. Yet the one-parent home is not necessarily pathological, and the two-parent family is not always healthy. Other research has concluded that the attitudes of a single parent are more important in determining the sexual attitudes of children than the fact of single parenthood itself; that children of unwed mothers are no more likely to be emotionally disturbed than children of married parents (C. Klein, 1973); that, in general, children grow up better adjusted when they have a good relationship with one parent than when they grow up in a two-parent home characterized by discord and discontent (Rutter, 1983); and that an inaccessible, rejecting, or hostile parent is more damaging than an absent one (Hetherington, 1980).

EMOTIONAL DISTURBANCES IN CHILDHOOD

Emotional disturbances in childhood are not uncommon. Between 5 and 15 percent of American children are estimated to have mental health problems, which take a variety of forms (U.S. Department of Health and Human Services, 1980) and which may or may not respond favorably to relatively brief treatment.

Disorders with Physical Symptoms

Some troubling behaviors may be caused by delays or abnormalities of development related to biological maturation. Children often outgrow these conditions but may suffer undesirable side effects in the meantime. For example, a little boy who wets his bed is handicapped in his social life because he cannot sleep over at a friend's house or go away to summer camp. A little girl who develops a facial tic is humiliated when other children make fun of her. Therefore the appearance of any of the following conditions calls for attention.

Bed-Wetting Although most children stay dry, day and night, by the age of 3 to 5 years, bed-wetting (*enuresis*) is the most common chronic condition seen by pediatricians (Starfield, 1978). Most children outgrow this common developmental problem without any special help. At age 3, about one-third of children wet their beds; at

age 6, ten to fifteen percent (Children's Hospital of Pittsburgh, 1987b); and by age 10, only 3 percent of boys and 2 percent of girls (DSM III, 1980). By age 18, only 1 percent of males and virtually no females wet the bed.

Fewer than 1 percent of bed-wetters have any physical disorder, and researchers have a wide range of theories about why the other 99 percent cannot stay dry at night (Bakwin, 1971c; Barker, 1979; Chapman, 1974; Children's Hospital of Pittsburgh, 1987b; Fergusson, Horwood, & Shannon, 1986; Starfield, 1978; M.A. Stewart & Olds, 1973):

- *Emotional disturbance or stress.* Children who wet the bed periodically tend to do so after some emotionally charged episode but have no other symptoms of psychological disturbance. Stress from the birth of a new sibling, moving to a new home, starting in a new school, or parents' separation may lead to increased bed-wetting.
- *Genetic factors.* Adults who wet the bed in childhood are more likely to have enuretic children. Also, identical twins are more likely than fraternal twins to be concordant for bed-wetting.
- *Physiological factors.* Enuretic children tend to have functionally small bladders. They often have an urge to urinate in the daytime, and they may wake up to urinate at night.
- *Improper toilet training.*
- *Delayed maturation of the nervous system.*

While the cause of bed-wetting is usually impossible to pinpoint, the treatment is fairly standard. First, children and parents need reassurance that the problem is common, that in itself it is not serious, and that the child should not be blamed or punished. Parents should not do anything unless children themselves see their bed-wetting as a problem. Some of the most effective measures for treating enuresis include rewarding the child for staying dry; using electric devices that ring bells or buzzers when the child begins to urinate; administering various drugs; and teaching the child to practice controlling the sphincter muscles that control bladder function (Chapman, 1974). Some physicians recommend medication only as a last resort, because of its potential side effects, the possibility of abuse, and the high relapse rates associated with its use (Children's Hospital of Pittsburgh, 1987b).

Tics Children often develop *tics*—repetitive, involuntary muscular movements, known as *stereotyped movement disorders*. They blink their eyes, hunch their shoulders, twist their necks, bob their heads, lick their lips, grimace, grunt, snort, and utter guttural or nasal sounds. About 12 to 24 percent of schoolchildren—more boys than girls—have a history of tics, which usually appear first between the ages of 4 and 10 and generally go away before adolescence, sometimes to reappear at times of stress (DSM III, 1980).

Tics may arise from stresses in the child's past or current relationships. Some psychiatrists feel that children release emotional tension in this way. One 8-year-old boy, for example, who exhibited several tics, was very passive and inhibited, apparently substituting the tics for the aggressive things he wanted to say and do. After a year of weekly psychotherapy sessions, he became more assertive and gradually lost about 95 percent of his tics (Chapman, 1974).

Stuttering *Stuttering*—involuntary repetition of sounds and syllables—runs in families and is at least 4 times as common in boys as in girls. It generally begins before the age of 12 but is especially common between the ages of 2 to 3½ and 5 to 7. Most children stop stuttering spontaneously, about 1 percent continue to stutter in adolescence, and some 2 million American adults continue to stutter (DSM III, 1980; Pines, 1977).

Theories about the causes of stuttering include physical explanations, such as faulty training in articulation and breathing, problems with brain functioning, or defective feedback; and emotional explanations, such as parental pressure to speak properly or deep-seated emotional conflicts (Barker, 1979; Pines, 1977).

Treatment may include psychotherapy and counseling, speech therapy, drugs, and various special techniques to train stutterers to unlearn the patterns of motor responses they have developed over the years. The children are taught to speak slowly and deliberately; to breathe slowly and deeply, using the abdominal muscles

rather than those of the upper chest; and to start up their voices gently, as opposed to the abrupt and forceful way in which many stutterers begin to speak. Computers to monitor the voice, videotape machines, and metronomes worn like hearing aids are among the battery of technological aids that help stutterers. One program that claims a good success rate has stutterers use the telephone, ask strangers for directions, and participate in other stressful speaking situations. However, success ultimately depends on how much the stutterer continues to practice the new skills after the course is over (Pines, 1977).

Nonphysical Disturbances

Acting-Out Behavior Children's emotional difficulties often surface in their behavior. They show by what they do that they need help. They fight, they lie, they steal, they destroy property, and they break rules laid down by parents, school, and other authorities. These are common forms of *acting-out behavior:* misbehavior that is an outward expression of emotional turmoil.

Of course, almost all children make up fanciful stories as a form of make-believe or lie occasionally to avoid punishment. But when children past the age of 6 or 7 continue to tell tall tales, they are often signaling a sense of insecurity. They may need to make up glamorous stories about themselves to secure the attention and esteem of others; or, when lying becomes habitual or transparently obvious, they may be showing hostility toward their parents (Chapman, 1974).

Similarly, occasional minor stealing is common among children. Although it needs to be dealt with, it is not necessarily a sign that anything is seriously wrong. But when children repeatedly steal from their parents or steal so blatantly from others that they are easily caught, they are again often showing hostility toward their parents and their parents' standards. In some cases, the stolen items appear to be "symbolic tokens of parental love, power, or authority" (Chapman, 1974, p. 158) of which the child feels deprived.

Any chronic antisocial behavior needs to be regarded as a possible symptom of deep-seated emotional upset. In Chapter 11, on personality and social behavior in adolescence, we'll discuss some extreme forms of misbehavior, those that get young people into trouble with the law.

Hyperactivity   Johnny cannot sit still, cannot finish a simple task, cannot keep a friend, and is always in trouble. His teacher says, "I can't do a thing with him." His family doctor says, "Don't worry; he'll grow out of it." And his next-door neighbor says, "He's a spoiled brat."

The syndrome that Johnny is probably suffering from, formally known as ***attention deficit disorder with hyperactivity*** (DSM III, 1980), has three major symptoms—inattention, impulsivity, and a great deal of activity at inappropriate times and in inappropriate places, like classrooms. These traits appear to some degree in all children; but in about 3 percent of school-age children (10 times more boys than girls), they are so pervasive that they interfere with the child's functioning in school and other aspects of daily life. These children are considered hyperactive (DSM III, 1980).

A conference of the National Institutes of Health in 1984 concluded that a combination of genetic, neurological, biochemical, and environmental factors probably cause this kind of behavior. In fact, there are so many possible causes of hyperactivity, and their symptoms are so similar, that it is difficult to diagnose the cause of any particular case. Without a proper diagnosis, it is hard to be certain of the proper treatment. Some cases are associated with premature birth, trauma to the head, and infections that may produce minor brain damage. Lead poisoning is another possible cause. Family stress is yet another (Hadley, 1984).

Parents and teachers can often help hyperactive children do better at home and in school. First, they have to understand and accept the child's basic temperament. Then they can teach the child how to break up his or her work into small, manageable segments; they can incorporate physical activity into the daily classroom schedule; and they can offer alternative ways for the child to demonstrate what he or she has learned, such as individual conferences or tape-recorded reports, instead of written reports (M.A. Stewart & Olds, 1973).

Sometimes a stimulant is prescribed to help a hyperactive child focus attention on the task at hand (Charles, Schain, Zelniker, & Guthrie, 1979). Stimulant drugs do not help all hyperactive children, though, and we don't know the long-range effects of using medication to mask the personalities of what many observers believe to be basically normal children; and so it is best to consider drugs only as a last resort.

A treatment that has received much attention recently is a diet free of artificial food colorings and flavorings. However, this seems to help only a small number of hyperactive children, and the National Institutes of Health does not recommend it in all cases (Hadley, 1984).

Although there is currently no cure for hyperactivity, some hyperactive children grow up to function normally, and only a few of these have significant psychiatric or antisocial disorders. But most hyperactive children continue to have trouble concentrating and to behave impulsively, and so they experience difficulties at work, strains in personal relationships, and loss of self-esteem (Hechtman & Weiss, 1983).

School Phobia   Becky wakes up complaining of nausea. Yesterday morning it was a headache, the day before it was a stomachache, and last week she vomited three mornings in a row. Yet as soon as her mother gives her permission to stay home from school, her symptoms disappear, and she spends the rest of the day happily playing in her room.

School phobia—unrealistic fear that keeps children away from school—is misnamed, according to many professionals who have studied this syndrome. The phobia has less to do with a fear of school itself than with a fear of leaving the mother. So many researchers are convinced that "separation anxiety" underlies this problem that virtually no research has been done on the school situation of school-phobic youngsters. We know very little about their perceptions of school or how they get along with their teachers and the other children. If there *is* a problem at school—a sarcastic teacher, a bully in the schoolyard, or overly difficult work—the child's fears may be *realistic* ones; it may be the environment that needs changing, not the child.

What do we know about school-phobic children? They are not truants; their parents usually know when they are absent. They tend to have average intelligence or higher and to be average or above-average students. Their ages are evenly distributed from 5 to 15, and they are equally likely to be boys or girls. Although they come from a variety of backgrounds, their parents are likely to be professionals.

Not all school phobias are the same. In the "neurotic" type, which largely affects children from kindergarten through fourth grade, the avoidance of school comes on suddenly, and the child continues to function well in other areas. In the "characterological" type, seen in early adolescence, the phobia comes on more gradually, the child is more deeply disturbed, and the outlook for the future is less hopeful.

The most important element in the treatment of a school-phobic child is an early return to school. The longer school-phobic children are out of school, the harder it is to get them back. They are often timid and inhibited away from home, but willful, stubborn, and demanding with their parents. Most experts advise getting the child back to school first, then going on with whatever other steps may be called for, such as therapy for the child, for one or both parents, and possibly for the entire family. Getting the child back in school breaks the phobic cycle by restoring the child to a more normal environment and reducing the extreme interdependence between mother and child. It also keeps the child from falling farther behind in schoolwork, which can aggravate the problem.

The return to school may be accomplished gradually. First the parents may drive the child to school and just sit in the car. Then they may get out and walk around the outside of the building together. Next the parent may go with the child to the principal's office, and finally have the child go to school alone—first, possibly, for an hour a day, then several hours, and eventually for an entire day. This approach requires working closely with school officials.

Usually children can be returned to school without too much difficulty once treatment is begun. The few studies that have followed up school-phobic children in later years are unclear, though, in determining how well treatment has helped their overall adjustment (D. Gordon & Young, 1976).

Everyone feels "blue" at times, but depression can be a danger signal and should be taken seriously, particularly when behavior shows marked change.

Childhood Depression "Nobody likes me" is a common complaint in middle childhood, when children tend to be popularity-conscious. But when these words were addressed to a school principal by an 8-year-old boy in Florida whose classmates had accused him of stealing from the teacher's purse, it was a danger signal. The boy vowed that he would never return to school—and he never did. Two days later, he hanged himself by a belt from the top rail of his bunk bed ("Doctors rule out," 1984).

Fortunately, depressed children rarely go to such lengths, though suicide among young people is on the increase (see Chapter 18). How can we tell the difference between a harmless period of the "blues" (which we all experience at times) and a major *affective disorder*—that is, a disorder of mood? The basic symptoms of an affective disorder are similar from childhood through adulthood; but some features are age-specific (DSM III, 1980).

Friendlessness is only one sign of *childhood depression.* This disorder is also characterized by inability to have fun, to concentrate, and to display normal emotional reactions. Depressed children are frequently tired, extremely active, or inactive. They talk very little, cry a great deal, have trouble concentrating, sleep too much or too little, lose their appetite, start doing poorly in school, look unhappy, complain of physical ailments, feel overwhelmingly guilty, suffer severe separation anxiety (which may take the form of school phobia), or think often about death or suicide (Malmquist, 1983; Poznanski, 1982).

Any four or five of these symptoms may support a diagnosis of depression, especially when they represent a marked change from the child's usual pattern. Parents do not always recognize "minor" problems like sleep disturbances, loss of appetite, and irritability as signs of depression, but children themselves are often able to describe how they feel (Children's Hospital of Pittsburgh, 1987a).

No one is sure of the exact cause of depression in children or adults. There is some evidence for a biochemical predisposition, which may be triggered by specific experiences (see Chapter 2). School-age children who are depressed are likely to lack social and academic competence; but it is not clear whether such incompetence causes depression or is caused by depression (Blechman, McEnroe, Carella, & Audette, 1986).

While moderate to severe depression is fairly easy to spot, milder forms are harder to diagnose. The presence of any of the above symptoms should, therefore, be followed closely, and if they persist, the child should be given psychological help.

Treatment Techniques

The choice of a specific mode of treatment for a particular disorder depends on many factors: the nature of the problem, the child's personality, the willingness of the family to participate, the availability of treatment in the community, the financial resources of the family, and, very often, the orientation of the professional first consulted.

Psychological Therapies We'll consider three forms of psychological therapy: individual psychotherapy, family therapy, and behavioral therapy.

INDIVIDUAL PSYCHOTHERAPY *Psychotherapy* is a treatment technique in which a therapist helps people gain insights into their personality and relationships, past and present, and helps them interpret their feelings and behavior. Individual psychotherapy, in which the therapist sees a child one on one, may take any of several forms:

- *Preventive therapy.* A therapist may see a child at a time of great stress, such as the death of a parent, even though the child has not exhibited any symptoms of disturbance.
- *Supportive therapy.* Occasional sessions offer a child the chance to talk about worries with a friendly, sympathetic person who can help the youngster cope more easily with stress.
- *Play therapy.* The therapist gets clues about what is bothering a child from the way he or she plays with a doll family or other toys.

To help children understand and cope with their feelings, a therapist must first accept those feelings. To get at underlying feelings, the therapist interprets what the child says and does, both in the therapy sessions and in everyday life, as reported at the sessions.

Child psychotherapy is usually much more effective when combined with counseling for the parents, who often feel guilty about having "caused" their child's problem and feel inadequate because they cannot deal with it on their own. A professional can help them focus on ways to cope most effectively with the situation.

FAMILY THERAPY In *family therapy,* the entire family is the client. The therapist sees the whole family together, observes the way family members act with one another, and points out to them their patterns of functioning—both the growth-producing patterns and the inhibiting or destructive ones.

Sometimes the child whose problem brings the family into therapy is, ironically, the healthiest member, responding to a sick situation. This was true in the case of a 10-year-old girl who threatened her parents with a kitchen knife after they told her that her dog had died, when in fact they had taken him to the Society for the Prevention of Cruelty to Animals. Therapy revealed an atmosphere of hostility and dishonesty that permeated all the family relationships, avoidance by all members of coming to grips with their problems, and, ultimately, a basic conflict between husband and wife that had set the stage for the girl's problems and those of her 16-year-old brother, who was getting into trouble at school. Through therapy the parents were able to confront their own differences and begin to resolve them—the first step toward solving the children's problems as well.

BEHAVIOR THERAPY **Behavior therapy,** also called *behavior modification,* uses principles of learning theory to alter behavior—to eliminate undesirable behaviors like bed-wetting and temper tantrums or to develop desirable ones like being on time and doing household chores. A behavior therapist does not look for underlying reasons for a child's behavior and does not typically try to offer the child insight into his or her situation, but aims simply to change the behavior itself. For example, the therapist may use operant conditioning to encourage a desired behavior, such as putting dirty clothes into the hamper. Every time the child does so, he or she gets a reward, like a piece of candy, words of praise, or a token that can be exchanged for toys.

This approach is effective in dealing with specific fears and behavior problems. When a child's problems are more deep-seated, though, behavior therapy needs to be supplemented by psychotherapy for the child, the parents, or both.

EVALUATING THE PSYCHOLOGICAL THERAPIES
A review of 75 well-designed studies of the use of various types of psychological therapy with children concluded that these therapies are generally effective (R. J. Casey & Berman, 1985). Just as adults who received therapy showed greater improvement than adults who did not, children who received treatment scored better on a variety of outcome measures (including self-concept, adjustment, personality, social skills, school achievement, cognitive function-

Therapists who work with troubled children often encourage them to express themselves through play, which helps bring out their emotions.

ing, and resolution of fears and anxieties) than children who received none. However, children gained less than adults in self-esteem and adjustment.

Children who were treated for such specific problems as phobias, impulsiveness, hyperactivity, and bed-wetting showed more improvement than children whose therapy aimed at better social adjustment. There was little evidence that any one form of therapy (play or nonplay, individual or group, "child-only" or treatment of child and parents) was superior to another.

An interesting sidelight is that, while parents, therapists, and researchers observed definite gains in treated children, teachers and peers tended not to notice much improvement; this suggests that their first impressions may be hard to overcome.

Drug Therapy Over the past 3 decades, the number of available prescription drugs has mushroomed: 90 percent of all the drugs available today were unknown 40 years ago (M. A. Stewart & Olds, 1973). With the proliferation of new drugs has come the use of **drug therapy**—a treatment technique that includes the administration of drugs—for emotional disorders in both adults and children. Today, antidepressants are commonly prescribed for bed-wetters, stimulants for hyperactive children, and a range of other medications for children with other psychological problems.

Giving pills to children in order to change their behavior is a radical step, especially since so many medicines have undesirable side effects. In some cases, the drugs relieve only the behavioral symptoms and do not get at the underlying causes. Drugs do have their place in the treatment of some emotional disturbances of childhood, but their use should not eliminate psychotherapy for troubled children.

STRESS AND RESILIENCE

Stressful events are part of every childhood. Illness, the birth of a new baby, sibling rivalry, frustration, and the temporary absence of parents are common childhood experiences. Other stresses are less common: divorce or death of parents, hospitalization, and the day-in, day-out grind of poverty affect the lives of many children, as do larger events like natural disasters and wars. Children in the twentieth century are subjected to new stresses, including the brutality of concentration camps and the threat of nuclear annihilation. One of the most stressful aspects of catastrophic events is children's realization that their parents are powerless to protect them.

There are also situations in which the parents themselves are a source of stress. We've already examined physical abuse in Chapter 5. Now we'll look at psychological maltreatment and then at pressure to grow up too soon. Finally, we'll consider why some children are better able than others to withstand these and other stresses.

Psychological Maltreatment

When a child is abused, the physical hurt may heal quickly, but the psychological scars may never go away. The same is true when a parent regularly "puts down" a child or turns away coldly from the child's pleas for affection and attention.

Physicians, legislators, and mental health professionals are becoming increasingly concerned about **psychological maltreatment,** which has been broadly (and somewhat vaguely) defined as action (or failure to act) that damages children's behavioral, cognitive, emotional, or physical functioning (Hart & Brassard, 1987). This syndrome may include rejecting, terrorizing, isolating, exploiting, missocializing, degrading, and corrupting children and being emotionally unresponsive to them (Hart & Brassard, 1987; Rosenberg, 1987). The resulting physical, emotional, mental, or social impairment may keep children from reaching their full potential as adults (Garrison, 1987).

Psychological maltreatment probably plays a part in almost all of the more than 2 million cases of child abuse and neglect. It also occurs without physical abuse. It has been linked to children's lying, stealing, low self-esteem, emotional maladjustment, dependency, underachievement, depression, failure to thrive, aggression, homicide, and suicide, as well as to psychological distress in later life, and it may also play a part in learning disorders (Hart & Brassard, 1987).

Psychological maltreatment occurs both in families and in institutions, such as schools, hospitals, day care centers, and juvenile justice programs. Schools have come a long way since "reading, 'riting, and 'rithmetic" were "taught to the tune of a hickory stick" and with a dunce cap as a "reward," but some schools still attempt to instill discipline through fear, intimidation, and degradation (Hart & Brassard, 1987). Programs to "resocialize" troubled youngsters have been known to strip them of privacy, dignity, and independence; place them in isolation; hold them incommunicado; forbid them to wear street clothes; force them to wear humiliating signs; and make them clean floors with toothbrushes (Melton & Davidson, 1987).

Such *institutional* maltreatment can sometimes be stopped by passing laws. But maltreatment by *parents* is more difficult to deal with. In most states, children may be taken from offending parents; however, the courts are often reluctant to take this step except in extreme cases, especially when it is unclear that institutional care will be more beneficial (Melton & Davidson, 1987). A more effective approach might be to encourage cooperation between families and social service agencies.

The best time for intervention is before a

child is born. High-risk parents can be instructed in child development, offered support services, and trained to increase their sensitivity to the needs (for example) of a crying baby. Ultimately, it may be possible to eliminate psychological maltreatment only in a less violent society that values children and does not subordinate their needs to those of parents or caretakers (Hart & Brassard, 1987).

The "Hurried Child"

Children today, even if they are not maltreated or subjected to unusual stresses, must cope with subtle pressures. Because families now are more mobile than those of earlier times, children are more likely to change schools and friends and less likely to know many adults well. They frequently hear words that were once taboo, and they know more about technology, sex, and violence than children of previous generations. In addition, single-parent homes and parents' work schedules bring adult responsibilities to many children (refer back to Box 9-2).

The child psychologist David Elkind has called today's child the "hurried child" (1981, 1987a, 1987b). Like a number of other thoughtful observers, he is concerned that the pressures of life today are making children grow up too soon and are making their shortened childhood too stressful. Today's children are pressured to succeed in school, to compete in sports, and often to meet their parents' emotional needs. On television and in real life, children are exposed to many adult problems before they have mastered the problems of childhood. Yet children are not small adults. They feel and think like children, and they need a period of childhood—not a premature adulthood—for healthy cognitive and emotional development.

Coping with Stress: The Resilient Child

Human behavior is not like a chemical reaction. A certain amount of stress does not necessarily yield a predictable outcome. For example, although stress on families can lead to child abuse and psychological maltreatment, many parents who are under great stress do not abuse or maltreat their children. And many maltreated children grow up to lead healthy, productive lives (Hart & Brassard, 1987; Rosenberg, 1987). What makes the difference?

Children's reactions to stressful events may depend on several factors (Rutter, 1984), including the event itself (for example, children's response to a parent's death is different from their response to divorce), the child's age (preschoolers and adolescents react to parents' divorce differently), and the child's sex (boys are more vulnerable than girls). Yet if two children of the same age and sex are exposed to the same stressful experience, one may crumble while the other comes through. Why?

Resilient children are youngsters who bounce back from circumstances that would blight the emotional development of most children. These are the children of the ghetto who go on to distinguish themselves in the professions. These are the neglected and abused children who go on to form intimate relationships and to lead fulfilling lives. In spite of the bad cards they have been dealt, these children are winners. They are creative, resourceful, independent, and enjoyable to be with. How do they do it?

Several studies have identified "protective factors" that may operate to reduce the effects of stressors, such as kidnapping or poor parenting (Anthony & Koupernik, 1974; Garmezy, 1983; Rutter, 1984). It has been suggested that several of these factors also protect children who are subjected to psychological maltreatment (Rosenberg, 1987).

One cluster of factors relates to the *child's personality*. Resilient children tend to be adaptable enough to cope with changing circumstances. They tend to be positive thinkers, friendly, sensitive to other people, and independent. They feel competent and have high self-esteem. Intelligence, too, may be a factor; good students appear to cope better (Rutter, 1984).

There has been little research on the possibility that differences in ability to handle stress are inherited or on the effect of differences in temperament, which seem to be at least in part genetic (Rutter, 1983). Are some children born with stress-proof personalities? Or must children *develop* resilience in response to environmental factors? Whether or not some protective characteristics are inherited, factors such as the following seem to contribute to children's resilience:

■ *The child's family.* Resilient children are likely to have good relationships with parents who are emotionally supportive to them and to each other, or, failing that, to have a close relationship with at least one parent. If they lack even this, they are likely to be close to at least one relative or other adult who expresses interest in them and obviously cares for them, and whom they trust.

■ *Learning experiences.* Resilient children are likely to have had experience solving social problems. They have observed positive models—parents, older siblings, or others—dealing with frustration and making the best of a bad situation. They have faced challenges themselves, have worked out solutions, and have learned that they can affect outcomes and exert a measure of control over their lives.

■ *Reduced risk.* Children who have been exposed to only one of a number of factors strongly related to psychiatric disorder (such as discord between the parents, low social status, overcrowding at home, a disturbed mother, a criminal father, and experience in foster care or institutions) are often able to overcome the stress; but when two or more of these factors are present, children's risk of developing an emotional disturbance goes up fourfold or more (Rutter, quoted in Pines, 1979). When children are not besieged on all sides, they can often cope with adverse circumstances.

■ *Compensating experiences.* A supportive school environment and successful experiences in sports, in music, or with other children can help make up for a dismal home life, and in adulthood a good marriage can compensate for poor relationships earlier in life.

All this research does not, of course, mean that what happens in a child's life does not matter. In general, children with unfavorable backgrounds have more problems in adjustment than do those with favorable backgrounds. The heartening promise of these findings, however, lies in the recognition that what happens in childhood does not necessarily determine the outcome of a person's life (Kagan, 1984), that many people do have the strength to rise above the most difficult circumstances, and that we are constantly rewriting the stories of our lives for as long as we live.

SUMMARY

The Self-Concept

■ Self-concept has three important aspects: understanding oneself, regulating one's behavior, and developing self-esteem. Self-concept develops greatly during middle childhood, as a result of cognitive growth, the influence of the peer group, and the development of skills.

1 Children begin to define themselves in psychological and social terms and to compare their real selves with their ideal selves.

2 As children develop moral reasoning and become aware of the views of others, they coordinate personal and social behavioral demands and values.

■ Self-esteem, which grows out of comparisons with others, is extremely important to success and happiness.

1 Four factors that may influence self-esteem are a sense of significance, competence, virtue, and power.

2 Parents of children with high self-esteem tend to have authoritative parenting styles.

■ Sexism—the belief that one sex is superior—can damage self-esteem, but it is no longer as strong an influence as in the past on gender-typing during middle childhood.

■ A number of theories give insights into the development of self-concept during middle childhood.

1 Freud saw middle childhood as a period of latency, or relative sexual calm. The development of the superego keeps the id under control, allowing the ego to deal with the outside world and resulting in rapid socialization and skill development.

2 Erikson's fourth crisis, which takes place dur-

ing middle childhood, is that of industry versus inferiority, and the "virtue" that should come out of this period is *competence*.

3 Social-learning theorists point to the influence of parents, teachers, and peers as models who become powerful shapers of self-concept.

4 Piaget's cognitive-developmental approach holds that the decline of egocentrism and the ability to decenter make children more sensitive to what others think of them and also more able to see themselves from different viewpoints.

5 According to the information-processing approach, children build, test, and modify self-schemata (hypotheses or knowledge structures about themselves) on the basis of experience. Many lasting self-schemata develop during middle childhood.

Aspects of Personality Development in Middle Childhood

■ Schoolchildren today spend more of their leisure time watching television and less time playing than in the past. As children move through elementary school, they do less pleasure reading. Many children are involved in sports and other organized activities.

■ The society of childhood mirrors changes in adult society. Many children today are from more mobile families and thus have weaker social bonds than children in previous generations, and so the peer group sometimes tends to substitute for kinship bonds.

■ The peer group is an important arena for the building of self-concept and self-esteem.

■ School-age youngsters are most susceptible to pressure to conform, which may encourage antisocial behavior in children who are too weak to resist.

■ Most children select peers who are like them in age, sex, race, and socioeconomic status. Racial prejudice among schoolchildren appears to be diminishing as a result of school integration.

■ The basis of friendship changes during middle childhood. Children choose friends they feel comfortable with, and they see their friendships as involving give-and-take.

■ Popularity influences self-esteem. Children who are not only ignored by their peers but rejected by them are at risk of emotional and behavioral problems. They need to learn social skills.

■ Although school-age children spend less time with their parents than with their peers, relationships with parents continue to be most important. Other important relationships are with grandparents, siblings, friends, and teachers. Different relationships serve different purposes for children.

■ New issues related to school and the use of leisure time arise during this period.

1 Although school-age children require less direct care and supervision than younger children, it is still important for parents to monitor their children's activities.

2 Although disciplinary methods evolve with children's cognitive development, there appears to be an underlying consistency in parents' child-rearing attitudes. There are some differences among social classes in parents' interactions with school-age children.

3 Coregulation is an intermediate stage in the transfer of control from parent to child, in which children make more of their own day-to-day decisions under their parents' general supervision.

■ Siblings exert a powerful influence on each other either directly (through their interactions) or indirectly (through their impact on each other's relationship with their parents).

■ Children grow up in a variety of family situations besides the traditional nuclear family. These include families in which mothers work outside the home (now a majority of families), families with divorced parents, and other one-parent families. In any of these, an atmosphere of love, support, and respect for family members will provide an excellent prognosis for healthy development.

1 Age affects children's reactions to both mothers' employment and divorce. Whether children make a successful adjustment to either situation depends largely on the way the parents handle it.

2 Children of employed mothers (particularly girls) may benefit from their mothers' enhanced self-esteem, from added family income, and from less stereotyped gender attitudes. However, sons may show some negative effects, and latchkey children may be at greater risk if they are not mature enough to care for themselves.

3 Children living with only one parent are under special stress and are at risk of lower achievement in school and other problems. These children do better in school when their parents are involved with the children's schooling.

Emotional Disturbances in Childhood

■ Emotional disturbances during childhood are not uncommon. These include disorders that cause physical symptoms, such as bed-wetting, tics, and stuttering; they also include nonphysical disturbances, such as acting-out behavior, hyperactivity, school phobias, and childhood depression.

■ Treatment techniques include individual psychotherapy, family therapy, behavior therapy, and drug therapy. Studies show that psychological therapy is generally effective.

Stress and Resilience

■ Normal childhood stresses take many forms and can affect the healthy emotional development of children. Unusual stresses, such as natural disasters and wars, also affect many children.

■ Psychological maltreatment of children appears to be widespread among both families and institutions. It results in damage to children's behavioral, cognitive, emotional, or physical functioning and may prevent them from fulfilling their potential.

■ As a result of advanced technology, family responsibilities, and pressure to grow up too soon, many children today are experiencing a shortened and stressful childhood.

■ Psychologists have studied factors that enable some children to withstand stress better than others. Resilient children are those who are able to "bounce back" from unfortunate circumstances.

KEY TERMS

acting-out behavior (page 327)
affective disorder (329)
attention deficit disorder with
   hyperactivity (328)
behavior therapy (331)
childhood depression (330)
coregulation (315)
drug therapy (331)
enuresis (326)
family therapy (330)
ideal self (301)

industry versus inferiority (305)
latchkey children (320)
latency period (304)
prejudice (308)
psychological maltreatment (332)
psychotherapy (330)
real self (301)
resilient children (333)
school phobia (328)
self-awareness (301)
self-concept (301)

self-definition (301)
self-esteem (302)
self-recognition (301)
self-schema (305)
sexism (304)
sociogram (310)
sociometric (310)
stuttering (327)
tics (327)
underachievers (314)

SUGGESTED READINGS

Ahrons, C. R., & Rodgers, R. H. (1987). *Divorced families: A multidisciplinary developmental view.* New York: Norton. This book, based on a comprehensive study of family functioning after divorce, views divorce as a normative developmental process, in which the nuclear family reorganizes itself as "binuclear." It describes challenges faced by families at different life stages and provides suggestions for ways society can help divorced families.

Bronfenbrenner, U. (1970). *Two worlds of child-hood: U.S. and U.S.S.R.* New York: Russell Sage. A comparative study of child-rearing methods in the United States and the Soviet Union.

Coopersmith, S. (1967). *The antecedents of self-esteem.* San Francisco: Freeman. A thorough and thought-provoking report of an in-depth study of 85 boys, 10 to 12 years old, which correlated the boys' levels of self-esteem with their parents' attitudes and child-rearing practices, as well as with other aspects of the boys' functioning.

Gurian, A., & Formanek, R. (1983). *The socially*

competent child: A parent's guide to social development—from infancy to early adolescence. Boston: Houghton Mifflin. Two psychologists draw on the latest research to provide practical suggestions for helping children to make friends with children their own age and to get along with adults. Many quotations and anecdotes about children make this lively reading.

Long, L., & Long, T. (1983). *The handbook for latchkey children and their parents.* New York: Berkley. A summation of the pros and cons of self-care, based on interviews with latchkey children, their parents, and adults who were latchkey children. The book includes practical advice and lists organizations that can help working parents create the best environment for their child.

Olds, S. W. (1986). *The working parents survival guide.* New York: Bantam. An in-depth manual for mothers and fathers that draws on up-to-date research to examine the concerns of working parents and their children. It offers practical solutions for a variety of problems, including finding and evaluating good child care, recognizing the appearance of emotional troubles, and helping children adjust to parents' separation.

Pogrebin, L. C. (1983). *Family politics.* New York: McGraw-Hill. A lively profamily book by a feminist who compares traditional and contemporary families, identifies the strengths and weaknesses of various kinds of families, and urges changes in light of the needs and interests of parents and children today.

Rimm, S. B. (1986). *Underachievement syndrome: Causes and cures.* Watertown, WI: Apple. A readable guidebook by a psychologist-educator, distilled from her clinical experience. Rimm shows how children come to be underachievers and how underachieving can be cured by giving attention to the child, the parents, and the school environment simultaneously. Many parents will recog-

nize such "types" as Manipulative Mary, Perfectionist Pearl, and Bully Bob.

Saunders, A., & Remsberg, B. (1984). *The stress-proof child: A loving parent's guide.* New York: Holt, Rinehart & Winston. A practical guide for parents to help children deal with stress. It provides suggestions for helping children develop self-esteem, as well as guidelines for recognizing signs of stress in children and techniques for dealing with it.

Shreve, A. (1987). *Remaking motherhood: How working mothers are shaping our children's future.* New York: Viking. A research-based book by an award-winning journalist that delves into the risks and rewards of "a new kind of mothering" and finds that children of working mothers, in general, are not "deprived," but enriched. The book covers the working mother as a new role model; the effects of mothers' employment on daughters and sons, including stresses and strains; the new working father; and the single working mother.

Stewart, M. A., & Gath, A. (1978). *Psychological disorders of children.* Baltimore: Williams & Wilkins. Two child psychiatrists have written this book to introduce doctors, nurses, and students to such problems as autism, schizophrenia, hyperactivity, depression, and retardation. Each chapter starts off with a quotation from a case history or a literary example and then briefly describes the particular problem and gives information about causes and treatment. There is an excellent checklist for parents to evaluate a child's behavior.

Stewart, M. A., & Olds, S. W. (1973). *Raising a hyperactive child.* New York: Harper & Row. A book for the lay reader that defines the characteristics of hyperactivity, explores possible causes, and offers practical suggestions to parents and teachers concerning day-to-day living with hyperactive children.

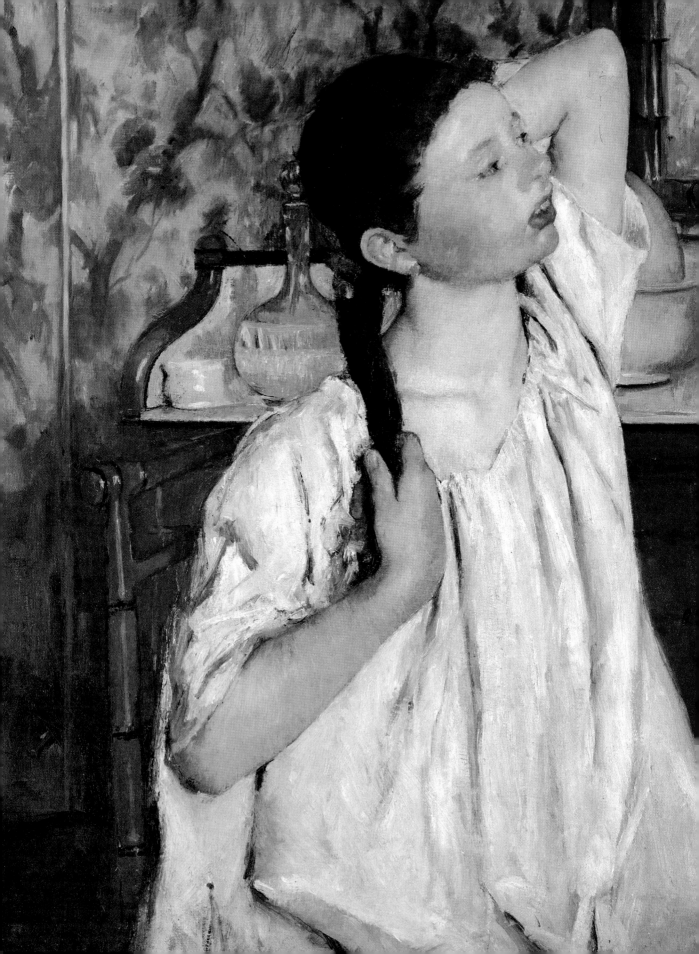

ADOLESCENCE

In adolescence, young people's appearance changes as a result of the hormonal events of puberty. Their thinking changes as they develop the ability to deal with abstractions. Their feelings change about almost everything. All areas of development converge as adolescents confront their major task, the establishment of adult identity.

■ In **Chapter 10,** we examine the dramatic physical and intellectual development that takes place during the years from about age 12 till about age 20. We see the impact of early and late maturation, we look at health problems that affect adolescents, and we see how their advances in intellectual competence help them consider abstract ideas, moral issues, and career choices. We look at the roles of school and work in teenagers' lives.

■ In **Chapter 11,** we see how adolescents incorporate their new appearance, their puzzling physical yearnings, and their new intellectual abilities into their sense of self. We examine the major task of adolescence—the achievement of identity, including sexual identity. We look at the relationships adolescents have with their parents, and we examine the peer group as the testing ground for teenagers' ideas about life and about themselves. We look at some problems that arise during the teens, as well as some of the personality strengths of adolescents.

10

CHAPTER

PHYSICAL AND INTELLECTUAL DEVELOPMENT IN ADOLESCENCE

I think what is happening to me is so wonderful, and not only what can be seen on my body, but all that is taking place inside.

Anne Frank,
The Diary of a Young Girl, 1952
(entry written January 5, 1944)

ASK YOURSELF

- What physical changes do adolescents experience, and how do these changes affect them psychologically?

- How prevalent are eating disorders, drug abuse, and sexually transmitted diseases, and what can be done about them?

- How does cognitive development affect the way adolescents solve problems and make moral judgments and life decisions?

- What factors affect the value of secondary schooling, and why do some adolescents drop out of school?

- What factors influence young people's vocational choices?

Apache Indians in the southwestern United States mark a girl's sexual maturation with a 4-day ritual of chanting from sunrise to sunset (see Box 10-1). Jewish people traditionally welcome 13-year-old boys into the adult community with a bar mitzvah celebration; in the twentieth century, a similar celebration, the bas (or bat) mitzvah, has been instituted for girls.

Such coming-of-age rites are common in many traditional societies in which *puberty*—the attainment of sexual maturity—is considered the beginning of adulthood. Rites of passage may include severe tests of strength and endurance; mutilation, such as circumcision of both boys and girls, piercing of ears, filing of teeth, or elaborate tattooing; religious blessings; separation from the family; or acts of magic.

In modern industrial societies, no single ritual marks the passage from childhood to adulthood. Instead, between childhood and adulthood we recognize a transitional stage of development known as *adolescence*.

This transitional period is so ingrained in our culture that it is hard to realize that the concept of adolescence as a developmental stage is a recent phenomenon. Before the twentieth century, adult responsibilities came with puberty, when children immediately entered an apprenticeship in the world of work. Now the change from childhood to adulthood takes longer, partly because puberty occurs earlier than it did a century ago and also because our complex society requires a longer period of education before a young person is ready for independence.

Adolescence begins at about age 12 or 13 and ends in the late teens or early twenties. It is easier to determine when childhood ends than to decide when adulthood has arrived. The first passage is heralded by unmistakable bodily changes; the second follows various socially defined developments.

Legal adulthood comes at different ages for different purposes: having a driver's license is allowed at age 16 in most states; voting, at age 18; enlisting in the army, at 17; marrying without parents' permission, usually at age 18; and being responsible for contracts, at age 18 to age 21, varying by state. Sociological adulthood is

BOX 10-1   WINDOW ON THE WORLD

AN APACHE GIRL COMES OF AGE

Among the Apache Indians of the American southwest, a girl's entrance into puberty is celebrated by a 4-day sunrise ceremony (actually, a ceremony of chanting from sunrise to sunset), which reenacts the tribe's version of how the world was created (Heard Museum, 1987).

According to Apache lore, the first woman on earth was a deity called Changing Woman, the mother of twins who cleansed the world of evil so that human beings could live well. During the puberty rite (also called "gifts of Changing Woman"), the deity's spirit is believed to enter the girl to prepare her for her role as mother and life giver. Among the gifts that Changing Woman is believed to bestow upon her are strength, even temperament, prosperity, and long life.

As male members of the tribe gather around, chanting, the girl approaches a ceremonial blanket laid out on the ground, on which a buckskin has been placed. She wears an abalone shell on her forehead and carries a staff that represents longevity and a cane that she will need when she is old. The buckskin upon which she stands symbolizes the hope that she will always have plenty of meat and not go hungry.

The girl kneels before the sun and is massaged to "mold" her body into adult form and to give her strength. On the last day of the ceremony, the girl is blessed with pollen, symbolizing her newfound reproductive powers.

In many traditional cultures, ceremonies like this one give community recognition to the importance and value of the physical changes that prepare a young person for an adult role in the society. Modern industrial societies, on the other hand, have no comparable single initiation rite; instead, the sexual aspects of "coming of age" are often only whispered about, and entrance into adulthood stretches over the period of approximately 7 or 8 years called *adolescence*.

(© Bill Gillette/Stock, Boston)

The Apache Indians of the American southwest celebrate a girl's entrance into puberty with a 4-day ritual that includes special clothing, a symbolic blanket, and singing from sunrise to sunset. In modern industrial societies, there is no single comparable initiation rite.

attained when young people become self-supporting, choose careers, marry, or found families. Psychological adulthood comes when they discover their identity, become independent from their parents, develop their own systems of values, and can form mature relationships of friendship and love. Some people never leave adolescence, no matter what their chronological age.

In this chapter we consider the dramatic physical changes of adolescence and the psychological reactions to them, which are greatly influenced by cultural standards. We look at how adolescents develop intellectually as they achieve the ability to think abstractly yet retain vestiges of egocentric thought. We see how their thinking processes affect their moral reasoning. Since cognitive development affects both education and career, we look at adolescents in school, at work, and in their search for vocational goals. We'll delve more deeply into the adolescent quest for identity in Chapter 11.

MATURATION IN ADOLESCENCE: PUBESCENCE TO PUBERTY

The biological changes that signal the end of childhood include rapid physiological growth, changes in bodily proportions, the budding of the breasts in girls and the deepening of the voice in both sexes, and the onset of menstruation in girls and the emergence of boys' ability to ejaculate semen. These changes do not take place overnight; they come about through the process of adolescent maturation: the progression from pubescence to puberty.

Pubescence is the stage during which the reproductive functions mature, rapid growth occurs in height and weight, the primary sex organs (shown in Figure 10-1) enlarge, and secondary sex characteristics (listed in Table 10-1) appear. Pubescence normally lasts about 2 years and ends at *puberty,* the point at which a boy or girl reaches full sexual maturity and is able to reproduce. Pubescence is the time in life of the greatest increase in sexual differentiation since the early prenatal stage.

Timing of Sexual Maturation: The Secular Trend

Any eighth- or ninth-grade class picture presents startling contrasts. Flat-chested little girls can be seen next to full-bosomed, full-grown young women. Skinny little boys are found next to broad-shouldered, mustached young men. This individual variability is normal. There is about a 6- to 7-year range in both boys and girls for both pubescence and puberty.

The *average* age for the beginning of pubescence in girls is 10 years (with puberty following at 12), but normal girls may show the first signs as early as 7 or as late as 14 (and may thus reach puberty from 9 to 16). The average age for boys' entry into pubescence is 12 (with puberty at 14),

Figure 10-1 Primary sex organs.

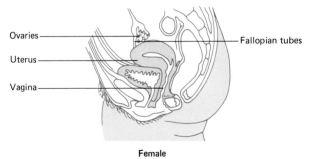

Female

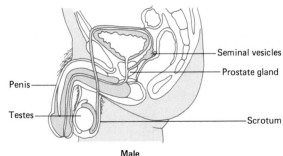

Male

TABLE 10·1 SECONDARY SEX CHARACTERISTICS

GIRLS	BOYS
Breasts	Pubic hair
Pubic hair	Axillary (underarm) hair
Axillary (underarm) hair	Facial hair
Increased width and depth of pelvis	Changes in voice
	Changes in skin
Changes in voice	Broadening of shoulders
Changes in skin	

with a normal range from 9 to 16 (and with puberty from 11 to 18) (Chumlea, 1982). As we'll see, whether a youngster is an early or a late maturer often has social and psychological consequences.

The various events leading to puberty unfold in a sequence that is much more consistent than their actual timing, though even their order varies somewhat from one person to another. The usual sequences are shown in Table 10-2.

It is not known why maturation begins when it does, or what precise mechanism triggers it. What is known is only that at some biologically determined time—a time apparently regulated by the interaction of genes, individual health, and environment—the pituitary gland sends a message to a young person's gonads, or sex glands. Upon receipt of that message, a girl's ovaries sharply step up their production of estrogen, and a boy's testes increase the manufacture of androgens, particularly testosterone. These hormones stimulate sexual maturation.

TABLE 10·2 USUAL SEQUENCE OF PHYSIOLOGICAL CHANGES IN ADOLESCENCE

GIRLS' CHARACTERISTICS	AGE OF FIRST APPEARANCE
Growth of breasts	8–13
Growth of pubic hair	8–14
Body growth	9.5–14.5 (average peak, 12)
Menarche	10–16.5 (average, 12.5)
Underarm hair	About 2 years after pubic hair
Increased output of oil- and sweat-producing glands (which may lead to acne)	About the same time as underarm hair

BOYS' CHARACTERISTICS	AGE OF FIRST APPEARANCE
Growth of testes, scrotal sac	10–13.5
Growth of pubic hair	10–15
Body growth	10.5–16 (average peak, 14)
Growth of penis, prostate gland, seminal vesicles	11–14.5 (average, 12.5)
Change in voice	About the same time as growth of penis
First ejaculation of semen	About 1 year after beginning of growth of penis
Facial and underarm hair	About 2 years after appearance of pubic hair
Increased output of oil- and sweat-producing glands (which may lead to acne)	About the same time as underarm hair

Body size in infancy may correlate with the timing of puberty, according to a recent longitudinal study (Mills, Shiono, Shapiro, Crawford, & Rhoads, 1986). When 78 healthy, well-nourished boys reached their fourteenth birthdays, those who had been heavier and more muscular at the age of 6 months were more advanced in sexual development. The differences were apparently not attributable to the boys' diets in infancy. It may be that both growth in infancy and the onset of puberty are genetically influenced, possibly through inherited differences in production of hormones. Since no females were included in the study, its findings may not apply to girls.

On the basis of historical sources, developmentalists have inferred the existence of a *secular trend* downward in the age at which young people reach adult height and sexual maturity (a secular trend, in the life sciences, is a trend that can be seen only by observing several generations). This trend began about 100 years ago and has occurred in the United States, western Europe, and Japan, but not in some other countries (Chumlea, 1982).

The most obvious explanation seems to be the influence of a higher standard of living. Children who are healthier, better nourished, and better cared for mature earlier and grow bigger. Evidence of this is the fact that in less developed countries, puberty comes later than in more industrialized cultures. In New Guinea, for example, girls do not begin to menstruate until sometime between 15.4 and 18.4 years of age (Eveleth & Tanner, 1976).

The secular trend appears to have ended, at least in the United States, probably as a reflection of higher living standards in most segments of our population (Schmeck, 1976). The leveling of the trend suggests that the age of puberty has now reached some genetically determined limit and that better nutrition is unlikely to bring the age still lower. This may explain why, in the study of boys' sexual development described above, diet did not affect the timing of puberty.

Physiological Changes of Adolescence

Let's look at the changes that lead up to puberty—the adolescent growth spurt, the beginning of menstruation for girls, the presence of sperm in the urine of males, the maturation of organs involved in reproduction, and the development of secondary sex characteristics—and when most young people in the United States experience them.

The Adolescent Growth Spurt   One of the early signs of maturation is the *adolescent growth spurt,* a sharp increase in height and weight that generally begins in girls between the

(© Michael Rizza/Stock, Boston)

Because girls experience the adolescent growth spurt earlier than boys do, girls are taller, heavier, and stronger from ages 11 to 13—a state of affairs that boys often find embarrassing because of the societal expectation that males should be bigger than females.

ages of 9½ and 14½ (usually at about age 10) and in boys between the ages of 10½ and 16 (usually at about age 12 or 13). Soon after the growth spurt ends, the young person reaches sexual maturity, and growth drops off. Most girls attain their adult height by age 14 or 15, and most boys by age 18 (Elkind, 1984).

Before the growth spurt, boys are typically only about 2 percent taller than girls. From age 11 to age 13, girls are taller, heavier, and stronger. After the growth spurt, boys are larger again, now by about 8 percent. Because the growth spurt in males begins later than that in females, boys have more time to grow at the prepubertal rate, which is faster than the rate of growth after puberty.

Boys and girls grow differently during adolescence. The male becomes larger overall, his shoulders are wider, his legs are longer relative to his trunk, and his forearms are longer relative to both his upper arms and his height. The female's pelvis widens during adolescence to make childbearing easier, and layers of fat are laid down just under the skin, giving her a more rounded appearance.

In both sexes, the adolescent growth spurt affects practically all skeletal and muscular dimensions. Even the eye grows faster during this period, so that myopia, or nearsightedness, increases among adolescents, since myopia results when the eyeball is so lengthened that it focuses images in front of the retina rather than on it. The lower jaw usually becomes longer and thicker; both it and the nose project more; and the incisors of both jaws become more upright. These changes are greater in boys than in girls and follow their own timetables. During this period different parts of the body may temporarily be out of proportion. The result is the familiar teenage awkwardness or gawkiness that accompanies unbalanced, accelerated growth.

Before adolescence, boys are slightly stronger on the average than girls, but the difference is tiny. After the adolescent growth spurt, the male's larger muscles, larger heart and lungs, and greater capacity for carrying oxygen in the blood confer considerably greater strength and endurance. Many adult women, however, are stronger than many men because of body build or a high rate of physical activity.

Primary Sex Characteristics The *primary sex characteristics* are the characteristics that are directly related to reproduction—specifically, the sex organs, including the female's ovaries, uterus, and vagina and the male's testes, prostate gland, penis, and seminal vesicles (see Figure 10-1). The gradual enlargement of these body parts occurs during pubescence, leading to sexual maturation.

Sperm in the urine is considered the principal sign of sexual maturation in boys, who become fertile as soon as sperm is present. Like the onset of menstruation, the timing of the appearance of sperm is highly variable. One longitudinal study found that only 2 percent of 11- to 12-year-old boys showed sperm in the urine compared with 24 percent of 15-year-olds (Richardson & Short, 1978).

Secondary Sex Characteristics The *secondary sex characteristics* (see Table 10-1) are physiological characteristics of the two sexes that are signs of sexual maturation but do not directly involve the sex organs. These include the breasts in females and the broadened shoulders in males. Other secondary sex characteristics appear in both sexes: the growth of hair in the pubic area, on the face, in the armpits, and on the body; and the adult skin and adult voices of men and women. The timing of these signs is variable, but the sequence is fairly consistent (see Table 10-2).

The first sign of pubescence for girls is generally the budding of the breasts. The nipples enlarge and protrude; the areolae, the pigmented areas surrounding the nipples, enlarge; and the breasts assume first a conical and then a rounded shape. The breasts are usually fully developed before menstruation begins. Much to their distress, some adolescent boys experience temporary breast enlargement; this is normal and may last from 12 to 18 months.

Various forms of hair growth, including pubic hair and axillary hair (hair in the armpits), also signal maturation. Adolescent boys usually welcome the appearance of hair on the face and chest, but girls are generally dismayed if a slight amount of hair appears on their faces and around their nipples, though this is normal.

The skin of adolescent boys and girls becomes coarser and oilier, and the increased activity of

Left, above: These young ballerinas show the budding breasts that are usually the first sign of pubescence for girls. Other secondary sex characteristics will soon follow.

Below: Facial hair is one of the most noticeable secondary sex characteristics in males, and boys usually welcome the need to shave as a sign of maturity.

the sebaceous glands gives rise to outbreaks of pimples and blackheads. Acne is more troublesome in boys than it is in girls and seems to be related to increased amounts of the male hormone testosterone. The voices of both boys and girls deepen, partly in response to the growth of the larynx and partly—especially in boys—in response to the production of male hormones.

A pubescent boy often awakens to find a wet spot or a hardened, dried spot in the bed, letting him know that while he was asleep he had a nocturnal emission (wet dream), an ejaculation of semen. Most adolescent boys who are neither having sexual intercourse nor masturbating on a fairly regular basis experience these emissions, which are perfectly normal and may or may not occur in connection with an erotic dream.

Menarche   The most dramatic sign of sexual maturation for girls is *menarche*—the first menstruation, or monthly shedding of tissue from the lining of the womb. Menarche occurs fairly late in the sequence of female development (see Table 10-2); on the average, a girl in the United States first menstruates at the age of 12½, about 2 years after her breasts begin to develop and her uterus begins to grow, and after her height spurt has slowed down.

Although in many cultures menarche is taken as the sign that a girl has become a woman, usually the early menstrual periods do not include ovulation, and many girls are unable to conceive for 12 to 18 months after menarche. Sometimes, however, ovulation and conception do occur in these early months; therefore, after menarche, girls should assume that if they have sexual intercourse without an effective contraceptive, they can become pregnant.

One interesting line of research, which is especially relevant in light of young women's increased participation in athletic activities in recent years, has pursued the relationship between exercise and menstruation. Serious athletes, dancers, and swimmers often begin to menstruate quite late, sometimes not till after 18 years of age (R. E. Frisch, Wyshak, & Vincent, 1980). This may be due to the reduction in body fat as the result of strenuous exercise, to the stress of the training, or to a diminished level of blood circulation. In any case, most female athletes do not experience menstrual irregularity, and those who do usually become regular when they stop training and can then go on to have normal childbearing experiences (Shangold, 1978). Research has confirmed this reversible effect of vigorous exercise on menstrual irregularity, especially when the exercise is accompanied by weight loss (Bullen, Skrinar, Beitins, von Mering, Turnbull, & McArthur, 1985).

Psychological Impact of Physical Changes

Adolescence is probably the most embarrassing time in the entire life span. At a time when people are acutely self-conscious and sure that everyone else is watching their every move, their bodies are constantly betraying them. Boys' voices squeak unexpectedly, and their penises become obviously erect at inopportune times. Girls worry about the size of their breasts and about getting menstrual blood on their clothes. It is not surprising that the dramatic physical changes of adolescence should have many psychological ramifications—including the need to manage the insistent sexual urges that come with puberty.

Effects of Early and Late Maturation One of the great paradoxes of adolescence is the conflict between a young person's yearning to find an individual identity—to assert a unique self—and an overwhelming desire to be exactly like his or her friends. Anything that obviously sets an adolescent apart from the crowd can be unsettling, and youngsters are often disturbed if they mature sexually either much earlier or much later than their friends. Though neither late maturing nor early maturing is necessarily advantageous or troublesome, studies (both classic and recent) have found that the timing of maturation can have significant psychological effects, especially on boys.

EFFECTS ON BOYS Some research has shown early-maturing boys to be more poised, more relaxed, more good-natured, less affected, more popular with peers, more likely to be school leaders, and less impulsive than late maturers, while other studies have found them to be more worried about being liked, more cautious, and more bound by rules and routines. Late maturers, for their part, have variously been found to feel more inadequate, rejected, and dominated; to be more dependent, aggressive, and insecure; to rebel more against their parents; and to think less of themselves (Mussen & Jones, 1957; Peskin, 1967, 1973; Siegel, 1982). Although some studies have shown that early maturers retain an edge in terms of intellectual performance (Gross & Duke, 1980; Tanner, 1978), many differences seem to disappear by adulthood (M. C. Jones, 1957).

We see advantages and disadvantages in both situations. The early maturers reap the benefits to self-esteem of having the edge in sports and in dating, but they may have problems living up to others' expectations that they should act more mature than they are. Furthermore, they may have too little time to prepare for the sudden and intense changes of adolescence. The late maturers may feel and act more childish, but they may benefit from the longer period of childhood, when they need not deal with the new and different demands of adolescence, and they may become more flexible as they adapt to the problems of being smaller and more childish-looking than their peers (Peskin, 1973).

EFFECTS ON GIRLS Advantages and disadvantages show up for girls too. Early-maturing girls have been found to be less sociable, expressive, and poised and to be more introverted and shy than later maturers (M. C. Jones, 1958; Peskin, 1973). However, they have also been found to make better adjustments in adulthood (M. C. Jones & Mussen, 1958; Peskin, 1973).

Since they are bigger than the boys and more bosomy than the other girls, early-maturing girls may have problems that stem from their feeling so conspicuous; the very process of working through these problems may give them valuable experience in dealing with problems later in life. It is also possible that their problems are a reaction to other people's concerns about their sexuality. Parents and teachers, for example, may treat girls who have physically mature bodies more strictly and more disapprovingly than they treat less developed girls.

Reactions to Menarche and Menstruation
Menarche is more than a physical event; it is "a concrete symbol of a shift from girl to woman" (Ruble & Brooks-Gunn, 1982, p. 1557). Girls who have begun to menstruate seem more conscious of their femaleness than girls of the same age who have not yet reached menarche. They are more interested in boy-girl relations and in adorning their bodies, and when they draw female figures, they show more explicit breasts. In addition, they seem more mature in certain personality characteristics (Grief & Ulman, 1982).

Unfortunately, in the past, the negative side of menarche—the sometimes unexpected discomfort and embarrassment that may accompany it—has been emphasized. Menstruation has been a forbidden subject of discussion in some circles of polite society and even within many families. Cultural taboos have reinforced negative attitudes and have prevented the development of rituals to welcome young girls to womanhood, like those among the Apaches and in some other societies (Grief & Ulman, 1982). One team of researchers concluded that our culture treats menarche not as a rite of passage but as a hygienic crisis, arousing girls' anxieties about staying clean and sweet-smelling, but not instilling pride in their womanliness (Whisnant & Zegans, 1975).

Today, although many girls have mixed feelings about menarche and menstruation, most take these events in stride. According to one survey of more than 600 schoolgirls in grades 5 through 12, girls do not find their first menstruation particularly painful, and they do not feel restricted in any way. They trade stories about symptoms and seem fairly relaxed even though a significant change has taken place in their lives (Ruble & Brooks-Gunn, 1982).

The better prepared a girl is for menarche, the more positive her feelings and the less the distress she experiences (Koff, Rierdan, & Sheingold, 1982; Ruble & Brooks-Gunn, 1982). Unfortunately, though, some girls have too little information or, worse yet, have misinformation, and as a result, some women remember their first menstruation negatively (Rierdan, Koff, & Flaherty, 1986). Those whose menarche comes early are most likely to find it disruptive (Ruble & Brooks-Gunn, 1982)—possibly because they are less prepared or because they simply feel out of step with their friends.

What can be done to make menstruation a more positive experience? Pubescent girls need information in terms that they can understand. Much that young people are taught about menstruation may be too technical and too impersonal. Girls need to be told about the body parts and processes involved and what they can expect. They need to realize that menstruation is a special, universal female experience, different from injury or disease.

Parents should bring up the subject as soon as a girl's breasts and pubic hair begin to develop. They should reassure a daughter that menstruation is normal and that she will be able to continue with all her usual activities, like sports, swimming, and taking baths. They should encourage her to ask questions, and all family members, including fathers and brothers, should try to maintain an open, matter-of-fact attitude. In some families, celebrating menarche with a family ritual underlines the positive meaning of this event in a girl's life.

Feelings about Physical Appearance Most young teenagers are more concerned about their physical appearance than about any other aspect of themselves, and many are dissatisfied with what they see in the mirror (Siegel, 1982). Boys want to be tall and broad-shouldered; girls want to be slim but shapely. Anything that makes boys think that they look feminine or girls think that they look masculine makes them miserable. Teenagers of both sexes worry about their weight, their complexion, and their facial features. Girls tend to be unhappier about their looks than boys of the same age, probably because of our culture's greater emphasis on women's physical attributes (Clifford, 1971; Siegel, 1982).

Adults often dismiss adolescents' preoccupation with their looks. But in a society in which people's personalities tend to be judged by their appearance (Dion, Berscheid, & Walster, 1972), young people's self-image can have long-lasting effects on their feelings about themselves.

Adults who considered themselves attractive during their teenage years have higher self-esteem and are happier than those who did not. Not until the mid-forties do the differences in self-esteem and happiness disappear (Berscheid, Walster, & Bohrnstedt, 1973).

HEALTH CONCERNS

For most people, adolescence is a healthy time of life. The most common problems—such as eating disorders, drug abuse, and sexually transmitted diseases—can be traced to personality or lifestyle factors, and the primary cause of death at this time is not illness, but misadventure—accidents, homicide, and suicide.

Whenever the body and spirit undergo changes as dramatic as those of adolescence, some risks seem inevitable. Let's see what they are.

Nutrition

When Carl devours one hamburger after another or drinks several glasses of milk, pausing only to ask for more, his parents shake their heads in amazement. Is this the same young person, they wonder, who, only a few years ago, had such a meager appetite and had to be wheedled to clean his plate?

Boys, who grow more during adolescence, need more calories than girls. On the average, a girl needs about 2200 calories per day, while a boy needs about 2800 (a difference of 600 calories, or about two hamburgers). Protein levels are important to sustained growth. Teenagers should avoid eating large amounts of "junk foods" like french fries, soft drinks, ice cream concoctions, and snack chips and dips.

The most common mineral deficiencies of adolescents are of calcium, iron, and zinc. The need for calcium, which supports bone growth, is best met by drinking large quantities of milk. Girls are especially prone to calcium deficiency, a problem that may haunt them later in the form of osteoporosis (thinning of the bones), which afflicts 1 in 4 postmenopausal women. Iron-deficiency anemia is common among American adolescents. The diet of the average American is iron-poor, and teenagers need a

Most young teenagers of both sexes are more concerned about their physical appearance than about any other aspect of themselves. Boys want to be tall, broad-shouldered, and masculine-looking. They are proud of their muscles as much for what they look like as for what they can do.

steady source of iron, such as iron-fortified breads, dried fruits, and leafy green vegetables. Even a mild zinc deficiency can delay sexual maturity. Good sources of zinc include meats, eggs, seafood, and whole-grain cereal products (E.R. Williams & Caliendo, 1984).

Eating Disorders

Some adolescents, especially girls, put on weight as they enter their teens, and many who do then begin a lifelong struggle to reduce for the sake of health and beauty. In recent years, two eating problems—*anorexia nervosa* and *bulimia*—have become more common. Both reflect our society's stringent standards of female beauty, exalting slenderness above all else. Both also reflect the individual pathologies of people who try to meet those standards through bizarre patterns of eating.

Obesity The most common eating disorder in the United States is obesity, defined as being 20 percent over one's ideal weight. By this standard some 15 percent of adolescents are obese. Particularly discouraging is the tendency of obese teenagers to become obese adults (Maloney & Klykylo, 1983).

Obesity is generally assumed to result from overeating, and obese adolescents and adults are widely regarded as suffering from some form of impaired "willpower." There are risk factors, however, that seem to make some people more likely than others to become obese. These factors include *genetic regulation* of the body's metabolism (obesity often runs in families), *developmental history* (some children do not learn to distinguish between the clues their body gives them about hunger and fullness, and some people develop an abnormally large number of fat cells during childhood), *physical inactivity, emotional stress,* and *brain damage.*

Even in adolescence, obesity poses risks to health. It is associated with degenerative disorders of the circulatory system and an increased likelihood of heart disease. We'll discuss the relationship between obesity, diet, and exercise in Chapter 12, when we consider the physical development of young adults.

Anorexia Nervosa Someone suggests to an adolescent girl that she could stand to lose a few pounds. She loses them—and then continues to diet obsessively, refusing to eat, until she has lost at least 25 percent of her original body weight. Meanwhile, she stops menstruating; thick, soft hair spreads over her body; and she becomes intensely overactive. She may eventually die of starvation.

This is a typical scenario for **anorexia nervosa,** or self-starvation, an eating disorder seen mostly in young white women. The disorder may affect people of both sexes from age 8 to the thirties or even older, but it is most likely to occur in a bright, well-behaved, appealing female between puberty and the early twenties, from a stable, well-educated, well-off family. An estimated 2 percent of the 26 million females in the United States between the ages of 12 and 25 develop this condition to some degree. About 6 percent of the patients are adolescent boys (American Psychological Association, APA, 1986; Dove, undated).

Anorexics are preoccupied with food—cooking it, talking about it, and urging others to eat—but they eat very little themselves. They have a distorted view of themselves: they literally cannot see how shockingly thin they are. They tend to be good students whom their parents describe as "model" children, but they also tend to be withdrawn, depressed, and obsessed with repetitive, perfectionist behavior. Their families, too, appear to be harmonious on the surface, but the family members are actually overdependent and excessively involved in each other's lives and have difficulty dealing with conflict (Dove, undated).

We don't know what causes anorexia. Various researchers have suggested that it may be a physical disorder caused by a deficiency of a crucial chemical in the brain or by a disturbance of the hypothalamus; a psychological disturbance related to depression, a fear of growing up, or an extremely malfunctioning family; or a reaction to extreme societal pressures to be slender. Some psychologists believe that anorexic young people, who usually do what will please their parents, use eating as the one area in which they can be independent and take control of their lives. So far, none of these hypotheses has been conclusively supported, and research continues (Dove, undated; Yager, 1982).

The immediate objective of treatment is to reestablish eating, but weight gain is often only temporary unless the patient also gains insight into the feelings that have led to anorexia. Therefore treatment may include nutritional and behavioral therapy, cognitive therapy (providing information on the disorder), individual and group psychotherapy, drug therapy, and family counseling.

One study followed 63 female patients who were treated with such a combination of therapies. An average of 27 months after completion of their treatment, most of them had continued to gain weight, had resumed menstruating, and could function successfully in school or at work. Still, they continued to have some problems with body image. Even though they averaged 8 percent below their ideal weight, most thought of themselves as being overweight and as having excessive appetites, and many felt depressed and lonely. Apparently, most patients with anorexia need long-term support, even after they have stopped starving themselves (Nussbaum, Shenker, Baird, & Saravay, 1985).

Although alcohol is illegal for most high school and college students, it is usually easy to get—and it is a serious problem nationwide, sometimes leading to automobile accidents or a lifelong drinking problem. Most teenagers start to drink because their friends are doing it, and it makes them feel more grown-up.

was about 15½, found that those who used marijuana heavily (more than twice a week) were more likely than nonusers to have poor dietary habits and deteriorating health. Signs of nutritional deficiencies included muscle weakness, bleeding gums, and fatigue. The users also had more frequent infections of the upper respiratory tract and other physical problems (Farrow, Rees, & Worthington-Roberts, 1987).

Tobacco Sneaking a cigarette behind the barn was once a humorous staple of adolescent lore. But adults' amused indulgence toward young people's use of tobacco has turned to concern, with new awareness of hazards to health. The publication in 1964 of the U.S. Surgeon General's report clearly brought out relationships between smoking and lung cancer, heart disease, emphysema, and other illnesses.

Many adolescents got the message, as shown in the decline in smoking. Between 1977 and 1980, the percentage of teenagers who smoked cigarettes daily dropped from 29 percent to less than 20 percent, and it has remained at about that level through 1986. Teenagers express concern about the effects of smoking on health, and smokers feel the disapproval of their peers. Still, almost 68 percent of high school seniors have tried cigarettes at some time, and nearly 30 percent report having smoked during the previous month (NIDA, 1987).

Today, more adolescent girls than boys are smoking (in the past, more boys than girls smoked). As a result, one type of equality women have now achieved is a death rate from lung cancer virtually equal to that of men, though about 2½ times as many men develop the disease (American Cancer Society, 1985).

Children who become smokers usually take their first puff between 10 and 12 years of age and continue to smoke even though they do not enjoy it at first. Smokers generally become physically dependent on nicotine around the age of 15. Youngsters are more likely to smoke if their friends and family do (McAlister, Perry, & Maccoby, 1979; National Institute of Child Health and Human Development, 1978).

Teenagers who smoke tend to be late maturers; they smoke in order to seem older. They also tend to be more rebellious, to perform less well in school, to be better able to tolerate ambiguity, and to go out less for sports than those who do not smoke (Clausen, 1978; McAlister et al., 1979). It is ironic that rebellious young people who see smoking as an adult activity take it up so eagerly, embracing the behavior of the adults they are rebelling against. Since peer pressure has been effective in inducing people to smoke, its influence in the other direction may be the best preventive mechanism (Johnston, Bachman, & O'Malley, 1982; McAlister et al., 1979).

Sexually Transmitted Diseases (STDs)

What Are STDs? *Sexually transmitted diseases (STDs),* also referred to as *venereal diseases,* are diseases transmitted by sexual contact. The greater sexual freedom of the past 3 decades has brought soaring rates of these diseases, especially among adolescents. Of the 8 million to 12 million new cases of STDs in the United States each year, 3 out of 4 occur among 15- to 24-year-olds (U.S. Department of Health and Human Services, USDHHS, 1980).

By far the most prevalent STD is chlamydia, which causes infections of the urinary tract, the rectum, and the cervix and can lead, in women, to pelvic inflammatory disease (PID), a serious abdominal infection. Other STDs, in order of decreasing incidence, are gonorrhea, genital or venereal warts, herpes simplex, syphilis, and acquired immune deficiency syndrome (AIDS).

AIDS, a failure in the body's immune system, opens the door to fatal illness, most commonly pneumonia, and, as of this writing, has no known cure. AIDS is transmitted through bodily fluids (principally blood and semen) and, in this country, so far appears to be contracted mainly from homosexual and bisexual men, especially those who have had many partners; from sharing of contaminated hypodermic needles; and from transfusions of infected blood or blood products. The condition may not surface for years after the initial infection (American Foundation for the Prevention of Venereal Disease, AFPVD, 1986).

In 1986, a significant increase in the incidence of AIDS—more than 40,000 cases since 1981, of whom 58 percent were known to have died—precipitated a public health crisis, with predictions of 270,000 cases by 1991 (Morbidity and Mortality Weekly Report, December 12, 1986). An estimated 1 million to 3 million Americans are carriers of the disease, and at least 5 percent of these may go on to develop AIDS or AIDS-related conditions (AFPVD, 1986). As yet, though, AIDS has far fewer victims than genital herpes (which is also incurable) and other STDs (which can be treated with penicillin or other antibiotics).

Box 10-2 lists steps that adolescents and adults can take to protect themselves from STDs. Table 10-4 (pages 358–359) summarizes the most common STDs and their incidence, causes, most frequent symptoms, treatment, and consequences.

Implications for Adolescents The reasons for the high rates of sexually transmitted diseases among young people are many: increased sexual activity, especially among teenage girls; use of oral contraceptives, which do not protect against STDs, instead of the condom, which does; the complacent belief that these diseases affect *other* people; and young people's willingness to take risks because they want to have sexual intercourse more than they fear contracting a disease.

Actually, young girls may be even more susceptible than mature women to infections of the upper genital tract caused by STDs, which can lead to serious, even dangerous, complications. Unfortunately, teenagers are more likely than adults to put off getting medical care, they are less likely to follow through with treatment, and STDs are more likely to be misdiagnosed in teenagers than in adults (Centers for Disease Control, 1983).

Most teenagers know the basic facts—that STDs are transmitted through sexual contact, that anyone can get them, and that they are serious (Sorensen, 1973). But teenagers are often reluctant to seek help because they are afraid that their parents will find out, and they are ashamed and embarrassed to alert their sexual partners when they do contract an STD. Most of the educational campaigns aimed at eradicating this group of diseases focus on diagnosing and treating them early. Not until at least equal prominence is given to preventing them and to the moral obligation to avoid passing them on will headway be made in stopping this epidemic.

Death in Adolescence

When adolescents die, violence is usually the cause. In 1980, eighty percent of all deaths among 15- to 24-year-olds were due to accidents, homicide, and suicide. In part, this fact reflects the general good health and vigor of young people (in 1980 the mortality rate for persons between the ages of 15 and 24 was 119 deaths per 100,000 people), but it also reflects their lifestyles.

In 1979 the death rates in this age group were

BOX 10-2 PRACTICALLY SPEAKING

PROTECTING AGAINST SEXUALLY TRANSMITTED DISEASES

How can people who are sexually active protect themselves against sexually transmitted diseases (STDs)? These guidelines (adapted from American Foundation for the Prevention of Venereal Disease, 1986, and Upjohn, 1984) will minimize the possibility of your acquiring an STD and will maximize your chances of getting adequate treatment if you do contract one.

■ Have regular medical checkups. All sexually active persons should request tests specifically aimed at diagnosing the presence of STDs.

■ Know your partner. The more discriminating you are, the less likely you are to be exposed to STDs. Partners with whom you develop a relationship are more likely than partners you do not know well to inform you of any medical problems they have.

■ Avoid having sexual intercourse with many partners, promiscuous persons, and drug abusers.

■ Avoid any sexual activity involving exchange of bodily fluids. Use a condom during intercourse.

■ Avoid anal intercourse.

■ Use a contraceptive foam, cream, or jelly; it will kill many germs and help to prevent certain STDs.

■ Learn the symptoms of STDs: vaginal or penile discharge; inflammation, itching, or pain in the genital or anal area; burning during urination; pain during intercourse; genital, body, or mouth sores, blisters, bumps, or rashes; pain in the lower abdomen or in the testicles; discharge from or itching of eyes; and fever or swollen glands.

■ Inspect your partner for any visible symptoms.

■ If you develop any of the symptoms yourself, get immediate medical attention.

■ Just before and just after sexual contact, wash genital and rectal areas with soap and water; males should urinate after washing.

■ Do not have any sexual contact if you suspect that you or your partner may be infected. Abstinence is the most reliable preventive measure.

■ Avoid exposing any cut or break in the skin to anyone else's blood, body fluids, or secretions.

■ Practice good routine hygiene: frequent, thorough hand washing and daily fingernail brushing.

■ If you contract any STD, notify all recent sexual partners immediately, so that they can obtain treatment and avoid passing the infection back to you, or on to someone else. Inform your doctor or dentist of your condition so that precautions can be taken to prevent transmission. Do not donate blood, plasma, sperm, body organs, or other body tissue.

For more information, contact American Foundation for the Prevention of Venereal Disease, 799 Broadway, Suite 638, New York, NY 10003.

---

3 times higher for males than for females and were 20 percent higher for black people than for white people. Although the differences between the death rates for young black people and young white people are lessening, the prime causes of death are different. The leading cause of death among young white people is automobile accidents, while among young black people it is homicide. The third leading cause of death among both black and white people in this age group is suicide.

Of the 20 percent of deaths among 15- to 24-year-olds that stemmed from natural causes in 1980, cancer was the most prevalent cause. Cancer deaths in this age group have declined since the 1960s (USDHHS, 1982).

TABLE 10-4 THE MOST COMMON SEXUALLY TRANSMITTED DISEASES

DISEASE	NEW CASES IN 1986	CASES (%) MALE/FEMALE	CAUSE	SYMPTOMS: MALE	SYMPTOMS: FEMALE	TREATMENT	CONSEQUENCES IF UNTREATED
Chlamydia	4.6 million	60/40	Bacterial infection	Pain during urination, discharge from penis.*	Vaginal discharge, abdominal discomfort.†	Tetracycline or erythromycin.	Can cause pelvic inflammatory disease or eventual sterility.
Gonorrhea	1.8 million	60/40	Bacterial infection	Discharge from penis, pain during urination.*	Discomfort when urinating, vaginal discharge, abnormal menses.†	Penicillin or other antibiotics.	Can cause pelvic inflammatory disease or eventual sterility; can also cause arthritis, dermatitis, and meningitis.
Genital warts	1.0 million	40/60	Viral infection	Painless growths that usually appear on penis, but may also appear on urethra or in rectal area.*	Small, painless growths on genitalia and anus; may also occur inside the vagina without external symptoms.*	Removal of warts.	May be associated with cervical cancer; in pregnancy, warts enlarge and may obstruct birth canal.
Herpes	500,000	40/60	Viral infection	Painful blisters anywhere on the genitalia, usually on the penis.*	Painful blisters on the genitalia, sometimes with fever and aching muscles; women with sores on cervix may be unaware of outbreaks.*	No known cure, but controlled with antiviral drug acyclovir.	Possible increased risk of cervical cancer.

DISEASE	NEW CASES IN 1986	CASES (%) MALE/FEMALE	CAUSE	SYMPTOMS: MALE	SYMPTOMS: FEMALE	TREATMENT	CONSEQUENCES IF UNTREATED
Syphilis	90,000	70/30	Bacterial infection	In first stage, reddish-brown sores on the mouth or genitalia or both, which may disappear, though the bacteria remain; in the second, more infectious stage, a widespread skin rash.*	Same as in men.	Penicillin or other antibiotics.	Paralysis, convulsions, brain damage, and sometimes death.
AIDS (acquired immune deficiency syndrome)	13,500	93/7	Viral infection	Extreme fatigue, fever, swollen lymph nodes, weight loss, diarrhea, night sweats, susceptibility to other diseases.*	Same as in men.	No known cure, but experimental drug AZT extends life.	Death, usually due to other diseases, such as cancer.

*May be asymptomatic.
†Often asymptomatic.

Source: Adapted from Centers for Disease Control, 1986; Morbidity and Mortality Weekly Report, 1987b.

The major element that sets adolescent thinking on a higher level than the thought processes of childhood is the concept of "what if. . . ." Adolescents can think in terms of what *might* be true, rather than just in terms of what they see in a concrete situation. Since they can imagine an infinite variety of possibilities, they are capable of hypothetical reasoning. While vestiges of egocentric thinking betray their cognitive immaturity, they are able to think in broader terms about moral issues and about plans for their own future.

ASPECTS OF INTELLECTUAL DEVELOPMENT IN ADOLESCENCE

Cognitive Development: Piaget's Stage of Formal Operations

Adolescence is the time when many people reach Piaget's highest level of intellectual development, that of *formal operations*. The formal operations stage is characterized by the ability to think abstractly.

What Are Formal Operations? The nature of formal operations can be seen in different reactions to a story told by Peel (1967):

> Only brave pilots are allowed to fly over high mountains. A fighter pilot flying over the Alps collided with an aerial cable-way, and cut a main cable causing some cars to fall to the glacier below. Several people were killed.

A child still at the Piagetian level of *concrete operations* said, "I think that the pilot was not very good at flying. He would have been better off if he went on fighting." Only one explanation occurred to the child: that the pilot was inept and was not doing his real job—fighting. By contrast, a young person who had reached the level of formal operations paid no attention to the designation *fighter pilot* and found a variety of possible explanations for what had happened: "He was either not informed of the mountain railway on his route, or he was flying too low; also, his flying compass may have been affected by something before or after takeoff, thus set-

ting him off course and causing the collision with the cable" (Peel, 1967).

Cognitive development can be traced from stage to stage by following the progress of a typical child whom we'll call Adam in dealing with a classical Piagetian problem in formal reasoning, the pendulum problem. Adam is shown the pendulum, which consists of an object hanging from a string, and is then shown how he can change the length of the string, the weight of the object, the height from which the object is released, and the amount of force he can use to push the object. He is then asked to determine which of these factors, either alone or combined with others, determines how fast the pendulum swings.

When Adam first sees the pendulum, he is not yet 7 years old and is in the preoperational stage. At this time he is unable to formulate a plan for attacking the problem, but instead tries one thing after another in a hit-or-miss manner. First he pushes a long pendulum with a light weight, then he swings a short pendulum with a heavy weight, and then he removes the weight entirely. Not only is his method completely slapdash, but he cannot even understand or report what has actually happened. He is convinced that his pushes make the pendulum go faster, and even though this is not so, he reports it as observed fact.

The next time Adam is faced with the pendulum, he is 11 years old and in the stage of concrete operations. His more advanced cognitive ability shows in the way he tackles the problem this time. He looks at some possible solutions, and he even hits upon a partially correct answer. But he fails to try out every possible solution in a systematic way. He varies the length of the string and the weight of the object, and he thinks that both length and weight affect the speed of the swing. But because he has varied both factors at the same time, it is impossible for him to assess the effect of either one independently of the other.

Not until Adam is confronted with the pendulum again when he is 15 years old does he attack the problem in a thorough, well-organized manner. He now realizes that any one of the four factors, or some combination of them, might affect the speed of the swing. Therefore he carefully designs an experiment to test all the possible hypotheses by varying one factor at a time while holding all the others constant. By carefully doing this, he is able to determine that one factor—the length of the string—is the only one that determines how fast the pendulum swings. (This description of age-related differences in the approach to the pendulum problem has been adapted from Ginsburg & Opper, 1979.)

Adam's last solution to the pendulum problem shows that he has arrived at the stage of formal operations, a cognitive level usually attained at about the age of 12. Adam can now think in terms of what might be true and not just in terms of what he sees in a concrete situation. Since he can imagine an infinite variety of possibilities, he is, for the first time, capable of hypothetical-deductive reasoning. Once he develops a hypothesis, he can construct a scientific experiment to test that hypothesis and to deduce whether it is true. He considers all the possible relationships that might exist and goes through them one by one, to eliminate the false and arrive at the true.

People in the stage of formal operations can apply this systematic reasoning process to all kinds of problems, from the mechanics of day-to-day living to the construction of elaborate political and philosophical theories. They can bring to bear what they have learned in the past to solve the problems of the present and to plan for the future.

What Brings About Cognitive Maturity? Inner and outer changes in the lives of adolescents combine to bring about cognitive maturation, according to Piaget: their brain structures have matured and their social environments are widening, giving them more opportunities for experimentation. Interaction between the two kinds of changes is essential: even if young people's neurological development is sufficient to allow them to reach the stage of formal reasoning, they may never attain it if they have not been encouraged by their cultural and educational environment. By the same token, children who are *guided* toward rational thinking may reach the stage of formal operations (as shown by ability to solve the pendulum problem) ear-

What determines how fast the pendulum swings—the length of the string or the weight of the object suspended from it? According to Piaget, an adolescent who has achieved the stage of formal operations can make a hypothesis and figure out a logical way to test it. In one study, however, about half of the teenage subjects and more than one-third of the adult subjects could not solve this problem.

lier than they would if they were left to discover the necessary processes on their own.

Apparently, a large proportion of American adults do not attain this stage at all. Kohlberg and Gilligan (1971) reached that conclusion on the basis of several studies of the degree of success attained by people of various ages on different tasks involving formal operations. In one experiment, 265 people were asked to solve the pendulum problem. Among 10- to 15-year-olds, 45 percent were successful; among 16- to 20-year-olds, 53 percent; among 21- to 30-year-olds, 65 percent; and among 45- to 50-year-olds, 57 percent. Anywhere from 35 percent to 43 percent of adults, then, may not reach the level of formal operations, at least as measured by the pendulum problem.

Incidentally, even though fewer 45- to 50-

year-olds solved the problem than 21- to 30-year-olds, we cannot conclude that there is a midlife decline in reasoning ability. Cross-sectional studies like this one let us see differences in performance of people who are currently in different age groups, but these studies do not tell us about any changes that may occur with age. To measure those, we would need to conduct longitudinal studies with the same subjects.

For the majority of people who *do* achieve formal operations in adolescence, the ability to think abstractly opens many new doors. Among other things, it enables them to analyze others' political and philosophical theories and to construct their own. This intellectual development has emotional ramifications: "Whereas earlier the adolescent could love his mother or hate a peer, now he can love freedom or hate exploitation. The adolescent has developed a new mode of life: the possible and the ideal captivate both mind and feeling" (Ginsburg & Opper, 1979, p. 201).

Moral Development: Kohlberg's Levels of Morality

Obviously, a person cannot have a moral code based on ideals before developing a mind that is capable of imagining ideals. In Kohlberg's theory, which we introduced in Chapter 8, moral reasoning is a function of cognitive development, and so moral development generally continues in adolescence, as the ability to think abstractly enables young people to understand universal moral principles. Of course, advanced cognition does not *guarantee* advanced morality, but—says Kohlberg—it must *exist* for moral development to take place.

Adolescents apply moral reasoning to many kinds of problems, from lofty social issues to personal life choices. Just as adolescents are not all at Piaget's stage of formal operations, they are not all at the same place on Kohlberg's moral ladder (see Table 8-4). As we pointed out in Chapter 8, in Kohlberg's view it is the reasoning underlying the conclusion a person reaches in response to a moral problem (like "Heinz's dilemma"), not the conclusion itself, that indicates the stage of development the person has

reached. Some adolescents may be found at each of Kohlberg's three levels.

Preconventional Level Some delinquents (as well as some nondelinquent adolescents and even some adults) are still at the preconventional level. They think in terms of fear of punishment or in terms of the magnitude of an act (stage 1), or they may think in terms of self-interest (stage 2)—concerns that are more characteristic of childhood thought. Preconventional adolescents might justify copying someone's answers on a test by saying that they had cheated only "a little bit," or that they needed a good grade to get into college; or they might refrain from cheating for fear of getting caught.

Conventional Level Most adolescents—like most adults—are at Kohlberg's conventional stage of moral development (level II). They conform to social conventions, are motivated to support the status quo, and think in terms of doing the right thing to please others (stage 3) or to obey the law (stage 4). A thinker at this level might be tempted to "share" answers on a test to help a friend, while another teenager at the same level would refuse because it is against the rules. Or we might imagine a teenager at level II smoking marijuana to follow the crowd, while another adolescent at level II refrains because it is against the law.

Postconventional Level Even though most adolescents are capable of abstract thought, not until young adulthood are they likely to move into Kohlberg's postconventional level of morality, in which they develop their own moral principles (as we'll see in Chapter 12). Before people can reach this level of autonomous moral thought, according to Kohlberg and Gilligan (1971), they must recognize the relative nature of moral standards; that is, they must come to understand that every society evolves its own definition of right and wrong and that the values of one culture may seem shocking to another culture. Many young people discover such cultural differences when they enter college, which explains why college students are most likely to score at the postconventional level on Kohlberg's tasks. This stress on typical influ-

If anything drives parents mad, it is adolescents' egocentrism—their refusal to take seriously views that are not their own, especially the views of authority figures. If anything maddens teenagers, it is their parents' refusal to respect their point of view. As the thought processes of these adolescents mature, they will be better able to form adult relationships.

ences of college also explains why some critics consider Kohlberg's theory elitist. Another objection, as we saw in Chapter 8, is its apparent advocacy of relativism, which some critics say can lead to moral chaos.

Research suggests that it is possible to help young people move to higher levels of moral reasoning. The most effective way to do this seems to be to give adolescents ample opportunities to talk about, interpret, and role-play moral dilemmas, and to expose them to people at a level of moral thinking slightly higher than their present one.

Egocentrism

We have seen how children develop from totally egocentric beings whose interest extends not much farther than the nipple to persons capable of solving complex problems, analyzing moral dilemmas, and envisioning ideal societies. Yet in some ways, adolescents' thought often remains oddly immature. Adolescents frequently lose touch with reality and feel that "thinking makes it so," that if they believe something strongly enough, they can make it come true without doing anything themselves. Adolescents tend to be extremely critical (especially of parents and other authority figures), argumentative, self-conscious, self-centered, indecisive, and apparently hypocritical.

Elkind (1984) describes several thought processes that underlie typical personality patterns in adolescence and reflect egocentrism. Let's consider each of these briefly.

Finding Fault with Authority Figures Young people have a new ability to imagine an ideal world. As they do so, they realize that the people they once nearly worshiped fall far short of their ideal, and they feel compelled to try to bring reality closer to fantasy by pointing out all the shortcomings they notice. Parents who do not take this criticism personally but rather look at it as a necessary stage in their teenagers' cognitive and social development will be able to answer such comments matter-of-factly, indicating that nothing—and nobody (not even a teenager!)—is perfect.

Argumentativeness Adolescents want to practice their new ability to see the many nuances in an issue. If adults encourage and take part in arguments about principles while carefully avoiding discussion of personality factors, they can help young people stretch their reasoning ability without getting embroiled in family feuding.

Self-Consciousness A boy who hears his parents whispering "knows" that they are talking about him, and a girl who passes some boys laughing raucously "knows" that they are ridiculing her. The extreme self-consciousness of young adolescents can be explained by the concept of the ***imaginary audience:*** an observer who exists only in their own minds and who is as concerned with their thoughts and behaviors as they are themselves.

Adolescents can put themselves into the mind of someone else—can think about someone else's thinking. Since they have trouble distinguishing what is interesting to them from what is interesting to someone else, however, they assume that everyone else is thinking about the same thing they are thinking about—themselves.

A study that confirmed the "existence" of the imaginary audience in early adolescence asked students in the fourth, sixth, eighth, and twelfth grades about such situations as finding a grease spot on their clothes at the beginning of the dressiest party of the year and being asked to get up in front of a class to talk. The eighth-graders—especially the girls—turned out to be more self-conscious than the older and younger students and less willing to speak to an audience (Elkind & Bowen, 1979).

The imaginary audience stays with us to a certain degree in adulthood. We may agonize over what to wear to an event, thinking that everyone else will actually care what clothes we have on—and then realize that most people are so busy thinking about the impression *they* are making that they hardly notice our carefully chosen outfit at all! Because this self-consciousness is especially agonizing in adolescence, Elkind emphasizes the importance of adults' avoiding any public criticism or ridicule of young teenagers.

Self-Centeredness The conviction that we are special, that our experience is unique—a belief that Elkind terms the ***personal fable***—is particularly strong in early adolescence. This sense of uniqueness leads young people to think that somehow they are not subject to the natural rules that govern the rest of the world. The personal fable accounts for a great deal of self-destructive behavior that occurs because teenagers think that they are magically protected from harm. A girl thinks that *she* cannot get pregnant; a boy thinks that *he* cannot get killed on the highway; youngsters who experiment with drugs think that *they* cannot become hooked. "These things happen only to other people, not to me" is the unconscious assumption that helps to explain much adolescent risk taking. Young people need to maintain their sense of specialness while developing a realistic awareness that they are not exempt from the natural order of things.

Indecisiveness Teenagers have trouble making up their minds about even the simplest things because they are suddenly aware of the multiplicity of choices in virtually every aspect of life.

Apparent Hypocrisy Young adolescents often do not recognize the difference between expressing an ideal and working toward it. Thus they can march against pollution while littering. Part of growing up involves the realization that "thinking does not make it so," that values have to be acted upon to bring about change.

As the thought processes mature, adolescents are better able to think about their own identities, to form adult relationships with other people, and to determine how and where they fit into their society. The more that adolescents talk about their personal theories and listen to those of other people, the sooner they arrive at a mature level of thinking (Looft, 1971). One place where this often happens is in high school.

HIGH SCHOOL

The first public high schools in the United States were established in the 1890s. Because there were no child labor laws, the children of poor, uneducated immigrants were flooding the factories and the streets of city slums. Crusaders against juvenile delinquency and exploitation of children were in the forefront of the movement for universal free secondary education.

Now, after a century, the movement has come to fruition. Today, almost three-fourths of young Americans earn high school diplomas, compared with about one-third in the 1930s and just over one-half in the 1950s. Since 1972, about 3 million students a year have graduated from high schools around the country. About

High school is the central organizing experience of most teenagers' intellectual and social lives. Laboratory experiments help adolescents develop their reasoning powers. Encouraging more young people to take science and math courses is part of a push for excellence in American high schools.

half of them have gone on to college or will do so, and about half of these have earned or will earn bachelor's degrees (National Center for Education Statistics, NCES, 1982, 1984).

In addition to its function of fostering intellectual development, high school is the central organizing experience in most adolescents' lives. It offers a preview of career choices and opportunities to participate in sports and get together with friends. It combines encounters with peers and encounters with a variety of adults.

The Quality of Secondary Schooling

In 1983, a national commission assessed the quality of American high schools and, after an 18-month study, gave them a failing grade. The report, which was widely publicized, found that American students' achievement compared poorly with that of students in other industrialized nations and, on the average, was lower than that of American students 26 years before. In fact, studies showed that about 13 percent of 17-year-olds (and up to 40 percent of young people in minority groups) were functionally illiterate (unable to read and write well enough to function in today's society), nearly 40 percent could not draw inferences, 80 percent could not write a persuasive essay, and about 65 percent could not solve a mathematical problem involving several steps (National Commission on Excellence in Education, 1983).

Although the commission attributed this state of affairs to several factors, including too many electives and too little homework, the roots of the problem went deeper. The decline in standards seemed to be, in part, a by-product of the democratic goal of educating an entire population through adolescence. The commission found that the average high school or college graduate today is "not as well-educated as the average graduate of 25 or 35 years ago, when a much smaller proportion of our population completed [schooling]," but the report also noted that *"the average citizen* today is better educated and more knowledgeable than the average citizen of a generation ago" (National Commission on Excellence in Education, 1983, p. 11).

The immediate result of this report and several similar reports was a greater emphasis on academic requirements. Among other improvements, there were signs of renewed interest in learning foreign languages (Maeroff, 1984).

The effort to achieve equality of educational opportunity for all young people without sacrificing educational excellence will continue to be a major task in the coming years.

Home Influences on Students' Achievement

Even though adolescents are more independent than elementary school children and are less likely to look to their parents for direct help with schoolwork, more subtle home influences still affect how well they do in school.

A survey of more than 30,000 high school

TABLE 10·5 PARENTS' INVOLVEMENT AND HIGH SCHOOL GRADES

SURVEY ITEM	SELF-REPORTED GRADES			
	MOSTLY A'S	MOSTLY B'S	MOSTLY C'S	MOSTLY D'S
Mother keeps close track of how well child does in school.	92%	89%	84%	80%
Father keeps close track of how well child does in school.	85%	79%	69%	64%
Parents almost always know child's whereabouts.	88%	81%	72%	61%
Child talks with mother or father almost every day.	75%	67%	59%	45%
Child lives in household with both parents.	80%	71%	64%	60%

Note: This table, based on a survey of more than 30,000 high school seniors, shows the percentage of students with various grade averages who gave positive answers to each survey item. In each instance, the higher the grades, the more likely the parents were to be involved with the child.

seniors in more than 1000 schools (NCES, 1985) showed that the students with the best grades tend to be those whose parents are most involved in their children's lives (see Table 10-5). This is particularly true of fathers, whose involvement is more variable than that of mothers: the less involved a father is, the worse his children fare. In this survey, 85 percent of the A students had fathers who kept close track of their school progress, while only 64 percent of D students had closely involved fathers.

Of course, these results do not prove that parents' involvement improves students' grades. The causal relationship could conceivably be the other way around: when children do well in school, their parents may take more interest in their activities. But it seems more likely that parents' involvement and concern stimulate their children to do better, a conclusion supported by many other studies (Henderson, 1987).

In addition to monitoring homework and grades, the most helpful parents appear to know what their children are doing *outside* of school. They talk with their children frequently and are available to them. Three-fourths of the youngsters with top grades had parents who talked with them almost every day, compared with only 45 percent of the D students (NCES, 1985).

What Is the Effect of Socioeconomic Status?
Many people attribute findings like those just mentioned to differences in socioeconomic sta-

tus. But in the NCES survey, the relationship between parents' influence and school grades was much the same even after socioeconomic status was taken into account—indicating that parents' involvement, not socioeconomic advantage, was the key factor.

A statistical analysis of 101 studies (K. R. White, 1982) also found that the correlation between socioeconomic status and academic achievement is much weaker than is generally assumed and that it decreases as students get older (possibly, in part, because schools are providing equalizing experiences). What does seem to make an important difference in achievement is a student's home atmosphere—for example, the amount of reading matter available, the parents' attitudes toward education, their aspirations for and academic guidance of the child, the quality of conversation and language used at home, family stability, and participation in cultural activities. Some parents of low socioeconomic status (traditionally defined by income, occupation, and education) seem able to create a home atmosphere that fosters learning, while others do not.

Varying definitions of socioeconomic status (some of which have included "home atmosphere") may be partially responsible for the misleading impression that socioeconomically advantaged children tend to do better in school. "Even though family background does have a strong relationship to achievement, it may be *how* parents rear their children . . . and not the parents' occupation, income, or education that really makes the difference" (K. R. White, 1982, p. 471).

How Do Family Relationships Affect School Performance? It is not surprising that the intellectual atmosphere of the home and the extent to which parents pay attention to their children's activities may influence children's learning. A recent study goes even further. It shows that young adolescents' school achievement or behavior may be affected by how well they get along with their parents, or even by a parent's emotional state (Forehand, Long, Brody, & Fauber, 1986).

The sample in this study consisted of 46 boys and girls, whose average age was 13½ years, and their parents. The students' achievement was measured by grade-point averages, and their behavior was rated by teachers according to a standardized checklist. Parents and students were asked to recall disagreements over such issues as cleaning up the bedroom, homework, television, and drugs, and the parents were assessed on marital conflict and depression.

The researchers found that adolescents who have intense conflict with either parent tend to act up in school. So, to a lesser extent, do those whose mothers are depressed, but not those whose fathers are depressed. On the other hand, conflict with the father seems more important than conflict with the mother. Young people who get along poorly with their fathers tend to have lower grades than those who have a better relationship with their fathers. The relationship with the mother does not influence grades; and conflict between the parents affects neither students' grades nor their school behavior.

Why is conflict with the father so upsetting to young adolescents? Perhaps it is because such conflicts arise less frequently than conflict with the mother and thus may be more disturbing when they do occur. However, the reason may be that fathers tend to become involved when grades drop, producing more conflict. In either case, these findings highlight the importance of adolescents' relationships with their fathers, which has often been ignored in previous studies.

We see, then, that what happens in one part of an adolescent's world—the family—affects another part, school.

Dropping Out

A persistent problem in a society that aims for universal education is the minority of students who do not finish high school. Students who decide to leave school before receiving a diploma make a crucial decision that reduces their opportunities. Dropping out of high school does not guarantee poverty, but dropouts do have to scramble harder to start their careers. Many employers require a high school diploma, and many jobs require the skills that come from a solid education.

Who Drops Out? More than half a million students—about 14 percent of those who were sophomores in 1980—left high school before graduation. About one-fourth of these dropped out during their sophomore year, almost half in their junior year, and the rest in their senior year. Boys were slightly more likely to drop out than girls. Among racial and ethnic groups, Asian-Americans had the lowest dropout rate (3.1 percent), followed by white students (12.2 percent), black students (17 percent), Hispanic students (18 percent), and native Americans (29.2 percent) (NCES, 1983, 1984).

Although some dropouts are gifted ("Fewer gifted," 1987), most tend to be low achievers. Sophomores who test in the lowest quartile are 6 times as likely to drop out as those in the highest quartile. There also seems to be a generational effect. The dropout rate is 3 times higher for students whose fathers did not graduate from high school than it is for those whose fathers are college graduates (NCES, 1983). (Here again, we see the influence of fathers.)

Why Do They Drop Out? The reasons dropouts give for their decision are not surprising, although they do not tell the whole story. When asked 2 years later why they had dropped out, one group of males pointed to poor grades (36 percent), not having liked school (25 percent), having been expelled or suspended (13 percent), or having had to support the family. Girls attributed dropping out to marriage or plans to marry (31 percent), feeling that "school isn't for me" (31 percent), poor grades (30 percent), pregnancy (23 percent), or a job (11 percent) (NCES, 1983).* There may, however, be other reasons underlying the stated ones. For example, more than half of the girls said that they had left school because of pregnancy or marriage. But they may have become pregnant or gotten married because they were not doing well or were not interested in school. Some researchers have attributed dropping out to such factors as a lack of motivation and self-esteem, minimal encouragement of education by parents, teachers' low expectations of students, and disciplinary problems at home and at school (Rule, 1981). And some have pointed out that many youngsters who drop out after doing poorly in high school have been set up for failure earlier in their school careers—perhaps as early as kindergarten or first grade.

What Happens to Dropouts? Dropouts have trouble getting jobs. In 1982, twenty-seven percent of male high school dropouts and 31 percent of female high school dropouts were looking for work (32 percent of the young women were not looking for work because they were full-time homemakers). Among those who were working, typical jobs were waiting on tables, doing manual labor, doing factory work, working as a clerk in a store, baby-sitting, doing clerical work, and working on a farm. More than half the dropouts regretted leaving school very soon after they did so, and a small percentage took part in educational programs (NCES, 1983).

How Can Dropping Out Be Prevented? In view of parents' crucial role in encouraging school achievement, current efforts to keep adolescents in school focus on family involvement. Most low-income parents care about their children's future; but they are often poorly educated themselves and may suffer from low self-esteem, just like their children. They tend not to understand how schools function and what is expected of their children. Influenced by their own negative experiences, they tend to be suspi-

cious of school personnel and to believe that school officials "look down on them" (Rioux, 1987). Such parents need guidance on how to go to bat for their children and how to make sure that they get the help they need.

The National Committee for Citizens in Education has established a dropout prevention center with a toll-free hot line (1–800–NETWORK). Callers get advice on helping students who face suspension, expulsion, reduction of grades, or withholding of credit because of absences—actions that cause students to fall farther behind and thus increase the likelihood that they will become frustrated and drop out.

It seems clear that the best way to prevent dropping out is to attack the factors that make young people do poorly in school and lose confidence in their abilities.

DEVELOPING A CAREER

"What are you going to be when you grow up?" This is something children ask each other almost from the time they are old enough to form the question. And it is something most adolescents ask themselves with more urgency as the high school years come to an end.

Stages in Vocational Planning

At the age of 6, Julie wanted to be an astronaut. By the time she was 12 years old, she realized that mathematics and science were her worst subjects and she would never make it into the space program. At 15, after doing some volunteer work at a hospital, she decided that she would like to help other people, possibly as a psychiatrist. But by her senior year in high school, she had given up the idea of medical school and instead was applying to colleges that offered 5-year programs leading to a master's degree in social work.

Julie's progression of goals was fairly typical. It followed three classic stages in career planning: the *fantasy* period, the *tentative* period, and the *realistic* period (Ginzberg et al., 1951). During the fantasy period, which corresponds roughly to the elementary school years, choices are active and exciting rather than realistic, and decisions are emotional rather than practical.

---

*The figures total more than 100 percent because the respondents could give more than one reason for dropping out of school.

The tentative period, which comes about the time of puberty, ushers in a somewhat more realistic effort to match interests with abilities and values. By the end of high school, students are in the realistic stage and can plan for the right education to meet their career requirements.

Many in late adolescence, however, are still not realistic in making educational and career plans. In one study, more than 6000 high school seniors in Texas were asked to name their top three career choices and to report on their educational plans. They were also asked about their preferred vocational styles—working alone or with others; working indoors or outdoors; and working with people, things, or ideas.

At a time in their lives when they had to make crucial choices about education and work, these students showed very limited knowledge about occupations. Not surprisingly, they tended to know more about their first choice and increasingly less about the next two. But even of those who felt that they had a good understanding of their first career choice, only about half planned to get the appropriate amount of education. Some seemed bent on schooling that would leave them overeducated for their chosen career and others were not planning on getting enough training. Furthermore, most of the students did not seem to be making good matches between their career choices and their own interests (Grotevant & Durrett, 1980).

Their career choices did appear to be somewhat related to market conditions. In 1972, nearly 11 percent of students aimed to become teachers; by 1980, fewer than 4 percent expressed that ambition, most likely reflecting awareness of conditions that made the teaching profession relatively unattractive. Meanwhile, the proportion of young people planning careers in business, where more financial opportunity existed, jumped from 13 percent in 1972 to nearly 24 percent in 1980. Still, more than 50 percent of the seniors in the latter year hoped for professional and technical careers at a time when such positions constituted less than 13 percent of the labor force—suggesting that adolescents' ambitions and expectations were less realistic than they might be (Grotevant & Durrett, 1980). Not until college or even later do many young people have a truly realistic picture of their career goals.

Reading the want ads is one way for a teenager to learn which jobs are most plentiful and which pay well. Many high school and college students have unrealistic career goals because of unawareness of market conditions that make some kinds of work more attractive than others.

Influences on Vocational Planning

How do adolescents make career choices? Many factors enter in, including individual ability and personality; education; socioeconomic, racial, or ethnic background; societal values; and the accident of particular life experiences.

One life experience which is often thought to have a positive effect on adolescents' vocational planning is part-time work. However, as we note in Box 10-3 (page 370), part-time work actually seems to be fairly useless as preparation for a career, and it may be harmful to high school students' academic achievement.

Two other important influences on vocational planning are parents and gender. Let's consider each of these.

Parents Parents' encouragement and financial support influence their children's aspirations and achievement. If parents do not encourage children to pursue higher education and do not help them financially, it is much harder for the children. Some work their way through school, take out loans, or win scholarships.

Parents' encouragement is a better predictor

BOX 10-3 FOOD FOR THOUGHT

IS PART-TIME WORK GOOD FOR ADOLESCENTS?

Many adults would give a quick, unqualified "yes" to the question "Does work help adolescent development?" They would probably come up with a raft of reasons: for example, paid work teaches young people to handle money responsibly and helps them develop good work habits, and it helps to guide them in choosing a career.

According to recent research, however, this conventional wisdom is mistaken. Work seems to be of little benefit to teenagers' educational, social, or occupational development (Greenberger & Steinberg, 1986).

A greater proportion of teenage students are working today than at any other time in the past 25 years—about half of all high school juniors and seniors, and almost one-third of ninth- and tenth-graders (S. Cole, 1980). Some adolescents work because their families need the income, and others because they want the independence that comes from earning their own money.

Yet it turns out that teenagers who work are no more independent in making financial decisions or other decisions than their classmates who do not hold jobs (Greenberger & Steinberg, 1986). Most students who work part time do not learn the kinds of skills that will be useful later in life (Hamilton & Crouter, 1980), and those who work during high school are not likely to earn any more money afterward than they would if they did not hold jobs during high school (Greenberger & Steinberg, 1986).

Moreover, work seems to undermine performance in high school, especially for teenagers who put in more than 15 or 20 hours of work per week. Their grades, their involvement in school, and their attendance decline. Thus, the experience gained by working is offset by the reduced school experience.

And there are other hidden costs. Some teenage workers spend the money they earn on alcohol or drugs, develop cynical attitudes toward working, and cheat or steal from their employers. Working teenagers tend to spend less time with their families and feel less close to them. Furthermore, they have little contact with adults on the job, and they are usually exposed to gender-stereotyped occupational roles (Greenberger & Steinberg, 1986).

Some of these undesirable tendencies may be caused not by working itself but by the factors that motivate some teenagers to take jobs—in particular, those teenagers who are already uninterested in school, alienated from their families, and prone to drink or take drugs whenever they can afford to. In any case, working does not seem to help such young people manage their lives any better.

Some teenagers, of course, do gain from work: they learn how to manage money and time, how to find employment, and how to get along with a variety of people. But because the kinds of jobs teenagers can get are usually of a menial, dead-end nature, unrelated to their life goals, work experience generally proves to be less beneficial than a solid academic foundation.

of high ambition than social class. When 2622 sixth-, eighth-, tenth-, and twelfth-grade black students and white students from all social strata were asked to describe their own expectations for their education and their fathers' and mothers' expectations for them, more than half the students agreed with the perceived goals of each parent. A greater level of agreement existed between student and mother than between student and father, possibly because of the greater amount of time that women have traditionally spent with their children (T. E. Smith, 1981).

What about the parents' own careers? How weighty is their influence? A review of the literature found that a man's occupation influences his son's career choices, but not his daughter's

(Conger & Peterson, 1984). Werts (1966, 1968), for example, found that 43.6 percent of doctors' sons chose to enter medicine, that 27.7 percent of attorneys' sons opted for the law themselves, and that the sons of physical and social scientists were similarly influenced in their career choices. Newer research indicates that college-educated daughters of working mothers have higher career aspirations and achieve more in their careers than daughters of homemakers (L. Hoffman, 1979).

Gender A woman who entered engineering school at Ohio State University in 1945 was one of six females in her class. Some 35 years later, about 30 percent of the entering class were women (R. D. Feldman, 1982).

Although traditional gender-typing in occupational choice has broken down to a great extent, gender still has an influence. For example, even though boys' edge over girls in mathematical prowess is very small and has been found not to show up until about the age of 12 (see Chapter 7), many adolescent girls shy away from courses in mathematics and science and from occupations that require those skills (Matlin, 1987).

Larger differences between boys and girls have appeared among mathematically gifted seventh- and eighth-grade students who took the mathematics portion of the Scholastic Aptitude Test (SAT). About twice as many boys as girls scored above 500; and about 13 times as many boys as girls scored above 700—a level that is attained by only about 1 in 10,000 students (Benbow & Stanley, 1980, 1983). Benbow and Stanley suggest that the differences in male and female performance were due to biological factors; other researchers believe that they may reflect differences in socialization, attitudes, and experience with mathematics, or that differences in mathematical ability may be related to the spatial nature of many mathematical problems (Matlin, 1987).

Researchers who have analyzed cognitive gender differences in detail have found that these differences do not go across an entire field but apply to *specific* skills (Deaux, 1985). While boys are better at algebra, girls are just as good as boys at arithmetic and geometry and better than boys at computation (Becker, 1983; Marshall, 1984). Boys can visualize an object better from different angles, but girls do just as well as boys at analysis and reasoning (Linn & Petersen, 1985).

Evidence of the role that socialization and training can play is that in the past 20 years, since attitudes toward gender differences began changing, the gap between males and females in verbal, mathematical, and spatial skills has narrowed significantly (Deaux, 1985). Thus parents and teachers should not assume that adolescents of one sex or the other lack specific abilities in any cognitive area. Nor should young people of either sex be discouraged from pursuing career goals typically chosen by members of the other sex. It does not matter whether most boys are better at mathematics or most girls at writing—it is how well a particular boy writes or how well a particular girl solves mathematical problems that will affect the boy's or the girl's chances of success in the chosen field.

The choice of a career is closely tied in with a central personality issue during adolescence: the continuing effort to define the self, to discover and mold an identity. The question "Who shall I be?" is very close to "What shall I do?" If we pick a career that we feel is worth doing and one that we can do well, we feel good about ourselves. On the contrary, if we feel that it wouldn't matter to anyone whether we did our work or not, or if we feel that we're not very good at it, the very core of our emotional well-being can be threatened.

How adolescents' sense of identity develops will be discussed in Chapter 11, along with other personality and social issues.

Maturation in Adolescence: Pubescence to Puberty

■ Adolescence is a period of transition between childhood and adulthood. It begins with pubescence, a period of rapid physical growth and sexual maturation. Pubescence lasts about 2 years, ending in puberty, the point at which a person is sexually mature and able to reproduce.

■ The end of adolescence is not clear-cut in western societies, since no single sign indicates that adulthood has been reached. In some nonwestern cultures, adulthood is regarded as beginning at puberty and is signified by puberty rites, which take a variety of forms.

■ The term *secular trend* means a trend that can be observed over several generations. A secular trend toward earlier attainment of adult height and sexual maturity began about 100 years ago, probably because of improvements in living standards; it seems to have ended in the United States.

■ Dramatic physiological changes mark adolescence.

1 Both sexes undergo an adolescent growth spurt: sharp growth in height, weight, and muscular and skeletal development.

2 Primary sex characteristics are the characteristics directly related to reproduction, namely, the female and male reproductive organs. These enlarge and mature during pubescence.

3 The secondary sex characteristics include the breasts in females, the broadened shoulders in males, and the adult voices, skin, and growth of body hair characteristic of men and women.

4 Menarche in females occurs at an average age of 12½ in the United States. Males experience sperm in their urine and nocturnal emissions.

■ An adolescent's rapid body changes and physical appearance affect self-concept and personality. The effect of early or late maturing is particularly pronounced during adolescence but generally disappears in adulthood.

■ Girls adjust better to menarche if they are prepared for it with accurate information.

Health Concerns

■ Adolescents are generally in good health. Eighty percent of deaths in this group are due to accidents, homicide, and suicide. However, health problems such as anorexia nervosa and bulimia, drug and alcohol abuse, and sexually transmitted diseases affect a sizable number of adolescents.

Aspects of Intellectual Development in Adolescence

■ Many adolescents attain Piaget's stage of formal operations, which is characterized by the ability to think abstractly.

1 People in the stage of formal operations can engage in hypothetical-deductive reasoning. They can think in terms of possibilities, deal flexibly with problems, and test hypotheses.

2 Since experience plays a more important part in the attainment of this cognitive stage than in that of previous Piagetian stages, not all people become capable of formal operations.

■ Most adolescents are at Kohlberg's conventional level (stages 3 and 4) of moral development. However, some young people in adolescence are at the preconventional stage and some are at the postconventional stage.

■ Although the adolescent is not egocentric in the sense that a younger child is, adolescents show egocentric tendencies. These include finding fault with authority figures, argumentativeness, self-consciousness, self-centeredness, indecisiveness, and apparent hypocrisy.

High School

■ With the achievement of virtually universal secondary education in the United States, high school is the central organizing experience—intellectually and otherwise—in the lives of most adolescents.

■ Efforts are being made to improve the quality of American high schools.

■ Home atmosphere, parents' involvement, and

family relationships appear to make more difference than socioeconomic status in how well children do in school.

■ Although most adolescents in the United States graduate from high school, some half a million students who were sophomores in 1980 dropped out before graduating. Efforts are being made to prevent dropping out by advising potential dropouts and by attacking the underlying causes.

Developing a Career

■ The search for identity is closely linked to vocational choice, which is influenced by several factors, including gender and parents' attitudes.

■ A greater number of adolescents are working today than at any time in the past 25 years. However, work seems to have little benefit for a teenager's educational, social, or occupational development.

KEY TERMS

adolescent growth spurt (page 346)
anorexia nervosa (352)
bulimia (353)
formal operations (360)
imaginary audience (364)

menarche (348)
personal fable (364)
primary sex characteristics (347)
puberty (342, 344)
pubescence (344)

secondary sex characteristics (347)
secular trend (346)
sexually transmitted (venereal) diseases (STDs) (356)

SUGGESTED READINGS

Boston Women's Health Book Collective. (1984). *The new our bodies, ourselves.* New York: Simon & Schuster. An absorbing discussion of a variety of topics concerning women and their bodies.

Colman, W. (1988). *Understanding and preventing AIDS.* Chicago: Children's Press. A detailed, profusely illustrated overview for teenagers and parents, including profiles of AIDS patients, a history of the epidemiology of AIDS, and a discussion of the immune system and how the AIDS virus attacks it.

Elkind, D. (1984). *All grown up and no place to go.* Reading, MA: Addison-Wesley. A thought-provoking book about the difficulties today of being a teenager and raising teenagers. Elkind argues that teenagers today are unprepared for the adult challenges they are asked to face, and so they exhibit many problem behaviors. The chapter relating formal operational thinking abilities to behaviors such as self-centeredness, self-

consciousness, and argumentativeness is outstanding.

Greenberger, E., & Steinberg, L. (1986). *When teenagers work.* New York: Basic Books. An absorbing and controversial analysis of research on the impact that working has on teenagers. The authors conclude that working during the teens entails a number of hidden costs that affect development negatively.

Inhelder, B., & Piaget, J. (1958). *The growth of logical thinking from childhood to adolescence.* Boston: Little, Brown. A classic account of Piaget's research written with his longtime collaborator Barbel Inhelder. The book traces cognitive development through its four stages.

Landau, E. (1983). *Why are they starving themselves?* New York: Messner. A practical guide to understanding anorexia nervosa and bulimia that includes numerous case studies and information about where to get help.

11

CHAPTER

PERSONALITY AND SOCIAL DEVELOPMENT IN ADOLESCENCE

It confuses the sprouting adolescent to wake up every morning in a new body. It confuses the mother and father to find a new child every day in a familiar body.

> Donald Barr, "What Did
> We Do Wrong?" 1967

ASK YOURSELF

■ How do different theories explain the development of personality in adolescence?

■ How do adolescents search for their identity?

■ How inevitable is the "adolescent rebellion," and how are adolescents' attitudes and behavior influenced by parents and peers?

■ What sexual practices and attitudes are current among adolescents?

■ What are the causes and consequences of teenage pregnancy and juvenile delinquency?

■ What are some special personality strengths of adolescents?

A central question in the drama of adolescence is, "Who am I?" The theme of these years—and a major theme for years to come—is the search for identity: what makes each person an individual unlike any other who has ever lived or will ever live.

The question "Who am I?" begins to form in infancy, when babies first discover their separateness from their mothers. Tentative answers gather as children learn the boundaries of self, shed much of their egocentric thinking, and size up their skills and values in the mirror of the peer group.

The quest for selfhood crests in adolescence, when physical, cognitive, and social and emotional development reach a peak. At the age of 15, for example, Meredith has the body of a woman. Now capable of adult sexual behavior and of advanced problem solving, she knows that she will soon be responsible for her own life. How will she choose to live it? What kind of work will she do? What decisions will she make

about sexual relationships and other relationships? What beliefs and values will she live by?

These are not easy choices, and they are often accompanied by emotional turmoil. Identity and intimacy are two of the preoccupations that underlie teenagers' alternating high and low spirits. Nor is their children's adolescence an easy time for parents. As adolescents try their wings, they are often as erratic and unpredictable as birds taking their first flights from the nest. They chafe at the ties that bind them to the older generation, often seeing mothers and fathers not as helpful but as inhibiting. Yet while teenagers look to their peers as companions in the struggle for independence, they still turn to their parents at important times for guidance and emotional support.

In this chapter, we first examine some fundamental issues of personality development in adolescence from the perspectives of theory and research. We discuss relationships with peers and parents and how adolescents come to terms with their sexuality. Next we turn to the serious problems of teenage pregnancy and juvenile delinquency. Finally, we sum up some of the special strengths of adolescents.

UNDERSTANDING PERSONALITY DEVELOPMENT

Theoretical Perspectives

What accounts for the emotional ups and downs of adolescence? Why do teenagers often come into conflict with adults? How do young people emerge from this period as unique, mature personalities? Many theories offer explanations about the nature of adolescence. Here are several of the important theories.

G. Stanley Hall ("Storm and Stress")   Hall, the first psychologist to formulate a theory of adolescence, proposed that the major physical changes of adolescence cause major psychological changes (Hall, 1904/1916). He believed that young people's efforts to adjust to their changing bodies ushered in a period of *storm and stress.* Hall saw adolescence as a period of intense, fluctuating emotions, from which young people may emerge morally stronger. Hall's view of adolescence as an invariably stormy period of life has been accepted by many observers of young people and hotly contested by others.

Sigmund Freud: The Genital Stage   Freud's psychosexual theory, like Hall's, views conflict as a result of the physical changes of adolescence. In Freud's view, this conflict is preparatory to the *genital stage,* the stage of mature adult sexuality.

According to Freud, the physiological changes of puberty reawaken the *libido,* the basic energy source that fuels the sex drive. The sexual urges of the earlier phallic stage—urges that go "underground" during the latency period of middle childhood—resurface. In the genital stage, sexual energy flows in socially approved channels, which Freud defined as heterosexual relations with partners outside the person's family.

Before adolescents can complete the transi-

"Who am I?" is the major question of adolescence, as young people pursue the search for identity and ponder their life choices.

tion to the genital stage, they must overcome their unresolved sexual feelings toward the mother or father. In what Freud called a *reaction formation*—a defense mechanism (see Chapter 1) in which a person expresses feelings opposite to his or her real feelings—sexual attachment is replaced by temporary hostility. Thus, in Freud's view, the onset of adolescence sets the stage for storm and stress within the family, part of the phenomenon known as *adolescent rebellion.* (As we'll see later in this chapter, such rebellion is not inevitable.)

In freeing themselves from sexual dependency upon the other-sex parent, Freud said, young adolescents typically go through a "homosexual" stage, which may take the form of excessive admiration of an adult of the same sex or a close friendship with another young person. Such a relationship is a forerunner of mature relationships with persons of the other sex.

Another transition of adolescence, according

to Freud, is the change in sexuality, from a desire for pure pleasure to a mature drive with the goal of reproduction. The need to masturbate becomes more urgent in early adolescence, preparing the young person for eventual sexual release with a partner; after this is achieved, masturbatory needs diminish. Girls (said Freud) need to switch from the immature clitoral orgasm (obtained from masturbation) to the mature vaginal orgasm (achieved in sexual intercourse) (S. Freud, 1925/1959, 1953).

Challenges to the latter aspects of Freud's theory have arisen from contemporary research. Masturbation does *not* decline with age and sexual experience. On the contrary, adolescents 16 years of age and older are more likely to masturbate than those who are under 16, and nonvirgins are more likely to masturbate than virgins (Sorensen, 1973). Furthermore, the clitoral orgasm, rather than being a leftover from childhood, characterizes the sexual response of many normal, well-adjusted adult women (Masters & Johnson, 1966).

Anna Freud: Ego Defenses of Adolescence

To Sigmund Freud, the psychosexual changes of adolescence represented the playing out of a drama begun in early childhood. His daughter, the psychoanalyst Anna Freud, places more emphasis on the adolescent years themselves and their contribution to character formation. According to Anna Freud (1946), the reactivated libido threatens the delicate balance of ego and id, which quieted the latency years. The resultant anxiety calls forth such ego defense mechanisms as intellectualization and asceticism.

Intellectualization—translation of sexual impulses into abstract thought—may be seen in adolescents' predilection for all-night discussions of religion, politics, and the meaning of life. Although other investigators relate these "bull sessions" to adolescents' search for identity or to their increased ability to deal with abstract thought, Anna Freud considers such intellectual speculations a defense because (she says) young people are not trying to solve real problems but are manipulating words and ideas to respond to instinctual needs of their changing bodies.

Anna Freud sees *asceticism* (self-denial) as a defense against adolescents' fear of losing control over their impulses. Because of this fear, some adolescents may overcontrol themselves by renouncing such simple pleasures as favorite foods or attractive clothing. Later in life, Anna Freud says, as people gain confidence in their ability to control their dangerous impulses, they tend to relax and to be less strict with themselves.

Margaret Mead: The Cultural Factor

Margaret Mead, an anthropologist who studied adolescence in the South Pacific islands of Samoa (1928) and New Guinea (1935), concluded that the way a culture handles the changes of adolescence determines the nature of the transition. In Samoa, for example, Mead observed no "storm and stress" but a serene, gradual transition from childhood to adulthood and an easy acceptance of the adult role. She concluded that when a society permits children to see adult sexual activity and to engage in sex play, to watch babies being born and to be intimately aware of death, to do important work, to exhibit assertive and even dominant behavior, and to know precisely what they will be expected to do as adults, adolescence is relatively stress-free. In societies like our own, however, the shift from childhood to adulthood is much more discontinuous and, as a result, much more stressful, according to Mead.

Mead's work on Samoa was recently criticized by D. Freeman (1983), who claimed that adolescence there is indeed tumultuous and stressful. Other analyses have defended Mead's findings (L. D. Holmes, 1987). In any case, the controversy, coming nearly 60 years after Mead's fieldwork, done in 1925, has had a muted impact. By 1983, storm and stress was no longer considered inevitable even for adolescents in the United States, as we shall see.

Erik Erikson: Crisis 5—Identity versus Identity Confusion

Erikson's fifth crisis reflects the struggles of his own youth. After completing his education, Erikson wandered around Europe, unsure of what career to follow. After trying painting and wood carving, he accepted an offer to teach art at a private school in Vienna for children whose parents were undergoing analysis at Freud's Psychoanalytic Institute, and the association with Freud led to Erikson's eventual decision to become a psychoanalyst. Then, as an immigrant to the United States, Erikson had a second "identity crisis." He later found evidence of similar crises in his work with adolescents and adults (see Chapter 1).

According to Erikson (1968), the chief task of adolescence is to resolve the conflict of *identity versus identity confusion.* The desirable outcome is a sense of oneself as a unique human being with a meaningful role to play in society. The active agent of identity formation is the ego, which puts together its knowledge of the person's abilities, needs, and desires and of what must be done to adapt to the social environment.

The search for identity is a lifelong search, which comes into focus during adolescence and may recur from time to time during adulthood. Erikson emphasizes that this effort to make sense of the self and the world is a healthy, vital process that contributes to the ego strength of the adult. The conflicts that are involved in the process serve to spur growth and development.

There are many aspects of the search for identity. One of the most significant during adolescence is deciding on a career. In the previous stage, that of *industry versus inferiority,* a child acquires the skills needed for success in the culture. Adolescents need to find ways to use these skills. Rapid physical growth and new genital maturity alert young people to their impending adulthood, and they begin to wonder about their roles in adult society.

Erikson sees the prime danger of this stage as identity (or role) confusion, which can express itself in a young person's taking an excessively long time to reach adulthood. (Erikson did not resolve his own youthful identity crisis until he was in his mid-twenties.) However, a certain amount of identity confusion is normal and (according to Erikson) accounts for the chaotic, volatile nature of much adolescent behavior, as well as teenagers' self-consciousness about their appearance.

Cliquishness and intolerance of differences— both hallmarks of the adolescent social scene— are defenses against identity confusion, according to Erikson. Adolescents may also express their confusion by regressing into childishness to avoid resolving conflicts or by committing themselves impulsively to poorly thought out

(© David W. Hamilton/Image Bank)

Adolescent infatuation, according to Erik Erikson, is an important route to self-discovery. As they express their most intimate thoughts and feelings to each other, adolescent sweethearts see themselves reflected in the mirror of the loved one and are better able to clarify their own identities.

courses of action. Unlike Anna Freud, however, Erikson does not claim that ideological commitment is an irrelevant defense mechanism. During the *psychosocial moratorium* (Erikson, 1950, p. 262), or "time out" period that adolescence and youth provide, many young people's efforts focus on a search for commitments to which they can be faithful. These commitments are both ideological and personal, and the extent to which young people can be true to them determines their ability to resolve the crisis of this stage.

Thus the fundamental "virtue" that arises from the identity crisis is the *virtue of fidelity*— sustained loyalty, faith, or a sense of belonging to friends and companions, to a loved one, or to a set of values, an ideology, a religion, a movement, or an ethnic group. Such an identification emerges from selective affirmation and repudiation of the identifications with which the child has grown up. Fidelity represents a higher level of the virtue of trust, developed in infancy: not only the capacity to trust others and oneself, but the capacity to be trustworthy. Also, trust is now transferred from the parents to other mentors and leaders. According to Erikson, failure to achieve fidelity results in such common adolescent attitudes as diffidence and defiance.

Erikson sees infatuation between adolescents as an avenue toward identity. By becoming intimate with another person and sharing thoughts and feelings, the adolescent offers up his or her own tentative identity, sees it reflected in the loved one, and is better able to clarify the self.

Adolescent intimacies differ from true intimacy, which involves commitment, sacrifice, and compromise and which (according to Erikson) cannot take place until after the achievement of a stable identity. (See Chapter 13 for a discussion of intimacy in young adulthood.) This sequence, however, pertains only to males. Females, in Erikson's view, achieve identity and intimacy at the same time: an adolescent girl puts identity issues aside for the time being as she prepares to identify with the man she will marry. Erikson's scheme, then, like Freud's, takes the male's development as the norm.

Some recent research explores differences between identity development in males and in females, and expands and clarifies Erikson's theory of identity formation as well. Let's see what that research tells us.

Research on Identity

Kate, Mark, Nicholas, and Andrea are all about to graduate from high school. Kate has weighed her interests and talents and has settled on her career choice—music therapy. After carefully researching colleges, she has applied to three that offer good programs. Mark knows exactly what he is going to do: his parents have always assumed that he would go into the family business, and he has never given much thought to doing anything else. Nicholas has no idea of what he wants to do, but he is not worried. He figures that he will go to college, have a good time, and see what happens. Andrea has not yet made a decision about her life goals and is agonizing over them. She thinks that she may be interested in something having to do with science, but she is torn between a premedical program and engineering school.

All four young people are involved in identity formation, yet the process—like the result—is different for each. What accounts for the differences?

Identity States The most prominent researcher on identity issues during adolescence is the psychologist James E. Marcia. Marcia defines identity as "an internal, self-constructed, dynamic organization of drives, abilities, beliefs, and individual history" (1980, p. 159). In research based on Erikson's theory, he has identified four identity states, or statuses, and has correlated them with other aspects of personality, such as anxiety, self-esteem, moral reasoning, and patterns of social behavior. These states are not *stages* in the identity search, since they do not form a progression; but they are not necessarily permanent. A person's identity status may change as he or she continues to develop (Marcia, 1979).

Marcia's four identity states (see Table 11-1) are determined by the presence or absence of the two elements which, according to Erikson, are crucial to forming identity: crisis and commitment. By *crisis,* Marcia means a period of conscious decision making, and he defines *commitment* as a personal investment in an occupation or a system of beliefs (ideology). To evaluate a person's identity status, Marcia (1966) developed a semistructured 30-minute interview (see Table 11-2 for sample questions and answers). On the basis of a person's answers, he or she is classified in one of the following four categories:

1 *Identity achievement* (crisis leading to commitment): People (like Kate) in this category have spent a great deal of time actively

TABLE 11-1 CRITERIA FOR IDENTITY STATUSES		
	POSITION ON OCCUPATION AND IDEOLOGY	
IDENTITY STATUS	CRISES (PERIOD OF CONSIDERING ALTERNATIVES)	COMMITMENT (ADHERENCE TO A PATH OF ACTION)
Identity achievement	Present	Present
Foreclosure	Absent	Present
Identity diffusion	Present or absent	Absent
Moratorium	In crisis	Present but vague

Source: Adapted from Marcia, 1980.

TABLE 11-2 IDENTITY-STATUS INTERVIEW

SAMPLE QUESTIONS	TYPICAL ANSWERS FOR THE FOUR STATUSES
About occupational commitment: "How willing do you think you'd be to give up going into ___ if something better came along?"	*Identity achievement.* "Well, I might, but I doubt it. I can't see what 'something better' would be for me." *Foreclosure.* "Not very willing. It's what I've always wanted to do. The folks are happy with it and so am I." *Identity diffusion.* "Oh sure. If something better came along, I'd change just like that." *Moratorium.* "I guess that if I knew for sure, I could answer that better. It would have to be something in the general area—something related. . . ."
About ideological commitment: "Have you ever had any doubts about your religious beliefs?"	*Identity achievement.* "Yes, I even started wondering whether there is a god. I've pretty much resolved that now, though. The way it seems to me is . . ." *Foreclosure.* "No, not really; our family is pretty much in agreement on these things." *Identity diffusion.* "Oh, I don't know. I guess so. Everyone goes through some sort of stage like that. But it really doesn't bother me much. I figure that one religion is about as good as another!" *Moratorium.* "Yes, I guess I'm going through that now. I just don't see how there can be a god and still so much evil in the world or . . ."

Source: Adapted from Marcia, 1966.

thinking about the important issues in their lives (that is, they have gone through the crisis period), they have made crucial choices, and they now express strong commitment to those choices. Identity achievers are characterized by *flexible strength:* they tend to be thoughtful, but not so introspective that they cannot do anything. They have a sense of humor, function well under stress, are capable of intimate relationships, and are open to new ideas while maintaining their own standards.

2 *Foreclosure* (commitment without crisis): People (like Mark) who are in the state of foreclosure have made commitments, but instead of considering alternative choices (going through crisis), they have accepted other people's plans for their lives. She becomes a devoutly religious homemaker because her mother was one, or he becomes a farmer and a Republican because his father was both of these. Foreclosures are characterized by *rigid strength:* they tend to be happy and self-assured, sometimes smug and self-satisfied, and to have a strong sense of family ties. They believe in law and order, like to follow a strong leader, and become dogmatic when their ideas are threatened.

3 *Identity diffusion* (no commitment): People (like Nicholas) in identity diffusion may or may not have gone through a period of considering alternatives (crisis), but in either case they have made no commitments. They may be either seemingly carefree people who have actively avoided commitment or aimless floaters. Drifting and centerless, they tend to be superficial or unhappy and often lonely because they have no genuinely intimate relationships.

4 *Moratorium* (in crisis): People (like Andrea) in moratorium are in a stage of ambivalent struggle. Currently in the process of making decisions, they seem to be heading for commitment and will probably achieve identity. They tend to be lively, talkative, and in conflict. They are close to the parent of the other sex and are competitive and anxious. They want intimacy and understand what it involves but are not necessarily in intimate relationships.

Gender Differences in Identity Formation

Freudian theory is based on the belief that biology is destiny. Psychologists today are more likely to emphasize the role of socialization in the formation of identity. Whatever the reasons, there are differences between the sexes in the struggle to define identity. Although early theorists like Freud and Erikson saw different paths toward identity development in males and females, only in recent years have researchers given much attention to the female's quest for identity.

Carol Gilligan (1982) has studied women in several contexts and has concluded that women define themselves less in terms of their achievement of a separate identity and more in terms of relationships with other people. They judge themselves on their responsibilities and on their ability to care for others as well as for themselves. They achieve identity less through competitive striving and more through cooperative effort.

Marcia (1979) modified his original interviews to plumb issues of female identity. One of the changes was the addition of questions about attitudes toward premarital intercourse, women's roles, and lifestyles. The results were surprising. Whereas the men in moratorium most closely resembled those who had achieved identity, the women who appeared closest to achieving identity were those in foreclosure.

Marcia surmised that because women are under pressure to uphold and transmit the values of society, *stability* of identity is so important for them that it is just as adaptive for them to achieve identity early in life without much effort on their own part as it is for them to struggle to forge their own identity. Marcia also maintains that women do not wait to develop the capacity for intimacy until after they have achieved identity, as in Erikson's male-based pattern, but that for them identity and intimacy develop together. This conclusion seems to build on other research indicating that intimacy is more important for girls than for boys, even in grade-school friendships (Cooke, 1979).

Part of the difference in male and female patterns may be due to different treatment of the sexes by parents. Several studies have found different child-rearing patterns to be associated with different identity statuses (Marcia, 1980).

An essential aspect of the search for identity is the need to assert independence of parental control, and an important arena for that search is the peer group. Let's examine adolescents' relationships with their parents and peers before taking a closer look at the development of sexual identity, which is related to both.

ASPECTS OF PERSONALITY DEVELOPMENT IN ADOLESCENCE

Relationships with Parents and Peers

The storm and stress that is sometimes associated with the teenage years in the United States and other western cultures has been called the **adolescent rebellion**—a rebellion that may encompass not only conflict within the family but a general alienation from adult society and hostility toward its values. Yet studies of adolescents typically find that fewer than 1 out of 5 fit the "classical" picture of the tumultuous teens (Offer & Offer, 1974).

Age does become a powerful bonding agent in adolescence—more powerful than race, religion, community, or sex. American teenagers spend much of their free time with people their own age, with whom they feel comfortable and can identify. They have their best times with their friends, feeling free, open, involved, excited, and motivated when with them; thus it is not surprising that these are the people they most want to be with. Young people are caught up in a "generational chauvinism": they tend to believe that most other adolescents share their personal values while most older people do not (Csikszentmihalyi & Larson, 1984; Sorensen, 1973).

Nevertheless, the rejection of the parents' values is often partial, temporary, or superficial. Teenagers' values remain closer to their parents' than many people realize, and the "adolescent rebellion" is often little more than a series of minor skirmishes.

Conflict with Parents Many young people do feel a constant conflict between wanting to break away from their parents and realizing how dependent they really are on them. The adolescent must give up the childhood identification of "the Smiths' little boy" or "the Browns' little girl" and establish a separate identity while

(Drawing by Ziegler; © 1985 The New Yorker Magazine, Inc.)

"While we're at supper, Billy, you'd make Daddy and Mommy very happy if you'd remove your hat, your sunglasses, and your earring."

Some adolescents feel the need to make Daddy and Mommy very unhappy by flaunting their rejection of their parents' behavioral standards and values. But although the search for a distinct identity is a vital part of adolescence, many teenagers can achieve separation from their parents without going to flamboyant extremes.

at the same time retaining ties with parents and family (Siegel, 1982).

Adolescents' ambivalent feelings are often matched by their parents' own ambivalence. Torn between wanting their children to be independent and wanting to keep them dependent, parents often find it hard to let go. As a result, parents may give teenage children "double messages," saying one thing but communicating just the opposite by their actions. One longitudinal study of 27 adolescent boys found that the conflict is particularly strong for the mother, who finds herself losing authority and power (Steinberg, 1981).

Still, one survey of the literature on conflict between parents and adolescents suggests that minor bickering is more typical than major battling. The survey—which summarizes its conclusions in its subtitle, "All Families Some of the Time and Some Families Most of the Time"— points out that conflict between parents and teenagers is normal and healthy (Montemayor, 1983). Most of the studies (which go back more than 50 years) found the majority of arguments between parents and adolescents to be over mundane matters like schoolwork, friends, chores, siblings, noise, curfews, and cleanliness (see Table 11-3, page 386). These arguments

may reflect the quest for independence (as is often speculated), or they may be just a continuation of the parents' effort to teach the child to conform to social rules. "This [socializing] task inescapably produces a certain amount of tension. . . . At this point it is simply not clear whether parent-adolescent conflict has a 'deeper meaning' than this" (Montemayor, 1983, p. 91).

Conflict seems to increase in early adolescence, stabilize in middle adolescence, and decrease again after about age 18. The decline may reflect the entry into adulthood or the tendency of 18-year-olds to move away from home.

The review concludes that a storm and stress view of adolescence is extreme. Conflict is a part of every relationship and is especially to be expected in a transitional period like adolescence, when the established parent-child relationship must be reconstructed. Most families manage the conflict of adolescence without too much discomfort (see Box 11-1, pages 384–385, for ways to keep communication open between parent and adolescent). Severe, unresolved conflicts may be over issues that arose earlier in childhood and may be associated with serious problem behavior. In such cases, intervention and counseling can often help.

BOX 11-1   PRACTICALLY SPEAKING

IMPROVING COMMUNICATION BETWEEN ADOLESCENTS AND PARENTS

Although adolescence can be a trying period for both the people who are going through it and the people who are living with them, the home need not become a battleground if parents and young people make special efforts to understand each other. The following guidelines (adapted from National Institute of Mental Health, NIMH, 1981) may help.

WHAT PARENTS CAN DO

- Give your undivided attention when your teenager wants to talk. Don't read, watch television, or busy yourself with other tasks.

- Listen calmly, and concentrate on hearing and understanding your teenager's point of view.

Communication between parents and adolescents may flow more naturally when they are engaged in a shared pursuit. Grinding corn in the traditional manner strengthens the bond between this Navajo mother and daughter.

(© Ruth Duskin Feldman)

- Speak to your teenager as courteously and pleasantly as you would speak to a stranger.

- Try to understand teenagers' feelings even if you don't always approve of their behavior. Try not to make judgments.

- Keep the door open on any subject. Be an "askable" parent.

- Avoid belittling and humiliating your teenager and laughing at what may seem to you to be naive or foolish questions and statements.

- Encourage teenagers to "test" new ideas in conversation by not judging their ideas and opinions, but instead by listening and then offering your own views as plainly and honestly as possible.

- Help teenagers build self-confidence by encouraging their participation in activities of their choice (not yours).

- Make an effort to commend your teenager frequently and appropriately.

- Encourage your teenager to participate in family decision making and to work out family concerns with you.

- Understand that teenagers need to challenge your opinions and your ways of doing things to achieve the separation from you that is essential for their own adult identity.

WHAT ADOLESCENTS CAN DO

- Avoid looking at your parents as the enemy. The chances are that they love you and have your best interests in mind, even if you don't necessarily agree with their way of showing that.

- Try to understand that your parents are human beings, with their own insecurities, needs, and feelings.

- Listen to your parents with an open mind and try to see situations from their point of view.

- Share your feelings with your parents so that they will be able to understand you better.

- Live up to your responsibilities at home and in school so that your parents will be more inclined to grant you the kind of independence you want and need.

- Bolster your criticisms of family, school, and government with suggestions for practical improvements.

- Behave as courteously and considerately toward your own parents as you would toward the parents of your friends.

TABLE 11-3 THREE MOST COMMON CAUSES OF ARGUMENTS WITH PARENTS ACCORDING TO ADOLESCENTS (SELECTED STUDIES, 1929–1982)

STUDY	SAMPLE	CAUSES OF ARGUMENTS
Lynd & Lynd (1929)	348 males, 382 females: grades 10–12	1 The time I get in at night. 2 Number of times I go out during school nights. 3 Grades at school.
Punke (1943)	989 males, 1721 females: high school students	1 Social life and friends. 2 Work and spending money. 3 Clothes.
Remmers (1957)	15,000 males and females: high school students	1 I'm afraid to tell parents when I've done wrong. 2 Parents are too strict about my going out at night. 3 Parents are too strict about the family car.
Johnstone (1975)	1261 males and females: ages 13–20	1 Studying. 2 Use of spare time. 3 School.
D. A. Rosenthal (1982)	630 males and females: ages 13–16	1 Drinking or smoking. 2 Time and frequency of going out. 3 Doing jobs around the house.

Source: Condensed from Montemayor, 1983.

The Role of the Peer Group   Adolescents are in one of life's most complex transitions, and they handle it with varying degrees of grace and ease. An important source of support for adolescents—as well as of pressure for behavior that parents may disapprove—is their growing involvement with their peers.

At a time when young people are experiencing rapid physical changes, they take comfort from being with other people who are going through similar changes. At a time when the surge toward social and emotional maturity demands that young people question the value of adult standards and the need for parental guidance, it is reassuring to be able to turn for advice to friends who can understand and sympathize because they are in the same position themselves. At a time when young people are "trying on" new values, they can test these ideas with their peers with less fear of being ridiculed or "shot down" than they might have with parents or other adults. The peer group is a source of affection, sympathy, and understanding; a place for experimentation; and a supportive setting for the achievement of autonomy and independence from parents (Coleman, 1980; P.R. Newman, 1982).

It is no wonder, then, that adolescents like to spend time with their peers.

HOW ADOLESCENTS SPEND THEIR TIME—AND WITH WHOM   What do teenagers do on a typical day? With whom do they do it? Where do they do it? And how do they feel about what they are doing?

For 1 week, 75 high school students in a suburb of Chicago carried beepers that rang at a random moment once every 2 hours during the day. The average student received and responded to 69 percent of the beeper signals by reporting on his or her activities. The students gave a total of 4489 self-reports, from which researchers described what it is like to be a teenager today (Csikszentmihalyi & Larson, 1984).

The results (see Figures 11-1, 11-2, and 11-3) showed the importance of the peer group. The adolescents spent more than half their waking hours with other teenagers—friends (29 percent of the time) and classmates (23 percent)—and only about 5 percent of their time with one

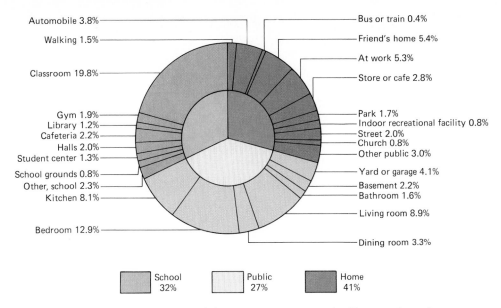

Figure 11-1 Where adolescents spend their time: percentage of self-reports in each location (N = 2734). Here and in Figures 11-2 and 11-3, 1 percentage point is equivalent to approximately 1 hour per week, spent in the given location or activity. (*Source:* Csikszentmihalyi & Larson, 1984, p. 59.)

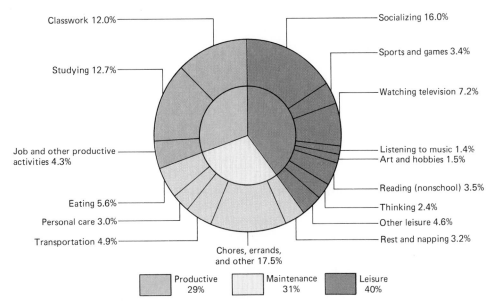

Figure 11-2 What adolescents spend their time doing. (*Source:* Csikszentmihalyi & Larson, 1984, p. 63.)

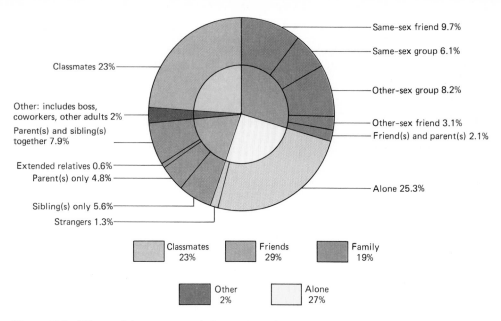

Figure 11-3 Whom adolescents spend their time with.
(*Source:* Csikszentmihalyi & Larson, 1984, p. 71.)

Chart labels:
- Same-sex friend 9.7%
- Same-sex group 6.1%
- Other-sex group 8.2%
- Other-sex friend 3.1%
- Friend(s) and parent(s) 2.1%
- Alone 25.3%
- Classmates 23%
- Other: includes boss, coworkers, other adults 2%
- Parent(s) and sibling(s) together 7.9%
- Extended relatives 0.6%
- Parent(s) only 4.8%
- Sibling(s) only 5.6%
- Strangers 1.3%

Legend:
- Classmates 23%
- Friends 29%
- Family 19%
- Other 2%
- Alone 27%

or both parents. (The teenagers did spend 41 percent of their time at home, but their favorite room was their own bedroom.) They were happier with friends (though not with classmates, whom they had not necessarily chosen as their friends) than with their families. That is probably because they had more fun with friends—joking, gossiping, and just passing the time aimlessly—than they did at home, where everyday activities tended to be more serious and more humdrum.

These adolescents reported that they felt good most (71 percent) of the time, despite rapid mood changes. They tended to be happiest when doing something active, productive, and challenging, like playing football or the piano, dancing, or trading jokes—something with rules to learn and something that gave them feedback on their competence. They were happier doing schoolwork or paid work than watching television, reading, thinking, or resting. They also liked to relax away from adult supervision—getting together informally with friends in the park or some other public place, at a friend's house, or at a student center.

FRIENDSHIPS "What *do* you talk about for so long?" an exasperated parent may ask a teenager who has been on the phone for an hour with the best friend he or she has seen no more than 2 hours before.

The most affectionate and supportive peer relationships are those with close friends. Friendships are likely to be closer and more intense in adolescence than at any other time in the life span (Berndt, 1982). The ability of close friends to share their innermost thoughts and feelings rests on cognitive development: adolescents are better able than younger children to express what they think and feel, and because they are less egocentric, they can be more sensitive to the thoughts and feelings their friends share with them.

Emotional support and sharing of confidences are particularly vital to friendships between females, in adolescence and throughout later life. Boys and men tend to count more people as friends than girls and women do, but male friendships are rarely as close as female friendships.

Although the intimacy and trust of a "best

Adolescents are happiest when they are doing something active and challenging that increases their feelings of competence. They have most fun with their friends, with whom they feel free, open, involved, excited, and motivated.

friendship" may fill the void created by the need to separate from the parents, girls who seek intimacy in friendship to compensate for lack of it at home seem least likely to find it. In a recent survey of 134 high school juniors and seniors (M. Gold & Yanof, 1985), the girls who had the strongest friendships also reported affectionate relationships with their mothers, viewed their mothers as democratic (nonauthoritarian), and wanted to be like them. In Erikson's terms, we might say that through their relationships with their mothers, these girls had developed enough trust and autonomy to be ready for intimacy. Girls who had poor relationships with their mothers tended to be less affectionate with their friends and less likely to model themselves after them, and in their friendships one young person or the other usually dominated. Thus the influence of parent-child relationships on friendships, which begins in early childhood, continues through adolescence, at least for girls.

How do adolescents choose their friends? They tend to pick friends who are already like them; and once young people become friends, they influence each other to become more alike (Berndt, 1982). Similarity is more important to friendship in adolescence than it is later in life, probably because teenagers are struggling to differentiate themselves from their parents and, as a result, need support from people who are like them in certain important ways (Weiss & Lowenthal, 1975).

This need is also evident in the tendency of adolescents to imitate each other's behavior and to be influenced by peer pressure. As a result, adolescents often find themselves in a tug-of-war between their parents and their peers.

Peer Pressure versus Parental Influence If the other girls in her group wear faded, patched jeans and running shoes, Amy will not come to school in a plaid skirt and penny loafers. If her crowd congregates at a drive-in restaurant at night, Amy will not—by choice—spend her evenings in the library. Her friends influence not only the way she dresses and wears her hair but also her social activities, sexual behavior, use or nonuse of drugs, pursuit or nonpursuit of academic achievement, and vocational aspirations—the basic patterns of her life.

"PEER POWER" Members of the peer group are constantly influencing and being influenced by each other. Even the most outspoken "nonconformists" are usually following very closely the customs of their chosen groups.

Still, "peer power" is not everything. Most teenagers have positive ties with their parents (J.P. Hill, 1980), and parents' views count more than teenagers realize. Peers tend to have more to say about such everyday issues as choice of wardrobe; parents have more influence regarding what job to take or what to do about a moral dilemma (Brittain, 1963; Emmerick, 1978).

As adolescents become surer of themselves, they become more autonomous; they are more likely to make up their own minds and to stick with their decisions in the face of disagreement from either parents or peers (P.R. Newman, 1982).

ADOLESCENTS WITH SINGLE PARENTS Are adolescents without fathers more vulnerable to peer pressure to engage in antisocial activities? The answer appears to be yes.

One study, using an unusually detailed, nationally representative survey of 6710 twelve- to seventeen-year-olds, concluded that teenagers living with a mother alone (regardless of socioeconomic status) are more likely than teenagers with two parents to be truant, to run away from home, to smoke, to have school discipline problems, or to be arrested or have repeated encounters with police. This tendency lessens, especially for boys, when another adult (such as a grandparent or a friend of the mother, but *not* a stepfather) lives in the home (Dornbusch et al., 1985).

These findings were based on data from a survey completed in 1970. A more recent study of 865 somewhat younger children (10 to 15 years of age) in schools in Madison, Wisconsin, came to similar conclusions, particularly with regard to stepfamilies. The researchers found that youngsters without biological fathers are susceptible to peer pressure for deviant behavior, regardless of whether there is a stepfather in the home. The students, who were predominantly white and of mixed socioeconomic backgrounds, were asked to choose between two hypothetical courses of action: one suggested by the child's friends; the other, what the young person "really" thought he or she should do. The answers showed that youngsters living with both natural parents were likely to be more autonomous (less influenced by peers) than those who were living in either single-parent households or stepfamilies. The presence of a stepparent was found to be a particularly weak deterrent to deviance among the oldest children sampled (Steinberg, 1987).

Of course, this study measured only hypothetical, not actual, behavior. But an earlier study of young people from the same schools found that responses to hypothetical problems were significantly related to youngsters' self-reports of actual misconduct (B.B. Brown, Classen, & Eicher, 1986). Thus it is probably fair to assume that adolescents growing up without their biological fathers are more likely to get into trouble.

"LATCHKEY ADOLESCENTS" Are "latchkey adolescents" especially vulnerable to peer pressure? They are not, according to an earlier study of the same 865 students that used the same method (the posing of hypothetical dilemmas). Rather, susceptibility seems to depend on the type of self-care situation and how much control is maintained by the absent parents (Steinberg, 1986).

The questionnaires showed that students who were home alone (where, presumably, they might check in with a parent by phone and might follow an agreed-upon schedule of homework and other activities) were no more influenced by peers than those who were home with adults or older siblings. The farther removed youngsters were from effective adult supervision, the more they were at risk. Those who were unsupervised at a friend's house were more likely to be influenced by peers than those who were at home alone, and those who were just "hanging out" with a group were most susceptible of all. Yet even in these riskier situations, students whose parents kept tabs on their whereabouts proved to be little more influenced by peers than youngsters who were supervised by adults.

Furthermore, the study showed that authoritative parenting (see Chapter 7) can lay a firm psychological foundation that enables adolescents to resist peer pressure. The less direct the supervision a young person has after school, the more important the effect of having been raised authoritatively.

However, we cannot infer causation from these results. We do not know whether susceptibility to peer pressure is increased when youngsters spend time away from adult supervision or whether adolescents who choose to spend more of their time with friends are already more subject to peer pressure. Both factors may be at work. Also, since the subjects of these studies were largely suburban young people, the results may not apply to urban or rural adolescents.

Making friends with members of the other sex is an important step in the development of sexual identity. The high school cafeteria is a center for social activity, where heterosexual peer groups (often based on shared interests and tastes, such as athletics or music) cluster in separate areas.

One theme comes through loud and clear from all these studies of peer pressure and parents' influence—a theme that has gathered force from middle childhood on. That theme is the importance of continued supervision by parents even after children reach an age when they are spending much of their time on their own.

Sex is one subject on which the influences of parents and peers often conflict. Let's see how adolescents achieve sexual identity and how they deal with their parents concerning this exciting yet troubling new aspect of their lives.

Achieving Sexual Identity

One of the most profound changes in an adolescent's life is the movement from close friendships with people of the same sex to friendships and romantic attachments with members of the other sex. The shift from unisexual to heterosexual peer-group membership is part of a normal, healthy progression on the route to adulthood. Seeing oneself as a sexual being, coming to terms with one's sexual stirrings, and developing an intimate, romantic relationship are important aspects of the achievement of sexual identity.

Adolescents' images of themselves and their relationships with peers and parents are bound up with their sexuality. Among adolescents, sexual activity—casual kissing, necking and pet-

ting, or genital contact—fulfills a number of needs, only one of which is physical pleasure. Teenagers may have sexual interaction to enhance intimacy, to seek new experience, to prove their maturity, to keep up with their peers, to find relief from pressures, or to investigate the mysteries of love.

Studying Adolescents' Sexuality Before we talk about what adolescents are saying and doing sexually these days, we need to think about the difficulties of doing sexual research, especially when it involves young people. Virtually every sex research project—from the 1940s, when Kinsey undertook his original surveys, down to the present day—has suffered from the criticism that it is not accurate because people who would voluntarily take part in such a project tend to be sexually active, interested in sex, and liberal about sex and therefore do not represent a true sampling of the population at large. Furthermore, critics charge that there is no way to corroborate what people say about their sex lives and that some may lie to conceal their sexual activities while others lie to exaggerate them.

When the subjects are young people being asked by older people about behaviors that have "traditionally been regarded as inappropriate and immoral, if not illegal and sinful" (Dreyer, 1982, p. 564), the problems multiply. Then, too, parental consent is often needed for the participation of legal minors, and parents who grant such permission may not be a cross section of the population.

All these objections have some validity. Still, such surveys have merit: even if we cannot generalize their findings to the population as a whole, within the groups that participate we can see trends over time, and these tell us something about changing sexual mores. We should bear in mind, however, that attitudes may be changing more than behavior. Although teenagers today *seem* to be more sexually active than teenagers a generation or two ago, it is possible that they are not acting much differently but are simply more willing to talk about their sexual activities.

Sexual Attitudes and Behavior   The subject of adolescents' sexuality is of course a large one. We'll consider masturbation, homosexuality and heterosexuality, and communication with parents about sex.

MASTURBATION   The subject of masturbation exemplifies some of the research issues that we have just pointed out. *Masturbation* (self-stimulation) is many young people's first sexual experience. Yet, perhaps because of the stigma traditionally attached to it, the subject has had little study. What research we do have shows an increase since the early 1960s in the number of adolescents who masturbate (Dreyer, 1982). But we do not know whether boys and girls are actually masturbating more than teenagers used to or whether they are merely more willing to admit it.

One recent survey found that by the age of 18 well over half of boys, but only a minority of girls, say that they have masturbated. Surprisingly for this "sexually liberated" era, most teenagers continue to regard masturbation as shameful; fewer than one-third say that they feel no guilt when they masturbate (Coles & Stokes, 1985).

Similarly, most adults in our society experience more anxiety in talking about self-stimulation than about any other aspect of sexuality (E.J. Roberts, Kline, & Gagnon, 1978). Yet contemporary educators stress that masturbation is normal and healthy, that it cannot result in physical harm, that it helps people learn how to give and receive sexual pleasure, and that it provides a way to fulfill sexual desire without entering into a relationship for which the person is not emotionally ready (Barbach, 1975; Kinsey, Pomeroy, Martin, & Gebhard, 1953; LoPiccolo & Lobitz, 1972).

SEXUAL PREFERENCE: HETEROSEXUALITY AND HOMOSEXUALITY   It is in adolescence that a person's *sexual orientation* is usually expressed: whether that person will—as most people do—become sexually interested in members of the other sex *(heterosexual)* or interested in persons of the same sex *(homosexual).*

Homosexuality   Many young people have one or more homosexual experiences during their growing-up years, usually before age 15 (Dreyer, 1982). Few, however, go on to make this a regular pattern. According to one report, only 3 percent of adolescent boys and 2 percent of girls have ongoing homosexual relationships, even though about 15 percent of the boys and 10 percent of the girls have had a homosexual contact during adolescence. Despite the fact that homosexuality is more visible today than it used to be, with more people openly declaring their preference for people of the same sex, research indicates that homosexual behavior has been stable or has declined during the past 30 years (Chilman, 1980).

What causes homosexuality? A number of hypotheses have been advanced to account for the existence of homosexuality. The oldest is that it represents a kind of mental illness. In a classic study, Hooker (1957) could find no evidence to support this contention. Her conclusions and those of other researchers (along with political lobbying and changes in public attitudes) eventually led the American Psychiatric Association to stop classifying homosexuality as a mental disorder.

Other theories include the possibility of a genetic factor, a hormonal imbalance, a family constellation with a dominating mother and a weak father (thought by some to cause male homosexuality), and a chance-learning situation, in which a young person who has been seduced by someone of the same sex then develops a preference for that sex. So far, no scientific support has been found for the family-constellation and chance-learning theories; and only tentative evidence has been found for the genetic and hormonal theories. (One recent study was the first to find a biological difference between heterosexual and homosexual men, a different hormone-response pattern to estrogen stimulation. Since the homosexual men in this study were at the extreme end of homosexual orientation, the findings may not apply to all homosexuals) (Gladue, Green, & Hellman, 1984).

Another hypothesis is that there are probably several different reasons why a person becomes heterosexual or homosexual, and that interaction among various hormonal and environmental events is crucial. This broad hypothesis seems to have garnered the most support (A.P. Bell, Weinberg, & Hammersmith, 1981; Durden-Smith & DeSimone, 1982; Masters & Johnson, 1979). It is interesting to note that homosexual behavior is one kind of sexual behavior which does not seem to have increased in incidence over the years and the incidence of which appears to be similar in a number of cultures (Hyde, 1986).

How do homosexual males feel about their sexual preference? There has been little research on homosexuals, and practically none on lesbians (homosexual females). One recent study found that most young homosexual males have no desire to change their sexual orientation, even though rejection and isolation by "straight" peers endanger their social, emotional, and physical health.

These conclusions were based on anonymous interviews with 29 young male volunteers in Minneapolis, of whom 79 percent described themselves as homosexual and 21 percent, bisexual. Their average age was 18, and they were predominantly white, middle-class, and Christian (Remafedi, 1987a, 1987b). Although the average age at which the youths had become aware of their homosexuality was 14, eight of them recalled feeling an attraction to men (which they defined as both physical and emotional, not exclusively sexual) by the age of 6. About half of them felt that they had been influenced in the direction of homosexuality by negative family and environmental situations in early childhood. Only 10 were still living with

one or both parents; a majority of the parents had split up.

Although their sexual preference was well established (only 6 of the 29 wanted to be heterosexual), many of these youths did not fully accept their homosexuality. They lacked self-esteem, viewed themselves as less masculine than other males, or were fearful of the future. Many suffered from negative attitudes of parents and friends; from the need to hide their sexual preference; from perceived discrimination in education, employment, or housing; from verbal abuse by peers; and from physical assaults—and this in a community that, unlike many others, has laws protecting the rights of male and female homosexuals.

Many of the youths had serious problems. Eight had dropped out of school (mainly because of sex-related conflicts), 24 had used illicit drugs, and about half had had at least one brush with the law, usually because of drug abuse, truancy, prostitution, or running away from home. Nearly three-fourths had seen psychiatrists, usually for problems related to their sexual identity, and almost one-third had been hospitalized for mental illness. All but one had contemplated suicide, and 10 had actually attempted it.

Younger homosexual males may be at the greatest psychological risk, "because of emotional and physical immaturity, unfulfilled developmental needs for identification with a peer group, lack of experience, and their dependence upon parents who may be unwilling or unable to provide emotional support around the issue of homosexuality" (Remafedi, 1987a, p. 336).

Only four of these subjects said that they had current medical problems; but nearly half of them had a history of sexually transmitted diseases, and only three underwent regular screening. The majority said that they would not go to their family doctors about sex-related problems but would prefer to go to clinics for homosexuals.

Heterosexuality Today's heterosexual teenagers are much more sexually active than previous generations were. In the past 2 decades there has been a great increase in the acceptance of premarital sex (especially among girls), along

Today's teenagers are more sexually active than earlier generations, and there is much more acceptance of premarital sex today than in the past. With the decline in the double standard for males and females, many girls now feel pressure to engage in sexual activity before they think they should. A girl's first sexual partner is likely to be her boyfriend, but a boy's is likely to be a casual acquaintance.

with a dramatic lowering of the age at which young people begin to engage in sex.

In 1969, most studies showed that fewer than half of college students approved of sex before marriage (Mussen, Conger, & Kagan, 1969); by 1979, ninety percent of college men and 83 percent of college women approved (Mahoney, 1983). And in a Harris poll taken in 1986, well over half of a nationally representative sample of 1000 white, black, and Hispanic teenagers— 61 percent of the boys and 53 percent of the girls—reported having had intercourse by the age of 17. Sexual activity increases rapidly with age, from 4 percent of 12-year-olds to 20 percent of 14-year-olds and 57 percent of 17-year-olds (Louis Harris & Associates, 1986).

A girl is likely to have her first sexual relations with a steady boyfriend, while a boy is likely to have his first intercourse with someone he knows casually. A girl's first partner is usually 3 years older than she is, while a boy's first partner tends to be about a year older (Dreyer, 1982; Zelnik, Kantner, & Ford, 1981; Zelnik & Shah, 1983).

Attitudes versus behavior: Most teenagers apparently become sexually active earlier than they say they should. In the 1986 Harris poll, the median age named as the "right age" to start having intercourse was 18, even though most of the 17-year-olds and nearly half of the 16-year-

olds were already sexually active. Interestingly, 78 percent of those polled said that they believed that most of their peers did not wait until the "right age."

Similarly, another study, of 3500 junior high and high school students, found that 83 percent of sexually active young people give a "best age for first intercourse" older than the age at which they experience it themselves and 88 percent of young mothers give an older "best age for first birth" than is true for them. As the authors observed, many adolescents hold "values and attitudes consistent with responsible sexual conduct, but not all of them are able to translate these attitudes into personal behavior" (Zabin, Hirsch, Smith, & Hardy, 1984). In other words, adolescents are like adults in that how they *say* they should behave sexually often differs from what they actually *do.*

Early sexual activity: Why do so many adolescents begin having sexual relations so early? With the near collapse of the old double standard, which held that premarital sex was all right for males but not for females, teenage girls (and, to a lesser extent, boys) find themselves under pressure to engage in activities that some of them do not feel ready for. Indeed, social pressure was the chief reason given by 73 percent of the girls and 50 percent of the boys in the Harris poll when asked why many teenagers do not wait for sex until they are older. One-fourth of the teenagers (28 percent of the girls) reported that they themselves had felt pressured to go farther sexually than they wanted to.

Both boys and girls also mentioned curiosity as a reason for early sex, while boys (more than girls) cited sexual feelings and desires. Only 6 percent of boys and 11 percent of girls mentioned being in love with the partner.

Although only 3 percent of the teenagers in the Harris poll said that they had been influenced toward sexual activity by the media, some professionals who deal with young people cite a study by the National Institute of Mental Health, *Television and Behavior,* as "strong evidence that television influences attitudes, values, behaviors, and socialization" (American Academy of Pediatrics Committee on Adolescence, 1986, p. 535). The Center for Population Options found in 1984 that teenagers spend an average of 24 hours a week watching television and 21 hours listening to the radio and are exposed to "more than 9,000 sexual references, innuendos, and behaviors each year" (American Academy of Pediatrics Committee on Adolescence, 1986, p. 535). Teenagers are also exposed to innumerable sexual images in movies.

A major reason for concern about the early age at which many teenagers begin sexual activity is the heightened risk of pregnancy (discussed in the next section) and of sexually transmitted infections (discussed in Chapter 10). Most adolescents do not plan ahead for their first intercourse, and 85 percent of nonvirgins have not sought advice about contraception or preventing infection. The earlier the first sexual experience, the longer the teenager tends to wait before seeing a doctor (American Academy of Pediatrics Committee on Adolescence, 1986).

It appears, then, that many young people at this confusing time of life are caught up in socially dictated behavior patterns that put them at risk of unwanted pregnancies and disease and may hamper their achievement of mature, autonomous sexual identity.

COMMUNICATING WITH PARENTS ABOUT SEX
Parents' attitudes toward teenagers' sexuality are more liberal than they used to be. Today's parents are less likely to punish or cast out a pregnant daughter and more likely to help her. Parents today may worry about where to put their daughter's boyfriend when she brings him home from college for a weekend; parents 20 years ago would not have admitted knowing that a daughter was sexually involved with a man (and she would not have told them).

An extensive survey of contemporary teenagers' views on and experiences with sex found that when parents give guidance, it is overwhelmingly positive. Only 3 percent of the teenagers recalled their parents' telling them that sex was not normal and healthy. Yet communication about sex remains a problem for many parents and young people. Parents often think that they have said more than their children have actually heard. One girl, already a mother at age 15, reported, "[My mother] told me that she'd told me to come to her when it was time for me to have sex and she'd get me some birth control, but she must have said it *very* softly" (Coles & Stokes, 1985, p. 37).

Indeed, the Harris poll found that almost one-third (31 percent) of American teenagers— 28 percent of those who are sexually active— have never talked with their parents about sex, and 42 percent are nervous or afraid to bring it up. Furthermore, almost two-thirds (64 percent) have never discussed birth control at home. This is important, because sexually active teenagers who *have* had discussions with their parents about sexual matters are more likely to use birth control consistently than adolescents who have not; and as we shall see in the next section, teenagers' confusion and ignorance on these subjects increases the risk of pregnancy. Boys, Hispanic teenagers, and young people whose parents are not college graduates are least likely to have talked about sex with their parents (Louis Harris & Associates, 1986).

Ironically, teenagers consider their parents to be the *best* possible source of information about sex and birth control. Yet a poll of adults found that many parents feel that they need outside help in teaching their children about sexual matters (Louis Harris & Associates, 1986).

Adolescents' ambivalent attitudes make it difficult for parents to discuss sex with them. Although they say that they would like to be open and frank with their parents about their sexual behavior, they often resent being questioned, and they tend to consider their sexual activities nobody else's business. On the other hand, when parents ignore obvious sexual activities on a teenager's part, the young person may become puzzled and angry. As one 16-year-old girl said, looking ahead to the time when *she* would be a parent:

> I'm not going to pretend that I don't know what's happening. If my daughter comes in at five in the morning, her skirt backwards and wearing some guy's sweater, I'm not going to ask her, "Did you have a nice time at the movies?" . . . I don't plan to fail! (Sorensen, 1973, p. 61)

SOME PROBLEMS OF ADOLESCENCE

Although most young people weather adolescence well, some serious problems may occur. Two problems that may have repercussions throughout life are unplanned pregnancies and juvenile delinquency.

It is important to remember that these problems are not "normal" or "typical." They are signs that a young person is in trouble and needs help.

Pregnancy

The teenage pregnancy rate in the United States is one of the highest in the world—nearly 10 percent for girls aged 15 to 19—and is still climbing. With about 60 percent of pregnancies in this age group ending in abortion (E.F. Jones et al., 1985), birthrates (especially for older teenagers and nonwhite teenagers) have fallen since 1970. But the birthrate for *unmarried* teenagers has taken an upswing (National Center for Health Statistics, 1984b). In 1982, according to the National Center for Health Statistics, 39 percent of babies born to white teenagers and 90 percent of those born to black girls were born out of wedlock, more than ever before (Brooks-Gunn & Furstenberg, 1986).

More than 9 out of 10 teenagers who do carry their babies to term choose, at least at first, to keep them rather than give them up for adoption or place them in foster care. Once these young mothers discover how demanding caring for a baby is, they may leave the infant unat-

tended for increasingly long periods. Children of teenagers often enter the state's foster care system. Years may pass before a foster child's final status is settled (Alan Guttmacher Institute, 1981).

Consequences of Teenage Pregnancy The consequences of pregnancy in adolescence are enormous for the girls and boys involved, their babies, and society at large.

Teenage girls are more prone to several complications of pregnancy, including anemia, prolonged labor, and toxemia (McKenry, Walters, & Johnson, 1979). Young mothers are twice as likely as older mothers to bear low-birth-weight and premature babies; they are also 2 to 3 times more likely to have babies who die in the first year; and they are 2.4 times more likely to bear children with neurological defects (McKenry et al., 1979).

A major reason for the health problems of teenage mothers and their children is social, not medical. Many teenage mothers are poor, do not eat properly, and get poor prenatal care—or none at all (S.S. Brown, 1985). In two large-scale studies done in university hospitals, one in this country and one in Denmark, teenagers' pregnancies turned out better than those of women in any other age group, leading the researchers to conclude that "if early, regular, and high quality medical care is made available to pregnant teenagers, the likelihood is that pregnancies and deliveries in this age group will not entail any higher medical risk than those of women in their twenties" (Mednick, Baker, & Sutton-Smith, 1979, p. 17).

Even with the best care, however, and the best of physical outcomes, the fate of teenage parents and their children is often not a happy one. Eighty percent of pregnant teenagers aged 17 and under, and 90 percent of those aged 15 and under, never finish high school; as a result, they often become unemployable and go on welfare, beginning or continuing a cycle of dependency that saps their motivation to achieve success in their work or in their personal lives (Furstenberg, 1976; Jaslow, 1982). Unmarried pregnant girls attempt suicide more often than other girls their age (McKenry et al., 1979).

The young father's life is also affected, of course. For one thing, a boy who becomes a fa-

One of the worst consequences of teenage pregnancy is the tendency for girls to drop out of school and to drift into lifelong financial dependency. These girls go to a school in Fort Worth, Texas, especially oriented toward pregnant students aged 12 to 21. Some of the girls keep their babies; other release them for adoption. Either way, the mothers can continue their education.

ther before the age of 18 is only two-fifths as likely to graduate from high school as a boy who postpones parenthood until a later age (Card & Wise, 1978).

The children of teenage parents are more likely than other children to have low IQ scores and do poorly in school (Baldwin & Cain, 1980), and the differences increase as the children grow older. Behavior problems, such as over-activity, lack of self-control, willfulness, and aggressiveness show up in the preschool years and foreshadow problems in school, such as inattention, distractibility, and failure to persist in tasks. By high school, the children of young parents tend to be low achievers, and they also tend to be at high risk of becoming delinquents or of becoming teenage parents themselves (Baldwin & Cain, 1980; Brooks-Gunn & Furstenberg, 1986).

Sons of teenage mothers appear to be more vulnerable than daughters to such effects, especially to those that show up early in the school years. This may be due in part to the absence of a father in the home, in part to boys' greater tendency toward aggressiveness and acting out, and in part to their general sensitivity to environmental conditions. Girls' problems tend to show up in the high school years, when they may drop out or become pregnant (Brooks-Gunn & Furstenberg, 1986).

Why Teenagers Get Pregnant Why, in an age of improved methods of contraception, do so many adolescent girls become pregnant? The most obvious reason is that they do not use contraceptives.

According to the Harris poll cited earlier, two-thirds of teenagers who are sexually active do not always use birth control, and 27 percent say that they *never* use it. The single reason that teenagers most commonly give for having unprotected sex is that the occasion for sex arose unexpectedly, with no time to prepare; 21 percent of those who usually have sexual intercourse without contraceptives state that reason (Louis Harris & Associates, 1986). Most teenagers who have had intercourse by the age of 17 say that their first experience was unanticipated (American Academy of Pediatrics Committee on Adolescence, 1986)—two-thirds, according to the Harris poll. Only 41 percent of sexually active teenagers use contraceptives the first time they have intercourse, and many fail to use them on subsequent occasions (Louis Harris & Associates, 1986), or fail to use them properly.

When asked why their *peers* do not use contraceptives, though, many adolescents tell a different story. Nearly 40 percent say that young people either prefer not to use birth control, do not think about it, do not care, enjoy sex more without it, or *want* to get pregnant (Louis Harris &

Associates, 1986). Other frequently mentioned reasons are lack of knowledge of contraceptives or lack of access to them (25 percent); young people's embarrassment about seeking contraception or fear that their parents will find out that they are having sex (24 percent); and the belief that pregnancy "won't happen to me" (14 percent). (The last is an example of the personal fable, explained in Chapter 10.)

Teenagers' opinions about why *other* teenagers do not take sexual precautions may reveal the subjects' own motivations. More than one study suggests, for example, that guilt feelings often underlie the familiar protest that sexual activity was unexpected. The old saying "I'm not that kind of girl" sums up the attitude of some girls who avoid birth control (Cassell, 1984). These girls feel that sexual intercourse is wrong and that they should not be engaging in it. Unpremeditated sex is acceptable, while carefully planned sex is something that only "bad" girls do.

The guiltier a girl feels about having premarital sex, the less likely she is to use an effective method of contraception (Herold & Goodwin, 1981). A girl who feels guilty is embarrassed to go to a birth control clinic and to have an internal physical examination, she is less likely than a girl who does not feel guilty to read about birth control on her own, and she is more likely to think that oral contraceptives are hard to obtain.

Who Is Likely to Get Pregnant? Disadvantaged adolescents—those who are most likely to be sexually active in the first place—are often least likely to protect themselves when they have sex. Black and Hispanic teenagers, teenagers who live with a single parent, and those whose parents are relatively uneducated tend not to use contraceptives (or not to use medically sound methods, like "the pill" or the diaphragm); while teenagers who make high grades, have ambitious career aspirations, or are involved in extracurricular activities or sports are likely to use birth control if they have intercourse (Ford, Zelnick, & Kantner, 1979; Louis Harris & Associates, 1986).

The age at which sexual activity begins is another risk factor. A survey of single women in their twenties found that 1 out of 3 sexually active white women and 7 out of 10 sexually active black women had had at least one pregnancy, and the younger the woman was at first intercourse, the more likely she was to have become pregnant (Tanfer & Horn, 1985).

Girls are particularly at risk in the first few months after they begin having intercourse. Half of first premarital pregnancies occur in the first 6 months after beginning intercourse, and 1 out of 5 occur in the first month (Zabin, Kantner, & Zelnik, 1979). Teenagers seldom seek advice about contraceptives until they have been sexually active for a year or more. The younger a girl is when she begins to have sex, the longer she waits before seeking help with contraception.

What about the boy's role? Studies done in the 1970s found that boys were less likely to assume responsibility for preventing pregnancy than boys in previous generations. In one survey, more than 60 percent of boys who had had intercourse during the preceding month said that they never used a condom (Sorensen, 1973), once the most commonly used contraceptive among young people. The increased use of condoms to prevent transmission of AIDS may help to prevent unwanted births as well.

Needs of Unmarried Teenage Parents Any pregnant woman needs to be reassured about her ability to bear and care for a child and about her continued attractiveness. She needs to express her anxieties and to receive sympathy and reassurance. The unmarried teenager is especially vulnerable. Whatever she decides to do about the pregnancy, she has conflicting feelings. During pregnancy, a time when a girl needs the most emotional support, she often gets the least. Her boyfriend may be frightened by the responsibility and turn away from her. Her family may be angry with her. She may be isolated from her friends if she does not attend school. To alleviate these pressures, the pregnant teenager should be able to discuss her problems with an interested, sympathetic, and knowledgeable counselor.

Programs that help pregnant girls stay in school can teach them job and parenting skills (Buie, 1987). A number of high schools operate day care centers for the children of unmarried students to help the mothers continue their schooling.

The value of training young people to be parents showed up in a program in which 80 low-income teenage mothers received training either through a biweekly visit to their homes (by a graduate student and a teenage aide) or through paid job training as teachers' aides in the infants' nursery of a medical school. When compared with babies in a control group, the infants of both parent-training groups did better. They weighed more, had more advanced motor skills, and interacted better with their mothers. The mothers who worked as teachers' aides and their children showed the most gains. These mothers had lower rates of additional pregnancies, more of them returned to work or school, and their babies showed the most progress (T.M. Field, Widmayer, Greenberg, & Stoller, 1982).

The mother bears the major impact of an out-of-wedlock pregnancy, but a teenage father's life is often affected as well. A boy who feels emotionally committed to the girl he has impregnated also has decisions to make. He may pay for her to have an abortion, at some financial sacrifice. He may marry his girlfriend, a move that will affect his educational and career plans. The adolescent father also needs someone to talk to, to help him sort out his own feelings so that he and his partner can make the best decision for themselves and the new life they have conceived.

Preventing Teenage Pregnancy Adolescents who have discussed sex, pregnancy, and contraception with their parents are more likely to use birth control. Teenagers who have had comprehensive sex education courses at school are more likely to use contraceptives all the time than teenagers who have not had comprehensive sex education courses. But while most American teenagers have had some kind of sex education, only 35 percent have had *comprehensive* courses that included information about various kinds of contraceptives and where to get them. Furthermore, many adolescents are confused or in doubt about basic facts. For example, only 40 percent know the time in a girl's menstrual cycle when she is most likely to become pregnant.

More effective sex education, along with more dialogue between parents and children,

may be helpful in preventing teenage pregnancies (Louis Harris & Associates, 1986), as could responsible portrayal of sexual issues and advertising of contraceptives on radio and television (AAP Committee on Adolescence, 1986). Concern over AIDS has brought a sharp increase in public support for sex education in elementary schools and for advertising condoms on television ("Sex study," 1987).

See Box 11-2, on pages 400–401, for other suggestions about how to prevent teenage pregnancy.

Juvenile Delinquency

There are two kinds, or categories, of juvenile delinquents. One category is the *status offender*. This is the young person who has been truant, has run away from home, has been sexually active, has not abided by parents' rules, or has done something else that is ordinarily not considered criminal—except when done by a minor. If Mark Twain's character Huckleberry Finn were alive and active today, he would fit into this category.

The second kind of juvenile delinquent is one who has done something that is considered a crime no matter who commits it—like committing robbery, rape, or murder. If the young person is under the age of 16 or 18 (depending on the state), he or she is usually treated differently from the way an adult criminal is treated. The court proceedings are likely to be secret, the offender is more likely to be seen and sentenced by a judge rather than a jury, and the punishment is usually more lenient. However, in some particularly violent crimes, minors are occasionally tried as adults.

Between 1985 and 1986, the number of arrests of people under the age of 18 rose 3 percent (U.S. Department of Justice, Federal Bureau of Investigation, FBI, 1987). Young people in this age group are responsible for more than their share of certain kinds of crimes. Although persons under the age of 18 constitute only about one-fourth of the total population, they account for about one-third of all crimes against property, including robbery, larceny, theft, motor vehicle theft, and arson (U.S. Department of Justice, FBI, 1986).

BOX 11-2 PRACTICALLY SPEAKING

PREVENTING TEENAGE PREGNANCY

Why is the United States the only industrial nation in the world where teenage pregnancy is increasing? Several factors commonly offered as causes—the prevalence of sexual activity among teenagers, an unusually large population of poor black teenagers, high unemployment among teenagers, and federal welfare programs that ease the financial pressure of premature parenthood—fail to explain the trend (E.F. Jones et al., 1985):

■ Rates of early intercourse are similar here and in the Netherlands, yet pregnancy and abortion rates for girls aged 15 to 19 are about 7 times as high in this country. In Sweden, where girls become sexually active much earlier, the rates of pregnancy and abortion are less than half the rates in the United States.

■ Pregnancy and abortion rates are far higher among both white and black American teenagers than they are for teenagers elsewhere.

■ Unemployment among teenagers is a serious problem in other industrial countries, too.

■ Industrial nations with more generous support programs for poor mothers have much lower teenage pregnancy rates than the United States.

What, then, are the reasons for other countries' success in preventing teenage pregnancy?

■ *Easy availability of free or inexpensive contraceptives on a confidential basis.* Adolescents in Britain, France, the Netherlands, and Sweden can get contraceptives free or at nominal cost from doctors or clinics. In Sweden, parents cannot be told that their

children have sought contraceptives; in the Netherlands, teenagers can request confidentiality (E.F. Jones et al., 1985). American teenagers say that making contraceptives free, keeping their distribution confidential, and making them easy to obtain would be the three most effective ways to encourage use of birth control. Establishment of clinics close to (but not in) schools is one step that teenagers suggest to make access easier (Louis Harris & Associates, 1986). Young teenagers cite confidentiality as an important consideration in choosing a birth control clinic. Many young people say they would not go to a clinic that insisted on notifying parents or obtaining their consent (Jaslow, 1982).

■ *Sex education and information about sex.* In

Boys are much more likely than girls to get into trouble with the law. For years, four or five boys were arrested for every girl, but recently the ratio has dropped to 3.5 to 1. Still, girls' crime rates are similar to boys' only for such status offenses as running away from home, incorrigibility, and engaging in sexual intercourse. Boys commit more of virtually all other delinquent offenses, especially violent ones. The increase among girls in such behaviors as drug use and running away from home apparently leads to activities that support them, like shoplifting, robbery, larceny, and prostitution (U.S. Department of Justice, FBI, 1986).

Personal Characteristics of Delinquents
What makes one child get into trouble when another who lives on the same street, or is even in the same family, remains law-abiding? Not surprisingly, children who get into trouble early in life are more likely to get into deeper trouble later on. Stealing, lying, truancy, and poor educational achievement are all important predictors of delinquency (Loeber & Dishion, 1983). Related to the last of these factors is a recent finding that delinquents have a slightly lower average IQ (92) than that of the general population (100). Deficits are most pronounced in verbal skills (Quay, 1987).

Sweden, sex education is compulsory at all grade levels. Dutch schools have no special sex education programs, but the mass media and private groups in the Netherlands provide extensive information about birth control, and Dutch teenagers are well informed (E.F. Jones et al., 1985). Realistic, comprehensive educational programs that include information on various means of contraception and how to obtain them are related to getting teenagers to use birth control consistently (Alan Guttmacher Institute, 1981). Girls tend to respond especially well to counseling by other girls close to their own age (Jay, DuRant, Shoffitt, Linder, & Litt, 1984). The main message to get across is that not using contraceptives is "dumb" (Louis Harris & Associates, 1986, p. 57).

Of course, delaying sexual activity is the most effective means of birth control. When parents discuss sex with children from an early age, communicate healthy attitudes, and are available to answer questions, the children are likely to wait for sex until an appropriate age (Jaslow, 1982). Community programs can help young people stand up against peer pressure to be more sexually active than they want to be (Howard, 1983). The two arguments for delaying sex that teenagers find most convincing are the danger of catching sexually transmitted diseases and the danger that a pregnancy will ruin a person's life (Louis Harris & Associates, 1986).

Specific messages that need to be communicated to young people include the following (S. Gordon & Everly, 1985):

■ If someone says to you "If you really love me, you'll have sex with me," it's always a line.

■ Sex is never a test of love.

■ It's not romantic to have sex without using a means of birth control—it's stupid.

■ "No" is a perfectly good oral contraceptive.

■ It is perfectly normal not to have sex.

■ Machismo is a way of hurting and exploiting people that a boy uses in order to feel more secure.

■ More than 85 percent of boys who impregnate teenage girls will eventually abandon them.

■ Girls who feel that they don't amount to anything unless a boy loves them won't amount to much even after they are loved—if they ever are.

■ The most important components of a relationship are love, respect, caring, having a sense of humor, and honest communication without violating the privacy of the other person's body, mind, and emotions.

One study of 55 delinquents who had been patients at the Illinois State Psychiatric Institute concluded that delinquency is not a class phenomenon but a result of emotional turmoil that affects young people from all levels of society. Delinquents from affluent families are taken to psychiatrists, while the ones from poor families are booked by the police. The study identified four kinds of delinquents: *impulsive* delinquents, who act without thinking and have no controls; *narcissistic* delinquents, who focus only on themselves, feel that they have been hurt, and see getting back at the people who have hurt them as their only way of maintaining self-esteem;

emotionally empty delinquents, who are passive, unfeeling loners; and *depressed* delinquents, who act out to relieve the pain of their internal conflicts (Offer, Ostrov, & Marohn, 1972).

The Delinquent's Family Several characteristics of parents are associated with delinquency in children. One study found that antisocial behavior in adolescents is closely related to parents' inability to keep track of their children's activities and to discipline them. The researchers concluded: "It seems that parents of delinquents are indifferent trackers of their sons' whereabouts, the kind of companions they keep, or the type of activities in which they engage" (Patterson & Stouthamer-Loeber, 1984, p. 1305). These investigators also found that parents of delinquent children are less likely to punish rule breaking with anything more severe than a lecture or a threat.

Similarly, an extensive analysis of studies of juvenile delinquency reported that the strongest predictor of delinquency was the extent of family supervision and discipline. The poorest predictor was socioeconomic status (Loeber & Dishion, 1983).

These findings support the discussion earlier in this chapter about adolescent rebellion. Much of the tension that is often considered a sign of adolescent rebellion may arise over the conflict between adolescents' desire for prompt gratification and parents' responsibility to socialize their children. When parents cannot or will not fill their socializing role, their children may become problems for society.

Dealing with Juvenile Delinquency How can we help young people lead productive, law-abiding lives? And how can we protect society from juvenile delinquents? So far, the answers to both these questions are unclear. Can young offenders be turned away from a life of crime by sentences that consider their youth, supplemented by probation and counseling? Or should young offenders be treated as adults, with sentences based on the seriousness of their offense rather than on their age?

One study suggests that the choice of treatment of juvenile delinquents is less important than simple maturity, and that except for a relatively small group of "hard-core" offenders, it is almost impossible to predict which young people will commit crimes in adulthood (L. W. Shannon, 1982). That study was a longitudinal analysis of police and court records along with interviews of 6000 young adults in Racine, Wisconsin, which found that many of those (especially men) who had been punished for delinquency as adolescents eventually got into more serious trouble, and so did many of those who had been referred to social workers. On the other hand, although the vast majority in the sample (90 percent of the men and 65 to 70 percent of the women) had committed some kind of violation in their youth (for which they were or were not stopped by police), very few (about 5 to 8 percent) had been booked for felonies later.

Why did most of these people become law-abiding adults? Fewer than 8 percent said that it was because they were afraid of getting caught. Most said that they realized that what had seemed like fun in their early years was no longer appropriate.

Most adolescents, then, outgrow their "wild oats." But society must continue to seek effective ways to help the small minority who do not.

PERSONALITY STRENGTHS OF ADOLESCENTS

The attention given to the minority of teenagers who get into serious trouble sometimes obscures the many positive aspects of adolescents' lives. With all its turbulence, normal adolescence is an exciting time, when all things seem possible. Teenagers are on the threshold of love, of life's work, and of participation in adult society. They are getting to know the most interesting people in the world: themselves. Yet few adolescents recognize and value their positive attributes.

Researchers who gave blank sheets of paper to 100 high school students and asked them to list their strengths found that out of a total of 19 categories generated (see Table 11-4), the average student listed only 7 strengths (Otto & Healy, 1966). In this they were very like adults, who in comparable studies have listed an average of 6 strengths but filled pages with lists of problems and weaknesses.

Most of the young people listed intellectual or emotional strengths or strengths in relationships. Although the listings of boys and girls differed somewhat, they were more alike than different. More girls listed strengths in social functioning and dependability, while more boys listed strengths in sports and other activities.

The researchers gave adolescents more credit for personality strengths than the young people did themselves, listing 16 "personality resources or strengths" of adolescents that differ qualitatively from those of adults:

1 Adolescents have considerable energy, or drive, and vitality.

TABLE 11-4 CATEGORIES OF ADOLESCENTS' STRENGTHS

TYPE	DESCRIPTION
Health	Being in general good health, promoting and maintaining health, and having energy and vitality.
Aesthetic strengths	Ability to enjoy and recognize beauty in nature, objects, or people.
Special aptitudes or resources	Special abilities or capacities such as skill for repairing things; the ability to make things grow, or a "green thumb"; and ability in mathematics or music.
Employment satisfaction	Enjoyment of work or duties, the ability to get along with coworkers, pride in work, and great satisfaction with work.
Social strengths	Having sufficient friends of both sexes, using humor in social relations, and having the ability to entertain others.
Spectator sports	Attending or being interested in football or baseball games, for example. The researchers included reading books and plays in this category.
Strengths through family and others	Getting along with brothers, sisters, and parents; being able to talk over problems with the father or mother; feeling close or loyal to the family.
Imaginative and creative strengths	Use of creativity and imagination in relation to school, home, or the family, and expression of creative capacity through writing, for example.
Dependability and responsibility	Being able to keep appointments, being trusted by other people, keeping promises, and persevering in bringing a task to its conclusion.
Spiritual strengths	Attending activities and meetings of church, synagogues, etc.; being a member of a religious organization; relying on religious beliefs; feeling close to God; using prayer or meditation.
Organizational strengths	Being able to lead clubs, teams, or organizations and to give or carry out orders; having long- or short-range plans.
Intellectual strengths	Interest in new ideas from people, books, or other sources; enjoyment of learning; interest in the continuing development of the mind.
Emotional strengths	Ability to give and receive warmth, affection, or love; the capacity to "take" anger from others and to be aware of the feelings of others; the capacity for empathy.
Expressive arts	Participating in plays, ballroom dancing, and other types of dancing; sculpting; or playing a musical instrument.
Relationship strengths	Getting along well with most teachers; being patient and understanding with people; helping others; accepting people as individuals regardless of sex, beliefs, or race; being confided in by other people.
Education, training, and related areas	Getting good grades and acquiring special skills, such as typing, selling, or mechanical drawing.
Hobbies and crafts	Having hobbies or interests such as stamp or coin collecting, sewing or knitting, or hairstyling.
Sports and activities	Participation in swimming, football, tennis, or basketball, for example, and enjoyment of or skill in these activities or outdoor activities such as camping and hiking.
Other strengths	Ability to take risks, liking adventure or pioneering, and the ability to grow through defeat or crisis.

Source: Adapted from Otto & Healy, 1966.

Normal adolescence is exciting. All things appear possible to a young person on the threshold of love, of work, and of participation in the broader society.

2   They are idealistic and have a real concern for the future of this country and the world.

3   They frequently exercise their ability to question contemporary values, philosophies, theologies, and institutions.

4   They have a heightened sensory awareness and perceptivity.

5   They are courageous, able to take risks themselves or stick their necks out for others.

6   They have a considerable feeling of independence.

7   They possess a strong sense of fairness and dislike intolerance.

8   More often than not, they are responsible and can be relied on.

9   They are flexible and adapt to change readily.

10 They are usually very open, frank, and honest.

11 They have an above-average sense of loyalty to organizations and causes.

12 They have a sense of humor, which they often express.

13 More often than not, they have an optimistic and positive outlook on life.

14 They often think seriously and deeply.

15 They have great sensitivity to, and awareness of, other people's feelings.

16 They are engaged in a sincere and ongoing search for identity.

If we can help more young people recognize and build on their strengths as they are about to enter adult life, adolescents' search for identity can bear richer fruit for them.

SUMMARY

Understanding Personality Development

■ G. Stanley Hall viewed adolescence as a time of storm and stress, marked by turbulent, contradictory emotions.

■ According to Sigmund Freud, before adolescents enter the genital stage, the stage of mature adult sexuality, they must overcome their unresolved sexual feelings toward their parents. This process can produce temporary hostility.

■ Anna Freud expanded Sigmund Freud's work on defense mechanisms. Two that she found particularly important during adolescence are intellectualization and asceticism.

■ Margaret Mead concluded from studies of South Pacific cultures that much of the stress of adolescence in western societies may be the result of cultural influences.

■ Erik Erikson's fifth psychosocial crisis is the conflict between identity and identity confusion.

The "virtue" that should arise from the identity crisis is fidelity.

■ The most important task during adolescence is the search for identity.

■ Research by James Marcia, based on Erikson's theory, examined the presence or absence of crisis and commitment in a person's identity formation. On the basis of these factors, Marcia identified four categories of identity formation: identity achievement, foreclosure, diffusion, and moratorium.

■ Marcia, Gilligan, and other researchers have found differences in the ways in which males and females achieve identity. Intimate relationships appear to be more important for women; achievement, for men.

Aspects of Personality Development in Adolescence

■ Although the relationships between adolescents and their parents are not always smooth, there is little evidence that a full-blown rebellion characterizes most of these relationships. Parents and their teenage children often hold similar values.

■ Adolescents spend most of their time with their peers, who play an important role in their development. Friendships become more intimate, and relationships develop with peers of the other sex.

■ Peer pressure influences some adolescents toward antisocial behavior, especially adolescents whose parents offer little supervision.

■ Adolescents' sexuality strongly influences their developing identity. Masturbation and occasional early homosexual experiences are common.

■ Sexual attitudes and behaviors are more liberal today than in the past. There is more acceptance of premarital sexual activity, and there has been a decline in the double standard.

■ Because of social pressure, many adolescents become sexually active sooner than they feel that they should. A majority have had intercourse by the age of 17.

■ Although many parents are more accepting of teenage sexuality than in the past, many adolescents have difficulty discussing sexual matters with their parents.

Some Problems of Adolescence

■ Pregnancy is a major problem among adolescents today. The adolescent pregnancy rate in the United States is one of the highest in the world.

■ Although most pregnant teenagers have abortions, 90 percent of those who have their babies keep them. Teenage pregnancy often has negative consequences for mother, father, child, and society.

■ Comprehensive sex education and more communication between parents and adolescents can encourage teenagers to delay sexual activity and to use contraceptives and can thus reduce the pregnancy rate.

■ Juvenile delinquents fall into the following two categories:

1 Young people (under 16 or 18 years) who have been arrested and found guilty of an offense punishable by law.
2 Status offenders, who commit acts (such as truancy and incorrigibility) that are not criminal for adults.

■ Young people under 18 account for more than their share of crimes, particularly crimes against property. However, the vast majority of youngsters who have juvenile police records grow up to be law-abiding.

Personality Strengths of Adolescents

■ Even with all the difficulties of establishing a personal, sexual, social, and vocational identity, adolescence is typically an interesting, exciting, and positive threshold to adulthood.

■ Adolescents generally seem to have more personality strengths than they give themselves credit for.

adolescent rebellion (page 382)
asceticism (378)
commitment (380)
crisis (380)
foreclosure (381)
genital stage (377)
heterosexual (392)

homosexual (392)
identity achievement (380)
identity diffusion (381)
identity versus identity confusion (379)
intellectualization (378)
libido (377)

masturbation (392)
moratorium (381)
reaction formation (377)
sexual orientation (392)
status offender (399)
storm and stress (377)

SUGGESTED READINGS

Coles, R., & Stokes, G. (1985). *Sex and the American teenager*. New York: Harper & Row. A detailed discussion of a survey of American teenagers' sexual behaviors and attitudes. Extensive quotations from interviews fill the book with remarks that are memorable for their candor and truth.

Csikszentmihalyi, M., & Larson, R. (1984). *Being adolescent: Conflict and growth in the teenage years*. New York: Basic Books. A detailed portrait of the day-to-day world of typical American middle-class teenagers: what they do, how they feel, and what they think about. The book is a readable account of what it is like to be an adolescent.

Erikson, E. H. (1968). *Identity: Youth and crisis*. New York: Norton. Erikson's classic discussion of the development of identity during adolescence.

Glenbard East Echo. (Compilers). (1984). *Teenagers themselves*. New York: Adama. Over 9000 teenagers voice their thoughts about their lives and their values. The book uses teenagers' own words to destroy the idea that teenagers are apathetic about the world beyond their private concerns.

Holmes, L. D. (1987). *Quest for the real Samoa: The Mead/Freeman controversy and beyond*. South Hadley, MA: Bergin & Garvey. An analysis of both Margaret Mead's and Derek Freeman's findings about Samoan life, which concludes that Mead was essentially correct in her descriptions of a coming-of-age that is remarkably free from the kind of storm and stress associated with adolescence in western industrial countries.

Hyde, J. (1986). *Understanding human sexuality* (3d ed.). New York: McGraw-Hill. An exceptionally readable textbook covering a wide range of topics in the area of sexuality: physical and hormonal factors, contraception, research on sex, variations in sexual behavior, sexual dysfunction, and the treatment of sex in religion, the law, and education.

Offer, D., Ostrov, E., & Howard, K. I. (1981). *The adolescent: A psychological self-portrait*. New York: Basic Books. A discussion of normal adolescents, focusing on their feelings about sexual relations, their families, their friends, and themselves. This book challenges the view that adolescence is a time of storm and stress.

Sarrel, L. J., & Sarrel, P. M. (1979). *Sexual unfolding: Sexual development and sex therapies in late adolescence*. Boston: Little, Brown. A detailed description, by a husband-wife team of sex therapists at Yale University, of sexual development in late adolescence and of ways in which professionals can help when problems arise. Case histories of college students illustrate contemporary sexual issues.

PART

PART

6

YOUNG ADULTHOOD

As will be seen in Chapters 12 and 13, people change and grow in many ways during the years from age 20 to age 40, the approximate boundaries we have set to define young adulthood. During these 2 decades, they make many of the decisions that will affect the rest of their lives, with regard to their health, their happiness, and their success. It is at this stage of life that most people leave their parents' home, take their first job, get married, and have and raise children—all major transitions. It is no wonder that many social scientists consider these years the most stressful in the life span.

■ How adults eat, how much they drink, whether they smoke, what kind of exercise they get, how they handle stress—all these lifestyle choices can have a major impact on both present and future physical functioning, as will be seen in **Chapter 12.** In that chapter we also discuss the ramifications of decisions about college and career, which are related to developments in intellectual functioning in early adulthood.

■ In **Chapter 13,** we discuss two different approaches to explaining social and emotional development in adulthood: the age-related theories of Erikson, which have inspired several intensive studies of adults; and the timing-of-events theory, which emphasizes life experiences more than chronological age in explaining why people feel and act as they do. With a background of both these theories, it is easier to understand the events of young adulthood that relate to some core choices: to marry or remain single, to have children or not, to select a sexual lifestyle, to make friends.

12

CHAPTER

PHYSICAL AND INTELLECTUAL DEVELOPMENT IN YOUNG ADULTHOOD

If . . . happiness is the absence of fever, then I will never know happiness. For I am possessed by a fever for knowledge, experience, and creation.

Diary of Anaïs Nin (1931–1934), written when she was between 28 and 31

ASK YOURSELF

■ How do the lifestyles and behavior of young adults affect their physical health?

■ In what ways do intellectual functioning and moral reasoning develop in young adulthood?

■ How does the college experience influence development?

■ What impact do age, gender, and family have on career development and work satisfaction?

For many people, the essence of young adulthood is captured in these words: "Time—there's never enough to do everything I want to do and everything I should do." They may be spoken by a college senior trying to fit in all the courses needed to prepare for medical school. They voice the feelings of a young woman newly hired as an attorney, who works 80 hours a week while trying to find time for her personal life, which includes seeing her fiancé and running 5 miles a day. They express the dilemma of a young man who has risen to middle-level management and whose boss questions his career commitment when he leaves work early enough to have dinner with his children. And they reflect the pressures on a single mother who, overwhelmed by the stresses of raising a baby alone and making ends meet, is driven to smoking too much and eating too little.

People in these situations and others set priorities every day of their lives. They make important decisions that affect their health, their careers, and their personal relationships. They are still maturing in many important ways. It is ironic, therefore, that at one time developmentalists characterized the years from the end of adolescence to the onset of old age as a relatively uneventful plateau.

Actually, as we'll see in this chapter and the chapters to come, the adult years hold great potential for intellectual, emotional, and even physical development. Important advances occur during young adulthood (which will be arbitrarily defined as the span between ages 20 and 40), throughout middle age (defined in this book as from age 40 to age 65), and through late adulthood (age 65 and over).

Some of these advances come about as the result of the new and significant roles that many people assume in adulthood: those of worker, spouse, and parent. These roles affect the way people think and the way they act; and the way they think and act affects the way they carry out these roles—or whether they carry them out at all.

The interactions among the various aspects of development—physical, intellectual, and social and emotional—are striking during this period, and we examine them in this chapter. We see, for example, how personality affects health when we examine the factors that incline some people to smoke, drink, or exercise, or that increase the risk of heart attack. We look at such intellectual issues as the measurement of adults' intelligence, whether there are adult stages of cognitive development, and whether men and women follow different routes to moral maturity. We also look at the college experience and the intellectual and personality development that occurs in college. We end the chapter with a discussion of one of the most important issues during this period of life, the choice of career, which will come up again in Chapter 13, when we examine personality development in adulthood and the choice of a personal lifestyle.

SENSORY AND PSYCHOMOTOR FUNCTIONING

The typical young adult is a good physical specimen. Strength, energy, and endurance are at their peak. From the middle twenties, when most body functions are fully developed, until about the age of 50, declines in physical capabilities are usually so gradual that they are hardly noticed.

Today's 20-year-olds tend to be taller than their parents because of the secular trend in growth, discussed in Chapter 10. Between the ages of 30 and 45, height is stable; then it begins to decline (Tanner, 1978).

The peak of muscular strength occurs sometime around 25 to 30 years of age; it is followed by a gradual 10 percent loss of strength between the ages of 30 and 60. Most of the weakening occurs in the back and leg muscles; a little less, in the arm muscles (Bromley, 1974). Manual dexterity is most efficient in young adulthood; agility of finger and hand movements begins to lessen after the mid-thirties (Troll, 1985).

The senses are also at their sharpest during young adulthood. Visual acuity is keenest at about age 20 and does not begin to decline until about age 40, when a tendency toward farsightedness makes many people resort to reading glasses. A gradual hearing loss typically begins before age 25; after age 25, the loss becomes more apparent, especially in the ability to hear higher-pitched sounds. Taste, smell, and sensitivity to pain and temperature generally show no diminution until about age 45 to age 50.

HEALTH

Health Status

Young adults are the healthiest people in the population. More than 9 out of 10 people aged 17 to 44 view their health as excellent, very good, or good (U.S. Department of Health and Human Services, USDHHS, 1986). People in this age group report getting far fewer colds and respiratory infections than they did as children; and when they do get colds, they usually shake them off easily. They tend to have outgrown childhood allergies, and they have fewer accidents than children have. Many young adults are never seriously sick or incapacitated.

(© Pierre Perrin/Sygma)

The typical young adult is a good physical specimen—though few display the extraordinary grace and control shown by the Olympic bronze medalist Debi Thomas.

(© Peter Menzel/Stock, Boston)

The leading cause of death for people aged 25 to 34 is accidents, primarily automobile accidents. This toll could be reduced markedly by two measures—wearing seat belts and avoiding driving after drinking.

Fewer than 1 percent are limited in their ability to get around and do things because of chronic conditions or impairment.

About half of all acute conditions experienced in young adulthood are respiratory, and another 20 percent are injuries. The most frequent chronic conditions, especially in low-income families, are back or spine problems, hearing impairments, arthritis, and hypertension. The most frequent reasons for hospitalization in these years are childbirth, accidents, and digestive and genitourinary system diseases (USDHHS, 1985). Black people are more likely than white people to suffer from hypertension in young adulthood (USDHHS, 1986).

One reason why war is so tragic is that it exacts its death toll largely from a segment of the population—young adults—that normally has very low death rates. People under the age of 35 rarely die of natural causes, and since 1950 the already-low death rate for 25- to 44-year-olds in the United States has dropped, largely because of a decline in deaths from heart disease and cancer (USDHHS, 1985).

Given the healthy state of most young adults, it is not surprising that accidents (primarily automobile accidents) are the leading cause of death for people aged 25 to 34. Next comes cancer, followed by heart disease, suicide, and homicide. Between the ages of 35 and 44, though, cancer and heart disease are the biggest killers.

The age of 35 represents a turning point—the first time since infancy when the chief cause of death is a physical illness.

Race and gender make a significant difference in both the rates and the causes of death in young adulthood. Black people are more than twice as likely as white people to die at this time, mostly because of higher homicide rates. Men in the age group 25 to 44 are twice as likely to die as women in this age range. Men are most likely to die in automobile crashes and women of cancer (USDHHS, 1986).

Influences on Health and Fitness

Good health is not just a matter of luck; it often reflects the way people live. Human beings are not passive victims or beneficiaries of their heredity; they can do a great deal to enhance their own health.

The Centers for Disease Control (1980) estimates that 50 percent of deaths from the 10 leading causes in the United States are linked with factors over which people have some control. Apart from such obviously risky or self-destructive behaviors as reckless driving, failure to use seat belts, association with dangerous people, and suicide, some of the things people do from day to day can either augment or sap their vigor and extend or shorten their lives.

Health, as defined by the World Health Orga-

nization, is "a state of complete physical, mental, and social well-being and is not merely the absence of disease and infirmity" (Danish, 1983). People can seek such a state of wellness by pursuing certain activities (like eating well and exercising regularly) and refraining from others (like smoking or drinking to excess).

A study of 7000 adults, aged 20 to 70, found that observance of seven basic habits concerning diet, sleep, exercise, smoking, and drinking is directly related to health. These habits are: eating breakfast, eating regular meals and not snacking, eating moderately to maintain normal weight, exercising moderately, sleeping regularly 7 to 8 hours a night, not smoking, and drinking alcohol moderately or not at all. People who follow all seven habits are the healthiest of all; the next-healthiest are those who follow six, then those who follow five, and so on (Belloc & Breslow, 1972). Other research shows that alcoholics, drug abusers, and people who are sexually promiscuous expose themselves to heightened risks of infectious disease (Pankey, 1983).

The link between behavior and health points up the interrelationship among the physical, intellectual, and emotional aspects of development. What people do affects how they feel. Even when people *know* the facts about good health habits, their personalities, their social settings, and their emotional states often outweigh their awareness of what they should do and lead them into unhealthy behavior.

Let's look at some of the behaviors that are strongly and directly linked with health (see the practical tips in Box 12-1, page 416–417) and at some factors that indirectly influence health: socioeconomic level, gender, and lifestyle.

Diet The popular saying "You are what you eat" sums up the great importance of diet for physical and mental health. The first three of the seven health habits just cited are related to diet. What people eat determines to a considerable extent how they look, how they feel physically, and how likely they are to suffer from various diseases. Such conditions as diabetes and gout, for example, are more common among people who eat rich foods.

WEIGHT In a society that values slenderness and judges people by their physical attractive-ness, being overweight can be a severe psychological problem. It also has adverse physical effects and carries risks of high blood pressure, heart disease, and certain cancers.

People who are 10 percent heavier than the "ideal" weight for their height and body build are considered *overweight,* while the term *obese* is generally reserved for those who are at least 20 percent over their desirable weight.

Obesity is such a serious health hazard that the National Institutes of Health (1985) urges that the 34 million Americans who have medically significant obesity receive the same kind of medical attention given to people with life-threatening disorders. Lower levels of overweight can also impair health, especially if there are other risk factors, like diabetes or hypertension.

Recent research has confirmed the dangers of being fat. Among 8006 Japanese men aged 45 to 68, death rates were highest for the fattest and the thinnest men. The thinnest ones, however, had lost weight since their twenties, probably because of the illnesses they eventually died from. Thus, people who are normally thin or who deliberately lose weight have a better prognosis than heavy people and people who lose weight involuntarily as a result of ill health (Rhoads & Kagan, 1983).

The effort to lose weight is such a constant preoccupation for so many people that every year some new diet book becomes a best-seller. Unfortunately, although many overweight people do lose weight on fad diets, most gain it back almost immediately after resuming their usual eating patterns. The most effective weight loss method is to cut down the amount of food eaten, to use behavior modification techniques so as to change eating patterns, and to exercise more. Young adults (adults under age 40) generally control their weight better than older adults do.

CHOLESTEROL Evidence has been mounting that high levels in the bloodstream of a fatty substance called *cholesterol* pose a risk of heart disease. Cholesterol creates fat deposits in blood vessels throughout the body, sometimes narrowing those vessels to a point at which the blood supply to the heart can be cut off, leading to a heart attack.

BOX 12-1 PRACTICALLY SPEAKING

WHAT YOU CAN DO TO IMPROVE YOUR HEALTH

As research cited in this chapter shows, how you feel and how long you live often depend on what you do. Evidence continues to mount underscoring the fact that people have a great deal of control over their health and their longevity. If you follow the recommendations listed below, you will be doing your part to maximize good health and long life.

■ *Eat for health.* Eat breakfast, eat regular meals, and don't snack. Eat moderately to maintain normal weight. Eat a diet low in cholesterol to help prevent heart disease: fish and poultry (without skin) rather than red meats; almost no high-fat and smoked meats such as bacon and sausage; low-fat or skim milk and yogurt made from it; no more than two to four egg yolks a week; less butter and other fats; and low-fat cheeses like low-fat cottage cheese, low-fat ricotta, and low-fat mozzarella instead of hard and creamy cheeses. Eat foods associated with lowered cancer rates: high-fiber fruits and vegetables and whole-grain cereals; citrus fruits and dark-green and yellow vegetables which will be high in vitamin A, vitamin C, or both; and vegetables in the cabbage family (such as cauliflower, broccoli, and brussels sprouts).

■ *Exercise regularly.* Find an exercise program that you will enjoy enough that you will stick with it. If possible, find someone who will exercise with you. It doesn't matter whether you run, bicycle, swim, walk briskly, or do aerobic dancing; what matters is doing one of these for at least 20 minutes at a stretch three times a week. You need to get your pulse up to 70 to 85 percent of its theoretical maximum rate (estimated by subtracting your age from 220). If you are under 16 or over 35, you should see your doctor before embarking on an exercise regime. In any case, build up gradually, and even when you are in a full-fledged program, be sure to warm up gradually at the beginning of each session and then to cool down afterward.

The link between cholesterol and heart disease, which was suspected for some time, has now been definitively established. In one large-scale study, almost 4000 middle-aged men with high cholesterol levels were observed for 7 years. All the men followed low-cholesterol diets, and some received a cholesterol-lowering drug. The most encouraging finding from this study is that reducing cholesterol levels can lower the risk of heart disease and death (Lipid Research Clinics Program, 1984a; 1984b).

Since the most important determinant of cholesterol levels seems to be the kinds and amounts of food people eat, the American Heart Association (1984) has proposed dietary recommendations for everyone from the age of 2 up (see Box 12-1). This diet emphasizes fish and poultry rather than red meat; low-fat or skim milk; low-fat yogurt and cottage cheese rather than hard cheeses; margarine and oil rather than butter; and a lowered intake of fats, oil in general, and egg yolks (no more than two to four yolks per week).

DIET AND CANCER Extensive research, worldwide, has pointed strongly to a link between dietary habits and the risks of certain kinds of cancer. Japanese-American women in the United States, for example, have higher rates of breast cancer than women in Japan. On the other hand, people in Japan have higher rates of cancer of the stomach and esophagus than Americans of Japanese descent. It is suspected that breast cancer is related to a high-fat diet and that stomach and esophageal cancers are associated with pickled, smoked, and salted fish (Gorbach, Zimmerman, & Woods, 1984).

These findings and other apparent associations between diet and the incidence of cancer led the American Cancer Society (1984) to issue

- *Use your seat belt.* It's very likely that at some time in your life you will be in an automobile accident. Your chances of being killed in a crash increase 25 times if you are thrown out of your car. Your belt doubles your chances of surviving a crash (Engelberg, 1984).

- *Don't smoke.* If you have never smoked, don't start. If you smoke now, stop immediately. The sooner you stop, the better it will be for your health and the health of any children you may bear and raise in the future. If you need help in stopping, you can go to one of a number of groups or professionals who offer support, or you can chew a gum specially designed for the purpose.

- *Drink alcohol in moderation or not at all.* If you don't drink, there's no reason to start. If you are a moderate social drinker who consumes no more than two to three drinks a day (of whiskey, beer, or wine), and if your drinking has not caused any problems for you, there's probably no need for you to stop. If you are drinking more heavily than this, or if your drinking has gotten you into trouble on the job, at home, or with the law, your life and those of others may depend on your giving up alcohol altogether. So far, the most effective way to do this seems to be through the organization Alcoholics Anonymous, which has chapters in communities around the world.

- *Avoid drugs.* Drugs, especially if used heavily, can harm your health, affect your mind, weaken your motivation to work, and sour your relationships, as well as get you into trouble with the law. Pregnant women who use drugs endanger their unborn children.

- *Learn how to cope with stress.* If you exhibit "Type A" behavior, make a deliberate effort to change your behavior patterns. Because hostility appears to be the harmful aspect of Type A behavior, look for a counseling program that can teach you to modify a hostile attitude.

- *Lead a healthy sexual life.* Avoid promiscuity, which has been linked to cervical cancer and to acquired immune deficiency syndrome (AIDS). Protect yourself from sexually transmitted diseases (see Box 10-2).

a set of nutritional guidelines to reduce the risk of cancer. Moderation in drinking alcohol is encouraged, as is weight control, since overweight people have higher rates of cancer. (See Box 12-1 for specific recommendations regarding food.)

Exercise The trendiest clothes these days are running shoes, warm-up suits, and leotards. In the desire to look good and feel good, Americans are flexing their muscles and are finding that exercising can be fun. Today's "fitness craze" has gone a long way toward improving Americans' health.

There has been a slight decline in the number of adults doing frequent strenuous exercise, which may signal that the exercise boom has peaked. Still, 1 in 3 adults exercise strenuously three or more times a week, and more than three-fourths get some sort of regular exercise—a figure that has not changed significantly in recent years. The strenuous exerciser is most likely to be a man under age 40 who is well educated, has a relatively high income and a high-status occupation, considers himself to be in excellent health, and believes that he has considerable control over his health (Prevention Research Center, 1986).

Whether they jog or jump, dance or swim, bike or bounce, people who exercise are reaping many benefits. They are maintaining desirable body weight; building muscles; strengthening heart and lungs; lowering blood pressure; protecting against heart attacks, cancer, and osteoporosis (a thinning of the bones that tends to affect older women, causing fractures); relieving anxiety and depression; and possibly lengthening their lives (P.R. Lee, Franks, Thomas, & Paffenberger, 1981; McCann & Holmes, 1984; Notelovitz & Ware, 1983).

One-third of American adults exercise strenuously three or more times a week, and more than three-fourths get regular exercise—some of them in company-sponsored programs like this one. Regular exercise helps people feel good and look good. It builds muscles, strengthens heart and lungs, keeps weight down, and protects against a variety of physical disorders.

(© Jim Wilson/Woodfin Camp)

Smoking People who smoke expose themselves to increased risk of cancer, heart disease, and a number of other disorders that are likely to shorten their lives. Smoking is related to lung cancer, as well as to cancer of the larynx, mouth, esophagus, bladder, kidney, pancreas, and cervix; to gastrointestinal problems, such as ulcers; to heart attacks; and to respiratory illnesses like bronchitis and emphysema (USDHHS, 1987).

Even people who do not smoke themselves often suffer because of *passive smoking*, that is, smoking that takes place around them. We noted in Chapter 2 the effects that a pregnant woman's smoking can have on her unborn child. Research shows that nonsmokers in households in which more than two packs of cigarettes are smoked daily inhale smoke equal to one or two cigarettes a day (Matsukura et al., 1984). Children of smoking mothers show diminished lung function (Tager, Weiss, Munoz, Rosner, & Speizer, 1983); nonsmokers married to heavy smokers and children of women who smoke are at a special risk of lung cancer (Correa, Pickle, Fontham, Lin, & Haenszel, 1983).

The effects of smoking on smokers themselves have been well known for many years, and, fortunately, many people have gotten the message. Today only one out of three 25- to 44-year-olds smoke, the lowest percentage since figures have been collected, beginning in 1955

(USDHHS, 1987). However, the number of women who smoke has risen, to the point where women now smoke as much as men. College graduates are less likely to smoke than people with less education (Prevention Research Center, 1986).

At least 90 percent of the people who stop smoking do so on their own; other people who want to break the habit turn to specific programs for help. The most promising programs combine a variety of techniques, including cognitive, behavioral, and aversive approaches. Use of nicotine chewing gum, along with information on the drawbacks of smoking, has been successful (USDHHS, 1987).

Alcohol The United States is a drinking society. Advertising in the news media links whiskey with the good life, and beer and wine with a good time. Drinking is considered the norm; two-thirds of adults say that they sometimes drink (Prevention Research Center, 1986). Most adults express hospitality by offering a glass of wine, a beer, or a cocktail, and a nondrinker is often pressed for explanations.

According to their own reports, 8 out of 10 adults who drink alcohol are light or moderate drinkers, consuming three drinks or fewer in a given day (Prevention Research Center, 1986). It is possible that moderate drinking protects against heart disease, but at this time claims to

that effect are still controversial (Haskell et al., 1984).

What is *not* controversial is the harmful effect that alcohol has upon millions of drinkers and the people around them. For some 1 out of 10 adults, alcohol can pose significant problems. Long-term excessive use may lead to such grave physical ills as cirrhosis of the liver, cancer, and heart failure (National Institute on Alcohol Abuse and Alcoholism, NIAAA, 1981). Besides liver damage, drinkers are likely to suffer from other gastrointestinal disorders (including ulcers), heart disease, nervous system damage, and other medical problems ("Alcoholism," 1978). And as we saw in Chapter 2, drinking by a pregnant woman can result in damage to the fetus.

Alcohol abuse is a major cause of deaths from automobile accidents (NIAAA, 1981), and although more than 70 percent of drivers never drive after drinking, 28 percent do so at least sometimes (Prevention Research Center, 1986). Alcohol is also implicated in deaths from drowning, suicide, fire, and falls and is a factor in many cases of family violence (NIAAA, 1981).

Despite the damage that alcohol can do to physical and psychological health, many people who have a drinking problem do not recognize it. Not until people acknowledge a problem themselves can they do anything about it. The most effective approach to alcoholism so far has been the group-oriented one of Alcoholics Anonymous, which emphasizes recognition of the problem, total abstinence, and the emotional support of other alcoholics (Zimberg, 1982).

Stress *Stress* is the organism's physiological and psychological reaction to demands made on it; a *stressor* is an event capable of causing stress. Whether or not an event becomes a stressor depends upon the way a person interprets that event.

Stress is, of course, an inevitable part of everyone's life. Some stress is essential, and some is actually energizing. As one leading stress researcher said, "Complete freedom from stress is death" (Selye, 1980, p. 128). But stress— or rather, the way people cope with stress—is coming under increasing scrutiny as a factor in causing or aggravating such diseases as hypertension, heart ailments, stroke, and ulcers.

Stress, or awareness of stress, seems to be on the rise. Sixty percent of adults—and a majority in every adult age group under 65—report that they feel under great stress at least once a week, and 27 percent feel it 3 days a week or more (Prevention Research Center, 1986). Seventy percent say that they consciously try to reduce stress. College graduates and people with high incomes are most likely to feel frequent stress— and to take steps to control it.

The most commonly reported physical symptoms of stress include headaches, muscle aches or tension, stomachaches, and fatigue. The most common psychological symptoms include nervousness, anxiety, tenseness, anger, irritation, and depression.

We will first examine some of the evidence for a connection between stressful life events and illness, and then we'll focus on personality factors that have been implicated in the link between stress and heart disease.

LIFE EVENTS AND ILLNESS When two psychiatrists looked at the life events that had preceded illness among 5000 hospital patients, they found strong evidence that the more changes had taken place in a person's life, the greater the likelihood of illness within the next year or two (T.H. Holmes & Rahe, 1976). Surprisingly, some of the stressful events that patients reported seemed positive—such as marriage, a new home, or an outstanding personal achievement. Even happy events, though, require adjustments to change. Change can induce stress, and some people react to stress by getting sick.

On the basis of people's assessments of the amount of adjustment various life events required, the researchers assigned numerical values to the events (see Table 12-1, page 420). About half of the people who scored between 150 and 300 life change units (LCUs) in a single year became ill, and about 70 percent of those with 300 LCUs did.

Although the documentation of the tie between stress and illness is important, there are some difficulties with Holmes and Rahe's conclusions. The biggest problem, perhaps, is in the view they present that human beings *react* rather than *act*. Their approach fails to consider the importance of someone's interpretation of a particular event, that is, the meaning it holds for

TABLE 12-1 LIFE EVENTS AND WEIGHTED VALUES

LIFE EVENT	VALUE
Death of spouse	100
Divorce	73
Marital separation	65
Jail term	63
Death of close family member	63
Injury or illness	53
Marriage	50
Being fired at work	47
Marital reconciliation	45
Retirement	45
Change in health of family	44
Pregnancy	40
Sex difficulties	39
Gain of new family member	39
Change in financial state	38
Death of close friend	37
Change of work	36
Change in number of arguments with spouse	35
Foreclosure of mortgage	30
Change of responsibility at work	29
Son's or daughter's leaving home	29
Trouble with in-laws	29
Outstanding personal achievement	28
Wife's beginning or stopping work	26
Beginning or ending school	26
Revision of habits	24
Trouble with boss	23
Change in work hours	20
Change in residence	20
Change in schools	20
Change in recreation	19
Change in social activity	18
Change in sleeping habits	16
Change in number of family get-togethers	15
Change in eating habits	15
Vacation	13
Minor violations of law	11

Source: Adapted from T. H. Holmes & Rahe, 1976.

the person. For example, divorce has different impact on the person who initiates it and on the one on whom it is imposed. Also, Holmes and Rahe do not address the fact that stress can result from *lack* of change—boredom, inability to advance at work, or unrewarding personal relationships. Finally, their findings do not tell us *how* stress produces illness, nor do they explain why some people get sick from stress while others seem to thrive on it.

THE IMPORTANCE OF CONTROL   One answer to these questions may lie in the element of control. When people feel that they can control

events, they are less likely to get sick. Research on both human beings and animals has found links between stressors perceived as uncontrollable and various kinds of illness, including cancer (Laudenslager, Ryan, Drugan, Hyson, & Maier, 1983; Matheny & Cupp, 1983; Sklar & Anisman, 1981).

Lack of control may also explain another finding based on a survey of 100 middle-class, middle-aged Californians—that the irritations of everyday life may be better predictors of physical and psychological problems than are the major events in people's lives (R.S. Lazarus, 1981). This might be because most people feel that they *should* be able to control the small things in life, such as avoiding traffic jams, safeguarding possessions so that they are not lost or stolen, and getting along with other people. When these "shoulds" do not operate, people feel at fault.

Some hospitals offer stress management workshops that teach people to control their reactions when faced with stressful situations and to turn stress into an opportunity for constructive change. One such program emphasizes "positive self-talk." For example, a mother who gets upset when her son brings home a poor report card can learn to stop blaming herself for failure as a parent and, instead, to tell herself that her son's grades are not entirely within her control. Then she may be able to turn her attention to how she *can* influence her son: build communication with him or offer to help him improve his study skills. In addition, such workshops frequently incorporate such techniques as relaxation, meditation, and biofeedback.

PERSONALITY FACTORS IN STRESS AND HEART DISEASE The tendency to experience stress, or the way people cope with stress, may reflect certain personality factors that have been implicated in heart disease. For example, in one study of 227 middle-aged men of whom 26 had had heart attacks, these 26 were more likely to have worried and to have felt sad, anxious, tired, and lacking in sexual energy in the year before the attack than were the other men (Crisp, Queenan, & D'Souza, 1984). Another study, of 2320 survivors of heart attacks, found that those men who were socially isolated and under stress were more likely to die within 3 years after their attacks than men who were more sociable and under less stress (Ruberman, Weinblatt, Goldberg, & Chaudhary, 1984). It is possible that the states of mind of the high-risk men in both these groups caused them to smoke more and to eat in unhealthy ways and also affected their hormonal systems in ways that brought about heart disease.

Is there a particular type of personality that is prone to heart attack? Research suggests that there may be.

People who have what has been called *"Type A" behavior patterns* are impatient, competitive, aggressive, and hostile. They act as if they are constantly racing against time and facing challenges. People with *"Type B" behavior patterns* are more relaxed, easygoing, and unhurried. They cope with their environment more realistically—they do not try to do the impossible, and they do not regard everything (even leisure activities) as a challenge to their control, the way Type A people do. A landmark study found that Type A people (who are mostly men) are more likely to suffer heart attacks in their thirties or forties, whereas Type B people almost never have heart attacks before age 70—even if they smoke, eat fatty foods, and do not exercise (Friedman & Rosenman, 1974).

Apparently because Type A people perceive their environment as challenging or threatening, their bodies react to the mildest events almost as if they were fighting for their lives, by secreting excessive amounts of noradrenaline, an adrenaline-like hormone. These secretions may damage the lining of the coronary arteries and encourage cholesterol deposits; may cause abnormal heart rhythms, increased heart rate, and higher blood pressure; or may trigger blood clots that cause heart attacks (Rosenman, 1983).

Recent research has challenged the relationship between Type A behavior and heart disease on several fronts. One study found that among men who have had heart attacks, Type A men are more likely to survive than Type B men (Ragland & Brand, 1988). Other studies have failed to confirm a close relationship between overall Type A behavior and the risk of having a heart attack. One line of research, however, suggests that one aspect of Type A behavior—hostility stemming from cynicism about other people's motives—does appear to be related to that risk (Barefoot, Dahlstrom, & Williams, 1983; R.B. Williams, Barefoot, & Shekelle, 1984). The researchers suggest that this hostility reflects an incomplete resolution of Erikson's first crisis, trust versus mistrust.

Not all Type A people are hostile, and this fact is important because hostility appears to be the "lethal" component of Type A behavior. The implication is that, in adults at least, competitiveness, intensity, and other aspects of the classic Type A pattern are not harmful and that treatment should focus only on reducing hostility.

A family's financial condition influences the physical condition of all its members. Unemployed parents—like these people lined up at a Salvation Army soup kitchen—may be unable to provide adequate health care or regular, nutritious meals for themselves or their children.

It may be possible to modify Type A behavior patterns in people who have suffered heart attacks and thus to prevent recurrences. Even more promising are indications that Type A behavior can be identified and modified *before* heart disease occurs. Type A people have been taught to temper their reactions to stress while retaining the energy and drive that impel them to succeed (Gill et al., 1985). Some specific suggestions are provided in Box 12-1.

Indirect Influences on Health Clearly, what people do or refrain from doing and the way they respond to life's changes and challenges can directly affect their health. Certain indirect influences—education, economic status, gender, and marital status—are also related to health and health-protective behavior.

SOCIOECONOMIC FACTORS As we saw in Chapter 6, a family's financial condition is a major influence on children's physical condition; thus it is not surprising that income affects adults' health as well. It is not clear whether it is better health care or a healthier lifestyle that helps to protect the more affluent, but both factors seem important.

Education is also an important factor. Adults who have not gone to college are at increased risk of developing chronic diseases like hypertension (high blood pressure) and cardiovascular (heart) disease. The less education people have had, the greater their chances of contracting such a disease, of being seriously affected by it, and even of dying from it. These findings—which hold true even when such factors as age, sex, race, and smoking or nonsmoking are controlled—come from a survey of a representative national sample of 5652 working people between the ages of 18 and 64 (Pincus, Callahan, & Burkhauser, 1987).

This does not mean, of course, that formal education *causes* good health, but merely that it is an indicator of other factors that may do so. These factors may include financial resources, diet and other health habits, and the ability to solve problems (including problems concerning personal health). People with more education tend to come from families with more money, and so they can afford to eat better and to get better preventive health care and better medical treatment. In addition, more affluent and better-educated people tend to have learned sensible personal habits and to be aware of the importance of a healthy way of life. They tend to exercise more and to eat more nutritiously. Finally, people with more schooling may have developed more self-confidence and may have learned to handle stress more effectively.

GENDER AND LIFESTYLE Who are healthier—women or men? Women have lower death rates throughout adulthood. Yet women report being ill more often than men, and they use health services more often.

What accounts for these differences? Several

BOX 12-2 FOOD FOR THOUGHT

EFFECTS OF THE MENSTRUAL CYCLE

Heart disease affects men to a much greater degree than women—at least women who have not reached menopause—quite possibly because of the hormonal protection women enjoy during the years their bodies are producing estrogen. This, then, may well be a major benefit of the female menstrual cycle, a powerful regulator of a number of different hormones that fluctuate in a woman's body for some 40 years of her life—from about age 12 until about age 50. An increasing amount of research has been conducted in recent years to determine the effects of these hormones on women's physiological, intellectual, and emotional states.

An indication of how pervasive these effects are is seen in the operation of the five senses—sight, hearing, taste, smell, and touch—at different phases of the menstrual cycle. Sight is keenest at the time of ovulation (usually midcycle), hearing peaks at the beginning of a menstrual period and again at ovulation, smell is most sensitive at midcycle and reduced during menstruation, and sensitivity to pain is lowest just before a period. No reliable patterns have emerged for taste (Parlee, 1983).

Women's cognitive abilities, unlike their sensory capacities, do not seem to be affected by the menstrual cycle. In one study that measured 50 women, aged 30 to 45, the women showed no statistically significant cyclic differences in tests of perception, memory, problem solving, inductive reasoning, concept formation, and creativity. Some women did show higher levels of anxiety and depression premenstrually, however—a finding that has emerged in a number of studies.

Although women and their doctors have been aware for centuries of various physiological changes during the menstrual cycle (which sometimes affect women's moods), only fairly recently have severe symptoms associated with such changes been described as a medical phenomenon. *Premenstrual syndrome (PMS)* is a disorder characterized by physical discomfort and emotional tension, which may appear up to 2 weeks before a menstrual period and which then decline during and after it. Estimates of the proportion of women with symptoms severe enough to interfere with their normal activities vary widely, from about 20 to 40 percent.

Symptoms may include headaches, swelling and tenderness of the breasts, abdominal bloating, weight gain, anxiety, fatigue, depression, irritability, acne, constipation, or other discomforts (American Council on Science and Health, 1985; Harrison, 1982; R. L. Reid & Yen, 1981). These symptoms are not distinctive in themselves; it is their timing that identifies PMS. Women who think that they may have PMS should keep a diary to document that the appearance of symptoms is cyclical.

We do not know exactly what causes PMS; it may be related to the hormonal and biochemical changes that come with the menstrual cycle, and there may be psychological causes as well. In fact, not all physicians agree that PMS exists, and among those who do, its treatment is controversial, since little information is available on the effectiveness of various regimes. The Food and Drug Administration has not approved the use of any drug specifically for the treatment of PMS. Some doctors prescribe progesterone, while others, concerned with possible long-term effects of this hormone, recommend vitamins and minerals. A healthy diet and an exercise regime are often recommended, and since these should be part of both sexes' daily life anyway, they constitute a sound prescription. In addition, treatment may aim at alleviating specific symptoms: for example, antidepressants for a woman who feels "blue" before her period, or diuretics for a woman who holds fluids. Until we know more about PMS, women troubled by premenstrual discomfort need to seek sympathetic practitioners who will help them find out what works best for them individually.

PMS is sometimes confused with dysmenorrhea, menstrual cramps. Cramps tend to afflict adolescents and young women; PMS is more typical in women in their thirties or older. Dysmenorrhea is caused by contractions of the uterus, which are now known to be set in motion by prostaglandin, a hormone-like substance; thus it can be treated with prostaglandin inhibitors.

reasons have been suggested, among them biological ones. Female hardiness at every stage of life has been attributed to the genetic protection afforded by the presence of two X chromosomes, and, in mature women, to the beneficial effects of female hormones (see Box 12-2). At the same time, menstruation and pregnancy tend to make women aware of the body and its functioning, and cultural standards encourage medical management of those processes. Women see doctors during pregnancy, while trying to become pregnant, and for such routine tests as the Pap smear, which detects cervical cancer; and they are more likely to be hospitalized than men, most often for surgery in connection with the reproductive system (Nathanson & Lorenz, 1982).

Behavioral and attitudinal differences between the sexes also seem to be important. Women's more frequent visits to their physicians reflect greater sensitivity to their bodies. They know more about health, think more and do more about preventing illness, are more aware of symptoms and susceptibility, and are more likely to express their medical fears and worries (Nathanson & Lorenz, 1982). Gender-role stereotyping may enter in: men may feel that illness is not masculine and may be less likely to admit it when they do not feel well.

Thus, the fact that women say more often than men that they are sick does not mean that women are in worse general health, nor does it necessarily mean that they are imagining ailments or that they have an unhealthy preoccupation with illness. It may well be that the better care women take of themselves helps them to live longer than men.

Another factor seems to be the traditionally different lifestyles of most men and women—as evidenced by the fact that as women's lifestyles have become more like men's, their vulnerability has become more like men's, too. Today more women than before are dying from lung cancer and heart attacks, probably because women are smoking more and drinking more and are under more stress.

Since more men than women do paid work, employment may be a factor in men's lower frequency of reported illness. Indeed, employed women report less illness than homemakers—possibly because employees need to protect their jobs, their salaries, and their image as healthy workers (Nathanson & Lorenz, 1982).

Marriage also comes into the picture. Marriage seems to be healthful for both women and men, as we'll see in Chapter 13, when we look at marriage and other lifestyle choices. (It is also possible that married people merely *seem* healthier than others, since family responsibilities discourage them from taking time off from work.)

The impact of such choices as marriage and employment on physical health illustrates, once again, the relationship between the various domains of human development. It will be interesting to see the changes that occur as women's and men's roles move closer to one another. By and large, women are health-conscious not only for themselves but for their families—their husbands, their children, and (eventually) their aging parents. In fact, according to C. Lewis and Lewis, women—more than physicians—may be "the principal determiners of the health status of all members of society" (1977). As these authors ask, "If females become more equal (i.e., like males), who will look after them?"

The changing roles of men and women need not result only in women's picking up more of the ills that formerly fell more heavily on males. It can mean men's taking on more "feminine" habits, including a heightened awareness of health and of what it takes to preserve and restore it.

INTELLECTUAL DEVELOPMENT

ASPECTS OF INTELLECTUAL DEVELOPMENT IN YOUNG ADULTHOOD

Common sense suggests that adults think differently from children—that adults can hold different kinds of conversations, can understand much more complicated material, and can solve problems beyond the capabilities of most children or even of many adolescents. But how correct is common sense? And if differences do exist, what is the basis for them?

In considering the intellectual aspects of adult life, we are concerned with such questions as these:

- What happens to intelligence as measured by standard IQ tests? Does it improve, decline, or stay the same throughout the adult years? If there are changes, why do they occur? Do different aspects of cognitive functioning change in different ways? Does the method of data collection affect the findings?
- Can adults' cognition be characterized in terms of qualitative stages, as children's was by Piaget?
- Is the use of tasks originally designed for children and adolescents valid in testing adults? Would other tasks be more appropriate?
- Do certain types of intelligence emerge or strengthen in adulthood?

Let's delve into some of these questions now, remembering that we'll continue our discussion of intellectual development in adults in Chapters 14 and 16, which deal with middle and late adulthood.

Intelligence and Cognition

Psychometrics   An obvious way to attempt to find out whether intelligence increases or declines during adulthood is to give adults of different ages psychometric tests similar to those that are used to measure intelligence in children. Let's see what the results of such testing have been.

CROSS-SECTIONAL VERSUS LONGITUDINAL STUDIES   Intellectual functioning is generally at a high level in young adulthood. For many years it was believed that general intellectual activity peaked at about the age of 20 and then declined. This conclusion was based on the results of cross-sectional studies, which gave intelligence tests to people in various age groups and found that young adults did best (Doppelt & Wallace, 1955; H. Jones & Conrad, 1933; Miles & Miles, 1932).

In any cross-sectional study, though, such differences may result from *cohort* differences rather than from the effects of age per se. That is, people born more recently may know more

and have more skills because they have had better or longer schooling. The superior intellectual performance of young people may not mean that intelligence diminishes with age but that today's young people have had different experiences and therefore have developed their intellectual abilities more than people born a generation earlier. If that is so, then cross-sectional studies that appear to present a bleak picture of the course of intellectual functioning in adulthood may actually underestimate the intellectual potential of older people.

Indeed, longitudinal studies, which test the same people periodically over the years, have shown an increase in general intelligence at least until the fifties (Bayley & Oden, 1955; Owens, 1966). But these studies also present problems in interpretation of their findings. Since subjects are tested more than once, their higher scores on subsequent tests may reflect such "practice effects" as feeling more comfortable in the testing situation or remembering how they have solved similar problems in previous testings. Thus, what looks like improvement may reflect a gain in performance rather than a real gain in abilities. We'll discuss the sequential approach of K. Warner Schaie, which tries to overcome the drawbacks of both these methods of collecting data, in Chapter 16, because the implications of an assumed decline in intelligence are especially relevant in late adulthood.

FLUID VERSUS CRYSTALLIZED INTELLIGENCE   The picture is complicated further by the existence of different kinds of intellectual abilities. R. B. Cattell (1965) and J. L. Horn (1967, 1968, 1970) proposed a distinction between "fluid" and "crystallized" intelligence. **Fluid intelligence** involves the processes of perceiving relations, forming concepts, reasoning, and abstracting. This type of intelligence is considered to be dependent on neurological development and relatively free from the influences of education and culture. It is therefore tested by tasks in which the problem posed is novel for everyone or else is an extremely common cultural element. For example, people may be asked to group letters and numbers, to pair related words, or to remember a series of digits. Fluid intelligence is measured by such instruments as the Raven Progressive Matrices, in which a person must

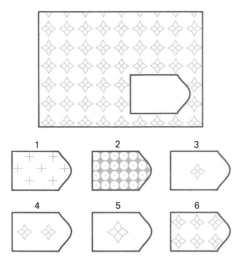

Figure 12-1 Item from the Raven Progressive Matrices Test. This test item is a measure of fluid intelligence, since it represents a novel task that does not ostensibly depend on knowledge. Even without instructions, a test-taker can understand what to do. However, people from a culture in which fill-in or matching exercises are common may do better on tests like this than people from other cultures. (*Source:* Raven, 1983.)

select a pattern that best completes a series of patterns (see Figure 12-1).

Crystallized intelligence, on the other hand, involves the ability to remember and use learned information and is therefore more dependent on education and cultural background. This type of intelligence is measured by tests of vocabulary, general information, and response to social dilemmas.

From an information-processing perspective, fluid intelligence depends on the ability to process *new* information. Crystallized intelligence depends on the use of stored information and on how *automatic* a person's information processing has become, especially in complex tasks like reading, which require a large number of mental operations (Sternberg, 1985a).

Fluid intelligence appears to reach full development in the late teens and begins to decline in early adulthood. However, people may continue to do better on tests of crystallized intelligence until near the end of life (J. L. Horn & Donaldson, 1980; see Figure 12-2). So far, though, much of the research on fluid and crystallized intelligence is cross-sectional, and so the reservations that were expressed in the preceding

section regarding cross-sectional studies need to be borne in mind. Data from longitudinal studies do show improvement in at least some of the abilities representing crystallized intelligence.

Rather than try to measure a *quantitative* increase or decline in adult intelligence, some developmentalists have looked for *qualitative* changes in the way people think as they mature. Let's turn now to K. Warner Schaie's theory of cognitive development in adulthood.

Theoretical Approaches In describing intellectual development from infancy through adolescence, we were concerned with the way cognitive abilities expand and progress through different qualitative levels. Piaget attributed these changes to a combination of maturation and experience. What happens, then, in an adult? As we might expect, experience plays an especially important role in intellectual functioning. But the experiences of an adult are different from and usually far broader than those of a child, whose world is defined largely by home and school. Because of the diversity of adult experiences, making generalizations about adults' cognition is extremely difficult (Flavell, 1970).

Still, some developmental psychologists have proposed ways to look at intellectual development in adulthood.

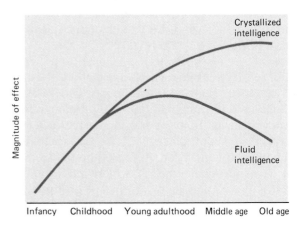

Figure 12-2 Changes in fluid and crystallized intelligence. Changes occur in two types of intelligence over a life span. While there is a decline in "fluid intelligence," there is a gradual increase in "crystallized intelligence." (*Source:* J. L. Horn & Donaldson, 1980.)

K. WARNER SCHAIE: STAGES OF COGNITIVE DEVELOPMENT IN ADULTHOOD One of the most interesting models describes five cognitive stages (Schaie, 1977–1978). According to this approach, intellectual development proceeds as a series of transitions from "what I need to know" (the acquisition of skills in childhood and adolescence), through "how I should use what I know" (the integration of these skills into a practical framework), to "why I should know" (the search for meaning and purpose that culminates in the "wisdom of old age"). Real-life experiences, then, are important influences on cognitive functioning. The sequence of stages in this model, described below, is shown in Figure 12-3.

1 *Acquisitive stage (childhood and adolescence):* Young people learn information and skills largely for their own sake, without regard for the context, to prepare for participation in society. They are likely to perform best on specific tests that give them a chance to show what they can do, even if the tasks themselves do not have meaning in their own lives.

2 *Achieving stage (late teens or early twenties to early thirties):* A shift from the acquisitive stage to the achieving stage occurs when people no longer merely acquire knowledge for its own sake but have to use what they know to achieve competence and establish independence. In this stage, people do best on tasks that are relevant to the life goals they have set for themselves.

3 *Responsible stage (late thirties to early sixties):* People in this stage are concerned with long-range goals and practical, real-life problems that are likely to be associated with the responsibility they bear for others (such as family members or employees).

4 *Executive stage (thirties or forties through middle age):* People in this stage are responsible for societal systems (such as governmental or business concerns) rather than just family units and need to integrate complex relationships on a number of levels.

5 *Reintegrative stage (late adulthood):* Older adults—who have relaxed their degree of societal involvement and responsibility, and whose cognitive functioning may be limited by biological changes—are more selective about the tasks on which they choose to expend effort. They are concerned about the purpose of what they do and are less likely than before to bother with tasks that have no meaning for them.

If adults do go through qualitative changes in intellectual functioning, the traditional psychometric tests may be inappropriate for them. The tasks of developing completely new strategies to measure intellectual competence in adults will be, says Schaie, "no less than that faced by Binet in initially measuring the intelligence of school children" (1977–1978, p. 135).

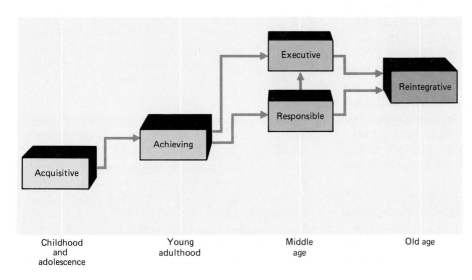

Figure 12-3 Stages of cognitive development in adults. (*Source:* Based on Schaie, 1977–1978.)

ROBERT STERNBERG: TRIARCHIC THEORY An-other way of looking at what distinguishes adults' intellectual functioning from that of children is in terms of certain kinds of thinking that become more important and more sophisticated in adult life. Let's look at an example.

Alice, Barbara, and Celia applied to graduate programs at Yale University. Alice had earned almost straight A's in college, scored extremely high on the Graduate Record Examination (GRE), and had excellent recommendations. Barbara's undergraduate grades were only so-so, and her GRE scores were low by Yale's exacting standards, but her letters of recommendation enthusiastically praised her exceptional research and creative ideas. Celia's grades, GRE scores, and recommendations were good but not among the best.

Alice and Celia got into the graduate program. Barbara did not, but the psychology professor Robert Sternberg hired her as a research associate, and she took graduate classes on the side.

Alice did very well the first year or so, but less well after that. Barbara confounded the admissions committee by doing work as outstanding as her letters of recommendation had predicted. Celia's performance in graduate school was only fair, but she had the easiest time getting a good job afterward (Trotter, 1986).

Three aspects of intelligence What explains these three stories? According to Sternberg (1985a, 1987), these women represent three different aspects of intelligence, which everyone has to a greater or lesser extent and which are particularly useful in different kinds of situations:

- ■ **Componential element:** how efficiently people process and analyze information. This is the *critical* side of intelligence, which tells people how to approach problems, how to go about solving them, and how to monitor and evaluate the results. People with strength in this area are good at taking intelligence tests and finding holes in arguments.
- ■ **Experiential element:** how people approach novel and familiar tasks. This is the *insightful* dimension of intelligence, which allows people to compare new information with what they already know or to come up with new ways of putting facts together—as Einstein did when he developed his theory of relativity. Automatic performance of familiar operations (like recognizing known words) is an important adjunct to insight, because it leaves the mind free to tackle unfamiliar tasks (like decoding new words).
- ■ **Contextual element:** how people deal with their environment. This is the *practical,* "real-world" aspect of intelligence, which becomes increasingly valuable in adult life; for example, in selecting a place to live or a field of work. It is the ability to size up a situation and figure out what to do: either adapt to it, change it, or find a new, more comfortable setting.

Applying Sternberg's theory to the three graduate students, then, we see that Alice's strong point was her componential ability. She was the kind of student who sails through the tests typically given in undergraduate schools. But in graduate school, where original thinking is expected, Barbara's superior experiential intelligence—her fresh insights and innovative ideas—began to shine. Celia, on the other hand, was strongest in practical, contextual intelligence—"street smarts." She knew her way around. She chose "hot" research topics, submitted her papers to the "right" journals, and knew where and how to apply for jobs.

Psychometric tests concentrate on tasks that measure componential (critical) intelligence. However, they do not normally assess experiential (insightful) or contextual (practical) abilities. Since these last two aspects of intelligence are particularly important in adult life, psychometric tests are even less useful in gauging adults' intelligence than in gauging children's.

Practical intelligence and tacit knowledge Practical intelligence involves the application of **tacit knowledge**—"inside" information, or "savvy," which is not formally taught or openly expressed (like knowing how to win a promotion or cut through red tape). Getting ahead often depends on knowing about self-management (understanding motivation and knowing how to organize time and energy), knowing about management of tasks (as in knowing how to write a

Success in business and professional life often depends on tacit knowledge—practical, "inside" information about how things are done, which is not openly expressed but must be gained from experience.

grant proposal), and knowing about management of others (as in knowing when to reward subordinates). Job performance typically shows only a weak correlation with IQ and employment tests; but one study in which hypothetical work-related scenarios were presented to experts and novices in psychology and business management found a significant relationship between job performance and the above three categories of tacit knowledge (Wagner & Sternberg, 1986).

This research raises interesting questions that need further exploration. How and when is tacit knowledge acquired? Why do some people seem to acquire it more efficiently than others? Are there ways to acquire it more rapidly? Can it be taught directly, or is it best picked up by observing mentors?

Moral Development

The most influential theorists in the field of moral reasoning hold that moral development in childhood and adolescence rests on cognitive development—the shedding of egocentric thought and the growing ability to think abstractly (see Chapters 8 and 10). We have seen, however, that many adolescents do not reach Kohlberg's highest stages of moral thinking. Fully principled, postconventional thinking at

Kohlberg's fifth and sixth stages often does not occur until at least the twenties—if ever. At this level of moral thought, development is chiefly a function of experience.

The Role of Experience in Moral Judgments

The adage "Live and learn" sums up adult moral development. Experience often leads people to reevaluate their criteria for judging what is right and fair. Usually the experiences that promote such change have a strong emotional component, which triggers rethinking in a way that hypothetical, impersonal discussions cannot. As people undergo such experiences, they are more likely to see other people's points of view with regard to social and moral conflicts.

It is often not until young adulthood—when the crises and turning points of identity revolve around moral issues—that people commit themselves to acting on their moral principles. Demonstrating against perceived wrongs like apartheid in South Africa helps college students translate their growing intellectual awareness into action.

STAGE	SUBJECT	QUESTION	ANSWER	INTERPRETATION
Stage 1	Tommy, at age 10	"Is it better to save the life of one important person or the lives of a lot of unimportant people?"	"All the people that aren't important, because one man just has one house, maybe a lot of furniture, but a whole bunch of people have an awful lot of furniture. . . . "	Tommy is confusing the value of people with the value of their property.
Stage 2	Tommy, at age 13	"Should a doctor 'mercy-kill' a fatally ill woman who is requesting death because of pain?"	"Maybe it would be good to put her out of her pain; she'd be better off that way. But the husband wouldn't want it; it's not like an animal. If a pet dies, you can get along without it—it isn't something you really need. Well, you can get a new wife, but it's not really the same."	Tommy thinks of the woman's value in terms of what she can do for her husband.
Stage 3	Tommy, at age 16	"Should a doctor 'mercy-kill' a fatally ill woman who is requesting death because of pain?"	"It might be best for her, but her husband—it's a human life—not like an animal; it just doesn't have the same relationship that a human being does to a family. . . . "	Tommy identifies with the husband's distinctively human empathy and love, but he still does not realize that the woman's life would have value even if her husband did not love her or even if she had no husband.
Stage 4	Richard, at age 16	"Should a doctor 'mercy-kill' a fatally ill woman who is requesting death because of pain?"	"I don't know. In one way, it's murder; it's not a right or privilege of man to decide who shall live and who should die. God put life into everybody on earth, and you're taking away something from that person that came directly from God, and you're destroying something that is very sacred; it's in a way part of God, and it's almost destroying a part of God when you kill a person."	Richard sees life as sacred because it was created by God, an authority.

TABLE 12-2
CONTINUED

STAGE	SUBJECT	QUESTION	ANSWER	INTERPRETATION
Stage 5	Richard, at age 20	"Should a doctor 'mercy-kill' a fatally ill woman requesting death because of pain?"	"There are more and more people in the medical profession who think it is a hardship on everyone—the person, the family—when you know that someone is going to die. When a person is kept alive by an artificial lung or kidney, it's more like being a vegetable than being a human. If it's her own choice, I think there are certain rights and privileges that go along with being a human being."	Richard now defines the value of life in terms of equal and universal human rights in a context of relativity, with consideration of the quality of that life and of the practical consequences.
Stage 6	Richard, at age 24	"Should a doctor 'mercy-kill' a fatally ill woman requesting death because of pain?"	"A human life takes precedence over any other moral or legal value, whoever it is. A human life has inherent value whether or not it is valued by a particular individual."	Richard now sees the value of human life as absolute and not as something derived from or dependent on social or divine authority. There is a universality to his thinking, which transcends cultural boundaries.

Source: Adapted from Kohlberg, 1968.

For example, Bielby and Papalia (1975) noted that some adults spontaneously offer personal experiences as reasons for their answers to Kohlberg's moral dilemmas such as Heinz's dilemma (discussed in Chapter 8). Someone who has had actual experience with cancer is more likely to condone a man's stealing a precious drug to save his dying wife than someone who has not, and to give as an explanation for condoning it his or her own illness or that of a loved one.

Two experiences that advance moral development, according to Kohlberg, are confronting conflicting values away from home (such as those encountered in college) and experiencing sustained responsibility for the welfare of other people (a reason why parenthood is such a significant transition). Kohlberg (1973) believes that the cognitive awareness of higher moral principles develops in adolescence but that most people do not commit themselves to acting upon these principles until adulthood, when the crises and turning points of identity often revolve around moral issues.

The cognitive stage, then, seems to set the upper limit for moral growth potential. Someone whose thinking is still at the level of concrete operations is unlikely to exhibit a sophisticated level of moral decision making. But someone at the cognitive stage of formal operations may not attain the highest level of moral thinking, either—until experience catches up with cognition.

Table 12-2 shows an example of Kohlberg's sequence of moral development—from childhood into young adulthood—in which subjects reveal their perception of the value of human life. (Remember that Kohlberg identifies one's stage of moral development by the reasons one gives for a conclusion rather than by the conclusion itself. Also, for many people, the ages given for stages 5 and 6 would be in the late twenties or even later.)

Are There Gender Differences in Moral Development? The question of gender differences in moral development has evoked one of the hottest controversies in developmental psychology. Many critics have assailed Freud's idea that women, because of their biological nature, are morally inferior to men. Kohlberg's theory of moral reasoning, too, has been attacked for its orientation toward values that are in general more important to males than to females. The basis for the criticism is that some studies of moral reasoning in adulthood have shown differences in the levels achieved by men and women, and these differences have consistently favored men.

A review of the literature on moral development, however, found no significant gender differences in the levels of moral reasoning across the life span. Only a few inconsistent differences showed up in childhood and adolescence. Small differences found in a few studies of adults did favor men, but the findings were not clearly gender-related, since the men in the studies generally had more education and higher-level jobs than the women. The author of the review concluded that "the moral reasoning of males and females is more similar than different" (Walker, 1984, p. 687).

An absence of gender differences in moral development does not mean, however, that men and women look at moral issues the same way. Indeed, there is evidence that they define morality differently and base their moral decisions on different values. Carol Gilligan (1982), one of the most prominent critics of Kohlberg's work, maintains that his approach fails to take into account women's major concerns and perspectives. While our society demands that men be assertive and use independent judgment, it expects women to be concerned with the well-being of others and to sacrifice themselves to ensure that well-being. Woman's central moral dilemma, then, is the conflict between herself and others, a conflict that does not emerge in Kohlberg's scheme.

To determine how women develop morally, Gilligan examined their reasoning regarding an area of their lives in which they have choices: the control of fertility. She interviewed and gave Kohlberg's dilemmas to 29 women referred by abortion and pregnancy counseling services. These women talked about whether they would terminate their pregnancies or allow them to continue, and how they were arriving at their decisions.

The women spoke "in a distinct moral language whose evolution traces a sequence of development," writes Gilligan (1982, p. 73). They saw morality in terms of selfishness versus responsibility and as an obligation to exercise care and avoid hurt. They viewed people who care for each other as the most responsible, and those who hurt someone else as selfish and immoral. Gilligan concluded that while men tend to think more in terms of abstract justice and fairness, women tend to think more about their responsibilities to specific people. Gilligan identified a sequence of moral development for women, shown in Table 12-3.

Gilligan provides a dramatic illustration of the two contrasting concepts of morality: Kohlberg's morality of rights on the one hand and her own morality of responsibility on the other. The abstract morality exemplified by Kohlberg's stage 6 led the biblical Abraham to be ready to sacrifice the life of his son when God demanded it as a proof of faith. Gilligan's person-centered morality can also be seen in the Bible, in the story of the woman who proved to King Solomon that she was a baby's mother when she agreed to give up the infant to another woman rather than see it harmed.

Acknowledging the female perspective on moral development enables us to appreciate the importance for both sexes of connections with other people and of the universal need for compassion and care.

THE COLLEGE EXPERIENCE

College can mean anything from a 2-year community college stressing vocational training or a small 4-year liberal arts school to a large state

TABLE 12-3 GILLIGAN'S LEVELS OF MORAL DEVELOPMENT IN WOMEN

STAGE	DESCRIPTION
Level 1: Orientation of individual survival	The woman concentrates on herself—on what is practical and what is best for her.
Transition 1: From selfishness to responsibility	The woman realizes her connection to others and thinks about what would be the responsible choice in terms of other people (such as the unborn baby), as well as herself.
Level 2: Goodness as self-sacrifice	This conventional feminine wisdom dictates sacrificing the woman's own wishes to what other people want—and will think of her. She considers herself responsible for the actions of others, while holding others responsible for her own choices. She is in a dependent position, one in which her indirect efforts to exert control often turn into manipulation, sometimes through the use of guilt.
Transition 2: From goodness to truth	She assesses her decisions not on the basis of how others will react to them, but on her intentions and the consequences of her actions. She develops a new judgment that takes into account her own needs, along with those of others. She wants to be "good" by being responsible to others, but also wants to be "honest" by being responsible to herself. Survival returns as a major concern.
Level 3: Morality of nonviolence	By elevating the injunction against hurting anyone (including herself) to a principle that governs all moral judgment and action, the woman establishes a "moral equality" between herself and others and is then able to assume the responsibility for choice in moral dilemmas.

Source: Adapted from Gilligan, 1982.

university with graduate divisions. Most colleges today are coeducational, but a few are still all-male or all-female. With such diversity, it is difficult to generalize about the college experience.

Who Goes to College?

Today's college classrooms include many different kinds of students. Bonnie, for example, entered directly from high school, having already decided on a premedical program. Jim worked for 2 years after high school and is now taking courses in music and journalism, unsure which to follow as a career. Seth wants a master's degree in business administration as his route to a six-figure salary. Marilyn, like her mother before her, has come to college looking for a husband. Elise interrupted her education to marry and to raise three children; now that her children are in college, she has come back to get her degree. Warren, retired from the hardware business after a lifetime of supporting a family, now has time to expand his intellectual horizons.

More than 12.2 million students are enrolled in American colleges and universities, 60 percent of them full-time and three-fourths at the undergraduate level. A majority—52 percent—are women, and an increasing proportion are returning students, aged 35 and older (U.S. Department of Education, 1987b; see Chapter 14).

In general, the ablest students go to college. Although socioeconomic status may affect access to a higher education, many superior students get scholarships or loans (U.S. Department of Education, 1987c). Still, about 1 out of 8 high school seniors of high ability never go to college (National Institute of Education, NIE, 1984).

Most students go to 4-year colleges or universities; a smaller number, to junior or community colleges. A still smaller minority, usually students of lower academic performance and socioeconomic level, attend vocational or technical schools. Public institutions draw the most students. White people are more likely than members of minority groups to attend private universities (U.S. Department of Education, 1987c).

Intellectual and Personality Development in College

College is often a time of intellectual discovery and personal growth. The traditional-age college student (who, of course, is no longer necessarily the *typical* student) is in transition from adolescence to adulthood. College offers the opportunity to question assumptions held over from childhood, which might otherwise interfere with the establishment of adult identity.

Students change in response to the diversity of the student body, which may pose challenges to long-held views and values; to the student culture itself, which is structured differently from the culture of society at large; to the curriculum, which may offer new insights and new ways of thinking; and to members of the faculty, who may take a personal interest in a student and provide new role models (Madison, 1969).

One avenue of self-discovery may be the exploration of new, more realistic career choices than the ambitions of childhood and adolescence. For example, a student who has been attracted to the adventurousness of a career in astronomy may find, after some experience in various academic disciplines, that his real leanings are toward working with people.

The academic and social challenges encountered in college often lead to intellectual and moral growth. In a widely cited study, based on interviews with 67 Harvard and Radcliffe students throughout their undergraduate years, the students progressed from extremely rigid thinking to flexibility and ultimately to freely chosen commitments (Perry, 1970):

- First, students see the world in polar terms: every question has a right answer known to an "authority," who must teach it.
- As students encounter a wide variety of ideas (from their studies and from other students), they accept the coexistence of several different points of view, and they also accept their own uncertainty. They consider this stage temporary, however, and expect to learn the "one right answer eventually."
- Next they see the relativism of all knowledge and values: they recognize that different societies, different cultures, and different individuals work out their own value systems.
- Finally they affirm their identity through the values and commitments they choose for themselves.

Recently, some critics have charged that American colleges foster relativistic thinking which promotes the idea that all values are equally valid, and that they thus fail to give students rational standards for weighing the merits of particular arguments, philosophies, or cultural practices (Bloom, 1987).

Debate about the purposes of college education is healthy, for it reaffirms society's concern with the intellectual and personality development of young adults. Most people would agree, though, that two basic purposes of a college education are to broaden young people's perspective and to encourage them to think for themselves.

Gender Differences in Development in College

Gone are the days when many college women quipped (only partly in jest) that they were there to get an "M.R.S." degree. Yet studies done as recently as the late 1970s showed that girls—who often outshone boys throughout elementary school and high school—slipped behind academically in higher education.

The studies found that female students, even the ablest ones, had lower self-esteem and more limited aspirations than males. Women tended to avoid academic risks and especially to steer away from mathematics (Sells, 1980). They overprepared for class and took careful notes, but panicked over assignments and examinations and felt less confident than their male classmates about their preparation for graduate study (Leland et al., 1979). Even highly gifted women tended to go to less selective colleges than men and were less likely to go on to prestigious graduate schools and high-status occupations (Kerr, 1985).

Female college students may develop more interest and confidence in studying anatomy when taught by a female instructor who serves as a role model. Although the number of women going into traditionally "masculine" fields has greatly increased since the 1970s, male students are still more likely to major in a physical science.

Some observers attributed these patterns to the ways girls are socialized, noting that during adolescence girls become more focused on relationships and boys become more focused on careers (Kerr, 1985). These observers pointed out that society gives girls subtle and not-so-subtle messages that emphasize the primacy of their roles as wife and mother and the difficulty or even impossibility of combining personal achievement with love and family. (Young men, of course, are given no reason to feel that their roles as future husbands and fathers interfere with developing their career potential.)

Other researchers looked into the college classroom itself for patterns of gender discrimination (such as male professors' calling on male students more often and "putting down" females), but their studies showed conflicting results (J. Bernard, 1976; Sternglanz & Lyberger-Ficek, 1975).

Today, the role of women in American society is changing rapidly, and the change is reflected in college enrollment, in the courses young women choose, and in their personal, educational, and occupational goals. In the 1970s, high school girls were less likely than boys to go to college and less likely to finish. Today girls are *more* likely than boys to go to college and about as likely to aim for advanced degrees (U.S. Department of Education, 1987c).

Women (unlike men) are getting more de-grees today than in the past. More than half of the bachelor's degrees awarded in 1984–1985, nearly half of the master's degrees (49.9 percent), and about one-third of the doctoral and professional degrees were awarded to women (U.S. Department of Education, 1987a). From 1974 to 1984, the percentage of women among students of dentistry, medicine, veterinary medicine, and law took large leaps (Congressional Caucus for Women's Issues, 1987; see Figure 12-4).

Yet some gender-based differences persist. Among students who took the Scholastic Apti-

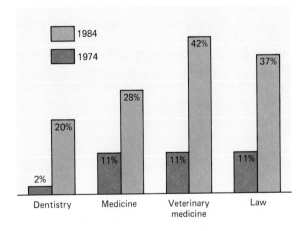

Figure 12-4 Percentage of women among graduate students pursuing advanced degrees in certain fields, 1974–1984. (*Source:* Associated Press, 1987.)

tude Test (SAT) for college admission in 1987, eighty-four percent of those who planned to study engineering were boys, while 79 percent of those considering teaching careers were girls. Girls were more interested than boys in visual and performing arts (62 percent), communications (65 percent), foreign languages (80 percent), health and allied fields (68 percent), home economics (88 percent), library science (74 percent), English (66 percent), and social sciences and history (65 percent). Boys were more likely than girls to major in architecture (63 percent), computer science (65 percent), military science (86 percent), and physical sciences (70 percent).

"Math phobia," though, appears to be on the wane: boys who planned to major in mathematics had only a slight edge (52 to 48 percent) over girls (Newhouse News Service, 1987).

More research is needed to determine how college women are dealing with the wider options available to them.

Leaving College

The college dropout is variously defined as a student who leaves a college and takes some time off before resuming studies at the same school ("stopping out"), or transfers to another school, or ends college studies altogether. About half of entering college students never get degrees at all (NIE, 1984).

There is no typical dropout. Students leave school for all sorts of reasons—marriage, the desire to be close to a loved one, a change in occupational status, or dissatisfaction with some aspects of the school they are enrolled in. Ability may be a factor to some extent; able students are more likely than they were in the early 1970s to remain in college (U.S. Department of Education, 1987c). But although most dropouts have lower average aptitude scores than those who stay in school, they are usually doing satisfactory work.

One study of 432 first-year students at a large university compared answers on orientation questionnaires of those who withdrew during the year and those who stayed. The withdrawers had been more dissatisfied with their lives at the time of admission. The men seemed to be following their parents' goals rather than their own and were less interested in their courses than

the continuers were. The women did not get along with their parents as well as the continuers did and were also more likely to feel lost, lonely, and socially isolated. For some of these students, withdrawal was an active step toward separating from their parents and forming their own identities (Timmons, 1978).

For some students, the decision to leave college temporarily may be a positive step. Many students gain more by working for a while, enrolling at a more compatible institution, or just allowing themselves more time to mature. Many colleges now make it easier for students to take leaves of absences, to study part-time, and to earn credit for independent study, life experiences, and work done at other institutions. Our main concern, then, is not with the "stopouts" but with those college students who never get degrees at all and who, as a result, may become seriously limited in their opportunities.

Formal education need not—and often does not—end in one's early twenties. It can and should continue throughout adulthood. An indication of the trend toward lifelong learning can be seen in the fact that, between 1972 and 1982, college enrollments for people aged 25 to 34 increased by 69.8 percent, and enrollments for those 35 and older increased an even higher 77.4 percent (Grant, 1984). We'll discuss the place of educational programs in the lives of mature adults in later chapters.

DEVELOPING A CAREER

Young adulthood is the time when most people embark upon their first full-time jobs, thus carving out an important aspect of their identity, achieving financial independence, and showing their ability to assume adult responsibilities. Long before this time, however, and long after it, work has played and will continue to play a major role in development. Children think about what they want to be when they grow up, and although their thoughts are often fanciful, many a career is born in a child's dream. Adolescents struggle with developing a vocational identity. People in midlife often question their career choices and make changes voluntarily—or are forced into them by unemployment—and many older adults need to deal with the issues of retirement.

Work is closely tied in with all aspects of development—intellectual, physical, and social and emotional. Factors in all these realms affect the kind of work people do, and their work can affect every other area of their lives, as we'll see when theories of adult personality development are discussed in Chapter 13. Right now, let's look at some important aspects of work in the lives of young adults: how age and gender affect attitudes and performance, and how working life and family life intersect (see Box 12-3, page 438).

Age-Related Attitudes and Behavior

How does a person's stage in life affect the way he or she thinks about work and performs on the job? A substantial body of research has found a number of age-related effects, as reported in a review of more than 185 studies (Rhodes, 1983).

How Young Adults Feel about Their Jobs By and large, younger workers (under age 40), who are in the process of carving out their careers, are less satisfied with their jobs overall than they will be later on, at least until age 60. They are less involved with their jobs, less committed to their employers, and more likely to change jobs than they will be in later life.

What accounts for the growth of job satisfaction with age? Researchers are not sure. There are no clear age differences in specific aspects of job satisfaction (satisfaction with promotion, supervision, and coworkers), and findings regarding satisfaction with pay have been mixed. It is possible that the relationship between age and overall job satisfaction may reflect the nature of the work itself. The longer people work at a specific occupation, the more rewarding the work may be (Rhodes, 1983).

Or it may be that younger people, who are still seeking the best path in life, are aware that they can change career directions more easily now than later. They may look at their jobs with a more critical eye than they will when they have made a stronger commitment.

Again, we must be cautious in interpreting differences that show up in cross-sectional studies. For example, older people have shown a greater belief in the "work ethic," the idea that people should work hard to develop character. It is likely that this is a difference in values between cohorts rather than an effect of how long people have lived. There may be more of a developmental difference, however, in personality needs that are associated with work. Younger workers, for example, are more concerned with the interest level of their work, with opportunities for developing their abilities, and with chances for advancement. Older workers care more about having friendly supervisors and coworkers and receiving help with their work.

How Young Adults Perform on the Job Findings about the relationship between age and job performance are mixed. Studies on absenteeism, for example, give conflicting results. But if we break the findings down to *avoidable* absences (the ones that seem to be voluntary on the worker's part and are not excused by the employer) and *unavoidable* ones (such as those caused by sickness), we do see some effects of age. Younger workers have more avoidable absences than older workers, possibly because of a lower level of job commitment. Older workers have more unavoidable absences, probably as a result of poorer health and slower recovery times from accidents.

When we look at how well people do their work, the picture again is not clear-cut. It is possible that the key issue is experience rather than chronological age: when older people perform better, it may be because they have been on the job longer, not because they are older.

As we'll see, many workers continue to be productive very late in life. In general, age differences in performance seem to depend largely on how performance is measured and on the demands of a specific kind of work. A job that requires quick reflexes, for example, is likely to be performed better by a young person; one that depends on maturity of judgment may be better executed by an older person.

Gender-Related Attitudes and Behavior

Today 1 out of every 3 economists, 1 out of every 4 computer programmers, 1 out of every 6 mail carriers, and 1 out of every 2 bartenders

BOX 12-3   FOOD FOR THOUGHT

HOW DUAL-EARNER COUPLES COPE

Never before have so many women worked outside the home: in close to 2 out of 3 homes in which the husband is working, the wife is out working, too (Conference Board, 1984). Marriages in which husband and wife both hold jobs outside the home represent a considerable change from traditional family patterns in American society and offer both advantages and disadvantages.

A major advantage, of course, is financial. Most first-time home buyers are dual-income families, and the wife's income often raises a family to middle-income status or even affluence. One out of every eight wives earn half or more of the family's total income; 1 out of every 3 earn between 30 and 50 percent (Conference Board, 1984).

The benefits are often not just financial. Intangible benefits may include:

■ More equal relationship between husband and wife

■ Sense of integrity for the woman

■ Closer relationship between a father and his children

■ Enhanced capacity for each partner to function and develop in both work and family roles

This way of life presents many stresses, too, for working couples. There are extra demands on time and energy, conflicts between work and family roles, possible competitive rivalry between husband and wife,

and anxiety and guilt over whether the children's needs are being met. One source of strain lies in the fact that a working husband and wife are part of three role systems— the work system of the wife, the work system of the husband, and the joint family system. Each role makes varying demands at different times, and couples have to decide which should take priority at each time. The family is most demanding when there are young children; career demands are especially stressful when a worker is getting established or being promoted. Unfortunately, both kinds of demands often occur around the same time: often in young adulthood.

Because of the transitional nature of the sweeping changes in family and career aspirations, today's hard-working, family-oriented men and women have few models to show them how to handle the role conflicts and other problems that arise. As couples work out their own solutions, they are bringing about changes in the way they divide the work within the home. Although women who work outside the home continue to assume the primary responsibility for homemaking and child care (Nock & Kingston, 1984), there is a trend toward more sharing of tasks (Maret & Finlay, 1984).

Besides sharing tasks, working couples call upon a wide range of coping mechanisms (Olds, 1986; D. A. Skinner, 1983). They use some of the extra income afforded

by their two jobs to hire help— for child care, for housekeeping chores, and for such timesaving and labor-saving alternatives as laundry service, take-out and restaurant meals, and microwave ovens. They call upon resources in the community, such as after-school, weekend, and summer programs for their children; friends who are living similar lifestyles and can offer emotional and practical support; and family members who give many kinds of help. They organize their lives to include time with their children, time with each other, and personal time. They expect the children to do more work within the home. They learn how to compartmentalize their lives, to leave work concerns at the office and family worries at home when they go from one sphere to the other. And they continually remind themselves of the benefits of this lifestyle, even when the strains of managing work and family seem overwhelming.

As more couples adopt this lifestyle, society will have to respond with institutional changes to alleviate the strains on dual-earner families. Living and working environments could be redesigned, for example, so that people could pool domestic services and thus split their time more easily between home and workplace. More jobs could be structured on a part-time basis; more employers could provide child-care services. Such changes would help parents, children, and society.

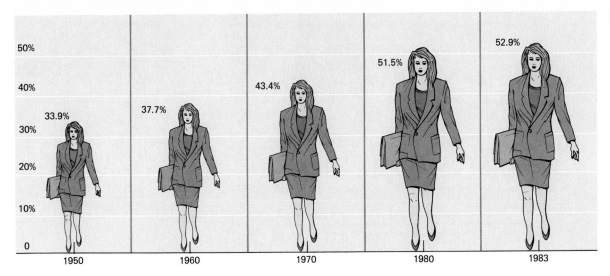

Figure 12-5 Percentage of American women in the labor force, 1950–1983. (*Source: Bianchi & Spain, 1986.*)

are women (Congressional Caucus for Women's Issues, 1987). Gender has less to do with vocational choice than 25 years ago, when most women—regardless of their individual interests and talents—planned to devote the bulk of their working lives to homemaking and child care. (Care of one's own home and children has rarely even been recognized as a vocational choice but has been seen as just something that women are "supposed to do.")

Even in previous generations, many women worked for pay outside of the home. Female participation in the labor force is now greater than ever: about 53 percent of women in 1983, compared with about one-third in 1950 (Bianchi & Spain, 1986; see Figure 12-5). More than 6 out of 10 mothers of children under 18 are employed (Hayghe, 1986; see Table 9-3).

Like men, women work to earn money, to achieve recognition, and to fulfill personal needs. About two-thirds of working women need to work because they are single, divorced, widowed, separated, or married to men earning less than $10,000 per year. The women's movement has inspired many women to seek challenging and satisfying jobs. Sociological trends toward later marriage and childbearing and smaller families have made it easier for many young women to pursue ambitious educational and career goals. And women who do have families are taking advantage of alternative work patterns such as part-time and flexible schedules, and job sharing (Maymi, 1982).

Laws providing for equal opportunity in employment underline the rights of both sexes to be considered for jobs equally, to be paid

Most women work because they need the money, but they also want nonfinancial benefits such as recognition and the satisfaction of using their abilities. The women's movement has inspired many women, like this cable splicer, to find jobs outside the traditional domain of "women's work."

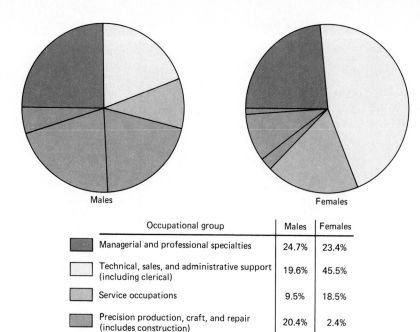

Occupational group	Males	Females
Managerial and professional specialties	24.7%	23.4%
Technical, sales, and administrative support (including clerical)	19.6%	45.5%
Service occupations	9.5%	18.5%
Precision production, craft, and repair (includes construction)	20.4%	2.4%
Operators, fabricators, and laborers	20.9%	9.1%
Farming, forestry, and fishing	4.9%	1.2%
Total	100.0%	100.1%

Figure 12-6 Employed persons by major occupational groups and sex. *Note:* Because of rounding, total for females is more than 100 percent. (*Source:* U.S. Department of Labor, 1985.)

equally, and to be promoted equally. Reality, however, still falls far short of equality. For every dollar that men earn, women earn only about 70 cents. The wage gap has narrowed slightly in the past few years—not so much because women are paid more but because men's earnings have dropped as highly paid manufacturing jobs have disappeared (Congressional Caucus for Women's Issues, 1987).

Although more women are getting better jobs these days (especially in business and the professions), a disproportionate number are still doing low-paid work of the types that have traditionally been done by women (and that tend to re-main low-paid largely *because* they are done by women). As Figure 12-6 shows, close to half of all employed women are clerks, salespersons, and the like; very few have skilled craft or construction jobs. As more women have entered the labor force, many have come in at low-paying, entry-level jobs, and often they do not advance as rapidly as men do. In part, this may reflect discrimination in the marketplace; in part, it may reflect the real conflicts that many women face as they try to juggle work and family roles.

In Chapter 13, we'll explore the effects of both work and relationships on young men's and women's personality development.

Sensory and Psychomotor Functioning

■ The typical young adult, from about 20 to 40 years of age, is in good health; physical and sensory abilities are usually excellent.

Health

■ Accidents are the leading cause of death for people from age 25 to age 34; cancer is the leading cause from 35 to 44.

■ Specific behavior patterns, such as eating habits, exercise, smoking, drinking alcohol, and ways of reacting to stress, can have a direct effect on health.

■ Good health is related to levels of education and income, gender, and lifestyle.

■ Women are more likely than men to report being ill, to use health services, and to be hospitalized. Women are more health-conscious than men and tend to arrange for the health services of their entire families.

■ Hormones of the menstrual cycle seem to affect women physically and emotionally, but not with regard to their intellectual functioning.

Aspects of Intellectual Development in Young Adulthood

■ Intellectual functioning is generally at a high level in young adulthood.

■ Horn and Cattell have proposed two types of intelligence: fluid and crystallized. Each is influenced by different factors and displays a different developmental course.

■ K. Warner Schaie has proposed five stages of cognitive development from childhood through late adulthood: acquisitive, achieving, responsible, executive, and reintegrative.

■ Robert Sternberg has proposed three aspects of intelligence: componential (critical), experiential (insightful), and contextual (practical). The second and third aspects develop and become particularly important in adulthood.

■ According to Lawrence Kohlberg, moral development in adulthood depends primarily on experience, but as before, moral thinking cannot exceed the limits set by cognitive development.

■ The issue of women's moral development has been explored by Carol Gilligan, who proposes that women have concerns and perspectives that are not tapped in Kohlberg's theory and research. Whereas men tend to think more about justice and fairness, women are more concerned with responsibilities to specific people.

The College Experience

■ The college experience affects intellect and personality, as college students question long-held assumptions and values.

■ In the past, girls often did better than boys in elementary school and high school, but that picture tended to change at the college level. Today, more women are going to college and are earning advanced degrees. The fields that men and women choose to study still differ markedly, however.

■ About 50 percent of college students never earn degrees.

Developing a Career

■ Career development is important during young adulthood. Younger workers are less committed to their present jobs than older workers.

■ Dual-earner families, in which both spouses work outside the home, are becoming more prevalent. Both society and the working couples have to make changes to alleviate the stresses associated with the potentially conflicting demands of work and family.

■ Women, like men, work for a variety of reasons—to earn money, to achieve recognition, and to fulfill personal needs. Women tend to earn less than men, and although more women are getting better jobs than in previous decades, most are still doing low-paid work. Today an increasing number of women are pursuing careers in business, law, medicine, and other traditionally male-dominated areas.

KEY TERMS

achieving stage (page 427)
acquisitive stage (427)
componential element (428)
contextual element (428)
crystallized intelligence (426)
executive stage (427)

experiential element (428)
fluid intelligence (425)
premenstrual syndrome (PMS) (423)
reintegrative stage (427)
responsible stage (427)

stress (419)
stressor (419)
tacit knowledge (428)
Type A behavior pattern (421)
Type B behavior pattern (421)

SUGGESTED READINGS

Bolles, R.N. (1984). *What color is your parachute? A practical manual for job-hunters and career changers.* Berkeley, CA: Ten Speed Press. A practical and entertaining step-by-step guide to deciding on life goals and finding the work that will help to implement them.

Chernin, K. (1985). *The hungry self.* New York: Times Books. A probing analysis of women's often troubled relationship with food. After looking at the cultural significance and personal consequences of eating disorders, the author concludes that eating problems often conceal identity problems that stem from troubled mother-daughter relationships.

Gilligan, C. (1982). *In a different voice.* Cambridge, MA: Harvard University Press. A discussion of the misrepresentation of women by the major theorists in developmental psychology, with an emphasis on women's moral development.

Kerr, B.A. (1985). *Smart girls, gifted women.* Columbus, OH: Ohio Psychology. A thought-provoking book that considers the question "Why don't gifted women achieve more in their careers?" Drawing on a variety of studies, the author lists principles for guiding gifted girls and offers specific ideas for parents.

Sternberg, R. (1985). *Beyond IQ.* Cambridge: Cambridge University Press. Sternberg's statement of the triarchic theory of intelligence.

Terkel, S. (1974). *Working.* New York: Random House. The subtitle of this powerful book tells its story: "People talk about what they do all day and how they feel about what they do." The book is made up of transcripts of interviews with workers in a wide range of occupations.

13

CHAPTER

13

CHAPTER

PERSONALITY AND SOCIAL DEVELOPMENT IN YOUNG ADULTHOOD

... The situation of the adult is by no means as different from that of the child as it is generally assumed [to be]. Every adult is in need of help, of warmth, of protection, in many ways differing [from] and yet in many ways similar to the needs of the child.

Erich Fromm, *The Sane Society*, 1955

ASK YOURSELF

■ Do adults' personalities develop in definite, predictable patterns, or does the course of development depend on what happens in people's lives?

■ How is personality development in young adulthood similar and different for males and females?

■ What are the effects of such lifestyle choices as marriage, divorce, single life, cohabitation, parenthood, stepparenthood, and nonparenthood?

■ What do love, sexuality, and friendship mean to young adults?

Looking back, most 40-year-olds would say that they are very different people from what they were at the age of 20, when they entered young adulthood. And by the age of 60 or 70, it is likely that even more important changes will have taken place. It is hard to believe, then, that until recently, students of human development paid little attention to the social and emotional development that takes place during the 50 or more years of adult life.

Today few people believe that personalities stop growing when bodies are fully grown. Most developmentalists are now convinced that human beings are capable of change and growth as long as they live. In this and succeeding chapters we discuss the body of theory and research in adult development that has arisen during the past few decades. Two principal approaches are the normative-crisis model and the timing-of-events model.

Erik Erikson's theory is an example of the *normative-crisis model,* which describes human development in terms of a definite sequence of age-related social and emotional changes. Erikson and others who follow this approach (such as Daniel Levinson and George Vaillant, whose work popularized the concept of the *midlife crisis*) believe that there is a built-in "ground plan" for human development, which everyone follows.

Proponents of the *timing-of-events model* see development not as the result of a set plan or schedule of crises but as a result of the times in people's lives when important events take place. Thus this model (of which Bernice Neugarten is a major advocate) allows for more individual variation. According to this view, if life events occur as expected, development proceeds smoothly; if they do not, stress can result, affecting development. Stress may occur either if an unexpected event occurs (such as a job layoff) or if an expected event happens earlier or later

(© Julie Houck 1986/Stock, Boston)

Intimacy, a major achievement of young adulthood, comes about through commitment to a relationship that may demand sacrifice and compromise. According to Erik Erikson, intimacy is possible only after each partner has achieved his or her own identity. Carol Gilligan and other researchers propose a different sequence for women, who, they say, often achieve intimacy first and then go on to find identity later, sometimes years later.

than usual or fails to happen (for example, if one is not yet married at age 35 or is already widowed at that age). This model, then, is concerned with chronological age only insofar as it relates to the norms that culture leads people to expect.

In this chapter we look at both of these approaches, each of which is backed by research. We also examine how young adults reach important decisions that frame their lives—decisions that revolve around love, sex, parenting, and friendship. Although the important area of work and career was discussed in Chapter 12, this realm is so vital to the issues explored in Chapter 13 that it comes up again here.

PERSONALITY DEVELOPMENT IN YOUNG ADULTHOOD: TWO MODELS

Normative-Crisis Model

Sigmund Freud and Erik Erikson each proposed a series of stages in which people need to resolve critical issues in their development. Freud did not take his theories of development beyond adolescence, but Erikson went on to propose three crises in adulthood: one in young adulthood, one in middle age, and one in late adulthood. (We discuss the latter two crises in Chapters 15 and 17.)

Inspired by Erikson, several researchers have studied adults to identify specific stages or phases of development. The longitudinal Grant study, reported by George E. Vaillant (1977), followed a large group of Harvard University students from age 18 into their fifties. In a smaller, biographical study, Daniel Levinson and his colleagues (1978) tested and interviewed 35- to 45-year-old men and identified key periods of change (see Table 13-1, page 448). We present the aspects of these studies that apply to young adulthood in this chapter and those that pertain to middle age in Chapter 15.

Erik Erikson: Crisis 6—Intimacy versus Isolation

The sixth of Erikson's eight crises—and what he considers to be the major issue of young adulthood—is *intimacy versus isolation.* According to Erikson, young adults need and want intimacy; that is, they need to make deep personal commitments to others. If they are unable or afraid to do this, they may become isolated and self-absorbed.

The ability to achieve an intimate relationship, which demands sacrifice and compromise, depends on the sense of identity, which is supposed to have been acquired in adolescence. A young adult who has developed a strong identity is ready to fuse it with that of another person.

Not until a person is ready for intimacy can

ERIKSON (1950)	VAILLANT (1977)	LEVINSON (1978, 1986)
Intimacy versus isolation (age 20 to age 40): Sense of identity, developed during adolescence, enables young adults to fuse their identity with that of others. Young adults resolve conflicting demands of intimacy, competitiveness, and distance and develop an ethical sense. They are ready to enter into a loving heterosexual relationship with the ultimate aim of providing a nurturing environment for children.	*Age of establishment (age 20 to age 30):* Moving from under the parents' dominance to autonomy; finding a spouse; raising children; developing and deepening friendships.	*Novice phase of early adulthood (age 17 to age 33):* Building a provisional life structure; learning its limitations. 1 *Early adult transition (age 17 to age 22):* Moving out of the parents' home; becoming more independent. 2 *Entry life structure for early adulthood (age 22 to age 28):* Building a first life structure; choosing an occupation; marrying; establishing a home and a family; joining civic and social groups; following a dream of the future and finding an older mentor to help find ways to achieve that dream.
	Age of consolidation (age 25 to age 35): Doing what has to be done; consolidating career; strengthening marriage; not questioning goals.	3 *Age-30 transition (age 28 to age 33):* Reassessing work and family patterns; creating the basis for the next life structure. *Culminating phase of early adulthood (age 33 to age 45):* Bringing to fruition the efforts of early adulthood. 1 *Culminating life structure for early adulthood (age 33 to age 40):* a "Settling Down": Building a second adult life structure; making deeper commitments to work and family; setting timetables for specific life goals; establishing a niche in society; realizing youthful aspirations. b "Becoming One's Own Man": Getting out from under other people's power and authority; seeking independence and respect; discarding the mentor.
	Age of transition (around age 40): Leaving the compulsive busywork of occupational apprenticeships to examine the "world within."	2 *Midlife transition (age 40 to age 45):* Ending early adulthood; beginning middle adulthood.

"true genitality" occur. Until this point, people's sex lives have been dominated either by the search for their own identity or by "phallic or vaginal strivings which make of sex-life a kind of genital combat" (1950, p. 264). Now, however, psychologically healthy people are willing to risk temporary loss of self in coitus and orgasm, as well as in very close friendships and other situations requiring self-abandon.

The young adult, then, can aspire to a "utopia of genitality"—mutual orgasm in a loving heterosexual relationship, in which trust is shared and the cycles of work, procreation, and recreation are regulated. The ultimate aim is to help the children of this union achieve satisfactorily all the stages of their own development. Thus, Erikson sees this not as a purely sexual utopia but as an all-encompassing accomplishment. He distinguishes sexual *intimacies*, which may take place in casual encounters, from *intimacy with a capital "I,"* characterized by mature mutuality that goes beyond sexuality (E. Hall, 1983).

The "virtue" that develops during young adulthood is the *virtue of love*, or *mutuality of devotion* between partners who have chosen to share their lives. People also need a certain amount of temporary isolation during this period in order to think through some important choices on their own. As young adults resolve the often-conflicting demands of intimacy, competitiveness, and distance, they develop an ethical sense, which Erikson considers the mark of the adult.

According to Erikson, a decision not to fulfill one's natural procreative urge has serious consequences for development, which we discuss in Chapter 15. Erikson, then, limits "healthy" development to loving heterosexual relationships that produce children. His exclusion of homosexual, celibate, and single lifestyles and other childless lifestyles from the realm of healthy development has been criticized, as has his focus on a male pattern of development. Also, his assertion that people find their identity in adolescence contradicts research that shows that the search for identity continues during adulthood.

George Vaillant: The Grant Study of Harvard University Men In adapting to life events and circumstances, people can change themselves, their surroundings, or both. What kinds of ad-

aptations are healthiest, and how do various adaptations affect the quality of life?

In 1938, a group of 268 Harvard undergraduates who were considered emotionally and physically healthy and especially self-reliant were selected for a study that has come to be called the *Grant Study*. In his report on the research, which followed 95 of the men into their fifties, Vaillant (1977) came to several important conclusions. He stated that lives are shaped not by isolated traumatic events, but by the quality of sustained relationships with important people; that people change and develop throughout life; and that the mechanisms people use to adapt to their life circumstances determine their level of mental health.

EGO DEFENSE MECHANISMS AND ADAPTATION TO LIFE Vaillant identified four types of *ego defense mechanisms,* or characteristic ways in which people adapt to life situations: *mature mechanisms,* for example, the use of humor or helping others; *immature mechanisms,* for example, developing aches and pains with no physical basis; *psychotic mechanisms,* in which people distort reality; and *neurotic mechanisms,* for example, repressing anxiety, intellectualizing, or developing irrational fears. Men who used the mature adaptive mechanisms were more successful in many ways. They were happier, got more satisfaction from their work, enjoyed richer friendships, made more money, were mentally and physically healthier, and seemed better adjusted all around.

CAREER CONSOLIDATION AND STAGES OF DEVELOPMENT According to Vaillant, the life histories of the men in the Grant Study support Erikson's developmental progression, with the addition of a stage that Vaillant calls *career consolidation.* This stage—which Vaillant places somewhere between the twenties and the forties and which he says pertains to both men and women—is characterized by preoccupation with strengthening one's career. In Erikson's scheme, it would fall between the sixth crisis—the development of intimacy—and the seventh crisis, which concerns generativity, or guiding the next generation. (We discuss Erikson's seventh crisis, which he places in middle age, in Chapter 15.)

The fact that career consolidation occurs after intimacy but before generativity may yield clues to why many marriages run into trouble at about the seventh year. A person may turn away from an established intimate relationship to focus his or her full attention upon career concerns; as a result, the relationship may wither from neglect. Problems may loom particularly large if the couple are at different points in this sequence, with one wanting to work on intimacy and the other on career, or with one wrapped up in a career while the other is ready to move on to generativity.

Vaillant found that the specific ages at which changes take place vary for different people, but he did observe a typical pattern as the bright, achieving men in the study moved from stage to stage.

At age 20, many of the men were still their mothers' sons, very much under parental dominance. The decade of the twenties—and sometimes the thirties—was spent winning autonomy from parents, marrying, having and raising children, and deepening friendships that had begun during adolescence. Ninety-three percent of those men who at age 47 were considered best adjusted had achieved stable marriages before age 30 and were still married at 50.

Between the ages of 25 and 35, these men worked hard at consolidating their careers and devoted themselves to their families. They did what had to be done, followed the rules, strove for promotions, accepted "the system." They rarely questioned whether they had chosen the right woman or the right career. The excitement, charm, and promise they had radiated as college students disappeared during these years, causing the anthropologist who interviewed them in 1950 and 1952 to describe them as "colorless, hardworking, bland young men in gray flannel suits" (Vaillant, 1977, p. 217).

The career consolidation stage ends, says Vaillant, when "at age 40—give or take as much as a decade—men leave the compulsive, unreflective busywork of their occupational apprenticeships, and once more become explorers of the world within" (p. 220). In Chapter 15 we return to the men in the Grant study and examine the discoveries of these midlife explorations.

Daniel Levinson: Life Structure Levinson (1978) and his colleagues at Yale University interviewed in depth and gave personality tests to 40 men aged 35 to 45, equally divided among four occupations: hourly workers in industry, business executives, academic biologists, and novelists. The interviews focused on all aspects of their lives—education, work, religion, politics, leisure, and relationships with parents, siblings, wives, children, and peers.

From this study, which was conducted by researchers with backgrounds in psychology, psychiatry, and sociology—and from other research, from biographical sources, and from his (as of this writing) unpublished studies of women, as well—Levinson has constructed a theory of development in adulthood.

LIFE STRUCTURE AND LIFE ERAS At the heart of Levinson's theory is the *life structure*—"the underlying pattern or design of a person's life at a given time" (1986, p. 6). This is an evolving framework that shapes and is shaped by a person's relationship with the environment. The life structure has both external and internal aspects. It includes the people, places, institutions, things, and causes that a person finds most important, as well as the values, dreams, and emotions that make them so.

Most people's life structures are built primarily around their work and their families. Other components may include race, religion, and ethnic heritage; such broad societal events as wars and economic depressions; or something as specific as an influential book or a favorite vacation spot.

People shape their life structures, says Levinson, during four overlapping eras of about 20 to 25 years each. The eras are connected by transitional periods of about 5 years, when people appraise the structures they have built and explore possibilities for restructuring their lives for the next era (see Figure 13-1). Within each era are shorter phases and periods, also linked by transitions. All in all, then, people spend nearly half their adult lives in transition (Levinson, 1986). Levinson believes (though it remains to be proved) that the same fundamental sequence occurs across culture and class boundaries and has occurred throughout history, even

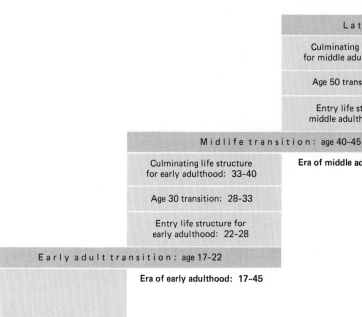

Late adult transition: age 60-65

Culminating life structure
for middle adulthood: 55-60

Era of late adulthood: 60-?

Age 50 transition: 50-55

Entry life structure for
middle adulthood: 45-50

Midlife transition: age 40-45

Culminating life structure
for early adulthood: 33-40

Era of middle adulthood: 40-65

Age 30 transition: 28-33

Entry life structure for
early adulthood: 22-28

Early adult transition: age 17-22

Era of early adulthood: 17-45

Era of preadulthood: 0-22

Figure 13-1 Levinson's ladder: phases in the life of a man. (*Source:* Levinson, 1986; adapted from Levinson, 1978.)

though the particular structures people build may be quite different (Levinson, 1986).

The four eras are:

1 *Preadulthood* (*age 0 to age 22*), the formative years from conception to the end of adolescence
2 *Early adulthood* (*age 17 to age 45*), in which people make significant life choices and exhibit the greatest energy but also experience the most stress
3 *Middle adulthood* (*age 40 to age 65*), when most people have somewhat reduced biological capacities but greater social responsibilities
4 *Late adulthood* (*age 60 on*), the final phase of life

These are not stages, in the sense that one is less advanced than the next, but "seasonal cycles" of development, each with its own tasks. At each time of life, a given person may have varying degrees of success in building a satisfying life structure (Levinson, 1986).

PERIODS OF EARLY ADULTHOOD Levinson divides the era of early adulthood into a novice phase, when a person builds an entry life structure; and a second phase, in which the person builds a culminating life structure for early adulthood (see Table 13-1). Let's look at these two phases and the transitions that lead up to them. (In Chapter 15, we examine the next era, middle adulthood.)

Early adult transition (ages 17 to 22*) During the early adult transition, which for any given individual may take 3 to 5 years, a man† needs to

*All ages are approximate.
†Levinson (1986) says that his conclusions apply to women, with some variations, but only his published studies of men are available as of this writing.

Finding a mentor—an older person who takes an interest in and guides a younger person's career—is an important task of the phase of life that Daniel Levinson has called "Entering the Adult World." This older doctor offering advice to two younger colleagues may be a vital factor in their success.

move out of preadulthood and into adulthood, to move out of his parents' home and become more independent both financially and emotionally. The youth who goes to college or into the army enters an institutional situation midway between being a child in the family and reaching full adult status.

Entry life structure for early adulthood (age 22 to age 28) During the novice phase, which Levinson has also called *"Entering the Adult World,"* the young person becomes an adult and builds the *entry life structure for early adulthood.* This may consist of relationships with the other sex, usually leading to marriage and children; involvement with work, leading to the choice of occupation; choosing a home; relationships with friends and family; and involvement with civic and social groups.

Two important features of the entry life structure are the "dream" and the "mentor." Men often enter adulthood with a ***dream*** of their future, couched in terms of a career. The vision of, say, becoming a famous writer or winning a Nobel Prize for scientific work spurs them on and vitalizes much of their adult development. But the all-too-common realization, generally in midlife, that the cherished dream will not be fulfilled may precipitate an emotional crisis (see Chapter 15). The way men face the need to reassess their goals and substitute more attainable ones determines how well they will cope with life.

A man's success is strongly influenced during these apprenticeship years by finding a ***mentor,*** that is, someone about 8 to 15 years older who takes an interest in him, offers guidance and inspiration, and passes on wisdom, moral support, and practical help in both career and personal matters.

Age-30 transition At about age 30, men take another look at their lives. They wonder whether the commitments they have made during the previous decade have been premature—or they make strong commitments for the first time.

Some men slide through this transition fairly easily; others experience developmental crises, in which they find their present life structures intolerable yet seem unable to form better ones. Problems with marriage are prevalent now, and the divorce rate peaks. The role of work shifts as a man changes jobs, is promoted, or settles down after a period of uncertainty. Some men enter psychotherapy to help them clarify their goals.

If the choices made now are sound, they provide a strong foundation for the next life structure. If they are poor, they may dangerously weaken it. No matter how good the structure, however, it will continue to change.

Culminating life structure for early adulthood (age 33 to age 40) The early thirties usher in what Levinson has called "*Settling Down,*" a concerted effort to realize one's youthful aspirations. The apprenticeship phase is over, and men are ready to build the *culminating life structure for early adulthood.* They make deeper commitments to work, family, and other important aspects of their lives. Men set specific goals for themselves (a professorship, a certain level of income, a one-person art show) with a set timetable, often hoping to pass some milestone by the age of 40. They work at establishing their niche in society—at digging in and anchoring their lives firmly in family, occupation, and community. At the same time, they continue to work at advancement—at building a better life, improving and using their skills, becoming more creative, and making more contributions to society. These two tasks are contradictory, since people cannot advance if they make too strong a commitment to stability, and so some juggling and a constant evaluation of priorities need to take place.

In the middle to late thirties, toward the end of the settling-down period, comes a period called "*Becoming One's Own Man*" (*BOOM*). A man now chafes under the authority of those who have power and influence over him and wants to break away and speak with his own voice; but he fears a loss of affirmation and respect. During "BOOM," a man often discards his mentor and is at odds with his wife, children, lover, boss, friends, or coworkers. The way a man resolves or fails to resolve the issues of this phase will affect the way he manages the midlife transition (discussed in Chapter 15).

Women's Development in Early Adulthood

Do women go through the same kinds of age-linked changes that Levinson's original studies found for men? Levinson (1986) says that they do, and there is some supporting evidence in a recent review of four unpublished dissertations, which used Levinson's method of in-depth biographical interviewing with small numbers of women. But the women handled the characteristic tasks of each period differently from men; their lives tended to be more conflict-filled and less stable (P. Roberts & Newton, 1987).

The four investigators (D. Adams, 1983; Droege, 1982; Furst, 1983; W. Stewart, 1977) interviewed a total of 39 women, from 28 to 53 years old. In one study (D. Adams, 1983), there were eight respondents, all black attorneys. In the other three studies, all the subjects were white, and not all of them (only from 36 to 91 percent) were employed. From 50 to 100 percent of each sample had been married at some time, and 25 to 87 percent were parents.

THE FOUR TASKS The review focused on the four tasks that Levinson identified for the novice phase of early adulthood: forming a dream, forming a mentor relationship, forming an occupation, and forming an enduring love relationship.

All but 6 of the 39 women were able to form dreams, but their dreams were more vague and complex and less motivating than men's, and their life structures tended to be tentative and temporary. Whereas men's dreams generally focused on achievement in work, most women seemed to have split dreams that involved both their own achievements and their relationships. They tended to define themselves in relation to others—husbands, children, or colleagues.

These findings are consistent with other writings that have pointed up a major difference between men's and women's paths to identity. Men have traditionally "found themselves" by separating from their families of origin, by becoming autonomous ("one's own man"), and by pursuing their individual interests. Several writers on women have proposed that women develop their identities not by breaking away from their relationships with other people but through the responsibility and attachment that characterize such ties (Baruch, Barnett, & Rivers, 1983; Chodorow, 1978; Gilligan, 1982).

All 39 women were concerned with the search for a "special man." But whereas the "special woman" in Levinson's scheme helps her man pursue his dream, these women tended to see themselves as supporting their husbands' goals. Husbands, in fact, were the major obstacles to women's realizing the individualistic portion of their dreams. (For example, the husband of one woman who considered applying for a Fulbright scholarship threatened to find another woman who would be more interested in her marriage.)

Many of the women identified role models during their twenties, but only four achieved true mentor relationships. According to Levinson's theory, we would expect many of the women to be hampered in their occupational advancement.

AGE-30 TRANSITION The task of forming an occupation—which for men often extends through the age-30 transition—stretched well into middle age for the women in the four studies. This was true not only for women who at first followed the traditional pattern of marriage and motherhood (and faced a 10- to 20-year disadvantage when they finally began pursuing their occupational dreams), but also for those who had formed specific career goals in their twenties and then interrupted their education or careers to care for children or to put their husbands through school.

During the age-30 transition, many women reversed their career and family priorities or at least paid more attention to the previously neglected half of their dreams: those who earlier had concentrated on marriage and motherhood now stressed individualistic goals, while those who had concentrated on career (like Adams's attorneys) now emphasized relationships. (These findings are quite different from Levinson's pattern for men, who appear to remain focused primarily on careers throughout early adulthood.) Also, during this period of reappraisal, women began making greater demands on their husbands to accommodate to the women's personal interests and goals. The women who found the age-30 transition most stressful were those who were unsatisfied with both their relationships and their occupational achievements during their twenties.

Along the same lines, a longitudinal study of 132 Mills College seniors found that women who *committed* themselves during their twenties to career, family, or both developed more fully than women who had no children and who chose work that was beneath their capabilities. Between the age of 27 and the early forties, women who had faced the challenges of career or parenthood became more disciplined, independent, hard-working, and confident and improved their "people skills." They were more dominant, more motivated to achieve, more emotionally stable, more goal-oriented, and more interested in what was going on in the world outside their families than were women who had made neither kind of commitment (Helson & Moane, 1987). This research suggests that a range of satisfactory life structures is possible for young women who form dreams and set about making them come true.

Evaluating the Normative-Crisis Approach
We offer a full critique of the normative-crisis approach in Chapter 15, but we want to make a few preliminary points here.

The theory that emerged from the Grant Study and from Levinson's research—that there is a predictable sequence of age-related changes throughout adult life—has been influential. But the concept of a universal pattern of development for adults, though intriguing, is questionable. It is true that children's ages do allow fairly accurate estimates of their place within the sequence of development, but adults' ages may reveal less than their personality and history reveal. As we will show in the next section, people's unique experiences do much to shape their development. Individual personality characteristics, which show some stability over the years, also affect the course of people's lives. Furthermore, it is misleading to look at adults' development as a series of stages or phases, since many of the same issues recur throughout adulthood.

Equally important, it is risky to generalize from studies that are so limited in their samples. Both the Grant Study and Levinson's studies were based on small groups of mostly white middle- to upper-middle-class men. Since all these men were born in the 1920s or 1930s, their development may have been influenced by societal events that did not affect people born earlier or later. And studies of women show patterns of development somewhat different from those experienced by men.

Probably the most important contribution made by these pioneering studies of adult development was their role in emphasizing—both to researchers and to the public at large—how much development actually takes place after adolescence. Although it is necessary to remember the limitations of this research, its findings are helpful in the identification of developmental threads that run through the lives of many people.

Timing-of-Events Model

Instead of looking at adults' development as a function of age, the timing-of-events model, which has gained favor in the past 2 decades, views life events as markers of development. According to this model, people develop in response to the specific events in their lives and the specific times when they occur.

Types and Timing of Life Events In childhood and adolescence, internal maturational events signal the transition from one developmental stage to another. A baby says the first word, takes the first step, loses the first baby tooth. A youngster's body changes to signal the entry into pubescence.

In adulthood, however, people move from "a biological to a social clocking of adult development" (Danish & D'Augelli, 1980, p. 111). Physiological and intellectual maturation are now less important to growth than are the effects of such external events as marriage, parenthood, divorce, widowhood, and retirement. For example, menopause is generally of less importance in a woman's life than a change in her job situation.

NORMATIVE VERSUS NONNORMATIVE EVENTS Life events are of two types: the ones people expect (*normative life events*) and the ones they ordinarily do not expect (*nonnormative life events*). Normative events include marriage and parenthood in early adulthood, and widowhood and retirement late in life. However, "the events of a person's life rarely are as orderly as the sociological study of the life span implies in emphasizing such regular status changes" (Brim & Ryff, 1980, p. 376). Thus, people's lives are punctuated by such nonnormative events as a traumatic accident, an unexpected promotion, the loss of a job, a lottery prize, a stock market crash, a notable achievement, or a notorious scandal.

Timing can affect the normativeness of an event. Traditionally, most adults have had strong feelings about the time in life when certain activities are acceptable (Neugarten, Moore, & Lowe, 1965). People are usually keenly aware of their own timing and describe themselves as "early," "late," or "on time" in marrying, having

According to the timing-of-events model, the age at which people experience such major life events as a first baby can have an important influence on development. A normative event like parenthood, which most people expect during young adulthood, may become nonnormative and thus more difficult to deal with if it occurs earlier or later.

children, settling on careers, or retiring. Such events, which are usually normative, become nonnormative when they are "off time"; for example, when a person marries at 14 or 41 or retires at 41 or 91.

In contrast to the normative-crisis school, the timing-of-events model holds that normative events, which come at expected times, are generally taken in stride; "it is the events that upset the expected sequence and rhythm of the life cycle that cause problems" (Neugarten & Neugarten, 1987, p. 33).

INDIVIDUAL VERSUS CULTURAL EVENTS Another distinction is that between an individual event and a cultural one. An *individual event* is something that happens to one person or one family, such as pregnancy or job promotion. A *cultural event* shapes the context in which individuals develop. Examples are an economic depression, an earthquake, a war, a famine, or an accident at a nuclear reactor or a chemical plant.

Cultural events affect people's "social clocks." A timetable that seems right and proper to people in one age cohort may feel jarring to members of the next generation. And the typical timing of such events as marriage varies from culture to culture (see Box 13-1, page 456).

BOX 13-1   WINDOW ON THE WORLD

THE MARRYING AGE

People in eastern Europe tend to marry early; Scandinavians tend to marry late. Variations in the typical "marrying age" in different cultures can tell us something about the cultures themselves (Bianchi & Spain, 1986).

The statistical differences are striking. In Hungary, for example, 70 percent of the young women and one-third of the young men aged 20 to 24 have already married, whereas in Nordic countries, 85 percent of the women and 95 percent of the men in this age group have not. Like other nations in the Soviet bloc, Hungary has a policy of encouraging births. In Scandinavia, on the other hand, cohabitation is popular among young adults. Although most Scandinavians do marry eventually, they do not marry in their early twenties.

Japan, too, has a high proportion of unmarried young adults. But young men and women in Japan do not cohabit, like those in

A Japanese bride and groom are likely to be older than a bride and groom in eastern Europe and to have lived at home with their parents before marriage, rather than cohabiting as many unmarried couples do in Scandinavian countries.

Scandinavia; they tend to live at home with their parents longer than young adults in other cultures.

Industrialized nations, in which increasing numbers of women go to college and enter the labor force, are experiencing a trend toward

delayed marriage. In the United States, Canada, Great Britain, and France, well over half of the women and three-fourths of the men between the ages of 20 and 24 have not yet been married (see Table 13-3 later in this chapter).

THE DECLINE OF AGE-CONSCIOUSNESS During the second half of the twentieth century, our society has become less age-conscious (Neugarten & Hagestad, 1976; Neugarten & Neugarten, 1987). The consensus that there is a "right time" to do certain things has narrowed. Middle-aged middle-class people in the 1950s, when asked the "best age" for finishing school, marrying, and retiring, showed far more agreement than their counterparts 2 decades later (see Table 13-2). Today people are more accepting of 40-year-old first-time parents and 40-year-old grandparents, 50-year-old retirees and 75-year-old workers, 60-year-olds in blue jeans, and 30-year-old college presidents.

Yet despite this "blurring of traditional life periods" (Neugarten & Neugarten, 1987, p. 32), there are still societal expectations about the appropriate ages for events to occur, and (though to a lessened extent) people do try to time their major life events (marriage, parent-hood, job changes) by this social clock. For example, a young woman who puts off marrying to get a foothood on the career ladder may then "hurry to catch up with parenthood" (p. 33).

Responding to Life Events No matter which type of event we are talking about—normative or nonnormative, individual or cultural—the key issue is how the individual responds to it. An event that energizes one person may lead to depression in another.

How a person reacts to events depends on several internal and external factors (Brim & Ryff, 1980; Danish & D'Augelli, 1980; Danish, Smyer, & Nowak, 1980). These include: antici-pation of the event (how well prepared the per-son is—for example, through classes for pro-

spective parents or seminars for planning retirement); cognitive understanding (how the person interprets the event); physical health (in-cluding the person's physical resources for han-dling stress); personality factors (flexibility and resilience); life history (including how well the person has previously coped with stressful events); and social support (including how much emotional support the person can get from others who understand what he or she is going through).

In the next section, we look at important life events of young adulthood that revolve around intimate relationships like marriage and parent-hood. We also examine some personal lifestyles in which some of the traditional life events do not take place.

TABLE 13-2 THE "RIGHT TIME" FOR LIFE EVENTS AND ACTIVITIES

ACTIVITY OR EVENT	APPROPRIATE AGE RANGE	LATE 1950s STUDY % WHO AGREE		LATE 1970s STUDY % WHO AGREE	
		MEN	WOMEN	MEN	WOMEN
Best age for a man to marry	20–25	80	90	42	42
Best age for a woman to marry	19–24	85	90	44	36
When most people should become grandparents	45–50	84	79	64	57
Best age for most people to finish school and go to work	20–22	86	82	36	38
When most people should be ready to retire	60–65	83	86	66	41
When a man has the most responsibilities	35–50	79	75	49	50
When a man accomplishes most	40–50	82	71	46	41
When a woman has the most responsibilities	25–40	93	91	59	53
When a woman accomplishes most	30–45	94	92	57	48

Note: Table shows the percentage of middle-aged middle-class people who agreed on a "right time" for major life events and achievements in two surveys, one taken in the late 1950s and the other in the late 1970s.
Source: Adapted from Rosenfeld & Stark, 1987; adapted, in turn, from Passuth, Maines, & Neugarten, 1984.

Lovers often resemble each other in appearance or personality, suggesting that a form of self-love plays a part in the choice of a partner. These two military cadets have common career goals.

INTIMATE RELATIONSHIPS AND PERSONAL LIFESTYLES

During the young adult years most people decide whether to marry, cohabit, or stay single and whether or not to have children. For most young adults, an intimate relationship—love—is a pivotal factor in their lives.

Love

Love has long been a favorite topic for poets, novelists, and songwriters. It has become increasingly popular with social scientists as well, who have come up with some illuminating findings about "this thing called love."

Do opposites attract? Or do most people tend to fall in love with someone like themselves? Some element of self-love must be involved in the selection of a loved one, since lovers tend to resemble each other in many traits: physical appearance and attractiveness, mental and physical health, intelligence, popularity, warmth, their own parents' marital and individual happiness, and such other family factors as socioeconomic status, race, religion, education, and income (Murstein, 1980). On the other hand, many people choose partners who offer something they themselves lack. For example, a very

intelligent young woman who has trouble getting along with people may value warmth and friendliness in a man even if he is less intellectual than she is.

Research on love has helped to dispel some of the myths about it. One study of 24 couples, who ranged in age from the teens to the seventies and who were described by acquaintances as "very much in love" (Neiswender, Birren, & Schaie, 1975), found that:

- Men and women do *not* experience love differently. Women, for example, are not more emotional, nor are men more physical.
- Married love is not qualitatively different from unmarried love. It is neither more realistic and mature nor less idealistic.
- Love is not only for the young. Although people of different ages do experience love somewhat differently, older people love just as much as younger people.

Four aspects of a relationship seem to be equally important: (1) emotional ("I feel complete because of him"), (2) cognitive ("I think she makes good decisions"), (3) physical ("Our sexual relationship is both powerful and tender"), and (4) verbal ("He finds it easy to confide in me"). Physical intimacy becomes steadily more important from adolescence to middle age and then abruptly less so. Young and middle-aged adults are the most realistic about their lovers' strengths and weaknesses; both adolescents and older adults tend to idealize their loved ones. (Of course, we must keep in mind that these findings are from a cross-sectional study, which measured differences among couples of different ages rather than changes in particular couples.)

The more evenly balanced a couple's individual contributions to a relationship, the happier the couple tends to be. When a man and a woman find that their relationship seems to favor one or the other of them, they usually either try to make the relationship fairer (the person who feels cheated demands more, or the one who has not contributed enough gives more) or talk themselves into believing that things are fairer than they seem, or end the relationship (Walster & Walster, 1978).

Marriage

Marriage is still in style. The marriage rate, which dropped sharply in the early 1970s, has stabilized; recently, more than 2.5 million American couples a year have married. Most adults marry, usually for the first time during young adulthood (National Center for Health Statistics, 1984a; Norton & Moorman, 1987).

People have been marrying at later and later ages. In 1986, according to the U.S. Bureau of the Census, the median age of the first-time bridegroom was 25.7 years and of the first-time bride, 23.1 years, compared with 24.7 and 22 years, respectively, in 1980.

Benefits of Marriage The ubiquity of marriage throughout history and around the world attests to the fact that it meets a variety of fundamental needs. Marriage is usually considered the best way to ensure orderly raising of children and thus the continuation of the species. In most societies marriage also has economic benefits, providing for an orderly division of labor and a viable consuming and working unit. It provides an available and regulated outlet for sexual activity. In a highly mobile, fragmented society like ours, marriage *ideally* provides a secure source of friendship, affection, and companionship. It offers the opportunity for emotional growth through a reciprocal relationship that is more mutual than the relationship with parents and more committed than the relationships with siblings, friends, or sweetheart. (The high divorce rate attests to the difficulty of attaining these ideals, but the high remarriage rate shows that many people keep trying.)

MARRIAGE AND HAPPINESS Studies done between the 1950s and the 1970s found that married people were happier than others—or that happy people tended to marry. In one study of 2000 adults around the country, married men and women of all ages reported more satisfaction than the single, the divorced, or the widowed. The happiest of all were married people in their twenties with no children—especially the women. Young wives reported feeling much less stress after marriage, while young husbands, although happy, said that they felt more stress (A. Campbell, Converse, & Rodgers, 1975). Apparently marriage was still seen as an accomplishment and a source of security for a woman but as a responsibility for a man.

However, this picture seems to be changing, according to surveys by the National Opinion Research Center (Glenn, 1987). Although a greater proportion of married people than of people who have never married still call themselves "very happy," the gap has narrowed dramatically—among 25- to 39-year-olds, from 31 percentage points in the early 1970s to 8 points in 1986. Apparently, never-married people (especially men) are happier today, while married people (especially women) are less happy.

A possible reason is that some of the benefits of marriage are no longer confined to wedlock. Single people can now get both sex and companionship outside of marriage, and marriage is no longer the sole (or even the most reliable) source of security for women. Also, since most women now continue their employment, marriage for them is likely to bring an *increase* rather than a decrease in stress.

MARRIAGE AND HEALTH Marriage, in general, seems to be healthful. Census data and other governmental health surveys show that married people tend to be healthier than people who are separated, divorced, or widowed (Verbrugge, 1979). Married people have fewer disabilities or chronic conditions that limit their activities; and when they need to go to the hospital, their stays are generally short. People who have never been married are the next-healthiest group, followed by the widowed and then by those who are divorced or separated.

The data do not tell us whether marriage confers health. Healthy people may attract mates more easily, be more interested in getting married, and be more satisfying marriage partners. Or married people may lead healthier, safer lives than single people. And because spouses can take care of each other, they may be less likely than unmarried adults to require hospitalization or institutionalization. Even in many less-than-ideal marriages, the partners provide company for each other, offer emotional support, and do many things that ease day-to-day life. The loss of these supports through death or separation may make the widowed and divorced more vulnerable to mental and physical disorders (Doherty & Jacobson, 1982).

Predicting Success in Marriage What is success in marriage? Researchers have relied on people's ratings of their own marriages, on the absence of marital counseling, or on the number of years a couple stay together. All these criteria are flawed: people are sometimes less than honest with themselves; some people find it easier to acknowledge problems and seek help; and some people will put up with unhappiness longer than others. Even so, these three criteria are still the best ones we have for rating marriages.

Age at marriage is an important predictor of success. Teenagers have high divorce rates for many reasons. Early marriage may affect career or educational aspirations, restrict both partners' potential for growth, and lock a couple into a relationship neither one is mature enough to handle. People who wait until their late twenties or later to marry have the greatest chances for success. The marriage also has a better chance if the bride is not pregnant and has not given birth before marriage. Black people, people who have not completed their education, and people whose parents were unhappily married or divorced are more likely than other people to fail in marriage (Kieren, Henton, & Marotz, 1975; Kimmel, 1980; Norton & Moorman, 1987; Troll, 1975).

The success of a marriage has much to do with the ways the partners learn to communicate and to deal with decision making and conflict. The patterns they set during young adulthood affect the quality of the marriage at midlife (marriage in midlife will be discussed in Chapter 15).

Violence between Spouses Some spouses, more often men, react to their personal or marital problems by becoming violent. Violence is more common among young, poor, and unemployed couples, whether married or living together without marriage (Lystad, 1975; Yllo & Straus, 1981). Men who abuse women tend to be social isolates, to have low self-esteem, to be sexually inadequate, to be inordinately jealous, and to deny and minimize the frequency and intensity of their violence, usually blaming the woman (J. L. Bernard & Bernard, 1984; R. Harris & Bologh, 1985).

Why do women stay with men who abuse them? Some have emotional problems them-

selves and feel that they deserve to be beaten. Some interpret physical violence as a sign of love or of masculinity. Some are financially dependent. Some are afraid to leave for fear that they will be caught and beaten again or even killed.

Women in this position often feel that they have nowhere to turn. In many states, a wife cannot sue her husband for assault, and police officers called to break up a fight between husband and wife rarely arrest the husband. Yet a study in Minneapolis showed that men who are arrested for family violence are less likely to continue to abuse their families (L. W. Sherman & Berk, 1984).

Today more attention is being paid to the plight of abused wives. Shelters now exist in many communities where battered wives can go with their children for refuge and counseling, and the legal system is becoming more responsive to the needs of families torn by violence. Programs are springing up to help abusive men stop their violent behavior, usually through group counseling (J. L. Bernard & Bernard, 1984; Feazell, Mayers, & Deschner, 1984).

Divorce

The dissolution of marriage is largely a phenomenon of young adulthood. The "seven-year itch" is more than folklore; this is a peak time for divorce.

The United States has one of the highest divorce rates in the world, with more than 1 million divorces a year (National Center for Health Statistics, 1984a). But the divorce rate, after a 2-decade rise, appears to have leveled off since 1980 (Glick & Lin, 1986b; Norton & Moorman, 1987).

Why Divorce Has Increased Divorce is more common today because of societal changes. Women are less financially dependent on their husbands now and so are less likely to stay in bad marriages. There are fewer legal obstacles and there is less religious opposition to divorce, and less social stigma attached to it. In the past, some couples stayed together "for the sake of the children"; today, that is not always considered the wisest course. And since a smaller proportion of couples *have* children these days, it may be easier to return to a single state (Berscheid & Campbell, 1981). Also, divorce rates are highest in times of national prosperity (Kimmel, 1980); in less prosperous times, couples may be more willing to put up with unhappy marriages because of the economic advantages of maintaining only one household.

Furthermore, people expect more from marriage now. As its economic and social bases have become less significant, its emotional importance has become more significant. More people live far from extended families—and want spouses to serve as parents and best friends, as well as lovers. People today expect their mates to enrich their lives, help them develop their potential, and be loving companions and passionate sexual partners. When a marriage falls short of expectations, few people consider it shameful or immoral to seek a divorce.

For all these reasons, people in unhappy marriages are less likely to accept the situation today than they might have been years ago. They are more likely to recognize that the marriage will not get better by itself and that the present situation is likely to damage the personalities of both spouses and their children. Some couples try professional marriage counseling. This may help them work out their difficulties and save the marriage, or it may help them to decide that separation is best for everyone and to handle it in the best way possible.

Reactions to Divorce Even if a marriage has been unhappy, ending it is always painful, especially when children are involved (see Chapter 9). A divorce brings feelings of failure, blame, hostility, and self-recrimination. Divorce has many aspects: the emotional (the deterioration of the marital relationship); the legal; the economic; the coparental (taking care of the children's needs); the communal (changes in relationships with people and institutions outside the family); and the psychic (the individual's need to regain personal autonomy). In a particular relationship, some of these aspects are more intense than others, but all cause stress (Bohannan, 1971).

The breakup of a marriage is rarely an overnight occurrence. In one longitudinal study that followed more than 4000 men for 5 years, those who were later to separate or divorce scored lower on measures of psychological well-being than did those who were still married when the study ended; the differences often showed up long before any marital disruption occurred (Erbes & Hedderson, 1984). Of course, we cannot be sure whether general well-being was affected by degree of satisfaction with marriage or whether satisfaction in marriage was affected by psychological state, or both.

A person's adjustment after divorce depends largely on feelings toward the self, toward the partner, and toward the way the divorce has been handled. The decision to separate may be a positive one that represents growth and maturity, a new understanding of oneself and one's needs, and a new appreciation of what one must do to make a marriage work. But no matter how "successful" the divorce, there is always a painful period of adjustment.

Divorced people tend to be lonely. They may be estranged from in-laws with whom they have been close and from friends who continue to see only the former partner. A divorced person faces a host of practical as well as emotional problems: caring for the children, paying the bills, making new friends, developing new romantic and sexual relationships, developing sources of social support, and coming to terms with the psychological significance of the divorce.

The person who takes the first step to end the marriage often does so not only with relief but also with sadness, guilt, apprehension, and anger. Nonetheless, he or she (more often she—women initiate divorce more often than men) is usually in better emotional shape in the early months of the separation than the other partner, who, in addition to many of these feelings, has to deal with the deep pain of rejection and the sense of being powerless over his or her life (J. B. Kelly, 1982; Pettit & Bloom, 1984). Anger, depression, and disorganized thinking and functioning often characterize the postdivorce period, balanced somewhat by feelings of relief, a continuing attachment to the separated spouse, and the hopeful feeling of having a fresh chance in life (J. B. Kelly, 1982).

Remarriage Most divorced people do not remain single. Until the late 1960s, the remarriage rate kept pace with the rising divorce rate; it declined sharply in the 1970s and more moderately in the 1980s, as more divorced adults began cohabiting outside of marriage or continued to live alone. Still, an estimated three-quarters of divorced women remarry, and men are even likelier to remarry than women of the same age. The more educated a woman is, the less likely she is to remarry, no matter how many children she has—perhaps because she has a better chance of supporting herself and her family. Redivorce, too, seems to have peaked in the late 1970s, when second marriages were more likely to dissolve than first marriages; now the incidence of redivorce is approaching that of first divorce (Glick & Lin, 1986b; Norton & Moorman, 1987).

Apparently, the high divorce rate is not a sign that people do not want to be married. It often represents the desire to be *happily* married and the conviction that the pain and trauma of divorce may be necessary to make way for a better life.

Single Life

The percentage of young men and women who have not yet married has increased dramatically during the past few decades in every age bracket from 20 to 34 (see Table 13-3). Some of these people will marry eventually, but it is possible that an increasing proportion never will.

Many young adults may postpone or avoid marriage because of the likelihood that it will end in divorce (Glick & Lin, 1986b). Such wariness may be wise, since, as we have seen, the younger people are when they first marry, the worse the chances for success.

People who once might have felt pressure to marry now seem to feel more freedom to stay single for a longer period of time. Some want the freedom to try new experiences and do not want to hedge this freedom by assuming the emotional and financial obligations of marriage. Since single persons do not need to consider how their actions will affect spouses and children, they are freer to take social, economic, and physical risks. They can decide more easily to move across the country or across the world, to take chances on new kinds of work, to further their education, or to engage in creative activities. Some people stay single because they like being alone.

More than 60 single men and women, aged 22 to 62, revealed in interviews a number of "pulls" (advantages of being single) and "pushes" (negative aspects of being married) that made many people opt for the single life. Among the "pulls," single people cited career opportunities; self-sufficiency; sexual freedom; exciting lifestyle; mobility; the freedom to change; and opportunities for sustained friendships, a variety of experiences, a plurality of roles, and psychological and social autonomy. Among the "pushes" were restrictions within a monogamous relationship (feeling trapped, obstacles to self-development, boredom, unhappiness, anger, and prescribed role-playing and the need to conform to expectations), poor communication,

TABLE 13-3 PERCENT OF MEN AND WOMEN NEVER MARRIED AT VARIOUS AGES, 1970–1986			
MEN	1970	1980	1986
20–24 years	54.7	68.8	75.5
25–29 years	19.1	33.1	41.4
30–34 years	9.4	15.9	22.2
WOMEN	1970	1980	1986
20–24 years	35.8	50.2	57.9
25–29 years	10.5	20.9	28.1
30–34 years	6.2	9.5	14.2

Source: U.S. Bureau of the Census, 1986.

sexual frustration, lack of friends, limited mobility, and limited availability of new experiences (Stein, 1976).

The problems of single people range from practical ones like finding a job, getting a place to live, and being totally responsible for themselves to the intangibles of wondering where they fit into the social world, how well they are accepted by friends and family, and how their single status affects their self-esteem.

Two common stereotypes of single people—that they are lonelier than married people and that they have many different sexual partners—do not hold up under research. When 400 never-married, divorced, and remarried Ohioans were interviewed, most of the never-married subjects did not express great feelings of loneliness and fewer than 20 percent had multiple sexual partners. On both these criteria, divorced people came closer to the stereotype than those who had never married (Cargan, 1981).

Cohabitation

A relatively recent social development is *cohabitation,* in which an unrelated man and woman live together. This arrangement prevailed in 1 out of every 40 households in 1986—a threefold increase since 1960 (U.S. Bureau of the Census, 1986).

Why do couples decide to live together? For one thing, the secular biological trend toward earlier maturation, combined with the recent societal trend toward extended education, creates a longer span between physiological and social maturity. Many young people want close sexual relationships and yet are not ready for marriage. Living with someone helps many young adults to know themselves better, to understand what is involved in an intimate relationship, and to clarify what they want in marriage and in a mate. Often the experience is a maturing one.

For many young people, living together is the modern equivalent of "going steady." It is not a trial marriage, nor does it seem to serve as practice for marriage. People who have lived together do not necessarily have better marriages than those who have not (J. M. Jacques &

Single life is increasingly common among young adults, for a variety of reasons. This 30-year-old man with a master's degree in business administration returned to his Illinois farming community to manage land that has been in his family for a century. As a rural bachelor, he meets few eligible women; he spends his evenings reading by a wood-burning stove, and when he gets lonely, he takes his dog for a walk.

Chason, 1979). In fact, one study found that during the first year of marriage, people who had not previously lived together (one-third of a sample of 168 people from the general community) got along better than those who had—possibly because the former had not been together long enough for problems to surface (R. E. L. Watson, 1983).

Some of the problems of cohabiting couples are similar to those of newlyweds: overinvolvement in the other person, the working out of a sexual relationship, the felt loss of personal identity, an overdependency on the other, and a growing distance from other friends. Other problems are specific to the nature of cohabitation: discomfort about the ambiguity of the situation, jealousy, and the desire for a commitment. Most newly married people express satisfaction with their premarital arrangement, whether they have cohabited or not; but when they do have regrets, women are more likely to regret having cohabited, while men regret not having done so (R. E. L. Watson, 1983).

(© Joel Gordon)

Most married couples have sexual relations more frequently during the first year of marriage than ever again, but sex can continue to be pleasurable and healthy throughout a couple's life together.

Sexuality

Underlying all these lifestyle decisions is the need for young adults to determine how they will express their sexual drive. As people enter their twenties, they face the task of achieving independence, competence, responsibility, and equality, all in relation to their sexuality. During the next few years, most people make major decisions about their sexual lifestyles: whether they will engage in casual, recreational sex or embrace monogamy and whether they will express their sexuality in heterosexual, homosexual, or bisexual activity. Many of the issues common in the thirties have sexual aspects—the decision to marry after a protracted singlehood, the decision to have a child, the foray into extramarital sex that often comes with the "seven-year itch," and the changes in sexual patterns following divorce.

Sexual Activity among Unmarried People

More and more young people are having sexual experiences before marriage; the later people marry, the less likely they are to be virgins on their wedding day. According to a recent report, premarital intercourse is usual for most American women. Eighty-two percent of

women in their twenties who had never been married had had intercourse, and more than half (53 percent) were sexually active at the time of the study (Tanfer & Horn, 1985).

Among younger people, sexual activity is generally bound up with an affectionate relationship, and there is little promiscuity. There is more casual sex among older single people and separated and divorced persons. Those young adults who do *not* engage in premarital sex hold back for a number of reasons: moral or religious scruples, fear of pregnancy or sexually transmitted diseases, fear of public opinion, or fear of how it will affect their marriages. Women express these fears more than men.

Sexual Activity in Marriage

It is surprising how little research exists about sex in marriage. We do know that most couples have sexual relations more frequently during the first year of marriage than they ever will again. The likelihood is that the more frequently they have intercourse during that first year, the more frequently they will in the future. After 10 years of marriage, 63 percent of couples make love at least once a week and 18 percent three times a week or more, compared with 83 percent and 45 percent, respectively, for couples married less than 2 years (Blumstein & Schwartz, 1983).

Husbands and wives have more frequent sexual intercourse than their counterparts in the same age brackets did in the past several decades. They also engage in more varied sexual activities. Most important, though, is that married people now seem to derive more pleasure from the sexual side of marriage (M. M. Hunt, 1974).

This change has come about as a result of a societal evolution from Victorian attitudes about the "wickedness" of sex to an acceptance of sexual activity—especially in marriage—as normal, healthy, and pleasurable. More information about sex has been available in the public press, in professional journals, and from practitioners of the profession of sex therapy pioneered by Masters and Johnson (1966).

The greater reliability of contraceptives and the availability of legal and safe abortion have also contributed to this change, freeing husbands and wives from fears of unwanted pregnancy. And the women's liberation movement has helped many women to acknowledge their sexuality.

Extramarital Sex   Some married people become involved in extramarital sex—especially after the first few years of a marriage, when the excitement and novelty of sex with the spouse wear off or problems in the relationship surface. One partner or the other, or both, may seek outside sex partners out of boredom or anger at the spouse, to recapture a remembered joy or to seek a more vital relationship, or out of a desire for sexual emancipation that the spouse may or may not share.

It is hard to know just how common extramarital sexual activity is, because there is no way to tell whether people are giving accurate information about their sexual practices. Some of the studies that have sought this information have used self-selected, skewed samples (such as readers of sexually liberal magazines like *Cosmopolitan* and *Playboy*). However, it looks as if more married people are having extramarital sex than in the past. They are having it at younger ages, and the increase is especially notable among women.

In Kinsey's surveys done in the 1940s and 1950s, 51 percent of men and 26 percent of women reported extramarital intercourse (Kinsey, Pomeroy, & Martin, 1948; Kinsey et al., 1953). Now, according to estimates based on several more recent studies, between one-half and three-fourths of married men have extramarital sex by age 40 or 50, and between 34 and 43 percent of married women do so (Nass, Libby, & Fisher, 1984; A. P. Thompson, 1983).

Parenthood and Nonparenthood

Choosing Parenthood   The birth of a baby marks a major transition in the parents' lives. Moving from an intimate relationship involving two people to one involving a third—who is helpless and totally dependent—changes people and changes marriages. Parenthood is a developmental experience, whether the children are biological offspring, are adopted, or are the children of only one spouse.

WHY PEOPLE HAVE CHILDREN   Having children has traditionally been regarded as "the fulfill-ment of a marriage, if not the primary reason for marriage" (McCary, 1975, p. 289). In preindustrial societies, families needed to be large; children helped with the family's work and eventually cared for their aging parents. And because the death rate in childhood was much higher than it is today, fewer children reached maturity.

Because the economic and social reasons for having children were so powerful, parenthood—and especially motherhood—had a unique aura. Today, though, the economic and cultural reasons for parenthood have lessened or have been reversed. In advanced societies, technological progress requires fewer workers, and improved medical care ensures the survival of most children. Overpopulation is a major problem in some parts of the world. In industrial countries, social security and other government programs help with care of the aged. Furthermore, as we'll see, it has become clear that children can have negative, as well as positive, effects on a marriage.

Still, most couples who have children choose to do so. One team of researchers studied 199 married couples who ranged from nonparents to parents of four. The chief motivations for childbearing were the desire for a close relationship with another human being and the wish to take part in educating and training a child. The major deterrents were the expenses connected with children and the parents' perceptions that a child would interfere with their educational and vocational goals (F. L. Campbell, Townes, & Beach, 1982).

Psychoanalytic theorists maintain that women have a deep instinctual wish to bear and nurture infants; that they thus replace their own mothers; and that their babies are a substitute for the penis they will never have. Ego psychologists like Erikson define parenthood in terms of growth in skills and personality resources; they see generativity, or a concern with establishing and guiding the next generation, as a basic developmental need. Functionalist sociologists attribute reproduction to people's needs for immortality, which they achieve by replacing themselves with their own children. Still another interpretation is that parenthood is a part of nature, common throughout the animal world. And there are still cultural pressures to have

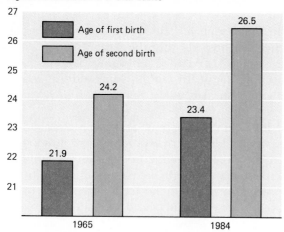

Age of mothers at birth of their babies

Figure 13-2 Age of mothers at birth of their first and second babies, 1965–1984. (*Source:* Rosenfeld & Stark, 1987.)

children, on the assumption that all normal people want them.

WHEN PEOPLE HAVE CHILDREN By and large, couples now have fewer children and have their children later in life (see Figure 13-2); many couples spend the early years of marriage finishing their education and establishing their careers. More women these days—twice as many as a generation ago—have their first children after the age of 30—a pattern that more closely resembles their grandmothers' than their mothers' (C. C. Rogers & O'Connell, 1984).

This pattern is apparently no accident: national surveys show that today's women believe in a later ideal age for first birth. The most recently married women, the better educated, and the most radically feminist choose the latest "ideal ages" (Pebley, 1981). More educated women actually do have their children later; educational level at the time of marriage is the most important predictor of a woman's age when she first gives birth (Rindfuss & St. John, 1983). (See Box 13-2 for advantages and disadvantages of having children early or late.)

The trend toward later motherhood appears to be a favorable one for babies. When 105 new mothers ranging in age from 16 to 38 were interviewed and observed interacting with their infants, the older mothers reported greater satisfaction with parenting and spent more time at

it. They were also more affectionate and sensitive to their babies and more effective in encouraging desired behavior (Ragozin, Basham, Crnic, Greenberg, & Robinson, 1982). One explanation may be that more mature mothers are better able to handle the transition to parenthood.

THE TRANSITION TO PARENTHOOD Both women and men undergo a great many conflicting feelings as they prepare to become parents. Those who have deliberately planned the pregnancy are usually excited about the forthcoming birth, but even they generally experience ambivalence. The pregnancy forces them to think about the responsibility of caring for a totally dependent child and imposes a sometimes frightening sense of permanence on the marriage. Pregnancy also has an impact on a couple's sexual relationship, sometimes enhancing the intimacy between them, sometimes creating barriers.

Indeed, parenthood represents a more abrupt and thoroughgoing alteration in a person's life than marriage does, both in everyday activities and in outlook. Early studies found that the birth or adoption of a first child creates a major upheaval for both parents and for the marital bond (Dyer, 1963; LeMasters, 1957). More recent research, however, has portrayed the event as a time of transition that involves some difficulty but is, by and large, a positive experience (Hobbs & Cole, 1976; Hobbs & Wimbish, 1977).

During the first pregnancy, both parents face such tasks as developing emotional attachments to the unborn child, coming to terms with their relationships with their own parents, resolving their own emotional needs to be cared for, and evaluating financial, housing, child-care, and other practical issues. These tasks help both of them develop a sense of themselves as persons and as parents (Valentine, 1982).

Two studies of a total of 139 well-functioning, mostly middle-class Pennsylvania families found that the transition to parenting can put strains on a marriage. The effect is particularly noticeable from 1 to 3 months after the birth of a first child, when the "honeymoon" period is over. Still, parenthood apparently does not drastically alter the quality of the marital relationship: couples who have the happiest marriages before the

BOX 13-2 PRACTICALLY SPEAKING

ADVANTAGES OF HAVING CHILDREN EARLY OR LATE

What is the best age to have children? There are certain advantages in having children *early*:

■ The parents are likely to have more physical energy. They can cope better with such things as getting up in the middle of the night, staying up all night with a sick baby, and keeping up with the heavy demands of a job and a family.

■ The mother is likely to have fewer medical problems with pregnancy and childbirth. Women who conceive after age 35 to 40 are statistically more likely to suffer from toxemia, high blood pressure, and kidney disorders, and they run a higher risk of bearing a child with a birth defect.

■ When the children are young, the parents will make more energetic companions. As the children become teenagers and then young adults, the parents will be more in tune with them psychologically.

■ The parents will be giving themselves a cushion of time if they have trouble conceiving immediately. (Some older couples who do not conceive right away

hear the clock ticking away. The more trouble they have, the more anxious they become, and this very anxiety may lead to further difficulty.)

■ The mother will have had fewer years to engage in activities that have been identified as risk factors in childbearing—such as drinking, smoking, and overeating. Furthermore, hypertension and related circulatory problems, glucose intolerance, and diabetes are more likely to develop in middle age.

■ The parents will not be as likely to have built up unrealistic expectations of their children, as do many couples who have waited years to have a family.

On the other hand, there are also advantages in having children *late*:

■ The parents will have had a chance to think more about their goals—what they want in life, from both their family and their careers.

■ The parents will be more mature and will have the benefits of their life experience to bring to their parenting.

■ The parents will be better established in their careers, and so they will not have to press so hard on the job at the very time when their children's needs are likely to be greatest.

■ The parents will already have proved to themselves that they can make it on the job, and so they will not feel as if their children are keeping them from attaining career success and they will be able to relax and enjoy their children.

■ The parents will be likely to have more money, which will make it easier to handle the expenses of children, buy timesaving and laborsaving services, and get more child care.

■ The parents will be in a stronger position to negotiate a favorable maternity or paternity leave, a part-time work schedule, an arrangement whereby they can do some work at home, or some other accommodation. Knowing their value to an organization, an employer will be more likely to make concessions to hold on to them.

Source: Adapted from Olds, 1986, pp. 30–31.

baby's arrival still have the happiest marriages afterward (Belsky, Lang, & Rovine, 1985; Belsky, Spanier, & Rovine, 1983).

With the intrusion of night feedings and dirty diapers, couples reported that marriage tended to become less romantic and more of a partnership. They expressed less affection, communicated less, and shared leisure activities less frequently. Wives, who performed most of the child-care tasks and thus experienced the great-

These parents are obviously enjoying the fun and stimulation of having children. But by now they have undoubtedly realized that parenthood also has other aspects. The physical, psychological, and financial stresses of rearing children contribute to the parents' own development. One of the best things about parenthood is that it is never predictable: parents must constantly meet the challenges of their children's changing needs.

est lifestyle change, showed a greater decline in marital satisfaction than their husbands—but then, the women were more satisfied than the men to begin with. Husbands became somewhat more involved in child care when the infants were 3 to 9 months old; and by the end of that time, the husbands' and wives' marital satisfaction approached a more nearly equal level.

A related study found that the couples who underwent the most stress were those whose experience with parenthood during the baby's first 3 months of life was not as good as they had expected. This finding bears out the view of the timing-of-events school of thought—that the way people respond to crucial life events depends on their anticipation of these events. Again, this effect was more pronounced for wives, who may not have realized the extent to which their lives would be changed by the physical exhaustion of both birth and the day-and-night routine of baby care (Belsky, 1985).

Another study, of 210 middle-class married women in Georgia, found that the sex of the child makes a difference. Mothers of boys—especially mothers with *two* boys, an infant and a preschooler—reported less marital satisfaction and cohesiveness than either mothers of girls or childless wives, who appeared to be equally happy in marriage. This may be because some parents find young boys to be more temperamentally difficult and rambunctious than girls

and conflict over managing a son's behavior can undermine a marriage (Abbot & Brody, 1985).

PARENTHOOD AS A DEVELOPMENTAL EXPERIENCE As difficult as it may be to take on the role of parent, sustaining it is even more demanding (B. C. Miller & Myers-Walls, 1983). As children develop, parents do too.

One of the best things about parenthood is that it is never boring. Just as parents are adjusting to the needs of caring for an infant, the baby turns into an adventuresome toddler who needs to be watched; just when parents have gotten used to this stage, the toddler becomes a preschooler. As a child's needs continue to unfold (see Table 13-4), parents may draw upon their own childhood experiences and may work out emotional issues that they have never resolved.

Parents also need to cope with conflicts between personal roles (parent versus spouse, parent versus employee). In doing so, most successful parents define their situation positively. They are clear that in any conflict, their parental responsibilities ultimately come first; they are able to compartmentalize (concentrate on one set of responsibilities at a time); and they are willing to compromise their standards (B. C. Miller & Myers-Walls, 1983; Myers-Walls, 1984; Paloma, 1972).

Unfortunately, some parents cannot meet the physical, psychological, and financial challenges

BOX 13-3 PRACTICALLY SPEAKING

COPING WITH STEPPARENTHOOD

The word *stepparent* conjures up vivid images from childhood tales—of wicked stepmothers and cruel stepfathers. These images may sabotage the efforts of the kindest stepparents to forge close, warm relationships with the children of their spouses. Yet many stepparents are making the effort, and many do succeed.

With today's high rate of divorce and remarriage, families made up of "yours, mine, and ours" are becoming more common. Some 35 million adults are now stepparents to 1 in every 5 children (Visher & Visher, 1983).

The stepfamily—also called the "blended," or "reconstituted," family—is different from the "natural" family. For one thing, it has a larger supporting cast, including former spouses, former in-laws, and absent parents, as well as assorted aunts, uncles, and cousins on both sides. Furthermore, it may be "contaminated with anger, guilt, jealousy, value conflicts, misperceptions, and fear" (Einstein, 1979, p. 64). It is, in short, burdened by much baggage not carried by an "original" family. Obviously, it cannot be expected to function in the same way.

Stepfamilies must deal with stress that arises from the losses (as a result of death or divorce) experienced by both children and adults, which can make them afraid to trust and to love. Stepfamilies look back on a welter of family histories, which may complicate present relationships. Previously established bonds between children and their biological parents or loyalty to an absent or dead parent may interfere with the formation of ties to the stepparent—especially when children go back and forth between two households. In addition, it is common to find a disparity in life experiences, as when a father of adolescents marries a woman who has never had a child (Visher & Visher, 1983).

Families cope with these stresses in a number of ways. Some of the most successful strategies include the following (C. Berman, 1981; Visher & Visher, 1983).

- *Having realistic expectations:* Members of stepfamilies have to remember that their family is different from a biological family. They have to allow time for loving relationships to develop. They need to see what is positive about their differences: instead of resisting the diversity in two households, for example, they can welcome it as an expansion of resources and experiences.

- *Developing new relationships within the family:* Families need to build new traditions and develop new ways of doing things that will be right for them in particular. They can plan activities to give the children some time alone with the biological parent, some time alone with the stepparent, and some time with both parents, and activities that provide time alone for the couple, too. They can move to a new house or apartment, one that does not hold memories of a past life.

- *Understanding children's emotions:* Parents need to be sensitive and responsive to children's fears, hurts, and resentments at a time when the adults may be euphoric about building a new life together.

- *Maintaining a courteous relationship with the former spouse:* Children adjust best after divorce when they maintain close ties with both their biological parents, when they are not used as weapons for angry parents to hurt each other, and when they are not subjected to the pain of hearing a parent or stepparent insult the absent parent.

- *Seeking social support:* Sharing feelings, frustrations, and triumphs with other stepparents and stepchildren often helps people to view their own situations more realistically and to benefit from the experiences of others.

For people who have been bruised by past losses, the stepfamily has the potential for providing the same benefits as any family that cares about all its members. Achieving complete caring within the family is not easy (it is not easy for biological families, either), but it can be done.

TABLE 13·4 STAGES OF PARENTING

WHAT CHILDREN OF DIFFERENT AGES NEED FROM THEIR PARENTS

INFANT AND TODDLER	PRESCHOOLER	SCHOOLCHILD	ADOLESCENT	YOUNG ADULT
Total care: feeding, clothing, bathing, protecting from harm, etc. Emotional attachment A sense of security arising from trust that they are being cared for The beginnings of a feeling of control over life, achieved from parents' responsiveness	Continuing care balanced with encouragement of independence and autonomy Help in channeling aggression Help in developing a good sense of gender identity Help in forming a healthy acceptance of their bodies Encouragement of intellectual abilities, especially language	Help in balancing information from the outside world with what is learned at home Help in forming goals to strive for Help in developing moral reasoning Encouragement of achievement (academic, athletic, social) Encouragement of special talents and skills Help in achieving high self-esteem	Help in handling sexual drive in positive way Help in achieving independence from parents and other adult authorities Encouragement to form own code of values Encouragement and help with educational and career goals	Encouragement of independence Awareness that parents can be consulted as older friends who will share their wisdom and experience without directing their children's lives from their own needs for vicarious success Role models for achieving intimacy, for integrating work and family roles, for finding fulfillment

HOW ADULTS DEVELOP AT DIFFERENT STAGES OF PARENTING

BEFORE BIRTH OF FIRST CHILD	PRESCHOOLER	SCHOOLCHILD	ADOLESCENT	YOUNG ADULT
Thinking about why they want children Planning their lives as parents **INFANT AND TODDLER** Resolving conflicts between individual goals (career, comfort, and convenience) and baby's needs Change in image of themselves from parents' children to children's parents Giving of self physically and emotionally Working through their relationship with their own parents—encouraging their role as grandparents, while not leaning on them for parenting decisions	Learning to change parenting behavior as child's needs change (permitting more independence, for example) Keeping the marital bond strong despite children's demands on time and energy Pursuing vocational goals more vigorously as child begins to move out of the house Learning how to consult books, media, child-rearing experts without being too dependent on them Forgiving themselves for not being perfect parents	Developing a realistic view of the child's abilities, separating their own achievement needs from the child's Appreciating the child for who he or she is, not for living out their own fantasies of being a genius or an athlete Learning how to be sensitive to the emotional needs of other people Participating in the child's school and extracurricular life to give of themselves in a public setting Recapturing the freshness of childhood by seeing things through the eyes of their child Rewriting their own childhood history by offering child opportunities they have never had	Reexamining values in response to child's questioning and testing of limits Learning how to be flexible Learning how to be strong in setting necessary limits Seeing the adolescent as an emerging adult with his or her own interests and not as a mirror of the parents Attending to own career goals, while not ignoring children's needs	Enjoying relationship with young adults who happen to be their children Accepting children as independent people who need to make their own decisions and learn from their mistakes Learning how to offer help without being intrusive or controlling Rebuilding their marriage (or single social life) on a new basis without children at home Rethinking individual life goals after work of parenting is complete Embracing grandparenthood without interfering with child's parenting of own children

of parenthood. They may abuse, neglect, maltreat, or abandon their children (see Chapters 5 and 9); or they may become physically or emotionally ill themselves. Most parents, however, do cope, sometimes with the help of family, friends, neighbors, books and articles about child rearing, and professional advice.

As we will see, adoptive parents have special challenges to meet; so do stepparents (see Box 13-3).

FINDING ALTERNATIVE WAYS TO PARENTHOOD

Infertility When Marcie and Jon got married, they planned to have a baby as soon as possible. It never occurred to them that they might have trouble conceiving; but as more than a year went by and no conception took place, they were forced to face the possibility that one or both of them might be infertile. Ten to fifteen percent of American couples experience the disappointment of **infertility**—inability to conceive after trying for 12 to 18 months (Francoeur, 1985; National Center for Health Statistics, 1984a).

Causes of infertility: Sometimes the cause of infertility lies with the man. He may be producing too few sperm; while only one is needed to fertilize the ovum, a sperm count lower than 60 to 200 million per ejaculation makes conception unlikely. Or his sperm may not be able to exit because of a blocked passageway, or they may not be able to swim well enough to reach the cervix. Or the problem may rest within the woman's body. She may not be ovulating (producing ova), she may be producing abnormal ova, or her fallopian tubes may be blocked, preventing the ova from reaching the uterus. Or the mucus in her cervix may prevent sperm from penetrating it, or a disease of her uterine lining may prevent implantation of the fertilized ovum.

Sometimes surgery can correct the problem. Sometimes hormones can raise the sperm count or enhance ovulation. In fact, some fertility drugs cause superovulation, producing two, three, or more babies at a time. In more than 1 in 10 cases, however, both man and woman seem perfectly normal, but still are not able to conceive.

Psychological effects of infertility: Infertility often burdens a marriage with psychological problems. People who have always assumed that they would be able to reproduce usually have trouble accepting the fact that they cannot do what seems to come naturally and easily to others. They tend to become angry with themselves, with each other, and with their doctors, and to feel empty, worthless, and depressed over their inability to control their lives. Their sexual relationship often suffers as sex becomes a matter of "making babies, not love" (J. Liebmann-Smith, personal communication, 1985; Porter & Christopher, 1984).

Couples who are unable to bear children often benefit from professional counseling or support from other infertile couples; Resolve, a national nonprofit organization with headquarters in Boston, offers such services. One outcome may be that the couple chooses to remain childless. In some cases, surgery may correct the problem. Another solution is to adopt a child.

Adoption The oldest solution to infertility is adoption, a system found in all cultures throughout history. Since 1970, more Americans—including single people, older people, working-class families, and two-earner couples—have been adopting children. Because advances in contraception and the legalization of abortion have reduced the supply of normal white American babies, children available for adoption are likely to be of foreign birth, to have some disability, or to be beyond infancy. Adoptions are more likely to be arranged independently—through private attorneys and doctors—than through agencies (E.B. Bolles, 1984).

Adoption has been well accepted in the United States, but prejudices about it have been accepted, too, such as the belief that adopted children are bound to have problems because they have been deprived of their biological parents. Such views were long reinforced by studies in which samples of adopted children were selected from among people who were seeking mental health services. However, a recent study of adopted children who had been placed by a New Jersey agency found that although there was a difference between the attitudes of adopted and nonadopted children, the positive differences were all on the adopted children's side. Contrary to expectations, they were more confident, viewed the world more positively, felt better able to control their lives, and saw their

Because increased use of contraception and abortion has drastically reduced the number of white American babies available for adoption, many couples are adopting foreign-born children like this Korean baby.

adoptive parents as more nurturing than the nonadopted children in a control group saw theirs (Marquis & Detweiler, 1985).

That is not to say that adopting a child is easier than bearing one. Quite the contrary: in addition to the developmental issues that biological parents face, adoptive parents have to deal with special challenges—the acceptance of their infertility (if this is the reason they have chosen to adopt), the awareness that they are not duplicating the experience of their own parents, the need to explain the adoption to their children, and the jealousy they may feel when their children express an interest in learning about their biological parents.

New methods of becoming a parent As the number of babies available for adoption dwindles, new means of conception are becoming popular. These procedures make it possible for couples to have children that are genetically at least half their own. Four controversial methods are artificial insemination, in vitro fertilization, donor eggs, and surrogate motherhood.

Artificial insemination: Some couples are able to produce children through **artificial insemination**—injection of a man's sperm directly into

the woman's cervix. If a husband seems to be infertile, a couple may choose artificial insemination by a donor (AID), a method that has been in use since the beginning of the twentieth century. Some 20,000 women a year are inseminated with the sperm of anonymous donors. The donor may be matched with the husband for physical and ethnic characteristics, and the husband's sperm may be mixed with the donor's so that the possibility will exist that the man who will raise the child is the biological father. Many couples who conceive in this way never tell the children or anyone else about the children's origins.

In vitro fertilization: In 1978, front-page headlines announced the birth of Louise Brown, the first "test-tube baby."* After 12 years of trying to conceive, Louise's parents had authorized their fertility specialist (a gynecologist) to extract an ovum from Mrs. Brown's ovary, allow it to mature in an incubator, and then fertilize it with Mr. Brown's sperm. The doctor then implanted the embryo in Mrs. Brown's uterus, where it grew in the normal way.

In vitro fertilization, fertilization that takes place outside the mother's body, is becoming increasingly common for women whose fallopian tubes are blocked or damaged. Usually several ova are fertilized and implanted, to increase the chances of success.

Donor eggs: Women who cannot produce normal ova may be able to bear children through the use of **donor eggs,** ova donated from fertile women—the female counterpart of AID. Two baby boys, born within months of each other, are examples of the two ways this can be done. In Australia, a baby was born after an ovum was taken from a donor's body and fertilized in the laboratory and the resulting embryo was implanted in another woman's uterus (Lutjen, Trounson, Leeton, Findlay, Wood, & Renou, 1984). In California a baby's birth was made possible by artificial insemination while the donor's egg was still in her body. Five days later, her uterus was flushed out, and a healthy embryo was retrieved and was inserted into the recipient's uterus (Bustillo et al., 1984).

*Actually, this popular term is a misnomer: the fertilization is seldom performed in a test tube anymore. Even the term *in vitro* is wrong. This phrase is Latin for "in glass," but most labs use plastic dishes.

Surrogate motherhood: In March 1986, Mary Beth Whitehead gave birth to a baby girl who became known as "Baby M." Ms. Whitehead had agreed, in return for $10,000, to bear a child for William and Elizabeth Stern and had been artificially inseminated with Mr. Stern's sperm. But after giving birth, Ms. Whitehead changed her mind and wanted to keep the baby. Following an emotional 7-week trial, a New Jersey judge awarded custody to Mr. Stern. He ruled that "Baby M" would be better off with the Sterns and stripped the biological mother of all parental rights. Later, however, a higher court invalidated the surrogacy contract. The court gave custody of the child to Mr. Stern, the father, but restored Ms. Whitehead's parental rights and granted her a liberal visitation arrangement.

The "Baby M" case is a dramatic example of the issues in **surrogate motherhood,** in which a woman who is not married to a man bears his baby and agrees to give the child to the father and his wife. Usually a couple resort to surrogate motherhood when the man is fertile and the woman is not. Usually the surrogate already has children of her own, and so it is most likely that she understands what giving up a baby means. However, the psychological impact of giving up a baby that a woman has nurtured in her body for 9 months can be more severe than anyone anticipates.

Ethical questions: The "Baby M" case brought a surge of efforts to outlaw or regulate surrogacy contracts. To many people, the most objectionable aspect, aside from the possibility of forcing the surrogate to relinquish the baby, is the payment of money, which can amount to as much as $30,000, including fees to a "matchmaker" and medical expenses. (Payment for adoption is forbidden in about 25 states as of this writing; but surrogate motherhood is not adoption, since the man involved is the biological father.) The idea of a "breeder class" of poor and disadvantaged women who carry the babies of the well-to-do strikes many people as wrong.

New and unorthodox means of conception raise many other questions. Must the people who use them be infertile, or should they be free to make such arrangements for convenience? Should single people and homosexual couples be able to use these methods? Should the children know about their parentage? Should chromosome tests be performed on all prospective donors and surrogates? What is the risk that children fathered or mothered by the same donor or surrogate (genetic half siblings) might someday meet and marry, putting their children at increased risk of birth defects? Can handling an embryo outside the human body injure it? If a test-tube baby is born with a major defect, is the physician liable? What happens if a couple who have contracted with a surrogate divorce before the birth?

One thing seems certain, though: as long as there are people who want children and who are unable to conceive or bear them, human ingenuity and technology will come up with new ways to satisfy their need.

Choosing Nonparenthood "When are you two going to have a baby?" This refrain is familiar—and annoying—to many childless couples. Some couples choose not to have children; others (as we have just discussed) would like to but cannot.

Some 5 to 7 percent of American couples are voluntarily childless, and the number appears to be rising (D.E. Bloom & Pebley, 1982). Couples who choose childlessness tend to follow one of two characteristic paths. They may decide before marriage never to have children. Or, more common, they may keep postponing conception until they finally reach a point when they decide that they do not want children at all.

What makes people come to this decision? Some couples conclude at an early age that they do not have what it takes to make good parents and that they would rather have contact with other people's children than full responsibility for their own. In some cases people have such heavy commitments to their careers that they do not want to take time away from them to raise a family. Some couples feel that having children might be an intrusion on their relationship. Some enjoy the freedom to travel or to make spur-of-the-moment decisions, and they do not want the financial burdens that children entail.

People who choose childlessness tend to be white educated city dwellers with relatively high incomes. They tend to have married relatively late, to have experienced marital disruption, and to have moved often—something they would not be as likely to do with children (D.E. Bloom & Pebley, 1982).

Some couples remain childless because they do not want to give up the freedom they enjoy together, and they feel that children might intrude on their relationship.

enjoyable activities together. (It is possible that parents do not need to do as much together or talk as much with each other because some of their interpersonal needs are met by their interactions with their children.)

The fact that both groups were generally happy in their marriages may reflect their deliberate choice of their lifestyles. Still, some people who want children are discouraged by the costs and the difficulty of combining parenthood with employment. Improved child-care arrangements and other support services might help more couples make truly voluntary decisions (D.E. Bloom & Pebley, 1982).

Although there is more acceptance now than there used to be of couples who decide not to have children, societal disapproval still exists, making such couples defensive and apologetic. Despite considerable evidence that voluntary childlessness has no ill effects on mental health (D.E. Bloom & Pebley, 1982), one study found that college students regard men as less healthy psychologically if they do not have children, and that they like women who are involuntarily childless better than those who are childless by choice (Calhoun & Selby, 1980).

In one study comparing 42 couples who had chosen either parenthood or childlessness, the two groups turned out to be quite similar in their family backgrounds and their levels of marital satisfaction, but different in the way they interacted with their spouses (H. Feldman, 1981). The childless couples had less traditional attitudes toward women and engaged in more

Friendship

During the young adult years, as people are falling in love and either marrying or living with someone, establishing themselves in their careers, and raising children, they often feel as if they do not have enough time to be with their friends. Friends, however, do play an important role in young adulthood. In fact, one study of friendships across the life span found that newlyweds have more friends than adolescents, the middle-aged, or the elderly (Weiss & Lowenthal, 1975).

Characteristics of Adult Friendship In an effort to identify the characteristics of a close friendship and to distinguish them from those of a romantic relationship, one team of researchers questioned 150 people, of whom two-thirds were students at a college and one-third members of the community (K.E. Davis, 1985). They found that friendships were characterized by trust, respect, enjoyment of each other's company, understanding and acceptance of each other, willingness to help and to confide in each other, and spontaneity, or feeling free to be oneself.

Romantic bonds included all of these plus sexual passion and extreme caring to the point of self-sacrifice. However, the people in the study saw best friendships as more stable than ties with a spouse or lover. Most people's close and best friends were of the same sex as they were; 27 percent listed members of the other sex as best friends.

Willingness to cross gender lines for friendship also showed up in another study, this one of upper-middle-class Americans and Australians whose average age was in the mid-thirties. By and large, the women in this study had more intimate, emotional friendships than the men did, and again, most people's closest friends were of the same sex. However, men and women in this sample who held unconventional attitudes had more in common with each other than with people of the same sex who were conventional in their beliefs and behaviors. The researcher defined nonconventionality in terms of the desire to influence change, to seek pleasure or greater happiness, and to exert more control over one's life, as well as an overall satisfaction with life combined with the willingness to take risks. Men and women who fit this description have more friends of both sexes and reveal more about themselves to their friends than those who do not. Friends of both sexes are important to them, but so is a measure of solitude; they do not need to be around people all the time (R.R. Bell, 1981).

Couple Friendships Newly married people often find that they do not care for each other's friends from single days, and then they have to decide whether they will see their friends separately, whether they will put up with each other's friends, or whether they can work out some sort of compromise. People may make friends as couples—a new element that makes forming friendships more complex. Very often people enjoy the friendship of one member of a marriage, but not the other. Yet in a couple-oriented society, it is difficult to see one without the other. Many couples solve this problem by allowing a kind of "discount" for couple friendships. That is, they do not expect the same level of intimacy they would look for in a single friendship. The friendship meets their needs for involvement with other people besides themselves and their families, allows them to avoid isolation and to see each other in outside situations, and offers an extra source of stimulation for each couple (Leefeldt & Callenbach, 1979).

The bonds forged in young adulthood with both friends and family members often endure throughout life. These relationships continue to influence people through middle age and into old age, and the changes they experience in their more mature years affect these relationships, as we'll discuss in the following chapters.

SUMMARY

Personality Development in Adulthood: Two Models

■ Studies of adults show that development continues throughout life. In young adulthood, people develop as they confront the issues of leaving their parents' home, deciding on careers, establishing relationships and families, and setting life goals.

■ Two important perspectives on adulthood are the normative-crisis model and the timing-of-events model.

■ The normative-crisis model, exemplified by the works of Erikson, Vaillant, and Levinson, proposes that there is a built-in ground plan for human development and that during each part of the life span, people must deal with a particular crisis or task.

1 Erikson's sixth psychosocial crisis is intimacy versus isolation. To develop successfully, according to Erikson, young adults must fuse their identities in a close, intimate heterosexual relationship that leads to procreation. Negative outcomes that may result during this period are self-absorption and isolation.

2 In the Grant Study of Harvard men, Vaillant found that men who used "mature" defenses were more successful in many ways than those who used less mature adaptive techniques. This study also revealed a period of career consolidation that characterized men in their thirties.

3 According to Levinson, the goal of adults' development is building the life structure. In his studies of men, Levinson found periods of transition and periods of stability alternating throughout adulthood. His four phases of early

adulthood are the early adult transition (17 to 22 years), the entry life structure for early adulthood (22 to 28 years), the age-30 transition (28 to 33 years), and the culminating life structure for early adulthood (33 to 40 years). Two important influences during young adulthood are a mentor and one's dream.

■ Studies of adult women suggest that gender differences exist in paths to identity. Males have traditionally defined themselves in terms of separation and autonomy; females seem to achieve identity through relationships and attachment.

1 Women often have split dreams, which involve both individual achievements and relationships. At the age-30 transition, their priorities often shift between the two aspects of the dream.

2 Women seldom find true mentors and often do not complete the formation of an occupation until middle age.

■ The timing-of-events model proposes that adult development is influenced by the specific important events that occur in a person's life, and that the timing of an event affects the person's reaction to it.

■ Life events may be of two types: expected (or normative) and unexpected (nonnormative). Timing can affect the normativeness of an event. Events that are perceived as being "off time" are generally more stressful than those that occur "on time."

■ Although our society has become less age-conscious, many people still try to time major life events such as marriage, occupational progression, and parenthood by "social clocks."

Intimate Relationships and Personal Lifestyles

■ The emotional, cognitive, physical, and verbal aspects of love tend to be about equally important in young adulthood, but their relative importance varies across the life span.

■ During young adulthood, many people decide whether and whom to marry. Americans have been marrying later than in the past. Successful marriages tend to occur between people in their late twenties or older.

■ People develop emotionally and socially during marriage. Married men and women generally report more satisfaction with their lives than single, divorced, or widowed people, but the difference is lessening.

■ The United States has one of the highest divorce rates in the world, with more than 1 million divorces each year. Although divorce usually entails a painful period of adjustment (even for the spouse who has initiated it), most divorced people remarry.

■ Today greater numbers of people feel free to remain single until a late age or never to marry. The advantages of being single include opportunities for career exploration, travel, and self-sufficiency. Possible negative aspects include the difficulties of being totally responsible for oneself and of finding social acceptance.

■ The number of men and women cohabiting has tripled since 1960. Cohabiting is in many ways a maturing experience, though there may be problems associated with it, such as dealing with the ambiguity of the situation, jealousy, and the desire for a commitment.

■ Most young adults make basic decisions about their sexual lifestyles. More young people today are having sexual experiences before marriage, and husbands and wives are having more frequent and more varied sexual activity than in previous generations. More married people, especially young married people, appear to be having sexual relationships outside of marriage.

■ Having a child marks a major transition in a couple's life, from sharing reciprocal responsibilities to having total responsibility for a new life. Parenthood has a mixed impact on marriages.

■ Couples who are infertile may suffer adverse psychological effects. Adoption is becoming more difficult because of a decreased supply of American babies, and more couples are trying artificial insemination, in vitro fertilization, use of donor eggs, and surrogate motherhood.

■ Many couples today opt for fewer children than in past decades or remain childless, and an increasing number of women, especially educated women, have children later in life.

■ Friendships are important during young adulthood. Now, people often make friends as couples, as well as individually. Although complex, couple friendships allow both partners to be involved with others and to avoid isolation, and they offer both couples an extra source of stimulation.

artificial insemination (page 472)   infertility (471)   nonnormative life events (455)
career consolidation (449)   intimacy versus isolation (447)   normative-crisis model (446)
cohabitation (463)   in vitro fertilization (472)   normative life events (455)
donor eggs (472)   life structure (450)   surrogate motherhood (473)
dream (452)   mentor (452)   timing-of-events model (446)
ego defense mechanisms (449)

SUGGESTED READINGS

Bellino, J.H., & Wilson, J. (1985). *You can have a baby.* New York: Crown. A full study of the way fertilization works, how it can go wrong, and what can be done to assist it. The book is written for the layperson but is as complete as a textbook.

Bernard, J. (1972). *The future of marriage.* New York: World. A controversial book that examines the impact of marriage on both sexes and concludes that marriage is more beneficial for men than for women.

Bingham, M., & Stryker, S. (1987). *More choices: A strategic planning guide for mixing career and family.* Santa Barbara, CA: Advocacy Press. This guidebook, in workbook format, provides much information and realistic encouragement to teenagers and young adults to prepare them for balancing work and family life in the context of long-range life goals.

Boston Women's Health Book Collective. (1978). *Ourselves and our children: A book by and for parents.* New York: Random House. A warm and intimate book, full of personal testimony about a wide range of parenting issues.

Corson, S.L. (1983). *Conquering infertility.* Norwalk, CT: Appleton-Century-Crofts. A practical guide about all aspects of infertility, written by a medical specialist in the treatment of infertility.

Masters, W.H., Johnson, V.E., & Kolodny, R.C. (1986). *Sex and human loving.* Boston: Little, Brown. An overall look at sexuality, summarizing for general readers the information in the earlier books of Masters and Johnson and adding material on a broad range of sexual issues.

Matlin, M.W. (1987). *Psychology of women.* New York: Holt. A comprehensive and readable review.

Merser, C. (1987). *"Grown-ups": A generation in search of adulthood.* New York: Putnam's. A highly readable account based on personal experience and research, by a member of the "baby-boom" generation of young adults, many of whom have not gone through the predictable life transitions their parents went through.

Olds, S.W. (1985). *The eternal garden: Seasons of our sexuality.* New York: Times Books. A description of sexual development throughout life, through personal accounts. Several people ranging in age from 20 to 83 tell of significant turning points in their own lives; their stories are then interpreted in the light of both classic and contemporary research.

Pogrebin, L.C. (1986). *Among friends: Who we like, why we like them, and what we do with them.* New York: McGraw-Hill. An absorbing analysis, for lay readers, of friendship in contemporary society. It illustrates findings from social science research with anecdotes gleaned from over 150 interviews and the author's own life. There are interesting sections on differences between men's and women's friendships and on the changing patterns of friendships from infancy through old age.

7 PART

MIDDLE ADULTHOOD

When does middle age begin? Is it at that birthday party when you summon up your breath to blow out 40 candles? Is it the day your daughter demolishes you on the tennis court or the day your son announces his engagement? Or is it the day when you notice that police officers are getting younger all the time? Middle adulthood, which in this book is defined roughly as the years from age 40 till age 65, has many markers. In Chapters 14 and 15, we will see what sets these years apart from the years that come before and afterward.

■ In **Chapter 14**, we examine health in middle adulthood, looking at menopause, the male climacteric, and the physical changes that appear in both sexes. We also look at ways in which adults' thinking processes differ from those of younger people. Finally, we examine the satisfactions that middle-aged people get from their work, as well as the effects of burnout, unemployment, and the challenge of changing careers at midlife.

■ In **Chapter 15**, we explore the famous "midlife crisis." Should all people get ready for it—or is it a figment of researchers' and journalists' imagination? We explore another controversial issue related to social and emotional development: whether personality is fixed early in adulthood or whether it changes over the years. Finally, we look at the relationships middle-aged adults have with the important people in their lives: their spouses, their friends, and the generations on either side of them—their children and their parents. These are richly textured years.

14

CHAPTER

PHYSICAL AND INTELLECTUAL DEVELOPMENT IN MIDDLE ADULTHOOD

The primitive, physical, functional pattern of the morning of life, the active years before forty or fifty, is outlived. But there is still the afternoon opening up, which one can spend not in the feverish pace of the morning but in having time at last for those intellectual, cultural, and spiritual activities that were pushed aside in the heat of the race.

Anne Morrow Lindbergh,
Gift from the Sea, 1955

ASK YOURSELF

■ What physical changes do men and women experience during the middle years, and how do they cope with them?

■ Does intellectual functioning in middle adulthood have a distinctive character?

■ Why do some people continue their education or change careers at midlife?

■ What benefits do middle-aged people get from their work?

alud, amor, y pesetas—y el tiempo para gustarlos. This Spanish toast ("Health, love, and money—and time to enjoy them") inspired the authors of a book about middle age to use it as a chapter title, finding it the "ideal summary of what middle age can offer" (B. Hunt & Hunt, 1974, p. 23).

Rather than think of middle age as a time of stodginess, paunches, aches and pains, and regrets about lost youth, many people in the middle years consider it the best time of their lives. In general, middle-aged people today are in good physical, financial, and psychological shape. They are likely to be in their peak earning years, and since their children are usually fully grown or nearly so, many are in the most secure financial position of their lives. As a group, today's 40- to 65-year-olds have substantial assets. Medical advances and awareness of preventive care and fitness are keeping the present generation of middle-aged people, by and large, in good physical health. And one of the greatest strengths of middle age stems from having lived long enough to acquire valuable social and professional experience and having opportunities to use that experience.

This "prime time" of life has its stresses, of course. The middle-aged adult realizes that his or her body is not what it once was. In a youth- and fitness-oriented society, wrinkles, sags, and muscle twinges are unwelcome signs of aging. Furthermore, signs of growing older can hurt people who are looking for jobs.

This is significant because the work that people do exerts a major influence on the way they feel about this time of life. Middle age is a time of taking stock. People reevaluate their earlier career aspirations and how well they have fulfilled them. Sometimes they modify their goals or embark on totally new careers.

Reevaluation—which extends to intimate relationships and other aspects of the lifestyle (as will be seen in Chapter 15)—comes about because of a shift in people's orientation in time.

Instead of thinking of their life span in terms of the years they have already lived, people begin to think of the time they have left to live (Neugarten, 1967). They begin to realize that they cannot possibly do everything they want to do, and they are eager—sometimes desperately so—to make the most of their remaining years. This realization prompts some people to switch careers, some to leave their spouses, and some to retire.

In this chapter, we discuss some of the physical and intellectual issues of middle age. We focus on health, on sensory and psychomotor functioning, and on the distinctive ways people think and learn at midlife. We look at adult education and at the role of work, considering its satisfactions and stresses and the stimulating challenge of a change in career. In Chapter 15, we explore the social and emotional issues and intimate relationships of this time of life.

PHYSICAL DEVELOPMENT

From young adulthood through the middle years, biological changes generally take place so gradually that they are hardly noticed—until one day a 45-year-old man realizes that he cannot read the numbers in the telephone directory without eyeglasses, or a 55-year-old woman has to admit that she is not as quick on her feet as she used to be.

Physical functioning and health are usually good in these years, though not at the peak level of young adulthood. Most people take changes in reproductive and sexual capacities—menopause and the male climacteric—in stride, but there may be some anxiety about a decline in physical attractiveness.

PHYSICAL CHANGES

Sensory and Psychomotor Functioning

Although changes in sensory and motor capabilities are real and affect people's concept of themselves and their interaction with others, these changes are usually fairly small, and most middle-aged people compensate well for them.

Vision, Hearing, Taste, and Smell As the lens of the eye becomes less elastic with age, its focus does not adjust as readily; as a result, many people develop *presbyopia*—the farsightedness associated with aging—and thus need reading glasses. Bifocals—eyeglasses in which lenses for reading are combined with lenses for distant vision—help people make the adjustment between near and far objects. Middle-aged people also experience a slight loss in sharpness of vi-

sion; and because the pupil of the eye tends to become smaller, they need about one-third more brightness to compensate for the loss of light reaching the retina (Belbin, 1967; Troll, 1985). Nearsightedness, though, tends to level off in these years.

There is also a gradual hearing loss during middle age, especially with regard to sounds at the upper frequencies; this condition is known as *presbycusis*. After about age 55, hearing loss is greater for men than for women (Troll, 1985). However, most hearing loss during these years is not even noticed, since it is limited to levels of

(© Stacy Pick 1986/Stock, Boston)

Many people become farsighted during middle age, to the point where they need reading glasses; but people who wore glasses for nearsightedness earlier in life sometimes find that they need them less now.

sound that are unimportant to behavior. Auditory aging occurs at much later ages among some African tribespeople than it does in Europe and the United States, possibly because people in western countries are suffering the effects of living in a high-noise environment (Timiras, 1972).

Taste sensitivity begins to decline at about age 50, particularly the ability to discriminate "finer nuances of taste" (Troll, 1985, p. 32). The number of taste buds declines after childhood, and since the tastebuds become less sensitive, foods that may be quite flavorful to a younger person may seem bland to a middle-aged person unless spices are added (Troll, 1985). Sensitivity to smells seems to hold up well; it is one of the last senses to decline (Troll, 1985).

Strength, Coordination, and Reaction Time

"Use it or lose it" is the motto of many middle-aged people, who have taken up jogging, racquetball, tennis, aerobic dancing, or other forms of physical exercise that often make them fitter, stronger, and more energetic than they were in their youth.

Although there is a gradual decline in strength and coordination during the middle years, the loss is so small that most people barely notice it. A 10 percent reduction in physical strength from its peak during the twenties does not mean much to people who rarely, if ever, exert their full strength in their daily lives.

Of course, the less people do, the less they *can* do. People who lead sedentary lives lose muscle tone and energy and so become even less inclined to exert themselves physically. People who make the effort to be active throughout adulthood reap the benefits of more stamina and resilience after the age of 60.

Simple reaction time slows by about 20 percent, on the average, between the ages of 20 and 60 (Birren, Woods, & Williams, 1980). Complex motor skills, which increase during childhood and youth, gradually decline after people have achieved their full growth. But the decline does not necessarily result in diminished performance. Driving, for example, requires several skills, including coordination, quick reaction time, and ability to tolerate glare. After the age of about 30 to 35, each of these individual abilities declines (DeSilva, 1938, cited in Soddy &

Kidson, 1967). And yet, driving ability is better in middle age than before (McFarland, Tune, & Welford, 1964). The improvement that comes with experience more than makes up for the decrements that come with age.

Similarly, skilled industrial workers in their forties and fifties are usually more productive than ever, partly because they are generally more conscientious and careful (Belbin, 1967). Furthermore, middle-aged workers are less likely than younger workers to have disabling injuries on the job—a result, no doubt, of experience and good judgment, which more than compensate for any diminution of coordination and motor skills (B. Hunt & Hunt, 1974).

Changes in Reproductive and Sexual Capacity

One of the fundamental changes of middle age—the decline of reproductive capacities—affects men and women differently. Women's ability to bear children comes to an end sometime during this period; men, although they can continue to father children, begin to experience a lessening of fertility and, in some cases, a decline in potency.

Menopause The biological event of *menopause* occurs when a woman stops ovulating and menstruating and can no longer bear children. This occurs at about age 50 on the average, but may quite normally happen several years earlier or later (Upjohn, 1983). A time span of some 2 to 5 years during which a woman's body undergoes the various physiological changes that bring on the menopause is known technically as the *climacteric.*

During the climacteric, a woman's body reduces its production of the female hormone *estrogen.* As a result, some women experience physical symptoms, which may include hot flashes (sudden sensations of heat that flash through the body), thinning of the vaginal lining (which can make sexual intercourse painful), or urinary dysfunction (caused by tissue shrinkage) (Ballinger, 1981). In 1 out of 4 post-menopausal women, the decrease in estrogen leads to *osteoporosis,* a condition in which the bones become thinner and more susceptible to fractures (see Figure 14-1 and Box 14-1).

BOX 14-1 **PRACTICALLY SPEAKING**

PREVENTING OSTEOPOROSIS

Thinning of the bones— *osteoporosis*—is a major cause of broken bones in old age (National Institute on Aging, 1983). This is largely a disorder of women, and it is most prevalent in white women, thin women, smokers, and women who do not get enough calcium or enough exercise. It also tends to occur in women whose menopause comes early as a result of surgical removal of the ovaries.

Osteoporosis seems to be preventable if women take certain steps in youth and middle age. The most important preventive measures are getting more calcium and more exercise, avoiding smoking, and (for some women) taking hormone supplements (NIH, 1984a).

Most American women drink little milk and eat few foods rich in calcium, and those who have osteoporosis tend to be those who consume even less of this important mineral. Women should get between 1000 and 1500 milligrams of calcium a day or even more, beginning in their youth. They can easily do so by taking care to consume such calcium-rich foods as the following:

■ Dairy foods. To get the benefits of calcium without the burden of cholesterol

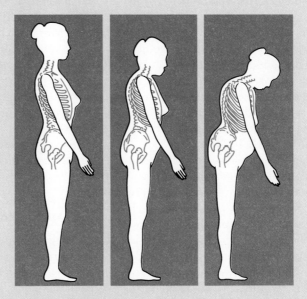

Figure 14-1 Osteoporosis. As osteoporosis weakens bones, fractures of vertebrae may cause women to become stooped from the waist up, with a height loss of 4 inches or more. (*Source:* Notelovitz & Ware, 1983.)

and calories, the best foods in this category are low-fat milk and low-fat yogurt.

■ Canned sardines and salmon (if eaten with the bones still present); and oysters, canned or fresh.

■ Such vegetables as broccoli, kale, and collard, dandelion, turnip, and mustard greens.

Exercise seems to stimulate new bone growth: it should become part of the daily routine early in life and should continue to some degree as long as possible throughout life. The best

exercises for increasing bone density are such weight-bearing activities as walking, running, jumping rope, aerobic dancing, and bicycling.

The National Institutes of Health (1984a) also recommends the administration of estrogen to women at particularly high risk of developing osteoporosis, such as those who have had the ovaries removed. This step, however, is more controversial than the dietary and exercise recommendations, which can be safely followed by all women.

The administration of artificial estrogen can often resolve some of the above problems dramatically. Although replacement of estrogen alone has been related to a higher risk of cancer of the lining of the uterus, research suggests that when artificial progesterone is given along with the estrogen, the risk of developing this kind of cancer falls below the level for women who receive no hormone at all (Bush et al., 1983; Hammond, Jelovsek, Lee, Creasman, & Parker, 1979). There is little information, however, about the safety of long-term combined estrogen and progesterone treatment (National Institutes of Health, NIH, 1984a).

For most women, menopause is a *none*vent psychologically. At one time, a number of psychological problems, especially depression, were blamed on the menopause, but recent research shows no reason to attribute psychiatric illness to this normal event. In one classic study in which several hundred women from 21 to 65 years old were asked about their attitudes toward menopause, women who had been through it had a much more positive view than women who had not (Neugarten, Wood, Kraines, & Loomis, 1963). One typical comment was, "I've been healthier and in much better spirits since the change of life. I've been relieved of a lot of aches and pains" (Neugarten, 1968, p. 200).

Psychological problems in midlife are more likely to be caused by negative societal attitudes toward aging. In cultures that value the older woman, few problems are associated with the menopause (Ballinger, 1981). A society's attitude toward aging seems to influence a menopausal woman's well-being far more than does the level of hormones in her body.

The Male Climacteric Although men can continue to father children till quite late in life, some middle-aged men experience a decrease in fertility and frequency of orgasm and an increase in impotence (Beard, 1975). Furthermore, middle-aged men seem to have cyclic fluctuations in the production of hormones (Kimmel, 1980).

The *male climacteric*—a period of physiological, emotional, and psychological change involving a man's reproductive system and other body systems—generally begins about 10 years later

than a woman's climacteric period, and the pattern of symptoms varies (Weg, 1987). About 5 percent of middle-aged men are said to experience such symptoms as depression, fatigue, sexual inadequacy, and vaguely defined physical complaints (Henker, 1981). Since researchers have found no relationships between hormone levels and mood changes (Doering, Kraemer, Brodie, & Hamburg, 1975), it is probable that most men's complaints are just as subject to environmental pressures as women's are. Some of the problems may be related to disturbing life events, such as illness of the man or his wife, business or job problems, children's leaving home, or death of parents.

Appearance and Sexual Adjustment: The Double Standard of Aging

Although both sexes suffer from our society's premium on youth, women are especially oppressed by the traditional double standard of

(© Gabe Palmer 1986/Stock Market)

Wrinkles and graying hair often imply that a man is "in the prime of life" but that a woman is "over the hill." This double standard of aging, which downgrades the attractiveness of middle-aged women but not of their husbands, can affect a couple's sexual adjustment.

aging. The gray hairs, coarsened skin, and "crow's feet" that are considered attractive as proofs of experience and mastery in men are regarded as telltale signs in women that they are "over the hill." The feminine look is "smooth, rounded, hairless, unlined, soft, unmuscled—the look of the very young; characteristics of the weak, of the vulnerable" (Sontag, 1972, p. 9). Once these signs of youth have faded, so (in many men's eyes) has a woman's value as a sexual and romantic partner and even as a prospective employee or business associate. Some homosexual men may also suffer from the loss of their appeal as they age (Berger, 1982). (Even heterosexual men, who historically have escaped societal penalties for showing the natural effects of aging, are sometimes at a disadvantage in the job and promotion market as they reach middle age.)

The double standard differentiates husbands' and wives' sexual adjustment, according to a recent study. The physical changes that often occur with age appear to have more effect on a husband's sexual responsiveness to his wife than on a wife's responsiveness to her husband (Margolin & White, 1987).

A nationwide random sample of 1509 married men and women 55 years old or less were interviewed by telephone. Three years later, in follow-up interviews, they were asked whether they or their spouses had gained weight or had become less shapely during the intervening period. They were also asked about sexual problems and attitudes. The conclusion was sadly predictable: "men who believe that their spouse is declining in physical attractiveness, but that they themselves are not, are more likely than other men to report sexual problems in their marriage. . . . No such pattern exists for women" (Margolin & White, 1987, p. 25). These men tend to become less interested in their wives sexually, less happy with their sexual relationships, and less likely to be faithful to their wives. This seems to be true regardless of age, economic circumstances, or how long the couple have been married.

The pressures created by a society which believes in looking young, acting young, and being young—added to the real physical losses that people may suffer as they get older—contribute to what has been called the *midlife crisis* (dis-

cussed in Chapter 15). Men and women who can withstand these pressures while staying as fit as possible, and who can appreciate the attainment of maturity as a positive achievement for both sexes, will be able to make the most of middle age—a time when both physical and intellectual functioning are likely to be at an impressively high level.

Loss of Reserve Capacity

Many of the health problems that arise in middle age are due to the loss of *reserve capacity,* that is, the ability of body organs and systems to put forth extra effort in times of stress or dysfunction.

Maintaining physical fitness can help stave off the body's loss of reserve capacity. Still, middle-aged runners need to pace themselves carefully, realizing that the heart of the average 40-year-old under stress pumps little more than half as much blood as the heart of a 20-year-old.

The commonest physical changes include:

- Diminished ability to pump blood
- Diminished kidney functioning
- Diminished enzyme secretion in the gastrointestinal tract, leading to indigestion and constipation
- Weakening of the diaphragm
- Enlargement of the prostate gland in the male (the organ surrounding the neck of the urinary bladder), often causing bladder and sexual problems

Some of these changes are a direct result of aging. Still, behavioral factors and lifestyle (as discussed in Chapter 12) can affect their timing and extent. People age at different rates, and the decline of the body systems is gradual.

HEALTH

Health Status

The typical middle-aged American is quite healthy. In a recent government survey, approximately 82 percent of people 45 to 64 years old reported their health to be good, very good, or excellent (U.S. Department of Health and Human Services, USDHHS, 1986). Only about 7 percent of people in this age range are unable to carry out important activities because of their health (USDHHS, 1985). College-educated people and white people rate their health better than do less-educated people and black people; the difference probably reflects the benefits of good health care and habits established earlier in life (USDHHS, 1982, 1985).

Health Problems

Diseases and Disorders The most common chronic ailments of the middle-aged are asthma, bronchitis, diabetes, nervous and mental disorders, arthritis and rheumatism, impairments of sight and hearing, and malfunctions or diseases of the circulatory, digestive, and genitourinary systems. These ailments do not necessarily come on in middle age, however; while three-fifths of 45- to 64-year-olds have these chronic conditions, two-fifths of people between ages 15 and 44 already suffer from them (Metropolitan

Women see doctors more than men do (probably because they are more health-conscious), and they tend to live longer. As women's lifestyles become more like men's, however, they become more susceptible to previously "male" ills like lung cancer. This woman's physician is explaining the importance of preventing lung disease by avoiding smoking.

Life Insurance Company, cited by B. Hunt & Hunt, 1974).

One major health problem in middle age is high blood pressure, also known as **hypertension.** This disorder, which is dangerous because it often predisposes people to heart attack or stroke, affects 1 out of 5 adult Americans. It is particularly prevalent among black people and poor people (USDHHS, 1982, 1985). Many deaths from heart disease and stroke have been prevented by blood pressure screening and the use of medication when indicated to bring down the pressure (USDHHS, 1985).

Death Rates and Causes of Death Today, when people tend to live longer, death in middle age seems premature but not as unexpected as in childhood or in young adulthood. Beginning at age 35, the death rate at least doubles for each of the next two decades. Death is now more likely to come from natural causes than from accidents or violence. The three leading causes of death between the ages of 35 and 54 are cancer, heart disease, and accidents; between ages 55 and 64, the leading causes are cancer, heart disease, and strokes (USDHHS, 1982).

Since 1950, there has been a 27 percent decline in mortality during midlife. This is due principally to a decreased likelihood of dying of heart disease at this time of life. There are also fewer fatal strokes. But there are more fatal cancers; a 250 percent jump in lung cancer fatalities has offset a decline in deaths from all other kinds of cancer.

As in young adulthood, death rates are higher for men than for women and higher for black people than for white people. Men aged 45 to 64 are twice as likely to die as women in this age bracket. Men are 3 times more likely to die from heart disease and 25 to 30 percent more likely to die from cancer or stroke. The leading cause of death for women aged 45 to 64 continues to be cancer, principally of the breast, the genital organs, or the lungs (USDHHS, 1982, 1986)—the

last related to increased smoking by women.

The death rate for middle-aged black people is 1.7 times that for white people—a smaller difference than that between black and white young adults. But 3 times as many black people as white people die of strokes, because of the greater prevalence of hypertension among black people. In addition, death rates of black people are 50 percent higher than those of white people from heart disease, 40 percent higher from cancer, and 70 percent higher from cirrhosis of the liver (USDHHS, 1982).

INTELLECTUAL DEVELOPMENT

The adage "You can't teach an old dog new tricks" does not apply to people. Middle-aged and older people can and do continue to learn new "tricks," new facts, and new skills, and they can remember those they already know well. There is no evidence of decline in many types of intellectual functioning before age 60, and there are even increases in some areas, such as vocabulary and general information. Middle-aged people can learn new skills—unless they think that they cannot. Furthermore, middle-aged people show a distinct advantage in solving the problems of everyday life, which arises from their being able to synthesize their knowledge and their experience.

ASPECTS OF INTELLECTUAL DEVELOPMENT IN MIDDLE ADULTHOOD

Intelligence and Cognition

As we discuss intelligence and cognition in maturity, we return to the questions we raised in Chapter 12 about the nature of intelligence and the way it is tested in adulthood: what standardized IQ tests can and cannot tell us about adults' intelligence, how appropriate these tests are for evaluating adults, and what kinds of intellectual abilities may improve through the years.

What Psychometric Tests Show According to traditional psychometric tests, patterns of intel-

ligence persist into middle age: adults who achieve relatively high IQ scores are generally those who have had high scores as children. Not surprising, they also tend to be healthier, better educated, and at higher socioeconomic levels than those with lower scores.

Standardized tests also show that performance on some kinds of tasks increases during adulthood, with different abilities peaking at different times. As we pointed out in Chapter 12, whereas fluid intelligence (the ability to handle new material or situations) typically declines during adulthood, crystallized intelligence (the ability to solve problems on the basis of automatic processing of stored information) often increases through middle age. For example, verbal abilities rise, especially among people who use their intellectual powers regularly, either on the job or through reading or other mental stimulation.

Nevertheless, the validity of the traditional IQ tests for adults seems questionable. Since many of the tests were originally designed for children, adults may find the questions and tasks silly. In addition, they may lack the motivation to do their best. Young people usually have a strong stake in testing well, partly to prove themselves and also partly because they hope for some payoff such as college admission. Adults, especially more mature ones, rarely have as strong a goal.

Finally, these tests may not tap the abilities that are most central to what intelligence means in adulthood, such as practicality and the ability to function well in various situations. Although the middle-aged may take somewhat longer to do certain tasks and may not be as adept at solving novel problems as younger people are, they may compensate by the judgment garnered from a range of experience wider than that of younger people. Thus when adults do not perform well on psychometric tests, it is not clear whether it is because their memory or reasoning ability is faltering or whether it is simply because this kind of test is inappropriate for their age group.

Changes in Cognition in Middle Adulthood
K. Warner Schaie, whose proposed stages of adult development were discussed in Chapter 12, is one of those who have criticized the use of conventional psychometric tests for adults. As he points out, adults are usually more concerned about how to use knowledge for practical purposes than about acquiring knowledge and skills for their own sake. In middle age, according to Schaie's model, adults in either the responsible or the executive stage use their intellectual abilities to solve real-life problems associated with family, business, or societal responsibilities. This cognitive development of middle age ties in with Erikson's belief (which will be discussed in Chapter 15) that middle-aged people are concerned with the task of generativity—responsibility for establishing and guiding the next generation.

CHARACTERISTICS OF MATURE THINKERS Piaget characterized the use of formal logic as the highest level of thought, but mature thinking is more complex and calls upon other resources. Apparent inconsistencies can exist side by side in the mind of an adult who is pursuing a practical goal. In the words of one psychologist, "Playful exercise of cognitive schemes, endless generating of 'ifs' and 'whens,' [may] no longer . . . be adaptive" (Labouvie-Vief, 1980, p. 153). Instead, when people focus their intellectual energies on solving real problems, they learn to accept contradiction, imperfection, and compromise as part of adult life.

Mature thinking, according to Labouvie-Vief (1985, 1986), contains a certain amount of subjectivity and reliance on intuition, rather than the pure logic characteristic of formal operational thought. Mature thinkers tend to personalize their reasoning, using the fruits of their experience when called upon to deal with ambiguous situations. Thus experience contributes to mature adults' superior ability to solve practical problems, which is sometimes called wisdom (see Chapter 16).

TESTING PRACTICAL PROBLEM SOLVING Which do you think you would handle better—playing a game of "twenty questions" or figuring out what to do about a flooded basement? In one study (Denney & Palmer, 1981), 84 adults between the ages of 20 and 79 were given two kinds of problems. One was similar to a game of "twenty questions" (and much like a traditional task on intelligence tests). Subjects were shown 42 pictures of common objects and were told to figure out which one the examiner was thinking of, by asking questions that could be answered "yes" or "no." Scoring was based on how many questions it took to get the answer and the percentage of questions that eliminated more than one item at a time ("Is it an animal?") rather than only one ("Is it the cow?").

Subjects were also asked what they would do in real-life situations like these: your basement is flooding; your refrigerator is not cold; you are stranded in a car during a blizzard; your 8-year-old is 1½ hours late coming home from school; the vacuum cleaner you bought from a door-to-door salesperson stopped working after 2 or 3 weeks. Solutions were scored on the degree to which they involved self-reliance rather than the aid of other people.

The results confirmed the central point we have been making about adult intelligence. The older the subjects were, the worse they did on "twenty questions"; but the *best* practical problem solvers were people in their forties and fifties, who based their answers on the experiences of everyday living.

What is the purpose of intelligence, anyway? Is it to play games, or to solve the many problems that face people every day? If it is the latter, then it is clear why the middle-aged are known as the *command generation,* the age group that wields the most authority in virtually all institutions in society. They have not solved all the problems, of course, but no one else seems better qualified to have the responsibility.

This Spanish-speaking man and woman studying English are among the 14 percent of adults in the United States enrolled in part-time educational programs. Mature learners, who most often take classes for job-related reasons, tend to be more motivated than younger students.

The Adult Learner

A woman marries at 17, bears and raises six children, and goes to college at 41 and to law school at 48; at 51 she is on the legal staff of the government of a major American city. A 56-year-old automotive mechanic takes a not-for-credit night course in philosophy. A 49-year-old physician signs up for a seminar in recent advances in endocrinology. These three people exemplify the boom in continuing education, the fastest-growing aspect of American education today.

Almost 14 percent of American adults aged 17 and over participate in part-time adult education courses. Half of these students are 35 years old or older, and 55 percent are women. Almost 92 percent have finished high school, more than 80 percent are employed, and nearly half have incomes over $30,000 (U.S. Department of Education, 1986a). And in the school year 1985–1986, 14 percent of college students were 35 years old and older, representing an 11 percent increase in number in 2 years (U.S. Department of Education, 1987b).

Why do adults go to school? Almost two-thirds of those who take part-time classes do so for reasons related to their jobs (U.S. Department of Education, 1986a). Some seek training that will help them do their work better; for example, professionals in fields of rapidly growing knowledge like law, medicine, and engineering need to keep up with new developments. Many people study to move up the career ladder or to prepare for different kinds of work. Some women who have devoted their young adult years to homemaking and parenting go back to school to prepare for midlife careers. People who see retirement approaching may want to expand their minds and their skills to make more productive and interesting use of their newfound leisure. And some adults simply enjoy learning and want to keep on doing it.

Mature learners tend to be more motivated than learners of traditional age. They have come to realize that learning is not limited to the classroom but also occurs informally—at home, on the job, and elsewhere. What they may lack in specific academic skills, they make up for in the richness and variety of the lessons of life, which they apply to the material they confront when they go back to school (Datan, Rodeheaver, & Hughes, 1987).

But adult learners are often more anxious and less self-confident than their younger classmates, who "know the ropes" because they have been going to school, usually without interruption, for the past 12 years or more. And older students have a number of practical problems that most younger students do not have. They may have trouble fitting classes into their busy schedules and juggling course work, parenting, and jobs. Transportation and child care may pose difficulties, and friends and family are not always supportive.

To help meet the needs of adult learners, an increasing number of colleges are granting credits for practical life experience. They are also becoming more flexible in scheduling, providing more opportunities for students to matriculate part time and to do much of their work independently. At many colleges, students may follow custom-designed academic syllabi, working at home and checking in from time to time with supervising tutors.

Colleges are not the only places, of course, that offer adult education courses. Public schools, community organizations, businesses, labor unions, professional societies, and government agencies do, too.

In today's complex society, education is never finished. And although not all learning takes place in school, more and more people are finding some sort of formal learning important to their keeping up with the challenges and opportunities of the world of work, as well as for developing their full intellectual potential.

WORK

Occupational Patterns

During middle adulthood, the typical worker is likely to fit one of two descriptions. He or she is either at the peak of a career chosen during young adulthood, earning more money, exerting more influence, and commanding more respect than at any other period in life; or on the threshold of a new vocation, possibly spurred by the reevaluation of self that takes place during midlife. A variation on this second pattern is that of some women, who enter or reenter the work force at this time of life or move into more demanding work because of the emptying of the nest or the need for money to put children through college.

People who follow the first pattern are reaping personal benefits and also letting society benefit from their years of experience in a chosen field. Most of them continue to enjoy the work they have settled into. And because of their accumulation of experience and wisdom, many of them attain positions of power and responsibility. Most officeholders, business leaders, academic giants, and other prominent persons in our society tend to be in their middle years; outstanding accomplishments of people much younger than 40 or much older than 65 usually rate special notice.

The top ranks of business, government, and the professions are still male-dominated, though women have made significant headway in these and other fields. In general, women earn less than men and face barriers in both hiring and advancement (Chacko, 1982; see Chapter 12). In addition, although about half of middle-aged women now do paid work compared with only about 20 percent in the 1920s (R. R. Bell, 1983), many of these women have just entered the work force for the first time in their adult lives or have reentered it after "dropping out" to concentrate on raising their children. Such women often face not only age and gender discrimination, but the real disadvantage of competing with people who have a 20-year head start. (Middle-aged men—who are more likely to have been in the work force throughout adult life—are less often at such a disadvantage.) This gender gap may narrow as the current generation of young adults, most of whom have been working straight through their child-rearing years, reach middle age.

People who follow the second career pattern are getting much attention these days as part of a trend toward a multicareer lifetime. Very shortly, we will look at some of the motivations that lead people to change jobs or careers, and then we'll see what kinds of work are most conducive to personal and intellectual growth.

Occupational Stress

When workers are dissatisfied with their jobs, it is often because of one of a variety of stressors (see Table 14-1). These stressors are related to a variety of physical and emotional complaints, although specific links are hard to establish.

Research has connected certain patterns with certain occupations. Persons in low-status health care occupations (such as technicians and aides) and personal service occupations (such as waiters and telephone operators) have particularly high rates of admission to community mental health centers (Colligan, Smith, & Hurrell, 1977). These may be related to the strains of being in a subordinate position, in which the worker experiences pressure and authoritarian treatment and cannot respond to it (Holt, 1982). Physicians, their spouses, and paramedics are especially prone to drug addiction and suicide (R. M. Murray, 1974), which may say more about their access to drugs than about anything else.

The specific stress of **burnout** is characterized by emotional exhaustion and a feeling that one can no longer accomplish anything on the job. It is especially common among people in the helping professions, such as medicine, teaching, social work, and police work, and it often strikes those practitioners who have been the most dedicated and who feel frustrated by their inability to help people as much as they would like to. The feeling of helplessness and lack of control is usually a response to day-in, day-out stress rather than the stress that is connected with an immediate crisis. Symptoms, which come on gradually, may include fatigue, insomnia, headaches, persistent colds, stomach troubles, alcohol or drug abuse, and trouble getting along

with people. The burned-out practitioner may quit a job suddenly, pull away from family and friends, and sink into depression (Briley, 1980; Maslach & Jackson, 1985).

Some measures that seem to help burned-out workers include cutting down on working hours and taking breaks, including long weekends and vacations. Other standard stress-reducing techniques—exercise, music, or meditation—often help.

Unemployment

The biggest work-related stressor of all is the sudden unexpected involuntary loss of a job. A substantial body of research on unemployment since the 1930s (concentrating almost entirely on male workers) has linked it to mental and

(© Rick Browne/Stock, Boston)

Unemployment can be devastating, as many industrial workers discovered when automobile and steel plants laid off employees, or shut down altogether, as a result of foreign competition. The loss of a paycheck can be integrally connected with a loss of identity and self-esteem. People of both sexes cope better with unemployment when they have adequate financial, psychological, and social resources to draw on.

physical illness and to problems in family functioning.

According to the research, two major sources of stress are the loss of income (with associated financial hardships) and the effect of this loss on the worker's feelings about himself. Workers who derive their identity from their work, men who define manhood as supporting a family, and people who define their worth in terms of the dollar value of their work lose more than their paychecks when they lose their jobs. They lose a piece of themselves and, with it, their self-esteem (Voydanoff, 1983).

The ability to cope with unemployment depends on various factors. Those who do best have some financial resources to draw on, either savings or the earnings of other family members. They do not blame themselves for being failures but see the job loss in more objective terms. They have the support of understanding, adaptive families and can draw on outside resources, like friends.

The importance of paid work to women's well-being has been increasingly recognized in recent years. In the past, women's relationships—especially with their husbands and children—were thought to be most important for their self-esteem. Newer research, however, such as one intensive study of about three hundred 35- to 55-year-old Boston-area women (discussed in Chapter 15), has found that a woman's sense of pride and power is more strongly related to her paid work than to her personal life, especially if she is in a high-prestige occupation (Baruch et al., 1983). Women are just as likely as men to feel economically, psychologically, and physically distressed at the loss of a job, as shown in a study of former employees of an Indiana plant that closed in 1982 (Perrucci & Targ, 1984). Both women and men reported such physical ailments after job loss as headaches, stomach trouble, and high blood pressure, and workers of both sexes felt less in control of their lives.

A crucial element in adjustment is the context in which a person sees the loss. Those who can look at such a forced change as an opportunity to do something else or as a challenge for growth can develop emotionally and professionally. They may not only change jobs, but change the entire direction of their careers.

Changing Careers in Midlife

At age 40, the president of a multimillion-dollar corporation left his prestigious position to go back to school to study architecture; eventually he opened his own architectural firm. At age 50, a homemaker who had held a variety of part-time jobs while her children were growing up enrolled in a school of social work; with her master's degree, she found a good job as a community organizer, which enabled her to draw on many of her past experiences.

Stories of midlife career changes abound these days as people seek new careers for a variety of reasons. With today's longer life expectancies, many middle-aged people—realizing that they do not want to keep doing the same thing for the next 20 years—strike out in totally new directions. Others are forced by unemployment with technological or economic causes to seek second careers. A middle-aged worker may feel pressured by younger workers moving up the career ladder and might rather change jobs entirely than deal with the competition. Another middle-aged person may think, "I'm in a rut," or, "I've gone as far as I can go with this company," and may seek the challenge of a job that offers more opportunity for advancement or personal growth.

Some common events of middle age affect people's life structures in general and their careers in particular. The emptying of the nest when the youngest child leaves home may lead to a reorientation from family concerns to career considerations. A woman's enthusiasm about her first job outside the home may inspire her husband to look for a new line of work that will provide similar excitement. Divorce or widowhood may force a woman to work from necessity rather than choice and perhaps to try to find a better-paying job. People who after years of work have paid off the mortgage or put the last child through college may feel free to take jobs with easier work loads, to switch to occupations that bring in fewer dollars but more satisfaction, or to go into risky but exciting business ventures. Other people suddenly realize that they are ill prepared for retirement and focus on accumulating a nest egg while they are still capable of substantial earnings.

How do career changers fare? The answer may depend in part on whether the change is free or forced. People who freely choose to make a change (and even some who are forced to, who seize on a layoff or forced retirement as an opportunity for growth) may enjoy their lives more while contributing their valuable experience to new organizations or ventures.

In one study, 37 "career dropouts"—people aged 30 to 55 who had chosen voluntarily to leave successful white-collar or professional careers—were happy with their new jobs and lifestyles, even though they generally earned less money and worked hard. They had left their jobs because they were bored, felt their jobs had no meaning, and often felt exploited by employers whose values were in conflict with theirs. All these people felt that the better quality of their new lives more than compensated for their lower incomes (Roberts, in Entine, 1974).

Career changers often benefit not only themselves but whomever and whatever they work for. People who opt for new careers in midlife tend to be particularly valuable employees. They "are better adjusted, have a higher need to achieve, and have a greater sense of self-esteem and ambition than those who remain in their first careers" (Schultz & Schultz, 1986, p. 321).

Education and counseling can help people who are considering midlife career changes to recognize the possibilities that are open to them and to understand how they can make the most of those possibilities. (Among the possibilities are new ways to balance education, work, and leisure. For one perspective on how to do so, see Figure 14-2 and Box 14-2, page 496.) The decision whether or not to stay in a job may hinge on the amount of intellectual and personal growth that the work provides.

How Work Enhances Personal and Intellectual Growth

Do people change as a result of the kind of work they do? Both common sense and research say yes: people seem to grow in jobs that challenge their capabilities.

What specific aspects of work affect psychological functioning? In an examination of 50 different aspects of the work experience, from the pace of the work to relationships with co-workers and supervisors, the aspect that turned out to have the strongest impact was the *substantive complexity* of the work itself: "the degree to which the work, in its very substance, requires thought and independent judgment" (Kohn, 1980, p. 197). A sculptor's work, for example, is more complex than a ditchdigger's, a lawyer's work is more complex than a clerk's, a computer programmer's work is more complex than a data processor's, and a research scientist's work is more complex than a druggist's. (This "substantive complexity" may have something to do with creativity, which is discussed in Box 14-3 on pages 497–498.)

A combination of cross-sectional and longitudinal studies revealed a reinforcing interplay between the substantive complexity of work and the worker's intellectual flexibility in coping with demanding situations. People with more complex work tend to become more flexible thinkers, not only on the job but in other areas of their lives. "They become more open to new experience. They come to value self-direction more highly. They even come to engage in more intellectually demanding leisure-time activities. In short, the lessons of work are directly carried over to nonoccupational realms" (Kohn, 1980, p. 204). At the same time, a person's intellectual flexibility influences the complexity of the work he or she will be doing 10 years down the road.

This circular relationship "may begin very early in life when children from culturally advantaged families develop skills and other qualities that result in their being placed in classroom situations and tracks that are relatively complex and demanding, which in turn contribute to further development of intellectual flexibility" (Smelser, 1980, p. 16). The spiral continues in adulthood, as people begin their careers—and the gap widens. More flexible thinkers tend to go into more complex jobs, which in turn enable them to grow in flexibility, qualifying them for even more complex work. Those who show less flexibility at the outset and obtain less complex work grow more slowly or not at all (Kohn, 1980).

One of the most significant points to emerge from this research is that what is most important about work is not income or status but what peo-

BOX 14-2 FOOD FOR THOUGHT

A NEW WAY TO PLAN A LIFE

The career counselor Richard N. Bolles, author of the best-selling career guide *What Color Is Your Parachute?* (1987), wrote another book called *The Three Boxes of Life* (1979). The boxes are three realms in people's lives—education, work, and leisure. According to Bolles, most of us view them as shown in Figure 14-2*a*, with the first 20 years or so of life taken up with education, the next 40 years given over principally to work, and the final years dedicated to leisure.

The problem with this approach is that by devoting themselves to one aspect of life at a time, people do not enjoy each period of life as much as they might. Equally important, they do not prepare themselves for the next phase. For example, by concentrating for many years on school and work, people may forget how to play. As a result, when they retire and have all the leisure time they want, too many people do not know what to do with it. But if people combined these three realms throughout their lives (as shown in Figure 14-2*b*), life would be richer and more fulfilling.

Some people have taken steps in this direction: college

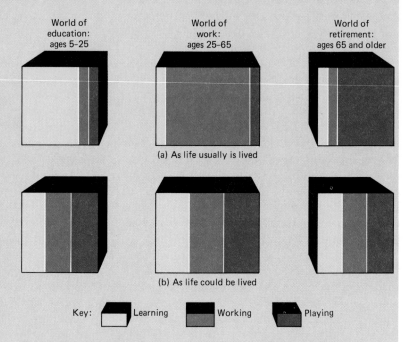

(a) As life usually is lived

(b) As life could be lived

Key: Learning   Working   Playing

Figure 14-2 The three "boxes" of life. (*Source:* Adapted from R. N. Bolles, 1979.)

students may take work-study programs or "stop out," either to work or to play; middle-aged adults may go back to school or take a year out to pursue a special interest; and retirees may devote their later years to study or to the pursuit of a new line of work. The people taking these steps are still pioneers, however. Most people have yet to climb out of the boxes society has constructed.

To make the integration of

learning, work, and play easier, societal instructions and values would have to undergo the kind of reevaluation to which many people subject their individual lives in middle age. People often find that such reevaluation helps them to redesign their lives in a more fulfilling way. Perhaps our culture, with a similar reevaluation, could be redesigned as well.

BOX 14-3 FOOD FOR THOUGHT

CREATIVITY TAKES HARD WORK

At age 40 or thereabouts, Frank Lloyd Wright designed Robie House in Chicago, Louis Pasteur developed the germ theory of disease, and George Eliot wrote the first of the several novels that were to give her a secure place in English literature. Charles Darwin was 50 when he presented his theory of evolution, and Leonardo da Vinci was 52 when he painted the *Mona Lisa*. These monumental achievements are examples of the creative productivity that is possible in middle age.

Just what goes into the cognitive processes of highly creative minds is a puzzle that many researchers have tried to solve. One, Howard Gruber (Gardner, 1981), a psychology professor at Rutgers University, has approached this question through intensive case studies of the intellectual lives of great scientists like Darwin.

To find out how Darwin's mind worked, Gruber pored over Darwin's notebooks, trying to map the changes that occurred in his thinking during the 18 months after his return from a 5-year voyage of exploration in which he had meticulously recorded his observations of fossils, plants, animals, and rocks along the coast of South America and in the Pacific islands.

There is a commonly held idea that the creative act involves sudden insight. But Gruber was struck by how long it took Darwin to think through a new idea. Darwin went down at least one blind alley before happening upon an essay by the English economist Thomas Malthus, which described how natural disasters and wars keep population increases under control. Malthus's description of the struggle for survival triggered Darwin's solution to the problem of how evolutionary changes come about. It occurred to him that in this struggle, some species—those whose characteristics were best adapted to the environment—would survive and others would not. But even then, it took Darwin several months after reading Malthus's essay to develop his principle of natural selection, which explains how adaptive traits tend to be passed on through reproduction. And it was not until 2 decades later that he finally published his theory and the supporting evidence.

Although each mind works somewhat differently, Gruber has found some common characteristics of highly creative people:

■ They work *painstakingly and slowly* to master the knowledge and skills they need to solve a problem. Darwin, for example, studied barnacles for 8 years—probably until he knew more about them than anyone else in the world.

■ They constantly *visualize* ideas. Darwin drew one

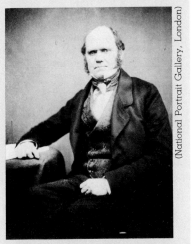

Charles Darwin was 50 years old when he proposed his theory of evolution. This original and controversial theory—evidence of the high level of creative productivity that can occur in middle age—represented the fruition of years of slow, careful, painstaking work.

particular image—a branching tree—over and over, as he refined his theory of how more complex, highly developed species evolve on the "tree" of nature.

■ They are *goal-directed*; they have a strong "sense of purpose, a feeling of where they are and where they want to go" (Gardner, 1981, p. 69).

■ They have *networks* of *enterprises*, often juggling several seemingly unrelated projects or activities.

■ They are able to "*bracket*" (set aside) problems they have insufficient information to solve and go on to something else, or to adopt working assumptions for the time being. Darwin did this when he got stuck on questions about heredity for which he had no reliable answers (Mendel's theories were not then known).

- They are *daring*. It took courage for Darwin to publish a theory that broke away from the entrenched ideas of his day.

- Rather than work in isolation (as they are sometimes thought to do), they *collaborate* or discuss their ideas with others—not within established groups and settings, but by choosing peers and designing environments that nurture their work.

- They *enjoy* turning over ideas in their minds "and would not dream of doing anything else" (Gardner, 1981, p. 70). Evidence of this is that Darwin was reading Malthus's essay for amusement.

- Through hard work, they *transform themselves*, until what would be difficult for someone else seems easy for them.

This last point, in particular, is reminiscent of Kohn's belief (1980) that substantively complex work, requiring deep thought and independent judgment, can contribute to intellectual growth—not only in a Darwin but in anyone.

ple actually do when they work. The other important finding is that people's minds do not stop developing at the end of adolescence or young adulthood—"intellectual flexibility continues to be responsive to experience well into midcareer" (Kohn, 1980, p. 202).

Why is the complexity of work tied in so closely with intellectual growth? One reason may be that—in a society in which work plays a central role in people's lives—mastery of complex tasks affects people's sense of self: it gives them a feeling of competence and teaches them that "the problems one encounters in the world are manageable" (Kohn, 1980, p. 205). Thus we see again a possible link between intellectual development and the social and emotional aspects of personality, to which we turn in Chapter 15.

SUMMARY

- Middle adulthood is a time of reevaluation. There is no single biological marker or behavioral sign denoting the beginning of middle age. In this book, *middle age* is defined as the period from 40 to 65 years of age.

Physical Changes

- Middle-aged adults experience some declines in sensory abilities and complex motor skills, but they can compensate for these declines with such aids as eyeglasses and with the application of experience and judgment.

- Menopause, the cessation of menstruation and reproductive ability in women, typically occurs around age 50. It occurs when a decrease in the production of estrogen brings about the end of ovulation, and it is associated with hot flashes, thinning of the vaginal lining, and urinary dysfunction. Osteoporosis, a condition in which the bones become thinner and more susceptible to fractures, affects 1 out of 4 postmenopausal women. There is no reason to attribute psychological problems to menopause.

- Although men can continue to father children until late in life, in some men the male climacteric brings a decline in fertility and in frequency of orgasm, an increase in impotence, and other symptoms.

- The "double standard of aging" in American society causes women (but not most men) to seem less desirable as they lose their youthful looks. For both sexes, the problems of getting older are often amplified by living in a society that places a premium on youth.

Health

■ Most middle-aged people are in good health. Many of the health problems that occur are due to loss in the reserve capacity of particular body systems, or the ability of those systems to put forth extra effort in times of stress or dysfunction.

■ Although death rates have declined in recent generations (especially death from heart disease and stroke), death rates increase throughout midlife. Death is more likely to occur in this period from natural causes than from accidents or violence. The leading causes of death are cancer, heart disease, accidents, and stroke. As in younger age groups, death rates are higher for males than for females and for black people than for white people.

Aspects of Intellectual Development in Middle Adulthood

■ Performance on many standardized intelligence measures increases during adulthood, especially for verbal abilities and tasks involving stored knowledge. However, the appropriateness of conventional IQ tests for adults is questionable.

■ Although middle-aged people may perform more slowly and may not be as adept at solving novel problems, some research suggests that the ability to solve practical problems based on experience peaks at midlife.

■ Continuing education for adults is the fastest-growing area of education in the United States.

■ Adults go to school for many reasons, but chiefly to improve their work-related skills and knowledge or to prepare for a change of career.

■ Adult learners tend to be more motivated but less self-confident than young students.

Work

■ Many middle-aged people are at the peak of their careers, but others are involved in career changes that may be triggered by the self-evaluation process of midlife. For some, occupational stresses such as burnout, unemployment, and specific working conditions affect physical and emotional well-being.

■ Combining education, work, and leisure throughout life can enrich the entire life span.

■ The kind of work adults do affects the degree to which they grow intellectually. There seems to be a direct relationship between the complexity of the work a person does and that person's intellectual flexibility.

■ Some people do extremely creative work in middle age. Studies of scientists show that creativity appears to have more to do with slow, painstaking work than with sudden inspiration.

SUGGESTED READINGS

Bolles, R. N. (1979). *The three boxes of life*. Berkeley, CA: Ten Speed Press. A compelling and entertaining argument for the integration of lifelong learning, working, and leisure, with suggestions for the kind of life and work planning that can bring it about.

Freudenberger, H. J., & Richelson, G. (1980). *Burnout: The high cost of high achievement*. Garden

City, NY: Anchor. A description of the syndrome experienced by frustrated high achievers, including a checklist for self-diagnosis, as well as suggestions for preventing and handling burnout. Extensive case histories are included.

Gross, R. (1982). *The independent scholar's handbook.* Reading, MA: Addison-Wesley. Lively, anecdotal manual on "how to turn your interest in any subject into expertise." The book offers advice on finding the right subject, doing research, getting grants, finding colleagues, writing and publishing your findings, and organizing an "independent scholar's roundtable" in any community.

John-Steiner, V. (1985). *Notebooks of the mind: Explorations of thinking.* Albuquerque: University of New Mexico Press. On the basis of interviews with more than 50 men and women prominent in the humanities, arts, and sciences and of extensive biographical research, the author, a psycholinguist, describes the psychology of creativity and thought.

Notelovitz, M., & Ware, M. (1983). *Stand tall: The informed woman's guide to preventing osteoporosis.* Gainesville, FL: Triad. A book of up-to-date information, by researchers at the University of Florida, on preventing and treating osteoporosis and on the pros and cons of hormone therapy, with guidelines for diet and exercise. A valuable resource for women from age 30 on up.

Troll, L. E. (1985). *Early and middle adulthood* (2d ed.). Monterey, CA: Brooks/Cole. A survey of research findings on physical status, personality, and intellectual functioning, by a leading developmental researcher.

15

CHAPTER

15

CHAPTER

PERSONALITY AND SOCIAL DEVELOPMENT IN MIDDLE ADULTHOOD

What happens to a dream deferred?
Does it dry up
Like a raisin in the sun? . . .
Maybe it just sags
Like a heavy load.
Or does it explode?

Langston Hughes, "Montage
of a Dream Deferred," 1951

ASK YOURSELF

■ How typical is the midlife crisis?

■ Is personality stable during adulthood, or does it change?

■ How similar are women's and men's development during middle age?

■ Do marriages become happier or less happy in middle age?

■ How do middle-aged people cope with teenage children, the "empty nest," and the care of aging parents?

When asked, "How are you?" a vivacious speech therapist replied, "I'm going to have my fortieth birthday in 2 weeks, and I can't talk to anyone without mentioning it. So I guess I'm having my midlife crisis. Isn't everybody?"

Personality and lifestyle changes during the middle years are often attributed to the **midlife crisis,** a potentially stressful period during the early to middle forties, which is precipitated by a review and reevaluation of one's past life and heralds the onset of middle age.

The concept of the midlife crisis burst into public consciousness in the late 1970s with the popularization of the findings of Vaillant and Levinson, who (along with Erikson) take a normative-crisis approach to human development. This view (introduced in Chapter 13) is that the human personality goes through a universal sequence of critical changes at certain ages.

The term *midlife crisis*—first enunciated by such psychoanalysts as Jacques and Jung—has become a trendy catchphrase, quick to pop up as an explanation for a bout of depression, an extramarital affair, or a career change. Such events are taken as signs of a shift from an outward orientation, or a concern with finding a place in society, to an inward orientation, a search for meaning within the self (Jung, 1966). This inward turn may be unsettling; as people question their life goals, they may temporarily lose their moorings.

What brings on the crisis, according to E. Jacques (1967), is awareness of mortality. The first part of adulthood is over, its tasks largely done. People have most likely formed their families and may be tasting freedom from the daily responsibilities of child care. They have established their occupations and may have attained a degree of success. They have achieved independence from their parents, who may now be turning to *them* for advice and help. They are in the prime of life, but now they realize that their time has become much shorter and they will not be able to fulfill all the dreams of their youth, or (if they have fulfilled them) that they have not found the hoped-for satisfaction.

This realization is not necessarily traumatic. For many people, this is just one more of life's many transitions, and although readjustments

"Goodbye, Alice. I've got to get this California
thing out of my system."

are called for, they are generally fairly easy. People can emerge from this time of questioning with more awareness and understanding of themselves and of others; with more wisdom, strength, and courage; and with a greater capacity for love and enjoyment.

In one way, talking about midlife crisis is helpful, because it calls attention to the dynamic nature of personality in middle age. In another way, it is unhelpful, since it can lead to a rigid notion that everyone has to undergo a crisis in order to successfully negotiate emotional development at midlife.

Today attention is shifting from the midlife crisis, and the normative-crisis model from which it springs, to the timing-of-events model of Bernice Neugarten and others (introduced in Chapter 13). According to this view, personality development is influenced less by age than by what events people experience and when they occur. Twenty or thirty years ago, the occurrence and timing of such significant events as marriage, first job, and births of children and grandchildren were fairly predictable. Now lifestyles are more diverse, people's "social clocks" tick at different rates, and a "fluid life cycle" has washed out the old boundaries between youth and adulthood, and between middle age and old age (Neugarten & Neugarten, 1987).

The timing-of-events model also recognizes that societal changes affect the significance of events and their impact on people's personalities. For example, when most of women's lives revolved around childbearing and child rearing, the end of the reproductive years meant something different from what it means now, when most women are only in their mid-thirties by the time their youngest child has started school. When people died earlier, survivors felt old earlier, since the deaths of friends, relatives, and prominent people close to their age were reminders that someday they, too, would die.

Whether a crisis takes place or not, a heightened awareness of life's limits often leads middle-aged people to recognize that if they wish to change direction, they must act quickly. Midlife is a time of stock taking, not only in regard to careers (as discussed in Chapter 14) but in intimate relationships.

In this chapter we look at middle adulthood through the prism of the normative-crisis model of development, and we also present a critique of that model. Then we look at important events in relationships. As we examine changes in marriage, sexuality, sibling bonds, and friendship, as well as relationships with maturing children and aging parents, we note variations in the shape and timing of these events. Two events

Coaching a Little League baseball team is one form of what Erik Erikson calls *generativity*. As middle-aged people begin to feel the end of their own lives approaching, they seek to guide the development of the next generation. Erikson views parenthood as an important, though not an essential, preparation for generativity.

that are taking place more frequently in middle age these days—retirement and becoming grandparents—are discussed primarily in Chapters 16 and 17.

NORMATIVE-CRISIS THEORY AND RESEARCH

Much of the major theoretical and research work on adult development done in the past few decades has come from a normative-crisis viewpoint. This perspective on middle adulthood is exemplified by Erikson's stage of generativity versus stagnation; Robert Peck's expansion of Erikson's work; and Vaillant's and Levinson's findings on men, introduced in Chapter 13. (See Table 15-1 for a summary of these four views.)

Erik Erikson: Crisis 7—Generativity versus Stagnation

At about age 40, according to Erikson, people go through their seventh crisis, that of **generativity versus stagnation.** Generativity is the concern of mature adults for establishing and guiding the next generation. Looking ahead to the waning of their lives, people feel a need to participate in the continuation of life. If this need is not met, Erikson says, people become stagnant (inactive or lifeless).

People's impulse to foster the development of the young is not limited to guiding their own children. It can be expressed through such activities as teaching and mentorship—a mutually fulfilling relationship that satisfies a younger protégé's need for guidance (see Chapter 13) as well as an older person's generativity needs. Generativity can also take the form of productivity or creativity (in the arts, for example) or of self-generation, the further development of personal identity.

As in Erikson's other stages, it is the *balance* of one trait over the other that is important. Even the most creative person goes through fallow periods, gathering energy for the next project; but too much stagnation can result in self-indulgence or even in physical or psychological invalidism.

The "virtue" of this period is *care*: "a widening commitment to *take care of* the persons, the products, and the ideas one has learned *to care for*" (Erikson, 1985, p. 67). (The task of generativity seems to correspond to Schaie's responsible stage and executive stage of midlife cognitive development, discussed in Chapters 12 and 14, which are characterized by practical problem solving in others' behalf.)

TABLE 15-1 FOUR VIEWS OF DEVELOPMENT IN MIDDLE ADULTHOOD

ERIKSON (1950)	PECK (1955): FOUR CRITICAL PSYCHOLOGICAL DEVELOPMENTS RELATED TO SUCCESSFUL ADJUSTMENT TO MIDDLE AGE	VAILLANT (1977): GRANT STUDY OF HARVARD UNIVERSITY MEN (CLASSES OF 1939–1944)	LEVINSON (1978, 1986): STAGES OF MIDLIFE DEVELOPMENT IN MEN
Crisis 7—Generativity versus stagnation The impulse to foster the development of the next generation leads middle-aged persons to become mentors to young adults. The wish to have children is instinctual, and so childless people must acknowledge their sense of loss and express their generative impulses in other ways, helping to care for other people's children directly or as protégés in the workplace. Some stagnation could provide a rest that leads to greater future creativity. Too much stagnation could lead to physical or psychological invalidism.	1 *Valuing wisdom versus valuing physical powers:* People realize that the knowledge they have gained through the years, enabling them to make their life choices wisely, more than makes up for their declining physical powers and youthful attractiveness. 2 *Socializing versus sexualizing in human relationships:* People learn to appreciate the unique personalities of others as they learn to value them as friends rather than as sex objects. 3 *Emotional flexibility versus emotional impoverishment:* Deaths of parents and friends force breaks in meaningful relationships. People must develop the ability to shift their emotional investments from one person to another. Physical limitations can require a change in activities. 4 *Mental flexibility versus mental rigidity:* Flexibility enables people to use their past experiences as provisional guides to the solution of new issues.	*Midlife transition (age 40—"give or take a decade"):* Midlife is stressful, as adolescence is stressful, because of the demands of entrance into a new stage of life. Much of the pain comes from having the maturity to face pain that was suppressed for years. Many men reassessed their past, reordered their attitudes toward sexuality, and seized one more chance to find new solutions to old needs. The best-adjusted men were the most generative and found these years (from 35 to 49) the happiest of their lives. *Tranquil fifties:* Males become more nurturant and expressive. Sexual differentiation lessens. The fifties are a generally mellower time of life.	*Midlife transition (age 40 to age 45):* Questioning one's life—values, desires, talents, goals; looking back over past choices and priorities; deciding where to go now; coming to terms with youthful dreams; developing a realistic view of self. *Entry life structure for middle adulthood (age 45 to age 50):* Reappraisal leads to a new life structure involving new choices. Some men retreat into a constricted—or well-organized, overly busy—middle age. *Age-50 transition* (age 50 to age 55):* Men who have not gone through their midlife crisis earlier may do so now. Others may modify the life structures they have formed in their mid-forties. *Culminating life structure for middle adulthood* (age 55 to 60):* Men complete middle adulthood; a time of great fulfillment. *Late adult transition* (age 60 to age 65):* Middle age ends; preparation for late adulthood begins.

*Projected.

Generativity, then, is a step beyond procreation and, according to Erikson, is not easily achieved by people who have not experienced parenthood. Erikson believes that those who either voluntarily or involuntarily remain childless need to acknowledge a sense of loss, or "generative frustration," and to find other outlets for their generative tendencies—for example, through assistance to children in developing countries. In Erikson's words, "... a new generative ethos may call for a more *universal care* concerned with a qualitative improvement in the lives of all children" (1985, p. 68).

Erikson's concept of generativity does seem to correspond to a common impulse at this time of life. Even so, many people who have cared for their own children for years may need to take care of themselves for a while before they can again focus on nurturing others. Furthermore, his view that people who have not had children have trouble achieving generativity is considered narrow by many psychologists today.

Robert Peck:
Four Developments of Middle Age

Expanding on Erikson's concepts, Peck (1955) specifies four psychological developments as critical to successful adjustment in middle age. Peck differs from other representatives of the normative-crisis approach in that he ties these developments not so much to chronological age as to the circumstances of a person's life, which determine the issues he or she is dealing with. For example, a 45-year-old single woman competing for a high-level executive job that would involve being transferred to a strange city is dealing with life issues different from those of a 45-year-old grandmother in an entry-level job whose recently separated daughter wants her to take care of the baby so that *she* can work. The way *both* of these women adjust to their circumstances, however, can be evaluated according to four criteria:

1 *Valuing wisdom versus valuing physical powers.* Wisdom, defined by Peck as the ability to make the best choices in life, appears to depend largely on sheer life experience and the opportunities of encountering a wide range of relationships and situations. Sometime between the late thirties and the late forties, most successfully adjusted people appreciate that the wisdom they have acquired more than makes up for their diminished physical strength, stamina, and youthful attractiveness.

2 *Socializing versus sexualizing.* People redefine the men and women in their lives, valuing them as individuals, as friends, and as companions rather than primarily as sex objects. In this way they can appreciate the unique personalities of others and can reach a greater depth of understanding.

3 *Emotional flexibility versus emotional impoverishment.* The ability to shift emotional investment from one person to another and from one activity to another becomes crucial during middle age. This is the time when people are likely to experience breaks in their relationships because of the deaths of parents and friends and because of the maturing and independence of children. They may also have to change their activities because of physical limitations.

4 *Mental flexibility versus mental rigidity.* By middle age, many people have worked out a set of answers to life's important questions. But when they let these answers control them rather than continue to seek out new answers, they become set in their ways and closed to new ideas. Those people who remain flexible use their experiences and the answers they have already found as provisional guides to the solution of new problems.

None of these developments need wait until middle age; some may already have occurred in the mature personality in early adulthood. If they do not take place by the middle years, however, Peck doubts that the person will be able to make a successful emotional adjustment.

George Vaillant: The Grant Study
of Harvard University Men

The longitudinal study known as the *Grant Study* (introduced in Chapter 13), which followed Harvard undergraduates from the classes of 1939 to 1944 into their fifties, identified a midlife transition at about age 40 ("give or take as much as a decade"). After the stage of career consolidation, which usually occurred during the thirties, many of the men abandoned the "compulsive, unreflective busywork of their occupational apprenticeships and once more [became] explorers of the world within" (Vaillant, 1977, p. 220). Neugarten (1977), a prominent advocate of the timing-of-events model, also observed this tendency toward introspection in the middle-aged, which echoes Jung's concept of an inward turning; but it seems to vary with personality. (This issue and the question of other personality changes in midlife are discussed in Box 15-1 on page 510.)

The midlife transition may be stressful, because of the demands of entrance into a new stage of life. These years are often marked by difficulties in getting along with teenage children and sometimes by overt depression. Much of the pain of midlife, according to Vaillant, is old, repressed pain, which surfaces now that men are mature and strong enough to deal with it. Once they have faced their repressed feelings, many men can use the transition period as one more chance to find new solutions to old needs. Thus, many men reassess their past, come to terms with long-suppressed feelings about their parents, and reorder their attitudes toward sexuality.

As troubling as the transition years sometimes were for the men in the Grant Study, the transition rarely assumed the dimensions of a crisis. Furthermore, these men were no more likely to get divorced, to be disenchanted with their jobs, or to become depressed at midlife than at any other time during the life span. By their fifties, the best-adjusted men in the group actually saw the years from 35 to 49 as the *happiest* in their lives.

This research reveals Erikson's influence in a number of ways, notably its attention to generativity. The best-adjusted of these men were also the most generative, as measured by their having responsibility for other people on the job, their giving money to charity, and their having raised children whose academic achievements equaled their fathers'.

Although the study yielded little information about the fifties, it did find them a generally mellower and more tranquil time of life than the forties. Vaillant observed some of the same traits noted by others: the lessening of sexual differentiation with advancing age (which Brim, 1974, refers to as the "normal unisex of later life") and the tendency for males to become more nurturant and expressive (again, see Box 15-1).

Daniel Levinson: Studies of Men[*]

Levinson and his associates (1978, 1980, 1986), whose work was also influenced by Erikson's concept of generativity, describe midlife as a time when life structures "always" change appreciably, "though the forms and degree of change vary enormously" (Levinson, 1986, p. 5). Change continues, to a lesser degree, throughout the subsequent era of middle adulthood, which is a calmer time. Although biological capacities are somewhat reduced, most people become "senior members" of their "own particular worlds" (p. 6), responsible for the work of others and for guiding the generation of young adults who will soon take their place.

Levinson divides middle adulthood into the following phases (refer back to Table 15-1 for a summary).

Midlife Transition (Age 40 to age 45) Like all of Levinson's transitional periods, the midlife transition is "both an ending and a beginning" (Levinson, 1986, p. 7): a person is completing the work of early adulthood while learning the ropes of middle adulthood. During this bridge period, men—now more acutely aware of their mortality—question virtually every aspect of their lives. Thirty-two of the forty men in Levinson's sample found this a time of moderate or severe crisis, during which they often felt upset and acted irrationally. Levinson believes that the midlife reappraisal has to involve emotional turmoil because of its challenge to virtually every value one has held. Such reevaluation is healthy, however, since in looking back over the choices they made earlier in life people have the opportunity to encourage aspects of themselves that may have been neglected. People who successfully negotiate this transition come to terms with

[*]Levinson says that women go through phases similar to those he described for men, but his studies of women have not been published as of this writing.

BOX 15·1   FOOD FOR THOUGHT

DOES PERSONALITY CHANGE IN MIDDLE AGE?

"I'm a completely different person now from the one I was twenty years ago," said the 47-year-old architect, as the six other people at the table, all in their forties and fifties, nodded in vigorous agreement.

Many people experience personality changes during adulthood, especially at midlife. Are these changes deep-seated, or are they surface changes? Is there a basic core of personality that remains stable throughout life?

These are controversial questions. For a long time, most psychologists believed that personality is set like plaster by young adulthood. Then in the 1970s, psychological thinking shifted to emphasize the seemingly limitless capacity for change throughout life (Z. Rubin, 1981). Now there are two camps: one believes that change will occur unless something interferes with development (Brim & Kagan, 1980); the other believes that personality will remain stable unless a specific change-producing event occurs (Costa & McCrae, 1981).

Both common sense and research suggest that people change in some ways and remain the same in others. Through experience and accomplishments, most adults gain in self-esteem and a sense of control over their lives, but basic temperament tends to remain constant (Brim & Kagan, 1980). Longitudinal studies suggest that bubbly junior high schoolers grow up

to be cheerful 40-year-olds; complaining adolescents turn into querulous adults; assertive 20-year-olds become outspoken 30-year-olds; and people who cope well with the problems of youth are equally able to handle the problems of later life (J. Block, 1981; Costa & McCrae, 1981; Eichorn, Clausen, Haan, Honzik, & Mussen, 1981; Haan & Day, 1974; Livson, 1976; Noberini & Neugarten, 1975).

Although people in general seem to become more introverted and introspective as they get older—Neugarten (1977) calls people's concern with their inner life *interiority*—those who are extroverts in their youth tend to remain more outgoing than other people. Indeed, extroversion, as well as neuroticism (a mild emotional disturbance arising from anxiety) and openness to new experience, remain remarkably stable throughout adulthood, according to a cross-sectional national sampling of more than 10,000 people 32 to 88 years old (Costa, McRae, Zonderman, Barbano, Lebowitz, & Larson, 1986). Certain traits do seem to soften with maturity. For example, impulsive children usually do grow up to be restless, impatient adults, but as adults they are less impulsive than they once were (Stewart & Olds, 1973).

One common change in midlife is the tendency to take on characteristics associated with the other sex. Men often become more open about their feelings, more interested in developing intimate

relationships, and more nurturing, while women tend to become more assertive, self-confident, and achievement-oriented (Chiriboga & Thurnher, 1975; Cytrynbaum, Bluum, Patrick, Stein, Wadner, & Wilk, 1980; Helson & Moane, 1987; Neugarten, 1968).

The reasons for these changes are in question. Some writers, citing observations of similar changes in earlier periods of history, suggest that hormonal changes may blur distinctions between the sexes (Rossi, 1980). Most social scientists, however, advance a cultural explanation based on men's and women's traditional roles: at the same time when a woman is freer—because her children have grown and left home—to develop her nonmaternal abilities and to seek career achievement, a man begins to wonder whether work is the most important thing in life after all (Gutmann, cited in Cytrynbaum et al., 1980).

Now that younger women are more achievement-oriented and more likely to combine working with mothering and younger men are assuming a larger role in child rearing, we may not see such a switch in midlife personalities. Indeed, the changes we have seen may have less to do with gender than with the questions middle-aged people ask themselves as they evaluate their lives: "Is this all there is to life? Shouldn't I try other options while I still have time?"

the dreams of their youth and emerge with a more realistic view of themselves.

An important task of midlife is to become more of an individual—"more compassionate, more reflective and judicious, less tyrannized by inner conflicts and external demands, and more genuinely loving of [oneself] and others" (Levinson, 1986, p. 5). People who fail in this task, says Levinson, lead increasingly trivial and stagnant lives.

A man at midlife, according to Levinson, needs to deal with opposite tendencies within himself. Although he feels older than the younger generation, he is not yet ready to call himself middle-aged. He must avoid clinging too much to youthful attitudes, which would keep him from finding his place in the world of middle adulthood; yet if his thinking becomes too "old," it will become "dry and rigid" (Levinson, 1980, p. 286). He must also try to integrate the "masculine" and "feminine" parts of his personality—his need for separateness and his need for attachment to others.

Entry Life Structure for Middle Adulthood (Age 45 to age 50) By his mid-forties, a man begins to build a new life structure that may involve new choices: perhaps a new career or a restructuring of his present work, or a new wife or a different way of relating to the same wife. Some people, according to Levinson, never resolve the tasks of midlife: they lead a boringly constricted middle age, or they keep busy, well organized—and unexcited. The most successful people often find middle age the most fulfilling and creative time of life, an opportunity to allow new facets of their personalities to flower.

Age-50 Transition (Age 50 to age 55)* Another chance to modify the life structure comes in the early fifties. Levinson and his colleagues (1978) initially held that "it is not possible to get through middle adulthood without having at least a moderate crisis" during either the midlife

transition or the age-50 transition (p. 62). He has since softened that view a bit, saying merely that the age-50 transition is "likely to be an especially difficult time" for men whose midlife transition has been relatively smooth (Levinson, 1980, p. 287).

Culminating Life Structure for Middle Adulthood (Age 55 to age 60) The culminating life structure for middle adulthood is a stable period when men finish building the framework of middle adulthood. Those who can rejuvenate themselves and thus enrich their lives find the fifties a time of great fulfillment.

Late Adult Transition (Age 60 to age 65) The early sixties are a major turning point, the time for ending middle age and preparing for late adulthood.

Women's Development in Middle Adulthood

The most influential normative-crisis theories of adult development—those of Erikson, Levinson,[†] and Vaillant—have all been male-oriented in theoretical concepts, research samples, or both. However, men's experience may not be an appropriate base from which to generalize about women. In recent years, other researchers have examined women's experience in middle age and have found some similarities to and some differences from the male-based models.

Do Women Undergo Levinsonian Changes? Droege's dissertation (1982), analyzed by P. Roberts and Newton (1987) and discussed in Chapter 13, applied Levinson's biographical interview technique to 12 women ranging in age from 44 to 53. For these women, the midlife transition appeared to be a less clear-cut dividing line than Levinson found for men. The women's lives continued to be unstable after the transition, perhaps because the women had not yet come to a point in their careers at which they could assess their achievements and make a definite change of direction.

Still, the women in Droege's study led different kinds of lives before and after the transition.

---

*This phase and the next two phases were projected for the men in Levinson's original sample, who were not followed into their fifties and sixties. In Levinson's recent writing (1986), he outlines these phases more definitively, presumably on the basis of a pilot sample of men and women interviewed for a forthcoming project on middle adulthood, as well as other biographical sources.

[†]As noted earlier, however, Levinson believes that women go through phases similar to those he attributes to men.

The change began in the late thirties, when the women began to identify themselves in a broader context than their own families, taking on roles of community leadership. This shift—comparable to that of men who seek more authority in midlife—can be called "Becoming One's Own Woman."

At midlife, women made changes in career and family commitments that appeared to be linked more to age, to the awareness of mortality, and to shifting roles and desires for self-expression than to any specific event. (The "emptying of the nest," for example, was a critical "marker" event only for women whose lives had been extremely family-centered.) Some took on paid or volunteer work; others reduced their work loads. Some altered their marital or other relationships or redefined basic values. This process appeared to be psychologically healthy: the women who took risks and made real structural changes in their lives escaped the depression that sometimes comes at midlife and showed higher self-esteem than those who did not build new structures for middle age.

Mastery and Pleasure as Indications of Well-Being A much larger study, of almost 300 women between the ages of 35 and 55, points to factors that contribute to women's healthy adjustment in the middle years (Barnett, 1985; Baruch et al., 1983). The investigators first interviewed 60 women, 10 from each of 6 groups: employed women who had never married, employed married women with children, employed married women without children, employed divorced women with children, married homemakers with children, and married homemakers without children. On the basis of what these women said about the pleasures, problems, and conflicts in their lives, the researchers then drew up a questionnaire and administered it to a random sample of 238 other women in the six categories. The subjects had an average educational level of 2 years beyond high school, and their incomes ranged from $4500 to more than $50,000.

Two elements appeared to influence a woman's mental health: how much mastery, or control, she felt she had over her life and how much pleasure she derived from life. Neither of these criteria was related to age: the older women in this sample felt just as good about themselves as the younger ones. Nor was there any evidence for a midlife crisis. Nor did simple relationships show up between well-being and whether a woman was married, had children, or was pre- or postmenopausal. What did emerge as vitally important was the combination of a woman's work and her intimate relationships.

Paid work was the single best predictor of mastery, a positive experience with husband and children (including a good sex life) was the best predictor of pleasure, and the single best key to psychological well-being was a challenging job that paid well and that gave a woman the opportunity to use her skills and make decisions. The women who scored highest overall on both mastery and pleasure were employed married women with children; the lowest scorers were unemployed childless married women. Thus, women's well-being seems to be enhanced by taking on multiple roles, despite the stress that goes along with active involvement in several important areas of life. It is even more stressful, apparently, to be underinvolved—to have too little to do, to have a job that is not challenging enough, or to have too few personal and occupational demands. These findings echo those of Helson & Moane (1987), discussed in Chapter 13, that women who commit themselves to career, family, or both show more personality growth between early and middle adulthood than those who do not make such commitments.

Evaluating the Normative-Crisis Model

The problem of trying to describe women's development by generalizing from findings regarding men is a critical limitation of Levinson's and Vaillant's studies. The applicability of these findings to people who differ from those in the samples in other ways is also questionable, as we mentioned in our preliminary critique of the normative-crisis model in Chapter 13. Additional objections have been raised concerning the universality of the midlife crisis and other age-linked divisions and the validity of the "healthy" male model of development portrayed in the studies.

Can the Findings Be Generalized to Other Populations? The subjects of these studies were, mostly, privileged white men. Vaillant's sample contained no black men; only 5 of Levinson's 40 subjects were black, and most of these were solidly middle- or upper-class. Furthermore, the middle-aged subjects were all born in the 1920s or 1930s. Thus, findings about them may not be applicable to men of other races, other socioeconomic levels, other cohorts, or other cultures, or to women.

The cohort issue is an interesting one. What we know about "normative" development in middle adulthood is based on research with people who either were born or grew up during the economic depression of the 1930s. These men were members of a small cohort that benefited from an expanding economy after World War II. They may have achieved work success far beyond their early expectations—and then burned out at an early age. Their development may, then, be unusual rather than typical (Rossi, 1980). If future cohorts experience alternating periods of education, work, and leisure throughout life, as Bolles (1979) has proposed (see Box 14-2), their course of development may be different, and a midlife career switch may be seen as routine rather than as a sign of crisis.

Finally, as Levinson himself notes, his theory has yet to be tested in other cultures—some of which do not even have a concept of middle age (see Box 15-2 on page 514).

How Typical Is the Midlife Crisis? The midlife crisis is an "artifact of the media," one psychologist told a television reporter recently. "Crisis, transition and change occur all through life" (Schlossberg, 1987, p. 74).

Many other writers have challenged the notion that crisis is a hallmark of midlife. The transition to middle age may be potentially stressful, but the stress does not necessarily take on crisis proportions (Brim, 1977; Farrell & Rosenberg, 1981; Rossi, 1980). Nor is this sort of transition necessarily limited to the middle years. For example, one group of men in their thirties who had achieved success quite young were already struggling with the kinds of issues commonly associated with middle age. These men were asking themselves questions like "Was it worth it?" "What next?" and "What shall I do with the rest of my life?" (Taguiri & Davis, 1982, cited in Baruch et al., 1983).

Research that calls into question the universality of the midlife crisis also bears out the timing-of-events view that crises arise in response to events, not birthdays. Events that used to be characteristic of a certain time of life are no longer so predictable; and their unpredictability may bring on crisis, catching people unprepared and unable to cope (Neugarten & Neugarten, 1987). Thus, whether a midlife transition (or any other transition) turns into a crisis appears to be less related to age than to the particular circumstances of a person's life and how the person deals with those circumstances; "one person may go from crisis to crisis while another . . . experience[s] relatively few strains" (Schlossberg, 1987, p. 74).

Differences in the way people handle the midlife transition may reflect their position in society, according to a much larger and more socioeconomically representative study of men than Levinson's (Farrell & Rosenberg, 1981). Comparing 300 men at midlife with 150 younger men, the researchers found that only 12 percent of the older men experienced full-blown midlife crises, though about two-thirds had some adjustment problems. Whereas Levinson found a virtually universal midlife crisis among his advantaged sample, Farrell and Rosenberg found that unskilled laborers were much more likely to show stress than were professional men or middle-class executives but the lower-class men were more likely to deny or avoid their problems or to express them through authoritarian attitudes.

It appears, then, that although adults do go through transitions at midlife, as well as earlier and later, the timing and acuteness of these transitions and the way people cope with them may be less reflective of their age than of their life circumstances and personalities.

Is Adult Development Age-Linked? The foregoing criticisms go to the heart of the normative-crisis approach: the idea that development follows a definite, age-linked sequence. Although Erikson and Vaillant are somewhat sketchy in assigning ages to their stages, Levin-

same time redefine what it means to be sons and daughters to their own parents, who may now need their help. We'll therefore examine how people in middle adulthood cope with being in the midlife "sandwich" between maturing children and aging parents.

Marriage and Divorce

Marriage in middle age today is very different from what it was in earlier times. When life expectancies were shorter, with women often dying in childbirth, it was the rare couple indeed who lived with each other for 25 or 30 or 40 years. The most common pattern was for marriages to be broken by death and for the survivors to remarry (often, they married others who had been widowed). In second marriages or in marriages in which the original partners did grow old together, households were usually alive with children. People had children early and late, had more of them, and expected them to live at home until they married. It was relatively rare for a middle-aged husband and wife to be alone together.

Today more marriages are ended by divorce, but couples who manage to stay together can often look forward to 20 or more years of married life after the last child has left the home.

Marital Satisfaction   What happens to the quality of a longtime marriage? Research has produced contradictory findings. Some early studies found that marital satisfaction declines through the years (Pineo, 1961), while others found more complex patterns, with a marriage improving in some respects but worsening in others (Burr, 1970).

Current literature suggests that marital satisfaction follows a U-shaped curve. From a high point early in the marriage, it declines until late middle age and then rises again through the first part of late adulthood (S.A. Anderson, Russell, & Schumm, 1983; Gilford, 1984; Gilford & Bengtson, 1979; Gruber-Baldini & Schaie, 1986). The least happy time seems to be the period when most couples are heavily involved in child rearing and careers. *Positive* aspects of marriage (such as discussion, cooperation, and shared laughter) seem to follow the U-shaped pattern, while *negative* aspects (such as sarcasm,

anger, and disagreement over important issues) decline from young adulthood through age 69 (Gilford, 1984; Gilford & Bengtson, 1979). This may be because more and more couples who have frequent marital battles divorce along the way.

The first part of the middle years, when many couples must deal with teenage children making their way toward independence, tends to be stressful. At this time, according to one recent study, a man's or woman's marital satisfaction has to do with the closeness of his or her relationship with an adolescent child of the same sex. The more distant a father and son or a mother and daughter are, the more discontent there is likely to be with the marriage. Also, the identity issues of midlife appear to affect wives' (but not husbands') feelings about their marriages; women become less satisfied with their marriages as the demands of child rearing diminish and their feelings of power and autonomy increase (Steinberg & Silverberg, 1987).

Typical personality changes of middle age, including the tendency of women to take on "masculine" characteristics and of men to take on "feminine" characteristics, can alter husbands' and wives' interaction and their expectations regarding their marital roles; and their ability to adjust to each other's changing needs can affect their satisfaction with married life (Zube, 1982). For example, the husband of a woman who goes to work for the first time may have difficulty accepting her as an equal partner in the marriage and as a worker with an outside life that does not include him.

The years immediately after the children leave home may bring as much contentment as the honeymoon (H. Feldman & Feldman, 1977). Husband and wife may breathe a sigh of relief. They have more privacy than they have had in years, the freedom to be spontaneous, fewer money worries, and a new opportunity to get to know each other as individuals. This "second honeymoon" may coincide with a "honeymoon stage" of retirement, which, unfortunately, may not last; research has found another drop in marital satisfaction after age 69 (Gilford, 1984; see Chapter 17).

The research on marital satisfaction has been criticized on methodological grounds. Much of the older research dealt with only the husband's or the wife's attitude, not with both. Also, virtually all studies have been cross-sectional; they show differences among couples of different age cohorts rather than exploring changes in the *same* couples. In addition, the samples have included only couples whose marriages have survived, omitting those who are divorced (Blieszner, 1986).

One recent study—a study of 175 couples—that confirmed the U-shaped curve (Gruber-Baldini & Schaie, 1986) used a quasi-longitudinal method to address some of the defects of cross-sectional research. However, only 22 of the 175 couples in the study were followed throughout its entire 30-year span; the rest were added at various points. (This particular study seems to support the common observation that spouses become more alike as years go by. The longer a couple were married, the more they resembled each other in their way of thinking and outlook on life—even in mathematical skills. But this tendency toward like-mindedness halted temporarily, along with the dip in marital satisfaction, during the child-rearing years.)

The years after children leave home may be comparable to the honeymoon; many couples find renewed romance in middle age. Freed from the responsibilities of child rearing, a husband and wife can concentrate on their relationship and explore new interests. This "second honeymoon" sometimes coincides with the early stage of retirement.

What Makes Middle-Aged Couples Split Up or Stay Together?

How a marriage fares in the middle years may depend largely on its quality up to those years. A marriage that has been basically good all along may be better than ever (Troll & Smith, 1976). The *passionate love* of newlyweds—the initial intense attraction with its wildly emotional ups and downs—fades as day-to-day life together dispels the sense of mystery. But in a strong marriage, *companionate love*—loving friendship marked by affection, attachment, commitment, and security—deepens as a couple share joys and sorrows, trust and loyalty, and an intimate knowledge of each other (E. Walster & Walster, 1978).

In a shaky marriage, though, the *"empty nest"*—the transition that occurs when the last child leaves home—may be a personal and marital crisis. With the children gone, a couple may realize that they no longer have much in common and may ask themselves whether they want to spend their remaining years together.

Although divorce is less common among the middle-aged than among young adults, the difference may be one of cohort rather than age. Women born in the years just after World War II were entering adulthood just when women's roles were changing most rapidly. These women, now in their late 30s, have a higher divorce rate than those who are 10 years older or 10 years younger; and as their generation enters middle age, it is projected that its divorce rate will rise still further (Norton & Moorman, 1987). (These census data on marital history cover women only; responses for men were considered unreliable, since they were often provided by someone other than the men themselves.)

Middle-aged couples are separating for many of the same reasons as younger couples—their greater expectations from marriage and their growing willingness to end an unsatisfactory relationship; the increased acceptance of divorce, even for older couples; and the less stringent divorce laws across the country.

Of course, divorce is rarely easy; and it can be especially traumatic for middle-aged and older people, who expect their lives to be relatively settled. People over the age of 50, particularly women, tend to suffer more distress than younger people when going through divorce

TABLE 15-2 WHY SPOUSES STAY TOGETHER

MEN	WOMEN
My spouse is my best friend.	My spouse is my best friend.
I like my spouse as a person.	I like my spouse as a person.
Marriage is a long-term commitment.	Marriage is a long-term commitment.
Marriage is sacred.	Marriage is sacred.
We agree on aims and goals.	We agree on aims and goals.
My spouse has grown more interesting.	My spouse has grown more interesting.
I want the relationship to succeed.	I want the relationship to succeed.
An enduring marriage is important to social stability.	We laugh together.
We laugh together.	We agree on a philosophy of life.
I am proud of my spouse's achievements.	We agree on how and how often to show affection.
We agree on a philosophy of life.	An enduring marriage is important to social stability.
We agree about our sex life.	We have a stimulating exchange of ideas.
We agree on how and how often to show affection.	We discuss things calmly.
I confide in my spouse.	We agree about our sex life.
We share outside hobbies and interests.	I am proud of my spouse's achievements.

Note: These are the reasons given most often by 351 couples married for 15 years or more. The reasons are listed in order of frequency.
Source: Lauer & Lauer, 1985.

(Chiriboga, 1982). But the stress of divorce appears to be less than that of living out a frustrating, conflict-filled relationship (Pearlin, 1980); and so, many people with unhappy marriages decide to end them.

Indeed, divorce has become so prevalent that sociologists are now studying why some marriages do *not* break up. One survey asked 351 couples who had been married at least 15 years (of whom 300 couples said that they were happily married) to select from a list of 39 statements the most important reasons for the longevity of their marriages. The responses of the men and the women were remarkably similar (see Table 15-2). The reasons most frequently given for lasting marriages were a positive attitude toward the spouse as a friend and as a person; belief in the commitment to, and sanctity of, marriage; and agreement on aims and goals in life. Also, happily married couples spent as much time together as they could and shared many activities (Lauer & Lauer, 1985).

Interestingly, although most of the happily married couples were generally satisfied with

their sex lives, this was not one of the uppermost reasons for their happiness. Sexual compatibility was far down on the women's list of priorities and not much higher on the men's. Some respondents reported a decline in their sexual activity; others said that their sex lives had remained stable or had improved. Those whose sexual relations were less than ideal found other, more compelling reasons for marital bliss.

These findings fit in with what we have learned in the past 2 decades or so regarding sexuality in middle adulthood. Let's turn to that often-misunderstood topic.

Sexual Relationships

Myths about sexuality in middle age (many of which were believed by the middle-aged themselves) have served in the past to diminish the enjoyment of this time of life for many people. Recent advances in health and medical care, more liberal attitudes toward sex throughout society, and new studies of sexual activity have reinforced the awareness that sex during middle age and the older adult years can be a vital part of life. National surveys of sexual activity in the United States have found that middle-aged people are engaging in sexual activity more often and in more varied ways than ever before (Brecher, 1984; M.M. Hunt, 1974; B.D. Starr & Weiner, 1981).

Sexual activity is different, however, during the middle years. Most men do not experience sexual tension as often as when they were younger. Men who eagerly sought sexual activity every other day may now be content to go 3 to 5 days between orgasms. Their erections arrive less often of their own accord and more often only with direct stimulation. Their orgasms come more slowly and sometimes not at all. And they require a longer recovery time after one orgasm before they can ejaculate again. After menopause, women may not become aroused as readily as before, and inadequate vaginal lubrication may make intercourse painful.

Very often a decrease in sexual activity can be attributed to nonphysiological causes: monotony in a sexual relationship, preoccupation with business or money worries, mental or physical fatigue, overindulgence in food or drink, physical and mental infirmities of either partner, or fear of failure to perform associated with or resulting from any of these causes (Masters & Johnson, 1966).

Couples who are aware of these potential blocks to sexual fulfillment, who recognize the normal changes of middle age, and who can design their sex life around them can still find great satisfaction. Measures that can enhance the sex life of middle-aged couples include the use of a lubricating substance when a woman's natural lubrication is inadequate, longer and more inventive foreplay to arouse both partners, close attention to overall physical condition, capitalizing on the longer sexual act made possible by the male's slower orgasm, and the continuation of regular and frequent sexual activity (B. Hunt & Hunt, 1974).

Relationships with Siblings

After Margaret V. was widowed in her fifties, her married brother, whom she had previously seen no more than once a month, made a point of seeing her every week. He helped her with home repairs and financial decisions, and he and his wife included her in their social activities.

Many middle-aged siblings stay in touch and stand ready to help each other in time of need. Relationships with siblings are the longest-lasting in most people's lives, and they become even more important as people grow older.

According to one survey, some 85 percent of middle-aged adults have at least one living brother or sister, and the average person has two. Although they may not see each other as frequently as they used to, siblings are likely to get together at least several times a year, and, in many cases, once a month or more. It is very unusual for them to lose touch completely (Cicirelli, 1980, cited in Cicirelli, 1982).

Although childhood rivalry may continue during adulthood, many siblings (especially sisters) become closer. More than two-thirds of people who are siblings feel close or extremely close to their brothers and sisters and derive considerable satisfaction from their relationship with them; more than three-fourths report that they get along well or very well (Cicirelli, 1980, cited in Cicirelli, 1982). Issues may arise, however, over the care of elderly parents and questions of inheritance, especially if the relationship between the siblings has not been good.

Friendships

Middle-aged people sometimes seem to have less time and energy for friendship than do people in other stages of life. They are often heavily involved with family—spouses, children, and aging parents; they are usually busy with their work; and they often want to spend whatever extra time they have building up security for impending retirement (Weiss & Lowenthal, 1975). As a result, people in middle adulthood tend to have fewer friends than either newly-weds or people about to retire, and their friendships seem less complex; that is, they use fewer adjectives to describe the dimensions of their friendships.

Yet friendships do persist throughout middle age and are a strong source of emotional support and well-being (Baruch et al., 1983). Many

Friends are a valuable source of companionship, support, and enjoyment in middle age. Being at the same stage of life and having similar interests are now the predominant factors in the choice of friends.

of the friends of middle age are old friends, though people do make some new friends, often through organizations they belong to. Chronological age is less a factor in making friends now than is similarity in life stage, such as age of children, duration of marriage, or occupational status (Troll, 1975).

What midlife friendships lack in quantity, they often make up for in quality as people turn to their friends for emotional support and practical guidance—for example, to help them deal with maturing children and aging parents.

Relationships with Maturing Children

Parenthood is a process of letting go. From the moment of birth, children follow a course of development that ultimately leads to independence from their parents. During the parents' middle age, most families are in the final throes of the process.

Issues for Parents of Adolescents   It is ironic that the people at the two times of life most popularly linked with emotional crisis—adolescence and middle age—frequently live in the same household. It is usually middle-aged adults who are the parents of adolescent children. While dealing with their own special concerns, they have to deal daily with young people who are undergoing their own great physical, emotional, and social changes. Sometimes parents' own long-buried adolescent fantasies resurface as they see their children turning into sexual beings. Furthermore, seeing their children at the brink of adulthood makes some parents realize even more sharply how much of their adulthood is behind them. The contrast in life stages sometimes creates resentment and jealousy on the part of the parent—and an overidentification with the child's fantasies (T. Vahanian, personal communication, January 23, 1980).

Another issue that middle-aged parents need to face is an acceptance of their children as they are—not as the people the parents have hoped and dreamed they would be. In coming to terms with this reality, parents must realize that they do not have total control over their children, that the children cannot be molded into carbon copies or improved models of the parents. Parents must face the fact that the directions their children choose may be very different from the ones the parents want them to follow.

This acceptance is so difficult for many parents, and the need to break away is so strong for many young people, that the years of adolescence can be hard on everyone in the family. The most frequent area of disagreement among the middle-aged couples interviewed in one study (Lowenthal & Chiriboga, 1972) was child rearing. As one father of three said, just after his youngest child had gone off to college, "They make the last couple of years at home so miserable that their going doesn't come as a trauma—it's a relief!"

The "Empty Nest"   For years, people have talked about the *"empty nest"* crisis—a difficult transition when the last child leaves home that supposedly afflicts women in particular. Recent research has shown, however, that although some women who have a heavy investment in mothering do experience problems at this time,

FEIFFER

they are far outnumbered by those who find it liberating not to have children in the home anymore (Barnett, 1985; Brecher, 1984; L.B. Rubin, 1979). There is some evidence that this stage is harder on fathers, who may react to their children's leaving with regrets that they did not spend more time with them when they were younger (L.B. Rubin, 1979). The empty nest also appears to be hard on parents whose children do not become independent when the parents expect them to (Harkins, 1978) and on women who have not prepared for the event by reorganizing their lives (through work or other involvements; Targ, 1979).

Among 54 middle- and lower-middle-class men and women whose youngest child was about to leave home, this transition stage represented the lowest point in life satisfaction for only three women and two men (Lowenthal & Chiriboga, 1972). And even among these five, none explained their low levels of happiness by referring to their children's imminent departures. On the other hand, 13 of the parents found their children's adolescence their most trying period, a time when they had problems with their children or conflicts with their spouses over the children.

The Not-So-Empty Nest What happens when (as is becoming the case more and more) the

nest does not empty when expected, or is refilled by fledgling adults returning home to live? As the timing-of-events model would predict, this phenomenon sometimes leads to tension as parents are forced to accommodate to the presence of their full-grown offspring (Lindsey, 1984).

In 1984, 37 percent of 18- to 29-year-olds in the United States (most of them in the lower end of this age bracket) were in households headed by their parents. About 7 percent of the men and 10 percent of the women were in school, and most had not yet married. About half of young black adults (54 percent of young black men) lived with their parents; a trend for an increasing number of black adults (who face widespread unemployment) to be living with parents has been continuous since 1940 (Glick & Lin, 1986a). Among other population groups, the return of young adults to the parents' home gathered momentum during the 1970s and 1980s, when the nation's economy slowed down. Jobs became harder to get, housing costs climbed, couples were postponing marriage, divorce and unwed parenthood were on the rise, and many young people had trouble maintaining a household on a single income (Clemens & Axelson, 1985; Glick & Lin, 1986a).

Two small studies of a total of 39 parents who had young adult children living with them

Parenting is not over when the youngest child graduates from college or gets a full-time job, but parents and children need to redefine their roles to reflect the children's independent status. Most families maintain frequent contact, and many middle-aged parents help young adult children get on their feet.

This situation creates a number of possible sources of psychological conflict. Adult children living with parents may fall into immature, dependent habits, while the parents continue or resume the role of caregivers. Furthermore, the young adult is likely to feel isolated from peers and to have difficulty establishing intimacy—according to Erikson, the major task of this age. Meanwhile, the parents may be deprived of long-postponed freedom to renew their own intimacy, to explore personal interests, and to resolve marital issues that were preempted by parental responsibilities. Almost half of the still-married parents complained of strains on their marriages, particularly when the child was over 21 (Clemens & Axelson, 1985).

A much larger and more recent study of 677 elderly couples in Boston whose children had been living with them for 1 to 44 years since becoming adults found little marital stress related to the mere presence of an adult child. Instead, it was the amount of conflict between parents and child that affected marital discord (Suitor & Pillemer, 1987).

Lifelong Parenting The difficulty many parents have in treating their offspring as adults is illustrated by a story that Elliott Roosevelt has told about his mother, Eleanor, who was seated next to him at a state dinner. When a friend later asked Elliott, then in his forties, what his mother had said to him when she leaned over to whisper in his ear, he answered, "She told me to eat my peas."

Even after the years of active parenting are over and all the children have flown the nest, parents are still parents. The midlife roles of parent to young adults and grandparent to their children raise new issues and call for new attitudes and behaviors.

Some studies indicate that young, newly married adults (especially daughters) are closely tied to their middle-aged parents, who often help them financially or with various services, like baby-sitting or helping them get their first homes in order. Parents and adult children often visit each other, and young couples spend a great deal of time talking about their parents.

Parents and adult children generally enjoy each other's company and get along well. They may maintain harmony by avoiding touchy in-

found that "fledgling adults are more welcome when they are under the age of 22 and their stay is relatively brief" (Clemens & Axelson, 1985, p. 263). Most of the parents surveyed were happy with the arrangement for the time being but wanted their offspring to get on their own feet. A little more than half saw no negative effects on their marriage. They found their grown children to be helpful with household chores and with caring for younger children and remarked that having them at home enhanced the family's closeness.

But more than 4 out of 10 of the parents in these studies reported serious conflict with their fledglings, often stemming from the hours the young people kept or the way they took care of (or failed to take care of) the family home and car. Disagreements also arose over dress and over lifestyle—particularly over sex, alcohol, drugs, and choice of friends.

tergenerational issues—a strategy one researcher has likened to the establishment of "demilitarized zones" (Hagestad, 1984).

Parents in the prime of life generally continue to give their children more than they get from them (Aldous, 1987; Troll, 1986; Troll, Miller, & Atchley, 1979). Their continuing support probably reflects the relative strength of middle-aged adults and the continuing needs of young adults, who are in what some psychologists consider to be the most stressful years in the life span (Pearlin, 1980). The balance of mutual aid tends to shift as the parents grow older (as we discuss in the next section).

Relationships with Aging Parents

A 45-year-old woman says, "My mother is my best friend. I can tell her anything." A 50-year-old man visits his retired father every evening, bringing him news and asking his opinions about problems in the family business. A 40-year-old divorced mother sees her parents more often now than she did in 15 years of marriage and needs their help more now than since her teens. A 55-year-old man, who cannot have a 10-minute phone conversation with his mother without an argument, says, "I wish she would die so I could feel guilty and get it over with." A couple in their early sixties find that the time they had hoped to spend traveling and playing with their grandchildren is being spent instead in caring for both their widowed mothers.

The relationships that middle-aged people have with their parents vary enormously, often reflecting the history of the bond (Leigh, 1982; Morgan, 1984). These ties are not static, however; they evolve constantly through the years.

During middle age, many people are able for the first time to look at their parents objectively, neither idealizing them nor blaming them for their mistakes and inadequacies. The coming of maturity helps people to see their parents as individuals with both strengths and weaknesses.

Something else happens during these years. One day a son or daughter looks at a mother or father—and sees an old person. The middle-aged child realizes that the parent is no longer a pillar of strength to lean on, but is now starting to lean on the child. Older adults often seek their children's help in making decisions. The

(© 1985 Phil Huber/Black Star)

By middle age, many people are able to look at their parents objectively, neither idealizing them nor exaggerating their shortcomings. This middle-aged daughter realizes that her mother is no longer a tower of strength but instead is beginning to lean on *her*. Mothers and daughters usually remain closer than any other combination of family members.

loss of physical faculties and earning powers may make them dependent on their children for the performance of daily tasks and for financial support. If they become ill, infirm, or mentally confused, their children may be called upon to assume total responsibility for managing their lives.

Contact with Parents The overall picture that emerges from a growing body of recent research on middle-aged children and their elderly parents is one of a strong bond growing out of attachment earlier in life—and continuing as long as both generations live (M.H. Cantor, 1983; Cicirelli, 1980; Lang & Brody, 1983; B. Robinson & Thurnher, 1981). Parents and children see and speak to each other frequently and generally get along well, with relatively little strain between them. In one study, 87 percent of adult children with elderly parents felt close or very close to their fathers, and 91 percent to their mothers (Cicirelli, 1981).

Since both generations want to be independent, adults and elderly parents usually do not live together unless that arrangement becomes absolutely necessary because the parent is too poor or too ill to live alone and has no other real option. Most older people (even those who are in difficult circumstances) do not want to burden their families; fewer than 1 percent of those now living alone say that they would rather live with their children (Commonwealth Fund, 1986).

With many people today living in smaller quarters than in the past, it is often inconvenient to absorb an extra person into a household, and everyone's privacy—as well as relationships—may suffer. Middle-aged children may resent having their parents looking over their shoulder; parents may resent having to account to their children for the ways they spend their time. Many older people feel that it would be difficult to live with their married children's families because it would be hard to refrain from giving advice, which they know would rarely be welcomed (Lopata, 1973).

However, the two generations often live *near* each other and see each other frequently. One study found that 8 out of 10 older persons had seen at least one of their children within the past week (Rabushka & Jacobs, 1980). Mothers and daughters are more likely to maintain close contact than any other combination of family members (Troll, 1986; Troll et al., 1979).

Mutual Help Although help flows back and forth between the generations, a classic study found that older parents are more likely to receive aid from both their middle-aged children and their grandchildren than to give it (R. Hill, 1965). "In general, parents give more services and money to their children throughout their life, and children give more emotional support, household help, and care during illness" (Troll, 1986, p. 23). Among working-class families, though, money is more likely to flow from child to parent (Troll et al., 1979).

Elderly parents tend to be somewhat selective, focusing their attention and aid on the child who needs them most. They may, for example, open their home to a child whose marriage has ended; and parents of handicapped children often maintain their protective roles as long as they live. Single adult children get more financial assistance and help with transportation from elderly parents than married adult children; adult children who are divorced are most likely to receive help with child care and housework and emotional support (Aldous, 1987). Unhappily married, divorced, and widowed children often become closer to their parents, getting from them the support that they are not getting from their spouses.

Caring for Aging Parents The generations get along best while the parents are healthy and vigorous. When older people become infirm—especially if they suffer from mental deterioration or personality changes—the burden of caring for them often strains the relationship. Daughters, in particular, become distressed, because they are the ones who generally have this responsibility—most often for aging, ailing mothers (Troll, 1986).

Even though mothers worry about losing their independence and being burdens on their children (Troll, 1986), the children are the ones to whom many elderly women turn first when in need of care. In one study, more than half of the adult children surveyed felt some strain, and one-third reported substantial strain, in connection with helping their elderly parents. The strain most often showed up in the form of physical or emotional exhaustion and the feeling that the parent was impossible to satisfy (Cicirelli, 1980).

One probable source of negative feelings is the disappointment, anger, and guilt that the middle-aged often feel when they realize that they, rather than their parents, now have to be the strong ones. In addition, their anxiety over the anticipated end of their parents' lives is likely to be tinged with worry about their own mortality (Cicirelli, 1980; Troll, 1986).

On a more practical level, there is the burden of time, money, and energy that this "generation in the middle"—torn between filial obligations and the need to help launch fledgling children—must spend on aging parents. If they have full-time jobs, they may devote a large portion of their nonworking hours to caring for parents, sometimes for years on end.

The needs of aging parents seem to fall into the category of nonnormative, unanticipated demands. New parents expect, for example, to assume the full physical, financial, and emotional care of their babies, with the assumption that such care will gradually diminish as children grow up. Somehow most people do not expect to have to care for their parents; they ignore the possibility of parents' infirmity and rarely plan ahead for it; and when it cannot be denied, they perceive it as interfering with other responsibilities and plans. Now that the fastest-growing group in our population is the frail elderly, aged 85 and over, many people in their fifties and sixties are finding themselves in a position that was quite rare in earlier generations.

Timing also enters in. Parents who are looking forward to or just experiencing the end of responsibility for their own children—and who now sense keenly that their own time on earth is limited—may feel that the need to care for their parents will deprive them of the chance to fulfill their own dreams. The sense of being "tied down," of not being able to take a vacation or make other plans, is, for some adult children, the hardest thing about caring for their elderly parents (B. Robinson & Thurnher, 1981).

Still, children do care for their parents; they do not abandon them (Troll, 1986). Parents and children alike feel better when the care comes from feelings of attachment and not duty (M.H. Cantor, 1983; B. Robinson & Thurnher, 1981). Therefore, one psychologist who has studied these intergenerational ties emphasizes that it is less effective to appeal to children's sense of obligation and more fruitful to encourage such attachment behaviors as visiting and telephoning (Cicirelli, 1980). When children are in touch with their parents, they can tell when their help is needed and they usually respond by giving it.

Elder Abuse In shocking contrast to the usually close ties between adults and aging parents is the phenomenon of *elder abuse*—neglect or physical or psychological abuse of dependent older persons, often by the children "taking care" of them. Just as child abuse emerged as a major social problem in the 1960s and violence between spouses in the 1970s, the mistreatment of growing numbers of frail elderly people has been a pressing social concern of the 1980s.

Abuse of the elderly can take the form of neglect, as in the withholding of food, shelter, clothing, medical care, money, or other assets. It can involve psychological torment in the form of tongue-lashings or threats of violence or abandonment. It can also appear as actual violence—in the beating, punching, or burning of old people who cannot protect themselves.

Because of problems in defining such abuse, as well as in reporting it, estimates of the number of cases of abuse of the elderly vary widely, from 600,000 to 1 million, involving about 4 percent of the older population (Eastman, 1984). It is probably as underreported as child abuse and violence between spouses.

The person most typically abused is a very old, infirm woman; the abuser is likely to be a middle-aged son or daughter who sees the mother as the source of overwhelming stress. There is some evidence that people who are now abusing their dependent parents are those who were abused themselves as children (Eastman, 1984; Pedrick-Cornell & Gelles, 1982).

Just as with child abuse and violence between spouses, the problem has to be approached by treating both victim and attacker (Hooyman, Rathbone-McCuan, & Klingbeil, 1982). Procedures have to be developed to identify and report abuse and to protect the victims. Prevention and treatment programs for abusers can reduce their stress and help them to be caregivers instead of pain givers. Some of these services offer education, emotional support, counseling, financial assistance, and substitute care to give them respite for a day, a weekend, or a week.

Reducing the Strain of Caregiving Of course, most people who have elderly parents do not abuse them. But even the most loving daughter or son may become frustrated, anxious, or resentful under the constant strain of having to meet an older person's seemingly endless needs—especially if there is no one else to turn to.

The pressure of financial support for elderly parents has been lessened considerably by such programs as social security, Supplemental Security Income, Medicare, and Medicaid. Other forms of societal support could be instituted and expanded, such as free or low-cost day care programs where older people can go from morning till dinnertime, transportation and escort services, such in-home services as meals and housekeeping, and respite care so that people who have elderly parents requiring their daily attention can get away for a few days. Flexible work schedules would benefit people with elderly dependents.

Counseling and self-help groups can offer much-needed emotional support, pass on information about community resources, and help sons and daughters develop skills for dealing with their aging parents (M.H. Cantor, 1983; Cicirelli, 1980; B. Robinson & Thurnher, 1981). One such program, which helped daughters realize the limits of their ability to meet their mothers' needs and the value of encouraging their mothers' own self-reliance, not only lifted the daughters' burdens somewhat but actually improved their relationships with their mothers, so that the mothers became less lonely (Scharlach, 1987).

As we'll see in Chapters 16 and 17, the needs of older adults in American society are assuming more and more importance as this segment of the population grows to unprecedented numbers.

SUMMARY

Normative-Crisis Theory and Research

■ Some personality traits remain stable in adulthood, but growth and change do occur. Middle-aged people tend to become more introspective, and both sexes tend to take on characteristics that are typically associated with the other sex.

■ Erikson's seventh psychosocial crisis, occurring during middle age, is generativity versus stagnation. The generative person is concerned with establishing and guiding the next generation. One who fails to develop a sense of generativity suffers from stagnation, self-indulgence, and perhaps physical and psychological invalidism.

■ Expanding on Erikson's concepts, Peck specified four psychological developments critical to successful adjustment during middle age: valuing wisdom versus valuing physical powers, socializing versus sexualizing, emotional flexibility versus emotional impoverishment, and mental flexibility versus mental rigidity.

■ The Grant Study of Harvard men (reported by Vaillant) and Levinson's study of 40 male biologists, novelists, business executives, and factory workers suggest that the early forties are a potentially stressful time of transition. Some people experience "crisis," although midlife does not necessarily signal a crisis.

■ Levinson's periods of middle adulthood include the midlife transition (age 40 to age 45), the entry life structure for middle adulthood (age 45 to age 50), the age-50 transition (age 50 to age 55), the culminating life structure for middle adulthood (age 55 to age 60), and the late adult transition (age 60 to age 65).

■ Because the Grant Study and Levinson's research focused mainly on privileged white men born in the 1920s or 1930s, their results may not be applicable to women, nonwhite people, and members of other cohorts and other cultures. The universality of age-linked phases of development in general, and of the midlife crisis in particular, is questionable.

■ Normative-crisis research on middle-aged women suggests that women, too, go through midlife changes but their subsequent lives are less settled than those of men.

■ Mastery and pleasure are important elements of well-being for middle-aged women. Both challenging, well-paid work and family commitments contribute to women's psychological health.

Personal Relationships and Timing of Events

■ The timing-of-events model suggests that development depends on the occurrence and timing of important events, which are often changes that take place in relationships.

■ Research on the quality of marriage in middle

- age is inconclusive. The most prevalent pattern appears to be a dip in marital satisfaction during the years of child rearing followed by an improved relationship after the children leave home.

- The most important factors in marital longevity seem to be positive feelings about the spouse, a commitment to long-term marriage, and shared aims and goals.

- Middle-aged couples today are engaging in sexual relations more often and in more varied ways than their counterparts in the past. Sexual compatibility is not the most important factor in a happy marriage, but sexual activity and sexual satisfaction can and often do continue throughout middle age and the older adult years.

- Bonds with siblings often become closer during middle age.

- Middle-aged people tend to invest less time and energy in developing friendships than younger adults do, since their energies are devoted to family, work, and building up security for retirement.

- Parents of adolescents need to come to terms with a loss of control over their children's lives.

- The postparental years—when children have left—are often among the happiest. The "emptying of the nest" may be stressful, however, for fathers who have not been involved with child rearing, parents whose children have not become independent when expected, and mothers who have failed to prepare for the event.

- Today more young adults are living with their parents, often for economic reasons. Conflict between the two generations can put strains on the parents' marriage.

- Middle-aged parents tend to remain involved with their young adult children and to continue giving them more than they get from them.

- Relationships between middle-aged adults and their parents are usually characterized by a strong bond of affection. Although older parents typically do not live with their adult children, they generally maintain frequent contact and offer and receive assistance.

- Middle-aged people, especially daughters, may have to become caregivers to ailing, aging parents. This can be a source of considerable stress and may even lead to elder abuse, a growing concern. Various support programs can help relieve the strain of caregiving.

KEY TERMS

companionate love (page 517)
elder abuse (525)
emotional flexibility versus emotional impoverishment (508)
empty nest (517, 520)

generativity versus stagnation (506)
interiority (510)
mental flexibility versus mental rigidity (508)
midlife crisis (504)

passionate love (517)
socializing versus sexualizing (508)
valuing wisdom versus valuing physical powers (508)

SUGGESTED READINGS

Baruch, G., Barnett, R., & Rivers, C. (1983). *Lifeprints.* New York: McGraw-Hill. A book based on research with 35- to 55-year-old women that explores women's happiness and self-esteem, emphasizing the dual elements of work and family. The authors stress the value of paid employment in helping a woman feel in control of her life and of multiple roles (work, marriage, motherhood) in achieving overall well-being.

Edinberg, M.A. (1987). *Talking with your aging parents.* Boston: Shambhala. The author, a clinical psychologist and director of the Center for the Study of Aging at the University of Bridgeport in Connecticut, suggests strategies for communicating with elderly parents about their special needs (for institutional care, extra help, and so on). The author also discusses how middle-aged children can cope with their own feelings of guilt regarding the burdens of family obligations.

Farrell, M.P., & Rosenberg, S.D. (1981). *Men at midlife.* Boston: Auburn. A research report about male development in middle age that describes four ways of experiencing middle age and concludes that not all men have a midlife crisis.

Halpern, J. (1987). *Helping your aging parents: A practical guide for adult children*. New York: McGraw-Hill. A well-written guidebook for the "sandwich generation" that includes a wealth of practical information and constructive advice, as well as psychological guidance, on the physiological changes of aging, the stress of caregiving, what to do when a parent moves in, deciding on a nursing home, dealing with death and dying, and more. It includes specific information on community resources and services.

Klagsbrun, F. (1985). *Married people: Staying together in the age of divorce*. New York: Bantam. A well-researched and sensitively written book that draws upon published research, interviews with happily married couples, and the author's exploration of her own long-term marriage to examine such topics as the transition from passionate to companionate love, competition between spouses, the influence of family (including children) and friends on a couple's relationship, and sexuality.

Porcino, J. (1983). *Growing older, getting better: A handbook for women in the second half of life*. Reading, MA: Addison-Wesley. A reassuring, straightforward guide that draws on research findings to provide information on such issues as family transitions (widowhood, the empty nest, grandmotherhood), new forms of living arrangements, physical and mental health, and career and financial issues.

Rubin, L.B. (1979). *Women of a certain age: The midlife search for self*. New York: Harper & Row. A report of in-depth interviews with 160 women covering such topics as the empty nest syndrome, menopause, depression, and sexuality. The many quotes from the interviewees make the book lively and give it a personalized flavor.

Smelser, N.J., & Erikson, E.H. (1980). *Themes of work and love in adulthood*. Cambridge, MA: Harvard University Press. A collection of articles by nine experts in adult development that consider the issues adults confront in attempting to create a meaningful life.

TABLE 16·1 LIFE EXPECTANCY BY SEX AND RACE

	WHITE PEOPLE	BLACK PEOPLE	ALL RACES
Males	71.8	65.3	71.2
Females	78.7	73.7	78.2
Both sexes			74.7

Note: In years, for a baby born in 1985.
Source: U.S. Department of Health and Human Services, USDHHS, 1986.

the average life span would be increased by only 2 or 3 years, but if we could eliminate heart and kidney ailments, the increase would be more than 11 years (Fries & Crapo, 1981).

Gender and Racial Differences in Life Expectancy

On the average, white Americans live longer than black Americans, and women live longer than men (see Table 16-1 and Figure 16-2).

The vulnerability of males observable in gestation continues throughout life and has important implications for the older segment of the population. In 1900, there was only a 2-year difference in life expectancy between the sexes, but because the decline in death rates has been twice as great for females as for males, the spread was 7 years for babies born in 1985 (U.S. Bureau of the Census, 1983; USDHHS, 1986). Among 65- to 69-year-olds, there are only 80 men to every 100 women, and among people over 85, the difference is even more dramatic: only 42 men to every 100 women. Thus the problems of aging are largely the problems of women; they tend to live longer than men, to be widowed, to remain unmarried, and to have more years of poor health (U.S. Bureau of the Census, 1983; Katz, Branch, Branson, Papsidero, Beck, & Greer, 1983).

Thus, far from being a bonus for women, their extra years may well be characterized by illness, poverty, dependency, loneliness, and institutionalization. When we talk about the *quality* of life rather than its *quantity*, men have the advantage. They keep their health longer, and so their years of *active* life expectancy and independence are greater (Katz et al., 1983). This male-dominated society might handle the problems of aging differently if the people facing these problems late in life were more likely to be men.

Why People Age: Two Theories

There are many theories of aging, but none has been universally accepted. We do not know exactly why, with advancing age, people's bodies function less efficiently. We do know that aging

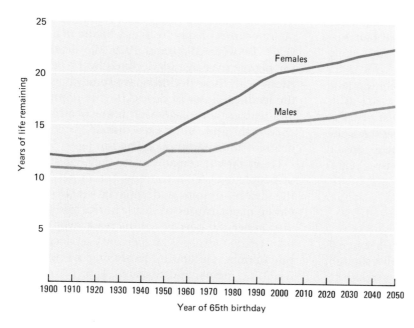

Figure 16-2 Life expectancy at age 65, 1900–2050 (projected). Because of medical advances, the number of additional years that people who reach the age of 65 can expect to live has been increasing throughout this century. The increase is greater for women, whose life expectancy is already longer than men's, and this gap is predicted to continue widening during the first half of the twenty-first century. Most gerontologists, however, believe that there is an upper limit to human life expectancy and that it will not continue to increase indefinitely. (*Source:* U.S. Bureau of the Census, 1983.)

The onset of *senescence*—the period of the life span marked by the declines in body functioning associated with aging—varies greatly. One 80-year-old man can hear every word of a whispered conversation, while another has trouble hearing words that are shouted at him. One woman in her seventies regularly runs 5-mile races, while another cannot walk around the block.

The lengthening of life in modern times has swelled the population of the aging and has focused attention on such questions as why senescence comes earlier for some people than for others. After discussing historical changes in life expectancy, we'll consider two theories of why aging occurs. After that, we'll examine some physical changes often associated with aging and some things that people can do to stay healthy and to minimize physical losses.

LONGEVITY AND THE AGING PROCESS

Eos, a mythological goddess, asked Zeus to allow Tithonus, the mortal she loved, to live forever. Zeus granted Tithonus immortality, and the lovers lived happily—but not forever. Tithonus began to grow old until he became so infirm that he could not move. Yet he was denied the gift of death. To this day he lives on, where Eos finally put him away, a helpless, driveling vegetable. Eos had made a grievous error—she had forgotten to ask Zeus to grant eternal youth along with eternal life.

In recognition of the tragedy of life too long extended, the Gerontological Society has as its motto: "To add life to years, not just years to life." The goal of research on the aging is not "extension of longevity per se, but the extension of our most vigorous and productive years" (Hayflick, 1974, p. 40).

Life Expectancy

Trends in Life Expectancy Today, most people can expect to grow old. Historically, though, a large population of the elderly is a relatively recent phenomenon.

The average child born in ancient Rome could expect to live no more than 20 to 30 years. By the turn of the twentieth century, babies born in the United States had an average life expectancy of about 47 years—so low, in part, because many died in infancy. By 1985, average life expectancy had risen to almost 75 years— about 3 times the life span of the ancient Roman (AARP, 1986; U.S. Department of Health and Human Services, USDHHS, 1986; Zopf, 1986). The 1980 census counted some 32,000 people over the age of 100 (U.S. Bureau of the Census, 1983), and this number is growing rapidly.

These gains in life expectancy result from two major avenues of medical progress. One is the dramatic decline in infant and child mortality rates that took place during the first half of the twentieth century. The other is the development of new drugs and medical procedures to treat many illnesses that used to be fatal. But this trend may be ending: Many gerontologists maintain that 110 years is about the upper limit of human longevity (despite some extravagant claims of people in certain societies that they are 140 or more), and that the average 80-year-old of today can expect to live only a little longer than 80-year-olds of previous centuries.

Death Rates and Causes of Death The dramatic increase in average longevity since the turn of the century reflects a sharp decline in death rates in the United States (the proportions of Americans of specific ages who die in a given year). Between 1950 and 1979, the death rate for people over age 65 declined by 17 percent. Along with these declines have come changes in the leading causes of death: for the population as a whole, there have been fewer deaths from childbirth and infectious disease and more deaths from conditions related to age.

Heart disease remains by far the biggest killer of people over 65, accounting for 45 percent of the deaths despite a decline in recent years. Other major causes of death in this age group are cancer (20 percent, an increase over previous years), stroke (11 percent, a decrease), pneumonia, influenza, hardening of the arteries, accidents, and diabetes (U.S. Bureau of the Census, 1983).

If cancer were eliminated as a cause of death,

BOX 16-3 **PRACTICALLY SPEAKING**

YOU AND THE OLDER PEOPLE IN YOUR LIFE

Many of the findings from the wealth of recent research on late adulthood can be applied to daily life. The following suggestions might make the lives of your parents, your grandparents, or other older people you care about happier and more comfortable.

■ *For persons with hearing problems:* Speak slightly louder than normally, but don't shout. Don't speak too fast. Speak at a distance of 3 to 6 feet, in good light, so that your lip movements and gestures can be used as clues to your words. Don't chew, eat, or cover your mouth while you're speaking. Turn off the radio and the television while you're talking. If the listener doesn't understand what you have said, rephrase your idea in short, simple sentences.

■ *For persons with vision problems:* Install bright lighting at the top of staircases (most falls occur on the step at the top of the landing). Help to analyze lighting in work and reading areas to see that it is directed for greatest efficiency. Keep floor areas clutter-free and don't rearrange furniture. Help to get rid of unnecessary items in cupboards and bookshelves and highlight often-used items with bright-colored markers. Good gifts include sunglasses (to wear outside, so that less of an adjustment needs to be made upon coming in from outdoors), a pocket or purse flashlight (to help read menus or theater programs), a magnifying glass to put in a pocket or hang on a chain, large-type reading matter, and a tape recorder and cassettes.

■ *Encourage physical activity:* Take part in shared activities that you both enjoy, like walking, bicycling, dancing, or skating. Make such activities a regular weekly event. Help by finding out what resources there are in the community—for example, at the local Y. Good gifts are pool and Y memberships and exercise accessories.

■ *Help with memory:* When giving information, try to present it in more than one way (write it down and give it orally, too). Be patient and reassuring about memory lapses, remembering that younger people forget things, too.

Learn and teach some memory tricks. Good gifts are a pocket notebook and pen (for immediately jotting down thoughts and things to do), a calendar (for writing down appointments), and a note pad to keep by the phone or in the kitchen (or both).

■ *Encourage mental alertness:* Play games that require thought, such as word games, "twenty questions," and card games. Go to movies and plays together. Read a book together and discuss it. Find out what adult education courses are offered locally. Ask questions about subjects the older person knows about. Good gifts are games, books, and tickets.

■ *Enrich yourself through the older person's experience:* Tape-record interviews with the older person in which you ask about childhood memories, descriptions of family members, experiences, subjects about which the person is knowledgeable, and opinions about life. You will enrich your own knowledge and awareness, and the older person will realize the value of his or her wisdom and memories.

THE OLDEST OLD

Since the number of healthy, vigorous people above the age of 65 is rapidly growing, we may soon begin to talk of old age as starting at 85. Although the age group over 85, which has been called the *oldest old*, is the fastest-growing segment of the population of the United States (increasing by 165 percent in 22 years), it has had little research attention. Now Charles Longino (1987), a gerontologist at the University of Miami, using 1980 census data, has drawn a portrait of these "remarkably diverse" people. In addition, we can learn about the lives of some people in this age bracket from a 1986 report by the National Institute on Aging (NIA; cited in Meer, 1987).

Who are the oldest old? Where and how do they live? How is their health? What do they like to do? The answers are predictable in some cases but unexpected in others.

Because of men's lower life expectancy, almost 70 percent of the oldest old are women, and 82 percent of the women are widowed (compared with only 44 percent of the men). Since high schools were a new phenomenon when these people were young, it is not surprising that most of them never went beyond eighth grade.

The states with the largest proportion of people over 85 are North Dakota, South Dakota, Nebraska, Kansas, Missouri, Iowa, Minnesota, Maine, Massachusetts, and Rhode Island. Far from being dependent on others, most of these people live in their own homes, and 30 percent live alone. One-fourth are in nursing homes, hospitals, or other institutions. Their average household income topped $20,000 in 1985. One out of six are poor.

Most of the people in the NIA studies spend considerable time with other people. More than half of a sample in Iowa belong to professional, social, recreational, or religious groups and go to services at least once a week. More than 3 out of 4 see their children or other close relatives once a month.

Many of these eldest citizens have health problems. Many have been seriously hurt in falls, and at least one-fourth in the NIA studies were hospitalized in the year preceding. Nationally, almost 10 percent are disabled and isolated—unable even to use public transportation (Longino, 1987). But a surprisingly large number need little medical care.

Thus, even at the latest stage of life, it is misleading to generalize about "the elderly." What emerges is a picture of individual human beings— some needy and frail, but most of them relatively independent, healthy, and involved.

an elderly client. Attitudes like these affect the way older people live and the way they feel about themselves. Many older people are among the most ardent believers in the myths of aging.

Nor are the positive stereotypes much more helpful—the picture of old age as a time of tranquillity, a "golden age" of peace and relaxation when people can harvest the fruits of their lifelong labors; or as a carefree second childhood, in which people idle away their hours playing golf or gin rummy.

The fact is that older people are an extremely diverse lot, with individual strengths and weaknesses. Late adulthood is a normal period of the life span, with its own special characteristics and its own developmental tasks. In this chapter we look at physical and intellectual changes at this time of life, and at some of the implications these changes hold for social and emotional well-being, discussed in detail in Chapter 17.

Learning about late adulthood can prepare you for what to expect when *you* get there and can suggest to you what you can do *now* to make your stay there as pleasant as possible. Knowing what the aging process is like can also help you get along with, and enrich the lives of, the older people in your life (see Box 16-3, page 538).

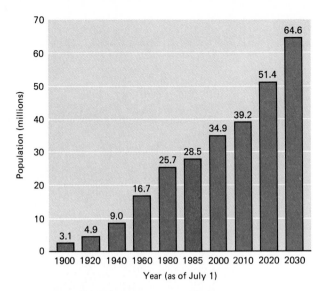

Figure 16-1 Population of the United States aged 65 and over, 1900–2030 (projected). Since the beginning of this century, the number of people aged 65 and over has continued to increase, both in absolute terms (as shown) and relative to the rest of the population. This trend is expected to continue through the aging of the "baby boom" generation. *Note:* Increments in years on horizontal scale are uneven. (*Source:* AARP, 1986.)

ple become eligible for full social security retirement benefits. But these days many people are already retired by the age of 55 (some of them starting on *new* careers), while some continue to work far into their 70s or even longer.

Not only are the older generation getting "younger"; they are also becoming more numerous. Between 1980 and 1985, the number of Americans over 65 years old grew almost 3 times as fast as the rest of the population. By 1985, there were 28.5 million people in this age bracket, 1 in every 8. It is projected that by the year 2030, more than 1 out of every 5 Americans will be over age 65 (see Figure 16-1). The fastest-growing age group are people 85 years old and older, who now number more than 1 percent of the population (AARP, 1986; U.S. Bureau of the Census, 1983; see Box 16-2).

The graying of the population has two basic causes. First, comparatively high birth rates in the late nineteenth century and the early to mid-twentieth century, combined with high immigration rates in this century, swelled the numbers of people now in the over-65 bracket. As the "baby boom" generation (born in the late 1940s and the 1950s) ages, the proportion of older Americans will peak, about a third of the way through the twenty-first century, after which it will drop again. Second, medical advances have lengthened the average life expectancy. Fewer people now die in childhood and early adulthood, and new medicines and procedures are keeping many people alive who once would have succumbed to a variety of illnesses.

As older people become more of a presence in our society, the need to help them make the most of their lives becomes more urgent, inspiring research in gerontology and *geriatrics,* the branch of medicine concerned with the aged and with aging. There is an increasing need for support services for the frail elderly, many of whom have outlived their savings and cannot pay for their own care. As the over-65 population becomes more influential at the polls and in the marketplace, we are likely to see changes in governmental programs, as well as in television programming, in new products, and in residential patterns.

High on the agenda of advocates for the elderly is the need to combat persistent misconceptions about aging. The list of inaccurate negative stereotypes is long: that old people are poorly coordinated, feel tired most of the time, and easily fall prey to infections; that they have many accidents in the home and spend most of their time in bed; that they tend to live in hospitals, nursing homes, or other institutions suitable for people whose health and abilities are steadily declining; that they are not so smart any more and are unable to remember the simplest things or to learn new facts and skills; that they have no interest in or desire for sexual relationships; that they become isolated from family and friends and sit around watching television or listening to the radio; that they do not spend their time productively; and that they have become grouchy, self-pitying, touchy, and cranky.

How do such ageist beliefs hurt older people? A physician who assumes that a 75-year-old heart patient is no longer interested in sex and who does not bring up the subject may be denying the patient a source of fulfillment. An adult child who is patronizing and overprotective encourages an aging parent to become infantile. A social worker who accepts depression as an expected part of growing old in effect abandons

BOX 16-1 WINDOW ON THE WORLD

AGING IN OTHER CULTURES

Every day an aged farmer in the Soviet Union climbs up and down steep hills to reach the fields to put in half a day's hard work. A wizened old Ecuadoran woman busily gathers strands of sheep wool and spins it into cloth. A Kashmiri of advanced age dances vigorously at a wedding. These three people are typical of the aged populations in three widely separated locations: Abkhazia, in the southern Soviet Union; Vilcabamba, an Andean village in Ecuador; and the principality of Hunza in Pakistani Kashmir (Leaf, 1973).

Initial reports that people in these societies routinely reached ages well over 100 and sometimes beyond 150 turned out, upon investigation, to be unsubstantiated; none of these people can be proved to be over 110 (about the upper limit in the United States), and there is no indication that there are any more people over 90 than in the United States (Fries & Crapo, 1981; Palmore, 1984). Still, we can learn important lessons from these three societies, in which older people are generally long-lived, vigorous, healthy, and respected and youth is thought to extend to the age of 80.

First, the social status of older people is high. They live with members of their families, who revere them and appreciate the useful contributions they make to the

family and the community. In Hunza, a council of wise elders meets every day to resolve disputes.

Second, there is no forced retirement. People work as long as they are able. On a regular, daily basis, very old people pick tea, feed poultry, weed, do laundry, clean house, tend animals, and care for small children.

A major physical difference between people in these societies and those in our society is their diet: they eat fewer than 2000 calories a day (only 1200 in Vilcabamba), and their diets are low in animal fat. Obesity is virtually nonexistent. Eating less meat and dairy products seems to delay development of atherosclerosis (clogging of the arteries leading to the heart), a frequent ailment among older people in the United States. Experts agree that people need fewer calories as they age, so long as their diets are nutritionally sound.

Another important factor contributing to health is a high level of physical activity. In all three cultures, such normal everyday activities as hiking over mountains, farming, sheepherding, and hunting promote good muscle tone and cardiovascular fitness.

Genetic factors may also be involved. Very old people in our country, as well as in these three cultures, are often the children of parents who have lived to advanced ages.

This elderly woman, who lives in the mountain village of Vilcabamba in Ecuador, crosses the Chamba River on her donkey every day on her way to work in the fields. We can learn important lessons from societies such as this one, in which old people are generally vigorous, healthy, and respected.

They may be lacking genes that carry predispositions to fatal or disabling diseases. Heredity becomes particularly important in small, isolated communities like Vilcabamba and Hunza, where there is a great deal of intermarriage.

The most important lesson we can learn from communities where very old people are so healthy is not how to reach a very old age but how to make old age a good age. At a time when more and more people are adding pages to their books of life, we need to look for ways to make their endings happier.

Old age is rather like another country. You will enjoy it more if you have prepared yourself before you go.

B. F. Skinner and M. E. Vaughan,
Enjoy Old Age, 1983

ASK YOURSELF

■ When does late adulthood begin, and what physical changes does this period bring?

■ What causes aging?

■ What influences the health of older people?

■ What are some reversible and irreversible mental and behavioral disorders?

■ What factors affect intellectual functioning in late adulthood, and how can intellectual performance be improved?

■ What can people do to make the most of retirement?

In Japan, where the average person lives longer than anywhere else in the world, a contest was held recently to come up with a new word to refer to old age—a term that would be descriptive of the active lives most older Japanese live today. The winner coined the word *jit-sunen,* meaning "age of fruition" (*Ageing International,* cited in American Association of Retired Persons, AARP, 1987a). Here in the United States, people advanced in years are called *senior citizens, golden-agers, elderly persons, persons in the harvest years* or *twilight years, older Americans,* or simply *elders.*

Why do people need euphemisms to discuss old age? One reason may be wishful thinking: everybody wants to live long, but nobody wants to grow old. Mostly, though, the sensitivity to terminology comes from concern about **ageism:** prejudice or discrimination based on age, most commonly against older persons. Too often, the image the word *old* brings to mind is that of a feeble person hobbling on a cane or dozing in a rocking chair.

If that stereotype ever was realistic, it is not anymore—not in the United States and not in Japan—and in many other societies it was cer-

tainly never true (see Box 16-1). **Gerontologists,** who study the aged and the process of aging, observe that many of today's 70-year-olds act and think as 50-year-olds did 10 or 20 years ago (Herz, cited in J.C. Horn & Meer, 1987). Many of the supposed negative characteristics of old age are actually due to improper eating habits, lack of exercise, or certain neurological diseases that may or may not accompany aging. A new category, the *young-old,* takes in the majority of older persons, those who—regardless of chronological age—are vital, vigorous, and active; while *old-old* refers to the frail, infirm minority (Neugarten & Neugarten, 1987).

Even more than between earlier phases of life, it is becoming harder to draw the line between the end of middle adulthood and the beginning of late adulthood. If, as the saying goes, "you're as young as you feel," how should we classify the 84-year-old man who talks about putting aside money for his "twilight years"?

Retirement—the traditional marker of old age—is no longer a reliable guide. Age 65, which we are considering in this book to be the beginning of late adulthood, has long been the customary retirement age, and that is when peo-

16

CHAPTER

PHYSICAL AND INTELLECTUAL DEVELOPMENT IN LATE ADULTHOOD

8

PART

LATE ADULTHOOD

Development continues during the years after 65, as adults in the last phase of life face challenges, both old and new, in highly individual ways.

■ In **Chapter 16,** we look at myths about aging and theories to explain the aging process. Most older people are in fairly good physical health, despite the changes that take place with age, and most are mentally sound as well. Some older persons do, of course, suffer physical or mental problems (or both), and these problems are

described, along with ways of preventing and treating them. We explore the controversy over intellectual functioning in late life and conclude that although some abilities may diminish with age, there is a great deal of evidence that older people who remain intellectually active retain their abilities and even increase their mental capacities in some ways.

■ In **Chapter 17,** we look at different patterns of successful aging, and we examine the important relationships in late

adulthood—with spouses, children, grandchildren, and siblings. We look at the ways people adjust to the loss of a spouse and at the role of sexuality in late life. We examine the ways older people live, either in the community or, for a small minority, in nursing homes. It becomes clearer than ever that—although there are certain common patterns in the human experience—each person is an individual, and that one's individuality becomes more pronounced in the later years of life.

8

PART

is a complex process influenced by heredity, nutrition, health, and various environmental factors.

Most theories of biological aging take one of two basic approaches. The **programmed-aging theory** maintains that bodies age in accordance with a normal developmental pattern built into every organism; this program, preset for each species, is subject to only minor modifications. The **wear-and-tear theory of aging,** on the other hand, holds that bodies age because of continuous use—that aging is the result of accumulated "insults" to the body.

Proponents of the programmed-aging theory reason that since each species has its own pattern of aging and its own life expectancy, this pattern must be predetermined and inborn. Leonard Hayflick (1974), who studied the cells of many different animals, found that there is a limit on the number of times normal cells will divide—about 50 times for human cells. He maintains that this limit controls the life span, which for humans seems to be about 110 years. People may be born with genes that become harmful later in life, causing deterioration. One area of deterioration may be the body's immune system, which seems to become "confused" in old age, so that it will attack the body itself.

Adherents of the wear-and-tear theory compare the human body to a machine, whose parts eventually wear out from long use. We know, for example, that the cells of the heart and brain can never replace themselves, even early in life. When they are damaged, they die. The same thing seems to happen to other cells later in life: as they grow older, they are less able to repair or replace damaged components. According to this theory, internal and external stresses (which include the accumulation of harmful materials, such as chemical by-products of metabolism) aggravate the wearing-down process.

The difference between these two approaches is not just theoretical. If people are programmed to age in a certain way, they can do little to retard the process; but if they age because of the stresses their bodies are subject to, they may be able to extend their lives by eliminating some of these stresses. The truth very likely lies in a combination of these two approaches: genetic programming may determine an outside limit for the length of human life, but wear and tear may influence how close a person gets to that limit.

Along the same lines, some gerontologists distinguish between **primary aging,** a gradual process of bodily deterioration that begins early in life and continues inexorably through the years; and **secondary aging,** "the results not of age but of disease, abuse and disuse—factors often under our own control" (Busse, 1987; J.C. Horn & Meer, 1987, p. 81). People may not be able to stop their reflexes from slowing down or their hearing from becoming less acute; but by eating properly and keeping active and physically fit, many older people can and do stave off the secondary effects of aging.

PHYSICAL CHANGES

Sensory and Psychomotor Functioning

Sensory and psychomotor abilities decline with age, but there is, of course, a great degree of individual variation.

Vision The farsightedness that affects most people in middle age stabilizes at about age 60. With the help of either glasses or contact lenses, most older people can see fairly well. Many people over 65, however, do have serious visual problems that affect their daily lives. Many have 20/70 vision or worse, have trouble perceiving depth or color and adapting to abrupt changes in lighting, are sensitive to glare, and cannot see well in the dark. They often develop cataracts, cloudy or opaque areas in the lens of the eye that prevent light from passing through and thus cause blurred vision. These problems are responsible for accidents in and out of the home, and they may keep older persons from driving—especially at night—and from enjoying activities like reading and hobbies that require close work.

When vision problems are not too severe, they can often be helped by corrective lenses, medical or surgical treatment, or changes in the environment (see Box 16-3). New surgical techniques allow removal of cataracts; patients may use special glasses or contact lenses following cataract surgery, or they may have plastic lenses implanted during the operation.

The hearing aid in this man's ear makes it easier for him to understand his young granddaughter's high-pitched speech, but it may also magnify distracting background noise. More than 10 million older Americans have some degree of hearing loss, but only about 1 in 20 wears a hearing aid. Medical treatment, surgery, or special training can also help people with hearing problems.

At worst, visual disorders and diseases can result in blindness. Half of the legally blind people in the United States are over 65, and retinal disorders are the leading cause of blindness among the elderly (National Institute on Aging, NIA, undated a; White House Conference on Aging, 1971).

Glaucoma, another frequent cause of blindness, occurs when fluid pressure builds up, damaging the eye internally. If this disease (which seldom has early symptoms) is detected through routine vision checkups, it may be treated and controlled with eye drops, medicine, laser treatments, or surgery.

Hearing Hearing loss is very common in late adulthood; about 3 out of 10 people between the ages of 65 and 74 and about half of those between the ages of 75 and 79 experience it to some degree. More than 10 million older people in the United States are hearing-impaired (NIA, undated b).

Because older people tend to have trouble hearing high-frequency sounds, they often cannot hear what other people are saying, especially when there is competing noise from radio or television, or the buzz of several people talking at once. To demonstrate how people with hearing losses may react in such situations, college students were hypnotically induced into a state of partial temporary deafness. The students began to feel as if other people were talking about them or were deliberately excluding them from conversations (Zimbardo, Andersen, & Kabat, 1981). It is easy to see, then, how people whose hearing is impaired may feel lonely and isolated and may develop personality quirks that make them hard to get along with, thus increasing their loneliness. We see once again how physical experience can affect emotional development.

Hearing aids can compensate for hearing loss to some degree, but only 5 percent of older people wear them (National Council on Aging, 1978). Hearing aids may be hard to adjust to, especially since they magnify background noises as well as the sounds the wearer wants to hear. Furthermore, many people feel that wearing a hearing aid is like wearing a sign saying "I'm getting old."

Medical treatment, special training, and surgery are other ways to help the hearing-impaired. People should have their hearing checked if they find it difficult to understand words; complain that other people are mumbling; cannot hear a dripping faucet or the high notes of a violin; hear continual hissing or ringing noises; or do not enjoy parties, television, or concerts because they miss much of what goes on (NIA, undated b).

Other Senses When older people complain that their food does not taste good anymore, this may be because they have fewer taste buds

Older people can do most of the things younger people can do, from reeling in a fish to reshingling a house. But older people take longer to do things because their reflex responses and information processing are slowed.

in the tongue—but also because the olfactory bulb (the organ in the brain that is responsible for the sense of smell) has withered. Taste is very often based on what people can smell. A recent study of almost 2000 people aged 5 to 99 found that the sense of smell is keenest between ages 30 and 60; it declines slightly from age 60 through age 80, and then there is a sharp drop. More than 4 out of 5 persons over 80 years old have major impairments in smell, and more than half have virtually no sense of smell at all (Doty, 1984). Because food loses its flavor, older people eat less and and are often undernourished.

The bodies of older people adjust less quickly to cold and become chilled more easily than those of younger people. Exposure to cold and to poor living conditions may cause abnormally low body temperature, a serious risk for the aged. Older people cannot cope as well with heat, either, and they cannot work as effectively in moderately high temperatures as younger people can.

Strength, Coordination, and Reaction Time
Older people do not have the strength they once had, and they are severely limited in activities requiring endurance or the ability to carry heavy loads. Otherwise, they can do most of the same things that younger people can, but they do them more slowly (Birren et al., 1980; Salthouse, 1985).

The general slowing down—which affects the quality of responses as well as the time taken for them—may result from environmental deprivation and depression, as well as from neurological changes (Butler & Lewis, 1982). Because older people's reflex responses are slowed, incontinence—loss of bladder or bowel control—sometimes occurs.

A major factor in older people's tendency to suffer falls and other accidents is the slowness with which they process information (Birren, 1974). It takes longer for them to assess their environment, take in all the appropriate factors, and make decisions. Slowness in information processing shows up in all aspects of older people's lives. As we'll see, it makes them do more poorly on intelligence tests, especially timed ones. It interferes with their ability to learn new information and to retrieve information from memory (Birren et al., 1980; Salthouse, 1985). It causes them to ask people to repeat information that has been presented too quickly or not clearly enough.

Combined with their slower reaction time, older people's decreased efficiency in sensorimotor coordination increases the risk of driving. People over age 65 have a disproportionate share of traffic accidents; evidently this is usually because of improper turning, failure to yield right-of-way, and sign violations (Sterns, Barrett, & Alexander, 1985), rather than speeding. Yet the ability to drive can make the difference between active participation in society and enforced isolation.

For their own protection and that of others, older drivers' vision, coordination, and reaction time should be retested regularly. Older workers who are capable of continuing to drive can compensate for any loss of ability by driving more slowly and for shorter distances, and by choosing the easiest routes (Sterns et al., 1985).

Most older people recognize the slowdown in their functioning and take special pains to exercise caution in their everyday activities. Society, too, needs to recognize this slowdown and the sensory changes that come with age and to redesign environments to help older adults manage their lives more safely and comfortably.

Other Physical Changes

Many of the physical changes that are often associated with aging are readily apparent to even the most casual observer. The skin becomes paler and more splotchy, taking on a parchment-like texture and losing some elasticity. Since some subcutaneous fat and muscle disappear, the inelastic skin tends to hang in folds and wrinkles. Varicose veins are more common. The hair becomes thinner in both men and women, and what is left turns gray or white.

Older people may shrink in size because the disks between their spinal vertebrae atrophy and the slight loss of stature that ensues may be exaggerated by the tendency to stoop. Osteoporosis, a thinning of the bone that affects some women after menopause, may cause a "widow's hump" at the back of the neck. (See Chapter 14.) Chemical composition of the bones changes, causing an increased chance of bone fractures.

Older people sleep less than younger ones, and men especially tend to wake up during the night and have difficulty falling back to sleep. Older people sleep more lightly than younger people and have fewer periods of deep sleep and dream sleep (Woodruff, 1985).

All the body systems and organs are more susceptible to disease, but the most serious change affects the functioning of the heart. After age 55, the rhythm of the heart becomes slower and more irregular; deposits of fat accumulate around it and interfere with its functioning; and

the blood pressure rises. On the whole, the digestive system remains relatively efficient. The smooth muscles of the internal organs continue to operate well, and the liver and gallbladder hold up well. When obesity is present, it affects the circulatory system, the kidneys, and sugar metabolism; it contributes to degenerative disorders and tends to shorten life.

Loss of Reserve Capacity

As mentioned in Chapter 14, the human body has the equivalent of money in the bank for a rainy day. Under normal circumstances, people do not use their organs and body systems to the limit, but extra capacity is available for extraordinary circumstances. This backup capacity, which allows body systems to function in times of stress, is called **reserve capacity** (or *organ reserve*); it enables each organ to put forth 4 to 10 times as much effort as usual. Reserve capacity helps to preserve homeostasis, the maintenance of vital functions within their optimum range (Fries & Crapo, 1981).

As people age, their reserve levels drop. Although the decline is not usually noticeable in everyday life, older people cannot respond to stressful demands as quickly as younger people. A person who used to be able to shovel snow and then go skiing afterward may now exhaust the capacity of the heart by the shoveling alone. Young people can almost always survive pneumonia; older people are likely to succumb.

People need reserve capacity just to survive as pedestrians. Because older people cannot call upon fast reflexes, vigorous heart action, and quick-responding muscles to get out of harm's way, they are more likely to be victims of traffic accidents. As reserve capacity diminishes, people may become less able to care for themselves and more dependent on others.

HEALTH

Despite the physical changes that come with age, most elderly people are reasonably healthy. According to a report by the U.S. Department of Health and Human Services published in 1986, about 68 percent of people 65 years old and older rate their health as good, very good, or excellent, while a little more than 30 percent describe their health as fair or poor.

Sixty percent of people over the age of 65 do not have to limit any major activities for health reasons, as compared with 80 percent of 45- to 64-year-olds. Not until age 85 do more than half the population report such limitations. Among people who are not in institutions, a majority of those 85 and over, three-fourths of 75- to 84-year-olds, and 86 percent of 65- to 74-year-olds can take care of their personal needs (such as eating, using the toilet, dressing, and bathing) and home chores (such as cooking, shopping, and housework) without assistance (AARP, 1986; U.S. Bureau of the Census, 1983). Thus the stereotype of the helpless, ill old person is not based on reality—not even for the very aged.

People with higher incomes are likely to be healthier than poorer people, rural residents are most likely to have chronic conditions (those of long duration) that limit their activity, and elderly white people tend to be healthier than black people. These differences probably reflect differences in lifestyles, preventive care, and access to good medical care (AARP, 1986; U.S. Bureau of the Census, 1983).

Influences on Health and Fitness

Shifts in the causes of death result from societal factors such as improvements in sanitation, immunization against many diseases that used to kill in childhood (like diphtheria and whooping cough), and the widespread use of antibiotics, which have taken some of the scare out of bronchitis, influenza, and pneumonia. The population as a whole has a higher standard of living, is eating better, and is more knowledgeable about health.

Along with these positive changes have come some negative ones—the increase in smoking and in carcinogenic agents in foods, in the workplace, and in the air we breathe, which lead to more deaths from cancer; and the faster pace of life, which contributes to hypertension and heart disease. The very fact that more people are now living to advanced ages means that they are more likely to contract conditions and diseases that are more likely to occur late in life.

The likelihood that an older person will be

These women and men working out on exercise bikes are deriving the benefits of regular physical exercise in old age. They may well avoid some of the physical changes commonly associated with "normal aging," which are now thought to be the result of inactivity.

reasonably healthy and fit and will be able to avoid the secondary effects of aging often depends on the extent to which he or she has followed and continues to follow the healthy lifestyle practices discussed in Boxes 12-1 and 16-1. These practices include eating moderately, eating regular meals (something that older people living alone may neglect to do), and avoiding cholesterol; not smoking; drinking alcohol in moderation or not at all; avoiding use of drugs; coping with stress; and getting regular exercise.

Exercise is just as valuable in the lives of older adults as it is in earlier phases of the life span, since many of the physical changes commonly associated with "normal aging" are now thought to be the result of inactivity. For this reason, the Council on Scientific Affairs of the American Medical Association (1984) recommends a lifelong program of physical exercise.

Regular physical exercise throughout adulthood seems to provide protection against both hypertension and heart disease. In addition, it seems to diminish losses in speed, stamina, and strength and in such basic functions as circulation and breathing. It improves joint and muscle

This elderly police officer is not unusual in continuing to pursue his work. Most older people are reasonably healthy and active; the stereotype of old age as a time of illness and helplessness is not based on reality. Workers over the age of 65 take no more time off the job because of illness than younger workers.

strength and flexibility, reducing the chance of injuries, and helps to prevent or relieve lower-back pain and symptoms of arthritis. It may also improve mental alertness and cognitive performance and may help relieve anxiety and mild depression (Birren et al., 1980; Blair, Goodyear, Gibbons, & Cooper, 1984; Bromley, 1974; Pardini, 1984).

Health Care and Health Problems

Medical Conditions Although most elderly people are in good health, chronic medical conditions do become more frequent with age and may cause disability. Most older people have at least one chronic condition; the most common conditions are arthritis, hypertension, hearing impairments, heart disease, cataracts, and impairments of the legs, hips, back, or spine (AARP, 1986). But people over 65 report fewer

colds, flu infections, and acute digestive problems than younger people. The danger, when older people do become ill, is that a minor illness—superimposed on a variety of chronic conditions and combined with the loss of reserve capacity—may have serious repercussions.

When acute illness does strike an older person, it generally entails more days of restricted activity than it would for a younger person. Even so, this amounts to an average of only 32 days (including 15 days sick in bed) in a year. Like younger workers, workers over 65 take off an average of only 4 or 5 days each year because of illness (AARP, 1986; Estes, 1969; U.S. Bureau of the Census, 1983).

Overall, older people need more medical care than younger people. They go to the doctor more often, are hospitalized more frequently, and stay in the hospital longer, and they spend more than 3 times as much money (an average of $4200 a year) on health care. Medicare (part of the social security system, available to everyone over age 65), Medicaid (available only to low-income people), and other government programs cover about two-thirds of this cost. About one-fourth of the cost comes out of people's own pockets (or their relatives'); private insurance covers very little (AARP, 1986; Binstock, 1987).

Contrary to the stereotype that most elderly people live in nursing homes, only 1 out of 20 people over 65 are institutionalized at any one time. The odds, however, are about 1 in 5 that a given person will spend some time in a nursing home. As might be expected, the proportion of nursing home patients rises with age—to almost 1 in 4 for people over 85 (AARP, 1986; American Health Care Association, 1984). Some people in nursing homes might be able to remain in the community if they had someone to help them with health care and daily activities. (We will discuss institutionalization again in Chapter 17.)

Dental Health Tooth and gum problems are common in late adulthood. Only a very small proportion of people keep all their teeth until very late in life. Tooth loss has serious implications for nutrition. People with poor or missing teeth find many foods unappealing and hard to chew; as a result, they eat less or shift to softer foods, which are often less nutritious (Wayler, Kapur, Feldman, & Chauncey, 1982).

Dental health is related to a combination of innate tooth structure and lifelong eating and dental health habits. Among people interviewed for a 1982 report, more than half of those 65 and over had not seen a dentist for 2 years or more (USDHHS, 1982). Extensive loss of teeth—especially serious among low-income groups—may reflect inadequate dental care (or a lack of dental care) more than the effects of aging.

Mental and Behavioral Disorders As the family and friends of a 76-year-old man watched him go downhill mentally for 8 months, they assumed that he was becoming senile. A neurologist, however, discovered that a blood clot was pressing on the man's brain. The clot was removed, and the man's behavior returned to normal.

Very often, the confusion, forgetfulness, and personality changes that are sometimes associated with old age have physiological causes. The general term for such apparent intellectual deterioration is *dementia.* The word *senility,* frequently used to describe dementia in older people, is not a true medical diagnosis but a "wastebasket" term for a wide range of symptoms.

Contrary to popular stereotype, dementia is not an inevitable part of aging. Although it does affect an estimated 3 million Americans (AARP, 1987b), most older people are in good mental health. Nor is moderate memory loss necessarily a sign of dementia. Furthermore, while some dementias are irreversible, others can be reversed with the right treatment. The most prevalent—and most feared—irreversible dementia is Alzheimer's disease.

IRREVERSIBLE CONDITIONS *Alzheimer's disease* A respected poet cannot remember her own name, much less her poetry. A former industrial tycoon, swathed in a diaper, spends hours polishing his shoes. These are among the approximately 6 percent of older people who are victims of *Alzheimer's disease,* a degenerative brain disorder that gradually robs people of intelligence, awareness, and even the ability to control bodily functions, and finally kills them (Reisberg, 1983). This dreaded malady occasionally

strikes in middle age, but most victims are over 65 years old. The disease is estimated to affect some 20 to 30 percent of those who live to their mid-eighties (Heston & White, 1983).

The cause of Alzheimer's disease is a mystery. Various theories have blamed a biochemical deficiency, a viral infection, a genetic tendency, a defect of the immune system, or even aluminum poisoning (Cohen, 1987). Early-appearing Alzheimer's disease has long been thought to be inherited, but it has been harder to detect a genetic tendency for the late-arriving form of Alzheimer's disease, since many potential victims may die of other causes earlier in life. Now a research team has suggested that this variety, too, may be inherited in much the same way as the early-onset type. In fact, by the age of 90, relatives of patients with Alzheimer's disease were found to have an almost 50 percent risk of getting the disease, about 4 times as high as the risk to a control group (Mohs, Breitner, Silverman, & Davis, 1987).

Symptoms and diagnosis: The first signs of Alzheimer's disease may not seem alarming and may even be overlooked: they may include a tendency to garble phone messages, an inability to play a game of cards or tennis, or sudden outbreaks of extravagance. The most prominent early symptom is memory loss, especially for recent events. More symptoms follow, such as confusion, irritability, restlessness, agitation, and impairments of judgment, concentration, orientation, and speech. As the disease progresses, the symptoms become more pronounced and disabling. By the end, the victim cannot understand or use language, does not recognize family members, and cannot eat without help.

Diagnosing Alzheimer's disease is difficult because the disorder is hard to distinguish from other forms of dementia. The only sure diagnosis so far depends on observation of tissue deep within the brain, which can be done only by autopsy after death. The brain of a person with Alzheimer's disease shows tangles of nerve fibers, cell loss, and other changes. These changes are also found to some extent in normal aging, but they are far more pronounced in people suffering from Alzheimer's disease, and they are more likely to occur in the area of the brain associated with memory (the hippocampus;

Three successive paintings of a windmill by the same artist show progressive mental deterioration associated with Alzheimer's disease, a brain disorder that affects all aspects of functioning. The artist did the first painting in his late sixties, at about the time that he began to show signs of the disease. In the second painting, done 7 years later, perspective is inaccurate, color sense is poor, and there is less attention to detail. When the artist made the third sketch, 2 years after the second, he could render only gross elements.

Hyman, Van Hoesen, Damasio, & Barnes, 1984).

Doctors usually diagnose Alzheimer's disease in a living person by ruling out other conditions that could account for the symptoms (Heston & White, 1983; Kokmen, 1984). A new technique, nuclear magnetic resonance scanning, may improve diagnostic accuracy (Summers, Majovski, Marsh, Tachiki, & Kling, 1986). Although Alzheimer's disease itself is incurable, more accurate diagnosis would allow treatment of similar ailments that are sometimes misdiagnosed as Alzheimer's disease.

Treatment: A great deal of research is going on, ranging from the testing of new drugs to improve memory (Harbaugh, Roberts, Coombs, Saunders, & Reeder, 1984; Thal, Fuld, Masur, & Sharpless, 1983) through grafting fetal brain tissue into the brains of aged impaired rats (Gage, Bjorklund, Stenevi, Dunnett, & Kelly, 1984). Drugs have been used to raise the levels of acetylcholine, a neurotransmitter (a chemical needed to transmit information through the nervous system) whose concentration is lowered in the brains of patients with Alzheimer's disease (Cohen, 1987). However, at this point no cure has been discovered.

Patients with Alzheimer's disease may be helped by drugs that relieve agitation, lighten depression, or help them sleep. Proper nourishment and fluid intake are important, and exer-cise and physical therapy may be beneficial. Memory aids can help everyday functioning. Probably the biggest help to both patient and family is the social and emotional support that can come through professional counseling and support groups (Heston & White, 1983; Kokmen, 1984; LaBarge, 1981; L.W. Lazarus, Stafford, Cooper, Cohler, & Dysken, 1981).[*]

Other irreversible conditions About 80 percent of dementia cases among older persons are caused either by Alzheimer's disease or by a series of small strokes (NIA, 1980). When symptoms come on in several sudden steps, rather than gradually, strokes are the likeliest explanation (AARP, 1987b). In cases of mixed dementia, both changes like those seen with Alzheimer's disease and strokes seem to occur (Reisberg, 1987). Small strokes can often be prevented by controlling hypertension through screening, low-salt diet, and medication (NIA, 1984).

REVERSIBLE CONDITIONS Many older people mistakenly believe that they can do nothing about their mental and behavioral problems because "you can't turn back the clock." Actually, some 100 conditions—including about 15 percent of dementia cases—can be cured or

[*]For more information, write to Alzheimer's Disease and Related Disorders Association, Inc., 360 North Michigan Ave., Chicago, IL 60601.

substantially alleviated *if* they are correctly diagnosed and treated. The most common are depression, intoxication caused by medically prescribed drugs, and metabolic or infectious disorders; the next most common are malnutrition, anemia, alcoholism, low thyroid functioning, and head injury (AARP, 1987b; NIA, 1980).

Overmedication Some apparent dementia turns out to be a side effect of drug intoxication. Many older people take as many as a dozen different medications prescribed by several different doctors. Because physicians do not always ask what medicines a patient is already taking, they may prescribe drugs that will interact with them in a harmful way. In addition, because of age-related changes in the body's metabolism and because an older person may be small and thin, a dosage that would be appropriate for a 40-year-old may constitute an overdose for an 80-year-old (Henig, 1979).

Depression Some mental and personality changes that seem to indicate brain disorders are actually the result of depression. Many older people suffer from a variety of more or less disabling aches and pains; have lost spouses, siblings, friends, and sometimes children; take medications that can cause alterations in mood; and feel that they have practically no control over their lives. It is not surprising, then, that at any given time about one-third of those over age 65 will experience a major depression within the next 3 years (Heston & White, 1983). Depressed people often become disorganized, absentminded, careless, apathetic, unable to concentrate, and uninterested in the world around them. They may fail to eat properly, and malnutrition or dehydration (especially in summer) may make them incoherent (AARP, 1987b; Cohen, 1981).

Support networks of family and friends can help older people to ward off depression or to find help when it occurs. Help is available from antidepressant medication, from psychotherapy, or from a variety of medical and community services (Cohen, 1981). Unfortunately, many older people do not get help. For one thing, private treatment is expensive, and low-cost mental health services are not offered in

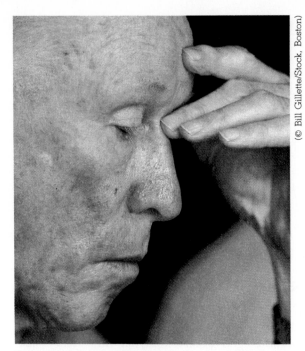

(© Bill Gillette/Stock, Boston)

Some old people become depressed as a result of physical and emotional losses, and some apparent "brain disorders" are actually due to depression. But depression can often be relieved if older people seek the help they need.

every community; but older people rarely use these services anyway. Only a very small percentage of persons seen in psychiatric clinics are over age 60, and only a small percentage of those seen in community health centers are over 65 (Butler & Lewis, 1982).

Some older people are too proud to admit that they need help; some are frightened of mental illness and feel that seeking help would mean they were "crazy"; some believe that they are "too old to change"; and some are unaware that psychiatric treatment need not be long and costly. Some people do not realize that their symptoms are treatable—especially when family members or insensitive clinicians dismiss reversible disorders as irreversible "senility." Often the true cause of a problem becomes obscured in a vicious circle. People who slow down because they are depressed may fear that their brain is degenerating, and that belief depresses them even more, contributing to the appearance of dementia; whereas, if they received treatment for the depression, they might begin acting "like themselves" again.

Most people do not deteriorate markedly in late adulthood. Do they, however, continue to learn and grow intellectually, or does intelligence now falter and decline? We'll examine this controversial question, and then we'll look at what happens to memory in normal, healthy adults. Finally, we'll see how some older people keep their minds sharp through continuing education and how they view work and retirement.

ASPECTS OF INTELLECTUAL DEVELOPMENT

Intelligence: Does Intelligence Decline in Late Adulthood?

Leah W., aged 75, was taken aback when a middle-aged woman told her how "alert" she seemed. The older woman considered the comment patronizing and gratuitous—as well she might.

Two Views of Intelligence Some psychologists argue that "general intellectual decline in old age is largely a myth" (Baltes & Schaie, 1974, p. 35, 1976; Schaie & Baltes, 1977). Others dismiss this interpretation as rosy (J.L. Horn & Donaldson, 1976, 1977).

To weigh these two points of view, we need to look at the results of intelligence tests that have been given to people of different ages, at the kinds of tests given, and at the ways in which data have been collected. But first we need to consider the kinds of intelligence being tested.

FLUID AND CRYSTALLIZED INTELLIGENCE—WHICH IS MORE IMPORTANT? The distinction between *fluid* and *crystallized* intelligence (described in Chapter 12) is crucial to this controversy. Horn (who helped to develop this distinction) and his colleagues consider fluid abilities (which are called on to solve novel problems and which decline in late adulthood, presumably because of neurological losses) to be at the heart of intelligence. Therefore they see intellectual aging, in this core area, as a downhill slide.

Schaie and Baltes, on the other hand, maintain that while some abilities (mostly fluid) de-

cline, other important abilities (mostly crystallized abilities, the kind that depend on learning and experience) either hold their own or increase in later life. Furthermore, they stress the emergence of *new* abilities, such as wisdom. Finally, studies suggest that performance on fluid tests can be improved with training. Thus, these researchers emphasize that any assumption of overall intellectual decline is unwarranted.

FLUID AND CRYSTALLIZED INTELLIGENCE—HOW ARE THEY TESTED? Three important aspects of testing fluid and crystallized intelligence are types of tests, influences on performance, and ways to improve older people's performance. Let's consider these.

Cross-sectional, longitudinal, and sequential testing As was pointed out in Chapter 12, cross-sectional and longitudinal testing designs show different kinds of changes in adult intelligence. The early cross-sectional tests (which tested different people of different ages all at a single time) found that intelligence increased throughout childhood, peaked in adolescence or very early adulthood, and then declined from middle age on. The longitudinal tests (which followed the *same* people over a period of time) found that intelligence increased up to age 50 and remained stable up to age 60 or so. However, both testing designs had disadvantages: chiefly, the cohort effect in cross-sectional studies and the effect of practice in longitudinal ones.

To overcome these disadvantages and to resolve the discrepancies between the two sets of data, Schaie and his colleagues developed a new approach to study changes in intellectual functioning independent of both cohort differences and practice effects (Baltes, 1985; Schaie, 1979, 1983; Schaie & Herzog, 1983; Schaie & Strother, 1968). In 1956, their now-classic sequential study began with a battery of tests of 500 randomly chosen volunteers from Seattle (25 men and 25 women in each 5-year age interval from 20 to 70 years). Every 7 years, the original subjects were retested and new subjects were added to the study; by 1984 more than 2000 people had been tested on such timed tasks as recognizing synonyms, understanding spatial relations (mentally rotating a figure in space), word fluency (writing as many words beginning with the letter *s* as possible in 5 minutes), and solving logical and numerical problems.

The major findings are that older people's intellectual functioning is characterized by variability and multidirectionality of change and is subject to cultural and environmental influences:

- *Variability:* Some people's intellectual abilities begin to decline during their thirties, others' not till their seventies; and about one-third of people over age 70 do better on intelligence tests than the average young adult. An individual person's functioning is influenced by such factors as health, kind of job, and education. Most fairly healthy adults in the United States do not experience any significant mental loss until about age 60, but if they live long enough, their intellectual functioning will begin to decline at some point.
- *Multidirectionality of change:* As described in Chapter 12, fluid intelligence begins to decline in the thirties, but crystallized intelligence remains stable or even increases into the seventies. After this time, crystallized intelligence also declines, but the decline may be due to older people's slower response time, not to their abilities.
- *Cultural and environmental influences:* Different cohorts show different patterns of intellectual functioning in maturity (just as they do earlier in life) as the result of different kinds of life experiences. For example, people who grew up more recently in the United States have more formal education, on the average; have been exposed to more information through television; have taken more tests and have taken them more recently; are in better health; and are likely to have jobs that depend on thinking rather than on physical labor. All these factors contribute to differences among cohorts.

Influences on performance on tests What older people *can* do is not known; what is known is only what they *do* do under certain conditions (Willis & Baltes, 1980). Studies that show a decline in test performance may or may not reflect an actual decline in intellectual competence. A number of physical and psychological factors may depress older people's test scores, leading to underestimation of their intelligence.

Because it is harder for older people to see and hear, they often have trouble getting instructions and actually doing the tasks. Performance also suffers because of poor coordination and agility. People who are physically fit and not fatigued and those who have relatively low blood pressure, less disease, and fewer negative neurophysiological indicators do best on intelligence tests (Furry & Baltes, 1973; Schaie & Gribbin, 1975).

Statistically, the poorer showings of older people in cross-sectional studies may be influenced by **terminal drop,** a sudden decrease in intellectual performance shortly before death. Terminal drop is not a function of age, since it is seen in people who die young; but it tends to bring down the average scores of an older sample, since more people in an older age bracket are likely to die in the near future.

In addition, as is true with young people (see Chapter 8), attitudes toward a testing situation can affect the results. Older people may be anxious, especially if they are unfamiliar with the testing situation and have not taken intelligence tests for a long time. They may lack confidence in their ability to solve test problems, and the expectation that they will not do well may become a self-fulfilling prophecy. Or they may lack motivation because performance on intelligence tests does not mean much to them.

The time limits on most intelligence tests are particularly unfair to older people, who are usually well aware that everything takes them longer than it once did. Since both physical and psychological processes slow down with age, it is not surprising that older subjects perform less well on timed tests than when they are allowed as much time as they need (J.L. Horn & Cattell, 1966; Schaie & Herzog, 1983). The emphasis on speed in western culture may result in automatically defining older people as less intelligent than younger ones.

Furthermore, as discussed in Chapters 12 and 14, tasks that are developed for children, to see whether they are acquiring the skills that characterize intellectual development during childhood and adolescence, may be inappropriate for testing the intelligence of older people,

Older people can join the computer age, as this woman (who is being taught by a high school student) demonstrates. Old people who are motivated and helped can put forth the extra effort needed to maintain or even expand their intellectual capacity.

which depends on how well they apply their skills to everyday life. The difference between the two kinds of intelligence showed up in a study in which a number of women, aged 65 to 87, gave "wrong" explanations of Piagetian conservation tasks because they related the questions to their real-life experience. For example, when asked whether there was the same amount of space in different-shaped houses made with the same number of blocks, one woman said, "When you start getting fancy, you always lose some space because [you] have to have a hallway upstairs as well as downstairs, which takes away space" (P. Roberts, Papalia-Finlay, Davis, Blackburn, & Dellmann, 1982, p. 191).

Until test developers devise ways to measure people's ability to deal with the kinds of real situations they are likely to encounter—tasks like balancing a checkbook, reading a railroad timetable, or making informed decisions about medical problems—we will not have an accurate picture of older people's intelligence (Schaie, 1976). We also need more research on the cognitive processes involved in intellectual functioning, and how the components of those processes may change with age. Such research may tell us why there is so much variation in findings on intelligence in late adulthood (Dixon & Baltes, 1986).

Helping older people to improve their intellectual performance Everyone has had the experience of performing a given task better at one time than another. The results of an exam may well show the effects of too little sleep the night before, of not feeling well, of a testing room that is too hot or too cold, of worries about something else in one's life, or of an "I don't care" attitude. Test performance may also be affected, of course, by how much and how well people study for a test and by their skills in taking tests (knowing, for example, when to guess on true-false questions and how much time to spend on a hard question before going on).

This variability, or modifiability, of a person's performance is called **plasticity.** The plasticity of older test-takers has been the subject of research that has helped older people do better on tests by identifying and modifying factors that influence their performance. Several studies have been based largely on the Adult Development and Enrichment Project (ADEPT), which originated at Pennsylvania State University (Blieszner, Willis, & Baltes, 1981; Plemons, Willis, & Baltes, 1978; Willis, Blieszner, & Baltes, 1981).

In one recent study based on ADEPT (Blackburn, Papalia, & Foye, 1986), 73 healthy volunteers whose average age was about 70 were randomly assigned to three groups, each of which met for about 5 hours in small subgroups. The first group received formal training in figural relations (rules for determining the next figure in a series). The second group worked with the same training materials and problems but were self-taught—that is, they had no formal instruction. The third group, a control group, received no training. Pretests and posttests contained some tasks similar to those in the training materials and other tasks that were markedly different. Both experimental groups improved more than the control group, but the people in the self-taught group maintained their gains better on a posttest after 1 year. Apparently the opportunity to work out their own solutions fostered more durable learning than being taught a set of rules.

Findings like these show that training and practice can improve older people's performance even on tests of fluid intelligence. Much as aging athletes can often call upon physical reserves, older people who get training, practice, and social support seem to be able to draw upon intellectual reserves. Late adulthood, then, need not be a time of intellectual decline if people are motivated and helped to put forth extra effort to maintain or enhance their mental powers (Dixon & Baltes, 1986).

A New View: Mechanics and Pragmatics of Intelligence Old age "adds as it takes away," said the poet William Carlos Williams in one of three books of verse written between his first stroke at the age of 68 and his death at 79.

In a review of new directions in research, Dixon and Baltes (1986) sketch a *dual-process model,* a picture of intellectual functioning in late adulthood that includes both those aspects of intelligence that are subject to deterioration and also those that may continue to advance but are unlikely to show up on psychometric tests. This model identifies and seeks to measure two dimensions of intelligence:

1 *Mechanics of intelligence* consist of "the content-free architecture of information processing and problem solving" (p. 221). This is the area of intellect in which there is often an age-related decline; it is similar to fluid intelligence.

2 *Pragmatics of intelligence* include such potential growth areas as practical thinking, the application of accumulated knowledge and skills, specialized expertise, professional productivity, and wisdom.

Older adults are likely to improve not on the basic cognitive "mechanics" they learned in childhood but rather on their "pragmatic" use of the information and know-how they have garnered from their education, their work, and their life experience. This pragmatic domain is far broader than crystallized intelligence (which is usually measured by tests of vocabulary and general information).

Pragmatic intelligence can help older people to maintain or enhance their intellectual functioning through *selective optimization with compensation.* By doing what they are good at, older people can use their special abilities to compensate for losses in other areas. This concept may help explain how artists like Pablo Picasso and Francisco Goya, writers like George Bernard Shaw, and composers like Giuseppe Verdi were able to produce some of their finest works in their seventies and eighties.

Wisdom is an important part of pragmatic intelligence. (It is also the "virtue" that emerges from Erikson's final crisis, discussed in Chapter 17.) Yet there has been little study of wisdom, perhaps because it is hard to define and test.

Wisdom goes beyond book learning, expertise, and factual knowledge, though it may rely on all of them. One attribute of wisdom is sound judgment, both in everyday conduct and in making hard decisions. Wisdom reminds older people of their capabilities and their limitations; it tells them what lessons to draw from their experiences; and it gives them perspective on how to use the time that remains (Dixon & Baltes, 1986).

Memory

"I can't remember whether or not I put the sugar in that cake," says Pauline B., at age 73 a professional caterer. "I guess I really am getting old if I'm this forgetful." Yet Pauline remembers the telephone numbers of a wide circle of friends, relatives, and customers; she never forgets an appointment; and she keeps most of her recipes in her head.

The Three Memory Systems Failing memory is often considered to be a sign of aging. The man who always kept his schedule in his head may now write it in an engagement calendar; the woman who takes several medicines may measure out each day's dosages and put them in a place where she is sure to see them.

Yet in memory, as in other respects, older people's functioning varies greatly. To understand why, we need to remember that there is not a single capacity called *memory*. Instead, as noted in Chapter 8, researchers believe that three different storage systems—sensory memory, short-term memory, and long-term memory—each serve distinct purposes. Aging usually has a significant effect only on long-term memory for recent events (Poon, 1985).

SENSORY MEMORY The brain records whatever a person sees, hears, smells, tastes, or touches—anything that comes in through the senses—and places the information in a temporary storage called **sensory memory,** where it stays very briefly. Images in sensory memory quickly fade unless transferred to short-term memory.

Iconic (visual) memory, the only type of sensory memory that has been studied in older people, seems to hold up fairly well (Poon, 1985). Without this ability to register visual images (such as an array of letters), people would be unable to read or to make sense of anything they saw.

SHORT-TERM MEMORY When a person looks up a telephone number in order to dial it, the number goes into **short-term memory,** which holds information for about 20 seconds. Researchers assess short-term memory by asking people to repeat a sequence of numbers, either in the order in which they have been presented or in reverse order. The number of digits a person can recall seems to be relatively unaffected by age, though it may take an older person a little longer to respond (Craik, 1977; Poon, 1985).

LONG-TERM MEMORY **Long-term memory** refers to the long-term storage of information. Research has distinguished between older people's long-term memory for newly learned information and their memory for information learned in the more distant past. The former drops off significantly with advancing age: over a period of hours or days, younger adults can remember such newly learned material as word pairs or paragraphs better than older people do (Craik, 1977; Poon, 1985). However, the ability to recall events from long ago is not generally affected by advanced age. When grandma reminisces about books she read in her youth, her memories are probably as reliable as those of younger adults (Poon, 1985).

Why Does Memory Decline? Investigators have offered several hypotheses to explain age differences, particularly in long-term memory for recent events.

BIOLOGICAL HYPOTHESES Some researchers point to neurological changes and other physiological changes connected with aging. Thus, the more a person deteriorated physically, the more memory loss would take place. So far, the biological approach appears to be more useful to explain memory impairment in people with brain damage or other pathological conditions than to explain memory loss in normal, healthy older adults (Poon, 1985).

PROCESSING HYPOTHESES A second approach focuses on the three steps required to process information in memory: encoding, storage, and retrieval. Older people seem to be less efficient than younger people at encoding information: preparing and "labeling" it for storage so that it will be easier to retrieve when needed. Older people are not as likely to think of ways to organize material to make it easier to remember (such as putting names in alphabetical order). But when given suggestions for organizing, older subjects remember just as well as younger subjects (Hultsch, 1971; Poon, 1985).

Older people often have trouble retrieving information from memory. In one study, older people had some trouble *recalling* items they had learned, but they did just as well as younger people in *recognizing* the items (Hultsch, 1971). In other words, if asked a question, they might have difficulty in coming up with the right answer themselves; but if presented with a multiple-choice problem, they could recognize the correct answer.

This 80-year-old student at Queens College, doing library research alongside her younger classmates, is one of a growing number of older persons enrolled in formal educational programs—whether to pursue new interests, develop new skills, keep their minds alert, keep up with societal changes, or just make their lives more interesting.

(© Tannenbaum/Sygma)

Older people are often slow at retrieval. When asked to memorize up to seven items and then to tell whether a certain item is on the list, older people are as accurate as young and middle-aged adults but are not as quick to come up with the answers. They seem to take longer to search their memories, to make a decision, and then to express the decision (T.R. Anders, Fozard, & Lillyquist, 1972). It is almost impossible, however, to separate poor retrieval from poor encoding. Someone who has difficulty retrieving information before being taught organizing strategies apparently has a problem with encoding, not retrieval (Poon, 1985).

CONTEXTUAL CONSIDERATIONS Some researchers have recently become interested in how "contextual" factors—factors determining how a particular person responds to a particular task—account for individual differences in recall. Such factors might include motivation, intelligence, learning habits, and degree of familiarity with test items, as well as the type of task.

Accordingly, the designers of one recent study reasoned that age differences in memory should be more pronounced when people are less intellectually able, flexible, and resourceful; when they are given little guidance in encoding and retrieval; or when the material is unfamiliar. The researchers compared three groups of 20 elderly volunteers (differing in socioeconomic status, verbal intelligence, and daily activ-

ity levels) with a group of 20 undergraduate students. All participants were tested individually on three verbal tasks, including recalling words from a list. The most intelligent, affluent, and socially active old people did best on all the tasks—about as well as the undergraduates—while the least intelligent, least economically advantaged, and least active ones did worst. As expected, there was less difference in performance when the subjects were given cues to jog their memories than when they were asked to recall the words on their own (Craik, Byrd, & Swanson, 1987).

This study shows that to speak of an across-the-board decline in memory is dangerously misleading. We need to ask: Which older people are we talking about? What tasks are they being asked to do? And how well prepared are they to do them?

Lifelong Learning

Why do some older people learn more and remember more than others? How can we maintain high levels of intelligence into late life?

One of the principal findings to come from the research is that the phrase "use it or lose it" seems applicable to mental ability as well as to physical ability. Continuing intellectual activity throughout life helps keep performance high, whether this activity takes the form of reading, taking part in stimulating conversation, doing crossword puzzles, playing bridge or chess or Scrabble—or going back to school, as more and more mature adults are doing.

Adult Education in Late Life Now that they have time to spare, many older people use it to educate themselves. Since people who were well educated in their earlier years are more inclined to seek more education later in life and since education rates have been rising steadily (U.S. Bureau of the Census, 1983), there will probably be continued increases in the number of older people enrolled in educational programs.

Older people go to school for many reasons: they want to understand and keep up with technological and sociocultural changes, to prepare for a new line of work, to make retirement more interesting and more meaningful, to develop skills for independent living, and to pursue interests they never had time for during the years of making a living and raising a family (Willis, 1985).

To accommodate the needs of this growing population, we need to expand adult education programs and to make them more accessible. Already many colleges offer tuition-free courses for older students. Low-cost summer Elderhostel programs offer 1- or 2-week minicourses in Shakespeare, geography, early American music, and a wide variety of other subjects. Some vocational programs give special attention to the needs of older women who have never worked for pay and who now must do so for either financial or emotional reasons. These are all steps in the right direction.

Helping Older People Learn Older people can learn new skills and information, but they learn better when the materials and methods take into account the physiological, psychological, and intellectual changes that older students may be going through. Older people learn best when material is presented slowly and over a longer period of time with intervals in between, rather than in concentrated form. Their ability to learn depends largely on the nature of the task, on how it relates to previous experiences, and on the teaching method. Older people cannot acquire as much speed in complex rhythmic tasks or in tasks that require sensorimotor coordination. It is particularly hard for them to learn

new skills that involve unlearning deeply ingrained habits. Older people may find it hard to learn from lectures in which material is presented quickly; they do much better when they have some control over the pace of their learning.

Older people may become discouraged in training programs because they do not learn as quickly as their younger classmates or as they themselves learned in their younger years. Instructors can encourage older students by assuring them that it may take them a little longer, but when they finish they will be just as capable as their younger colleagues.

Other ways to help older people learn are to provide reading matter that has fairly large print and audiovisual materials that are clear and easily understandable by students whose physical faculties are not as keen as they once were. Programmed teaching aids that use repetition and allow adequate time for responses are excellent tools for older learners. Pressure can be eliminated by minimizing competition and deemphasizing grades.

WORK AND RETIREMENT

A 77-year-old furniture salesman loses his job because of the death of his employer, and he gets three offers of employment, one of which he takes. A 65-year-old woman is the only physician in her community to continue to make house calls.

Perhaps because people like these—older people doing productive paid work—represent only 3 percent of the work force (Schick, 1986), they are less visible than the stereotyped carefree retirees "sallying forth from Florida condominiums every morning to frolic on the golf course" (Pollack, 1985, p. A27). Although almost 3 million people over 65 were working or looking for work in 1985, they represented a far smaller percentage of their age group than their counterparts in the past. About two-thirds of older men were in the labor force in 1900 and almost half in 1950, but only 1 out of 6 are today (AARP, 1986; Bird, 1987; U.S. Bureau of the Census, 1983).

Early retirement and a decline in self-employment are the chief explanations for the dramatic decline in older men's participation in the work force. The proportion of older women who work has decreased more modestly, from about 10 percent (during the 1950s) to 7 percent. These smaller figures probably reflect the fact that fewer women in this age group worked earlier in life and that those who did tended to retire as early as possible because they were limited in the kinds of work they could do (AARP, 1986; Bird, 1987).

Retirement does not necessarily mean stopping work altogether. Many healthy retirees spend part of their time in gainful employment; in fact, part-timers account for a little more than half (53 percent) of older workers. Although there are probably some people over the age of 65 in virtually every known occupation, 3 out of 4 older workers are white-collar and about 1 out of 4 are self-employed (AARP, 1986; Bird, 1987; Schick, 1986).

By using her leisure time to do volunteer work as a tutor, this elderly woman is not only helping her student but helping herself to keep intellectually active and to feel useful. Many communities have established programs like this one, to tap the valuable resources that retired people have to offer.

Feelings about Retirement

With almost two-thirds of all workers now retiring before they reach age 65, the average man[*] can expect to spend one-fifth of his life in retirement (Schick, 1986). How do people feel about retirement?

Some, of course, eagerly await retirement, while others dread it. The way workers react to giving up their jobs depends on many factors, including how much they like their work, how much they need the money, whether they have chosen to retire or have been forced to do so, whether they have planned ahead for the change, and what interests they have besides their work. Generally, the higher the level of education and job status, the less eager workers are to retire and the more likely they are to continue working after age 65. People with tedious, low-level jobs that require hard physical labor are often eager to stop working, and when they do, their health is apt to improve (Butler & Lewis, 1977; Shanas, Townsend, Wedderburn, Friis, Milhoj, & Stehouwer, 1968). About one-third of workers aged 65 and over are forced to retire because of company rules, because they are in poor health, or because they cannot find work.

The way a person feels about retirement usually revolves around money and health. Not surprisingly, retirees who feel well and who do not have financial worries are more satisfied with retirement than are those who do not feel well enough to enjoy their leisure time and who miss the income (Barfield & Morgan, 1974, 1978; Streib & Schneider, 1971).

Use of time is another important factor. Just after retirement, many people relish the first long stretches of leisure time they have had since childhood. They enjoy spending time with family and friends and exploring new interests they never had time for before. As time goes on, some retirees begin to feel bored, restless, and useless. The most satisfied retirees tend to be those who are physically fit and who are doing part-time paid or volunteer work that lets them use their skills (Schick, 1986).

Making the Most of Retirement

Retirement is one of the major transitions of old age. What can be done to help more people enjoy it? Adjustment to retirement generally depends on how well people have prepared beforehand and on how they use their time.

[*]Studies on the impact of retirement have focused largely on male workers; with the increased role of work in women's lives, this imbalance is being corrected.

Planning Ahead Planning for retirement, which should ideally begin by middle age, includes structuring life to make it enjoyable and productive, providing adequately for financial needs, anticipating any physical or emotional problems, and discussing with a spouse how the retirement will affect him or her. Many community organizations and financial institutions offer preretirement workshops; self-help books on retirement appear regularly; and a growing number of companies recognize that informed decisions about retirement can boost employees' morale and productivity (Ossofsky, 1979).

Using Leisure Time Well Some retired people relish being able to sleep late, go fishing, or take in an afternoon movie. But for those who get more gratification from using the fruits of their professional and personal experience in a more structured, "worklike" way, programs have sprung up to tap this valuable resource. In several cities, retired business people share their experience with budding entrepreneurs. On college campuses, retirees tutor, counsel, and offer career advice to undergraduates. Older persons often serve as "foster" grandparents to children whose own grandparents are not available. Retired workers have been enlisted as teachers and supervisors in such technical fields as drafting, car repair, electronics, and computer technology.

Retirement could be made easier and more satisfying by restructuring the life course. Young adults usually plunge into education and careers; middle-agers use most of their energy earning money; and older people have trouble filling their time. If people wove work, leisure, and study into their lives in a more balanced way at all ages (as suggested in Chapter 14), young adults would feel less pressure to establish themselves early, middle-aged people would feel less burdened, and older people would be more stimulated and would feel—and be—more useful.

SUMMARY

- Because the number and proportion of older people in the United States are greater than ever, there is an increased interest in the aging process. Gerontology is the study of aging, and geriatrics is the branch of medicine concerned with the aged.

- The fastest-growing group in the population of the United States are those over the age of 85.

- Negative stereotypes about old people reflect ageism—prejudice or discrimination based on age. Such attitudes toward the elderly affect older people's feelings about themselves as well as society's treatment of them.

- Aging may have as much to do with health and attitude as with years of living. Today many older people are healthy, vigorous, and active. These people are referred to as the *young-old*, and the frail and infirm as the *old-old*.

Longevity and the Aging Process

- Senescence, the period in the life span when people begin to grow old, begins at different ages for different people. The designation of age 65 as the beginning of late adulthood is based on the traditional age of retirement, even though many people retire earlier these days (and some retire later).

- Life expectancy has increased dramatically since 1900. Children born in 1985 have an average life expectancy of almost 75 years. Black people tend to die earlier than white people, and men tend to die younger than women.

- The death rate for older people has declined. Today, heart disease, cancer, and stroke are the three leading causes of death for people over age 65.

- Most theories of why people age physically fall into two categories: aging as a programmed process and aging as a result of wear and tear to the body. Most likely both of these factors influence aging.

- Some gerontologists distinguish between primary aging, an inevitable process of bodily deterioration; and secondary aging, which results from the way people use their bodies and thus is largely preventable.

Physical Changes

■ Sensory and perceptual abilities decline during late adulthood, with vast individual differences in the timing and extent of decline.

■ Older people experience a general slowing down of responses and of information processing. This slowdown requires them to make adjustments in many aspects of their lives.

■ A number of other physical changes occur with advancing age, including some loss of skin coloring, texture, and elasticity; thinning and graying or whitening of hair; shrinkage of body size; and thinning of bones.

■ People tend to sleep less and more lightly in old age than in their youth.

■ Most body systems generally continue to function fairly well, but the heart, in particular, becomes more susceptible to disease because of its decreased efficiency. The reserve capacity of the heart and other organs declines.

Health

■ Exercise has many physical and psychological benefits. A program of regular physical exercise is recommended throughout life.

■ Most older people are reasonably healthy, but the incidence of illness and number of days of hospitalization is proportionally higher among older people than among younger people. Although most older people have one or more chronic conditions, many are not severely hampered by them.

■ Loss of teeth and gum problems are common in late adulthood, especially when dental care has been inadequate. Very few people keep all their teeth until late in life.

■ Most older people are in good mental health. Dementia, or intellectual deterioration, affects a minority of people of advanced age.

■ Some forms of dementia, such as those brought on by Alzheimer's disease or by multiple strokes, are irreversible; others, such as those caused by overmedication and depression, can be reversed with proper treatment.

Aspects of Intellectual Development

■ A major controversy concerns whether intelligence declines in late adulthood. Fluid intelli-gence, the ability to solve novel problems, does appear to decline; but crystallized intelligence, which is based on learning and experience, does not.

■ Early cross-sectional research using psychometric tests of intelligence indicated decline; longitudinal studies indicated stability up to age 60 or so. Schaie's sequential studies suggest a more complex picture: intellectual functioning in late adulthood is marked by variability, multidirectionality, and susceptibility to cultural and environmental influences.

■ Physical and psychological factors and test conditions can influence intellectual performance. Therefore, performance on intelligence tests may not be a precise measure of intellectual competence.

■ Older people show considerable cognitive plasticity (modifiability) in intellectual performance. Their positive response to an intellectually supportive environment demonstrates that they can and do learn.

■ Some aspects of intelligence seem to increase with age. Dixon and Baltes propose a dual-process model: the mechanics of intelligence often decline, but the pragmatics of intelligence (practical thinking, specialized knowledge and skills, and wisdom) continue to grow. Successful aging, according to this theory, involves selective optimization with compensation (using special abilities to compensate for losses).

■ While sensory, short-term, and remote long-term memory appear to be nearly as efficient in older adults as in younger people, long-term memory for recently learned information is often less efficient, probably because of problems with encoding (organization) and retrieval. Recognition is easier than recall.

■ Contextual factors—factors determining how a particular person responds to a particular task—may account for individual differences in recall. Like intelligence, memory functioning in older individuals varies greatly: more intelligent people may show little or no memory decline.

■ Continuing mental activity may be critical to keep older people mentally alert. Adult education programs can be designed to meet their needs.

■ Learning and memory are interrelated. Older people can learn new skills and information provided that it is presented slowly and over a longer period of time with intervals between exposures.

Work and Retirement

- Some older people continue to work for pay, but the vast majority are retired. There is a trend toward retirement before the age of 65. However, many retired people find part-time paid or volunteer work.

- Retirement is a major transition of old age. This transition can be eased by planning for retirement and by learning how to use leisure time.

KEY TERMS

ageism (page 534)
Alzheimer's disease (547)
dementia (547)
dual-process model (553)
geriatrics (536)
gerontologists (534)
long-term memory (554)
mechanics of intelligence (553)

plasticity (552)
pragmatics of intelligence (553)
primary aging (541)
programmed-aging theory (541)
reserve capacity (544)
secondary aging (541)
selective optimization with
   compensation (553)

senescence (539)
sensory memory (554)
short-term memory (554)
terminal drop (551)
wear-and-tear theory of aging
   (541)

Brown, D. S. (1984). *Handle with care: A question of Alzheimer's.* Buffalo, NY: Prometheus. A sensitive and practical book about Alzheimer's disease written by a woman whose mother was a victim.

Butler, R. N. (1975). *Why survive?* New York: Harper & Row. An angry book by a noted gerontologist who details the problems of being old in the United States today. This book, which won a Pulitzer Prize, offers suggestions on both personal and societal levels, gives case histories, and provokes thought on major social issues.

Herr, J. J., & Weakland, J. H. (1979). *Counseling elders and their families.* New York: Springer. A practical guide to the problems of the elderly. The book is written primarily for health professionals, but other readers will also find it useful in problem solving.

Heston, L. L., & White, J. A. (1983). *Dementia: A practical guide to Alzheimer's disease and related disorders.* San Francisco: Freeman. A very readable guidebook about all aspects of dementias. The authors provide information about current theories, treatment possibilities, and practical concerns.

Maddox, G. L. (Ed.) (1987). *The encyclopedia of aging.* New York: Springer. A comprehensive, authoritative, concise reference on hundreds of topics related to late adulthood. Articles, arranged alphabetically, were written by prominent scholars in biology, medicine, nursing, psychology, psychiatry, sociology, and other fields.

Springer, D., & Brubaker, T. H. (1984). *Family caregivers and dependent elderly.* Beverly Hills, CA: Sage. A guide for caregivers of dependent older persons that translates findings of research into practical applications. The book includes examples and exercises to help families deal with everyday problems of caregiving.

17

CHAPTER

PERSONALITY AND SOCIAL DEVELOPMENT IN LATE ADULTHOOD

There is still today
And tomorrow fresh with dreams:
Life never grows old

Rita Duskin, "Haiku,"
Sound and Light, 1987

ASK YOURSELF

- What important psychological tasks of late adulthood have been identified by Erikson and Peck?

- What personality and lifestyle patterns contribute to successful aging?

- How can society help older people deal with issues such as financial need and housing?

- How do older people receive emotional support from their relationships with family and friends?

Dexter T., 83, looks adoringly at his 81-year-old wife. "I always thought sunsets were more spectacular than sunrises, anyway," he says. "Now we're having some beautiful times in the evening of our lives." After each had been widowed and had lived alone for some time, the two met at a dance for older adults. Now, after having been married for 2 years, Liz T. says, "This is the most well-rounded relationship I've ever had. Dexter and I are intellectual equals and we have a lot of laughs together. I feel we're fortunate that we've reached this point in life, and our story shows that it's never too late to find love and sex."

Love and sex are among the most important social and personality issues throughout life. Their importance continues in late adulthood, and they can go far to help people enjoy this time. The losses that Dexter and Liz suffered from widowhood are typical at this time of life. But so are the vigor and openness that enabled them to begin a new relationship with each other.

Late adulthood is the developmental stage during which people clarify and find use for what they have learned through the years (But-

ler & Lewis, 1982). Growth and adaptation can occur now, as in all other phases of life, if people are flexible and realistic—if they learn how to conserve their strength, how to adjust to change and loss, and how to use these years productively. At this time of life, certain feelings come to the fore. People have a new awareness of time, a desire to leave a legacy to their children (or to the world), and a wish to pass on the fruits of their experience, to validate their lives as having been meaningful.

People who feel well, who have opportunities to demonstrate competence, and who feel in control of their lives are likely to have a strong enough sense of self to cope with the problems and losses of these years—the death of loved ones, the loss of work roles, and the loss of bodily strength and sensory acuity. Successful aging *is* possible and many people *do* experience the last stage of life positively.

In this chapter, we look at two theories of psychological development in late adulthood and we examine some attempts to define *successful aging.* We discuss some social issues related to aging and the ways older people's lives are affected by where and how they live. Finally, we look at relationships older people have with

Many older people reexamine their lives and decide to use their remaining time for things they always wanted to do but somehow did not. Elderhostel is an educational program for older adults who want to expand their horizons. The men and women on this Elderhostel field trip are examining a tidal pool.

family and friends, which greatly influence the quality of these last years of life.

THEORY AND RESEARCH ON PERSONALITY DEVELOPMENT

If I had my life to live over again, I'd try to make more mistakes the next time. I would relax. I would limber up. I would be sillier than I have been this trip. I know of very few things I would take seriously. I would be crazier. I would be less hygienic. I would take more chances. I would take more trips. I would climb more mountains, swim more rivers, and watch more sunsets. I would burn more gasoline. I would eat more ice cream and fewer beans. I would have more actual problems and fewer imaginary ones. (Stair, undated)

Nadine Stair—a participant in the Colorado Outward Bound School, which encourages adults of all ages to examine their lives and their values in the context of an outdoor experience—wrote these lines at the age of 85. Late adulthood is the time when many people reexamine their lives, looking not only backward but forward, and decide how best to use the time that remains. Let's see what theory and research can tell us about this final phase of the search for self-knowledge.

Erik Erikson: Crisis 8—Integrity versus Despair

In his eighth and final crisis, *integrity versus despair,* Erikson sees older people as confronting the need to accept the way they have lived their lives in order to accept approaching death. They struggle to achieve a sense of integrity, of the coherence and wholeness of their lives, rather than give way to despair over their inability to relive their lives differently.

People who succeed in this final, integrative task—building on the outcomes of the seven previous crises—gain a sense of the order and meaning of their lives within the larger social order, past, present, and future. The "virtue" that develops during this stage is *wisdom,* an "informed and detached concern with life itself in the face of death itself" (Erikson, 1985, p. 61). Thus wisdom is an important psychological resource of late adulthood as well as an intellectual strength, as discussed in Chapter 16.

Wisdom, according to Erikson, includes acceptance of the life one has lived, without major regrets for what could have been or for what one should have done differently. It includes acceptance of one's parents as people who did the best they could and thus are worthy of love, even though they were not perfect. It implies

Older people, according to Robert Peck, need to find new interests and sources of self-esteem to take the place of their former work roles and to make up for physical losses. An elderly person like the painter shown here, who can focus on relationships and absorbing activities, can often overcome physical discomforts.

acceptance of one's death as the inevitable end to a life lived as well as one knew how to live it. It implies acceptance of the imperfections of oneself, one's parents, and one's life.

The person who does not achieve such acceptance is overwhelmed by despair, realizing that time is too short to try out alternative roads to integrity. While integrity must outweigh despair for the successful resolution of this crisis, some despair is inevitable, according to Erikson—a sense of mourning not only for the misfortunes and lost opportunities of one's own life but for the vulnerability and transience of the human condition.

Yet late life is also a time to play, to recapture a childlike quality, which is essential for creativity. Although the time for procreation is over, creation can still take place. Even as the body's functions weaken and sexual energy diminishes, says Erikson, people can enjoy "an enriched bodily and mental experience" (1985, p. 64).

Robert Peck: Three Crises of Late Adulthood

Peck (1955), in his expansion of Erikson's discussion of psychological development in late life, emphasized three major crises that older people must resolve for healthy psychological functioning. The successful resolution of these crises allows a person to move beyond the concern with work, physical well-being, and mere existence to a broader understanding of self and of life's purpose.

The three crises are:

1   *Broader self-definition versus preoccupation with work roles.* The issue in this crisis, which Peck calls ***ego differentiation versus work-role preoccupation,*** is the degree to which a person is defined by the work he or she does. Each person must ask: "Am I a worthwhile person only insofar as I can do a full-time job; or can I be worthwhile in other, different ways— as a performer of several other roles, and also because of the kind of person I am?" (Peck, 1955, cited in Neugarten, 1968, p. 90).

Especially upon retirement, people need to redefine their worth as human beings beyond their work roles. People who can find other personal attributes to be proud of are more likely to succeed in maintaining their vitality and sense of self. The woman whose major work was as a wife and parent faces this issue when her children leave home or her husband dies. Whether a career was centered on the marketplace or the home, people adjusting to loss of their work roles need to explore themselves and find other interests to take the place of those that formerly gave direction and structure to life. They need to recognize that their egos are richer and more diverse than the sum of their tasks at work.

2 *Transcendence of the body versus preoccupation with the body.* The physical decline that generally accompanies aging signals a second crisis: the need to overcome concerns about one's physical condition and to find other, compensating satisfactions. Peck calls this **body transcendence versus body preoccupation.** People who have emphasized physical well-being as the basis of a happy life may be plunged into despair by any diminution of their faculties or by aches and pains. Those who can instead focus on relationships with people and on absorbing activities that do not depend on perfect health can overcome physical discomfort.

An orientation away from preoccupation with the body should be developed by early adulthood, but it is critically tested in late life. One goal throughout life may well be the cultivation of mental and social powers that can increase with age, as well as those attributes—such as strength, beauty, muscular coordination, and other hallmarks of physical well-being—that are likely to diminish over the years.

3 *Transcendence of the ego versus preoccupation with the ego.* Probably the most difficult task older people confront is to transcend their concern with themselves and their lives here and now and to accept the certainty of their coming death. Peck describes this crisis as **ego transcendence versus ego preoccupation** and believes that successful adaptation to the prospect of death "may well be the most crucial achievement of the elder years" (Peck, 1955, cited in Neugarten, 1968, p. 91).

How can people feel positive about their own death? They can do so by recognizing that the way they have led their lives will allow them to achieve enduring significance—through the children they have raised, the contributions they have made to the culture, and the personal relationships they have forged. Essentially, they transcend the ego by contributing to the happiness or well-being of others, which, says Peck, "more than anything else, differentiates human living from animal living" (Peck, 1955, cited in Neugarten, 1968, p. 91).

Research on Changes in Personality

Although basic personality traits (such as extroversion, neuroticism, and openness to new experiences) are generally stable throughout life (see Box 15-1), research suggests that values and outlook do change in ways consistent with those Erikson proposed. In several studies by Carol Ryff and her associates (1982; Ryff & Baltes, 1976; Ryff & Heincke, 1983), men and women in various stages of adult life reported themselves to have been most concerned with intimacy in young adulthood, with generativity in middle adulthood, and with integrity in late adulthood, though they felt that other aspects of their personalities—such as impulsiveness, humility, and orderliness—had not changed. Between the middle and later years, women also noted a change from instrumental values (such as ambition, courage, and capability) to terminal values (such desirable end states of existence as a sense of accomplishment, freedom, and playfulness). Their focus changed, then, from doing to being. (Men did not show this kind of change; middle-aged men were already focused on the terminal values, possibly indicating that in these cohorts, men made this shift of values earlier in life.)

Although people tend to become more introspective from middle age onward, this tendency does not necessarily result in the self-transcendence that Peck describes. Indeed, many older people become more preoccupied with meeting their own needs. This may be a reaction to a lifetime of caring for and about other people; it may also reflect the fact that personal needs actually are greater in old age.

AGING

Aging Successfully

Is an older person who tranquilly watches the world go by from a rocking chair on the front porch making as healthy an adjustment to aging as one who is busy and involved from morning till night? There is more than one way to age successfully, and the patterns that people follow vary with their individual personalities and unique life circumstances.

Let's look at two theories that advance contrasting models for successful aging—disengagement theory and activity theory—and then examine research findings about how people actually age.

Disengagement Theory   Samuel G. used to be active in several political organizations, and even after retirement from his job as a civil engineer he kept busy for a while going to meetings, writing for newsletters, and getting together for a weekly card game with old friends. Then he dropped out of one group after another and, eventually, even from his Friday night poker game. He was pursuing the pattern of *disengagement,* long considered by some to be the "right" way to age (Cumming & Henry, 1961).

According to **disengagement theory,** aging is characterized by mutual withdrawal. The older person voluntarily cuts down activities and commitments, while society encourages segregation by age by pressuring people to retire, among other things. The theory maintains that this pattern is normal, as is the older person's increased preoccupation with the self and decreased emotional investment in others. The decline in social interaction helps older people to maintain their equilibrium and is beneficial both to the individual and to society. Since the older person welcomes this withdrawal and voluntarily contributes to it, morale is high.

The theory of disengagement has generated considerable research, much of which has failed to support its prediction that low morale would accompany high activity and its contention that disengagement is inevitable, universal, and sought by older people themselves (Maddox, 1968; Reichard, Livson, & Peterson, 1962).

Critics maintain that disengagement seems to

be related less to age than to factors *associated* with aging, such as poor health, widowhood, retirement, and impoverishment. Instead of being a predictable result of aging, it is influenced by the social environment. For example, when people work (and are, thus, economically engaged), they continue their work-related associations—involvement with trade unions, professional friendships, reading in the field, and the like. When they lose or give up their jobs, however, they tend to give up these activities.

Disengagement may be more common when people feel that they are close to death. One research team measured degrees of engagement among 80 older people and then more than 2 years later compared the engagement levels they had recorded for the people who had died in the meantime with those for the people who were still alive. The people who had died had shown signs of disengagement 2 years before their death; the survivors had not. These researchers concluded that disengagement does exist, but that it is a short-lived process, taking about 2 years rather than the 25 or 30 originally proposed (Lieberman & Coplan, 1970).

Those who feel that the facts about older people do not support the disengagement theory contend that it is rationalization by a culture that wants to put older people "on the shelf." By stating that older people *themselves* want to disengage, society justifies its lack of attention to their needs (Hochschild, 1975).

Activity Theory   After selling the business that neither of her children wanted to carry on, Charlotte L. turned her energy and attention to community projects. She started a local chapter of the Gray Panthers, an activist group promoting the interests of the elderly; she became the area chairwoman for coordinating sales of UNICEF cards; and she volunteered at her local public library. After her husband died, she met a man she had known 50 years before and resumed a relationship with him, taking several trips with him each year.

Charlotte L.'s life is representative of *activity theory,* which holds that the more active older people remain, the more successfully they age. In this model, unlike disengagement theory, the older person remains as much as possible like a middle-aged person, keeping up as many activities as possible and finding substitutes for those that have been lost through retirement or the death of spouse or friends. Advocates of this view hold that a person's roles (as worker, spouse, parent, and so on) are the major source of satisfaction in life, and that the greater the loss of roles through retirement, widowhood, distance from one's children, infirmity, or other causes, the lower the person's satisfaction with life will be.

According to some studies, it is not being active per se but *what* older people do that makes the difference. In interviews with 411 people, aged 52 to over 75, researchers found that activity in and of itself bore little relationship to satisfaction with life (Lemon, Bengtson, & Peterson, 1972). But a later study showed that the *kind* of activity does matter. Researchers asked more than 1000 older people from three different kinds of communities (public housing, a planned retirement village, and a community with a large proportion of retirees) about their activities and their satisfaction with life. The happiest were the ones most involved in *informal* activities—doing things with friends and family. *Solitary* activities, such as reading, watching television, and pursuing hobbies alone, had no effect one way or the other; and *formal* activity (structured group activities) actually had a negative effect (Longino & Kart, 1982).

It is possible that people who are dissatisfied with life seek out more formal activity. Another explanation is that group interactions arouse dissatisfaction by encouraging older people to compare their lives with those of their age-mates—and to find their own lives less satisfying.

Patterns of Aging The main problem with both activity theory and disengagement theory is their attempt to characterize successful aging as following a single pattern. Actually, according to a classic study, the way people adapt to aging depends on their personalities and the ways they have adapted to situations throughout life rather than on their levels of activity and involvement.

The Kansas City Studies of Adult Life analyzed styles of aging by looking at personality, activity level, and life satisfaction. Intensive interviews with 159 men and women aged 50 to

(© Dennis Brack/Black Star)

Maggie Kuhn, founder of the Gray Panthers, exemplifies successful aging as described by activity theory. In helping older people to become a powerful political force in the United States, she has developed her own leadership qualities and has continued to bring out new abilities in herself.

90 yielded four major personality types: the *integrated,* the *armor-defended,* the *passive-dependent,* and the *unintegrated.* Researchers correlated these types with varying levels of activity in 11 social roles (parent, spouse, grandparent, kin-group member, worker, homemaker, citizen, friend, neighbor, club or association member, and church member). They then rated the subjects according to their levels of life satisfaction. Analysis of the data for the 70-year-olds to 79-year-olds in the study yielded eight patterns of aging that fit 50 out of the 59 people in this age group (Neugarten, Havighurst, & Tobin, 1968).

The predominant pattern of successful aging was characterized by a fairly high level of activity—though this was not the only pattern. In general, as people aged, they tended to experience a "shrinkage in social life space" (Neugarten, 1973, p. 325). That is, they were less socially active and filled fewer roles.

Here are the four major personality types, subdivided into the eight patterns of aging:

1   *Integrated* (17 of the 59 people): These people were functioning well and had complex inner lives, competent egos, intact cognitive abilities, and high levels of life satisfaction. They fell into three life patterns:
    a   *Reorganizers* were highly active; they had reorganized their lives, substituting new interests for old, and they engaged in a wide variety of activities.
    b   *Focused* people showed medium levels of activity; they had become selective, devoting energy to and gaining satisfaction from one or two roles (like the retired man now preoccupied with his roles as homemaker, parent, and husband).
    c   *Disengaged* people showed low levels of activity; by personal preference, they had withdrawn into self-contained lives and were content.

2   *Armor-defended* (15 of the 59 people): These people were achievement-oriented, striving, and tightly controlled.
    a   People in a *holding-on* pattern retained the lifestyle of middle age as long as possible. They engaged in high or medium levels of activity and were high in life satisfaction.
    b   *Constricted* people tried hard to defend themselves against aging by limiting expenditure of energy, social interaction, and experience. They achieved high or medium life satisfaction while showing either low or medium activity.

3   *Passive-dependent* (11 of the 59 people): These people fell into one of two life patterns—succorance-seeking or apathetic.
    a   *Succorance-seeking* people needed to be dependent on others; as long as they could lean on one or two people, they could maintain high or medium life satisfaction. They engaged in high or medium levels of activity.
    b   *Apathetic* people seemed to have been passive all their lives; they did little, and they achieved medium or low life satisfaction.

4   *Unintegrated* (7 of the 59 people): These people showed a disorganized pattern of aging. They had gross defects in psychological functioning, poor control over their emotions, and deterioration in thought processes. They managed to stay in the community, but with low activity and low life satisfaction.

These varied patterns of aging (most of which can be termed successful, at least for the particular people who practiced them) show that people differ greatly in the way they live the later years of life. Older people (like young people) are influenced by such situational factors as health, work status, financial resources, and family status. Their personalities determine the way they react to these factors. They choose the kinds of activities that make them feel good about themselves—that fit in with their abilities or their values—and they have different capacities to cope with life's stresses.

Furthermore, people tend to react to life in much the same way they have reacted to it through the years. Research conducted by Bernice Neugarten and her associates indicates that people who cope well early in life cope well in later life, too—and the reverse (1968, 1973; Neugarten et al., 1968). As Neugarten writes, "Aging is not a leveler of individual differences except, perhaps, at the very end of life. In adapting to both biological and social changes, the aging person continues to draw upon that which he has been, as well as that which he is" (1973, p. 329).

Social Issues Related to Aging

The ability to cope with life's challenges may be sorely tested in late adulthood. On top of the physical problems that may accompany aging, the social circumstances in which many older people find themselves are extremely trying, or even overwhelming. Three common issues are financial hardship, living arrangements, and vulnerability to crime.

Income   Many older people are anxious about money. Some are living on fixed incomes; as prices rise, their dollars do not go as far as they did at the time of retirement. Social security is the largest single source of income for older people in the United States; 92 percent receive social security benefits, which in 1984 accounted for 35 percent of older people's income. Pensions accounted for 14 percent; assets, 26 percent; and earnings from work, 23 percent (American Association of Retired Persons, AARP, 1986; Commonwealth Fund, 1986).

Older people who live alone or with nonrelatives tend to be worse off financially than those who are members of family households. In 1985, single individuals had a median income of only $7568, compared with $19,162 for families (usually couples) headed by persons aged 65 or older (AARP, 1986).

Thanks to such government programs as social security and Medicare, fewer old people live in poverty today—1 out of 8 in 1985, compared with 1 out of 4 in 1959. In fact, the poverty rate for people aged 65 and up is slightly less than the rate for younger people. Still, there are about 3.5 million poor elderly people, and more than one-fifth of the older population are classified as poor or near-poor. Women, minorities (see Box 17-1, page 572), single people, and people who did unskilled or service jobs during their working years are likeliest to be poor (AARP, 1986; Commonwealth Fund, 1986).

Many older people are facing poverty for the first time in their lives. When they were younger, they were able to earn enough to meet their needs. Now, they cannot work, and inflation has eroded their savings and pensions. Many infirm or disabled people have outlived their savings at a time when their medical bills are soaring. Some of them receive help from such public assistance programs as Supplemental Security Income, subsidized housing, Medicaid, and food stamps. Others, however, either are not eligible or for some other reason are not taking part in these programs—often because they do not know about the programs or do not know how to apply for them.

Our society's medical progress enables people to live longer; we need to make economic progress to allow more older people to live decently. Butler (1975) recommends a universal pension system that would "incorporate under one umbrella all private and public pension plans, including Social Security." It would allow for rises in the cost of living; two-thirds would be fi-

nanced from general federal tax revenues and one-third from trust funds. Such a plan would ensure that older people would not have to face poverty along with the other problems of aging.

Living Arrangements   There is a stereotyped view of older people as residents of institutions. On the contrary, however, 95 percent live in the community. Of this group, about two-thirds live in families—most with spouses, the rest with children or other relatives. (The latter group tend to be in poor health; it is possible that they have moved in with their relatives because they cannot care for themselves.) The remaining one-third live alone or with people to whom they are not related; the odds of living alone increase with age (AARP, 1986; Commonwealth Fund, 1986; see Figure 17-1 for a comparison of men's and women's living arrangements).

Almost three-fourths of older people live in metropolitan areas, and more than half of these live in suburbs rather than central cities. Three-quarters of the homes in which older people live are their own, and the mortgages are usually paid up. Still, older people as a group spend a larger proportion of their income on housing than younger people do; and their homes tend to be older and slightly less adequate (AARP, 1986).

The more than 8 million older people who live alone—a 64 percent increase since 1970—

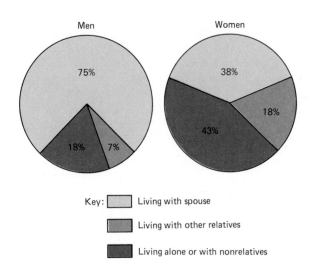

Figure 17-1   Living arrangements of people aged 65 and over, 1985. (*Source:* AARP, 1986; based on data from U.S. Bureau of the Census.)

BOX 17·1   WINDOW ON THE WORLD

AGING IN MINORITY CULTURES

In 1964, the National Urban League described the plight of the black aged as a state of "double jeopardy," in which they suffered from discrimination based on both age and race. More than 20 years later, that description is still all too true. Furthermore, it could be applied just as well to other subgroups in our population, such as Mexican-Americans, native Americans, and Puerto Ricans.

All the typical problems of aging are even more troublesome for older members of minority groups, who make up about 10 percent of the elderly population. First of all, they tend to be poorer. Families headed by older black people had a median income of only $11,937 in 1985, about 37 percent below the national median. Almost one-third of older black people and one-fourth of older Hispanic people were below the poverty line (AARP, 1986). Minority-group elderly people are more likely to become ill and less likely to get treatment. They tend to be less educated, to have histories of unemployment or underemployment, to live in poorer housing, and to have shorter life expectancies than white people in their age group. Their needs for social and medical services are greater, but they live in areas where services are least available.

A particular irony is that many minority-group workers do not benefit from the social security and Medicare benefits they have earned. Often, after having contributed to these funds during their working years, they die too soon to collect benefits. Furthermore, since many of the jobs held by minority-group workers are not covered by social security, elderly people in minority groups are more likely than other older persons to be on Old Age Assistance.

Older people among various ethnic groups in the United States, and especially those who were born in other countries, often do not take advantage of community and government services for which they are eligible. They may not know what services are available; they may be too proud to accept assistance because they regard it as a form of charity; they may be reluctant to travel outside their own neighborhood or may be without the means to do so; and they may feel uncomfortable dealing with people who do not understand their ways of doing things— with regard, for example, to diet, housing patterns, or family traditions. Agencies that serve older people, therefore, should be sensitive to these concerns and should reach out to elderly people in need when these people do not seek help themselves (Gelfand, 1982).

Some minority subcultures differ from the dominant culture in patterns of family life and standards of behavior.

Among Hispanic families, for example, older people have traditionally received a great deal of respect, and grandparents have played an important role in child rearing and have exerted considerable influence over family decisions. In recent years, with assimilation, this pattern has been breaking down, so that the relations between the generations are becoming more like those in the population as a whole. Still, there seems to be more of an extended-family pattern among Hispanic people than among other groups in the population, and the position of elderly people is still relatively high. Mexican-Americans, for example, have "strong helping networks with their children." But those who rely heavily on their children tend to have low levels of psychological well-being, possibly due to their dependency (Markides & Krause, 1986).

Black families also have extensive kinship networks, through which the generations help each other with financial aid, child care, advice, and other supports. This help usually supplements formal assistance from community and governmental agencies for the neediest family members (R.C. Gibson, 1986; Mindel, 1983).

Many minority-group elderly people, then, gain strength and resilience from their extended families and their friends.

are at special risk. Almost 8 out of 10 are women, 80 percent are widowed, and almost one-half either have no children or have none living near them. Those who live alone are older and poorer on the average than elderly people who live with someone else, and they are likely to be apartment renters rather than homeowners. They are also more likely to suffer from depression and fears about the future. Yet almost 9 out of 10 value their independence and *prefer* to be on their own (Commonwealth Fund, 1986).

LIVING INDEPENDENTLY Faye W.'s dream during the last years of her life, when she was in a nursing home, was to live in a room in a private home, so that she could regain the independence she missed. However, because she required an unusual level of care and it was not possible to find an appropriate house, she remained in the nursing home until her death.

Mrs. W.'s desire to live in the community is shared by most older people. Those living in the community report higher levels of well-being than those in institutions, even when health levels are about the same (Chappell & Penning, 1979). But living arrangements often become a major problem as people age. One of a couple may become too infirm to manage three flights of rickety steps. A neighborhood may deteriorate, and frail-looking older people may become prey to young thugs. Mental or physical disability may keep a person who lives alone from being able to manage.

A person in this situation sometimes goes to an institution, but in recent years creative social planning has enabled growing numbers of older people to make use of alternative living arrangements in the community.

Sometimes the provision of relatively minor supports, such as meals, transportation, and home health aides, can help an older person remain in his or her own home. Sometimes, however, a change needs to be made for those older people who do not need or want to have their lives totally managed for them but who have an impairment that makes it hard, if not impossible, to manage on their own. They usually want to be in the neighborhood where they have been living, to be as independent as possible, to have privacy, to feel safe, and to have

Residents of group retirement homes enjoy socializing with others their age and get help with shopping, cooking, and cleaning, while caring for their own personal needs and maintaining a sense of self-reliance. Such homes, usually run by social agencies, are among an array of alternatives available to elderly persons who do not need nursing care but who are unable to be completely self-sufficient.

some social contacts (E. M. Brody, 1978; Lawton, 1981). A number of different kinds of living arrangements, some traditional and some innovative, can help those people who fall between self-sufficiency and complete dependency (Hare & Haske, 1983–1984; Lawton, 1981). These include:

- *Retirement and life-care communities:* These are available only to people with considerable funds. They often offer independent living units, with services such as cleaning, laundry, and meals. As residents age, they may use more extensive services, including health care in a nursing facility.
- *Sharing a house:* In a number of communities, social agencies match people who need a place to live with people who have houses or apartments with extra rooms. Each person usually has a private room but shares living, eating, and cooking areas.
- *Group homes:* This kind of arrangement is almost always set up by a social agency, which may own or rent the house. The agency brings together the elderly residents—usually between 4 and 12—and often hires help to shop, cook, do heavy cleaning, drive residents, and offer professional counseling. Res-

idents care for their own personal needs and take some responsibility for day-to-day tasks.

- *Cooperatives and communes:* These group living arrangements, managed totally by the residents with no agency involvement, are very rare because they require more continuous commitment from their members than most old people can offer.
- *Accessory housing:* Independent units ("granny flats") are created so that an older person can live in a remodeled single-family home or in temporary quarters set up in the yard of a single-family home. These units provide privacy for both parties, cut travel time and expense for caregivers, and offer security as well as care for the elderly residents.

It is estimated that up to 40 percent of the people who go into nursing homes do not actually need nursing care but have no better alternative (Baldwin, cited in Hinds, 1985). There are good humane and economic reasons, therefore, to explore alternatives like the ones described here.

LIVING IN INSTITUTIONS Most older people do not want to live in an institution, and most families do not want to place their parents in one. The older person often feels that placement amounts to outright rejection by the children, and the children usually place their parents reluctantly, apologetically, and with great guilt. Sometimes, though, because of the older person's needs or the family's circumstances, such a placement seems to be the only solution.

Although only 5 percent of people over 65 years old are institutionalized at any one time, the proportion increases dramatically with age, rising to 23 percent for those 85 years old and over. The single most important factor keeping people *out* of institutions is being married (Health Care Finance Administration, 1981). Most of the 1.3 million residents of institutions are widows, less than half can get around by themselves, more than half are mentally impaired, and one-third are incontinent (AARP, 1986; Moss & Halamandaris, 1977; U.S. Bureau of the Census, 1983). As the population ages and wives' life expectancy continues to increase faster than husbands', the number of residents of institutions will probably grow even more.

Nursing homes vary in quality and in the type and level of care offered. One essential element is opportunity for residents to make decisions and exert some control over their daily lives.

That conclusion emerged from an experiment in which 91 residents of a highly rated nursing home were divided into two groups (Langer & Rodin, 1976). Forty-seven of the people were told that they were responsible for seeing that they got good care, for making decisions about how they spent their time, and for changing things they did not like. They were also asked to choose and care for a plant. The 44 people in the second group were told that the staff was responsible for caring for them and for making them happy. They were each handed a plant and were told that the nurses would water and care for it.

The results—according to questionnaires filled out by the residents before and 3 weeks after the experiment, and according to ratings by nurses who knew nothing of the experiment—were dramatic. Among the first group (those encouraged to take more responsibility), 93 percent became more active, more alert, and happier, and they became involved in many different kinds of activities. But among the group that had been encouraged to be passive, 71 percent became weaker and more disabled. These findings suggest that loss of control over one's life can lead to depression and even death.

Other essentials of a good nursing home are a professional staff who specialize in the care of the elderly, an adequate government insurance program, and a coordinated structure that can provide various levels of care as needed (Kayser-Jones, 1982). The ideal home should be lively, homelike, safe, hygienic, and attractive. It should offer stimulating activities and opportunities to socialize with people of both sexes and all ages. It should also provide enough privacy that residents who want to be sexually active will have the opportunity; and it should offer a full range of social, therapeutic, and rehabilitative services. The residents will be happier in such a place, and so will their visitors. (For suggestions on visiting someone in a nursing home, see Box 17-2.)

But many nursing homes are far from ideal. In 1987, one-third of the nation's nursing homes did not meet minimum standards

BOX 17-2 PRACTICALLY SPEAKING

VISITING SOMEONE IN A NURSING HOME

It is often difficult to visit someone in a nursing home. It is painful for family members to witness the deterioration of mental faculties that were once keen, to hear complaints that may have less to do with their apparent content than with the physical and emotional losses the older person has experienced, and to feel the depths of the depression from which the older person may be suffering. One survey of family visitors found that many of them enjoyed fewer than half of their visits, mostly for these reasons (York & Calsyn, 1977).

Visitors cannot change most of these realities, but they can do something about another major problem—the lack of anything to do on visits. It is possible to engage the nursing home resident in activities that can be stimulating and comforting even if he or she has suffered mental and sensory losses. The following suggestions can be adapted to the level of functioning of the resident (B.W. Davis, 1985; A. Ferber, personal communication, 1985):

■ *Call on the older person's strengths.* Ask him or her for advice in an area of expertise, such as cooking, fishing, or crafts.

■ *Provide the opportunity to make decisions.* Ask the resident where he or she wants to go if you are going out for lunch or for a drive; ask what he or she wants to

Visitors to residents of nursing homes can enliven their visits with stimulating activities that call on the older person's strengths, interests, and memories.

(© 1986 Blair Seitz/Photo Researchers)

wear; ask advice on a gift to buy for a family member.

■ *Be a good listener.* When the older person wants to talk, pay attention even if you have heard the stories before. Do not judge or argue. Listen to the feelings beneath the words. Hear complaints without feeling that you need to do anything about them. Sometimes just being a sympathetic listener who understands how the speaker feels is enough.

■ *Call on the older person's reserves of old memories.* A person who forgets what happened 5 minutes ago may have vivid memories of the distant past. You might ask the resident to sing old songs with you; to

tell you what his or her siblings were like; or to describe childhood celebrations, getting the first job, or meeting his or her spouse.

■ *Start a project together and talk about it as you work.* You could put together a scrapbook or a photo album, arrange flowers, make Christmas ornaments, do simple sewing or knitting, or do a jigsaw puzzle.

■ *Tape-record the older person.* You will be creating your own oral history to pass down to the older person's descendants. At the same time, the older person will probably appreciate the opportunity to review his or her life, to give some structure to it, and to think about some of its high points. Some of the questions you might ask could cover decisions and turning points in the person's life, achievements he or she is proud of, wisdom that can be passed along, and events that he or she experienced or witnessed.

■ *Stimulate the senses.* You can enhance the older person's experience of the world by wearing and talking about bright colors, bringing in beautifully illustrated books and calendars, and putting up seasonal decorations; by playing favorite musical selections; by wearing perfume or scented after-shave lotion and bringing some for the resident; by bringing favorite foods (that have been cleared with the nursing home staff); and, most important, by hugging, holding hands, and touching the older person in other comforting ways.

Your visits are important to a person who lives in a nursing home, away from the familiar places and people of earlier life. You will enjoy them more yourself by following these guidelines.

adopted into federal law late in that year. The legislation—an effort to upgrade institutional care, protect the rights of patients, and help ensure their social, psychological, physical, and mental well-being—provides for denial of Medicare and Medicaid payments to nursing homes found to be substandard in three consecutive annual inspections.

Crime Many older people do not go out after dark, do not carry any money, and do not use public transportation because of their fear of crime. This fear is a serious obstacle to mobility, affecting daily life and mental health. The fears of older people are based partly on their recognition of their frailty and diminished ability to protect themselves. The actual rates of victimization for the three most serious violent crimes—murder, rape, and assault—are quite low among older Americans, but 25 percent of older people still report that fear of crime is a serious problem of aging (National Institute on Aging, NIA, 1982).

The kinds of crime that most commonly affect older people are fraud, theft of checks from the mail, vandalism, purse snatching, and harassment by teenagers (NIA, 1982). Many older people are taken in by "con" artists who defraud them of their savings, sometimes leaving them virtually penniless; and many of the incidents of fraud go unreported because of the victim's fear or embarrassment.

PERSONAL RELATIONSHIPS

The importance of close relationships with family and friends continues in late adulthood. In a study of 800 people aged 45 to 89 who were living in the community (not in nursing homes or other institutions), almost all (96 percent) were very close to at least one family member and often more, and 85 percent had at least one close friend (Babchuk, 1978–1979). The number of such important relationships dwindled after age 70, probably as the result of age-mates' deaths and the hesitancy some older people felt about forming new bonds. Married people tended to have more close ties than single people, women more than men, and people in high-status occupations more than blue-collar or unskilled workers. By and large, though, it is clear that most older people are not isolated but lead lives that are enriched by the presence of people who care about them and to whom they feel close.

The family is still the primary source of emotional support, and the late-life family has several special characteristics (Brubaker, 1983). First of all, it is likely to be multigenerational. Most older people's families include at least three generations; many—with very old parents and very young great-grandchildren—span four or five generations. The presence of so many people brings a richness of experience, as well as special pressures. Second, the late-life family has a long history, which also has its positive and negative aspects. Long experience of coping with stresses can give older people confidence in dealing with whatever life sends their way. On the other hand, many older people are still resolving unfinished business of childhood or early adulthood. Finally, a number of life events are especially characteristic of older families (though they sometimes occur in middle adulthood): becoming a grandparent or great-grandparent, retiring from work, and coping with widowhood after a long marriage.

Let's look at the relationships that older people have with others of their own generation—spouses, siblings, and friends—and with their children and grandchildren. We'll also examine the lives of older adults who are divorced or widowed, have never married, or are childless.

Marriage

"One wonderful thing about being married now," said a 79-year-old woman, "is that Bill and I can have a 'show and tell' session every morning when we tell each other about our aches and pains and know that the other one really cares how we feel. Then we can go through the day without boring anyone else with them!"

The long-term marriage is a relatively novel phenomenon; most marriages, like most people, used to have a shorter life span. It was not uncommon for a man to lose one or more wives in childbirth, or for either a man or a woman to lose one or more mates to influenza. Today, fiftieth anniversaries are more common, though many marriages are still severed earlier by death or divorce. Because life expectancy and social expectations differ for men and women, 75 percent of older men are married and living with their spouses, compared with only 38 percent of older women (see Figure 17-1).

Marital Happiness Couples who are still together in their sixties are more likely than middle-aged couples (though not than young couples) to find their marriages satisfying, and many report that their marriages have gotten better over the years (Gilford, 1986). One likely reason is that, since divorce has been easier to

Many couples who are still together late in life, especially in the middle to late sixties, say that they are happier in marriage than they were in their younger years. The most rewarding aspects of marriage at this age include companionship and the ability to express feelings. Romance, fun, and sensuality have their place, too, as this couple in a hot tub demonstrate.

obtain in recent decades, spouses who are still together in late adulthood are those who have chosen to stay together. The decision to divorce usually comes in the early years of a marriage, and couples who stay together despite difficulties are often able to work out their differences and eventually arrive at mutually satisfying relationships.

Another possible explanation for the reports of greater marital satisfaction in late adulthood is that people of this age are more satisfied with life in general. Their satisfaction may stem from factors other than the marriage, such as work, the alleviation of the pressures of raising children, or more comfortable financial circumstances. Another possibility is that people may unconsciously feel that they have to justify having remained in a marriage for many years by saying that they are happy.

People aged 70 to 90 consider themselves less happily married than those aged 63 to 69; perhaps advancing age and physical ailments aggravate the strains on marriage. Also, women, who generally expect more warmth and intimacy from marriage than men do, tend to be less satisfied with their marriages (Gilford, 1986).

Strengths and Strains in Marriage The ability of married people to handle the ups and downs of late adulthood with comparative serenity may be a result of their mutual supportiveness, which in turn reflects three important advantages that marriage confers, particularly at this time of life: intimacy (both sexual and emotional), interdependence (sharing of tasks and resources), and a sense of belonging to each other (Atchley, 1985; Gilford, 1986).

By and large, the changes that occur with aging have a mellowing effect on marriage. As husband and wife shed the roles of breadwinner and child rearer, many couples become more interested in each other's personality than in each other's function, and enjoyment of each other's company becomes a prime element of the marriage (Zube, 1982).

According to one study, being in love is still the most important factor in success in marriage in late adulthood. Older spouses also value companionship and the opportunity to express their feelings openly, as well as respect and common interests. The most common problems arise from differences in values, interests, and philosophies (Stinnett, Carter, & Montgomery, 1972).

Some of these problems may be due to the personality changes that often occur in middle age, leading women and men to develop in opposite directions (Zube, 1982); and the success of marriage in late adulthood may depend on a couple's ability to adjust to these changes. As the husband becomes less involved with work and more interested in intimacy, the wife may be feeling a stronger desire for personal growth and self-expression. One woman, describing her husband's recent retirement and her insistence that he find some kind of work, said, "There was just a little bit too much togetherness. . . . I told him I'd married him for better or worse, but not for lunch" (Weenolsen, 1988, p. 114).

In one study, women who had not worked outside the home cited both pros and cons of their husbands' retirement. They missed their personal freedom, felt too many demands on

their time, and had more togetherness than they wanted. On the other hand, they felt needed in their new "job" and their morale was high (Keating & Cole, 1980).

Role adjustments may involve arguments over who does what household chores. Many wives in marriages lasting till late adulthood feel that they have gained power; this gain may reflect societal changes in women's roles and status, rather than changes due to age alone.

Ill health (usually the husband's) can be another source of strain and a severe test of a marriage's strength. Spouses (especially wives) who must care for disabled mates may suffer isolation, anger, and frustration and are often in poor health themselves (Gilford, 1986).

Never before have so many couples remained together long enough "to encounter the constellation of life-changing events that the last stages of the marital career now bring." Some marriages become overburdened by the stress caused by these changes; others "have built reserves of intimacy and belongingness on which to draw" (Gilford, 1986, p. 19).

Divorce

Divorce in late life is rare; if a couple are going to take this step, they usually do it much earlier. In the past 20 years there has been an increase in the number of divorced older people, but

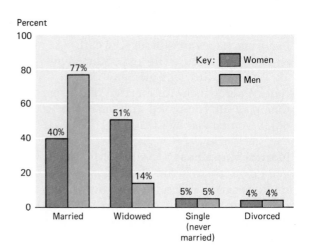

Figure 17-2 Marital status of persons aged 65 and over, 1985. (*Source:* AARP, 1986; based on data from U.S. Bureau of the Census.)

only 4 percent of elderly men and women are divorced and not remarried (AARP, 1986; see Figure 17-2). Given the high divorce rates for younger age groups in recent decades, however, the proportion is likely to rise in the future.

People aged 50 to 79 who divorce have more trouble adjusting to the change than people aged 20 to 49, and the older group tend to have less hope for the future (Chiriboga, 1982). Divorced and separated men and women express considerably less satisfaction with family life than do the married, widowed, or never-married. The men are less satisfied with friendships and activities not related to work than are men in the other categories, but this does not hold true for women. For both sexes, however, rates for mental illness and death are higher, perhaps because social support networks for older divorced people are inadequate (Uhlenberg & Myers, 1981).

Widowhood

"As long as you have your husband, you're not old," said a recently widowed 75-year-old woman. "But once he dies, old age sets in fast."

Widowhood is widespread in late adulthood, and it is a burden that women are far likelier to carry than men. Half of the women in the United States over the age of 65 are widowed, compared with only 1 out of every 7 men in this age group (AARP, 1986; see Figure 17-2). This is largely because women tend to live longer than men and usually marry men who are older. In fact, about half of all women become widows before they are 56 (Balkwell, 1981). There are more than 5 times as many older widows as older widowers, and so women are less likely than men to marry again; that is why most of the 8 million older people who live alone are women.

We discuss mourning in Chapter 18. Here, we look at what losing a spouse in late adulthood can mean for the day-to-day life of the survivor.

Adjusting to the Death of a Spouse   A man whose marriage of 56 years ended with the sudden death of his wife said, "One of the hardest things for me now is feeling that I'm not *important* to one other person. My children love me, but they have their own families and their own

(© Mimi Forsyth/Monkmeyer)

Family photographs and memories help fill the void created by death. A widow who had built her life around the care and companionship of her husband may have a difficult emotional adjustment to make. Women who are used to pursuing their own interests and who know how to manage the financial and practical details of their lives usually make the best adjustment to living alone.

lives to lead. I have good friends, but they're not the same either. Nobody can take Lil's place."

The widowed survivor of a long marriage faces a host of emotional and practical problems. If the marriage has been good, there is a great emotional void: the survivor has lost a lover, a confidant, a good friend, and a steady companion. Even in a bad marriage, the loss is felt. For one thing, the role of spouse no longer exists. This is especially hard for the person who has structured his or her life around the care and companionship of the spouse, but it also affects working people who now do not have a partner to come home to and retired people who no longer have anyone around to talk to or argue with.

Social life also changes. Friends and family usually rally to the mourner's side immediately after the death, but eventually they all return home and go about their own lives, leaving the survivor alone to carve out an entirely new life structure. Married friends sometimes become upset when bereaved people talk about their grief, because they cannot deal with the thought that this could happen to them, too. As a result, they may avoid the widowed when their friendship is most sorely needed.

Men and women generally adjust differently to widowhood and have different problems, though both often feel like a "fifth wheel" among couples they have been friendly with for years. Men are more likely to see other women and to remarry, whereas women usually become friendly with other widows but have a hard time meeting and forming relationships with men (Brecher, 1984; Lopata, 1977, 1979).

The widowed of both sexes have higher rates of mental illness, especially depression, than the married (Balkwell, 1981). Men are more likely to die within 6 months of a wife's death (Parkes, Benjamin, & Fitzgerald, 1969), and women are more likely to have disabling chronic conditions (Verbrugge, 1979).

One of the serious problems faced by both sexes is economic hardship. When the husband has been the main breadwinner, his widow is deprived of his income. The widowed man, on the other hand, has to buy many of the services his wife provided. When both spouses have been employed, the loss of one income is often a major blow (Lopata, 1977, 1979).

Like any life crisis, widowhood affects people differently, depending on their personalities and life circumstances. It always takes time for the pain of loss to heal (see Chapter 18), but people can prepare themselves better for widowhood (and for life in general) if they begin early to develop a strong sense of their own identity and a sturdy measure of self-sufficiency. A woman is less likely to be devastated by her husband's death if she is used to pursuing her own interests and knows how to manage the financial and practical details of her life. A man will cope better if he knows how to cook, do laundry, and make his own social plans.

Living as a Widow or Widower Those people who seem to make the best adjustment to widowhood are the ones who keep busy, develop new roles (taking on new paid or volunteer activities, for example), or become more deeply involved in activities in which they already take part. They see their friends quite a bit (which seems more helpful than frequent visits with their children) and take advantage of such community programs as widow support groups (Balkwell, 1981; C. J. Barrett, 1978; Vachon, Lyall, Rogers, Freedmen-Letofky, & Freeman, 1980).

Most widows, however, do not join formal organizations; they rely on their own informal support systems. According to a summary of research, the loneliest widows are those who have few or no children, who are in poor health, who lost their husbands suddenly or unexpectedly or at a relatively early age, who have been widowed for less than 6 years, or who have few friends or social activities (Lopata, Heinemann, & Baum, 1982).

Many studies have found older people to be better adjusted to widowhood than younger people, but often the investigators have not considered the length of time a person has been widowed. One study, which did so, found that being widowed early does *not* generally have a long-term effect on morale. Nor is it easier or harder to lose a husband or wife at an earlier or a later age—grief is grief, no matter when the loss occurs. Older widows and widowers interviewed did tend to have somewhat higher morale than younger ones, no matter how long they had been widowed—which led the investigator to suggest that the crucial factor might be the availability of companions, especially widowed peers, who do not make the widowed person feel inferior or different (Balkwell, 1985).

The *quality* of a widowed person's relationships may be more important than the frequency of social contacts. Different relationships serve different purposes; a widow is more likely to seek out her children when she is worried or depressed but will turn to her brothers or sisters for financial help (T. B. Anderson, 1984).

Remarriage

After Norah L.'s friend Alice B. died, Mrs. B.'s widowed husband moved out of town. Some years later, back in town on a visit to his son, he called on Norah L., now widowed herself, and took her to lunch. She recalls:

> We began to write, and he called me up. Before I knew it, we decided to get married. I guess I didn't think I ever would [get married]. I didn't think I wanted to. [But] as he came, I kind of missed him

when he didn't come, see? The more we saw of each other, the better we liked each other. It just worked into something. (Vinick, 1978, p. 361)

Norah L.'s story is unusual—but her new husband's is not. Elderly widowers are more likely to remarry than widows, and men (of any age) are more likely than women to remarry after a divorce. Remarriage rates among divorced older women, which drop sharply with age, have declined from 9 out of 1000 in 1975 to 6 out of 1000 in 1982 (Glick & Lin, 1986b). The higher rate of remarriage among men is probably due primarily to the greater availability of potential partners. Furthermore, older men seem to feel more need to remarry; women tend to be more able to take care of their own household needs, are sometimes reluctant to give up pension rights they have as widows, or fear having to care for a terminally ill husband, perhaps for the second time.

In an effort to find out more about "remarital" relationships, Vinick (1978) interviewed 24 older couples who had remarried when both partners were over 60 years of age. In many ways, the courtship and remarriage of Norah L. were typical of those in the study. Most of the remarried couples in this study had been widowed rather than divorced; most had known each other during their previous marriages or had been introduced by friends or relatives; and in most, the man had taken the initiative in beginning the relationship. Although most couples had not fallen in love at first sight, more than half of them had married less than a year after they had begun seeing each other as single people.

Why had these older people decided to marry again? Most sought companionship and relief from loneliness. Men were most likely to cite these reasons, while women were somewhat more likely to mention their feelings toward or the personal qualities of the men they had married. Most had the approval of their adult children, though some had received negative feedback from their friends, sometimes because the friends felt abandoned or envious.

Almost all of these people—who had been remarried for 2 to 6 years—were very happy in their marriages, except for a very small minority, most of whom felt that they had been forced into these marriages by circumstances beyond their control. The typical response was like this one:

> We're like a couple of kids. We fool around—have fun. We go to dances and socialize a lot with our families. We enjoy life together. When you're with someone, you're happy. (Vinick, 1978, p. 362)

The women's happiness tended to be tied to external factors—their friends' approval, enough money, and satisfactory housing. The men's satisfaction was related more to internal states—how they had felt about remarriage beforehand, how they had gotten along with their children, and their present state of mental and physical health. These marriages tended to be calmer than marriages earlier in life; the partners had a "live and let live" attitude. Much of the serenity seemed to stem from the absence of some of the strains found in early marriages, such as raising children, striving for career success, and getting along with in-laws.

In another study, of 100 couples who had married when the men were at least 65 years old and the women at least 60 years old and who had been married for at least 5 years, several clues to successful marriage emerged (McKain, 1972). Most of the spouses had known each other before either partner had been widowed, and the ones who had known each other well before marriage were happiest afterward. The happiest couples also had the approval of their friends and relatives, had enough money, did not live in a house either had occupied with the former spouse, and had adjusted well to the role changes brought by aging (such as retirement, departure of adult children, and the inability to drive).

In addition to enhancing the lives of the two people involved, remarriage in late adulthood can lighten a societal burden, since older people living alone are more likely at some point to need help from community agencies or to have to enter institutions. Thus it would be wise on pragmatic as well as humanitarian grounds to encourage remarriage (by letting people retain their pensions and social security benefits) or at least to foster shared living for older men and women, such as the group housing arrangements described earlier in this chapter.

(© Bill Pierce—Time/Sygma)

Sexual relationships can be a vital part of life in late adulthood; they are by no means only a memory or an occasional foray into pleasures of the past. People who were sexually active when younger usually continue to be sexually active in late life, if partners are available. Sexuality can be expressed in closeness, touching, affection, and intimacy as well as sexual intercourse.

Single Life: The "Never Marrieds"

Only 5 percent of older men and women have never married (AARP, 1986; see Figure 17-2). These people may constitute a "distinct type of social personality" that does not seem to need such an intimate relationship (Gubrium, 1975). When 22 never-married people, aged 60 to 94, were interviewed about their attitude toward getting old, they expressed less loneliness than the typical person of their age. They also seemed to be less affected by aging; they were more independent, had fewer social relationships, and were generally satisfied with their lives.

Sexual Relationships

Until very recently, most comments about sexuality in late life seemed to reflect either of two attitudes: "Aren't they cute?" or "Dirty old man (woman)." One of our most prevalent stereotypes has been that older people *are* sexless and *should be* sexless, and that those who are *not* are perverted. However, as researchers have gath-

ered information on sexual behavior of older adults, they have found that sexuality can be a vital force throughout life.

Human beings are sexual beings from birth until death. Their sexuality can be expressed in many ways other than genital contact—in touching, in closeness, in affection, in intimacy (Kay & Neelley, 1982). Even though illness or frailty may prevent older people from acting upon their sexual feelings, the feelings persist. Sex serves many purposes besides the purely physical. An active sexual relationship assures each partner of the other's love and affection and assures both of their own continuing vitality.

Although the physical part of sex represents a healthy aspect of adult functioning, it was not scientifically recognized as a normal element of the lives of older people until the 1960s, with the pioneering sexual research of William H. Masters and Virginia E. Johnson and the findings of the Duke University Longitudinal Study. More recent reports also show a rich panorama of sexual experience well into late adulthood (Brecher, 1984; B. D. Starr & Weiner, 1981).

After interviewing men and women over age 60, Masters and Johnson (1966, 1981) concluded that people who have had active sexual lives during their younger years are likely to continue to be sexually active in later life. The most important factor in the maintenance of effective sexuality is consistent sexual activity over the years. A healthy man who has been sexually active can usually continue some form of active sexual expression into his seventies or eighties. Women are physiologically able to be sexually active as long as they live. A major bar to a fulfilling sexual life for older women is the unavailability of interested partners.

Sex is, of course, somewhat different in late adulthood from what it is earlier in life. Older people do not feel as much sexual tension, are likely to have less frequent sexual relations, and experience some diminution in the intensity of the experience. Healthy older men have lower levels of testosterone (a male sex hormone) than normal, healthy men in their twenties (Bremner, Vitiello, & Prinz, 1983). An older man takes longer to develop an erection and longer to ejaculate. Some of the physiological signs accompanying arousal, such as sexual flush and increased muscle tone, are present but less intense. Sexual responses of older women are similarly affected. Breast engorgement, nipple erection, increased muscle tone, clitoral and labial engorgement, and other signs of sexual arousal are less intense than before; but older women are still able to reach orgasm, especially if they have been sexually active through the years.

Despite these changes, both men and women can enjoy their sexuality in late life. Sexual expression can be an even more significant part of the lives of older people if both young and old recognize that such expression is normal and healthy at this time of life: if older people accept their own sexuality without shame or embarrassment and if younger people avoid ridiculing or patronizing older persons who show evidence of healthy sexuality. Housing arrangements for older people can be designed to provide opportunities for men and women to socialize, with enough privacy that those who are interested in sexual relationships can pursue them. Medical and social workers can take older people's sexual needs into account when prescribing therapies (avoiding, when possible, drugs that interfere with sexual functioning) and can matter-of-factly discuss sexual activity—for example, with a heart patient who may be embarrassed to bring it up.

Relationships with Siblings

"When I die, don't you dare let my brother Pete come to my funeral," Leah W. told her daughter. "If he won't make up while I'm alive, I don't want him to do it after I'm dead." But a sister intervened as a peacemaker, and Mrs. W. and her brother reestablished the close ties they had known before the argument that had estranged them for years. They were a source of great comfort to each other in their last years of life.

Sibling relationships are the longest-lasting relationships in most people's lives (Cicirelli, 1980). Since more than 75 percent of people aged 65 and older have at least one sibling, brothers and sisters play important roles in the support networks of older people (Scott & Roberto, 1981).

The small body of research on elderly siblings suggests that in late adulthood siblings maintain

relationships of the kind they have had in middle age. Very often they become closer in early or middle adulthood, after establishing their own identities through career and family, than they were while growing up together. They often make special efforts to renew their ties after their children leave the nest, and although some rivalry may persist, it tends to be offset by emotional closeness and affection (Cicirelli, 1980; Ross, Dalton, & Milgram, 1980; Scott & Roberto, 1981).

Looking back over their lives, older people who feel close to their brothers or sisters express a sense of peace with life and with themselves, while those who are estranged from their siblings often feel upset, as if they have failed their family value systems. Siblings who have reestablished ties with each other generally feel that they have accomplished something important (Ross et al., 1980). Sisters are especially important in maintaining family relationships; they challenge and stimulate each other and are emotionally supportive to their brothers. Older men with sisters feel better about life and worry less about aging than men without sisters (Cicirelli, 1977).

Although older people feel closer to their children and their grandchildren than to their siblings and are more likely to get help from children than from siblings, they usually turn to siblings before they turn to anyone else. As more people choose to have only one or two children, or none at all, relationships with siblings during late life will probably become increasingly important as a source of emotional support and practical help (Cicirelli, 1980; Scott & Roberto, 1981).

Friendships

Most older people have close friends, and those who have active circles of friends are more satisfied with life (Babchuk, 1978–1979; Lemon et al., 1972). Older people choose their friends largely on the same bases as younger people. Friends are likely to live close by and to be of the same sex, same marital status, same race, and same socioeconomic status, and of about the same age. Middle-class people typically have more friends than working-class people, and they are more likely to distinguish between

BOX 17-3   FOOD FOR THOUGHT

PETS

An elderly person said, "Sadie doesn't care how we look or how old we are. She just wants to love us" (Schmall & Pratt, 1986, p. 44).

Sadie is not a daughter or a sister, but a pet; yet that fact makes her no less precious to her owners. Although pets—dogs, cats, birds, or goldfish—cannot take the place of human companions, they meet important emotional needs for people of all ages, and perhaps especially for older people who live alone (Schmall & Pratt, 1986):

■ *Pets build self-esteem.* They do not carp or criticize; they just make their owners feel wanted, as Sadie does.

■ *Pets provide intimacy.* Many people talk to and confide in their pets as if they were members of the family. In fact, at least 70 percent of pet owners think of them as just that (Carmack, 1985). Many older people "believe their pets are sensitive to their moods and feelings" (Schmall & Pratt, 1986, p. 44).

■ *Pets give affection*—the simple sort of affection that parents get from their young children and often miss when the children grow up (Beck & Katcher, 1983). A pet provides a warm body to hug and to hold on one's lap—an element missing from many older people's lives.

■ *Pets make older people feel needed.* Pets, like children, need care (Beck & Katcher, 1983). Being responsible for a pet may motivate an older person to take better care of himself or herself, too.

■ *Pets are relaxing.* Talking to and stroking a dog or cat can lower an older person's blood pressure (Katcher, 1984).

■ *Pets are icebreakers.* It is easier to start up a conversation with a stranger while walking a dog (Erickson, 1985).

In view of the important role that pets play in older people's lives, it should not surprise us that people often grieve over the loss of a pet

An animal may literally be a person's best friend. Pets meet important emotional needs for people of all ages, but perhaps especially for elderly people who live alone. This woman's dog provides a living thing to stroke, hug, take care of, and talk to.

much as they do over the loss of a relative. Bereaved pet owners need to talk about their feelings and to have those feelings taken seriously. When older people who have pets go into a hospital or nursing home, plans need to be made for care of the pet in order to relieve the owner's worry. If possible, some sort of continuing contact should be arranged.

---

friends and neighbors. Working-class people, on the other hand, tend to make friends with people who live in their neighborhood and to make little or no distinction between friends and neighbors (Babchuk, 1978–1979; Rosow, 1970).

People who are widowed or who retire earlier than most of their friends often find their social lives restricted (Blau, 1961). Widows and widowers tend to feel out of place among couples; and early retirees find that most of their friends are unavailable during the day. Retirees are also likely to feel left out when the conversation revolves around their friends' work. As their friends' statuses change, both widows and retired persons come back into the social swim. On the other hand, aging people often lose friends as a result of death or may be less able to spend time with them because of illness or incapacity

Older people often enjoy the time they spend with friends more than the time they spend with family members. The openness and excitement of relationships with friends help older men and women rise above worries and problems. Intimate friendships give older people a sense of being valued and wanted and help them deal with the changes and crises of aging.

(B. B. Brown, 1981). (See Box 17-3 for a discussion of older people's nonhuman friends—their pets.)

Friendship is different from other relationships because of the fact that people *choose* their friends. The element of choice may be especially important to older people, who often feel their control over their lives slipping away (R. G. Adams, 1986).

Although family members provide more reliable emotional support, older people report that they enjoy the time they spend with their friends more than the time they spend with their families. Researchers (Larson, Mannell, & Zuzanek, 1986) asked 92 retired adults (52 women and 40 men) between the ages of 55 and 88 to wear beepers for one week. The subjects were paged at approximate 2-hour intervals; at those times, they filled out reports on what they were doing and with whom, and what they were thinking and feeling.

When people were with their friends, they tended to report being more alert, excited, and emotionally aroused than when they were with family members, including spouses. (However, when married people were with *both* spouses and friends, their emotional state was more positive than when they were with friends alone or spouses alone.) The explanation, in part, appears to be that older people tend to engage in more active leisure pursuits with friends, whereas much of their time with family members is spent on routine household tasks or watching television. Older people have a sense of openness and reciprocity with their friends, and the lightheartedness and spontaneity of friendships enables them to rise above ordinary daily concerns.

Still, spending more time with friends apparently does not result in higher overall life satisfaction, whereas spending more time with a spouse does. It may be the very brevity and infrequency of the time spent with friends that gives it its special flavor. Friends are a powerful source of *immediate* enjoyment, while family provides a greater underlying sense of security and support.

Other studies emphasize different aspects of friendship: common interests, social involvement, and mutual help (R. G. Adams, 1986). Intimacy is especially important to older adults, who need to know that they are still valued and wanted despite physical and other losses. In this respect, friends and neighbors often take the place of family members who are far away. People who have close, stable relationships with friends in whom they can confide their deepest feelings and thoughts—with whom they can talk about their worries and pain—deal better with the changes and crises of aging (Genevay, 1986; Lowenthal & Haven, 1968). The support of friends significantly reduces the impact of stress on physical and mental health (Cutrona, Russell, & Rose, 1986).

Parenthood

In our society, the relationship between older people and their adult children is complex. Unfortunately, both for the old (who have reserves of experience and wisdom to draw on) and for the young (who have much to learn), people in our society rarely look to their elders for advice, especially when those elders are their parents. A spirit of independence, a feeling that one needs to learn from one's own mistakes, and the idea that older people's experiences lose their relevance have interfered with the age-old cycle in which the old taught and counseled the young.

Nor do people in our society fall naturally into the cycle of care, common in some traditional societies, in which older people can expect to be cared for in their children's homes just as the children once received their parents' care. As was pointed out in Chapter 15, when middle-aged children must care for aging parents, the children are often torn between love and resentment, between duty toward parents and obligations toward spouse and children, and between wanting to do the right thing and not wanting one's present style of life to change.

Still, most adult children and elderly parents do help each other in many ways. The two generations often remain close, seeing each other frequently. Most older people live near at least one of their children, and they tend to turn first to their children (especially their daughters) for assistance (see Chapter 15).

Childlessness

Many parents say that one of the advantages of having children is to be assured of care and companionship in their old age. As we have seen, however, having children is not complete assurance. The big difference in level of satisfaction and care in late adulthood comes not from the presence of children, but from the presence of a spouse. Married people are much less likely than single people to be institutionalized; the presence or absence of children does not seem to make much of a difference (Johnson & Catalano, 1981).

What is life like for the more than 5 million childless people who make up about 20 percent of the population over 65? Research has found little evidence of any important drawbacks to nonparenthood in late life. Older people without children are no lonelier, no more negative about their lives, and no more afraid of death than those with children. Most older adults' morale depends more on how often they see their friends than on how often they see their children (Glenn & McLanahan, 1981; Johnson & Catalano, 1981; Keith, 1983; Rempel, 1985).

Parents do turn to their children for help, however. What do nonparents do? Even though people without children see a larger circle of friends and neighbors than do parents, they do not go to these people when they are sick. Ultimately, "blood is blood": they usually go to their brothers or sisters, or if none are alive or able to help, to *their* children—the nieces and nephews—or to more distant relatives (Johnson & Catalano, 1981). These more distant relatives are not as committed as children and siblings, but they do step in to coordinate services for their older relatives, often out of respect for their own parents.

Grandparenthood

Today's grandparents are more likely to be designing rocking chairs than sitting in them, to be marketing cookies than baking them, and to be wearing jogging suits than wearing aprons. This is partly because people usually become grandparents for the first time in middle age, at an average age of 50 for women and 52 for men (Troll, 1983). It is also because the role of grandparent is usually secondary to other roles in an older person's life, despite a societal tendency to identify grandparenting status even when it is totally irrelevant—as in "Two grandmothers . . . spent more than four days in jail for refusing to tell . . . where another woman had hidden her money" ("Two women," 1984).

One child psychiatrist claims that today's grandparents "have turned their backs on an entire generation" (Kornhaber, 1985, p. 159)—that they feel that they put in their time raising their own children and are now entitled to enjoy themselves rather than get involved with their grandchildren. Other researchers respond that the facts do not bear out that indictment.

Grandparenting *is* important to the 75 per-

This woman helping her grandson fix his bicycle typifies today's active grandparent. The grandparent-grandchild tie can bring a special element of fun, warmth, and caring, without the strain of child-rearing responsibilities. Grandparents are important sources of wisdom and symbols of continuity of family life.

cent of people over 65 who have grandchildren, as well as to their children and the grandchildren themselves. It must be, since 75 percent of the grandparents see their grandchildren at least once a week, which means that one generation or the other is making the effort to visit (Troll, 1983).

A major study (consisting of interviews, group discussions, and case studies of a three-generational, nationally representative sample) found that "grandparents play a limited but important role in family dynamics" and that grandparents have strong emotional ties to their grandchildren (Cherlin & Furstenberg, 1986a, p. 26). In fact, the grandparents in the study—whose average age was 66—reported that they were closer to their grandchildren than they had been to their own grandparents.

In most cases, the bond is expressed not through direct intervention in the raising of the children (which both parents and grandparents usually see as undesirable because both value their independence) but through casual, frequent contact and companionship—even when the grandparents and the parents do not get along. When grandparents and grandchildren do *not* see each other often, it is usually because they live too far apart.

The tacit "norm of noninterference" (p. 27) evaporates in times of trouble, when grandpar-

ents become a ready resource. Lillian E. Troll, who has done extensive studies of families in later life, maintains that grandparents perform the role of family "watchdogs" (1980, 1983). They stay on the fringes of the lives of their children and grandchildren, with varying degrees of involvement, but rarely play strong roles in the lives of the younger generation—unless they *need* to. At times of crisis, such as after a divorce or during illness or money troubles, they step in and become more active with their grandchildren. In good times, while it may seem that they are not closely involved, they are still watching to be sure that things are going well. Black grandparents, though, are more likely to act like parents even when there is no crisis (Cherlin & Furstenberg, 1986a; see Box 17-1).

Gender differences exist in grandparenting. Grandmothers tend to have closer, warmer relationships and to serve more often as surrogate parents than grandfathers do. The mother's parents are likely to be closer to the grandchildren than the father's parents, and the mother's mother is usually named by children as the favorite grandparent. The maternal grandparents are more likely to become involved during a crisis (Cherlin & Furstenberg, 1986a; Hagestad, 1978, 1982; Kahana & Kahana, 1970).

Crisis or no, grandparents are important to their grandchildren. They are sources of wisdom, companions in play, connectors to the past, and symbols of the continuity of family life. Grandparenting may be seen as the ulti- mate generative function: an expression of the human longing to transcend mortality by invest- ing oneself in the lives of future generations.

SUMMARY

Theory and Research on Personality Development

■ The eighth and final crisis of Erikson's theory of psychosocial development is integrity versus despair. Older people need to accept their lives and impending death; if they fail, they become overwhelmed with the realization that time is too short to begin another life and therefore are unable to accept death.

■ Peck specified three pairs of psychological alter- natives critical to successful old age: ego differ- entiation versus work-role preoccupation, body transcendence versus body preoccupation, and ego transcendence versus ego preoccupation.

While some aspects of personality appear to remain stable in late adulthood, there are shifts in other areas.

Aging

■ Two theories of successful aging are disengage- ment theory and activity theory.

1 Disengagement theory holds that normal aging is characterized by mutual withdrawal between society and the older person.

2 Activity theory maintains that the more active elderly people remain, the more successfully they age.

■ Research points to a variety of patterns of suc- cessful (and unsuccessful) aging, including inte- grated, armor-defended, passive-dependent, and unintegrated patterns.

■ Older people tend to have lower incomes than younger adults. Although the financial situation for older people has improved, some 3.5 million of them live in poverty. Many become poor for the first time after retirement.

■ Most older people live with members of their families. Of the 95 percent who are not institu- tionalized, one-third live alone, and most of these prefer to be on their own.

■ Developing housing alternatives to institution- alization is a major challenge. Possibilities in- clude retirement and life-care communities, sharing a house, group homes, cooperatives and communes, and accessory housing.

■ Only 5 percent of people over 65 years old are institutionalized at any one time. Most likely to be institutionalized are very old, frail women.

■ Many older people fear crime. The most frequent crimes with elderly victims are fraud, theft of checks from the mail, vandalism, purse snatch- ing, and harassment by teenagers.

Personal Relationships

■ Relationships are very important for older peo- ple, as they are for people of all ages.

■ As life expectancy increases, so does the poten- tial longevity of marriage. Marriages that last into late adulthood (especially the early part of that period) tend to be relatively satisfying; but strains that arise from personality and role changes may require adjustment by both part- ners.

■ Divorce is relatively uncommon among older people.

■ Remarriage in late adulthood tends to be a posi- tive experience.

■ People who reach late life without marrying seem to be of a more independent sort and tend to be less lonely than the typical person of their age.

■ People are sexual beings throughout life. Many older people are sexually active, though the degree of sexual tension and the frequency and intensity of sexual experience are generally lower than for younger adults.

■ Often relationships between siblings become closer in later life than they were in earlier adulthood. Sisters in particular make the effort to maintain these ties.

■ Friendships are important for immediate enjoy- ment, for intimacy, and for support in meeting the problems of aging.

- Although elderly parents and their adult children do not typically live together, they frequently see or contact each other and offer each other assistance.

- The presence or absence of children is not associated with important psychological or material rewards in old age.

- Grandparents have close ties with their grandchildren and see them frequently unless they live too far away. Generally, grandparents today do not interfere with the way their grandchildren are raised but take a more active role in time of crisis.

KEY TERMS

activity theory (page 568)
armor-defended (569)
body transcendence versus body preoccupation (567)
disengagement theory (568)

ego differentiation versus work-role preoccupation (566)
ego transcendence versus ego preoccupation (567)
integrated (569)

integrity versus despair (565)
passive-dependent (569)
unintegrated (569)

SUGGESTED READINGS

Averyt, A. C. (1987). *Successful aging: A sourcebook for older people and their families.* New York: Ballantine. A concise handbook that covers planning for retirement, preparing for widowhood or divorce, finances, independent living, keeping active and healthy, community resources, and much more, while dispelling myths about aging.

Brecher, E. M., & the Editors of Consumer Reports Books. (1984). *Love, sex, and aging.* Boston: Little, Brown. A comprehensive study of sexual attitudes and behaviors of Americans over 50, with many lively quotations. The findings and anecdotes reported demolish the stereotypes of a sexually inactive later life.

Cherlin, A. J., & Furstenberg, F. F., Jr. (1986b). *The new American grandparent: A place in the family, a life apart.* New York: Basic Books. A rich, often eloquent, and sometimes troubling portrait of grandparenthood in the United States today by two prominent sociologists, based on the first representative nationwide study of grandparents. The book contains many quotations and anecdotes.

Doress, P. B., & Siegal, D. L. (Eds.). (1987). *Ourselves, growing older: Women aging with knowledge and power.* New York: Simon & Schuster. A collaborative effort sponsored by the Boston Women's Health Book Collective that gives women the knowledge they need to take control of their physical and emotional health in middle and late adulthood. The book, addressed to all women regardless of income, ethnic background, or sexual preference, emphasizes the positive side of aging. It is a no-nonsense compendium of frank information on such topics as diet, exercise, body image, relationships, sexuality, illnesses, problems in the medical care system, housing alternatives, and finances.

Seligman, M. (1975). *Helplessness.* San Francisco: Freeman. A fascinating account of Seligman's theory that anxiety and depression arise from learned helplessness, that is, loss of control, a situation that characterizes many elderly in the United States today. Seligman makes the case that allowing people some control in their lives guards against helplessness.

9

PART

THE END OF LIFE

Human beings are individuals. They enjoy distinctive life experiences and enjoy them in different ways. One experience that everyone undergoes is the ending of life. The better people can understand and approach this inevitable event, the more fully they can live.

■ In **Chapter 18,** the final chapter in this book, we examine some important issues relating to death: how people in different stages of life think about it and feel about it, how people face their own impending death, how they deal with the death of those they love, and what can be done to make their adjustment easier. We also look at the "right to die" and what this means with relation to "mercy" killing and suicide. We see that death is an integral element of the life span and that understanding the end of life helps us understand the whole of life.

18

CHAPTER

DEATH AND BEREAVEMENT

> . . . The key to the question of death unlocks the door of life.
>
> Elisabeth Kübler-Ross,
> *Death: The Final Stage of Growth*, 1975

■ How do attitudes toward death, dying, and bereavement change across the life span?

■ What psychological changes often accompany the last period of life?

■ How do people face their own death and the death of their loved ones?

■ What can be done to help people cope with death, dying, and bereavement?

■ Are there circumstances in which the intentional ending of a life may be justified?

■ Why is suicide increasing, particularly among teenagers, and what can be done to prevent it?

■ How can people find meaning and purpose in death as a normal part of human development?

Death was once very much a part of daily life. People expected some of their children (or their sisters and brothers) to die in infancy or childhood. They saw family and friends succumb to an array of fatal illnesses at an early age. Before modern times, some 50 people out of every 1000 died in a typical year; and during periods of plague or natural disaster, death rates reached 40 percent. More than one-third of all babies died in infancy, and half of all children died before their tenth birthday (Lofland, 1986).

Since about the turn of the twentieth century, advances in medicine and sanitation have brought a "mortality revolution" in modern, developed countries (Lofland, 1986, p. 60). Death rates are typically below 9 percent; infant mortality has fallen to about 1 percent in the United States and even lower in much of Europe (Lofland, 1986).

The result is that life expectancy has greatly increased (see Chapter 17): children are more likely to reach adulthood, adults are more likely to reach old age, and older people are able to overcome illnesses that were once almost sure to be fatal. Death, then, has become largely a phenomenon of late adulthood. People in the early part of life rarely have to face the immediacy of death, as their forebears did; when people reach the time of life when death becomes a more constant presence, they are likely to be ill prepared (Lofland, 1986).

As death has become something that happens mostly to the old and infirm, it has assumed a peripheral place in younger people's consciousness. People in the last stages of life may live in separate retirement communities or nursing homes. Care of the dying and the dead, once a familiar aspect of family life, has become the province of professionals. People go to hospitals to die, and undertakers prepare their bodies for burial. People rarely even speak directly of death; instead, they use euphemisms like *passing away, passing on,* and *going to meet one's maker.* Young and even middle-aged people seldom meet death face to face, and people may go through a large part of their lives without giving a great deal of thought to their own death.

But while direct encounters with death are less frequent these days, death is a constant presence in the media. The tendency in the American popular culture to deny the personal reality of death is coupled with a "pornographic" obsession with fantasies of violent death, as seen in horror movies and violent television shows. Deaths in battle, in fires, and in other disasters become "impersonal statistics" on the evening news, "removed from the realm of feeling" (Feifel, 1977, p. 5); only a frightening event like an airplane crash, a suicide wave among teenagers, or an epidemic such as the spread of AIDS brings death to the forefront of public awareness.

Recently, a healthier attitude toward death seems to have been emerging. People are beginning to seek to understand death; to explore the emotional, moral, and practical issues surrounding it; and to try to make this inevitable outcome of every person's life as positive as possible. *Thanatology*, the study of death and dying, is arousing a great deal of interest as people recognize the importance of integrating death into life.

The terminal stage of life is a significant and valuable portion of the life course. If people live long enough, they are all bound to have to deal with the deaths of persons who are close to them. Furthermore, the awareness that they themselves must die one day can impart a special appreciation of life's pleasures and can make them think about the values they live by.

People can prepare themselves for the last stage of life by observing others who are close to death, by seeing how death is treated in literature and the arts, and by studying death and talking about it. By considering death in this way, people can enhance life. They can live in the knowledge that each day may be their last, giving them a final chance to express their best qualities and to savor the sweetness of life.

All deaths are different, just as all lives are different. The experience of dying is not the same for an accident victim, a person with terminal cancer, a suicide, and a person who dies instantaneously of a heart attack; nor is the experience of bereavement the same for their survivors. Yet all people are human; and just as there are commonalities in their lives, there are commonalities in death.

In this chapter we look at the biological, social, and psychological aspects of death (the state) and dying (the process). We examine the ways in which people in different phases of life think about death. We explore efforts to ease the process of dying and the pain of bereavement through education about death, hospices for the terminally ill, and support organizations for the dying and their families. We see the various forms grief can take, and we consider ways to help survivors handle their bereavement. We also look at such controversial issues as the use of heroic measures to prolong life, euthanasia ("mercy" killing), and suicide, and especially at recent increases in suicide among adolescents. Finally, we look at how people can accept death by finding purpose in life.

THREE ASPECTS OF DEATH

There are at least three aspects of dying: the *biological,* the *social,* and the *psychological,* all of which have become increasingly controversial.

The legal definition of *biological* death varies from state to state, but in general, biological death is considered the cessation of bodily processes. A person may be pronounced dead when the heart stops beating for a significant period of time or when electrical activity in the brain ceases. The criteria for death have assumed more complex dimensions with the development of medical apparatus that can prolong the basic signs of life indefinitely. People in a deep coma can be kept alive for years, even though they may have suffered irreversible brain damage and may never regain consciousness. Later in this chapter we will discuss the issue of whether or when such life supports may be withheld or removed.

The *social* aspects of death revolve around funeral and mourning rituals and the legal arrangements for redistribution of power and wealth. A major problem in present-day American society is a lack of widely accepted conventions of behavior for people who know that they are dying, for those around them, and for the survivors after the death of a loved one. Several conventions which do exist and which are rarely helpful for either dying people or those close to them are to isolate the dying in a hospital or nursing home, to refuse to discuss their condition with them, to separate from them before death by visiting less often, and thus to leave them alone to cope with imminent death.

The *psychological* aspects of death involve the way people feel both about their own death as it draws near and about the death of those close to them. Most people today have a great deal of trouble coming to terms with the meaning of death. We need a more positive acceptance of the reality of death as a natural and expected phase of life.

FACING DEATH

Attitudes toward Death and Dying across the Life Span

One topic of interest to thanatologists and developmentalists alike is the way people of different ages think and feel about death, and how they are influenced by their cognitive, emotional, and experiential development.

Childhood A girl in the first grade, grieving for a classmate who had died after a violent beating, said, "I'll make a picture of Lisa and put it on her coffin and she'll sit up and become alive again" (Neuffer, 1987). This little girl, like most young children, thought that death was a temporary state. It is usually not until sometime between the ages of 5 and 7 that children come to understand that death is *irreversible*—that a dead person, animal, or flower cannot come to life again.

At about the same age, children realize two other important concepts about death: first, it is *universal* (all living things inevitably die); second, a dead person is *nonfunctional* (all life functions end at death). Before then, children may believe that certain groups of people (such as teachers, parents, and children) do not die, that a person who is smart enough or lucky enough can avoid death, and that they themselves will be able to live forever. They may also believe that a dead person can still think and feel, even though the person clearly cannot eat or speak.

These observations about children's views of death emerge from a review of 40 studies that have been done since the 1930s, most of them based on interviews with children (Speece & Brent, 1984). Because all three concepts—irreversibility, universality, and the cessation of functions—usually develop at the time when, according to Piaget, children move from preoperational to concrete operational thinking (see

Most young children believe that death is temporary and that a dead animal, person, or flower will come back to life. The discovery of a dead bird offers a natural opportunity to help children develop a more realistic understanding of death.

Chapter 8), it seems likely that this cognitive achievement lays the groundwork for a mature understanding of death.

Children who are still caught up in egocentric thinking usually cannot understand death, because it is beyond their personal experience. But preschool-age children who are terminally ill often *do* realize the imminence of their own death. Cultural experience, too, influences attitudes toward death. Children from poor families are more likely to associate death with violence, while middle-class children connect it with disease and old age (Bluebond-Langner, 1977).

Children can be helped to understand death if they are introduced to the concept at an early age in the context of their own experience and given opportunities to talk about the issues surrounding it. The death of a pet or of flowers may provide a natural opportunity. (Later in this chapter we'll discuss other ways to teach children about death.)

Adolescence Adolescents tend to have highly "romantic" ideas about death: "adolescents make brave soldiers because they do not fear annihilation" so much as they are concerned about being "brave and glorious" (Pattison, 1977, p. 23). In their drive to discover and live out their identities, they are concerned not with how long they will live but with *how* they will live. Perhaps this partially explains the appeal of suicide in adolescence.

Furthermore, many adolescents are still thinking in egocentric ways and are in the grip of the *personal fable* (which was described earlier, in Chapter 10). They feel that they can take virtually any kind of risk without danger. They hitchhike, they drive recklessly, and they experiment with potent drugs—very often with tragic results.

When adolescents are terminally ill, they face death "in the contradictory and perplexing ways adolescents seem to face life" (Feifel, 1977, p. 177). The mysticism and intense interest in religion that are common in adolescence often become heightened. At the same time, mortally ill young people may deny their real condition and talk as if they are going to recover when, in fact, they know that they are not. Denial, and the accompanying repression of emotions, is a

(© Mary Ellen Mark/Archive)

These adolescents at a camp for cancer patients must face their own mortality, a subject to which many young people give little thought. Terminally ill adolescents handle the approach of death in varying ways that reflect their personalities. Some become angry, some turn to mysticism, and some deny the situation.

useful device that helps many sick young people deal with this crushing blow to their expectations for life. Ill teenagers are far more likely to be angry than depressed. They think about suicide much less than adults in similar circumstances and are much more likely to cast about looking for someone to blame. Their anger at the unfairness of their fate often erupts toward their parents, their doctors, their friends, or the world in general.

Of course, there is no one way in which dying adolescents act; the way they handle the imminence of death reflects their individual personalities.

Young Adulthood Most young adults—having finished their education, training, and courtship and having recently embarked on careers, marriage, or parenthood—are eager to live the lives they have been preparing for. When young adults are suddenly taken ill or badly injured, they are likely to feel more intensely emotional about imminent death than people in any other period of life (Pattison, 1977). They feel extremely frustrated at the inability to fulfill their dreams. They have worked terribly hard—for nothing. Their frustration turns to rage, and that rage often makes young adults difficult hospital patients.

They are troublesome patients for another reason as well—the fact that the hospital staff members responsible for their care are usually young adults themselves, who find it difficult dealing with the thought of death for a person around their own age. Much of adults' thought about death is evasive: people do not like to think about the possibility of their own death (Kastenbaum, 1977).

Middle Adulthood

Once, when Saul Alinsky, a community organizer in Chicago, was asked what had made him decide to devote his life to organizing working-class people, he recalled a time when he had been gravely ill:

> I realized then that I was going to die. I had always known that in some abstract sense, of course, but for the first time I really *knew* it deep inside me. And I made up my mind that before I died I would do something that really made a difference in the world. (S. A. Alinsky, personal communication, 1966)

It is in middle age that most people really *know* deep inside themselves that they are indeed going to die. With the death of their parents, they are now the oldest generation. As they read the obituary pages—which they are likely to do more regularly at this age than they used to—they find more and more familiar names. Their bodies send them signals that they are not so young, agile, and hearty as they once were.

With this inner knowledge, the way middle-aged people perceive time undergoes a change. Previously, they have thought of their lives in terms of the number of years they have lived since birth, but now they think of the number of years left to them until death and how to make the most of those years (Neugarten, 1967; see Chapter 15).

The realization that death is certain is often an impetus for making a major life change. People take stock of their careers, their marriages, their relationships with their children, their friendships, their values, and the ways they spend their time.

Late Adulthood

The 79-year-old woman looked very small and frail in the middle of the hospital bed. "Don't feel sorry for me when I'm gone," she told her daughter. "I'm not afraid of death—I'm only afraid of living like this."

This woman—lonely since the death of her husband and her closest friends, sick and unable to pursue the activities she had enjoyed, and concerned about becoming a burden on her children—was ready to embrace death.

In general, older people are less anxious about death than middle-aged people (Bengtson, Cuellar, & Ragan, 1975). Through the years, as people lose friends and relatives, they gradually reorganize their thoughts and feelings to accept their own mortality. Their physical problems and some of the other troubles of old age may diminish their pleasure in living. Those who feel that their lives have been meaningful are usually more able to accept the prospect of death than those who are still wondering about the point of having lived at all.

Some, though—like the 82-year-old woman who wrote the following lines within a few days before her second, and fatal, heart attack—have complex feelings:

> . . . I refuse to believe I am a piece of dust scuttering through uncaring space. I believe I count—that I have work to do—that there is need of me. I have a place. I want to live. The moment is Now—Now is my forever. I am still somebody—somebody on whom nothing is lost. With my last breath, I sing a psalm. (R. Duskin, personal communication, February 1986)

Thus acknowledgment of death may be mixed with affirmation of the preciousness of the life that is slipping away.

Confronting One's Own Death

How do people face the approach of their own death? By what processes do they accept the fact that their lives will end soon? What kinds of psychological changes do they undergo when death is imminent? Professionals have closely observed persons close to death and have evolved theories to explain some of the psychological changes that occur as death approaches.

Psychological Changes Preceding Death

Psychological changes often begin to take place even before physiological signs indicate that a person is dying. In Chapter 16 we noted a terminal drop in intellectual functioning often experienced shortly before death. Personality changes, too, may show up during the terminal period.

In one study, 80 people aged 65 to 91 were studied during a 3-year period and were given a battery of psychological tests. Afterward, the researchers compared the scores of those subjects who had died within a year after the last testing session with the scores of those who had lived an average of 3 years beyond that session (Lieberman & Coplan, 1970).

The subjects who died within the year had lower scores on cognitive tests. They were also less introspective, less aggressive, and more docile. Those who were dealing with some sort of crisis and were close to death were more afraid of and more preoccupied with death than were people who were beset by similar crises but were not close to death. (Persons who were close to death but whose lives were relatively stable at the time showed neither special fear of nor preoccupation with death.) These observations suggest a psychosomatic relationship, in which physiological changes in the body trigger psychological changes. The changes, though, are not simply effects of disease, since people who recovered from acute illnesses did not show the same pattern of personality decline as people who later died from the same kinds of illnesses.

The people in this study talked quite freely about death. Many of them had worked out its meaning to them and had integrated it into their outlook on life. (At the end of this chapter, we'll discuss the life review, a technique for consciously finding meaning and purpose in life.)

Elisabeth Kübler-Ross: Stages of Dying

Elisabeth Kübler-Ross, a psychiatrist who works with dying people, is widely credited with hav-

Elisabeth Kübler-Ross has been a pioneer in arousing popular and medical interest in death and dying. A psychiatrist who works with dying patients, she encourages them to talk about themselves and their feelings about impending death. On the basis of these discussions, she has theorized that there are five stages in coming to terms with death.

ing sparked the current interest in the psychology of death and dying. She has found that most patients welcome an opportunity to speak openly about their condition, and that most are aware of their closeness to death even when they have not been told about it.

After speaking with some 500 terminally ill patients, Kübler-Ross (1969) proposed that there are five stages in coming to terms with death: (1) denial (refusal to accept the reality of what is happening); (2) anger; (3) bargaining for extra time; (4) depression; and (5) ultimate acceptance. Kübler-Ross (1970) gives examples from case histories to illustrate each stage (see Table 18-1, pages 600–601). A similar progression may characterize the feelings of people who face imminent bereavement (Kübler-Ross, 1975).

Other professionals who work with dying patients point out that Kübler-Ross's "stages" are not true stages, as the term is commonly used in other theories like Piaget's. Although the emotions that Kübler-Ross describes do commonly occur, not everyone goes through all five stages,

TABLE 18·1 KÜBLER-ROSS'S STAGES OF DYING

STAGE	EXPLANATION	EXAMPLE
Denial	Most people respond with shock to the knowledge that they are about to die. Their first thought is, "Oh, no, this can't be happening to me." When people around the patient also deny reality, he or she has no one to talk to and, as a result, feels deserted and isolated. When allowed some hope along with the first announcement and given the assurance that they will not be deserted no matter what happens, people can drop the initial shock and denial rather quickly.	Mrs. K., 28, a mother of two young children, was hospitalized with a terminal liver disease. After visiting a faith healer, she told the hospital chaplain, "It was wonderful. I have been healed. I am going to show the doctors that God will heal me. I am all well now" (1970, p. 43). Eventually, she showed that she was no longer denying her illness when, holding the doctor's hand, she said, "You have such warm hands. I hope you are going to be with me when I get colder and colder" (1970, p. 45).
Anger	After realizing that they are dying, people become angry. They ask, "Why me?" They become envious of those around them who are young and healthy. They are really angry not at these people, but at the youth and the health that they themselves do not have. They need to express their rage to get rid of it.	Mr. O., a successful businessman who had been a dominant, controlling person all his life, became enraged as Hodgkin's disease took away his control over his life. His anger dissipated somewhat after his wife and the hospital nurses gave him back a measure of control by consulting him on time and length of family visits and times for various hospital procedures.
Bargaining	The next thought may be, "Yes, it's happening to me—*but*." The *but* is an attempt to bargain for time. People may pray to God, "If you just let me live to see my daughter graduated . . . or my son married . . . or my grandchild born . . . I'll be a better person . . . or I won't ask for anything more . . . or I'll accept my lot in life." These bargains represent the acknowledgment that time is limited and life is finite. When people drop the *but*, they are able to say, "Yes, me."	A woman in great pain was very sad at the thought that she would not be able to attend the wedding of her oldest and favorite child. With the aid of self-hypnosis, she controlled her pain; and during the period before the wedding she promised that she would ask no more if she could live only long enough to be there. She did attend, a radiant mother of the groom, and when she returned to the hospital, despite her fatigue she told the doctor, "Now don't forget I have another son!" (1970, p. 83).
Depression	In this stage, people need to cry, to grieve for the loss of their own life. By expressing the depths of their anguish, they can overcome depression much more quickly than if they feel pressured to hide their sorrow.	Mr. H., who had enjoyed singing in the choir, teaching Sunday school, and doing other church and community work, was no longer able to carry out these activities, because of his illness. He said, "The one thing that makes life worthless right now is the fact that I looked upon myself . . . as not ever being able to go back to these things" (1970, p. 103). Other elements in his depression were his feeling that his wife did not appreciate his involvement in these nonpaying activities that he considered valuable, and the fact that he had never completed the mourning process for his parents and a daughter who had died. After he reviewed his feelings with the doctor and the chaplain and his wife reassured him that she did appreciate him, his depression lifted.

TABLE 18·1 CONTINUED

STAGE	EXPLANATION	EXAMPLE
Acceptance	Finally, people can acknowledge, "My time is very close now, and it's all right." This is not necessarily a happy time, but people who have worked through their anxieties and anger about death and have resolved their unfinished business end up with a feeling of peace with themselves and the world.	Mrs. W., 58, was facing the pain and the knowledge of abdominal cancer with courage and dignity—until her husband begged the surgeons to do an operation that could prolong her life. She changed radically, becoming restless and anxious, asking often for pain relief, and screaming and hallucinating in the operating room so that the surgery did not take place. After husband and wife spoke separately with the doctor, it became clear that Mrs. W. was ready to die but felt that she could not until her husband was able to accept her illness and let her go. When he finally saw that his need to keep her alive conflicted with her need to detach herself from the world (including him) and die, both partners were able to share their feelings and accept her death.

Source: Kübler-Ross, 1969, 1970.

and people may go through the stages in different sequences. A person may go back and forth between anger and depression, for example, or may feel both at once. Instead of the orderly progression in the theoretical model, dying people may show "a jumble of conflicting or alternating reactions running the gamut from denial to acceptance, with a tremendous variation affected by age, sex, race, ethnic group, social setting, and personality" (Butler & Lewis, 1982, p. 370). Unfortunately, some health professionals take the theory as "gospel" and feel that they have failed if if they cannot bring a patient to "the ultimate goal, the big number 5— 'acceptance' of death" (Leviton, 1977, p. 259).

Dying is an individual experience, as living is. For some people, denial or anger may be a healthier way to face death than calm acceptance. Thus Kübler-Ross's model—useful as it is in helping us understand the feelings of people facing the end of life—should not be held up as a criterion for "the good death."

Bereavement, Mourning, and Grief

Death is often very hard not only on the dying person but also on the survivors. In our fast-paced, death-denying culture, survivors are expected to be brave, to suppress their fears, and to get on with the business of living. Yet feelings of loss run deep. They need to be expressed before survivors can accept what has happened, heal their wounds, and reorganize their lives.

What is meant by the terms *bereavement, mourning,* and *grief*? **Bereavement** is the objective *fact* of loss: the survivor's change in status, for example, from a wife to a widow or from a child to an orphan. **Mourning** refers to the *behavior* that the bereaved and the community engage in after a death: the all-night Irish wake, at which friends and family keep vigil and toast the memory of the dead person; the week-long Jewish *shiva*, when the family remains at home to receive visitors (see Box 18-1, page 602); or flying a flag at half-mast to observe the death of a pub-

BOX 18-1 WINDOW ON THE WORLD

MOURNING CUSTOMS AMONG TRADITIONAL JEWS

Customs concerning death, dying, and bereavement are a reassuring anchor amid the turbulence of loss. One example is found in traditional Jewish culture. Rituals prescribed by Jewish law allow death to occur with dignity and provide a wholesome, humane outlet for the feelings of those who are dying or bereft. Although most Jewish people no longer observe all the guidelines for dying and mourning (A. Gordon, 1975; Heller, 1975), these customs do speak to important psychological needs and may be thought-provoking for Jews and non-Jews alike.

GUIDELINES FOR DYING

Jewish tradition views death as a natural part of life, to be faced directly and realistically.

■ During a terminal illness, loved ones stay with the patient as much as

An Orthodox Jewish funeral is simple, unostentatious, and realistic, and it is meant to help the bereaved face their loss. The community provides emotional support and afterwards helps mourners begin the process of recovery by serving a communal meal at their home. Traditional cultures like this one help people deal with death and grief through rituals that have generally understood, culturally accepted meanings.

possible, offering comfort and support while encouraging him or her to prepare for the end. By

never leaving the dying person alone, the survivors alleviate guilt, since they will know that they have

---

lic figure. **Grief** is the *emotional response* of the bereaved, which can be expressed in many ways, from rage to a feeling of emptiness.

Traditional cultures help people deal with bereavement and grief in a structured way, through mourning rites that are universally understood and have accepted meanings. In our diversified culture, many mourners lack such satisfying, reassuring structures. As old customs fall into disuse, the bereaved lose valuable supports for coping with their grief.

Forms of Grief Professionals who work with the bereaved have identified several forms of

grief: *anticipatory grief,* which may begin before the death occurs; *normal grief* following the death; and *morbid grief,* in which the person shows symptoms of emotional disturbance.

ANTICIPATORY GRIEF The family and friends of a person who has been ill for a long time often prepare themselves for the loss by experiencing symptoms of grief while the person is still alive. This often helps the survivors, enabling them to handle the actual death more easily when it does come (J. T. Brown & Stoudemire, 1983). If such anticipatory grief, however, makes the survivors disengage them-

done everything they could. The deathbed vigil also keeps mourners from denying the reality of the death, since they see it taking place.

■ Dying persons are treated as living persons, fully able to handle their own affairs and participate in relationships until the moment of death.

■ To the extent possible, a dying person puts material and spiritual affairs in order by giving away possessions, blessing loved ones and giving them last words of instruction or advice (the "ethical will"), and making a deathbed confession, or repentance of wrongdoing. These communications with dear ones represent a last contact with the familiar as the person is about to enter the unknown.

GUIDELINES FOR MOURNING
Instead of repressing natural feelings (and thus producing delayed grief), Judaism encourages mourners to express their grief and sorrow openly as a first step toward healing. A traditional Jewish funeral is simple and unostentatious and is kept realistic to prevent mourners from denying the implications of death. Jewish funerals are likely to be attended by children who were close to the deceased. The coffin, by tradition, is very simple and is kept closed.

■ Mourners make immediate plans for burial, thus expressing concern and respect for the dead person and carrying out the natural wish to do all that they can for their loved one.

■ By tearing their clothes before the funeral, mourners symbolize the severing of the relationship with the dead person.

■ The eulogy gives mourners an opportunity to reflect on their loss and to pour out their grief in tears.

■ At the cemetery, mourners are encouraged to shovel dirt into the hole themselves. This is a final act of love and concern in putting their loved one to rest.

■ The year of mourning corresponds roughly to the stages of grief: "three days of deep grief, seven days of mourning, thirty days of gradual readjustment, and eleven months of remembrance and healing" (A. Gordon, 1975, p. 51). After the funeral, the community helps the mourners begin the recovery process by serving a meal at their home. This ushers in the week of *shiva*. As they visit with each other and with friends throughout that week, mourners can talk about the details of the death, share memories, and vent emotions, while being reminded that life goes on. During the year that follows, the bereaved are gradually drawn back into the life of the community.

selves from the dying person while he or she is still alive, it can create a devastating sense of isolation for the terminally ill person.

NORMAL GRIEF Grieving usually follows a fairly predictable pattern. In order to resolve grief in a healthy way, the bereaved person must accept the painful reality of the loss, gradually let go of the bond with the dead person, readjust to life without that person, and develop new interests and relationships. This process of "grief work" generally takes place in three phases—though, as with Kübler-Ross's stages, they may vary (J. T. Brown & Stoudemire, 1983; Schulz, 1978):

1 The initial phase, which may last for several weeks (especially after a sudden or an unexpected death), is *shock and disbelief*, which may protect the bereaved from intense reactions. Survivors often feel lost, dazed, and confused. Shortness of breath, tightness in the chest or throat, nausea, and a feeling of emptiness in the abdomen are common. As the awareness of loss sinks in, the initial numbness gives way to overwhelming feelings of sadness, which may be expressed by frequent crying.

2 The second phase, which may last 6 months or longer, is *preoccupation with the memory of the dead person*. The survivor, left alone to

cope with the resumption of everyday life, tries to come to terms with the death but cannot yet accept it. Frequent crying continues, and the bereaved person may suffer from insomnia, fatigue, or loss of appetite. A widow, for example, may relive her husband's death and their entire relationship, going over all the details in her mind and in her conversation, in an obsessive search for the meaning of his death. From time to time she may be seized by a feeling that her dead husband is present: she will hear his voice, sense his presence in the room, even see his face before her. She may have vivid dreams of him and suddenly waken to again realize her loss. These sensations diminish with time, though they may recur—perhaps for years—on such occasions as the anniversary of their marriage or of his death.

3 The final phase, *resolution,* has arrived when the bereaved person resumes interest in everyday activities—when memories of the dead person bring fond feelings (mingled with sadness) rather than sharp pain and longing. A widower still misses his dead wife, but he knows that life must go on, and he becomes more active socially, getting out more, seeing people, resuming old interests, and perhaps discovering new interests. Many survivors feel a surge of strength and are proud to have recovered.

MORBID GRIEF   When the reactions associated with normal grief become unusually intense or last unusually long, they are usually considered pathological. Morbid grief is thought to be more likely to occur if the bereaved person has a history of personality disorders, lost a parent in childhood, had an especially dependent or hostile relationship with the dead person, or was going through a number of crises at the time of the death. Grieving is also likely to become morbid if the death was sudden and unexpected or was the result of murder, suicide, or other unusual circumstances; or if the survivor does not get enough support from family and friends (J. T. Brown & Stoudemire, 1983).

Morbid grief may be either delayed or distorted. In delayed grief, the bereaved person at first seems to be holding up unusually well;

friends may marvel at his or her strength. But by denying grief, the person forces it inward and may develop physical problems like asthma or colitis or may experience shattering grief later on.

Distorted grief may take the form of compulsive overactivity, identification with the dead person, physical deterioration, withdrawal from social contact, or severe depression. A person who reacts in such ways may be extremely angry at the dead person over some unresolved issue or may feel guilty, blaming himself or herself for the death (J. T. Brown & Stoudemire, 1983).

Recently, mental health professionals have questioned whether there is a "normal" timetable for grief—whether grief goes through clearly defined stages—and whether grief that departs from such a pattern is a sign of mental illness. Studies show considerable differences in people's reactions to bereavement. The resolution of grief does not necessarily follow a straight line from shock to resolution, and mourning may continue for years, surfacing on anniversaries or other dates that are important to the bereaved person. As one psychiatry professor warns, we "should be wary of pegging 'deviant' labels on grieving behavior" (Kleinman, cited in Joyce, 1984).

Grief Therapy   Most bereaved people are able to work through their grief, with the help of family and friends, and to resume normal lives. For some, however, *grief therapy*—a program to help the bereaved cope with their losses—seems indicated (Schulz, 1978).

Professional therapists focus on helping bereaved people express their sorrow and their feelings of loss and guilt, of hostility and anger. They encourage their clients to review their relationships with the deceased and to integrate the fact of the death into their lives so that they can be freed to develop new relationships and new ways of behaving toward surviving friends and relatives.

Such lay organizations as Widow to Widow, Catholic Widow and Widowers Club, and Compassionate Friends (for parents whose children have died) emphasize the practical and emotional help that one person who has lost someone close can give to another.

We need to be able to accept the eventual coming of death to those whom we love, just as we need to realize that our own time on earth is limited.

Helping People Deal with Dying and Bereavement

With the growing realization that death can be faced better if people understand it, several movements have arisen to help make dying and bereavement more humane. These include programs of death education, hospices to care for the terminally ill, and support groups and services for the dying and their families.

Death Education "Why did my guinea pig die? When will it be alive again?"

"What can I say to my friend when she says she's going to kill herself?"

"How much should I tell terminally ill patients about their true situation?"

These are just a few of the questions that are dealt with in *death education:* programs aimed at various age levels and groups of people to teach them about dying and grief and to help them deal with these issues in their personal and professional lives.

Educators have realized that it is important for people to explore their attitudes toward death, to be familiar with ways various cultures handle it, and to be sensitive to its emotional ramifications, for both the person who dies and the people who survive. Courses about death are being offered to high school and college students; to social workers, doctors, nurses, and other professionals who work with dying people and their survivors; and to the community. Even early childhood teachers are introducing discussions about death at appropriate times, when they fit into the curriculum or into the children's experience. Learning about death helps people of all ages.

GOALS OF DEATH EDUCATION What, specifically, can death education accomplish? The goals vary according to the ages and needs of the students, but some are important for everyone. Some of the important aims, applicable to people of different ages and with different interests, are as follows (Leviton, 1977):

- To help children grow up with as few death-related anxieties as possible
- To help people develop their own individual belief systems about life and death
- To help people see death as a natural end to life
- To help people prepare for their own death and the death of those close to them
- To help people feel comfortable around the dying and treat them humanely and intelligently for as long as they live
- To help both laypeople and health-care professionals, such as doctors and nurses, get a realistic view of the professional and his or her obligation to the dying and their families
- To understand the dynamics of grief and the ways in which people of different ages typically react to loss
- To understand and be able to help a suicidal person
- To help consumers decide what kind of funeral services they want for themselves and their families and to show them how to purchase them wisely
- To make dying as positive an experience as possible by emphasizing the importance of minimizing pain; offering warm, personal care; involving family and close friends in the care of the dying person; and being sensitive to that person's wishes and needs

TEACHING CHILDREN ABOUT DEATH Children are usually interested in talking about death with caring adults. They should talk in a warm, supportive atmosphere with an adult who is aware of children's varying cognitive levels and who is sensitive to their individual feelings and experiences (Koocher, 1973).

Death education can help children to allay their anxieties on two levels—the relatively impersonal, cognitive level and the more personal, emotional level. On the cognitive level, teachers can raise the topic in social studies classes, by having students compare funeral practices and religious beliefs about death; or in science class, where they can talk about the difference between what is "alive," what is "not alive," and what is "dead." On the feeling level, teachers can respond to the death of a pet, the death of a class member's relative, or the death of a public figure, giving the children support for their

(© Bill Binzen/Photo Researchers)

By teaching her son about death, this mother can help allay his anxieties about it. Parents and teachers who discuss death with children need to be warm, supportive, and sensitive to their feelings. It is also important to remember that children vary in their cognitive readiness to understand death.

feelings. Children may be encouraged to write short sympathy notes when appropriate. Teachers and parents need to walk a thin line to help children deal with a difficult topic like death without increasing their anxiety.

The Hospice Movement "I had a fast-growing conviction," writes Norman Cousins in *Anatomy of an Illness* (1979), "that a hospital is no place for a person who is seriously ill" (p. 29). Many who are concerned with the terminally ill are convinced that for these patients hospitals are even less the right place. The typical hospital is set up to treat acute illness, with the goal of curing people and sending them home well; and this goal is bound to be thwarted when a patient is terminally ill. Dying patients are often subjected to needless tests and useless treatment, are given less attention than patients whose chances of recovery are better, and are constrained by hospital rules that have no relevance for them.

The hospice movement began in response to a need for special facilities and care for these patients. *Hospice care*—warm, personal patient- and family-centered care for the terminally ill—

(Cynthia Johnson/TIME Magazine)

A volunteer working with terminally ill cancer patients and their relatives at a hospice in New Jersey is part of a growing movement to ease the pain and fear of dying patients and their families. The main feature of hospice programs is warm, personal care to help with a range of physical, social, and emotional problems related to dying.

Volunteers at a Shanti group meeting in San Francisco join hands to give emotional support to patients with AIDS or related diseases. The Shanti Project, whose name comes from the Sanskrit word for "inner peace," was founded by a psychologist to offer compassionate care to the terminally ill and their families.

can be given in a hospital or another institution, at home, or through some combination of home and institution. Doctors, nurses, social workers, psychologists, aides, clergy, friends, family members, and volunteers of a variety of ages and backgrounds work together to ease the pain and treat the symptoms of patients, to keep them as comfortable and alert as possible, to take an interest in them and their families and show them kindness, and to help the families deal with the patients' illnesses and death.

In one study comparing standard hospital care and hospice care for terminally ill cancer patients who were randomly assigned to one or the other, the main difference was found to be in the frame of mind of the patients and their families. The hospice patients and the family members most involved with their day-to-day care were more satisfied than were the hospital patients and *their* relatives. There were no differences between the two groups, however, in pain, symptoms, activities of daily living, emotional states, or expense. The difference, then, seems to reflect the fact that the hospice teams spent more time with patients and their families in helping them cope with impending death (Kane, Wales, Bernstein, Leibowitz, & Kaplan, 1984).

Support Groups and Services Orville Kelly, a man who had been diagnosed as suffering from terminal cancer, wrote:

The death rate for any generation is 100 percent. We *all* die. However, I know what will probably kill me, while most people do not. We have no guarantee of how long we will live. But I believe it is truly the quality of life, not the quantity, that is most important. [O. Kelly, 1978, p. 63]

Spurred by his own initial difficulty in dealing with his diagnosis, Kelly founded Make Today Count, an organization where seriously ill patients and their families can talk about their feelings and the problems of living with terminal illness.

The Shanti Project, another support group, whose name derives from the Sanskrit word for "inner peace," was founded in the San Francisco Bay area by Charles Garfield, a psychologist deeply concerned with offering compassionate care for the dying and their families. The project's hot-line number is likely to ring at any hour of the day or night, with requests from all over the country. One caller may ask for a volunteer to break the news to an elderly woman and her family that the woman is dying; a second, for someone to counsel a man about to undergo chemotherapy so that he will know what to expect and to support him through the ordeal; and a third, to help the wife of a dying man cope with her own feelings so as to be as helpful as possible to her husband. (Currently, the Shanti Project is devoting almost all its resources to help support terminally ill AIDS patients.)

Shanti volunteers are of all ages—from young adults to the elderly—and come from many different personal and religious backgrounds. The major requisite is that they have "the willingness, emotional strength, training, and sensitivity to confront humanely the realities of death and dying without resorting to evasion and denial" (Garfield & Clark, 1978, p. 364).

CONTROVERSIAL ISSUES OF DEATH AND DYING

Immediately after birth, a baby boy is found to have several disabilities. One is Down syndrome, a genetic defect characterized by mild to moderate mental retardation (see Chapter 2). Another is an obstruction that makes it impossible for him to swallow and thus to eat. The physician asks the infant's parents whether he should perform an operation to remove the obstruction. If he does not, the baby will die.

A little girl has been so badly beaten by her stepfather that, according to a team of neurosurgeons, her brain has died. There is no chance, they say, that she could ever walk, speak, or even think. The stepfather's attorney is attempting to prevent the hospital from disconnecting the respirator as the mother has requested, so that his client cannot be tried for murder. If hospital personnel do turn off the machines that are maintaining the child's breathing and heart action, who is responsible for her death—the stepfather, or the hospital employees?

A 55-year-old woman is suffering from terminal cancer. With medical care she may live another couple of years, but the likelihood is that she will become so weak that she will be confined to her bed most of the time. She is likely to be in great pain. She asks her physician to give her a potent drug. He knows that an overdose will bring death, and he strongly suspects that the woman plans to end her life at a time of her own choosing.

These are only a few examples of the hard choices that may face patients, families, and physicians these days: choices between the quality of life and its length. Many of these issues arise from technological advances: antibiotics that enable older patients to survive one dread

illness only to succumb to another; respirators that keep people alive and breathing when they are in a coma and show no brain activity or other physiological function; organ transplants that may achieve "miracles" at great risk.

The questions are endless. When a medicine can relieve pain but may shorten the patient's life, should the doctor prescribe the drug? In a traumatic childbirth, if a doctor can save only one life, whose should it be—the mother's, or the baby's? Is abortion a medical procedure, or is it murder?

Do people have the right to take their own life? If so, under what circumstances may they do it? What is the legal liability of someone who helps a person commit suicide?

How should a doctor who has diagnosed a terminal illness tell his or her patient? Should patients be given an estimate of how long they have to live, so that they can put their affairs in order and prepare for death? Or will knowing the prognosis hasten death, becoming a self-fulfilling prophecy?

Who makes the decision that a life is not worth prolonging? Who decides when to stop treatment? What abuses are possible? How can they be prevented?

None of these questions has a simple answer. Each requires soul-searching by everyone involved. Each situation is unique, and therefore each solution must be unique.

Euthanasia and the Right to Die

On March 18, 1983, a 79-year-old man visited his 62-year-old wife in the nursing home where she was living. The wife, who had once been a successful businesswoman, was now suffering from advanced Alzheimer's disease and was confined to her bed. She screamed constantly and was unable or unwilling to speak. The husband pushed his wife's wheelchair into a stairwell, where he killed her with a pistol shot. The district attorney who prosecuted the husband called his act "classic first-degree murder." The grand jury refused to indict, and the man went free (Malcolm, 1984).

The husband in this case was practicing *euthanasia,* or mercy killing. His act was an example of **active euthanasia,** action deliberately taken with the purpose of shortening a life in order to

TABLE 18-2 PUBLIC OPINION ON PROLONGING LIFE BY MACHINE

TOTAL	YES (77)	NO (15)	DON'T KNOW (8)
Male	78	15	7
Female	77	14	9
18–44 years old	80	14	6
45 and older	73	16	11
$12,499 or less	69	19	12
$12,500–$24,999	75	17	8
$25,000–$34,999	84	12	4
$35,000–$49,999	83	11	4
$50,000 or more	83	13	4
Not high school graduate	66	20	14
High school graduate	78	15	7
Some college	87	9	4
College graduate	81	13	5
Living in northeast	75	16	9
Midwest	77	16	7
South	73	9	
West	85	8	7
White	80	13	7
Black	60	30	9
Liberal	88	11	3
Moderate	77	15	3
Conservative	76	17	7

Note: Table shows responses in percent to a poll taken in June 1984 among 1593 adults, who were asked, "Medical technology now enables doctors to prolong the lives of many people who are terminally ill. Do you believe doctors should stop using these techniques if the patient asks, even if that means the patient will die?"
Source: New York Times/CBS News Poll, 1984.

end suffering or to carry out the wishes of a terminally ill patient. ***Passive euthanasia*** describes those situations in which mercy killing takes the form of withholding treatment that might extend life, such as medication, life-support systems, or feeding tubes.

Although active euthanasia is highly controversial, most people are not in favor of preserving life in all cases. In a *New York Times*–CBS poll taken in 1984, 77 percent of the respondents said that doctors should not use advanced medical technology to prolong the lives of the terminally ill against their wishes (see Table 18–2).

In 1983 the President's Commission for the Study of Ethical Problems in Medicine and Biomedical and Behavioral Research proposed that mentally competent patients and families acting on behalf of incompetent patients be allowed to halt medical treatment that keeps them alive without any hope of curing or improving their condition. The commission said that ending a life intentionally was forbidden but that doctors could give pain-relieving drugs that were likely to shorten life if the reason for administering the drugs was to relieve pain (Schmeck, 1983).

In recent years many people have made out ***living wills*** (see Box 18-2, pages 610–611), documents stating their own wishes about the kinds of measures they want—or do not want—taken if they become terminally ill. Such documents, which are legally valid in some states but not in others, are meant to ensure that decisions made

BOX 18-2 ■ PRACTICALLY SPEAKING

THE LIVING WILL

People who receive extraordinary measures to prolong life are often unconscious or mentally incompetent by the time these measures are put into effect. Therefore, by making crucial decisions ahead of time about the kind of care desired and communicating these decisions to others, people can do much to ensure that they receive the extent of care that they want. One way to do this is through a document known as a *living will*. The following suggestions for implementing such a will come from the organization Concern for Dying (250 West 57th Street, New York, NY 10107), which will send free copies of its "Living Will" on request. (If your state has adopted living will legislation, it may be wise to use the legally approved wording.)

My Living Will
To My Family, My Physician, My Lawyer, and All Others Whom It May Concern

Death is as much a reality as birth, growth, maturity and old age—it is the one certainty of life. If the time comes when I can no longer take part in decisions for my own future, let this statement stand as an expression of my wishes and directions, while I am still of sound mind.

If at such a time the situation should arise in which there is no reasonable expectation of my recovery from extreme physical or mental disability, I direct that I be allowed to die and not be kept alive by medications, artificial means or "heroic measures." I do, however, ask that medication be mercifully administered to me to alleviate suffering even though this may shorten my remaining life.

This statement is made after careful consideration and is in accordance with my strong convictions and beliefs. I want the wishes and directions here expressed carried out to the extent permitted by law. Insofar as they are not legally enforceable, I hope that those to whom this Will is addressed will regard themselves as morally bound by these provisions.

(Specific provisions, if any, would be listed here.)

Durable Power of Attorney (optional)

I hereby designate_____to serve as my attorney-in-fact for the purpose of making medical treatment decisions. This power of attorney shall remain effective in the event that I become incompetent or otherwise unable to make such decisions for myself.

Optional notarization:

"Sworn and subscribed to

before me this_____day

of_____, 19_____."

_____
Notary Public
(seal)

Signed_____

Date_____

Witness_____

_____
Address

Witness_____

_____
Address

*Copies of this request have been given to*_____

_____

(Optional) My Living Will is registered with Concern for Dying (No._____)

while a person is healthy and competent will be followed.

However, doctors and hospitals have not always honored requests not to use "heroic" life-support measures. Beginning in 1988, the Joint Commission on Accreditation of Hospitals, a national accrediting agency, is requiring hospitals and nursing homes to establish written policies regarding when and how lifesaving treatment may be withheld.

Sometimes, of course, people who are ill want to live as long as possible, regardless of their condition. In such cases, too, patients' wishes must be respected.

Suicide

Many people find life so precious that they have trouble understanding why anyone would voluntarily end it. Yet every 20 minutes, on the average, between 1970 and 1980, someone in the United States committed suicide. Suicide is increasing among males and decreasing among females, and white people are almost twice as likely to kill themselves as black people. The average age of people who commit suicide has dropped dramatically; in 1980, half of all suicides were between the ages of 15 and 39, and more than one-third of the males were less than 30 years old. The increasing use of guns instead of poison or other less sure methods indicates that more people who commit suicide are determined to succeed (Morbidity and Mortality Weekly Report, MMWR, 1985; see Figure 18-1, on page 612, for suicide rates by age since 1950).

Statistics probably understate the number of suicides, since many go unreported and some "accidental" deaths may actually be self-inflicted. Furthermore, the figures do not in-

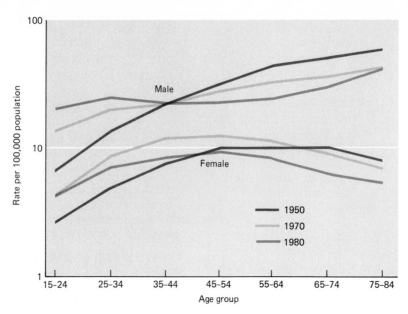

Figure 18-1 Suicide rates by age group and sex, United States, 1950–1980. Suicide rates for younger people, especially males, have increased greatly since 1950, while rates for older people have decreased. Nonetheless, men are still most likely to commit suicide in old age, and women are more likely to do so in middle age. (*Source:* Morbidity and Mortality Weekly Report, 1985.)

clude suicide *attempts*. There are about 6000 documented suicides a year among young people; some mental health professionals estimate that each year 400,000 children and teenagers try to kill themselves and fail (National Committee for Citizens in Education, NCCE, 1986).

Suicide among Children "It wasn't an accident. I figured if I died it wouldn't hurt as much as if I lived." These were the words of a dying 5-year-old child (Turkington, 1983).

It is painful and difficult to believe that young children can be so unhappy that they take their lives. Yet a recent study strongly suggests that many "accidents" involving preschoolers may actually be deliberate attempts at suicide, attempts that go unrecognized as child abuse once did (P. A. Rosenthal & Rosenthal, 1984). Sixteen children aged 2½ to 5 who had seriously injured themselves or had tried to do so (13 of them more than once) were compared with 16 preschoolers who were having serious behavioral problems. The children diagnosed as suicidal were more aggressive, seemed more depressed, had more morbid ideas, ran away more, and were less likely to cry after being hurt than were the other children. Most of the suicidal children had parents who did not want them and who abused or neglected them; six had been separated from parents through divorce, foster

placement, adoption, or death; and all of them showed disturbed attachment behavior (see Chapter 5). Through play therapy, it became apparent that the children's reasons for trying to do away with themselves were either to punish themselves, to escape or remedy their painful situations, or to be reunited with a loved, nurturing person (such as a dead father).

The psychiatrists who conducted this study recommend asking preschoolers about the circumstances of their accidents to try to uncover underlying psychological causes. Very young children may be particularly at risk because they generally believe (as did half of the children in this study) that death is reversible.

Suicide among Adolescents A 16-year-old girl, constantly at odds with her parents because they disapprove of her boyfriend, breaks up with the boy. The next morning, her sister discovers the girl's lifeless body next to an empty bottle of sleeping pills. An 18-year-old boy, despondent after a traffic accident that results in the junking of his car, the revocation of his driving license, and an upcoming trial, jumps off an icy bridge to his death.

These two teenagers are among a growing number of young people who have seen no way out of a bad time in their lives other than ending them. Suicide rates among teenagers—

especially among boys—have soared; in 1983, suicide was the second most frequent cause of death among 15- to 19-year-olds, taking 1700 lives yearly. The top cause of death was accidents, some of which may have actually been suicides (National Center for Health Statistics, cited in L. Eisenberg, 1986).

Between 1950 and 1977, the suicide rate at first quadrupled for adolescent boys and doubled for girls and then remained at approximately the level it had reached (see Figure 18-1). The overall increase for adolescents was about 60 percent between 1970 and 1980; during the same period, the rate for the population as a whole actually fell slightly. Even more alarming is the likelihood (based on cohort studies) that today's young people will continue to be more suicide-prone as they get older (L. Eisenberg, 1980, 1986; MMWR, 1985; G. E. Murphy & Wetzel, 1980).

WHY TEENAGERS ATTEMPT SUICIDE What makes life intolerable to so many young people? People who attempt suicide generally feel lonely, isolated, and alienated and consider themselves unloved by parents and peers. Some child-study professionals believe that suicide rates among teenagers have risen because today's adolescents are under much more stress than their counterparts in earlier days (Elkind, 1984). Many young people who attempt suicide under stress do not want to die, however. They only want to change their lives, and their suicide attempts are desperate pleas for attention and help. Through impulsiveness or strategic miscalculation, they often die before help can reach them.

Three studies of young people who tried to kill themselves—two of them atypical in that most or all of the subjects were women—provide some clues to the personality of the would-be suicide. In the first, a study of forty 12- to 19-year-old males and females who were receiving psychiatric treatment after suicide attempts, it turned out that *all* had been emotionally ill *before* trying to end their lives. Depression, drug abuse, and unstable personality were the most common diagnoses. These young people tended to react severely to a loss, to have poor control over their rage, and to be impulsive (Crumley, 1979).

"Suicide High" was what people in Omaha, Nebraska, began calling Bryan High School after three students there committed suicide within 5 days. Several "clusters" of teenage suicides have occurred in the United States, where suicide has become the second leading cause of death among adolescents (the first being accidents)—perhaps because many young people feel worthless or under intolerable pressure to achieve. Seeking to stem the tide of hysteria aroused by the deaths of classmates, guidance counselors like the one shown here urge students to "choose life." *(Ted Kirk/*TIME* Magazine)*

The second study found similar characteristics—impulsiveness and low tolerance for frustration and stress—in a group of young women who had attempted suicide, many of whom were firstborns. They were often in conflict with their parents, unable to call upon them for support, and unable even to communicate with their fathers, who in many cases had left during the women's adolescence (P. Cantor, 1977).

In the third study, 75 percent of the subjects were female. The report covered sixty-five 7- to 19-year-olds (with a median age of 16) in a suicide prevention program in a hospital serving a low-income inner-city black population. Half of these young people were described as "loners." Three-fourths were doing very poorly in school; many had failed one or more grades or were dropouts or chronic truants. Another 35 percent had behavior or discipline problems. Among 25 who received psychological testing, 60 percent were judged to suffer from minimal brain dysfunction, with attendant learning difficulties and the poor self-image and feelings of hopelessness that often accompany academic failure. Their families were troubled; a high proportion of these teenagers had parents who were separated, divorced, or alcoholic, or who did not live with them.

This study confirms other research which has found that adolescents who try to kill themselves have experienced very different patterns of life from other young people. On the other hand, a national survey of top high school juniors and seniors found that 31 percent had considered suicide and 4 percent had tried it (*Who's Who Among American High School Students,* cited in NCCE, 1986). Whereas low achievers may turn to suicide because they feel that their lives are worthless, high achievers may do so because they feel under tremendous pressure to perform. Depressed adolescents often abuse alcohol and other drugs, which play a part in some 50 percent of teenage suicide attempts (NCCE, 1986).

PREVENTING SUICIDE IN ADOLESCENCE What can parents do to prevent teenagers from becoming part of these frightening statistics? First of all, they can make clear that their love is unconditional, not contingent upon behavior and school achievement. They can include teenagers in family decisions and give them household chores that make them feel valued and responsible. Because adolescents have not lived long enough to realize that rejection and disappointment are often transitory, it may help for parents to point out situations in which they or someone else (like a movie star or an athlete) came through a difficult time. A parent's sharing his or her own grief and hurt over painful losses may encourage an adolescent to open up and do the same (NCCE, 1986). See Box 18-3 for more suggestions.

Suicide among Adults Patrons at a recent Metropolitan Opera performance of Verdi's *Macbeth* were horrified during intermission when an elderly man plunged to his death from an upper balcony. This man—an 82-year-old singing coach named Bantcho Bantchevsky—had been lively and gregarious and had lived for his music and his friends until his health began to deteriorate a few months before. His depres-

sion grew until he took his life, dying in the theatrical manner in which he had lived (Okun, 1988).

Suicide among adults often occurs in conjunction with depression or with debilitating physical illness. Although in absolute numbers most suicides occur among young white males (aged 15 to 34), the highest *rate* of suicide in the entire population is among white men over the age of 65, and the rate increases as they get older. For white women, the rates are highest in middle age; black men and black women are most vulnerable as young adults (25 to 35) (MMWR, 1985; USDHHS, 1982).

The suicide rates for adults may be even larger than they seem, since many deaths may not be recognized as self-inflicted. Some may look like traffic accidents or the consequences of accidental overdoses of drugs or the forgetful failure to take life-preserving medicine. Older people who take their own lives seem to plan carefully and to know just what they are doing, as can be judged from the fact that 1 out of every 2 attempts in old age end in loss of life, compared with only 1 out of every 7 among adolescents (National Council on Aging, 1978).

Why do older adults commit suicide? One explanation is despair over a progression of irreversible losses that they are helpless to stop: losses of work, of friends, of a spouse, of children, of memory, of health, and finally of self-esteem and hope. Perhaps at a certain point the only control they seem to have over their lives is to end them.

A likely explanation for the high rates of self-destruction among older white men is that after the sometimes lofty achievements of their youth, it is harder for them to face the deprivations of old age. Another contributing factor may well be their overidentification with their work roles, which leaves them without identity after they have stopped working.

Often psychotherapy, medication, or increased social contact can help to lift a person's feeling of isolation and depression and restore an interest in life. At other times—especially when an older person has a disabling or painful illness—all efforts fail.

The Ethical Issue In some quarters, ending one's life is seen as a rational decision, given cer-

BOX 18-3 PRACTICALLY SPEAKING

HELPING TO PREVENT SUICIDE

After a person has committed suicide, family and friends are usually overwhelmed with guilt, along with their grief. They ask themselves, "Why didn't I know? Why didn't I do something?" Very often the person intent on suicide carefully keeps his or her plans from everyone, but at other times the signals appear well before the deed. In fact, sometimes the attempt at suicide is a call for help, and some people die because they are more successful than they intended to be. People who want to help prevent suicides need to learn to recognize the warning signals of suicide and need to know the kinds of actions that are often effective in heading it off.

WARNING SIGNS OF SUICIDE

- Withdrawal from family or friends

- Talking about death, the hereafter, or suicide

- Giving away prized possessions

- Drug or alcohol abuse

- Personality changes, such as unusual anger, boredom, or apathy

- Unusual neglect of appearance

- Difficulty concentrating on work or school

- Staying away from work, school, or other usual activities

- Complaints of physical problems when nothing is organically wrong

- Sleeping or eating much more or much less than has been customary

- Loss of self-esteem

- Feelings of helplessness, hopelessness, extreme anxiety, or panic

WHAT A CONCERNED PERSON CAN DO

- Talk to the person about his or her suicidal thoughts. Bringing up the subject will not put ideas into the mind of someone who has not already thought of suicide, and it will bring feelings out into the open.

- Tell others who are in a position to do something— the person's parents or spouse or other family members, a close friend, or a therapist or counselor. It's better to break a confidence than to let someone die.

- Do as much as possible to relieve the real-life pressures that seem intolerable, whether that means calling a rejecting lover, lending money, or interceding with an employer.

- Show the person that he or she has other options besides death, even though none of them may be ideal.

- Press for gun control legislation. Suicide rates declined in England and Wales between 1960 and 1975, apparently as a result of the elimination of natural gas, which had been a popular method. In this country and in Australia, the number of barbiturate-caused suicides declined in proportion to the number of prescriptions written. The number of suicides involving guns has risen in recent years; gun control legislation would probably decrease such deaths. Many suicides are impulsive; if a convenient means is not at hand, the depressed person may not go any further, or may at least defer the action long enough to get help. Furthermore, a person who leans toward one method may be reluctant to use another (L. Eisenberg, 1980).

Most communities and hospitals have suicide prevention hot lines—some operating 24 hours a day— where people can call to talk with someone about their problems. Most college counseling departments provide suicide prevention services. A state-by-state listing of such programs is available from the National Committee on Youth Suicide Prevention, 666 Fifth Avenue, 13th Floor, New York, NY 10103.

tain circumstances, such as terminal illness; and suicide is considered a right to be defended. There is growing support for "right to die" legislation, which removes the criminal connotations from suicide and gives mature people the right to end their lives when they see fit.

Another view is that while we can empathize with a person who has committed suicide, we should try to thwart a suicide that has not yet been successfully carried out. This viewpoint holds that suicide is not so much a wish for death as a desire to avoid unbearable pain, either physical or emotional, and that what is needed is to find ways to reduce the pain. Box 18–3 lists some ways in which the family, friends, and therapists of potential suicides can help them.

FINDING A PURPOSE IN LIFE AND DEATH

For most of us, death comes at a time and in a way not of our choosing. Its coming is the inevitable end to the journey that began at the moment of conception. As death approaches, people tend to look back over what they have made of themselves—how they have changed and grown. They ask themselves about the purpose of life and death and try to sum up what their lives have meant.

The Meaning of Death

The central character of Tolstoy's short story "The Death of Ivan Ilyich" is racked by an illness that he knows will be fatal. In despair, he asks himself over and over again what meaning there is to his agony. Even greater than his physical suffering is Ivan Ilyich's mental torture as he lies dying and becomes more and more convinced that he has wasted his life, that his life has been without purpose, and therefore that his death is equally pointless.

What Tolstoy dramatized in literature, contemporary social scientists are finding to be true in life. Viktor Frankl (1965), a psychoanalyst who survived a Nazi death camp during World War II, observed that people need to find meaning in their own death if they are to feel that life

is meaningful. Conversely, the greater purpose they find in their lives, the less they fear death. A researcher who tested this hypothesis by administering attitudinal scales to 39 women whose average age was 76 found that those who saw the most purpose in life did indeed have the least fear of death (Durlak, 1973).

"There is no need to be afraid of death," Kübler-Ross has written (1975, p. 164). Awareness of death, she says, is the key to personal growth and to the development of human potential:

It is the denial of death that is partially responsible for [people's] living empty, purposeless lives; for when you live as if you'll live forever, it becomes too easy to postpone the things you know that you must do. In contrast, when you fully understand that each day you awaken could be the last you have, you take the time *that day* to grow, to become more of who you really are, to reach out to other human beings. . . . For only when we understand the real meaning of death to human existence will we have the courage to become what we are destined to be. (pp. 164, 165)

Reviewing a Life

The old doctor who is the hero of the classic Ingmar Bergman film *Wild Strawberries* dreams and thinks about his past and his coming death. Realizing how cold and unaffectionate he has been, he becomes warmer and more open in his last days. This film underscores the fact that personality can change at any time in the life span, no matter how late.

The doctor in *Wild Strawberries* was able to make his life more purposeful through a *life review,* a process of reminiscence that enables a person to see the significance of his or her life.

Older people's natural tendency to talk about the people, events, and feelings of previous years is an important part of the life-review process. Life-review therapy can help make the review more conscious, deliberate, and efficient (Butler, 1961; M. I. Lewis & Butler, 1974). Some of the techniques for evoking memories that are used in life-review therapy are presented in Box 18-4.

By going over their lives, people may see their experiences and actions in a new light. They

BOX 18-4   PRACTICALLY SPEAKING

EVOKING MEMORIES FOR A "LIFE REVIEW"

The following methods (adapted from M. I. Lewis & Butler, 1974) for uncovering hidden memories are used in life-review therapy. These methods are often useful and enjoyable and can be used fruitfully outside a therapeutic situation. When engaged in as part of an ongoing project with younger family members or friends, they can build a bridge between the generations, help older persons experience a creative ordering of their lives, and give younger people information and insights that may help them in their own old age.

■ *Written or taped autobiographies.* The incidents, experiences, and people included in these autobiographies are significant. It is also important to be aware of what is *not* here. (One successful professional man put together an extensive record of his life, with practically no mention of his two middle-aged children. When the therapist delved into this omission, the man revealed that he was estranged from both his children and used the therapy to examine his feelings about them.)

■ *Pilgrimages (in person or through correspondence).* When possible, older people can take trips back to the locations of their birth, childhood, youth, and young adult life. They can take photos and notes to put their thoughts in order. If they cannot do this in reality, they can often contact people still living in these places. Failing that, they can summon up their memories. (One woman, who was still angry with her parents for forbidding her to go into the attic and had for years fantasized about what they were hiding from her, now discovered that there had never been any stairs and that the prohibition was for her safety.)

■ *Reunions.* Getting together with high school and college classmates, family members, or members of a religious or civic organization lets people see themselves next to their peers and other important people in their lives.

■ *Genealogy.* Developing a family tree can give a person a sense of continuity in history and can also help to relieve the fear of death by the awareness of how

many family members have already died. The search is interesting in itself as older persons put ads in newspapers, visit cemeteries, and pore over town records, family Bibles, and records of a church, a synagogue, or some other religious organization.

■ *Scrapbooks, photo albums, old letters, and other memorabilia.* The items that people have kept usually have a special, pleasurable meaning in their lives. By talking about them, older people can often recall long-forgotten events, acquaintances, and emotional experiences.

■ *Summation of lifework.* By summing up what they regard as their contributions to the world, older people get the sense that they have participated meaningfully in it. Some older people's summations have grown into published books, poems, and music.

■ *Focus on ethnic identity.* By concentrating on special traditions and experiences they enjoyed as members of their ethnic groups, older persons can appreciate their heritage and pass it on.

Participating in a class reunion—sharing memories with people who played a part in formative experiences—is one way to review a life. Life review can help people see important events in a new light and can motivate them to seek a sense of closure by rebuilding damaged relationships or completing unfinished tasks.

may have a chance to complete unfinished tasks, such as reconciling with estranged family members or friends. The sense of completion after accomplishing these tasks can be a comfort as people round out the time that remains to them. Of course, there is also the risk that a life review can make people feel that they have wasted their lives, have injured others, and now have no chance to compensate for the past or improve on it. More often, though, they can make a balanced assessment, recognizing both successes and failures and "bequeathing" their values to those who may be able to carry them on.

Within our limited life span, none of us can realize all our capabilities, gratify all our desires, engage all our interests, or experience all the richness that life has to offer. The tension between virtually infinite possibilities for growth and a finite time in which to do the growing defines human life from beginning to end. By choosing which possibilities to pursue and by following them as far as we can in the time we have, each of us contributes to the unfinished story of human development.

SUMMARY

■ Recently there has been an upsurge in interest, in American society, in the topic of death. Thanatology is the study of death and dying.

Three Aspects of Death

■ There are at least three aspects of dying: the biological (cessation of body processes), the social (mourning customs and legal implications of death), and the psychological (emotional reactions to death).

Facing Death

■ Sometime between the ages of 5 and 7, most children develop the understanding that death is irreversible and universal and that all life functions end at death.

■ Adolescents tend to have romantic conceptions of death and to be caught up in the personal

fable, believing that they can take risks without danger.

■ Young adults who are about to die resent their inability to fulfill the dreams they have worked to achieve.

■ It is usually in middle age that people fully realize the inevitability of their own death and begin thinking about how to make the most of their remaining years.

■ In late adulthood, many people accept the prospect of death more tranquilly, especially if they feel that they have led meaningful lives.

■ People often undergo both intellectual and personality changes shortly before death.

■ Elisabeth Kübler-Ross, a pioneer in the study of death and dying, proposes that there are five stages in coming to terms with death: denial, anger, bargaining, depression, and acceptance. However, these stages do not necessarily represent the healthiest progression for all persons.

■ Bereavement is the objective change in status of

a survivor following a death. Mourning is the behavior followed by the bereaved person after a death. Grief is the emotional response of the bereaved.

■ Three forms of grief are anticipatory grief (grief preceding the actual loss), normal grief, and morbid (unhealthy) grief.

■ Some bereaved people need help through formal grief therapy or from support groups in order to cope with grief.

■ Death education helps people to understand their attitudes toward death, to become familiar with the ways various cultural groups deal with death, and to be aware of the needs of dying persons and survivors.

■ The hospice movement has developed to provide patient- and family-centered care for persons with terminal illnesses and their loved ones. Hospice care can be given in a hospital, in another institution, or at home.

■ Support groups and services can help people deal with death, dying, and bereavement.

Controversial Issues of Death and Dying

■ Active euthanasia is deliberate action that is taken to shorten a life in order to end suffering.

Passive euthanasia is the withholding of treatment that might extend the life of a terminally ill patient.

■ Most people do not favor using advanced medical technology to prolong the lives of the terminally ill against their wishes. People can sign "living wills" stating their wishes about the kinds of measures they want or do not want taken in case of terminal illness.

■ The highest suicide rate is among white men over the age of 65. Suicide is increasing among teenagers, especially boys, and is the second leading cause of death in adolescence. The leading cause of death among adolescents is accidents, but many presumed "accidents" (even among preschoolers) may actually be suicides or attempted suicides.

Finding a Purpose in Life and Death

■ Evidence suggests that the more purpose and meaning people find in their lives, the less they fear death.

■ Life review is a process of reminiscence that helps people to prepare for death by assessing the significance of their lives and also gives them a last chance to make changes or to complete unfinished tasks.

KEY TERMS

active euthanasia (page 608)
anticipatory grief (602)
bereavement (601)
death education (605)
grief (602)

grief therapy (604)
hospice care (606)
life review (616)
living wills (609)
morbid grief (602)

mourning (601)
normal grief (602)
passive euthanasia (609)
thanatology (595)

SUGGESTED READINGS

Klagsbrun, F. (1976). *Too young to die.* Boston: Houghton Mifflin. A straightforward, readable account of the myths and realities of suicide among young people that explores motives, describes symptoms of depression, and suggests ways to help those thinking about ending their lives.

Kübler-Ross, E. (1969). *On death and dying.* New York: Macmillan. A moving book that inspired a new interest in death. The author draws upon case studies and actual dialogues with dying patients to back up her pioneering concept that there are five stages in the outlook of the dying patient.

Kübler-Ross, E. (Ed.). (1975). *Death: The final stage of growth.* Englewood Cliffs, NJ: Prentice-Hall. This book, the most accessible of Kübler-Ross's works, treats death as a normal part of human development. It offers a spectrum of views from clergy, doctors, nurses, sociologists, terminally ill patients, and survivors and compares the ways our culture and other cultures treat death and dying.

Lerner, G. (1978). *A death of one's own.* New York: Simon & Schuster. The story of the death of the author's husband from a brain tumor, the decision by husband and wife to face the death together at home, and the meaning of the experience for the author.

Lopata, H. Z. (1979). *Women as widows: Support systems.* New York: Elsevier. A report based on a study of over 1000 widows in the Chicago area, examining the effects of age, educational level, race, and social supports on women's ability to cope with widowhood.

Mitchell, P. (1976). *Act of love: The killing of George Zygmaniak.* New York: Knopf. A powerful tale of a real-life "mercy killing," which describes the events leading up to the shotgun killing of one brother by another, recreates the trial, and in the process raises legal and moral questions.

GLOSSARY

accommodation Piagetian term for a change in an existing cognitive structure to cope with new information. (24)

achieving stage Second of Schaie's five cognitive stages, in which young adults use knowledge to gain competence and independence and do best on tasks relevant to life goals they have established for themselves. (427)

acquired adaptations In Piagetian terminology, reorganized schemes for particular behaviors, learned by accommodation. (127)

acquisitive stage First of Schaie's five cognitive stages, characterized by the child's and adolescent's learning of information and skills largely for their own sake. (427)

acting-out behavior Misbehavior (such as lying or stealing) spurred by emotional turmoil. (327)

active euthanasia Deliberate action taken to shorten the life of a terminally ill person in order to end suffering or to carry out the wishes of the patient; also called *mercy killing*. Compare with *passive euthanasia*. (608)

activity theory Theory of aging that holds that in order to age successfully a person must remain as active as possible. Compare with *disengagement theory*. (568)

adaptation Piagetian term for effective interaction with the environment (problem solving) through the complementary processes of assimilation and accommodation. (23)

adolescent growth spurt Sharp increase in height and weight that precedes sexual maturity. (346)

adolescent rebellion "Storm and stress" characteristic of some but not all adolescents, encompassing both conflict within the family and a general alienation from adult society and its values. (382)

affective disorder Disorder of mood. (329)

ageism Prejudice or discrimination against a person (most commonly an older person) based on age. (534)

aggressive behavior Hostile assault, physical or verbal, intended to hurt the recipient or establish dominance. (243)

alleles Pair of inherited genes (similar or different) that affect a particular trait. (45)

Alzheimer's disease Irreversible dementia (degenerative brain disorder) characterized by deterioration in memory, awareness, and control of bodily functions, eventually leading to death. (547)

ambivalent attachment Pattern of attachment in which an infant becomes anxious before the primary caregiver leaves, is extremely upset during his or her absence, and both seeks and resists contact upon his or her return; also called *resistant attachment*. (164)

amniocentesis Prenatal medical procedure in which a sample of amniotic fluid is withdrawn and analyzed to determine whether any of certain genetic defects are present. (69)

anal stage According to Freudian theory, the psychosexual stage of toddlerhood (12–18 months to 3 years), in which the chief source of sensual gratification is moving the bowels; toilet training forces the child to delay this gratification. (150)

androgynous Personality type integrating positive characteristics typically thought of as masculine with positive characteristics typically thought of as feminine. (233)

animism Attribution of life to inanimate objects; according to Piaget, characteristic of preoperational thought. (204)

anorexia nervosa Eating disorder, seen mostly in young women, in which people starve themselves. (352)

anoxia Lack of oxygen, which may cause brain damage. (90)

anticipatory grief Grief that begins before an expected death and helps family and friends to prepare for bereavement. (602)

Apgar scale Standard measurement of a newborn's condition; it assesses appearance, pulse, grimace, activity, and respiration. (88)

apnea Temporary cessation of breathing. (95)

armor-defended Personality type in late adulthood described by Neugarten et al. Armor-defended people are achievement-oriented, striving, and tightly controlled; their life patterns are characterized as either holding on or constricted. (569)

artificial insemination Injection of sperm into a woman's cervix in order to enable her to conceive. (472)

asceticism Defense mechanism typical of adolescence, described by Anna Freud, which is characterized by self-denial as a defense against adolescents' fear of loss of control over their impulses. (378)

assimilation Piagetian term for the incorporation of new information into an existing cognitive structure. (24)

attachment Active, affectionate reciprocal relationship specifically between two persons (usually infant and parent), in which interaction reinforces and strengthens the link. (164)

attention deficit disorder with hyperactivity Syndrome characterized by inattention, impulsivity, and considerable activity at inappropriate times and places. (328)

authoritarian parents In Baumrind's terminology, parents whose child-rearing style em-
phasizes the values of control and obedience and who use forceful punishment to make children conform to a set standard of conduct. Compare with *authoritative parents* and *permissive parents*. (250)

authoritative parents In Baumrind's terminology, parents whose child-rearing style blends respect for a child's individuality with an effort to instill social values in the child. Compare with *authoritarian parents* and *permissive parents*. (250)

autonomy Independence; self-determination. (151)

autonomy versus shame and doubt According to Erikson, the second critical pair of alternatives in psychosocial development (from 12–18 months to 3 years), in which toddlers develop a balance of autonomous control (independence, self-determination) over shame and doubt. (151)

autosomes The 22 pairs of nonsex chromosomes. (44)

avoidant attachment Pattern of attachment in which an infant rarely cries when separated from the primary caregiver and avoids contact upon his or her return. (164)

basic trust versus basic mistrust According to Erikson's theory, the first critical balancing of alternatives in psychosocial development (from birth to 12–18 months), in which the infant develops a sense of whether or not the world can be trusted; the quality of interaction with the mother in feeding is a primary determinant of the outcome of this stage. (151)

battered child syndrome Pattern of child abuse and neglect first identified in 1962. (175)

Bayley Scales of Infant Development Standardized test for measuring the intellectual development of infants; the test consists of a mental scale and a motor scale, each of which yields a development quotient (DQ), computed by comparing what a particular baby can do at a certain age with the performance of a large number of previously observed babies at the same age. (125)

behaviorism School of psychology that emphasizes the study of observable behaviors and events and the role of environment in causing behavior. (18)

behavior modification Therapeutic approach using principles of learning theory to encourage desired behaviors or eliminate undesired ones; also called *behavior therapy*. (247)

behavior therapy Alternative term for *behavior modification*. (331)

bereavement Loss due to death, which leads to a change in the survivor's status (for example, from wife to widow). (601)

birth trauma Birth-related brain injury caused by oxygen deprivation, mechanical injury, or infection or disease at birth. (90)

body transcendence versus body preoccupation Psychological issue of late adulthood, described by Peck, which is occasioned by the need to overcome concerns about one's physical condition and to find compensating satisfactions. (567)

Brazelton Neonatal Behavioral Assessment Scale Neurological and behavioral test to measure neonates' response to the environment; it assesses interactive behaviors, motor behaviors, physiological control, and response to stress. (90)

bulimia Eating disorder in which a person regularly eats huge quantities of food and then purges the body by laxatives or induced vomiting; most common in young women. (353)

burnout Syndrome of emotional exhaustion and a sense that one can no longer accomplish anything on the job, often experienced by people in the helping professions. (493)

career consolidation Stage, described by Vaillant, occurring between the twenties and forties and characterized by preoccupation with strengthening one's career. (449)

case studies Scientific studies, each covering a single case or life, based on notes taken by observers or on published biographical materials. (26)

castration complex Phenomenon described by Freud in which a male child, seeing that girls do not have a penis and overwhelmed by guilt about his Oedipal feelings and fear of his father's power, becomes fearful that he will be castrated by his father. (226)

causality Piagetian term for the recognition that certain events cause other events. (127)

centration In Piaget's theory, a limitation of preoperational thought that leads the child to focus on one aspect of a situation and neglect others, often leading to illogical conclusions. (202)

cephalocaudal principle Principle that development proceeds in a head-to-toe direction, i.e., that upper parts of the body develop before lower parts. (96)

cerebral cortex Upper layer of the brain, responsible for thinking and problem solving. (84)

cesarean section Delivery of a baby by surgical removal from the uterus. (74)

childhood depression Affective disorder characterized by a child's inability to form and maintain friendships, have fun, concentrate, and display normal emotional reactions. (330)

chorionic villus sampling Prenatal diagnostic procedure in which tissue from villi (hairlike projections of the membrane surrounding the embryo) is analyzed for birth defects. (70)

chromosomes Segments of DNA that carry the genes, the transmitters of heredity; in the normal human being, there are 46 chromosomes. (42)

circular reactions In Piaget's terminology, processes by which the infant learns to reproduce desired occurrences originally discovered by chance. Piaget described three types of circular reactions: primary, secondary, and tertiary. (127)

classical conditioning Kind of learning in which a previously neutral stimulus (a neutral stimulus is one that does not elicit a particular response) acquires the power to elicit a response after the stimulus is repeatedly associated with another stimulus that ordinarily does elicit the response. (18)

classification Ability to sort stimuli into categories according to characteristics (for example, color and shape). (205)

climacteric Period of 2 to 5 years during which a woman's body undergoes physiological changes that bring on menopause. (484)

clinical method Technique of observation in which subjects are questioned in a flexible, individualized way, with the interviewer asking follow-up questions to explore the responses and gain insight into the subjects' thought processes. (27)

cognitive development Changes in thought processes that result in a growing ability to acquire and use knowledge. (22, 126)

cognitive play Forms of play that reveal and enhance children's cognitive development. (238)

cohabitation Living together and maintaining a sexual relationship without being legally married. (463)

commitment In Marcia's terminology based on Erikson's theory, an element of identity formation consisting of personal investment in an occupation or system of beliefs. (380)

companionate love Loving friendship marked by affection, attachment, commitment, and security; this kind of love tends to deepen with the passage of time. Compare with *passionate love*. (517)

componential element In Sternberg's triarchic theory, the analytic aspect of intelligence, which determines how efficiently people process information and solve problems. (428)

concordant In genetics, similar with respect to a trait. (51)

concrete operations Third stage of Piagetian cognitive development (approximately from age 5–7 to age 11), during which children develop logical but not abstract thinking. (269)

conditioned response In classical conditioning, a response that comes to be elicited by a conditioned stimulus. (19, 118)

conditioned stimulus In classical conditioning, an initially neutral stimulus that, after repeated pairing with an unconditioned stimulus, elicits a response similar to that elicited by the unconditioned stimulus. (19, 118)

conservation In Piaget's terminology, awareness that two objects of equal size remain equal in the face of perceived alteration (for example, a change in shape) so long as nothing has been added to or taken away from either object. (202, 269)

contextual element In Sternberg's triarchic theory, the practical aspect of intelligence, which determines how effectively people deal with their environment. (428)

control group In an experiment, a group of people who are similar to the people in the experimental group but who do not receive the treatment whose effects are to be measured. The results obtained with the control group are compared with the results obtained with the experimental group. (29)

convergent thinking Thinking aimed at finding the one "right" answer to a problem; traditional thinking. Compare with *divergent thinking*. (294)

coregulation Transitional stage during middle childhood in which parent and child share power over the child's behavior, the parent exercising general supervision and the child regulating his or her own specific activities. (315)

correlational studies Research that shows the direction and magnitude of relationships between variables but cannot establish cause-and-effect relationships. (28)

crisis In Marcia's terminology based on Erikson's theory, a period of conscious decision making that may precede identity formation. (380)

critical period Specific time during development when a given event will have the greatest impact. (10)

cross-sectional study Study design in which people of different ages are assessed on one occasion, providing comparative information about different age cohorts. Compare with *longitudinal study*. (31)

cross-sequential study Study design that combines cross-sectional and longitudinal techniques by assessing people in a cross-sectional sample more than once. (31)

crystallized intelligence Type of intelligence, proposed by Cattell and Horn, involving the ability to remember and use learned information; it is relatively dependent on education and cultural background. Compare with *fluid intelligence*. (426)

culture-fair Describing an intelligence test that deals with experiences common to various cultures, in an attempt to avoid placing test-takers at an advantage or disadvantage due to their cultural background. Compare with *culture-free*. (283)

culture-free Describing an intelligence test that would have no culturally linked content if it were possible to design. Compare with *culture-fair*. (283)

data Information that is obtained through research. (13)

death education Programs to educate people about dying and grief to help them deal with these issues in their personal and professional lives. (605)

decenter In Piagetian terminology, to consider all significant aspects of a situation simultaneously. Decentration is characteristic of operational thought. (202, 269)

deduction Type of logical reasoning that proceeds from a general premise to an implied conclusion about a situation. (203)

defense mechanisms According to Freudian theory, ways in which people unconsciously combat anxiety by distorting reality. (16)

deferred imitation In Piaget's terminology, reproduction of an observed behavior after the passage of time by calling up a stored symbol of it. (201)

dementia Apparent intellectual and personality deterioration sometimes associated with old age and caused by a variety of irreversible and reversible physiological conditions; sometimes called *senility*. (547)

Denver Developmental Screening Test Test given to children 1 month to 6 years old to determine whether or not they are developing normally; it assesses gross motor skills, fine motor skills, language development, and personal and social development. (105)

dependent variable In an experiment, the factor that may or may not change as a result of manipulation of the independent variable. (28)

depression Emotional disturbance characterized by feeble responses to stimuli, low initiative, and sullen or despondent attitudes. (56)

difficult child Child whose temperament is characterized by irritable mood, irregular biological rhythms, and intense responses to situations. Compare with *easy child* and *slow-to-warm-up child*. (158)

disengagement theory Theory of aging that holds that successful aging is characterized by mutual withdrawal between the older person and society. Compare with *activity theory*. (568)

divergent thinking Thinking that produces a variety of fresh, diverse possibilities; creative thinking. Compare with *convergent thinking*. (294)

dizygotic twins Twins conceived by the union of two different eggs with two different sperm cells within a brief period of time; also called *fraternal*, or *two-egg*, *twins*. (43)

DNA (deoxyribonucleic acid) Genetic substance that controls the makeup and functions of body cells. (42)

dominant inheritance Pattern of inheritance, described by Mendel, in which only the dominant trait of two competing traits is expressed. (45)

donor eggs Method of conception in which an ovum of a fertile woman is implanted in the uterus of a woman who cannot produce normal ova. (472)

Down syndrome Most common chromosomal disorder, usually caused by an extra twenty-first chromosome and characterized by mild or moderate mental retardation, and by such physical signs as a downward-sloping skin fold at the inner corners of the eyes; also called *Down's syndrome*. (49)

dream According to Levinson, the vision that spurs young adults and vitalizes their development; failure to fulfill the dream may precipitate a midlife crisis. (452)

drug therapy Therapeutic technique that includes administration of drugs. (331)

dual-process model Model of intellectual functioning in late adulthood, proposed by Baltes, which identifies and seeks to measure two dimensions of intelligence: the mechanics of intelligence and the pragmatics of intelligence. (553)

dyslexia Common learning disability involving inability to learn to read or difficulty in doing so. (292)

easy child Child whose temperament is characterized by a happy mood, regular biological rhythms, and readiness to accept new experiences. Compare with *difficult child* and *slow-to-warm-up child*. (158)

ego In Freudian theory, an aspect of personality that develops during infancy and operates on the reality principle, seeking acceptable means of gratification in dealing with the real world. (150)

egocentrism In Piaget's terminology, a characteristic of preoperational thought consisting of inability to consider another's viewpoint; a form of egocentrism is also characteristic of adolescents. (203)

ego defense mechanisms Psychological mechanisms to adapt to life circumstances, classified by Vaillant as mature, neurotic, immature, or psychotic. (449)

ego differentiation versus work-role preoccupation Psychological issue of late adulthood, described by Peck, centering on the degree to which the person defines himself or herself by work roles as opposed to other personal attributes. (566)

ego transcendence versus ego preoccupation Psychological issue of late adulthood, described by Peck, centering on the need to accept the certainty of oncoming death by transcending concern with one's own life. (567)

elder abuse Neglect or physical or psychological abuse of dependent older persons, often by their own children as a result of the stress of caring for the parents. (525)

Electra complex According to Freudian theory, the female counterpart of the Oedipus complex, in which the young girl in the phallic stage feels sexual attraction for her father and rivalry toward her mother. (226)

electronic fetal monitoring Monitoring of fetal heartbeat by machine in labor and delivery. (71)

embryonic stage Second stage of gestation (2 to 8–12 weeks), characterized by rapid growth and development of major body systems and organs. (60)

emotional flexibility versus emotional impoverishment One of four psychological developments described by Peck as critical to successful adjustment in middle age: the ability to shift emotional investment from one person or activity to another when such a shift is necessitated by physical limitations or life events. (508)

emotions Subjective feelings such as sadness, joy, and fear, which arise in response to situations and experiences and are expressed through some kind of altered behavior. (152)

empty nest Term for the transitional phase of parenting following the last child's leaving the parents' home. (517, 520)

enuresis Bed-wetting. (326)

environmental influences Nongenetic influences on development attributable to experiences with the outside world. (9)

equilibration In Piagetian terminology, the tendency to strive for equilibrium (balance) among cognitive elements within the organism and between it and the outside world. (24)

estrogen Female hormone; its reduction during the climacteric may result in hot flashes, thinning of the vaginal lining, and urinary dysfunction. (484)

executive stage Fourth of Schaie's cognitive stages, in which the middle-aged person responsible for societal systems integrates complex relationships on several levels. (427)

experiential element In Sternberg's triarchic theory, the insightful, creative aspect of intelligence, which determines how effectively people approach both novel and familiar tasks. (428)

experiment Rigorously controlled, replicable (repeatable) procedure in which the researcher manipulates variables to assess their effect on each other. (28)

experimental group In an experiment, the group receiving the treatment under study; any changes in these people are compared with changes in the control group. (29)

extinction Cessation of a response, or its return to the baseline level, when the response is no longer reinforced. (20)

failure to thrive An apparently healthy, well-fed baby's failure to grow, often as a result of emotional neglect. (176)

family therapy Therapeutic technique in which the whole family is treated together. (330)

fertilization Union of sperm and ovum to produce a zygote. (41)

fetal alcohol syndrome (FAS) Mental, motor, and developmental abnormalities (including stunted growth, facial and bodily malformations, and disorders of the central nervous system) affecting the offspring of some women who drink heavily during pregnancy. (65)

fetal stage Final stage of gestation (8–12 weeks to birth), characterized by increased detail of body parts and greatly elongated body size. (62)

fetal tobacco syndrome Growth retardation of offspring of some women who smoke heavily during pregnancy. (67)

fixation In Freudian theory, an arrest in development that occurs because a child has been gratified too much or too little during a particular psychosexual stage. (14)

fluid intelligence Type of intelligence, proposed by Cattell and Horn, involving ability to perceive relations, form concepts, and reason abstractly. It is considered dependent on neurological development and relatively free from influences of education and culture and is thus tested by novel problems or tasks with common cultural elements. Compare with *crystallized intelligence*. (425)

foreclosure Identity status described by Marcia in which a person who has not spent time considering alternatives (that is, has not been in crisis) is committed to other people's plans for his or her life. (381)

formal operations According to Piaget, the final stage of cognitive development, reached by some adolescents, which is characterized by the ability to think abstractly. (360)

gamete Sex cell (sperm or ovum). (41)

gender Significance of being male or female. (225)

gender conservation Realization that one's sex will always stay the same. (230)

gender differences Differences between males and females that may or may not be based on biological differences. (231)

gender identity Awareness, developed in early childhood, that one is male or female. (225, 230)

gender roles Behaviors, interests, attitudes, and skills that a culture considers appropriate for males and females and expects them to fulfill. (232)

gender stereotypes Exaggerated generalizations about male or female role behavior. (233)

gender-typing Socialization process by which a child, at an early age, learns the appropriate gender role. (232)

gene Basic functional unit of heredity, which determines an inherited characteristic. (42)

generativity versus stagnation According to Erikson, the seventh critical alternative of psychosocial development, in which the mature adult develops a concern with establishing and guiding the next generation or else experiences stagnation (a sense of inactivity or lifelessness). (506)

genetic counseling Clinical service that advises couples of their probable risk of having children with particular hereditary defects. (52)

genetics Study of hereditary factors affecting development. (42)

genital stage According to Freud, the psychosexual stage of mature sexuality, achieved during adolescence. (377)

genotype Underlying genetic composition that causes certain traits to be expressed; may vary without causing changes in phenotype, because of the presence of recessive genes. (46)

geriatrics Branch of medicine concerned with the aged and with aging. (536)

germinal stage First 2 weeks of prenatal development, characterized by rapid cell division and increasing complexity; the stage ends when the conceptus attaches itself to the wall of the uterus. (57)

gerontologists Persons engaged in gerontology, the study of the aged and the process of aging. (534)

giftedness Exceptional potential in any of the following areas: general intellectual ability, specific academic aptitudes, lead-

ership, talent in the arts, creativity, psychomotor ability. (292)

grief Emotional response of the bereaved to a death. (602)

grief therapy Program to help the bereaved cope with loss. (604)

habituation Simple type of learning in which familiarity with a stimulus results in loss of interest and reduces or stops the response. (103, 117)

heredity Inborn influences on development, carried on the genes inherited from the parents. (9, 42)

heterosexual Describing a person whose sexual orientation is toward the other sex. (392)

heterozygous Possessing two dissimilar alleles for a trait. (45)

holophrase Single word that conveys a complete thought; the typical speech form of children aged 12 to 18 months. (137)

homosexual Describing a person whose sexual orientation is toward the same sex. (392)

homozygous Possessing two similar alleles for a trait. (45)

horizontal décalage Piagetian term for a child's inability to transfer learning about one type of conservation to other types, because of which the child masters different types of conservation tasks for the first time at different ages (for example, learning substance conservation before either weight or volume conservation). (269)

hospice care Warm, personal patient- and family-centered care for a person with a terminal illness. (606)

hospitalism Decline in a child's intellectual and psychological functioning resulting from long-term institutionalization. (173)

human development Scientific study of quantitative and qualitative ways in which people change over time. (4)

humanistic perspective View of humanity that sees people as having the ability to foster their own positive, healthy development through the distinctively human capacities for choice, creativity, and self-realization. (24)

hypertension High blood pressure. (488)

hypothesis Possible explanation for a phenomenon, used to predict the outcome of an experiment. (13)

id In Freudian theory, the instinctual aspect of personality (present at birth) that operates on the pleasure principle, seeking immediate gratification. (150)

ideal self Person's concept of who he or she would like to be; compare with *real self*. (301)

identification Process by which a person acquires characteristics, beliefs, attitudes, values, and behaviors of another person or of a group; an important personality development of early childhood. (225)

identity achievement Identity status, described by Marcia, which is characterized by commitment to choices made following a crisis period, or period spent in thinking about alternatives. (380)

identity diffusion Identity status, described by Marcia, which is characterized by absence of commitment and may or may not follow a period of considering alternatives (crisis). (381)

identity versus identity confusion According to Eriksonian theory, the fifth critical alternative of psychosocial development, in which an adolescent must determine his or her own sense of self (identity), including the role he or she is to play in society. (379)

imaginary audience Observer who exists only in an adolescent's mind and is as concerned with the adolescent's thoughts and actions as is the adolescent himself or herself. (364)

imprinting Instinctive form of learning in which, after a single encounter, an animal recognizes and trusts one particular individual. (162)

independent segregation Mendel's law that hereditary traits are transmitted separately. (45)

independent variable In an experiment, the variable over which the experimenter has control. Compare *dependent variable*. (28)

induction Type of logical reasoning in which a generalization is made on the basis of particular observations. (203)

industry versus inferiority In Erikson's theory, the fourth critical alternative of psychosocial development, occurring during middle childhood, in which children must learn the productive skills their culture requires or else face feelings of inferiority. (305)

infantile autism Developmental disorder that begins within the first 2½ years of life and is characterized by lack of responsiveness to other people. (56)

infant mortality Death during the first year of life. (90)

infertility Inability to conceive after 12 to 18 months. (471)

information-processing approach Study of intellectual development by analyzing the mental processes that underlie intelligent behavior: the manipulation of symbols and perceptions to acquire information and solve problems. (122, 132)

initiative versus guilt According to Erikson, the third crisis of psychosocial development, occurring between the ages of 3 and 6, in which children must balance the urge to form and carry out goals with their moral judgments about what they want to do. Children develop initiative when they try out new things and are not overwhelmed by failure. (227)

integrated Personality type in late adulthood described by Neugarten and her associates. Integrated people function well and have complex inner lives, competent egos, intact cognitive abilities, and high levels of life satisfaction; their life patterns are characterized as either reorganized, focused, or disengaged. (569)

integrity versus despair According to Erikson, the eighth and final critical alternative of psychosocial development, in which people in late adulthood

either accept their lives as a whole and thus accept death or yield to despair that their lives cannot be relived. (565)

intellectualization Defense mechanism typical of adolescence, described by Anna Freud, which is characterized by translation of sexual impulses into abstract intellectual discussions. (378)

intelligence quotient (IQ) Measurement of intelligence obtained by dividing a person's mental age (MA) by his or her chronological age (CA) and multiplying the result by 100. (123)

intelligent behavior Behavior that is goal-oriented (conscious and deliberate) and adaptive (used to identify and solve problems). (122)

interiority In Neugarten's terminology, a concern with inner life (introversion or introspection), which generally increases as people grow older. (510)

interview method Research technique in which people are asked to state their attitudes, opinions, or histories. (28)

intimacy versus isolation According to Erikson, the sixth critical alternative of psychosocial development, in which young adults either make commitments to others or face a possible sense of isolation and consequent self-absorption. (447)

introjection In Freudian theory, the process by which the superego takes into the child's personality societal values represented by the parents. (227)

invisible imitation Imitation with parts of one's body that one cannot see, e.g., the mouth. (132)

in vitro fertilization Fertilization of an ovum outside the mother's body. (472)

irreversibility In Piaget's theory, a limitation on preoperational thinking consisting of failure to understand that an operation can be reversed, restoring the original condition. (202)

karyotype Chart in which photomicrographs of a prospective parent's chromosomes are arranged according to size and

structure to reveal any chromosomal abnormalities. (53)

language acquisition device In Chomsky's nativist theory, an inborn mental structure that enables children to build linguistic rules by analyzing the language they hear. (139)

lanugo Fuzzy prenatal body hair, which drops off within a few days after birth. (83)

latchkey children Children who care for themselves at home without adult supervision because both parents work outside the home or because they have a single custodial parent who works outside the home. (320)

latency period In Freudian theory, a period of relative psychosexual calm that occurs during middle childhood after the Oedipus or Electra complex has been resolved and the superego has developed. (304)

learning Long-lasting change in behavior that occurs as a result of experience. (116)

learning disabilities Disorders that interfere with specific aspects of learning and school achievement. (291)

learning theory Theory that behavior is learned from experience. The two major branches are traditional learning theory (behaviorism) and social-learning theory. (138)

libido In Freud's terminology, the source of energy that fuels the sex drive. (377)

life review Reminiscence about one's life in order to determine its significance. (616)

life structure According to Levinson, the basic pattern of a person's life at a given time, consisting of internal and external aspects that shape and are shaped by the person's relationship with the environment. (450)

linguistic speech Speech designed to convey meaning. (137)

living will Document specifying the type of care wanted by the maker in the event of terminal illness. (609)

longitudinal study Study design in which data are collected about the same people over a period of time, to assess developmental changes that occur with age. Compare with *cross-sectional study*. (31)

long-term memory Store of permanent or long-lasting memories, which may be retrieved with varying degrees of ease depending on the efficiency of organization and storage. Long-term memory for newly learned information diminishes with aging, but long-term memory for memories acquired in the distant past does not generally diminish appreciably. Compare with *short-term memory*. (277, 554)

low-birth-weight babies Babies who weigh less than 5½ pounds at birth because they are premature or small for date. (90)

mainstreaming Integration of disabled and nondisabled children in the classroom. (289)

male climacteric Period of physiological, emotional, and psychological change involving a man's reproductive system and other body systems. (486)

masturbation Sexual self-stimulation. (392)

maternal blood test Prenatal diagnostic procedure to detect the presence of fetal abnormalities, used particularly when the fetus is at risk of defects in the central nervous system. (70)

maturation Unfolding of a biologically determined, age-related sequence of behavior patterns programmed by the genes, including the readiness to master new abilities. (51, 117)

mean length of utterance (MLU) Average number of morphemes in a child's utterance. (137)

mechanics of intelligence In the dual-process model of Baltes, the abilities to process information and solve problems, irrespective of content; the area of intellect in which there is often an age-related decline. Compare with *pragmatics of intelligence*. (553)

mechanistic perspective View of humanity that sees development as an automatic response to external stimuli or events. (18)

meconium Fetal waste matter, excreted during the first few days after birth. (84)

medicated delivery Childbirth in which the mother receives anesthesia. (72)

menarche First menstruation. (348)

menopause Cessation of menstruation and of ability to bear children, typically around age 50. (484)

mental age (MA) Assessment of intellectual ability determined by matching a child's score on an intelligence test with the average age of those in a sample group who have scored similarly. (123)

mental flexibility versus mental rigidity One of four psychological developments described by Peck as critical to successful adjustment in middle age: the ability to use experience as a guide to solving new problems rather than becoming set in one's ways and closed to new ideas. (508)

mentor According to Levinson, an older person whose guidance and advice in both career and personal matters strongly influence a young adult's prospects for success. (452)

metacommunication Understanding of the processes involved in communication; metacommunication increases during middle childhood. (280)

metamemory Understanding of how memory works. (277, 279)

midlife crisis Potentially stressful life period precipitated by the review and reevaluation of one's past, typically occurring in the early to middle forties. (504)

mnemonic strategies Mental devices to aid memory. (277)

monozygotic twins Twins resulting from the division of a single zygote after fertilization; also called *identical*, or *one-egg*, *twins*. (43)

morality of autonomous moral principles In Kohlberg's system, the highest level of moral development, normally reached after the age of 12 (if it is ever reached at all), in which people follow internally held moral principles and make choices between conflicting moral standards. (275)

morality of constraint First of Piaget's two stages of moral development, characterized by rigid, simplistic judgments; also called *heteronomous morality*. (271)

morality of conventional role conformity Second of Kohlberg's three levels of moral reasoning, normally reached between the ages of 10 and 13, in which children have internalized the standards of authority figures and obey rules to please others or to maintain order. (275)

morality of cooperation Second of Piaget's two stages of moral development, characterized by moral flexibility; also called *autonomous morality*. (271)

moratorium Identity status, described by Marcia, in which a person is currently considering alternatives (in crisis) and seems headed for commitment. (381)

morbid grief Grief that is unusually intense or long-lasting and is believed to indicate emotional disturbance or pathology. (602)

morphemes The smallest meaningful elements of speech. (137)

mother-infant bond A mother's feeling of close, caring connection with her newborn. (162)

mourning Behavior of the bereaved and the community after a death. (601)

multifactorial inheritance Pattern of inheritance in which a single trait is affected by a combination of genetic and environmental factors. (47)

multiple alleles Genes that have three or more alternative forms. (46)

nativism Theory that views human beings as having an inborn capacity for language acquisition. (138)

natural childbirth Method of childbirth, developed by Dr. Grantly Dick-Read, that seeks to prevent pain by eliminating the mother's fear of childbirth. (73)

naturalistic observation Method of research in which people's behavior is studied in natural settings without the observer's intervention or manipulation. (26)

neonatal period First 4 weeks of life, a time of transition from intrauterine dependency to independent existence. (82)

neonate Newborn baby. (82)

neutral stimulus In classical conditioning, a stimulus that ordinarily does not elicit a particular reflex response. (19, 118)

nonnormative life events In the timing-of-events model, life experiences which are unusual and thus not normally anticipated or are ordinary but come at unexpected times, and which may thus have major impact on development. (455)

normal grief Grief that follows a death, usually in a fairly predictable pattern consisting of three phases: initial shock and disbelief, preoccupation with the memory of the dead, and resolution. Compare with *morbid grief*. (602)

normative-crisis model Theoretical model, typified by the work of Erikson, Levinson, and Vaillant, that describes social and emotional development in terms of a definite sequence of age-related changes. Compare with *timing-of-events model*. (446)

normative life events In the timing-of-events model, expected life experiences that occur at customary times. (455)

object permanence In Piaget's terminology, the understanding that a person or object still exists when out of sight. (127)

Oedipus complex Phenomenon described by Freud, in which the young boy in the phallic stage feels sexual attraction for his mother and rivalry toward his father. (226)

operant conditioning Form of learning in which a response continues to be made because it has been reinforced or stops being made because it has been punished; also called *instrumental conditioning*, because the learner is instrumental in changing the environment to bring about either reinforcement or punishment. (19, 119)

operational thinking In Piaget's terminology, mental manipula-

tion of symbols and signs to carry out logical operations. (269)

oral stage According to Freudian theory, the psychosexual stage of infancy (birth to 12–18 months), characterized by sensual gratification in the oral region, chiefly through food. (149)

organismic perspective View that sees people as active agents of their own development and sees development as occurring in a sequence of qualitatively different stages. (22)

organization Piagetian term for integration of knowledge into a system to make sense of the environment. (23)

osteoporosis Condition affecting 1 in 4 postmenopausal women, in which the bones become thinner and more susceptible to fractures. (484)

Otis-Lennon Mental Ability Test Group intelligence test for kindergarten to twelfth grade, covering classification, verbal and numerical concepts, general information, and ability to follow directions. (281)

ovulation Expulsion of ovum from ovary, which occurs about once every 28 days from puberty to menopause. (41)

passionate love Initial intense attraction of lovers, which often brings wild emotional ups and downs; this kind of love tends to fade with the passage of time. Compare with *companionate love*. (517)

passive-dependent Personality type in late adulthood described by Neugarten and her associates. Passive-dependent people have life patterns that are characterized as either succorance-seeking or apathetic. (569)

passive euthanasia Deliberate withholding of life-prolonging treatment from a terminally ill person in order to minimize suffering or carry out the wishes of the patient. Compare with *active euthanasia*. (609)

penis envy Phenomenon, described by Freud, in which a girl envies the male's penis and wants one of her own. (226)

permissive parents In Baum-

rind's terminology, parents whose child-rearing style emphasizes the values of self-expression and self-regulation. Compare with *authoritarian parents* and *authoritative parents*. (250)

personal fable Conviction, typical in adolescence, that one is special, unique, and not subject to the rules that govern the rest of the world. (364)

personality Person's collective pattern of character, behavioral, temperamental, emotional, and mental traits. (55)

phallic stage According to Freudian theory, the stage of psychosexual development between the ages of 3 and 6, in which the child receives gratification chiefly in the genital area. (226)

phenotype Observable characteristic of a person; may be unvarying even with differences in underlying genotype. (46)

phobias Irrational, involuntary fears inappropriate to the real situation. (242)

physiological jaundice Common and reversible condition caused by immaturity of the liver and characterized by yellowing of skin and eyeballs shortly after birth. (84)

Piagetian approach Study of intellectual development by describing qualitative stages, or typical changes, in children's and adolescents' cognitive functioning; proposed by Jean Piaget. (122, 126)

plasticity Variability or modifiability of a given person's performance. (552)

pleasure principle In Freudian theory, the operating principle of the id: the attempt to obtain immediate gratification of instinctual needs. Compare with *reality principle*. (150)

pragmatics of intelligence In the dual-process model of Baltes, the dimension of intelligence that tends to grow with age and includes practical thinking, application of accumulated knowledge and skills, specialized expertise, professional productivity, and wisdom. Compare with *mechanics of intelligence*. (553)

preconventional morality According to Kohlberg, the first level of moral development, in which children aged approximately 4 to 10 years obey rules or standards set by others, in order to gain rewards or avoid punishment. (275)

prejudice Negative attitude toward someone because of his or her membership in a group, often a racial group. (308)

prelinguistic speech Forerunner of linguistic speech; includes crying, cooing, babbling, and accidental and deliberate imitation of sounds without understanding their meaning. (136)

premenstrual syndrome (PMS) Disorder producing symptoms of physical discomfort and emotional tension before a menstrual period. (423)

preoperational stage In Piaget's theory, the second major period of intellectual development (approximately from age 2 to age 7), in which children can think about things not physically present by using mental representations but are limited by their inability to use logic. (200)

prepared childbirth Method of childbirth, developed by Dr. Ferdinand Lamaze, that uses instruction, breathing exercises, and social support to remove fear and pain. (73)

presbycusis Gradual loss of hearing that occurs during middle age, especially with regard to sounds at the upper frequencies. (483)

presbyopia Farsightedness associated with aging, resulting when the lens of the eye becomes less elastic. (483)

pretend play Play involving imaginary situations; also called *fantasy play*, *dramatic play*, or *imaginative play*. (240)

preterm babies Babies born before thirty-seventh week of gestation, dated from the mother's last menstrual period; also called *premature babies*. (92)

primary aging Gradual process of bodily deterioration that begins early in life and continues

through the life span. Compare with *secondary aging*. (541)

primary circular reactions Simple repetitive acts centered on the infant's body, designed to reproduce pleasant sensations originally discovered by chance; characteristic of the second substage of the sensorimotor stage described by Piaget. (127)

primary sex characteristics Characteristics directly related to reproduction; specifically, the male and female sex organs. These enlarge and mature during adolescence. See *secondary sex characteristics*. (347)

private speech Talking aloud to oneself with no intent to communicate; common in early and middle childhood. (209)

programmed-aging theory Theory that bodies age in accordance with a normal development pattern built into every organism of a particular species; compare with *wear-and-tear theory of aging*. (541)

Project Head Start Compensatory preschool education program begun in the United States in 1965. (216)

prosocial behavior Behavior intended to help others without external reward. (245)

proximodistal law Principle that development proceeds from within to without, i.e., that parts of the body near the center develop before the extremities. (97)

psychoanalytic perspective View of humanity concerned with the unconscious forces motivating human behavior. (13)

psychological maltreatment Action or failure to act that damages children's behavioral, cognitive, emotional, or physical functioning and may keep children from realizing their full potential as adults. (332)

psychometric approach Study of intellectual development by attempting to measure quantitatively the factors that appear to make up intelligence. (122, 123)

psychosexual development In Freudian theory, an unvarying sequence of stages of personality development during childhood and adolescence, in which

gratification shifts from the mouth to the anus and then to the genitals. (14)

psychosocial-development theory Theory of Erikson that societal and cultural influences play a major part in healthy personality development. According to this theory, development occurs in eight maturationally determined stages throughout the life span, each revolving around a particular crisis or turning point in which the person is faced with achieving a healthy balance between alternative positive and negative traits. (17)

psychotherapy Therapeutic technique in which a therapist helps people gain insight into their personalities and relationships, past and present, by helping them interpret their feelings and behavior. (330)

puberty Time at which a person attains sexual maturity and is able to reproduce. (342, 344)

pubescence Period of development preceding puberty and characterized by rapid physiological growth, maturation of reproductive functioning, enlargement of the sex organs, and appearance of the secondary sex characteristics. (344)

punishment In operant conditioning, a stimulus that, when administered following a particular behavior, decreases the probability that the behavior will be repeated. (19)

qualitative changes Changes in kind, structure, or organization, such as changes in the nature of a person's intelligence or the way the mind works. (4)

quantitative changes Changes in the number or amount of something, such as height, weight, or vocabulary. (4)

random sampling Type of sampling that ensures representativeness because each member of the population has an equal chance to be selected. (29)

reaction formation In Freudian theory, a defense mechanism characterized by the replacement of an anxiety-producing feeling by the expression of its opposite. (377)

reaction range Potential variability in the expression of a hereditary trait, depending on environmental conditions. (51)

reality principle In Freudian theory, the operating principle of the ego: the search for acceptable and realistic ways to obtain gratification. (150)

real self Person's concept of who he or she actually is. Compare with *ideal self*. (301)

recall Ability to reproduce material from memory without being presented with it again. Compare with *recognition*. (199)

recessive inheritance Expression of a recessive (nondominant) trait, which, according to Mendel, occurs only if the offspring receives the same recessive gene from each parent. (45)

recognition Ability to identify previously learned material when presented with it again; tested by asking a person to choose the correct answer from among several possibilities. Compare with *recall*. (119)

reflex behaviors Automatic responses to external stimulation. Reflexes—by their presence or disappearance—are early signs of an infant's neurological growth. (85)

reinforcement In operant conditioning, a stimulus that, when administered following a particular behavior, increases the probability that the behavior will be repeated. (19, 119)

reintegrative stage Fifth of Schaie's cognitive stages, in which older people choose to focus energy on tasks that have meaning for them. (427)

reliability Consistency of a test in measuring performance. (281)

reliable Describing a test that is consistent in measuring performance. (123, 125)

representational ability Capacity to remember (mentally represent) objects and experiences without needing a stimulus, largely through the use of symbols and signs. (127)

reserve capacity Ability of body organs and systems to put forth 4 to 10 times as much effort as usual in times of stress or dys-

function; also called *organ reserve*. (487, 544)

resilient children Children who are able to "bounce back" from circumstances that would have a highly negative impact on the emotional development of most children. (333)

responsible stage Third of Schaie's five cognitive stages, in which middle-aged people are concerned with long-range goals and practical problems often related to their responsibility for others. (427)

Rh factor Protein substance in the blood of most people; when it is present in the blood of a fetus but not in the mother, death of the fetus can result. (68)

role-taking Ability to imagine another person's situation or point of view. (272)

sample In an experiment, the group of subjects chosen to represent the entire population under study. (29)

schema In Bem's cognitive-social theory, a mentally organized pattern of behavior that helps a child sort out information about the environment. (230)

scheme In Piaget's terminology, a basic cognitive structure that an infant uses to interact with the environment; an organized pattern of thought and behavior. (23, 127)

schizophrenia Psychological disorder characterized by loss of contact with reality and such symptoms as delusions, hallucinations, and thought disturbances. (55)

school phobia Unrealistic fear of school, probably reflecting separation anxiety. (328)

scientific method System of established principles of scientific inquiry, including careful observation and recording of data, testing of alternative hypotheses, and widespread dissemination of findings and conclusions so that other scientists can learn from, analyze, repeat, and build on the results. (26)

secondary aging Aging processes that result from disease and bodily abuse and disuse, factors that may be subject to the

person's own control. Compare with *primary aging*. (541)

secondary circular reactions An infant's intentional repetition of actions to reproduce desired effects discovered in the environment outside the body; characteristic of the third substage of the sensorimotor stage described by Piaget. (129)

secondary sex characteristics Physiological characteristics of the sexes which develop during adolescence (and do not involve the sex organs), including breasts in females, broadened shoulders in males, growth of body hair in both sexes, and adult skin and adult voices of men and women. See *primary sex characteristics*. (347)

secular trend Trend that can be seen only by observing several generations. A secular trend toward earlier attainment of adult height and sexual maturity began a century ago and appears to have ended in the United States. (346)

secure attachment Attachment pattern in which an infant can separate readily from the primary caregiver and actively seeks out the caregiver upon return. (164)

selective optimization with compensation In the dual-process model of Baltes, the ability of older people to maintain or enhance their intellectual functioning through the use of special abilities to compensate for losses in other areas. (583)

self-awareness Realization, beginning in infancy, of separateness from other people and things, allowing reflection on one's own actions in relation to social standards. (154, 301)

self-concept Sense of self, including self-understanding and self-control or self-regulation. (301)

self-control Child's ability to alter or delay an action when the caregiver is not present, on the basis of knowing what behavior is socially acceptable. (180)

self-definition External and psychological characteristics by which a person describes himself or herself. (301)

self-esteem Person's self-evaluation or self-image. (302)

self-fulfilling prophecy Expectation or prediction of behavior that tends to come true because it leads people to act as if it were already true. (288)

self-recognition Children's ability to recognize their own physical image; occurs at about 18 months. (154, 301)

self-regulation Child's independent control of behavior to conform to understood social expectations. (179)

self-schema According to the information-processing approach, the self-concept: a set of knowledge structures, or hypotheses, based on social experience, which organize and guide the processing of information about the self and help children decide how to act and imagine what they may become. (305)

senescence Period of the life span during which people experience decrements in bodily functioning associated with aging; begins at different ages for different people. (539)

sensorimotor stage First of Piaget's stages of cognitive development, when infants (from birth to 2 years) learn through their developing senses and motor activities. (127)

sensory memory Fleeting awareness of images or sensations, which disappears quickly unless transferred to short-term memory. (277, 554)

separation anxiety Distress shown by an infant, usually beginning in the second half of the first year, when a familiar caregiver leaves; it is commonly a sign that attachment has occurred. (170)

sex chromosomes Pair of chromosomes that determines sex: XX in the normal female, XY in the normal male. (44)

sex differences Physical differences between males and females. (231)

sexism Prejudice against a person because of sex; judging one sex, usually the male, as superior. (304)

sex-linked inheritance Pattern of inheritance in which certain characteristics carried on the sex chromosomes (usually the X chromosome) are transmitted differently to males and females. (46)

sexually transmitted diseases (STDs) Diseases transmitted by sexual contact; also called *venereal diseases*. (356)

sexual orientation Sexual interest either in the other sex (heterosexual orientation) or in the same sex (homosexual orientation), usually expressed during adolescence; also called *sexual preference*. (392)

shaping In operant conditioning, a method of bringing about a new response by reinforcing responses that are progressively more like it. (20)

short-term memory Working memory, the active repository of information currently being used; its capacity is limited but increases rapidly during middle childhood and is relatively unaffected by aging. Material in short-term memory disappears after about 20 seconds unless transferred to long-term memory. (277, 554)

sign In Piaget's terminology, a conventional mental representation of an abstraction, such as a word or numeral. (201)

slow-to-warm-up child Child whose temperament is characterized by mild intensity of response and hesitancy to accept new experiences. Compare with *difficult* and *easy child*. (158)

small-for-date babies Babies whose birth weight is less than that of 90 percent of babies of the same gestational age, as a result of slow fetal growth. (92)

socialization Process of learning the behaviors considered appropriate in one's culture. (161)

socializing versus sexualizing One of four psychological developments described by Peck as critical to successful adjustment in middle age: the appreciation of other people as friends and companions rather than as sex objects. (508)

social-learning theory Theory, proposed chiefly by Bandura, that behaviors are learned by observing and imitating models and are maintained through reinforcement. (20)

social play Play in which children interact with other children, commonly regarded as a sign of social competence. (238)

social speech Speech intended for a listener. (207)

sociogram Diagram of social relationships among members of a group. (310)

sociometric Describing quantitative techniques for the study of interpersonal relationships. (310)

spontaneous abortion Natural expulsion from the uterus of a conceptus that cannot survive outside the womb; also called *miscarriage*. (60)

standardized norms Standards for determining mental age of persons who take an intelligence test, obtained from scores of a large, representative sample of children who took the test while it was in preparation. (123)

Stanford-Binet Intelligence Scale Individual intelligence test used primarily with children to measure practical judgment, memory, and spatial orientation. (210)

states Periodic variations in an infant's daily cycles of wakefulness, sleep, and activity. (97)

status offender Juvenile charged with committing an act that would not be considered criminal if the offender were older (for example, being truant, running away from home, or engaging in sexual intercourse). (399)

"storm and stress" In Hall's terminology, the idea that adolescence is necessarily a time of intense, fluctuating emotions; see *adolescent rebellion*. (377)

stranger anxiety Phenomenon that often occurs during the second half of a child's first year (in conjunction with separation anxiety), when the infant becomes wary of strange people and places; commonly a sign that attachment has occurred. (169)

stress The organism's physiological and psychological reaction to demands made on it. (419)

stressor Event capable of causing stress. (419)

stuttering Involuntary repetition of sounds and syllables. (327)

substantive complexity Degree to which the nature of a kind of work requires thought and independent judgment. (495)

sudden infant death syndrome (SIDS) Sudden and unexpected death of an apparently healthy infant. (95)

superego According to Freudian theory, the aspect of personality representing values that parents and other agents of society communicate to a child. It develops around the age of 5 or 6 as a result of resolution of the Oedipus or Electra complex. (227)

surrogate motherhood Method of conception in which a woman who is not married to a man agrees to bear his baby and then give the child to the father and his wife. (473)

symbol In Piaget's terminology, an idiosyncratic mental representation of a sensory experience. (200)

symbolic function In Piaget's terminology, ability to learn by using mental representations (symbols or signs) to which a child has attached meaning; this ability, characteristic of preoperational thought, is shown in deferred imitation, symbolic play, and language. (200)

symbolic play In Piaget's terminology, play in which a child makes an object stand for something else. (201)

systematic desensitization Therapeutic technique for treating a phobia through gradual exposure to the feared object. (242)

tacit knowledge Information that is not formally taught or openly expressed but is necessary to get ahead; includes self-management and management of tasks and of others. (428)

telegraphic Describing linguistic utterances that omit many parts of speech but still convey meaning. (137)

temperament Person's characteristic style of approaching and reacting to people and situations. (55, 157)

teratogenic Capable of causing birth defects. (62)

terminal drop Sudden decrease in intellectual performance shortly before death. (551)

tertiary circular reactions A baby's purposeful variations of behavior to test novel ways of producing desired results; characteristic of the fifth substage of the sensorimotor stage described by Piaget. (130)

thanatology Study of death and dying. (595)

theory Set of related statements about data that helps scientists to explain, interpret, and predict behavior. (13)

tics Repetitive, involuntary muscular movements. (327)

timing-of-events model Theoretical model, advocated by Neugarten, that describes adult social and emotional development as a response to whether the occurrence and timing of important life events is expected or unexpected. Compare with *normative-crisis model*. (496)

transduction In Piaget's terminology, a preoperational child's tendency to mentally link particular experiences without the use of inductive or deductive logic, sometimes resulting in false conclusions. (203)

transitional objects Objects—commonly soft, cuddly ones—used repeatedly at bedtime to help a child make the transition from dependence to independence. (197)

"Type A" behavior pattern Competitive, aggressive, impatient, hostile behavior pattern; the element of hostility in this pattern appears to be associated with a risk of early coronary disease. See also *"Type B" behavior pattern*. (421)

"Type B" behavior pattern Relaxed, easygoing, unhurried behavior pattern found to be associated with less risk of early coronary disease than is the more hostile "Type A" behavior pattern. (421)

ultrasound Prenatal medical procedure using high-frequency sound waves to detect the outline of a fetus, judge gestational age, detect multiple pregnancies, detect abnormalities or death of the fetus, and determine whether the pregnancy is progressing normally. (70)

unconditioned response In classical conditioning, an automatic, unlearned response to a particular stimulus; also called *unconditioned reflex*. (19, 118)

unconditioned stimulus In classical conditioning, a stimulus that automatically elicits an unlearned (unconditioned) response. (19, 118)

underachievers Adults or children who perform below their apparent potential. (314)

unintegrated Personality pattern in late adulthood described by Neugarten and her associates. Unintegrated people show disorganized patterns of aging and have gross defects in psychological functioning, poor emotional control, intellectual deterioration, low activity levels, and low life satisfaction. (569)

valid Describing a test that has validity. (123)

validity Degree to which a test measures what it is supposed to measure. (281)

valuing wisdom versus valuing physical powers One of four psychological developments described by Peck as critical to successful adjustment in middle age: the appreciation that the ability to make wise choices based on life experience compensates for diminished physical strength, stamina, and youthful attractiveness. (508)

vernix caseosa Oily substance on a neonate that protects against infection and dries within a few days after birth. (83)

visible imitation Imitation with parts of one's body that one can see, such as the hands and the feet. (132)

visual cliff Apparatus designed

to give an illusion of depth and used to assess depth perception in infants. (104)

visual preference An infant's tendency to look longer at certain stimuli than at others, which depends on the ability to differentiate between sights. (104)

visual-recognition memory Ability to remember and recognize a visual stimulus. (133)

wear-and-tear theory of aging Theory that bodies age because of continuous use and accumulated "insults." Compare with *programmed-aging theory*. (541)

Wechsler Intelligence Scale for Children (WISC-R) Individual intelligence test for school children that yields separate scores for verbal and performance subtests and a total score. (281)

Wechsler Preschool and Primary Scale of Intelligence (WPPSI) Individual intelligence test for children aged 4 to 6½ that includes verbal and performance subtests. (281)

zygote One-celled organism resulting from the union of sperm and ovum. (41)

BIBLIOGRAPHY

Abbott, D. A., & Brody, G. H. (1985). The relation of child age, gender and number of children to the marital adjustment of wives. *Journal of Marriage and the Family, 47*(1), 77–84.

Abramovitch, R., Corter, C., & Lando, B. (1979). Sibling interaction in the home. *Child Development, 50,* 997–1003.

Abramovitch, R., Corter, C., Pepler, D., & Stanhope, L. (1986). Sibling and peer interactions: A final follow-up and comparison. *Child Development, 57,* 217–229.

Abramovitch, R., Pepler, D., & Corter, C. (1982). Patterns of sibling interaction among preschool-age children. In M. E. Lamb (Ed.), *Sibling relationships: Their nature and significance across the lifespan.* Hillsdale, NJ: Erlbaum.

Abravanel, E., & Sigafoos, A. D. (1984). Exploring the presence of imitation during early infancy. *Child Development, 55,* 381–392.

Abroms, K., & Bennett, J. (1979). *Paternal contributions to Down's syndrome dispel maternal myths.* ERIC.

Abroms, K., & Bennett, J. (1981). Changing etiological perspectives in Down's syndrome: Implications for early intervention. *Journal of the Division for Early Childhood, 2,* 109–112.

Abt Associates. (1978). *Children at the center: Vol. 1. Summary findings and policy implications of the National Day Care Study.* Washington, DC: U.S. Department of Health, Education, and Welfare.

Action for Children's Television. (undated). *Treat TV with T.L.C.* One-page flyer. Newtonville, MA: Author.

Adams, D. (1983). *The psychosocial development of professional black women's lives and the consequences of careers for their personal happiness.* Unpublished doctoral dissertation, Wright Institute, Berkeley, CA.

Adams, R. G. (1986). Friendship and aging. *Generations, 10*(4), 40–43.

Adebonojo, F., & Sherman, W., with Jones, L. C. (1985). *How baby grows: A parent's guide to nutrition.* New York: Arbor.

Adler, A. (1928). *Understanding human nature.* London: Allen & Unwin.

Adler, M. J. (Ed.). (1984). *The paideia program: An educational syllabus.* New York: Macmillan.

Ahrons, C.R., & Rodgers, R. H. (1987). *Divorced families: A multidisciplinary developmental view.* New York: Norton.

Ainsworth, M. D. S. (1969). Object relations, dependency, and attachment: A theoretical review of the infant-mother relationship. *Child Development, 40,* 969–1025.

Ainsworth, M. D. S. (1979). Infant-mother attachment. *American Psychologist, 34*(10), 932–937.

Ainsworth, M. D. S. (1982). Attachment: Retrospect and prospect. In C. M. Parkes & J. Stevenson-Hinde (Eds.), *The place of attachment in human behavior.* New York: Basic Books.

Ainsworth, M. D. S., & Bell, S. (1970). Attachment, exploration, and separation: Illustration by the behavior of one-year-olds in a strange situation. *Child Development, 41,* 49–67.

Ainsworth, M. D. S., & Bell, S. (1977). Infant crying and maternal responsiveness: A rejoinder to Gewirtz and Boyd. *Child Development, 48,* 1208–1216.

Ainsworth, M. D. S., Blehar, M. C., Waters, E., & Wall, S. (1978). *Patterns of attachment: A psychological study of the strange situation.* Hillsdale, NJ: Erlbaum.

Alan Guttmacher Institute. See under *Guttmacher.*

Alcoholism (Part II). (1978). *Harvard Medical School Health Letter, 3*(10), 1–2.

Aldous, J. J. (1987). Family life of the elderly and near-elderly. *Journal of Marriage and the Family, 49*(2), 227–234.

Alemi, B., Hamosh, M., Scanlon, J. W., Salzman-Mann, C., & Hamosh, P. (1981). Fat digestion in very low-birth-weight infants: Effects of addition of human milk to low-birth-weight formula. *Pediatrics, 68*(4), 484–489.

Almy, M., Chittenden, E., & Miller, P. (1966). *Young children's thinking: Some aspects of Piaget's theory.* New York: Teachers College Press.

Altemeir, W. A., O'Connor, S. M., Sherrod, K. B., & Vietze, P. M. (1985). Prospective study of antecedents for nonorganic failure to thrive. *Journal of Pediatrics, 106,* 360–365.

Alvarez, W. F. (1985). The meaning of maternal employment for mothers and their perceptions of their three-year-old children. *Child Development, 56,* 350–360.

American Academy of Pediatrics. (1973). The ten-state nutrition survey: A pediatric perspective. *Pediatrics, 51*(6), 1095–1099.

American Academy of Pediatrics. (1978). Juice in ready-to-use bottles and nursing bottle caries. *News and Comment, 29,* 1.

American Academy of Pediatrics. (1986a). *Day care facts and figures.* Elk Grove Village, IL: Author.

American Academy of Pediatrics. (1986b). *How to be your child's TV guide: Guidelines for constructive viewing.* Elk Grove Village, IL: Author.

American Academy of Pediatrics. (1986c). *Positive approaches to day care dilemmas: How to make it work.* Elk Grove Village, IL: Author.

American Academy of Pediatrics Committee on Adolescence. (1986). Sexuality, contraception, and the media. *Pediatrics, 78*(3), 535–536.

American Academy of Pediatrics Committee on Drugs. (1978). Effects of medication during labor and delivery on infant outcome. *Pediatrics, 62*(3), 402–403.

American Academy of Pediatrics Committee on Drugs. (1980). Marijuana. *Pediatrics, 65*(3), 652–656.

American Academy of Pediatrics Committee on Drugs. (1982). Psychotropic drugs in pregnancy and lactation. *Pediatrics, 69*(2), 241–243.

American Academy of Pediatrics Committee on Fetus and Newborn. (1986). Use and abuse of the Apgar score. *Pediatrics, 78*(6), 1148–1149.

American Academy of Pediatrics Committee on Nutrition. (1981). Nutritional aspects of obesity in infancy and childhood. *Pediatrics, 68*(6), 880–883.

American Academy of Pediatrics Committee on Nutrition. (1986). Prudent life-style for children: Dietary fat and cholesterol. *Pediatrics, 78*(3), 521–525.

American Academy of Pediatrics Committee on Pediatric Aspects of Physical Fitness, Recreation, and Sports. (1981). Competitive athletics for children of elementary school age. *Pediatrics, 67*(6).

American Academy of Pediatrics Task Force on Infant Mortality. (1986). Statement on infant mortality. *Pediatrics, 78*(6), 1155–1160.

American Association for Protecting Children. (1987a, October 23). *National estimates of child abuse and neglect reports, 1976–1986.* Denver: American Humane Association.

American Association for Protecting Children. (1987b, October 25). *Child abuse reports continue to increase.* Denver: American Humane Association.

American Association of Retired Persons (AARP). (1986). *A profile of older Americans.* Brochure. Washington, DC: Author.

American Association of Retired Persons (AARP). (1987a, April-May). Let's change the word "elderly." *Modern Maturity,* p. 16.

American Association of Retired Persons (AARP). (1987b, October). When the mind falters: Medical sleuths, caring professionals may find simple and reversible cause. *AARP News Bulletin,* pp. 6–7.

American Cancer Society. (1984, November). Diet, nutrition, and cancer prevention: A guide to food choices (NIH Publication No. 85-2711). Washington, DC: Public Health Service.

American Cancer Society. (1985). *1985 cancer facts and figures.* Pamphlet. Washington, DC: Author.

American Council on Science and Health. (1985). *Premenstrual syndrome.* Pamphlet. Summit, NJ: Author.

American Foundation for the Prevention of Venereal Disease (AFPVD). (1986). *Sexually transmitted disease (STD): Prevention for everyone* (13th ed.). Pamphlet. New York: Author.

American Health Care Association. (1984). *Facts in brief on long-term health care.* Washington, DC: Author.

American Heart Association. (1984). *Eating for a healthy heart: Dietary treatment of hyperlipidemia.* Dallas: Author.

American heritage dictionary of the English language. (1971). W. Morris (Ed.). Boston: Houghton Mifflin.

American Medical Association Council on Scientific Affairs. (1984). Exercise programs for the elderly. *Journal of the American Medical Association, 252*(4), 544–546.

American Psychological Association (APA). (1982). *Ethical principles in the conduct of research with human participants.* Washington, DC: Author.

American Psychological Association (APA). (1985, February 22). *Psychologists warn of potential dangers in TV violence.* Position statement. Washington, DC: Author.

American Psychological Association (APA). (1986, November 17). *Eating disorders linked to family relations, study finds.* [Press release]. Washington, DC: Author.

Ames, L. B. (1984, March). Kindergarten—not for four-year-olds! *Instructor,* pp. 32, 37.

Anastasi, A. (1958). Heredity, environment, and the question "how?" *Psychological Review, 65*(4), 197–208.

Anastasi, A. (1968). *Psychological testing.* New York: Macmillan.

Anastasi, A. (1976). *Psychological testing* (4th ed.). New York: Macmillan.

Anders, T., Caraskadon, M., & Dement, W. (1980). Sleep and sleepiness in children and adolescents. In I. Litt (Ed.), Adolescent medicine. *Pediatric Clinics of North America, 27*(1), 29–44.

Anders, T. R., Fozard, J. L., & Lillyquist, T. D. (1972). Effects of age upon retrieval from short-term memory. *Developmental Psychology, 6*(2), 214–217.

Anderson, J. N. (1972). Attachment behavior out of doors. In N. Blurton Jones (Ed.), *Ethological studies of child behavior.* London: Cambridge University Press.

Anderson, S. A., Russell, C. S., & Schumm, W. R. (1983). Perceived marital quality and family life-cycle categories: A further analysis. *Journal of Marriage and the Family, 45,* 127–139.

Anderson, T. B. (1984). Widowhood as a life transition: Its impact on kinship ties. *Journal of Marriage and the Family, 46,* 105–114.

Andrews, S. R., Blumenthal, J. B., Johnson, D. L., Kahn, A. J., Ferguson, C. J., Lasater, T. M., Malone, P. E., & Wallace, D. B. (1982). The skills of mothering—a study of parent-child development centers. *Monograph of the Society for Research in Child Development, 47*(6, Serial No. 198).

Anthony, E. J., & Cohler, B. J. (Eds.). (1987). *The invulnerable child.* New York: Guilford.

Anthony, E. J., & Koupernik, C. (Eds.). (1974). *The child in his family: Children at psychiatric risk.* (Vol. 3). New York: Wiley.

Apgar, V. (1953). A proposal for a new method of evaluation of the newborn infant. *Current Research in Anesthesia and Analgesia, 32,* 260–267.

Archer, C. J. (1984). Children's attitudes toward sex-role division in adult occupational roles. *Sex Roles, 10,* 1–10.

Arend, R., Gove, F., & Sroufe, L. A. (1979). Continuity of individual adaptation from infancy to kindergarten: A predictive study of ego-resiliency and curiosity in preschoolers. *Child Development, 50,* 950–959.

Aries, P. (1962). *Centuries of childhood.* New York: Vintage.

Arnon, S., Midura, T., Damus, K., Wood, R., & Chin, J. (1978, June 17). Intestinal infection and toxin production by *Clostridium botulinum* as one cause of SIDS. *The Lancet,* pp. 1273–1276.

Ash, P., Vennart, J., & Carter, C. (1977, April). The incidence of hereditary disease in man. *The Lancet,* pp. 849–851.

Asher, S., Hymel, S., & Renshaw, P. (1984). Loneliness in children. *Child Development, 55,* 1456–1464.

Asher, S., Renshaw, P., Geraci, K., & Dor, A. (1979, March). *Peer acceptance and social skill training: The selection of program content.* Paper presented at the meeting of the Society for Research in Child Development, San Francisco.

Aslin, R. N., Pisoni, D. B., & Jusczyk, P. W. (1983). Auditory development and speech perception in infancy. In P. H. Mussen (Ed.), *Handbook of child psychology* (4th ed., pp. 573–687). New York: Wiley.

Associated Press. (1987, July 23). Women on the move. *Chicago Sun-Times.*

Atchley, R. (1985). *Social forces and aging* (4th ed.). Belmont, CA: Wadsworth.

Atkinson, R. C., & Shiffrin, R. M. (1968). Human memory: A proposed system and its control processes. In K. W. Spence & J. T. Spence (Eds.), *The psychology of learning and motivation: Advances in research and theory* (Vol. 2). New York: Academic.

Atkinson, R. C., & Shiffrin, R. M. (1971). The control of short-term memory. *Scientific American, 225,* 82–90.

Averyt, A. C. (1987). *Successful aging: A sourcebook for older people and their families.* New York: Ballantine.

Azrin, N., & Foxx, R. M. (1981). *Toilet training in less than a day.* New York: Pocket Books.

Babchuk, N. (1978–1979). Aging and primary relations. *International Journal of Aging and Human Development, 9*(2), 137–151.

Babson, S. G., & Clark, N. G. (1983).

Relationship between infant death and maternal age. *Journal of Pediatrics, 103*(3), 391–393.

Baillargeon, R. (1987). Object permanence in 3½- and 4½-month-old infants. *Developmental Psychology, 23*(5), 655–664.

Baird, P. A., & Sadovnick, A. D. (1987). Life expectancy in Down syndrome. *Journal of Pediatrics, 110,* 849–854.

Bakwin, H. (1970, August 29). Sleepwalking in twins. *The Lancet,* pp. 446–447.

Bakwin, H. (1971a). Car-sickness in twins. *Developmental Medicine and Child Neurology, 13,* 310–312.

Bakwin, H. (1971b). Constipation in twins. *American Journal of Diseases of Children, 121,* 179–181.

Bakwin, H. (1971c). Enuresis in twins. *American Journal of Diseases of Children, 121,* 222–225.

Bakwin, H. (1971d). Nail-biting in twins. *Developmental Medicine and Child Neurology, 13,* 304–307.

Baldwin, W., & Cain, V. S. (1980). The children of teenage parents. *Family Planning Perspectives, 12,* 34.

Balkwell, C. (1981). Transition to widowhood: A review of the literature. *Family Relations, 30,* 117–127.

Balkwell, C. (1985). An attitudinal correlate of the timing of a major life event: The case of morale in widowhood. *Family Relations, 34,* 577–581.

Ballinger, C. B. (1981). The menopause and its syndromes. In J. G. Howells (Ed.), *Modern perspectives in the psychiatry of middle age* (pp. 279–303). New York: Brunner/Mazel.

Baltes, P. B. (1985). *The aging of intelligence: On the dynamics between growth and decline.* Unpublished manuscript.

Baltes, P. B., Reese, H. W., & Lipsitt, L. (1980). Life-span developmental psychology. *Annual Review of Psychology, 31,* 65–110.

Baltes, P. B., & Schaie, K. W. (1974). Aging and IQ: The myth of the twilight years. *Psychology Today, 7*(10), 35–38.

Baltes, P. B., & Schaie, K. W. (1976). On the plasticity of intelligence in adulthood and old age: Where Horn and Donaldson fail. *American Psychologist, 31,* 720–725.

Bandura, A., & Huston, A. (1961). Identification as a process of incidental learning. *Journal of Abnormal and Social Psychology, 63*(12), 311–318.

Bandura, A., Ross, D., & Ross, S. A. (1961). Transmission of aggression through imitation of aggressive models. *Journal of Abnormal and Social Psychology, 63,* 575–582.

Bandura, A., Ross, D., & Ross, S. A. (1963). Imitation of film-mediated aggressive models. *Journal of Abnormal and Social Psychology, 66*(1), 3–11.

Bane, M. J. (1980). A profile of the family in the 1980's. In *Focus on the family: New images of parents and children in the 1980's.* Boston: Wheelock College Center for Parenting Studies.

Barbach, L. G. (1975). *For yourself: The fulfillment of female sexuality.* Garden City, NY: Doubleday.

Bardouille-Crema, A., Black, K. N., & Feldhusen, J. (1986). Performance on Piagetian tasks of black children of differing socioeconomic levels. *Developmental Psychology, 22*(6), 841–844.

Barefoot, J. C., Dahlstrom, W. G., & Williams, R. B. (1983). Hostility, CHD incidence, and total mortality: A 25-year follow-up study of 255 physicians. *Psychosomatic Medicine, 45*(1), 59–63.

Barfield, R. E., & Morgan, J. N. (1974). *Early retirement: The decision and the experience and a second look.* Ann Arbor, MI: Institute for Social Research.

Barfield, R. E., & Morgan, J. N. (1978). Trends in satisfaction with retirement. *Gerontologist, 18*(1), 19–23.

Barker, P. (1979). *Basic child psychiatry* (3d ed.). Baltimore: University Park Press.

Barnes, A., Colton, T., Gunderson, J., Noller, K., Tilley, B., Strama, T., Townsend, D., Hatab, P., & O'Brien, P. (1980). Fertility and outcome of pregnancy in women exposed in utero to diethylstilbestrol. *The New England Journal of Medicine, 302*(11), 609–613.

Barnes, K. E. (1971). Preschool play norms: A replication. *Developmental Psychology, 5*(1), 99–103.

Barnett, R. (1985, March 2). *We've come a long way—but where are we and what are the rewards?* Presentation at conference, Women in Transition, New York University's School of Continuing Education, Center for Career and Life Planning, New York.

Barrett, C. J. (1978). Effectiveness of widows' groups in facilitating change. *Journal of Counseling and Clinical Psychology, 46*(1), 20–31.

Barrett, D. E., Radke-Yarrow, M., & Klein, R. E. (1982). Chronic malnutrition and child behavior: Effects of early caloric supplementation on social and emotional functioning at school age. *Developmental Psychology, 18,* 541–556.

Baruch, G. K., & Barnett, R. C. (1986). Fathers' participation in family work and children's sex-role attitudes. *Child Development, 57,* 1210–1223.

Baruch, G., Barnett, R., & Rivers, C. (1983). *Lifeprints.* New York: McGraw-Hill.

Bass, M., Kravath, R. E., & Glass, L. (1986). Death-scene investigation in sudden infant death. *The New England Journal of Medicine, 315,* 100–105.

Battelle, P. (1981, February). The triplets who found each other. *Good Housekeeping,* pp. 74–83.

Bauer, D. (1976). An exploratory study of developmental changes in children's fears. *Journal of Child Psychology and Psychiatry, 17,* 69–74.

Baughman, E. E. (1971). *Black Americans.* New York: Academic.

Baumrind, D. (1971). Harmonious parents and their preschool children. *Developmental Psychology, 41*(1), 92–102.

Baumrind, D. (1977). Some thoughts about childrearing. In S. Cohen & T. Comiskey (Eds.), *Child development: Contemporary perspectives.* Itasca, IL: Peacock.

Baumrind, D., & Black, A. E. (1967). Socialization practices associated with dimensions of competence in preschool boys and girls. *Child Development, 38*(2), 291–327.

Bayley, N. (1933). Mental growth during the first three years. *Genetic Psychology Monographs, 14,* 1–93.

Bayley, N. (1965). Comparisons of mental and motor test scores for age 1-15 months by sex, birth order, race, geographic location, and education of parents. *Child Development, 36,* 379–411.

Bayley, N. (1969). *Bayley scales of infant development.* New York: Psychological Corporation.

Bayley, N., & Oden, M. (1955). The maintenance of intellectual ability in gifted adults. *Journal of Gerontology, 10,* 91–107.

Beard, R. J. (1975). The menopause. *British Journal of Hospital Medicine, 12,* 631–637.

Beautrais, A. L., Fergusson, D. M., & Shannon, F. T. (1982). Life events and childhood morbidity: A prospective study. *Pediatrics, 70*(6), 935–940.

Beck, A., & Katcher, A. (1983). *Between pets and people.* New York: Putnam.

Beck, J. (1986). *How to raise a brighter child: The case for early learning.* New York: Pocket Books.

Becker, B. J. (1983). *Item characteristics and sex differences on the SAT-M for mathematically able youths.* Paper presented at the annual meeting of the American Educational Research Association, Montreal.

Behrman, R. E. (1985). Preventing low birth weight: A pediatric perspective. *Journal of Pediatrics, 107*(6), 842–854.

Behrman, R. E., & Vaughan, V. C. (Eds.). (1983). *Nelson textbook of pediatrics* (12th ed.). Philadelphia: Saunders.

Beit-Hallahmi, B., & Rabin, A. I. (1977). The kibbutz as a social experiment and as a child-rearing laboratory. *American Psychologist, 32,* 532–541.

Belbin, R. M. (1967). Middle age: What happens to ability? In R. Owen (Ed.), *Middle age.* London: BBC.

Bell, A. P., Weinberg, M. S., & Hammersmith, S. K. (1981). *Sexual preference: Its development in men and women.* Bloomington: Indiana University Press.

Bell, R. R. (1981). Friendships of women and men. *Psychology of Women Quarterly, 5*(3), 402–417.

Bell, R. R. (1983). *Marriage and family interaction* (6th ed.). Homewood, IL: Dorsey.

Bell, S., & Ainsworth, M. D. S. (1972). Infant crying and maternal responsiveness. *Child Development, 43,* 1171–1190.

Bellinger, D., Leviton, A., Watermaux, C., Needleman, H., & Rabinowitz, M. (1987). Longitudinal analyses of prenatal and postnatal lead exposure and early cognitive development. *The New England Journal of Medicine, 316* (17), 1037–1043.

Bellino, J. H., & Wilson, J. (1985). *You can have a baby.* New York: Crown.

Belloc, N. B., & Breslow, L. (1972). Relationship of physical health status and health practices. *Preventive Medicine, 1*(3), 409–421.

Belsky, J. (1979). Mother-father-infant interaction: A naturalistic observational study. *Developmental Psychology, 15,* 601–607.

Belsky, J. (1980). A family analysis of parental influence on infant exploratory competence. In F. A. Pedersen (Ed.), *The father-infant relationship: Observational studies in a family setting.* New York: Praeger.

Belsky, J. (1984). Two waves of day care research: Developmental effects and conditions of quality. In R. Ainslie (Ed.), *The child and the day care setting.* New York: Praeger.

Belsky, J. (1985). Exploring individual differences in marital change across the transition to parenthood: The role of violated expectations. *Journal of Marriage and the Family, 47*(4), 1037–1044.

Belsky, J. (1987, August). *Mother care, other care, and infant-parent attachment security.* Paper presented at the annual meeting of the American Psychological Association, New York.

Belsky, J., Lang, M. E., & Rovine, M. (1985). Stability and change in marriage across the transition to parenthood: A second study. *Journal of Marriage and the Family, 47*(4), 855–865.

Belsky, J., Spanier, G. B., & Rovine, M. (1983). Stability and change in marriage across the transition to parenthood. *Journal of Marriage and the Family, 45*(3), 567–577.

Beltramini, A. U., & Hertzig, M. E. (1983). Sleep and bedtime behavior in preschool-aged children. *Pediatrics, 71*(2), 153–158.

Bem, S. L. (1974). The measurement of psychological adrogyny. *Journal of Consulting and Clinical Psychology, 42,* 155–162.

Bem, S. L. (1976). Probing the promise of androgyny. In A. G. Kaplan & J. P. Bean (Eds.), *Beyond sex-role stereotypes: Readings toward a psychology of androgyny.* Boston: Little, Brown.

Bem, S. L. (1983). Gender schema theory and its implications for child development: Raising gender-aschematic children in a gender-schematic society. *Signs, 8,* 598–616.

Bem, S. L. (1985). Androgyny and gender schema theory: A conceptual and empirical integration. In T. B. Sonderegger (Ed.), *Nebraska Symposium on Motivation, 1984. Psychology and gender.* Lincoln: University of Nebraska Press.

Benbow, C. P., & Stanley, J. C. (1980). Sex differences in mathematical ability: Fact or artifact? *Science, 210,* 1262–1264.

Benbow, C. P., & Stanley, J. C. (1983). Sex differences in mathematical ability: More facts. *Science, 222,* 1029–1031.

Benderly, B. L. (1987). *The myth of two minds: What gender means and doesn't mean.* New York: Doubleday.

Bengtson, V., Cuellar, J. A., & Ragan, P. (1975, October 29). *Group contrasts in attitudes toward death: Variation by race, age, occupational status and sex.* Paper presented at the annual meeting of the Gerontological Society, Louisville, KY.

Benn, R. K. (1986). Factors promoting secure attachment relationships between employed mothers and their sons. *Child Development, 57,* 1224–1231.

Bennett, F. C., Robinson, N. M., & Sells, C. J. (1983). Growth and development of infants weighing less than 800 grams at birth. *Pediatrics, 71*(3), 319–323.

Berenda, R. W. (1950). *The influence of the group on the judgments of children.* New York: King's Crown.

Berger, R. M. (1982). *Gay and gray: The older homosexual male.* Urbana: University of Illinois Press.

Berk, L. E. (1986). Private speech: Learning out loud. *Psychology Today, 20*(5), 34–42.

Berk, L. E., & Garvin, R. A. (1984). Development of private speech among low-income Appalachian children. *Developmental Psychology, 20*(2), 271–286.

Berman, C. (1981). *Making it as a stepparent: New roles/new rules.* New York: Bantam.

Berman, S. M., MacKay, H. T., Grimes, D. A., & Binkin, N. J. (1985). Deaths from spontaneous abortion in the United States. *Journal of the American Medical Association, 253,* 3119–3123.

Bernard, J. (1972). *The future of marriage.* New York: World.

Bernard, J. (1976). Where are we now? Some thoughts on the current scene. *Psychology of Women Quarterly, 1,* 21–32.

Bernard, J. L., & Bernard, M. L. (1984). The abusive male seeking treatment: Jekyll and Hyde. *Family Relations, 33,* 543–547.

Bernbaum, J. C., Pereira, G., Watkins, J. B., & Peckham, G. J. (1983). Nonnutritive sucking during gavage feeding enhances growth and maturation in premature infants. *Pediatrics, 71*(1), 41–45.

Berndt, T. J. (1982). The features and effects of friendship in early adolescence. *Child Development, 53,* 1447–1460.

Berscheid, E., & Campbell, B. (1981). The changing longevity of heterosexual close relationships. In M. J. Lerner & S. C. Lerner (Eds.), *The justice motive in social behavior.* New York: Plenum.

Berscheid, E., Walster, E., & Bohrnstedt, G. (1973). The happy American body: A survey report. *Psychology Today, 7*(6), 119–131.

Bertenthal, B. L., & Campos, J. J. (1987). New directions in the study of early experience. *Child Development, 58,* 560–567.

Bianchi, S. M., & Spain, D. (1986). *American women in transition.* New York: Russell Sage Foundation.

Bielby, D., & Papalia, D. (1975). Moral development and perceptual roletaking egocentrism: Their development and interrelationship across the life span. *International Journal of*

Aging and Human Development, 6(4), 293–308.

Bierman, K. L., & Furman, W. (1984). The effects of social skills training and peer involvement on the social adjustment of preadolescents. *Child Development, 55,* 151–162.

Biller, H. B. (1981). The father and sex role development. In M. E. Lamb (Ed.), *The role of the father in child development.* New York: Wiley.

Bingham, M., & Stryker, S. (1987). *More choices: A strategic planning guide for mixing career and family.* Santa Barbara, CA: Advocacy.

Bingol, N., Fuchs, M., Diaz, V., Stone, R. K., & Gromisch, D. S. (1987). Teratogenicity of cocaine in humans. *Journal of Pediatrics, 110,* 93–96.

Binstock, R. H. (1987). Health care: Organization, use and financing. In G. L. Maddox (Ed.), *The encyclopedia of aging* (p. 308). New York: Springer.

Bird, C. (1987, June–July). The shape of work to come. *Modern Maturity,* pp. 33–45.

Birns, B. (1976). The emergence and socialization of sex differences in the earliest years. *Merrill-Palmer Quarterly, 22,* 229–254.

Birren, J. E. (1974). Translations in gerontology—from lab to life: Psychophysiology and speed of response. *American Psychologist, 29*(11), 808–815.

Birren, J. E., Woods, A. M., & Williams, M. V. (1980). Behavioral slowing with age: Causes, organization, and consequences. In L. W. Poon (Ed.), *Aging in the 1980s.* Washington, DC: American Psychological Association.

Blackburn, J. A., Papalia, D. E., & Foye, B. (1986). *Fluid ability training: Comparison of treatment procedures.* Paper presented at the annual meeting of the American Psychological Association, Washington, DC.

Blair, S. N., Goodyear, N. N., Gibbons, L. W., & Cooper, K. H. (1984). Physical fitness and incidence of hypertension in normotensive men and women. *Journal of the American Medical Association, 252*(4), 487–490.

Blakeslee, S. (1984, November 11). Brain studies shed light on disorders. *The New York Times,* Section 12, p. 45.

Blau, Z. S. (1961). Structural constraints on friendship in old age. *American Sociological Review, 26,* 429–439.

Blauvelt, H. (1955). Dynamics of the mother-newborn relationship in goats. In B. Schaffner (Ed.), *Group*

processes. New York: Macy Foundation.

Blechman, E. A., McEnroe, M. J., Carella, E. T., & Audette, D. P. (1986). Childhood competence and depression. *Journal of Abnormal Psychology, 95*(3), 223–227.

Blieszner, R. (1986). Trends in family gerontology research. *Family Relations, 35,* 555–562.

Blieszner, R., Willis, S. L., & Baltes, P. B. (1981). Training research on induction ability: A short-term longitudinal study. *Journal of Applied Developmental Psychology, 2,* 247–265.

Block, J. (1981). Some enduring and consequential structures of personality. In A. I. Rabin et al. (Eds.), *Further explorations in personality.* New York: Wiley.

Block, J. H. (1978). Another look at sex differentiation in the socialization behaviors of mothers and fathers. In F. Wenmark & J. Sherman (Eds.), *Psychology of women: Future direction of research.* New York: Psychological Dimensions.

Bloom, A. (1987). *The closing of the American mind.* New York: Simon & Schuster.

Bloom, B. S. (1985). *Developing talent in young people.* New York: Ballantine.

Bloom, D. E., & Pebley, A. R. (1982). Voluntary childlessness: A review of the evidence and its implications. *Population Research and Policy Review, 1,* 203–234.

Bluebond-Langner, M. (1977). Meanings of death to children. In H. Feifel (Ed.), *New meanings of death* (pp. 47–66). New York: McGraw-Hill.

Blumstein, P., & Schwartz, P. (1983). *American couples: Money, work, sex.* New York: Morrow.

Bohannon, P. (1971). The six stations of divorce. In P. Bohannon (Ed.), *Divorce and after.* New York: Anchor.

Bolles, E. B. (1982). *So much to say.* New York: St. Martin's.

Bolles, E. B. (1984). *The Penguin adoption handbook.* New York: Viking.

Bolles, R. N. (1979). *The three boxes of life.* Berkeley, CA: Ten Speed Press.

Bolles, R. N. (1987). *What color is your parachute?* Berkeley, CA: Ten Speed Press.

Bornstein, M. H. (1985). How infant and mother jointly contribute to developing cognitive competence in the child. *Proceedings of the National Academy of Science, 82,* 7470–7473.

Bornstein, M. H., & Sigman, M. D. (1986). Continuity in mental development from infancy. *Child Development, 57,* 251–274.

Boston Women's Health Book Collective. (1978). *Ourselves and our children: A book by and for parents.* New York: Random House.

Boston Women's Health Book Collective. (1984). *The new our bodies, ourselves.* New York: Simon & Schuster.

Bower, T. G. R. (1976). Repetitive processes in child development. *Scientific American, 235*(5), 38–47.

Bower, T. G. R. (1977). *The perceptual world of the child.* Cambridge, MA: Harvard University Press.

Bowes, W., Brackbill, Y., Conway, E., & Steinschneider, A. (1970). The effects of obstetrical medication on fetus and infant. *Monographs of the Society for Research in Child Development, 35,* 3–25.

Bowlby, J. (1958). The nature of the child's tie to his mother. *International Journal of Psychoanalysis, 39,* 1–23.

Bowlby, J. (1960). Separation anxiety. *International Journal of Psychoanalysis, 41,* 89–113.

Bowman, J. A., Sanson-Fisher, R. W., & Webb, G. R. (1987). Intervention in preschools to increase the use of safety restraints by preschool children. *Pediatrics, 79,* 103–109.

Brackbill, Y., & Broman, S. H. (1979). *Obstetrical medication and development in the first year of life.* Unpublished manuscript.

Bracken, M., Holford, T., White, C., & Kelsey, J. (1978). Role of oral contraception in congenital malformations of offspring. *International Journal of Epidemiology, 7*(4), 309–317.

Brazelton, T. B. (1973). *Neonatal behavioral assessment scale.* Philadelphia: Lippincott.

Brecher, E., & the Editors of Consumer Reports Books. (1984). *Love, sex, and aging: A Consumers Union report.* Boston: Little, Brown.

Bremner, W. J., Vitiello, M. V., & Prinz, P. N. (1983). Loss of circadian rhythmicity in blood testosterone levels with aging in normal men. *Journal of Clinical Endocrinology and Metabolism, 56,* 1278–1281.

Brewster, A. B. (1982). Chronically ill hospitalized children's concepts of their illness. *Pediatrics, 69,* 355–362.

Bridges, K. M. B. (1932). Emotional development in early infancy. *Child Development, 3,* 324–341.

Briley, M. (1980, July-August). Burnout stress and the human energy crisis. *Dynamic Years,* pp. 36–39.

Brim, O. G. (1974). *Theories of the male mid-life crisis.* Address at the Annual Convention of the American Psychological Association, New Orleans.

Brim, O. G. (1977). Theories of the male mid-life crisis. In N. Schlossberg & A. Entine (Eds.), *Counseling adults.* Monterey, CA: Brooks/Cole.

Brim, O. G., & Kagan, J. (Eds.). (1980). *Constancy and change in human development.* New York: Wiley.

Brim, O. G., & Ryff, C. D. (1980). On the properties of life events. In P. B. Baltes & O. G. Brim (Eds.), *Life-span development and behavior* (Vol. 3). New York: Academic.

Bringuier, J. (1980). *Conversations with Jean Piaget.* Chicago: University of Chicago Press.

Brittain, C. (1963). Adolescent choices and parent-peer cross-pressures. *American Sociological Review, 28,* 385–391.

Brodbeck, A. J., & Irwin, O. C. (1946). The speech behavior of infants without families. *Child Development, 17,* 145–156.

Brody, E. B., & Brody, N. (1976). *Intelligence.* New York: Academic.

Brody, E. M. (1978). Community housing for the elderly. *Gerontologist, 18*(2), 121–128.

Brody, J. (1981, March 10). Sperm found especially vulnerable to environment. *The New York Times,* p. C1 ff.

Brody, L. R., Zelazo, P. R., & Chaika, H. (1984). Habituation-dishabituation to speech in the neonate. *Developmental Psychology, 20,* 114–119.

Bromley, D. B. (1974). *The psychology of human aging* (2d ed.). Middlesex, England: Penguin.

Bronfenbrenner, U. (1970). *Two worlds of childhood: U.S. and U.S.S.R.* New York: Russell Sage Foundation.

Bronfenbrenner, U. (1974). Developmental research, public policy, and the ecology of childhood. *Child Development, 45,* 1–5.

Bronfenbrenner, U., Alvarez, W. F., & Henderson, C. R. (1984). Working and watching: Maternal employment and parents' perceptions of their three-year-old children. *Child Development, 55,* 1362–1378.

Bronfenbrenner, U., Belsky, J., & Steinberg, L. (1977). *Daycare in context: An ecological perspective on research and public policy.* Review prepared for Office of the Assistant Secretary for Planning and Evaluation, U.S. Department of Health, Education, and Welfare.

Bronson, F. H., & Desjardins, C. (1969). Aggressive behavior and seminal vesicle function in mice: Differential sensitivity to androgen given neonatally. *Endocrinology, 85,* 871–975.

Brooks, J., & Lewis, M. (1976). Infants' responses to strangers: Midget, adult, child. *Child Development, 47,* 323–332.

Brooks-Gunn, J., & Furstenberg, F. F. (1986). The children of adolescent mothers: Physical, academic, and psychological outcomes. *Developmental Review, 6,* 224–251.

Brophy, J. E., & Good, T. L. (1974). *Teacher-student relationships.* New York: Holt.

Brown, B. B. (1981). A life-span approach to friendship: Age-related dimensions of an ageless relationship. In H. Z. Lopata (Ed.), *Research on the interweave of social roles: Friendship.* Greenwich, CT: JAI.

Brown, B. B., Classen, D. R., & Eicher, S. A. (1986). Perceptions of peer pressure, peer conformity dispositions, and self-reported behavior among adolescents. *Developmental Psychology, 22,* 521–530.

Brown, D. S. (1984). *Handle with care: A question of Alzheimer's.* Buffalo, NY: Prometheus.

Brown, J., LaRossa, G., Aylward, G., Davis, D., Rutherford, P., & Bakeman, R. (1980). Nursery-based intervention with prematurely born babies and their mothers: Are there effects? *Journal of Pediatrics, 97*(3), 487–491.

Brown, J. E. (1983). *Nutrition for your pregnancy.* Minneapolis: University of Minnesota Press.

Brown, J. L. (1987). Hunger in the U.S. *Scientific American, 256*(2), 37–41.

Brown, J. T., & Stoudemire, A. (1983). Normal and pathological grief. *Journal of the American Medical Association, 250,* 378–382.

Brown, P., & Elliott, H. (1965). Control of aggression in a nursery school class. *Journal of Experimental Child Psychology, 2,* 103–107.

Brown, R. (1973a). Development of the first language in the human species. *American Psychologist, 28*(2), 97–106.

Brown, R. (1973b). *A first language: The early stages.* Cambridge, MA: Harvard University Press.

Brown, R., Cazden, C. B., & Bellugi, U. (1969). The child's grammar from I to III. In J. P. Hill (Ed.), *Minnesota symposia on child psychology* (Vol. 2). Minneapolis: University of Minnesota Press.

Brown, S. S. (1985). Can low birth weight be prevented? *Family Planning Perspectives, 17*(3), 112–118.

Browne, A., & Finkelhor, D. (1986). Impact of child sexual abuse: A review of research. *Psychological Bulletin, 99*(1), 66–77.

Brubaker, T. (1983). Introduction. In T. Brubaker (Ed.), *Family relationships in later life.* Beverly Hills, CA: Sage.

Bühler, C. (1933). *Der menschliche, Lebenslauf al psychologisches Problem.* Leipzig: Verlag von S. Herzel.

Bühler, C. (1968). The development structure of goal setting in group and individual studies. In C. Bühler & F. Massarek (Eds.), *The course of human life.* New York: Springer.

Buie, J. (1987, April 8). Pregnant teenagers: New view of old solution. *Education Week,* p. 32.

Bullen, B. A., Skrinar, G. S., Beitins, I., von Mering, G., Turnbull, B. A., & McArthur, J. W. (1985). Induction of menstrual disorders by strenuous exercise in untrained women. *The New England Journal of Medicine, 312,* 1349–1353.

Burke, B. S., Beal, V. A., Kirkwood, S. B., & Stuart, H. C. (1943). Nutrition studies during pregnancy. *American Journal of Obstetrics and Gynecology, 46,* 38–52.

Burr, W. (1970). Satisfaction with various aspects of marriage over the life cycle. *Journal of Marriage and the Family, 32*(1), 29–37.

Bush, T. L., Cowan, L. D., Barrett-Connor, E., Criqui, M. H., Karon, J. M., Wallace, R. B., Tyroler, H. A., & Rifkind, B. M. (1983). Estrogen use and all-cause mortality: Preliminary results from the Lipid Research Clinics program follow-up study. *Journal of the American Medical Association, 249*(7), 903–906.

Busse, E. W. (1987). Primary and secondary aging. In G. L. Maddox (Ed.), *The encyclopedia of aging* (p. 534). New York: Springer.

Bustillo, M., Buster, J. E., Cohen, S. W., Hamilton, F., Thorneycroft, I. H., Simon, J. A., Rodi, I. A., Boyers, S., Marshall, J. R., Louw, J. A., Seed, R., & Seed, R. (1984). Delivery of a healthy infant following nonsurgical ovum transfer. *Journal of the American Medical Association, 251*(7), 889.

Butler, R. (1961). Re-awakening interests. *Nursing Homes: Journal of American Nursing Home Association, 10,* 8–19.

Butler, R. (1975). *Why survive? Being old in America.* New York: Harper & Row.

Butler, R., & Lewis, M. (1977). *Aging and mental health* (2d ed.). St. Louis: Mosby.

Butler, R., & Lewis, M. (1982). *Aging and mental health* (3d ed.). St. Louis: Mosby.

Butterfield, E., & Siperstein, G. (1972). Influence of contingent auditory stimulation upon nonnutritional suckle. In J. Bosma (Ed.), *Oral sensation and perception: The mouth of the infant.* Springfield, IL: Thomas.

Calderone, M. S., & Johnson, E. W. (1981). *The family book about sexuality.* New York: Harper & Row.

Calhoun, L. G., & Selby, J. W. (1980). Voluntary childlessness, involuntary childlessness, and having children: A study of social perceptions. *Family Relations, 29*(2), 181–183.

Campbell, A., Converse, P. E., & Rodgers, W. L. (1975). *The quality of American life: Perceptions, evaluations, and satisfactions.* New York: Russell Sage Foundation.

Campbell, F. L., Townes, B. D., & Beach, L. R. (1982). Motivational bases of childbearing decisions. In G. L. Fox (Ed.), *The childbearing decision: Fertility, attitudes, and behavior.* Beverly Hills, CA: Sage.

Campos, J. J., Langer, A., & Krowitz, A. (1970). Cardiac responses on the visual cliff in prelocomotor human infants. *Science, 170,* 196–197.

Cantor, M. H. (1983). Strain among caregivers: A study of experience in the United States. *Gerontologist, 23*(6), 597–604.

Cantor, P. (1977). Suicide and attempted suicide among students: Problem, prediction and prevention. In P. Cantor (Ed.), *Understanding a child's world.* New York: McGraw-Hill.

Caplan, T., & Caplan, F. (1983). *The early childhood years.* New York: Bantam.

Card, J. J., & Wise, L. L. (1978). Teenage mothers and teenage fathers: Impact of early childbearing on the parents' personal and professional lives. *Family Planning Perspectives, 10,* 199.

Cargan, L. (1981). Singles: An examination of two stereotypes. *Family Relations, 30,* 377–385.

Carlson, B. E. (1984). The father's contribution to child care: Effects on children's perceptions of parental roles. *American Journal of Orthopsychiatry, 54*(1), 123–136.

Carmack, B. J. (1985). The effects on family members and functioning after the death of a pet. In M. B. Sussman (Ed.), *Pets and the family* (pp. 149–161). New York: Haworth.

Carroll, J. L., & Rest, J. R. (1982). Moral development. In B. Wolman (Ed.), *Handbook of developmental psychology.* Englewood Cliffs, NJ: Prentice-Hall.

Carter, D., & Welch, D. (1981). Parent-

ing styles and children's behavior. *Family Relations, 30,* 191–195.

Casey, P. H., Bradley, R., & Wortham, B. (1984). Social and nonsocial home environment of infants with nonorganic failure-to-thrive. *Pediatrics, 73*(3), 348–353.

Casey, R. J., & Berman, J. S. (1985). The outcome of psychotherapy with children. *Psychological Bulletin, 98*(2), 388–400.

Cassell, C. (1984). *Swept away.* New York: Simon & Schuster.

Cassidy, J. (1986). The ability to negotiate the environment: An aspect of infant competence as related to quality of attachment. *Child Development, 57,* 331–337.

Cattell, R. B. (1965). *The scientific analysis of personality.* Baltimore: Penguin.

Centers for Disease Control. (1980). Risk factor update. Atlanta: U.S. Department of Health and Human Services.

Centers for Disease Control. (1983). *CDC Surveillance Summaries* (Vol. 32). Atlanta: Author.

Centers for Disease Control. (1986). Statistical information. Atlanta: Author.

Chacko, T. I. (1982). Women and equal employment opportunity: Some unintended effects. *Journal of Applied Psychology, 67,* 119–123.

Chance, P., & Fischman, J. (1987). The magic of childhood. *Psychology Today, 21*(5), 48–58.

Chapman, A. H. (1974). *Management of emotional problems of children and adolescents* (2d ed.). Philadelphia: Lippincott.

Chappell, N. L., & Penning, M. J. (1979). The trend away from institutionalization. *Research on Aging, 1*(1), 161–187.

Charles, L., Schain, R. J., Zelniker, T., & Guthrie, D. (1979). Effects of methylphenidate on hyperactive children's ability to sustain attention. *Pediatrics, 64*(4), 412–418.

Chasnoff, I. J., Burns, W. J., Schnoll, S. H., & Burns, K. A. (1985). Cocaine use in pregnancy. *The New England Journal of Medicine, 313,* 666–669.

Chasnoff, I. J., Hunt, C., Kletter, R., & Kaplan, D. (1986). Increased risk of SIDS and respiratory pattern abnormalities in cocaine-exposed infants. *Pediatric Research, 20,* 425A.

Cherlin, A., & Furstenberg, F. F. (1986a). Grandparents and family crisis. *Generations, 10*(4), 26–28.

Cherlin, A. J., & Furstenberg, F. F. (1986b). *The new American grandparent: A place in the family, a life apart.* New York: Basic Books.

Chernin, K. (1985). *The hungry self.* New York: Times Books.

Chess, S. (1983). Mothers are always the problem—or are they? Old wine in new bottles. *Pediatrics, 71*(6), 974–976.

Chess, S., & Thomas, A. (1982). Infant bonding: Mystique and reality. *American Journal of Orthopsychiatry, 52*(2), 213–222.

Chess, S., Thomas, A., & Birch, H. G. (1965). *Your child is a person: Psychological approach to parenthood without guilt.* New York: Viking.

Child Welfare League of America. (1986). *Born to run: The status of child abuse in America.* Washington, DC: Author.

Children's Hospital of Pittsburgh. (1987a, November). Depression in children. *Kidstuff,* p. 1.

Children's Hospital of Pittsburgh. (1987b, September). Nighttime worries. *Kidstuff,* p. 2.

Chilman, C. S. (1980). *Adolescent sexuality in a changing American society: Social and psychological perspectives* (NIH Publication No. 80–1426). Bethesda, MD: National Institutes of Health.

Chiriboga, D. A. (1982). Adaptation to marital separation in later and earlier life. *Journal of Gerontology, 37,* 109–114.

Chiriboga, D. A., & Thurnher, M. (1975). Concept of self. In M. F. Lowenthal, M. Thurnher, & D. A. Chiriboga & Associates (Eds.), *Four stages of life: A comparative study of women and men facing transitions.* San Francisco: Jossey-Bass.

Chisholm, J. S. (1983). *Navajo infancy: An ethological study of child development.* New York: Aldine.

Chodorow, N. (1978). *The reproduction of mothering.* Berkeley: University of California Press.

Chomsky, C. S. (1969). *The acquisition of syntax in children from five to ten.* Cambridge, MA: Massachusetts Institute of Technology (MIT) Press.

Chomsky, N. (1972). *Language and mind* (2d ed.). New York: Harcourt Brace Jovanovich.

Chumlea, W. C. (1982). Physical growth in adolescence. In B. B. Wolman (Ed.), *Handbook of developmental psychology.* Englewood Cliffs, NJ: Prentice-Hall.

Cicirelli, V. G. (1976a). Family structure and interaction: Sibling effects on socialization. In M. F. McMillan & S. Henao (Eds.), *Child psychiatry: Treatment and research.* New York: Brunner/Mazel.

Cicirelli, V. G. (1976b). Siblings teaching siblings. In V. L. Allen (Ed.), *Children as teachers: Theory and research on tutoring.* New York: Academic.

Cicirelli, V. G. (1977). Relationship of siblings to the elderly person's feeling and concerns. *Journal of Gerontology, 12*(3), 317–322.

Cicirelli, V. G. (1980, December). *Adult children's views on providing services for elderly parents.* Report to the Andrus Foundation.

Cicirelli, V. G. (1981, April). *Interpersonal relationships of siblings in the middle part of the life span.* Paper presented at the biennial meeting of the Society for Research in Child Development, Boston.

Cicirelli, V. G. (1982). Sibling influence throughout the lifespan. In M. E. Lamb & B. Sutton-Smith (Eds.), *Sibling relationships: Their nature and significance across the lifespan.* Hillsdale, NJ: Erlbaum.

Clarke-Stewart, A. (1977). *Child care in the family: A review of research and some propositions for policy.* New York: Academic.

Clarke-Stewart, A. (1978). And daddy makes three: The father's impact on mother and young child. *Child Development, 49,* 466–478.

Clausen, J. A. (1978). Adolescent antecedents of cigarette smoking: Data from the Oakland growth study. *Social Science and Medicine, 1,* 357–382.

Clemens, A. W., & Axelson, L. J. (1985). The not-so-empty nest: Return of the fledgling adult. *Family Relations, 34,* 259–264.

Clement, J., Schweinhart, L. J., Barnett, W. S., Epstein, A. S., & Weikart, D. P. (1984). *Changed lives: The effects of the Perry Preschool Program on youths through age 19.* Ypsilanti, MI: High/Scope.

Clifford, E. (1971). Body ratification in adolescence. *Perceptual and Motor Skills, 33,* 119–125.

Cobrinck, P., Hood, R., & Chused, E. (1959). Effects of maternal narcotic addiction on the newborn infant. *Pediatrics, 24,* 288–290.

Cohen, G. D. (1981). *Depression and the elderly.* (DHHS Publication No. ADM 81–932). Washington, DC: U.S. Government Printing Office.

Cohen, G. D. (1987). Alzheimer's disease. In G. L. Maddox (Ed.), *The encyclopedia of aging* (pp. 27–30). New York: Springer.

Cohn, V. (1975, November 5). New method of delivering babies cuts down "torture of the innocent." *Capital Times.*

Colby, A., Kohlberg, L., Gibbs, J., & Lieberman, M. (1983). A longitudinal study of moral development. *Monographs of the Society for Research in Child Development, 48*(1–2, Serial No. 200).

Cole, C., & Rodman, H. (1987). When school-age children care for themselves: Issues for family life educators and parents. *Family Relations, 36,* 92–96.

Cole, S. (1980). Send our children to work? *Psychology Today, 14*(2), 44 ff.

Coleman, J. (1980). Friendship and the peer group in adolescence. In J. Adelson (Ed.), *Handbook of adolescent development.* New York: Wiley.

Coles, R. (1986). *The moral life of children.* Boston: Atlantic Monthly.

Coles, R., & Stokes, G. (1985). *Sex and the American teenager.* New York: Harper & Row.

Colligan, M. J., Smith, M. J., & Hurrell, J. J. (1977). Occupational incidence rates of mental health disorders. *Journal of Human Stress, 3,* 34–39.

Collins, R. C., & Deloria, D. (1983). Head Start research: A new chapter. *Children Today, 12*(4), 15–19.

Collins, W. A. (Ed.). (1984). *Development during middle childhood: The years from six to twelve.* Washington, DC: National Academy.

Colman, W. (1988). *Understanding and preventing AIDS.* Chicago: Children's Press.

Commonwealth Fund Commission on Elderly People Living Alone. (1986). *Problems facing elderly Americans living alone.* New York: Louis Harris & Associates.

Condon, W., & Sander, L. (1974). Synchrony demonstrated between movements of the neonate and adult speech. *Child Development, 45,* 456–462.

Condry, J. C., & Condry, S. (1974). *The development of sex differences: A study of the eye of the beholder.* Unpublished manuscript, Cornell University, Ithaca, NY.

Condry, J. C., Siman, M. L., & Bronfenbrenner, U. (1968). Characteristics of peer- and adult-oriented children. Unpublished manuscript, Cornell University, Department of Child Development, Ithaca, NY.

Conference Board, Inc. (1984). *The working woman: A progress report.* New York: Consumer Research Center.

Conger, J. J., & Peterson, A. C. (1984). *Adolescence and youth.* New York: Harper & Row.

Congressional Caucus for Women's Issues. (1987). *The American woman, 1987–88.* Washington, DC: Author.

Connecticut Early Childhood Education Council (CECEC). (1983). *Report on full-day kindergarten.* Author.

Cooke, S. (1979). *A comparison of identity formation in preadolescent girls and boys.* Unpublished master's thesis, Simon Fraser University, Toronto.

Coons, S., & Guilleminault, C. (1982). Development of sleep-wake patterns and non-rapid eye movement sleep stages during the first six months of life in normal infants. *Pediatrics,* 69(6), 793–798.

Coopersmith, S. (1967). *The antecedents of self-esteem.* San Francisco: Freeman.

Corbin, C. (1973). *A textbook of motor development.* Dubuque, IA: Brown.

Corman, H. H., & Escalona, S. K. (1969). Stages of sensorimotor development: A replication. *Merrill-Palmer Quarterly,* 15, 351–361.

Correa, P., Pickle, L. W., Fontham, E., Lin, Y., & Haenszel, W. (1983, September 10). Passive smoking and lung cancer. *The Lancet,* 595–597.

Corson, S. L. (1983). *Conquering infertility.* Norwalk, CT: Appleton-Century-Crofts.

Corter, C. M. (1976). The nature of the mother's absence and the infant's response to brief separation. *Developmental Psychology,* 12(15), 428–434.

Corter, C. M., Rheingold, H. L., & Eckerman, C. O. (1972). Toys delay the infant's following of his mother. *Developmental Psychology,* 6, 138–145.

Costa, P. T., & McCrae, R. R. (1981). Still stable after all these years: Personality as a key to some issues in adulthood and old age. In P. B. Baltes & O. G. Brim (Eds.), *Lifespan development and behavior* (Vol. 3). New York: Academic.

Costa, P. T., McCrae, R. R., Zonderman, A. B., Barbano, H. E., Lebowitz, B., & Larson, D. M. (1986). Cross-sectional studies of personality in a national sample: 2. Stability in neuroticism, extraversion, and openness. *Psychology and Aging,* 1(2), 144–149.

Costanzo, P. R., & Shaw, M. E. (1966). Conformity as a function of age level. *Child Development,* 37, 967–975.

Cousins, N. (1979). *Anatomy of an illness as perceived by the patient.* New York: Norton.

Cowan, M. W. (1979). The development of the brain. *Scientific American,* 241, 112–133.

Cox, J., Daniel, N., & Boston, B. O. (1985). *Educating able learners:*

Programs and promising practices. Austin: University of Texas Press.

Craik, F. I. M. (1977). Age differences in human memory. In J. E. Birren & K. W. Schaie (Eds.), *Handbook of the psychology of aging.* New York: Van Nostrand Reinhold.

Craik, F. I. M., Byrd, M., & Swanson, J. M. (1987). Patterns of memory loss in three elderly samples. *Psychology and Aging,* 2(1), 79–86.

Cratty, B. (1979). *Perceptual and motor development in infants and children* (2d ed.). Englewood Cliffs, NJ: Prentice-Hall.

Crisp, A. H., Queenan, M., & D'Souza, M. F. (1984). Myocardial infarction and the emotional climate. *The Lancet,* 1(8377), 616–618.

Croake, J. W. (1973). The changing nature of children's fears. *Child Study Journal,* 3(2), 91–105.

Crumley, F. (1979). Adolescent suicide attempts. *Journal of the American Medical Association,* 241(22), 2404–2407.

Csikszentmihalyi, M., & Larson, R. (1984). *Being adolescent: Conflict and growth in the teenage years.* New York: Basic Books.

Cuckle, H. S., Wald, N. J., & Lindenbaum, R. H. (1984). Maternal serum alpha-fetoprotein measurement: A screening test for Down's syndrome. *The Lancet,* 926–929.

Cumming, E., & Henry, W. (1961). *Growing old.* New York: Basic Books.

Cutrona, C., Russell, D., & Rose, J. (1986). Social support and adaptation to stress by the elderly. *Journal of Psychology and Aging,* 1(1), 47–54.

Cytrynbaum, S., Bluum, L., Patrick, R., Stein, J., Wadner, D., & Wilk, C. (1980). Midlife development: A personality and social systems perspective. In L. Poon (Ed.), *Aging in the 1980s.* Washington, DC: American Psychological Association.

Daniels, D., & Plomin, R. (1985). Origins of individual differences in infant shyness. *Developmental Psychology,* 21(1), 118–121.

Danish, S. J. (1983). Musings about personal competence: The contributions of sport, health, and fitness. *American Journal of Community Psychology,* 11(3), 221–240.

Danish, S. J., & D'Augelli, A. R. (1980). Promoting competence and enhancing development through life development intervention. In L. A. Bond & J. C. Rosem (Eds.), *Competence and coping during adulthood.* Hanover, NH: University Press of New England.

Danish, S. J., Smyer, M. A., & Nowak,

C. A. (1980). Developmental intervention: Enhancing life-event processes. In P. B. Baltes & O. G. Brim (Eds.), *Life-span development and behavior* (Vol 3). New York: Academic.

Datan, N., Rodeheaver, D., & Hughes, F. (1987). Adult development and aging. *Annual Review of Psychology,* 38, 153–180.

Davidson, J. E., & Sternberg, R. J. (1984). The role of insight in intellectual giftedness. *Gifted Child Quarterly,* 28(2), 58–64.

Davis, B. W. (1985). *Visits to remember: A handbook for visitors of nursing home residents.* University Park: Pennsylvania State University Cooperative Extension Service.

Davis, K. E. (1985, February). Near and dear: Friendship and love compared. *Psychology Today,* 19, 22–30.

Deaux, K. (1985). Sex and gender. *Annual Review of Psychology,* 36, 49–81.

DeCasper, A., & Fifer, W. (1980). Newborns prefer their mothers' voices. *Science,* 208, 1174–1176.

Decker, M. D., Dewey, M. J., Hutcheson, R. H., & Schaffner, W. (1984). The use and efficacy of child restraint devices. *Journal of the American Medical Association,* 252(18), 2571–2575.

DeFrain, J., & Ernst, L. (1978). The psychological effects of sudden infant death syndrome on surviving family members. *Journal of Family Practice,* 6(5), 985–989.

DeFrain, J., Montens, L., Stork, J., & Stork, W. (1986). *Stillborn: An invisible death.* Lexington, MA: Heath.

DeFrain, J., Taylor, J., & Ernst, L. (1982). *Coping with sudden infant death.* Lexington, MA: Heath.

Denney, N. W. (1972). Free classification in preschool children. *Child Development,* 43, 1161–1170.

Denney, N. W., & Palmer, A. M. (1981). Adult age differences on traditional and practical problem-solving measures. *Journal of Gerontology,* 36(3), 323–328.

Dennis, W. (1960). Causes of retardation among institutional children: Iran. *Journal of Genetic Psychology,* 96, 47–59.

Denny, F. W., & Clyde, W. A. (1983). Acute respiratory tract infections: An overview. In W. A. Clyde & F. W. Denny (Eds.), Workshop on acute respiratory diseases among children of the world. *Pediatric Research,* 17, 1026–1029.

deRegt, R. H., Minkoff, H. L., Feldman, J., & Schwartz, R. H. (1986). Relation of private or clinic care to the cesarean birth rate. *The New England Journal of Medicine, 315,* 619–624.

deVilliers, P. A., & deVilliers, J. (1979). *Early language.* Cambridge, MA: Harvard University Press.

DeVries, R. (1969). Constancy of generic identity in the years three to six. *Monographs of the Society for Research in Child Development, 34*(3, Serial No. 127).

Diagnostic and statistical manual of mental disorders (DSM III). (1980). Washington, DC: American Psychiatric Association.

Dickson, W. P. (1979). Referential communication performance from age 4 to 8: Effects of referent type, context, and target position. *Developmental Psychology, 15*(4), 470–471.

Dietz, W. H., & Gortmaker, S. L. (1985). Do we fatten our children at the television set? Obesity and television viewing in children and adolescents. *Pediatrics, 75,* 807–812.

DiMaio, M. S., Baumgarten, A., Greenstein, R. M., Saal, H. M., & Mahoney, M. J. (1987). Screening for fetal Down's syndrome in pregnancy by measuring maternal serum alpha-fetoprotein levels. *The New England Journal of Medicine, 317,* 342–346.

Dion, K. K., Berscheid, E., & Walster, E. (1972). What is beautiful is good. *Journal of Personality and Social Psychology, 24,* 285–290.

Dixon, R. A., & Baltes, P. B. (1986). Toward life-span research on the functions and pragmatics of intelligence. In R. J. Sternberg & R. K. Wagner (Eds.), *Practical intelligence: Nature and origins of competence in the everyday world.* New York: Cambridge University Press.

Doctors rule out transplant from organs of hanged boy. (1984, November 23). *The New York Times,* p. A26.

Doering, C. H., Kraemer, H. C., Brodie, H. K. H., & Hamburg, D. A. (1975). A cycle of plasma testosterone in the human male. *Journal of Clinical Endocrinology and Metabolism, 40,* 492–500.

Doherty, W. J., & Jacobson, N. S. (1982). Marriage and the family. In B. Wolman (Ed.), *Handbook of developmental psychology.* Englewood Cliffs, NJ: Prentice-Hall.

Donaldson, M. (1979). *Children's minds.* New York: Norton.

Doppelt, J. E., & Wallace, W. L. (1955). Standardization of the Wechsler Adult Intelligence Scale for older persons. *Journal of Abnormal and Social Psychology, 51,* 312–330.

Doress, P. B., & Siegal, D. L. (Eds.). (1987). *Ourselves, growing older: Women aging with knowledge and power.* New York: Simon & Schuster.

Dornbusch, S. M., Carlsmith, J. M., Bushwall, S. J., Ritter, P. L., Leiderman, H., Hastorf, A. H., & Gross, R. T. (1985). Single parents, extended households, and the control of adolescents. *Child Development, 56,* 326–341.

Doty, R. L. (1984, December). Smell identification ability: Changes with age. *Science, 226,* 1441–1443.

Dove, J. (undated). *Facts about anorexia nervosa.* Bethesda, MD: National Institutes of Health, Office of Research Reporting, National Institute of Child Health and Human Development.

Dreyer, P. H. (1982). Sexuality during adolescence. In B. B. Wolman (Ed.), *Handbook of developmental psychology.* Englewood Cliffs, NJ: Prentice-Hall.

Droege, R. (1982). *A psychosocial study of the formation of the middle adult life structure in women.* Unpublished doctoral dissertation, California School of Professional Psychology, Berkeley, CA.

Dunn, J. (1983). Sibling relationships in early childhood. *Child Development, 54,* 787–811.

Dunn, J. (1985). *Sisters and brothers.* Cambridge, MA: Harvard University Press.

Dunn, J., & Kendrick, C. (1982). *Siblings: Love, envy and understanding.* Cambridge, MA: Harvard University Press.

DuPont, R. L. (1983). Phobias in children. *Journal of Pediatrics, 102*(6), 999–1002.

Durden-Smith, J., & DeSimone, D. (1982, April). The sex signals. *Playboy,* pp. 144–146, 226–242.

Durlak, J. A. (1973). Relationship between attitudes toward life and death among elderly women. *Developmental Psychology, 8*(1), 146.

Dyer, E. (1963). Parenthood as crisis: A re-study. *Marriage and Family Living, 25,* 196–201.

Easterbrooks, M. A., & Goldberg, W. A. (1984). Toddler development in the family: Impact of father involvement and parenting characteristics. *Child Development, 55,* 740–752.

Eastman, P. (1984). Elders under siege. *Psychology Today, 18*(1), 30.

Eckerman, C. O., & Stein, M. R. (1982). The toddler's emerging interactive skills. In K. H. Rubin & H. S. Ross (Eds.), *Peer relationships and social skills in childhood.* New York: Springer-Verlag.

Edinberg, M. A. (1987). *Talking with your aging parents.* Boston: Shambhala.

Edwards, C. P. (1977). The comparative study of the development of moral judgment and reasoning. In R. Monroe, R. Monroe, & B. B. Whiting (Eds.), *Handbook of cross-cultural human development.* New York: Garland.

Egbuono, L., & Starfield, B. (1982). Child health and social status. *Pediatrics, 69*(5), 550–557.

Egeland, B., & Farber, E. A. (1984). Infant-mother attachment: Factors related to its development and changes over time. *Child Development, 55,* 753–771.

Egeland, B., & Sroufe, L. A. (1981). Attachment and early maltreatment. *Child Development, 52,* 44–52.

Egertson, H. A. (1987, May 20). Recapturing kindergarten for 5-year-olds. *Education Week,* p. 28, 19.

Ehrhardt, A. A., & Money, J. (1967). Progestin induced hermaphroditism: I.Q. and psychosexual identity. *Journal of Sexual Research, 3,* 83–100.

Eichorn, D. H., Clausen, J. A., Haan, N., Honzik, M. P., & Mussen, P. H. (1981). *Present and past in midlife.* New York: Academic.

Eiger, M. S., & Olds, S. W. (1987). *The complete book of breastfeeding.* New York: Workman.

Eimas, P. (1985). The perception of speech in early infancy. *Scientific American, 252*(1), 46–52.

Eimas, P., Siqueland, E., Jusczyk, P., & Vigorito, J. (1971). Speech perception in infants. *Science, 171,* 303–306.

Einstein, E. (1979, April). Stepfamily lives. *Human Behavior,* pp. 63–68.

Eisenberg, A., Murkoff, H. E., & Hathaway, S. E. (1984). *What to expect when you're expecting.* New York: Workman.

Eisenberg, L. (1980). Adolescent suicide: On taking arms against a sea of troubles. *Pediatrics, 66,* 315–320.

Eisenberg, L. (1986). Does bad news about suicide beget bad news? *The New England Journal of Medicine, 315,* 705–706.

Eisenson, J., Auer, J. J., & Irwin, J. V. (1963). *The psychology of communication.* New York: Appleton-Century-Crofts.

Elkind, D. (1981). *The hurried child.* Reading, MA: Addison-Wesley.

Elkind, D. (1984). *All grown up and no place to go.* Reading, MA: Addison-Wesley.

Elkind, D. (1987a). *Miseducation.* New York: Knopf.

Elkind, D. (1987b). Superkids and

super problems. *Psychology Today, 21*(5), 60–61.

Elkind, D., & Bowen, R. (1979). Imaginary audience behavior in children and adolescents. *Developmental Psychology, 15*(1), 38.

Emanuel, I., Sever, L., Milham, S., & Thuline, H. (1972). Accelerating aging in young mothers of children with Down's syndrome. *The Lancet, 2,* 361–363.

Emmerich, W., Goldman, K. S., Kirsch, B., & Sharabany, R. (1976). *Development of gender constancy in economically disadvantaged children.* Princeton, NJ: Educational Testing Service.

Emmerich, W., Goldman, K. S., Kirsch, B., & Sharabany, R. (1977). Evidence for a transitional phase in the development of gender constancy. *Child Development, 48,* 930–936.

Emmerick, H. (1978). The influence of parents and peers on choices made by adolescents. *Journal of Youth and Adolescence, 7*(2), 175–180.

Engelberg, S. (1984, September 26). Why motorists won't buckle up. *The New York Times,* pp. C1, C8.

Entine, A. (1974). *Americans in middle years: Career options and educational opportunities.* California: Ethel Percy Andrus Gerontological Center.

Epstein, J. L. (1983). *Effects on parents of teacher practices of parent involvement* (Report No. 346). Baltimore: Johns Hopkins University Center for Social Organization of Schools.

Epstein, J. L. (1984, May). Single parents get involved in children's learning [Summary]. *CSOS Report.* Baltimore, MD: Johns Hopkins University Center for Social Organization of Schools (CSOS).

Epstein, J. L. (1987). Effects on student achievement of teachers' practices of parental involvement. In S. Silvers (Ed.), *Literacy through family, community and school interaction.* Greenwich, CT: JAI.

Erbes, J. T., & Hedderson, J. J. C. (1984). A longitudinal examination of the separation/divorce process. *Journal of Marriage and the Family, 46*(4), 937–941.

Erickson, R. (1985, March/April). Companion animals and the elderly. *Geriatric Nursing,* pp. 92–96.

Erikson, E. H. (1950). *Childhood and society.* New York: Norton.

Erikson, E. H. (1963). *Childhood and society* (2d ed.). New York: Norton.

Erikson, E. H. (1964). *Insight and responsibility.* New York: Norton.

Erikson, E. H. (1968). *Identity: Youth and crisis.* New York: Norton.

Erikson, E. H. (1973). The wider identity. In K. Erikson (Ed.), *In search of common ground: Conversations with Erik H. Erikson and Huey P. Newton.* New York: Norton.

Erikson, E. H. (1985). *The life cycle completed.* New York: Norton.

Eron, L. D. (1980). Prescription for reduction of aggression. *American Psychologist, 35*(3), 244–252.

Eron, L. D. (1982). Parent-child interaction, television violence, and aggression in children. *American Psychologist, 37*(2), 197–211.

Espenschade, A. (1960). Motor development. In W. R. Johnson (Ed.), *Science and medicine of exercise and sports.* New York: Harper & Row.

Espenshade, T. J. (1979). The economic consequences of divorce. *Journal of Marriage and the Family, 41*(3), 615–625.

Estes, E. H. (1969). Health experience in the elderly. In E. Busse & E. Pfeiffer (Eds.), *Behavior and adaptation in late life.* Boston: Little, Brown.

Evans, G. (1976). The older the sperm . . . *Ms., 4*(7), 48–49.

Evans, J., & Ilfeld, E. (1982). *Good beginnings: Parenting in the early years.* Ypsilanti, MI: High/Scope.

Evans, R. I. (1967). *Dialogue with Erik Erikson.* New York: Harper & Row.

Eveleth, P. B., & Tanner, J. M. (1976). *Worldwide variation in human growth.* London: Cambridge University Press.

Eysenck, H. J., & Kamin, L. (1981). *The intelligence controversy.* New York: Wiley.

Eysenck, H. J., & Prell, D. B. (1951). The inheritance of neuroticism: An experimental study. *Journal of Mental Science, 97,* 441–466.

Fagan, J. F. (1982). Infant memory. In T. M. Field, A. Huston, H. Quay, L. Troll, & G. Finley (Eds.), *Review of human development.* New York: Wiley.

Fagan, J. F., & McGrath, S. K. (1981). Infant recognition memory and later intelligence. *Intelligence, 5,* 121–130.

Falbo, T., & Polit, D. F. (1986). Quantitative review of the only child literature: Research evidence and theory development. *Psychological Bulletin, 100*(2), 176–189.

Fallot, M. E., Boyd, J.L., & Oski, F. A. (1980). Breast-feeding reduces incidence of hospital admissions for infection in infants. *Pediatrics, 65*(6), 1121–1124.

Fantz, R. L. (1963). Pattern vision in newborn infants. *Science, 140,* 296–297.

Fantz, R. L. (1964). Visual experience in infants: Decreased attention to familiar patterns relative to novel ones. *Science, 146,* 668–670.

Fantz, R. L. (1965). Visual perception from birth as shown by pattern selectivity. In H. E. Whipple (Ed.), New issues in infant development. *Annals of the New York Academy of Science, 118,* 793–814.

Fantz, R. L., Fagan, J., & Miranda, S. B. (1975). Early visual selectivity. In L. Cohen & P. Salapatek (Eds.), *Infant perception: From sensation to cognition: Vol. 1. Basic visual processes* (pp. 249–341). New York: Academic.

Fantz, R. L., & Nevis, S. (1967). Pattern preferences and perceptual-cognitive development in early infancy. *Merrill-Palmer Quarterly, 13,* 77–108.

Farrell, M. P., & Rosenberg, S. D. (1981). *Men at midlife.* Boston: Auburn.

Farrow, J. A., Rees, J. M., & Worthington-Roberts, B. S. (1987). Health, developmental, and nutritional status of adolescent alcohol and marijuana abusers. *Pediatrics, 79*(2), 218–223.

Father Gander. (pseudonym for D. W. Larche). See D. W. Larche.

Feagans, L.(1983). A current view of learning disabilities. *Journal of Pediatrics, 102*(4), 487–493.

Feazell, C. S., Mayers, R. S., & Deschner, J. (1984). Services for men who batter: Implications for programs and policies. *Family Relations, 33,* 217–223.

Feifel, H. (1977). *New meanings of death.* New York: McGraw-Hill.

Fein, G. (1981). Pretend play in childhood: An integrative review. *Child Development, 52,* 1095–1118.

Feinberg, M., Smith, M., & Schmidt, R. (1958). An analysis of expressions used by adolescents at varying economic levels to describe accepted and rejected peers. *Journal of Genetic Psychology, 93,* 133–148.

Feldman, H. (1981). A comparison of intentional parents and intentionally childless couples. *Journal of Marriage and the Family, 43*(3), 593–600.

Feldman, H., & Feldman, M. (1977). *Effect of parenthood at three points on marriage.* Unpublished manuscript.

Feldman, H., Goldin-Meadow, S., & Gleitman, L. (1979). Beyond Herodotus: The creation of language by linguistically deprived deaf children. In A. Lock (Ed.), *Action, gesture and symbol: The emergence of language.* New York: Academic.

Feldman, R. D. (1982). *Whatever happened to the quiz kids: Perils and profits of growing up gifted.* Chicago: Chicago Review Press.

Feldman, R. D. (1985, October). The pyramid project: Do we have the answer for the gifted? *Instructor*, pp. 62–71.

Feldman, R. D. (1986, April). What are thinking skills? *Instructor*, pp. 34–39.

Fergusson, D. M., Horwood, L. J., & Shannon, F. T. (1986). Factors related to the age of attainment of nocturnal bladder control: An 8-year longitudinal study. *Pediatrics, 78*, 884–890.

Fetterly, K., & Graubard, M. S. (1984, March 23). Racial and educational factors associated with breast-feeding—United States, 1969 and 1980. *Morbidity and Mortality Weekly Report*, (MMWR), pp. 153–154.

Fewer gifted drop out than believed. (1987, June). *Gifted Children Monthly*, pp. 3–4.

Field, D. (1977). The importance of the verbal content in the training of Piagetian conservation skills. *Child Development, 52*, 326–334.

Field, D. (1981). Can preschool children really learn to conserve? *Child Development, 52*, 326–334.

Field, T. M. (1978). Interaction behaviors of primary versus secondary caretaker fathers. *Developmental Psychology, 14*, 183–184.

Field, T. M. (1986). Interventions for premature infants. *Journal of Pediatrics, 109*(1), 183–190.

Field, T. M., & Roopnarine, J. L. (1982). Infant-peer interaction. In T. M. Field, A. Huston, H. C. Quay, L. Troll, & G. Finley (Eds.), *Review of human development.* New York: Wiley.

Field, T. M., Sandberg, D., Garcia, R., Vega-Lahr, N., Goldstein, S., & Guy, L. (1985). Pregnancy problems, postpartum depression, and early mother-infant interactions. *Developmental Psychology, 21*(6), 1152–1156.

Field, T. M., Widmayer, S., Greenberg, R., & Stoller, S. (1982). Effects of parent training on teenage mothers and their infants. *Pediatrics, 69*(6), 703–707.

Fiske, E. B. (1984, November 11). Learning disabled: A new awareness. *The New York Times*, Sec. 12, pp. 1, 44, 58.

Fitness Finders. (1984). *Feelin' good.* Spring Arbor, MI: Author.

Flavell, J. H. (1963). *The developmental psychology of Jean Piaget.* New York: Van Nostrand Reinhold.

Flavell, J. H. (1970). Cognitive changes in adulthood. In L. R. Goulet & P. B. Baltes (Eds.), *Life-span developmental psychology: Research & theory.* New York: Academic.

Flavell, J. H. (1977). *Cognitive development.* Englewood Cliffs, NJ: Prentice-Hall.

Flavell, J. H., Beach, D., & Chinsky, J. (1966). Spontaneous verbal rehearsal in a memory task as a function of age. *Child Development, 37*, 283–299.

Flavell, J. H., Speer, J. R., Green, F. L., & August, D. L. (1981). The development of comprehension monitoring and knowledge about communication. *Monographs of the Society for Research in Child Development, 46*(5, Serial No. 192).

Fomon, S. J., Filer, L. J., Anderson, T. A., & Ziegler, E. E. (1979). Recommendations for feeding normal infants. *Pediatrics, 63*(1), 52–59.

Ford, J., Zelnik, M., & Kantner, J. (1979, November). *Differences in contraceptive use and socioeconomic groups of teenagers in the United States.* Paper presented at the meeting of the American Public Health Association, New York.

Forehand, R., Long, N., Brody, G. H., & Fauber, R. (1986). Home predictors of young adolescents' school behavior and academic performance. *Child Development, 57*, 1528–1533.

Forman, M. R., Graubard, B. I., Hoffman, H. J., Beren, R., Harley, E. E., & Bennett, P. (1984). The Pima infant feeding study: Breast feeding and gastroenteritis in the first year of life. *American Journal of Epidemiology, 119*(3), 335–349.

Foundation for Child Development. (1981). Panel survey of "Time allocation in American households." In *Interim report to the Foundation for Child Development: Demographic differences in parents' and children's time use.* Ann Arbor: University of Michigan.

Francoeur, R. T. (1985). Reproductive technologies: New alternatives and new ethics. *SIECUS Report, 14*, 1–5.

Frankenburg, W. K. (1978). *Denver developmental screening test.* Denver: University of Colorado Medical Center.

Frankenburg, W. K., Dodds, J. B., Fandal, A. W., Kazuk, E., & Cohrs, M. (1975). *The Denver developmental screening test: Reference manual.* Denver: University of Colorado Medical Center.

Frankl, V. (1965). *The doctor and the soul.* New York: Knopf.

Freedman, D. G. (1979, January). Ethnic differences in babies. *Human Nature*, pp. 15–20.

Freeman, D. (1983). *Margaret Mead and Samoa.* Cambridge, MA: Harvard University Press.

Freud, A. (1946). *The ego and the mechanism of defense.* New York: International Universities Press.

Freud, S. (1959). An autobiographical study. In J. Strachey (Ed. and Trans.), *The standard edition of the complete psychological works of Sigmund Freud* (Vol. 20). London: Hogarth, 1959. (Original work published 1925)

Freud, S. (1953). *A general introduction to psychoanalysis* (J. Riviere, Trans.). New York: Perma-books.

Freudenberger, H. J., & Richelson, G. (1980). *Burn-out: The high cost of high achievement.* Garden City, NY: Anchor.

Fried, P. A. (1983). *Pregnancy and life-style habits.* New York: Beaufort.

Fried, P. A., Watkinson, B., & Willan, A. (1984). Marijuana use during pregnancy and decreased length of gestation. *American Journal of Obstetrics and Gynecology, 150*, 23–27.

Friedman, M., & Rosenman, R. H. (1974). *Type A behavior and your heart.* New York: Knopf.

Fries, J. F., & Crapo, L. M. (1981). *Vitality and aging.* San Francisco: Freeman.

Frisch, H. (1977). Sex stereotypes in adult-infancy play. *Child Development, 48*, 1671–1675.

Frisch, R. E., Wyshak, G., & Vincent, L. (1980). Delayed menarche and amenorrhea in ballet dancers. *The New England Journal of Medicine, 303*, 17–19.

Frueh, T., & McGhee, P. (1975). Traditional sex role development and amount of time spent watching television. *Developmental Psychology, 11*(1), 109.

Fuchs, D., & Fuchs, L. S. (1986). Test procedure bias: A meta-analysis of examiner familiarity effects. *Review of Educational Research, 56*, 243–262.

Fuchs, F. (1980). Genetic amniocentesis. *Scientific American, 242*(6), 47–53.

Fuchs, L. S., & Fuchs, D. (1986). Effects of systematic formative evaluation of student achievement: A meta-analysis. *Exceptional Children, 53*, 199–205.

Furman, W. (1982). Children's friendships. In T. M. Field, A. Huston, H. C. Quay, L. Troll, & G. E. Finley (Eds.), *Review of human development.* New York: Wiley.

Furman, W., & Bierman, K. L. (1983). Developmental changes in young children's conceptions of friendship. *Child Development, 54*, 549–556.

Furman, W., & Buhrmester, D. (1985). Children's perceptions of the personal relationships in their social networks. *Developmental Psychology, 21*(6), 1016–1024.

Furry, C. A., & Baltes, P. B. (1973). The effect of age differences in ability-extraneous performance variables on the assessment of intelligence in children, adults, and the elderly. *Journal of Gerontology, 28*(1), 73–80.

Furst, K. (1983). *Origins and evolution of women's dreams in early adulthood.* Unpublished doctoral dissertation, California School of Professional Psychology, Berkeley, CA.

Furstenberg, F. F. (1976). The social consequences of teenage parenthood. *Family Planning Perspectives, 8*(4), 148–164.

Gaensbauer, T., & Hiatt, S. (1984). *The psychobiology of affective development.* Hillsdale, NJ: Erlbaum.

Gage, F. H., Bjorklund, A., Stenevi, U., Dunnett, S. B., & Kelly, P. A. T. (1984). Intrahippocampal septal grafts ameliorate learning impairments in aged rats. *Science, 22*, 533–536.

Gamble, T. J., & Zigler, E. (1986). Effects of infant day care: Another look at the evidence. *American Journal of Orthopsychiatry, 56*(1), 26–42.

Gamer, E., Thomas, J., & Kendall, D. (1975). Determinants of friendship across the life span. In F. Rebelsky (Ed.), *Life: The continuous process.* New York: Knopf.

Gansberg, J. M., & Mostel, A. P. (1984). *The second nine months.* New York: Pocket Books.

Gardner, H. (1979, March 29). Exploring the mystery of creativity. *The New York Times*, pp. C1, C17.

Gardner, H. (1981, July). [Interview with Howard Gruber]. Breakaway minds. *Psychology Today*, pp. 64–71.

Gardner, H. (1983). *Frames of mind: The theory of multiple intelligences.* New York: Basic Books.

Gardner, R. (1973). *Understanding children.* New York: Aronson.

Garfield, C., & Clark, R. (1978). The Shanti Project: A community model of psychosocial support for patients and families facing life-threatening illness. In C. Garfield (Ed.), *Psychosocial care of the dying patient* (pp. 355–364). New York: McGraw-Hill.

Garmezy, N. (1983). Stressors of childhood. In N. Garmezy & M. Rutter. (Eds.), *Stress, coping and development in children.* New York: McGraw-Hill.

Garn, S. M. (1966). Growth and devel-

opment. In E. Ginzberg (Ed.), *The nation's children* (pp. 24–42). New York: Columbia University Press.

Garrison, E. G. (1987). Psychological maltreatment of children: An emerging focus for inquiry and concern. *American Psychologist, 42*(2), 157–159.

Garvey, C. (1977). *Play.* Cambridge, MA: Harvard University Press.

Garvey, C., & Hogan, R. (1973). Social speech and social interaction: Egocentrism revisited. *Child Development, 44*, 562–568.

Gavotos, L. A. (1959). Relationships and age differences in growth measures and motor skills. *Child Development, 30*, 333–340.

Geber, M. (1962). Longitudinal study and psychomotor development among Baganda children. *Proceedings of the Fourteenth International Congress of Applied Psychology, 3*, 50–60.

Geber, M., & Dean, R. F. A. (1957). The state of development of newborn African children. *The Lancet, 1*, 1216–1219.

Gelfand, D. E. (1982). *Aging: The ethnic factor.* Boston: Little, Brown.

Geller, E., Ritvo, E. R., Freeman, B. J., & Yuwiler, A. (1982). Preliminary observations of the effect of fenfluramine on blood serotonin and symptoms in three autistic boys. *The New England Journal of Medicine, 307*(3), 165–169.

Gelman, R., Bullock, M., & Meck, E. (1980). Preschoolers' understanding of simple object transformations. *Child Development, 51*, 691–699.

Gelman, R., Spelke, A., & Meck, E. (in press). [Work on animism in children].

General Mills, Inc. (1977). *Raising children in a changing society.* Minneapolis, MN: Author.

General Mills, Inc. (1981). *The General Mills American family report 1980–81: Families at work: Strengths and strains.* Minneapolis, MN: Author.

Genevay, B. (1986). Intimacy as we age. *Generations, 10*(4), 12–15.

Gesell, A. (1929). Maturation and infant behavior patterns. *Psychological Review, 36*, 307–319.

Getzels, J. W. (1964). Creative thinking, problem-solving and instruction. In *Yearbook of the National Society for the Study of Education* (Part I, pp. 240–267). Chicago: University of Chicago Press.

Getzels, J. W. (1984, March). *Problem-finding and creativity in higher education* [The Fifth Rev. Charles F. Donovan, S.J., Lecture]. Boston College, School of Education, Boston.

Getzels, J. W., & Jackson, P. W. (1962). *Creativity and intelligence: Explorations with gifted students.* New York: Wiley.

Gewirtz, H. B., & Gewirtz, J. L. (1968). Caretaking settings, background events, and behavior differences in four Israeli childrearing environments: Some preliminary trends. In B. M. Foss (Ed.), *Determinants of infant behavior* (Vol. 4). London: Methuen.

Gibson, E. J., & Walk, R. D. (1960). The "visual cliff." *Scientific American, 202*, 64–71.

Gibson, R. C. (1986). Older black Americans. *Generations, 10*(4), 35–39.

Gil, D. G. (1971). Violence against children. *Journal of Marriage and the Family, 33*(4), 637–648.

Gilford, R. (1984). Contrasts in marital satisfaction throughout old age: An exchange theory analysis. *Journal of Gerontology, 39*, 325–333.

Gilford, R. (1986). Marriages in later life. *Generations, 10*(4), 16–20.

Gilford, R., & Bengtson, V. (1979). Measuring marital satisfaction in three generations: Positive and negative dimensions. *Journal of Marriage and the Family, 41*, 387–398.

Gill, J. J., Price, V. A., Friedman, M., Thoresen, C. E., Powell, L. H., Ulmer, D., Brown, B., & Drews, F. R. (1985). Reduction of Type A behavior in healthy middle-aged American military officers. *American Heart Journal, 110*(3), 503–514.

Gilligan, C. (1982). *In a different voice: Psychological theory and women's development.* Cambridge, MA: Harvard University Press.

Ginsburg, H., & Opper, S. (1979). *Piaget's theory of intellectual development* (2d ed.). Englewood Cliffs, NJ: Prentice-Hall.

Ginzberg, E., et al. (1951). *Occupational choice: An approach to a general theory.* New York: Columbia University Press.

Gladue, B. A., Green, R., & Hellman, R. E. (1984). Neuroendocrine response to estrogen and sexual orientation. *Science, 225*, 1496–1499.

Gleitman, L. R., Newport, E. L., & Gleitman, H. (1984). The current status of the motherese hypothesis. *Journal of Child Language, 11*, 43–79.

Glenbard East Echo. (Compilers). (1984). *Teenagers themselves.* New York: Adama.

Glenn, N. D. (1987). Marriage on the rocks. *Psychology Today, 21*(10), 20–21.

Glenn, N. D., & McLanahan, S. (1981). The effects of offspring on the psychological well-being of older adults. *Journal of Marriage and the Family, 43*(2), 409–421.

Glick, P. C., & Lin, S.-L. (1986a). More young adults are living with their parents: Who are they? *Journal of Marriage and the Family, 48,* 107–112.

Glick, P. C., & Lin, S.-L. (1986b). Recent changes in divorce and remarriage. *Journal of Marriage and the Family, 48*(4), 737–747.

Golbus, M., Loughman, W., Epstein, C., Halbasch, G., Stephens, J., & Hall, B. (1979). Prenatal genetic diagnosis in 3000 amniocenteses. *The New England Journal of Medicine, 300*(4), 157–163.

Gold, D., & Andres, D. (1978a). Developmental comparison between adolescent children with employed and non-employed mothers. *Merrill-Palmer Quarterly, 24,* 243–254.

Gold, D., & Andres, D. (1978b). Relations between maternal employment and development of nursery school children. *Canadian Journal of Behavioral Science, 10,* 116–129.

Gold, D., Andres, D., & Glorieux, J. (1979). The development of Francophone nursery-school children with employed and nonemployed mothers. *Canadian Journal of Behavioral Science, 11,* 169–173.

Gold, M., & Yanof, D. S. (1985). Mothers, daughters, and girlfriends. *Journal of Personality and Social Psychology, 49*(3), 654–659.

Goldberg, S., & Divitto, B. A. (1983). *Born too soon: Preterm birth and early development.* San Francisco: Freeman.

Golden, M., Birns, B., & Bridger, W. (1973). *Review and overview: Social class and cognitive development.* Paper presented at the meeting of the Society for Research in Child Development, Philadelphia.

Goldschmid, M. L., & Bentler, P. M. (1968). The dimensions and measurement of conservation. *Child Development, 39,* 787–815.

Goldsmith, M. F. (1985). Possible herpes virus role in abortion studies. *Journal of the American Medical Association, 251,* 3067–3070.

Goldstein, H., & Tanner, J. (1980, March 15). Ecological considerations in the creation and the use of child growth standards. *The Lancet,* pp. 582–585.

Goodenough, F. L. (1949). *Mental testing: Its history, principles, and applications.* New York: Rinehart.

Goodman, G. S. (1984). The child witness: An introduction. *Journal of Social Issues, 40,* 1–7.

Gorbach, S. L., Zimmerman, D. R., &

Woods, M. (1984). *The doctors' anti-breast cancer diet.* New York: Simon & Schuster.

Gordon, A. (1975). The Jewish view of death: Guidelines for mourning. In E. Kübler-Ross (Ed.), *Death: The final stage of growth.* Englewood Cliffs, NJ: Prentice-Hall.

Gordon, D., & Young, R. (1976). School phobia: A discussion of etiology, treatment, and evaluation. *Psychological Bulletin, 39,* 783–804.

Gordon, J. (1975). Nutritional individuality. *American Journal of Diseases of Children, 129*(4), 422–424.

Gordon, S., & Everly, K. (1985). Increasing self-esteem in vulnerable students: A tool for reducing pregnancy among teenagers. In *Impact '85.* Syracuse, NY: Ed-U Press.

Gottesman, I. I. (1962). Differential inheritance of the psychoneuroses. *Eugenics Quarterly, 9,* 223–227.

Gottesman, I. I. (1963). Heritability of personality: A demonstration. *Psychology Monographs, 77*(9, Whole No. 572).

Gottesman, I. I. (1965). Personality and natural selection. In S. G. Vandenberg (Ed.), *Methods and goals in human behavior genetics* (pp. 63–80). New York: Academic.

Gottesman, I. I., & Shields, J. (1966). Schizophrenia in twins: 16 years consecutive admission to a psychiatric clinic. *British Journal of Psychiatry, 112,* 809–818.

Gould, R. (1978). *Transformations.* New York: Simon & Schuster.

Grant, W. V. (1984). Trends in college enrollments: 1972 to 1982. In *Statistical highlights of the National Center for Educational Statistics* (Publication No. NCES 84-403). Washington, DC: U.S. Department of Education.

Gray, J. A., Lean, J., & Keynes, A. (1969). Infant androgen treatment and adult open-field behavior: Direct effects and effects of injections of siblings. *Physiology and Behavior, 4*(2), 177–181.

Graziano, A. M., & Mooney, K. C. (1982). Behavioral treatment of "nightfears" in children: Maintenance and improvement at 2½ to 3-year follow-up. *Journal of Counseling and Clinical Psychology, 50*(4), 598–599.

Green, B. (1984). *Good morning, Merry Sunshine.* New York: Atheneum.

Greenberg, M. (1985). *The birth of a father.* New York: Continuum.

Greenberg, M., & Morris, N. (1974). Engrossment: The newborn's impact upon the father. *American Journal of Orthopsychiatry, 44*(4), 520–531.

Greenberg, S. B. (1972). *Attitudes to-*

ward increased social, economic and political participation by women as reported by elementary and secondary students. Paper presented at the American Educational Research Association convention, Chicago.

Greenberger, E., & Steinberg, L. (1986). *When teenagers work.* New York: Basic Books.

Greenfield, P. M. (1984). *Mind and media.* Cambridge, MA: Harvard University Press.

Grief, E. B., & Ulman, K. J. (1982). The psychological impact of menarche on early adolescent females: A review of the literature. *Child Development, 53,* 1413–1430.

Gross, R. (1982). *The independent scholar's handbook.* Reading, PA: Addison-Wesley.

Gross, R. T., & Duke, P. (1980). The effect of early versus late physical maturation on adolescent behavior. In I. Litt (Ed.), *Symposium on adolescent medicine. Pediatric Clinics of North America, 27*(1), 71–78.

Grossmann, B., & Wrighter, J. (1948). The relationship between selection-rejection and intelligence, social status, and personality among sixth grade girls. *Sociometry, 11,* 346–355.

Grotevant, H., & Durrett, M. (1980). Occupational knowledge and career development in adolescence. *Journal of Vocational Behavior, 17,* 171–182.

Gruber-Baldini, A., & Schaie, K. W. (1986, November 21). *Longitudinal-sequential studies of marital assortativity.* Paper presented at the annual meeting of the Gerontological Society of America, Chicago.

Gruen, G., Korte, J., & Baum, J. (1974). Group measure of locus of control. *Developmental Psychology, 10*(5), 683–686.

Gubrium, F. F. (1975). Being single in old age. *International Journal of Aging and Human Development, 6*(1), 29–41.

Guilford, J. P. (1959). Three faces of intellect. *American Psychologist, 14,* 469–479.

Gurian, A., & Formanek, R. (1983). *The socially competent child: A parent's guide to social development—from infancy to early adolescence.* Boston: Houghton Mifflin.

Gurucharri, C., & Selman, R. (1982). The development of interpersonal understanding during childhood, preadolescence, and adolescence: A longitudinal follow-up study. *Child Development, 53,* 924–927.

Guttmacher, A. F. (1973). *Pregnancy, birth, and family planning.* New York: Viking.

Alan Guttmacher Institute. (1981).

Teenage pregnancy: The problem that hasn't gone away. New York: Viking.

Haan, N., & Day, D. (1974). A longitudinal study of change and sameness in personality development: Adolescence to later adulthood. *International Journal of Aging and Human Development, 5*(1), 11–39.

Hadley, J. (1984, July–August). Facts about childhood hyperactivity. *Children Today,* pp. 8–13.

Hagestad, G. O. (1978). *Patterns of communication and influence between grandparents and grandchildren in a changing society.* Paper presented at the meeting of the World Conference of Sociology, Uppsala, Sweden.

Hagestad, G. O. (1982). *Issues in the study of intergenerational continuity.* Paper presented at the National Council on Family Relations Theory and Methods Workshop, Washington, DC.

Hagestad, G. O. (1984). The continuous bond: A dynamic, multigenerational perspective on parent-child relations between adults. In M. Perlmutter (Ed.), *Minnesota symposium on child psychology.* Hillsdale, NJ: Erlbaum.

Haith, M. M. (1986). Sensory and perceptual processes in early infancy. *Journal of Pediatrics, 109*(1), 158–171.

Hall, E. (1983). A conversation with Erik Erikson. *Psychology Today, 17*(6), 22–30.

Hall, E. G., & Lee, A. M. (1984). Sex differences in motor performance of young children: Fact or fiction? *Sex Roles, 10,* 217–230.

Hall, G. S. (1916). [Originally published 1904]. *Adolescence.* New York: Appleton.

Hall, G. S. (1922). *Senescence: The last half of life.* New York: Appleton.

Halpern, J. (1987). *Helping your aging parents: A practical guide for adult children.* New York: McGraw-Hill.

Hamilton, S., & Crouter, A. (1980). Work and growth: A review of research on the impact of work experience on adolescent development. *Journal of Youth and Adolescence, 9*(4), 323–338.

Hammond, C. B., Jelovsek, F. R., Lee, K. L., Creasman, W. T., & Parker, R. T. (1979). Effects of long-term estrogen replacement therapy. II: Neoplasia. *American Journal of Obstetrics and Gynecology, 133,* 537–547.

Harbaugh, R. E., Roberts, D. W., Coombs, D. W., Saunders, R. L., & Reeder, T. M. (1984). Preliminary report: Intercranial cholinergic drug infusion in patients with Alzheimer's disease. *Neurosurgery, 15,* 514–518.

Hardy-Brown, K., & Plomin, R. (1985). Infant communicative development: Evidence from adoptive and biological families for genetic and environmental influences on rate differences. *Developmental Psychology, 21*(2), 378–385.

Hardy-Brown, K., Plomin, R., & DeFries, J. C. (1981). Genetic and environmental influences on rate of communicative development in the first year of life. *Developmental Psychology, 17,* 704–717.

Hare, P. H., & Haske, M. (1983–1984, December–January). Innovative living arrangements: A source of long-term care. *Aging,* pp. 3–8.

Harkins, E. (1978). Effects of empty nest transition on self-report of psychological and physical well-being. *Journal of Marriage and the Family, 40*(3), 549–556.

Harlow, H. F., & Harlow, M. K. (1962). The effect of rearing conditions on behavior. *Bulletin of Menninger Clinic, 26,* 213–224.

Harlow, H. F., & Zimmerman, R. R. (1959). Affectional responses in the infant monkey. *Science, 130,* 421–432.

Harmon, R., Suwalsky, J., & Klein, R. (1979). Infant's preferential response for mother versus unfamiliar adult. *Journal of the American Academy of Child Psychiatry, 18*(3), 437–449.

Harris, B. (1979). Whatever happened to little Albert? *American Psychologist, 34*(2), 151–161.

Harris, L., & Associates. (1986). *American teens speak: Sex, myths, TV and birth control: The Planned Parenthood poll.* New York: Planned Parenthood Federation of America.

Harris, R., & Bologh, R. W. (1985). The dark side of love: Blue- and white-collar wife abuse. In *Victimology,* in press.

Harrison, M. (1982). *Self-help for premenstrual syndrome.* Cambridge, MA: Matrix.

Hart, S. N., & Brassard, M. R. (1987). A major threat to children's mental health: Psychological maltreatment. *American Psychologist, 42*(2), 160–165.

Hartley, R. E. (1959). Sex-role pressures and the socialization of the male child. *Psychological Reports, 5,* 457–468.

Hartmann, E. (1981). The strangest sleep disorder. *Psychology Today, 15*(4), 14–18.

Hartshorne, H., & May, M. A. (1928–1930). *Studies in the nature of character* (Vols. 1–3). New York: Macmillan.

Hartup, W. W. (1970). Peer relations. In T. D. Spencer & N. Kass (Eds.), *Perspectives in child psychology: Research and review.* New York: McGraw-Hill.

Hartup, W. W. (1984). The peer context in middle childhood. In W. A. Collins (Ed.), *Development during middle childhood: The years from six to twelve.* Washington, DC: National Academy.

Haskell, W. L., Camargo, C., Williams, P. T., Vranizan, K. M., Krauss, R. M., Lindgren, F. T., & Wood, P. D. (1984). The effect of cessation and resumption of moderate alcohol intake on serum high-density-lipoprotein subfractions. *The New England Journal of Medicine, 310*(13), 805–810.

Haswell, K., Hock, E., & Wenar, C. (1981). Oppositional behavior of preschool children: Theory and prevention. *Family Relations, 30,* 440–446.

Haugh, S., Hoffman, C., & Cowan, G. (1980). The eye of the very young beholder: Sex typing of infants by young children. *Child Development, 51,* 598–600.

Hay, D. F., Pedersen, J., & Nash, A. (1982). Dyadic interaction in the first year of life. In K. H. Rubin & H. S. Ross (Eds.), *Peer relationships and social skills in children.* New York: Springer.

Hayden, A., & Haring, N. (1976). Early intervention for high risk infants and young children: Programs for Down's syndrome children. In T. D. Tjossem (Ed.), *Intervention strategies for high risk infants and young children* (pp. 573–607). Baltimore: University Park Press.

Hayes, L. A., & Watson, J. S. (1981). Neonatal imitation: Fact or artifact? *Developmental Psychology, 17*(5), 655–660.

Hayflick, L. (1974). The strategy of senescence. *Gerontologist, 14*(1), 37–45.

Hayghe, H. (1986, February). Rise in mothers' labor force activity includes those with infants. *Monthly Labor Review,* pp. 43–45.

Health Care Finance Administration. (1981). *Long term care: Background and future directions.* Washington, DC: U.S. Department of Health and Human Services.

Heard Museum of Anthropology and Primitive Art. (1987). [Curatorial notes for exhibit on Apache sunrise ceremony]. Phoenix, AZ.

Hechinger, F. M. (Ed.). (1986). *A better start: New choices for early learning.* Ypsilanti, MI: High/Scope.

Hechtman, L., & Weiss, G. (1983). Long-term outcome of hyperactive children. *American Journal of Ortho-psychiatry, 53,* 532–541.

Heller, Z. I. (1975). The Jewish view of dying: Guidelines for dying. In E. Kübler-Ross (Ed.), *Death: The final stage of growth.* Englewood Cliffs, NJ: Prentice-Hall.

Helson, R., & Moane, G. (1987). Personality change in women from college to midlife. *Journal of Personality and Social Psychology, 53*(1), 176–186.

Henderson, A. (1987). *The evidence continues to grow: Parent involvement improves student achievement.* Columbia, MD: National Committee for Citizens in Education.

Henig, R. M. (1979). Ageism's angry critic. *Human Behavior, 8*(1), 43–46.

Henig, R. M. (1986, September 2). Smart kids, hard questions: The challenge of the gifted child. *Washington Post Health,* pp. 13–16.

Henker, F. O. (1981). Male climacteric. In J. G. Howells (Ed.), *Modern perspectives in the psychiatry of middle age.* New York: Brunner/Mazel.

Henly, W. L., & Fitch, B. R. (1966). Newborn narcotic withdrawal associated with regional enteritis in pregnancy. *New York Journal of Medicine, 66,* 2565–2567.

Herbst, A. L., Kurman, R. J., Scully, R. E., & Poskanzer, D. D. (1971). Clear-cell adenocarcinoma of the genital tract in young females. *The New England Journal of Medicine, 287*(25), 1259–1264.

Herold, E. S., & Goodwin, M. S. (1981). Premarital sexual guilt and contraceptive attitudes and behavior. *Family Relations, 30,* 247–253.

Herr, J. J., & Weakland, J. H. (1979). *Counseling elders and their families.* New York: Springer.

Heston, L. L. (1966). Psychiatric disorders in foster-home-reared children of schizophrenic mothers. *British Journal of Psychiatry, 112,* 819–825.

Heston, L. L., & White, J. A. (1983). *Dementia.* New York: Freeman.

Hetherington, E. M. (1965). A developmental study of the effects of sex of the dominant parent on sex role preference, identification and imitation in children. *Journal of Personality and Social Psychology, 2,* 188–194.

Hetherington, E. M. (1980). Children and divorce. In R. Henderson (Ed.), *Parent-child interaction: Theory, research and prospect.* New York: Academic.

Hetherington, E. M., Cox, M., & Cox, R. (1975). *Beyond father absence: Conceptualizing effects of divorce.* Paper presented at the meeting of the Society for Research in Child Development, Denver.

Hetherington, E. M., & Parke, R. (1979). *Child psychology: A contemporary viewpoint* (2d ed.). New York: McGraw-Hill.

Heyns, B., & Catsambis, S. (1986). Mother's employment and children's achievement: A critique. *Sociology of Education, 59,* 140–151. [See also Reply to Milne, Myers, & Ginsburg, 154–155.]

Hier, D. B., & Crowley, W. F. (1982). Spatial ability in androgen-deficient men. *The New England Journal of Medicine, 20,* 1202–1205.

Hill, C. R., & Stafford, F. P. (1980). Parental care of children: Time diary estimate of quantity, predictability, and variety. *Journal of Human Resources, 15,* 219–239.

Hill, J. P. (1980). The family. In *Yearbook of National Society for Study of Education.* Chicago: University of Chicago Press.

Hill, R. (1965). Decision making and the family life cycle. In E. Shanas & G. Streib (Eds.), *Social structure and the family: Generational relations.* Englewood Cliffs, NJ: Prentice-Hall.

Hinds, M. deC. (1985, January 31). For older people, communal living has its rewards. *The New York Times,* pp. C1, C8.

Hingson, R., Alpert, J. J., Day, N., Dooling, E., Kayne, H., Morelock, S., Oppenheimer, E., & Zuckerman, B. (1982). Effects of maternal drinking and marijuana use on fetal growth and development. *Pediatrics, 70*(4), 539–546.

Hirsch, J. (1972). Can we modify the number of adipose cells? *Postgraduate Medicine, 51*(5), 83–86.

Hobbs, D., & Cole, S. (1976). Transition to parenthood: A decade replication. *Journal of Marriage and the Family, 38*(4), 723–731.

Hobbs, D., & Wimbish, J. (1977). Transition to parenthood by black couples. *Journal of Marriage and the Family, 39*(4), 677–689.

Hochschild, A. (1975). Disengagement theory: A critique and proposal. *American Sociological Review, 40,* 553–569.

Hofferth, S. L. (1979). Day care in the next decade: 1980–1990. *Journal of Marriage and the Family, 41*(3), 649–658.

Hoff-Ginsberg, E. (1985). Relations between discourse properties of mothers' speech and their children's syntactic growth. *Journal of Child Language, 12,* 367–385.

Hoff-Ginsberg, E. (1986). Function and structure in maternal speech: Their relation to the child's development of syntax. *Developmental Psychology, 22*(2), 155–163.

Hoff-Ginsberg, E., & Shatz, M. (1982). Linguistic input and the child's acquisition of language. *Psychological Bulletin, 92*(1), 3–26.

Hoffman, L. (1979). Maternal employment. *American Psychologist, 34*(10), 859–865.

Hoffman, L. (1986). Work, family, and the child. In M. S. Pallak & R. O. Perloff (Eds.), *Psychology and work: Productivity, change, and employment.* Washington, DC: American Psychological Association.

Hoffman, M. (1970). Moral development. In P. H. Mussen (Ed.), *Carmichael's manual of child psychology.* New York: Wiley.

Hoffman, M. (1977). Sex differences in empathy and related behaviors. *Psychological Bulletin, 84,* 712–722.

Hoffman, M., & Hoffman, L. W. (Eds.). (1964). *Review of child development research.* New York: Russell Sage Foundation.

Hogge, W. A., Schonberg, S. A., & Golbus, M. S. (1986). Chorionic villus sampling: Experience of the first 1000 cases. *American Journal of Obstetrics and Gynecology, 154,* 1249–1252.

Hollingsworth, J. (1986). *Unspeakable acts.* New York: Congdon & Weed.

Holmes, L. (1978). Genetic counseling for the older pregnant woman: New data and questions. *The New England Journal of Medicine, 298*(25), 1419–1421.

Holmes, L. D. (1987). *Quest for the real Samoa: The Mead-Freeman controversy and beyond.* South Hadley, MA: Bergin & Garvey.

Holmes, T. H., & Rahe, R. H. (1976). The social readjustment rating scale. *Journal of Psychosomatic Research, 11,* 213.

Holt, R. R. (1982). Occupational stress. In L. Goldberger & S. Breznitz (Eds.), *Handbook of stress.* New York: Free Press.

Honzik, M. P., Macfarlane, J. W., & Allen, L. (1948). The stability of mental test performance between two and 18 years. *Journal of Experimental Education, 17,* 309–323.

Hooker, E. (1957). The adjustment of the male overt homosexual. *Journal of Projective Techniques, 21,* 18–31.

Hooyman, N. R., Rathbone-McCuan, E., & Klingbeil, K. (1982). Serving the vulnerable elderly. *Urban and Social Change Review, 15*(2), 9–13.

Horn, J. (1983). The Texas adoption project: Adopted children and their intellectual resemblance to biological and adoptive parents. *Child Development*, *54*, 268–275.

Horn, J. C., & Meer, J. (1987). The vintage years. *Psychology Today*, *21*(5), 76–90.

Horn, J. L. (1967). Intelligence—Why it grows, why it declines. *Transaction*, *5*(1), 23–31.

Horn, J. L. (1968). Organization of abilities and the development of intelligence. *Psychological Review*, *75*, 242–259.

Horn, J. L. (1970). Organization of data on life-span development of human abilities. In L. R. Goulet & P. B. Baltes (Eds.), *Life-span developmental psychology: Theory and research*. New York: Academic.

Horn, J. L., & Cattell, R. B. (1966). Age differences in primary mental ability factors. *Journal of Gerontology*, *21*, 210–220.

Horn, J. L., & Donaldson, G. (1976). On the myth of intellectual decline in adulthood. *American Psychologist*, *31*, 701–719.

Horn, J. L., & Donaldson, G. (1977). Faith is not enough: A response to the Baltes-Schaie claim that intelligence does not wane. *American Psychologist*, *32*, 369–373.

Horn, J. L., & Donaldson, G. (1980). Cognitive development II: Adulthood development of human abilities. In O. G. Brim & J. Kagan (Eds.), *Constancy and change in human development*. Cambridge, MA: Harvard University Press.

Horowitz, F. D., & O'Brien, M. (1986). Gifted and talented children: State of knowledge and directions for research. *American Psychologist*, *41*(10), 1147–1152.

Householder, J., Hatcher, R., Burns, W., & Chasnoff, I. (1982). Infants born to narcotic-addicted mothers. *Psychological Bulletin*, *92*, 453–468.

Howard, M. (1983). Postponing sexual involvement: A new approach. *SIECUS Report*, *11*(4), 5–6, 8.

Hoyenga, K. B., & Hoyenga, K. T. (1979). *The question of sex differences*. Boston: Little, Brown.

Hudson, J. L., Pope, H. G., & Jonas, J. M. (1983). Treatment of bulimia with antidepressants: Theoretical considerations with clinical findings. In A. J. Stunkard & E. Stellar (Eds.), *Eating and its disorders*. New York: Raven.

Hughes, M. (1975). *Egocentrism in preschool children*. Unpublished doctoral dissertation, Edinburgh University, Edinburgh.

Hultsch, D. F. (1971). Organization and memory in adulthood. *Human Development*, *14*, 16–29.

Humphrey, L. L. (1986). Structural analysis of parent-child relationships in eating disorders. *Journal of Abnormal Psychology*, *95*(4), 395–402.

Hunt, B., & Hunt, M. (1974). *Prime time*. New York: Stein & Day.

Hunt, C. E., & Brouillette, R. T. (1987). Sudden infant death syndrome: 1987 perspective. *Journal of Pediatrics*, *110*(5), 669–678.

Hunt, M. M. (1974). *Sexual behavior in the 1970's*. New York: Dell.

Hutt, C. (1972). *Males and females*. Middlesex, England: Penguin.

Hyde, J. S. (1981). How large are cognitive gender differences? A meta-analysis using omega squared and d. *American Psychologist*, *36*(8), 892–901.

Hyde, J. S. (1986). *Understanding human sexuality* (3d ed.). New York: McGraw-Hill.

Hyman, B. T., Van Hoesen, G. W., Damasio, A. R., & Barnes, C. L. (1984). Alzheimer's disease: Cell-specific pathology isolates hippocampal formation. *Science*, *225*, 1168–1170.

Ingram, D. D., Makuc, D., & Kleinman, J. C. (1986). National and state trends in use of prenatal care, 1970–1983. *American Journal of Public Health*, *76*(4), 415–423.

Inhelder, B., & Piaget, J. (1958). *The growth of logical thinking from childhood to adolescence*. Boston: Little, Brown.

Inhelder, B., & Piaget, J. (1964). *The early growth of logic in the child*. New York: Norton.

Inouye, E. (1965). Similar and dissimilar manifestations of obsessive-compulsive neuroses in monozygotic twins. *American Journal of Psychology*, *121*, 1171–1175.

Institute for Social Research. (1985). How children use time. In *Time, goods and well-being*. Ann Arbor: University of Michigan.

Ioffe, F., Childiaeva, R., & Chernick, V. (1984). Prolonged effect of maternal alcohol ingestion on the neonatal electroencephalogram. *Pediatrics*, *74*(3), 330–335.

Iosub, S., Bamji, M., Stone, R. K., Gromisch, D. S., & Wasserman, E. (1987). More on human immune deficiency virus embryopathy. *Pediatrics*, *80*, 512–516.

Iwamura, S. G. (1980). *The verbal games of pre-school children*. New York: St. Martin's.

Iwanaga, M. (1973). Development of interpersonal play structures in 3, 4, and 5 year old children. *Journal of Research and Development in Education*, *6*, 71–82.

Izard, C. E. (1971). *The face of emotions*. New York: Appleton-Century-Crofts.

Izard, C. E. (1977). *Human emotions*. New York: Plenum.

Izard, C. E., Huebner, R. R., Resser, D., McGinness, G. C., & Dougherty, L. M. (1980). The young infant's ability to produce discrete emotional expressions. *Developmental Psychology*, *16*(2), 132–140.

Jacobson, J. L., Jacobson, S. W., Fein, G. G., Schwartz, P. M., & Dowler, J. K. (1984). Prenatal exposure to an environmental toxin: A test of the multiple effects model. *Developmental Psychology*, *20*(4), 523–532.

Jacobson, J. L., & Wille, D. E. (1984). Influence of attachment and separation experience on separation distress at 18 months. *Developmental Psychology*, *20*(3), 477–484.

Jacobson, J. L., & Wille, D. E. (1986). The influence of attachment pattern on developmental changes in peer interaction from the toddler to the preschool period. *Child Development*, *57*, 338–347.

Jacques, E. (1967). The mid-life crisis. In R. Owen (Ed.), *Middle age*. London: BBC.

Jacques, J. M., & Chason, K. J. (1979). Cohabitation: Its impact on marital success. *Family Coordinator*, *28*(1), 35–39.

Janerick, D., & Jacobson, H. (1977, March 5). Seasonality in Down's syndrome: An endocrinological explanation. *The Lancet*, pp. 515–516.

Janos, P. M., & Robinson, N. M. (1985). Psychosocial development in intellectually gifted children. In F. D. Horowitz & M. O'Brien (Eds.), *The gifted and talented: Developmental perspectives* (pp. 251–295). Washington, DC: American Psychological Association.

Jarvik, L. F., Kallmann, F., & Klaber, N. M. (1957). Changing intellectual functions in senescent twins. *Acta Genetic Statistca Medica*, *7*, 421–430.

Jaslow, C. K. (1982). *Teenage pregnancy* (ERIC/CAPS Fact Sheet). Ann Arbor, MI: Counseling and Personnel Services Clearinghouse.

Jay, M. S., DuRant, R. H., Shoffitt, T., Linder, C. W., & Litt, I. F. (1984). Effect of peer counselors on adolescent compliance in use of oral contraceptives. *Pediatrics*, *73*(2), 126–131.

Jeffcoate, J. A., Humphrey, M. E., & Lloyd, J. K. (1979). Disturbance in the parent-child relationship following preterm delivery. *Developmental Medicine and Child Neurology*, *21*, 344–352.

Jelliffe, D., & Jelliffe, E. (1974). *Fat*

babies: Prevalence, perils and prevention. London: Incentive Press.

Jelliffe, D., & Jelliffe, E. (1983). Recent scientific knowledge concerning breastfeeding. *Rev. Epidem. et Sante Publ., 31*, 367–373.

Jensen, A. R. (1969). How much can we boost IQ and scholastic achievement? *Harvard Educational Review, 39*, 1–123.

Jersild, A. T., & Holmes, F. (1935). Children's fears. *Child Development Monographs, 6*(Whole No. 20).

Johnson, C. L., & Catalano, D. J. (1981). Childless elderly and their family supports. *Gerontologist, 21*(6), 610–618.

John-Steiner, V. (1985). *Notebooks of the mind: Explorations of thinking.* Albuquerque: University of New Mexico Press.

Johnston, L. D., Bachman, J. G., & O'Malley, P. M. (1982). *Student drug use, attitudes, and beliefs: National trends 1975–1982.* Rockville, MD: National Institute on Drug Abuse.

Johnstone, J. W. C. (1975). Social change and parent-youth conflict: The problem of generations in English and French Canada. *Youth and Society, 7*, 3–26.

Jones, E. (1961). *The life and work of Sigmund Freud* (Edited and abridged by L. Trilling & S. Marcus). New York: Basic Books.

Jones, E. F., Forrest, J. D., Goldman, N., Henshaw, S. K., Lincoln, R., Rosoff, J. I., Westoff, C. F., Wulf, W., & Wulf, D. (1985). Teenage pregnancy in developed countries: Determinants and policy implications. *Family Planning Perspectives, 17*, 53–63.

Jones, H., & Conrad, H. (1933). The growth and decline of intelligence: A study of a homogeneous group between the ages of 10 and 60. *Genetic Psychology Monographs, 13*, 223–298.

Jones, M. C. (1957). The late careers of boys who were early—or late—maturing. *Child Development, 28*, 115–128.

Jones, M. C. (1958). The study of socialization patterns at the high school level. *Journal of Genetic Psychology, 93*, 87–111.

Jones, M. C., & Mussen, P. H. (1958). Self-conceptions, motivations, and interpersonal attitudes of early- and late-maturing girls. *Child Development, 29*, 491–501.

Jost, H., & Sontag, L. (1944). The genetic factor in autonomic nervous system function. *Psychosomatic Medicine, 6*, 308–310.

Joyce, C. (1984). A time for grieving. *Psychology Today, 18*(11), 42–46.

Jung, C. G. (1966). Two essays on analytic psychology. In *Collected Works* (Vol. 7). Princeton, NJ: Princeton University Press.

Jung, C. G. (1968). *The archetypes and the collective unconscious* (Bollingen Series, Vol. 20, 2d ed.). Princeton, NJ: Princeton University Press.

Kagan, J. (1958). The concept of identification. *Psychological Review, 65*(5), 296–305.

Kagan, J. (1971). *Personality development.* New York: Harcourt Brace Jovanovich.

Kagan, J. (1979). Overview: Perspectives on human infancy. In J. Osofsky (Ed.), *Handbook of infant development.* New York: Wiley.

Kagan, J. (1982). Canalization of early psychological development. *Pediatrics, 70*(3), 474–483.

Kagan, J. (1984). *The nature of the child.* New York: Basic Books.

Kahana, B., & Kahana, E. (1970). Grandparents from the perspective of the developing grandchild. *Developmental Psychology, 3*(1), 98–105.

Kallman, F. J. (1953). *Heredity in health and mental disorder.* New York: Norton.

Kamin, L. J. (1974). *The science and politics of IQ.* Potomac, MD: Erlbaum.

Kamin, L. J. (1981). Commentary. In S. Scarr (Ed.), *Race, social class, and individual differences in I.Q.* Hillsdale, NJ: Erlbaum.

Kandel, D. B., Davies, M., Karus, D., & Yamaguchi, K. (1986). The consequences in young adulthood of adolescent drug involvement. *Archives of General Psychiatry, 43*, 746–754.

Kane, R. I., Wales, J., Bernstein, L., Leibowitz, A., & Kaplan, S. (1984, April 21). A randomized controlled trial of hospice care. *The Lancet*, pp. 890–894.

Kaplan, H., & Dove, H. (1987). Infant development among the Ache of East Paraguay. *Developmental Psychology, 23*(2), 190–198.

Kastenbaum, R. (1977). The kingdom where nobody dies. In S. Zarit (Ed.), *Readings in aging and death: Contemporary perspectives.* New York: Harper & Row.

Katcher, A. H. (1984, September-October). Are companion animals good for your health? *Aging*, pp. 2–3.

Katz, S., Branch, L. G., Branson, M. H., Papsidero, J. A., Beck, J. C., & Greer, D. S. (1983). Active life ex-

pectancy. *The New England Journal of Medicine, 309*, 1218–1224.

Kay, B., & Neeley, J. N. (1982). Sexuality and the aging: A review of current literature. *Sexuality and Disability, 5*, 38–46.

Kayser-Jones, J. S. (1982). Institutional structures: Catalysts of or barriers to quality care for the institutionalized aged in Scotland and the U.S. *Social Science Medicine, 16*, 935–944.

Kearsley, R. B. (1981). Cognitive assessment of the handicapped infant: The need for an alternative approach. *American Journal of Orthopsychiatry, 51*(1), 43–54.

Keating, N., & Cole, P. (1980). What do I do with him 24 hours a day? Changes in the housewife role after retirement. *Gerontologist, 20*, 84–89.

Keeney, T. J., Canizzo, S. R., & Flavell, J. H. (1967). Spontaneous and induced verbal rehearsal in a recall task. *Child Development, 38*, 953–966.

Keith, P. M. (1983). A comparison of the resources of parents and childless men and women in very old age. *Family Relations, 32*, 403–409.

Kelly, D. H., Golub, H., Carley, D., & Shannon, D. C. (1986). Pneumograms in infants who subsequently died of sudden infant death syndrome. *Journal of Pediatrics, 109*, 249–254.

Kelly, J. B. (1982). Divorce: The adult perspective. In B. Wolman (Ed.), *Handbook of developmental psychology.* Englewood Cliffs, NJ: Prentice-Hall.

Kelly, O. (1978). Living with a life-threatening illness. In M. C. Garfield (Ed.), *Psychosocial care of the dying patient* (pp. 59–66). New York: McGraw-Hill.

Kempe, C. H., et al. (1962). The battered child syndrome. *Journal of the American Medical Association, 181*(Part 1), 17–24.

Kempe, C. H., & Helfer, R. E. (Eds.). (1987). *The battered child* (4th ed.). Chicago: University of Chicago Press.

Kerr, B. A. (1985). *Smart girls, gifted women.* Columbus, OH: Ohio Psychology.

Kieren, D., Henton, J., & Marotz, R. (1975). *Hers and his.* Hinsdale, IL: Dryden.

Kimmel, D. C. (1980). *Adulthood and aging* (2d ed.). New York: Wiley.

Kinsey, A. C., Pomeroy, W., & Martin, C. E. (1948). *Sexual behavior in the human male.* Philadelphia: Saunders.

Kinsey, A. C., Pomeroy, W., Martin, C. E., & Gebhard, P. H. (1953). *Sex-*

ual behavior in the human female. Philadelphia: Saunders.

Klagsbrun, F. (1976). *Too young to die.* Boston: Houghton Mifflin.

Klagsbrun, F. (1985). *Married people: Staying together in the age of divorce.* New York: Bantam.

Klaus, M. H., & Kennell, J. H. (1976). *Maternal-infant bonding.* St. Louis: Mosby.

Klaus, M. H., & Kennell, J. H. (1982). *Parent-infant bonding* (2d ed.). St. Louis: Mosby.

Klaus, M. H., & Klaus, P. H. (1985). *The amazing newborn: Making the most of the first weeks of life.* Reading, MA: Addison-Wesley.

Klein, C. (1973). *The single parent experience.* New York: Walker.

Klein, N., Hack, M., Gallagher, J., & Fanaroff, A. A. (1985). Preschool performance of children with normal intelligence who were very low-birth-weight infants. *Pediatrics, 75,* 531–537.

Klein, R. P., & Durfee, J. T. (1975). *Infants' reactions to strangers versus mothers.* Paper presented at the meeting of the Society for Research in Child Development, Denver.

Kleinberg, F. (1984). Sudden infant death syndrome. *Mayo Clinic Proceedings, 59,* 352–357.

Kleinman, J. C., Cooke, M., Machlin, S., & Kessel, S. S. (1983). *Variations in use of obstetric technology* (DHHS Publication No. PHS 84-1232). Washington, DC: U.S. Government Printing Office.

Koff, E., Rierdan, J., & Sheingold, K. (1982). Memories of menarche: Age, preparation, and prior knowledge as determinants of initial menstrual experience. *Journal of Youth and Adolescence, 11,* 1–9.

Kohlberg, L. (1966). A cognitive-developmental analysis of children's sex-role concepts and attitudes. In E. E. Maccoby (Ed.), *The development of sex differences.* Stanford, CA: Stanford University Press.

Kohlberg, L. (1968). The child as a moral philosopher. *Psychology Today, 2*(4), 25–30.

Kohlberg, L. (1969). Stage and sequence: The cognitive-developmental approach to socialization. In D. A. Goslin (Ed.), *Handbook of socialization theory and research.* Chicago: Rand McNally.

Kohlberg, L. (1973). Continuities in childhood and adult moral development revisited. In P. Baltes & K. W. Schaie (Eds.), *Life-span developmental psychology: Personality and socialization.* New York: Academic.

Kohlberg, L., & Gilligan, C. (1971, Fall). The adolescent as a philosopher: The discovery of the self in a postconventional world. *Daedalus,* pp. 1051–1086.

Kohlberg, L., Yaeger, J., & Hjertholm, E. (1968). Private speech: Four studies and a review of theories. *Child Development, 39,* 691–736.

Kohn, M. L. (1980). Job complexity and adult personality. In N.J. Smelser & E. H. Erikson (Eds.), *Themes of work and love in adulthood.* Cambridge, MA: Harvard University Press.

Kokmen, E. (1984). Dementia—Alzheimer type. *Mayo Clinic Proceedings, 59,* 35–42.

Kolata, G. (1986). Obese children: A growing problem. *Science, 232,* 20–21.

Koocher, G. (1973). Childhood, death, and cognitive development. *Developmental Psychology, 9,* 369–375.

Kopp, C. B. (1982). Antecedents of self-regulation. *Developmental Psychology, 18*(2), 199–214.

Kopp, C. B., & McCall, R. B. (1982). Predicting later mental performance for normal, at-risk, and handicapped infants. In P. B. Baltes & O. G. Brim (Eds.), *Life-span development and behavior* (Vol. 4). New York: Academic.

Korner, A. F., Zeanah, C. H., Linden, J., Berkowitz, R. I., Kraemer, H. C., & Agras, W. S. (1985). The relationship between neonatal and later activity and temperament. *Child Development, 56,* 38–42.

Kornhaber, A. (1985). Grandparenthood and the new social contract. In V. L. Bengtson & J. F. Robertson (Eds.), *Grandparenthood.* Beverly Hills, CA: Sage.

Kotelchuck, M. (1973, March). *The nature of the infant's tie to his father.* Paper presented at the meeting of the Society for Research in Child Development, Philadelphia.

Kotelchuck, M. (1975, September). *Father caretaking characteristics and their influence on infant-father interaction.* Paper presented at the meeting of the American Psychological Association, Chicago.

Kramer, J., Hill, K., & Cohen, L. (1975). Infants' development of object permanence: A refined methodology and new evidence for Piaget's hypothesized ordinality. *Child Development, 46,* 149–155.

Krauss, R., & Glucksberg, S. (1977). Social and nonsocial speech. *Scientific American, 263*(2), 100–105.

Kreutzer, M., & Charlesworth, W. R. (1973, March). *Infant recognition of emotions.* Paper presented at the meeting of the Society for Research in Child Development, Philadelphia, PA.

Kreutzer, M., Leonard, C., & Flavell, J. (1975). An interview study of children's knowledge about memory. *Monographs of the Society for Research in Child Development, 40*(1, Serial No. 159).

Kübler-Ross, E. (1969). *On death and dying.* New York: Macmillan.

Kübler-Ross, E. (1970). *On death and dying* (paperback ed.). New York: Macmillan.

Kübler-Ross, E. (Ed.). (1975). *Death: The final stage of growth.* Englewood Cliffs, NJ: Prentice-Hall.

Kupfersmid, J., & Wonderly, D. (1980). Moral maturity and behavior: Failure to find a link. *Journal of Youth and Adolescence, 9*(3), 249–261.

LaBarge, E. (1981, November). Counseling patients with senile dementia of the Alzheimer type and their families. *Personnel & Guidance Journal,* pp. 139–142.

Labouvie-Vief, G. (1980). Beyond formal operations: Uses and limits of pure logic in life-span development. *Human Development, 23*(3), 141–161.

Labouvie-Vief, G. (1985). Intelligence and cognition. In J. E. Birren & K. W. Schaie (Eds.), *Handbook of the psychology of aging* (2d ed.). New York: Van Nostrand Reinhold.

Labouvie-Vief, G. (1986). Modes of knowledge and the organization of development. In M. L. Commons, L. Kohlberg, F. Richards, & J. Sinnott (Eds.), *Beyond formal operations 3: Models and methods in the study of adult and adolescent thought.* New York: Praeger.

Lagercrantz, H., & Slotkin, T. A. (1986). The "stress" of being born. *Scientific American, 254*(4), 100–107.

Lamb, M. E. (1977). Father-infant and mother-infant interaction in the first year of life. *Child Development, 48,* 167–181.

Lamb, M. E. (1978). Influence of the child on marital quality and family interaction during the prenatal, perinatal, and infancy periods. In R. Lerner & G. Spanier (Eds.), *Child influences on marital and family interaction: A life-span perspective.* New York: Academic.

Lamb, M. E. (1981). The development of father-infant relationships. In M. E. Lamb (Ed.), *The role of the father in child development* (2d ed.). New York: Wiley.

Lamb, M. E. (1982a). The bonding phenomenon: Misinterpretations and their implications. *Journal of Pediatrics, 101*(4), 555–557.

Lamb, M. E. (1982b). Early contact

and maternal-infant bonding: One decade later. *Pediatrics, 70*(5), 763–768.

Lamb, M. E., Campos, J. J., Hwang, C. P., Leiderman, P. H., Sagi, A., & Svejda, M. (1983). Maternal-infant bonding: A joint rebuttal. *Pediatrics, 72*(4), 574–575.

Landau, E. (1983). *Why are they starving themselves?* New York: Messner.

Landesman-Dwyer, S., & Emanuel, I. (1979). Smoking during pregnancy. *Teratology, 19*, 119–126.

Lang, A. M., & Brody, E. M. (1983, February). Characteristics of middle-aged daughters and help to their elderly mothers. *Journal of Marriage and the Family, 45*(1), 193–202.

Langer, E., & Rodin, J. (1976). The effects of choice and enhanced personal responsibility in an institutional setting. *Journal of Personality and Social Psychology, 34*(2), 191–198.

Larche, D. W. (Father Gander, pseudonym). (1985). *Nursery rhymes: The equal rhymes amendment.* Santa Barbara, CA: Advocacy.

Larson, R., Mannell, R., & Zuzanek, J. (1986). Daily well-being of older adults with friends and family. *Psychology and Aging, 1*(2), 117–126.

Laudenslager, M. L., Ryan, S. M., Drugan, R. C., Hyson, R. L., & Maier, S. F. (1983). Coping and immunosuppression: Inescapable but not escapable shock suppresses lymphocyte proliferation. *Science, 221*, 568–570.

Lauer, J., & Lauer, R. (1985). Marriages made to last. *Psychology Today, 19*(6), 22–26.

Lawson, A., & Ingleby, J. D. (1974). Daily routines of preschool children: Effects of age, birth order, sex and social class, and developmental correlates. *Psychological Medicine, 4*, 399–415.

Lawton, M. P. (1981). Alternate housing. *Journal of Gerontological Social Work, 3*(3), 61–79.

Lazarus, L. W., Stafford, B., Cooper, K., Cohler, B., & Dysken, M. (1981). A pilot study of an Alzheimer's patients' and relatives' discussion group. *Gerontologist, 21*(4), 353–357.

Lazarus, R. S. (1981). Little hassles can be hazardous to health. *Psychology Today, 15*(7), 58–62.

Leach, P. (1983). *Babyhood* (2d ed.). New York: Knopf.

Leaf, A. (1973). Every day is a gift when you are over 100. *National Geographic, 143*(1), 93–118.

Leahy, R. (1976). Development of preference and processes of visual scanning in the human infant during the

first three months of life. *Developmental Psychology, 12*(3), 250–254.

Leboyer, F. (1975). *Birth without violence.* New York: Random House.

Lee, P. R., Franks, P., Thomas, G. S., & Paffenberger, R. S. (1981). *Exercise and health: The evidence and its implications.* Cambridge, MA: Oelgeschlager, Gunn, & Hain.

Lee, R. V. (1973, September 16). What about the right to say "no"? *The New York Times Magazine.*

Leefeldt, C., & Callenbach, E. (1979). *The art of friendship.* New York: Pantheon.

Lehman, H. C. (1953). *Age and achievement.* Princeton, NJ: Princeton University Press.

Lehtovaara, A., Saarinen, P., & Jarvinen, J. (1965). *Psychological studies of twins: 1. GSR reactions.* Helsinki: University of Helsinki, Psychological Institute.

Leib, S., Benfield, G., & Guidubaldi, J. (1980). Effects of early intervention and stimulation on the preterm infant. *Pediatrics, 66*, 83–90.

Leigh, G. K. (1982). Kinship interaction over the family life span. *Journal of Marriage and the Family, 44*(1), 197–208.

Leland, C., et al. (1979). *Men and women learning together: Co-education in the 1980's.* Findings presented at conference, Men/Women/College, The Educational Implications of Sex Roles in Transition. December 1-2, 1978, at Brown University. Report published by Ford, Rockefeller, and Carnegie Foundations.

LeMasters, E. E. (1957). Parenthood as crisis. *Marriage and Family Living, 19*, 352–355.

Lemon, B., Bengtson, V., & Peterson, J. (1972). An exploration of the activity theory of aging: Activity types and life satisfaction among inmovers to a retirement community. *Journal of Gerontology, 27*(4), 511–523.

Lenneberg, E. H. (1967). *Biological functions of language.* New York: Wiley.

Lenneberg, E. H. (1969). On explaining language. *Science, 164*(3880), 635–643.

Lepper, M. R. (1985). Microcomputers in education. *American Psychologist, 40*, 1–18.

Lerner, G. (1978). *A death of one's own.* New York: Simon & Schuster.

Lerner, J. V., & Galambos, N. L. (1985). Maternal role satisfaction, mother-child interaction, and child temperament: A process model. *Developmental Psychology, 21*(6), 1157–1164.

Lerner, R., & Lerner, J. (1977). Effects of age, sex, and physical attractive-

ness on child-peer relations, academic performance, and elementary school adjustment. *Developmental Psychology, 13*(6), 585–590.

Lesko, M., & Lesko, W. (1984). *The maternity sourcebook: 230 basic decisions for pregnancy, birth, and baby care.* New York: Warner.

Lester, B. M. (1979). A synergistic process approach to the study of prenatal malnutrition. *International Journal of Behavioral Development, 2*, 377–394.

Lester, R., & Van Theil, D. H. (1977). Gonadal function in chronic alcoholic men. *Advances in Experimental Medicine and Biology, 85A*, 339–414.

Leveno, K. J., Cunningham, F. G., Nelson, S., Roark, M., Williams, M. L., Guzick, D., Dowling, S., Rosenfeld, C. R., & Buckley, A. (1986). A prospective comparison of selective and universal electronic fetal monitoring in 34,995 pregnancies. *The New England Journal of Medicine, 315*, 615–619.

Levine, M. D. (1987). *Developmental variation and learning disorders.* Cambridge, MA: Educators Publishing.

Levine, R. (1980). Adulthood among the Gusii of Kenya. In N. J. Smelser & E. H. Erikson (Eds.), *Themes of work and love in adulthood* (pp. 77–104). Cambridge, MA: Harvard University Press.

Levinson, D. (1980). Toward a conception of the adult life course. In N. J. Smelser & E. H. Erikson (Eds.), *Themes of work and love in adulthood* (pp. 265–290). Cambridge, MA: Harvard University Press.

Levinson, D. (1986). A conception of adult development. *American Psychologist, 41*(1), 3–13.

Levinson, D., with Darrow, C., Klein, E., Levinson, M., & McKee, B. (1978). *The seasons of a man's life.* New York: Ballantine.

Leviton, D. (1977). Death education. In H. Feifel (Ed.), *New meanings of death,* pp. 253–272. New York: McGraw-Hill.

Levy, D. M. (1966). *Maternal overprotection.* New York: Norton.

Lewis, C., & Lewis, M. (1977). The potential impact of sexual equality on health. *The New England Journal of Medicine, 297*(11), 863–869.

Lewis, M., & Brooks, J. (1974). Self, other, and fear: Infants' reactions to people. In H. Lewis & L. Rosenblum (Eds.), *The origins of fear: The origins of behavior* (Vol. 2). New York: Wiley.

Lewis, M. I., & Butler, R. N. (1974). Life-review therapy: Putting memories to work in individual and group psychotherapy. *Geriatrics, 29,* 165–173.

Lickona, T. (1973, March). *An experimental test of Piaget's theory of moral development.* Paper presented at the meeting of the Society for Research in Child Development, Philadelphia.

Lickona, T. (Ed.). (1976). *Moral development and behavior.* New York: Holt.

Lieberman, M., & Coplan, A. (1970). Distance from death as a variable in the study of aging. *Developmental Psychology, 2*(1), 71–84.

Liebert, R. M. (1972). Television and social learning: Some relationships between viewing violence and behaving aggressively. In J. P. Murray, E. A. Rubinstein, & G. A. Comstock (Eds.), *Television and social behavior* (Vol. 2). Washington, DC: U.S. Government Printing Office.

Lindsey, R. (1984, January 15.) A new generation finds it hard to leave the nest. *The New York Times,* p. 18.

Linn, M. C., & Petersen, A. C. (1985). Emergence and characterization of gender differences in spatial ability: A meta-analysis. *Child Development, 56,* 1479–1498.

Lipid Research Clinics Program. (1984a). The lipid research clinic coronary primary prevention trial results: I. Reduction in incidence of coronary heart disease. *Journal of the American Medical Association, 251,* 351–364.

Lipid Research Clinics Program. (1984b). The lipid research clinic coronary primary prevention trial results: II. The relationship of reduction in incidence of coronary heart disease to cholesterol lowering. *Journal of the American Medical Association, 251,* 365–374.

Lipsitt, L. (1982). Infant learning. In T. M. Field, A. Huston, H. Quay, L. Troll, & G. Finley (Eds.), *Review of human development.* New York: Wiley.

Lipsitt, L. (1986). Learning in infancy: Cognitive development in babies. *Journal of Pediatrics, 109*(1), 172–182.

Lipsitt, L., & Werner, J. S. (1981). The infancy of human learning processes. In E. S. Gollin (Ed.), *Developmental plasticity.* New York: Academic.

Livson, F. (1976). *Sex differences in personality development in the middle adult years: A longitudinal study.* Paper presented at the annual meeting of the Gerontological Society, Louisville, KY.

Loda, F. A. (1980). Day care. *Pediatrics in Review, 1*(9), 277–281.

Loeber, R., & Dishion, T. (1983). Early predictors of male delinquency: A review. *Psychological Bulletin, 94,* 68–99.

Loehlin, J., Lindzey, G., & Spuhler, J. (1975). *Race differences in intelligence.* San Francisco: Freeman.

Lofland, L. H. (1986). When others die. *Generations, 10*(4), 59–61.

Long, L. (1984). *On my own: The kids' self-care book.* Washington, DC: Acropolis.

Long, L., & Long, T. (1983). *The handbook for latchkey children and their parents.* New York: Berkley.

Longino, C. F. (1987). *The oldest Americans: State profiles for database planning.* Coral Gables, FL: University of Miami Department of Sociology.

Longino, C. F., & Kart, C. S. (1982). Explicating activity theory: A formal replication. *Journal of Gerontology, 37*(6), 713–721.

Long-term outlook for children with sex chromosome abnormalities. (1982, July 3). *The Lancet,* p.27.

Looft, W. R. (1971). *Toward a history of life-span developmental psychology.* Unpublished manuscript, University of Wisconsin, Madison.

Lopata, H. (1973). Living through widowhood, *Psychology Today, 7*(2), 87–98.

Lopata, H. (1977, September–October). Widows and widowers. *Humanist,* pp. 25–28.

Lopata, H. (1979). *Women as widows.* New York: Elsevier.

Lopata, H., Heinemann, G. D., & Baum, J. (1982). Loneliness: Antecedents and coping strategies in the lives of widows. In L. A. Peplau & D. Perlman (Eds.), *Loneliness: A sourcebook of current theory, research, and therapy* (pp. 310–326). New York: Wiley.

LoPiccolo, J., & Lobitz, C. (1972). The role of masturbation in the treatment of sexual dysfunction. *Archives of Sexual Behavior, 2,* 163–171.

Lorenz, K. (1957). Comparative study of behavior. In C. H. Schiller (Ed.), *Instinctive behavior.* New York: International Press.

Lott, I. T., Bocian, M., Pribram, H. W., & Leitner, M. (1984). Fetal hydrocephalus and ear anomalies associated with maternal use of isotretinoin. *Journal of Pediatrics, 105,* 597–600.

Louis Harris & Associates. See Harris, L., & Associates.

Lowenthal, M., & Chiriboga, D. (1972). Transition to the empty nest: Crisis, challenge, or relief? *Archives of General Psychiatry, 26,* 8–14.

Lowenthal, M., & Haven, C. (1968). Interaction and adaptation: Intimacy as a critical variable. In B. Neugarten (Ed.), *Middle age and aging.* Chicago: University of Chicago Press.

Lozoff, B., Wolf, A. W., & Davis, N. S. (1985). Sleep problems seen in pediatric practice. *Pediatrics, 75,* 477–483.

Lustick, M. J. (1985). Bulimia in adolescents: A review. *Pediatrics, 76*(4), 685–690.

Lutjen, P., Trounson, A., Leeton, J., Findlay, J., Wood, C., & Renou, P. (1984). The establishment and maintenance of pregnancy using in vitro fertilization and embryo donation in a patient with primary ovarian failure. *Nature, 307,* 174–175.

Lynd, R. S., & Lynd, H. M. (1929). *Middletown.* New York: Harcourt, Brace.

Lynn, R. (1982). IQ in Japan and the United States shows a growing disparity. *Nature, 297,* 222–223.

Lystad, M. (1975). Violence at home: A review of literature. *American Journal of Orthopsychiatry, 45*(3), 328–345.

Maccoby, E. (1980). *Social development.* New York: Harcourt Brace Jovanovich.

Maccoby, E. (1984). Middle childhood in the context of the family. In W. A. Collins (Ed.), *Development during middle childhood: The years from six to twelve.* Washington, DC: National Academy.

Maccoby, E., & Jacklin, C. (1974). *The psychology of sex differences.* Stanford, CA: Stanford University Press.

Macfarlane, A. (1975). Olfaction in the development of social preferences in the human neonate. In *Parent-infant interaction* (CIBA Foundation Symposium, 33). Amsterdam: Elsevier.

Maddox, G. (1968). Persistence of life style among the elderly. In B. Neugarten (Ed.), *Middle age and aging.* Chicago: University of Chicago Press.

Maddox, G. (Ed.). (1987). *The encyclopedia of aging.* New York: Springer.

Madison, P. (1969). *Personality development in college.* Reading, MA: Addison-Wesley.

Maeroff, G. I. (1984, October 29). Interest in learning foreign languages rises. *The New York Times,* p. A1.

Mahoney, E. R. (1983). *Human sexuality.* New York: McGraw-Hill.

Malcolm, A. H. (1984, September 23). Many see mercy in ending empty lives. *The New York Times,* pp. 1, 56.

Malmquist, C. P. (1983). Major depression in childhood: Why don't we know more? *American Journal of Orthopsychiatry, 53*(2), 262–268.

Maloney, M. J., & Klykylo, W. M. (1983). An overview of anorexia nervosa, bulimia, and obesity in children and adolescents. *Journal of the American Academy of Child Psychiatry, 22*, 99–107.

Mamay, P. D., & Simpson, P. L. (1981). Three female roles in television commercials. *Sex Roles, 7*(12), 1223–1232.

Mansfield, R. S., & Busse, T. V. (1981). *The psychology of creativity and discovery: Scientists and their work.* Chicago: Nelson-Hall.

Maratsos, M. (1973). Nonegocentric communication abilities in preschool children. *Child Development, 44,* 697–700.

March of Dimes Birth Defects Foundation. (1983a). *Drugs, alcohol, tobacco abuse during pregnancy.* White Plains, NY: Author.

March of Dimes Birth Defects Foundation. (1983b). *Genetic counseling.* White Plains, NY: Author.

March of Dimes Birth Defects Foundation. (undated). *Low birthweight.* Public health education information sheet.

Marcia, J. E. (1966). Development and validation of ego identity status. *Journal of Personality and Social Psychology, 3*(5), 551–558.

Marcia, J. E. (1979, June). *Identity status in late adolescence: Description and some clinical implications.* Address given at a symposium on identity development, Rijksuniversitat Groningen, Netherlands.

Marcia, J. E. (1980). Identity in adolescence. In J. Adelson (Ed.), *Handbook of adolescent psychology.* New York: Wiley.

Maret, E., & Finlay, B. (1984, May). The distribution of household labor among women in dual-earner families. *Journal of Marriage and the Family, 46*(2), 357–364.

Margolin, L., & White, L. (1987). The continuing role of physical attractiveness in marriage. *Journal of Marriage and the Family, 49*(1), 21–27.

Marion, R. W., Wiznia, A. A., Hutcheon, G., & Rubinstein, A. (1986). Human T-cell lymphotropic virus type III (HTLV-III) embryopathy. *American Journal of Diseases of Children, 140,* 638–640.

Markides, K. S., & Krause, N. (1986). Older Mexican Americans. *Generations, 10*(4), 31–34.

Markus, H. (1980). The self in thought and memory. In M. Wegner & R. R. Vallacher (Eds.), *The self in social psychology.* New York: Oxford University Press.

Markus, H., & Nurius, P. S. (1984). Self-understanding and self-regulation in middle childhood. In W. A. Collins (Ed.), *Development during middle childhood: The years from six to twelve.* Washington, DC: National Academy.

Marland, S. P. (1972). *Education of the gifted and talented.* Washington, DC: U.S. Government Printing Office.

Marquis, K. S., & Detweiler, R. A. (1985). Does adopted mean different? An attributional analysis. *Journal of Personality and Social Psychology, 48,* 1054–1066.

Marshall, S. P. (1984). Sex differences in children's mathematic achievement: Solving computations and story problems. *Journal of Educational Psychology, 76,* 194–204.

Martin, G. B., & Clark, R. D. (1982). Distress crying in neonates: Species and peer specificity. *Developmental Psychology, 18*(1), 3–9.

Martin, J., Martin, O., Lund, C., & Streissguth, A. (1977). Maternal alcohol ingestion and cigarette smoking and their effects on newborn conditioning. *Alcoholism: Clinical and Experimental Research, 1,* 243–247.

Martinez, G. A., & Kreiger, F. W. (1985). The 1984 milk-feeding patterns in the United States. *Pediatrics, 76,* 1004–1008.

Marwick, C., & Simmons, K. (1984). Changing childhood disease pattern linked with day-care boom. *Journal of the American Medical Association, 215*(10), 1245–1251.

Maslach, C., & Jackson, S. E. (1985). Burnout in health professions: A social psychological analysis. In G. Sanders & J. Suls (Eds.), *Social psychology of health and illness.* Hillsdale, NJ: Erlbaum.

Maslow, A. (1954). *Motivation and personality.* New York: Harper & Row.

Maslow, A. (1968). *Toward a psychology of being.* Princeton, NJ: Van Nostrand Reinhold.

Masnick, G., & Bane, M. J. (1980). *The nation's families, 1960–1990.* Cambridge, MA: Joint Center for Urban Studies of MIT and Harvard University.

Masson, J. M. (1984). *The assault on truth: Freud's suppression of the seduction theory.* New York: Farrar, Straus & Giroux.

Masters, W. H., & Johnson, V. E. (1966). *Human sexual response.* Boston: Little, Brown.

Masters, W. H., & Johnson, V. E. (1979). *Homosexuality in perspective.* Boston: Little, Brown.

Masters, W. H., & Johnson, V. E. (1981). Sex and the aging process. *Journal of the American Geriatrics Society, 29,* 385–390.

Masters, W. H., Johnson, V. E., & Kolodny, R. C. (1986). *Sex and human loving.* Boston: Little, Brown.

Matas, L., Arend, R., & Sroufe, L. A. (1978). Continuity of adaptation in the second year: The relationship between quality of attachment and later competence. *Child Development, 49,* 547–556.

Matheny, K. B., & Cupp, P. (1983). Control, desirability, and anticipation as moderating variables between life change and illness. *Journal of Human Stress, 9*(2), 14–23.

Matlin, M. W. (1987). *The psychology of women.* New York: Holt, Rinehart, & Winston.

Matsukura, S., Taminato, T., Kitano, N., Seino, Y., Hamada, H., Uchihashi, M., Nakajima, H., & Hirata, Y. (1984). Effects of environmental tobacco smoke on urinary cotinine excretion in nonsmokers. *The New England Journal of Medicine, 311*(13), 828–832.

Maurer, D., & Salapatek, P. (1976). Developmental changes in the scanning of faces by young children. *Child Development, 47,* 523–527.

Maxwell, L. (1987, January). *Eight pointers on teaching children to think* (Research in Brief, IS 87-104 RIB). Washington, DC: U.S. Department of Education, Office of Educational Research and Improvement.

Mayer, J. (1973). Fat babies grow into fat people. *Family Health, 5*(3), 24–26.

Maymi, C. R. (1982). Women in the labor force. In P. W. Berman & E. R. Ramey (Eds.), *Women: A developmental perspective* (NIH Publication No. 82-2298). Washington, DC: U.S. Department of Health and Human Services.

Maziade, M., Boudreault, M., Cote, R., & Thivierge, J. (1986). Influence of gentle birth delivery procedures and other perinatal circumstances on infant temperament: Developmental and social implications. *Journal of Pediatrics, 108*(1), 134–136.

McAlister, A. L., Perry, C., & Maccoby, N. (1979). Adolescent smoking: Onset and prevention. *Pediatrics, 63*(4), 650–658.

McCall, R. (1977). Challenges to a science of developmental psychology. In S. Chess & A. Thomas (Eds.), *Annual progress in child psychiatry and child development* (pp. 3–23). New York: Brunner/Mazel.

McCall, R. B., Appelbaum, M. I., & Hogarty, P. S. (1973). Developmental changes in mental performance. *Monographs of the Society for Research in Child Development, 38* (Serial No. 150).

McCann, I. L., & Holmes, D. S. (1984). Influence of aerobic exercise on depression. *Journal of Personality and Social Psychology, 46*(5), 1142–1147.

McCartney, K. (1984). Effect of quality of day care environment on children's language development. *Developmental Psychology, 20*(2), 244–260.

McCary, J. L. (1975). *Freedom and growth in marriage.* Santa Barbara, CA: Hamilton.

McClelland, D., Constantian, C., Regalado, D., & Stone, C. (1978). Making it to maturity. *Psychology Today, 12*(1), 42–53, 114.

McFarland, R. A., Tune, G. B., & Welford, A. (1964). On the driving of automobiles by older people. *Journal of Gerontology, 19,* 190–197.

McGraw, M. B. (1940). Neural maturation as exemplified in achievement of bladder control. *Journal of Pediatrics, 16,* 580–589.

McGuinness, D. (1986, February 5). Facing the "learning disabilities" crisis. *Education Week,* pp. 28, 22.

McKain, W. C. (1972). A new look at older marriages. *Family Coordinator, 21*(1), 61–69.

McKenry, P. C., Walters, L. H., & Johnson, C. (1979). Adolescent pregnancy: A review of the literature. *Family Coordinator, 23*(1), 17–28.

McKinley, D. (1964). *Social class and family life.* New York: Free Press.

McKinney, K. (1987, March). *A look at Japanese education today* (Research in Brief, IS 87-107 RIB). Washington, DC: U.S. Department of Education, Office of Educational Research and Improvement.

Mead, M. (1928). *Coming of age in Samoa.* New York: Morrow.

Mead, M. (1935). *Sex and temperament in three primitive societies.* New York: Morrow.

Mead, M., & Heyman, K. (1971). *Family.* New York: Collier-Macmillan.

Mednick, B. R., Baker, R. L., & Sutton-Smith, B. (1979). *Teenage pregnancy and perinatal mortality* (Contract No. 1-117-82807). Unpublished paper reporting on a study supported by the U.S. Department of Health, Education, and Welfare.

Medrich, E. A., Roizen, J. A., Rubin, V., & Buckley, S. (1982). *The serious business of growing up.* Berkeley: University of California Press.

Meer, J. T. (1987). The oldest old: The years after 85. *Psychology Today, 21*(5), 82.

Melnick, S., Cole, P., Anderson, B. A.,

& Herbst, A. (1987). Rates and risks of diethylstilbestrol-related clear-cell adenocarcinoma of the vagina and cervix. *The New England Journal of Medicine, 316,* 514–516.

Melton, G. B., & Davidson, H. A. (1987). Child protection and society: When should the state intervene? *American Psychologist, 42*(2), 172–175.

Meltzoff, A. N., & Moore, M. K. (1983). Newborn infants imitate adult facial gestures. *Child Development, 54,* 702–709.

Meredith, N. V. (1969). Body size of contemporary groups of eight-year-old children studied in different parts of the world. *Monographs of the Society for Research in Child Development, 34*(1).

Merrow, J. (1983). *One family's story* (Audiocassette #AV405). Columbia, MD: National Committee for Citizens in Education.

Merser, C. (1987). *"Grown-ups": A generation in search of adulthood.* New York: Putnam.

Miles, C., & Miles, W. (1932). The correlation of intelligence scores and chronological age from early to late maturity. *American Journal of Psychology, 44,* 44–78.

Miller, B., & Gerard, D. (1979). Family influences on the development of creativity in children: An integrative review. *Family Coordinator, 28*(3), 295–312.

Miller, B. C., & Myers-Walls, J. A. (1983). Parenthood: Stresses and coping strategies. In H. I. McCubbin & C. R. Figley (Eds), *Stress and the family: Vol. 1. Coping with normative transitions.* New York: Brunner/Mazel.

Miller, C. A. (1985). Infant mortality in the U.S. *Scientific American, 253,* 31–37.

Miller, E., Cradock-Watson, J. E., & Pollock, T. M. (1982, October 9). Consequences of confirmed maternal rubella at successive stages of pregnancy. *The Lancet,* pp. 781–784.

Miller, G. A. (1956). The magical number seven, plus or minus two: Some limits on our capacity to process information. *Psychological Review, 63,* 81–97.

Miller, J. F., Williamson, E., Glue, J., Gordon, Y. B., Grudzinskas, J. G., & Sykes, A. (1980). Fetal loss after implantation: A prospective study. *The Lancet,* pp. 554–556.

Miller, L. B., & Bizzel, R. P. (1983). Long-term effects of four preschool programs: Sixth, seventh, and eighth grades. *Child Development, 54,* 727–741.

Miller, P. H. (1983). *Theories of devel-*

opmental psychology. San Francisco: Freeman.

Miller, P. M., Danaher, D. L., & Forbes, D. (1986). Sex-related strategies in coping with interpersonal conflict in children aged five and seven. *Developmental Psychology, 22*(4), 543–548.

Miller, V., Onotera, R. T., & Deinard, A. S. (1984). Denver developmental screening test: Cultural variations in southeast Asian children. *Journal of Pediatrics, 104*(3), 481–482.

Mills, J. L., & Graubard, B. I. (1987). Is moderate drinking during pregnancy associated with an increased risk for malformations? *Pediatrics, 80*(3), 309–314.

Mills, J. L., Graubard, B. I., Harley, E. E., Rhoads, G. G., & Berendes, H. W. (1984). Maternal alcohol consumption and birth weight: How much drinking is safe during pregnancy? *Journal of the American Medical Association, 252,* 1875–1879.

Mills, J. L., Shiono, P. H., Shapiro, L. R., Crawford, P. B., & Rhoads, G. G. (1986). Early growth predicts timing of puberty in boys: Results of a 14-year nutrition and growth study. *Journal of Pediatrics, 109,* 543–547.

Milne, A. M., Myers, D. E., & Ginsburg, A. (1986). Comment on Heyns and Catsambis's "Mother's employment and children's achievement: A critique." *Sociology of Education, 59,* 152–154; [See also rejoinder, 155.]

Milne, A. M., Myers, D. E., Rosenthal, A. S., & Ginsburg, A. (1986). Single parents, working mothers, and the educational achievement of school children. *Sociology of Education, 59,* 125–139.

Minde, K., Shosenberg, N., Marton, P., Thompson, J., Ripley, J., & Burns, S. (1980). Self-help groups in a premature nursery: A controlled evaluation. *Journal of Pediatrics, 96,* 933–940.

Mindel, C. H. (1983). The elderly in minority families. In T. H. Brubaker (Ed.), *Family relationships in later life.* Beverly Hills, CA: Sage.

Mirga, T. (1984, August 29). Emerging interest in reasoning skills marks meeting on "critical thinking." *Education Week,* pp. 1, 10.

Mitchell, P. (1976). *Act of love: The killing of George Zygmaniak.* New York: Knopf.

Mittler, P. (1969). *Psycholinguistic skills in four-year-old twins and singletons.* Unpublished doctoral dissertation, University of London.

Mittler, P. (1971). *The study of twins.* Baltimore: Penguin.

Mohs, R. C., Breitner, J. C. S., Silverman, J. M., & Davis, K. L. (1987).

Alzheimer's disease: Morbid risk among first-degree relatives approximates 50% by 90 years of age. *Archives of General Psychiatry, 44,* 405–408.

Money, J., & Ehrhardt, A. (1972). *Man and woman, boy and girl.* Baltimore: Johns Hopkins University Press.

Money, J., Ehrhardt, A., & Masica, D. N. (1968). Fetal feminization induced by androgen insensitivity in the testicular feminizing syndrome: Effect on marriage and maternalism. *Johns Hopkins Medical Journal, 123,* 105–114.

Montemayor, R. (1983). Parents and adolescents in conflict: All families some of the time and some families most of the time. *Journal of Early Adolescence, 3,* 83–103.

Moore, A. U. (1960). *Studies on the formation of the mother-neonate bond in sheep and goats.* Paper presented at the meeting of the American Psychological Association.

Moore, K., & Meltzoff, A. (1975). *Neonate imitation: A test of existence and mechanism.* Paper presented at the meeting of the Society for Research in Child Development, Denver.

Moore, N., Evertson, C., & Brophy, J. (1974). Solitary play: Some functional reconsiderations. *Developmental Psychology, 10*(5), 830–834.

Morbidity and Mortality Weekly Report (MMWR). (1985, June 21). *Suicide—U.S., 1970–1980.*

Morbidity and Mortality Weekly Report (MMWR). (1986, December 12). *Update: Acquired immunodeficiency syndrome—United States.*

Morbidity and Mortality Weekly Report (MMWR). (1987a, January 16). *Infant mortality among blacks.*

Morbidity and Mortality Weekly Report (MMWR). (1987b, August 14). *Update: Acquired immunodeficiency syndrome—United States.*

Morgan, L. (1984). Changes in family interaction following widowhood. *Journal of Marriage and the Family, 46*(2), 323–331.

Morland, J. (1966). A comparison of race awareness in northern and southern children. *American Journal of Orthopsychiatry, 36,* 22–31.

Moskowitz, B. A. (1978). The acquisition of language. *Scientific American, 239*(5), 92–108.

Moss, F., & Halamandaris, V. (1977). *Too old, too sick, too bad.* Germantown, MD: Aspen Systems.

Murphy, C. M., & Bootzin, R. R. (1973). Active and passive participation in the contact desensitization of snake fear in children. *Behavior Therapy, 4,* 203–211.

Murphy, D. P. (1929). The outcome of

625 pregnancies in women subjected to pelvic radium roentgen irradiation. *American Journal of Obstetrics and Gynecology, 18,* 179–187.

Murphy, G. E., & Wetzel, R. D. (1980). Suicide risk by birth cohort in the United States, 1949 to 1974. *Archives of General Psychiatry, 37,* 519–523.

Murray, A. D., Dolby, R. M., Nation, R. L., & Thomas, D. B. (1981). Effects of epidural anesthesia on newborns and their mothers. *Child Development, 52,* 71–82.

Murray, R. M. (1974). Psychiatric illness in doctors. *The Lancet, 151,* 1211–1213.

Murstein, B. I. (1980). Mate selection in the 1970s. *Journal of Marriage and the Family, 42,* 777–792.

Mussen, P. H., Conger, J. J., & Kagan, J. (1969). *Child development and personality.* New York: Harper & Row.

Mussen, P. H., & Eisenberg-Berg, N. (1977). *Roots of caring, sharing, and helping: The development of prosocial behavior in children.* San Francisco: Freeman.

Mussen, P. H., & Jones, M. C. (1957). Self-conceptions, motivations, and interpersonal attitudes of late- and early-maturing boys. *Child Development, 28,* 243–256.

Mussen, P. H., & Rutherford, E. (1963). Parent-child relations and parental personality in relation to young children's sex role preferences. *Child Development, 34,* 589–607.

Myers, J. K., Weissman, M. M., Tischler, G. L., Holzer, C. E., Leaf, P. J., Orvaschel, H., Burke, J. D., Kramer, M., & Stoltzman, R. (1984). Six-month prevalence of psychiatric disorders in three communities. *Archives of General Psychiatry, 41*(10), 959–967.

Myers, N., & Perlmutter, M. (1978). Memory in the years from 2 to 5. In P. Ornstein (Ed.), *Memory development in children.* Hillsdale, NJ: Erlbaum.

Myers-Walls, J. A. (1984). Balancing multiple role responsibilities during the transition to parenthood. *Family Relations, 33,* 267–271.

Nadi, N. S., Nurnberger, J. I., & Gershon, E. S. (1984). Muscarinic cholinergic receptors on skin fibroblasts in familial affective disorder. *The New England Journal of Medicine, 311,* 225–230.

Naeye, R. L., & Peters, E. C. (1984). Mental development of children whose mothers smoked during pregnancy. *Obstetrics and Gynecology, 64,* 601.

Nakanishi, N. (1982). A report on "How do people spend their time"

survey in 1980. *Studies of Broadcasting, 18,* 93–113.

Nass, G. D., Libby, R. W., & Fisher, M. P. (1984). *Sexual choices: An introduction to human sexuality* (2d ed.). Monterey, CA: Wadsworth Health.

Nathanson, C. A., & Lorenz, G. (1982). Women and health: The social dimensions of biomedical data. In J. Z. Giele (Ed.), *Women in the middle years.* New York: Wiley.

National Assessment of Educational Progress. (1981, October). *Reading, thinking and writing: Results from the 1979–80 national assessment of reading and literature* (Report No. 11-L-01). Denver: Education Commission of the States.

National Assessment of Educational Progress. (1982). *Reading comprehension of American youth: Do they understand what they read?* (Report No. 11-R-02). Denver: Education Commission of the States.

National Assessment of Educational Progress. (1985). *The reading report card.* Washington, DC: U.S. Department of Education, National Center for Educational Statistics.

National Center for Education Statistics (NCES). (1982). *Digest of educational statistics 1982* (Publication No. NCES-82-407). Washington, DC: U.S. Government Printing Office.

National Center for Education Statistics (NCES). (1983). High school dropouts: Descriptive information from high school and beyond. *NCES Bulletin.* Washington, DC: U.S. Department of Education.

National Center for Education Statistics (NCES). (1984). *The condition of education* (Publication No. NCES-84-401). Washington, DC: U.S. Government Printing Office.

National Center for Education Statistics (NCES). (1985). *The relationship of parental involvement to high school grades* (Publication No. NCES-85-205b). Washington, DC: U.S. Department of Education.

National Center for Education Statistics (NCES). (1986). *Education statistics: A pocket digest* (Publication No. CS-86-401). Washington, DC: U.S. Department of Education Center for Statistics.

National Center for Health Statistics. (1984a). *Annual summary of births, deaths, marriages, and divorces: U.S., 1983* (DHHS Publication No. PHS 84–1120). Hyattsville, MD: Public Health Service.

National Center for Health Statistics. (1984b). *Trends in teenage childbearing. United States, 1970–1981* (Series 21, No. 41, Stock No.

01702200–851–3). Washington, DC: U.S. Government Printing Office.

National Center for Health Statistics. (1986). *Maternal weight gain and the outcome of pregnancy, United States, 1980. Vital Statistics* (DHHS Publication No. 86–1922). Washington, DC: U.S. Government Printing Office.

National Coalition on Television Violence. (undated). *Action alert: War toys/cartoons more violent.* Champaign, IL: Author.

National Commission on Excellence in Education. (1983, April). *A nation at risk: The imperative for educational reform* (Stock No. 065–000–00177–2). Washington, DC: U.S. Government Printing Office.

National Commission for the Protection of Human Subjects of Biomedical and Behavioral Research. (1978). Report.

National Committee for Citizens in Education (NCCE). (1986, Winter Holiday). Don't be afraid to start a suicide prevention program in your school. *Network for Public Schools,* pp. 1, 4.

National Council on Aging. (1978). *Fact book on aging: A profile of America's older population.* Washington, DC: Author.

National Institute on Aging (NIA). (1980). *Senility: Myth or madness.* Washington, DC: U.S. Government Printing Office.

National Institute on Aging (NIA). (1982). *Crime and the elderly.* Washington, DC: U.S. Department of Health and Human Services, Public Health Service.

National Institute on Aging (NIA). (1983). *Age page: Osteoporosis: The bone thinner.* Bethesda, MD: U.S. Government Printing Office.

National Institute on Aging (NIA). (1984). *Be sensible about salt.* Washington, DC: U.S. Government Printing Office.

National Institute on Aging (NIA). (undated a). *Age Page: Aging and your eyes.* Bethesda, MD: U.S. Government Printing Office.

National Institute on Aging (NIA). (undated b). *Age Page: Hearing and the elderly.* Bethesda, MD: U.S. Government Printing Office.

National Institute on Alcohol Abuse and Alcoholism (NIAAA). (1981, October). *Fact sheet: Selected statistics on alcohol and alcoholism.* Rockville, MD: National Clearinghouse for Alcohol Information.

National Institute on Alcohol Abuse and Alcoholism (NIAAA). (1986). *Media alert: FAS awareness campaign: My baby . . . strong and healthy.* Rockville, MD: National Clearinghouse for Alcohol Information.

National Institute of Child Health and Human Development. (1978). Smoking in children and adolescents. *Pediatric Annals,* 7(9), 130–131.

National Institute on Drug Abuse (NIDA). (1987). Cocaine use remains steady, other drug use declines among high school seniors. *NIDA Notes,* 2(2), 1.

National Institute of Education (NIE). (1984). *Involvement in learning: Realizing the potential of American higher education.* Washington, DC: Author.

National Institute of Mental Health (NIMH). (1981). *Plain talk about adolescence.* Washington, DC: U.S. Government Printing Office.

National Institute of Mental Health (NIMH). (1982). *Television and behavior: Ten years of scientific progress and implications for the eighties, Vol. 1: Summary report* (DHHS Publication No. ADM 82–1195). Washington, DC: U.S. Government Printing Office.

National Institutes of Health (NIH). (1979). NIH Consensus Development Conference. *Clinical Pediatrics,* 18(9), 535–538.

National Institutes of Health (NIH). (1984a). *Osteoporosis* (1984–421–132:4652). Consensus Development Conference Statement, 5(3). Bethesda, MD: U.S. Government Printing Office.

National Institutes of Health (NIH). (1984b, February 6–8). *The use of diagnostic ultrasound imaging in pregnancy.* Consensus Development Conference Statement. Bethesda, MD: U.S. Government Printing Office.

National Institutes of Health (NIH). (1985). *Health implications of obesity.* Consensus Development Conference Statement, 5(9). Washington, DC: U.S. Government Printing Office.

Neal, J. H. (1983). Children's understanding of their parents' divorces. In L. A. Kurdek (Ed.), *Children and divorce: New directions for child development* (No. 19). San Francisco: Jossey-Bass.

Neiswender, M., Birren, J., & Schaie, K. W. (1975). *Age and the experience of love in adulthood.* Paper presented at the annual meeting of the American Psychological Association, Chicago.

Nelson, K. (1973). Structure and strategy in learning to talk. *Monographs of the Society for Research in Child Development,* 38(1–2).

Nelson, K. (1981). Individual differences in language development: Implications for development and language. *Developmental Psychology,* 17(2), 170–187.

Nelson, N., Enkin, M., Saigal, S., Bennett, K., Milner, R., & Sackett, D. (1980). A randomized clinical trial of the Leboyer approach to childbirth. *The New England Journal of Medicine,* 302(12), 655–660.

Neuffer, E. (1987, November 14). School parents wrestle with Lisa's death. *The New York Times,* p. 29.

Neugarten, B. (1967). The awareness of middle age. In R. Owen (Ed.), *Middle age.* London: BBC.

Neugarten, B. (1968). Adult personality: Toward a psychology of the life cycle. In B. Neugarten (Ed.), *Middle age and aging.* Chicago: University of Chicago Press.

Neugarten, B. (1973). Personality change in late life: A developmental perspective. In C. Eisdorfer & M. P. Lawton (Eds.), *The psychology of adult development and aging.* Washington, DC: American Psychological Association.

Neugarten, B. (1977). Personality and aging. In J. Birren & K. W. Schaie (Eds.), *Handbook of the psychology of aging* (pp. 626–649). New York: Van Nostrand Reinhold.

Neugarten, B., & Hagestad, G. (1976). Age and the life course. In H. Binstock & E. Shanas (Eds.), *Handbook of aging and the social sciences.* New York: Van Nostrand Reinhold.

Neugarten, B., Havighurst, R., & Tobin, S. (1968). Personality and patterns of aging. In B. Neugarten (Ed.), *Middle age and aging.* Chicago: University of Chicago Press.

Neugarten, B., Moore, J. W., & Lowe, J. C. (1965). Age norms, age constraints, and adult socialization. *American Journal of Sociology,* 70, 710–717.

Neugarten, B., & Neugarten, D. A. (1987). The changing meanings of age. *Psychology Today,* 21(5), 29–33.

Neugarten, B., Wood, V., Kraines, R., & Loomis, B. (1963). Women's attitudes toward the menopause. *Vita Humana,* 6, 140–151.

Newhouse News Service. (1987, September 25). Sex still factor in student job goals. *Chicago Sun-Times,* p. 37.

Newman, H. H., Freeman, F. H., & Holzinger, K. J. (1937). *Twins: A study of heredity and environment.* Chicago: University of Chicago Press.

Newman, P. R. (1982). The peer group. In B. Wolman (Ed.), *Handbook of developmental psychology*. Englewood Cliffs, NJ: Prentice-Hall.

Newson, J., Newson, E., & Mahalski, P. A. (1982). Persistent infant comfort habits and their sequelae at 11 and 16 years. *Journal of Child Psychology and Psychiatry, 23,* 421–436.

New York Times/CBS News Poll. (1984, September 23). Prolonging life by machine. *The New York Times,* p. 56.

Nieburg, P., Marks, J. S., McLaren, N. M., & Remington, P. L. (1985). The fetal tobacco syndrome. *Journal of the American Medical Association, 253,* 2998–2999.

Nilsson, L., Ingelman-Sundberg, A., & Wirsen, C. (1966). *A child is born: The drama of life before birth.* New York: Delacorte.

Nisan, M., & Kohlberg, L. (1982). Universality and variation in moral judgment: A longitudinal and cross-sectional study in Turkey. *Child Development, 53,* 865–876.

Noberini, M., & Neugarten, B. (1975). *A follow-up study of adaptation in middle-aged women.* Paper presented at the annual meeting of the Gerontological Society, Portland, OR.

Nock, S. L., & Kingston, P. W. (1984). The family work day. *Journal of Marriage and the Family, 46*(2), 333–343.

Norton, A. J., & Moorman, J. E. (1987). Current trends in marriage and divorce among American women. *Journal of Marriage and the Family, 49*(1), 3–14.

Notelovitz, M., & Ware, M. (1983). *Stand tall: The informed woman's guide to preventing osteoporosis.* Gainesville, FL: Triad.

Nussbaum, M., Shenker, I. R., Baird, D., & Saravay, S. (1985). Follow-up investigation in patients with anorexia nervosa. *Journal of Pediatrics, 106,* 835–840.

Oates, R. K., Peacock, A., & Forrest, D. (1985). Long-term effects of nonorganic failure to thrive. *Pediatrics, 75,* 36–40.

O'Bryant, S. L., & Corder-Boltz, C. R. (1978). The effects of television on children's stereotyping of women's work roles. *Journal of Vocational Behavior, 12,* 233–244.

O'Connor, M. J., Cohen, S., & Parmelee, A. H. (1984). Infant auditory discrimination in preterm and full-term infants as a predictor of 5-year intelligence. *Developmental Psychology, 20,* 159–165.

Offer, D., & Offer, J. B. (1974). Normal adolescent males: The high school and college years. *Journal of the American College Health Association, 22,* 209–215.

Offer, D., Ostrov, E., & Howard, K. I. (1981). *The adolescent: A psychological self-portrait.* New York: Basic Books.

Offer, D., Ostrov, E., & Marohn, R. C. (1972). *The psychological world of the juvenile delinquent.* New York: Basic Books.

Okun, S. (1988, January 29). Opera coach died in his "house of worship." *The New York Times,* pp. B1, B3.

Olds, S. W. (1985). *The eternal garden: Seasons of our sexuality.* New York: Times Books.

Olds, S. W. (1986). *Working parents' survival guide.* New York: Bantam.

Orenberg, C. L. (1981). *DES: The complete story.* New York: St. Martin's.

Ossofsky, J. (1979). *Retirement preparation: Growing corporate involvement.* New York: Ruder & Finn.

Ostrea, E. M., & Chavez, C. J. (1979). Perinatal problems (excluding neonatal withdrawal) in maternal drug addiction: A study of 830 cases. *Journal of Pediatrics, 94*(2), 292–295.

Oswald, P. F., & Peltzman, P. (1974). The cry of the human infant. *Scientific American, 230*(3), 84–90.

Otto, H., & Healy, S. (1966). Adolescents' self-perception of personality strengths. *Journal of Human Relations, 14*(3), 483–490.

Owens, W. A. (1966). Age and mental abilities: A second adult follow-up. *Journal of Educational Psychology, 57*(6), 311–325.

Paffenberger, R. S., Hyde, R. T., Wing, A. L., & Steinmetz, C. H. (1984). A natural history of athleticism and cardiovascular health. *Journal of the American Medical Association, 252*(4), 491–495.

Page, D. C., et al. (1987). The sex-determining region of the human Y chromosome encodes a finger protein. *Cell, 51,* 1091–1104.

Palmore, E. B. (1984). Longevity in Abkhazia: A reevaluation. *Gerontologist, 24*(1), 95–96.

Paloma, M. M. (1972). Role conflict and the married professional woman. In C. Safilious-Rothschild (Ed.), *Toward a sociology of women.* Lexington, MA: Xerox.

Pankey, G. A. (1983, October 5). *Life style compromised patients.* Paper presented to Medical Writers Seminar, New York.

Papalia, D. (1972). The status of several conservation abilities across the life-span. *Human Development, 15,* 229–243.

Papalia, D., & Tennent, S. (1975). Vocational aspirations in preschoolers: A manifestation of early sex-role stereotyping. *Sex Roles, 1*(2), 197–199.

Papousek, H. (1959). A method of studying conditioned food reflexes in young children up to age six months. *Pavlovian Journal of Higher Nervous Activity, 9,* 136–140.

Papousek, H. (1960a). Conditioned motor alimentary reflexes in infants: 1. Experimental conditioned sucking reflex. *Ceskoslovenska Pediatrie, 15,* 861–872.

Papousek, H. (1960b). Conditioned motor alimentary reflexes in infants: 2. A new experimental method of investigation. *Ceskoslovenska Pediatrie, 15,* 981–988.

Papousek, H. (1961). Conditioned head rotation reflexes in infants in the first months of life. *Acta Paediatrica, 50,* 565–576.

Pardini, A. (1984, April–May). Exercise, vitality and aging. *Aging,* pp. 19–29.

Paris, S. G., & Lindauer, B. K. (1976). The role of influence in children's comprehension and memory for sentences. *Cognitive Psychology, 8,* 217–227.

Parke, R. D. (1977). Some effects of punishment on children's behavior—revisited. In E. M. Hetherington & R. D. Parke (Eds.), *Contemporary readings in child psychology.* New York: McGraw-Hill.

Parke, R. D., & Tinsley, B. R. (1981). The father's role in infancy: Determinants of involvement in caregiving and play. In M. E. Lamb (Ed.), *The role of the father in child development* (2d ed.). New York: Wiley.

Parkes, C. M., Benjamin, B., & Fitzgerald, R. (1969). Broken heart: A statistical study of increased mortality among widowers. *British Medical Journal, 4,* 740–743.

Parlee, M. B. (1983). Menstrual rhythms in sensory processes: A review of fluctuations in vision, olfaction, audition, taste, and touch. *Psychological Bulletin, 93*(3), 539–548.

Parmelee, A. H. (1986). Children's illnesses: Their beneficial effects on behavioral development. *Child Development, 57,* 1–10.

Parmelee, A. H., Wenner, W. H., & Schulz, H. R. (1964). Infant sleep patterns: From birth to 16 weeks of age. *Journal of Pediatrics, 65,* 576.

Parten, M. (1932). Social play among preschool children. *Journal of Abnormal and Social Psychology, 27,* 243–269.

Passuth, P., Maines, D., & Neugarten, B. L. (1984, April). *Age norms and age constraints twenty years later.*

Paper presented at Midwest Sociological Society meeting, Chicago.

Patterson, G. R., & Stouthamer-Loeber, M. (1984). The correlation of family management practices and delinquency. *Child Development, 55*, 1299–1307

Pattison, E. M. (1977). The experience of dying. In E. M. Pattison (Ed.), *The experience of dying.* Englewood Cliffs, NJ: Prentice-Hall.

Pearlin, L. I. (1980). Life strains and psychological distress among adults. In N. J. Smelser & E. H. Erikson (Eds.), *Themes of work and love in adulthood.* Cambridge, MA: Harvard University Press.

Pebley, A. R. (1981). Changing attitudes toward the timing of first birth. *Family Planning Perspectives, 13*(4), 171–175.

Peck, R. C. (1955). Psychological developments in the second half of life. In J. E. Anderson (Ed.), *Psychological aspects of aging.* Washington, DC: American Psychological Association.

Pedersen, F. A., Cain, R., & Zaslow, M. (1982). Variation in infant experience associated with alternative family roles. In L. Laosa & I. Sigel (Eds.), *The family as a learning environment.* New York: Plenum.

Pedersen, F. A., Rubenstein, J. L., & Yarrow, L. J. (1973, March–April). *Father absence in infancy.* Paper presented at the meeting of the Society for Research in Child Development, Philadelphia.

Pedersen, F. A., Rubenstein, J. L., & Yarrow, L. J. (1979). Infant development in father-absent families. *Journal of Genetic Psychology, 135*, 51–61.

Pederson, E., Faucher, T. A., & Eaton, W. W. (1978). A new perspective of the effects of first-grade teachers on children's subsequent adult status. *Harvard Educational Review, 48*, 1–31.

Pedrick-Cornell, C., & Gelles, R. J. (1982). Elder abuse: The status of current knowledge. *Family Relations, 31*, 457–465.

Peel, E. A. (1967). *The psychological basis of education* (2d ed.). Edinburgh: Oliver & Boyd.

Peery, D., Jensen, L., & Adams, G. (1984). *Relationships between parents' attitudes regarding child rearing and the sociometric status of their preschool children.* Unpublished manuscript, Brigham Young University, Salt Lake City.

Pelz, D. C., & Andrews, F. M. (1966). *Scientists in organizations: Produc-*

tive climates for research and development. New York: Wiley.

Pepler, D., Corter, C., & Abramovitch, R. (1982). Social relations among children: Siblings and peers. In K. Rubin & H. Ross (Eds.), *Peer relationships and social skills in childhood.* New York: Springer-Verlag.

Perrin, E. C., & Gerrity, P. S. (1981). There's a demon in your belly: Children's understanding of illness. *Pediatrics, 67*, 841–849.

Perrucci & Targ. (1984). Study on effects of unemployment.

Perry, W. G. (1970). *Forms of intellectual and ethical development in the college years.* New York: Holt.

Persson-Blennow, I., & McNeil, T. F. (1981). Temperament characteristics of children in relation to gender, birth order, and social class. *American Journal of Orthopsychiatry, 51*, 710–714.

Peskin, H. (1967). Pubertal onset and ego functioning. *Journal of Abnormal Psychology, 72*, 1–15.

Peskin, H. (1973). Influence of the developmental schedule of puberty on learning and ego functioning. *Journal of Youth and Adolescence, 2*, 273–290.

Petri, E. (1934). Untersuchungen zur Erbedingtheir der Menarche. *Z. Morph. Anthr., 33*, 43–48.

Pettigrew, T. F. (1964). Negro American intelligence. In T. F. Pettigrew (Ed.), *Profile of the Negro American* (pp. 100–135). Princeton, NJ: Van Nostrand Reinhold.

Pettit, E. J., & Bloom, B. L. (1984). Whose decision was it? The effects of initiator status on adjustment to marital adjustment. *Journal of Marriage and the Family, 46*(3), 587–595.

Piaget, J. (1928). *Judgment and reasoning in the child.* New York: Harcourt, Brace.

Piaget, J. (1932). *The moral judgment of the child.* New York: Harcourt, Brace.

Piaget, J. (1951). *Play, dreams, and imitation* (C. Gattegno & F. M. Hodgson, Trans.). New York: Norton.

Piaget, J. (1952). *The origins of intelligence in children.* New York: International Universities Press.

Piaget, J. (1955). *The child's construction of reality.* London: Routledge.

Piaget, J. (1962). Comments on Vygotsky's critical remarks concerning *The language and thought of the child,* and *Judgment and reasoning in the child.* In L. S. Vygotsky, *Thought and language.* Cambridge, MA: Massachusetts Institute of Technology (MIT) Press.

Piaget, J., & Inhelder, B. (1967). *The*

child's conception of space. New York: Norton.

Piaget, J., & Inhelder, B. (1969). *The psychology of the child.* New York: Basic Books.

Pincus, T., Callahan, L. F., & Burkhauser, R. V. (1987). Most chronic diseases are reported more frequently by individuals with fewer than 12 years of formal education in the age 18–64 United States population. *Journal of Chronic Diseases, 40*(9), 865–874.

Pineo, P. (1961). Disenchantment in the later years of marriage. *Marriage and Family Living, 23*, 3–11.

Pines, M. (1977, February 13). St-st-st-st-st-st-stuttering. *The New York Times Magazine*, pp. 261ff.

Pines, M. (1979). Superkids. *Psychology Today, 12*(8), 53–63.

Pines, M. (1983, November). Can a rock walk? *Psychology Today,* pp. 44–54.

Placek, B. (1986). Commentary: Cesarean rate still rising statistic. *Statistical Bulletin, 67*, 9.

Plemons, J., Willis, S., & Baltes, P. (1978). Modifiability of fluid intelligence in aging: A short-term longitudinal training approach. *Journal of Gerontology, 33*(2), 224–231.

Plomin, R. (1983). Developmental behavioral genetics. *Child Development, 54*, 253–259.

Pogrebin, L. C. (1980). *Growing up free: Raising your child in the 80's.* New York: Bantam.

Pogrebin, L. C. (1983). *Family politics.* New York: McGraw-Hill.

Pogrebin, L. C. (1986). *Among friends: Who we like, why we like them, and what we do with them.* New York: McGraw-Hill.

Pollack, R. F. (1985, March 14). A wrong way to see the aged. *The New York Times,* p. A27.

Pomeranz, V. E., with Schultz, D. (1984). *The first five years: The relaxed approach to child care.* New York: St. Martin's.

Poon, L. W. (1985). Differences in human memory with aging: Nature, causes, and clinical implications. In J. E. Birren & K. W. Schaie (Eds.), *Handbook of the psychology of aging* (2d ed.). New York: Van Nostrand Reinhold.

Pope, H. G., Hudson, J. L., Jonas, J. M., & Yurgelun-Todd, D. (1983). Bulimia treated with imipramine: A placebo-controlled, double-blind study. *American Journal of Psychiatry, 140*, 554–558.

Porcino, J. (1983). *Growing older, getting better: A handbook for women* in the second half of life. Reading, MA: Addison-Wesley.

Porter, N. L., & Christopher, F. S. (1984). Infertility: Towards an awareness of a need among family life practitioners. *Family Relations, 33,* 309–315.

Power, T. G., & Chapieski, M. L. (1986). Childrearing and impulse control in toddlers: A naturalistic investigation. *Developmental Psychology, 22*(2), 271–275.

Poznanski, E. O. (1982). The clinical phenomenology of childhood depression. *American Journal of Orthopsychiatry, 52*(2), 308–313.

Prechtl, H. F. R., & Beintema, D. J. (1964). *The neurological examination of the full-term newborn infant: Clinics in developmental medicine* (No. 12). London: Heinemann.

Prevention Research Center. (1986). *Prevention index '86: A report card on the nation's health* [Summary Report]. Emmaus, PA: Rodale.

Pryor, K. (1985). *Don't shoot the dog: The new art of teaching and training.* New York: Bantam.

Punke, H. H. (1943). High school youth and family quarrels. *School and Society, 58,* 507–511.

Putallaz, M. (1987). Maternal behavior and children's sociometric status. *Child Development, 58,* 324–340.

Quay, H. (1987). Intelligence. In H. C. Quay (Ed.), *Handbook of juvenile delinquency.* New York: Wiley.

Quinby, N. (1985, October). On testing and teaching intelligence: A conversation with Robert Sternberg. *Educational Leadership,* pp. 50–53.

Rabushka, A., & Jacobs, B. (1980, February 15). Are old folks really poor? Herewith a look at some common views. *The New York Times,* p. A29.

Rachal, J. V., Guess, L. L., Hubbard, R. L., Maisto, S. A., Cavanaugh, E. R., Waddell, R., & Benrud, C. H. (1980). *Adolescent drinking behavior: Vol. 1. The extent and nature of adolescent alcohol and drug use.* Research Triangle Park, NC: Research Triangle Institute.

Radin, N. (1981). The role of the father in cognitive, academic, and intellectual development. In M. E. Lamb (Ed.), *The role of the father in child development.* New York: Wiley.

Ragland, D. R., & Brand, R. J. (1988). Type A behavior and mortality from coronary heart disease. *The New England Journal of Medicine, 318*(2), 65–69.

Ragozin, A. S., Basham, R. B., Crnic, K. A., Greenberg, M. T., & Robinson, N. M. (1982). Effects of maternal age on parenting role. *Developmental Psychology, 18*(4), 627–634.

Raskin, P. A., & Israel, A. C. (1981). Sex-role imitation in children: Effects of sex of child, sex of model, and sex-role appropriateness of modelled behavior. *Sex Roles, 1,* 1067–1076.

Rassin, D. K., Richardson, J., Baranowski, T., Nader, P. R., Guenther, N., Bee, D. E., & Brown, J. P. (1984). Incidence of breast-feeding in a low socioeconomic group of mothers in the United States: Ethnic patterns. *Pediatrics, 73,* 132–137.

Raven, J. C. (1983). *Raven progressive matrices test.* San Antonio, TX: Psychological Corporation.

Ravitch, D. (1983). The education pendulum. *Psychology Today, 17*(10), 62–71.

Read, M. S., Habicht, J.-P., Lechtig, A., & Klein, R. E. (1973, May). *Maternal malnutrition, birth weight, and child development.* Paper presented at the International Symposium on Nutrition, Growth and Development, Valencia, Spain.

Reese, H. W. (1961). Relationships between self-acceptance and sociometric choices. *Journal of Abnormal and Social Psychology, 62,* 472–474.

Reese, H. W. (1977). Imagery and associative memory. In R. V. Kail & J. W. Hagen (Eds.), *Perspectives on the development of memory and cognition.* Hillsdale, NJ: Erlbaum.

Reeves, R. (1984, October 1). Journey to Pakistan. *New Yorker,* pp. 39–105.

Reichard, S., Livson, F., & Peterson, P. (1962). *Aging and personality: A study of 87 older men.* New York: Wiley.

Reid, J. R., Patterson, G. R., & Loeber, R. (1982). The abused child: Victim, instigator, or innocent bystander? In D. J. Berstein (Ed.), *Response structure and organization.* Lincoln: University of Nebraska Press.

Reid, R. L., & Yen, S. S. C. (1981). Premenstrual syndrome. *American Journal of Obstetrics and Gynecology, 139*(1), 85–104.

Reisberg, B. (Ed.). (1983). *Alzheimer's disease.* New York: Free Press.

Reisberg, B. (1987). Senile dementia. In G. L. Maddox (Ed.), *The encyclopedia of aging* (pp. 594–600). New York: Springer.

Remafedi, G. (1987a). Adolescent homosexuality: Psychosocial and medical implications. *Pediatrics, 79,* 331–337.

Remafedi, G. (1987b). Male homosexuality: The adolescent's perspective. *Pediatrics, 79,* 326–330.

Remmers, H. H. (1957). *The American teenager.* Indianapolis: Bobbs-Merrill.

Rempel, J. (1985). Childless elderly: What are they missing? *Journal of Marriage and the Family, 47*(2), 343–348.

Rendina, I., & Dickerscheid, J. D. (1976). Father involvement with first born infants. *Family Coordinator, 25,* 373–379.

Renzulli, J. S., & McGreevy, A. M. (1984). *A study of twins included and not included in gifted programs.* Storrs: University of Connecticut School of Education.

Rest, J. R. (1975). Longitudinal study of the Defining Issues Test of moral judgment: A strategy for analyzing developmental change. *Developmental Psychology, 11*(16), 738–748.

Restak, R. (1984). *The brain.* New York: Bantam.

Restak, R. (1986). *The infant mind.* Garden City, NY: Doubleday.

Rheingold, H. L. (1956). The modification of social responsiveness in institutionalized babies. *Monographs of the Society for Research in Child Development, 21*(Serial No. 63).

Rheingold, H. L. (1985). Development as the acquisition of familiarity. *Annual Review of Psychology, 36,* 1–17.

Rheingold, H. L., & Eckerman, C. O. (1970). The infant separates himself from his mother. *Science, 168,* 78–83.

Rhoads, G. G., & Kagan, A. (1983, March 5). The relationship of coronary disease, stroke, and mortality to weight in youth and middle age. *The Lancet,* pp. 492–495.

Rhodes, S. R. (1983). Age-related differences in work attitudes and behaviors: A review and conceptual analysis. *Psychological Bulletin, 93*(2), 328–367.

Rice, B. (1979). Brave new world of intelligence testing. *Psychology Today, 13*(4), 27–41.

Rich, D. (1985). *The forgotten factor in school success—the family: A policymaker's guide.* Washington, DC: Home and School Institute.

Richards, M. P. M. (1971). Social interaction in the first week of human life. *Psychiatria, Neurologia, Neurochirugia, 74,* 35–42.

Richardson, D. W., & Short, R. V. (1978). Time of onset of sperm production in boys. *Journal of Biosocial Science, 5,* 15–25.

Ridenour, M. V. (1982). Infant walkers: Development tool or inherent danger. *Perceptual & Motor Skills, 55,* 1201–1202.

Rieder, M. J., Schwartz, C., & Newman, J. (1986). Patterns of walker use and walker injury. *Pediatrics, 78*(3), 488–493.

Rierdan, J., Koff, E., & Flaherty, J. (1986). Conceptions and misconceptions of menstruation. *Women and Health, 10*(4), 33–45.

Rieser, J., Yonas, A., & Wilkner, K. (1976). Radial localization of odors by human newborns. *Child Development, 47*, 856–859.

Rimm, S. B. (1985, September). How to reach the underachiever. *Instructor*, pp. 73–76.

Rimm, S. B. (1986). *Underachievement syndrome: Causes and cures.* Watertown, WI: Apple.

Rindfuss, R. R., & St. John, C. (1983). Social determinants of age at first birth. *Journal of Marriage and the Family, 45*, 553–565.

Rioux, J. W. (1987, Summer). Parents & dropout prevention. *Network for Public Schools*, pp. 7–8.

Ritvo, E. R., Freeman, B. J., Mason-Brothers, A., Mo, A., & Ritvo, A. M. (1985). Concordance for the syndrome of autism in 40 pairs of afflicted twins. *American Journal of Psychiatry, 142*, 74–77.

Roberts, E. J., Kline, D., & Gagnon, J. (1978). *Family life and sexual learning: A study of the role of parents in the sexual learning of children.* New York: Project on Human Sexual Development, Population Education.

Roberts, G. C., Block, J. H., & Block, J. (1984). Continuity and change in parents' child-rearing practices. *Child Development, 55*, 586–597.

Roberts, M. (1987). Class before birth. *Psychology Today, 21*(5), 41.

Roberts, P., & Newton, P. M. (1987). Levinsonian studies of women's adult development. *Psychology and Aging, 2*(2), 154–163.

Roberts, P., Papalia-Finlay, D., Davis, E. S., Blackburn, J., & Dellmann, M. (1982). "No two fields ever grow grass the same way": Assessment of conservation abilities in the elderly. *International Journal of Aging and Human Development, 15*(3), 185–195.

Robertson, L. F. (1984, November). Why we went back to half-days. *Principal*, pp. 22–24.

Robinson, B., & Thurnher, M. (1981). Taking care of aged parents: A family cycle transition. *Gerontologist, 19*(6), 586–593.

Robinson, M. J., et al. (1974). In S. M. Gellis (Ed.), *The yearbook of pediatrics.* Chicago: Yearbook Medical Publishers.

Robson, K. S. (1967). The role of eye-to-eye contact in maternal-infant attachment. *Journal of Child Psychology and Psychiatry, 8*, 13–25.

Roche, A. F. (1981). The adipocyte-number hypothesis. *Child Development, 52*, 31–43.

Rodman, H., & Cole, C. (1987). Latchkey children: A review of policy and resources. *Family Relations, 36*, 101–105.

Rogers, C. C., & O'Connell, M. (1984). Childspacing among birth cohorts of American women: 1905–1959. *Current Population Reports*, Ser. P-20, No. 385.

Rogers, M. F. (1985). AIDS in children: A review of the clinical, epidemiological and public health aspects. *Pediatric Infectious Disease, 4*(3), 230–236.

Roopnarine, J., & Field, T. (1984). Play interaction of friends and acquaintances in nursery school. In T. Field, J. Roopnarine, & M. Segal (Eds.), *Friendships in normal and handicapped children.* Norwood, NJ: Ablex.

Roopnarine, J., & Honig, A. S. (1985, September). The unpopular child. *Young Children*, pp. 59–64.

Rose, R. J., & Ditto, W. B. (1983). A developmental-genetic analysis of common fears from early adolescence to early adulthood. *Child Development, 54*, 361–368.

Rose, R. M., Gordon, T. P., & Bernstein, I. S. (1972). Plasma testosterone levels in the male rhesus: Influences of sexual and social stimuli. *Science, 178*(4061), 643–645.

Rose, S. A., & Wallace, I. F. (1985). Visual recognition memory: A predictor of later cognitive functioning in preterms. *Child Development, 56*, 843–852.

Rosenberg, M. S. (1987). New directions for research on the psychological maltreatment of children. *American Psychologist, 42*(2), 166–171.

Rosenfeld, A., & Stark, E. (1987). The prime of our lives. *Psychology Today, 21*(5), 62–72.

Rosenman, R. H. (1983, June). *Type A behavior in corporate executives and its implications for cardiovascular disease.* Paper presented at a seminar-workshop, Coping with Corporate Stress: Avoiding a Cardiovascular Crisis, New York.

Rosenthal, D. A. (1982, August). *The influence of ethnicity on parent-adolescent conflict.* Paper presented at the Second National Child Development Conference, Melbourne, Australia.

Rosenthal, M. K. (1982). Vocal dialogues in the neonatal period. *Developmental Psychology, 18*(1), 17–21.

Rosenthal, P. A., & Rosenthal, S. (1984). Suicidal behavior by preschool children. *American Journal of Psychiatry, 141*(4), 520–525.

Rosenthal, R., & Jacobson, L. (1968). *Pygmalion in the classroom.* New York: Holt.

Rosenzweig, M. R. (1984). Experience, memory, and the brain. *American Psychologist, 39*, 365–376.

Rosenzweig, M. R., & Bennett, E. L. (Eds.). (1976). *Neural mechanisms of learning and memory.* Cambridge, MA: Massachusetts Institute of Technology (MIT) Press.

Rosetti-Ferreira, M. C. (1978). Malnutrition and mother-infant asynchrony: Slow mental development. *International Journal of Behavioral Development, 1*, 207–219.

Rosow, I. (1970). Old people: Their friends and neighbors. *American Behavioral Scientist, 14*, 59–69.

Ross, H. G., Dalton, M. J., & Milgram, J. I. (1980, November). *Older adults' perceptions of closeness in sibling relationships.* Paper presented at annual meeting of the Gerontological Society, San Diego, CA.

Rossi, A. S. (1980). Aging and parenthood in the middle years. In P. B. Baltes & O. G. Brim (Eds.), *Life-span development and behavior* (Vol. 3). New York: Academic.

Rovee-Collier, C., & Fagen, J. W. (1976). Extended conditioning and 24-hour retention in infants. *Journal of Experimental Child Psychology, 21*, 1.

Rovee-Collier, C., & Fagen, J. W. (1981). The retrieval of memory in early infancy. In L. P. Lipsitt (Ed.), *Advances in infancy research* (Vol. 1). Norwood, NJ: Ablex.

Rovee-Collier, C., & Lipsitt, L. (1982). Learning, adaptation, and memory in the newborn. In P. Stratton (Ed.), *Psychobiology of the human newborn.* New York: Wiley.

Ruberman, W., Weinblatt, E., Goldberg, J. D., & Chaudhary, B. S. (1984). Psychosocial influences on mortality after myocardial infarction. *The New England Journal of Medicine, 311*, 552–559.

Rubin, A. (1977, September). Birth injuries. *Hospital Medicine*, pp. 114–130.

Rubin, D. H., Krasilnikoff, P. A., Leventhal, J. M., Weile, B., & Berget, A. (1986, August 23). Effect of passive smoking on birth-weight. *The Lancet*, pp. 415–417.

Rubin, K. (1982). Nonsocial play in preschoolers: Necessary evil? *Child Development, 53*, 651–657.

Rubin, K., Maioni, T. L., & Hornung, M. (1976). Free play behaviors in middle-class and lower-class preschoolers: Parten and Piaget revisited. *Child Development, 47*, 414–419.

Rubin, K., & Ross, H. S. (1982). *Peer relationships and social skills in childhood.* New York: Spring-Verlag.

Rubin, K., Watson, K., & Jambor, T.

(1978). Free-play behaviors in preschool and kindergarten children. *Child Development, 49*, 534–536.

Rubin, L. B. (1979). *Women of a certain age.* New York: Harper & Row.

Rubin, Z. (1981). Does personality really change after 20? *Psychology Today, 15*(3), 18–27.

Ruble, D. N., & Brooks-Gunn, J. (1982). The experience of menarche. *Child Development, 53*, 1557–1566.

Rule, S. (1981, June 11). The battle to stem school dropouts, *The New York Times*, pp. A1, B10.

Russell, L. B., & Russell, W. L. (1952). Radiation hazards to the embryo and fetus. *Radiology, 58*(3), 369–376.

Rutter, M. (1971). Parent-child separation: Psychological effects on the children. *Journal of Child Psychology and Psychiatry, 12*, 233–260.

Rutter, M. (1974). *The qualities of mothering: Maternal deprivation reassessed.* New York: Aronson.

Rutter, M. (1979a). Maternal deprivation, 1972–1978: New findings, new concepts, new approaches. *Child Development, 50*, 283–305.

Rutter, M. (1979b). Separation experiences: A new look at an old topic. *Pediatrics, 95*(1), 147–154.

Rutter, M. (1983). Stress, coping, and development: Some issues and some questions. In N. Garmezy & M. Rutter (Eds.), *Stress, coping, and development in children.* New York: McGraw-Hill.

Rutter, M. (1984). Resilient children. *Psychology Today, 18*(3), 57–65.

Ryerson, A. J. (1961). Medical advice on child rearing, 1550–1900. *Harvard Educational Review, 31*, 302–323.

Ryff, C. D. (1982). Self-perceived personality change in adulthood and aging. *Journal of Personality and Social Psychology, 42*(1), 108–115.

Ryff, C. D., & Baltes, P. B. (1976). Value transition and adult development in women: The instrumentality-terminality sequence hypothesis. *Developmental Psychology, 12*(6), 567–568.

Ryff, C. D., & Heincke, S. G. (1983). Subjective organization of personality in adulthood and aging. *Journal of Personality and Social Psychology, 44*(4), 807–816.

Sachs, B. P., McCarthy, B. J., Rubin, G., Burton, A., Terry, J., & Tyler, C. W. (1983). Cesarean section. *Journal of the American Medical Association, 250*(16), 2157–2159.

Sadowitz, P. D., & Oski, F. A. (1983). Iron status and infant feeding practices in an urban ambulatory center. *Pediatrics, 72*(1), 33–36.

Sagi, A., & Hoffman, M. (1976). Em-

pathic distress in newborns. *Developmental Psychology, 12*(2), 175–176.

Salapatek, P., & Kessen, W. (1966). Visual scanning of triangles by the human newborn. *Journal of Experimental Child Psychology, 3*, 155–167.

Salthouse, T. A. (1985). Speed of behavior and its implications for cognition. In J. E. Birren & K. W. Schaie (Eds.), *Handbook of the psychology of aging.* New York: Van Nostrand Reinhold.

Sameroff, A. (1971). Can conditioned responses be established in the newborn infant? *Developmental Psychology, 5*, 1–12.

Samuels, M., & Samuels, N. (1979). *The well baby book.* New York: Summit.

Sandler, D. P., Everson, R. B., Wilcox, A. J., & Browder, J. P. (1985). Cancer risk in adulthood from early life exposure to parents' smoking. *American Journal of Public Health, 75*, 487–492.

Sanford, L. T. (1982). *The silent children: A parent's guide to the prevention of child sexual abuse.* New York: McGraw-Hill.

Sarrel, L. J., & Sarrel, P. M. (1979). *Sexual unfolding: Sexual development and sex therapies in late adolescence.* Boston: Little, Brown.

Saturday News Quiz (1984, July 7). *The New York Times*, pp. 16, 40.

Saunders, A., & Remsberg, B. (1984). *The stress-proof child: A loving parent's guide.* New York: Holt, Rinehart & Winston.

Scarr, S. (1984). *Mother care/other care.* New York: Basic Books.

Scarr, S., & Weinberg, R. (1983). The Minnesota adoption study: Genetic differences and malleability. *Child Development, 54*, 260–267.

Schaeffer, H. R., & Emerson, P. (1964). The development of social attachments in infancy. *Monographs of the Society for Research in Child Development, 29*(3).

Schaie, K. W. (1976). *External validity in the assessment of intellectual development in adulthood.* Paper presented at the annual meeting of the American Psychological Association, Washington, DC.

Schaie, K. W. (1977–1978). Toward a stage theory of adult cognitive development. *Journal of Aging and Human Development, 8*(2), 129–138.

Schaie, K. W. (1979). The primary mental abilities in adulthood: An exploration in the development of psychometric intelligence. In P. B. Baltes & O. G. Brim (Eds.), *Life-span development and behavior* (Vol. 2). New York: Academic.

Schaie, K. W. (1983). The Seattle longitudinal study: A twenty-one-year investigation of psychometric intelligence. In K. W. Schaie (Ed.), *Longitudinal studies of adult personality development.* New York: Guilford.

Schaie, K. W., & Baltes, P. B. (1977). Some faith helps to see the forest: A final comment on the Horn-Donaldson myth of the Baltes-Schaie position on adult intelligence. *American Psychologist, 32*, 1118–1120.

Schaie, K. W., & Gribbin, K. (1975). Adult development and aging. *Annual Review of Psychology, 26*, 65–96.

Schaie, K. W., & Herzog, C. (1983). Fourteen-year cohort sequential analyses of adult intellectual development. *Developmental Psychology, 19*(4), 531–543.

Schaie, K. W., & Strother, C. (1968). A cross-sequential study of age changes in cognitive behavior. *Psychological Bulletin, 70*, 671–680.

Schanberg, S. M., & Field, J. M. (1987). Sensory deprivation illness and supplemental stimulation in the rat pup and preterm human neonate. *Child Development, 58*, 1431–1447.

Scharlach, A. E. (1987). Relieving feelings of strain among women with elderly mothers. *Psychology and Aging, 2*(1), 9–13.

Schick, F. L. (Ed.). (1986). *Statistical handbook on aging Americans.* Phoenix, AZ: Oryz.

Schickedanz, J. A. (1986). *More than the ABCs: The early stages of reading and writing.* Washington, DC: National Association for the Education of Young Children.

Schlossberg, N. K. (1987). Taking the mystery out of change. *Psychology Today, 21*(5), 74–75.

Schmall, V. L., & Pratt, C. (1986). Special friends: Elders and pets. *Generations, 10*(4), 44–45.

Schmeck, H. M. (1976, June 10). Trend in growth of children lags. *The New York Times*, p. 13.

Schmeck, H. M. (1983, March 22). U.S. panel calls for patients' right to end life. *The New York Times*, pp. A1, C7.

Schmitt, B. D. (1986). The prevention of sleep problems and colic. *Pediatric Clinics of North America, 33*(4), 763–774.

Schmitt, B. D., & Kempe, C. H. (1983). Abusing neglected children. In R. E. Behrman & V. C. Vaughn (Eds.), *Nelson textbook of pediatrics* (12th ed.). Philadelphia: Saunders.

Schmitt, M. H. (1970). Superiority of breast-feeding: Fact or fancy? *American Journal of Nursing*, 1488–1493.

Schuckit, M. A. (1985). Genetics and the risk for alcoholism. *Journal of the American Medical Association*, *254*(18), 2614–2617.

Schuckit, M. A. (1987). Biological vulnerability to alcoholism. *Journal of Consulting and Clinical Psychology*, *55*(3), 301–309.

Schulman, M., & Mekler, E. (1985). *Bringing up a moral child*. Reading, MA: Addison-Wesley.

Schultz, D. P., & Schultz, S. E. (1986). *Psychology and industry today* (4th ed.). New York: Macmillan.

Schulz, R. (1978). *The psychology of death, dying, and bereavement*. Reading, MA: Addison-Wesley.

Schweinhart, L. U., Weikart, D. P., & Larner, M. B. (1986). A report on the High/Scope preschool curriculum comparison study. *Early Childhood Research Quarterly, 1*, 15–45.

Scott, J. P. (1958). *Animal behavior*. Chicago: University of Chicago Press.

Scott, J. P., & Roberto, K. A. (1981, October). *Sibling relationships in late life*. Paper presented at the annual meeting of the National Council on Family Relations, Milwaukee.

Sears, P. (1977). *Life satisfaction of Terman's gifted women: 1927–72. Comparison with the gifted men and with normative samples*. Paper presented at the fifth annual conference, School of Education, University of Wisconsin, Madison.

Sears, P., & Barbee, A. (1978). Career and life satisfaction among Terman's gifted women. In *The gifted and the creative: A fifty-year perspective*. Baltimore: Johns Hopkins University Press.

Sears, R. R., Maccoby, E. E., & Levin, H. (1957). *Patterns of child rearing*. New York: Harper & Row.

Secunda, V. (1984). *By youth possessed: The denial of age in America*. New York: Bobbs-Merrill.

Seligman, M. (1975). *Helplessness*. San Francisco: Freeman.

Sells, L. W. (1980). The mathematics filter and the education of women and minorities. In L. H. Fox, L. Brody, & I. Tobin (Eds.), *Women and the mathematical mystique*. Baltimore: Johns Hopkins University Press.

Selman, R. L. (1973, March). *A structural analysis of the ability to take another's social perspective: Stages in the development of role-taking ability*. Paper presented at the meeting of the Society for Research in Child Development, Philadelphia.

Selman, R. L., & Selman, A. P. (1979). Children's ideas about friendship: A new theory. *Psychology Today, 13*(4), 71–80, 114.

Selye, H. (1980). The stress concept today. In I. L. Kutash, L. B. Schlesinger, & Associates (Eds.), *Handbook on stress and anxiety* (pp. 127–143). San Francisco: Jossey-Bass.

Sex study by young gains favor. (1987, April 12). *Chicago Sun-Times*, p. 22.

Sexton, M., & Hebel, R. (1984). A clinical trial of change in maternal smoking and its effect on birth weight. *Journal of the American Medical Association, 251*(7), 911–915.

Shanas, E., Townsend, P., Wedderburn, D., Friis, H., Milhoj, P., & Stehouwer, J. (Eds.). (1968). *Old people in three industrial societies*. New York: Atherton.

Shangold, M. (1978, May 14). Female runners advised to follow common sense. *The New York Times*, Sec. 5, p. 2.

Shannon, D. C., & Kelly, D. H. (1982a). SIDS and near-SIDS (Part 1). *The New England Journal of Medicine, 306*(16), 959–965.

Shannon, D. C., & Kelly, D. H. (1982b). SIDS and near-SIDS (Part 2). *The New England Journal of Medicine, 306*(17), 1022–1028.

Shannon, L. W. (1982). *Assessing the relationship of adult criminal careers to juvenile careers*. Iowa City, IA: University of Iowa, Iowa Urban Community Research Center.

Shatz, M., & Gelman, R. (1973). The development of communication skills: Modifications in the speech of young children as a function of listener. *Monographs of the Society for Research in Child Development, 38*(5, Serial No. 152).

Shaywitz, S., Cohen, D., & Shaywitz, B. (1980). Behavior and learning difficulties in children of normal intelligence born to alcoholic mothers. *Journal of Pediatrics, 96*(6), 978–982.

Shepherd-Look, D. L. (1982). Sex differentiation and the development of sex roles. In B. B. Wolman (Ed.), *Handbook of developmental psychology*. Englewood Cliffs, NJ: Prentice-Hall.

Sherman, A., Goldrath, M., Berlin, A., Vakhariya, V., Banoom, F., Michaels, W., Goodman, P., & Brown, S. (1974). Cervical-vaginal adenosis after in utero exposure to synthetic estrogen. *Obstetrics and Gynecology, 44*(4), 531–545.

Sherman, L. W., & Berk, R. A. (1984, April). The Minneapolis domestic violence experiment. *Police Foundation Reports*, pp. 1–8.

Shinn, M. (1978). Father absence and children's cognitive development. *Psychological Bulletin, 85*, 295–324.

Shreve, A. (1987). *Remaking motherhood: How working mothers are shaping our children's future*. New York: Viking.

Siegel, O. (1982). Personality development in adolescence. In B. B. Wolman (Ed.), *Handbook of developmental psychology*. Englewood Cliffs, NJ: Prentice-Hall.

Siegler, R. S., & Richards, D. (1982). The development of intelligence. In R. Sternberg (Ed.), *Handbook of human intelligence*. London: Cambridge University Press.

Signorielli, N., Gross, L., & Morgan, M. (1982). Violence in television programs: Ten years later. In D. Pearl, L. Bouthilet, & J. Lazar (Eds.), *Television and behavior: Ten years of scientific progress and implications for the eighties: Technical reviews* (Vol. 2). Washington, DC: National Institute of Mental Health.

Silver, L. B. (1984). *The misunderstood child*. New York: McGraw-Hill.

Simner, M. L. (1971). Newborn's response to the cry of another infant. *Developmental Psychology, 5*(1), 135–150.

Simon, S. B., & Olds, S. W. (1977). *Helping your child learn right from wrong*. New York: McGraw-Hill.

Simons, C. (1987, March). They get by with a lot of help from their *kyoiku* mamas. *Smithsonian*, pp. 44–52.

Singer, S. (1985). *Human genetics* (2d ed.). New York: Freeman.

Singleton, L., & Asher, S. (1979). Racial integration and children's peer preferences: An investigation of developmental and cohort differences. *Child Development, 50*, 936–941.

Skeels, H. M. (1966). Adult status of children with contrasting early life experiences. *Monographs of the Society for Research in Child Development, 31*(Serial No. 3).

Skeels, H. M., & Dye, H. B. (1939). A study of the effects of differential stimulation on mentally retarded children. *Program of the American Association of Mental Deficiency, 44*, 114–136.

Skinner, B. F. (1938). *The behavior of organisms: An experimental approach*. New York: Appleton-Century.

Skinner, D. A. (1983). Dual-career families: Strains of sharing. In H. I. McCubbin & C. R. Figley (Eds.), *Stress and the family: Vol 1. Coping with normative transitions*. New York: Brunner/Mazel.

Sklar, L. S., & Anisman, H. (1981).

Stress and cancer. *Psychological Bulletin, 89*(3), 369–406.

Slater, E., with Shields, J. (1953). *Psychotic and neurotic illnesses in twins* (Medical Research Council Special Report, Ser. No. 278). London: Stationery Office.

Slobin, D. I. (1971). Universals of grammatical development in children. In W. Levelt & G. B. Flores d'Arcais (Eds.), *Advances in psycholinguistic research.* Amsterdam: New Holland.

Smelser, N. J. (1980). Issues in the study of work and love in adulthood. In N. J. Smelser & E. H. Erikson (Eds.), *Themes of work and love in adulthood.* Cambridge, MA: Harvard University Press.

Smelser, N. J., & Erikson, E. H. (1980). *Themes of work and love in adulthood.* Cambridge, MA: Harvard University Press.

Smilansky, S. (1968). *The effects of sociodramatic play on disadvantaged preschool children.* New York: Wiley.

Smith, D. W., & Wilson, A. A. (1973). *The child with Down's syndrome (mongolism).* Philadelphia: Saunders.

Smith, T. E. (1981). Adolescent agreement with perceived maternal and paternal educational goals. *Journal of Marriage and the Family, 43,*85–93.

Smollar, J., & Youniss, J. (1982). Social development through friendship. In K. H. Rubin & H. S. Ross (Eds.), *Peer relationships and social skills in childhood.* New York: Springer-Verlag.

Snarey, J. R. (1985). Cross-cultural universality of social-moral development: A critical review of Kohlbergian research. *Psychological Bulletin, 97,* 202–232.

Snarey, J. R., Reimer, J., & Kohlberg, L. (1985). Development of social-moral reasoning among kibbutz adolescents: A longitudinal cross-cultural study. *Development Psychology, 21,* 3–17.

Snow, C. E. (1972). Mother's speech to children learning language. *Child Development, 43,* 549–565.

Snow, C. E. (1977). Mother's speech research: From input to interaction. In C. E. Snow & C. A. Ferguson (Eds.), *Talking to children: Language input and acquisition.* London: Cambridge University Press.

Snow, C. E., Arlman-Rupp, A., Hassing, Y., Jobse, J., Joosten, J., & Verster, J. (1976). Mothers' speech in three social classes. *Journal of Psycholinguistic Research, 5,* 1–20.

Snow, M. E., Jacklin, C. N., & Maccoby, E. E. (1983). Sex-of-child differences in father-child interaction at one year of age. *Child Development, 54,* 227–232.

Soddy, K., & Kidson, M. (1967). *Men in middle life, cross-cultural studies in mental health.* Philadelphia: Lippincott.

Solomons, H. (1978). The malleability of infant motor development. *Clinical Pediatrics, 17*(11), 836–839.

Sontag, S. (1972, September 23). The double standard of aging. *Saturday Review.*

Sorensen, R. C. (1973). *Adolescent sexuality in contemporary America.* Tarrytown, NY: World.

Sorensen, T., Nielsen, G., Andersen, P., & Teasdale, T. (1988). Genetic and environmental influence of premature death in adult adoptees. *The New England Journal of Medicine, 318,* 727–732.

Sostek, A. J., & Wyatt, R. J. (1981). The chemistry of crankiness. *Psychology Today, 15*(10), 120.

Speece, M. W., & Brent, S. B. (1984). Children's understanding of death: A review of three components of a death concept. *Child Development, 55,* 1671–1686.

Spiegler, D., Malin, H., Kaelber, C., & Warren, K. (1984, January 13). Fetal alcohol syndrome: Public awareness week. *Morbidity and Mortality Weekly Report,* pp. 1–2.

Spiro, M. E. (1958). *Children of the kibbutz.* Cambridge, MA: Harvard University Press.

Spitz, R. A. (1945). Hospitalism: An inquiry in the genesis of psychiatric conditioning in early childhood. In D. Fenschel et al. (Eds.), *Psychoanalytic studies of the child* (Vol. 1, pp. 53–74). New York: International Universities Press.

Spitz, R. A. (1946). Hospitalism: A follow-up report. In D. Fenschel et al. (Eds.), *Psychoanalytic studies of the child* (Vol. 1, pp. 113–117). New York: International Universities Press.

Spock, B. (1976). *Baby and child care.* New York: Pocket Books.

Spock, B., & Rothenberg, M. B. (1985). *Baby and child care.* New York: Pocket Books.

Springer, D., & Brubaker, T. H. (1984). *Family caregivers and dependent elderly.* Beverly Hills, CA: Sage.

Squire, S. (1983). *The slender balance.* New York: Putnam.

Sroufe, L. A. (1977). Wariness of strangers and the study of infant development. *Child Development, 48,* 731–746.

Sroufe, L. A. (1979). Socioemotional

development. In J. Osofsky (Ed.), *Handbook of infant development.* New York: Wiley.

Sroufe, L. A. (1983). Individual patterns of adaptation from infancy to preschool. In M. Perlmutter (Ed.), *Proceedings of Minnesota symposium on child psychology.* Hillsdale, NJ: Erlbaum.

Sroufe, L. A., Fox, N. E., & Pancake, V. R. (1983). Attachment and dependency in a developmental perspective. *Child Development, 54,* 1615–1627.

Sroufe, L. A., & Waters, E. (1976). The ontogenesis of smiling and laughter: A perspective on the organization of development in infancy. *Psychological Review, 83,* 173–189.

Sroufe, L. A., & Wunsch, J. (1972). The development of laughter in the first year of life. *Child Development, 43,* 1326–1344.

Stacey, M., Dearden, R., Pill, R., & Robinson, D. (1970). *Hospitals, children and their families: The report of a pilot study.* London: Routledge.

Stair, N. (undated). [Course reading]. Denver: Colorado Outward Bound School.

Stamps, L. (1977). Temporal conditioning of heart rate responses in newborn infants. *Developmental Psychology, 13*(6), 624–629.

Starfield, B. (1978). Enuresis: Focus on a challenging problem in primary care. *Pediatrics, 62,* 1036–1037.

Starfield, B., Katz, H., Gabriel, A., Livingston, G., Benson, P., Hankin, J., Horn, S., & Steinwachs, D. (1984). Morbidity in childhood—a longitudinal view. *The New England Journal of Medicine, 310,* 824–829.

Starr, A., Amlie, R. N., Martin, W. H., & Sanders, S. (1977). Development of auditory function in newborn infants revealed by auditory brain stem potentials. *Pediatrics, 60,* 831.

Starr, B. D., & Weiner, M. B. (1981). *The Starr-Weiner report on sex and sexuality in the mature years.* New York: Stein & Day.

Staub, S. (1973). *The effect of three types of relationships on young children's memory for pictorial stimulus pairs.* Unpublished doctoral dissertation, Harvard University Graduate School of Education, Cambridge, MA.

Stearns, M. S., & Peterson, S. (1973). *Parent involvement in compensatory education programs: Definitions and findings.* Palo Alto, CA: Stanford Research Institute.

Stein, P. J. (1976, September 3). *Being single: Bucking the cultural impera-*

tive. Paper presented at the annual meeting of the American Sociological Association.

Steinberg, L. (1981). Transformations in family relations at puberty. *Developmental Psychology, 17*, 833–840.

Steinberg, L. (1986). Latchkey children and susceptibility to peer pressure: An ecological analysis. *Developmental Psychology, 22*(4), 433–439.

Steinberg, L. (1987). Single parents, stepparents, and the susceptibility of adolescents to antisocial peer pressure. *Child Development, 58*, 269–275.

Steinberg, L., & Silverberg, S. B. (1987). Influences on marital satisfaction during the middle stages of the family life cycle. *Journal of Marriage and the Family, 49*, 751–760.

Steiner, J. E. (1979). Human facial expressions in response to taste and smell stimulation. *Advances in Child Development and Behavior, 13*, 257.

Stenchever, M. A., Williamson, R. A., Leonard, J., Karp, L. E., Ley, B., Shy, K., & Smith, D. (1981). Possible relationship between in utero diethylstilbestrol exposure and male fertility. *American Journal of Obstetrics and Gynecology, 140*(2), 186–193.

Stern, D. (1977). *The first relationship: Infant and mother.* Cambridge, MA: Harvard University Press.

Sternberg, R. J. (1982). Who's intelligent? *Psychology Today, 16*(4), 30–39.

Sternberg, R. J. (1984, September). How can we teach intelligence? *Educational Leadership*, pp. 38–50.

Sternberg, R. J. (1985a). *Beyond IQ: A triarchic theory of human intelligence.* New York: Cambridge University Press.

Sternberg, R. J. (1985b, November). Teaching critical thinking, Part I: Are we making critical mistakes? *Phi Delta Kappan*, pp. 194–198.

Sternberg, R. J. (1986). *Intelligence applied: Understanding and increasing your intellectual skills.* San Diego: Harcourt Brace.

Sternberg, R. J. (1987, September 23). The uses and misuses of intelligence testing: Misunderstanding meaning, users over-rely on scores. *Education Week*, pp. 28, 22.

Sternglanz, S., & Lyberger-Ficek, S. (1975). *An analysis of sex differences in academic interactions in the college classroom.* Paper presented at the biennial meeting of the Society for Research in Child Development, Denver.

Sternglanz, S., & Serbin, L. (1974). Sex role stereotyping in children's

television programs. *Developmental Psychology, 10*, 710–715.

Sterns, H. L., Barrett, G. V., & Alexander, R. A. (1985). Accidents and the aging individual. In J. E. Birren & K. W. Schaie (Eds.), *Handbook of the psychology of aging.* New York: Van Nostrand Reinhold.

Stevens, J. H., & Bakeman, R. (1985). A factor analytic study of the HOME scale for infants. *Developmental Psychology, 21*(6), 1106–1203.

Stevenson, H. W., Stigler, J. W., Lee, S., Lucker, G. W., Kitamura, S., & Hsu, C. (1985). Cognitive performance and academic achievement of Japanese, Chinese, and American children. *Child Development, 56*, 718–734.

Stevenson, M., & Lamb, M. (1979). Effects of infant sociability and the caretaking environment on infant cognitive performance. *Child Development, 50*, 340–349.

Stewart, M. A., & Gath, A. (1978). *Psychological disorders of children.* Baltimore: Williams & Wilkins.

Stewart, M. A., & Olds, S. W. (1973). *Raising a hyperactive child.* New York: Harper & Row.

Stewart, R. B. (1983). Sibling attachment relationships: Child-infant interactions in the strange situation. *Developmental Psychology, 19*(2), 192–199.

Stewart, W. (1977). *A psychosocial study of the formation of the early adult life structure in women.* Unpublished doctoral dissertation, Columbia University, New York.

Stinnett, N., Carter, L., & Montgomery, J. (1972). Older persons' perceptions of their marriages. *Journal of Marriage and the Family, 34*, 665–670.

Stjernfeldt, M., Berglund, K., Lindsten, J., & Ludvigsson, J. (1986, June 14). Maternal smoking during pregnancy and risk of childhood cancer. *The Lancet*, pp. 1350–1352.

Stone, L. J., Smith, H. T., & Murphy, L. B. (1973). *The competent infant: Research and commentary.* New York: Basic Books.

Strauss, M., Lessen-Firestone, J., Starr, R., & Ostrea, E. (1975). Behavior of narcotics-addicted newborns. *Child Development, 46*, 887–893.

Streib, G. F., & Schneider, C. J. (1971). *Retirement in American society: Impact and process.* Ithaca, NY: Cornell University Press.

Streissguth, A. P., Martin, D. C., Barr, H. M., Sandman, B. M., Kirchner, G. L., & Darby, B. L. (1984). Intrauterine alcohol and nicotine expo-

sure: Attention and reaction time in 4-year-old children. *Developmental Psychology, 20*(4), 533–541.

Strickland, D. M., Saeed, S. A., Casey, M. L., & Mitchell, M. D. (1983). Article in *Science, 220*, 521–522.

Stuart, M. J., Gross, S. J., Elrad, H., & Graeber, J. E. (1982). Effects of acetylsalicylic-acid ingestion on maternal and neonatal hemostasis. *The New England Journal of Medicine, 307*, 909–912.

Stunkard, A. J., Foch, T. T., & Hrubec, Z. (1986). A twin study of human obesity. *Journal of the American Medical Association, 256*(1), 51–54.

Suitor, J. J., & Pillemer, K. (1987). The presence of adult children: A source of stress for elderly married couples? *Journal of Marriage and the Family, 49*, 717–725.

Sullivan, H. S. (1953). *The interpersonal theory of psychiatry.* New York: Norton.

Sullivan, M. W. (1982). Reactivation: Priming forgotten memories in infants. *Child Development, 53*, 516.

Summers, W. K., Majovski, L. V., Marsh, G. M., Tachiki, K., & Kling, A. (1986). Oral tetrahydroaminoacridine in long-term treatment of senile dementia, Alzheimer's type. *The New England Journal of Medicine, 315*(20), 1241–1245.

Suomi, S., & Harlow, H. (1972). Social rehabilitation of isolate-reared monkeys. *Developmental Psychology, 6*(3), 487–496.

Tabor, A., Philip, J., Madsen, M., Bang, J., Obel, E. B., & Norgaard-Pedersen, B. (1986, June 7). Randomized controlled trial of genetic amniocentesis in 4606 low-risk women. *The Lancet*, pp. 1287–1293.

Tager, I. B., Weiss, S. T., Munoz, A., Rosner, B., & Speizer, F. E. (1983). Longitudinal study of the effects of maternal smoking on pulmonary function in children. *The New England Journal of Medicine, 309*, 699–703.

Tanfer, K., & Horn, M. C. (1985). Contraceptive use, pregnancy and fertility patterns among single American women in their 20's. *Family Planning Perspectives, 17*(1), 10–19.

Tanner, J. M. (1973). Growing up. *Scientific American, 229*(3), 35–43.

Tanner, J. M. (1978). *Fetus into man: Physical growth from conception to maturity.* Cambridge, MA: Harvard University Press.

Targ, D. B. (1979). Toward a reassessment of women's experience at middle-age. *Family Coordinator*,

28(3), 377–382.

Tatelbaum, J. (1980). *The courage to grieve*. New York: Lippincott.

Tautermannova, M. (1973). Smiling in infants. *Child Development, 44*, 701–704.

Tavris, C., & Offer, C. (1977). *The longest war: Sex differences in perspective* (2d ed.). New York: Harcourt Brace.

Tellegren, A., Lykken, D. T., Bouchard, T. J., Wilcox, K. J., Segal, N. L., & Rich, S. (in press). Personality similarity in twins reared apart and together. *Journal of Personality and Social Psychology*.

Teller, D. Y., & Bornstein, M. H. (1987). Infant color vision and color perception. In P. Salapatek & L. B. Cohen (Eds.), *Handbook of infant perception: Vol. 1. From sensation to perception* (pp. 185–236). Orlando, FL: Academic.

Terkel, S. (1974). *Working*. New York: Random House.

Terman, L. M., & Oden, M. H. (1959). *Genetic studies of genius: Vol 5. The gifted group at mid-life*. Stanford, CA: Stanford University Press.

Thal, L. J., Fuld, P. A., Masur, D. M., & Sharpless, N. S. (1983). Oral psycostigmine and lechithin improve memory in Alzheimer disease. *Annals of Neurology, 13*, 491–496.

Thomas, A., & Chess, S. (1977). *Temperament and development*. New York: Brunner/Mazel.

Thomas, A., & Chess, S. (1984). Genesis and evolution of behavioral disorders: From infancy to early adult life. *American Journal of Orthopsychiatry, 141*(1), 1–9.

Thomas, A., Chess, S., & Birch, H. G. (1968). *Temperament and behavior disorders in children*. New York: New York University Press.

Thomas, D. (1985). The dynamics of teacher opposition to integration. *Remedial Education, 20*(2), 53–58.

Thomas, R. (1979). *Comparing theories of child development*. Belmont, CA: Wadsworth.

Thompson, A. P. (1983). Extramarital sex: A review of the research literature. *Journal of Sex Research, 19*(1), 1–22.

Thompson, R. A., Lamb, M. E., & Estes, D. (1982). Stability of infant-mother attachment and its relationship to changing life circumstances in an unselected middle-class sample. *Child Development, 53*, 144–148.

Thompson, S. K. (1975). Gender labels and early sex-role development. *Child Development, 46*, 339–347.

Tiger, L., & Shepher, J. (1975). *Women in the kibbutz*. New York: Harcourt Brace.

Timiras, P. S. (1972). *Developmental physiology and aging*. New York: Macmillan.

Timmons, F. (1978). Freshman withdrawal from college: A positive step toward identity formation? A follow-up study. *Journal of Youth and Adolescence, 7*(2), 159–173.

Tomasello, M., Mannle, S., & Kruger, A. C. (1986). Linguistic environment of 1- and 2-year-old twins. *Developmental Psychology, 22*(2), 169–176.

Tonkova-Yompol'skaya, R. V. (1973). Development of speech intonation in infants during the first two years of life. In C. A. Fergusin & D. Slobin (Eds.), *Studies of child language development*. New York: Holt.

Tribich, D., & Klein, M. (1981). On Freud's blindness. *Colloquium, 4*, 52–59.

Trickett, P. K., & Kuczynski, L. (1986). Children's misbehaviors and parental discipline strategies in abusive and nonabusive families. *Developmental Psychology, 22*(1), 115–123.

Troll, L. E. (1975). *Early and middle adulthood*. Monterey, CA: Brooks/Cole.

Troll, L. E. (1980). Grandparenting. In L. W. Poon (Ed.), *Aging in the 1980s*. Washington, DC: American Psychological Association.

Troll, L. E. (1983). Grandparents: The family watchdogs. In T. H. Brubaker (Ed.), *Family relationships in later life*. Beverly Hills, CA: Sage.

Troll, L. E. (1985). *Early and middle adulthood* (2d ed.). Monterey, CA: Brooks-Cole.

Troll, L. E. (1986). Parents and children in later life. *Generations, 10*(4), 23–25.

Troll, L. E., Miller, S., & Atchley, R. (1979). *Families in later life*. Belmont, CA: Wadsworth.

Troll, L. E., & Smith, J. (1976). Attachment through the life span. *Human Development, 3*, 156–171.

Tronick, E. (1972). Stimulus control and the growth of the infant's visual field. *Perception and Psychophysics, 11*, 373–375.

Tronick, E., & Field, T. (Eds.). (1986). Maternal depression and infant disturbance. In W. Damon (Ed.), *New directions for child development* (No. 34). San Francisco: Jossey-Bass.

Trotter, R. J. (1983). Baby face. *Psychology Today, 17*(8), 14–20.

Trotter, R. J. (1986). Profile: Robert J. Sternberg: Three heads are better than one. *Psychology Today, 20*(8), 56–62.

Trotter, R. J. (1987). You've come a long way, baby. *Psychology Today, 21*(5), 34–45.

Tsai, M., & Wagner, N. (1979). Incest and molestation: Problems of childhood sexuality. *Resident and Staff Physician*, 129–136.

Tuddenham, R. D. (1951). Studies in reputation: 3. Correlates of popularity among elementary school children. *Journal of Educational Psychology, 42*, 257–276.

Turkington, C. (1983, May). Child suicide: An unspoken tragedy. *APA Monitor*, p. 15.

Two women go to jail to protect another's cash. (1984, April 10). *The New York Times*, p. A19.

Uhlenberg, P., & Myers, M. A. P. (1981). Divorce and the elderly. *Gerontologist, 21*(3), 276–282.

Ungerer, J., Brody, L. R., & Zelazo, P. R. (1978). Long-term memory for speech in 2- to 4-week-old infants. *Infant Behavioral Development, 1*, 127.

Upjohn Company. (1983). The menopausal woman: An enlightened view. *Writer's guide to menopause*. Kalamazoo, MI: Author.

Upjohn Company. (1984). *Writer's guide to sex and health*. Kalamazoo, MI: Author.

U.S. Bureau of the Census. (1982). Statistics.

U.S. Bureau of the Census. (1983). *America in transition: An aging society* (Current Population Reports, Series P-23, No. 128). Washington, DC: U.S. Government Printing Office.

U.S. Bureau of the Census. (1984). *Marital status and living arrangements: March 1983* (Current Population Reports: Population characteristics, Series P-20, No. 389). Washington, DC: U.S. Government Printing Office.

U.S. Bureau of the Census. (1985). Statistics.

U.S. Bureau of the Census. (1986). Statistics.

U.S. Bureau of the Census. (1987). *Who's minding the kids? Child care arrangements: Winter 1984–85* (Current population reports: Household economic studies, Series P-70, No.9). Washington, DC: U.S. Government Printing Office.

U.S. Department of Education. (1986a). *Participation in adult education, May, 1984* (Office of Educational Research and Improvement Bulletin CS 86–308B). Washington, DC: Center for Education Statistics.

U.S. Department of Education. (1986b). *What works: Research about reading and learning*. Washington, DC: Office of Educational Research and Improvement. (Available from What Works, Pueblo, CO 81009)

U.S. Department of Education. (1987a). *Bachelor's and higher de-*

grees awarded in 1984–85 (Office of Educational Research and Improvement Bulletin CS 87–329B). Washington, DC: Center for Education Statistics.

U.S. Department of Education. (1987b). Enrollment in colleges and universities, Fall 1985 (Office of Educational Research and Improvement Bulletin CS 87–311B). Washington, DC: Center for Education Statistics.

U.S. Department of Education. (1987c). Transition from high school to postsecondary education: Analytical studies (Office of Educational Research and Improvement Publication No. CS 87–309C). Washington, DC: U.S. Government Printing Office.

U.S. Department of Health, Education, and Welfare (USDHEW). (1976). Health, United States, 1975 (DHEW Publication No. HRA 76–1232). Rockville, MD: National Center for Health Statistics.

U.S. Department of Health and Human Services (USDHHS). (1980). The status of children, youth, and families, 1979 (DHHS Publication No. OHDS 80–30274). Washington, DC: U.S. Government Printing Office.

U.S. Department of Health and Human Services (USDHHS). (1981a). The prevalence of dental caries in U.S. children, 1979–1980. Survey (NIH Publication No. 82–2245). Washington, DC: U.S. Government Printing Office.

U.S. Department of Health and Human Services (USDHHS). (1981b). Statistics on incidence of depression.

U.S. Department of Health and Human Services (USDHHS). (1982). Prevention '82 (DHHS [PHS] Publication No. 82–50157). Washington, DC: U.S. Government Printing Office.

U.S. Department of Health and Human Services (USDHHS). (1983). Health: United States. Washington, DC: U.S. Government Printing Office.

U.S. Department of Health and Human Services (USDHHS). (1984). Child sexual abuse prevention: Tips to parents. Washington, DC: Office of Human Development Services, Administration for Children, Youth, and Families. National Center on Child Abuse and Neglect.

U.S. Department of Health and Human Services (USDHHS). (1985). Health, United States, 1985. (DHHS Publication No. PHS 86–1232). Washington, DC: U.S. Government Printing Office.

U.S. Department of Health and Human Services (USDHHS). (1986). Health, United States, 1986 and Prevention Profile (DDH Publication No. PHS 87–1232). Washington, DC: U.S. Government Printing Office.

U.S. Department of Health and Human Services (USDHHS). (1987). Smoking and health: A national status report (HHS/PHS/CDC Publication No. 87–8396). Washington, DC: U.S. Government Printing Office.

U.S. Department of Health and Human Services (USDHHS). (1988, June 21). HHS News.

U.S. Department of Justice, Federal Bureau of Investigation (FBI). (1986, December). Age-specific arrest rates and race-specific arrest rates for selected offenses 1965–1985. Uniform Crime Reporting Program. Washington, DC: U.S. Government Printing Office.

U.S. Department of Justice, Federal Bureau of Investigation (FBI). (1987, July 25). Press release on crimes in 1986.

U.S. Department of Labor. (1985). Employed persons by major occupational groups and sex. Statistics. Washington, DC: U.S. Government Printing Office.

Uzgiris, I. C. (1972). Patterns of cognitive development in infancy. Merrill-Palmer Institute Conference on Infant Development, Detroit.

Uzgiris, I. C., & Hunt, J. (1975). Assessment in infancy. Urbana: University of Illinois Press.

Vachon, M., Lyall, W., Rogers, J., Freedmen-Letofky, K., & Freeman, S. (1980). A controlled study of self-help intervention for widows. American Journal of Psychiatry, 137(11), 1380–1384.

Vaillant, G. E. (1977). Adaptation to life. Boston: Little, Brown.

Valdes-Dapena, M. (1980). Sudden infant death syndrome: A review of the medical literature, 1974–1979. Pediatrics, 66(4), 597–614.

Valentine, D. P. (1982). The experience of pregnancy: A developmental process. Family Relations, 31(2), 243–248.

Vandenberg, S. G. (1967). Hereditary factors in normal personality traits (as measured by inventories) (1965). In J. Wortes (Ed.), Recent advances in biological psychiatry (Vol. 9, pp. 65–104). New York: Plenum.

Vaughan, V., McKay, R. J., & Behrman, R. (1979). Nelson textbook of pediatrics (11th ed.). Philadelphia: Saunders.

Verbrugge, L. (1979). Marital status and health. Journal of Marriage and the Family, 41, 467–485.

Vinick, B. (1978). Remarriage in old age. Family Coordinator, 27(4), 359–363.

Visher, E., & Visher, J. (1983). Stepparenting: Blending families. In H. I. McCubbin & C. R. Figley (Eds.), Stress and the family: Vol 1. Coping with normative transitions. New York: Brunner/Mazel.

Voydanoff, P. (1983). Unemployment: Family strategies for adaptation. In C. R. Figley & H. I. McCubbin (Eds.), Stress and the family: Vol II. Coping with catastrophe. New York: Brunner/Mazel.

Vuori, L., Christiansen, N., Clement, J., Mora, J., Wagner, M., & Herrera, M. (1979). Nutritional supplementation and the outcome of pregnancy: 2. Visual habituation at 15 days. Journal of Clinical Nutrition, 32, 463–469.

Vygotsky, L. S. (1962). Thought and language. Cambridge, MA: Massachusetts Institute of Technology (MIT) Press.

Wachs, T. (1975). Relation of infants' performance on Piaget's scales between 12 and 24 months and their Stanford Binet performance at 31 months. Child Development, 46, 929–935.

Wagner, R. K., & Sternberg, R. J. (1986). Tacit knowledge and intelligence in the everyday world. In R. J. Sternberg & R. K. Wagner (Eds.), Practical intelligence: Nature and origins of competence in the everyday world. Cambridge: Cambridge University Press.

Wald, E. R., Dashevsky, B., Byers, C., Guerra, N., & Taylor, F. (1988). Frequency and severity of infections in day care. Journal of Pediatrics, 112, 540–546.

Waldrop, M., & Halverson, C. (1975). Intensive and extensive peer behavior: Longitudinal and cross-sectional analyses. Child Development, 46, 19–26.

Walker, L. J. (1984). Sex differences in the development of moral reasoning: A critical review. Child Development, 55, 677–691.

Wallach, M. A., & Kogan, N. (1965). Modes of thinking in young children: A study of the creativity-intelligence distinction. New York: Holt.

Wallach, M. A., & Kogan, N. (1967). Creativity and intelligence in children's thinking. Transaction, 4(1), 38–43.

Wallerstein, J. S. (1983). Children of divorce: The psychological tasks of the child. American Journal of Orthopsychiatry, 53(2), 230–243.

Wallerstein, J. S., & Kelly, J. B. (1980). Surviving the break-up: How children actually cope with divorce. New York: Basic Books.

Walster, E., & Walster, G. W. (1978).

A new look at love. Cambridge, MA: Addison-Wesley.

Wasserman, A. L. (1984). A prospective study of the impact of home monitoring on the family. *Pediatrics, 74,* 323–329.

Watson, J. B. (1919). *Psychology from the standpoint of a behaviorist.* Philadelphia: Lippincott.

Watson, J. B., & Rayner, R. (1920). Conditioned emotional reactions. *Journal of Experimental Psychology, 3,* 1–14.

Watson, R. E. L. (1983). Premarital cohabitation vs. traditional courtship: Their effects on subsequent marital adjustment. *Family Relations, 32*(1), 139–147.

Wayler, A. H., Kapur, K. K., Feldman, R. S., & Chauncey, H. H. (1982). Effects of age and dentition status on measures of food acceptability. *Journal of Gerontology, 37*(3), 294–299.

Webb, W. B., & Bonnet, M. (1979). Sleep and dreams. In M. E. Meyer (Ed.), *Foundations of contemporary psychology.* New York: Oxford University Press.

Weenolsen, P. (1988). *The transcendence of loss over the life span.* New York: Harper & Row.

Weg, R. (1987). Menopause: Biomedical aspects. In G. L. Maddox (Ed.), *The encyclopedia of aging* (pp. 433–437). New York: Springer.

Wegman, M. E. (1983). Annual summary of vital statistics—1982. *Pediatrics, 72*(6), 755–764.

Wegman, M. E. (1986). Annual summary of vital statistics—1985. *Pediatrics, 78*(6), 983–994.

Weiffenback, J., & Thach, B. (1975). *Taste receptors in the tongue of the newborn human: Behavioral evidence.* Paper presented at the meeting of the Society for Research in Child Development, Denver.

Weiss, L., & Lowenthal, M. (1975). Life-course perspectives on friendship. In M. Lowenthal, M. Thurner, & D. Chiriboga (Eds.), *Four stages of life.* San Francisco: Jossey-Bass.

Weitkamp, L. R., & Schacter, B. Z. (1985). Transferrin and HLA: Spontaneous abortion, neural tube defects, and natural selection. *The New England Journal of Medicine, 313*(15), 925–932.

Weitzman, L., Eifler, D., Hokada, E., & Ross, C. (1972). Sex-role socialization in picture books for preschool children. *Journal of Sociology, 77*(6), 1125–1150.

Wellman, H., & Lempers, J. (1977). The naturalistic communicative abilities of two-year-olds. *Child Development, 48,* 1052–1057.

Werner, E. E. (1985). Stress and protective factors in children's lives. In A. R. Nichol (Ed.), *Longitudinal studies in child psychology and psychiatry.* New York: Wiley.

Werner, E. E., Bierman, L., French, F. E., Simonian, K., Connor, A., Smith, R., & Campbell, M. (1968). Reproductive and environmental casualties: A report on the 10-year follow-up of the children of the Kauai pregnancy study. *Pediatrics, 42*(1), 112–127.

Werner, J. S., & Siqueland, E. R. (1978). Visual recognition memory in the preterm infant. *Infant Behavior and Development, 1,* 79–94.

Werts, C. E. (1966). Social class and initial career choice of college freshmen. *Sociology of Education, 39,* 74–85.

Werts, C. E. (1968). Paternal influence on career choice. *Journal of Counseling Psychology, 15,* 48–52.

West Berlin Human Genetics Institute. (1987). Study on effects of nuclear radiation at Chernobyl on fetal development.

Whisnant, L., & Zegans, L. (1975). A study of attitudes toward menarche in white middle class American adolescent girls. *American Journal of Psychiatry, 132*(8), 809–814.

White, B. L. (1971, October). *Fundamental early environmental influences on the development of competence.* Paper presented at the Third Western Symposium on Learning: Cognitive Learning, Western Washington State College, Bellingham, WA.

White, B. L. (1975). *The first three years of life.* Englewood Cliffs, NJ: Prentice-Hall.

White, B. L., Kaban, B., & Attanucci, J. (1979). *The origins of human competence.* Lexington, MA: Heath.

White, K. R. (1982). The relation between socioeconomic status and academic achievement. *Psychological Bulletin, 91*(3), 461–481.

White House Conference on Aging. (1971). *Aging and blindness.* Special Concerns Session Report. Washington, DC: U.S. Government Printing Office.

Wideman, M. V., & Singer, J. F. (1984). The role of psychological mechanisms in preparation for childbirth. *American Psychologist, 34,* 1357–1371.

Williams, E. R., & Caliendo, M. A. (1984). *Nutrition: Principles, issues, and applications.* New York: McGraw-Hill.

Williams, J., Best, D., & Boswell, D. (1975). The measurement of children's racial attitudes in the early school years. *Child Development, 46,* 494–500.

Williams, R. B., Barefoot, J. C., & Shekelle, R. B. (1984). The health consequences of hostility. In M. A. Chesney, S. E. Goldston, & R. H. Rosenman (Eds.), *Anger: Hostility and behavior medicine.* New York: Hemisphere/McGraw-Hill.

Willis, S. L. (1985). Towards an educational psychology of the older adult learner: Intellectual and cognitive bases. In J. E. Birren & K. W. Schaie (Eds.), *Handbook of the psychology of aging.* (2d ed.). New York: Van Nostrand Reinhold.

Willis, S. L., & Baltes, P. B. (1980). Intelligence in adulthood and aging. In L. W. Poon (Ed.), *Aging in the 1980s.* Washington, DC: American Psychological Association.

Willis, S. L., Blieszner, R., & Baltes, P. B. (1981). Intellectual training research in aging: Modification of performance on the fluid ability of figural relations. *Journal of Educational Psychology, 73,* 41–50.

Wilson, G., McCreary, R., Kean, J., & Baxter, J. (1979). The development of preschool children of heroin-addicted mothers: A controlled study. *Pediatrics, 63*(1), 135–141.

Wilson, R. S. (1983). The Louisville twin study: Developmental synchronies in behavior. *Child Development, 54,* 298–316.

Winick, M. (1981, January). Food and the fetus. *Natural History,* pp. 16–81.

Winick, M., Brasel, J., & Rosso, P. (1972). Nutrition and cell growth. In M. Winick (Ed.), *Nutrition and development.* New York: Wiley.

Wittrock, M. C. (1980). Learning and the brain. In M. C. Wittrock (Ed.), *The brain and psychology.* New York: Academic.

Wolfe, D. A. (1985). Child-abusive parents: An empirical review and analysis. *Psychological Bulletin, 97*(3), 462–482.

Wolff, P. H. (1963). Observations on the early development of smiling. In B. M. Foss (Ed.), *Determinants of infant behavior* (Vol. 2). London: Methuen.

Wolff, P. H. (1966). The causes, controls, and organizations of behavior in the newborn. *Psychological Issues, 5*(1, Whole No. 17), 1–105.

Wolff, P. H. (1969). The natural history of crying and other vocalizations in early infancy. In B. M. Foss (Ed.), *Determinants of infant behavior* (Vol. 4). London: Methuen.

Wood, D., McMahon, L., & Cranstoun, Y. (1980). *Working with under fives.* Ypsilanti, MI: High/Scope.

Woodruff, D. S. (1985). Arousal, sleep and aging. In J. E. Birren & K. W. Schaie (Eds.), *Handbook of the psychology of aging.* New York: Van Nostrand Reinhold.

Working Women Education Fund. (1981). *Health hazards for office workers.* Cleveland, OH: Author.

Wright, J. T., Waterson, E. J., Barrison, I. G., Toplis, P. J., Lewis, I. G., Gordon, M. G., MacRae, K. D., Morris, N. F., & Murray Lyon, I. M. (1983, March 26). Alcohol consumption, pregnancy, and low birthweight. *The Lancet,* pp. 663–665.

Yager, J. (1982). Family issues in the pathogenesis of anorexia nervosa. *Psychosomatic Medicine,* 44(1), 43–60.

Yarrow, L. (1961). Maternal deprivation: Toward an empirical and conceptual reevaluation. *Psychological Bulletin,* 58, 459–490.

Yarrow, M. R. (1978, October 31). *Altruism in children.* Paper presented at the program, Advances in Child Development Research, New York Academy of Sciences, New York.

Yllo, K., & Straus, M. A. (1981). Interpersonal violence among married and cohabiting couples. *Family Relations,* 30, 339–347.

Yogman, M. J., Dixon, S., Tronick, E., Als, H., & Brazelton, T. B. (1977, March). *The goals and structure of face-to-face interaction between infants and their fathers.* Paper presented at the meeting of the Society for Research in Child Development, New Orleans.

York, J. L., & Calsyn, R. J. (1977).

Family involvement in nursing homes. *Gerontologist,* 17(6), 500–505.

Young, K. T., & Zigler, E. (1986). Infant and toddler day care: Regulations and policy implications. *American Journal of Orthopsychiatry,* 56(1), 43–55.

Youniss, J., & Volpe, J. (1978). A relational analysis of children's friendship. In W. Damon (Ed.), *Social cognition* (pp. 1–22). San Francisco: Jossey-Bass.

Zabin, L. S., Hirsch, M. B., Smith, E. A., & Hardy, J. B. (1984). Adolescent sexual attitudes and behavior: Are they consistent? *Family Planning Perspectives,* 15, 16, 185.

Zabin, L. S., Kantner, J. F., & Zelnik, M. (1979). The risk of adolescent pregnancy in the first months of intercourse. *Family Planning Perspectives,* 11(4), 215–222.

Zakariya, S. B. (1982, September). Another look at the children of divorce: Summary report of the study of school needs of one-parent children. *Principal,* pp. 34–37.

Zelazo, P. R. (1981). An information-processing approach to infant cognitive assessment. In *Developmental disabilities in preschool children.* Englewood Cliffs, NJ: Spectrum.

Zelazo, P. R., Kotelchuck, M., Barber, L., & David, J. (1977, March). *Fathers and sons: An experimental facilitation of attachment behaviors.* Paper presented at the meeting of the Society for Research in Child Development, New Orleans.

Zelnik, M., Kantner, J. F., & Ford, K. (1981). *Sex and pregnancy in adolescence.* Beverly Hills: CA: Sage.

Zelnik, M., & Shah, F. K. (1983). First

intercourse among young Americans. *Family Planning Perspectives,* 15(2), 64–72.

Zeskind, P. S., & Iacino, R. (1984). Effects of maternal visitation to preterm infants in the neonatal intensive care unit. *Child Development,* 55, 1887–1893.

Zeskind, P. S., & Ramey, C. T. (1981). Preventing intellectual and interactional sequelae of fetal malnutrition: A longitudinal, transactional, and synergistic approach to development. *Child Development,* 52, 213–218.

Zimbardo, P., Andersen, S., & Kabat, L. (1981). Induced hearing deficit generates experimental paranoia. *Science,* 212(26), 1529–1531.

Zimberg, S. (1982). Psychotherapy in the treatment of alcoholism. In E. M. Pattison & E. Kaufman (Eds.), *Encyclopedia handbook of alcoholism.* New York: Gardner.

Zimmerman, I. L., & Bernstein, M. (1983). Parental work patterns in alternate families: Influence on child development. *American Journal of Orthopsychiatry,* 53(3), 418–425.

Zopf, P. E. (1986). *America's older population.* Houston, TX: Cap and Gown Press.

Zube, M. (1982). Changing behavior and outlook of aging men and women: Implications for marriage in the middle and later years. *Family Relations,* 31(1), 147–156.

Zuckerman, B. S., & Beardslee, W. R. (1987). Maternal depression: A concern for pediatricians. *Pediatrics,* 79(1), 110–117.

Zuckerman, D. M., & Zuckerman, B. S. (1985). Television's impact on children. *Pediatrics,* 75(2), 233–240.

ACKNOWLEDGMENTS

PART-OPENING ART

Part One: Will Barnet, *Elena and Ona* (1961). Three Lions/Photo Source.

Part Two: Pierre-Auguste Renoir, *Gabrielle and Jean*. Art Resource.

Part Three: Diego Rivera, *Muchacho Mexicano*. Three Lions/Photo Source.

Part Four: Theodore Robinson, *The Girl with the Dog* (c. 1880). Cincinnati Art Museum, gift of Mrs. A. M. Adler.

Part Five: Mary Cassatt, *Girl Arranging Her Hair* (1886). National Gallery of Art, Washington, DC, Chester Dale Collection.

Part Six: Pablo Picasso, *The Reading of the Letter* (1921). Art Resource.

Part Seven: Will Barnet, *Self-Portrait* (1966). Museum of Fine Arts, Boston, anonymous gift.

Part Eight: Laura Wheeler Waring, *Anna Washington Derry* (1927). National Museum of American Art, Smithsonian Institution, gift of the Harmon Foundation.

Part Nine: Georges de la Tour, *Magdalena with Lamp*. Three Lions/Photo Source.

CHAPTER 1

Chapter-opening photograph: © Michael Philip Mannheim/Stock Market.

Figures

Figure 1-3: Maslow, A. (1954). *Motivation and personality* (3d ed.). Revised by Robert Frazer et al. Copyright 1954, 1987 by Harper & Row, Publishers, Inc. Copyright © 1970 by Abraham Maslow. Reprinted by permission.

CHAPTER 2

Chapter-opening photograph: © Chris Clarke/Photo Researchers.

Chapter-opening quotation: Sexton, Anne (1966). Little girl, my string bean, my lovely woman. In *Live or die.* Copyright © 1966 by Anne Sexton. Reprinted by permission of Houghton Mifflin Company.

Boxes

Box 2-4: Eisenberg, A., Murkoff, H. E., & Hathaway, S. E. (1984). *What to expect when you're expecting.* Copyright © by A. Eisenberg, H. E. Murkoff, & S. E. Hathaway. Reprinted by permission of Workman Publishing. All rights reserved.

Figures

Figures 2-6, 2-7, and 2-8: March of Dimes Birth Defects Foundation.

(1987). *Genetic counseling: A public health information booklet* (rev. ed.) Adapted by permission.

Figure 2-11: Fuchs, F. (1986). Genetic amniocentesis. *Scientific American, 242*(6), 47–53. Copyright © 1980 by Scientific American, Inc. All rights reserved. Adapted by permission.

Figures 2-12 and 2-13: Lagercrantz, H., & Slotkin, T. A. (1986). The stress of being born. *Scientific American, 245*(40), 104–105. Copyright © 1986 by Scientific American, Inc. All rights reserved. Adapted by permission.

Figure 2-14: By permission of Everett Davidson.

Tables

Table 2-1: Nilsson, L. (1977). *A child is born* (2d ed.) New York: Dell.

Photos on pages 60–61: 4-week-old fetus, 3-month-old fetus, and 5-month-old fetus—© Lennart Nilsson, *A Child Is Born*; English translation © 1966, 1977 by Dell Publishing Company, Inc. 4-month-old fetus—© Lennart Nilsson, *Behold Man*; English translation © by Albert Bonniers Forlag, Stockholm. 7-month birth—© Petit Format/Nestle/Science Source/Photo Researchers, Inc.

Quotations in Text

Page 55: Definition of *personality.* Copyright © 1985 by Houghton

Mifflin Company. Reprinted by permission from *The American Heritage Dictionary*, 2d College Edition.

CHAPTER 3

Chapter-opening photograph: © Mimi Cotter/International Stock Photo.

Chapter-opening quotation: Fraiberg, Selma. (1959). *The magic years*. Copyright © 1959 by Selma Fraiberg.

Figures

Figure 3-1: Restak, R. (1984). *The brain*. Copyright © 1984 by Educational Broadcasting Company and Richard M. Restak, M.D. Reprinted by permission of Bantam Books. All rights reserved.

Figure 3-2: Brown, J. L. (1987). Hunger in the United States. *Scientific American*, *256*(2), 37–41. Copyright © 1987 by Scientific American. All rights reserved.

Tables

Table 3-1: Timiras, P. S. (1972). *Developmental physiology and aging*. Copyright © 1972 by P. S. Timiras. Reprinted by permission of Macmillan Publishing Company.

Table 3-3: Apgar, V. (1953). A proposal for a new method of evaluation of the newborn infant. *Current Researches in Anesthesia and Analgesia*, *32*, 260–267. Reprinted by permission of International Anesthesia Research Society.

Table 3-4: Brown, S. S. (1985). Can low birth weight be prevented? *Family Planning Perspectives*, *17*(3). Adapted by permission of Alan Guttmacher Institute and the author.

Table 3-6: Denver Developmental Materials, Inc. (1969). *Denver Developmental Screening Test*. Copyright © 1969, William K. Frankenburg, M.D., & Josiah B. Dodds, Ph.D., University of Colorado Medical Center. Adapted by permission.

CHAPTER 4

Chapter-opening photograph: Suzanne Szasz/Photo Researchers.

Figures

Figure 4-1: Fagan, J. F. (1982). Infant memory. In Field, T. M., Huston, A.,

Quay, H., Troll, L., & Finley, G. (Eds.), *Review of human development*. Copyright © 1982. Reprinted by permission of John Wiley & Sons, Inc.

Tables

Table 4-2: Lenneberg, E. H. (1969). On explaining language. *Science*, *164*(3880), 635–643. Copyright 1969 by American Association for the Advancement of Science.

CHAPTER 5

Chapter-opening photograph: © Marie Taglienti/Image Bank.

Chapter-opening quotation: Hartford, John. (1971). Life prayer. In *Word movies*. Copyright © 1968 by Ensign Music Corporation.

Photograph on page 180: Henry Francis Du Pont Winterthur Museum, Joseph Downs Collection, no. 71x247.13.

Figures

Figure 5-1: Used by permission of American Humane Association.

Tables

Table 5-1: Sroufe, L. A. (1979). Socioemotional development. In Osofsky, J. (Ed.), *Handbook of infant development*. Copyright © 1979. Reprinted by permission of John Wiley & Sons, Inc.

Table 5-2: Trotter, R. J. (1983). Baby face. *Psychology Today*, *17*(8), 14–20. Copyright © 1983 by American Psychological Association. Reprinted by permission.

Table 5-3: Thomas, A., & Chess, S. (1984). Genesis and evolution of behavioral disorders: From infancy to early adult life. *American Journal of Psychiatry*, *141*(1), 1–9. Copyright © 1984 American Psychiatric Association. Adapted by permission.

Quotations in Text

Page 151: Erikson, E. H. (1950). *Childhood and society*. Copyright 1950, © 1963, W. W. Norton & Company, Inc. Reprinted by permission.

CHAPTER 6

Chapter-opening photograph: © George E. Jones III/Photo Researchers.

Chapter-opening quotation: From the Danish poet Adam G. Oehlenschlager, 1779–1850.

Figures

Figure 6-1: Brown, J. L. (1987). Hunger in the United States. *Scientific American*, *256*(2), 37–41. Copyright © 1987 by Scientific American, Inc. All rights reserved.

Figure 6-3: Gelman, R., Bullock, M., & Meck, E. (1980). Preschoolers' understanding of simple object transformations. *Child Development*, *51*, 691–699. © Society for Research in Child Development, Inc.

Figure 6-5: Field, D. (1977). The importance of the verbal content in the training of Piagetian conservation skills. *Child Development*, *52*, 326–334. © Society for Research in Child Development, Inc.

Tables

Table 6-1: Corbin, C. B. (1973). *A textbook of motor development*. © 1973 by William C. Brown Publishers, Dubuque, Iowa. All rights reserved. Adapted by permission.

Table 6-2: Bolles, E. B. (1982). *So much to say*, p. 93. Copyright © 1982 by Edmund Blair Bolles. Published by St. Martin's Press, Inc.

CHAPTER 7

Chapter-opening photograph: © Lowell Georgia/Photo Researchers.

CHAPTER 8

Chapter-opening photograph: © Lawrence Migdale 1986/Photo Researchers.

Chapter-opening quotation: Mead, Margaret. (1971). *Family*. Reprinted by permission of Institute for Intercultural Studies.

Photograph on page 294: Watercolor by Carmontelle; reproduced by permission of the Trustees, National Gallery, London.

Figures

Figure 8-1: Wallach, M. A., & Kozar, N. (1967). Creativity and intelligence in children's thinking. *Transaction, 4*(1), 38–43. Copyright © 1967 by Transaction, Inc. Reprinted by permission.

Tables

Table 8-1: Cratty, B. J. (1979). *Perceptual and motor development in infants and children* (2d ed.), p. 222. © 1979. Reprinted by permission of Prentice-Hall, Inc., Englewood Cliffs, New Jersey.

Table 8-2: Kohlberg, L. (1964). The development of moral character and moral ideology. In Hoffman, M., & Hoffman, L. (Eds.), *Review of child development research, 1.* © 1964 by Russell Sage Foundation. Adapted by permission.

CHAPTER 9

Chapter-opening photograph: © 1982 Mark Bolster/International Stock Photo.

Chapter-opening quotation: Nash, Ogden. (1956). The absentees. In *Verses from 1929 on.* Copyright 1942 by Ogden Nash. First appeared in *The Saturday Evening Post.* Reprinted by permission of Little, Brown & Company.

Boxes

Box 9-3: Olds, S. W. (1980, June 10). When parents divorce. *Woman's Day,* 70, 108, 110. Adapted by permission of *Woman's Day* and Julian Bach, agent for the author.

Tables

Table 9-1: Chance, P., & Fischman, J. (1987). The magic of childhood. *Psychology Today, 21*(5), 48–58. Copyright © 1987 American Psychological Association. Reprinted by permission. Data from Institute for Social Research. (1985). How children use time. *Time, goods, and well-being.* Reprinted by permission of J. Eccles et al.

Quotations in Text

Page 305: Erikson, E. H. (1950, 1963). *Childhood and society.* Copyright 1950, © 1963, W. W. Norton & Company, Inc. Reprinted by permission.

Page 304: Hartley, R. E. (1959). Sex role pressures and the socialization of the male child. *Psychological Reports,* 5, 457–468. Reprinted by permission of the author and publisher.

CHAPTER 10

Chapter-opening photograph: © Melchior DiGiacomo/Image Bank.

Chapter-opening quotation: Frank, Anne. (1952). *The diary of a young girl.* Copyright 1952 by Otto H. Frank, 1952 by American Jewish Committee.

Quotations in Text

Page 360: Peel, E. A. (1967). *The psychological basis of education* (2d ed.). Reprinted by permission of the author.

CHAPTER 11

Chapter-opening photograph: © 1986 John Lawler/Stock Market.

Chapter-opening quotation: Barr, Donald. (1967). What did we do wrong? *The New York Times.* Copyright © 1967 by The New York Times Company.

Boxes

Box 11-3: Gordon, S., & Everly, K. (1985). Increasing self-esteem in vulnerable students: A tool for reducing pregnancy among teenagers. *Impact '85.* Copyright 1985 by S. Gordon, Institute for Family Research and Education, Syracuse University.

Figures

Figures 11-1, 11-2, and 11-3: Csikszentmihalyi, M., & Larson, R. (1984). *Being adolescent: Conflict and growth in the teenage years.* Copyright © 1984 by Basic Books, Inc., Publishers. Reprinted by permission.

Tables

Table 11-1: Marcia, J. E. (1980). Identity in adolescence. In Adelson, J. (Ed.), *Handbook of adolescent psychology.* Copyright © 1980. Reprinted by permission of John Wiley & Sons, Inc.

Table 11-2: Marcia, J. E. (1966). Development and validation of ego identity status. *Journal of Personality and Social Psychology, 3*(5), 551–558. Copyright 1966 by American Psychological Association. Adapted by permission of the author.

Table 11-4: Otto, H., & Healy, S. (1966). Adolescents' self-perception of personality strengths. *Journal of Human Relations, 14*(3), 483–490. Adapted by permission.

CHAPTER 12

Chapter-opening photograph: © Craig Aurness 1984/Woodfin Camp.

Chapter-opening quotation: *Diary of Anaïs Nin, 1931–1934.* (1978). New York: Harcourt Brace Jovanovich.

Figures

Figure 12-1: *Raven Standard Progressive Matrices,* A5. Reprinted by permission of J. C. Raven, Ltd.

Figure 12-2: Horn, J., & Donaldson, G. (1980). Cognitive development II: Adulthood development of human abilities. In Brim, O. G., & Kagan, J. (Eds.), *Constancy and change in human development.* Reprinted by permission of Harvard University Press.

Figure 12-3: Schaie, K. W. (1977–1978). Toward a stage theory of adult cognitive development. *International Journal of Aging and Human Development, 8*(2), 129–138. © 1977–1978 by Baywood Publishing Company, Inc.

Figure 12-4: Reprinted by permission of Associated Press.

Figure 12-5: Bianchi, S. M., & Spain, D. (1986). *American women in transition.* Copyright 1986 by Russell Sage Foundation. Reprinted by permission.

Tables

Table 12-2: Kohlberg, L. (1968). The child as a moral philosopher. *Psychology Today, 2*(4), 25–30. Copyright © 1968 by American Psychology Association. Adapted by permission.

CHAPTER 13

Chapter-opening photograph: © Sepp Seitz 1984/Woodfin Camp.

Chapter-opening quotation: Fromm, Erich. (1955). *The sane society.* New York: Holt, Rinehart & Winston.

Boxes

Box 13-2: Olds, S. W. (1986). *The working parents' survival guide.* Copyright © 1978, 1979, 1980, 1982, 1983 by Sally Wendkos Olds. Adapted by permission of Bantam Books, Inc. All rights reserved.

Figures

Figure 13-1: Levinson, D. J. (1986). A conception of adult development. *American Psychologist, 41*(1), 3–13. Reprinted by permission.

Tables

Table 13-2: Passuth, P., Maines, D., & Neugarten, B. L. (1984). In Rosenfeld, A., & Stark, E. (1987), The prime of our lives. *Psychology Today, 21*(May), 62–64, 66, 68–72. Copyright © 1987 by American Psychological Association. Adapted by permission.

CHAPTER 14

Chapter-opening photograph: © Gabe Palmer/Stock Market.
Chapter-opening quotation: Lindbergh, A. M. (1955). *Gift from the sea.* Copyright © 1955 by Anne Morrow Lindbergh. Reprinted by permission of Pantheon Books, a division of Random House, Inc.

Figures

Figure 14-1: Notelovitz, M., & Ware, M. (1982). *Stand tall: The informed woman's guide to preventing osteoporosis.* Illustration © 1982 by Triad Publishing Company.
Figure 14-2: Bolles, R. N. (1979). *The three boxes of life.* Copyright © 1978, 1981 by Richard N. Bolles. Published by Ten Speed Press, Berkeley, California. Adapted by permission.

Tables

Table 14-1: Working Women Education Fund. (1981). *Warning! Health hazards for office workers.* Copyright 1981 by Working Women Education Fund, Cleveland, Ohio. Adapted by permission.

CHAPTER 15

Chapter-opening photograph: © Adamsmith Productions/Woodfin Camp.
Chapter-opening quotation: Hughes, L. (1951). Montage of a dream deferred. *The panther and the lash.* Copyright 1951 by Langston Hughes. Reprinted by permission of Alfred A. Knopf, Inc.

Tables

Table 15-2: Lauer, J., & Lauer, R. (1985). Marriages made to last. *Psychology Today, 19*(60), 22–26. Copyright © 1985 American Psychological Association. Reprinted by permission.

Quotations in Text

Pages 506, 508: Erikson, E. (1985). *The last stage: The life cycle completed.* Reprinted by permission of W. W. Norton & Company, Inc.

CHAPTER 16

Chapter-opening photograph: © Sybil Shelton/Peter Arnold.
Chapter-opening quotation: Skinner, B. G., & Vaughan, M. E. (1938). *Enjoy old age.* New York: Appleton-Century-Crofts.

CHAPTER 17

Chapter-opening photograph: © Junebug Clark/Photo Researchers.
Chapter-opening quotation: Duskin, Rita. (1987). Haiku. In *Sound and light.* Copyright 1987 Ruth Duskin Feldman and Bunny L. Shuch.

Boxes

Box 17-2: Adapted in part from David, B. W. (1985). *Visits to remember: A handbook for visitors of nursing home residents.* Adapted by permission of Pennsylvania State University Cooperative Extension Service. Adapted in part from Ferber, A. (1985). Personal communication to S. W. Olds.

Quotations in Text

Page 565: Stair, N. (Undated). Course materials for Colorado Outward Bound School. Reprinted by permission.
Pages 580–581: Vinick, B. (1978). Remarriage in old age. *Family Coordinator, 27*(4), 359–363. Copyright 1978 by National Council on Family Relations, St. Paul, Minnesota. Reprinted by permission.

CHAPTER 18

Chapter-opening photograph: © Dennis Stock/Magnum.
Chapter-opening quotation: Kübler-Ross, Elisabeth. (1975). *Death: The final stage of growth.* Copyright © 1975 by Elisabeth Kübler-Ross. Reprinted by permission of Simon & Schuster, Inc.

Boxes

Box 18-2: Concern for Dying. (Undated). *The living will.* Reprinted by permission of Concern for Dying, an Educational Council.

Tables

Table 18-1: Kübler-Ross, E. (1969). *On death and dying.* © 1969 by Elisabeth Kübler-Ross. Reprinted by permission of Macmillan Publishing Company.
Table 18-2: Many see mercy in ending empty life. (1984, September 23). *The New York Times.* Copyright © 1984 by The New York Times Company. Reprinted by permission.

Quotations in Text

Page 598: Alinsky, S. (1966). Personal communication to S. W. Olds.
Page 598: Duskin, R. (1986). Personal communication.
Page 607: Kelly, Orville (1978). Living with a life threatening illness. In Garfield, M. C. (Ed.), *Psychosocial care of the dying patient.* © 1978. Reprinted by permission of McGraw-Hill Book Company.
Page 616: Kübler-Ross, E. (1975). *Death: The final stage of growth.* Copyright © 1975 by Elisabeth Kübler-Ross. Reprinted by permission of Simon & Schuster, Inc.

INDEXES

Name Index

Martin, C. E., 392, 465, 652–653
Martin, D. C., 65, 67, 667
Martin, G. B., 178, 656
Martin, J., 67, 656
Martin, O., 67, 656
Martin, W. H., 103, 666
Martinez, G. A., 100, 656
Marton, P., 95, 657
Marwick, C., 656
Masica, D. N., 235, 658
Maslach, C., 493, 656
Maslow, Abraham, 25, 656
Masnick, G., 161, 656
Mason-Brothers, A., 56, 663
Masson, J. M., 17, 35, 227, 656
Masters, William H., 378, 393, 464, 477, 519, 582, 656
Masur, D. M., 548, 668
Matas, L., 166, 656
Matheny, K. B., 420, 656
Matlin, M. W., 227, 232, 371, 477, 656
Matsukura, S., 418, 656
Maurer, D., 104, 656
Maxwell, L., 287, 656
May, M. A., 276, 649
Mayer, J., 102, 656
Mayers, R. S., 460, 645
Maymi, C. R., 439, 656
Maziade, M., 74, 656
Mead, Margaret, 35, 88–89, 262, 378, 657
Meck, E., 204, 647
Mednick, B. R., 396, 657
Medrich, E. A., 306, 307, 657
Meer, J., 534, 541, 651
Meer, J. T., 537, 657
Mekler, E., 665
Melnick, S., 65, 657
Melton, G. B., 332, 657
Meltzoff, A. N., 29n., 132, 657, 658
Mendel, Gregor, 45, 46
Meredith, N. V., 264, 657
Merrow, J., 291, 657
Merser, C., 477, 657
Metropolitan Life Insurance Company, 488
Michaels, W., 65, 665
Michotte, 127
Midura, T., 95, 637
Miles, C., 425, 657
Miles, W., 425, 657
Milgram, J. I., 583, 663
Milham, S., 49, 645
Milhoj, P., 557, 665
Miller, B., 295, 657
Miller, B. C., 468, 657
Miller, C. A., 90, 91, 657
Miller, E., 68, 657
Miller, G. A., 277, 657
Miller, J. F., 60, 657
Miller, L. B., 217, 657
Miller, P., 270, 636
Miller, P. H., 5, 17, 21, 657
Miller, P. M., 231, 232n., 657
Miller, S., 523, 524, 668
Miller, V., 88, 657
Mills, J. L., 65, 346, 657
Milne, A. M., 319, 321, 324, 657
Milner, R., 74, 659
Minde, K., 95, 657
Mindel, C. H., 572, 657
Minkoff, H. L., 74, 643–644

Miranda, S. B., 104, 118, 645
Mirga, T., 286, 657
Mitchell, M. D., 71, 667
Mitchell, P., 620, 657
Mittler, P., 54, 56, 657
Mo, A., 56, 663
Moane, G., 454, 510, 512, 650
Mohs, R. C., 547, 657–658
Money, J., 234, 235, 644, 658
Montaigne, Michel Eyquem de, quoted, 224
Montemayor, R., 383, 386n., 658
Montens, L., 79, 643
Montessori, Maria, 215, 216
Montgomery, J., 578, 667
Mooney, K. C., 198, 648
Moore, A. U., 162, 658
Moore, J. W., 455, 659
Moore, K., 29n., 132, 657, 658
Moore, N., 238, 658
Moorman, J. E., 459, 460, 462, 517, 660
Mora, J., 62, 669
Morbidity and Mortality Weekly Report (MMWR), 90, 91, 356, 359n., 611, 612n., 613, 614, 658
Morelock, S., 66, 650
Morgan, J. N., 557, 637
Morgan, L., 523, 658
Morgan, M., 244, 665
Morland, J., 309, 658
Morris, N., 167, 648
Morris, N. F., 67, 671
Moskowitz, B. A., 140, 658
Moss, F., 574, 658
Mostel, A. P., 113, 647
Mozart, Wolfgang Amadeus, 294n.
Munoz, A., 418, 667
Murkoff, H. E., 63n., 79, 644
Murphy, C. M., 242, 658
Murphy, D. P., 68, 658
Murphy, G. E., 613, 658
Murphy, L. B., 173, 667
Murray, A. D., 72, 658
Murray, R. M., 493, 658
Murray Lyon, I. M., 67, 671
Murstein, B. I., 458, 658
Mussen, P. H., 229, 246, 247, 349, 394, 510, 644, 652, 658
Myers, D. E., 319, 321, 324, 657
Myers, J. K., 56, 658
Myers, M. A. P., 579, 668
Myers, N., 199, 200, 658
Myers-Walls, J. A., 468, 657, 658

Nader, P. R., 100, 662
Nadi, N. S., 57, 658
Naeye, R. L., 67, 658
Nakajima, H., 418, 656
Nakanishi, N., 285, 658
Napoleon I (Napoleon Bonaparte), quoted, 162
Nash, A., 178, 649
Nash, Ogden, quoted, 300
Nass, G. D., 465, 658
Nathanson, C. A., 424, 658
Nation, R. L., 72, 658
National Assessment of Educational Progress (NAEP), 286, 287, 306, 658
National Center for Education Statistics (NCES), 215n., 365–368, 658

National Center for Health Statistics, 64, 396, 459, 460, 471, 613, 658–659
National Clearinghouse for Human Genetic Diseases, 53
National Coalition on Television Violence, 245, 659
National Commission on Excellence in Education, 292, 365, 659
National Commission for the Protection of Human Subjects of Biomedical and Behavioral Research, 32, 659
National Committee for Citizens in Education (NCCE), 368, 612, 614, 659
National Committee on Youth Suicide Prevention, 615
National Council on Aging, 542, 614, 659
National Education Association, 290
National Institute on Aging, 485, 537, 542, 548, 549, 576, 659
National Institute on Alcohol Abuse and Alcoholism (NIAAA), 65, 66, 354, 419, 659
National Institute of Child Health and Human Development, 355, 659
National Institute on Drug Abuse (NIDA), 353–355, 659
National Institute of Education (NIE), 433, 436, 659
National Institute of Mental Health (NIMH), 66, 245, 247, 384, 395, 659
National Institutes of Health (NIH), 12, 47, 71, 213, 328, 415, 485, 486, 659
National Library of Medicine, 41n.
National Opinion Research Center, 459
National Urban League, 572
Neal, J. H., 322, 659
Needleman, H., 69, 638
Neelley, J. N., 582, 652
Neiswender, M., 458, 659
Nelson, K., 137, 139, 659
Nelson, N., 74, 659
Nelson, S., 71, 654
Neuffer, E., 596, 659
Neugarten, Bernice, 12, 446, 455, 456, 457n., 483, 486, 505, 509, 510, 513, 534, 566, 567, 569–570, 598, 659–661
Neugarten, D. A., 455, 456, 505, 513, 534, 659
Nevis, S., 104, 645
Newhouse News Service, 436, 659
Newman, H. H., 54, 659
Newman, J., 109, 662
Newman, P. R., 386, 390, 660
Newport, E. L., 141, 647
Newson, E., 198, 660
Newson, J., 198, 660
Newton, P. M., 453, 511, 663
New York Times–CBS poll, 609, 659
Nieburg, P., 67, 660
Nielsen, G., 54, 666
Nilsson, L., 79, 660
Nin, Anaïs, quoted, 412

Nisan, M., 276, 660
Noberini, M., 510, 660
Nock, S. L., 438, 660
Noller, K., 65, 637
Norgaard-Pedersen, B., 70, 667
Norton, A. J., 459, 460, 462, 517, 660
Notelovitz, M., 417, 485n., 500, 660
Nowak, C. A., 457, 643
Nurius, P. S., 301, 302, 305, 656
Nurnberger, J. I., 57, 658
Nussbaum, M., 352, 660

Oates, R. K., 176, 660
Obel, E. B., 70, 667
O'Brien, M., 292, 294, 295, 651
O'Brien, P., 65, 637
O'Bryant, S. L., 237, 660
O'Connell, M., 466, 663
O'Connor, M. J., 134, 660
O'Connor, S. M., 177, 636
Oden, M., 425, 638
Oden, M. H., 293, 668
Oehlenschlager, Adam G., quoted, 190
Offer, C., 227, 668
Offer, D., 382, 401, 406, 660
Offer, J. B., 382, 660
Okun, S., 614, 660
Olds, S. W., 100, 113, 297, 320, 325n., 326, 328, 331, 337, 438, 467n., 477, 510, 644, 660, 665, 667
O'Malley, P. M., 355, 652
Onotera, R. T., 88, 657
Oppenheimer, E., 66, 650
Opper, S., 145, 361, 362, 647
Orenberg, C. L., 79
Orvaschel, H., 56, 658
Oski, F. A., 100, 101, 645, 664
Ossofsky, J., 558, 660
Ostrea, E., 66, 660, 667
Ostrov, E., 401, 406, 660
Oswald, P. F., 154, 660
Otto, H., 402, 403n., 660
Owens, W. A., 425, 660

Paffenberger, R. S., 417, 654, 660
Page, David, C., 44, 660
Palmer, A. M., 490, 643
Palmore, E. B., 535, 660
Paloma, M. M., 468, 660
Pancake, V. R., 166, 666
Pankey, G. A., 415, 660
Papalia, D., 31, 233, 431, 552, 639, 660
Papalia-Finlay, D., 552, 663
Papousek, H., 120, 660
Papsidero, J. A., 540, 652
Pardini, A., 546, 660
Paris, S. G., 200, 278, 660
Parke, R., 650
Parke, R. D., 169, 249, 660
Parker, R. T., 486, 649
Parkes, C. M., 580, 660
Parlee, M. B., 423, 660
Parmelee, A. H., 98, 134, 193, 660
Parten, Mildred, 238, 239n., 660
Passuth, P., 457n., 660–661
Pasteur, Louis, 497
Patrick, R., 510, 643

Subject Index

Science
Activities
for Children

Science Activities for Children

VOLUME ONE

Ninth Edition

George C. Lorbeer
California State University - Northridge

•

Leslie W. Nelson
California State University - Los Angeles

WCB **Wm. C. Brown Publishers**

Book Team

Editor *Paul L. Tavenner*
Developmental Editor *Ann Shaffer*
Production Coordinator *Carla D. Arnold*

 Wm. C. Brown Publishers

President *G. Franklin Lewis*
Vice President, Publisher *Thomas E. Doran*
Vice President, Operations and Production *Beverly Kolz*
National Sales Manager *Virginia S. Moffat*
Group Sales Manager *John Finn*
Executive Editor *Edgar J. Laube*
Director of Marketing *Kathy Law Laube*
Marketing Manager *Pam Cooper*
Managing Editor, Production *Colleen A. Yonda*
Manager of Visuals and Design *Faye M. Schilling*
Production Editorial Manager *Julie A. Kennedy*
Production Editorial Manager *Ann Fuerste*
Publishing Services Manager *Karen J. Slaght*

WCB Group

President and Chief Executive Officer *Mark C. Falb*
Chairman of the Board *Wm. C. Brown*

Cover design by Elaine G. Allen

Cover photo from the Stock Market © Palmer/Kane, Inc.

Some of the laboratory experiments included in this text may be
hazardous if materials are handled improperly or if procedures are
conducted incorrectly. Safety precautions are necessary when you are
working with chemicals, glass test tubes, hot water baths, sharp
instruments, and the like, or for any procedures that generally require
caution. Your school may have set regulations regarding safety
procedures that your instructor will explain to you. Should you have any
problems with materials or procedures, please ask your instructor for
help.

Drawings by: Dick Lane, Harry Horowitz, Ruth Jerneka, Dave
Hawbecker, George Lorbeer, and Shawn Keehne.

This ninth revision of *Science Activities for Children* has been
exclusively developed by George C. Lorbeer.

Contents

PART 1: PHYSICAL WORLD

PART II: ENERGY

PART III: PLANTS

PART IV: ANIMALS

PART V: HEALTH

PART VI: ECOLOGY

PART VII: EARTH AND SPACE

PART VIII: AVIATION, SATELLITES, AND SPACE TRAVEL

Preface

This Ninth Revision of *Science Activities for Children,* Volume One, has been greatly enlarged, updated, and improved in many ways. In addition to Volume One, a second volume is now available for *Science Activities for Children:* Volume Two. The volumes can be used alone or in conjunction with each other; Volume One features basic, introductory activities while Volume Two contains more rigorous, higher level activities. Each activity has been expanded to include three new parts: 1. "Related Activities," 2. "Vocabulary Building-Spelling Words," and 3. "Thought for Today." These provide a more interdisciplinary approach and make science more interesting and challenging to the student. Each activity is explained in clear, non-technical language. A photograph, sketch, or drawing accompanies each activity to help the teacher and/or student get an overall idea of the activity before reading the detailed information provided.

The basic emphasis of this book is a "hands-on" approach. Every activity has materials listed and procedures to follow to make scientific learning more meaningful to the student. Dewey's famous statement, "We learn by doing," is certainly psychologically sound and very practical. It is the backbone of this book. Children learn best by direct, first-hand experiences. Listening to a teacher's interpretation of natural phenomena might be interesting to the teacher, but it lacks substance and meaning for the students.

This book has been designed to provide teachers, teachers-in-training, student teachers, and students with a complete lesson so that even the neophyte in science can perform each activity successfully. The materials suggested are usually common, inexpensive items found around the home, local store, or in the classroom. Activities can be carried out as a student experiment, group activity, or a teacher demonstration. In addition, this book can also be used by curriculum workers, science supervisors, other school administrators, or even parents, to enrich science school programs.

Not since Sputnik has there been such an emphasis on science. The United States of America is awakening to the realization that many of her educated population are illiterate in science and that many of the advances in the field of technology are stemming from foreign countries. We are fast losing our lead in the field of science at a time when scientific knowledge is vital to the average citizen as well as to the science specialist. The problem stems from the fact that we are NOT providing our school children with the scientific background and problem solving techniques that will keep America strong and progressing. This book can help us reverse the trend of our scientific back-sliding, so let's get on with it!

What is Science?

1. Science is the study of the biological environment from the tiniest living organism to the largest life form, and the physical environment from the smallest speck of matter to the immense universe.
2. Science is a method of problem solving which requires using all means necessary—no holds barred. It is not a predetermined, sequential step-by-step process. If it were, all the world's problems would have already been solved! It includes hypothesizing and investigating, using all the resources and skills available, and reaching conclusions based on objective evidence.
3. Science is an attitude based on facts.
4. Science is an art, producing internal satisfactions.
5. Science is a pragmatic philosophy.

In planning any science program, the first step for the teacher is to determine what are the desired objectives. While the individual teacher may want to develop a personal list of goals, the authors recommend that as a start, teachers consider the following vital objectives for science education.

1. Developing personal strengths
2. Becoming aware of the social realities and natural phenomena
3. Having fun in games, hobbies, and recreation
4. Enjoying artistic experiences
5. Living healthfully and safely
6. Recognizing vocational potentials
7. Learning scientific facts and principles (concepts)
8. Developing a scientific attitude
9. Becoming proficient in the use of the scientific method
10. Building a sound personal and social philosophy of life.

Expanded Discussion of Objectives

1. Personal strengths include not only the bases of reading, writing, and arithmetic, but also communication skills, socializing activities, critical attitudes of work, problem solving skills, and satisfying social and psychological needs. All these strengths can be developed in a good science program. Students must communicate orally and in writing about their investigations. Discussions take place continuously and provide not only resource information, but also develop oral skills and build scientific vocabularies. Pupils learn to be critical of their work by comparing their activities with those found in readings and discussions with others. Students involved in science activities have many of their social and psychological needs met, e.g., recognition, affection, security, belongingness, etc.

2. The ability to interpret social realities and natural phenomena alleviates misconceptions and unreasoning fears. The child who understands the cause of thunder and has demonstrated this in a small but meaningful way by clapping his/her hands, is not likely to be afraid of the noise. When he/she knows that animals are not apt to sting or bite except in self-defense, he/she is less susceptible to the fears of animals, carried by many children into adult life. Children are naturally curious about their environment and will do almost anything to learn something about it—if we don't stifle their individual initiative. Children are continually asking, Why? How? When? What? and many other questions. The wise teacher, with little effort, can direct students down the discovery path to acquire skills and knowledge. We, as educators, should use this natural curiosity as a prime motivating device in inspiring students to learn not only about science, but all the other disciplines as well.

3. Science is fun! Children enjoy creating projects and performing experiments. Much science can be learned through games and contests. Many students have hobbies that involve science—collecting butterflies, raising pets, and planning a space trip are a few activities that illustrate this point. Recreational activities such as swimming, back-packing, baseball, racquetball, skating, outdoor cooking, and crafts all have science educational implications.

4. Science is an art, and like an art, it provides many enjoyable internal satisfactions. A student who has constructed a simple telegraph is an artist and reaps as much internal satisfaction as another pupil who has composed a simple melody or painted an imperfect picture. The student who derives satisfaction from the color and form of a beautiful butterfly will enjoy it even more after seeing it pass through its transformation from pupa to adult. Science activities can produce intrinsic satisfactions just as enjoyable as any other art form—don't discount this phase of science education.

5. Everyone needs to live healthfully and safely. Science educators can help children do this by having them learn about food, rest, exercise, accident prevention, first aid, diseases, the avoidance of drugs, etc. No one, from the very young to the very old, can help but benefit from activities involving health and safety. The child's understanding of the cause and prevention of disease helps prevent careless exposure, both

personal and social to common colds and other contagious diseases. Indoctrination about drugs can mean the difference between success and disaster, life and death—even to young children.

6. Every vocation involves science in one way or another. A policeman is concerned with sounds, light, mechanics, health, safety, etc. A musician is concerned with sounds, electricity, health, air, matter, etc. A gardener is involved with plants, animals, health, air, water, soil, etc. No vocation is void of science. Our society is becoming more scientific and it is education's responsibility to induct our youth into this technological society.

7. Science enables elementary school students to learn some of the basic facts about their biological and physical environments. By building on basic facts, students begin to acquire concepts which expand with each new related fact. Concepts are built from facts, not vice versa. The problem in teaching is to select pertinent facts which develop desired concepts.

8. Elementary school science education helps students develop a scientific attitude. They begin to learn cause and effect relationships, increase their natural curiosity, suspend judgment, develop the desire to search for answers, approach problems with an open mind, and accept the scientific method as a basic approach to solve "factual" problems. A scientific attitude can eliminate superstitions, remove unfounded fears, and prevent individuals from jumping to erroneous conclusions.

9. While the scientific method cannot solve all the problems people face, learning the basic procedures in the scientific method can help individuals with many problems. It will enable the student to sense problems, hypothesize about them, devise possible solutions, conduct tests, make accurate observations, collect data, eliminate red herrings, and possibly come up with the right answers—if not on the first attempt, then on subsequent studies of the problem. The scientific method can never solve problems on the level of "values." It can help find facts, never values. Science can never determine what is good or bad, right or wrong, better or worse—these are value judgments whose answers must be left to the philosophers. Science can help each student in the solving of personal problems by having each of them develop a strategy of inquiry and investigation. Problems stimulate thinking and never before has critical thinking been so sorely needed.

10. We all need a sound philosophy of living. Science can aid in this major objective by yielding information about life itself, the difference between living and non-living matter, the elements that make a healthy organism, and the dangers to living individuals from external sources or self-imposed deleterious substances and behaviors.

In summarizing the objectives of science, we know that this discipline helps us understand our environment. It enables us to solve problems with an open mind, helps us appreciate the natural order and beauty of the universe, aids us to live in a more intelligent manner, teaches us respect for all things, and encourages us to conserve our natural resources for the good of all mankind, now and for generations to come.

Science should be for each student a "rediscovery of the known by the uninformed." Students are not like sponges. They cannot automatically absorb knowledge. They are individuals who learn best by firsthand experiences.

The school science program promotes good mental health in that it helps students face daily living experiences without evasions, benefits them in improving their self-images, increases their ability to work with others, assists them in adjusting to disappointments and failures, aids them in analyzing situations, and develops sound emotional responses.

Through science education, the student can achieve many objectives, from the improvement of reading skills to developing creativity. Don't sell science education short! Our society is becoming more technologically oriented than ever before and consequently, we must teach *more* science in our schools, not less—to do otherwise is to cheat our students in their ability to live in a complex world.

As far as the physical make-up of this book, there are many fine features which make it especially easy for teachers to use. It is divided into eight major parts which include the broad areas of science. Each part contains many carefully selected activities and each activity has nine major divisions:

1. **Problem**

   Each *problem* is stated in the form of a typical question which could be raised by a student. This enables the teacher to select the appropriate activity.

2. **Materials**

   The *materials* are supplies and equipment needed to perform the activity.

3. **Procedure**

   The *procedure* is the step-by-step process in utilizing the materials. These procedures are the "junior scientists'" techniques, especially if the teacher encourages hypothesizing, suggesting test procedures, and anticipating suspected conclusions.

4. **Results**

   The *results* are the observed conclusions of the stated procedure which, incidentally, also serve as a double-check for the teacher.

5. **Supplemental Information**

   The *supplemental information* regarding each activity includes more scientific information, references, safety precautions, scientific principles involved or suggestions for further study.

6. **Thought Questions**

   Thought questions are included so that the teacher may add stimulating questions, especially if they prefer the "inquiry" techniques, to challenge the "junior scientists" to think about the possible solutions to related problems. This encourages students and teachers to do more critical thinking and perform "open-ended experiments," if they so choose.

7. **Related Activities**

   These *related activities* have been added to enrich each area of study. Activities can be correlated to show the interrelationships of science activities, and consequently, the students will gain a better comprehension of each area and not view each activity as an isolated idea.

8. **Vocabulary Builders—Spelling Words**

   The *vocabulary builders—spelling words* category has been developed to integrate Science and Language Arts—particularly spelling. We need to help students improve their language skills in every way possible, and science instruction should provide a vehicle for this effort.

9. **Thought for Today**

   The *thought for today* has been added to provide enjoyment as well as thought to each lesson, a philosophical and/or humorous statement has been added to each activity. This technique has been used in classrooms for years and has proven to be an excellent initiatory activity.

This book is not designed to cover all the science activities for any one grade level. Instead, it attempts to select typical, effective, proven activities from the various areas of science to give a teacher sufficient ideas to start a good program of science education with a feeling of confidence. A teacher at any level of instruction can modify any activity up or down, making it more complex or easier, depending upon the age and maturity of the students in the class. If properly used, it will create interest and stimulate activity in science. When students participate in these activities, either individually or in small groups, they will learn more science and also have fun seeing what happens when they follow the simple instructions. It must be remembered that these activities are for elementary school students who are full of curiosity and do like to have fun! Some of the activities in this book were prepared to raise scientific questions in the minds of students. Other activities were designed to answer simple questions which arise in daily living. When children fly kites, they are inclined to ask "What causes a kite to stay up in the air?" On the other hand, when they ask, "What is air pressure?" a simple demonstration can show that it is powerful enough to crush a can. This gives rise to many other scientific questions which can be answered by other activities in this book, e.g., What is gas? How does heat travel? What is sound? etc.

Science experiences which are encountered in the everyday lives of students are especially emphasized in this book. The knowledge gained from such activities will help prepare them for more formal work in junior high, high school, and college or university.

The science teacher should be a director of learning, an agent of interaction, a stimulator, a guide, a resource person, and rarely if ever, a "story teller." The teacher must recognize that students differ in experiences, learning rates, interests, abilities, etc., and must take these factors into account so as not to frustrate any potential "junior scientist."

Much of the current science education thinking lies in the "process approach" with "hands-on" activities. These major focuses can be accomplished by challenging students to find out how they will solve the particular problems cited and comparing them with the "Procedures" given in the text. Encouraging the students to adopt procedures is recommended regardless of whether they succeed or not. If the students arrive at similar procedures, then the "Results" cited in the text can be omitted until the students have finished the activity. Then students can compare the results they found with those given in the text. By using modifications, teachers can use these science activities with any particular approach they desire. Regardless of what emphasis the teachers use, the stress should be on the students in:

1. experimenting to gather data and make observations
2. gathering facts by means of direct observation under controlled conditions
3. interpreting and organizing data
4. measuring and recording findings
5. looking for irregularities, deviations, or exceptions
6. seeking assistance of others who are considered "experts"
7. using books, periodicals, etc. as sources to gather data
8. speculating and making hypotheses
9. verifying data by any reliable source
10. testing results through new applications
11. predicting on the basis of gathered information
12. checking cause and effect relationships
13. utilizing new tools and techniques
14. inquiring into new strategies of problem solving, etc.
15. developing "models"
16. clarifying problems
17. reporting findings accurately.

Two key points for the science teacher are: "GET YOUR STUDENTS ACTIVELY INVOLVED" and "KEEP YOUR STUDENTS ACTIVELY INVOLVED." If you do, your rewards will be unlimited.

George C. Lorbeer
Leslie W. Nelson

Science
Activities
for Children

Part I

Physical World

Section A: Matter

Activity   IA1

A. Problem: *What Are the Three States of Matter?*

B. Materials:
1. Chalkboard
2. Chalk
3. Collection of materials: (solids, liquids, and gases)

C. Procedure:
1. Make a chart showing the three states of matter as illustrated.
2. Briefly describe the three states of matter, i.e., solids, liquids, and gases.
3. Have the children classify each of the materials by its state.
4. Add as many other items to each heading until you are sure the children have learned the differences among the states of matter.

D. Result:
The children will learn the different states of matter as they develop the chart.

E. Supplemental Information:
Each state of matter has its own unique characteristics and can be readily distinguished. Solids have definite shapes; liquids assume the exact shape of the containers they occupy; and gases expand to fill the space of the container.

F. Thought Questions:
1. What are some other differences among solids, liquids, and gases?
2. Is ice a liquid or a solid?
3. Can we change the states of matter, that is, can we change a solid to a liquid or a liquid to a gas?
4. How can you change water from a liquid to a solid?
5. How can you change water from a liquid to a gas?

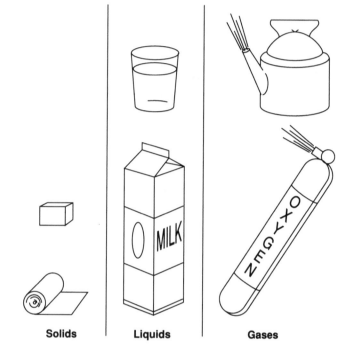

Solids   Liquids   Gases

G. Related Topics and Activities:
1. Blow air into a paper or cellophane bag and study it.
2. Put a straw into a glass of water, blow into it, and describe what happens.
3. See all Activities in this Section.

H. Vocabulary Builders—Spelling Words:
1) **solids**   2) **liquids**   3) **gases**   4) **steam**
5) **oxygen**

I. Thought for Today:
"The American Dream is not over; America is an adventure."

Activity

A. Problem: *Can Matter be Changed from One State to Another?*

B. Materials:
1. Heat source
2. Sauce pan
3. Regular ice (small pieces)
4. Dry ice
5. Old plate or pie tin

C. Procedure:
1. Put the regular ice in the sauce pan and apply heat.
2. Continue applying heat until the ice is melted.
3. Continue applying heat until the water evaporates.
4. Put dry ice in the sauce pan and apply heat.

D. Results:
1. The ice will change to water.
2. The water will change to steam.
3. The dry ice will change directly to a gas.

E. Supplemental Information:

Heat causes molecules of substances to move faster and farther apart. Sufficient heat can change a solid to a liquid and then to a gas. Various substances have different melting points and different boiling points. The melting point is the point at which a solid changes to a liquid. The boiling point is the temperature at which a liquid changes to a gas. Some substances change directly from a solid to a gas. This is called "sublimation." These are physical changes. See Activities I-A-8 and I-A-9 for chemical changes.

F. Thought Questions:
1. Can all matter exist in three states?
2. Is heat, or the reduction of heat, a cause of the change of state of matter?
3. Can you name any other matter, except water, that exists as a solid, liquid, and a gas?

G. Related Topics and Activities:
1. Mothballs can be placed in the room and observed daily. They change from a solid to a gas at room temperature.
2. Changes in matter can be reversed and shown by condensation on a cold object and then freezing water with ice and table salt. Take temperatures as this is done.
3. See all Activities in this Section.

H. Vocabulary Builders—Spelling Words:
1) **sublimation**   2) **physical**   3) **chemical**
4) **change**   5) **molecules**   6) **melting**
7) **boiling**   8) **point**

I. Thought for Today:
"The family fireside is the best of schools."

A. Problem: *Can a Gas Change to a Liquid? A Liquid to a Gas? A Gas to a Solid? What is Condensation? Dew?*

B. Materials:
   1. Water
   2. Crushed ice
   3. Salt (table)
   4. Paper towels
   5. Glass jar
   6. Test tube
   7. Heat source
   8. Sauce pan
   9. Pane of glass
   10. Gloves (for handling hot materials)

C. Procedure One:
   1. Fill a glass jar with crushed ice.
   2. Mix a generous amount of salt in the ice.
   3. Place a water-filled test tube upright in the ice.
   4. Wrap paper toweling or other insulation around the glass jar.

   Procedure Two:
   1. Partly fill a sauce pan with water.
   2. Apply heat till the water boils.
   3. Hold the sheet of glass over the boiling water.

D. Results:
   1. After several minutes the water in the test tube will be frozen. (Procedure A)
   2. Drops of water will condense and collect on the cold glass. (Procedure B)

E. Supplemental Information:
Ice around the test tube will cool the water. Salt in the ice lowers the water temperature below the freezing point of water. When the water temperature is cooled to its freezing point (0°C. or 32°F.) the water will freeze (turn into ice). The wrapper helps prevent outside heat from warming the ice-salt mixture. *Note:* Put distilled water in the test tube for best results. The "snow" from a freezer or refrigerator is a good source of mineral-free water. A cool sheet of glass, or a cool lid, held several inches above boiling water will cool the vapor rising above the boiling water enough to condense the vapor, i.e., change its state from gas to liquid by lowering the temperature of the gas.

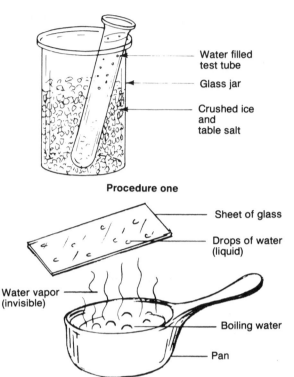

Water filled test tube
Glass jar
Crushed ice and table salt

Procedure one

Sheet of glass
Drops of water (liquid)
Water vapor (invisible)
Boiling water
Pan

Procedure two

F. Thought Questions:
   1. Is this principle used in making homemade ice cream?
   2. Why is the insulation wrapped around the jar?
   3. What makes an object hot or cold?
   4. What is meant by "dew point"?
   5. Does pressure effect condensation?
   6. Could we convert salt water to freshwater using this technique?

G. Related Topics and Activities:
   1. Wet a piece of cloth and hang it out to dry.
   2. Make some ice in a refrigerator freezer at school or have students make some at home.
   3. Boil some water. Add several tablespoons of salt. What happens immediately? (stops boiling)
   4. See all Activities in this Section.

H. Vocabulary Builders—Spelling Words:
   1) **liquid**   2) **solid**   3) **condensation**   4) **dew**
   5) **crushed**   6) **sauce**

I. Thought for Today:
   "All that mankind has done, thought, gained, or been, can be found in the pages of books."

Activity

A. Problem: *Do All Solids Melt at the Same Temperature?*

B. Materials:
1. Glasses, water
2. Double boiler or frying pan
3. Source of heat
4. Crushed ice
5. Thermometer (cooking)
6. Butter
7. Wax
8. Sugar
9. Other substances to be tested
10. Gloves (for handling hot materials)

C. Procedure:
1. Put the ice into a glass and record temperatures as ice melts.
2. Pour the water out.
3. Have students wear gloves as a safety precaution as some substances may splatter when heating.
4. Put the butter in the double boiler or frying pan.
5. Heat it until the butter melts.
6. Have a student note the temperature at which the butter melts.
7. Continue this process with other substances to be tested.
8. Make a graph or table showing the melting point of each of the substances used in the experiments.

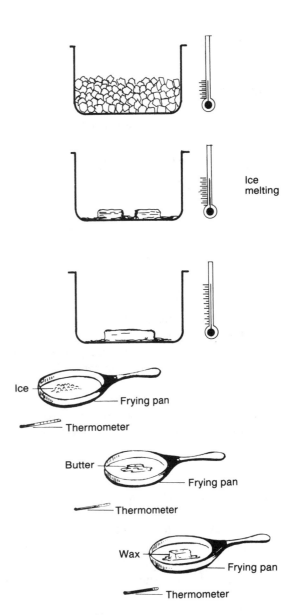

D. Result:
Each substance melts at a different temperature.

E. Supplemental Information:
1. Various materials require different amounts of heat before melting begins.
2. Care must be used in taking the temperatures of these melting points. Several attempts should be made on each trial to insure accuracy.
3. The melting point is a characteristic which is used to help identify each substance.
4. Melting is a process used in industry to separate and purify materials.

F. Thought Questions:
1. Does iron have a melting point?
2. Can dry ice be melted?
3. Do you know any solid substance which cannot be melted?

G. Related Topics and Activities:
1. Discuss the temperature at which snow melts.
2. Discuss the temperature at which some candy melts.
3. See all Activities in this Section.

H. Vocabulary Builders—Spelling Words:
1) **splattering** 2) **physical** 3) **change**
4) **boiling point** 5) **melting point**

I. Thought for Today:
"An ounce of prevention is worth a pound of cure."

Activity   I A 5

A. Problem: *Do All Liquids Boil at the Same Temperature?*

B. Materials:
   1. Large glass jars or beakers
   2. Heat source (Do not use open flame.)
   3. Water
   4. Test tube or small glass container
   5. Rubbing alcohol
   6. Thermometer
   7. Gloves

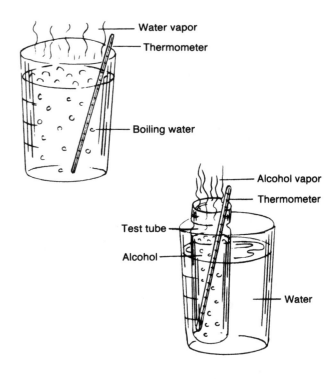

C. Procedure:
   1. Use gloves as a safety precaution.
   2. Boil some water.
   3. Record the temperature of the water when it boils.
   4. Pour water to the depth of several inches in glass jar or beaker.
   5. Put some alcohol into a small container and then place that small container in the water in the beaker.
   6. Place these two containers over heat. (Be sure the alcohol vapor is not exposed to open flame.)
   7. Record the temperature at which the alcohol boils.

D. Result:
The two liquids boil at different temperatures.

E. Supplemental Information:
   1. At standard pressure, water boils at 100°C. (212°F.). Rubbing alcohol's boiling point varies because it is a mixture. It usually boils around 78°C. (173°F.).
   2. Each substance has its own boiling point.
   3. Each substance has its own melting point.
   4. Scientists use these points to help identify different substances.

F. Thought Questions:
   1. Can all substances be changed into gases?
   2. What would happen in this experiment if the water and alcohol were mixed in one container and heated?
   3. What is meant by "fractional distillation"?

G. Related Topics and Activities:
   1. Determine the boiling points of ice and water.
   2. Test to find out if milk boils at the same temperature as water.
   3. See all Activities in this Section.

H. Vocabulary Builders—Spelling Words:
   1) **distillation**   2) **fractional**   3) **boiling point**
   4) **mixture**   5) **alcohol**

I. Thought for Today:
   "The written word can be erased; not the spoken one."

Activity

A. Problem: *What Are Atoms? Molecules?*

B. Materials:
1. Three glasses
2. Medicine dropper
3. Ink or food coloring
4. Water
5. Coffee crystals
6. Two jars, same size
7. Cover for one jar above
8. Two mothballs

C. Procedure:
1. Briefly explain the three different states of matter: solids, liquids, and gases.
2. Define and describe atoms and molecules.
3. Show examples and models of atoms such as iron, copper, zinc, etc.
4. Show examples and models of molecules such as water, salt, baking soda, oxygen gas (O_2), nitrogen gas (N_2).
5. Have students blow against their hands and describe what they feel.
6. Fill one of the glasses two-thirds full of water.
7. Pick up some ink with medicine dropper and place several drops on the surface of the water. Set it to one side and observe after several hours.
8. Place some coffee crystals at the bottom of a container or beaker of water.
9. Slowly pour water over the crystals and let stand. Observe results immediately and after several hours.
10. Place four or five mothballs in each of two containers, capping one of them.
11. Let stand for several days or weeks and note any changes.

D. Results:
1. When children blow air against their hands they are making molecules in a gaseous state move.
2. When drops of ink are placed on the surface of the water, the molecules in a liquid state (ink) move through the water.
3. When some coffee crystals are placed in a glass of water, the molecules in a solid state (coffee) move through water.

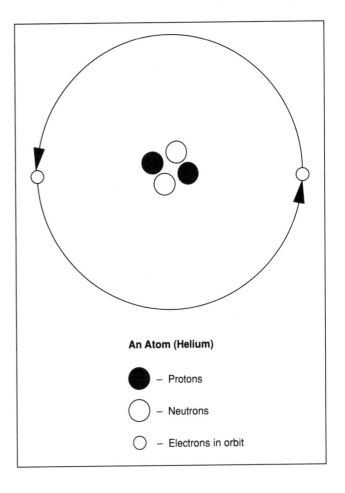

An Atom (Helium)

⬤ – Protons

◯ – Neutrons

◯ – Electrons in orbit

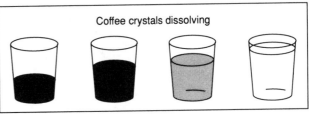

Coffee crystals dissolving

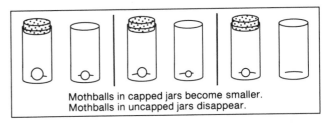

Mothballs in capped jars become smaller.
Mothballs in uncapped jars disappear.

4. In the last activities with mothballs, the mothballs in the uncovered jar will eventually disappear completely. The mothballs in the covered jar will become smaller. In the former case, the molecules in a solid state move through air.

E. Supplemental Information:

1. Molecules are so small that we cannot see them.
2. Molecules are in constant motion regardless of whether they are in a solid, liquid, or gaseous state.
3. In these activities we can think of the ink or food coloring, coffee crystals, or mothballs as clumps of molecules.
4. The smallest particle of matter that can be divided and still retain the properties of matter is called a molecule.
5. Atoms are the basic components of molecules. They are the smallest units of the elements.
6. Molecules are combinations of atoms.
7. There are now 109 known elements. The last ones have been synthesized in laboratories.
8. A million atoms or molecules are about the size of a pinhead.

F. Thought Questions:

1. If molecules didn't move, could clothes be dried outside?
2. Is all matter composed of molecules?
3. If all molecules are in motion, why don't all solids dissipate and disappear?

G. Related Topics and Activities:

1. Students should make models of atoms and molecules or draw sketches.
2. Have students make mobiles of atoms and molecules. Let the mobiles hang from the ceiling.
3. See all Activities in this Section.

H. Vocabulary Builders—Spelling Words:

1) **atoms**   2) **molecules**   3) **elements**
4) **electrons**   5) **protons**   6) **neutrons**
7) **orbits**   8) **evaporation**

I. Thought for Today:

"Do not put off until tomorrow what you can do today."

Activity

A. Problem: *What Are Elements? Compounds? Mixtures?*

B. Materials:
   1. Glass jar
   2. Bits of paper
   3. Paper clips
   4. Spoon
   5. Water
   6. Marbles
   7. Tacks
   8. Sand
   9. Salt
   10. Sugar
   11. Iron filings
   12. Copper pennies
   13. Magnifying glass

C. Procedure:
   1. Define terms:
      a. **Element**—basic unit of matter consisting of electrons, protons, and neutrons.
      b. **Compound**—combination of atoms with fixed chemical properties.
      c. **Mixture**—any physical combination of substances without changing chemical compositions.
   2. Identify each of the substances listed and tell what it is.
   3. Put the paper clips, bits of paper, marbles, and tacks into a half-filled glass of water.
   4. Stir vigorously.
   5. Look at the sand with a magnifying glass. Do all the particles look the same?
   6. Look at the sugar with a magnifying glass. Do all particles look the same?

D. Results:
   1. All of the materials in the glass retained their individual identities.
   2. Looking at the sand, the particles were varied in appearance.
   3. Looking at the sugar, the particles were identical in appearance.

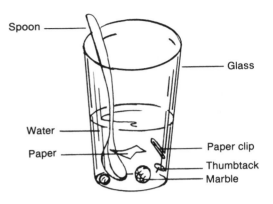

E. Supplemental Information:
A mixture is a combination of two or more ingredients, not in a fixed proportion, with each part retaining its identity.

F. Thought Questions:
   1. Is a mixture a physical change or a chemical change?
   2. How does a mixture differ from a solution?
   3. How many mixtures can you name?
   4. Is air a mixture or a compound?

G. Related Topics and Activities:
   1. Have students make a chart of the first ten elements in the periodic table showing differences in atomic number, weight, number of protons, number of electrons, number of neutrons, and the number of electrons in the outer ring.
   2. Discuss what elements, compounds, and mixtures are found in sea water.
   3. See all Activities in this Section.

H. Vocabulary Builders—Spelling Words:
   1) **elements**   2) **compounds**   3) **mixtures**   4) **iron**
   5) **copper**   6) **sand**   7) **sugar**   8) **marbles**

I. Thought for Today:
"Education is not training but rather the process that equips you to entertain yourself, a friend, and an idea."

Activity

A. Problem: *How Do Materials Combine?*

B. Materials:
1. Sulfur powder
2. Iron filings
3. Two test tubes
4. Magnet
5. Hot plate or Bunsen burner
6. Saucer
7. Ring stand
8. Paper towels
9. Hammer

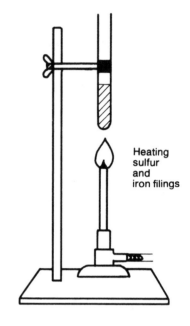

Heating sulfur and iron filings

C. Procedure:
1. Mix sulfur and iron filings in a test tube.
2. Shake the two elements together.
3. Pour them out onto a saucer.
4. Using a magnet, separate the iron filings from the sulfur.
5. Put twice as much sulfur as iron filings into a second test tube.
6. Heat this one over a hot plate or Bunsen burner. (Only the teacher or older student under the supervision of the teacher should do this part.)
7. Let cool.
8. Wrap the test tube in paper towels.
9. With hammer, break it as gently as possible.
10. Using the magnet, try to separate the iron filings from the sulfur.

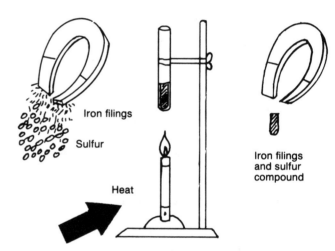

Iron filings

Sulfur

Heat

Iron filings and sulfur compound

D. Results:
1. When the iron and sulfur were mixed in the first test tube, the magnet attracted all the iron filings.
2. When the iron and sulfur were mixed in the second test tube and heated, a change in color occurred. The magnet was unable to separate the iron filings from the sulfur. They had chemically combined to form iron sulfide.

E. Supplemental Information:

A mixture is the placing together of two or more elements with each element retaining its individual properties. A compound is the union of two or more elements by chemical change; each element no longer retaining its original characteristics.

F. Thought Questions:
1. How do we know a chemical change has taken place?
2. What is the difference between a chemical and a physical change?

3. Why won't the magnet attract the iron sulfide compound?

G. Related Topics and Activities:
1. Study home food recipes for mixtures.
2. Study mineral ores for compounds.
3. See all Activities in this Section.

H. Vocabulary Builders—Spelling Words:
1) **materials**   2) **combine**   3) **elements**
4) **compounds**   5) **mixtures**   6) **ores**
7) **magnet**   8) **sulfur**

I. Thought for Today:

"Those who do not learn from the mistakes of the past are condemned to repeat them."

Activity

A. Problem: *What is Meant by a Chemical Change?*

B. Materials:
   1. Heat source (Bunsen burner, Sterno, alcohol lamp)
   2. Tablespoon
   3. Cube of sugar
   4. Tongs or clothespin

C. Procedure:
   1. Hold tablespoon with tongs or clothespin (safety precaution).
   2. Place the sugar in the spoon.
   3. Hold it over the flame.
   4. Notice the changes that take place in the sugar.

When sugar is heated it changes chemically and becomes a new substance.

D. Result:

The sugar first turns to dark brown and then to black.

E. Supplemental Information:

The heat causes a chemical change in the sugar. Actually the sugar molecules are broken down and they lose their hydrogen and oxygen which are contained in the original sugar molecule. The black substance which is left on the spoon is mainly carbon. Chemical changes may or may not involve heat.

F. Thought Questions:
   1. Will heat cause chemical changes to take place in other substances such as salt or sand?
   2. How does the change in the sugar compare with melting a substance such as melting a lump of ice?
   3. How many chemical changes can you name?

G. Related Topics and Activities:
   1. Name some chemical changes in which heat is involved.
   2. The teacher can separate mercury from mercuric oxide by heating.
   3. Examine some iron rust and discuss whether this is a chemical change. (Iron rust can be made quickly by placing steel wool in a solution of water, bleach, and vinegar.)
   4. Demonstrate how yeast is used in cooking and describe the chemical change that takes place.

H. Vocabulary Builders—Spelling Words:
   1) **molecules**   2) **decomposition**   3) **dehydration**
   4) **tablespoon**   5) **clothespin**

I. Thought for Today:

"The difference between genius and stupidity is that genius has limits."

Activity

A. Problem: *What is a Physical Change?*

B. Materials:
   1. Water glass
   2. Paper napkins
   3. Teaspoon
   4. Measuring cup
   5. Sugar
   6. Clean sand
   7. Iron filings
   8. Magnet
   9. Water

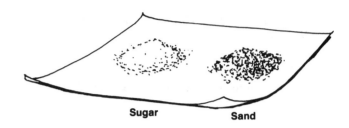

Sugar   Sand

C. Procedure:
   1. Mix two teaspoons of sugar with two teaspoons of sand on a paper napkin.
   2. Fill the measuring cup half-full with water.
   3. Put the mixture of sugar and sand into the water, and stir for a few moments.
   4. Let the mixture settle until the solution is clear.
   5. Pour the liquid part of the solution into the glass.
   6. Taste the solution in the glass.
   7. Mix the iron filings and the sand.
   8. Use a magnet and remove the iron filings.
   9. Discuss other examples of physical change such as:
      a. blowing up bicycle tires
      b. turning on a light bulb
      c. mowing the lawn.

Sugar solution

D. Results:
   1. With the sand and the sugar mixture, the sand was not dissolved in the solution, and when the stirring was stopped it settled to the bottom.
   2. Sugar remains in the solution, and the water tastes sweet. The sugar dissolves.
   3. The iron filings are extracted by the magnet.

E. Supplemental Information:
   1. The sugar can be recovered to its solid state by placing the solution over heat and evaporating the water slowly. (See Activity I-A-11.) Crystals of sugar will form in the bottom of the pan.
   2. Physical changes do not change the basic physical material(s), but may change its shape, condition, etc.
   3. A mixture is a combination of materials which changes none of the substances of which it is made.

F. Thought Questions:
   1. How can we separate a mixture of iron filings and sand?
   2. How can we separate a mixture of golf balls and tennis balls?
   3. Is air a mixture?

G. Related Topics and Activities:
   1. Put dissolved materials aside and let the water or solvent naturally evaporate.
   2. Discuss more examples of physical change found in the classroom:
      a. sharpening a pencil
      b. writing with pens
      c. tossing paper in the wastebasket
   3. See all Activities in this Section.

H. Vocabulary Builders—Spelling Words:
   1) **solvents**   2) **solute**   3) **evaporate**   4) **iron**
   5) **filings**

I. Thought for Today:
   "Technological progress has given society a more efficient way of going backwards."

Activity

A. Problem: *What is a Solution?*

B. Materials:
   1. Water
   2. Glass container
   3. Powdered milk
   4. Sugar
   5. Powdered chocolate, instant coffee, or dried soft drink powders
   6. Heat source
   7. Pie pan

Sugar dissolving in water

C. Procedure:
   1. Put a spoonful of sugar into the glass container; stir thoroughly.
   2. Note that nothing settles to the bottom.
   3. Pour all of the material out of the jar and notice that no residue is left on the bottom.
   4. Repeat the experiment with the powdered material selected above.
   5. Pour a solution of water sweetened with a lot of sugar into a pie pan.
   6. Heat and observe results.

D. Results:
   1. The sugar appears to become a part of the liquid and there will be no residue left in the bottom of the glass container.
   2. When the same experiment is done using the other powdered substance the same result is evident.
   3. When the sugar water is heated, the water evaporated and the solute (the sugar) is left behind. (Note this is a physical change—the sugar was not changed.)

E. Supplemental Information:
Whenever a solid substance is homogeneously mixed with a liquid and does not precipitate out, it is known as *dissolving* the substance in the liquid. The resulting liquid is a combination of the original liquid, plus the solid, which has been dissolved in it. This is known as a solution. Liquids can hold only so much dissolved material for each temperature.

F. Thought Questions:
   1. Will all materials dissolve in water?
   2. Are there some materials which will not dissolve in water, but will dissolve in alcohol or some other liquids?
   3. Is milk a solution?
   4. Why do some window and floor cleaners contain ammonia?

G. Related Topics and Activities:
   1. Test other materials to see if they will dissolve in water.
   2. Test other materials to see if they will dissolve in alcohol.
   3. Put materials in the bottom of a glass container and slowly pour water over them. Do they dissolve immediately?
   4. See all Activities in this Section.

H. Vocabulary Builders—Spelling Words:
   1) **dissolve**   2) **precipitate**   3) **solvent**   4) **solute**
   5) **solution**

I. Thought for Today:
   "A person without dreams is an individual without a future."

A. Problem: *What Matter is Acidic or Alkaline?*

B. Materials:
1. Three glasses
2. Red litmus paper
3. Blue litmus paper
4. Vinegar
5. Ammonia or baking soda solution
6. Salt
7. Water

Salt water

Red and blue litmus paper remain the same

Vinegar

Blue litmus paper turns red

Ammonia

Red litmus paper turns blue

C. Procedure:
1. Prepare a saltwater solution and put into one glass.
2. Dip a piece of red and a piece of blue litmus paper into the solution.
3. In a second glass pour a small amount of vinegar.
4. Dip a piece of blue litmus paper into the solution.
5. In a third tumbler pour a small amount of ammonia or baking soda solution.
6. Dip a piece of red litmus paper into this solution.
7. Repeat steps 4 and 6 using other colored litmus paper.

D. Results:
1. In the saltwater solution the red and blue litmus papers do not change colors.
2. In the vinegar solution the blue litmus paper turned red.
3. In the ammonia or baking soda solution the red litmus paper turned blue.
4. See "Supplemental Information" for other test results.

E. Supplemental Information:
1. Ions are atoms or molecules without their outer electrons or a gain of electrons from other atoms or molecules.
2. Solutions usually have hydrogen or hydroxide ions. If they have hydrogen ions they are acidic. If they have hydroxide ions they are alkaline (basic).

3. Litmus paper turns blue in the presence of alkaline solutions and red in the presence of acids. We can conclude that vinegar is acidic and that ammonia is alkaline (basic). Other liquids can be tested to determine if they are acidic or basic.
4. Some tap water may be naturally acidic or basic, and if so, then bottled or distilled water will have to be used.

F. Thought Questions:
1. Why do we need to know whether a substance is acid or alkaline?
2. If acid is spilled, how can we prevent it from causing damage?
3. What would happen if we placed red litmus paper in the vinegar? Blue litmus in the ammonia or baking soda solution?

G. Related Topics and Activities:
1. Test other liquids to determine if they are acidic or alkaline.
2. Research other chemical tests for determining acidity or alkalinity of liquids.
3. See all Activities in this Section.

H. Vocabulary Builders—Spelling Words:
1) **acidic** 2) **alkaline** 3) **alkalinity** 4) **basic**
5) **litmus paper**

I. Thought for Today:
"If people learn from their mistakes, many are getting a fantastic education."

A. Problem: *How Does a Fire Extinguisher Work?*

B. Materials:

1. Clear pint or quart bottle
2. Cork stopper
3. Vinegar water (one tbsp. vinegar in one cup water)
4. Baking soda
5. Paper napkin, small
6. Spoon and cup for measuring
7. Thread
8. Cloth or toweling

C. Procedure:

1. Fill bottle about one-third full of vinegar.
2. Wrap one teaspoonful of baking soda in a napkin.
3. Tie thread around napkin and suspend by fitting cork to neck of bottle.
4. Place cork in bottle so that it may be removed with minimum effort.
5. Wrap bottle with cloth or toweling as a safety precaution.
6. When fire extinguisher is set to use, point the top of the bottle toward the ceiling or toward a solid wall. *Be very careful not to point it toward anything which might break or cause injury.*
7. Invert the bottle momentarily and the solution will soften the napkin; the soda will be released to drop into the vinegar solution.
8. Keep class members at least six feet away from bottle.

D. Result:

When the vinegar reacts with the baking soda, carbon dioxide is given off. The carbon dioxide builds up pressure and the cork is forced out of the bottle with great force.

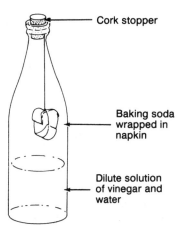

Cork stopper

Baking soda wrapped in napkin

Dilute solution of vinegar and water

E. Supplemental Information:

1. Carbon dioxide does not support combustion.
2. It drives out some of the oxygen which is needed for burning.
3. Three items are required for fires (burning): a) combustible material, b) oxygen, and c) heat.
4. If any one of the three items above are removed, then no burning can take place.

F. Thought Questions:

1. Why do we wrap the baking soda in a paper napkin?
2. How does carbon dioxide stop fires from burning?
3. Do all gases slow down fires?

G. Related Topics and Activities:

1. Design a fire extinguisher using different materials or procedures.
2. Have a fire department representative talk to class.
3. See all Activities in this Section.

H. Vocabulary Builders—Spelling Words:

1) **extinguisher**   2) **vinegar**   3) **napkin**
4) **fire**   5) **oxygen**   6) **combustible**

I. Thought for Today:

"He who hesitates is sometimes saved."

A. Problem: *How Can We Make Invisible Ink?*

B. Materials:
1. Lemon
2. Toothpick
3. Shallow dish
4. Paper
5. Heat source (light bulb)

Secret writing

C. Procedure:
1. Squeeze the juice from half a lemon.
2. Put the juice in a dish.
3. Use the juice to write. (A toothpick makes a good pen for invisible ink.)
4. Set aside the paper with the writing on it to dry.
5. Heat the paper by holding it over a light bulb.
6. Move the paper around so that all the invisible writing gets warm.

D. Results:
1. As the lemon juice dries it becomes invisible.
2. As the paper heats, the writing becomes visible.

E. Supplemental Information:
The heat causes a chemical change in the lemon juice which makes it turn brown. The writing therefore becomes visible. This system can be used to send "secret messages."

F. Thought Questions:
1. Will sugar in water have the same result as the lemon juice?
2. Will white vinegar yield the same result?
3. What other substances change color when heated?
4. Will plain water work?

G. Related Topics and Activities:
1. Students can write secret spelling words or answers to math problems using this procedure.
2. See Activity I-A-9.
3. See all Activities in this Section.

H. Vocabulary Builders—Spelling Words:
1) **invisible**   2) **secret**   3) **ink**   4) **lemon**
5) **toothpick**

I. Thought for Today:
"A person who doesn't read books has no advantage over the person who can't read."

Section B: Air

Activity   1B1

A. Problem: *Does Warm Air Rise or Fall?*

B. Materials:
1. Thread or string
2. Yardstick or meterstick
3. Pencil
4. Several books
5. Table
6. Two paper bags of equal size and weight
7. Candle
8. Matches
9. Coat hanger (wire)
10. Wooden block
11. Paper, thin, 4″ × 4″
12. Scissors
13. Cutting pliers
14. Staples or small nails

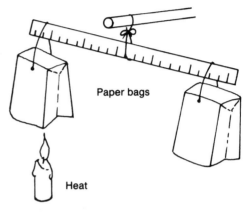

Paper bags

Heat

Procedure one

C. Procedure One:
1. Make a loop out of a foot long piece of thread or string and use it to support the yardstick or meterstick at the half-way mark.
2. Tie the other end of the thread in a loop and attach over a pencil, supported under several books set near the end of the table.
3. Make two pin-sized holes in the bottom of each of the bags, run a piece of thread through the holes and make the thread into a loose loop.
4. Hang both bags on the yardstick or meterstick as shown in the diagram. If the bags are exactly the same weight, they should make the yardstick or meterstick balance when they are placed one inch from each end. You may have to adjust one bag slightly until you get them balanced.
5. Hold a lighted candle a foot or more below the mouth of one open bag until the air inside is warmed. *Be careful with flame!*
6. Remove the candle and extinguish the flame.

Procedure Two:
1. Cut a circular piece of paper about four inches in diameter.
2. Starting from the outside of the circle cut a continuous strip about an inch wide.
3. Cut the wire coat hanger so that you have one long straight piece.
4. Staple or nail this to the base board bending the end at right angles for support.
5. Place one end of the spiral on the top of wire without puncturing the strip.
6. Light a candle beneath the strip.

D. Results:
1. The bag with the warm air will rise.
2. When the candle is removed and the warm air is dissipated (in a few seconds) the bags will again be balanced.
3. With the spiral cut-out, as the air is warmed, it sets up a convection current updraft that turns the "paper snake."

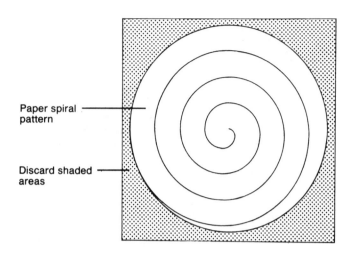

Paper spiral pattern

Discard shaded areas

Procedure two

E. Supplemental Information:

The bag with the warm air rises, therefore, it must be lighter than the air in the other bag. Heat causes air to expand. As air expands it becomes lighter because there are less molecules per volume. Cold causes air to contract. As air contracts it becomes heavier. Air has weight. Air has pressure because it has weight and movement. Most draft furnaces in houses operate on this heat principle. As the air is heated it becomes lighter and rises. Cold air comes in from the sides or below and thus a circulation of air takes place. This is very different from the principle of radiant heating by which the house is heated by radiation instead of air circulation.

F. Thought Questions:
   1. What problems do people have who fly hot air balloons?
   2. What happens to tires on a car or bicycle when the tires heat up or cool down?
   3. Can you think of any other ways that warm or hot air works for us?

G. Related Topics and Activities:
   1. Check the air temperature in different places around the school.
   2. Discuss what causes winds. See Activity VII-E-2.
   3. Check air movement in your classroom.

H. Vocabulary Builders—Spelling Words:
   1) **ascend** 2) **descend** 3) **convection** 4) **candle**
   5) **matches** 6) **spiral**

I. Thought for Today:
   "A teacher affects eternity; no one can tell where his influence stops."—Henry Adams

Activity

A. Problem: *Can Air Pressure Lift Heavy Objects?*

B. Materials:

1. Brick or other similar object
2. Small rubber balloon
3. Piece of glass tubing
4. String
5. Tire pump
6. Hot water bottle
7. Board, approximately 12″ × 18″

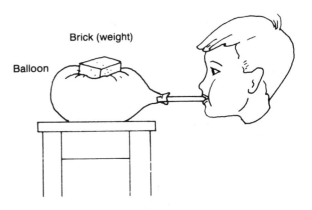

Procedure one

C. Procedure One:

1. Place the glass tubing in the neck of the balloon.
2. Put the brick on top of the deflated balloon.
3. Secure the neck with string.
4. Inflate the balloon by blowing into it.

Procedure Two:

1. Attach an air pump to the rubber tubing of a hot water bottle.
2. Place a board on the top of the empty hot water bottle.
3. Have a student stand on the board.
4. Pump air into the hot water bottle.

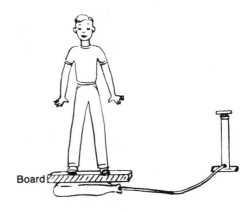

Procedure two

D. Results:

1. The balloon will expand by air pressure, and as it inflates it will lift the brick.
2. The air forced into the hot water bottle exerts enough pressure to lift the board and the student several inches.

E. Supplemental Information:

The rubber balloon has elastic sides and, therefore, when air is blown into it, it will expand. Because the walls of the balloon expand, the air pressure inside is almost the same as that outside of the balloon. The only difference lies in the extra pressure needed to expand the elastic of the balloon. Air pressure is used to inflate automobile and bicycle tires.

F. Thought Questions:

1. What happens if too much air is put into the balloon?
2. If the weight is extra heavy, will the boy have to blow harder to raise the object? Why?
3. In what other ways are heavy objects raised?
4. Where is air used to lift heavy objects?

5. Why is it smoother to ride on a tire filled with air than one which is not?
6. How are cars lifted in service stations when they are to be lubricated?
7. Does the pump get hot or cold? Why?

G. Related Topics and Activities:

1. Check an electric fan. Does it exert pressure?
2. Check the exhaust side of a vacuum cleaner. Does it exert pressure?
3. See all Activities in this Section.

H. Vocabulary Builders—Spelling Words:

1) **elastic**   2) **pump**   3) **balloon**   4) **tire**
5) **board**   6) **pressure**

I. Thought for Today:

"The mediocre teacher tells.
The good teacher explains.
The superior teacher demonstrates.
The great teacher inspires."

Activity

A. Problem: *Will Air Pressure Crush a Can?*

B. Materials:
1. One (or two) gallon tin can
2. Stopper to fit can
3. Pair of pot holders
4. Hot plate, gas burner, or canned heat
5. Water

C. Procedure:
1. Put about a quarter inch of water in the can.
2. Heat the can over heat source until the water reaches the boiling point and steam comes out of the opening.
3. Using pot holders, remove the can from the heat and close the opening with the stopper; make sure this is an airtight fit. *This is very important.*
4. Watch carefully as can cools after removing from heat source.

D. Result:

The can will slowly crinkle and collapse.

E. Supplemental Information:
1. The air pressure inside and outside were equal at the start, when the water was added, and when the water was steaming.
2. The steam forces most of the air out of the can.
3. After the can was sealed, the steam condensed causing a partial vacuum; the volume of air and steam was reduced causing the inside pressure to decrease. (One c.c. of water will make about 1500 c.c. of steam.) (c.c. stands for cubic centimeter.)
4. The condensation reduces the pressure inside, and the outside pressure, being greater, crushes the can.
5. If any outside air is let into the can, a balance of forces will take place, causing the can to remain intact.

F. Thought Questions:
1. How is a partial vacuum created on the inside of a can?
2. Why is it necessary to boil the water before sealing the can?
3. Why must the can be airtight?

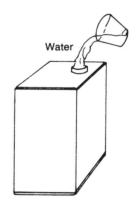

Water

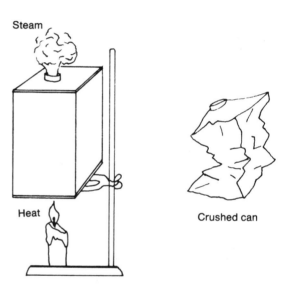

Steam

Heat

Crushed can

4. If air has a pressure of 14.7 pounds per square inch, how much pressure was exerted on this can? (Hint: How many surfaces does a can have?)

G. Related Topics and Activities:
1. Place a thimble full of water in a can with a push down top or use a loosely fitted cork. Place over heat source. Take precautions, for the cork will be blown out of can.
2. See all Activities in this Section.

H. Vocabulary Builders—Spelling Words:
1) **vacuum**   2) **condensation**   3) **precautions**
4) **steam**   5) **boiling point**

I. Thought for Today:

"It is harder to conceal ignorance than to acquire knowledge."

Activity

A. Problem: *What is Suction?*

B. Materials:
1. Two plungers
2. Small amount of water
3. Chair
4. Piece of porous material such as wire screen

C. Procedure:
1. Wet the rubber portions of the plungers and push ends together.
2. Have two members of class try to separate plungers, pulling straight out. (It is a good idea to have another student stand behind each in case they come apart quickly and forcibly.)
3. Observe results.
4. Have one student press a plunger against the seat of a chair.
5. Try to lift chair with the plunger.
6. Observe results.
7. Try to lift porous material.
8. Observe results.

D. Results:
1. When a partial vacuum is created on the inside of the two plungers by pushing them together, the pressure on the outside will be great enough so that two pupils of ordinary strength cannot pull them apart.
2. The chair can be lifted with the plunger.
3. The plunger will not be able to lift porous materials.

E. Supplemental Information:
The expulsion of air from the inside of the plunger reduces the pressures within and a greater relative pressure is exerted without. These activities prove that suction is really a differential in air pressure.

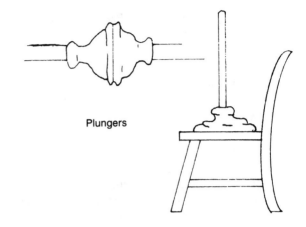

Plungers

F. Thought Questions:
1. What is a vacuum?
2. Can you think of any other ways in which rubber suction cups are used?
3. How do we use vacuums to help us?
4. Is there any other way we can get the plungers apart?

G. Related Topics and Activities:
1. Explain how a plunger works.
2. Place a straw in some colored water. Lift the straw out. Repeat putting finger on top before withdrawing.
3. See Activity I-B-11.

H. Vocabulary Builders—Spelling Words:
1) **suction**   2) **partial**   3) **vacuum**
4) **plunger**   5) **porous**

I. Thought for Today:
"Children need love, especially when they don't deserve it."

Activity

A. **Problem:** *How Does Air Pressure Hold Water in a Can?*

B. Materials:
1. Small metal can, complete with removable top or cork
2. Water

C. Procedure:
1. Punch a small hole near bottom of the can.
2. Put finger over hole and fill can with water.
3. With top off can, remove finger from hole and watch water flow from it in a steady stream.
4. Refill can with finger over hole.
5. Fasten top to it securely. (Finger must be over hole while refilling.)
6. Remove finger from hole and observe results.

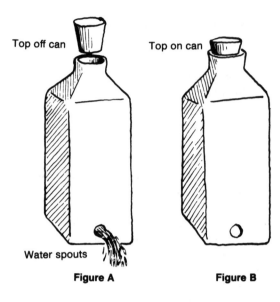

Top off can   Top on can

Water spouts

Figure A   **Figure B**

D. Results:
1. On first attempt with top off the can, water flows from the hole in a steady stream.
2. On second attempt, and with top on the can, water does not flow from the hole.

E. Supplemental Information:
When the can has no top on it, the weight of the water and air pressure will force the water out of the small hole in a steady stream. When the top is on, the air pressure cannot exert a downward force on the water in the can. Air pressure acting against the water in the hole does not permit any water to escape.

F. Thought Questions:
1. Does altitude have any effect on this experiment?
2. Why do we punch two holes on the top of any can holding a liquid?
3. Can water ever run uphill?

G. Related Topics and Activities:
1. What would happen in this experiment if we punched a series of holes in the can in a vertical position?
2. Test what would happen if the holes were punched in a horizontal line rather than vertical.
3. See all Activities in this Section.
4. See also Section VII-E, "Weather."

H. Vocabulary Builders—Spelling Words:
1) **atmospheric**   2) **pressure**   3) **stream**
4) **punched**   5) **finger**

I. Thought for Today:
"Without experience one gains no wisdom."

Activity

A. Problem: *Can Air Pressure Hold Water in a Tumbler?*

B. Materials:

1. Glass, water
2. Water
3. Piece of cardboard
4. Basin or sink

C. Procedure:

1. Fill the glass tumbler completely full of water.
2. Place a piece of stiff paper or cardboard on top of the glass and hold it in place with your hand.
3. Over a basin or sink being careful not to let any bubble of air enter between the cardboard and the glass, invert the tumbler while holding the cardboard in place.
4. Remove your hand carefully from below the paper or cardboard, being careful not to jar either the glass or the paper.

D. Result:

The cardboard and the water will remain in place.

E. Supplemental Information:

1. The water is held in the tumbler because the pressure of the air outside the glass against the cardboard was greater than the pressure of the water against the cardboard. It is important to seal the cardboard tightly against the glass. If any air gets in between the cardboard and the edge of the glass, this will not work.
2. The tumbler has only the weight of the water in it. Atmospheric pressure is excluded from the inside of the tumbler. Outside atmospheric pressure (14.7 lbs. per square inch at sea level) has only the weight of a tumbler of water to work against and therefore *pushes* the cardboard firmly against the tumbler.

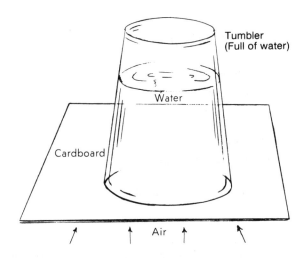

F. Thought Questions:

1. How much does air weigh?
2. What would happen if the drinking glass were only half-full?
3. What would happen if the drinking glass and cardboard were turned sideways after the cardboard adheres to the glass?

G. Related Topics and Activities:

1. Study the pressures working on a submarine.
2. What would be necessary for people to work under water constructing a tunnel or tube?
3. See other Activities in this Section.

H. Vocabulary Builders—Spelling Words:

1) **pressure**   2) **drinking**   3) **air**   4) **atmospheric**
5) **exerted**

I. Thought for Today:

"Perseverance is not a long race; it is many short races one after another."—Walter Elliott

Activity

A. Problem: *How Does Air Pressure in a Bicycle Tire Hold Up the Bicycle?*

B. Materials:
   1. Bicycle tire on bicycle
   2. Hand tire pump

C. Procedure:
   1. Deflate bicycle tire.
   2. Feel tire.
   3. Attach hose of hand pump to air valve of bicycle.
   4. Inflate the tire using hand pump.
   5. Stop when inflated tire has normal appearance.
   6. Have students feel the bicycle tire and the tire pump.

D. Results:
   1. Pupils can see and feel that air pressure does hold up the bicycle tire.
   2. The pump gets hot due to the compression of the air by the pump.

E. Supplemental Information:
   1. Automobile tires work in the same way (as above).
   2. Air pressure can hold up heavy objects. Some types of lifts use this principle. If time permits, you may wish to have pupils study how an air pump works.
   3. See Activity I-B-2.

F. Thought Questions:
   1. Why does a bicycle tire get flat only on the bottom?
   2. What might cause a tire to go flat?
   3. Is the air pressure in the tire greater than the air pressure outside the tire?
   4. How is air pressure measured?

G. Related Topics and Activities:
   1. Try the same test with an automobile tubed tire if one is available.
   2. Try the same test with an air mattress.
   3. Try the same test with a beach ball.

H. Vocabulary Builders—Spelling Words:
   1) **bicycle**   2) **tire**   3) **inflate**   4) **deflate**
   5) **attach**

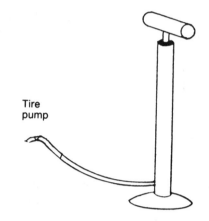

Tire pump

Bicycle

I. Thought for Today:
   "A mistake is evidence that someone has tried to do something."

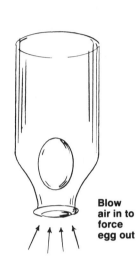

Blow air in to force egg out

A. Problem: *Can an Egg Be Put into a Small-Mouthed Bottle Without Breaking the Egg?*

B. Materials:
1. Small-mouthed bottle (slightly smaller than the egg)
2. Medium-sized wad of paper
3. Matches
4. Hard-boiled egg with shell removed

C. Procedure:
1. Show the pupils that the egg will not fit into the bottle without being crushed.
2. Light the wad of paper and insert it into the bottle.
3. Place the egg into the mouth of the bottle immediately.
4. Have students observe the results.

D. Result:

The egg will bob up and down, then slowly descend into the neck of the bottle, and finally pop into the bottle with a loud plunk.

E. Supplemental Information:
1. The bobbing up and down of the egg is due to the fact that as the heated air expands, the air bubbles out from beneath the egg. When the paper stops burning, the air within the bottle cools and the inside pressure is reduced. However, the normal air pressure on the top and sides of the egg remains unchanged. The egg, therefore, is forced into the bottle.
2. A good challenging question is how to get the egg back out without breaking the egg. This can be accomplished by inverting the bottle and blowing hard into its mouth; the increased air pressure on the inside will force the egg out. (Don't forget to duck or move head quickly to the side.)

F. Thought Questions:
1. What would happen to the egg if you tried to push it into the bottle with your hands?
2. Is the egg "sucked" into the bottle or is it pushed in by the outside air pressure?
3. Why aren't soft things crushed by the "heavy" air pressure which surrounds them?

G. Related Topics and Activities:
1. Place a candle in a shelled, hard-boiled egg. Light the candle and place the inverted bottle over the egg and the lighted candle.
2. See other Activities in this Section.

H. Vocabulary Builders—Spelling Words:
1) **expand**   2) **descend**   3) **bottle**   4) **hard-boiled**
5) **breaking**

I. Thought for Today:
"Education is what survives when what was learned has been forgotten."—B. F. Skinner

A. Problem: *How Does Air Move About a Burning Candle?*

B. Materials:
1. Funnel
2. Saucer
3. Several nails or small pieces of wood
4. Candle
5. Piece of cotton or woolen cloth
6. Matches
7. Nails or small pencils

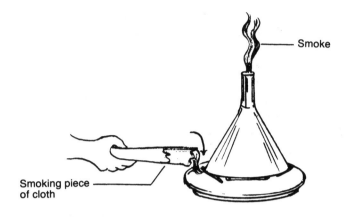

Smoke

Smoking piece of cloth

C. Procedure:
1. Fasten a small candle in an upright position on the saucer. (The candle must be short enough so that the funnel will fit over it.)
2. Light the candle.
3. Place the funnel over the candle in such a way so that the edge of the funnel sits directly on the saucer. Note what happens to the flame.
4. Remove the funnel.
5. Light the candle again.
6. Lay some nails or small pencils around the saucer in such a way that the funnel when replaced over the candle will not rest directly on the saucer.
7. Light the cotton or the cloth.
8. As soon as it begins to burn, blow it out.
9. Bring the smoking piece of cotton or cloth by the lower edge of the funnel and note how the smoke from the burning material travels.

D. Results:
When the funnel is placed over the candle without any air space underneath, the candle is immediately extinguished. When the funnel is placed over the candle in such a manner so that the air may travel underneath, the air travels underneath the funnel and the smoke comes out of the opening at the upper end of the funnel.

E. Supplemental Information:
When no air is allowed to come underneath the funnel, the candle is extinguished because the oxygen required to support combustion is not available. As soon as air is allowed to enter under the candle, the path of air can be traced and this indicates that air travels into the funnel and out the top and as long as air reaches the candle, it continues to burn.

F. Thought Questions:
1. With vertically opening windows, why do people open them both at the top and at the bottom?
2. Does hot air rise or fall? Why?
3. What is smoke?

G. Related Topics and Activities:
1. Shake a little talcum powder in the air and see what happens. Now using a heat source that has been on for a few minutes, shake some fine talcum powder over it. What does it do? Rise or fall? Why?
2. Discuss why heavy hot air balloons rise.

H. Vocabulary Builders—Spelling Words:
1) **extinguish** 2) **combustion** 3) **candle**
4) **funnel** 5) **saucer**

I. Thought for Today:
"A laugh at your own expense costs you nothing."—Mary H. Waldrip

Activity

A. Problem: *How Do We Drink with a Straw?*

B. Materials:
1. Drinking glass
2. Red food coloring or red ink
3. Water
4. Glass tubing or clear drinking straw

C. Procedure:
1. Mix some red coloring in a glass of water.
2. Holding tubing with finger on top, immerse in water container.
3. Observe portion of tubing under water.
4. Lift finger off top of tubing.
5. Observe what happens in tubing.
6. With finger off top of tubing, again immerse in container.
7. Observe what happens in tubing.
8. With tubing in water, cover the top of tubing with finger.
9. Lift tubing above the container.
10. Release finger off the top of tubing.

D. Results:
1. The water will not rise in the tubing until the finger has been removed.
2. When tubing is immersed and finger is released, water will rise in the tubing.
3. When colored water has risen, the finger placed over the top and the tube removed from the water, the water will stay in tube until the finger is released.

E. Supplemental Information:
Air pressure in the tube keeps the water out in the first part. Air pressure outside holds the water up in the second part because the finger prohibits the air pressure from acting down on the water. Water is forced out in the last activity by the weight of the water. (Air pressure is equal on top and bottom.) Sodas are drunk by reducing the air pressure in the mouth, and the air pressure outside forces the soda to move into the mouth.

F. Thought Questions:
1. Why won't the water enter the tube when the finger is on top of it?
2. Does this principle have anything to do with skin diving?
3. What happens to the air in the straw when we drink sodas?

G. Related Topics and Activities:
1. Discuss why water moves through a garden hose.
2. Discuss why water moves through a kitchen faucet.
3. Try drinking with two straws, but only one in the liquid.
4. See other Activities in this Section.

H. Vocabulary Builders—Spelling Words:
1) **drinking** 2) **straw** 3) **tubing** 4) **finger**
5) **coloring**

I. Thought for Today:
"Nothing makes a person more productive than the last minute."

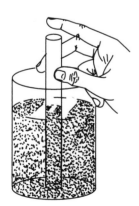
Place tube in water.

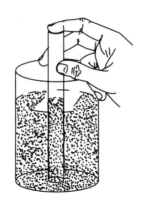
Place finger on tube.

Remove finger from glass.

Lift finger from tube.

Activity

A. Problem: *How Does a Siphon Work?*

B. Materials:
1. Three feet of plastic or rubber tubing
2. Two glass jars
3. Water

C. Procedure:
1. Fill one jar with water and place it on a level higher than the other jar.
2. Fill rubber tubing with water (must be completely filled).
3. Cover each end with one thumb.
4. Insert one end of tubing into the water in the higher jar and the other end into the lower jar. (Be sure that the end of the tube in the empty jar is below the water level in the water jar.)
5. Remove thumb from the end of the tubing in lower jar.

D. Result:
The water will flow from the full jar to the empty jar until the water is at the same level in both jars even though the quantity in the jars may not be the same.

E. Supplemental Information:
In the "Before" sketch the water will flow downward due to the force of gravity and the atmospheric pressure, P. As the water flows down, this will create a partial vacuum in the tube. The atmospheric pressure P exerted on the surface of the water L will force water up the tube and along the tube in direction D. This will cause a continuous flow of water as long as the level of M is lower than the level of L.

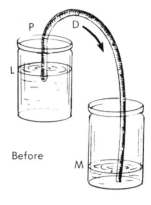
Before

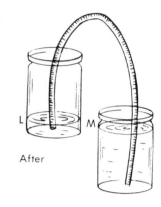
After

F. Thought Questions:
1. What will happen if the jars are alternately raised and lowered?
2. Will this siphon work if one of the jars becomes empty?
3. Why won't the siphon work if some air gets in the tubing?
4. Do water pumps use this principle? How?
5. Are there other ways to start a siphon?

G. Related Topics and Activities:
1. Practice siphoning your classroom aquarium when it needs cleaning.
2. Discuss the dangers of siphoning gasoline from an automobile.
3. See following Activity I-B-12.

H. Vocabulary Builders—Spelling Words:
1) **siphon** 2) **vacuum** 3) **pressure** 4) **plastic**
5) **tubing** 6) **thumb**

I. Thought for Today:
"School is a place where children live."

Activity

A. Problem: *How Can We Make a Fountain Siphon?*

B. Materials:
1. Two glass jars or beakers
2. Two-hole stopper to fit one jar or beaker
3. Two pieces of glass tubing (one long with pointed end, one short)
4. Two pieces of plastic or rubber tubing to fit glass tubing
5. Water colored with ink or food coloring
6. Ring stand
7. Pan or bucket

C. Procedure:
1. Put colored water in both jars or beakers.
2. Put a short piece of rubber tubing on the long glass tubing with pointed end up and place in one of the holes in the rubber stopper. (Wet stopper for easier insertion.)
3. Put long pieces of plastic or rubber tubing on short glass tubing and place in other hole.
4. Holding long pieces of plastic or rubber tubing above level of stoppered jar, turn jar upside down, placing short plastic or rubber tubing in bottom of the jar or beaker containing water.
5. Slide jar with tubing into ring stand by inverting jar and pinching the tubing.
6. Put the lower end of long plastic or rubber tubing in empty pan or bucket below the level of the jar or beaker which contains water.
7. Release plastic or rubber tubing. (Stop pinching.)

D. Result:
Water will run out of the long plastic or rubber tubing and at the same time other water will spurt into upper jar from the lower jar.

E. Supplemental Information:
The weight of the water in the upper jar or beaker will make the water flow downward into the lower pan or bucket, leaving a partial vacuum in the upper jar or beaker.

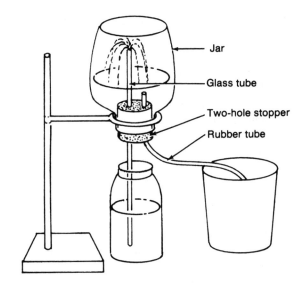

Jar

Glass tube

Two-hole stopper

Rubber tube

The outside air pressure will force the water upward through the tubing. Water comes up with such force that it forms a spray in the open space in the upper jar or beaker.

F. Thought Questions:
1. Can this fountain siphon be made to operate indefinitely?
2. If no water is added to the supply in the jar, when will the fountain stop operating?
3. With a sink and running water available, how could this run continuously?

G. Related Topics and Activities:
1. See previous Activity I-B-11.
2. See other Activities in this Section.

H. Vocabulary Builders—Spelling Words:
1) **siphon** 2) **fountain** 3) **pressure**
4) **tubing** 5) **plastic** 6) **rubber**

I. Thought for Today:
"How a person feels is more important than what a person knows."

Activity

A. Problem: *How Does Air Pressure Affect Boiling Water?*

B. Materials:
1. Pyrex flask
2. Stopper (cork or rubber)
3. Ring stand
4. Heat source
5. Glass
6. Cold water
7. Pot holders (or gloves)

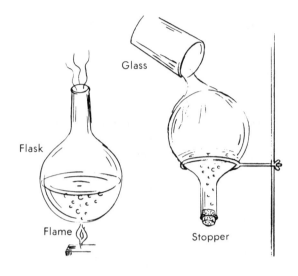

C. Procedure:
1. Boil water in the flask until the steam drives out all the air (about ten seconds after briskly boiling).
2. Shut off heat source.
3. Using pot holders or gloves, stopper flask tightly. (Water will stop boiling.)
4. Invert flask on ring stand using pot holders.
5. Pour cold water into glass and then over flask.
6. Wait until apparatus is completely cooled before trying to remove cork. Teacher should remove as reduced pressure causes a very tight fit.

D. Results:
1. Water in the flask boils, then stops boiling.
2. When cold water is poured over the inverted flask, the water inside will start to boil again.

E. Supplemental Information:
As cold water is poured over the flask, the steam which is formed by the boiling water is condensed, leaving a partial vacuum, and the water boils at a lower temperature. Air pressure affects boiling point temperatures.

F. Thought Questions:
1. Does water always boil at the same temperature?
2. Why does it take longer to cook an egg on a high mountaintop than it does at sea level?
3. How could you make water boil without increasing its temperature?
4. Could water ever boil at room temperature?
5. Why does water boil at a lower temperature on Pike's Peak or Mount Wilson?

G. Related Topics and Activities:
1. Discuss how a pressure cooker works.
2. See other Activities in this Section.
3. See Section VII-E, "Weather."

H. Vocabulary Builders—Spelling Words:
1) **invert** 2) **boiling** 3) **temperature**
4) **point** 5) **elevation**

I. Thought for Today:
"You can't have everything—where would you put it?"

Activity

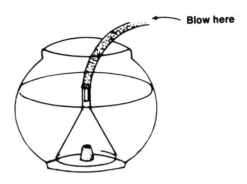

Blow here

A. Problem: *How Can People Work Under Water?*

B. Materials:
   1. Large glass container
   2. Water
   3. Cork
   4. Glass funnel
   5. Plastic tubing

C. Procedure:
   1. Fill the container about two-thirds full of water.
   2. Place the cork on water's surface.
   3. Place funnel over the cork.
   4. Push funnel to the bottom of the container and hold it there.
   5. Blow air into end of plastic tubing.

D. Results:
   1. Water will be forced out of the funnel.
   2. The cork will descend to the bottom.
   3. Air bubbles will rise to the surface.

E. Supplemental Information:

Air pressure may displace water in an enclosed underwater area. This area will remain dry as long as the pressure is maintained. Under actual working conditions, pressure must be increased and decreased very slowly, a process requiring several hours. People can work in a compressed air chamber only a short time.

F. Thought Questions:
   1. What will happen to people in an underwater chamber if the air hose breaks?
   2. If the air hose is sealed tightly, will the people suffocate or drown? Why?
   3. How do divers get their air? What are the dangers?
   4. What causes an object to sink or float?
   5. Why does gaseous air hold the liquid water out?

G. Related Topics and Activities:
   1. Push a drinking glass down over a cork floating in a glass container.
   2. How do deep sea divers work under water?
   3. See all Activities in this Section.

H. Vocabulary Builders—Spelling Words:
   1) **suffocate**   2) **compression**   3) **displace**
   4) **bottom**   5) **funnel**

I. Thought for Today:
   "Failing is not the worst possible outcome; not trying is."

Activity

A. Problem: *What is Sideways Air Pressure?*

B. Materials:
1. Wooden spool
2. Thin cardboard
3. Common pin or thumbtack

C. Procedure:
1. Cut a piece of cardboard approximately two inches square.
2. Push the pin or tack through the center of the cardboard.
3. Place this over one end of the spool with the pin inside the hole in the spool. (This keeps the card from sliding sideways.)
4. Blow a steady stream of air into the opposite end of the spool as card is held as shown in sketch.
5. Release the cardboard but continue to blow.

D. Results:
1. The cardboard seems to cling to the spool.
2. The harder you blow, the tighter the cardboard clings to the spool.
3. When the blowing stops, the cardboard falls.

E. Supplemental Information:
The blown air moves out the sides between the spool and cardboard, and not downward. The more air going out the side, the less pressure is exerted downward. The normal air pressure from below pushes upward, keeping the cardboard near the spool. When the blowing is stopped, the weight of the cardboard causes it to drop because the air pressure above and below is then equal and gravity takes over.

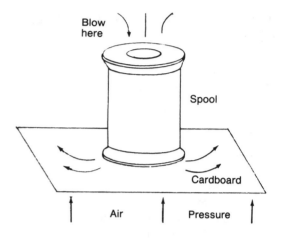

F. Thought Questions:
1. Is this experiment related to two passing trains?
2. If two automobiles pass too close to each other, what might happen?
3. Would children on passing bicycles be affected by this phenomenon?

G. Related Topics and Activities:
1. Look up "Bernoulli's Principle" and describe it in simple terms.
2. Place a ping-pong ball in a funnel holding the stem downward and blow through the stem of the funnel.
3. Place a ping-pong ball in a funnel with the stem pointing directly upward and try to blow the ball out of the funnel.
4. See other Activities in this Section.

H. Vocabulary Builders—Spelling Words:
1) **sideways** 2) **pressure** 3) **spool**
4) **wooden** 5) **thumbtack**

I. Thought for Today:
"Give a man a fish and he eats for a day; teach him to fish and he eats for a lifetime."

Activity

A. Problem: *In Which Direction Does Moving Air Exert the Most Pressure?*

B. Materials:
1. 5″ × 7″ card
2. Soda straw
3. Two ping-pong balls
4. Scotch tape
5. Thread
6. Two books
7. Desk or tabletop

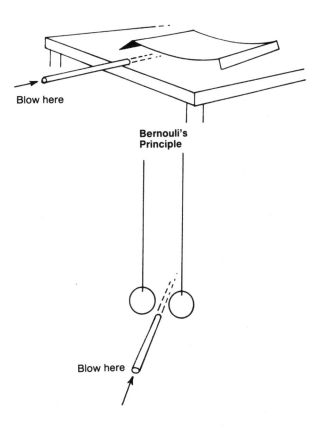

Blow here

Bernouli's Principle

Blow here

C. Procedure:
1. Fold the card so that one-half inch at each end of the card is perpendicular to the card itself.
2. Place the card on the table so that the folded card makes a little platform.
3. Using the soda straw, blow vigorously through the straw and underneath the card.
4. Scotch tape the thread to the two ping-pong balls and support them by placing thread underneath books on desk or tabletop.
5. Have a student using the soda straw again blow vigorously between the two balls to try to blow them apart.

D. Results:
1. The harder one blows and the faster the air moves underneath the card, the more the card bends down toward the current of air.
2. The harder one blows between the ping-pong balls, the closer they will move together.

E. Supplemental Information:
A rapidly moving current of air reduces the upward pressure in the "card activity," thus the normal pressure above the card is greater and pushes the card down. With the ping-pong balls, the normal air pressure between the balls is reduced thus the outside pressure forces the balls closer together. This is called "Bernoulli's Principle."

F. Thought Questions:
1. What happens if you stand close to a rapidly moving train?
2. What would happen if a person got too close to the jet stream of an airplane?
3. What happens when two automobiles pass close together?

G. Related Topics and Activities:
1. Hold a sheet of paper in front of your lips, let it droop, then blow briskly over the top.
2. How does this principle affect airplanes?
3. See other Activities in this Section.

H. Vocabulary Builders—Spelling Words:
1) **Bernoulli**   2) **principle**   3) **direction**
4) **exert**   5) **pressure**

I. Thought for Today:
"It is useless to try to reason a person out of a thing that he was never reasoned into."

Activity

A. Problem: *How Does an Atomizer Work?*

B. Materials:
1. Drinking straw
2. Scissors
3. Glass or cup
4. Water

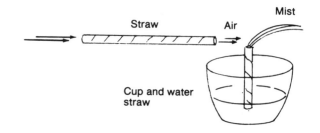

C. Procedure:
1. Cut off about two inches of the drinking straw with a pair of scissors.
2. Insert this piece into a cup of water holding it slightly off the bottom of the glass or cup.
3. Hold the remainder of the straw in a horizontal position as shown, and blow directly over the top of the short piece but not quite touching it.

D. Result:
When you have it just right, a mist or spray will form. Several trials are usually necessary for adjusting the straws.

E. Supplemental Information:
This model atomizer operates because the stream of air moving over the top of the short tube reduces the pressure over the straw in the cup of water. Normal air pressure, therefore, forces the water up the tube. When it gets to the top it is blown off in tiny droplets producing the desired spray. A spray gun works on the same principle. Bernoulli's Principle states that when air is moving rapidly in one direction, the sidewise air pressure is reduced.

F. Thought Questions:
1. Why does the liquid rise vertically in the tube?
2. Why doesn't the stream of air force the liquid back down into the tube?
3. Could other liquids be used?

G. Related Topics and Activities:
1. Examine a commercial air sprayer. Does it work the same way?
2. Do all sprayers work this way?
3. See other Activities in this Section.

H. Vocabulary Builders—Spelling Words:
1) **atomizer**   2) **mist**   3) **droplets**
4) **sideways**   5) **velocity**

I. Thought for Today:
"The only thing you can get in a hurry is trouble."

Activity

A. Problem: *How Much Oxygen is in the Air?*

B. Materials:
1. Widemouth jar (quart size)
2. Pyrex dish or metal pan
3. Matches
4. Candle
5. Water to fill dish halfway (color water if desired)

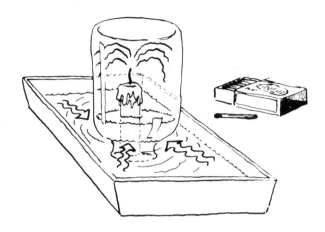

C. Procedure:
1. Light candle, set candle on melted drippings in center of dish or pan.
2. Fill pan half-full of water.
3. Place widemouth jar over lighted candle.
4. Observe results.

D. Results:
1. The candle will cease burning.
2. Water will rise in the jar.

E. Supplemental Information:
The candle flame has removed most of the oxygen from the air in the jar. The pressure of the air left inside the jar has been reduced below that of the air outside. Carbon dioxide, CO_2, is also formed. Air heated by the candle escapes under the lip of the jar. Water rises in the jar about one-fifth of the way so that we can conclude that oxygen makes up about 20% of the air. This is a rough estimate only since there are several other factors which must be taken into account such as heat, incomplete combustion, etc. Most of the rest of the air is nitrogen which makes up about 79% of the total air constituency.

F. Thought Questions:
1. Why does the candle go out?
2. Why does the water rise in the jar?
3. Is there any change in water level if the jar partially filled with water is allowed to remain for awhile? Why? Check level(s) with rubber band(s) around the jar.
4. What are the "products of combustion"?
5. Do they have any effect in this activity?

G. Related Topics and Activities:
1. Discuss how welders use oxygen.
2. Discuss how oxygen is a vital factor in space exploration.
3. See other Activities in this Section.

H. Vocabulary Builders—Spelling Words:
1) **oxygen**   2) **nitrogen**   3) **carbon**
4) **escapes**   5) **combustion**

I. Thought for Today:
"Education makes people easy to lead but difficult to drive; easy to govern but impossible to enslave."

A. Problem: *How Do We Detect Carbon Dioxide?*

B. Materials:

1. Limewater or slaked lime (purchase at a lumber yard or pharmacy)
2. Water
3. Clear soft drink (carbonated)
4. Glass fruit jar with cover
5. Small candle
6. Small bottle
7. Tubing, rubber or plastic
8. Rubber stopper, one hole (to fit soft drink bottle)
9. Glass tubing
10. Drinking straw

C. Procedure:

1. Use limewater or dissolve a tablespoon of slaked lime in a quart of water. Shake well. Let stand till nearly clear; remove and pour off the clear solution leaving the white solid in bottom undisturbed.
2. Place a one-inch layer of this lime solution in the jar and blow through the solution. (Fig. 1)
3. Place a candle in a glass jar; light the candle; and place the lid over the jar. (Fig. 2)
4. As soon as the candle goes out, remove the lid and candle and quickly add one-quarter (¼) inch of the lime solution. Cap the jar and shake well.
5. Add soft drink to jar with limewater solution. Shake well. (Fig. 3)
6. Wet the rubber stopper and insert tubing.
7. Place stopper in bottle that is half-filled with soft drink. (Fig. 4)
8. Attach plastic or rubber tubing to glass tubing.
9. Shake well holding plastic or rubber tubing tightly, then release over candle.

D. Results:

1. If carbon dioxide is present in sufficient strength, it will turn the limewater milky due to the formation of calcium carbonate.
2. Exhaled air from the human body contains carbon dioxide and will turn limewater milky or cloudy.
3. A burning candle gives off carbon dioxide; carbon dioxide does not support combustion.
4. The carbon dioxide present in a soft drink will turn milky in the presence of limewater.
5. Carbon dioxide will extinguish the candle as it does not support combustion.

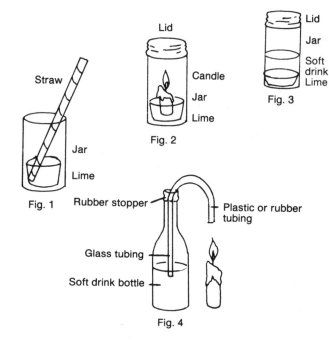

Fig. 1 — Straw, Jar, Lime

Fig. 2 — Lid, Candle, Jar, Lime

Fig. 3 — Lid, Jar, Soft drink, Lime

Fig. 4 — Rubber stopper, Plastic or rubber tubing, Glass tubing, Soft drink bottle

E. Supplemental Information:

1. Most soft drinks contain carbonic acid produced by dissolving carbon dioxide in water.
2. When oxygen and a substance containing carbon are heated to the kindling point, oxidation takes place and carbon dioxide is formed.
3. Limewater is calcium hydroxide. When calcium dioxide is added to this, calcium carbonate is formed. Since this does not dissolve well, it precipitates out, hence the liquid becomes milky.

F. Thought Questions:

1. What is the source of carbon dioxide in all these experiments?
2. What are some properties of carbon dioxide?
3. Is carbon dioxide heavier than air?
4. In fighting fires, is this an advantage or disadvantage?

G. Related Topics and Activities:

1. Study the characteristics of carbon dioxide.
2. Study the effects of adding extra carbon dioxide to the atmosphere.
3. See other Activities in this Section.

H. Vocabulary Builders—Spelling Words:

1) **detect**   2) **carbon dioxide**   3) **limewater**
4) **dissolve**   5) **solution**

I. Thought for Today:

"All that is necessary for evil to triumph is for good men to do nothing."—Edmund Burke

Section C: Water

Activity

A. Problem: *What Objects Float or Sink?*

B. Materials:
1. Pan of water
2. Twigs, leaves, cork
3. Small square of paper
4. Wooden and plastic buttons
5. Piece of glass
6. Aluminum cup
7. Metal jar lid
8. Water
9. Medicine bottle with eyedropper
10. Other small objects to test

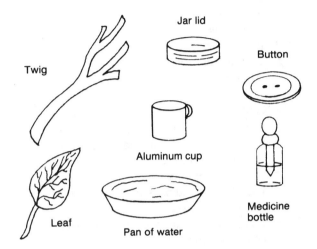

Twig — Jar lid — Button — Aluminum cup — Medicine bottle — Leaf — Pan of water

C. Procedure:
1. Place articles in pan of water, one at a time.
2. Observe which of them floats.
3. Place aluminum cup right-side up in the water, then upside down.
4. Do the same thing with the screw type top jar lid.
5. Place empty medicine bottle with eyedropper in the pan of water.
6. Remove from water.
7. Add a little water to medicine bottle and close with eyedropper.
8. Place in the pan of water.
9. Repeat steps six, seven, and eight until the bottle with eyedropper sinks.
10. Other small objects may be tested for flotation.

D. Results:
1. The twigs and the cork will float.
2. Leaves and paper will float until they become waterlogged.
3. Wooden buttons float; most plastic buttons sink.
4. The aluminum cup and the bottle cover will float when their open ends are up, but when inverted they will fill with water and sink.
5. The closed medicine bottle floats with some water, but when more water is added, it will become too heavy and sink.

E. Supplemental Information:
Objects float in water if they are lighter than an equal volume of water. Some objects sink after they become waterlogged because the light air is replaced by heavier water.

F. Thought Questions:
1. Why do leaves and paper float for a brief time and then sink?
2. How does a submarine submerge? rise? stay half-submerged?
3. Why do other objects sink?

G. Related Topics and Activities:
1. Test other objects for flotation such as sponges, bars of soap, pieces of cloth, hair clips, etc.
2. Check with pupils to see if they can float in swimming areas.
3. See all Activities in this Section.

H. Vocabulary Builders—Spelling Words:
1) **buoyancy**   2) **flotation**   3) **medicine**
4) **eyedropper**   5) **twig**

I. Thought for Today:
"The only ones who don't change their opinions are the dead and the foolish."

Activity

A. Problem: *What is Buoyancy?*

B. Materials:
   1. Citric acid
   2. Baking soda
   3. Mothballs
   4. Food coloring
   5. Two jars or clear bowls
   6. Toy ship

C. Procedure:
   1. In a large jar make a solution using one teaspoon of citric acid and one teaspoon of baking soda for every quart of water.
   2. Add food coloring.
   3. Pour 5 or 6 mothballs into this solution.
   4. Observe the results.
   5. Place the toy ship in second bowl which contains water only.

D. Results:
   1. When the mothballs are placed into the solution, they sink to the bottom. After a few moments, one by one, they slowly rise to the top. As they come to the surface, they roll over again and sink. A moment or two on the bottom and they rise again.
   2. The ship will float on the water.

E. Supplemental Information:
The mothballs are heavier than the solution. When they are dropped in, they sink to the bottom. A chemical reaction takes place with citric acid and soda which causes carbon dioxide to form. The bubbles of carbon dioxide collect on the mothballs and these bubbles lift the mothballs to the surface of the water. As the balls reach the surface, the bubbles of gas disappear into the air and the mothballs drop again to the bottom. A light ship or a heavy ship will not sink because it is lighter than the volume of water it has displaced. A ship's weight includes the metal, wood, and air.

F. Thought Questions:
   1. Does this principle of buoyancy have anything to do with submarine submersion?
   2. As the bubbles of gas form, why don't the bubbles of gas rise to the surface instead of collecting on the mothball?
   3. Is carbon dioxide heavier or lighter than air?

G. Related Topics and Activities:
   1. Cover the first bowl tautly with plastic wrap. Does this affect the test in any way?
   2. In a tall jar or graduated cylinder add some water, then some corn oil, then some rubbing alcohol, then baby oil and observe what happens. (Each layer should float on the earlier addition.)
   3. See other Activities in this Section.

H. Vocabulary Builders—Spelling Words:
   1) **citric acid**   2) **baking soda**   3) **mothball**
   4) **submarine**   5) **chemical reaction**

I. Thought for Today:
   "As spring approaches, the boys begin to feel more gallant, and the gals more buoyant."

Activity

A. Problem: *Why Can We Swim Easier in Salt Water?*

B. Materials:
   1. Four glasses two-thirds full of water
   2. Two pencils
   3. Two hard-boiled eggs
   4. Two thumbtacks
   5. Two tablespoons of salt

C. Procedure:
   1. Dissolve the salt in two of the glasses of water.
   2. Place one egg in freshwater, the other egg in salt water.
   3. Stick thumbtacks in rubber tips of pencils.
   4. Place one pencil in freshwater, the other pencil in salt water, tack ends down.

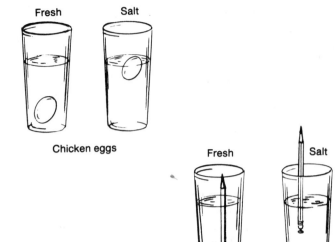

Chicken eggs

Pencil with thumbtack

D. Results:
   1. The egg placed in the freshwater will sink, but the egg in the salt water will be partially buoyed up.
   2. The pencil in salt water will float higher than the one in freshwater.

E. Supplemental Information:
   1. This is a simple hydrometer—a device for measuring the density of a liquid. The denser the water, the greater the buoyancy. Buoyancy is determined by the density of the liquid involved. Battery hydrometers use this principle. The denser the liquid, the stronger the battery.
   2. If you have ever swum in the ocean, you have found out that it is easier to keep afloat in salt water than it is in freshwater. The reason for this is that salt water is denser than freshwater. The heavier the liquid, the greater the buoyancy. A solid iron bar will float in liquid mercury.

F. Thought Questions:
   1. Is salt water denser (heavier) than freshwater?
   2. Is salt water denser (heavier) than an egg?
   3. Why is salt water heavier than freshwater?
   4. Why is water mixed with alcohol lighter than freshwater?

G. Related Topics and Activities:
   1. Have class relate experiences in swimming in salt water and freshwater.
   2. Compare densities of different liquids: oil, molasses, alcohol, mercury, etc.
   3. Make a simple hydrometer using a plastic straw, sealing it at one end, and adding sand to it until it acts like the pencil (or egg) described in the activity.

H. Vocabulary Builders—Spelling Words:
   1) **buoyancy**   2) **density**   3) **hard-boiled**
   4) **tablespoons**   5) **afloat**   6) **hydrometer**

I. Thought for Today:
   "A school is a building with four walls with tomorrow inside."—Len Waters

A. Problem: *What Makes a Submarine Go Up and Down?*

B. Materials:
1. Tall tumbler or one-quart canning jar
2. Eyedropper
3. Water
4. Rubber balloon
5. Rubber band

C. Procedure:
1. Fill the water up to about ½″ from the very top of the tumbler or jar.
2. Place the eyedropper in the water with enough water in it so that it just barely floats. (You'll have to make several trials to adjust it properly.)
3. Observe the air pocket inside.
4. Cut the balloon and make a rubber cap for the jar. Secure with a rubber band.
5. Push cap down and release.

D. Result:
The eyedropper goes into its dive when the rubber top is depressed. When the balloon is elevated the eyedropper floats near the surface of the water.

E. Supplemental Information:
The increase in air forces more water into the eyedropper making it heavier, consequently it sinks to the bottom. When the top of the balloon is elevated, the air pressure is decreased in the jar. The air in the eyedropper then forces the water out and the eyedropper becomes lighter and consequently rises.

Open end

Cartesian diver

F. Thought Questions:
1. Why is it important to adjust the eyedropper so that it just barely floats at the beginning of the experiment?
2. Can you do this experiment without having a little air in the eyedropper?
3. How do submarines use this principle?
4. What happens to the water level in the eyedropper?

G. Related Topics and Activities:
1. Discuss what makes any object sink or float.
2. Study deep sea diving and how divers descend and ascend.
3. See other Activities in this Section.

H. Vocabulary Builders—Spelling Words:
1) **submarine**   2) **eyedropper**   3) **rubber**
4) **ascend**   5) **descend**

I. Thought for Today:
"Every adult needs a child to teach; it's the best kind of adult education."

Activity

A. **Problem:** *Does Cooling Cause Liquids to Contract?*

B. Materials:
1. Hot water
2. Cold water
3. Two jars with covers
4. Labels or marking pens

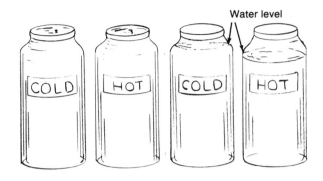

C. Procedure:
1. Fill one jar with hot water.
2. Fill the second jar with cold water.
3. Label one jar "COLD."
4. Label the other jar "HOT."
5. Cover the bottles and set them aside until the next day.
6. Observe water level in each of the bottles.

D. Result:

The bottle marked HOT will show a lower water level than the one marked COLD.

E. Supplemental Information:

The hot water has cooled so that it is at the same temperature as the cold water, and when cool, it does not occupy as much space as when it was hotter. The molecules have moved closer together.

F. Thought Questions:
1. Is this principle true of all liquids?
2. Does water ever expand when cooled?
3. Why does ice float if water normally contracts and gets heavier (per volume) as it cools?

G. Related Topics and Activities:
1. Have students check level of any liquids in the refrigerator and then again when they have warmed up to room temperature.
2. Does water always contract as it gets colder?
3. What causes water pipes to freeze?
4. See other Activities in this Section.

H. Vocabulary Builders—Spelling Words:
1) **molecules**   2) **liquid**   3) **label**   4) **bottle**
5) **temperature**

I. Thought for Today:

"It is easier to build a child than to repair a man or woman."

Activity

A. Problem: *At What Temperature Does Water Freeze?*

B. Materials:
1. Paper towel
2. Beaker or glass jar
3. Crushed ice
4. Salt
5. Test tube
6. Water
7. Thermometer

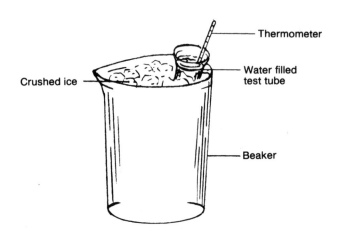

C. Procedure:
1. Fill the beaker or glass jar with crushed ice.
2. Put some water in the test tube.
3. Put a thermometer in the test tube in such a manner that it can be read. Observe temperature.
4. Place the test tube in the ice in the beaker.
5. Stir a generous amount of salt into the crushed ice. Note the temperature of the water in the test tube.
6. Immerse the test tube in the mixture of crushed ice and salt. Let it stand for several minutes, then note the temperature.

D. Result:

As long as the water in the test tube is immersed in the beaker or jar with crushed ice, the temperature will not go below 32°F. or 0°C. and cause the water to freeze. As the water in the test tube is placed in the mixture of salt and ice, the temperature of the water is lowered below the freezing point and the water in the test tube will freeze. The temperature at the time the water freezes is 32°F. or 0°C.

E. Supplemental Information:

Salt lowers the freezing point of water. This causes the water in the test tube to freeze.

F. Thought Questions:
1. Will a large amount of salt added to ice create a lower temperature than a small percentage of salt added to the ice?
2. Why is salt used in making homemade ice cream?
3. Do you think salt lowers or raises the boiling point of water?

G. Related Topics and Activities:
1. See Activity I-C-7, "Expansion or Contraction of Water when it Freezes."
2. See Activity II-B-1, "Temperatures" and Activity II-B-10, "Heating Water."
3. See all Activities in this Section.

H. Vocabulary Builders—Spelling Words:
1) **crushed**   2) **beaker**   3) **test tube**
4) **freezing**   5) **mixture**

I. Thought for Today:
"Education is a chest of tools."—Herbert Kaufman

Activity

A. Problem: *When Water Freezes Does it Expand or Contract?*

B. Materials:
1. Two small cans
2. Water
3. Refrigerator

C. Procedure:
1. Fill the two cans exactly to the top.
2. Place one can in the freezing compartment of a refrigerator.
3. Place the second can in the cold (regular) compartment.
4. Let the cans stand until the next day (or until the one placed in the freezing compartment is frozen).

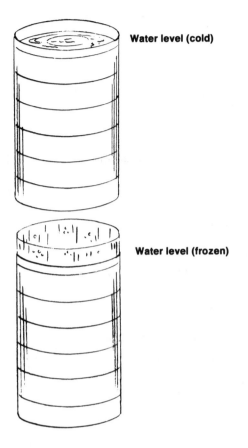

Water level (cold)

Water level (frozen)

D. Result:
The water placed in the cold (regular) compartment will have contracted so it is not quite to the top of the can. The water which has frozen will be pushed out so that it extends above the top of the can.

E. Supplemental Information:
Water expands when it freezes. During freezing, this expansion exerts extreme pressure. If the can in the freezer has a tight stopper, the force will be great enough to split the can.

F. Thought Questions:
1. What happens when water in an automobile radiator freezes without antifreeze?
2. What does antifreeze do when added to water in a radiator?
3. Why do icebergs float?
4. What causes some water pipes to break in cold weather?

G. Related Topics and Activities:
1. Repeat the experiment, only use old capped jars enclosed in cellophane containers.
2. Discuss how ice cream is made at home and why salt is added to the ice.
3. See other Activities in this Section.

H. Vocabulary Builders—Spelling Words:
1) **freezing**   2) **compartment**   3) **temperature**
4) **expand**   5) **contract**

I. Thought for Today:
"The art of teaching is the art of assisting discovery."—Mark Van Doren

Activity

A. Problem: *Do All Liquids Evaporate in an Equal Amount of Time?*

B. Materials:
1. Rubbing alcohol
2. Water

C. Procedure:
1. Place some rubbing alcohol on the back of one hand.
2. Place some water on the back of the other hand.
3. Notice the difference in feeling.

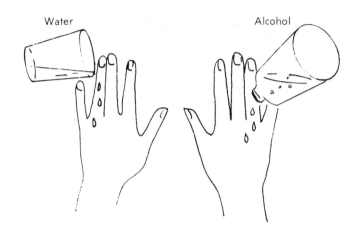
Water   Alcohol

D. Result:

The hand with rubbing alcohol will feel cool compared to the hand with water, and the alcohol will evaporate faster than the water.

E. Supplemental Information:

The faster liquids evaporate, the greater the cooling effect, consequently we can tell that alcohol evaporates faster than water. On hot days, a nurse may give a patient an alcohol rub to make him feel cool. In emergencies if a person has a very high temperature, alcohol rubs are helpful.

F. Thought Questions:
1. Will alcohol boil at a lower temperature than water?
2. Does the boiling point have anything to do with the rate of evaporation?
3. Why does alcohol evaporate faster than water?

G. Related Topics and Activities:
1. Test the evaporation of other household liquids such as hand lotions, after-shave lotions, vinegar, etc.
2. Discuss factors involved in speeding up evaporation rates.
3. See other Activities in this Section.

H. Vocabulary Builders—Spelling Words:
1) **liquids**   2) **alcohol**   3) **evaporate**
4) **amount**   5) **time**

I. Thought for Today:

"If you want children to improve, let them hear the nice things you say about them to others."—Haim Ginott

Activity

A. Problem: *Does Heat Cause Water to Evaporate Faster?*

B. Materials:
1. Two teaspoons
2. Candle
3. Matches
4. Water
5. Clothespin or tongs

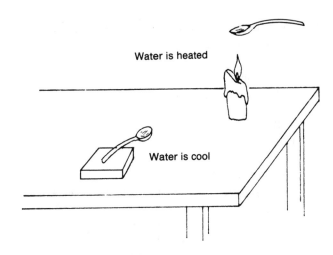

Water is heated

Water is cool

C. Procedure:
1. Place one teaspoon of water on the table as shown in drawing.
2. Using clothespin or tongs, hold a second teaspoon of water over a candle.

D. Result:
The water over the flame will evaporate more quickly than the water which remains unheated.

E. Supplemental Information:
The higher the temperature, the faster the rate of evaporation. This principle is used in clothes dryers.

F. Thought Questions:
1. Why does the heated water evaporate faster?
2. Does boiling water evaporate faster than hot water that is not boiling?
3. Besides heating, what other methods could be used to make water evaporate faster?

G. Related Topics and Activities:
1. Substitute ice cubes for regular water.
2. See other Activities in this Section.

H. Vocabulary Builders—Spelling Words:
1) **heat**   2) **evaporate**   3) **teaspoon**
4) **candle**   5) **temperature**

I. Thought for Today:
"Whatever is worth doing is worth doing well."

Activity

A. Problem: *How Does Area Affect the Rate of Evaporation?*

B. Materials:
1. Two teaspoons
2. Water
3. Book
4. Table

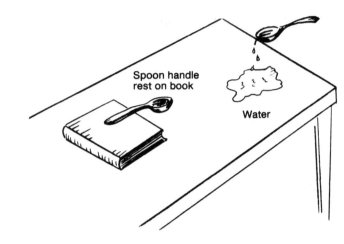

Spoon handle rest on book

Water

C. Procedure:
1. Spread one teaspoon of water over as wide an area as possible on a tabletop.
2. Place a book on the tabletop.
3. Place a second teaspoon, full of water, on the tabletop using the book for support.
4. Observe the rate of evaporation of each.

D. Result:

The water on the table will evaporate and disappear quickly. The water in the spoon will remain for a much longer period of time.

E. Supplemental Information:

Water evaporates faster when it is exposed to air on a larger surface. This has many practical applications. For example, in building reservoirs, a small, deep one will not lose as much water by evaporation as will a large shallow one. If a tennis court has pools of water from a rainstorm, it will dry much faster if the water is spread over a greater area of the court with a broom. In drying clothes, the larger the area exposed to the air, the faster will be the drying time.

F. Thought Questions:
1. Why does water evaporate faster when a larger surface is exposed to the air?
2. If people hang out their clothes to dry, why do they spread them out as far as possible?
3. Does humidity affect the rate of evaporation?

G. Related Topics and Activities:
1. Compare the rate of evaporation of various liquids.
2. See other Activities in this Section.

H. Vocabulary Builders—Spelling Words:

1) **evaporation**   2) **surface**   3) **reservoir**   4) **area**
5) **humidity**   6) **teaspoon**

I. Thought for Today:

"If all the world is a stage, a lot of people need lessons on how to act."

Activity

A. Problem: *Does Wind Help Drying?*

B. Materials:
   1. Fan
   2. Water
   3. Pot or pan

C. Procedure:
   1. Wet both hands with water.
   2. Place one hand in front of a fan.
   3. Let the other wet hand remain still and away from the breeze.
   4. Feel the difference in your hands.

Wind dries hands.

D. Result:
The wet hand placed in the path of the moving air will become cool and will dry more rapidly. The other hand will remain wet for a much longer period of time.

E. Supplemental Information:
Moving air produces faster evaporation than still air because of the increase in movement of the water molecules. This is why clothes will dry faster on a windy day than on a calm day.

F. Thought Questions:
   1. Why does the hand in front of the fan dry more rapidly?
   2. Why does the same hand get much colder than the other hand?
   3. When swimming at the beach, why does one seem colder on a windy day even if the temperature is about the same?

G. Related Topics and Activities:
   1. Have students discuss with their parents how they dry clothes outside.
   2. See Activities I-C-9 and I-C-10.
   3. See other Activities in this Section.

Wind dries clothes.

H. Vocabulary Builders—Spelling Words:
1) **moist**   2) **moisture**   3) **temperature**
4) **wind**   5) **drying**

I. Thought for Today:
"We all admire the wisdom of people who come to us for advice."

Activity

A. Problem: *How Can We Measure the Volume of Irregularly Shaped Objects?*

B. Materials:
   1. Glass measuring cup or graduate
   2. Irregular object (rock, nut, seashell, etc.)
   3. Water

C. Procedure:
   1. Fill the container with water to about two-thirds full (less if a large object is used).
   2. Record the reading (volume).
   3. Place the object gently in the container.
   4. Record the reading (volume).
   5. Subtract the first reading from the last.
   6. The difference is the volume of the object.

D. Results:
   1. Water will rise in the container.
   2. The difference in water level tells you the volume of the irregular object.

E. Supplemental Information:
   1. Objects which sink displace water equal to their volume.
   2. The increase in water volume equals the volume of the irregular object.
   3. Archimedes discovered this principle when he was taking a bath and the water overflowed.

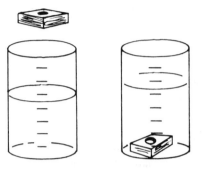

Water level rises.

F. Thought Questions:
   1. Does weight in this activity make any difference?
   2. How can you measure the volume of an irregularly shaped object that floats?
   3. Can you accurately measure tablespoons of butter in a cooking recipe by this procedure?

G. Related Topics and Activities:
   1. Measure the volume of many irregularly shaped objects.
   2. Use both our system and the metric system for reporting answers.

H. Vocabulary Builders—Spelling Words:
   1) **irregular** 2) **shape** 3) **Archimedes' Principle**
   4) **volume** 5) **measure** 6) **metric system**

I. Thought for Today:
   "Not only is there an art in knowing a thing, but also a certain art in teaching it."—Cicero

Section D: Magnetism

Activity 1D1

A. Problem: *What Kinds of Substances Do Magnets Attract?*

B. Materials:
1. Magnet
2. Nails
3. Pins
4. Pencils
5. Copper
6. Aluminum
7. Dime
8. Table
9. Other small objects

C. Procedure:
1. Place the objects on the table.
2. Touch the magnet against each object.
3. Observe the results.

D. Result:

Objects made of iron and steel will be attracted by the magnet.

E. Supplemental Information:

Magnets attract iron and steel objects, but do not attract wood, copper, silver, or other objects which do not contain iron. We still don't know what causes magnetic attraction and repulsion.

F. Thought Questions:
1. How can we test a metal to see if it contains iron?
2. How could a magnet be used to find a lost needle?
3. Why are magnets often used to separate iron or steel from wood or other nonmagnetic materials?
4. Does it make any difference what shape the magnet has?

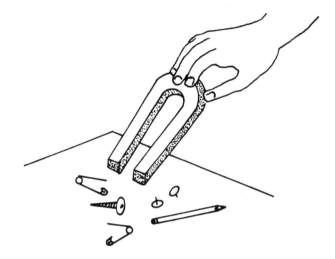

G. Related Topics and Activities:
1. Test other objects made of rubber, brass, paper, etc.
2. Test to determine if both ends of a horseshoe magnet have the same or different poles.
3. See other Activities in this Section.

H. Vocabulary Builders—Spelling Words:

1) **attraction** 2) **magnets** 3) **magnetism**
4) **repulsion** 5) **aluminum** 6) **copper**

I. Thought for Today:

"I have never let schooling interfere with my education."—Mark Twain

Activity 1D2

A. Problem: *Do Like Poles on Magnets Attract or Repel Each Other?*

B. Materials:
1. Two bar magnets
2. String, one foot in length
3. Means of suspension
4. Compass
5. Marking pens or pencils

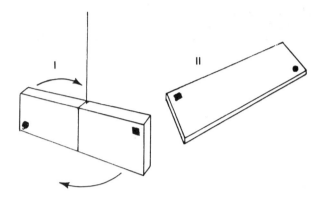

C. Procedure:
1. Suspend magnet I so that it will swing freely.
2. Put a large dot on the end of this magnet, and a square on the other end.
3. Approach the first magnet with a second magnet, end to end.
4. If the edges of the two magnets swing close together, place the opposite sign (dot or square) on this edge and the other sign on the opposite edge.
5. Repeat, approaching magnet with opposite ends and each end of the suspended magnet, noting whether the dot ends and the square ends repel or attract each other.
6. Use a compass to determine what poles are represented by the squares.
7. Use the compass again to determine what poles are represented by the dots.

D. Results:
1. The squares will repel each other.
2. The dots will repel each other.
3. Unlike signs (poles) will attract each other.
4. The north pole of the compass will be attracted to the south pole on the magnet. The north pointer on the compass is really a north-seeking compass. The north pole of a magnet is really a north-seeking edge. Consequently, the north pointer of a compass will be repelled by the north edge of the magnet.

E. Supplemental Information:
1. This proves one of the laws of magnetism: unlike magnetic poles attract; like magnetic poles repel.
2. Many games and home devices use magnetism.

F. Thought Questions:
1. How can you test an unmarked magnet to see which is the north and south pole?
2. Is a freely swinging bar magnet like a compass?
3. Why do compasses always point toward the north?

G. Related Topics and Activities:
1. A good follow-up activity is to determine whether the dots or squares are north or south poles.
2. Test a bar magnet with a horseshoe magnet in checking poles.
3. Rub a rubber rod briskly and place between two closely suspended pith balls.
4. See all Activities in this Section.

H. Vocabulary Builders—Spelling Words:
1) **magnets**   2) **horseshoe magnet**   3) **attraction**
4) **repulsion**   5) **repel**   6) **north-seeking**
7) **south-seeking**   8) **pith**

I. Thought for Today:
"The clash of ideas is the sound of freedom."

Activity ID3

A. Problem: *What Substances Do Magnetic Lines of Force Pass Through?*

B. Materials:
1. U-shaped magnet
2. Paper clip
3. Thin pieces of wood, glass, leather, iron, rubber, paper, cloth, copper, steel, aluminum, etc.
4. Large wide-mouthed jar
5. Iron filings
6. Water
7. Cup hook

C. Procedure:
1. Make a wooden support like that in Fig. 1.
2. Attach cup hook to the top.
3. Attach thread or string to the base.
4. Attach a paper clip about halfway to the top with thread or string from the wooden support.
5. Hang horseshoe (U-magnet) from the top so that there is a strong attraction to the paper clip but still enough room to insert test materials.
6. Insert test materials between the magnet and the paper clip.
7. Place filings in jar and cover with water to a depth of several inches. (The depth will depend on the strength of the magnet.) See Fig. 2.
8. Hold magnet just above the water.

D. Results:
1. The magnet will attract through paper, cloth, glass, thin plywood, rubber, and nonferrous materials.
2. The magnet will not attract through metals that are composed of iron or steel.
3. The iron filings will be attracted through the water.

E. Supplemental Information:
1. Several other metals besides iron are capable of becoming magnetized. Among them are cobalt and nickel.
2. Most metals are not magnetic.
3. Sometimes magnetic boards are used in a classroom. If a teacher wants to make a combination magnet and flannel board, steel screening can be placed underneath the flannel. Because magnetic lines of force travel through the flannel, magnets can still be used on the flannel board. It is suggested that a number of additional experiments can be conducted to determine the effects of thickness of objects and strength of magnets, on the ability of magnets to attract objects through other substances.

F. Thought Questions:
1. Why will a magnet attract an iron object through a piece of paper?
2. Can you think of any places in your home that have magnets?
3. Do motors have magnets?
4. Does a sucking coil use electromagnetism?

G. Related Topics and Activities:
1. Many commercial products use magnets. Have students do some research in this area.
2. Discuss how iron and steel objects could be located under water.
3. See all Activities in this Section.

H. Vocabulary Builders—Spelling Words:
1) **attract**   2) **lines of force**   3) **support**
4) **iron filings**   5) **paper clip**

I. Thought for Today:
"The primary purpose of a liberal education is to make one's mind a pleasant place in which to spend one's leisure."

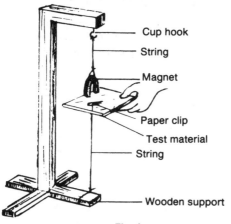

Cup hook
String
Magnet
Paper clip
Test material
String
Wooden support

Fig. 1

Fig. 2

Activity

A. **Problem:** *What is a Magnetic Field of Force?*

B. Materials:
1. Bar magnet
2. Sheet of paper or thin cardboard
3. Iron filings
4. Compass
5. Table

C. Procedure:
1. Lay a bar magnet flat on a table.
2. Cover the magnet with a thin cardboard or paper.
3. Sprinkle iron filings on the cardboard evenly.
4. Shake or tap the cardboard lightly.
5. Use a compass and plot lines of force and direction.

D. Result:
The iron filings will arrange themselves along the magnetic lines of force. Note that the filings seem to stand on end at the poles of the magnet.

E. Supplemental Information:
1. A magnet has a field of force. This will be shown by the iron filings being drawn together in lines, extending along the magnet. A little farther away from the magnet the iron filings will look just as they did when they were sprinkled on the cardboard. The force of the magnet did not move them. The force becomes weaker the farther we get from the magnet, finally becoming so weak it will not move the filings at all.
2. When a bar magnet is bent into a "U" shape it is called a "horseshoe magnet." This type of magnet will have greater attraction power because of its greater size. This is because the two poles are close together and the lines of force are closer together.

F. Thought Questions:
1. Does the strength of the magnet have any effect on the magnetic field?

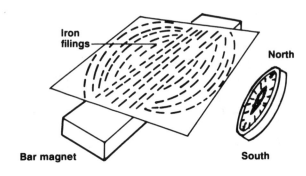

North pole

Iron filings

North

Bar magnet

South pole

South

Compass

Compass to check direction

2. How does the magnetic field of the bar magnet differ from that of the horseshoe magnet?
3. Where in your home can you find practical uses for magnets?

G. Related Topics and Activities:
1. Repeat test with a horseshoe magnet.
2. Pencil or ink lines can be drawn near iron filings for a permanent record.
3. See all Activities in this Section.

H. Vocabulary Builders—Spelling Words:
1) **iron filings**   2) **magnetic field**
3) **lines of force**   4) **horseshoe magnet**
5) **bar magnet**

I. Thought for Today:
"Part of the problems of the world is that people mistake sex for love, money for brains, and television for living."

Activity

A. **Problem:** *How Can We Support a Paper Clip Without Touching It?*

B. **Materials:**
1. Paper clips
2. Permanent magnet (preferably a bar magnet)
3. Piece of thread
4. Ring stand and a clamp
5. Small box

C. **Procedure:**
1. Support the magnet in the ring stand and clamp as shown in the diagram at right.
2. Secure a paper clip to a piece of thread and secure the thread to the base of the ring stand. The thread should be just long enough so that the paper clip cannot quite touch the tip of the magnet.
3. Cover the magnet with a small box so that class can't see the top of the apparatus.
4. Drop several paper clips away from apparatus and have class note that they fall.
5. Raise paper clip with thread close to box and have class note it does not fall.
6. Ask class why? Is this magic?
7. If class guesses correctly, then remove box.

D. **Result:**
If the magnet is reasonably strong, the paper clip will be held in the position shown.

E. **Supplemental Information:**
A magnet can attract a magnetic substance without touching it. Magnetic lines of force surround any magnet.

F. **Thought Questions:**
1. Does the strength of the magnet make any difference in this experiment?
2. Does the paper clip have to be magnetized?

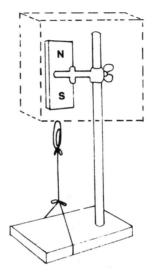

Box hides suspended magnet

3. Will it make any difference whether the north or south pole of the magnet is used?
4. Can this experiment be used to help determine how strong a magnet really is?
5. How far can the magnet be moved from the paper clip before the clip will fall?

G. **Related Topics and Activities:**
1. A good follow-up activity is I-D-3 on "What substances do Magnetic Lines of Force Pass Through?"
2. See Section II-G on "Current Electricity."
3. See all Activities in this Section.

H. **Vocabulary Builders—Spelling Words:**
1) **magnet** 2) **paper clip** 3) **thread**
4) **suspension** 5) **magic**

I. **Thought for Today:**
"One of the things a person notices when he visits a "backward" country is that the children still obey their parents."

Activity

A. Problem: *Can Iron and Steel Substances Be Magnetized?*

B. Materials:
1. Bar magnet
2. Steel knife
3. Test tube
4. Iron filings
5. Small magnetic compass

C. Procedure One:
1. Check knife to be magnetized with compass to be sure it hasn't been previously magnetized.
2. Dip knife into iron filings.
3. Check results. Do iron filings cling to knife?
4. Magnetize the knife by rubbing in one direction only with the end of the permanent magnet.
5. Dip into iron filings again.
6. Check results.

Procedure Two:
1. Fill the test tube nearly full with iron filings.
2. Move the end of the test tube around the compass.
3. Stroke the tube in one direction, with the bar magnet using one pole of the magnet only. While stroking the tube, be very careful not to jar it.
4. Move the test tube around the edges of the compass.
5. Notice any differences between the first and the second tests.
6. Shake the test tube.
7. Retest with compass.

D. Results:
1. The knife will be magnetized in the second test only and will pick up iron filings.
2. In most cases when iron filings are poured into a test tube and tested for magnetism by checking with a compass by noting its deflection, there will be little or no change.
3. When the iron filings are magnetized by stroking with a permanent magnet, the compass needle will strongly follow the test tube.
4. When the filings are jarred, the needle of the compass will not follow the test tube.

E. Supplemental Information:
When the north pole of a magnet is brought near a piece of iron or steel, it will establish a south pole at one end in the metal. The main point in creating a new magnet is to stroke the metal in one direction toward one end.

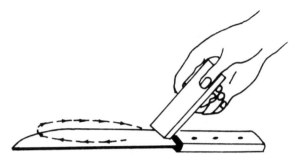

Procedure one

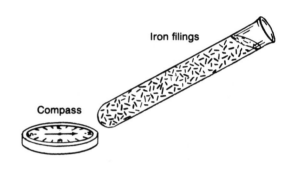

Iron filings

Compass

Procedure two

F. Thought Questions:
1. Can this procedure be used to make a magnet with any kind of metal?
2. Will this be a permanent magnet? Why?
3. What is the difference between a permanent and a temporary magnet?
4. Why is it necessary to stroke the tube in one direction only when making the iron filings into a magnet?
5. What would happen if filings were stroked both ways?
6. What changes, if any, would occur, if the opposite end of the bar magnet were used?

G. Related Topics and Activities:
1. Practice magnetizing other iron and steel objects such as knitting needles, nails, etc.
2. See all Activities in this Section.

H. Vocabulary Builders—Spelling Words:
1) **shake** 2) **compass** 3) **magnet**
4) **deflection** 5) **temporary** 6) **permanent**

I. Thought for Today:
"Ignorance doesn't kill you but it makes you sweat a lot."—Haitian proverb

Activity

A. Problem: *How Can We Make a Compass?*

B. Materials:

1. Magnet
2. Paper clips, brads, tacks, etc.
3. Needle
4. Cork
5. Dish of water
6. Square sheet of paper (two inches longer than the diameter of the dish)
7. Magnetic compass
8. Knife

C. Procedure:

1. Stroke a needle in one direction with a magnet until the needle becomes magnetized. Test it with a compass.
2. Trim slice of a cork and float it in the dish of water.
3. Place the needle across the cork.
4. Mark one corner of the paper "N" for North, the opposite "S" for South, the corner on your right "E" for East, and the one on your left "W" for West.
5. Set the saucer on the paper and allow the needle to come to rest.
6. Lift the saucer without disturbing the needle and move the paper around until the N for North and the point of the needle are in line.
7. Move the cork and the needle so that they point to various directions; release so the cork and needle swing freely.

D. Results:

1. The needle and cork will swing to a north-south line. (This can be tested by the magnetic compass.)
2. The floating magnetized needle will become a simple compass.

E. Supplemental Information:

1. A needle can be magnetized by rubbing it on a magnet in one direction only.
2. It acts as a compass in that it continues pointing north as the dish is moved.

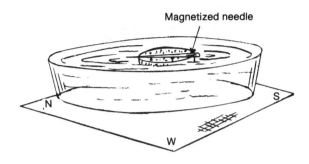

Magnetized needle

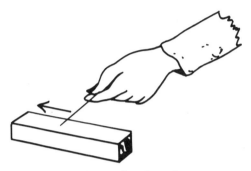

Rub needle in one direction only.

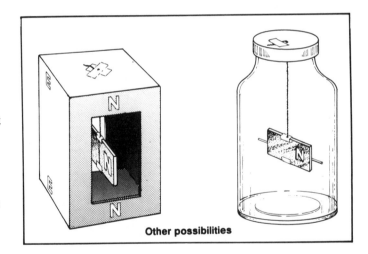

Other possibilities

F. Thought Questions:

1. Why must the needle be placed on a cork on the water?
2. Will a magnet held close to a compass keep the compass from pointing north and south?
3. Why does the magnetized needle point north and south instead of east and west?

G. Related Topics and Activities:
   1. Magnetize a needle. Cut it in two very carefully with cutting pliers. Check each piece for magnetic poles.
   2. Make a map of the schoolyard using a compass, protractors, and measuring tape.
   3. Make the two compasses shown above.
   4. See all Activities in this Section.

H. Vocabulary Builders—Spelling Words:
   1) **bowl**   2) **needle**   3) **compass**
   4) **measuring tape**   5) **protractor**

I. Thought for Today:
   "If two people agree on everything, you may be sure that one of them is doing all the thinking."

Section E: Static Electricity

Activity 1E1

A. Problem: *What is Static Electricity?*

B. Materials:
1. Two thin books
2. Piece of heavy glass
3. Small torn bits of tissue paper
4. Piece of silk cloth

C. Procedure:
1. Place books parallel on table leaving a space between them.
2. Place torn bits of paper on table between the books.
3. Place glass on books over the paper bits.
4. Rub glass briskly with silk cloth.

D. Result:
The pieces of paper dance or attach themselves to the glass when the cloth is rubbed on the glass.

E. Supplemental Information:
1. Electricity can be produced by rubbing silk on glass. Rubbing the glass with silk causes the electrons to be rubbed off the glass and the glass becomes positively charged. This attracts the negative charges of the neutral paper and hence, unlike charges attract.
2. Some static on radio and snow on television is caused by static electricity. Lightning is a huge spark of static electricity being generated in the air. The relationship of weather to the success of the experiments can be discussed; dry weather gives the best results. Students can divide into groups and experiment with combing their hair briskly and picking up tissue paper with the comb. They may try rubbing materials other than silk on the glass. Have them rub a piece of tissue paper against a blackboard. Many other experiments which illustrate static electricity can be tried.

F. Thought Questions:
1. Will it make any difference if a different kind of cloth is used in this experiment?

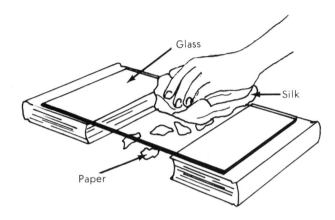

2. Does the direction the glass is rubbed make any difference, i.e., up and down, or across, or in a circular motion?
3. What are the differences between static electricity and regular (moving) electricity?

G. Related Topics and Activities:
1. Rub a comb through your hair briskly and then quickly hold it over torn bits of paper. (Hair gives up electrons to the comb and this attracts the positive charges of the neutral paper.) Actually the electrons of the paper move to the opposite side.
2. Suspend two (2) balloons from a common point with light thread. Rub each facing side of the balloons with wool or silk. (They will repel each other, i.e., move apart.)
3. See all Activities in this Section.

H. Vocabulary Builders—Spelling Words:
1) **static**   2) **electricity**   3) **positive**
4) **negative**   5) **neutral**   6) **spark**
7) **briskly**   8) **parallel**   9) **circular**

I. Thought for Today:
"A generation ago most men who finished a day's work needed rest; now they need exercise."

Activity

A. Problem: *Do Like Charges Repel or Attract Each Other?*

B. Materials:
1. Pith balls (Can be obtained at school supply houses or made from dry cornstalks.)
2. Thread
3. Glue
4. Tubing
5. Sealing wax rod
6. Wooden support

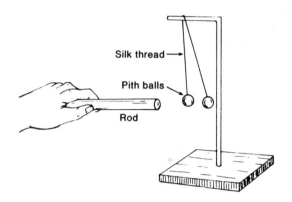

C. Procedure:
1. Fasten a pith ball to each end of a thread about twelve inches long, sewing them with a needle or using a little glue.
2. Hang them from a support made of wood, bent glass tubing, or wire, as shown in the accompanying illustration.
3. Bring the balls near to rubber rod which has been rubbed with fur or wool. Such a rod is charged negatively.

D. Result:

The balls will be first attracted to the rod, and then after a little while they will be repelled. Sometimes it is necessary to allow the balls to roll along the rod and to rub the rod several times. Soon both the balls secure the same charge as the rod, and they are repelled by the rod and by each other.

E. Supplemental Information:

Substances with like charges repel each other. Substances with unlike charges attract each other. The charge of any substance is determined by the electrons (negative) on the surface of the materials. If the electrons are rubbed off, the substance loses negative charges and becomes positively charged. If the surface picks up electrons it becomes negatively charged.

F. Thought Questions:
1. What is the difference between negative and positive charges of static electricity?
2. How are negative and positive charges of static electricity involved in lightning storms?
3. How can one tell what is positively charged and what is negatively charged?

G. Related Topics and Activities:
1. Blow up several balloons. Rub them briskly against your clothing. Try adhering them to a wall.
2. Have children discuss times they have walked across rugs and touched a metallic object and received a little shock.
3. See all Activities in this Section.

H. Vocabulary Builders—Spelling Words:
1) **repel**   2) **attract**   3) **pith balls**
4) **sealing wax**   5) **support**

I. Thought for Today:

"The greatest resource any country can have is its children."—Danny Kaye

Activity

A. Problem: *Does Static Electricity Affect Water Flow?*

B. Materials:
1. Rubber comb
2. Bits of paper
3. Stream of water
4. Head of hair

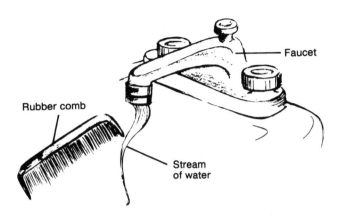

Faucet

Rubber comb

Stream of water

C. Procedure:
1. Vigorously comb your hair.
2. Hold the comb near a faucet with a thin, steady stream of water coming from it.
3. Observe the water.
4. Again comb hair and hold the comb near bits of paper. Notice that it is much easier to produce static electricity on cold, dry days.

D. Results:
1. When the comb is rubbed it will become negatively charged.
2. Running water has neutral charges. When the negatively charged comb is placed near the water, the electrons on the atoms of the water move to the opposite side, leaving the side nearest the comb positively charged. The attraction between the negatively charged comb and the positively charged side of the atoms of the water cause the water to "bend" toward the comb.

E. Supplemental Information:
1. Static electricity is caused by rubbing the electrons of atoms of one material and causing them to move towards other materials that have fewer electrons closest to them.
2. Lightning is one form of static electricity.
3. Static electricity is easier to produce on dry, cold days.

F. Thought Questions:
1. How do lightning rods work?
2. Where does the electricity come from that is in the clouds?
3. Can you make a balloon cling to a wall by rubbing it briskly against your clothing and then placing it on a wall?

G. Related Topics and Activities:
1. Suspend one comb. Rub a second comb briskly and bring near the first one.
2. See Section II-G, "Current Electricity."
3. See all Activities in this Section.

H. Vocabulary Builders—Spelling Words:
1) **static**   2) **comb**   3) **faucet**   4) **vigorously**
5) **briskly**   6) **stream**

I. Thought for Today:
"The bigger a person's head gets, the easier it is to fill his/her shoes."—Anne Bancroft

Activity

A. Problem: *Can Static Electricity be Produced by Friction?*

B. Materials:
1. Two rubber balloons
2. Piece of thread
3. Piece of wool cloth
4. Piece of manila paper
5. Candle or heat source

C. Procedure:
1. Inflate balloons and tie them together with thread.
2. Space them so that they can swing and touch each other freely.
3. Rub balloons with wool.
4. Have student raise a hand directly over balloons.
5. Dry manila paper with heat.
6. Rub paper with wool.
7. Place paper against wall or blackboard, observe what happens.

D. Result:

In the first experiment, the balloons follow the student's arm after the balloons are rubbed with wool. In the second experiment, the manila paper will cling to the board firmly for several minutes.

E. Supplemental Information:
1. The paper has a charge, but the wall is neutral. It should be remembered that before carrying out this experiment the manila paper should be thoroughly dry for best results. It can be concluded from the experiments that electricity can be produced by friction. This static electricity is the result of producing electric charges by rubbing materials briskly, which moves the outer electrons of atoms.
2. By rubbing any object briskly, usually the outer electrons are removed and picked up by another object. One object becomes positive and the other becomes negative. Either will attract a neutral object because the latter will move most of its electrons to one side and it becomes positive on one side and negative on the other.

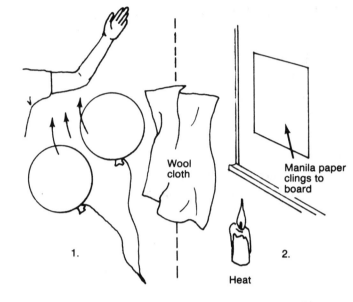

1.   2.

Wool cloth

Manila paper clings to board

Heat

F. Thought Questions:
1. How can you determine which materials rubbed together will cause static electricity?
2. What makes your hair crackle when you comb it briskly?
3. When one walks on carpeting and then touches a metal object a "crackle" is heard and a tiny spark is seen. What causes this?

G. Related Topics and Activities:
1. Test any material by rubbing it briskly and checking to see if it can pick up paper bits.
2. Study lightning and find the causes of its existence.
3. Make two pith balls out of corn stalks and test them by stringing them together and then charging them with a comb after it has been rubbed briskly. (See Activity I-E-1.)
4. See all Activities in this Section.

H. Vocabulary Builders—Spelling Words:
1) **electron**   2) **charges**   3) **positive**
4) **negative**   5) **attraction**   6) **repel**

I. Thought for Today:

"If you can tell the difference between good advice and bad advice, you don't need advice."

Part II

Energy

Section A: Sources

Activity   II **A** 1

A. Problem: *What Are Some Sources of Power?*

B. Materials:
   1. Batteries
   2. Flashlight
   3. Hot plate
   4. Pan
   5. Matches
   6. Flat metal tray
   7. Flat stick
   8. Photometer

C. Procedure:
   1. Discuss some of the sources of our present energy.
   2. Discuss some of the problems with our ever-increasing demand for power:
      a. fossil fuels burning causes air pollution
      b. coal burning causes air pollution
      c. population is increasing
      d. power demands are going up
      e. limitations to the number of dams that can be built as they destroy many local biotic communities
   3. Discuss some possible new sources of power.
   4. Show how a flashlight uses "chemical energy."
   5. Discuss how generators work. (See Activity II-F-3 on Steam Turbines.)
   6. Fill flat metal tray with water.
   7. Move water with flat stick illustrating wave action.
   8. Demonstrate how photometer moves by solar (light) radiation.
   9. Discuss solar batteries (used by astronauts).
   10. Turn on any electric appliance (light switch, projector, etc.) and discuss where the energy originated.
   11. Discuss nuclear energy and some of the problems that have occurred with its use and production.

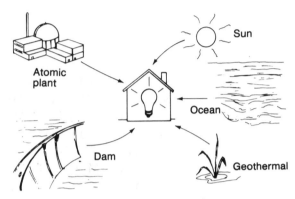

What will light our homes?

D. Results:
   1. Flashlight light is energy.
   2. Steam generators produce energy.
   3. Some countries are already using energy from ocean waves.
   4. Solar batteries are here but need to be perfected for greater economy.
   5. Most of our energy originates from the sun, even our fossil fuels.
   6. The use of nuclear (atomic) energy has been increasing throughout the world and so have the associated problems.

E. Supplemental Information:
   1. One of the urgent needs of the next 25 years is the source of new power as our population is greatly increasing, and our demands for more power are increasing about seven percent per year.
   2. New, nonpolluting power or residuals are needed.
   3. There are hot rock areas in the earth where we could tap geothermal energy.

F. Thought Questions:
1. Can you think of any possible new sources of power?
2. Do you think the winds could be harnessed for power?
3. How could we get more power out of our present systems?
4. Can ocean tides, currents, or waves be used as a source of power?

G. Related Topics and Activities:
1. See Section VII-C, "Earth's Crust."
2. See Part VI, "Ecology."
3. See all Activities in this Section.

H. Vocabulary Builders—Spelling Words:
1) **batteries**   2) **flashlight**   3) **photometer**
4) **fossil fuels**   5) **geothermal**   6) **solar**
7) **nuclear**

I. Thought for Today:
"One thing most children save for a rainy day is energy."

Activity

A. Problem: *Is There an Energy Crisis?*

B. Materials:
1. Can of oil
2. Picture of a gas appliance
3. Piece of coal or picture of coal
4. Picture of dam
5. Picture or model of a nuclear power plant
6. Picture of the sun

C. Procedure:
1. Describe the energy problems:
   a. Dependence on foreign oil
   b. Costs of foreign oil
   c. Demand for more energy by Americans (7% more/year)
   d. Estimated sources of present energy supplies:
      (1) oil—40%
      (2) nuclear—18%
      (3) coal—28%
      (4) natural gas—10%
      (5) hydroelectric—4%
   e. We are running out of oil in the continental United States.
   f. We have found oil in the North Slope of Alaska, but if we continue our present demand rate, this additional 2 million barrels of oil a day will be depleted.
2. Describe how we use oil:
   a. Gasoline
   b. Home heating, diesel fuel
   c. Industry, utilities
   d. Natural gas (industry, farms)
   e. Jet fuel
   f. Kerosene
   g. Lubricants
   h. Plastics
   i. Miscellaneous
3. Describe where we might get future energy supplies.
   a. Increase coal production.
   b. Increase nuclear power plants.
   c. Develop shale oil industry.
   d. Increase drilling explorations for oil and gas.
   e. Offshore drilling on our continental shelves.
   f. Reclaim oil wells that were formerly too costly.
4. Describe ways of more efficient use of energy resources.

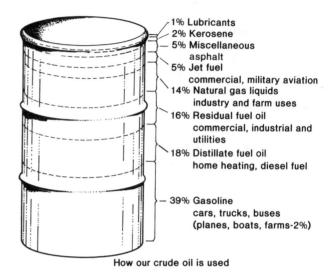

1% Lubricants
2% Kerosene
5% Miscellaneous asphalt
5% Jet fuel commercial, military aviation
14% Natural gas liquids industry and farm uses
16% Residual fuel oil commercial, industrial and utilities
18% Distillate fuel oil home heating, diesel fuel
39% Gasoline cars, trucks, buses (planes, boats, farms-2%)

How our crude oil is used

D. Result:

Students will learn that we are in an energy crisis condition and that we have little prospect of easing the situation in the immediate future. Most utility companies have raised their rates in order to slow the consumption of natural gas, electricity, and in some areas water, too.

E. Supplemental Information:
1. New sources of energy that could be most helpful are solar energy, geothermal, ocean tides, waves, and winds.
2. At the present rate of use, Arabian oil is expected to last only about 35 years.
3. Every day over four kilowatt hours of solar energy fall on each square foot on our planet earth at the latitude of Los Angeles. This is clean energy, no pollution, no destruction of land resources.

F. Thought Questions:
1. Do we need to think about conserving our energy as well as producing more?
2. Do you think the use of nuclear energy should be increased or decreased?
3. How would you solve the energy crisis?

G. Related Topics and Activities:
1. See Section II-G, "Current Electricity."
2. See Part VI, "Ecology."
3. See all Activities in this Section.

H. Vocabulary Builders—Spelling Words:
1) **oil**   2) **nuclear**   3) **hydroelectric**
4) **natural gas**   5) **coal**

I. Thought for Today:
"There are three ways to get things done: do it yourself, hire someone to do it, or forbid your kids to do it."

Activity

A. Problem: *How Can We Use Solar Energy?*

B. Materials:
1. Pan of cold water
2. Thermometer
3. Panel of darkened glass
4. Direct, bright sunlight

C. Procedure:
1. Record the temperature of the cold water.
2. Place the pan of cold water in direct sunlight.
3. Place the panel of darkened glass between the sun and the water.
4. Move the glass each 30 minutes so that the sun always shines directly on the glass.
5. Record the temperature of the water every 30 minutes.

D. Result:
The darkened glass acts as a solar cell and heats the water.

E. Supplemental Information:
There are many uses of solar energy. The universe has a great variety of forms of energy. Among the best known is radiant energy. In our solar system, the sun is the most important source of this kind of energy. Heat is also a form of radiant energy. We use heat for warming water and house heating. Solar energy saves a high percentage of energy costs.

F. Thought Questions:
1. How can solar energy be stored for use when the sun does not shine?
2. In what areas of the U.S. would solar energy devices be most efficient?
3. Can we use solar energy to generate steam?

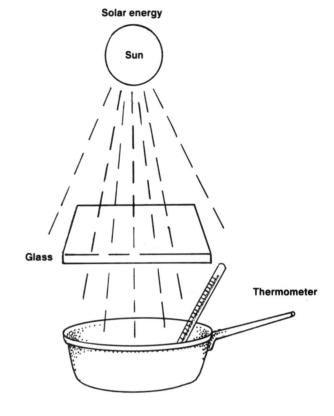

G. Related Topics and Activities:
1. See Section II-B, "Fire and Heat."
2. See Section VII-B, "Solar System."
3. See other Activities in this Section.

H. Vocabulary Builders—Spelling Words:
1) **solar** 2) **radiation** 3) **panel**
4) **air conditioners** 5) **radiant**

I. Thought for Today:
"In 40 minutes the sun delivers to the earth's surface as much energy as humans use in a year."

A. Problem: *Is Wind a Good Source of Energy?*

B. Materials:
1. Wooden stick about six inches long
2. Straight pin
3. Construction paper

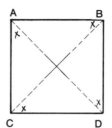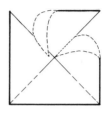

C. Procedure:
1. Cut a piece of construction paper making a 6″ square.
2. Draw diagonal lines from A to D and from B to C. (See sketch.)
3. Cut to within ½ inch of center point from four corners along these diagonal lines.
4. Fold points X to center and put the pin through the center where lines cross.
5. Attach pinwheel to the end of the wooden stick by forcing the point of the pin into the stick.
6. Blow into the center of the pinwheel or hold pinwheel in any current of air.

D. Result:
Students will learn to make a small paper windmill.

E. Supplemental Information:
1. Wind (moving air) causes pinwheel to whirl.
2. When the same principle is used on a large scale, the wind can be made to do beneficial work.
3. In some areas where winds are prevalent, many windmills have been constructed for providing energy to nearby communities.

F. Thought Questions:
1. How does wind make this paper windmill operate? What makes it turn?
2. Is this kind of windmill able to do work?
3. What kinds of work are ordinarily done with regular windmills?
4. Where do sailboats get their energy to move?
5. How do windmills work?

G. Related Topics and Activities:
1. Compare the workings of a regular fan to this paper windmill.
2. Compare this windmill to a propeller on a boat.
3. See Part VI, "Ecology."
4. See other Activities in this Section.

H. Vocabulary Builders—Spelling Words:
1) **windmill** 2) **construction** 3) **diagonal**
4) **center** 5) **pinwheel**

I. Thought for Today:
"The most called-upon prerequisite of a friend is an accessible ear."

Section B: Fire and Heat

Activity II B 1

A. Problem: *What Is the Difference Between a Celsius (Centigrade) and Fahrenheit Temperature Scale?*

B. Materials:
1. Fahrenheit thermometer
2. Celsius (Centigrade) thermometer
3. Water
4. Ice
5. Hot plate or heating device
6. Small drinking glass
7. Pan
8. Stirring rod or spoon

C. Procedure:
1. Put ice in glass of water and stir well.
2. Put thermometers in ice water and take readings.
3. Record findings.
4. Put water in pan and heat gently for about two minutes.
5. Place thermometers in water and record findings.
6. Return water to pan and heat again for several minutes.
7. Record findings again.
8. Return water to pan and heat water until it is boiling.
9. Place thermometers in water and record temperatures.
10. Have one student volunteer and take his body temperature orally.
11. Record findings.

D. Results:
1. Students will learn that temperatures can be measured on different scales.
2. Pupils might be able to determine the difference between the two readings. (One degree Celsius [Centigrade] = 1.8 degrees Fahrenheit).
3. Students will learn that ice melts (or water freezes) at 0°C. or 32°F.
4. Students will learn that water boils at 100°C. or 212°F.

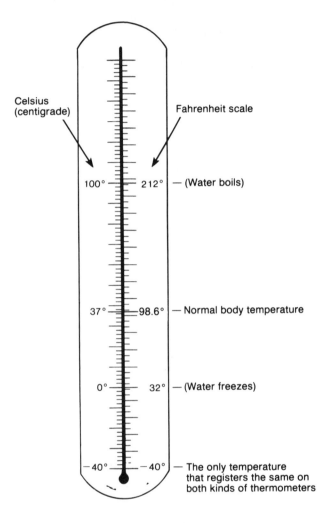

Celsius (centigrade)

Fahrenheit scale

100° — 212° — (Water boils)

37° — 98.6° — Normal body temperature

0° — 32° — (Water freezes)

−40° — −40° — The only temperature that registers the same on both kinds of thermometers

E. Supplemental Information:

Scientists sometimes use an Absolute or Kelvin scale. Its degrees are the same size as Celsius but it begins at a point in which there is no movement of the molecules. This point is zero on the Absolute or Kelvin scale, −273.16 on the Celsius or Centigrade scale and −459.69 on the Fahrenheit scale.

F. Thought Questions:
1. Why does the red colored mercury move in a thermometer?
2. Do all liquids boil at the same temperature?
3. What is normal room temperature in Fahrenheit? Celsius? Absolute?

G. Related Topics and Activities:

1. A mock-up of a thermometer can be made by using a tall piece of tagboard and a red ribbon that can be moved up and down. With Fahrenheit readings on one side and Centigrade on the other side, students can quickly compare readings. Slits can be made at the top and bottom of the scales and a ribbon can be made that is half-white and half-red to fit in slits making a circle of ribbon that can be easily moved to any temperature reading.

2. Check room temperatures and discuss comfort ranges.

3. Discuss areas students have visited that are "very hot" or "very cold."

4. For upper level students, challenge them to devise a formula for changing Celsius to Fahrenheit and another for converting Fahrenheit to Celsius.

5. See other Activities in this Section.

H. Vocabulary Builders—Spelling Words:

1) **Fahrenheit**   2) **Celsius**   3) **Centigrade**
4) **Absolute**   5) **Kelvin**   6) **thermometer**

I. Thought for Today:

"We must learn to live together as brothers or we will perish together as fools."

Activity

A. Problem: *How Does Heat Affect Solids?*

B. Materials:

1. Brass expansion ring (or wooden expansion ring with three long brass screws set in as shown in sketch). (See Supplemental Information.)
2. Brass expansion ball, sizes of "hole"
3. Heating equipment
4. Water
5. Tongs

C. Procedure:

1. Adjust the three screws on the ring so that the cold ball will barely pass through the opening.
2. Heat the ball.
3. Handling the warm ball with tongs, try to pass it through the ring.
4. Dip the ball in cold water, then try to pass it through the ring.

D. Results:

1. Without heat, the ball will be snug in the ring.
2. The heated ball will not go through the ring.
3. When the ball is cooled, the ball will easily pass through the ring.

E. Supplemental Information:

1. Inexpensive commercial equipment is available for this activity.
2. Solids expand when heated and contract when cooled.

F. Thought Questions:

1. How do people try to remove tight metal caps from bottles using this principle?
2. If a nut is stuck on a bolt, will heating the nut help to remove it?
3. Do all metals expand at the same rate?

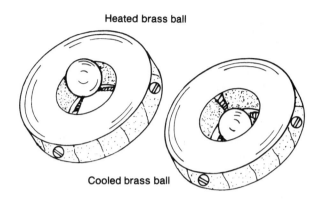

Heated brass ball

Cooled brass ball

G. Related Topics and Activities:

1. Have students check with parents on the difficulty of removing hot radiator caps from automobile radiators.
2. See Section I-B, "Air."
3. See other Activities in this Section.

H. Vocabulary Builders—Spelling Words:

1) **solids**   2) **expansion**   3) **contraction**
4) **metals**   5) **brass**

I. Thought for Today:

"Obstacles are what you see when you take your eyes off your goal."

Activity

A. Problem: *How Do Heating and Cooling Change the Length of a Wire?*

B. Materials:
   1. Piece of uninsulated iron or copper wire
   2. Weight
   3. Ruler
   4. Two stands or points to which wire can be stretched
   5. Candle

C. Procedure:
   1. Stretch the wire between two points.
   2. Tie a weight in the center of the wire.
   3. Measure the distance from the wire to the table.
   4. Use a candle to heat the wire.
   5. Move the candle back and forth along the wire so that the wire becomes heated throughout its entire length.
   6. Measure the distance from the wire to the table again.

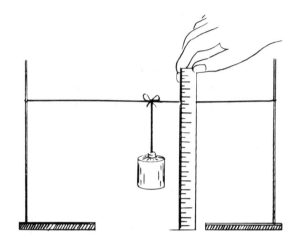

D. Result:
When the wire is heated, the weight will move closer to the table. This indicates that the wire expands when heated.

E. Supplemental Information:
Most metals expand when heated. In the case of the wire, this means that the wire becomes longer when it is heated. Sometimes this principle is used to remove tight nuts from bolts.

F. Thought Questions:
   1. Will the wire stretch tighter when it is cooled?
   2. Do telephone lines sag more on a hot day?
   3. If you had to string metal wire, would it be better to string it on a hot or a cold day?
   4. How do railroad tracks allow for expansion and contraction?

G. Related Topics and Activities:
   1. See Section I-B, "Air."
   2. See Section II-A, "Energy Sources."
   3. See other Activities in this Section.

H. Vocabulary Builders—Spelling Words:
   1) **heating**   2) **cooling**   3) **length**
   4) **weight**   5) **candle**

I. Thought for Today:

EVERYBODY, SOMEBODY, ANYBODY, AND NOBODY
This is a story about four people named Everybody, Somebody, Anybody and Nobody. There was an important job to be done and Everybody was sure that Somebody would do it. Anybody could have done it, but Nobody did it. Somebody got angry about that, because it was Everybody's job. Everybody thought Anybody could do it, but Nobody realized that Everybody wouldn't do it.
It ended up that Everybody blamed Somebody when Nobody did what Anybody could have done!
—Source unknown.

Activity

A. Problem: *Does Heat Travel in Solids? Do All Substances Conduct Heat at the Same Rate?*

B. Materials:
   1. Clamping device
   2. Thin steel rod
   3. Beeswax or candle wax
   4. Heat source
   5. Aluminum wire
   6. Copper wire
   7. Iron or steel wire
   8. Wood block, 2″ × 2″ × 6″
   9. Staples

C. Procedure One:
   1. Support the thin steel rod in the clamping device as shown in sketch.
   2. Make several small balls of beeswax or candle wax and stick them on the underside of rod at equal intervals.
   3. Apply heat to the unsupported end.

   Procedure Two:
   1. Staple wires to the top of the wooden block as shown in sketch.
   2. Attach beeswax or candle wax to the underside of each wire.
   3. Apply heat to the joined ends of the wires about an inch below wires.

D. Results:
   1. As the heat is conducted along the rod, the beeswax or candle wax will melt and drop off. The time of drop will become greater as the wax balls become farther away from source of heat.
   2. The beeswax or candle wax will drop off at different times: aluminum first, copper second, and steel third.

E. Supplemental Information:
   1. Heat is conducted more rapidly near the flame but more slowly as it is carried farther and farther away, because of heat loss due to radiation. If a rod is long enough, a point will

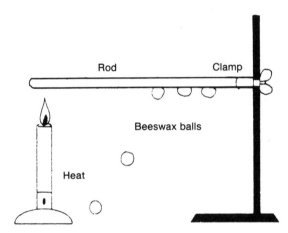

Procedure one

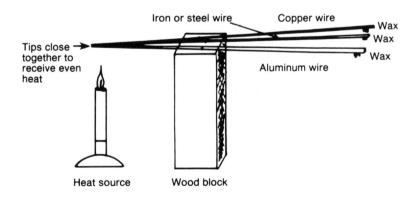

Procedure two

be reached where no wax balls will fall off because the heat of radiation is faster than the heat of conduction. If the melting point of the wax is known, it is possible to calculate the speed of conduction from point to point.

2. Solids expand as they become hotter and contract as they become colder. Of the three metals tested, aluminum conducts heat the fastest and steel, the slowest. Conduction of heat is correlated with the conduction of electricity.

F. Thought Questions:

1. How can you determine if copper conducts heat faster than steel?
2. Why does steel conduct heat faster than wood?
3. What are different ways objects may be heated?

G. Related Topics and Activities:

1. See previous Activity II-B-3 on heating and cooling a wire.
2. See Section I-B, "Air."
3. See other Activities in this Section.

H. Vocabulary Builders—Spelling Words:

1) **conduction**   2) **radiation**   3) **expansion**
4) **aluminum**   5) **copper**   6) **iron**

I. Thought for Today:

"It is a great thing to win the admiration of people, but a greater thing to gain their love."

Activity

A. Problem: *Do Some Substances Conduct Heat Faster Than Others?*

B. Materials:
1. China, aluminum, and wooden cups or bowls
2. Boiling water
3. Crushed ice
4. Thermometer

C. Procedure:
1. Put boiling water in each of the three containers.
2. Feel the outside of the containers.
3. Allow to stand for fifteen minutes.
4. Check the temperature in each of the three containers.
5. Put the same amount of crushed ice in each cup or bowl every five minutes.
6. Record the temperatures.
7. Empty and dry containers thoroughly.
8. Let stand at room temperature for fifteen minutes or use similar cups or bowls.
9. Fill each container about one-third full with an equal amount of water.
10. Place an equal amount of crushed ice in each container.
11. Check the temperature every five minutes for fifteen minutes.
12. Record the readings.
13. Compare the results.

D. Results:
1. The temperature of the containers will all feel different.
2. As the containers cool, the containers will all feel different; the cup or bowl that felt hottest will then feel coldest.
3. When crushed ice is added to the cups, the wooden bowl or cup will hold the temperature longer; the aluminum will lose its coldness faster as aluminum is the best conductor of heat.

E. Supplemental Information:
1. Aluminum is a much better conductor of heat than is either china or wood.
2. China is a better conductor of heat than wood.

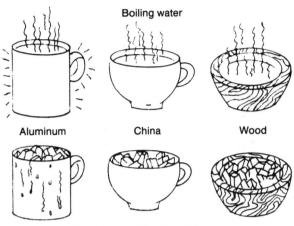

Boiling water

Aluminum   China   Wood

Containers with chipped ice

F. Thought Questions:
1. If you want coffee to stay hot, would you put it in an aluminum cup?
2. Why does hot coffee, when served in a metal cup, seem hotter at first, but much colder after a few minutes?
3. Will a cool drink stay cold longer in a metal can or a wooden bowl?
4. How does a thermos bottle keep hot liquids hot and cold liquids cold?

G. Related Topics and Activities:
1. Test other materials for conduction such as plastic and steel.
2. See Section I-B, "Air."
3. See other Activities in this Section.

H. Vocabulary Builders—Spelling Words:
1) **aluminum**   2) **china**   3) **wood**
4) **plastic**   5) **steel**   6) **conduct**

I. Thought for Today:
"Experience should be a guiding post not a hitching post."

Activity

A. Problem: *How Do We Make a Simple Thermometer?*

B. Materials:
   1. Small mouth bottle
   2. Rubber stopper, one hole to fit bottle
   3. Glass tubing
   4. Classroom thermometer, preferably with both Fahrenheit and Celsius (Centigrade) scales (or two thermometers)
   5. Two drinking glasses
   6. Heating device
   7. Water (clear and colored)
   8. Ice
   9. Two bowls
   10. Marking pencil or pen

Bottle and colored water

Warm water in glass

C. Procedure:
   1. Teach the pupils to read the scales on the thermometers. Explain the difference between the two scales.
   2. Have the students read and record the room temperature on any scale.
   3. Warm some water and place in glass.
   4. Read and record this temperature.
   5. Put ice in another glass of water.
   6. Read and record this temperature.
   7. If you have an aquarium in your classroom, read and record the water temperature.
   8. Mix equal amounts of warm water and ice water.
   9. Read and record this temperature.
   10. Fill the small mouth bottle with colored water.
   11. Insert glass tubing in rubber stopper. (Be sure stopper is wet before inserting.)
   12. Twist the stopper down in bottle until water rises an inch or so above stopper.
   13. With marking pencil or pen make a crude scale. (Circles on tubing.)
   14. Place this thermometer in a bowl of warm water.
   15. Read the temperature. Mark the level.
   16. Place this thermometer in a bowl of ice water.
   17. Read this thermometer. Note marking.
   18. Take temperatures by windows (inside and out).
   19. Make charts and graphs of different temperatures during the school day.

D. Results:
   1. Children will learn there are different scales for measuring temperature.
   2. Students will make a simple thermometer.
   3. Pupils will learn how to read a simple thermometer.

E. Supplemental Information:
   1. Heat is a result of molecules in motion. The faster they move the more heat is involved.
   2. Thermometers are instruments for measuring heat.

F. Thought Questions:
   1. Which degrees on a thermometer are larger? Celsius or Fahrenheit?
   2. Which moves more in thermometers—mercury or water?
   3. What is normal body temperature?

G. Related Topics and Activities:
   1. See Activity II-B-1, "Temperature Scales."
   2. See Section I-B, "Air."
   3. See other Activities in this Section.

H. Vocabulary Builders—Spelling Words:
   1) **thermometer**   2) **simple**   3) **Celsius**
   4) **Fahrenheit**   5) **Centigrade**

I. Thought for Today:
   "Few people travel the road to success without a puncture or two."

Activity

A. Problem: *Does Heat Affect Gases?*

B. Materials:
1. Glass flask
2. Rubber toy balloon
3. Heating apparatus

C. Procedure:
1. Blow balloon up to stretch rubber.
2. Let air out.
3. Place balloon over top of glass flask.
4. Heat glass flask slowly until balloon is inflated.
5. Set flask aside to cool. Note change in shape of balloon.

D. Result:
The balloon will inflate as the flask is heated, and deflate when allowed to cool.

E. Supplemental Information:
Gases expand when heated, contract when cooled.

F. Thought Questions:
1. Will the balloon expand more if a larger glass flask is used?
2. When the balloon is expanded, will it contract if the flask is placed in cold water?
3. Do automobile tires expand and contract?
4. Do bicycle tires expand and contract?

G. Related Topics and Activities:
1. Place an empty bottle in a refrigerator over night. Put a balloon over its neck. Let stand in warm room temperature.
2. See Section I-B, "Air."
3. See other Activities in this Section.

H. Vocabulary Builders—Spelling Words:
1) **expand**   2) **contract**   3) **balloon**
4) **flask**   5) **temperature**

I. Thought for Today:
"Science teachers teach 'what is.' Philosophy teachers teach 'what should be.'"

Activity

A. Problem: *What Causes a Candle to Burn?*

B. Materials:
   1. Candle
   2. Match
   3. Several pieces of paper or 4″ × 5″ cards
   4. Tongs or clothespin

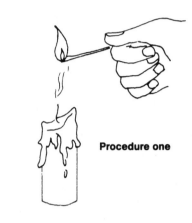

Procedure one

C. Procedure One:
   1. Light candle, let it burn, and then snuff it out.
   2. Immediately after snuffing out candle, hold a lighted match about an inch or less over the extinguished candle.

Procedure Two:
   1. Light candle.
   2. Holding the paper with tongs or clothespin, thrust it quickly about ¼ inch above the wick with little disturbance. *Caution:* Have a safe place to dispose of paper in case it bursts into flames. A small bucket with a little water in it is excellent.
   3. Remove as soon as it begins to scorch.
   4. Try several kinds of paper.

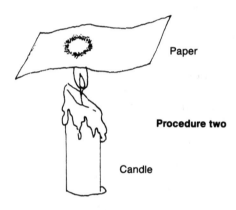

Paper

Procedure two

Candle

D. Results:
   1. The candle will again become lighted.
   2. A distinct charred ring will form with an unscorched center.

E. Supplemental Information:
   1. There is still a supply of inflammable gas immediately after you blow out a candle.
   2. The heated candle gas is burnable regardless of whether or not the candle happens to be lighted. This is proved when the candle again becomes ignited. Actually it is the gaseous material that burns, not the solid candle. The flame (heat) changes the solid candle to a gas and it is this gas that burns.
   3. In the second part, the flame (burning gases) is hollow and rather cool just above the wick. The sides of the flame's merging point can be determined by placing the paper at varying heights. The gas from the burning candle forms a cone shape, consequently the charred area will vary depending upon the height of the paper.

F. Thought Questions:
   1. Do any or all liquids burn?
   2. Do any or all solids burn?
   3. Do any or all gases burn?
   4. When gasoline burns, is it the liquid that burns or a gas which is given off by the liquid?
   5. Why is a charred *ring* formed instead of a charred *spot?*
   6. Why does the size of the charred ring vary with the height at which the paper is held?
   7. Where is the hottest part of the flame?
   8. Where does the carbon come from?

G. Related Topics and Activities:
   1. See Section I-B, "Air."
   2. See Section II-A, "Energy Sources."
   3. See other Activities in this Section.

H. Vocabulary Builders—Spelling Words:
   1) **flame**   2) **thrust**   3) **caution**   4) **wick**
   5) **dispose**

I. Thought for Today:
   "It is better to light one candle than to curse the darkness."

Activity

A. Problem: *What is Smoke?*

B. Materials:
1. Candle
2. Matches
3. Tablespoon
4. Newspaper
5. Flat pan
6. Non-burnable pad
7. Paper toweling
8. Clothespin

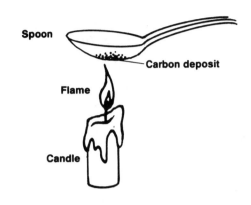

C. Procedure:
1. Light a candle and observe it closely as it burns.
2. Hold tablespoon in candle flame for a few seconds. (Hold with clothespin.)
3. Wipe clean with paper toweling.
4. Crumple up a piece of newspaper.
5. Place in baking pan.
6. Place pan on pad.
7. Light newspaper.

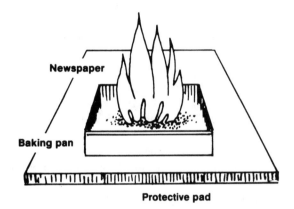

D. Results:
1. Black material collects on the spoon.
2. The newspaper leaves charred black ashes.

E. Supplemental Information:

The main part of the flame is bright yellow, and is due to actual particles of black carbon or soot which become nearly white in the flame before they finally burn. The black material which collects on the object is carbon which was removed from the flame before it had a chance to burn. Smoke is actually small solid particles of unburned carbon. The charred newspaper is essentially unburned carbon plus some mineral ashes.

F. Thought Questions:
1. Why doesn't all of the carbon burn?
2. How does the carbon get from the candle up to the spoon?
3. Where does the carbon come from in the charred newspaper?
4. What is necessary for complete combustion?

G. Related Topics and Activities:
1. See Activity I-A-3, "Changes in State."
2. See Activity II-B-12, "Fire Needs Oxygen."
3. See other Activities in this Section.

H. Vocabulary Builders—Spelling Words:

1) **combustion**   2) **smoke**   3) **carbon**
4) **candle**   5) **newspaper**

I. Thought for Today:

"There are two ways of spreading light: be the candle or the mirror that reflects it."

Activity

A. Problem: *Will Water Temperature Rise if Water is Heated While it Has Ice in it?*

B. Materials:
1. Pyrex coffee pot or other glass jar that can be heated easily and safely
2. Thermometer
3. Supply of ice
4. Electric hot plate or other heat source

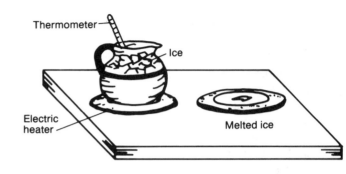

C. Procedure:
1. Put some water in the coffee pot or glass jar.
2. Put a generous supply of ice in the water.
3. Dip the thermometer in the ice water and keep stirring it until the temperature on the thermometer goes down to 32° Fahrenheit or 0° Celsius. (freezing point of water).
4. Apply heat slowly to the ice water.
5. Keep stirring the ice water gently until all the ice is gone, noting the temperature every half minute.
6. When the ice has melted note if there are any temperature changes for three or four minutes.

D. Results:
1. The temperature will not rise until the ice has melted.
2. When the ice has melted, the temperature will rise.

E. Supplemental Information:
The reason why the temperature doesn't rise can be found in the conditions that govern the freezing of water and the melting of ice. We have to have enough heat removed from the water to change its state from liquid to solid. The reverse is also true. We must add heat to change from a solid to a liquid. It requires eighty (80) calories of heat for each gram of water to melt the ice. This is why the temperature will not rise until all the ice has been melted.

F. Thought Questions:
1. After you have cooled a soft drink by adding ice to it and stirring, do you still have to add more ice in order to make it colder?
2. Will an ice-cold drink on a hot day be hotter than an ice-cold drink on a colder day?

G. Related Topics and Activities:
1. See Activity I-A-2, "Change of State of Matter."
2. See Section I-C, "Water."
3. See other Activities in this Section.

H. Vocabulary Builders—Spelling Words:
1) **temperature** 2) **melt** 3) **liquid**
4) **freezing** 5) **solid**

I. Thought for Today:
"Most minds are like concrete—all mixed up and permanently set."

A. Problem: *Can Water Be Heated in a Paper Container?*

B. Materials:
1. Paper cup, non-waxed
2. Ring stand
3. Clamp support
4. Wire screen
5. Water
6. Candle, burner, or Sterno
7. Safety pail
8. Tongs

C. Procedure:
1. Discuss what conditions must be present in order to have burning:
   a. fuel
   b. oxygen
   c. high temperature (kindling point of fuel).
2. Place the wire screen on the ring stand.
3. Place the cup on the wire screen.
4. Place the cup on the stand.
5. Fill the cup about one-third full of water.
6. Light the candle or burner and place below the cup so that the tip is just touching the bottom of the cup.
7. Have class observe the activity.
8. Discuss what conditions were present.
9. Remove the water from the cup.
10. Have tongs and a safety pail handy to dispose of burning paper if necessary.
11. Apply the flame again.
12. Observe the results.
13. Discuss what conditions were present.

D. Result:
The paper cup might char but will not burn as long as there is water in the cup because the water keeps the cup below its kindling point and conducts heat away from the paper cup. When the water is removed, the cup burns.

E. Supplemental Information:
This demonstration could be conducted over a sink or some other surface that will not be hurt by spilling water or by burning paper. Children should be kept at a safe distance.

F. Thought Questions
1. What conditions are necessary for wood to burn? gas to burn?
2. Would it make any difference if a waxed carton were used instead of a plain paper cup?
3. If something is burning what "condition(s)" must be removed to stop the burning?

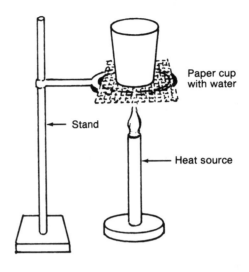

Paper cup with water

Stand

Heat source

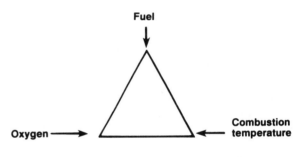

Fuel

Oxygen →

Combustion temperature

The fire triangle

G. Related Topics and Activities:
1. See Section I-C, "Water."
2. See Activity II-B-1, "Temperatures."
3. See Activity II-B-4, "Heat."

H. Vocabulary Builders—Spelling Words:
1) **kindling point**   2) **ring stand**
3) **oxygen**   4) **fuel**   5) **heat source**

I. Thought for Today:
"If something goes wrong it is more important to talk about who is going to fix it than who is to blame."

Activity

A. Problem: *Do Fires Need Oxygen?*

B. Materials:
1. Candle
2. Match
3. Glass jar

C. Procedure:
1. Strike the match and light the candle.
2. Let some of the candle wax drop on the table.
3. Place candle on melted wax so that it stands alone.
4. Discuss the fire triangle. (See Activity II-B-11.)
5. Place jar completely over candle.
6. Observe results.
7. Discuss what happened.

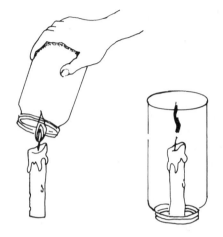

D. Result:

The candle flame will become weaker and weaker and will finally be extinguished.

E. Supplemental Information:

Fires need oxygen in order to burn. A burning flame (fire) may be extinguished by removing its supply of oxygen.

F. Thought Questions:
1. If you have a gas heater in your house should it be vented (accessed to air) or unvented? Why?
2. In order to have a fire, three conditions or things must be present. What are they?
3. Which one of these is usually the most easily removed or altered?

G. Related Topics and Activities:
1. See Section I-B, "Air."
2. See Activity VI-D-6, "Public Attractions."
3. See all Activities in this Section.

H. Vocabulary Builders—Spelling Words:
1) **vented**   2) **unvented**   3) **oxygen**
4) **extinguished**   5) **melted**

I. Thought for Today:

"The heaviest burden a man can carry is the chip on his shoulder."

Activity

A. Problems: *Is Carbon Dioxide Heavier Than Air? Will Carbon Dioxide Gas Support Combustion (Burning)?*

B. Materials:
1. Large glass jar
2. Baking soda and vinegar or dry ice (solid form of carbon dioxide)
3. Three candles
4. Wood or cardboard trough
5. Glass

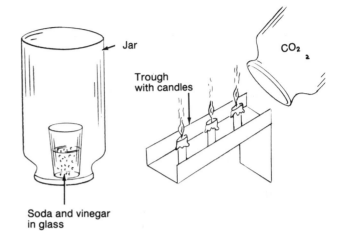

C. Procedure:
1. Attach candles in trough as shown in sketch.
2. Use prop to tilt one end.
3. Light candles.
4. If you are using baking soda and vinegar, place a handful of baking soda in glass.
5. Add a half cup of vinegar. (Carbon dioxide is formed when soda and vinegar are mixed.)
6. Place jar over the glass or place a piece of dry ice in the jar and cap it.
7. Wait several minutes so that the jar will fill with carbon dioxide.
8. Remove the lid and gently "pour" the carbon dioxide gas out of the jar and just over the top candle as shown in sketch.

D. Result:

As the carbon dioxide floats down the trough, the candles go out one by one.

E. Supplemental Information:
1. Carbon dioxide is heavier than air and thus can be "poured" from the bottle. Carbon dioxide is effective as a fire extinguisher because it is heavier than air and settles around the flame, shutting off the oxygen supply. This is what happens when the carbon dioxide is poured down the trough.
2. This activity proves that carbon dioxide is heavier than air and it does not support combustion.

F. Thought Questions:
1. Why is carbon dioxide applied above the flame instead of below the flame?
2. If you knew an excess of carbon dioxide was in the air, would it be better to breathe at the top or at the bottom of the room? Why?
3. Do you know any other way of making carbon dioxide?
4. Do our bodies give off carbon dioxide?
5. What would happen if oxygen was used instead of carbon dioxide?

G. Related Topics and Activities:
1. See all Activities with candles.
2. See Activity I-B-19, "Detecting Carbon Dioxide."
3. See other Activities in this Section.

H. Vocabulary Builders—Spelling Words:
1) **support**   2) **carbon dioxide**   3) **combustion**
4) **vinegar**   5) **baking soda**   6) **trough**

I. Thought for Today:
"The key to wisdom is a knowledge of our own ignorance."

Section C: Light and Color

Activity II C 1

A. Problem: *Can We See a Light Beam?*

B. Materials:
1. Glass jar with smaller opening at top than the rest of the jar
2. Crumpled paper
3. Matches
4. Cap or covering for the glass jar
5. Ice pick or carpenter's punch

C. Procedure:
1. Punch a hole about half the diameter of a dime in the cap.
2. Set fire to the crumpled piece of paper.
3. Push the burning paper into the bottle.
4. Put the cap with the hole on top of the bottle.
5. Hold the bottle at an angle which lets the cap face the sun. Continually adjust the angle of the bottle until the sun shines directly through the hole into the bottom of the bottle.

D. Result:
As the sun shines through the hole, the ray of light from the sun will be easily visible as it passes through the smoke.

E. Supplemental Information:
This is a variation of a natural condition we have seen many times when dust in the air clearly outlines a shaft of light. We actually see the reflection from the smoke particles or dust particles which the air contains.

F. Thought Questions:
1. Can you see the light beam from a movie projector in a theater?
2. Can sunlight pass through water?
3. What would the earth be like if there were no sunlight?

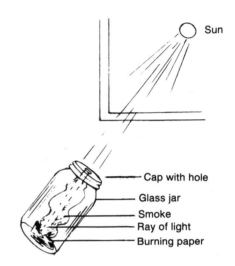

G. Related Topics and Activities:
1. See Activity II-C-4, "Colors in Sunlight."
2. See Part VII-B, "Solar System."
3. See other Activities in this Section.

H. Vocabulary Builders—Spelling Words:
1) **beam**   2) **crumpled**   3) **carpenter's punch**
4) **diameter**   5) **burning**

I. Thought for Today:
"There is no need to tie bells to fools."

Activity

A. Problem: *Does Light Travel Only in a Straight Line?*

B. Materials:
   1. Cardboard strips
   2. Candle or flashlight
   3. Candle holder
   4. Match
   5. Piece of rubber hose

C. Procedure:
   1. Make small, equal-sized holes in the center of four strips of cardboard (about ¼″ in diameter).
   2. Arrange the cardboard strips so that the holes are in a straight line.
   3. Fasten candle to candle holder.
   4. Light candle or turn on flashlight.
   5. Look through holes toward the candle or flashlight.
   6. Move one cardboard out of line and look toward the candle or flashlight.
   7. Look through hose toward candle or flashlight.
   8. Keeping the far end of the hose intact, bend the other end.
   9. Look at the candle or flashlight.

D. Results:
   1. With the cardboard strips in a straight line the candle or flashlight will be seen. When one cardboard strip is moved out of line, the light will not be seen.
   2. With the rubber hose, the light is visible only as long as the hose is perfectly straight. As soon as the hose is bent, the light cannot be seen.

E. Supplemental Information:
This experiment proves that light rays travel only in straight lines. For advanced students you might want to discuss light waves.

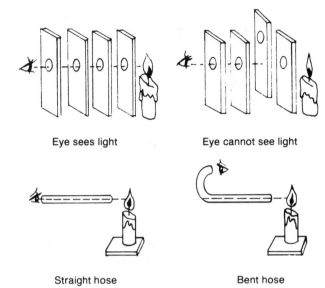

Eye sees light   Eye cannot see light

Straight hose   Bent hose

F. Thought Questions:
   1. Where does light come from?
   2. Do mirrors make light rays curve or bend?
   3. What is the difference between source light, reflected light, and refracted light?
   4. Why can't we see around a corner?

G. Related Topics and Activities:
   1. See Activity II-C-3, "Periscopes."
   2. See Activity II-C-4, "Sunlight."
   3. See other Activities in this Section.

H. Vocabulary Builders—Spelling Words:
   1) **travel**   2) **intact**   3) **flashlight**
   4) **bent**   5) **straight**

I. Thought for Today:
   "He who falls in love with himself will have no rivals."

Activity

A. Problem: *How Can We Make a Periscope? Can Light Be Bent?*

B. Materials:
1. Cardboard
2. Razor blade
3. Small pocket mirrors (two, four, or six)
4. Cellophane tape
5. Cardboard box (See Procedure Two)

C. Procedure One:
1. Fold the cardboard and cut diagonal slots in it as shown in the sketches.
2. Place the mirrors in the slot as shown and fasten them securely with cellophane tape. These should be at 45° angles.
3. Cut a square hole for the viewing section.

Procedure Two:
1. Cut cardboard box as shown in sketch.
2. Attach mirrors with cellophane tape with reflecting surfaces facing the inside of the box at 45° angles.
3. Put the top on the box.
4. Place the candle in front of one opening.

D. Results:
1. If procedures are followed, a periscope as shown in illustration will be completed.
2. Students will be able to "see through" solid objects.

E. Supplemental Information:
1. Light travels in straight lines if unhindered.
2. Light rays can be reflected by mirrors.
3. Silver plastic material from greeting cards may be substituted for mirrors.

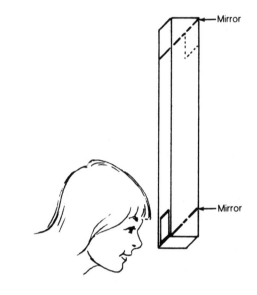

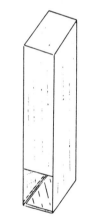

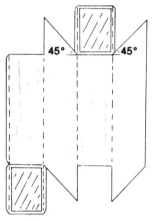

Periscope pattern
how to make a periscope

Completed periscope

Procedure one

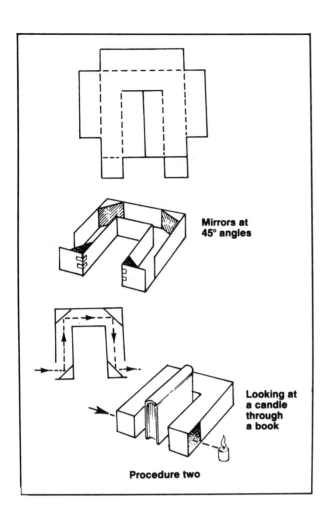

Mirrors at 45° angles

Looking at a candle through a book

Procedure two

F. Thought Questions:
1. How tall can we make a periscope?
2. Does light travel *from* our eyes or *to* our eyes? How can we prove this?
3. Where can periscopes be used?

G. Related Topics and Activities:
1. See Activities V-B, 2-8, "Eyes."
2. See Section I-B, "Air."
3. See all Activities in this Section.

H. Vocabulary Builders—Spelling Words:
1) **periscope**   2) **mirror**   3) **apparent**
4) **pattern**   5) **diagonal**

I. Thought for Today:
"It is better to keep your mouth shut and appear to be stupid than open it and remove all doubts."

Activity

A. Problem: *What Colors of Light Are in Sunlight?*

B. Materials:
1. Prism
2. Window
3. Strong sunlight
4. Any movable flat surface

C. Procedure:
1. Select window with strong sunlight passing through.
2. Allow sunlight to pass through prism so that a rainbow is formed on the flat surface.

D. Result:

Sunlight will split into the following sequence of colors: red, orange, yellow, green, blue, indigo, and violet.

E. Supplemental Information:

From an experiment such as this one, it can be shown that white light, such as sunlight, is composed not of a single color but of many colors. Whenever light passes at an angle from one substance into another of different density, it is bent; that is, its direction is changed. The different colors are bent differently, the violet being bent most and the red least. Hence, when the light comes out of the prism, the different colors are traveling in somewhat different directions, and they do not strike the flat surface in the same place. This is how the rainbow is produced. The droplets of falling water have the same effect as the prism. All the colors in combination are called the spectrum.

F. Thought Questions:
1. Why can we see various colors?
2. Are there other kinds of light rays which we don't see?
3. If we put two prisms together in opposite directions, what kind of light would appear?

G. Related Topics and Activities:
1. On a bright day, fill a glass bowl with water and set it on the edge of a counter so the sunlight can strike the water. Place a white sheet of paper so that the refracted light will strike it. Results: sunlight will be broken into its component colors.

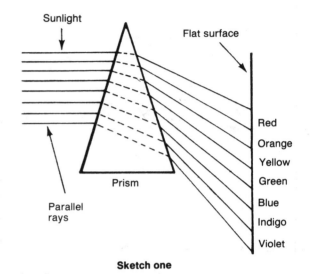

Sketch one

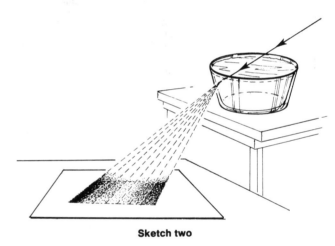

Sketch two

2. Cut glass with beveled edges also breaks sunlight into its spectrum.
3. See all Activities in this Section.

H. Vocabulary Builders—Spelling Words:
1) **prism**   2) **refraction**   3) **rainbow**   4) **angles**
5) **spectrum**

I. Thought for Today:
"Some speakers who don't know what to do with their hands should clamp them over their mouths."

Activity

A. Problem: *Are Some Colors Warmer Than Others?*

B. Materials:
1. Cotton swabs
2. Water
3. Paper cups
4. Six cups of tempera paint (black, white, red, yellow, blue, and green)
5. Cardboard lids for each
6. Paper towels
7. Scrap paper
8. Color wheel
9. Paint brushes
10. Thermometer

C. Procedure One:
1. Place cups of different colors of paint (primary colors) on the table: red, yellow, and blue.
2. Divide the class into 4 to 6 groups.
3. Instruct the children to be careful of their clothing.
4. Explain that with the primary colors all other colors can be created.
5. Have the children try mixing different primary colors to see what the secondary color would be.
6. Give each group an opportunity to mix the paints.
7. Have the students mix secondary colors: green, orange, purple.
8. Show the pupils the color wheel. They might make one for themselves as they progress.

Procedure Two:
1. Paint each cup a separate color.
2. Paint a lid to match each cup.
3. Put ¾ cup of cold water in each cup.
4. Take temperature of each cup with a thermometer. All cups should have the same temperature.
5. Set the cups in sunlight.
6. Record the temperature of the water in each cup at half hour periods.

D. Results:
1. The students will see that by mixing two of the primary colors, a third color (secondary color) is obtained. Yellow and blue make green.

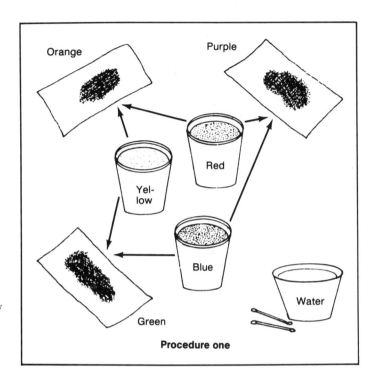

Procedure one

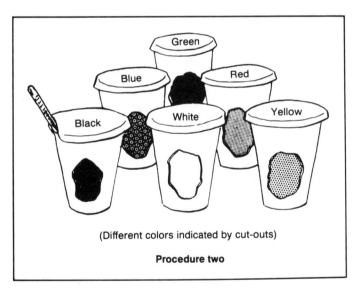

(Different colors indicated by cut-outs)

Procedure two

Yellow and red will make orange. Red and blue will make purple. Two secondary colors when mixed will produce a tertiary color.
2. The water in the black cup will get warmest in the shortest time.

E. Supplemental Information:

1. The primary colors of paint are different from the primary colors of light.
2. The so-called "hot" color red is not nearly as warm as black. White is the coolest color of all.

F. Thought Questions:

1. What will happen if primary colors are mixed together in unequal amounts?
2. How can colors be darkened? lightened?
3. What color clothing should one wear on hot days? cold days? Why?
4. If two objects are exposed to the sun, which one would become hotter; a light colored one or a dark colored one?
5. Can a person get sunburned on a cloudy day? How?

G. Related Topics and Activities:

1. Combine color making with art work.
2. Mix different food colorings.
3. Make colored disks that can be attached to a hand drill using various combinations of colors. Disks can be rotated quickly and colors will seem to blend.
4. See all Activities in this Section.

H. Vocabulary Builders—Spelling Words:

1) **primary**   2) **secondary**   3) **tertiary**
4) **different**   5) **darkened**   6) **lightened**

I. Thought for Today:

"Love most the unlovable."

Activity

A. Problem: *What is the Difference Between Source Light and Reflected Light?*

B. Materials:

1. Light bulb
2. Mirror
3. Reflector

C. Procedure:

1. Tell the students that you are going to show them two different types of light.
2. Demonstrate source light by lighting the light bulb and having the students watch the light directly.
3. Next, using the reflector to hide the light bulb from the students' view, turn the bulb on so that the light is reflected by the mirror.
4. Have the students look at the mirror.
5. Discuss the differences involved in direct light and reflected light.

D. Results:

1. The light will come from the bulb directly.
2. The light from the mirror will be reflected light from the bulb.

E. Supplemental Information:

1. We receive light by two means: direct and reflected. This activity will help children to understand light and darkness. Many things are visible because they give off their own light such as the sun, and electric light, candle, and a flashlight; these are all luminous.
2. Most substances are visible because they reflect light from one of the luminous sources. We can see in the light because of reflections from luminous objects, but we can't see the same objects if it is dark.

F. Thought Questions:

1. Why is reflected light from the mirror practically the same strength as direct light?
2. Is the sun direct (source) light?
3. Is the moon direct light or reflected light?

G. Related Topics and Activities:

1. Have students set up sketch two as nearly as possible. Have them discuss source (direct) (luminous) and reflected (indirect) light.

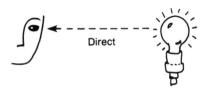

Sketch one

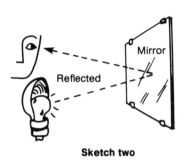

Sketch two

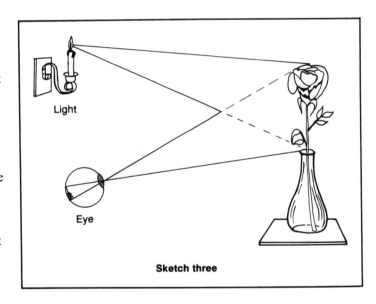

Sketch three

2. See Activity II-C-2, "How Light Travels."
3. See other Activities in this Section.

H. Vocabulary Builders—Spelling Words:

1) **source**   2) **reflected**   3) **emit**
4) **direct**   5) **indirect**   6) **luminous**

I. Thought for Today:

"Bad officials are elected by people who don't vote."

Activity

A. Problem: *Does Water Have Magnifying and Refractive Qualities?*

B. Materials:
1. Glass tumbler
2. Water
3. Teaspoon
4. Mirror

C. Procedure:
1. Hold spoon up to mirror and observe its appearance.
2. Put water in glass tumbler.
3. Put spoon in glass tumbler.
4. Look at the spoon and tumbler from a distance of several feet.

D. Results:
1. The spoon will be seen in the mirror and appears to be of the same size and unbroken.
2. The spoon will seem to be broken at the surface of the water.
3. The part of the spoon which is in the water will seem to be enlarged.

E. Supplemental Information:

Light rays striking the surface of the water are refracted because of the different densities of air and water. This makes the spoon appear to be bent as it enters the water. The curvature of the glass acts as a lens. This causes enlargement. The mirror may be omitted but this makes it more interesting.

F. Thought Questions:
1. Would this principle be important in shooting or spearing a fish in the water?
2. Would this refraction occur with other liquids?
3. What would be the appearance of a spoon if we had two different layers of liquids as clear salad oil on top of water?
4. Why does the sun look larger early in the morning and late in the evening?

(In the morning we actually see the sun rise over the horizon before it actually does and in the evening we actually see the sun set after it actually does because of refraction caused by the refraction from air molecules.)

G. Related Topics and Activities:
1. Take a wide glass jar about four inches wide and four inches high, set it on a sheet of white paper over a drawn, black line. Observe from the top and all angles at the side.
2. Put a penny in a teacup. Look at it from the side in the lowest possible position. Have someone add water to the cup and see the penny float to the top.
3. See all Activities in this Section.

H. Vocabulary Builders—Spelling Words:
1) **refraction**   2) **reflection**   3) **tumbler**
4) **broken**   5) **surface**   6) **magnifying**

I. Thought for Today:

"As tools become rusty, so does the mind; a garden uncared for soon becomes smothered in weeds; a talent neglected withers and dies."—Ethel R. Page

Activity

A. Problem: *What Causes a Shadow?*

B. Materials:

1. White sheet
2. Rope or heavy string, tacks, and safety pins (or device to support sheet)
3. Extension cord with socket, light bulb, and reflector, or filmstrip projector
4. If no filmstrip projector or reflector is available, a reflector can be made by cutting a piece of cardboard in an 18″ circle and making a small 1½″ hole in the middle. Secure with cellophane tape and place behind bulb.
5. Flashlight (if no projector available)
6. Yardstick or meter stick
7. Cardboard circle the same size as flashlight or projector lens.

C. Procedure:

1. Secure rope across the room and pin sheet to rope, or tack sheet over a doorway.
2. Hold light or place it on floor about seven or eight feet in front of sheet.
3. Place child in back of light.
4. Place child between sheet and light.
5. Have child move closer to sheet.
6. Have child move farther away from sheet.
7. Tape cardboard circle to end of stick.
8. Darken room.
9. Turn on flashlight or projector aiming toward wall or sheet.
10. Have student stand in front of flashlight or projector holding the circle over the lens.
11. Have the child move slowly away from lens and towards the sheet or wall.

D. Results:

1. The child will not cast a shadow when he stands in back of light.
2. The child will cast a shadow when he stands in front of sheet.
3. The circle shadow will become smaller as the child approaches the sheet.

E. Supplemental Information:

Light rays do not pass through the child, therefore, a shadow is cast on the screen when he stands in front of the light. This also demonstrates that light travels in straight lines. Some teachers like to make shadows with their hands forming various animals, objects, etc. Children love to do this as well. An opaque object will not permit light to pass through, consequently a shadow is formed.

Sketch one

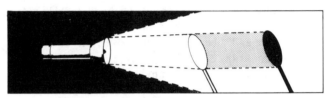

Does shadow get smaller, larger, or stay the same size as object moves closer to the screen?

Sketch two

F. Thought Questions:

1. How can you increase or decrease the height of a shadow?
2. Will moving the light closer to the boy cause the shadow to be larger or smaller? Why?
3. How does a sundial work?

G. Related Topics and Activities:

1. Change the position of the light or projector and observe size of shadow.
2. Change the size of the circles on the stick, but keep the same distance and observe the changes in size of shadow.
3. Have children write a play using shadow characters.
4. See all Activities in this Section.

H. Vocabulary Builders—Spelling Words:

1) **shadow**   2) **projector**   3) **flashlight**
4) **screen**   5) **sheet**   6) **wall**

I. Thought for Today:

"A winner never quits; a quitter never wins."

Activity

A. Problem: *How Can We Make a Simple Magnifying Glass?*

B. Materials:
1. One piece of flat glass which has been carefully cleaned
2. Medicine dropper
3. Piece of cloth
4. Other objects to examine
5. Nail (large), or dowel (small)
6. Copper wire, 6" approx.
7. Water

C. Procedure One:
1. Hold the glass in a horizontal position.
2. Use the medicine dropper to place a small drop of water on the lower side of the glass. (Do not attempt to place the drop of water on the upper side and then turn the glass over; the water will run off the edge.)
3. The surface of this hanging water drop is like the surface of a glass lens. Use it to examine the piece of cloth.
4. Place your eye very close to the glass and just above the water drop.
5. Hold the cloth just below the glass and very close to the water drop, but do not let them touch.
6. Slowly move the cloth downward until the image is as clear as possible.

Procedure Two:
1. Make several turns of wire around the nail or dowel.
2. Remove the wire from nail or dowel.
3. Dip the loop into water or use medicine dropper to place water in hole.

D. Result:
The water drop will magnify the cloth.

E. Supplemental Information:
These are simple and effective devices. Each child in the class can make one or both.

F. Thought Questions:
1. Why does the drop of water act like a magnifying glass?
2. Does the water bend the light rays?
3. How does a magnifying glass magnify?

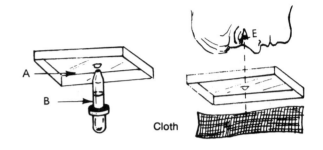

Procedure one

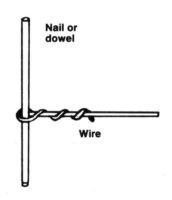

Procedure two

Wire magnifier drop

G. Related Topics and Activities:
1. If a regular microscope is available, use it to examine many objects. Care should be taken with regular microscopes because they are expensive—especially the lenses.
2. See all Activities in this Section.

H. Vocabulary Builders—Spelling Words:
1) **magnifying**   2) **medicine dropper**
3) **eye dropper**   4) **horizontal**   5) **lens**   6) **lenses**

I. Thought for Today:
"We can do anything we want to do if we stick to it long enough."

Activity

A. Problem: *How Does a Camera Work?*

B. Materials:
1. Convex lens or ordinary magnifying glass lens
2. Small cardboard box
3. Masking tape
4. Ground glass or thin white tissue paper (translucent)
5. Black paint
6. Paint brush
7. Magnifying glass
8. White surface
9. Darkened room
10. Source of light (either an open window or an electric light)
11. Scissors

C. Procedure One:
1. Paint the inside of the cardboard box black.
2. Cut a small round hole about the size of a pencil in one end of the box.
3. Tape a lens in the box behind the hole. (Be sure that the tape does not overlap into the hole.)
4. Put the ground glass or piece of translucent paper in the opposite end of the box.
5. Point the end of the box which contains the lens toward a tree or other object and see what happens on the ground glass or translucent paper.

Procedure Two:
1. Put the lens directly between the source of light and the white surface.
2. Move the lens toward the white surface until the source of light focuses on the white surface. This may require moving the lens backward and forward a little until an exact focus is obtained.

D. Results:
1. You will see the image from the outside of the box. *Note:* You may have to put a hood over your head in order to make the object appear darker and clearer on the ground glass or translucent paper.
2. The exact image of the source of light will be focused on the white surface.

E. Supplemental Information:
1. Light travels in straight lines.

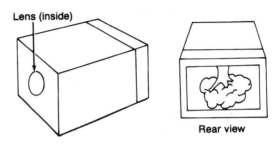

Lens (inside)

Rear view

Procedure one

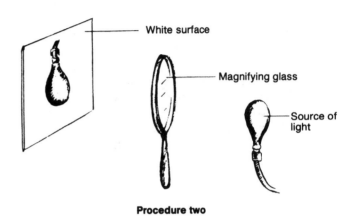

White surface

Magnifying glass

Source of light

Procedure two

2. Light rays can be made to bend if they pass through lenses. This is because the glass of the lens varies in thickness (density).

F. Thought Questions:
1. Why are distant objects always in focus and close-up objects not in focus?
2. How could you make the image larger? smaller?
3. Can you explain why the image is upside down?
4. Does the power of the lens have anything to do with the size of the image which appears on the white surface?

G. Related Topics and Activities:
1. See Activity II-C-2, "Light Travels."
2. See Activity II-C-11, "Pinhole Camera."
3. See other Activities in this Section.

H. Vocabulary Builders—Spelling Words:
1) **focus**   2) **camera**   3) **inverted**
4) **translucent**   5) **image**

I. Thought for Today:
"The world's most disappointed people are those who get what's coming to them."

Activity

A. Problem: *How Can We Make a Pinhole Camera?*

B. Materials:
1. Two paper cups or cylindrical cartons
2. Safety pin or punch (for making a tiny hole)
3. Translucent paper
4. Cellophane tape

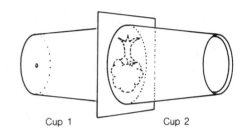

Cup 1   Cup 2

C. Procedure:
1. Punch a small hole in the center of the bottom of one paper cup (cup 1).
2. Cover the open end of this paper cup with a piece of translucent paper taping it to the cup.
3. Cut the bottom out of a second paper cup and place the large end next to the translucent paper and cellophane tape the two cups together.
4. Point the tiny hole end of the first cup at a well-lighted object and look at the translucent paper, using the second cup as a shade for the paper.

D. Result:
An image of the object will show on the translucent paper. The image will be upside down.

E. Supplemental Information:
This illustrates the principle of the camera. The light is reflected from the object, through the hole, and onto the translucent paper. The light rays are stopped by the paper and the image becomes visible.

F. Thought Questions:
1. Could you design a "pinhole camera" so that you could use regular film in it?
2. Why does the object appear upside down on the translucent paper?
3. If the lenses in our eyes work the same way, why don't we see everything upside down?

G. Related Topics and Activities:
1. See Activity II-C-1, "Light Beam."
2. See Activity II-C-2, "Light Travels."
3. See Activity II-C-6, "Sources of Light."
4. See Activity II-C-10, "How Camera Works."
5. See other Activities in this Section.

H. Vocabulary Builders—Spelling Words:
1) **camera**   2) **pinhole**   3) **translucent**
4) **cellophane**   5) **image**

I. Thought for Today:
"Children are like wet cement; whatever falls on them makes an impression."

Section D: Sound

Activity   II D 1

A. Problem: *What Causes Sound?*

B. Materials:
1. Blade of grass
2. Piece of paper
3. Tissue paper over comb
4. Rubber band
5. Toy guitar, or other musical instrument (string)
6. Any noisemaker (dried gourd, tonette, rattle, whistle, blocks of wood)

C. Procedure:
1. Have students hold a blade of grass or piece of paper between their thumbs and blow.
2. Have pupils place tissue paper over a comb, hold it to their lips, and hum.
3. Have pupils stretch a rubber band; pluck it; listen to it.
4. Stop the vibrations and listen again.
5. Have pupils pluck a musical stringed instrument, listen to it; stop vibrations and listen again.
6. Make sounds with noisemaker(s).
7. Ask the class if they know what all these sounds have in common.

D. Results:
1. These tests will produce vibrations which cause sound.
2. When vibrations cease, sounds will stop.

E. Supplemental Information:
1. Sounds travel in air at about 1,600 feet per second.
2. Sound travels faster in water and through solid objects.
3. One aspect of sound is *frequency* or *pitch*. It is the number of vibrations (cycles) per second.

Average person's hearing graph: (white area)

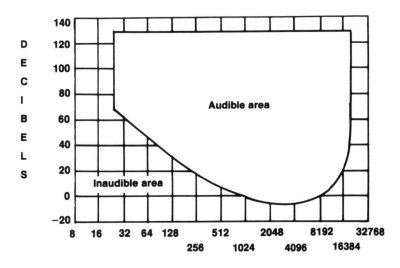

Frequency (pitch) in cycles per second

The more vibrations or cycles, the higher the pitch.

4. Another characteristic of sound is *intensity* or *amplitude*. The greater this is, the louder the sound.

5. The average person has a very limited hearing range and scope. (See previous page.)

6. The normal range is between 20 and 20,000 vibrations per second.

7. Through these experiences, pupils will learn that sound is caused by vibrations, i.e., vibrations produce sound.

F. Thought Questions:

1. What other vibrating objects will cause sound?
2. Are noises caused by vibrations?
3. Are there any vibrations we can't hear?
4. What is an echo?

G. Related Topics and Activities:

1. Study the sounds of music.
2. Listen to the sounds of birds, insects, and other animals.
3. Place finger on throat and hum.
4. See all Activities in this Section.

H. Vocabulary Builders—Spelling Words:

1) **frequency**   2) **pitch**   3) **intensity**
4) **sound**   5) **vibrations**   6) **cycles**

I. Thought for Today:

"Learning is the original and greatest of all 'do it yourself' projects."

Activity

A. Problem: *What Things Make Sound?*

B. Materials:
   1. Several different size tuning forks
   2. Desk top or table
   3. Pan
   4. Water

C. Procedure:
   1. Discuss the many sounds around us.
   2. Strike one tuning fork against the side of desk top or table.
   3. Listen to it.
   4. Strike another tuning fork against the side of desk top or table.
   5. Listen to it.
   6. Strike a tuning fork again, only this time place it on the desk top or table.
   7. Listen again.
   8. Fill the pan with water.
   9. Strike the tuning fork again and place it in the pan of water.

D. Results:
   1. When a tuning fork is struck, a sound is emitted.
   2. Different tuning forks emit different sounds.
   3. When the tuning fork is placed on the table, the sound appears to be louder. Solids transmit sound better than gases or liquids.
   4. When a tuning fork is placed in water, the water is splattered.

E. Supplemental Information:
   1. When a tuning fork is vibrated in air, it makes the molecules of air move back and forth. Sound transmission can be thought of as wave ripples from the source of any vibrating object. When the tuning fork is immersed in water it makes the molecules of water move back and forth.
   2. The softest sound we can hear is an almost quiet whisper. The loudest sound ever heard was in August of 1883 when the volcano Krakatoa, near Java erupted and the sound was heard 3,000 miles away. Scientists estimated that it reached 190 decibels.
   3. Sounds vary in volume, pitch, and harmonics (combinations).

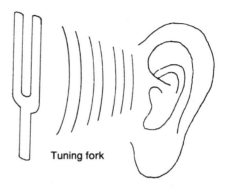

Tuning fork

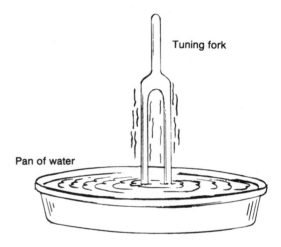

Tuning fork

Pan of water

F. Thought Questions:
   1. Why does the sound intensity increase when the handle is placed on a table or desk?
   2. Will a larger tuning fork make a lower pitched sound? Why?
   3. What determines the pitch of a tuning fork? length? width? both?

G. Related Topics and Activities:
   1. See Activity II-D-1, "Causes of Sound."
   2. See Activity II-D-3, "Pitch."
   3. See Activity II-D-6, "Sound and Solids."
   4. See Activity II-D-7, "Simple Telephone."
   5. See other Activities in this Section.

H. Vocabulary Builders—Spelling Words:
   1) **tuning fork**   2) **vibrations**   3) **different**
   4) **harmonics**   5) **splatter**

I. Thought for Today:
   "Thinking is like loving and dying; each of us must do it for ourself."

Activity

A. Problem: *What Causes Sounds to Vary in Pitch?*

B. Materials:
1. Wooden box or shoe box open at top
2. Rubber bands of varied lengths and thicknesses
3. String
4. Wire

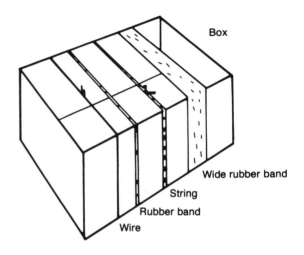

C. Procedure:
1. Using only one band, place on box and pluck.
2. Tighten band by pulling band out to the side but keeping top taut and pluck again.
3. Place bands of same lengths but different widths on box and pluck each band.
4. Place bands of same thickness but different lengths around box and pluck each band.
5. Place string, wire, and a band around box and pluck each one.

D. Results:
1. Short bands will have a higher pitch than long bands.
2. Tight bands will have a higher pitch than loose bands.
3. Thin bands will have a higher pitch than thick bands.
4. Light materials will have a higher pitch than heavy materials.

E. Supplemental Information:

By observing closely, students will learn that high pitches result from many vibrations and low pitches result from few vibrations.

F. Thought Questions:
1. Why won't a heavy band vibrate as rapidly as a light band?
2. Why will stretching a rubberband or a piece of catgut tight cause it to vibrate faster?
3. What does this have to do with tuning a violin or guitar?

G. Related Topics and Activities:
1. See Activity II-D-4, "Vibrating Wires."
2. See Activity II-D-6, "Sound Travels."
3. See Activity II-D-11, "Pop Bottle Music."
4. See other Activities in this Section.

PITCH SCALE (VIBRATIONS PER SECOND)

FREQUENCY	EXAMPLES (SOUND, MUSIC, HEARING)	
0 – 15	Below human capabilities	
16 – 20	Lower limit of human capabilities	
21 – 200	Deep bass tones	
256	Middle C = "DO"	
278	C-Sharp, D-Flat	
294	D = "RE"	
312	D-Sharp, E-Flat	
330	E = "ME"	
349	F = "FA"	Musical
370	F-Sharp, G-Flat	Scale
392	G = "SO"	
416	G-Sharp, A-Flat	
440	A = "LA"	
466	A-Sharp, B-Flat	
494	B = "TI"	
512	C = "DO"	
500 – 3,000	Normal conversation	
About 4,000	Highest musical tone	
About 8,000	Highest pitch, shrill tone	
About 20,000	Upper limit of human hearing	
About 30,000	Upper limit of dogs and cats	
About 100,000	Upper limit for bats	

H. Vocabulary Builders—Spelling Words:
1) **decibel** 2) **threshold** 3) **pain**
4) **whisper** 5) **eardrum**

I. Thought for Today:
"Intelligence is like a river—the deeper it is the less noise it makes."

Activity IID4

A. **Problem:** *How do Vibrating Wires Make Different Sounds?*

B. Materials:
1. Four wires of the same length:
   a. Two steel wires, same thickness (A & B)
   b. One steel wire, thinner than above two (C)
   c. One copper wire, same thickness as single steel wire (D)
2. Frame as illustrated
3. One light weight and three much heavier weights to keep wires taut

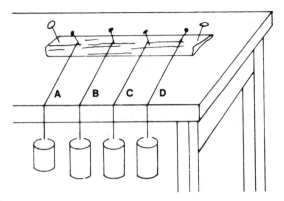

C. Procedure:
1. Arrange the four wires on a frame like the one in the sketch. A and B are made of steel of the same length and thickness. A has the light weight on it, B has a heavier weight. When the wire is stretched, we say it has tension. C is also made of steel wire but is not as thick as A or B. D is made of copper wire which is lighter than steel wire.
2. Pluck the various wires and note the differences in pitch produced.
3. Pluck any one wire and remember the pitch.
4. Press the same wire firmly to the table with your finger and pluck it again.
5. Repeat with the other wires. Listen carefully.

D. Result:

Different pitches will be produced.

E. Supplemental Information:

We know now that four different characteristics regulate the pitch of vibrating strings:
1. *The tension*—The higher the tension the higher the pitch. (Same thickness, length, and materials)
2. *The thickness*—The thinner the wire the higher the pitch. (Same material, same length and tension)
3. *The material*—The lighter the material the higher the pitch. (Same length, tension, and thickness)
4. *The length*—The shorter the wire the higher the pitch. (Same material, thickness, and tension)

F. Thought Questions:
1. Does this experiment have anything to do with tuning a piano? Pianos have wires that are struck.
2. If we double the weight, do we double the volume? pitch?
3. Do we hear the strings vibrating or the air molecules moving?

G. Related Topics and Activities:
1. Design some toy musical instruments using wires.
2. Design some method for increasing their pitch.
3. Design some method for increasing their volume.
4. See other Activities in this Section.

H. Vocabulary Builders—Spelling Words:
1) **vibrating**   2) **tension**   3) **material**
4) **length**   5) **width**

I. Thought for Today:

"The only reason some people listen to reason is to give them time for a rebuttal."

Activity

A. Problem: *Can We See and Feel Sound?*

B. Materials:
1. Steel knitting needle or ruler
2. Rubber band
3. Table
4. Sounding board (flat board with one nail protruding upwards toward each end) (See Sketch)

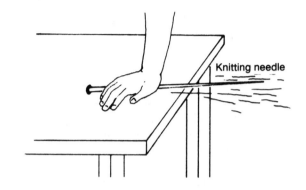

Knitting needle

C. Procedure:
1. Define the word "vibration" before the activity is started.
2. Give several examples of "vibrations" and "vibrating objects."
3. Stretch a rubber band between the two nails. Notice if there is any sound.
4. Pluck the rubber band and listen.
5. Lay one end of a steel knitting needle or ruler on the edge of the table.
6. Holding the end on the table with one hand, snap the needle or ruler up or down with the other hand.
7. Feel the air just above the needle without touching the needle.
8. Put your fingers on your throat when you talk.

Sounding board

D. Results:
1. The rubber band will produce no sound until it has vibrated.
2. Students will see the needle vibrating.
3. Pupils will feel the air above the needle moving.
4. Students observe that sound vibrations are produced in different ways.

E. Supplemental Information:
1. Sound vibrations can be felt and heard.
2. Sounds vary in pitch, volume, and quality (harmonics).
3. When the needle or ruler vibrates, it causes the air molecules to vibrate in unison with it. What the students see is the object moving. What the pupils feel is the movement of the air.

F. Thought Questions:
1. Can an object vibrate so fast that the ear will not hear the sound produced?
2. How can we find out the vibration range of the normal ear?
3. What three senses are involved in this activity?

G. Related Topics and Activities:
1. See Activity II-D-1, "Causes of Sound."
2. See Activity II-D-3, "Pitch."
3. See Activity II-D-4, "Vibrations."
4. See Activity II-D-6, "Sound Travels."
5. See Activity II-D-11, "Pop Bottle Music."
6. See other Activities in this Section.

H. Vocabulary Builders—Spelling Words:
1) **vibrations**   2) **harmonics**   3) **needle**
4) **ruler**   5) **pluck**

I. Thought for Today:
"If at first you don't succeed you're like most other people."

Activity

A. Problem: *Does Sound Travel Through Solids?*

B. Materials:

Three or four yardsticks or metersticks

C. Procedure:

1. Students in the class should pair off so that two students working together can be involved in this experiment.
2. Have one pupil hold the yardstick or meterstick close to his ear. *Caution:* both students must handle the yardstick carefully to avoid injury.
3. Have one pupil scratch the far end of the stick.
4. Have students tap the yardstick or meterstick at various distances.
5. Move the yardstick or meterstick away from the ear and repeat the last two steps.

D. Results:

1. When the yardstick or meterstick is held close to the ear the sound will be quite audible.
2. When the stick is held away from the ear the sound diminishes in direct proportion to the distance from the ear.
3. If the stick is moved a few inches away from the ear there is no audible sound.

E. Supplemental Information:

1. Actually the sound travels through the wood molecules much more easily than it does through the air because there are more molecules per given volume.
2. The normal human being can hear sounds between 20 and 20,000 vibrations (cycles) per second.

3. About 10% of all pupils have some hearing loss.
4. In order to have sound, some medium must carry the sound. This could be a *solid* as in this activity, a *liquid* such as water or a *gas* such as air.

F. Thought Questions:

1. Why did some Indians put their ears to the ground when hunting or tracking?
2. When a guitar is played, what substances do the sounds pass through?
3. How do you think fish communicate?

G. Related Topics and Activities:

1. Test other materials for sound conduction.
2. See Activity II-D-1, "Causes of Sound."
3. See Activity II-D-2, "Objects Cause Sound."
4. See Activity II-D-7, "Tin Can Telephone."
5. See other Activities in this Section.

H. Vocabulary Builders—Spelling Words:

1) **conduction**   2) **vibrations**   3) **molecules**
4) **liquids**   5) **solids**

I. Thought for Today:

"Happiness consists of being happy with what we have got and with what we haven't got."

Activity

A. Problem: *Can We Make a Simple Telephone?*

B. Materials:
1. Two empty cans
2. String (or waxed dental floss)
3. Wax (not necessary but desirable)
4. Two buttons
5. Ice pick or can opener

C. Procedure:
1. Punch a small hole in the center of each can at the bottom.
2. Cut string desired length and run wax up and down the string.
3. Put waxed string through the holes in the cans.
4. Tie a button on each end of the string to hold them firmly in the cans.
5. Keep the strings taut.
6. Have one student talk into one can and another student listen at the other can.

D. Result:
When a student talks into the can, the vibrations from the vocal chords cause the air to vibrate and this makes the bottom of the can vibrate. These vibrations are carried along the waxed string. When they reach the other can, the bottom of the can vibrates causing the adjacent air to vibrate. When the vibrations reach a person's eardrum at the other end of the string, they reproduce the sound of the voice.

E. Supplemental Information:
Sound must have a medium to vibrate. In this activity we can trace the vibrations through the different media from the vocal chords to the air to the can to the string to the other can to the eardrum.

F. Thought Questions:
1. Why does it help to wax the string in order to make this tin can telephone?
2. Would fine wire, stretched between the cans, be better than the string?
3. Would this telephone work around corners? Why?

G. Related Topics and Activities:
1. See Activity II-D-1, "Vibrations."
2. See Activity II-D-2, "Objects."
3. See Activity II-D-5, "Sensing Sound."
4. See Activity II-D-6, "Sounds and Solids."
5. See other Activities in this Section.
6. Compare this phone with a regular telephone.

H. Vocabulary Builders—Spelling Words:
1) **string**   2) **waxed**   3) **listen**   4) **taut**
5) **center**   6) **vocal chords**

I. Thought for Today:
"In quarreling, the truth is always lost."

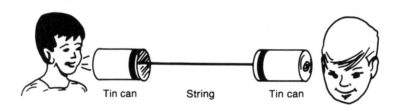

Tin can   String   Tin can

Activity

A. Problem: *Does Sound Travel in a Vacuum?*

B. Materials:

1. Flask or large bottle
2. One-holed rubber stopper
3. Round stick or rod
4. Miniature bells
5. Rubber band or masking tape
6. Source of heat (candle or hot plate)
7. Half cup of water

C. Procedure:

1. Secure bells to the bottom of rod with rubber band or masking tape after you have placed rod through the one-holed rubber stopper.
2. Fit stopper snugly into the flask or bottle.
3. Shake the jar and listen.
4. Put one-third cup of water in bottom of flask.
5. Boil water in the bottle for several minutes without stopper. Steam drives the air out leaving only a little liquid water and steam.
6. Remove bottle from the source of heat and immediately plug it with the prepared stopper, making sure the bells are in the wide part of the bottle (see diagram).
7. After cooling, shake the bottle and listen.

D. Results:

1. Sound will be heard when there is air in flask.
2. Sound will not be heard (or will be faintly heard) when flask contains a partial vacuum.

E. Supplemental Information:

Sound is a vibration of molecules and travels through solids, liquids, and gases. When a vacuum (no molecules) is established, sound cannot travel for there is no substance to conduct sound. If sound could pass through a vacuum, then there would be some sound that could be heard even if the glass flask "masked" some of it.

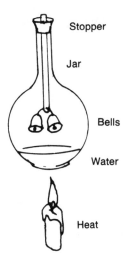

Stopper

Jar

Bells

Water

Heat

F. Thought Questions:

1. Why is it necessary to seal the bottle after it has been removed from the heat?
2. Could this be a test for a "vacuum"?
3. Can we see steam? (No, we see molecules of liquid water.)

G. Related Topics and Activities:

1. See Activity II-D-1, "Vibrations."
2. See Activity II-D-2, "Objects."
3. See Activity II-D-6, "Sound in Solids."
4. See Activity V-B-10, "Ears and Hearing."
5. See other Activities in this Section.

H. Vocabulary Builders—Spelling Words:

1) **flask**　2) **vacuum**　3) **snugly**　4) **steam**
5) **bottle**

I. Thought for Today:

"The best education is to be found in gaining the utmost information from the simplest apparatus."

A. Problem: *Can Sound be Produced by Friction?*

B. Materials:
1. Tin can
2. String (2′–3′)
3. Ice pick or nail
4. Button
5. Wax

C. Procedure:
1. Obtain an empty tin can with bottom intact.
2. Punch a small hole with an ice pick or nail through the center of the bottom of the can.
3. Take a piece of string two or three feet long and run it through the hole in the can.
4. Now put a button on the end of the string and tie a knot in the end of the string. This will keep the string from pulling out of the can when it is pulled.
5. Put wax on the string.
6. Hold the can in one hand.
7. Hold the string tightly between the fingers of the other hand and pull the hands apart letting the string slip through the fingers.

D. Result:
Sound will be produced.

E. Supplemental Information:
As the string passes through the hand, sound is produced in the can because the finger causes the string to vibrate and this causes the bottom of the can to vibrate by varying tensions of the string on the bottom of the can.

F. Thought Questions:
1. If we put grease on the string instead of resin, what would be the effect of the sound?
2. Why is resin put on violin bows?
3. How could the pitch of the sound be changed?
4. How is this similar to a bow being pulled across the strings of a cello or a bass viol?

G. Related Topics and Activities:
1. Compare this with several stringed musical instruments.
2. See Activity V-B-10, "Ears and Hearing."
3. See all Activities in this Section.

H. Vocabulary Builders—Spelling Words:
1) **friction** 2) **empty** 3) **button**
4) **tight** 5) **instruments**

I. Thought for Today:
"The trouble with doing nothing is not knowing when you are done."

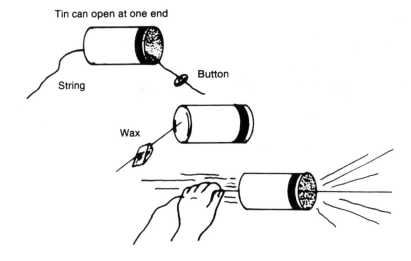

Tin can open at one end

String

Button

Wax

Activity

A. Problem: *How Does a Stethoscope Work?*

B. Materials:
1. Three pieces of rubber or plastic tubing, each 8″ long
2. Three medium size funnels
3. "Y" joint (glass tubing)
4. Some lightweight wire, string, or rubber bands
5. Vibrating devices

C. Procedure:
1. Take one piece of rubber or plastic tubing and put one of the funnels on one end.
2. Follow the same procedure for the other two tubing ear pieces.
3. Now join the three pieces of tubing with funnels together, using "Y" joint; tie all connections.
4. Have students listen with this homemade stethoscope to vibrating objects. The ear pieces can be held by other students or by rubber bands over the head and under the chin.
5. Listen to a student's heartbeat.
6. Have the student do some heavy exercise for two minutes and listen to heartbeat again.
7. Design apparatus as shown in Figure Two.
8. Make a noise in one part of room.
9. Have student guess where sound originates.

D. Results:
1. The funnels and tubes will intensify the vibrations of the heart by channeling sound waves through the tubes directly to the ears and eliminating outside noises. Children will get a better concept of how sound can be channeled and intensified.
2. The students will learn that the heart beats more frequently (and louder) after exercise.
3. In reversing funnels, sounds appear to be coming from opposite directions.

E. Supplemental Information:
Through experiments with the stethoscope, students will learn about sound, about their own bodily functions such as their heartbeat before and after exercise, and will overcome fear of the doctor.

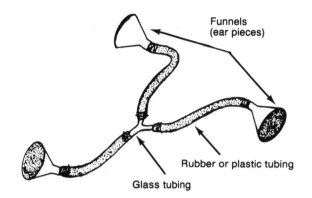

Figure One

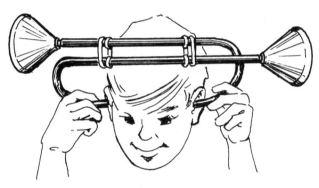

Figure Two

F. Thought Questions:
1. How does this instrument compare with the doctor's stethoscope?
2. How do you think stethoscopes help doctors?
3. Using this stethoscope, do all sounds have the same volume? pitch? quality?

G. Related Topics and Activities:
1. See Activities in Section V-B, "Senses."
2. See Section V-D, "Personal Health."
3. See all Activities in this Section.

H. Vocabulary Builders—Spelling Words:
1) **stethoscope** 2) **tubing** 3) **funnel**
4) **plastic** 5) **rubber**

I. Thought for Today:
"Parents were invented to make children happy by giving them something to ignore."

Activity

A. Problem: *How Can We Make Pop Bottle Music?*

B. Materials:
1. Eight pop bottles of the same size and type
2. Water
3. Stick or rod

C. Procedure:
1. Fill one bottle full of water.
2. Lower the depth of the water in the second bottle until the next note of the scale is obtained.
3. Continue lowering the level of water in each successive bottle about an inch each time.
4. This will give the eight tones of the scale which can be tested by blowing on the bottles or striking them with a stick or rod.
5. Add or remove water until each bottle has correct pitch.
6. Have eight children blow on or strike their own bottle.
7. Create or duplicate some simple tunes.

D. Results:
1. By having children blow on the bottles or strike them, notes can be sounded.
2. When the notes are put together simple tunes will be played.

E. Supplemental Information:

The pitch and tone produced from blowing over the pop bottles are due to the size of the resonating chamber within the bottle. The tone and pitch can also be affected by the shape of the chamber and by the material from which the bottle is made.

C   D   E   F   G   A   B   C

F. Thought Questions:
1. Why does enlarging the air chamber change the pitch?
2. Would a large jug produce a lower or higher pitch than a pop bottle? Why?
3. Does a pipe organ have similar resonating chambers?

G. Related Topics and Activities:
1. Integrate this lesson with music lessons.
2. See Section V-B, "Senses."

H. Vocabulary Builders—Spelling Words:
1) **resonating** 2) **hearing** 3) **depth**
4) **tone** 5) **scale**

I. Thought for Today:

"Peace comes not from the absence of conflict in life but upon the ability to cope with it."

Section E: Simple Machines

Activity

II E 1

A. Problem: *How Do the Wheel and Axle Help Us Do Work?*

B. Materials:

1. Two boxes of the same size, one with wheels and one without
2. Some heavy materials such as sand, books, etc.
3. Spring scale

C. Procedure:

1. Place the sand or heavy material in the box without wheels.
2. Attach the scale to one end of the box.
3. Holding the other end of the scale, drag the box a distance of about one yard.
4. Make a note of the number of ounces or pounds indicated by the pointer on the spring scale while the dragging was in progress.
5. Transfer the load to the box with wheels.
6. By the same process move this box the same distance and record the pull indicated on the spring scale.

D. Result:

The difference in readings indicated will show the increased amount of energy saved to move the box with the wheels and axle.

E. Supplemental Information:

1. Wheels help things move easily.
2. More energy was needed to drag the box without wheels than the box with wheels because the entire surface of the base of the box without wheels had to overcome friction, whereas the wheels of the other box reduced the contact area and subsequently had less friction to overcome. The wheel and the axle are very important in reducing friction. In fact, they are considered to be among man's most important inventions. The applications in automobiles, railroads, and almost every other phase of transportation are evident everywhere.
3. The mechanical advantage of a wheel and axle is the diameter of the wheel divided by the diameter of the axle. (Corresponding radii or circumferences may be used.)

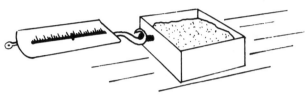

Dragging with flat surface

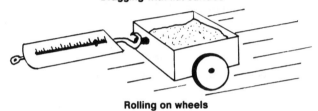

Rolling on wheels

F. Thought Questions:

1. Is a ball bearing device an example of using a wheel and axle?
2. Why is it important to use grease or oil in connection with the wheel and axle?
3. Cite some examples around or in your home where the wheel and axles are used.
4. Does the handle in a water well use a wheel and axle?

G. Related Topics and Activities:

1. Find out how many wheel and axles there are on a bicycle.
2. Can you find any wheel and axles in your classroom?
3. Make a spoolmobile by notching an empty spool of thread and inserting a rubber band through the center securing it with a small stick on one end and a long projecting stick on the other end.
4. See all Activities in this Section.

H. Vocabulary Builders—Spelling Words:

1) **wheel and axle**   2) **friction**   3) **grams**
4) **kilograms**   5) **scale**

I. Thought for Today:

"Human history becomes more and more a race between education and catastrophe."—H. G. Wells

Activity

A. Problem: *How Do Levers Make Work Easier?*

B. Materials:
  1. Heavy book
  2. Yardstick
  3. Hammer
  4. Nutcracker
  5. Several walnuts
  6. Scissors
  7. Tweezers
  8. Chart showing 1st, 2nd, and 3rd class levers

C. Procedure:
  1. Explain that every lever has three important points: the fulcrum, the force, and the weight or resistance.
  2. Allow the children to try to do, by hand, some kinds of work which can be easier by the use of levers such as: crack a nut by hand, pull a nail with the fingers, or lift a heavy object.
  3. Allow the children to perform these jobs with the use of simple machines and levers.
  4. Have children identify the class of lever from the sketches shown.

D. Result:

Children will learn about levers and be able to identify the class of each lever.

E. Supplemental Information:

The force required can be determined by multiplying the weight and the distance to the fulcrum and dividing by the distance the force is applied from the fulcrum. The lever is a form of a simple machine. Several tools use compound levers. (Nutcrackers and scissors are good examples.)

F. Thought Questions:
  1. How can a seesaw or teeter-totter be adjusted to accommodate children of different weights?
  2. What class of levers are scissors, wheelbarrows, and hammers?
  3. What levers can you name that you have in your home?

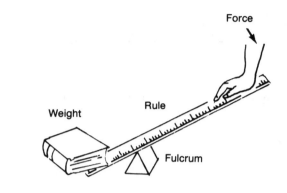

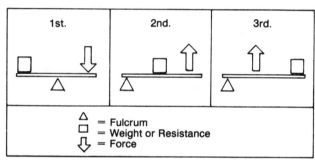

△ = Fulcrum
□ = Weight or Resistance
⇩ = Force

Classes of levers

G. Related Topics and Activities:
  1. Classify the following objects as to their class of lever:
     a. automobile jack
     b. bottle opener
     c. wheelbarrow
     d. pliers
     e. tongs
     f. knife
     g. hammer
     h. can opener
  2. Study the human body for different classes of levers. (We have all three types in the feet and arms.)
  3. See all Activities in this Section.

H. Vocabulary Builders—Spelling Words:

1) **force**   2) **weight**   3) **heavy**   4) **fulcrum**
5) **resistance**

I. Thought for Today:

"Some teen-agers are so delinquent that they could go to reform school on a scholarship."

Activity

A. Problem: *How Do Inclined Planes Help Us?*

B. Materials:
1. Boards of different lengths (See sketches for examples)
2. Toy wagon—(roller skates may be used)
3. Spring scale
4. Cord
5. Books or weights

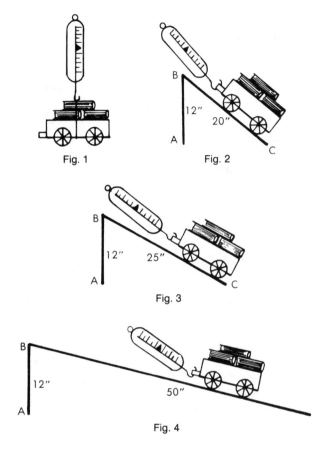

Fig. 1   Fig. 2

Fig. 3

Fig. 4

C. Procedure:
1. Put books or weights in the toy wagon for weight and secure with cord (Fig. 1).
2. Weigh the wagon and books. The weight represents the amount of force required to lift wagon and books.
3. Make an inclined plane with the shortest board (lengths approximately as shown in sketch).
4. Haul wagon up incline as shown in Figure 2 checking spring scale for reading (force).
5. Record this.
6. Use another (longer) inclined plane (Fig. 3).
7. Haul loaded wagon up inclined plane checking scale for reading.
8. Record this.
9. Use a third inclined plane using longest board, (Fig. 4).
10. Haul loaded wagon up, checking force required to lift.
11. Record this.
12. Compare results.

D. Result:

Using the same height, 12 inches, the student will find that the sharper the incline, the greater amount of force will be required. Or, putting it in another way, as the distance is increased, less force is required to pull the wagon up the same height.

E. Supplemental Information:

While the inclined plane makes it possible to move heavier objects, they must be moved over a longer distance. The total amount of force required to move the object up twelve inches therefore, is equal under all circumstances, if friction is disregarded. The advantage in the inclined plane thus comes in the fact that the force required is less than the weight.

F. Thought Questions:
1. What would happen if we used a sliding object instead of a wagon?
2. What are some ways in which we can lessen friction in working on an inclined plane?
3. Is it easier to walk straight up a steep hill or circle up it?
4. Is the wedge really an inclined plane?

G. Related Topics and Activities:
1. Repeat the experiment but use a roller skate or skateboard.
2. See Part II, "Energy."
3. See all Activities in this Section.

H. Vocabulary Builders—Spelling Words:
1) **inclined plane**   2) **force**   3) **resistance**
4) **scale**   5) **mechanical advantage**

I. Thought for Today:
"A bargain is something that costs less than the last time you didn't need it either."

A. Problem: *How Do Pulleys Help Us in Lifting Weights?*

B. Materials:

1. Two or more single-wheel pulleys (spools could be used)
2. Weight (weighted pail or other heavy object)
3. Light rope (or strong cord)
4. Set of draw scales
5. Supporting device

C. Procedure:

1. Lift up weight by cord and draw scales.
2. Record reading.
3. Put a small rope in the pulley. Be sure the rope is long enough to touch the floor or table. Tie one end of the rope securely to the handle of the pail. Attach the draw scale to the other end of the rope. Pull down on scale and note reading. (See Figure 1.)
4. Attach a pulley to the pail and loop the cord through this pulley and also through the top pulley. (See sketch.) Attach the scale to the other end of the rope and pull until it raises the pail. (See Figure 2.)

D. Results:

1. In the first experiment, the actual weight is determined.
2. In the second set-up with one fixed pulley, the force required is the same as the weight if friction is omitted. This merely changes the direction of pull.
3. In the third activity, with one movable pulley and one fixed pulley, the force to move weight is halved but the distance of the rope pulled is doubled.

E. Supplemental Information:

1. Fixed pulleys and movable pulleys help us in many ways.
2. The more pulley wheels there are, the easier it is to lift weights.
3. This principle is used for some hoists in garages so that one man can lift heavy automobile engines or even a whole car.
4. Pulleys are used for handling heavy freight on docks and on shipboard.

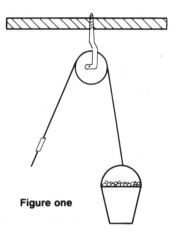

Figure one

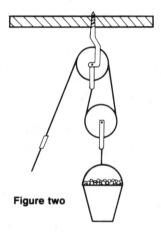

Figure two

5. Pulleys are used in cranes and derricks to lift heavy loads such as big pieces of steel, etc.
6. The mechanical advantage equals the number of movable ropes attached to the pulley or pulleys.

F. Thought Questions:

1. With a two-pulley arrangement, how much weight would a 100-pound pull lift?
2. How many single-wheeled pulleys would an average man have to use to lift a 500-pound object with a 100-pound pull?
3. Could you figure the amount of extra force that is required to overcome friction in all the activities cited?
4. Have you ever seen pulleys used in the construction of tall buildings? How?

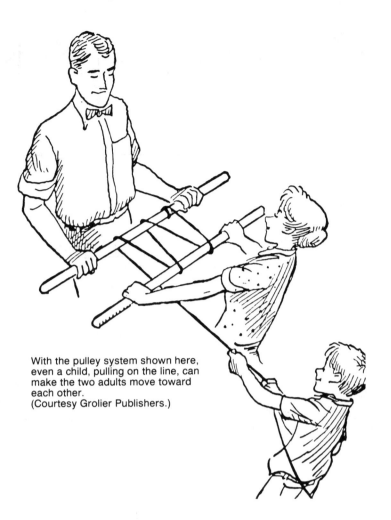

With the pulley system shown here, even a child, pulling on the line, can make the two adults move toward each other.
(Courtesy Grolier Publishers.)

G. Related Topics and Activities:

1. Have two adults each hold a broomstick horizontally. Have a child wrap a clothesline around the broomsticks four or five times leaving one end loose and tying the other end to one broomstick. When the adults try to pull apart, the child should pull on the loose end and will be able to force adults together.

2. See all Activities in this Section.

H. Vocabulary Builders—Spelling Words:
1) **pulley**   2) **scale**   3) **mechanical**
4) **advantage**   5) **weight**

I. Thought for Today:
"What we know is very little; what we don't know is immense."

Section F: Movement and Resistance

Activity II F 1

A. Problem: *What is Inertia? Momentum?*

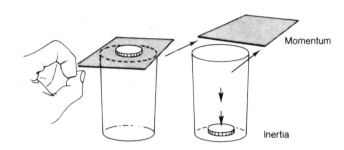

B. Materials:
1. Glass
2. Card, approximately 4″ × 4″
3. Coin

C. Procedure:
1. Explain inertia. (A body in motion tends to stay in motion or a body at rest tends to stay at rest unless acted on by some outside force.)
2. Explain momentum. (The force with which a body moves.)
3. Place card on glass.
4. Place coin in the middle of card.
5. Give the card a quick flip as shown in sketch.

D. Results:
1. The card will be knocked off the glass.
2. The coin will fall into the glass.

E. Supplemental Information:
1. The force on the card produced enough momentum to have the card knocked off the glass.
2. The inertia of the coin (the tendency to stay at rest) kept the coin from moving sideways and when it lost its support, gravity caused it to fall into the glass.
3. Momentum is equal to the mass times the velocity.
4. The greater the mass or the greater the speed, the greater will be the momentum of a moving object. The greater the momentum, the greater will be the force required to stop the object.

F. Thought Questions:
1. When a person first gets on a bicycle to ride it does he/she have any inertia? momentum?
2. When he/she is underway riding the bicycle does he/she have any inertia? momentum?
3. When brakes are applied to an automobile in motion, why doesn't it stop instantly?

G. Related Topics and Activities:
1. See Activity II-F-2, "Force of Steam."
2. See Activity II-F-3, "Steam Turbine."
3. See Activity II-F-4, "Steam Toys."
4. See Section VII-D, "Gravity."
5. See other Activities in this Section.

H. Vocabulary Builders—Spelling Words:
1) **inertia**   2) **momentum**   3) **body**
4) **rest**   5) **force**

I. Thought for Today:
"The teacher opens the door—you enter by yourself."

Activity

A. Problem: *Does Steam Exert a Tremendous Force?*

B. Materials:

1. Piece of pipe six inches long, ¾″ wide, and threaded on at least one end
2. Cap to fit the threaded end
3. Cork to fit in the other end
4. Bunsen burner or canned heat
5. Tablespoon of water
6. Ring stand and clamps

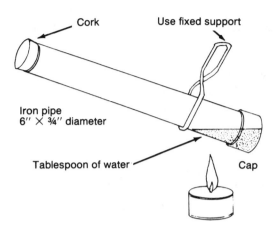

Cork   Use fixed support

Iron pipe
6″ × ¾″ diameter

Tablespoon of water   Cap

C. Procedure:

(Use extreme caution.)

1. Tighten the cap securely on the end of the pipe.
2. Place a tablespoon of water in the pipe. (See drawing.)
3. Place a cork stopper tightly in the opening of the other end.
4. *Be sure to point the pipe away from people, windows, or other fragile objects. Never hold pipe in hand.*
5. Secure the pipe at an angle to the stand with a clamp.
6. Heat the pipe at the capped end containing the water.
7. Aim toward a padded box, safe wall, or outside.

D. Result:

When the pipe has been heated, it will change the water to steam. The steam pressure creates a terrific pressure which forces the stopper out of the "cannon," usually with a loud noise and moderately high velocity.

E. Supplemental Information:

Steam exerts tremendous force. One cannot be too cautious in working with steam pressure.

F. Thought Questions:

1. Why do automobile radiators sometimes blow the cap off?
2. How can you prevent a hot water heater from exploding?
3. How is steam harnessed for the benefit of all of us?

G. Related Topics and Activities:

1. Boil water in a tea kettle without stopping up the spout.
2. Boil water in a pot with a lid on it.
3. Examine a steam engine or steam turbine or do research on each.
4. See Activity II-F-3, "Steam Generator."
5. See other Activities in this Section.

H. Vocabulary Builders—Spelling Words:

1) **threaded**   2) **safety**   3) **precautions**
4) **force**   5) **steam**

I. Thought for Today.

"The foundation of every nation is the education of its youth."

Activity

A. Problem: *How Does a Steam Turbine Work?*

B. Materials:
1. Three-inch cork disc
2. Eight strips of tin (½″ by 1½″)
3. Flat board (4″ square)
4. Long nail or dowel
5. Glass test tube
6. Gas burner or heat source
7. Glass tube bent at right angles
8. Rubber cork, single hole
9. Pyrex bottle
10. Tripod
11. Water

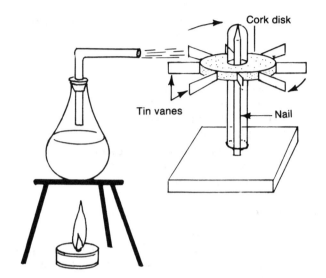

C. Procedure:
1. Assemble the materials as shown.
2. Space the tin vanes evenly; curve each slightly.
3. Adjust the glass tube so the end is as close to the vanes as possible.
4. Fill Pyrex bottle half full of water.
5. Heat the water.

D. Result:

The steam will be forced out of the flask and against the vanes causing the "turbine" to rotate.

E. Supplemental Information:

The steam turbine is capable of developing a great amount of power. Steam generators use this principle to generate electricity. The generators in atomic plants use steam turbines to turn the generators. The steam comes from water heated into steam by the nuclear reactors.

F. Thought Questions:
1. Why do the blades on the turbine have to be curved?

2. Why does the jet of steam need to be played on the turbine at an angle?
3. What other uses could steam turbines have?
4. Is inertia and/or momentum involved in this activity?

G. Related Topics and Activities:
1. Compare steam generators to gasoline engines.
2. Visit a steam generator power plant at a local utility.
3. See Activity II-F-2, "Force of Steam."
4. See other Activities in this Section.

H. Vocabulary Builders—Spelling Words:
1) **turbine**   2) **vanes**   3) **generate**   4) **power**
5) **Pyrex**

I. Thought for Today:
"A soft answer turns away wrath."

Activity

A. Problem: *How Can We Make Steam Propelled Toys?*

B. Materials: (Toy One, See drawing.)
1. Small can with lid
2. Soap dish
3. Small candle
4. Some pipe cleaners or wires
5. Water
6. Large dishpan or sink
7. Awl
8. Matches

Materials: (Toy Two, See drawing.)
1. Hollow eggshell
2. Coat hanger or heavy wire
3. Piece of thin plyboard or heavy cardboard
4. Candle
5. Matches
6. Toy wheels

C. Procedure One:
1. With an awl, punch a small hole near the top edge of the small can.
2. Place some water in the can.
3. Mount the can so that it will stand horizontally by twisting the pipe cleaner stems or wires around the can in such a way that they will support the can in the soap dish. (See drawing.)
4. Place this (steam boiler) carefully over a candle in the soap dish boat.
5. Place the soap dish on the water in a tub or large container.
6. Light the candle.

Procedure Two:
1. Construct toy as shown in sketch.
2. Fill egg half full of water using as small a hole as possible.
3. Place candle under supported eggshell.
4. Place apparatus in open space.
5. Light candle.

D. Results:
1. As the candle heats the water in the can it will change the water to steam. The steam squirts out the hole in the can which causes the whole boat to move in the opposite direction.
2. The toy eggshell will scoot around.

E. Supplemental Information:
The reason the boat moves forward is because the steam shooting out from the can creates a propulsion force which

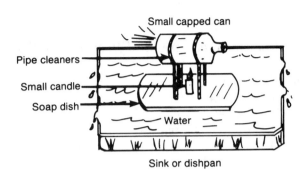

Steamboat (Toy one)

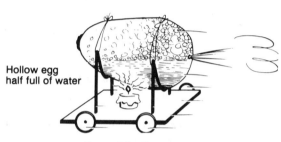

Eggmobile (Toy two)

causes the boat to move in the opposite direction. This is the same principle that permits a rocket to lift off from a launching pad. The fuel in the rocket pushes down on the pad with force which propels the rocket into space.

F. Thought Questions:
1. What are the different ways people use to transport themselves?
2. What kinds of propellant systems are used?
3. Do people use the same systems for propelling themselves on land, in the water, and in the air?

G. Related Topics and Activities:
1. Study Newton's Third Law of Motion: "For every action there is an equal and opposite reaction."
2. Study different means of transportation.
3. See Activity II-F-3, "Steam Generators."
4. See all Activities in this Section.

H. Vocabulary Builders—Spelling Words:
1) **steam**   2) **force**   3) **action**   4) **reaction**
5) **propulsion**

I. Thought for Today:
"We judge ourselves by what we are capable of doing, while others judge us by what we have already done."—Longfellow

Activity

A. Problem: *What are the Effects of Friction?*

B. Materials:
   1. Sandpaper
   2. Matches
   3. Two books for support
   4. Toy car
   5. Flat board
   6. Soap or wax
   7. Small wood block (same size as toy car)
   8. Two wooden blocks (3" × 4")

C. Procedure:
   1. Hold hands in front of you, palms facing each other—rub hands together.
   2. Strike a match.
   3. Rub a piece of sandpaper on a block of wood.
   4. Take 2 blocks of wood (3" × 4") and slide them together.
   5. Rub surfaces of blocks with soap or wax, and repeat above operation.
   6. Place a flat board in a position so that one end is higher than the other.
   7. Place a wooden block about the same size as the car on the top of the flat, inclined board.
   8. Place a toy car on the higher end and release the car.

D. Results:
   1. Hands, match, and wood will become warm.
   2. There will be less heat and friction when a lubricant is used.
   3. The block will not slide.
   4. The car will roll freely.

E. Supplemental Information:
   1. Friction produces heat and causes wear.
   2. Lubrication reduces friction.
   3. Rolling friction is less than sliding friction because there is less surface area contact.
   4. Ball bearings and roller bearings are examples of using rolling objects to reduce friction.

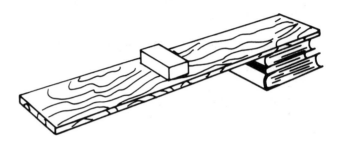

Sliding friction

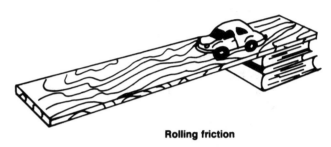

Rolling friction

F. Thought Questions:
   1. What are some other experiments you can devise to compare rolling friction to sliding friction?
   2. Why does lubrication reduce friction?
   3. Can water be used as a lubricant?
   4. How is friction lessened in engines?

G. Related Topics and Activities:
   1. Study a skate or skateboard wheel and determine how it reduces friction.
   2. Repeat block experiment but use a lubricating oil on its base.
   3. Try and locate ways in which friction helps us.
   4. See all Activities in this Section.

H. Vocabulary Builders—Spelling Words:
   1) **friction**   2) **block**   3) **lubrication**
   4) **rolling**   5) **wooden**

I. Thought for Today:
   "Science solves everything. When they found out they couldn't open windows on railroad cars, they air-conditioned the whole train."

Activity

A. Problem: *How Do We Overcome Friction?*

B. Materials:
1. Two rough blocks of wood (see sketch)
2. Small amount of light lubricating oil
3. Small spring scale
4. Two or three round pencils
5. Thumbtack or eyescrew
6. Heavy weight
7. String

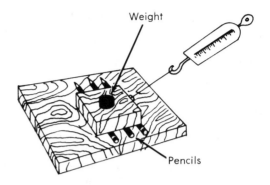

Weight

Pencils

C. Procedure:
1. Attach a tack or eyescrew to one side of a wooden block.
2. Attach a string to this.
3. Attach a small scale to string.
4. Place the weight on the block.
5. Pull scale slowly and record scale reading when block begins to move.
6. Repeat steps four (4) and five (5) except, insert pencils between the two blocks.
7. Record reading again as block begins to move.
8. Repeat steps four (4) and five (5) except this time spread a thin sheet of oil between the blocks.
9. Again record readings as block begins to move.

D. Result:
The readings will vary according to the amount of friction. The greater the friction, the greater the force necessary to get the block and weight moving.

E. Supplemental Information:
More friction is evident when there are large rough surfaces. Friction between rough surfaces can be reduced by the use of oil. Bearings change sliding friction to rolling friction. Pencils, in this case, are a form of rolling friction.

F. Thought Questions:
1. Why are ball bearings put in the wheels of a bicycle?
2. What other ways can friction be reduced on wagons, skateboards, bicycles, etc.?
3. Is friction ever helpful? How and when?
4. Do different materials have different surfaces that affect friction?

G. Related Topics and Activities:
1. Devise ways that a bicycle could reduce friction.
2. Discuss how ice skates are designed to reduce friction.
3. See all Activities in this Section.

H. Vocabulary Builders—Spelling Words:
1) **sliding**   2) **friction**   3) **rolling**
4) **lubricant**   5) **lubricated**

I. Thought for Today:
"What lies behind us and what lies ahead of us is nothing compared to what lies within us."

A. Problem: *How Does Friction Vary with Pressure?*

B. Materials:

Yardstick or meterstick

C. Procedure:

1. Spread your hands about 20 inches apart and ask someone to place the stick on top of your two pointed forefingers so that one end of the yardstick or meterstick is very close to one hand. The other hand will be about two-thirds down the other end of the yardstick (as illustrated in the sketch).
2. Estimate at what point which end of the yardstick will fall off your hands if you move your two hands together at exactly the same rate for each hand.
3. After you have made the estimate push your two hands together very slowly.
4. With stick still on fingers and both hands together move hands slowly apart.

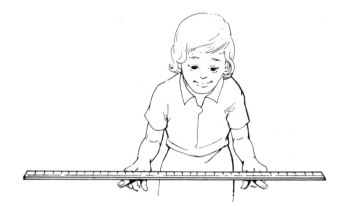

D. Results:

1. The stick will not fall either way, it will end up balanced on the two hands which always meet in the middle of the stick.
2. When moved outward, the hands will end up very close to the edges of the stick.

E. Supplemental Information:

The heavier the weight the greater the friction. The side that is longer (and heavier) will remain stationary until the other side becomes heavier. Then this (the other side) will move until the first side becomes heavier. This will keep up until the forefingers meet in the exact center of the yardstick or meterstick.

F. Thought Questions:

1. Why does the stick slide faster over one hand than the other?
2. Can you make the hands meet not in the center of the stick by putting a little oil on one hand and a little rosin or high friction material on the other?
3. What do you think will happen if you start with three fingers on one side and one finger on the other side?
4. What do you think will happen if you place a little weight in the middle of the stick before you start?

G. Related Topics and Activities:

1. See Section VII-D, "Gravity."
2. See Section II-E, "Simple Machines."
3. See all Activities in this Section.

H. Vocabulary Builders—Spelling Words:

1) **meterstick**   2) **friction**   3) **pressure**
4) **forefinger**   5) **stationary**

I. Thought for Today:

"The recognition of ignorance is the first spark of enlightenment."

Section G: Current Electricity

Activity   II**G**1

A. Problem: *How Can We Determine Which is the Positive Terminal of a Battery?*

B. Materials:
  1. Battery
  2. Potato (raw)
  3. Copper wires (2)
  4. Stripping pliers

C. Procedure:
  1. Strip all ends of the copper wires.
  2. Connect wires to the battery.
  3. Cut the potato to have a large flat slice.
  4. Put the ends of the wire into the cut side of the potato about *one inch* apart.

D. Result:
A green color will appear in the potato around one wire and bubbles will come from the potato around the other wire.

E. Supplemental Information:
  1. The green color appears where the positive wire enters the potato. This green color is due to the fact that the negative ions from the solution in the potato are neutralized at the anode (positive terminal) and form a green copper salt.
  2. Where the negative wire enters the potato, a small amount of hydrogen gas is formed (cathode or negative side).

F. Thought Questions:
  1. What will happen if the wires are too far apart in the potato?
  2. Would this work faster if we had several batteries instead of just one?

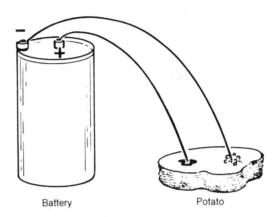

Battery   Potato

  3. Can anything else other than the potato be used in this experiment?
  4. What do you think is meant by a cathode ray tube in a television set?

G. Related Topics and Activities:
  1. Reverse the terminals in this activity and note results.
  2. Reverse the points of insertion in this activity and note results.
  3. See Section I-E, "Static Electricity."
  4. See all Activities in this Section.

H. Vocabulary Builders—Spelling Words:
  1) **positive**   2) **anode**   3) **cathode**
  4) **negative**   5) **terminals**

I. Thought for Today:
"Students are getting the new math and bringing home the old grades."

Activity

A. Problem: *What Materials Conduct Electricity?*

B. Materials:
1. Two 1½ volt batteries
2. Several feet of #20 wire
3. Several pieces of cloth, wood, glass, plastic, rubber, nails, pins, water, and paper
4. Flashlight bulb and socket
5. Knife switch
6. Short piece of wire to check test terminals
7. Block of wood
8. Tacks

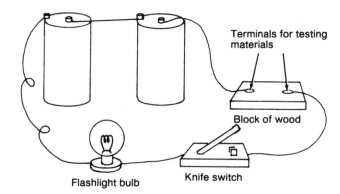

Terminals for testing materials

Block of wood

Flashlight bulb   Knife switch

C. Procedure:
1. Make the following wire connections:
    a. Center (positive) cell of one battery to the second battery
    b. Positive cell of second battery to one terminal on block of wood (under tack)
    c. Second terminal on block of wood to knife switch.
    d. Knife switch to one terminal on lamp
    e. Second terminal on lamp to negative terminal on first battery
2. Place a piece of wire across the test terminals.
3. Close the knife switch to see if lamp glows and all connections are tight.
4. Open knife switch.
5. Remove test wire.
6. Place a piece of cloth across test terminals.
7. Close knife switch.
8. Record whether lamp glows.
9. Open knife switch.
10. Remove cloth and replace with another test material.
11. Close knife switch.
12. Record whether lamp glows.
13. Repeat procedure for each test material.

D. Results:
1. The lamp will glow when the nail and pin are used.
2. The lamp will not glow when paper, wood, glass, plastic, cloth, or rubber are used.

E. Supplemental Information:
1. Metal (nails and pins) will conduct electric current, whereas nonmetals such as glass, plastic, rubber, wood, paper, and cloth do not conduct electrical current. If you wish, test

wires on test terminals, the wires can be left free to touch test materials since there is very little flow of electricity and usually cannot even be felt.
2. Materials that allow electricity to flow through them are called conductors. Those that do not are called insulators.
3. More batteries can be added for more potential flow.

F. Thought Questions:
1. Why is it necessary to know which materials are conductors of electricity?
2. How can you determine whether some conductors are more efficient than others?
3. Are human bodies conductors of electricity?
4. What would happen if the test wires were in a glass of distilled water? tap water? regular water? salt water?

G. Related Topics and Activities:
1. With wires in a glass of distilled water, close knife switch to test.
2. Repeat with tap water, and then with salt water.
3. Test other materials.
4. If you have an "electric identifier" in your classroom, this makes an excellent current tester.
5. See all Activities in this Section.

H. Vocabulary Builders—Spelling Words:
1) **conductor**   2) **insulator**   3) **terminal**
4) **socket**   5) **bulb**

I. Thought for Today:
"Good teachers cost more. Poor teachers cost most."

Activity

A. Problem: *How Does a Fuse Work?*

B. Materials:

1. Two dry cells (No. 6 preferably)
2. Four feet of insulated wire
3. Six thin strips of tin foil from chewing gum wrappers (Cut as shown in sketch.)
4. One piece of wood, 4″ × 4″
5. Knife switch
6. Rubber cement or nail
7. Cork
8. Staples or tape
9. Stripping pliers

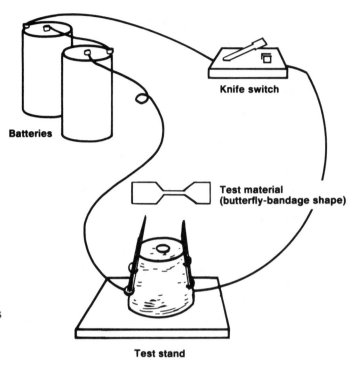

Batteries

Knife switch

Test material
(butterfly-bandage shape)

Test stand

C. Procedure:

1. Connect the two dry cells in a series as shown in sketch.
2. Cement or nail cork to block of wood.
3. Staple or tape wires to cork after stripping ends of wire.
4. Connect one wire from cork to dry cell.
5. Connect a second wire from cork to knife switch.
6. Connect last wire from knife switch to terminal on battery.
7. Open knife switch.
8. Put small test strip of foil between the upright stripped ends of the wires on the cork.
9. Close knife switch.

D. Result:

When the knife switch is closed, the circuit will be completed and electricity will flow through the fuse. The fuse will not be strong enough to carry the electricity and will overheat, melt, and "blow out" (break).

E. Supplemental Information:

Care should be taken when touching the wires connected to the dry cell. Sometimes these wires will get hot if the current is left on too long. Fuses and/or circuit breakers are always installed in electric wiring in homes or industry. The fuse or circuit breaker is made so that it will stop the flow of current when it becomes too strong for the safe operation of lights and/or appliances. Many homes have burned down because pennies have been placed in the fuse box and permitted electric wires to get too hot until a fire started. Newer homes use circuit breakers instead of fuses.

F. Thought Questions:

1. Why is it necessary to protect wiring systems with fuses?
2. Should all electric circuits have fuses or circuit breakers?
3. Do automobiles have fuses?

G. Related Topics and Activities:

1. Test materials to see if they would make good fuses.
2. Find out how a circuit breaker works.
3. Demonstrate a short circuit by bypassing the knife switch.
4. See all Activities in this Section.

H. Vocabulary Builders—Spelling Words:

1) **fuse**   2) **circuit breaker**   3) **insulated**
4) **terminal**   5) **short circuit**

I. Thought for Today:

"Always behave like a duck—keep calm on the surface but paddle like heck underneath."

Activity

A. Problem: *How Can We Make a Current Detector (Homemade Galvanometer)?*

B. Materials:
1. Twenty feet of #28 or smaller insulated wire
2. Adhesive, masking, or cellophane tape
3. Tongue depressor
4. Small pocket-size compass
5. Small bottle or wood dowel about an inch in diameter
6. Battery

C. Procedure:
1. Wrap about 50 turns of the insulated wire around the small bottle or cylinder. Wrap this in one direction only and wrap loosely. Leave enough of the two ends loose so they can be connected to battery.
2. Carefully slide the coil from the bottle or dowel and put three strips of tape around the coil as shown in the illustration.
3. Place a compass in the center of the coil as shown in the illustration.
4. Momentarily connect the terminals of the battery to the ends of the wire coil.
5. Observe compass.
6. Disconnect one wire from battery.

D. Result:
When the electric current passes through the coil, a magnetic field will be created which will deflect the compass needle from its regular position.

E. Supplemental Information:
If the coil is left connected to the battery for any length of time, serious damage will be done to the battery and also to the coil. Therefore, be sure that the connections are made only momentarily. When a current passes through the coil, the magnetic field which is created causes a deflection in the needle of the compass. The same technique can be used to detect any kind of an electric current.

F. Thought Questions:
1. Can this technique be used to find out whether a battery is dead or not?
2. Is this the principle on which commercial current detectors are based?
3. Which way did the compass needle point? Why?

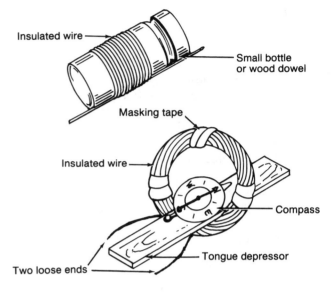

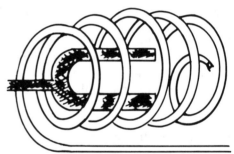

Simple galvanometer

G. Related Topics and Activities:
1. Make another coil like the first. Attach the two together with two wires. Place a compass in one and move a magnet in and out of the second. (Shows that a magnet produces an electric current.)
2. Suspend a magnetized razor blade from the top of a galvanometer and check results when connected to a battery.
3. See all Activities in this Section.

H. Vocabulary Builders—Spelling Words:
1) **galvanometer**   2) **current**   3) **detector**
4) **compass**   5) **cylinder**

I. Thought for Today:
"A father is usually more pleased to have his son look like him than act like him."

Activity

A. Problem: *What is a Series Circuit?*

B. Materials:
1. Two dry cell batteries
2. Light switch or a single knife switch
3. Four three-inch lengths of wire
4. Two nine-inch lengths of wire
5. Flashlight bulbs
6. Small bulb bases

C. Procedure:
1. Attach wires as shown in drawing.
   a. Center terminal (positive) on one battery to outside (negative terminal on second battery)
   b. Center terminal (positive) on second battery to one light base
   c. First light base to second light base
   d. Second light base to third light base
   e. Third light base to fourth light base
   f. Fourth light base to knife switch
   g. Knife switch to outside terminal of other battery
2. With light bulbs attached, close knife switch.
3. Observe lights.
4. Open knife switch.
5. Remove one light from base.
6. Close knife switch.
7. Observe remaining lights.

D. Results:
1. If all lights are connected and knife switch is closed, the lights will be on.
2. If one light is removed and knife switch closed, the remaining light will be off. (Removing the light breaks the circuit and no electricity will flow.)

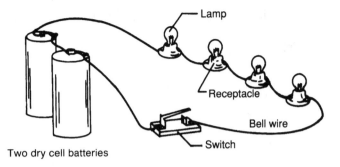

Two dry cell batteries

Labels: Lamp, Receptacle, Bell wire, Switch

E. Supplemental Information:
In a series circuit, only one wire connects with each light, so if any one light is taken out, the circuit is broken and all of the lights will go out.

F. Thought Questions:
1. If you have one bad bulb, how can you check to determine which one it is?
2. How can you check to determine if the battery is dead?
3. Why are some sets of lights able to burn even when one bulb is burned out?
4. What is the difference between a series circuit and a parallel circuit?

G. Related Topics and Activities:
1. Double the number of batteries to see how it affects the brilliance of the lights.
2. See all Activities in this Section.

H. Vocabulary Builders—Spelling Words:
1) **series**   2) **circuit**   3) **batteries**
4) **knife switch**   5) **parallel**

I. Thought for Today:
"Dancing is wonderful for girls; it's the first way they learn to guess what a boy is going to do before he does it."

Activity

A. Problem: *What is a Parallel Circuit?*

B. Materials:
1. Two dry cell batteries
2. Knife switch
3. Wire, #22 or #24, six feet long
4. Stripping pliers
5. Four small light bases
6. Four small flashlight bulbs

C. Procedure:
(Strip wires at each connection where wires are joined.)
1. Attach wires as shown in sketch.
2. Insert the bulbs.
3. Close the knife switch.
4. Observe results.
5. Loosen one bulb at a time keeping the others tight in socket.
6. Record observations.
7. Loosen various combinations of two bulbs keeping the remaining bulb tight in the socket.
8. Record observations.
9. Open knife switch.
10. Try to draw conclusions.

D. Results:
1. All the bulbs will light when the batteries are connected and the switch is closed.
2. If one or two bulbs are loosened or removed the light(s) will go out but the remaining one(s) will continue to burn.

E. Supplemental Information:
Any bulb(s) in a parallel circuit will continue to burn as long as a circuit is complete. When a single bulb is taken out, the electricity will bypass the one bulb and the electricity continues to operate the other bulbs, for it is able to complete the circuit which is necessary for electricity to flow.

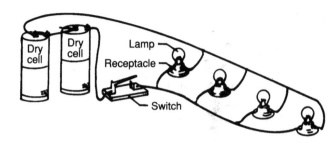

F. Thought Questions:
1. What makes a complete circuit?
2. What is the difference between wiring bulbs in *parallel* and wiring them in *series*?
3. In the above diagram which bulb(s) will go on and which one(s) will be off if the knife switch is moved to a position on one of the parallel light lines?

G. Related Topics and Activities:
1. Test a different number of batteries.
2. Test using a different number of lights.
3. Connect two lights in parallel and two in series. Observe. Remove one light anywhere and observe results. Repeat with other bulbs.
4. See all Activities in this Section.

H. Vocabulary Builders—Spelling Words:
1) **parallel** 2) **circuit** 3) **removed**
4) **stripping** 5) **pliers**

I. Thought for Today:
"An expert is one who is just beginning to understand his/her subject."

Activity

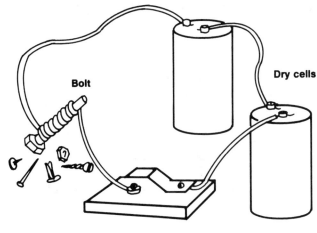

A. Problem: *How Can We Make an Electromagnet?*

B. Materials:

1. Two dry cell batteries
2. Iron or steel bolt about 2″ long
3. Twelve feet of insulated copper wire (#24)
4. Assortment of nails, nuts, bolts, pins, tacks, etc.
5. Pocket knife or cutting pliers for stripping wire
6. Knife switch

C. Procedure:

1. Show that the 2″ bolt is not magnetized by attempting to pick up some of the assorted nuts, pins, etc.
2. Strip the ends of the wires that connect the batteries and knife switch.
3. Connect the two batteries and knife switch as shown in drawing. Remove the insulation from both ends of the wire and connect the center terminal of one battery to the outside terminal of the other battery.
4. Wind the remaining wire around the 2″ bolt, leaving about one foot of free wire at both ends of wire.
5. Strip the insulation from both ends of the wire.
6. Connect one end to the outside terminal of one battery and the other end of the wire to the knife switch.
7. Hold the wired bolt close to the assorted nails, nuts, pins, etc.

D. Result:

The wire-wound bolt will attract the iron and steel objects as does a permanent magnet.

E. Supplemental Information:

Electricity can be used to create a temporary magnet. This magnet can be strengthened by increasing the number of turns on the bolt or by adding additional dry cells. A knife switch can be made with a metal strip and a screw mounted as shown in drawing.

F. Thought Questions:

1. Why does increasing the number of wraps around the bolt strengthen the magnet?
2. If the insulated wire is wrapped around a cardboard cylinder, what will happen to an iron bar placed in the cylinder? See Activity II-G-9, "Sucking Coil."
3. Would a thicker wire produce more or less magnetic strength?
4. How do junkyards use electromagnets?
5. What is the advantage of using an electromagnet?

G. Related Topics and Activities:

1. Demonstrate the difference between an electromagnet and a permanent one.
2. Devise an electromagnet game where objects are moved by an electromagnet such as a football player, a train, checkers, etc.
3. See all Activities in this Section.

H. Vocabulary Builders—Spelling Words:

1) **electromagnet**   2) **temporary**   3) **permanent**
4) **magnetized**   5) **insulated**

I. Thought for Today:

"None of us is as smart as all of us."

Activity

A. Problem: *How Can We Make a Model Telegraph?*

B. Materials:
   1. Small flat board
   2. Small block of wood
   3. Thin "T" strip of tin cut from a coffee ("tin") can
   4. Iron nails
   5. Two thumbtacks or screws
   6. Short strip of copper or brass
   7. Some light insulated copper wire (#16, #18, or #20)
   8. Two dry cell batteries
   9. Hammer

C. Procedure:
   1. Make the signal key by using a thin metal strip and securing it with a screw (see drawing).
   2. Place a tack underneath it for the key contact.
   3. Nail in "T" on block.
   4. Drive two nails into the flat board so their heads are just below the tin "T" strip.
   5. Nail small wood block on the flat board.
   6. Wrap one wire from the dry cell around the two nails and connect to the movable part of the key.
   7. Connect the second wire to the stationary part of the key which is the thumbtack or screw.
   8. Connect wire from key to batteries as shown in drawing.
   9. Press key down and release.

D. Result:
When the key is depressed the current will flow through the strip of metal. It will flow through the wire wrapped around two nails. An electromagnet will be made by the nails and the "T" strip of tin (tin plated iron) being subject to magnetism will click against the nails. As soon as the key is released the electric circuit is broken, the electromagnet is destroyed, and the "T" springs back up.

E. Supplemental Information:
Several sets can be hooked together to enable pupils to send and receive coded messages. This principle is used in commercial telegraph sets, which are fast becoming obsolete, but it makes a good toy and shows one the application of an electromagnet. To set up two sets, remember that the second key must be depressed to complete the circuit. In the Morse Code, "Dots" (quick depressions) and

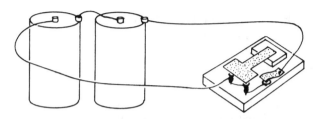

MORSE INTERNATIONAL TELEGRAPH CODE			
A	. —	N	— .
B	— . . .	O	— — —
C	— . — .	P	. — — .
D	— . .	Q	— — . —
E	.	R	. — .
F	. . — .	S	. . .
G	— — .	T	—
H	. . . .	U	. . —
I	. .	V	. . . —
J	. — — —	W	. — —
K	— . —	X	— . . —
L	. — . .	Y	— . — —
M	— —	Z	— — . .

Numbers:

1	. — — — —	7	— — . . .
2	. . — — —	8	— — — . .
3	. . . — —	9	— — — — .
4	. . . . —	0	— — — — —
5	. . . . .	Period	. — . — . —
6	—	Comma	— — . . — —

"Dashes" (long depressions) are used. The Morse Code alphabet and numbers are shown.

F. Thought Questions:
   1. What causes the nails to become magnetized?
   2. Why does the metal "T" have to be spaced quite close to the nail heads?
   3. Will more wraps of wire around the nails enable the set to work better?

G. Related Topics and Activities:
   1. Discuss other ways that people can communicate on a person-to-person basis.
   2. Send messages in other ways such as:
      a. semaphore flags
      b. gestures
      c. mirrors
      d. walkie-talkies
   3. See all Activities in this Section.

H. Vocabulary Builders—Spelling Words:
1) **telegraph**   2) **model**   3) **Morse Code**
4) **key**   5) **dots**   6) **dashes**

I. Thought for Today:
"Success comes in cans, not cannots."

Activity

A. Problem: *How Do We Make a Sucking Coil?*

B. Materials:
   1. Wire
   2. Small hollow tube made of cardboard or glass
   3. Long finishing nail
   4. Dry cell battery
   5. Knife switch

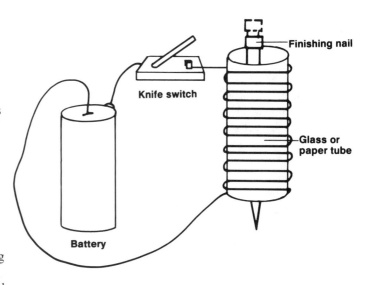

C. Procedure:
   1. Wind the wire around the hollow tube of cardboard or glass leaving two long ends.
   2. Place the hollow tube over the finishing nail (one with a small head) which is about as long as the sucking coil.
   3. Attach one of the end wires to the dry cell and the other wire to the switch (see drawing).
   4. Complete circuit by adding a wire from the push button or knife switch to the remaining terminal of the battery.
   5. Close the switch and observe the action of the nail.

D. Result:
When the coil is connected to a dry cell or toy transformer, the nail will first be pulled upward as shown by the dotted line. Then it will return to a resting position with the center of the nail nearly at the center of the coil.

E. Supplemental Information:
Magnetic lines of force created by the electric current pull the nail with such force that it jumps. We can make an electric chime by placing a bell so that the nail will strike it as it is pulled up by the sucking coil. Most musical door chimes use this principle.

F. Thought Questions:
   1. If the terminals are reversed will it change the direction of the movement?
   2. If the nail is reversed will it change the direction of the movement?
   3. What other ways could we use a sucking coil?

G. Related Topics and Activities:
   1. Make an electric chime using this principle of a "sucking coil" and devising some means of a sounding object.
   2. See especially Activity II-G-7, "Electromagnet."
   3. See all Activities in this Section.

H. Vocabulary Builders—Spelling Words:
   1) **sucking coil**   2) **finishing nail**
   3) **knife switch**   4) **chime**   5) **cardboard**

I. Thought for Today:
   "The most beautiful thing we can experience is the mysterious. It is the source of true art and science."—Albert Einstein

Activity

A. Problem: *How Does an Electric Doorbell Work?*

B. Materials:
   1. Electric doorbell
   2. Button switch
   3. Two dry cells

C. Procedure:
   1. Remove the cover of the doorbell so that working parts can be observed.
   2. Connect the two dry cells in series to the doorbell and the push button. See drawing. (Note that the center terminal of one dry cell is connected to the outside terminal of the second.) The push button can be placed anywhere in the circuit.
   3. Push the bell button down and hold for several seconds.

D. Result:

When the current is connected and is flowing through the wires of the electromagnets (a) they will become magnetized and will attract the iron bar (armature) (d). The armature is pulled toward the electromagnet and the clapper hits the bell. As the armature is pulled away from the contact point (b) which is fastened to it, it is pulled away from the fixed contact point (c). The circuit is broken. Since there is no current flowing through the electromagnets, they no longer attract the armature and it flies back. When the armature goes back the contact points again touch, the circuit is completed, and current flows again through the electromagnets. This attracts the armature to the electromagnets again and the whole cycle of operations is repeated. This continues rapidly as long as the button is pushed and the batteries are strong.

E. Supplemental Information:

This electric doorbell is one of the most common examples of what happens in creating and destroying magnetic lines of force with electricity. When the current flows, there is

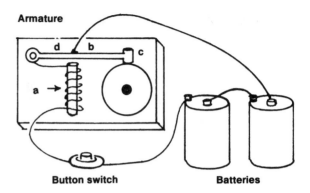

Armature **Button switch** **Batteries**

a magnet. Without the current, the magnetic lines of force disappear. Alternately applying the current and removing it thus makes the hammer vibrate. This principle is applied to many other household and commercial objects.

F. Thought Questions:
   1. How many things can you discover that use electromagnets in their operation?
   2. How can you increase the rapidity with which the vibration takes place?
   3. How does a doorbell differ from a door chime in operation?

G. Related Topics and Activities:
   1. Repeat activity but vary the number of batteries.
   2. Repeat activity but vary the winds on the armature.
   3. See all Activities in this Section.

H. Vocabulary Builders—Spelling Words:
   1) **doorbell**   2) **push button**   3) **terminal**
   4) **clapper**   5) **switch**

I. Thought for Today:
   "Horse sense is found in stable situations."

Activity

A. Problem: *Does an Electric Current Produce a Magnetic Field?*

B. Materials:
 1. Piece of heavy copper wire, 6 to 10 inches long (#10 or #12)
 2. Iron filings
 3. Dry cell battery (1.5 volts)
 4. A three-foot piece of #22 insulated wire (thin)
 5. Small magnetic compass

C. Procedure:
 1. Connect the heavy piece of copper wire directly across to the terminals of a dry cell making a loop as shown in sketch.
 2. Quickly dip a loop of the wire into the iron filings.
 3. Break the current by disconnecting the wire otherwise it will "short-circuit" the battery.
 4. Connect a three-foot piece of #22 insulated wire across the terminals of a dry cell. Arrange the wire so that one length of it is vertical or horizontal.
 5. Move a small magnetic compass around this wire.
 6. Switch the wires on the poles.
 7. Move the compass around.
 8. Observe results.
 9. Disconnect wire from terminals.

D. Results:
 1. In the first experiment the iron filings are attracted because of a magnetic field around the current.
 2. When the current is broken, the iron filings fall.
 3. In the second experiment, the compass will point to or away from the wire. The magnetic compass shows that the region around an electric current contains a magnetic field.
 4. When the current is reversed, the compass pointer will also be reversed.

E. Supplemental Information:
 1. Do not permit the wire to complete the circuit for prolonged periods of time, as this will damage the dry cell by reducing its electrical potential.

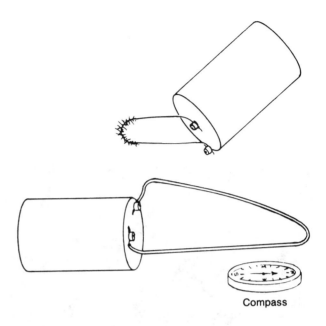

Compass

 2. Every electric current produces a magnetic field around the flow of electricity.

F. Thought Questions:
 1. What will happen if the wires used in this experiment are too short?
 2. What will happen if the wire is too fine?
 3. What will happen if the wires are left connected to the battery?

G. Related Topics and Activities:
 1. See Activity II-G-1, "Batteries."
 2. See Activity II-G-4, "Galvanometer."
 3. See Activity II-G-7, "Electromagnet."
 4. See Activity II-G-9, "Sucking Coil."
 5. See other Activities in this Section.

H. Vocabulary Builders—Spelling Words:
 1) **electric** 2) **compass** 3) **short-circuit**
 4) **reverse** 5) **current**

I. Thought for Today:
 "There is no comparison between that which is lost by not succeeding and that which is lost by not trying."

Part III

Plants

Section A: Parts and Classification

Activity IIIA1

A. Problem: *What Kinds of Trees Are Found in Our Neighborhood?*

B. Materials:
Wooded area around school or in neighborhood

C. Procedure:
1. Examine the trees you see and answer the following questions.
   a. What is a tree?
   b. Do all the trees have the same shape?
   c. Do they have the same kinds of leaves?
2. Have students draw sketches of different kinds of trees.
3. Discuss how trees differ from other plants.

D. Result:
Children observe that there are many kinds of trees.

E. Supplemental Information:
1. A tree is a special kind of green plant. It has a wooden stem covered with bark. We call the tree stem a trunk. Each tree has a different shape. Each shape is a different kind of tree. Trees are the biggest plants on our earth. Sequoia trees are giant plants found in California.
2. Trees provide homes for animals, especially birds.
3. Trees provide seeds, nuts, and fruits for animals, including people.
4. Some trees live to be thousands of years old.
5. Deciduous trees are the ones that lose their leaves every year.
6. Trees differ in height, shape, buds, twigs, bark, deciduous, or evergreen, etc.
7. Horizontal cuts on trees show rings. Each ring is a year's growth.
8. Some trees have stamens and pistils on different plants. In these it is necessary to have two different trees for reproduction.
9. Trees provide us with about 25% of our fresh oxygen supply.

F. Thought Questions:
1. How do trees differ from each other?

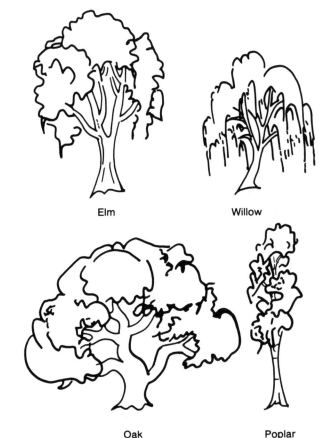

Elm   Willow

Oak   Poplar

2. Do some trees stay green all the time?
3. Why do some branches break off of trees?
4. Why do some trees become uprooted?

G. Related Topics and Activities:
1. Compare deciduous and evergreen trees.
2. Have students discuss forests and hiking experiences concerning trees.
3. Discuss forest fires. See Activity VI-D-6, "Keeping Forests, etc. Attractive."
4. Discuss the value of fruit trees.

H. Vocabulary Builders—Spelling Words:
1) **deciduous**   2) **evergreen**   3) **elm**
4) **oak**   5) **poplar**   6) **willow**

I. Thought for Today:
"There are two ways to get to the top of an oak tree. You can climb it or sit on an acorn."

Activity

A. **Problem:** *What Are the Main Parts of Plants?*

B. **Materials:**
 1. Potted plants
 2. Pictures of plants
 3. Specimens of plant parts

C. **Procedure:**
 1. Discuss the various plant parts.
 2. Have students identify the plant parts in the plants, pictures, and specimens.
 3. Have each student draw a picture of a specific plant labeling its main parts.

D. **Result:**
Students will learn the various plant parts and their main functions. These are:
 1. Roots—absorb water and minerals; anchor plants.
 2. Stems—paths for water and minerals to travel up and down; holds leaves.
 3. Leaves—produce food from sunlight.
 4. Flowers—attract pollinators to form seeds.
 5. Seeds—reproduce plant.
 6. Fruit—houses seeds.

E. **Supplemental Information:**
The roots, leaves, stems, flowers, fruit, and seeds are parts of a plant. Each of these parts may look different on the different kinds of plants, but each kind of plant has these same parts.

All plants need food. Leaves make the food for the plant. Leaves need air, sunshine, and water to do this work. All green plants are alike because they need sunshine, water, and air to make their food and to grow.

F. **Thought Questions:**
 1. How do plants get their food?
 2. Is a tree a plant?
 3. What foods do we eat from each part of the plant?
 4. Do plants attract animals?

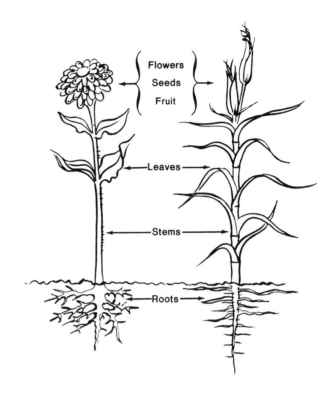

G. **Related Topics and Activities:**
 1. Study grasses.
 2. Watch plants grow from season to season.
 3. Study the main purpose of each plant.
 4. Dissect weeds and study their plant parts.
 5. See all Activities in this Section.

H. **Vocabulary Builders—Spelling Words:**
 1) **roots** 2) **stems** 3) **leaves** 4) **flowers**
 5) **seeds** 6) **fruit**

I. **Thought for Today:**
"When the going gets tough, the tough get going."

Activity

A. Problem: *Do All Plants Change in the Fall?*

B. Materials:
1. Leaves
2. Dried corn
3. Pumpkins
4. Hay
5. Other things collected by the children that are evidences of the fall season

C. Procedure:
1. During the fall season ask questions such as: What did you see on the way to school this morning that reminded you of the fall season?
2. Discuss with class such questions as:
   a. What happens to leaves in the fall?
   b. Why is the season called fall?
3. Observe the color of leaves and when they fall.
4. Find out what happens to birds and other animals in this season.
5. Discover how various plants and animals get ready for winter.
6. Observe what plants change in the fall season.
7. Observe if there are any plants that do not change in the fall season.

D. Result:
A better understanding of the fall season will be gained. Students will learn that some plants change drastically while others do not change at all. Deciduous trees are the most obvious plants that change in the fall. Evergreen trees keep their foliage all year long.

E. Supplemental Information:
It is important to know the seasons so that we can prepare for them. Ask the students what people do to prepare for each season. Other seasons and their characteristics can also be studied.

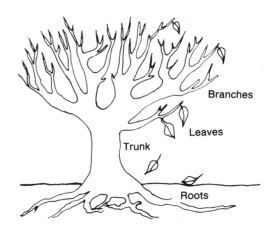

F. Thought Questions:
1. What causes the change in seasons?
2. Is it the same season everywhere on the earth at the same time?
3. Does the moon have seasons?
4. What happens to the fallen leaves?
5. What changes in plants do you see in the spring?

G. Related Topics and Activities:
1. See Activity VII-B-5, "Seasons."
2. See Activities III-F-6 and III-F-7, "Leaves."
3. See all Activities in Part III.

H. Vocabulary Builders—Spelling Words:
1) **deciduous** 2) **evergreens** 3) **fall**
4) **spring** 5) **seasons**

I. Thought for Today:
"The worst area of unemployment is between the ears."

Section B: Roots, Stems, and Leaves

Activity   III B 1

A. Problem: *In Which Direction Do Roots Grow?*

B. Materials:

1. Small rectangular glass container
2. Small, young plant
3. Piece of cardboard big enough for large side of container (see drawing)
4. A piece of cardboard large enough to cover one side so that roots can be observed
5. Second piece of cardboard to cover soil if loose
6. Potting soil or humus

C. Procedure:

1. Place plant in soil against one side of the container.
2. Place cardboard on the outside of the container to protect roots from light.
3. After four days turn container on its side using a second piece of cardboard if necessary to keep soil from falling out of container.
4. After four more days turn container right side up.
5. More advanced students might want to experiment with turning the box on its side and even upside down.
6. Movements may be repeated as many times as necessary.
7. Remove cardboard and observe at each turning.
8. Replace cardboard after each observation.

D. Result:

The roots will grow downward regardless of the position of the container.

E. Supplemental Information:

The course of growth for all roots, regardless of the position of the plant, is generally downward. Check the direction of the main root. This predisposition is called geotropism.

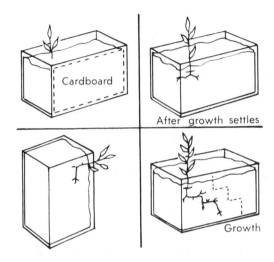

Cardboard

After growth settles

Growth

F. Thought Questions:

1. What would happen to root growth if rocks were placed in its path?
2. What would happen to root path if after several turnings of container the cardboards were left off?
3. Do all plant roots follow the same general path?

G. Related Topics and Activities:

1. Check to study the growth of roots on hillsides. In which direction do they grow?
2. See Activities in Section VII-C, "Earth's Crust."
3. See all Activities in this Section.

H. Vocabulary Builders—Spelling Words:

1) **geotropism**   2) **container**
3) **cardboard**   4) **soil**   5) **roots**

I. Thought for Today:

"Saying it with flowers doesn't mean throwing bouquets at yourself."

Activity

A. Problem: *Do Roots Seek Water?*

B. Materials:
1. Medium-sized plant box
2. Two-inch flower pot
3. Soil
4. Lima bean seeds (40–50) (They grow fast.)
5. Water

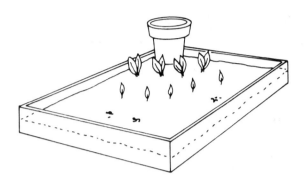

C. Procedure:
1. Place the pot close to one corner of the box.
2. Fill the box with soil.
3. Plant a number of seeds close to the flower pot working them down with a finger.
4. Plant about ten seeds at each measured distance from the flower pot. Distances that work well are three, six, nine, twelve, etc. inches.
5. Fill the flower pot one-half full of water. Do not put any water directly on the soil. The only source of water must come from the flower pot.
6. Keep the soil close to the flower pot slightly moist by adding water to the flower pot as necessary.
7. Check one plant about every three days from each measured distance from the flower pot beginning around the tenth day, noting particularly the direction of the growth of the roots and root hairs in relation to the flower pot.
8. Keep a record of these observations.

D. Results:
1. The seeds nearest the water will germinate first, the next row out germinate next, and so on outwards. The seeds farthest out usually do not germinate because of lack of water.
2. After ten days to two weeks, the roots can be detected growing toward the source of water.
3. After a month the plants closest to the flower pot should have many roots surrounding them.

E. Supplemental Information:
1. Water dissolves minerals in the soil.
2. Roots grow toward water.
3. Roots pick up water and dissolved materials.

F. Thought Questions:
1. Why do roots surround and sometimes infiltrate clay sewer pipes?
2. Do all seeds under the same conditions germinate at the same time?
3. Why do some seeds produce longer roots?

G. Related Topics and Activities:
1. See Activities in Section I-C, "Water."
2. See Activities in Section VII-C, "Earth's Crust."
3. See all Activities in this Section.

H. Vocabulary Builders—Spelling Words:
1) **root**   2) **water**   3) **lima beans**
4) **flower**   5) **pot**

I. Thought for Today:
"Get acquainted with your neighbors, you might like them."

Activity

A. Problem: *How Do Roots Absorb Water?*

B. Materials:
1. Glass
2. Molasses or syrup
3. Carrot
4. Glass tube
5. One-hole rubber stopper
6. Coring knife (apple corer)
7. Wax (or paraffin)

C. Procedure:
1. Remove the top of the carrot.
2. With apple corer, cut hole down from the top about three-fourths of its length and about one-half its diameter (to fit the one-holed stopper).
3. Fill the hole with syrup or molasses (to take up the part of the food stored in the root) and insert a long glass tube through a one-holed rubber stopper. (See drawing.)
4. Carefully seal the rubber stopper in the carrot by using melted wax or paraffin around the edges.
5. Then insert the carrot into a glass of water with the water covering about three-quarters of the carrot.
6. Observe the results daily.

D. Result:

Over a period of several hours to a few days the water from outside the root (see drawing) will be absorbed (by osmosis) by the root and will cause the liquid to move up the tube.

E. Supplemental Information:

There are many ways of setting up a demonstration of root absorption of water (osmosis). We are interested in learning about osmosis in plant roots because our food crops depend on it.

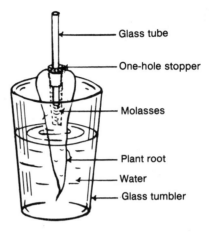

Carrots and turnips work well. The one precaution in this activity is to make sure the stopper is sealed tight, otherwise the liquid will not rise in the tube.

In securing the glass tube in the rubber stopper, moisten stopper and rotate glass tube back and forth or apply gentle pressure on the tube at the point of insertion.

F. Thought Questions:
1. Do our bodies use osmosis?
2. Do other liquids have the same kind of action?
3. What would happen if the top of the capillary tube were sealed?

G. Related Topics and Activities:
1. See Section I-C, "Water."
2. See Section VII-C, "Earth's Crust."
3. See all Activities in this Section.

H. Vocabulary Builders—Spelling Words:
1) **molasses**   2) **syrup**   3) **coring**
4) **wax**   5) **paraffin**

I. Thought for Today:
"People are never too busy to talk about how busy they are."

Section C: Seeds and Reproduction

Activity III C 1

A. Problem: *Where Do Seeds Come From?*

B. Materials:
1. Tomato
2. Grapefruit
3. Apple
4. Strawberry
5. Avocado
6. Grapes
7. Watermelon
8. Cantaloupe
9. Other seed-bearing fruits and vegetables
10. Seed packets from local nurseries

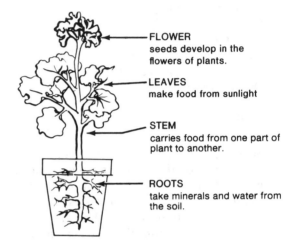

FLOWER
seeds develop in the flowers of plants.

LEAVES
make food from sunlight

STEM
carries food from one part of plant to another.

ROOTS
take minerals and water from the soil.

C. Procedure:
1. Discuss parts of plants.
2. Discuss the function of seeds.
3. Have students report on their experiences with seeds.
4. Divide class into groups of students and have them locate, describe, and cite the basic information they have gained about seeds.

D. Result:
Students will learn that there are many kinds of seeds and that seeds are a developing part of the plant itself.

E. Supplemental Information:
1. Some of the seeds might be planted to test their germination.
2. Seeds should be kept moist for germination.
3. Some plants do not have seeds.

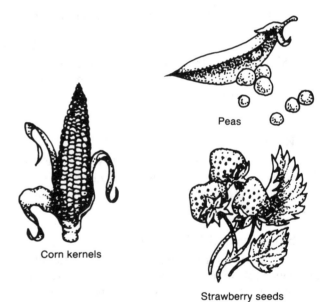

Peas

Corn kernels

Strawberry seeds

F. Thought Questions:
1. Which seeds can be seen outside of the plants?
2. Do small seeds grow into small plants and big seeds into big plants?
3. What prevents some seeds from germinating?

G. Related Topics and Activities:
1. Make a collection of seeds. (Many can be gathered from local nurseries.)
2. Plant some seeds and watch them develop.
3. Classify nut seeds.
4. See all Activities in this Section.

H. Vocabulary Builders—Spelling Words:
1) **seeds**   2) **pods**   3) **grain**   4) **flower**
5) **nursery**

I. Thought for Today:
"It costs more to amuse children now than it used to cost to educate their parents."

142   *Seeds and Reproduction*

Activity

A. Problem: *How Do Seeds Travel?*

B. Materials:
1. Different types of wild seeds
2. Printed materials about seeds
3. Chart materials

C. Procedure:
1. Have the students visit a garden to observe the growth of new seeds.
2. Ask students to gather information concerning seed travel.
3. Have them bring different types of seeds to class.
4. See if students can observe which seeds are more likely to travel by air, water, animals, or people.
5. Have them make charts of their findings.

D. Result:
Students will learn that seeds travel in many ways.

E. Supplemental Information:
On land, seeds are carried by man and animals. Parachute-type seeds, as well as seeds that come from bursting pods, travel by air. Some float on the surface of the water, while others roll on the ground or are stored in the ground by animals. Some seeds called burrs are carried on the clothing of man or on the fur of animals. Wild seeds can be carried by the forces of nature and by chance contact with men and animals. This activity is particularly effective in the fall season.

F. Thought Questions:
1. How does seed travel help maintain a plant species?
2. Can you name some seeds that people eat?
3. Can you name some seeds that animals eat?

Seeds travel in many ways.

G. Related Topics and Activities:
1. Classify seeds in any way the students want (doesn't have to be scientific). They might start with color, shape, size, texture, or whatever.
2. There are many unusual facts about seeds which children can collect. For example, you might ask, "Which fruit has its seeds on the outside?" (Answer: strawberry) or "Which fruit has a very large seed?" (Answer: avocado).
3. See all Activities in this Section.

H. Vocabulary Builders—Spelling Words:
1) **burrs**   2) **parachute**   3) **bursting**
4) **travel**   5) **pods**

I. Thought for Today:
"Teachers' successes are measured by their students' failures."

Activity

A. Problem: *What Conditions Lead to Mold Growth?*

B. Materials:
   1. Bread
   2. Water
   3. Cellophane, or some other airtight covering
   4. Magnifying glass

C. Procedure:
   1. Take two moist samples of bread. Seal one in cellophane; expose the other to air.
   2. Expose two more samples of bread, one in strong light, one in the dark.
   3. Expose two more samples of bread; keep one very dry, the other moderately moist.
   4. Expose two more samples, one in a warm dark place, the other in a cold dark place such as a refrigerator.
   5. Examine the samples each day with a magnifying glass and record any changes in appearance.

D. Result:
Molds will develop on some of the samples.

E. Supplemental Information:
Molds grow best in warm, dark, and moist conditions. Light, cold, and dryness discourage the growth of molds.

F. Thought Questions:
   1. Where and how should bread be stored to keep it free from molds?
   2. What other foods do you think might have molds if left exposed?

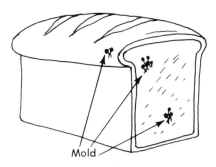

Mold

   3. What are ways that people have learned to preserve their foods?
   4. Are all plants green?
   5. How do mold seeds get on the food? (Answer: "Airborne.")

G. Related Topics and Activities:
   1. Discuss other food products on which molds grow.
   2. Discuss ways of preserving food.
   3. Have students examine molds under a magnifying glass and then draw pictures of the molds.
   4. See all Activities in this Section.

H. Vocabulary Builders—Spelling Words:
   1) **molds**   2) **moist**   3) **samples**
   4) **moderately**   5) **magnifying**

I. Thought for Today:
"A person who asks a question is a fool for five minutes. A person who does not, is a fool forever."

Activity

A. Problem: *How Do Bees Help Plant Reproduction?*

B. Materials:
   1. Nasturtiums, honeysuckles, roses, etc.
   2. Flower chart with parts labeled

C. Procedure:
   1. Divide class into small groups.
   2. Pass out flowers to the students.
   3. Have them identify the different parts of the flowers such as petal, stamen, pistil, and sepal.
   4. Examine the pistil. (The anther is on the end of the pistil.)
   5. Ask them to touch the pollen with their fingers gently and see what actually happens.
   6. Ask them if they know what happens when a bee perches in the flower in an effort to extract nectar.

D. Results:
   1. Students will learn the names of plant parts.
   2. The pollen will stick to the fingers of the sudents.

E. Supplemental Information:
   1. It has been shown that pollen will stick to the fingers, thus it will stick to the bees' legs and wings also. When pollen from one flower is carried to the stamen of another flower, cross-pollination has taken place.
   2. Pollination occurs only in seed-bearing plants.
   3. Seeds are carried by many insects and birds.
   4. Pollination is the transfer of male's reproductive units to the female's reproductive structures.
   5. Pollen is usually yellow or orange.

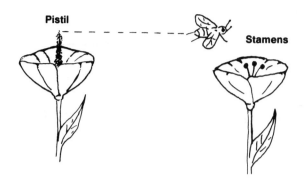

F. Thought Questions:
   1. What other insects might carry pollen from flower to flower?
   2. Can people carry pollen intentionally?
   3. How could we show that cross-pollination is part of plant reproduction?

G. Related Topics and Activities:
   1. Check flower shops for old flowers to study.
   2. Flowers can be dissected.
   3. Flowers can be pressed after studying.
   4. See all Activities in this Section.

H. Vocabulary Builders—Spelling Words:
   1) **bees**   2) **reproduction**   3) **pistil**   4) **stamen**
   5) **anther**

I. Thought for Today:
   "Use what talents you possess; the woods would be very silent if no birds sang except those who sang best."

Section D: Soils and Germination

Activity   III D 1

A. Problem: *Do All Plants Germinate and Grow at the Same Rate in Different Types of Soil?*

B. Materials:
   1. Eight lima bean seeds
   2. Four flowerpots or similar containers
   3. Four different types of soil: mainly sand, clay, loam, humus

C. Procedure:
   1. Fill each container with one type of soil and label it.
   2. Plant two seeds in each container. (Seeds sprout more rapidly if soaked overnight.)
   3. Keep soil moist.
   4. Place pots near window.
   5. Keep a chart record of plant growth as soon as the plants appear above the ground.

D. Result:
Different types of soil vary so greatly in texture and fertility that a wide variety of results can be expected. However the usual results are as follows: Those plants in the sand stopped growing after the food in the bean was consumed because the sand did not furnish the food necessary for continued plant growth.

E. Supplemental Information:
Rich garden soil can be used for loamy soil. Humus is newly decomposed materials. Leaves, twigs, and old parings can be used. Students can experiment with other types of soil such as gravel, rocks, or even mixtures of various soils mentioned. Additional beans can be planted and the beans dissected at various stages and in different types of soil. Using these methods, the best type of soil for each plant can be determined. Soil is being treated with more chemicals than ever as herbicides are replacing weeding.

F. Thought Questions:
   1. How would knowing the best kind of soil for each plant help farmers?
   2. What would happen if a specific plant used up most of a mineral needed for its growth?
   3. Is a mixture of soils better than any one type? How can you find out?

G. Related Topics and Activities:
   1. Many tests can be conducted on soils and germination. In any test be sure to have only one variable.
   2. See all Activities in this Section.
   3. See Section VII-C, "Earth's Crust."

H. Vocabulary Builders—Spelling Words:
   1) **germination**   2) **rate**   3) **soil**   4) **humus**
   5) **loam**

I. Thought for Today:
"In 1851 the modern bathtub was invented; the telephone, not until 1876. Just think, for 25 years you could take a bath without the phone ringing."

Activity

A. Problem: *Are Some Soils Better Than Others for Holding Water?*

B. Materials:
1. Five clay flowerpots, same size
2. Five glass jars, with mouths big enough for the flowerpots to be set in
3. Soils:
   a. Clay
   b. Silt
   c. Sand
   d. Loam
   e. Humus
4. Measuring cup
5. Water
6. Watch with second hand

C. Procedure:
1. Place each type of soil in a different flowerpot.
2. Place flowerpots in the glass jars.
3. Pour equal amounts of water into each flowerpot.
4. Observe the amount of water that runs off from each pot, the amount of dirt carried through with the water, and the length of time for the water to seep through.

D. Results:
1. There will be little or no runoff with the humus.
2. With clay, little soil is washed off.
3. Some sand and loam are carried off.
4. Silt is washed away in great quantities.

E. Supplemental Information:
1. Soil with vegetation will hold water longer and tends to prevent erosion. Leaf matter, remains from trees, holds water and becomes the best watershed materials.
2. The five test soils are:
   a. Sand—fine particles of disintegrated rock or seashells.

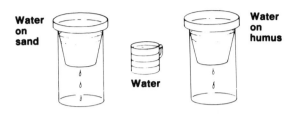

b. Humus—remains of dried plants and animals.
c. Loam—composition of gravel, sand, and clay.
d. Silt—very fine soil and sand deposited by running streams and rivers.
e. Clay—stiff, sticky kind of earth that can be molded.
3. The first eight inches of most farms' soils is called "topsoil." It takes about five hundred years to make one inch of topsoil. Modern farming practice is causing the loss of some topsoil.

F. Thought Questions:
1. What is a watershed?
2. How important is watershed to us?
3. Can farmers with steep slopes on their farms change their soil type?

G. Related Topics and Activities:
1. Study soil erosion and methods of prevention.
2. Study how farmers enrich or improve their soils.
3. See Activities in Part VI, "Ecology."
4. See all Activities in this Section.

H. Vocabulary Builders—Spelling Words:
1) **humus**   2) **loam**   3) **clay**   4) **silt**
5) **sand**

I. Thought for Today:
"A weed is a plant whose virtues are yet to be discovered."

Activity

A. Problem: *How Does Water Affect Germination?*

B. Materials:
1. Small flowerpots
2. Water glasses
3. Soil, humus
4. Bean seeds
5. Radish seeds
6. Paper towels
7. Water

C. Procedure A:
1. Plant bean seeds in small flowerpots in wet soil and dry soil.
2. Label one pot "Dry" and the other "Wet."
3. Keep temperature, light, and ventilation normal and equal for both pots.
4. Keep "Wet" pot moist, but do not water "Dry" pot.

Procedure B:
1. Place two folded paper towels in the bottom of each of two glasses.
2. Sprinkle some radish seeds on each pad and cover with another paper towel.
3. Label one glass "Dry" and the other "Wet."
4. Keep the towel in the "Wet" glass moist and the towel in the other glass dry.
5. Maintain temperature, light, and ventilation as in procedure "A."

D. Result:
In both procedures, only the seeds that were well watered germinated and grew.

E. Supplemental Information:
Water is necessary for seed germination. Sponge or cotton may be substituted for paper towels. Mustard seed or mixed birdseed may be substituted for radish seeds.

Procedure A

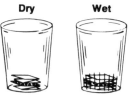

Procedure B

F. Thought Questions:
1. Do all seeds require the same amount of water for germination?
2. How do farmers control the amount of water they use after planting their seeds?
3. Is ocean water (salt water) good for germination?

G. Related Topics and Activities:
1. Test seeds using one group with soil and the other with no soil and an equal amount of water in each.
2. See all Activities in this Section.
3. See Section I-C, "Water."

H. Vocabulary Builders—Spelling Words:
1) **germination**   2) **flowerpot**
3) **temperature**   4) **moist**
5) **ventilation**

I. Thought for Today:
"It's nice to be important, but it's more important to be nice."

Activity III D 4

A. Problem: *How Does Air Affect Germination?*

B. Materials:
1. Lima bean seeds
2. Radish seeds
3. Four jars or two jars and two plastic cups
4. Soil, humus
5. Cotton
6. Water

C. Procedure A:
1. Plant lima bean seeds in jars.
2. Water both soils fairly well. When air bubbles cease to rise the air has been expelled from the soil.
3. Cap the first jar. This cuts off the air supply to the planting.
4. Keep the second planting moist by watering as needed.

Procedure B:
1. Fill the other two jars or cups with water.
2. On one place a cotton pad on top and some radish seeds on the cotton. (This will keep the seeds moist.)
3. Drop seeds into the water of the second container thus eliminating the air.
4. Keep the temperature and light the same for both jars.

D. Result:
In both procedures, where air is eliminated, the seeds will not germinate. In the first experiment, the seeds might germinate, but the new plant will quickly die from lack of oxygen in the air.

E. Supplemental Information:
Air is essential to germination and growth. It is the oxygen in the air that is required for photosynthesis, the process whereby plants manufacture their own food for their growth.

F. Thought Questions:
1. What other ways might air be eliminated from the jars?

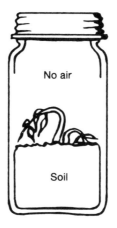

Procedure A

Cotton pad
Seed

Procedure B

2. Is too much air ever a problem to the farmer?
3. Would the same results occur with different types of seeds?

G. Related Topics and Activities:
1. See Section III-E, "Plant Growth."
2. See all Activities in this Section.
3. See other Activities in this Part.

H. Vocabulary Builders—Spelling Words:
1) **germination**   2) **lima bean**   3) **oxygen**
4) **radish**   5) **plastic**

I. Thought for Today:
"None is so tall as one who stoops to help a child."

Activity

A. Problem: *How Does Light Affect Germination?*

B. Materials:
1. Bean seeds
2. Grass seeds
3. Small flowerpots or cut-out milk cartons
4. Soil
5. Sponges
6. Bowls
7. Water

Procedure A   **Procedure B**

C. Procedure A:
1. Plant bean seeds in flowerpots.
2. Label one pot "Dark" and the other "Light."
3. Place the appropriately labeled one in the dark, and the other in the light.
4. Keep both pots well watered and ventilated, temperature normal.

Procedure B:
1. Wet two sponges and place in two bowls.
2. Add water to one-half inch depth.
3. Sprinkle each with grass seeds.
4. Place one in the dark and one in the light (not direct sunlight).
5. Keep the temperature and ventilation the same for both.

D. Result:

Seeds germinated in the light and also in the dark.

E. Supplemental Information:

Light is not necessary for germination. In some cases it may even be detrimental. After germination, when growth starts, most plants need light for normal growth.

F. Thought Questions:
1. Why are some flowers planted on the south side of homes? On the north side?
2. Where do grass seeds get their food to germinate?
3. Do you think all seeds need water to germinate?
4. How could you prevent germination of weed seeds in your garden?
5. Where does our natural light come from?

G. Related Topics and Activities:
1. Test different soils for the effects of light.
2. See all Activities in this Section.
3. See Section III-C, "Seeds and Reproduction."

H. Vocabulary Builders—Spelling Words:
1) **light**   2) **germination**   3) **flower**
4) **grass**   5) **sponges**

I. Thought for Today:

"If you have a job to do you might just as well do it right the first time."

Activity

A. Problem: *How Do We Test Germination Percentages of Seeds?*

B. Materials:
1. One square yard of cotton flannel
2. One hundred radish seeds
3. Pan of water
4. Thermometer

C. Procedure:
1. Dampen flannel with water.
2. Place 100 radish seeds over flannel.
3. Roll flannel into rather loose roll.
4. Place one end of roll in a pan of water.
5. Place thermometer and rolled flannel in a pan of water in an open window for ten days, adding water in pan as needed.
6. Record temperature daily.
7. After ten days unroll flannel and count number of seeds that sprouted.

D. Result:
Some of the seeds have sprouted; some have not.

E. Supplemental Information:
The ratio of the seeds that have sprouted to the total number of seeds planted can be determined. By finding the ratio it can be seen how many seeds would sprout if actually planted. This would tell the condition and probable age of the seeds and their growth expectation. This could lead to a discussion of how farmers estimate the amount of seed to plant under various circumstances. Also, many seed distributors report in percent the guaranteed germination of seeds if planted before a given date. A test for larger seeds can be conducted by placing a seed or seeds between a glass and a blotter curled up inside as shown in the bottom drawing.

F. Thought Questions:
1. Do all seeds need to be fresh to germinate?
2. Do all seeds of similar age have the same germination potential?
3. Where do farmers get their seeds?

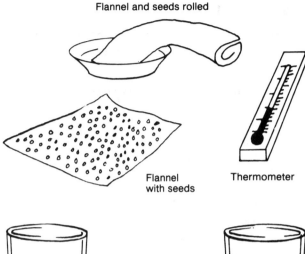

Flannel and seeds rolled

Flannel with seeds

Thermometer

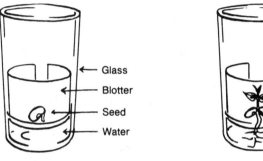

Plant a seed between glass and blotter.

Watch it grow.

G. Related Topics and Activities:
1. Test to determine if size of seeds has anything to do with time of germination.
2. See other Activities in this Part.
3. See Section III-C, "Seeds and Reproduction."
4. See all Activities in this Section.

H. Vocabulary Builders—Spelling Words:
1) **germination**   2) **percentages**   3) **ratio**
4) **thermometer**   5) **radish**

I. Thought for Today:
"The chicken that cackles the loudest is the first to lose its head."

Section E: Growth

Activity III E 1

A. Problem: *How Do Plants Grow?*

B. Materials:
1. Lima bean seeds
2. Five milk cartons
3. Good soil
4. Water
5. Paper towels
6. Spatula

C. Procedure:
1. Wash cartons. Cut four cartons to the height of 4″ and the other carton to 1″.
2. Put soil in the 4″ cartons.
3. Plant several beans in carton one, labeling with planting date.
4. Repeat with cartons two, three, and four, planting one carton each week.
5. Place in light sunny spot and keep soil damp.
6. One week after the last planting, put several seeds in the 1″ carton.
7. Add a small amount of water to sprout the seeds.
8. When plants have reached desired level of growth, uproot them carefully. Wash soil from roots (gently).
9. Place one plant from each stage of growth on a paper towel for each group of children to examine, compare, and discuss.

D. Result:
Plants will be at different stages of growth.

E. Supplemental Information:
1. Each seed has the potential for developing into a full grown plant if it is planted in good soil, watered, and kept in the sun. Some plants do not have seeds and reproduce by "vegetative propagation" where some part of the plant develops into a new plant. This may be a root, stem, or leaf. Gardeners and nurserymen use some of these possibilities in budding and grafting.

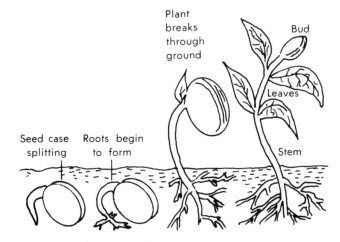

2. Corn grows fast. It takes 8 weeks to grow from a seed to a full plant with over 1,400 square inches of leaves. It establishes a root system which, if stretched out in one long line would measure 7 miles. There is a saying that "you can hear the corn grow." Well, some corn plants grow as much as 4 inches in one day.

F. Thought Questions:
1. How fast do the bean plants grow?
2. Do they grow faster during their first week, second week, third week, or fourth week?
3. Do all plants grow at the same speed?

G. Related Topics and Activities:
1. Have students describe some growth of plants they have seen.
2. Discuss ways to get rid of unwanted plants.
3. See all Activities in this Section.
4. See all Activities in this Part.

H. Vocabulary Builders—Spelling Words:
1) **growth** 2) **cartons** 3) **beans** 4) **label**
5) **sprout**

I. Thought for Today:
"Visits always give pleasure—if not coming, then the going."

A. Problem: *Do Plants Need Sunshine?*

B. Materials:
1. Growing plant with large leaves
2. Vaseline or grease
3. Black construction paper
4. Paper clips

C. Procedure A:
1. Place green plant in well-lighted place where it can be seen without being handled by class members.
2. Carefully cover *both* sides of several leaves with Vaseline or grease.
3. Observe these leaves each day and compare them with uncoated leaves. Notice color and freshness.

Procedure B:
1. Cut out a pattern on one side of a folded piece of black construction paper. (See "Mask" in Procedure "B.")
2. Clip the pattern on the leaf and leave it attached for several days.
3. After several days remove the construction paper and observe the results.

D. Results:
1. Procedure A:
The coated leaves will die and drop off.
2. Procedure B:
The masked portions will turn a pale green or brown while the unmasked portions will retain their normal color.

E. Supplemental Information:
The Vaseline or grease seals the tiny pores in the surface of the leaf and keeps the air out of the leaf. The leaf needs to respire to keep alive, to manufacture food by photosynthesis, thus supplying the total plant the nourishment it needs to survive. Without sunshine, the leaves will die. Leaves are required for plant survival.

F. Thought Questions:
1. What would happen if only the topside were coated? the bottom side?
2. Would a leaf continue to die if the coating were removed after one day?
3. What would happen if only half the leaf were covered (half of the topside and half of the bottom side)?
4. What happens to the plant leaf after the mask is removed? Observe for several days.

Procedure A

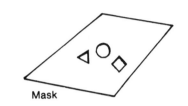

Mask

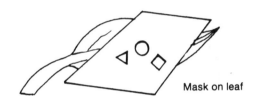

Mask on leaf

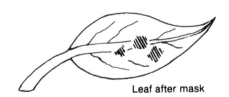

Leaf after mask

Procedure B

G. Related Topics and Activities:
1. See Activity III-F-5, "Splatter Prints."
2. Look at leaves of plants to see what damage has been done by insects.
3. See all Activities in this Section.

H. Vocabulary Builders—Spelling Words:
1) **sunshine**   2) **leaf**   3) **leaves**   4) **respire**
5) **grease**

I. Thought for Today:
"What society needs are broad people sharpened to a point."

Activity

A. Problem: *How Does Temperature Affect Growth?*

B. Materials:
1. Three young plants in separate flowerpots
2. Water
3. Soil, humus

C. Procedure:
1. Have students place one pot in an extremely cold place.
2. Have students place one pot in a moderately cool place.
3. Have students place the other in a warm place.
4. Label or classify these pots as cold, cool, and warm.
5. Pour enough water in each pot to keep the soil moist.
6. Keep other environmental factors equal.

D. Results:
1. After about one week, differences in sizes of plants will be noticed.
2. In the warm climate, the young plant should have grown the most.
3. In the cool climate the plant should have shown some growth but not as much as the former.
4. In the cold climate the plant should have shown very little growth and even signs of dying.

E. Supplemental Information:
Plants grow differently in varying conditions. A thermometer can be used to record the temperature in each pot. Try to use water at the same temperature the plant is located to reduce variables.

F. Thought Questions:
1. Will seeds germinate in a cold environment?
2. Do plants thrive better in warm or cold climates?
3. Do animals thrive better in warm or cold climates?

G. Related Topics and Activities:
1. If possible try and place another pot in a very hot place, such as next to a furnace or heater.
2. Check seeds for germination by varying temperature.
3. See all Activities in this Section.

Cold

Cool

Warm

H. Vocabulary Builders—Spelling Words:
1) **temperature** 2) **growth** 3) **extremely**
4) **moderately** 5) **environment**

I. Thought for Today:
"One sure way to lose ground is by slinging mud."

Activity

A. Problem: *Can Plants Live Without Water?*

B. Materials:
1. Bean seeds
2. Two small flowerpots
3. Water
4. Soil, humus

C. Procedure:
1. Plant some bean seeds in each of the small pots.
2. Place both plants in the sunshine.
3. Water plant "A" lightly each day.
4. Do not water plant "B."

D. Result:
Plant "A" will grow large and healthy. Plant "B" will soon die.

E. Supplemental Information:
All plants need water to live. Both water and sunshine are essential to the life of a plant. Sunshine or water alone is not enough. This activity works well as a follow-up of Activity III-E-1, "How do Plants Grow?"

F. Thought Questions:
1. Would the same results be possible with different kinds of seeds?
2. Is it possible to give a plant too much water?
3. How can a farmer tell if a plant is receiving enough water? not enough water? too much water?

G. Related Topics and Activities:
1. Start four lima bean seed plants. Vary the amount of water on each.
2. Add different liquids to different plants such as vinegar, clorox, salt water, etc., to see if it makes any difference in plant growth.
3. See all Activities in this Section.

Before

A is watered

B is not watered

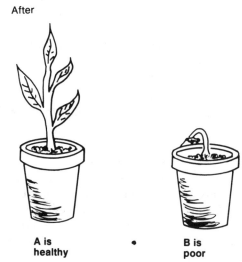

After

A is healthy

B is poor

H. Vocabulary Builders—Spelling Words:
1) **water**   2) **healthy**   3) **plants**   4) **liquids**
5) **vinegar**

I. Thought for Today:
"The easiest way to teach children the value of money is to borrow it from them."

Activity

A. **Problem:** *How Quickly Does Water Move in Stems?*

B. **Materials:**
   1. Plate
   2. Six wooden matches or toothpicks
   3. Water

C. **Procedure:**
   1. Break five matches half through at the middle.
   2. Arrange the five matches symmetrically on a dry plate around a circle about ¾ of an inch in diameter as shown in drawing.
   3. Dip a sixth match into water and wet each of the five match breaks with a drop or two of water.
   4. Leave the matches on the plate for a short time.

D. **Result:**
The matches partially straighten and thus form the shape of a five-pointed star.

E. **Supplemental Information:**
Water enters the dry wood cells in the bends of the matches and swells the cells. This swelling and movement, in turn, tends to straighten the matches and makes the ends move apart to form a five-pointed star. Capillarity is the movement of a liquid when in contact with dry cells in plants. In this case it moves quite quickly.

F. **Thought Questions:**
   1. Can you think of other examples of water movement in plants?
   2. Is this the same reaction that causes water pipes to burst in winter?
   3. What are the relationships among the terms capillarity, osmosis, and surface tension?

G. **Related Topics and Activities:**
   1. See Activity III-E-6, "Water Movement in Plants."
   2. See other Activities in this Section.
   3. See other Activities in this Part.

Plate

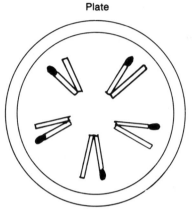

Wet the broken ends
of these matches

Matches form a
five-pointed star

H. **Vocabulary Builders—Spelling Words:**
   1) **capillarity**   2) **symmetrical**   3) **star**
   4) **straighten**   5) **liquid**

I. **Thought for Today:**
"Keep your words soft and sweet because you'll never know when you will have to eat them."

Activity

A. Problem: *How Does Water Move in Plants?*

B. Materials:
1. Carrots, celery, or flowers
2. Calla lilies or white carnations
3. Ink or food coloring
4. Tall glass or bottle
5. Knife
6. Eyedropper
7. Water

C. Procedure:
1. Color water with ink or food coloring.
2. Let carrot, celery, or flower stand in solution for one hour.
3. Remove and make crosscuts to show colored streaks.
4. Leave some calla lilies or white carnations in colored liquid for several hours and note results.

D. Result:
The colored fluid travels upward from the roots or stems leaving a telltale path.

E. Supplemental Information:
Plants have well-defined passageways through which liquids travel. By using a colored solution we can trace these channels through the plant. These tubes are formed by xylem cells in the plants.

F. Thought Questions:
1. What would happen if the stalk were split into two parts and each part dipped in a different colored solution?
2. What functions do you think the stems and stalks have other than transporting water?
3. What happens to plants during dry seasons? in summer time?

G. Related Topics and Activities:
1. See previous Activity III-E-5, "Osmosis."
2. See other Activities in this Section.
3. See other Activities in this Part.

H. Vocabulary Builders—Spelling Words:
1) **xylem** 2) **calla lilies** 3) **colored**
4) **knife** 5) **eyedropper**

Carrot

Celery

Flower

I. Thought for Today:
"Facility of speech is not always accompanied by fertility of thought."

Activity

A. Problem: *Do Plants Give Off Water?*

B. Materials:
1. Large leaf
2. Four water glasses
3. Cardboard
4. Water

C. Procedure:
1. Put water into a water glass (about one-third full).
2. Cut a hole in a piece of cardboard big enough for the stem of the leaf to slip through.
3. Place cardboard across the top of glass and arrange the leaf so that the stem is in the water and the blade is above the cardboard.
4. Set a second glass over the blade of the leaf.
5. Set up a similar piece of apparatus but do not put a leaf in this one.
6. Observe the inside of both upper glasses.

D. Result:
The glass on top of the leaf will soon contain droplets of water. The other top glass with no leaf in it will not have any droplets.

E. Supplemental Information:
The water which is transpired from the leaf condenses on the upper glass. This indicates that plants give off moisture. A small plant can be substituted for the large leaf. The surface of the leaf determines its rate of transpiration.

F. Thought Questions:
1. What kind of leaves give off the most water?
2. Does size or color have any effect on the amount of water transpired?
3. Does climate have any effect on transpiration?
4. Do all plants transpire at the same rate?

G. Related Topics and Activities:
1. See especially Activities III-E-5 and III-E-6, "Water in Plants."
2. Students should check different size leaves and plants.
3. See all Activities in this Section.

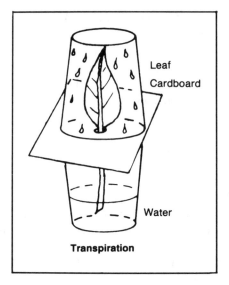

Leaf
Cardboard
Water
Transpiration

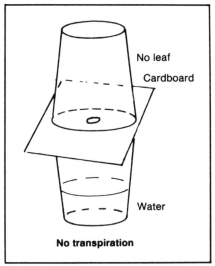

No leaf
Cardboard
Water
No transpiration

H. Vocabulary Builders—Spelling Words:
1) **transpire** 2) **cardboard** 3) **apparatus**
4) **similar** 5) **droplets**

I. Thought for Today:
"Live your life fully—this life is not a dress rehearsal."

Activity

A. Problem: *Is Light Necessary for Continued Growth of Plants? Can We Show the Effects of Photosynthesis?*

B. Materials:
1. Two flowerpots, plastic cups or cans filled with soil (humus)
2. Bean seeds
3. Paper bag

C. Procedure:
1. Soak bean seeds overnight to speed germination.
2. Plant seeds and allow plants to break through the soil. This may take one to two weeks.
3. Keep one pot in direct sunlight (Fig. 1).
4. Cover the other pot with a paper bag (Fig. 2).
5. Observe for several weeks removing bag for observation period only.

D. Result:
The covered plant will be stunted and pale while the plant which has received sunlight will be hearty and green. The covered plant will receive a little light through the paper bag and during periods of observation.

E. Supplementary Information:
Photosynthesis is the process whereby plants convert water and carbon dioxide in the presence of sunlight to plant food. Without any of these three factors, plants cannot manufacture food for their growth and development. The simplified formula for photosynthesis is:

Carbon dioxide + water + sunlight ⟶ sugar (food) + oxygen

This is usually stated, "Carbon dioxide and water in the presence of sunlight produces sugar (food) and oxygen."

F. Thought Questions:
1. What would happen if the paper bag were switched in the middle of the test period?
2. What would happen if a heavy, clear cellophane bag were placed over one plant instead of an opaque paper bag?
3. Is there any difference during the first few days when both plants break through the soil?

G. Related Topics and Activities:
1. Repeat tests, only expose to electric lights instead of sunlight.

Fig. I   Fig. II

Fig. I   Fig. II

2. See all Activities in this Section.
3. See other Activities in this Part.

H. Vocabulary Builders—Spelling Words:
1) **photosynthesis** 2) **sunlight** 3) **carbon dioxide**
4) **oxygen** 5) **sugar** 6) **presence**

I. Thought for Today:
"When your work speaks for itself, don't interrupt."

Activity

A. Problem: *Do Plants Grow Towards Light?*

B. Materials:
   1. Bean seeds
   2. Flowerpot or plastic cup
   3. Soil, humus
   4. Cardboard box

C. Procedure:
   1. Plant the bean seeds in flowerpot or plastic cup.
   2. Water them daily.
   3. After seeds have begun to sprout, place pot in a lightproof box with a window cut in one end. (See drawing.) The only light entering the box should come through the window.
   4. Observe daily.

D. Result:
The plant turns toward the light and continues to grow in the direction of the window.

E. Supplemental Information:
When school plants are placed near windows they should be turned occasionally to prevent one-sided growth. This tendency in plants is called phototropism.

F. Thought Questions:
   1. What would happen to the plant if the pot were rotated 180° after the first few weeks?
   2. What would happen if the hole were sealed?
   3. What would happen if colored cellophane were placed over the hole?

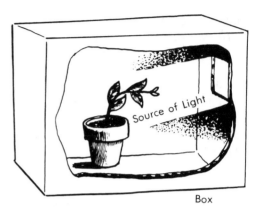

Box

G. Related Topics and Activities:
   1. Cut several holes at various places in the box. Open only one hole at a time until there is movement there. Then close this hole and open another one.
   2. Test sunlight against artificial light.
   3. See all Activities in this Section.

H. Vocabulary Builders—Spelling Words:
   1) **phototropism**   2) **humus**   3) **rotated**
   4) **sprout**   5) **lightproof**

I. Thought for Today:
"Rivers and people get crooked by following the line of least resistance."

Activity

A. Problem: *Do Land Plants and/or Water Plants Give Off Oxygen?*

B. Materials:

1. Two large glass jars
2. Live potted plants
3. Two candles
4. Matches
5. Grease or wax
6. Aquarium with water plant
7. Glass funnel
8. Test tube
9. Several splinters of wood

C. Procedure A (For Land Plants):

1. Place a lighted candle in an inverted jar. It will soon go out indicating that most of the oxygen has been chemically combined (Fig. 1).
2. To further prove this, raise the jar and insert a flaming splinter. Notice that it will quickly go out.
3. Place a live, green plant in another inverted jar (Fig. 2).
4. Place a lighted candle beside the plant.
5. When the candle goes out, put grease or wax around the mouth of the jar in order to keep air from seeping in (Fig. 3).
6. After 3 or 4 days, quickly insert a flaming splinter to test for oxygen.

Procedure B (For Water Plants):

1. Place a glass funnel over the plants in the aquarium.
2. Over the funnel put a test tube completely filled with water.
3. Wait until about one-third of the water has been displaced by gas in the tube.
4. Burn the end of the splinter then blow out the flame so that the end is still glowing.
5. Remove test tube carefully and insert the glowing end of the splinter into it.

D. Results:

1. In Procedure A:
   The candles go out because most of the oxygen has been converted to carbon dioxide.
2. In Procedure B:
   The glowing end of the splinter will burst into flame.

Grease

Procedure A

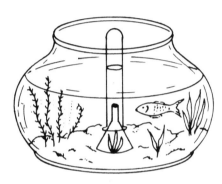

Procedure B

E. Supplementary Information:

1. Glowing splinters will burst in flames in the presence of oxygen.
2. Since both splinters burst in flames, it is evident that both land and water plants give off oxygen.
3. All animals, with few exceptions, require oxygen for survival.

F. Thought Questions:

1. What is the difference between air and oxygen?
2. Do plants give off oxygen at night when there is no sunshine?
3. Would the splinter burst into flames if the test tube contained air? carbon dioxide?
4. How does giving off oxygen help water animals?
5. Are water plants similar to land plants in giving off oxygen?
6. What special characteristics do plants have that live in the water?

G. Related Topics and Activities:
   1. See Activities on "Candles."
   2. See Section I-B, "Air."
   3. Determine how plants reproduce in water.
   4. See other Activities in this Section.

H. Vocabulary Builders—Spelling Words:
   1) **potted**   2) **wax**   3) **grease**   4) **test tube**
   5) **inverted**   6) **flaming**   7) **splinter**

I. Thought for Today:
   "Never close your lips to those to whom you have opened your heart."

Activity

A. **Problem:** *Do Plants Give Off Carbon Dioxide in Darkness?*

B. **Materials:**
1. Large canning jar (gallon size preferable)
2. Potted plant (almost touch top of jar)
3. Limewater
4. Cup
5. Lightproof cover for jar (tagboard or heavy cloth)

C. **Procedure:**
1. Place a small potted plant under a large canning jar and allow it to remain in darkness for a day. (Cover it during daylight.)
2. Carefully remove the jar and pour one-half cup of limewater into it.
3. Cover the jar and shake it well.

D. **Result:**
The limewater turns milky due to the presence of carbon dioxide.

E. **Supplemental Information:**
Plants give off oxygen during the day and carbon dioxide when placed in darkness. These processes are called respiration. This process is necessary for the plants to use the food they have produced.
The simplified formula is:

sugar (food) + oxygen → carbon dioxide (to the air) + water + energy

F. **Thought Questions:**
1. Where does the carbon come from in carbon dioxide?
2. Do you know what solid carbon dioxide is?
3. Can you name any other gases by their chemical names?

G. **Related Topics and Activities:**
1. See Activity III-E-10, "Oxygen."
2. See Activity I-B-19, "Carbon dioxide."
3. See all Activities in this Section.

H. **Vocabulary Builders—Spelling Words:**
1) **respiration** 2) **carbon dioxide**
3) **oxygen** 4) **limewater** 5) **darkness**

I. **Thought for Today:**
"Although there are many trial marriages, there are no such things as trial children."

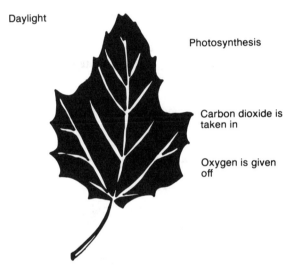

Daylight

Photosynthesis

Carbon dioxide is taken in

Oxygen is given off

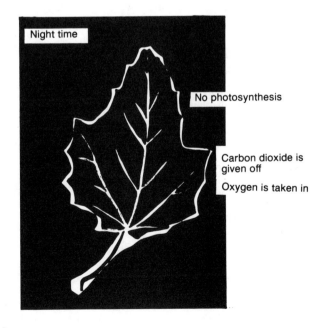

Night time

No photosynthesis

Carbon dioxide is given off

Oxygen is taken in

Section F: Fun with Plants

Activity III F 1

A. Problem: *How Do We Make a Decorative House Plant with a Sweet Potato?*

B. Materials:
1. Quart jar
2. Thin pins, toothpicks, or thin nails
3. Sweet potato
4. Water
5. Supporting device for hanging (if desired)

Early growth

C. Procedure:
1. Wash sweet potato carefully as some are treated to preserve them.
2. Note eyes or buds which indicate top of potato.
3. Place potato in jar about two-thirds of the way down.
4. Support with pins, toothpicks, or thin nails.
5. Fill the jar with water so that potato is half submerged.
6. Support or place on shelf near window.

D. Result:

An attractive classroom plant will develop.

E. Supplemental Information:
1. The sweet potato must be kept watered.
2. The sweet potato should have good sunlight for maximum growth.

F. Thought Questions:
1. Do you think an avocado seed can be made to sprout in the same way?
2. What other plants might be started in this fashion?
3. What is hydroponics?

Full growth

G. Related Topics and Activities:
1. Charts can be kept on the number of leaves and roots.
2. The roots can be studied both macroscopically and microscopically.
3. Plant leaves can be studied for size, shape, growth rates, etc.
4. See other Activities in this Section.

H. Vocabulary Builders—Spelling Words:
1) **decorative**   2) **sweet potato**
3) **supporting**   4) **device**   5) **preserve**

I. Thought for Today:

"If necessity is the mother of invention; discontent is the father of progress."

Activity

A. Problem: *How Do We Make a Carrot Basket?*

B. Materials:
   1. Fresh, large carrot
   2. Apple corer
   3. String
   4. Supporting device

C. Procedure:
   1. Cut the carrot in half horizontally.
   2. Using the lower half, hollow out the central core of the carrot about halfway down.
   3. Make a sling to support the carrot.
   4. Hang on supporting device.
   5. Keep hollowed-out portion full of water.

D. Results:
   1. Roots will sprout from the bottom.
   2. The roots will continue to grow until food from the carrot is gone.

E. Supplemental Information:
   1. Carrot must be kept watered or plant will die. (This is a plant.)
   2. It is always a good idea to make several of these and compare.

F. Thought Questions:
   1. What other types of vegetables could be grown in this manner?
   2. What type of plants have similar food storages?
   3. What part(s) of a plant are shown in this activity?

Carrot basket

G. Related Topics and Activities:
   1. Try this with other vegetables such as onions, turnips, and beets.
   2. See all Activities in this Section.
   3. See Activity III-F-1, "Sweet Potato Plant."
   4. See Activity III-E-6, "Water Moves in Plants."

H. Vocabulary Builders—Spelling Words:
   1) **carrot**   2) **basket**   3) **supporting**
   4) **string**   5) **hollow**

I. Thought for Today:
   "The biggest thing college prepares young people for is the knowledge of what it's like to be broke."

Activity

A. Problem: *How Do We Make a Simple Plant Terrarium?*

B. Materials:
1. Glass container and lid
2. Different small plants
3. Sufficient soil to fill one-third of container
4. Small trowel
5. Decorative rocks or driftwood
6. Water can

Glass container

C. Procedure:
1. Plan with class the setting of the terrarium (a wooded area, a desert scene, a farm, or other) and the planting arrangement.
2. Fill container with 3 inches of soil.
3. Demonstrate proper method of removing plants from pots. (Gently tap sides and bottom with trowel until soil is loosened enough to lift plant from pot.)
4. Plant the plants in container.
5. Arrange rocks and other decorative material.
6. Lightly sprinkle garden.
7. Place lid to one side on terrarium allowing air to get to plants.

D. Result:
Class will have created an artistic terrarium.

E. Supplemental Information:
1. A small dish garden or terrarium needs little or no water, as it uses the evaporation which condenses as moisture on the underside of the lid.
2. The terrarium should be given sufficient sunlight, and the air should be allowed to reach the plants. The terrarium should last for weeks and can be kept indefinitely by replacing the dead plants with live ones. Children will not only learn how to make a terrarium, but will also enjoy watching the plants develop.

F. Thought Questions:
1. What are the differences between a terrarium, a vivarium, and an aquarium?
2. Why are some plants more suited to a terrarium than others?
3. What would happen if the terrarium lid were kept on?

G. Related Topics and Activities:
1. Collect weeds around the school and plant them in the terrarium.
2. Plant grasses.
3. Plant radish seeds.
4. See other Activities in this Section.

H. Vocabulary Builders—Spelling Words:
1) **terrarium**   2) **vivarium**   3) **aquarium**
4) **trowel**   5) **decorative**

I. Thought for Today:
"It is by logic that we prove, but by intuition that we discover."

A. Problem: *How Can We Make Mounts for Plants?*

B. Materials:
1. Shallow cardboard box of any desired dimensions
2. Piece of glass, plastic, or heavy cellophane to fit under cover of cardboard box
3. Cotton
4. Razor blade or knife
5. Adhesive tape, masking tape, or glue
6. Dry plants and/or specimens

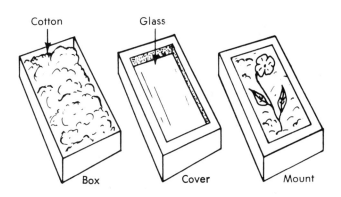

C. Procedure:
1. Draw ½-inch margin along all sides of cover.
2. Cut out along these lines with razor blade or knife. (Be very careful.)
3. Fit glass, plastic, or cellophane cover taping or gluing it to the bottom side of box cover.
4. Place enough cotton in box to nearly fill it.
5. Arrange the specimen, and label.
6. Replace cover.
7. Paint box if desired.

D. Result:

An attractive Riker-type box for storing plant and small animal specimens is made.

E. Supplemental Information:
1. An inexpensive Riker-type box for mounting leaves, pressed flowers, branches or stems, butterflies, or other insects, shells, etc., for display is easily made.
2. Attractive and durable display boxes can be made from inexpensive or discarded materials.
3. Only a minimum of time and work is needed to make the boxes.
4. Label should contain:
   a. scientific name of specimen
   b. common name of specimen
   c. where found
   d. date
   e. collector's name

F. Thought Questions:
1. What kind of plant specimens could be placed in these mounts?
2. What kind of animals could be placed in this type of mount?
3. What would cause spoilage of specimens in this Riker mount? What could be done to help eliminate this source or sources of trouble? (Answer: mothballs or flakes)

G. Related Topics and Activities:
1. Collect and mount insects.
2. Collect and mount butterflies.
3. See other Activities in this Section.

H. Vocabulary Builders—Spelling Words:
1) **Riker box**   2) **plastic**   3) **specimen**
4) **label**   5) **cellophane**

I. Thought for Today:
"Snowflakes are one of nature's most fragile things, but just look at what they can do when they stick together."

Activity

A. Problem: *How Can We Make a "Splatter Print"?*

B. Materials:

1. White or colored construction paper, size 9" × 12"
2. Old toothbrush
3. Scissors blade
4. Large leaf with a distinctive outside edge
5. Poster paint with consistency of thick cream (If your background paper is white, your paint should be dark enough in color for a good contrast. If you use colored paper, use a very dark color in harmony with it.)
6. Pins (enough to fasten leaf points)
7. Newspaper

C. Procedure:

1. Place several thicknesses of newspaper on a working surface.
2. Place construction paper on newspaper.
3. On top of this place the leaf.
4. Pin the leaf points to keep leaf from moving.
5. Dip toothbrush into poster paint.
6. Remove excess paint by shaking brush or rubbing on newspaper. (Too much paint makes blobs.)
7. Stand a little in front of leaf; begin splatter work by rubbing the scissors blade or your thumbnail against the bristles of the brush away from leaf so paint will splatter back.
8. Cover the entire surface. The strength of the color upon the print will depend upon the amount of splattering. Good work, free from blots, requires time, patience, and practice.
9. Remove actual leaf.

D. Result:

The leaf shape will be silhouetted in the same color as the construction paper against a dark splatter background.

E. Supplemental Information:

Another way to apply paint is to put mounting in box and cover with a fine wire screen. Brush can then be run over wire screen. Spray paint, lightly applied, can also be used.

G. Related Topics and Activities:

1. See Activities III-F-6 and III-F-7, "Plants, Leaves."
2. Make hearts for Valentine's Day, pumpkins for Halloween, turkeys for Thanksgiving, etc.
3. See all Activities in this Section.

H. Vocabulary Builders—Spelling Words:

1) **splatter** 2) **print** 3) **colored**
4) **construction** 5) **harmony**

I. Thought for Today:

"The only thing most people do better than anyone else is read their own handwriting."

Activity

A. Problem: *How Can We Make Blueprints of Leaves?*

B. Materials:

1. Piece of window glass
2. Piece of stiff cardboard or plywood
3. Wide adhesive or masking tape
4. Blueprint paper (cut desired size)
5. Pan of water
6. Leaf or fern frond

C. Procedure:

1. Place the glass upon the piece of stiff cardboard.
2. Fasten these together at the top with a piece of adhesive or masking tape. This is your printing frame.
3. Lift up the glass cover and place a piece of blueprint paper face up on the cardboard.
4. Lay the leaf (or fern) to be printed on top of the blueprint paper.
5. Cover all with the glass top.
6. Expose the frame to the sun for a few minutes.
7. Remove blueprint paper and soak print in a pan of water.

D. Result:

The last step brings out the blue color of the print and makes it permanent. The strength of the sunlight will determine the length of exposure. It will be necessary to experiment several times for best results.

E. Supplementary Information:

Blueprints are used extensively in the construction business for showing room and building plans.

F. Thought Questions:

1. What other methods can be used to duplicate plans, drawings, or small, flat objects?
2. What other plant parts can be shown in blueprints?
3. Are there any ways that leaves can be duplicated and magnified by some graphic means?

G. Related Topics and Activities:

1. See Activity III-F-5, "Splatter Printing."
2. See Activity III-F-7, "Artistic Leaf Rubbing."
3. See Activity III-E-11, "Leaves and Carbon Dioxide."
4. See all Activities in this Section.

H. Vocabulary Builders—Spelling Words:

1) **blueprint**   2) **window**   3) **leaf**
4) **fern**   5) **frond**   6) **masking**

I. Thought for Today:

"It's what guests say as they swing out of the driveway that really counts."

A. Problem: *How Can We Make an Artistic Leaf Rubbing on a Piece of Cloth?*

B. Materials:

1. Sheer white silk or cotton, a square 18″ × 18″ (a half-yard of 36″ material will make two squares)
2. Scissors
3. Wax crayons
4. Damp cloth
5. Twelve leaves or more of the same size with heavy veins
6. Drawing board or heavy board covered with cloth
7. Electric iron
8. Several sheets of plain white paper 18″ × 18″
9. Hard lead pencil
10. Thumbtacks

Trace

C. Procedure:

1. Plan arrangement of leaves on one sheet of paper first. Choose your best idea.
2. Draw around the edges of each leaf.
3. Remove actual leaves.
4. Upon the cloth-covered board, place this sheet of paper with sketched leaves.
5. Over this paper, place the sheet white cloth square tracing the leaf outlines *very* lightly with a hard lead pencil.
6. Lift up the cloth and replace the leaves in exact location on top of your paper design. Keep the vein side up.
7. With the leaves in position underneath, thumbtack the cloth to the drawing board.
8. With sharp-pointed crayon, very carefully rub over the cloth-covered leaves. All strokes must be very close together and in one direction. The rubbing, if carefully done, will bring out the leaf veining and leaf form.
9. To set the crayon, place a damp cloth over the fabric with the design uppermost.
10. Press with a hot iron.

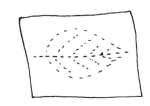

Cloth over tracing

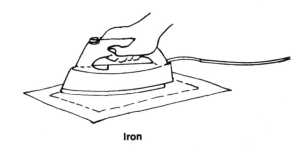

Iron

D. Result:

A handkerchief or neckerchief with a permanent leaf design.

E. Supplementary Information:

The finished cloth design can be preserved by placing it between two sheets of wax paper and ironing.

F. Thought Questions:

1. What is the purpose of heat in this activity?
2. Is this method similar to that done to put designs on T-shirts?
3. Can items other than leaves be used?

G. Related Topics and Activities:

1. See Activities III-F-5, III-F-6, "Plants, Leaves."
2. Make T-shirts with school logo.
3. See all Activities in this Section.

H. Vocabulary Builders—Spelling Words:

1) **artistic**   2) **rubbing**   3) **scissors**
4) **tracing**   5) **leaves**

I. Thought for Today:

"People generally quarrel because they can't argue."

Part IV

Animals

Section A: Classification

Activity IV A 1

A. Problem: *What Is the Difference between Living and Nonliving Things?*

B. Materials:
1. Books
2. Pencils
3. Rocks
4. Classroom plants
5. Classroom animals
6. Pictures of class's pets
7. Miscellaneous items

C. Procedure:
1. Have class make a list of nonliving things.
2. Make a list of the characteristics of living things.
3. Have them make a list of plants.
4. Have them make a list of animals.
5. Have them cite the differences between these three groups.

D. Results:
1. The pupils will recognize the differences between living and nonliving things and between plants and animals.
2. They will understand that most known living things are classified as either plants or animals.
3. Students will learn that many scientists today classify all living things in five main kingdoms.
   a. Monera
   b. Protista
   c. Fungi
   d. Plants
   e. Animals

E. Supplemental Information:
1. Living things are alike in some respects and different in others.
2. Nonliving things have very few characteristics of living things.
3. Animals move about; plants can't.
4. Animals have senses for locating food and the means of locomotion to obtain it.
5. Most plants make their own food.

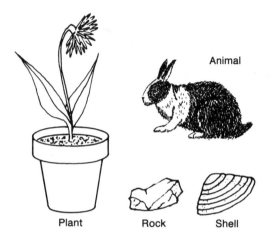

Animal

Plant   Rock   Shell

6. Living things will have the following characteristics:
   a. reproduce
   b. feed
   c. react to stimuli (irritability)
   d. grow
   e. develop
   f. get energy
   g. have cells (or are one)
   h. respire (breathe)
   i. have complex structure (protoplasm)
   j. die (may omit for younger children)

F. Thought Questions:
1. How do some nonliving things move?
2. What is the biggest living thing you know about? the smallest?
3. What is the largest nonliving thing? the smallest?
4. Do nonliving things ever affect other nonliving things?

G. Related Topics and Activities:
1. Look at some nonliving things with a microscope or magnifying glass.
2. Do some research on the biggest and smallest living things and nonliving things.

3. Younger children can collect pictures about plants and others about animals.
4. See Activity IV-A-2, "Animal Classification."
5. See all Activities in this Section.

H. Vocabulary Builders—Spelling Words:

1) **animals** 2) **plants** 3) **living**
4) **nonliving** 5) **locomotion** 6) **stimuli**
7) **respiration** 8) **protoplasm** 9) **irritability**

I. Thought for Today:

"One of the secrets of a long and fruitful life is to forgive everybody everything every night before you go to bed."—Ann Landers

Activity

A. Problem: *How Are Animals Classified?*

B. Materials:
1. Pictures of bacteria, fungi, and algae
2. Pictures of a wide variety of plants
3. Pictures, specimens, and stuffed animals

C. Procedure:
1. Describe the five main living kingdoms and give examples of each:
   a. **Monera**—bacteria, some blue-green algae
   b. **Protista**—amoebas, diatoms, euglena
   c. **Fungi**—molds, mildews, mushrooms
   d. **Plants**—mosses, liverworts, ferns, shrubs, trees
   e. **Animals**—jellyfish, worms, mollusks, centipedes, frogs, fish, rodents, birds, mammals
2. Have students try to classify any group of things such as books, hats, shoes, or clothing in any sub-classifications they choose (size, color, weight, function).
3. Have the students prepare their own classification of animals.
4. Describe how scientists classify living things in the following sub-classifications:
   kingdom
     phylum
       class
         order
           family
             genus
               species

5. Depending on the age of students, the depth of classification should be determined. Older students may want a book on animal taxonomy (technical animal classification). Younger students can use common, general sub-divisions as those mentioned above in Procedure. Middle grade students may want to subdivide these a little further.

D. Result:
Students will become aware of the complex nature of animal classification.

E. Supplemental Information:
Classification is a very difficult task and all scientists are not agreed as to classification schemes. Most problems of classification arise from tiny organisms.

F. Thought Questions:
1. Can all living things be classified?
2. Can automobiles be classified?
3. Can rocks be classified?

G. Related Topics and Activities:
1. See Activity IV-A-3, "What Animal am I?"
2. See Part VI, "Ecology."
3. See all Activities in this Section.

H. Vocabulary Builders—Spelling Words:
1) **kingdoms**   2) **phylum**   3) **order**
4) **class**   5) **family**   6) **genus**

I. Thought for Today:
"A child, like your stomach, doesn't need all you can afford to give it."

Activity

A. Problem: *What Animal Am I?*

B. Materials:
1. A flannel board with blue background, about 18″ × 24″
2. Flannel cutouts: A white rabbit and other familiar animals; strips of brown for ground, strips of green for grass, and an orange-colored carrot topped with green leaves; or original drawings of pictures from a picture book, mounted on cardboard and backed with strips of sandpaper or flocking to make them adhere to the flannel board.

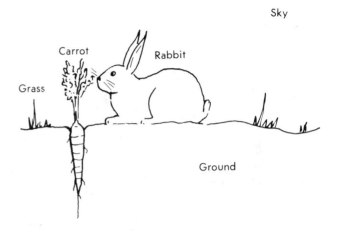

C. Procedure:
1. Place ground and grass strips on flannel board.
2. "Plant" carrot between ground strips.
3. Place rabbit near carrot on ground.
4. Have children learn the name of the animal, where it lives, and what it eats.
5. Change the animal and its setting.
6. For each animal find out:
   a. where it lives
   b. what it eats
   c. what preys on it
   d. how it has its young (eggs, live births)
   e. how important it is to us

D. Result:
Children will learn to identify common animals, their habitats, and their food.

E. Supplemental Information:
This activity can be used to integrate other subjects such as language arts or social studies by adding printed words on cards or including studies on farm, food, health, etc.

F. Thought Questions:
1. Can we get information about animals by their size? color? shape?
2. Can we get information about animals by where they live?
3. What information can't we get by a flannel board study that we could get if we were to see the animal in real life?

G. Related Topics and Activities:
1. See Activity IV-A-2, "Animal Classification."
2. See Activity VI-A-5, "Animal Extinction."
3. See other Activities in this Section.

H. Vocabulary Builders—Spelling Words:
1) **animal**   2) **flannel**   3) **cutouts**
4) **grass**   5) **carrot**

I. Thought for Today:
"Grow angry slowly, there's plenty of time."

Section B: Pets

Activity $\quad\quad\quad\quad$ IVB1

A. Problem: *What Kind of Pet Should I Have?*

B. Materials:
1. Pictures of various pets
2. Actual pets belonging to the students

C. Procedure:
1. Have a discussion about pets in general and those owned by the students.
2. Make a list of pets that the students suggest.
3. Group pets according to major characteristics such as:
   a. fish
   b. birds
   c. dogs and cats
   d. farm pets
   e. field animals, etc.
4. Let the students choose the category in which they are interested. Use this as a basis for committee study.
5. Each committee should make a notebook to record its findings, formulate a list of questions about the group of pets it has selected, and then research answers to questions that have been formulated.
6. Have a sharing time for the committees to report findings.
7. Items might include pets for watchdogs, friends, something beautiful to look at, companionship, or???

D. Results:
1. Students will develop a better knowledge of animals.
2. They will learn how to care for their pets.
3. They will learn how animals feed and protect themselves.
4. They will learn that some animals are hatched from eggs; others are born live from their mothers.

E. Supplemental Information:
1. Students can obtain information about pets in many ways such as:
   a. visiting pet stores
   b. talking to veterinarians
   c. observing their pets
   d. talking to neighbors about their pets.
2. Responsibilities for the care of pets must always be assigned whether at home or at school so that pets do not suffer from lack of food, exercise, or physical comfort.
3. It is important that the whole family share in the discussion of what kinds of pets should be kept in and/or around the home.

F. Thought Questions:
1. Why do people want pets?
2. Should people keep exotic pets (animals out of their natural environment)?
3. What should be done with stray pets? lost pets?

G. Related Topics and Activities:
1. Find out whether pets are naturally prey or predator.
2. For art work, draw a pet and use the drawing for a workbook cover.
3. Look for interesting articles about pets, and report to class.
4. Students can bring in pictures of their pets.
5. Do research on training of pets.
6. See all Activities in this Section.

H. Vocabulary Builders—Spelling Words:
1) **pets** 2) **dogs** 3) **cats** 4) **farm**
5) **field**

I. Thought for Today:
"If dogs could talk, they wouldn't be such good friends."

Activity

A. **Problem:** *How Do We Care for Dogs and Cats?*

B. **Materials:**
1. Pictures of cats
2. Pictures of dogs
3. Selected dogs and cats of students

C. **Procedure:**
1. Discuss the different breeds of dogs and cats the students have as pets.
2. Describe other breeds of dogs and cats.
3. Have each student tell how his particular pet is cared for:
   a. feeding
   b. exercising
   c. excretion needs
   d. cleaning
   e. sleeping
   f. protecting
   g. shots for disease prevention
4. Have each student also tell about the pet's:
   a. problems
   b. idiosyncrasies
   c. tricks
   d. manners
   e. association with other animals, etc.
5. Have a student or resource person talk about showing dogs at dog shows or cats at cat shows. (Feed stores or veterinary clinics may supply printed materials about care of pets.)

D. **Results:**
1. Students will learn about the care and feeding of dogs and cats.
2. They will become more appreciative of all living things.

E. **Supplementary Information:**
1. Animal shelters are full of dogs and cats that are lost, strayed, or abandoned because people have not taken proper care of their pets. Every class should have some classroom pet(s): fish, birds, small animals, etc.
2. Cats should have scratching pads (carpet-covered two-by-four).
3. Squirt catnip near the base of the scratching pad.

4. Newly acquired cats should be kept indoors for 10 days to become acquainted with their new home.
5. Litter boxes should be cleaned twice each week.
6. All pets should have proper vaccinations.
7. Most people know how to take care of dogs.
8. Cats are a different species with different needs.

F. **Thought Questions:**
1. What ways are dogs and cats like people?
2. What ways are dogs and cats different from people?
3. Do most owners take proper care of their dogs and cats?

G. **Related Topics and Activities:**
1. Check with a veterinarian about the care and feeding of dogs and cats.
2. Visit an animal shelter (pound).
3. See all Activities in this Section.

H. **Vocabulary Builders—Spelling Words:**
1) **feeding**   2) **exercising**   3) **excreting**
4) **cleaning**   5) **sleeping**   6) **caring**

I. **Thought for Today:**
"Nothing in the world is friendlier than a wet dog."

Activity

A. Problem: *How Do We Care for Hamsters, Guinea Pigs, Gerbils, and/or Mice?*

B. Materials:
1. Male animal
2. Female animal of same species
3. Two wire mesh pens, about 3′ × 2′ in area, with sides at least 16″ high
4. Four pans for food and water

C. Procedure:
1. Select students for specific duties, such as feeding the animals, cleaning the pens, or recording observations.
2. Place the two animals in the same pen and in time they will mate.
3. Feed the animals a variety of foods such as greens, bread, milk, etc.
4. Keep fresh water in the pen at all times.

D. Results:
1. Students will learn about the care and feeding of animals.
2. Pupils will discover some of the elements of breeding and caring for young animals.

E. Supplemental Information:
1. All life comes from life, and each species reproduces its own kind of living organism.
2. Life is dependent upon certain materials and conditions.
3. Most animals need food, water, exercise, fresh air, and sunshine.
4. Use caution in handling the females for a short time preceding and following the birth of a litter.
5. Hamsters are usually the most easily available rodent.
6. Mice are unusual pets and a lot of fun.
   a. They are near-sighted and timid.
   b. They are nocturnal and love to explore.
   c. They can produce up to 17 litters a year with 6 to 12 young in each litter.
   d. They eat about two ounces of food a day which should include seeds, bird seed, nuts, dry dog food, bread, cheese, and green vegetables.

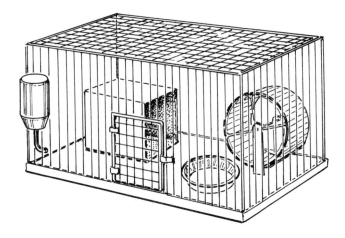

   e. Mice should have a litter box which should be cleaned every two days.
7. Responsibilities must always be assigned to students so that the pets do not suffer from lack of food, exercise, or physical comfort.

F. Thought Questions:
1. What are some common characteristics of pets?
2. What are the natural habitats of these animals?
3. How do these animals differ from dogs and cats?
4. Should animals be raised for fur coats and/or scientific research?

G. Related Topics and Activities:
1. Stories can be collected about pets.
2. Students can write creative stories about pets.
3. Students can relate their art work to these activities.
4. See all Activities in this Section.

H. Vocabulary Builders—Spelling Words:
1) **hamster**   2) **guinea pigs**   3) **gerbils**
4) **mice**   5) **rodents**

I. Thought for Today:
"Strolling through the back alley the seventy-four pound mouse cried, 'Here Kitty, Kitty, Kitty.'"

A. Problem: *How Do We Study Common Insects?*

B. Materials:

1. Collections of several kinds of insects that are common in a locality
2. Chart which shows the characteristics of the more common orders of insects

C. Procedure:

1. Students should carefully examine all the insects that are available. The common characteristics to look for are:
   a. number of legs
   b. whether the insect has wings
   c. shape of the body
   d. kind of head
   e. special characteristics or features of insects:
      1) outside skeleton (exoskeleton)
      2) bilateral symmetry
      3) three body parts:
         a. head
         b. thorax
         c. abdomen
2. Using the supplemental information which is attached to this activity, the students will try to classify the insects which they have at hand.

D. Results:

1. Students will learn common characteristics of insects.
2. Students may want to make insect collections.

E. Supplemental Information:

1. Insects make up one of the largest groups of animal life.
2. This is a highly motivating activity for individuals or groups.
3. Characteristics of the more common insect **orders** and selected representatives are:
   Coleoptera—sheath wings: beetles
   Two pairs wings; outer hard covering, membranous hind wings, complete metamorphosis, biting mouthparts
   Hemiptera—half or no wings: true bugs, aphids, and scale insects.
   Three types:
   a. Forewings thickened at base, thin ends overlap
   b. Forewings thickened throughout, roof-shaped over back
   c. No wings at all
   Metamorphosis incomplete, sucking mouthparts
   Lepidoptera—scale wings: Butterflies and moths
   a. Two pairs wings—often showy—covered with scales (spicules)
   b. Complete metamorphosis, adult mouthparts sucking
   Hymenoptera—membrane wings: Bees, wasps, ants, etc.
   a. Two pairs wings, membranous wings, sometimes hooked together
   b. Metamorphosis complete, mouthparts biting, sometimes modified
   Diptera—two wings: True flies, flies, mosquitoes, midges
   a. One pair membranous wings, complete metamorphosis
   b. Mouthparts biting or sucking
   Neuroptera—nerve wings: equal numerous cross-veins: Aphis lions, mayflies. Both complete and incomplete metamorphosis, biting mouthparts
   Orthoptera—straight wings: Grasshoppers, crickets, etc.
   a. Two pairs wings, outer straight over back, somewhat thickened
   b. Hind wings for flight, folded under forewings, metamorphosis incomplete, mouthparts biting
4. Make collecting equipment:
   a. insect nets
   b. killing jar (carbon tetrachloride)
   c. spreading board
   d. mounts
   e. collecting cages
   f. display cages
   g. ant colony

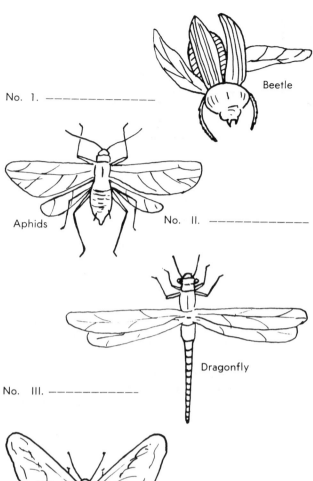

No. 1. _____ Beetle

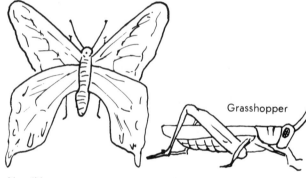

Aphids

No. II. _____

Dragonfly

No. III. _____

Grasshopper

No. IV. _____ No. V. _____

Bee

Fly

No. VI. _____ No. VII. _____

5. Some insects are harmful to people and carry diseases.
6. Some insects are helpful because they feed on plants and other animals that are harmful to people.
7. Insects develop from eggs.
8. Over 850,000 different species of insects have been named by scientists.
9. There are 25 groups of insects (orders).

F. Thought Questions:
1. What are some common insects found around our homes? our school? our community?
2. What are the main characteristics of insects?
3. Are spiders insects?
4. How do insects help us? hurt us?

G. Related Topics and Activities:
1. Younger students can describe major differences in insects.
2. Older students may make collections of insects.
3. Study metamorphosis.
4. See all Activities in this Section.

H. Vocabulary Builders—Spelling Words:
1) **beetle** 2) **aphid** 3) **dragonfly**
4) **grasshopper** 5) **butterfly** 6) (**other insects by name**)

I. Thought for Today:
"Ants and mosquitoes know in advance if it is going to rain. That's why they never miss a picnic."

Activity

A. Problem: *How Do Ants Live?*

B. Materials:
1. Twelve to fourteen ants
2. Large jar with screen
3. Loose soil
4. Water
5. Black paper
6. Small moist sponge
7. Honey or sugar
8. Magnifying glass
9. String or masking tape

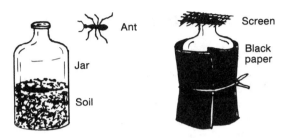

C. Procedure:
1. Fill the jar with loose soil.
2. Dampen soil lightly.
3. Leave sponge in jar (at the top).
4. Place ants and small amount of sugar in jar.
5. Cover jar with fine wire screen.
6. Tie or scotch-tape black paper around the jar. (Leave about an inch at the top of the jar without paper.)
7. Slip the black paper off for a short period each day to observe the ants at work.
8. It is necessary that ants have water daily.
9. Feed bread crumbs, meat crumbs, honey, and sugar. Caution—too much food will cause mold and odor in the colony.
10. Have students observe ants under a magnifying glass and draw a simple sketch of main body parts.

D. Results:
1. The students can see the progress ants make in building tunnels and storerooms.
2. Students will learn the major anatomical parts of ants.

E. Supplemental Information:
1. Ants work together to build homes and carry on life processes. They live in a specialized animal society, that is, some ants are workers, some royalty, and some cows.
2. Queens and males both have wings.

3. A simple ant house can be constructed out of glass. The large sides should be one foot square each and the small sides one foot high and two inches wide each. The base can be cut to size of any hard material. This ant house provides good viewing of ant tunnels. Black paper must still be used to keep ant house dark.

F. Thought Questions:
1. How do ants behave differently in their natural environment than they do in a classroom ant house?
2. What kinds of food have you seen ants carry to their natural homes?
3. Are ants strong animals? How much weight in comparison with their body weight have you seen them carry?
4. Can ants see? Have you seen two ants meet head-on?

G. Related Topics and Activities:
1. Carefully observe ants in their natural habitat.
2. Locate and describe the different kinds of ants.
3. Learn the difference between insects and spiders.
4. See all Activities in this Section.

H. Vocabulary Builders—Spelling Words:
1) **ants**   2) **aunts**   3) **screen**   4) **paper**
5) **society**

I. Thought for Today:
"We need society and we need solitude just as we need summer and winter, day and night, exercise and rest."—Philip Gilbert Hamerton

Activity

A. Problem: *How Do Bees Live?*

B. Materials:
   1. Glass bee house
   2. Dead bee
   3. Large picture of bees
   4. Books containing information about bees
   5. Magnifying glass
   6. Honeycomb (or jar of honey if honeycomb is unavailable)

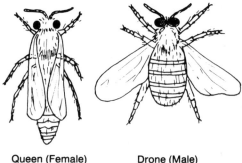

Queen (Female)   Drone (Male)

C. Procedure:
   1. Interest is stimulated by bringing to class a bee house, honeycomb or honey, and a dead bee.
   2. The class should list questions about bees and group them around broad areas such as "food," "habits," "structure," etc.
   3. The class should then attempt to find answers to their questions by observation and reading.
   4. Observe a bee under a magnifying glass.
   5. Pupils should draw a simple sketch of the main anatomical parts of a bee.

 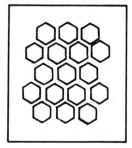

Worker   Honeycomb

D. Results:
   1. Students will learn about the community life of bees.
   2. Students will learn about the main body parts of bees.

E. Supplemental Information:
   1. Bees are insects.
   2. Life in a beehive is complex, orderly, and interesting. Each bee has its own work to do for the welfare of the entire colony.
   3. Children often confuse bees, wasps, hornets, and yellow-jackets.
   4. Precautions should be cited if live bees are investigated.
   5. There are 20,000 species of bees.
   6. Bees communicate where nectar is by "dancing maneuvers" (turning and waggling).

F. Thought Questions:
   1. How does the society of a bee compare with that of an ant?
   2. How are different flavors of honey made possible?
   3. What are the specific jobs of the specialized work of bees?

G. Related Topics and Activities:
   1. Study how beeswax is used (candles, cosmetics, pharmaceuticals, dental impressions, etc.).
   2. Discuss keeping bees with a local beekeeper.
   3. See all Activities in this Section.

H. Vocabulary Builders—Spelling Words:
   1) **queen**   2) **drone**   3) **worker**   4) **honey**
   5) **honeycomb**

I. Thought for Today:
   "Friendships multiply joys and divide griefs."—H. G. Bohn

Activity IV C 4

A. Problem: *Do Caterpillars Change to Butterflies? Do Larvae Change to Moths?*

B. Materials:
1. Live caterpillars
2. Pictures
3. Informational books
4. Live moths
5. Mounted moths and/or butterflies

C. Procedure:
1. Have a brief, general discussion about caterpillars and butterflies.
2. Have the students who are interested form a study committee.
3. The committee should find live caterpillars and plan how they will care for them.
4. As the caterpillars pass through the different stages, the members of the committee can report to the class by showing the stages and telling what they have observed.

D. Result:
The students will learn about each phase of the life cycle of a butterfly and/or a moth.

E. Supplemental Information:
1. Caterpillars eat specific types of food. If you are not sure about the food to feed the caterpillars, use the leaves or grass from where they were found.
2. Caterpillars and moths pass through four stages in their life cycles:
   a. First—eggs (adults lay them)
   b. Second—larvae (caterpillars)
   c. Third—chrysalis (pupae in cocoons)
   d. Fourth—butterflies or moths
3. The larva of the gypsy moth is one of the worst pests of man. It devours the leaves of the apple, oak, gray birch, alder, willow, and many other deciduous trees.
4. Butterflies are the most beautiful of all insects and youngsters love to collect and mount them.

F. Thought Questions:
1. How does the life cycle of a butterfly compare with the life cycles of other animals?

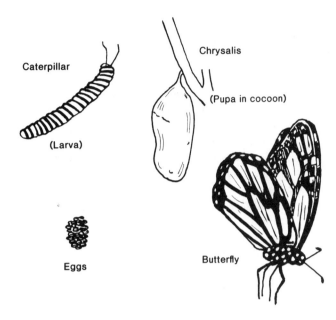

Caterpillar

(Larva)

Chrysalis

(Pupa in cocoon)

Eggs

Butterfly

2. How are the caterpillars going to be kept in class to insure their health and safety?
3. What are the differences between a moth and a butterfly?

G. Related Topics and Activities:
1. Study the differences between moths and butterflies.
   a. Butterflies have thin bodies; moths are fat.
   b. Butterflies fly during the day; moths fly at night.
   c. Butterflies' antennae are knobby; moths' antennae are feathery.
   d. Both migrate; some, long distances.
   e. We get silk from a silkworm moth's cocoon.
2. It is fun to search for these creatures.
3. Make a collection of them. They are beautiful.
4. See Activity IV-C-5, "Collecting Insects."

H. Vocabulary Builders—Spelling Words:
1) **eggs**   2) **larva**   3) **chrysalis**
4) **butterfly**   5) **moth**

I. Thought for Today:
"To know what is right and not do it is the worst form of cowardice."

Activity IV\,C\,5

A. Problem: *How Can We Preserve Insects or Make a Butterfly Collection?*

B. Materials:

1. Insects collected on a field trip
2. Insect pins (size 2 or 3) (or common pins)
3. Forceps
4. Cardboard insect boxes
   (See Activity III-F-4 on constructing Riker-type mounts.)
5. Glue
6. White card
7. Fine point pen
8. Spreading board, sheet of cork, or cardboard
9. Relaxing jar
10. Formalin (or fingernail polish remover which contains acetone)

C. Procedure:

1. Insects must be mounted with insect or common pins.
2. Place older specimens in a relaxing jar, a widemouthed jar with wet sand on the bottom. Add to this a few drops of formalin or acetone. Place the insects in the jar on the sand, and close the jar tightly. A small dish with sand may be substituted. The specimens will be soft enough to handle in a few days.
3. Hold the specimen between the fingers of one hand while putting the pin in vertically with the other hand. Push the specimen up toward the head of the pin three-eights of an inch for grasping the pin with the fingers. Use forceps for pushing the insects upon the pin.
4. Put the pin through the center of the stoutest part of the body, but never through a joint that lies between two parts of the insect.
5. Beetles must be pinned through on one of the hard shell wings, just to the right of the midline down through where the two wings meet on the body.
6. True bugs will need to be pinned through the small, triangular piece that is attached to the hind end of the thorax.
7. Keep specimen in most natural position. Place those with slender abdomens low on the pin. Spread out legs and antennae and let dry, then push to proper place on the pin.
8. Some insects should have wings spread in mounting. To save space, sometimes the wings on one side are spread to save room in the

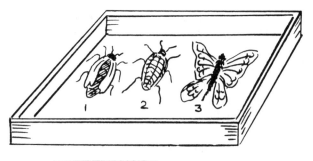

1	Bee
2	Beetle
3	Butterfly

insect box. A spreading board is best to use, but a sheet of cork can also be used.

9. Insects too small to pin are best glued to the tips of small cardboard points. Use a card as thick as a library bureau card. Cut it into strips about ⅜″ in width. Then make crosscuts across the strip at slight angles to make slender triangular points ⅜″ long and about ⅛″ wide at the base. These points can be made more quickly with a punch secured from an entomological supply house.
10. Now lay out the small insects on a clean sheet of paper so they rest on their right sides with their wings extending to your left, and with their heads toward you. Any other position will make it more difficult to examine the mounted specimen.
11. Put glue on the paper and pick up a cardboard point with the forceps, touch its smaller tip to the glue, and touch the point to the uppermost side of the insect. The insect will be fastened to the point with the right side up and its head away from you, when it is turned over. Put pin through the base of triangular point, letting the specimen extend to the left of the pin.
12. When labeling the specimen put a number on every insect pin. Make a label as small as it can possibly be made and still contain as much data as possible. Too many insect collections contain more paper labels than insects. Try making the labels as small as ½″ × ⁵⁄₁₆″.
13. Each specimen should be labeled with the locality, town and state, date, month, day, and year, (written 3.9.91 rather than March 9, 1991) and name of the collector. Add any other information you can as to the sort of place in which the insect was found, what it was doing, etc.

14. Specimens must be preserved in an airtight box (called a Schmitt box) if you hope to keep certain small beetles called museum pests from getting in and eating them up. You may want to keep a few specimens in a cigar box or some other similar container, but you will surely be disappointed if you try to keep them for any length of time. If the school has Schmitt boxes for its collection, they will probably appreciate any gifts you care to make to them, and the classes for years to come will profit from your skill and care in mounting these specimens.

15. Add moth balls or flakes for best preservation.

D. Result:

Students will learn common and scientific names of insects and proper collecting and mounting techniques.

E. Supplemental Information:

If these steps are used for mounting and preserving these specimens which have been collected, you will have a collection which you will be proud of and may keep safely for years to come.

F. Thought Questions:

1. Where would be the best locations to look for insects?
2. Is there a best time of day or season to try to collect insects?
3. What materials are needed to catch insects?

G. Related Topics and Activities:

1. Children love to collect things and these make beautiful collections.
2. See especially Activities IV-C-4, "Metamorphosis" and IV-C-5, "Collecting Insects."
3. See other Activities in this Section.

H. Vocabulary Builders—Spelling Words:

1) **preserve**   2) **forceps**   3) **spreading board**
4) **relaxing jar**   5) **abdomen**   6) **thorax**

I. Thought for Today:

"The butterfly counts not months but moments and has time enough."

Section D: Reptiles

Activity

A. Problem: *What Are Some Unusual Characteristics of Snakes?*

B. Materials:
1. Pictures of snakes (king, gopher, garter, bull, coral, and rattle)
2. Plaster specimens may be borrowed from local museums, colleges, or universities
3. Pamphlets, books, and other literature about snakes

C. Procedure:
1. Gather materials and data on snakes from the United States Department of Agriculture.
2. Post pictures on the bulletin board to arouse interest and discussion. Invariably the discussion will lead to poisonous snakes and common misconceptions concerning snakes.
3. Guide the discussion and if possible, ask for volunteers to do some research and present their findings to the class.

D. Result:
Better understanding of snakes helps to correct misconceptions; results in less fear of snakes, and helps to protect useful snakes.

E. Supplemental Information:
There are many more harmless than harmful snakes. Many snakes are helpful to people and should be protected. Most snakes, including poisonous ones, are timid and flee from people if they can. They are not as cunning as many people believe.
1. Characteristics of common snakes:
   a. Of the 136 species of recognized snakes in North America only about 4 species are poisonous. They are: rattlesnakes, coral snakes, copperheads, and water moccasins.
   b. Many of the harmless snakes are helpful to society and should be protected.
      1) Gopher and bull snakes eat mice, rats, and gophers, helping the farmers.
      2) Black snakes eat moles, frogs, and grasshoppers.

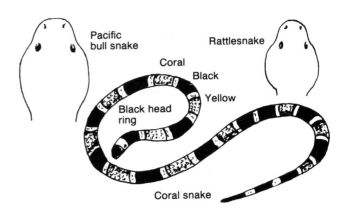

3) King snakes eat rodents and kill rattlesnakes.
4) Worm, ring-necked, and green snakes eat insects.
5) Whip, racers, pilot, and indigo snakes eat rodents and birds.
6) Garter, water, and hog-nosed snakes eat harmful birds and amphibians.
   c. Rattlesnakes (pit-viper family) can be recognized by the rattles on their tails and their triangular-shaped heads.
   d. The coral snake is about 15 inches long and has black rings that are bordered on each side by yellow ones; it has a black-tipped head.
   e. A snake's tongue is used primarily for smelling. It contains no poison.
   f. At most, a snake strikes about half its length.
2. First aid measures to take in case of snakebites:
   a. Call a doctor.
   b. Tie a tourniquet around the limb above the bite.
   c. Cut an X across the bite to help the bleeding and let the venom out.

F. Thought Questions:
1. What are some common characteristics of all snakes?
2. What are some common superstitions about snakes which are untrue?
3. What snake is most numerous in your locality?

G. Related Topics and Activities:
1. Compare snakes with other reptiles.
2. See all Activities in this Section.
3. See Activity IV-D-2, "Terraria for Reptiles."

H. Vocabulary Builders—Spelling Words:
1) **rattlesnakes**   2) **coral**   3) **poisonous**
4) **harmless**   5) **harmful**

I. Thought for Today:
"Silence is one of the hardest arguments to refute."

Activity

A. Problem: *How Do We Make a Terrarium for Reptiles?*

B. Materials:
1. Large glass box for terrarium
2. Plate glass cover
3. Masking tape
4. Sand
5. Small, dry twigs, rocks
6. Material for a hiding place
7. Shallow dish or saucer
8. Reptiles
9. Electric light (small, 25-watt bulb for heating)

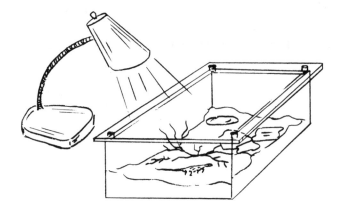

C. Procedure:
1. Fill the bottom of glass box with two inches of sand.
2. Place saucer inside.
3. Add twigs, rocks.
4. Design a place for reptile(s) to hide.
5. Add water to saucer.
6. Tape corners to raise corner height so that when glass cover is placed on top air will be able to pass under cover to reptile(s).
7. Put cover in place.
8. Put reptile(s) in terrarium.
9. Feed the reptiles with worms, live insects, and earthworms.
10. Place light over cover to maintain warm temperature.

D. Result:

Class will learn about reptiles and their care.

E. Supplemental Information:
1. Do not use poisonous varieties for classroom.
2. The best temperature for a terrarium is about 80° F.
3. Ants and flies are good food for lizards.
4. Feed them live food once a week.
5. Reptiles love to eat soft-bodied insects.

F. Thought Questions:
1. Are reptiles helpful to people?
2. What are some distinct characteristics of reptiles?
3. How do snakes shed their skin?

G. Related Topics and Activities:
1. Discuss with students their experiences with snakes.
2. Discuss with students their experiences with other reptiles.
3. Visit a zoo and look for reptiles.
4. See all Activities in this Section.

H. Vocabulary Builders—Spelling Words:
1) **terrarium** 2) **masking** 3) **twig**
4) **reptile** 5) **saucer**

I. Thought for Today:

"If you wouldn't write it and sign it, don't say it."

Section E: Water Animals (Fishes and Frogs)

Activity IV E 1

A. Problem: *How Do We Care for a Freshwater Aquarium?*

B. Materials:
1. Glass tank and cover
2. Sand
3. Plants, water
4. Paper
5. Sprinkling can
6. Fish (inexpensive tropical fish are good to start)
7. Snails
8. Air pump
9. Thermometer, water

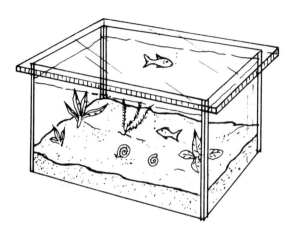

C. Procedure:
1. Wash glass tank thoroughly. A tank with a rectangular metal frame and a slate or glass bottom is most satisfactory. It is less likely to break than an all-glass tank without a frame, is easily repaired when broken, provides a large surface area for oxygen absorption, and offers an undistorted view of the fish. A tank 10″ × 10″ × 16″ or more is advisable, as it is difficult to keep a smaller tank in good condition. Globes or goldfish bowls prevent adequate observation of the occupants and do not provide enough surface on the bottom for the plant growth or the sand that is needed.
2. Wash sand till water is clear. Coarse sand is best for the aquarium.
3. Place a two-inch layer of sand at the bottom of the aquarium. Large pebbles and rocks, as well as ornamental castles, seashells, and the like should never be placed in the aquarium. Uneaten food settles and decays under them, polluting the water. Living fish are sufficient ornaments.
4. If the tank is not already in its permanent position, place it there now. (Moving the aquarium after it is filled with water may cause a leak.) The tank should be placed in a position that ensures a liberal supply of diffused light. An ideal position is one with an exposure of one to two hours of direct sunlight daily. This will result in the active process of photosynthesis, in which the plants use the carbon dioxide given off by the fish and release oxygen needed by the fish.

   Too much light encourages growth of algae and weeds which crowd out cultivated plants. If kept in a window, the tank should have a dark paper pasted on the outer side to prevent the growth of algae on the glass.
5. The tank should not be placed near a radiator because a high temperature is injurious to most fish. Cold-water fish, including goldfish, thrive at temperatures from 59° to 65° F. Tropical fish require temperatures of 70° to 80° F.
6. Pour water from a sprinkling can into the tank, taking care to disturb the sand as little as possible. The slow pouring of water from a sprinkling can allows it to become aerated.
7. Disinfect plants by putting them in a salt solution (four ounces of salt to the gallon) for one minute, then washing them in freshwater. All plants, native or purchased, should be disinfected.
8. Put plants in sand. When the roots are long, they should be pruned. Roots should be spread and well covered with sand.

   Plants should not be scattered over the whole aquarium but should be placed so as to leave an open space in which the fish can swim freely. Plants of like species are best grouped together. A planting plan of the bottom of the aquarium can be made on paper before the actual planting. Floating plants may be added later if desired. They are sometimes not recommended because they shut out light. Several kinds of plants are valuable as oxygenators. Sagittaria, Vallisneria, Elodea, Anacharis, Ludwigia, Myriophyllum, and Cabomba are all suitable and ornamental and may be rooted in the sand. It is often possible to obtain native plants entirely suitable for the aquarium. These should be thoroughly washed to prevent disease. Search in ponds and streams where minnows and other life are found and hunt for the small green plants under the water. Discover by investigation what plant life is at hand that will keep water pure, for the ponds grow their own aerating plants.

In the newly planted aquarium, algae may develop and freshwater may become cloudy. Even if cloudiness is considerable, the water should not be changed unless blue-green algae cover plants, sand, and windows with a dark slimy coat. Normally, blue-green algae will not disturb the aquarium. Soon the cloudiness disappears and an attractive light brown color replaces the crystal clear water of the newly planted aquarium.

When tap water is used, the tank should be allowed to stand at least 24 hours before putting in the animals. This allows the water to clear and become thoroughly oxygenated, the plants to take root, and any unwanted gases to dissipate. An air pump should be attached and utilized to continue proper oxygenation of aquarium.

9. After this time place fish and snails in the aquarium. The water in the aquarium should be approximately the same temperature as that from which the fish are taken. The fish should not be touched with the hands or dropped into the water, as this may injure their scales and lead to development of a fungus disease. They should be allowed to swim out of the container into the tank. A dip net may be used to transfer the fish from one container to another. Care must be taken that the size and species of the fish are such that the larger ones do not eat the smaller ones!

Freshwater snails are, for all purposes, the best scavengers. A snail to every gallon of water is recommended. Native species are usually preferred. They can be gathered from streams or ponds or bought. Certain small fish such as the "weather fish" and catfish are valuable in preventing food from settling to the bottom.

10. Feed fish sparingly. It is well to remember that prepared fish food is highly concentrated. Fish should be given only what they can eat within 15 minutes. If food remains at the bottom, too much has been given. Uneaten food should be removed.

Feedings should be regular. Twice a week is usually sufficient in cold weather—three times a week in warm seasons.

Prepared food can be obtained at aquarium supply stores, pet stores, and grocery stores. This may be supplemented by occasional fresh foods such as scrapings of raw beef and chopped lettuce. Live food such as Artemia is also satisfactory.

11. Remove immediately any fish showing signs of illness. Overfeeding, insufficient oxygen, and sudden changes in temperature are the chief causes of sickness among fish. Congested reddish fins, white fungus on the body, or wobbly body movement are signs of illness.

Treatment with saltwater has been found best for general use. For a weak bath, one teaspoonful salt to a gallon of water is recommended. For a strong bath, use one tablespoon salt to a gallon of water. A sick fish should be left in the weak bath for 24 hours. This treatment is continued with a new solution until the fish becomes healthy. The fish are left in the strong solution for only 15 to 20 minutes at a time. Saltwater treatment is not effective in all types of illness. Consult an aquarium book.

Gaping of fish at the top of the water may be due to an excess of carbon dioxide in the water or a lack of oxygen. If the water is oversaturated or undersaturated with oxygen, the excess or lack is quickly adjusted by exposure with the air above the water. However, since carbon dioxide passes from water to air and air to water very slowly, it takes much longer for an excess of carbon dioxide to pass off. It has been found that fish cannot take in oxygen at the gills if too much carbon dioxide is in the water. For this reason, fish can suffocate even when plenty of oxygen is present. Plants use carbon dioxide when actively engaged in photosynthesis and make the aquarium more habitable by reducing the amount of carbon dioxide in the water.

12. After fish have been placed in the aquarium, cover the aquarium with glass in order to prevent evaporation and the collecting of dust.

D. Result:

The aquarium will continue to provide material for discussion and research into the coexistence of various kinds of life and also what is required to support life in various circumstances.

E. Supplemental Information:

The experience of making an aquarium and caring for live animals in the classroom is both interesting and educational. The types of tank, sand, animals, and plants selected all are factors to be considered. Aging and proper temperature of the water, and the daily care and observation of the animals and plants are also important items. The students become aware of the interrelationship between plants and animals. The oxygen needed by the animals is provided by plants and the carbon dioxide needed by the plants is provided by animals. When the oxygen-carbon dioxide relationship is well-balanced, it is unnecessary to change the water in the aquarium. If a glass aquarium isn't available, a plastic box can be utilized.

F. Thought Questions:

1. What are the little dots that form on the sides of the aquarium that look as if they were covered with thin cellophane?
2. Which type of green plants survive best?
3. What are the advantages of bushy type plants?

G. Related Topics and Activities:

1. Construct and stock a saltwater aquarium. (Find specific directions. Saltwater fish are more varied and more beautiful.)
2. Raise guppies. They are easy to raise and quite prolific.
3. See all Activities in this Section.

H. Vocabulary Builders—Spelling Words:

1) **aquarium**   2) **sprinkling**   3) **snails**
4) **coarse**   5) **decay**   6) **algae**

I. Thought for Today:

"This would be a fine world if people showed as much patience as they do when waiting for fish to bite."

Activity

A. Problem: *Do Tadpoles Become Frogs?*

B. Materials:
1. Frog in jar or terrarium
2. Tadpoles in class aquarium
3. Sketches of different stages of development on chalkboard
4. Books with pictures of frog's development
5. Literature (booklets, pamphlets, etc.)

C. Procedure:
1. Let children observe tadpoles and frogs in science corner.
2. Have students read literature about frogs.
3. Have a question and answer period and pose such questions as:
   a. How far can a frog jump?
      Answer—20 times its own length.
   b. How many kinds of frogs are there?
      Answer—1,700 different species
   c. How long do they live?
      Answer—Many live as long as 30 years.
   d. What are the differences between frogs and toads?
      Answer—There are few visible differences, but the main ones are:
      Frogs:
         Skin: Soft, moist, smooth.
         Teeth: Small.
         Movement: Fast.
         Habitat: Mostly in water.
      Toads:
         Skin: Tough, dry with bumps (bumps give off a secretion which is harmful to animals). Toad skin has been used as a substitute for leather.
         Teeth: None.
         Habitat: On land and water.
4. Ask students if they would like to study what happens to fishlike tadpoles.
5. Have students observe the changes that occur in the tadpoles.
6. As a culmination, the teacher and pupils might cooperate in the making of a chart entitled:
   Frogs Are Valuable:
   a. They eat insects.
   b. Used by scientists in laboratories—their bodies work like ours do.

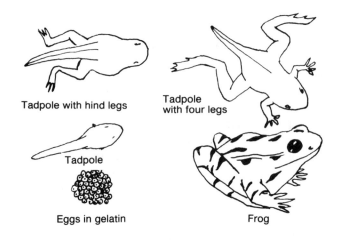

Tadpole with hind legs

Tadpole with four legs

Tadpole

Eggs in gelatin

Frog

D. Results:
1. Children gain firsthand experience observing the various phases of metamorphosis.
2. Children learn the characteristics of frogs and toads.

E. Supplemental Information:
1. Frogs are amphibians. They breathe through their skin under water. Frogs and tadpoles are within the experiences of many students. They can be observed as they develop in the classroom; they make interesting specimens for learning. When the aquarium is first set up, let the water stand for twenty-four hours before placing tadpoles in it. If aquarium is kept in the classroom, be sure to change water frequently or the tadpoles will die. They can be fed fish food, lettuce, and bits of hardboiled eggs. Frogs should be fed worms, mealworms, and flies. If the students want to keep a frog at home, they should dig a deep hole in the backyard in which is placed a large basin. Frogs should be fed live insects. All eggs are not fertile and those which are not, die. Tadpoles sometimes eat each other.
2. The best time to collect the eggs and tadpoles of frogs and toads is during the early summer. Eggs can be found floating on or near the surface of water among plants, particularly in shallow ponds and marshy places close to shore. Toads' eggs look like strings of jelly attached to plants, whereas frogs' eggs look like a mass of jelly. To collect them it is best to use a pail, wide-mouth jar, or even nets to scoop them up.

Add water plants that have been found nearby. Tadpoles look like those in the sketch and can best be collected in nets and put in large glass containers.

F. Thought Questions:

1. How do scientists classify (group) animals?
2. Where would frogs and tadpoles be placed?
3. How many animals do you know that live in and around the water?

G. Related Topics and Activities:

1. Have students draw pictures of the different stages of the metamorphosis of frogs.

2. Study the differences between frogs and toads.
3. Visit a pond or lake.
4. See all Activities in this Section.

H. Vocabulary Builders—Spelling Words:

1) **eggs**   2) **gelatin**   3) **tadpoles**   4) **frogs**
5) **toads**

I. Thought for Today:

"When you are in deep water, it's a good idea to keep your mouth shut."

Section F: Birds

Activity IV F 1

A. Problem: *How Do Birds Differ from Other Animals?*

B. Materials:
1. Pictures of various birds
2. Chart paper to list the characteristics of birds
3. Bird books
4. Stuffed birds if available

C. Procedure:
1. Place pictures of birds around the room. Have the bird books on the library table. If stuffed birds are obtainable, display them also.
2. When a question arises, guide the discussion so that the students will want to find out more about birds.
3. Have students study pictures, books, and specimens.
4. After the study period, list the characteristics of birds on chalkboard as students state them.
5. Have students notice that birds have feathers, wings, and beaks; lay eggs; have no teeth, etc.
6. The students should make a chart with the data they have discussed.

D. Result:
The students will learn some of the general characteristics of birds.

E. Supplemental Information:
1. Birds are warm-blooded animals. They have special characteristics which adapt them for food searching, protection, and flight.
2. There are many good bird feeders and birdbaths which the students might want to build.

F. Thought Questions:
1. How do the bones of birds differ from the bones of other land animals?

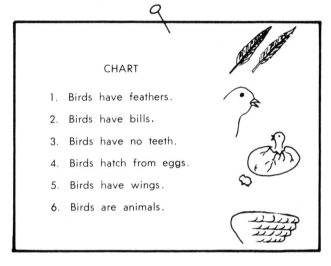

CHART
1. Birds have feathers.
2. Birds have bills.
3. Birds have no teeth.
4. Birds hatch from eggs.
5. Birds have wings.
6. Birds are animals.

2. Do birds need much energy for flight? How do they adjust to their energy requirements?
3. How are the wings of birds similar to the wings of airplanes? how different?
4. Are some birds threatened with extinction?
5. What is the biggest bird? the smallest?
6. Do farmers raise birds?

G. Related Topics and Activities:
1. Study game birds (birds that are hunted).
2. Visit a zoo or aviary to learn about exotic birds.
3. See all Activities in this Section.

H. Vocabulary Builders—Spelling Words:
1) **feathers**   2) **wings**   3) **beaks**   4) **eggs**
5) **teeth**

I. Thought for Today:
"You can't be a night owl and an early bird."

Activity

A. Problem: *How Do We Classify Common Birds?*

B. Materials:
1. Notebook
2. Pencil
3. Bird identification book

C. Procedure:
Take bird study trip and write identification information as follows:

1. *Coloration:* Striking colors or lack of them; contrasting color areas; spots at tip of tail, bars on wings or tail, or both, flashed in flight; rumppatch.
2. *Habitat* or place where bird is found.
3. *Outline and Movements:* Motionless: proportions of entire silhouette; of bill and shoulders; of tail to body; of head to body. Hopping or running: carriage of feet; frequency of changing pose of body; various mannerisms; such as twitching of wings and dipping of tail in flight; soaring; gliding; undulating; buzzing; whirring; "set" of wings.
4. *Notes:* Song of the male—various call notes of both adults; food calls of the young.

Field study will teach pupils to observe:

1. Beak	8. Bell
2. Throat	9. Breast
3. Nape	10. Tail
4. Crown	11. Wings
5. Eye color	12. Legs
6. Back	13. Feet
7. Rump	

Suggested chart for recording observations:

Name ....
Date ....Locality .... Length of bird ....

Beak:
Color .... Length................ Slender, wide or hooked................

Color:
Most striking .... Crown ....
Nape .... Back .... Rump..............
Throat .... Breast........................ Belly...............
Eye streak .... Eye color.......................

Tail:
Long or short.............. Square at end, V-shaped.........
Pointed .... General color ....
Crossbars or bands; marked by spots..........................
Color(s) ....

Wings:
Long, narrow; wing bars: none, one, or two.................
Color .... Outer primaries.....................

Legs:
Very long........ long......... medium .... short.........
Color...................

Feet:
Webbed ....Clawed.........Color .... Length ....

D. Result:
Students will learn to organize procedures for studying any kind of animal.

E. Supplemental Information:
1. Some birds fly straight, others dart about, others constantly sail or soar.
2. Nesting habits of birds are all designed to take advantage of protecting the eggs while hatching and also to protect the young after they are hatched.
3. Singing habits or the sounds which birds make have special significance in mating and in communication with other birds.

F. Thought Questions:
1. What are some behaviors of birds that are harmful to people?
2. How do birds help us?
3. What do birds eat?

G. Related Topics and Activities:
1. Make bird feeder. If you keep it stocked, you will see many different kinds of birds.
2. Take a field trip to a nearby wooded area and look for birds.
3. See all Activities in this Section.

H. Vocabulary Builders—Spelling Words:
1) **feathers**   2) **bills**   3) **wings**
4) **beaks**   5) **talon**

I. Thought for Today:
"Even the woodpecker owes its success to the fact that it uses its head and keeps pecking away until it finishes the job it starts."

Activity

A. Problem: *How Can We Hatch Chicken Eggs?*

B. Materials:
1. Fresh eggs (one for every four students)
2. Six to ten fertilized eggs
3. Chicken incubator
4. Saucers
5. Thermometer
6. Pencil and/or crayons
7. Paper
8. Calendar
9. Slide projector
10. Books, pamphlets on egg-hatching
11. Light or thermostat

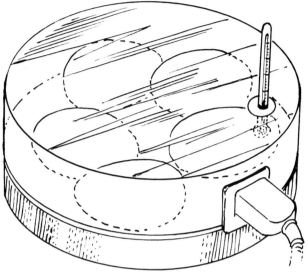

C. Procedure:
1. Study what embryos need for full development (food, water, air, and protection).
2. Have students break one egg per group of four students and examine it for its main parts (shell, yolk, albumen, air sac).
3. Study the function of each part:
   a. shell—protection
   b. yolk—food
   c. albumen—water
   d. air sac—air
4. Discuss what an egg must have from its environment in order to hatch. Discuss how these needs are met using an incubator.

Needs:	*How met in incubator:*
a. moisture	—pan of water
b. warmth	—light (temperature should be 100° F.)
c. protection	—container
d. rotation	—people (students)

5. Place fertilized eggs in incubator.
6. Place small pan of water inside incubator to keep eggs moist.
7. Mark eggs lightly with pencil or crayons so that when eggs are rotated daily, positions will be noted.
8. Turn the incubator on.
9. Regulate temperature to about 100° F. (38° C.).
10. Rotate eggs daily about one-third the way around.
11. Check temperature and moisture daily.
12. Between the 7th and 10th days, eggs can be "candled." (Candling is observing the inside of

eggs with the aid of a strong light.) Use the slide projector for the strong light.
13. Study eggs.
14. Draw sketches of observations.
15. Between the 17th and 20th days, eggs should be candled again.
16. Study the eggs.
17. Draw sketches of observations. Check books and pamphlets for corroborating evidence.
18. Around the 21st day, the eggs will hatch at various intervals of time.
19. The chicks will peck their way through the egg shells.

D. Results:
1. Students will learn the parts of an egg.
2. Students will learn the functions of the various parts of an egg.
3. Students will learn that many life forms develop from eggs.

E. Supplemental Information:

This is one of the most exciting activities in which students can become involved. Teachers can compare hen eggs to other animal eggs. The motivation from this activity will carry over to many related activities in science and other disciplines.

F. Thought Questions:

1. Are all eggs fertilized?
2. Do all eggs have the same incubation period?
3. Do all animals produce eggs?

G. Related Topics and Activities:

1. Compare chickens with other animals that hatch from eggs.
2. See Section IV-D, "Reptiles."
3. See all Activities in this Section.

H. Vocabulary Builders—Spelling Words:

1) **incubator**   2) **fertilized**   3) **thermostat**
4) **candling**   5) **moisture**

I. Thought for Today:

"A scientist recently crossed a carrier pigeon with a woodpecker. The bird not only carries messages, but also knocks on the door."

Section G: Mammals

Activity   IV G 1

A. **Problem:** *How Do Mammals Differ from Other Animals?*

B. Materials:
1. Pictures of many mammals
2. Books on mammals
3. Filmstrips or motion pictures about mammals

C. Procedure:
1. Review Activity IV-A-2, "How Animals Are Classified."
2. Discuss mammals. Mammals are members of the phylum Chordota (animals with backbones).
3. Discuss the common characteristics of mammals such as:
   a. backbones
   b. large brains
   c. warm-blooded
   d. born alive (few rare exceptions are born from eggs)
   e. suckle milk from milk glands
   f. body hair
4. Discuss various animals that fall into this classification such as:
   a. platypus
   b. anteater
   c. wallaby
   d. shrew
   e. lemur
   f. bat
   g. sloth
   h. gorilla
   i. jack rabbit
   j. whale
   k. walrus
   l. aardvark
   m. elephant
   n. wart hog
   o. tiger
   p. man
5. View filmstrip and movies that are accessible regarding mammals.

6. Discuss the fact that some mammals are meat eaters while others are primarily vegetarians. (Meat eaters must be strong, swift, and smart.) (Vegetarians spend a lot of time searching for leaves, twigs, and tender plant shoots.)
7. Discuss the wide habitats of mammals: equator to poles, land to water, high to low elevations, etc.
8. If possible plan a trip to the zoo.

D. Result:
Students will learn about mammals and that man is in this animal classification.

E. Supplemental Information:
There are many sources of information that can be obtained from a variety of resources such as:
1. pet stores
2. veterinarians
3. medical workers
4. psychologists
5. zoo keepers
6. farmers
7. feed stores
8. travel agencies, etc.

F. Thought Questions:
1. How do mammals differ from other animals?
2. How are mammals similar to other animals?
3. What mammals are very important to man? Why?
4. Is the bat a mammal? (Yes!!)

G. Related Topics and Activities:
1. Compare mammals with other members of the phylum Chordota.
2. Have each student research or report on one particular species in this phylum.
3. See all Activities in this Section.

H. Vocabulary Builders—Spelling Words:
Use the animals listed in Procedure.

I. Thought for Today:
"Frustration is not having anyone else to blame but yourself."

Activity

A. Problem: *What Are Some Common Jungle, Farm, and Sea Mammals?*

B. Materials:
1. Pictures of animals in these classifications
2. Filmstrips or motion pictures of these animals
3. Books, pamphlets about these animals

C. Procedure:
1. Review Activity IV-G-1, "How Do Mammals Differ from Other Animals?"
2. Organize three groups of students.
3. Have each group make a thorough study of one of the three groups cited in the problem.
4. Other areas could be included or substituted such as mountain, prairie, or desert.
5. The jungle group could study lions, tigers, elephants, zebras, rhinoceroses, hippopotamuses, leopards, etc.
6. The farm group could study horses, cows, pigs, hogs, goats, sheep, rabbits, etc.
7. The sea group could study whales, porpoises, dolphins, narwhals, and grampuses.
8. Show filmstrips and motion pictures concerning these animals.

D. Results:
1. Students will learn that mammals within a certain environment have common characteristics which are necessary for their survival.
2. Students can begin to realize the bases of animal classification.

E. Supplemental Information:
1. The age, maturity, and interests of the students will determine the depth of study of this activity.
2. Studies of mammals lead up to a study of human beings.

F. Thought Questions:
1. What are some of the environmental factors that determine where certain groups of mammals live?
2. Which area studied has the greatest number of mammals?
3. Which mammal out of each group would you rather be? Why?

Animals   205

G. Related Topics and Activities:
1. Study the ecological factors of each species.
2. Make predictions on the future of each species.
3. See all Activities in this Section.

H. Vocabulary Builders—Spelling Words:
1) **mountain**   2) **prairie**   3) **desert**
4) **jungle**   5) **farm**

I. Thought for Today:
"The wishbone will never replace the backbone."

A. Problem: *Are Human Beings Mammals?*

B. Materials:
1. Pictures of many mammals
2. Pictures of man in many activities
3. Books, pamphlets about mammals

C. Procedure:
1. Review Activities on "How are Animals Classified?" IV-A-2 and "How Do Mammals Differ from Other Animals?" IV-G-1.
2. Discuss the main characteristics of mammals:
    a. backbones
    b. large brains
    c. warm-blooded
    d. born alive (few hatch from eggs)
    e. suckle milk from milk glands
    f. body hair
    g. breathe with lungs
    h. seven neck bones
3. Compare these characteristics of humans with other mammals.

D. Result:
Students will learn that humans are part of the animal kingdom and are mammals.

E. Supplementary Information:
1. One of the shocking experiences of most children is the realization that they are animals.
2. The teacher can explain that humans are the highest order of animals in that they have three major biological characteristics that set them apart from other animals and they are:
    a. Complex brain (complex reasoning power, creative, problem-solver). For example, humans have created many "new foods" and "new tools."
    b. Prehensile hand (enables humans to be tool-using) (opposable thumb). This has enabled humans to communicate through writing and sign language.
    c. Well-developed voice box (gives humans the power to utter many sounds and consequently complex communication).
3. Mammals are a Class in animal classification. They have mammary glands.
4. Humans are omnivores because we eat meats and plants. We eat seeds (parts of plants) such as corn, wheat, rice, oats, barley, and rye.
5. Humans live everywhere on our planet. There are no races of humans, just ethnic differences.

6. The fact that people can and sometimes do interbreed proves that we are all members of one race—the Human Race.
7. Humans have the longest period of infant care of any mammal.
8. Humans need food and shelter too.
9. Humans are affected by the pranks of nature the same as any other animal: droughts, floods, severe weather, etc.
10. Fertilization takes place within the body as with other mammals. The fertilized egg develops into an embryo.

F. Thought Questions:
1. What mammals are people most like?
2. Do other mammals ever kill their own kind?
3. Which has the greatest effect on humans, biological inheritance or cultural environment?

G. Related Topics and Activities:
1. Discuss how humans cope with varied environments: swimming, flying, space travel, etc.
2. See especially Section V-C, "Nutrition."
3. See all Activities in this Section.

H. Vocabulary Builders—Spelling Words:
1) **mammal**   2) **backbone**   3) **creative**
4) **prehensile**   5) **complex**   6) **mammary**

I. Thought for Today:
"Humans are the only animal that can be skinned more than once."

Section H: Storages

Activity

A. Problem: *How Do We Build a Small Simple Cage?*

B. Materials:
   1. Screen 3" × 3"
   2. Wide-mouth jar and open lid
   3. Caterpillar or other insect
   4. A little soil, leaves, and small twigs

C. Procedure:
   1. Cut screen to fit jar lid; it replaces center of lid.
   2. Place soil, leaves, twigs, and insect inside of jar and replace screen lid. Fasten securely.

D. Result:

A small, simple cage is made.

E. Supplemental Information:
   1. Children have opportunity to participate in making cage and caring for insects. They can also watch various developmental changes which can be used as the basis for classroom discussions.
   2. This type of cage is easily kept clean and is adapted to different insects. The all-around view gives children a clear observation of the insect. This cage is very easy to make, and the size of the jar can be varied according to the need.

F. Thought Questions:
   1. What other small animals might be kept in such a cage?

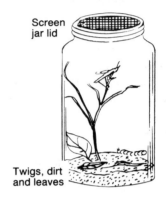

Screen jar lid

Twigs, dirt and leaves

   2. What are some precautions that must be taken in order to keep the animals alive?
   3. Could we test which foods these animals prefer to eat?

G. Related Topics and Activities:
   1. See Activity IV-C-1, "Insect Study."
   2. See Activity IV-A-2, "Animal Classification."
   3. See Activity IV-H-2, "Wire Cage."
   4. See all Activities in this Section.

H. Vocabulary Builders—Spelling Words:
   1) **cage**   2) **container**   3) **wide-mouth**
   4) **caterpillar**   5) **insect**

I. Thought for Today:
   "Have you noticed that even the busiest people are never too busy to take time to tell you how busy they are."

Activity

A. Problem: *How Do We Make a Wire Cage for Small Animals?*

B. Materials:

1. Pie plates, oatmeal box with cover, or cut out coffee can with lid
2. Wire screen, fine mesh, to fit inside base of cage, about 6 inches high
3. Plaster of Paris
4. Branch and leaves from shrubbery where animal was found
5. Wire cutters
6. Masking or cellophane tape
7. Heavy cardboard or leather hinge for top

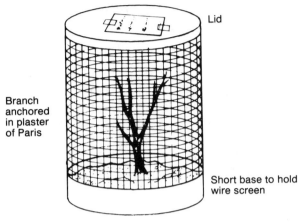

Lid

Branch anchored in plaster of Paris

Short base to hold wire screen

C. Procedure:

1. Pull one piece of wire from the screen to use as a lace.
2. Shape screen into circle to fit the plate or can.
3. Wind wire ends to edge of inner screen to outer screen to secure screen in fixed position.
4. Mix plaster of Paris and put in bottom of can.
5. Place branch in the desired position and let plaster dry.
6. Cover the plaster with leaves and the cage is completed.
7. The lid placed on top of the screen keeps the animal(s) inside the cage.

D. Result:

A small wire cage is made.

E. Supplemental Information:

1. This is an easy method by which the students can build an inexpensive cage. It will be useful in their observations of small animals because it is easy to view. It is exceptionally fine for caterpillars. Measure the circumference of the can before cutting the screen so that it will not overlap more than 1″. Any kind of a can with a lid will do for the bottom and the top of the cage.

2. Every cage should be provided with a shelter area into which the animal(s) can retire to sleep or to hide when excited or fearful. Warm and safe shelters should be provided for female animals that are expecting young.

F. Thought Questions:

1. What kind of animals can best be kept in such a cage?
2. What precautions should be taken to keep them alive?
3. What are some "natural" enemies of the animal(s) that you have collected?

G. Related Topics and Activities:

1. See Section IV-A, "Animal Classification."
2. See Section IV-B, "Pets."
3. Study care and feeding of animals to be collected.
4. See all Activities in this Section.

H. Vocabulary Builders—Spelling Words:

1) **wire**   2) **cage**   3) **screen**
4) **plaster**   5) **twig**

I. Thought for Today:

"Oddly enough, it's the person who knows everything who has the most to learn."

Activity

A. Problem: *How Can We Make a Cage for Medium-sized Animals?*

B. Materials:
1. Galvanized screen (about 1″ or 2″ mesh)
   a. 2 pieces 30″ × 26″—(sides)
   b. 2 pieces 20″ × 26″—(ends)
   c. 1 piece 21″ × 31″—(top)
2. Wire-cutter pliers
3. ⅜″ plywood for floor (21″ × 31″ if desired)
4. Wire flooring (optional) (21″ × 31″)
5. Saw

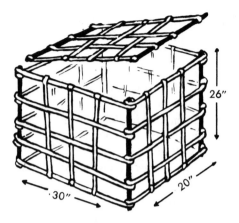

C. Procedure:
1. Cut pieces of wire to specifications.
2. The sides can be fastened together by either one of the following methods:
   a. Use galvanized wire to tie corners together, spacing the ties about 6 inches apart. Wind wire around three times.
   b. When cutting sides of cage, leave 1-inch projections of wire on front and back sides. These can be bent back around the wire of sides of cage.
3. The top is fastened in the same manner.
4. If a bottom is desired, the four corner wires could be secured to a baseboard by nailing them down or drilling holes through the board and fastening by nails; the cage could be placed over a cookie tray or other flat metal surface, or another piece of screen the size of the lid can be placed on the bottom.
5. Sand can be placed on the bottom of the cage for ease in cleaning.

D. Result:
A sturdy, practical classroom cage is made.

E. Supplemental Information:
1. This cage is collapsible for convenience in storing and carrying.
2. The tying of the edges together allows for folding of the cage when not in use.
3. This cage can be used for any of the larger pets such as rabbits, setting hens, squirrels, or raccoons in the classroom.

4. Each animal should have:
   a. enough space to move around and be comfortable
   b. an environment as close as possible to that of its own
   c. a shelter to hide or rest
   d. proper food
   e. fresh water
   f. good ventilation
   g. clean cage
   h. sufficient food and water during weekends and short vacation periods
   i. provision for care and feeding during long vacation periods

F. Thought Questions:
1. What kind of animals could be kept in this cage?
2. What modifications of this cage could be made that would make watering, feeding, and cleaning easier?
3. Could other types of animal cages be utilized?

G. Related Topics and Activities:
1. Students can chart growth of small animal(s).
2. See Section IV-A, "Animal Classification."
3. See all Activities in this Section.

H. Vocabulary Builders—Spelling Words:
1) **medium**   2) **size**   3) **pliers**   4) **plywood**
5) **galvanizing**

I. Thought for Today:
"Some minds are like concrete—thoroughly mixed and permanently set."

Activity

A. Problem: *How Can We Make a Simple Vivarium?*

B. Materials:

1. Aquarium
2. Glass cover
3. Charcoal
4. Small rocks
5. Soil
6. Plants
7. Watering can
8. Animal(s) desired

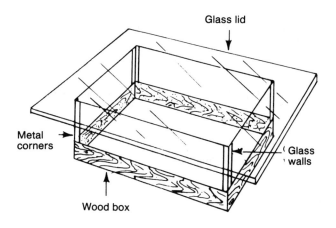

C. Procedure:

1. Clean the aquarium thoroughly.
2. Place a handful of charcoal at the bottom—this will help keep the soil sweet.
3. Put in a handful of small irregularly shaped rocks.
4. Place soil to depth of 1½" to 2" in the bottom of the aquarium over charcoal and rocks.
5. Use plants that thrive in a shady place and humid air.
6. Use a small or dwarf variety of slow growing plant.
7. Use a small sprinkling can for watering.
8. Place in a north window out of direct sunlight, but where it receives a reasonable amount of light.
9. Remove glass cover once a week, airing for about five minutes.
10. Frogs, toads, turtles, and lizards are suitable animals for this vivarium.
11. Reproduce animal's natural habitat as closely as possible.

D. Result:

Students will learn about plant environment and the habits of the animal(s).

E. Supplemental Information:

A vivarium is a helpful and interesting way to study animals and plants in their own environment. A homemade vivarium can be made from window panes, wooden supports, and heavy masking tape.

F. Thought Questions:

1. How does a vivarium differ from a terrarium?
2. What experiments could be done with several similar vivaria?
3. What plants or animals would probably not survive in vivaria?

G. Related Topics and Activities:

1. See Section IV-D, "Reptiles."
2. See Activity III-F-3, "Terrarium."
3. See all Activities in this Section.

H. Vocabulary Builders—Spelling Words:

1) **vivarium**   2) **aquarium**   3) **terrarium**
4) **charcoal**   5) **habitat**

I. Thought for Today:

"If you carry too many large bundles in both arms at the same time, it will cause your nose to itch."—John A. Norment

A. Problem: *What Should We Feed Captured Animals?*

B. Materials:
   1. Appropriate food for animal(s) as cited below
   2. Natural food

C. Procedure:
   1. Identify the animal(s).
   2. Look up appropriate feed for it (them).

D. Result:

Animals will be fed appropriate diets.

Carrots

Commercially prepared foods

E. Supplemental Information:
   1. Animals should be kept in an environment as similar to their natural environment as possible.
   2. The temperature range must be considered for each species.
   3. Animals should have adequate ventilation.
   4. Sunlight should be as close to their natural environment as possible.
   5. ANIMAL(S):   SUGGESTED MENUS:

Lettuce

Celery

ANIMAL(S):	SUGGESTED MENUS:
a. Ants	Grated dry dog food, dead insects and spiders, food scraps, especially products "sweetened" with sugar or honey
b. Birds	Wild bird seed, breadstuffs, pieces of raw vegetables and fruits, hard-boiled eggs, vegetable greens
c. Butterflies	Honey, thick sugar solution, nectar
d. Caterpillars	Leaves of plants where animals were found
e. Chickens	Scrap meat, grit, bird seed, corn
f. Earthworms	Finely ground leaves, grasses, and meat
g. Frogs and Toads	Soft-bodied insects, worms, caterpillars
h. Gerbils	Dry dog food, seeds, lettuce, carrots, grasses
i. Goldfish	Commercial goldfish food, ground dry dog food, oatmeal
j. Grasshoppers	Leaves where animals were found, celery, lettuce
k. Guinea pigs	Dog or rabbit food, lettuce, celery, carrots
l. Guppies	Commercially prepared tropical food; babies require tiny portions
m. Hamsters	Grains, dog biscuits, common vegetables, nuts
n. Lizards	Soft-bodied insects, flies, meal worms
o. Mice	Grated dry dog food, bread, meat leftovers, cheese
p. Rabbits	Commercial foods, most common vegetables
q. Snails	Most soft, green vegetables and leaves
r. Snakes	Soft-bodied insects, earthworms, small pieces of meat (irregular eaters, may go days without food)
s. Tadpoles	Fine guppy food, water plants, finely ground meat in small quantities

Cheese

Nuts

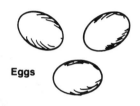

Eggs

Insects

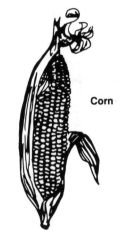

Corn

t. Turtles .... Soft-bodied insects, commercial foods, earthworms, lettuce, hard-boiled eggs

F. Thought Questions:

1. Why is natural food best for all animals?
2. Is water just as important as food in caring for animals?
3. How can you tell if an animal is sick?

G. Related Topics and Activities:

1. See Activity IV-A-2, "Animal Classification."
2. See Part III, "Plants."
3. See all Activities in this Section.

H. Vocabulary Builders—Spelling Words:

Use list of animals cited in Supplemental Information.

I. Thought for Today:

"To teach is to learn twice."

Activity   IV I 1

A. **Problem:** *What Products Do We Get from Animals?*

B. Materials:
1. Pictures of animals and illustrations of their usefulness to man; also illustrations of milk, wool, leather, etc.
2. Chart of various animals
3. Bulletin board

C. Procedure:
1. Introduce the lesson or unit by discussion of farm life.
2. Have the students identify the animals on the chart.
3. Have the students classify the animals into three groups: those that contribute food, those that work for us, and those that protect us.
4. Use the following questions as guides:
   a. How do animals help supply us with food?
   b. How do animals help supply us with clothing?
   c. How do animals help us do our work?
   d. How do animals protect us?
   e. How do animals help us in other ways?
5. Develop a bulletin board of animals and their resources.

D. Result:
Students will gain a greater understanding of domestic animals.

E. Supplemental Information:
Animals play vital roles in our daily lives.

F. Thought Questions:
1. What animals do people use other than farm animals?
2. How many animals are used in advertising? Why do you think the advertiser selected each animal for his advertisement or trade name?
3. What animal products do we use that come from foreign countries?

Milk

Clothing

Leather

G. Related Topics and Activities:
1. See Section V-C, "Nutrition."
2. See Part VI, "Ecology."
3. See other Activities in Part IV, "Animals."
4. See all Activities in this Section.

H. Vocabulary Builders—Spelling Words:
1) **products**   2) **resources**   3) **illustration**
4) **advertising**   5) **foreign**

I. Thought for Today:
"Education is the training that enables people to get along without intelligence."

Part V

Health

Section A: Body Structure and Function

Activity vA1

A. Problem: *What Are Cells, Tissues, and Organs?*

B. Materials:
1. Onion
2. Strip of bacon
3. Picture of heart, liver, and/or spleen
4. Microscope or magnifying glass
5. Pictures of mouth, windpipe, lungs (cross-sectional if possible)
6. Tongue depressor

C. Procedure:
1. Discuss how a body is like an automobile or a house. Each is a complete unit but made up of smaller and smaller parts or sections.
   a. Automobile has body, tires, motor, etc. Each of these has component parts.
   b. House has rooms; each room has component parts: windows, floors, walls, ceilings, etc..
2. Discuss the body beginning with the cell.
3. Cut an onion and slice one layer of it very thin.
4. Look at this one layer under a microscope or magnifying glass.
5. Scrape inside the cheek for cheek cells with the tongue depressor.
6. Examine these under a microscope.
7. Describe how the body is composed of:
   a. cells—which form
   b. tissues—which form
   c. organs—which are part of
   d. systems—which form the
   e. whole body.

D. Results:
1. Students will see cells under the microscope.
2. Pupils will learn that the body is composed of many parts all working in unison.

E. Supplemental Information:
1. The body is composed of trillions of cells.
2. The main kinds of tissue are muscle, skin, and organ.

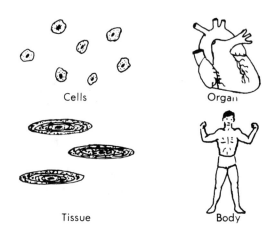

Cells

Organ

Tissue

Body

3. The main organs of the body are heart, spleen, liver, kidneys, reproductive organs, pancreas, stomach, etc..
4. The main systems of the body are the muscular, reproductive, circulatory, lymphatic, digestive, respiratory, and nervous systems.

F. Thought Questions:
1. Which systems are involuntary and which are voluntary? (Voluntary are those which individuals can control consciously.)
2. Do all animals have the same kinds of systems?
3. Do plants have the same kinds of systems?

G. Related Topics and Activities:
1. Study the main purpose of each body group.
2. Study how the structures of humans differ from the structures of other animals.
3. Study the parts of an individual body cell.
4. See all Activities in this Section.

H. Vocabulary Builders—Spelling Words:
1) **heart**   2) **spleen**   3) **liver**
4) **automobile**   5) **house**

I. Thought for Today:
"One learns much from one's teachers, more from one's colleagues, and most from one's pupils."

Activity

A. Problem: *What Are the Different Systems in Our Body?*

B. Materials:
1. Pictures
2. Books
3. Magazines
4. Puppets (optional)
5. Clay (optional)
6. Art supplies

C. Procedure:
1. Discuss with class the different systems of the body and their main purpose:
   a. respiratory—breathing
   b. digestive—eating
   c. muscular—moving
   d. excretory—eliminating
   e. circulatory—supplying
   f. skeletal—supporting
   g. lymphatic—protecting
   h. reproductive—reproducing
   i. nervous—sensing
   j. external protective—protecting (skin, hair, nails)
2. Have students collect pictures showing different systems in action. (Respiratory could be a runner breathing hard, digestive could be a person eating, muscular could be a weight lifter, etc.)
3. Have the students discuss what changes or modifications they would make in a person's construction to make him/her perfect.
4. Have them draw such changes. (See drawing for example.)
5. By reconstructing this perfect person, what health problems might be encountered?

D. Results:
1. Students will learn there are many different systems in the body.
2. All the systems are important.

E. Supplemental Information:
1. Each system has many component parts; for example, the circulatory system has the heart, arteries, veins, and many smaller vessels.
2. Stress should be placed on the interdependence of all systems.

F. Thought Questions:
1. Which system do you think is the most important?
2. Which system is the most complex?
3. Which system is the most important for growth?

G. Related Topics and Activities:
1. Compare our systems to an automobile, house, or mechanical robot (person).
2. Discuss how we can take better care of each of our systems.
3. See Section V-D, "Personal Health."
4. See all Activities in this Section.

H. Vocabulary Builders—Spelling Words:
Use the words listed under Procedure.

I. Thought for Today:
"If you are not afraid to face the music, someday you may lead the band."

A. Problem: *What Different Kinds of Bones and Joints Do We Have?*

B. Materials:
1. Pictures or drawings of human skeleton
2. Bones or joints from any source

C. Procedure:
1. Discuss that the main functions of bones in the body are to support it and help it in its movements.
2. Discuss the different types of movements the body can perform.
3. Ask if any of the students have ever broken a bone. If so, how did the doctor help to fix it?
4. Ask the class if they have ever found a bone in a field, in the woods, or anywhere.
5. Ask the class how many different kinds of movements the body can make.
6. Study the main bones of the body.
7. If chicken bones can be obtained, try to reconstruct a chicken skeleton.
8. Ask at local meat markets to supply whole bones of animals, and then study them for their location and function.
9. Discuss the function of bone marrow (supplies red blood cells).

D. Results:
1. Students will learn that the body has specialized bones and each part adds to body mobility.
2. Students will learn about the different kinds of joints:

Kind of Joint:	Location:
Ball-and-socket	Shoulder, hip
Hinge	Elbow, knee, finger
Pivot	Head on spine
Gliding	Vertebra
Angular	Wrist, ankle
Partially movable	Ribs to spine
	Hip to sacrum
Almost immovable	Cranium, adult

3. Students learn that the body has about 208 different bones, in four main groups:
   a. chest
   b. head
   c. arms and legs
   d. extremities (fingers and toes)

Fingers	Leg	Shoulder	Skull
Hinge joints	**Sliding joint**	**Ball and socket joint**	**Almost immovable joint**

E. Supplemental Information:
1. Bones are made of calcium. Growing children should have an adequate source of this vital substance.
2. Besides muscles and bones involved in body movement, there are also tendons, cartilages, blood supply, nerves, etc.
3. Good posture is determined by proper alignment of bones.
4. More than half of your body's 208 bones are in your hands and your feet.

F. Thought Questions:
1. Why do many people suffer from back problems?
2. Why can boys run faster than girls?
3. What do crossbones mean?
4. Do all animals have bones?
5. How can we take better care of our bones?

G. Related Topics and Activities:
1. Students can bring in bones they find from small animals.
2. Soak a bone in vinegar for several days and then examine it.
3. Older students may want to study the bones in one part of the body such as the arms, legs, or head.
4. String together empty thread spools to simulate the vertebra.
5. See all Activities in this Section.

H. Vocabulary Builders—Spelling Words:
Use the words listed under *Kind of Joint* in Results.

I. Thought for Today:
"Nature does make mistakes; sometimes she puts all the bones in the head and none in the back."

Activity   v A 4

A. Problem: *How Does Our Heart Work?*

B. Materials:

1. Model of heart
2. Pictures, posters, and/or charts showing the chambers of the heart and the circulatory system

C. Procedure:

1. Discuss the four chambers of the heart:
   a. Left Ventricle—starts the blood moving to all parts of the body.
   b. Right Atrium—receives blood from all parts of the body.
   c. Right Ventricle—starts blood moving to the lungs to be oxygenated.
   d. Left Ventricle—receives oxygenated blood from the lungs.
2. Have the students make a simple drawing of where the blood goes and the main blood vessels the body has to transport the blood.
3. Describe the pumping action of the heart.
4. Define the terms:
   a. Systolic—how hard the heart works (contracting).
   b. Diastolic—blood pressure when the heart relaxes (dilating).
5. Blood pressure is usually reported by citing the systolic pressure followed by the diastolic. Thus a reading of 120/80 (one twenty over eighty) are the pressures in millimeters of mercury.

D. Result:

Pupils can better understand how a four-chambered human heart circulates blood throughout the body.

E. Supplemental Information:

1. Blood circulates to the lungs to give off carbon dioxide and to get oxygen. It then returns to the heart to be pumped to all parts of the body. Our heart pumps about 100,000 times a day and pumps about 3,000 gallons of blood through 60,000 miles of arteries, veins, and capillaries. In a lifetime it pumps about 73,000,000 gallons of blood.
2. The blood is composed of serum (the liquid part) and white cells, red cells, and platelets (the solid parts). The white cells fight infection, the red cells distribute oxygen and pick up

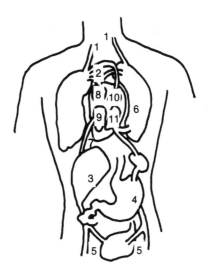

Major concentrations of blood:
1. Vessels of head and neck
2. Circulation to lungs
3. Liver
4. Stomach
5. Vessels of the lower limbs
6. Lungs
7. Vena cava
8. Right atrium
9. Right ventricle } Heart
10. Left atrium
11. Left ventricle

carbon dioxide, and the platelets help in blood clotting.
3. There are four types of blood: Types A, B, AB, and O. These must be matched in blood transfusions.
4. There is also an "Rh" factor that concerns blood clotting (agglutinogen). If a person has it, it is called "Rh Positive;" if not, it is called "Rh Negative."
5. The heart is about the size of a closed fist and weighs about 12 ounces in men and 9 ounces in women. There are valves which control the flow of blood during pumping motions.
6. The blood starts from the heart in large arteries and ends up in small capillaries smaller than the diameter of a human hair.
7. The blood delivers food to every cell in the human body.

F. Thought Questions:

1. What is heart disease?
2. How serious is heart disease?
3. Is there such a thing as "athlete's heart"?
4. How can we take better care of our hearts?

G. Related Topics and Activities:
   1. Discuss what happens during accidents which cause bleeding.
   2. See Section V-F, "First Aid."
   3. See all Activities in this Section.

H. Vocabulary Builders—Spelling Words:
   1) **artery**   2) **vein**   3) **capillary**
   4) **atrium**   5) **ventricle**   6) **platelets**

I. Thought for Today:
   "To be conscious that you are ignorant is the first step to knowledge."

Activity

A. Problem: *How Can We Find Our Pulse?*

B. Materials:
  1. Pictures, charts, or sketches of:
     a. human body
     b. forearm
     c. blood vessels in the arm
     d. point where pulse should be taken
  2. Clock or watch with second hand

C. Procedure:
  1. Briefly explain about the circulatory system.
  2. Discuss how the heart pumps food and oxygen to the cells and gets rid of wastes from all our cells.
  3. Describe how most blood vessels are deep within the body for protection.
  4. Show the chart of the forearm where pulse is to be located (radial artery).
  5. Divide class in pairs.
  6. Show class, on a student, where pulse can be taken.
     a. forearm
     b. nearest thumb side (radial side)
     c. in cavity between bones (radial and ulna)
     d. about two inches below joint of hand
  7. Cite how pulse is taken:
     a. use two of the three middle fingers (never thumb)
     b. press down until throbbing is felt
  8. Have students count the number of times the pulse beats (pulsates) for one-half minute.
  9. Multiply this number by two.
  10. Have students do some exercises and retake pulses.
  11. Have students take their pulses three minutes after exercises and compare findings with previous ones.
  12. Have students rest for five minutes and retake pulses.

D. Results:
  1. Students will learn something about the circulatory system.
  2. Pupils will learn how to take a pulse.
  3. Students will learn that the heart beats faster during exercise.

E. Supplemental Information:
  1. While the heartbeat will average around 72 beats per minute, pulse rate ranges are considered normal from 65–85.

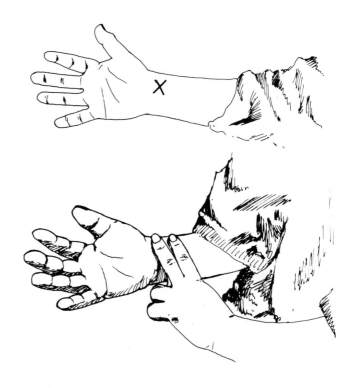

  2. Doctors look for not only the number of beats, but also if they are equal in strength and time duration.
  3. If students have problems locating pulse on arm, then have them feel for pulse on the neck, slightly forward of the midline using the three middle fingers.

F. Thought Questions:
  1. Does the heart beat faster in higher altitudes?
  2. What is an "athlete's heart"?
  3. Why does the heart beat faster when we exercise?
  4. How much blood does the heart pump every minute?
  5. Does the heart get any rest?

G. Related Topics and Activities:
  1. See Activity V-A-4, "The Heart."
  2. See Activity V-A-2, "Systems of the Body."
  3. See all Activities in this Section.

H. Vocabulary Builders—Spelling Words:
  1) **pulse** 2) **forearm** 3) **vessels**
  4) **midline** 5) **radial artery**

I. Thought for Today:
  "The heart is happiest when it beats for others."

Activity

A. Problem: *How Do Our Lungs Work?*

B. Materials:
1. Gallon jar with the bottom cut out
2. A one-hole stopper
3. Glass tubing branched at one end
4. Two small rubber balloons
5. Rubber diaphragm large enough to fit over the open end of the gallon jar (large piece of rubber balloon)
6. Heavy rubber band or string
7. Lungs (or pieces of) from meat market or meat packing house, or pictures of lungs

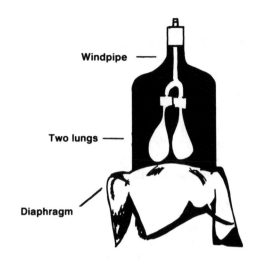

Diaphragm moves up and down

C. Procedure:
1. Attach the rubber balloons to the two ends of the glass tubing. Put the single end of the glass tubing through the rubber stopper and secure the rubber stopper in the top of the jar. Wet the glass tubing before insertion into the rubber stopper.
2. Put the piece of rubber over the large open end of the jar and secure tightly around the edges with heavy rubber band or tie tightly with a piece of string.
3. Push the rubber diaphragm in, making the chamber inside the bottle smaller, then pull the rubber diaphragm out, making the chamber inside the glass jar larger. Note what happens to the rubber balloons on the ends of the glass tubing.
4. Compare the apparatus demonstrated to actual lungs.
5. Relate breathing rate to exercise and rest.

D. Result:
As the diaphragm is pushed in and pulled out, the rubber balloons will alternately fill up with air and lose the air. Students will learn about breathing and how exercise influences the rate of breathing.

E. Supplemental Information:
1. The rubber balloons on the ends of the glass tubing can represent the lungs and the large glass jar will represent the thoracic cavity. The rubber shape on the large open end represents the diaphragm at the bottom of the thoracic cavity. This apparatus illustrates exactly what happens in breathing.
2. The surface area of adult lungs is about 1,000 square feet which is 20 times greater than the surface area of your skin.

3. Oxygen, drawn in when we breathe passes through the nose and/or mouth to the pharynx, larynx, trachea, and bronchi to the lungs. It is absorbed by the red blood cells as blood passes through the lungs.
4. Carbon dioxide is delivered to the lungs by the red blood cells in the blood and is expired during expiration (exhaling).
5. The lungs hold about 0.7 gallons of air (2.5 liters).
6. A normal breath is about 15 ounces or 500 milliliters of air.

F. Thought Questions:
1. What will happen if there is a hole in the rubber diaphragm?
2. What will happen if the opening in the end of the glass tubing is plugged up with a cork or with the finger?
3. Why does the breathing rate speed up during exercise?

G. Related Topics and Activities:
1. Relate this activity to the heart and exercise.
2. Discuss how smokers destroy some lung tissue and then can't perform as well due to a decrease in oxygen and food to every cell in the body.
3. See all Activities in this Section.

H. Vocabulary Builders—Spelling Words:
1) **breathe**   2) **diaphragm**   3) **lungs**
4) **thoracic**   5) **cavity**   6) **larynx**

I. Thought for Today:
"The greatest bankruptcy is the mind that has lost its enthusiasm."

Activity

A. Problem: *How Can We Show That the Body Uses Oxygen and Gives Off Carbon Dioxide?*

B. Materials:
1. Two quart jars
2. Plastic tube
3. Two candles
4. Glass bowl
5. Match
6. Water
7. Four ½" bolts
8. Limewater

C. Procedure:
1. Fill the glass bowl with water.
2. Fill a quart jar with water. Cover the open end of the bottle with the hand and insert the neck of the bottle under the surface of a bowl of water; the water will remain in the bottle after the hand has been removed.
3. Place the four bolts under the neck of the jar to give it support and also so tubing can be inserted.
4. Insert one end of a plastic tube into the filled bottle of water.
5. Blow air through the tube into the bottle until the water has been replaced with *exhaled* air. (Do not inhale through tube.)
6. Remove the bottle and set it upside down on the table gently and quickly.
7. Light two candles side by side.
8. Place the jar filled with exhaled air over one candle and at the same time place a jar filled with ordinary air over the other candle.
9. Repeat steps one through five.
10. Test exhaled air for carbon dioxide by quickly adding limewater, capping, and shaking.

D. Results:
1. The candle which is covered with the bottle of exhaled air will go out first; it does not contain as much oxygen as the bottle of ordinary air.
2. The exhaled air when tested for carbon dioxide will turn slightly milky. (See Activity III-E-11.)

E. Supplemental Information:
The body requires oxygen. Exhaled air has less oxygen than does inhaled air. The body uses about 5% of each inhalation of oxygen. Normal exhalations will produce

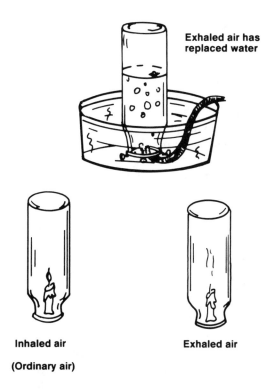

Exhaled air has replaced water

Inhaled air
(Ordinary air)

Exhaled air

better results than forced blowing in the tube. (See previous Activity.)

F. Thought Questions:
1. Where did the oxygen go that was lost from the air?
2. Test the exhaled air and regular air for carbon dioxide. What did you find?
3. Do plants use oxygen and carbon dioxide?

G. Related Topics and Activities:
1. Test your lung capacity by taking a full breath and blowing it into an inverted gallon container filled with water as described in Procedure.
2. Count the times students breathe normally in a minute and compare this with the number of times the students breathe after exercise.
3. See all Activities in this Section.

H. Vocabulary Builders—Spelling Words:
1) **oxygen**   2) **carbon dioxide**   3) **inhale**
4) **exhale**   5) **inhalation**   6) **exhalation**

I. Thought for Today:
"Sometimes the person of action is the one who just got both feet into hot water."

A. Problem: *Are All Fingerprints Different?*

B. Materials:
1. Pictures of people
2. Pictures of different kinds of fingerprints
3. Picture of hands
4. Magnifying glass
5. Carbon paper or ink stamp pad
6. Clean, white paper
7. Paper towels to clean fingers

C. Procedure:
1. Look at your fingerprints through a magnifying glass.
2. With carbon paper or ink stamp pad place a finger on it and then on a piece of clean, white paper.
3. Draw this fingerprint.
4. Repeat with all other fingers.
5. Compare your fingerprints with those of the pictures to identify the main kind.
6. See if you find any major type of fingerprint: a) whorl, b) arch, or c) loop (elongated balloon shape).

D. Results:
1. Students will learn the basics of fingerprints.
2. They will discover that no two fingerprints are identical.
3. They will see that even their own fingers have different prints.

E. Supplemental Information:
1. There are many types of fingerprints.
2. Fingerprints are a good form of identification in case of accidents.
3. Fingerprints are good clues in police work and are as good as leaving one's name and address.
4. These papillary ridges are also found on the soles and on the palms of the hands.
5. Even identical twins have different sets of fingerprints.
6. The right hands of individuals differ from the left hands.
7. With the aid of a computer, a fingerprint can be traced to 1 of 250,000,000 individuals, close to the population of the United States, in 4 seconds.

Tented arch

Loop

Whorl

8. Focal points in ridgeline patterns are deltas and cores:
   a. delta is the point concerned with divergence.
   b. core is the approximate center point.

F. Thought Questions:
1. Do you think everybody should be required to have their fingerprints on record?
2. Do fingerprints change if one skins his finger and the skin grows back?
3. Can fingerprints be changed?
4. Could fingerprints be used to locate a lost child?

G. Related Topics and Activities:
  1. See Activity V-A-1, "Cells, Tissues, and Organs."
  2. Might have police officer talk to class on crime and the use of fingerprints in investigations.
  3. See all Activities in this Section.

H. Vocabulary Builders—Spelling Words:
  1) **fingerprint**   2) **loop**   3) **whorl**
  4) **arch**   5) **identify**   6) **delta**   7) **core**

I. Thought for Today:
  "When it comes to picking up dirt, the vacuum cleaner can't compare with the telephone."

Section B: Senses

Activity vB1

A. Problem: *How Many Senses Do We Have? How Do We Receive Information from Our Environment?*

B. Materials:
1. Chart or notebook paper
2. Pen, pencil, marking pen
3. Pictures of sense organs (optional)

C. Procedure:
1. Talk to class about how we know what is in our environment (surroundings).
2. Have students list various sensations or feelings such as:
   a. warm clothing
   b. smell the flowers
   c. loud radio
   d. feel the rain
   e. sweet candy bar
   f. juicy orange
   g. clean hair
   h. fuzzy toy
   i. see a star
   j. taste the fruit
   k. listen to the drums
   l. sweep the floor

D. Result:
Students will develop a list that might include:
   a. touch
   b. pressure
   c. heat
   d. cold
   e. pain
   f. smell
   g. taste (sweet, sour, bitter, salty)
   h. sight
   i. hearing
   j. balance
   k. flavor (taste and smell)

E. Supplemental Information:
1. We have five main organs of sensation:
   a. skin
   b. nose
   c. ears
   d. eyes
   e. tongue

2. The skin has five sensory nerve endings; each can produce only one kind of sensation.
   a. touch
   b. pressure
   c. heat
   d. cold
   e. pain
3. Nasal mucus dissolves chemicals in the air.
4. Eyes blink for protection and to spread fluid.

F. Thought Questions:
1. Could we detect our surroundings if we lost all of our senses?
2. If a person loses one sense, are there any ways that it can be replaced?
3. Do you, or any of your friends or family wear glasses, contact lenses, or a hearing aid? How did these help change your or their life?

G. Related Topics and Activities:
1. Have students identify 10 objects in a paper sack just using their sense of touch.
2. Discuss what could affect our senses.
3. See all Activities in this Section.

H. Vocabulary Builders—Spelling Words:
Use the words listed in Result.

I. Thought for Today:
"A child is a thing that stands halfway between an adult and a television screen."

Activity

A. Problem: *How Well Do We See?*

B. Materials:
1. Snellen chart (lettering chart)
2. Astigmatic test chart
3. Color-blind chart

C. Procedure:
1. Discuss the fact that our eyes are among our most important possessions.
2. Discuss how people differ in their ability to see just as they differ in their ability to run or hear.
3. Test each of the students through the above charts to determine how well each can see. (In most cases the school nurse or school doctor would be happy to administer and discuss eye tests. If not, try a local optometrist or ophthalmologist.)

D. Results:
1. Some students will be found to have astigmatism.
2. Some students will be found to have visual problems in reading the letters at various distances.
3. Some students will be found to be color-blind.

E. Supplemental Information:
1. We do not see with the eye but with the brain and nervous system.
2. Some people use one eye more than the other and turn their head to see better.
3. About 25% of all students have some visual difficulties, and about 10% should be wearing glasses or contact lenses to see properly to do their classwork.
4. Glasses or contact lenses correct most visual problems.
5. Don't take your eyes for granted. Be sure your sight is right; have frequent check-ups.
6. No one should watch television from a distance closer than 8 feet.
7. Eyes can distinguish almost 5,000,000 differences in color.

F. Thought Questions:
1. What are some ways that we can protect our eyes?
2. If red-green color blindness is most common, should our traffic lights be red and green?

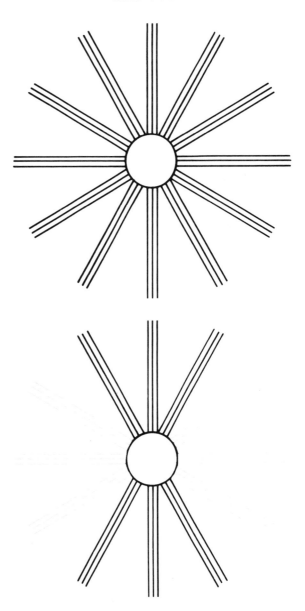

Snellen chart

3. Since good sight is related to good health, should we try to keep as healthy as possible so that we can see better and keep our eyes free from disease?

4. Should the light from the classroom windows come from the back, sides, or front of the room?

G. Related Topics and Activities:

1. See Activity V-B-3, "Pupils of Eye Change Size."
2. See Activity V-B-4, "Blending Colors."
3. See Activity V-B-5, "Seeing Motion."
4. See other Activities in this Section.

H. Vocabulary Builders—Spelling Words:

1) **Snellen**   2) **astigmatism**   3) **color blindness**
4) **problems**   5) **contact lenses**

I. Thought for Today:

"Motivation is the pulse of good teaching."

Activity

A. Problem: *Why Do the Pupils of Our Eyes Change Size?*

B. Materials:
   1. Flashlight
   2. Drawings of eyes with pupils dilated and contracted

C. Procedure:
   1. Define and point out the iris and the pupil of the eye.
   2. Have some students stand in a brightly lighted part of the room for one or two minutes and let some others observe the size of the pupils of their eyes.
   3. Move the students to a darker area of the room and have the observers report any changes in the size of their pupils.
   4. Have students cover their eyes with their hands for a few seconds and then quickly remove them.
   5. Discuss what observers saw when this was done.
   6. Cover one eye with one hand and repeat. Does one eye react or both?
   7. In groups of three, have one student be a test student, a second to alternately shine and remove the flashlight from shining in the eyes of the first student, and the third student should be the observer to note changes.
   8. Repeat step 7 shining the flashlight on only one eye. Did one eye react or both?

D. Result:
The pupils dilate when there is little light and contracts when light approaches the eye. Both eyes react to light stimulation of one eye.

E. Supplemental Information:
   1. Contraction of the pupil of the eye protects it from excessive light. Dilation allows more light to enter when it is dark.

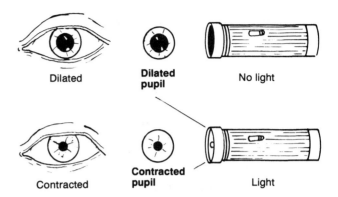

Dilated   **Dilated pupil**   No light

Contracted   **Contracted pupil**   Light

   2. Ideas to save your eyes:
      a. Have a good light when you read.
      b. When viewing television, have other lights on in room.
      c. Don't face the window on a bright day when reading.
      d. Don't read fine print excessively.
      e. Don't look at the sun.
      f. If you have frequent headaches, see a doctor.
      g. Don't read in bright sunlight.

F. Thought Questions:
   1. Are our pupils large or small when we watch television?
   2. Does the color of our eyes have anything to do with our ability to see?
   3. Why do some people wear dark glasses?

G. Related Topics and Activities:
   1. Should all automobile drivers take eye tests?
   2. Should bicycle drivers take eye tests?
   3. Stand in front of a mirror and open and close your eyes. Observe pupils.
   4. See all Activities in this Section.

H. Vocabulary Builders—Spelling Words:
   1) **iris** 2) **pupil** 3) **dilate**
   4) **contract** 5) **flashlight**

I. Thought for Today:
   "You can lead children to education but you can't make them learn."

A. Problem: *How Do Our Eyes Blend Separate Colors?*

B. Materials:
1. A disc (6″ in diameter)
2. A spindle (tack on pencil or dowel)
3. Three glass jars with lids
4. Two colors of paint powder

C. Procedure:
1. Divide the flat area of the disc into four equal spaces.
2. Mix small amounts of paints from each of the colors.
3. Using one color of paint, paint the two opposite quarters of the disc.
4. Spin the disc rapidly and note the appearance.
5. Using the other color of paint, apply paint to the other quarters of the disc.
6. Spin the disc rapidly and note the appearance.
7. Mix a small portion of the two paints in a third jar.
8. Observe results.

D. Results:
1. When the disc has only one color on it and is spun, the apparent color is slightly lighter than the original color (blends the color with white).
2. When the disc with the two colors spins, the colors appear to blend into each other—thus producing a third color. The blending of color (1) and color (2) will produce an entirely different color (3).
3. When the paints are mixed beforehand the same color (color 3) appears.

E. Supplemental Information:
Students can mix colors themselves. This gives them the opportunity to use paints that they themselves have mixed, gives added incentive to the students, and creates motivation. The variety of colors resulting from the students' individual blendings will result in more colorful pictures. When a light and dark color paint are blended, the dark color should be added to the light color for best results.

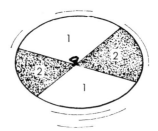

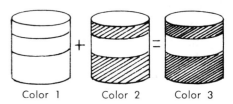

Color 1   Color 2   Color 3

F. Thought Questions:
1. Why do the colors appear to blend when we spin the disc?
2. Can you figure out what color will be produced before you spin the disc?
3. Will it make any difference how fast the disc is spun?
4. What would happen if we used three colors on the disc?

G. Related Topics and Activities:
1. Mix various combinations of three colors of paint.
2. Discuss what colors make a new color.
3. See especially Activity V-B-5, "Visual Persistency."
4. See all Activities in this Section.

H. Vocabulary Builders—Spelling Words:
1) **blending**   2) **primary**   3) **secondary**
4) **disc**   5) **spindle**

I. Thought for Today:
"It's not the I.Q., but the I WILL that's important in education."

Activity

A. Problem: *How Do We See Motion?*

B. Materials:

1. Heavy white cardboard 2½″ × 3″
2. Fine string, 36 inches long
3. India ink or black paint
4. Punch, one hole
5. Marking pen
6. Scissors

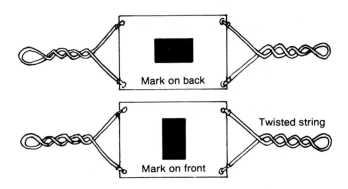

Mark on back

Mark on front

Twisted string

C. Procedure:

1. Punch four holes in the card as shown in the diagram.
2. Cut string in half.
3. Thread each string through two holes on one side of card securing ends well (see drawing).
4. Use black ink to make heavy vertical line on one side of the card.
5. Use black ink to make heavy horizontal line on the opposite side of the card.
6. Wind up the string and card by rotating card 20 to 30 times.
7. Spin the card rapidly by pulling the two loops outwardly.

D. Result:

The two marks will appear to blend, forming a cross.

E. Supplemental Information:

1. We may conclude that vision persists for a short time in the eye after the object is gone from view. This principle is called "visual persistency."
2. This principle is used in motion pictures and television.
3. We receive light sensations with our eyes and interpret these with our brain.

F. Thought Questions:

1. Could you design a test to determine how long a vision persists?
2. What percent of our population has visual handicaps?
3. What percent of our population should be wearing glasses or contact lenses?
4. Do motion pictures move?

G. Related Topics and Activities:

1. Draw various combinations on front and back of card such as a bird on one side and a cage on the other.
2. Look at the actual film of a motion picture film.
3. See all Activities in this Section.

H. Vocabulary Builders—Spelling Words:

1) **visual**   2) **persistency**   3) **vertical**   4) **horizontal**
5) **cardboard**

I. Thought for Today:

"Few people ever get dizzy from doing too many good turns."

Activity   vB6

A. Problem: *Do Our Eyes Get Tired?*

B. Materials:
1. Flashlight or slide projector
2. White surface
3. Red sheet of paper
4. Blue circular cut-out

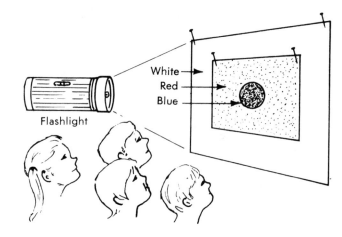

Flashlight

White →
Red →
Blue →

C. Procedure:
1. Place the red sheet of paper over the white surface.
2. Place the blue cut-out in the middle of the red sheet.
3. Darken the room.
4. Have the students face the display.
5. Flash the light on the blue design.
6. Have the students stare at the design for three minutes.
7. After three minutes, remove the red sheet of paper revealing only the white surface.

D. Result:
The students will see a yellow dot on a green background instead of the original colors.

E. Supplemental Information:
1. The eyes do get tired by steady gazing intently at one color.
2. The complementary color replaces it in their vision.
3. The term complementary colors means those two colors which when mixed together produce white. Tired eyes in this experiment could no longer see the red rays in the white light, so they saw the complementary color, green, and similarly the dot appeared as "yellow."

F. Thought Questions:
1. Can all people see red and green?
2. What is color blindness?
3. Can all animals see colors?
4. Do you think it is good to stare at T.V.? (The average child watches about 25,000 hours of television before graduating from high school. Students spend about 20,000 hours in school.)

G. Related Topics and Activities:
1. Try other combinations of colors.
2. See Activity V-B-8, "Optical Illusions."
3. See all Activities in this Section.

H. Vocabulary Builders—Spelling Words:
1) **complimentary** 2) **complementary** 3) **color blindness** 4) **mixed** 5) **circular** 6) **experiment**

I. Thought for Today:
"Few people have good enough eyesight to see their own faults."

Activity

A. Problem: *Are There Blind Spots in Our Eyes?*

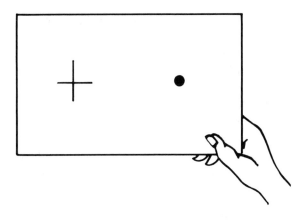

B. Materials:

1. 3″ × 5″ cards, plain (one for each student)
2. Pencils
3. Rulers

C. Procedure:

1. Have each student reproduce the card in the sketch using a dark pencil.
2. Have each student hold the card at arm's length with the right hand.
3. Have each student close his left eye or cover it with his hand.
4. Have each student stare at the cross and slowly move his hand holding the card towards his right eye.

D. Result:

When the card is about halfway toward the right eye, if the student has followed the procedures carefully, the dot will disappear.

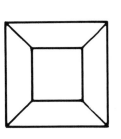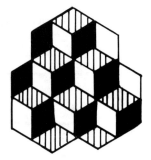

Starting at this figure the inner square appears to be first in the back then in front.

How many blocks do you see? Six or seven?

E. Supplemental Information:

1. This blind spot is where the image of the object seen would focus on the retina (optic nerve). Since there are no light sensitive cells there, the eye blanks out.
2. Here are two pictures that have double perceptions. What do you see?

F. Thought Questions:

1. How large a dot can each student make disappear? This can be tested by gradually increasing the size of the dot with a pencil.
2. Why don't we see the blind spot when we are using both eyes?
3. Do our eyes ever deceive us? See Activity V-B-8, "Optical Illusions."

G. Related Topics and Activities:

1. Collect other optical illusions.
2. Study a model of the eye.
3. See all Activities in this Section.

H. Vocabulary Builders—Spelling Words:

1) **blind spot**   2) **length**   3) **cover**
4) **cross**   5) **outwardly**

I. Thought for Today:

"If at first you don't succeed, you're running about average."

Activity

A. Problem: *Do Our Eyes Ever Deceive Us?*

B. Materials:

Charts of the illustrations depicted

C. Procedure:

1. Briefly describe how our eyes see. (Our eyes receive light and the light impulses travel to the brain via our optic nerves. The brain interprets these impulses and sometimes is confused.)
2. Have the students look at the sketches and report what they see. Which line is longer? Which ladder is taller?
3. Discuss the problems of interpreting three-dimensional objects on a two-dimensional plane.

D. Result:

Students will enjoy these optical illusions but more important, realize why the illustrations can be interpreted several ways.

E. Supplemental Information:

Start a collection of optical illusions. They are always good for a rainy day.

F. Thought Questions:

1. How can two people see the same thing but interpret it differently?

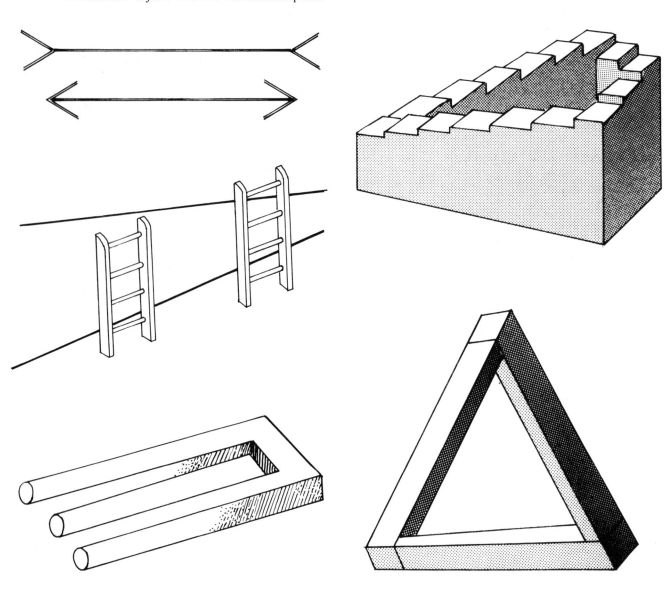

2. Are witnesses to accidents always able to describe the facts accurately?
3. Which are more important in seeing, our eyes or our brains?

G. Related Topics and Activities:
1. Study the cause of optical illusions.
2. Run other tests on the eyes and seeing. See Activities V-B-2, V-B-5, and V-B-6.
3. See other Activities in this Section.

H. Vocabulary Builders—Spelling Words:
1) **optical**   2) **illusion**   3) **interpreting**
4) **brain**   5) **problems**

I. Thought for Today:
"Heredity determines the color of a child's eyes, but it is the environment that lights them up."

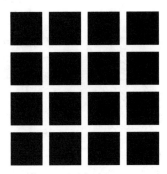

Are there any tiny gray squares at the intersections?

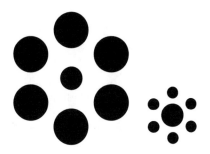

Which center dot is larger?

Activity

A. Problem: *How Do We Use a Microscope?*

B. Materials:
1. Microscope
2. Glass slides
3. Cover glasses
4. Onion skin
5. Leaves
6. Carrot
7. Water samples from various sources

C. Procedure:
1. Place a microscope where the outside light will hit mirror.
2. Place materials on slides with slide covers.
3. Focus by lowering slowly and carefully until the lens almost hits the cover glass and then focus sharply by slowly raising lens.

D. Results:
1. A whole new world will be realized by students.
2. Microscopic techniques will be learned.

E. Supplemental Information:
More advanced students can study blood circulation by using a goldfish carefully wrapped in wet cotton and placing tail under microscope. The lens is the most expensive part of the microscope so treat it with extreme care.

F. Thought Questions:
1. Why do doctors use a microscope?
2. How can microscopically small things live?

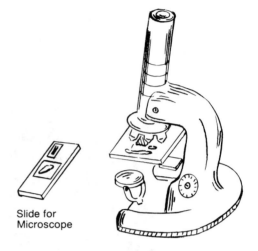

Slide for
Microscope

3. What are some essentials for all living things?
4. Why do laboratory technicians use a microscope?

G. Related Topics and Activities:
1. Compare what can be seen with a magnifying glass and a microscope.
2. Compare a microscope and a telescope.
3. See all Activities in this Section.

H. Vocabulary Builders—Spelling Words:
1) **microscope**   2) **onion**   3) **leaves**
4) **samples**   5) **lowering**

I. Thought for Today:
"We should all be concerned about the future because we have to spend the rest of our lives there."—Charles Kettering

Activity

A. Problem: *How Well Do We Hear?*

B. Materials:
1. Tape line
2. List of words to be used
3. Clock

C. Procedure A:
1. Have a student measure a distance of twenty feet by drawing a chalk line on the floor.
2. Have the pupil come to the front of the room to be tested. Explain carefully what you are going to do.
3. The student is to turn his/her back and repeat after you the words whispered at a distance of twenty feet. Care should be taken to whisper in a natural voice, not a forced whisper.

Procedure B:
1. Have the student hold his/her hand over his/her right ear.
2. Have another student hold a clock to the left ear and then move slightly away from him/her.
3. When the student being tested can no longer hear the ticking of the clock, she is to call, "Stop."
4. Have another student measure the distance between the tested student's ear and the clock.
5. Double check by walking toward the student to see when he/she begins to hear the ticking.
6. Repeat for right ear.

D. Result:
In most cases, the degree of hearing varies between the left and right ear. People do not all hear the same. The distance at which the student hears words and the ticking of the clock determines relative hearing ability.

E. Supplemental Information:
1. If the average student hears the clock or whisper at twenty feet, then hearing and correctly repeating the words scores 20–20.
2. If the student cannot hear at twenty feet, tester moves forward until he/she can hear, and the hearing is rated accordingly, i.e., 10–20, etc. Words have different pitches. Let pupils place their hands on their throats to discover

vibrations of whispered words—low pitch: 9, 19, 29; medium: 4, 40; highest pitched words: 6, 16, 60.
3. Our sense of balance is accomplished by nerves within the inner ear.

F. Thought Questions:
1. What are the different types of hearing losses?
2. How well do hearing aids re-establish "natural" hearing?
3. What percent of our population has hearing losses? What percent requires hearing aids?
4. What is the most beautiful sound you have ever heard?

G. Related Topics and Activities:
1. Discuss ways that our hearing can be impaired (sudden loud blasts, loud rock music, etc.).
2. What can we do to protect our ears from loud noises?
3. Have class close their eyes for several minutes being very quiet, and then report on noises heard.
4. See all Activities in this Section.

H. Vocabulary Builders—Spelling Words:
1) **measure**   2) **distance**   3) **whisper**
4) **ticking**   5) **clock**

I. Thought for Today:
"Mother nature is wonderful. Years ago she didn't know we were going to wear glasses, yet look at the way she placed our ears."

A. Problem: *What Makes Our Ears Pop When We Go Up or Down a Hill?*

B. Materials:
1. Quart jar
2. Rubber balloon
3. String or rubber bands

C. Procedure:
1. Ask students if they ever experienced their ears popping when they have been in cars travelling up or down high hills or mountains.
2. Have them recount their activities in these situations and ask if they know why.
3. Cut the rubber balloon to get maximum area.
4. Place the balloon over the quart jar.
5. Tie the balloon to the jar by string or fasten with rubber bands.
6. Raise the center of the balloon and release.

D. Result:
Students will hear a pop.

E. Supplemental Information:
1. The pop that is heard is the equalization of air pressure when the air moves from one area of concentration to another.
2. A drum makes a sound in the same way. The drumstick compresses the air within the drum suddenly. This makes a sound or pop.
3. In back of the eardrum lies the Eustachian tube which is filled with air. This opens up in the pharynx.
4. Sudden changes in air pressure, either higher or lower on the eardrum will cause the eardrum to move suddenly and make the eardrum pop like a drum. To avoid eardrums from popping, one can swallow air frequently, yawn, or yell. This opens up the Eustachian tube and equalizes the air pressure on the eardrum.
5. When we blow our nose, we should gently close one nostril to prevent the building up of air pressure, then repeat with the other nostril.

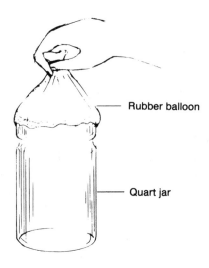

Rubber balloon

Quart jar

F. Thought Questions:
1. Are all sounds really small pops?
2. How can we protect our ears from injuries?
3. Can an excess noise actually break our eardrum as a very hard beat would break the drum skin?
4. How many people have hearing losses? (about 10%)
5. How many students need hearing aids? (about 3%)

G. Related Topics and Activities:
1. See previous Activity, V-B-10, "Hearing."
2. Discuss loud music and subsequent hearing loss.
3. See other Activities in this Section.

H. Vocabulary Builders—Spelling Words:
1) **Eustachian tube**   2) **eardrum**   3) **pharynx**
4) **swallow**   5) **yawn**

I. Thought for Today:
"To entertain some people all you have to do is listen."

A. Problem: *How Can We Learn About Our Sense of Touch?*

B. Materials:
   1. Table full of individual objects which can be handled and provide different sensations of touch. Such objects might include toothbrush, feather, orange, piece of cloth, fur, spoon, etc.
   2. Paper bag containing ten objects such as marbles, small ball, closed safety pin, spoon, eraser, button, shoelace, pine cones, etc.

C. Procedure:
   1. Have students write on the chalkboard different sensations they have felt and how experienced. For example, these might include such items as:
      a. softness—touching a sponge
      b. hardness—touching a rock
      c. coldness—touching ice
      d. warmness—washing with hot water
      e. mushiness—playing in mud
      f. stickiness—working with paste
      g. sharpness—cutting a finger
      h. roughness—feeling sandpaper
      i. smoothness—feeling marble
      j. smallness—pencil point
      k. bigness—house
      etc.
   2. Have students go to the touch table and report on how each of the objects felt. (See "Materials 1.")
   3. Without looking in the paper bag ("Materials 2") have some students feel inside and see if they can tell what the objects are. For added fun pass the bag around and see if each student can remember and list what was in the bag.

D. Results:
   1. Students will learn that the sense of touch includes many sensations and is very helpful in learning about our environment.
   2. Students will be able to identify some of the objects in the paper bag by their sense of touch.

E. Supplemental Information:

Our sense of touch is not only located in our fingers, but we have touch sensations all over our body. These are nerve endings in the skin which send messages to the brain. These

cutaneous senses include the specific senses of pressure, touch, pain, heat, and cold. All feeling sensations are combinations of these.

F. Thought Questions:
   1. When are we totally dependent on our sense of touch for information?
   2. When can our sense of touch warn us of dangers?
   3. Do babies like to be touched? Why?
   4. How important is the sense of touch to blind people?
   5. How do blind people read?

G. Related Topics and Activities:
   1. Discuss what we have learned through our sense of touch.
   2. Younger children can discuss sensations in playing with blocks, working with clay, etc.
   3. Discuss why we don't feel pain when we get a haircut.

H. Vocabulary Builders—Spelling Words:
Use the words listed in Procedure.

I. Thought for Today:
"Friendship is the only cement that will ever hold the world together."—Woodrow Wilson

Activity

A. Problem: *How Do We Use Our Sense of Smell?*

B. Materials:
1. Perfume or cologne in spray bottle
2. Soap
3. Cinnamon
4. Coffee
5. Onion
6. Cloves
7. Vanilla
8. Mint
9. Garlic
10. Lemon abstract
11. Sage
12. Fresh flowers
13. Chart paper

C. Procedure:
1. Have class close their eyes.
2. Tell them to raise their hands quietly if they can smell anything different.
3. Spray a small amount of perfume or cologne around the room.
4. Check the distance that fragrance can be detected.
5. Ask class if fragrance can be detected in areas where spray was not seen.
6. Have several volunteers close their eyes and see if they can identify different substances by their smell.
   a. soap
   b. cinnamon
   c. coffee
   d. onion
7. Record their findings.

D. Results:
1. Very, very small parts of perfume or cologne which we call molecules moved about the class. These small parts were too tiny to be seen.
2. These small parts (molecules) could be detected by our sense of smell.
3. Tiny, tiny parts of soap, cinnamon, coffee, and onion were detected by our sense of smell. These molecules drift around the room by air movements.

Our sense of smell can give us a lot of pleasure.

E. Supplemental Information:
1. A molecule is the smallest part of a substance that retains the properties of that substance.
2. We detect odors when molecules of certain substances reach nerve receptors inside our nose.
3. Molecules move through the air and some come in contact with the nerves in our nose.
4. This activity can also be used to detect air movement.

F. Thought Questions:
1. Can you tell what is cooking on the stove at home without looking?
2. Can you smell two things at the same time?
3. Can you smell anything if it is in a closed container?

G. Related Topics and Activities:
1. Discuss smoke detectors (molecules in movement during fires).
2. There are many other odors that can be detected with our eyes closed: garlic, herbs, ammonia, etc.
3. Discuss how air smells different after a rain.
4. See all Activities in this Section.

H. Vocabulary Builders—Spelling Words:
Use the words listed in Materials.

I. Thought for Today:
"Experience is a hard teacher because she gives the test first; the lessons come afterwards."

Activity

A. Problem: *How Many Different Tastes Do We Have?*

B. Materials:
   1. Pieces of:
      a. onion
      b. apple
      c. potato
      d. pickle
      e. pear
      f. carrot
   2. Salt
   3. Sugar
   4. Lemon juice
   5. Cotton swabs
   6. Instant coffee granules
   7. Other items of your choice
   8. Paper to draw and record findings
   9. Crayons
   10. Pencils
   11. Blindfolds
   12. Nose plugs (or students can hold noses)

C. Procedure:
   1. Have students draw a large outline of the tongue on paper.
   2. Have the students draw in areas of the tongue which roughly show:
      a. the tip of the tongue
      b. the middle of the tongue
      c. the sides of the tongue (see illustration).
   3. With blindfolds (or closed eyes) and with nose plugs (or holding noses) have groups of students taste each of the items cited in materials and place test items on each area of the tongue cited above. Use the four tastes only:
      a. sour
      b. bitter
      c. sweet
      d. salty
   4. Use a color for each of the above: for example:
      a. sour—red
      b. bitter—blue
      c. sweet—green
      d. salty—brown
   5. Record findings by writing the word of the item in its appropriate color in the area of the tongue taste noted.

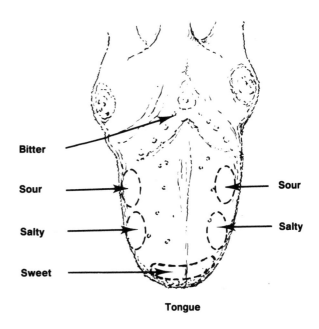

Tongue

D. Results:
   1. Sweet items will be noted in front of the tongue.
   2. Bitter items will be noted in back (center) of tongue.
   3. Salty items will be noted on front sides of tongue.
   4. Sour items will be noted on back sides of tongue.

E. Supplemental Information:

There are a few taste buds found on the soft palate and the epiglottis. Unless a substance is dissolved in the mouth, it cannot be tasted. Ordinarily the saliva in the mouth is sufficient to dissolve most substances. The tongue is also sensitive to touch, cold, heat, and pain.

Physiologists claim there are only four basic tastes: those involved in this activity. A few physiologists also list a fifth taste: alkalinity.

F. Thought Questions:
   1. If you had a choice between senses would you choose the sense of taste or the sense of smell?
   2. What can dull the sense of taste?
   3. Can we taste solid ice cream?
   4. Does our tongue have other senses, too? (Has anybody ever bitten his/her tongue?)
   5. Why do smokers have a diminished sense of taste?

G. Related Topics and Activities:

1. Discuss the many things we sense as taste that really are a combination of taste and smell.
2. Discuss our sense of taste when we are sick or have bad colds.
3. Close your eyes and hold your nose while biting into an apple or an onion. Can you taste what you are eating?
4. See all Activities in this Section.

H. Vocabulary Builders—Spelling Words:

1) **bitter**   2) **sweet**   3) **sour**   4) **salty**
5) **tongue**

I. Thought for Today:

"A sharp tongue is the only edged tool which grows keener with constant use."

SECTION C: NUTRITION

Activity

vC1

A. Problem: *What Kinds of Foods Do Our Bodies Need?*

B. Materials:
1. Items, containers, cans, etc., of each of major food groups:
   a. Milk
   b. Meat
   c. Bread-Cereal
   d. Vegetable-Fruit
2. Magazines with food pictures
3. Books about food

C. Procedure:
1. Divide class into four groups; one group representing each of the four major food groups.
2. Have each group:
   a. identify common characteristics of group
   b. reasons for eating that group of foods
   c. calories of average serving
   d. vitamins
   e. minerals
   f. costs, etc.
3. Each group may produce a notebook showing various foods found in their food group.
4. Have the class as a whole plan a balanced diet for a week. (If the students are old enough and want to, this could be an individual project.)

D. Results:
1. The students will learn that the body needs carbohydrates, fats, proteins, minerals, vitamins, and water.
2. The reasons for eating are body building materials, repair, heat and energy, and regulation.
3. Foods such as cereal, bread, and potatoes are fuels which furnish energy for work and play and keep our bodies warm. Foods such as lean meat, eggs, and beans furnish materials for body repair and growth. Foods such as tomatoes, milk, and carrots contain vitamins and minerals which keep our bodies in good working order.

Bread   Meat   Tomato

Potato   Eggs   Lettuce

E. Supplemental Information:
1. Everyone must eat enough of the right kinds of food every day in order to have a healthy body. The right kinds of foods include those which provide for energy, for body repair and growth, and for the proper functioning of body organs. This should include some items from each basic food group.
2. The average American consumes about 40 tons (36.3 metric tons) of food in a lifetime.

F. Thought Questions:
1. Is candy good for us to eat?
2. What should people be careful of when they diet?
3. What are some diseases of malnutrition?

G. Related Topics and Activities:
1. Discuss why breakfast should be the largest meal of the day.
2. Discuss the problems of cholesterol.
3. Discuss the importance of frequent medical checkups.
4. See all Activities in this Section.

H. Vocabulary Builders—Spelling Words:
1) **milk**   2) **bread**   3) **cereal**
4) **tomatoes**   5) **vitamins**   6) **minerals**

I. Thought for Today:
"If life hands you a lemon, make lemonade."

Activity

A. Problem: *What Are Good Sources of Vitamins and Minerals?*

B. Materials:
1. Empty vitamin bottles
2. Pictures of different foods cited below
3. Paper and pencils—to plan a perfect diet

C. Procedure:
1. Discuss the value of vitamins and minerals.
2. Describe how the foods we are eating are gradually losing some of the essential vitamins and minerals that we need for good health.
3. Students can make a collection of articles, newspaper accounts, and advertising relative to vitamins and minerals.
4. Have students develop a vitamin and mineral chart showing "Sources" and "Essential For" categories.
5. Have class plan for a perfect diet that would include all the necessary vitamins and minerals without taking supplements.
6. Discuss the value of taking supplements.

D. Result:
Students develop an understanding of mineral and vitamin requirements.

E. Supplemental Information:
1. The chart on the following page shows body requirements, and sources of vitamins and minerals.
2. Organic means containing carbon, i.e., made from living material.
3. Natural means not artificial (not manufactured).

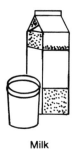

| Milk | Meat | Oranges | Sun |

4. Nutrition in plants is due primarily to genetics, not soil.
5. Vitamins and minerals help regulate body functions.

F. Thought Questions:
1. What is the difference between being underfed and undernourished?
2. How many people starve to death in the world each year?
3. Are people on strict diets usually undernourished?

G. Related Topics and Activities:
1. Discuss different body shapes and sizes.
2. Discuss which foods are best: natural or processed.
3. See all Activities in this Section.

H. Vocabulary Builders—Spelling Words:
1) **vitamins**   2) **minerals**   3) **deficiency**
4) **sources**   5) **essential**   6) **organic**
7) **natural**

I. Thought for Today:
"Food cures hunger; study cures ignorance."

VITAMIN:	BEST SOURCES:	ESSENTIAL FOR:
A	Liver, Dark green vegetables Deep yellow fruits and vegetables	Bone growth Night vision Healthy skin
B–1 (Thiamine)	Milk Seafood Whole grains	Healthy nerves Aids digestion Organ functions
B–2 (Riboflavin)	Meat, eggs Soybeans Green vegetables	Clear vision Healthy skin Healthy mouth
(Niacin)	Meat, fowl Fish, tomatoes Leafy vegetables	Skin Digestion Mental health
C (Ascorbic Acid)	Citrus fruits Tomatoes Leafy vegetables	Healthy gums Healing wounds Cement body cells
D	Sunlight Fish liver oil Fortified milk	Bone growth Strong teeth
Calcium	Asparagus Beans, milk Cauliflower	Bones Teeth Blood clotting
Chlorine	Bread Eggs Table salt	Osmosis Enzymes Hydrochloric acid
Cobalt	Liver Seafood Sweetbreads	Appetite Growth Muscle tone
Copper	Bran, cocoa Liver Oysters	Hemoglobin Tissues Repair
Iodine	Shrimp Broccoli, fish, Iodized salt	Forms thyroxin Regulates body metabolism
Iron	Almonds, egg yolk, Meat, Soybeans	Hemoglobin (carries oxygen to all cells)
Magnesium	Beans, bran, Corn, chocolate Peanuts	Muscular activity Enzyme activity
Phosphorus	Beans, cheese, Oatmeal, peas	Teeth, bones Buffers in blood Muscles
Potassium	Beans, bran, Molasses, olives Potatoes, spinach	Growth, osmosis Buffers, regulates heartbeat
Sodium	Beef, bread, Cheese, oysters Wheat germ	Regulates osmosis Buffers prevent water loss
Sulphur	Beans, bran Cheese, cocoa Fish, eggs	Formation of proteins
Zinc	Beans, cress, Lentils, liver Peas	Growth, tissue

Activity

A. Problem: *What Parts of Plants Do We Eat?*

B. Materials:

Pictures of food representing plant parts:
   1. Roots: carrots, radishes, beets, turnips, etc.
   2. Stems: asparagus, celery, etc.
   3. Seeds: corn, oats, wheat, rice, etc.
   4. Leaves: lettuce, spinach, cabbage, etc.

C. Procedure:
   1. Discuss with students the plant parts we eat.
   2. Divide the class into four groups. One group looks up information in books about those plants which provide us food in the form of seeds, the second group on roots, the third group on stems, and the fourth group on leaves.
   3. After the information is gathered, each group presents its findings to the rest of the class.
   4. Make a survey of grocery markets to find out how edible plants are processed to sell (disassembled, cooked, canned, cleaned, chopped, etc.).
   5. Have the students make a survey of their homes to find out how plant parts are prepared to make them more palatable.

D. Result:
   1. Students learn that people eat only certain parts of specific plants.
   2. Students will learn that grocery stores prepare plant foods to look nice to sell.
   3. Students learn that there are many ways plant foods can be prepared to eat.

E. Supplemental Information:

People do not eat the whole plant. Other parts may taste good and be nutritionally wholesome, but custom has led us to believe that only some parts of the plant are good for us.

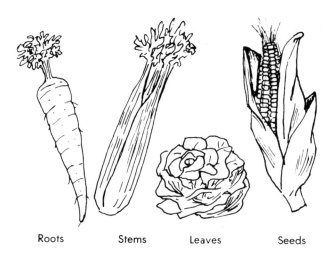

Roots   Stems   Leaves   Seeds

F. Thought Questions:
   1. What plants do we eat that have more than one edible part?
   2. Why should we eat vegetables?
   3. Does cooking help or hurt the food value of plant foods?

G. Related Topics and Activities:
   1. See Part III, "Plants."
   2. See Section V-D, "Personal Health."
   3. See all Activities in this Section.

H. Vocabulary Builders—Spelling Words:

1) **roots**   2) **stems**   3) **seeds**   4) **prepare**
5) **leaves**

I. Thought for Today:

"Happiness is not a station you arrive at, but a manner of traveling."

Activity

A. Problem: *What Foods Contain Carbohydrates (Starches and Sugars)?*

B. Materials:

1. Several 2″ × 4″ pieces of wax paper
2. One 4″ × 6″ piece of white paper for each kind of food to be tested
3. Iodine, tincture (diluted)
4. Foods to be tested: ham, corn, potatoes, flour, crackers, celery, bread, sugar, candy, etc.
5. Twelve test tubes
6. Benedict's Solution

C. Procedure:

1. Spread out papers, properly labeled with name of food on the table.
2. Place iodine and foods to be tested on the table.
3. Test each specimen by putting a drop of iodine on it.
4. Place each specimen on correctly labeled paper.
5. Place a sample of each food in a test tube.
6. Add Benedict's Solution to each.

D. Results:

1. When iodine is placed on the corn, flour, potatoes, crackers, and bread, the touched areas turn purplish-blue. The ham and celery areas remain a reddish-brown color.
2. Benedict's Solution turns a dark blue-green color in the presence of foods with sugar.

E. Supplemental Information:

Corn, potatoes, flour, crackers, and bread contain starch since they turned a purplish-blue in the area where iodine was placed. The ham and celery do not contain starch as the iodine remained a reddish-brown when placed on them. If Benedict's Solution is unavailable, Clinitest tablets are available at your local pharmacy. They are used by diabetic people to indicate if starch is converted to sugar in the body.

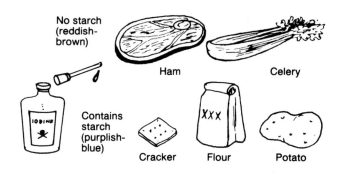

F. Thought Questions:

1. What other foods contain starch?
2. Where do most starches come from?
3. How much starch should a person consume daily?

G. Related Topics and Activities:

1. Make a list of common food items that contain starch.
2. Make a list of common food items that contain sugar.
3. See Part III, "Plants."
4. See all Activities in this Section.

H. Vocabulary Builders—Spelling Words:

1) **sugar**   2) **starch**   3) **carbohydrates**
4) **iodine**   5) **Benedict's Solution**

I. Thought for Today:

"Minds are like parachutes; they only function when they are open."

A. Problem: *How Do We Digest Carbohydrates (Starches and Sugars)?*

B. Materials:
1. Unleavened bread
2. Two test tubes
3. Benedict's Solution (test for sugar)
4. Two glasses of water
5. One-half teaspoon of sugar
6. One-half teaspoon of starch

C. Procedure:
1. Try to dissolve one-half teaspoon of starch in a glass of water.
2. Try to dissolve one-half teaspoon of sugar in a glass of water.
3. Take a piece of bread, soak it in warm water to soften, place it in a test tube and add Benedict's Solution.
4. Take a piece of bread, chew it a few minutes, place it in a clean test tube and add some Benedict's Solution. If students are squeamish about this then have students collect saliva in a test tube and then mix in small pieces of bread or cracker.

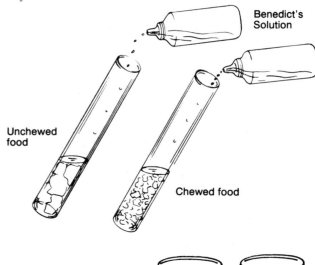

Benedict's Solution

Unchewed food

Chewed food

½ Teaspoon sugar

½ Teaspoon starch

Water

Bread

D. Results:
1. Starch is not soluble in water.
2. Sugar is soluble in water.
3. The bread that was tested for the presence of sugar without being chewed turned a light blue-green.
4. The bread that was chewed first and then tested for the presence of sugar turned a very dark blue-green.

E. Supplemental Information:
Benedict's Solution is used in testing for the presence of sugar. The reaction is stronger after the saliva has reacted on the bread, since starch has been changed into sugar. This shows that digestion of food begins in the mouth by changing insoluble starch to soluble sugar.

F. Thought Questions:
1. Why is it important to chew our food for a long time?
2. Is it healthful to eat a great many sugary foods?

3. What could be done to improve the Benedict's Solution test? (Maybe saliva contains sugar?)

G. Related Topics and Activities:
1. Compare starches with fats and proteins for food values.
2. Check local breads for food additives.
3. See all Activities in this Section.

H. Vocabulary Builders—Spelling Words:
1) **digest** 2) **carbohydrates** 3) **sugars**
4) **starches** 5) **chewed**

I. Thought for Today:
"Education is about the only thing lying around loose in the world, and it's about the only thing people can have as much of as they're willing to haul away."

Activity

A. **Problem:** *How Do We Test Foods for Fat?*

B. **Materials:**
1. Small piece of bacon
2. Peanuts
3. Olive oil or mayonnaise
4. Butter or butter substitute
5. Leafy vegetable
6. Bread
7. Six sheets of paper toweling

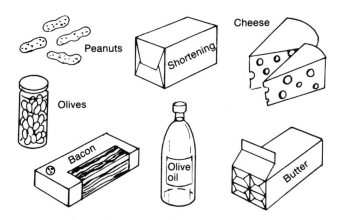

C. **Procedure:**
1. Firmly rub the food to be tested on a sheet of paper toweling.
2. Hold paper up to the light and notice the spot where rubbed.

D. **Result:**
If a translucent grease spot appears fat is present.

E. **Supplemental Information:**
1. Some foods contain much fat and others contain very little. Too many fatty foods in the diet can contribute to intestinal and heart disorders.
2. There are tests for proteins but these are usually too dangerous and, therefore, not recommended.

F. **Thought Questions:**
1. What is the difference between a fat and a protein?
2. How much fat should we have for a balanced diet?
3. What is cholesterol? What are the latest findings about this substance?

G. **Related Topics and Activities:**
1. See especially Activity V-C-5, "Carbohydrates."
2. See also Activity "V-C-7," "Butter."
3. See other Activities in this Section.

H. **Vocabulary Builders—Spelling Words:**
1) **mayonnaise** 2) **absorbent** 3) **grease**
4) **protein** 5) **translucent**

I. **Thought for Today:**
"To many of today's parents, youth is stranger than fiction."

Activity

A. Problem: *How Do We Make Butter?*

B. Materials:
1. One-half pint of whipping cream
2. One or more jars with lids
3. Colander
4. Salt
5. Crackers

Whipping cream

C. Procedure:
1. Discuss various kinds of dairy products.
2. Put cream into a pint jar.
3. Tighten lid and shake cream until butter forms. (Have students take turns shaking the jar.)
4. Pour buttermilk into separate jar (liquid part).
5. Wash the chunks of butter by placing them in a colander and running water over them.
6. Taste the unsalted butter.
7. Add salt to the butter and taste.
8. Put butter on crackers and have a class party.

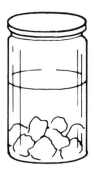
Shake jar vigorously.

D. Results:
1. Butter is formed when the cream is shaken.
2. Buttermilk is the by-product of the process of making butter.

Colander

E. Supplemental Information:
1. Butter is food. It contains fat and cholesterol.
2. Cream is lighter than milk. It rises to the top.

F. Thought Questions:
1. What is the difference in caloric value between margarine and butter?
2. What is the difference in the fat and protein value of each?
3. What is "butterfat"?

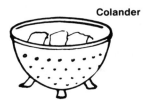
Wash thoroughly.

G. Related Topics and Activities:
1. Study how cheese is made.
2. Study how cottage cheese is made.
3. See all Activities in this Section.

H. Vocabulary Builders—Spelling Words:
1) **butter**   2) **whipping**   3) **cream**
4) **colander**   5) **chunks**   6) **buttermilk**

I. Thought for Today:
Baby octopus to mother: "All I want to know is which are my hands and which are my feet?"

Activity

A. Problem: *How Is Food Preserved?*

B. Materials:
1. Canned food
2. Dried food
3. Picture of frozen food
4. Salted food
5. Smoked food
6. Pasteurized milk
7. Canned milk

C. Procedure:
1. Discuss the problems of shortages of food throughout the world.
2. Discuss the problems of food production, distribution, and consumption.
3. Discuss how food must be preserved to ship from the producer to the consumers.
4. Discuss the problems of spoilage, bacteria.

D. Results:
1. Students learn that many people in the world are starving and underfed.
2. Pupils learn the problems of sending food abroad.
3. Students learn the problems of obtaining the food in one season and eating it in another.
4. Pupils will learn that salting, drying, and smoking removes the liquid and retards bacterial growth.

E. Supplemental Information:
1. There are over 5,000,000,000 people in the world today.
2. About 18 million people starve annually because of a lack of food.
3. The main problem today is a lack of distribution rather than production.
4. The world's population is expected to double in the next sixty years and this will require twice as much food; there is not that much agricultural land available.

F. Thought Questions:
1. How can we improve our distribution of food supplies?
2. How can we produce more and more food with less and less land?
3. Are our lands becoming polluted so that our foods are becoming contaminated?

G. Related Topics and Activities:
1. Study population projections and food increases.
2. Study why so many people in the world are starving.
3. See all Activities in this Section.

H. Vocabulary Builders—Spelling Words:
1) **canned**   2) **dried**   3) **frozen**
4) **salted**   5) **smoked**   6) **pasteurized**
7) **irradiated**

I. Thought for Today:
"The farmer doesn't go to work. He wakes up every morning surrounded by it."

SECTION D: PERSONAL HEALTH

Activity vD1

A. Problem: *How Can We Keep Healthy?*

B. Materials:

Pictures of:
- a. Nutritious foods
- b. Healthful exercises
- c. Wholesome relaxations
- d. Clean people

C. Procedure:
1. Discuss proper foods. (From International Society for Research on Nutrition and the Diseases of Civilization.)
   See especially Activity V-C-1.
2. Discuss proper exercise:
   - a. periodic examinations by doctor
   - b. simple exercises
   - c. progressive (slowly increasing muscle work)
   - d. balanced (heart, muscles, and lungs)
   - e. fresh air
     1) Air is a mixture of nitrogen, oxygen, carbon dioxide, and a few other gases.
     2) Relative humidity of about 60% is best for health and comfort.
     3) Ideal temperature is between 68° and 72° Fahrenheit.
3. Discuss proper rest:
   - a. 8 to 10 hours of sleep depending on age
   - b. adequate ventilation
   - c. rest periods during the day
4. Discuss cleanliness:
   - a. daily light washing (heavy soaps and detergents wash out natural oils and cause dry skin conditions)
   - b. cleansing creams

D. Results:
1. Students will learn that it takes a lot of careful thinking, planning, and exercising to be healthy.
2. Pupils will learn that we mustn't take health for granted.

E. Supplemental Information:
1. Mental and emotional health are just as important as physical health.
2. More people occupy hospital beds for the mentally ill than the physically ill.

F. Thought Questions:
1. What do some people do that impairs their health?
2. Do you think it is wise to have regular checkups by a doctor?
3. How do athletes train to get in top physical shape?

G. Related Topics and Activities:
1. See especially Activity V-D-2, "How Body Protects Itself."
2. See other Activities in this Part.
3. See other Activities in this Section.

H. Vocabulary Builders—Spelling Words:
1) **healthy**　2) **nutrition**　3) **exercise**
4) **cleanliness**　5) **emotional**　6) **physical**

I. Thought for Today:
"Jumping to conclusions is about the only exercise some people get."

A. Problem: *How Does Our Body Protect Itself?*

B. Materials:

Pictures of healthy children, men, and women

C. Procedure:

1. Discuss with class all the ways the body prevents or reduces sickness, accidents, or other bodily harm.
   a. blood clotting
   b. white blood cells
   c. skin
   d. blood
   e. perspiration
   f. muscles (run from danger)
   g. good eyesight
   h. good hearing ability
   i. tears
   j. hair
   k. nails
2. Older or advanced students may discuss some of the mental defenses people use:
   a. rationalization
   b. sublimation
   c. substitution
   d. compensation
   e. identification
   f. projection, etc.
3. Stress the importance of keeping your body clean.
4. Discuss ways that the common cold can be prevented.
   a. Stay away from people who are coughing.
   b. Keep up your body strength.
   c. Get plenty of rest.
   d. Drink 6 to 8 glasses of water daily.

D. Results:

1. Students will learn that the body has many defense mechanisms.
2. The pupils will learn that the body has internal and external protective devices.

E. Supplemental Information:

1. You can't see germs but they are in the air you breathe, the food you eat, and on everything you touch.
2. Germs cause illness.

3. Many people used to die of simple injuries such as cuts, wounds, and infected teeth. Doctors and dentists treat these once deadly infections with life-saving antiseptics and antibodies.
4. Modern science has increased our average life expectancy; it has not increased our maximum life span—yet.
5. In order for the body to properly defend itself, it must have a good source of food.
6. Parts of the body are growing and being renewed all the time.
7. People who can solve their problems rationally remain mentally healthy.

F. Thought Questions:

1. What would happen to us if any one of our defense mechanisms or protective devices failed us?
2. Can you think of any way that you might better protect yourself from disease or injury?
3. How are our protective mechanisms the same as other animals? How are they different?

G. Related Topics and Activities:
   1. Discuss good health practices.
   2. Clip out articles from the newspapers on health.
   3. Find out which germs cause which disease.
   4. See all Activities in this Section.

H. Vocabulary Builders—Spelling Words:
   1) **sickness**   2) **accident**   3) **perspiration**
   4) **rational**   5) **mechanism**

I. Thought for Today:
   "One who has health has hope and one who has hope has everything."

Activity

A. Problem: *How Do We Properly Care for Our Teeth?*

B. Materials:
1. Model of toothbrush or regular, soft, multi-tufted toothbrush
2. Dental floss
3. Colored wall chart of teeth
4. Water irrigating device for teeth

C. Procedure:
1. Discuss some facts about teeth:
   a. There are no substitutes for brushing, water irrigating devices, and flossing.
   b. There is no substitute for professional dental care.
   c. There is no such thing as all-day protection.
   d. There are no visible shields.
   e. Brushing alone does not prevent bad breath (halitosis); there are many causes.
   f. Mouthwashes are effective only for a short period of time.
   g. Salt and water and/or baking soda and water are as effective as many toothpastes and have no caustic, toxic, or abrasive effects.
2. Demonstrate how:
   a. upper teeth are brushed downward.
   b. lower teeth are brushed upward.
   c. surfaces of the teeth are brushed in a scooping scrubbing motion.
   d. the gumline of the teeth is brushed at a 45° angle down at gumline.
   e. dental floss is properly used.
3. Make tooth powder: mix one part salt to two parts baking soda.
4. Always use a soft multi-tufted brush; a hard brush may damage the gums.
5. Use dental floss. The most effective method of disrupting plaque between the teeth and at the gum line is the proper use of dental floss. It can remove up to 80% of plaque and is the most vital part of plaque control. It's a good idea to show students how to use dental floss making sure they use "C's" around the teeth as well as probing between the teeth.

D. Result:
Students will learn how:
   a. the surface of the teeth is cleaned.
   b. food is dislodged from between the teeth.
   c. plaque, the scum that builds up around the gums, is reduced or removed.

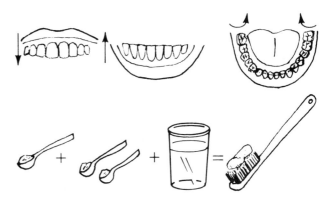

Salt, baking soda, and water make toothpaste

E. Supplemental Information:
1. Decay originates when bacteria react on food particles between the teeth and form an acid that destroys the tooth enamel and causes cavities.
2. Plaque is composed of mucous food particles and bacteria. It is the primary cause of tooth decay.
3. Ninety-five percent (95%) of people over 5 years of age have tooth decay.
4. By the age of 60 the average American has only 10 of his (her) 32 permanent teeth left.

F. Thought Questions:
1. How could you set up a test to show that acids cause tooth decay?
2. How could you test the relative effectiveness of different kinds of toothpastes and powders?
3. What kind of brushing does your dentist recommend? Does he/she recommend any brand names? Why or why not?

G. Related Topics and Activities:
1. Have a dentist or oral hygienist talk to the class about tooth care.
2. Have students relate visits to dentists.
3. Discuss, or have a professional show, how teeth can be straightened.
4. See all Activities in Part V, "Health."

H. Vocabulary Builders—Spelling Words:
1) **brushing**   2) **flossing**   3) **upward**
4) **downward**   5) **hygienist**

I. Thought for Today:
"The main difference between a human and a dog is that if you pick up a starving dog and make him prosperous he will not bite you."

Activity

A. Problem: *Why Do We Have to Wash Our Hands before Eating?*

B. Materials:
   1. Two unpeeled potatoes
   2. Paring knife
   3. Two glass jars that can be sterilized and sealed

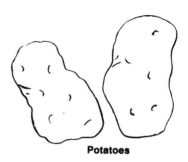

Potatoes

C. Procedure:
   1. Have two students volunteer to help with the experiment.
   2. Send one of the students to the washroom to wash his/her hands thoroughly.
   3. Leave the second student with his/her hands unwashed.
   4. Have both students peel a clean potato and place them in the sterile jars.
   5. Label the jars with either "Hands washed" or "Hands unwashed" as the case may be.
   6. Place the jars on the science table and observe from day-to-day to note if any changes occur.

D. Results:
   1. The jar labeled "Hands unwashed" will show mold growth on the potato.
   2. The jar labeled "Hands washed" will show little or no growth on the potato.

E. Supplemental Information:

Germs grow in dirt and therefore get on the hands. Hands should be washed before handling food. This helps eliminate germs that cause disease.

F. Thought Question:
   1. What are some sources of germs?
   2. How do people help keep their food clean?
   3. How do people preserve their food?

G. Related Topics and Activities:
   1. See Section V-C, "Nutrition."
   2. Discover why doctors scrub before operations.
   3. Discuss cleanliness at school and at home.
   4. See all Activities in this Section.

H. Vocabulary Builders—Spelling Words:
   1) **washed**   2) **unwashed**   3) **sterile**
   4) **volunteer**   5) **germs**   6) **disease**

I. Thought for Today:
   "Instruction ends in the classroom, but education ends with life."

Activity

A. Problem: *Are Bacteria Good or Bad?*

B. Materials:
   1. Empty cottage cheese carton
   2. Soap (hand and packaged)
   3. Toothpaste and toothbrush
   4. Food produced by bacteria (cheese, pickle, sauerkraut, etc.)
   5. Books, pamphlets, and pictures of bacteria
   6. Pictures of flies or mosquitos

C. Procedure:
   1. Ask a member of the class to describe a previous infection from a wound or cut.
   2. Show the class several examples of food or drink that has been aided by bacteria. (Fermentation is caused by bacteria.)
   3. Show class the soap and toothpaste.
   4. Ask the class if they know what causes sickness.
   5. Ask the class if they know what all these have in common.
   6. Show the pictures of flies or insects and ask why we are concerned with household insects.
   7. Let the students read printed materials about bacteria.
   8. Students should visit stores and describe different ways food is preserved and kept fresh.
   9. Older students can study bacteria by using gelatin to set up agar type Petri dishes.

D. Results:
   1. Students will learn about bacteria.
   2. Pupils will learn the importance of keeping clean and healthy.

E. Supplemental Information:
   1. There is a visible world which we can see and an invisible world which we cannot see in which bacteria live.
   2. Bacteria are small, invisible, colorless, one-celled plants which need food, water, and warmth for growth.
   3. Some bacteria are helpful, some harmful.
   4. The helpful ones speed the disposal of dead plants and animals and return needed elements to the soil for new growth. If it were not for these we would all starve due to lack of food. They also help produce some of our foods: sour cream, butter, cheese, pickles, sauerkraut, etc.

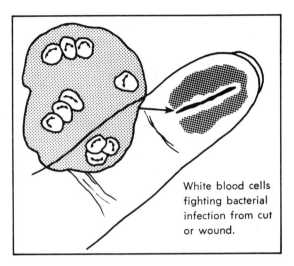

White blood cells fighting bacterial infection from cut or wound.

5. The harmful bacteria cause communicable diseases, cause food to spoil, meat to decompose, and teeth to decay.
6. Teeth should be shiny and smooth. Any rough spots or holes enable bacteria to live, produce acids, make bigger cavities, and allow more bacteria to live, consequently causing tooth decay.
7. Bacteria can double every fifteen minutes under ideal conditions.
8. The temperature where most harmful bacteria will die is 140°F. if left for ½ hour (used in pasteurizing milk). Shorter periods of time require higher temperatures. (Dishwashing should use 180°F.)
9. Drying, salting, and smoking were man's first attempt to preserve food even though he didn't know why (removes moisture and kills harmful bacteria).
10. Our bodies have three defenses against bacteria:
    a. Skin—needs to be healthy, clean, and unbroken.
    b. White blood cells—devour bacteria at points of infection.
    c. Antitoxins—body has or makes to control poisons (toxins) from bacteria.
11. Bacteria are hitchhikers; they cannot travel by themselves. This is why we should stay away from people who are sick and sneeze, cough, spit, or breathe near us.

12. Four things are necessary for bacteria to cause disease:
    a. must be carried by some vehicle
    b. must gain entrance to the body
    c. must be able to live and grow
    d. must cause injury to the body
13. Very few items are free of bacteria.
14. There are now many antibacterial medicines and drugs that doctors are using to control bacteria and reduce infection.

F. Thought Questions:

1. When a person is sick in your home, what precautions should you take to prevent bacteria or viruses from spreading?
2. How can floods cause disease?
3. What must be done to get rid of our solid and liquid garbage wastes from our homes?

G. Related Topics and Activities:

1. See all Activities in Part III, "Plants."
2. See Activity V-D-1, "Keeping Healthy."

3. Older students can study bacterial growth in Petri dishes involving:
    a. students biting their fingernails
    b. pupils using dirty handkerchiefs
    c. students coughing
4. Study clover, alfalfa, and/or soybeans for nitrogen fixation bacteria. (These yield more nitrogen.)
5. See all Activities in this Section.

H. Vocabulary Builders—Spelling Words:

1) **bacteria**   2) **helpful**   3) **harmful**
4) **cheese**   5) **pickle**   6) **sauerkraut**

I. Thought for Today:

"So far we've managed to confine germ warfare to television commercials."

Activity

A. Problem: *Is Caffeine Bad for Us?*

B. Materials:
   1. Coffee cup
   2. Tea pot
   3. Soda bottle or can
   4. Chocolate candy
   5. Pill bottle

C. Procedure:

Discuss caffeine citing some key points such as:
   a. mild stimulant
   b. one of the most widely used drugs
   c. is in coffee, tea, and chocolate
   d. gives a psychological lift
   e. improves alertness
   f. possible link in birth defects
   g. contained in many over-the-counter drugs
      including some headache relievers
   h. increases heartbeat
   i. increases basic metabolism rate
   j. mildly addictive
   k. many soft drinks contain caffeine

D. Result:

Students will learn about caffeine, and in particular, that many soft drinks contain caffeine.

E. Supplemental Information:
   1. Most of the caffeine taken out of coffee is sold to the soft drink industry.
   2. Soft drinks have replaced coffee as the number one drink.
   3. Most decaffeinated coffee has 97% of the caffeine removed.
   4. A teaspoon of tea leaves contains more of the stimulant drug caffeine than a teaspoon of ground coffee, but the caffeine in tea is usually more diluted when served (50%–70%).

F. Thought Questions:
   1. Do you think it is wise to drink beverages which contain caffeine?
   2. Is chocolate a good food?
   3. Should tired automobile and truck drivers use caffeine to stay awake?

G. Related Topics and Activities:
   1. Study decaffeinated coffee and determine whether it is good or bad.
   2. Study anti-sleeping pills to see if they contain caffeine.
   3. See all Activities in this Section.

H. Vocabulary Builders—Spelling Words:
   1) **caffeine**   2) **coffee**   3) **chocolate**
   4) **tea**   5) **stimulant**   6) **addictive**
   7) **drug**

I. Thought for Today:
   "A person wrapped up in himself makes a pretty small bundle."

Activity

A. Problem: *Is Smoking Bad for Our Health?*

B. Materials:

1. A quart size wide-mouthed jar with a two-hole stopper
2. Glass tubing
3. Rubber or plastic tubing
4. Three or four cigarettes
5. Water
6. Insect or small rodent

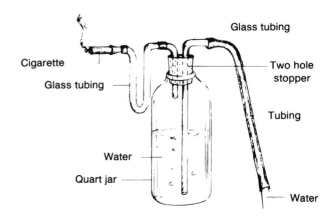

C. Procedure:

1. Make a smoking machine as illustrated in the diagram.
2. Fill a glass jar with water so that one of the tubes runs nearly to the bottom of the jar.
3. Attach a lighted cigarette to the end of the tubing as illustrated in the diagram.
4. Start the siphon by sucking on the tubing which extends below the bottom of the jar as illustrated in the diagram.
5. As the water is siphoned from the jar, air is sucked in through the glass or tubing holding the cigarette. If the cigarette is lighted, this apparatus will smoke the cigarette and collect the cigarette smoke in the jar. Some of the nicotine may be collected in the depression of the glass tubing before the smoke enters the jar. When the water is all gone the jar will be full of cigarette smoke. Next insert an insect or a small rodent into the jar and let them stand for a while. Next, observe what happens to the insect or small rodent.

D. Result:

The insect or rodent will die in a short time. If you are testing with a rodent and do not want it to die, you should remove the rodent from the jar after it becomes groggy, and quickly expose it to fresh air.

E. Supplemental Information:

1. The end of the rubber tubing can be pinched and held for a while better simulating the burning action of smoking a cigarette.
2. What happens to the insect or rodent is quite extreme because the concentration of the cigarette smoke in the bottle is greater than would be found even in the most concentrated smoke-filled room that you can imagine. But the fact that cigarette smoke is detrimental to

health, both in the lungs and the circulatory system has been demonstrated so conclusively that there is no doubt whatever about the harmful effects of cigarette smoke.

3. Specifically cigarette smoking:
   a. impairs the sense of taste
   b. impairs the sense of smell
   c. causes the smoker's breath to become very strong
   d. slows down circulation by constricting blood vessels so the heart has to pump harder and this causes a rise in blood pressure
   e. robs the body of 10% of its oxygen carrying capacity
   f. contains tars (like paving material used on a highway) and they are carcinogens
   g. contains over 15 known carcinogens
   h. has 3 deadly agents: 1) nicotine, 2) tars, and 3) carbon monoxide
   i. has enough nicotine in one pack of cigarettes to kill a person if all the nicotine was in a single dose
   j. causes stomach to secrete acids, producing ulcers
   k. causes 300,000 premature deaths every year
   l. causes 52,000 new cases of lung cancer each year
   m. has crippled the lungs of 50,000,000 people in the United States
   n. entices 1,000,000 new teenagers to start smoking every year
   o. harms tissue in the mouth, throat, breathing tubes, and lungs
   p. has almost the same harmful effects for those who inhale "second-hand" smoke

q. is involved in the sale of 565,000,000,000 cigarettes a year in the United States
r. causes bad breath (smokers' breath)
s. produces a hacker's cough
t. leads to emphysema
u. leads to heart disease
v. can cause cancer and lung disease
w. produces carbon monoxide which is deadly and the carbon monoxide takes the place of oxygen in the blood. (hemoglobin)
x. stains teeth
y. leaves nicotine odor in clothing, hair, drapes, upholstered furniture, etc.

F. Thought Questions:

1. What can be done with the nicotine which is collected in the depression in the glass tubing?
2. Is nicotine the only harmful ingredient in cigarette smoke?
3. Can you think of a way in which you can demonstrate the harmful effects of the nicotine which is collected?
4. Have you ever been in close quarters with people who are smoking? How did you feel about it? What do you think about it?

G. Related Topics and Activities:

1. List the disadvantages of smoking.
2. List the advantages (if any) of smoking.
3. Compare lists.
4. Have a smoker take a big drag on a cigarette and exhale it on a clean white handkerchief. (A big, brown stain will appear.) Ask students if they would like to have lots of this in their lungs.
5. Open a cigarette filter to examine its insides.
6. See all Activities in this Section.
7. Have students discuss any experiences they have had in a smoked-filled room.

H. Vocabulary Builders—Spelling Words:

1) **nicotine**   2) **smoking**   3) **cigarette**
4) **carcinogen**   5) **emphysema**

I. Thought for Today:

"The most incredible creation in the universe is your body. Don't you help to destroy it."

Activity

A. Problem: *Is Marijuana Bad for Our Health?*

B. Materials:
  1. Simulated marijuana cigarette (Roll your own "make-believe.")
  2. Crushed alfalfa

C. Procedure:
  1. The best method would be to have an outside speaker such as a doctor, police officer, or narcotics officer make the presentation.
  2. If unable to get expert resource person discuss the perils of smoking "pot."
      a. Causes birth defects, psychological addiction, sexual problems, brain damage, etc.
      b. It interferes with cell division and can cause abnormalities. (In young children and adolescents this can result in users becoming old before their time.)
      c. Reduces the number of cell divisions. (This is comparable to people later in life.)
      d. The more "pot" is used, the more it is needed; the more it is needed, the more dangerous it becomes.
      e. Marijuana smokers have about a 40% reduction in white blood cells. Lessens the body's ability to fight disease.
      f. Can cause cancer.
      g. The genetic mutations reduce the number of chromosomes that carry our hereditary characteristics.
      h. Impairs reproductive capability.
      i. Miscarriages increase.
      j. Despite what many believe, longtime users can get hooked by developing psychic dependence.
      k. Withdrawals lead to personality upsets: quarrelsome, anxious, impulsive, etc.
      l. The main point to drive home is that users have altered perceptions and impaired judgment. It is a hallucinogen.
      m. Smell the crushed alfalfa. (It resembles marijuana in this respect.)
      n. Not an innocuous drug.
      o. There were about 10,000,000 pounds of marijuana smoked last year in the United States.

The reason why there are no old addicts.

D. Results:
  1. Students should learn that use of "pot" leads to other deadly drugs.
  2. Almost all heroin addicts start with smoking tobacco, then marijuana.

E. Supplemental Information:
  1. Cannabis is the dried parts of the hemp plant from which marijuana is derived.
  2. Marijuana usage has increased about tenfold over the last eight years and younger and younger children are using it.
  3. Drug use is primarily a health and social problem which has become a police problem.
  4. We must make the outside world more attractive than the inside world.

F. Thought Questions:
  1. Should we abuse the only body that we will ever have?
  2. Why do you think people smoke, drink alcoholic beverages, and take mood altering pills?
  3. Have you ever been in closed quarters with people who are smoking? How did you feel? What did you think?
  4. Would you like to lose control of your body?
  5. Would you like to lose control of your mind?

G. Related Topics and Activities:
   1. See especially Activity, V-D-7, "Smoking Cigarettes."
   2. Compare marijuana and heroin.
   3. See all Activities in this Section.

H. Vocabulary Builders—Spelling Words:
   1) **marijuana**   2) **heroin**   3) **psychic**
   4) **dependency**   5) **abnormalities**   6) **hallucinogen**

I. Thought for Today:
   "Freedom is the right to be wrong, not the right to do wrong."— John G. Diefenbach

Activity

A. Problem: *Is Alcohol Bad for Our Health?*

B. Materials:
 1. Empty beer can
 2. Empty wine bottle
 3. Empty whiskey bottle
 4. Rubbing alcohol
 5. Earthworm
 6. Saucer

C. Procedure:
 1. Have students relate experiences with drinking people without citing names.
 2. Discuss why some young people drink:
    a. they think they are grown up
    b. to show off
    c. to escape from reality
    d. peer pressure
 3. Describe the different drinks that contain alcohol.
 4. Tell how it is not what you drink but how much alcohol is consumed that affects the person and can make him/her drunk or cause death.
 5. Place some alcohol in saucer.
 6. Place earthworm in the saucer.
 7. Observe results.

D. Results:
 1. The earthworm will die.
 2. Students will learn about the harmful effects of drinking.

E. Supplemental Information:
 1. Alcoholism is a serious major health problem in the United States.
 2. Beer contains 2–5% alcohol; wines, 8–17%.
 3. Whiskey, gin, rum contain 40–50% alcohol.
 4. Alcohol is a depressant, not a stimulant.
 5. Alcohol dulls the nerve centers in the brain.
 6. Muscular coordination is affected.
 7. Visual acuity is reduced.
 8. Forty percent of all automobile fatalities are caused by drinking drivers.
 9. Drinking by drivers and pedestrians is said to cause 30,000 highway deaths a year.
 10. Alcohol leads to brain damage usually to delirium tremens (horrifying hallucinations).
 11. Seventy percent of all adults drink.
 12. There are 13,000,000 alcoholics in the United States. (compulsive drinkers)

 13. All alcoholic drinks contain ethyl alcohol (C_2H_5OH).
 14. Ninety percent of alcohol gets into the bloodstream in an hour.
 15. If a 150 pound person drinks two beers, the alcohol level in his/her blood = 0.05%
    .10% affects motor activity
    .20% affects the midbrain (sleep)
    .50% could produce death from respiratory failure.
 16. Alcohol affects the liver and leads towards cirrhosis of the liver.
 17. Alcohol is involved in 31% of the homicides and 36% of the suicides.
 18. Half of all the crimes are committed by people under the influence of alcohol.
 19. "Don't let peer pressure lead to beer pressure."

F. Thought Questions:
 1. Are there any good arguments for drinking?
 2. Do you think some people drink for social reasons?
 3. Do you think some people drink because they are persuaded by friends? advertisements? peers?

G. Related Topics and Activities:
 1. See especially Activities on all drugs.
 2. Visit a grocery store and observe the liquor section.
 3. Have the school nurse discuss the problems of alcohol.
 4. Have a lecture from a recovering alcoholic.
 5. See all Activities in this Section.

H. Vocabulary Builders—Spelling Words:
   1) **alcohol**   2) **drinking**   3) **beer**   4) **wine**
   5) **whiskey**   6) **earthworm**

I. Thought for Today:
   "If you drink like a fish, swim, don't drive."

A. Problem: *Are Illicit Drugs Bad for Our Health?*

B. Materials:
1. Simulated pills
   a. Capsules from drugstore
   b. Food coloring added to salt, sugar
2. Pictures of real pills
3. Pictures of drugged individuals
4. Newspaper articles about drugs

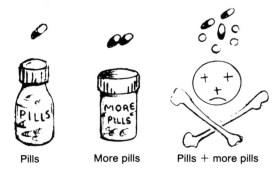

Pills   More pills   Pills + more pills

C. Procedure:
1. Discuss the rise of the use of drugs among young people.
2. Discuss why the drugs are used:
   a. profit
   b. peer pressure
   c. taking a dare
   d. false sense of reality
   e. escape from problems
3. Show students the simulated pills and briefly describe each:
   a. stimulants (uppers) amphetamines, cocaine
      1) deaden body's normal warning systems
      2) Methedrine (speed) can cause brain damage, paranoia
         a) person becomes jittery
         b) false sense of bravado
      3) street names are "A," bennies, pep pills, dexies, co-pilots, crystals, coke, snow
   b. depressants (downers) barbiturates
      1) overdose can paralyze breathing center
      2) drowsiness or escape (false)
      3) defective judgment can lead to falls, accidents, etc.
      4) street names are yellow-jackets, red birds, purple-hearts, blue heaven, etc.
   c. hallucinogens
      1) altered perceptions
      2) impaired judgment
      3) common street names: pot, grass, joint
   d. narcotics (opium, morphine, heroin)
      1) loss of appetite
      2) painful withdrawal symptoms
      3) temporary impotency or sterility
      4) common street names: "M," Miss Emma, "H," horse, junk, smack

D. Results:
1. Students will learn correct information about illicit drugs from their teacher; not from their peers.
2. Pupils will realize that adults know about drugs and the problems associated with their use.

E. Supplemental Information:
1. Drug use is becoming more prevalent among our young children.
2. If they don't get honest information from the homes and schools, they will believe the street information.
3. Over half of the amphetamines find their way to the illegal market.
4. Many students who take pep pills to cram for exams lack the coordination to take the exam.
5. Over 3,000 deaths per year in the U.S. result from the use of barbiturates.
6. Don't let street names fool you—all illicit drugs are potentially killers—sooner or later.
7. Drug use is primarily a health and social problem, but has become a police problem.
8. Most people take drugs to relieve anxieties. They're not pursuing pleasure; they want to hurt less.
9. The solution is education, not prisons.
10. Drug users can be detected by:
    a. change in behavior
    b. new questionable friends
    c. drowsiness
    d. callousness
    e. lack of concentration
    f. falling down in grades at school

F. Thought Questions:
   1. If you know anybody who is on drugs why do you think she/he is taking them?
   2. Do you think youngsters take drugs for kicks, curiosity, rebellion—or what?
   3. Why are potent drugs prescribed only by doctors?

G. Related Topics and Activities:
   1. Compare alcohol to drugs.
   2. Best education is to have a former drug addict talk to class.
   3. See all Activities in this Section.

H. Vocabulary Builders—Spelling Words:
   1) **illicit**   2) **drugs**   3) **hallucinogens**
   4) **stimulants**   5) **depressants**   6) **narcotics**

I. Thought for Today:
   "Dare to say NO to drugs."

Section E: Public Health

Activity

vE1

A. Problem: *How Are Diseases Spread?*

B. Materials:
1. Pictures of:
   a. bacteria
   b. fungi
   c. viruses
   d. people
   e. white blood cells
   f. doctors
   g. hospitals
2. Empty medicine bottles

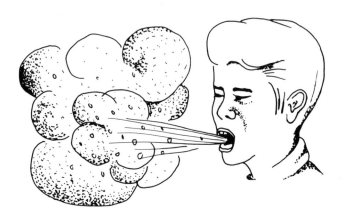

C. Procedure:
1. Ask the class if they have ever been sick. Have each student describe an illness: symptoms, length of time, methods of cure, etc.
2. Teach the pupils that:
   a. All communicable diseases are caused by microorganisms.
   b. Microorganisms are too small to be seen with the naked eye.
   c. Microorganisms grow in unsanitary conditions.
   d. Bacteria, one-celled plants, are microorganisms.
   e. Some bacteria are helpful to people, others cause disease.
   f. Most fungi, like bacteria, are tiny plants and some are helpful and some are harmful.
   g. Yeast is a type of fungi; so are molds.
   h. Viruses are another kind of microorganism which cause colds, chicken pox, measles, etc., and are so small that they can live inside bacteria.
   i. All microorganisms must enter the body some way to cause disease (mouth, nose, cut, bites).
   j. Some diseases are spread through air, water, milk, and other food.
   k. Some diseases are spread by animals and people.
   l. Medicine should only be taken on the advice of a doctor.

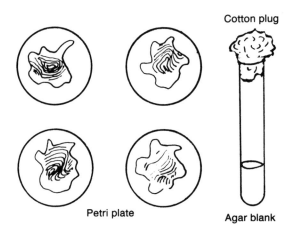

Cotton plug

Petri plate

Agar blank

3. For older students, or a teacher demonstration obtain three Petri dishes (plates) and agar, and in a water bath, melt the agar blanks.
4. Pour agar into Petri plates, taking care not to expose to air.
5. Invert the Petri plates and allow the agar to set.
6. Divide one plate into quarters by making marks with a pencil.
7. Taking care not to expose to air longer than necessary, have four students place the tips of their fingers in each of the four quarters. Re-cover the plate.
8. Have one student cough in the second Petri plate and re-cover.
9. Leave third Petri dish unexposed.
10. Incubate all Petri dishes at 37° C. for 24 hours.

D. Results:

1. Students will learn how diseases are spread.
2. Students will be better able to protect themselves from disease.
3. Bacteria will grow in Petri dishes exposed to touch or cough.

E. Supplemental Information:

1. The first line of defense against microorganisms is the skin and nasal and mouth membranes.
2. The white blood cells form the second line of defense.
3. The third line of defense is the body's antitoxins.
4. The last line of defense is the medical doctor.
5. Since the nutrient agar plates were sterile before the exposures, then any bacteria growth observed will be due to the fact that bacteria were present on the fingers and in the expired air of the cough. This should demonstrate the necessity for washing the hands and for covering the mouth when coughing.
6. A violent sneeze scatters some 20,000 water droplets through the air. If these carry rhinoviruses, the kind associated with the common cold, then nearby people may join the millions each year who catch cold and spend billions of dollars on remedies that so far have done little more than to psychologically minimize symptoms.

F. Thought Questions:

1. Are there unsanitary conditions in your home, neighborhood, and city?
2. Who should be responsible for cleanliness in your home, neighborhood, and city?
3. Do you think we can ever eliminate disease?
4. Where else are bacteria likely to be?
5. Are all bacteria bad?
6. Are there bacteria in the air?

G. Related Topics and Activities:

1. Study and/or discuss digging the Panama Canal and the problems workers encountered with disease.
2. Study and/or discuss the Black Plague that hit Europe in the Middle Ages (14th and 15th centuries).
3. See all Activities in this Section.

H. Vocabulary Builders—Spelling Words:

1) **diseases**   2) **spread**   3) **bacteria**
4) **fungi**   5) **viruses**

I. Thought for Today:

"A cold is both positive and negative, sometimes the eyes have it, sometimes the nose." —William Lyon Phelps

Activity

A. Problem: *How Does the Government Protect Our Health and Safety?*

B. Materials:
1. Toy cars
2. Empty medicine bottle
3. Glass of water
4. Empty, clean can with label
5. Pictures of meat, food
6. Pictures of unsanitary conditions
7. Toy fire engine
8. Toy ambulance
9. Model of street traffic control lights

C. Procedure:
1. Describe to the class how important it is to be healthy and to practice safety.
2. There are hundreds of examples of governmental regulations that can be effectively used in a lesson on health and safety. A few examples might be:
   a. Automobile speed limits
   b. Traffic controls: lights, lanes, rules
   c. Unsafe drinking water (Only about 50% of our drinking water is relatively safe.)
   d. Honest weights (meat, cans, gasoline)
   e. Licenses (for competent services)
   f. Fire protection
   g. Accident help (ambulance, hospital, paramedics)
   h. Inspections for health and safety
   i. Keeps records
   j. Maintains clinics
3. Have the principal of the school discuss health services and safety inspections.
4. Discuss why government conducts inspections and establishes health laws.

D. Results:
1. Students will learn that the government helps to protect our health and safety.
2. Pupils should learn that the best health and safety precaution is their own behavior.

E. Supplemental Information:
1. The United States Food and Drug Administration attempts to keep our foods and drugs safe. Unfortunately they are understaffed and cannot be as effective as they should be.
2. In threats of specific diseases, the government frequently offers free immunizations.

Government Inspected

3. The government is always trying to reduce our traffic casualties. There are about 50,000 deaths and several million injuries per year due to automobile accidents.

F. Thought Questions:
1. What do you think would happen to us if the government stopped protecting us from impure foods and drugs and unsafe conditions?
2. Would you eat in any public eating place if you thought the food might be unclean?
3. Should children on bicycles know and obey the traffic signals?
4. Do school custodians protect your health and safety?

G. Related Topics and Activities:
1. Discuss public health dangers.
2. Find out what governmental agencies in your community are concerned with health.
3. See all Activities in this Section.

H. Vocabulary Builders—Spelling Words:
1) **government**   2) **health**   3) **safety**
4) **inspections**   5) **clinics**

I. Thought for Today:
"Today is the tomorrow you worried about yesterday, and all is well."

Activity

A. Problem: *How Is Water Purified?*

B. Materials:
1. Large jar as illustrated
2. Stopper
3. Three-inch piece of glass tubing
4. Clean gravel
5. Coarse clean sand
6. Very fine sand
7. Charcoal paste (carbon and water)
8. Paste
9. Glass bowl
10. Dirty water
11. Supporting device

C. Procedure:
1. Insert glass tube into center of stopper.
2. Put stopper with tube in the small end of jar.
3. Fill the jar with the following layers in this order:
   a. two inches of clean gravel (A)
   b. two inches coarse, clean sand (B)
   c. one-half inch fine sand (C)
   d. one-half inch charcoal paste (D)
4. Pour some dirty water solution into jar. Save some for comparison.

D. Result:
The muddy water drains through the filter, leaving the foreign particles behind and yielding clean water.

E. Supplemental Information:
Impurities have been held back by the sharp edges of the ingredients as the water seeped through each layer, thus giving us the filtered water. Filtration is part of the procedure used in purifying water. Unclean drinking water can carry many diseases. Among the most common are dysentary, cholera, and bacterial infections. It is estimated that 60 million Americans are now drinking water of questionable standards. In the event of a natural disaster water should be boiled for at least five minutes. Many

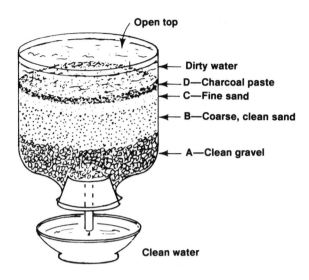

Americans are now buying bottled water or using water from their regular pipes which have had a filter added.

F. Thought Questions:
1. What other methods do we use to keep our water clean?
2. What are some possible contaminants?
3. Is it possible to get fresh water from the sea?

G. Related Topics and Activities:
1. See Section I-C, "Water."
2. Check with the local health department on the status of your community's water purity.
3. Check with the same department on the effectiveness of home water filtering systems.
4. See all Activities in this Section.

H. Vocabulary Builders—Spelling Words:
1) **purified**   2) **gravel**   3) **charcoal**
4) **impurities**   5) **ingredients**

I. Thought for Today:
"If you don't think cooperation is necessary, watch what happens to a wagon if one wheel comes off."

Section F: First Aid

Activity

vF1

A. Problem: *What Are the Main Procedures of First Aid?*

B. Materials:
1. Compresses
2. Tourniquets
3. Vaseline
4. Bactine
5. Disinfectant
6. Soap
7. Band Aids
8. Cotton swabs
9. Roller bandages
10. First aid kit
11. Red Cross First Aid Book

C. Procedure:

The teacher, doctor, school nurse, or a qualified first aid instructor could demonstrate the following:
1. Have class list the ways that they have seen people injured.
2. Discuss what was done in each of these cases.
3. Demonstrate the proper kind of first aid in each instance.
4. Discuss other injuries and discomforts that people have suffered.
5. Discuss the order of treating patients with multiple first aid problems.

D. Results:
1. Students should learn the proper procedures for:
   a. object in the eye
   b. fainting
   c. convulsions
   d. overdose of sleeping pills
   e. burns
   f. poisons
   g. drowning
   h. insect bites
   i. scratches, cuts, wounds
   j. bruises
   k. epileptic seizures
   l. nosebleed
   m. bleeding
2. Students will develop skills in treating minor injuries.

How would you help a girl who has fainted?

E. Supplemental Information:
1. Stress should be on the fact that first aid is only a temporary treatment until a doctor is available.
2. In drowning and loss of breathing, mouth-to-mouth resuscitation should be taught. If children are squeamish about putting their mouths on another, a plastic square with a hole cut in the center can be used.

F. Thought Questions:
1. Which of the items listed in Results is most dangerous and, therefore, should be administered to first?
2. Can police and firemen help in administering first aid?
3. What is the role of paramedics?

G. Related Topics and Activities:
1. Have a fireman, paramedic, school nurse, or school doctor discuss first aid procedures.
2. Take a field trip with selected students to visit a hospital's emergency facilities.
3. See all Activities in this Section.

H. Vocabulary Builders—Spelling Words:
1) **first aid** 2) **compresses** 3) **tourniquet**
4) **sterile** 5) **fainting** 6) **burns**
7) **abrasions** 8) **other terms in Results**

I. Thought for Today:
"The life of the party may be death on the highway."

Activity

A. Problem: *How Can Breathing Be Restored in Drowning or Shock?*

B. Materials:
1. Student volunteers
2. Handkerchiefs
3. Plastic squares
4. American Red Cross First Aid Book

C. Procedure:

The teacher, doctor, school nurse, or members of the fire department rescue squad could conduct the following activity:
1. Discuss ways that breathing might be stopped or impaired: drowning, poisonous gases, shock, choking, etc.
2. Discuss different ways that artificial respiration has been done in the past. (rolling over logs, holding legs up, etc.) (Death comes quickly if air doesn't get into the lungs.)
3. Demonstrate mouth-to-mouth resuscitation as preferred method.
   a. Start as quickly as possible.
   b. Bend neck back, keep one hand underneath.
   c. Pinch nose, keep closed.
   d. Cover mouth with handkerchief or plastic square with hole in it. (In real cases, must use mouth if no cover is available.)
   e. Take a deep breath and blow into victim's mouth. (If you cannot, blow into victim's nose.)
   f. If a small child, blow into both.
   g. After blowing in, remove your mouth and listen for air exhalation.
   h. Repeat about 12 times a minute for adults, 20 times a minute for children.
   i. Keep respiration going until breathing is restored or there is no possibility of recovery.

D. Results:
1. Students will learn how to do mouth-to-mouth resuscitation.
2. Students will gain confidence in attempting this procedure.

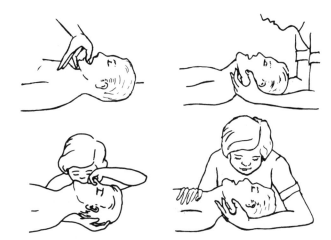

E. Supplemental Information:
1. A doctor, fire department members, or paramedics should be summoned as quickly as possible.
2. Many needless deaths occur because no one has administered artificial respiration or CPR effectively and soon enough.
3. Cardiopulmonary Resuscitation (CPR) should also be taught to older students. Everyone should learn this technique.

F. Thought Questions:
1. Should people ever swim alone?
2. What would cause people to be in a state of shock?
3. Which should be done first, restore breathing or stop bleeding?

G. Related Topics and Activities:
1. Doctors, nurses, paramedics can present this Activity effectively.
2. Check with Red Cross for appropriate pamphlets.
3. See all Activities in this Section.

H. Vocabulary Builders—Spelling Words:
1) **breathing** 2) **drowning** 3) **resuscitation**
4) **artificial** 5) **victim**

I. Thought for Today:
"A young person is a theory; an old person is a fact." — Ed Howe

Activity

A. Problem: *How Can Severe Bleeding Be Stopped?*

B. Materials:
   1. Sterile bandages
   2. Ruler or stick
   3. Multi-sensory aids on first aid

C. Procedure:
   1. Make believe one student is injured and losing blood.
   2. Determine area injured (face, head, arm, body, leg).
   3. If more than one area is injured, determine the most severe.
   4. This should include recognition of type of wound (vein or artery) and reason why knowledge is essential (to prevent excessive loss of blood). Consider these points:
      a. Arterial blood will spurt; venous blood will ooze or run steadily.
      b. Tourniquets are used *only* for severe arterial wounds on arms or legs.
      c. Tourniquets should be applied and released periodically to prevent permanent injury to member from loss of circulation.
      d. Sterile compresses are used for all other types of bleeding.
      e. It is important to keep bandages from sticking to wounds.
      f. Puncture wounds should be allowed to bleed to cleanse wound if bleeding is not excessive.
      g. Cleanliness is important.
   5. Discuss the nature of blood and the reasons why blood will clot on small wounds.
   6. Students should be given opportunity to use tourniquets and compresses.
      Caution: Do not allow tourniquet to stop flow of blood to any area for more than a very short time.

D. Result:
Students will learn the correct methods of stopping bleeding.

E. Supplemental Information:
Stopping loss of blood through excessive bleeding may save a life. That life may be the pupil's own. Almost all areas

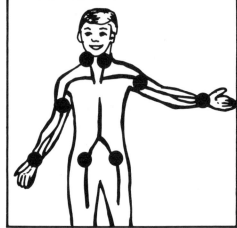

Pressure points to help stop severe bleeding

of the body can be self-treated in an emergency. The dangers of tourniquets are lessened through knowledge of what may happen through improper use. Students should realize that they can use these techniques on themselves in an emergency.

F. Thought Questions:
   1. What are pressure points?
   2. Why should compresses be sterile?
   3. Should tourniquets be placed above or below the wound for arterial bleeding? for venous bleeding? Why? How can you tell the difference?

G. Related Topics and Activities:
1. Visit a pharmacy for possible first aid supplies.
2. Talk to pharmacists.
3. See all Activities in this Section.

H. Vocabulary Builders—Spelling Words:
1) **bleeding**   2) **compresses**   3) **tourniquet**
4) **vein**   5) **artery**

I. Thought for Today:
"I seldom think of the future; it comes soon enough."

Activity

A. Problem: *How Can We Help a Person with Injuries on the Arms or Legs?*

B. Materials:
1. Triangular bandage
2. Roller bandages
3. Sterile compresses
4. First aid pamphlets

C. Procedure:
1. Discuss why first aid should be learned.
2. Demonstrate some of the uses of triangular bandages.
3. Show how to apply roller bandages.
4. Illustrate the uses of sterile compresses.
5. Let the students practice, using each type of first aid material.
6. Let the students check each other's bandages for correct application (with the teacher overseeing, of course).

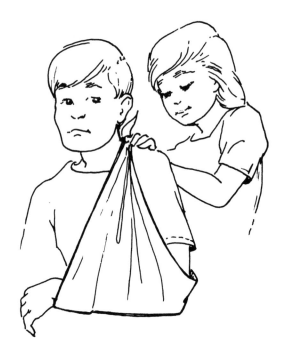

D. Result:

The students will learn some of the correct techniques for administering first aid.

E. Supplemental Information:
1. It in never too early to learn how to take care of ourselves and to aid others when accidents occur. Students should learn when to and when not to use bandages. The American Red Cross has excellent printed materials on first aid.
2. If you suspect dislocation(s), don't try to "put it back." Get help. If bone(s) return or snap back, still see a doctor because frequently there is damage to the ligaments and blood vessels.

F. Thought Questions:
1. What is the first thing a person should do in case of a serious accident?
2. What is the danger in moving a broken limb?
3. In a multiple injury, how do you determine which injury is most serious?

G. Related Topics and Activities:
1. See the following Activities:
   a. Activity V-A-3, "Kinds of Bones."
   b. Activity V-A-4, "How Heart Works."
   c. Activity V-A-5, "Finding Pulse."
2. Simulate aftermath of earthquakes, tornadoes, or auto accidents.
3. See all Activities in this Section.

H. Vocabulary Builders—Spelling Words:
1) **triangular**   2) **roller**   3) **sterile**
4) **compresses**   5) **bandages**

I. Thought for Today:
"We are all faced with a series of great opportunities disguised as insoluble problems."

Activity

A. Problem: *Why Do We Use Medicine and Pills?*

B. Materials:
1. Two Petri dishes with nutritive materials
2. Antiseptic
3. Adhesive tape
4. Cotton
5. Gauze

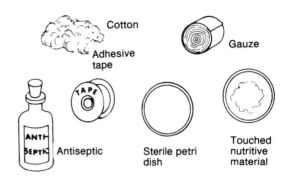

Cotton
Adhesive tape
Gauze
Antiseptic
Sterile petri dish
Touched nutritive material

C. Procedure:
1. Discuss reasons medicines, drugs, and pills are prescribed by doctors.
2. Have a student volunteer pretend she/he has an open wound or cut on his/her finger.
3. Touch skin surrounding the make-believe wound to the sterile Petri dish containing nutritive material and cover the dish.
4. Use antiseptic on the finger and repeat Petri dish experiment touching the dish with the part of the finger that has become sterilized.
5. Label both Petri dishes: one labeled "No Antiseptic" and the other, "Sterilized."
6. Store Petri dishes in a warm, dark place.
7. After three or four days, uncover both Petri dishes and examine contents.

D. Results:
1. The Petri dish marked "Sterilized" will have little or no bacterial growth.
2. The other Petri dish will show positive bacterial growth.

E. Supplemental Information:
1. On the skin there are many bacteria that grow and multiply.
2. Wounds should be disinfected to kill bacteria which otherwise would enter the wound and cause infection.
3. It is wise to avoid pills except on doctor's prescription(s).
4. Some pills do more harm than good.
5. Some pills are addictive:
   a. Aspirin—slightly (could cause ulcers) (also bleeding in sensitive people)
   b. Codeine
   c. Some nasal sprays
6. Medicinal sprays with Freon are destroying our ozone shield causing an excessive amount of

ultraviolet light to strike our planet, thus inducing the possibility of more skin cancer.
7. Mouthwashes don't help. They may kill good and bad bacteria. The good bacteria are our first line of defense.
8. Most diet pills don't work. They reduce the water content of the body thus giving people a psychological lift.
9. There are over 100,000 over-the-counter drugs and pills. No one knows for sure how they will interact with other body chemicals.

F. Thought Questions:
1. What would happen if your finger were touched to a Petri dish and an antiseptic was added over the touched area?
2. What are some good antiseptic agents?
3. What are bacteria? Are they all bad?

G. Related Topics and Activities:
1. Have a pharmacist talk to the class about drugs and medicine.
2. Discuss the dangers of "street drugs." See Activity V-D-10.
3. Discuss the damages that can be done to the body's chemical factory by putting unprescribed chemicals into it.
4. See all Activities in this Section.

H. Vocabulary Builders—Spelling Words:
1) **medicine**   2) **drugs**   3) **pills**
4) **antiseptic**   5) **sterilize**   6) **Petri dish**

I. Thought for Today:
"Trying to squash a rumor is like trying to unring a bell."

Section G: Safety

Activity

vG1

A. Problem: *How Can We Prevent Accidents?*

B. Materials:
1. Pictures of traffic accidents
2. Empty drug bottles
3. Empty gasoline can
4. Matches
5. Empty garden poison containers
6. Knife
7. Pictures or write-ups of swimming accidents
8. Bulletin board

C. Procedure:
1. The most effective way to teach accident prevention is to keep a running record of each accident found in the media or occurring to a class member. Some clippings or notices should be kept on the bulletin board. Some typical accidents might be:
   a. traffic accidents
   b. falls
   c. fires
   d. burns
   e. poisons (medicine cabinet and garage)
   f. contaminated or spoiled food
   g. cuts and wounds
   h. swimming accidents, etc.
2. Teacher should lead discussion on each type of accident.
3. Students should make suggestions on how each type of accident might have been prevented.
4. A safety check of the homes can be conducted: See Activity V-G-4 on "How safe are our homes?"
5. This activity could be part of a health unit on first aid.

D. Result:
Students will become more conscious of accident potentials and hopefully reduce the number of accidents occurring to young people.

E. Supplemental Information:
1. Accidents are the leading cause of death and injury to young people.

2. Resource people provide added emphasis to this vital area. They might include the school nurse, firefighter, police officer, doctor, member of emergency rescue team, etc.
3. Types of Home Fatalities for Young Children:
   a. Fires, burns 50%
   b. Firearms 23%
   c. Falls 6%
   d. Poisons 3%
   e. Miscellaneous 18%
4. The primary cause of fatalities of children outside the home is automobile accidents.

F. Thought Questions:
1. What kinds of accidents could occur at school? in the homes? on the playground? in swimming pools?
2. What kind of accidents could kill people?
3. Who are the people who are employed to take care of people who have accidents?

G. Related Topics and Activities:
1. Have a member of the paramedics or rescue squad talk to class.
2. Interview a nurse in a hospital emergency service.

3. Divide class in four sections and have each section work on one of the four main areas of accidents:
   a. highways
   b. work
   c. play
   d. home
4. Visit a fire station.
5. See all Activities in this Section

H. Vocabulary Builders—Spelling Words:
   1) **accident**   2) **prevent**   3) **traffic**
   4) **burns**   5) **falls**   6) **swimming**

I. Thought for Today:
   "Accident statistics prove the road to heaven is paved."

Activity

A. Problem: *What Traffic Signals Should We Know?*

B. Materials:
   1. Area of the playground with chalk-marked traffic lanes
   2. Traffic light mock-up (or red, yellow, and green cut-out circles)
   3. Railroad signal gate-guard mock-up
   4. Charts with "WALK," "DON'T WALK," and "WAIT" on them
   5. Chalk
   6. Mock-up stop sign
   7. Pictures of traffic with:
      a. automobiles
      b. bicycles and/or
      c. pedestrians

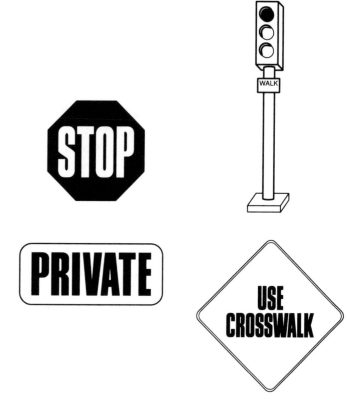

C. Procedure:
   1. Teacher marks an intersection with chalk on the playground. This should include traffic lanes and pedestrian crosswalks.
   2. Discuss rules for stop sign.
   3. Teacher discusses the following traffic color signals:
      a. Red—stop
      b. Yellow—caution (or slow)
      c. Green—go
   4. Teacher discusses lanes for automobiles and pedestrian crosswalks.
   5. Using the street layout, the teacher uses the traffic light mock-up or the circle cut-outs to have each student react to various traffic signals by walking, stopping, or waiting.
   6. The teacher repeats the activity using only the "WALK," "DON'T WALK," and "WAIT" cards.
   7. For older students the teacher can explain the function of railroad signal drop-gates.
   8. When class is back inside pictures of traffic can be studied for safe and unsafe practices.
   9. If the school has school crossing guards the teacher should play this role and have students walk through typical situations.

D. Result:
Students will learn the rules of the road and traffic safety procedures.

E. Supplemental Information:
   1. In the United States the number one cause of death and injury among people from birth through twenty-four years of age is traffic accidents.
   2. Most traffic signals are on a 60-second cycle and the students should be taught patience and safety in waiting.
   3. Most pedestrian accidents occur after school hours between 3 p.m. and 6 p.m.
   4. A traffic safety bulletin board is always an effective supplement to this activity.
   5. A felt board demonstration can also be used as a supplemental aid.

F. Thought Questions:
   1. Could a pedestrian be right and still be injured or killed in a traffic accident?
   2. What precautions should a pedestrian take if there are no traffic signals or pedestrian crossing lanes?
   3. How can traffic accidents be reduced?

G. Related Topics and Activities:
   1. Have students draw a simple traffic light and color appropriate signals.
   2. Collect pictures of traffic accidents and post on bulletin board.
   3. Discuss controlled and uncontrolled intersections.
   4. Play act out traffic hazards. (Shoe boxes can be pretend automobiles or bicycles.)

H. Vocabulary Builders—Spelling Words:
   1) **traffic**   2) **signal**   3) **walk**
   4) **wait**   5) **stop sign**   6) **caution**

I. Thought for Today:
   "Drive as if you owned the other car."

Activity

A. Problem: *What Safety Precautions Should I Take When Riding a Bicycle?*

B. Materials:
  1. Bicycle
  2. Area on the playground marked off with traffic lanes
  3. Model of traffic light

C. Procedure:
  1. Discuss with students problems that might happen to bicycles such as:
     a. brake failure
     b. broken chain
     c. troubled gears
     d. flat tire, etc.
  2. Teach and/or review directional arm signals for drivers of bicycles and cars.
  3. Teach and/or review traffic signals.
  4. Describe bicycle accessories that help with bicycle safety such as:
     a. reflectors
     b. lights
     c. horns
     d. viewing rods with flags
  5. Simulate normal traffic signals and have a student demonstrate by walking a bicycle through the correct procedures at intersections for each sequence of lights.
  6. Have one student walk a bicycle and a second student walk by his side to demonstrate proper arm signals for each type of turn and stop.
  7. Discuss with students what should be done if a serious problem happens to the bicycle.
  8. Discuss the do's and don't's of bicycle riding.
     a. Do watch for other vehicles.
     b. Do practice safety riding.
     c. Do follow the rules of the road.
     d. Don't be a show-off on a bicycle.
     e. Don't ride on the sidewalk.
     f. Don't ride at night without lights, etc.

D. Result:
Students will learn about bicycle safety in a safe area.

E. Supplemental Information:
Bicycle accidents and traffic deaths among youngsters are far too high and most are due to carelessness and lack of bicycle safety education.

F. Thought Questions:
  1. Should bicycle riders be licensed the same as automobile drivers?
  2. Should bicycle riders who break the law be given traffic violation tickets?
  3. Can bicycles be legally ridden on sidewalks in your community?

G. Related Topics and Activities:
  1. Discuss bicycle problems at uncontrolled intersections.
  2. Discuss the concept of right of way.
  3. See all Activities in this Section.

H. Vocabulary Builders—Spelling Words:
  1) **safety**   2) **precaution**   3) **bicycle**
  4) **intersection**   5) **uncontrolled**

I. Thought for Today:
"In large cities, the rush hour is when the traffic is almost at a standstill."

Activity

A. Problem: *How Safe Are Our Homes?*

B. Materials:
1. Bottles marked "Poison"
2. Sample bottles from medicine cabinet
3. Cooking pan with handle
4. Poisonous insect spray cans
5. Dirty rags, etc.

C. Procedure:
1. Have class discuss how they have been hurt around the house.
2. Have class discuss how others have been injured around their homes by such accidents as burns, scalds, falls, fire, drinking unprescribed medicines, etc.
3. Have each child become a "Home Health and Safety Inspector" for a day to see if anything that is potentially dangerous can be found.
4. Discuss the possible results of carelessness around the home.
5. Discuss the benefit of smoke and fire alarms in the home.
6. Discuss ways that homes can be made safe from burglars. (alarm systems, dead bolts, vacation precautions, etc.)

D. Result:

Students will become more aware of hazards around the home and the consequences if left unattended or uncorrected.

E. Supplemental Information:
1. Accidents around the home are one of the leading causes of deaths and severe injuries of young children.
2. There are many potentially dangerous practices around the home:
   a. Cooking with pots whose handles are not turned toward center of stove.
   b. Medicines, sprays, insecticides within easy reach of children.
   c. Anywhere there are fires or heat is a potential danger area: fireplace, stove, kerosene type heater, water heater, furnace, etc.
3. Unfortunately, crime is on the increase and students should be made aware of not only crime prevention but also what they might do to help prevent such incidents.

F. Thought Questions:
1. How can our homes be made safer?
2. How can our homes be made healthier?
3. What are other potentially dangerous areas in our homes? garages? cars? yards?

G. Related Topics and Activities:
1. Have students make a list of items in the home that can be used for emergencies such as:
   a. first aid kit
   b. fire extinguisher
   c. flashlight
   d. portable radio
   e. shut-off valves
   f. circuit breakers, etc.
2. Have students discuss how their homes are prepared for emergencies such as fire, floods, earthquakes, tornadoes, etc.
3. Ask students what they would do in each of the above cases.
4. Have each student make a list of phone numbers that could be used in an emergency.

H. Vocabulary Builders—Spelling Words:
1) **safety** 2) **inspector** 3) **health**
4) **poison** 5) **alarm** 6) **drinking**

I. Thought for Today:
"Some of our schools have gone modern. The kids who once cleaned erasers now dust the computers."

A. Problem: *How Can I Be Safe in the Water if I Get Tired or Can't Swim Well?*

B. Materials:
   1. Glass aquarium
   2. Inexpensive, flexible doll

C. Procedure:
   1. Discuss some of the dangers of:
      a. boating
      b. swimming
      c. wading
      d. surfing
      e. undertows
      f. scuba diving
   2. Discuss the human body in a water environment:
      a. buoyancy
      b. motion
      c. relaxation
      d. breathing
   3. Survey the class and find out how many can swim and how far.
   4. Fill the aquarium with water.
   5. With the flexible doll, demonstrate the Survival Floating Technique.
      a. Try to get a lung full of air.
      b. Place head in water and let feet and arms and head hang down.
      c. When air is needed, push hands down and raise head above water.
      d. When air is obtained, return to initial position.
   6. Have students stand up and go through motions.

D. Results:
   1. Students will learn this survival technique.
   2. Students will become aware of some of the dangers of water.

E. Supplemental Information:
   1. Most drownings involve young children who cannot swim.
   2. This technique could save thousands of lives each year if children knew how to keep afloat until help arrives.
   3. The Red Cross has printed material about this technique. See or obtain their Swimming and Water Safety manual.

F. Thought Questions:
   1. How long can a person live without air?
   2. What factors determine how long a person could live in water? (salt, temperature, etc.)
   3. What are some ways to reduce drownings?

G. Related Topics and Activities:
   1. Have children discuss some accidents in the water they know about.
   2. If possible talk to lifeguards about their experiences.
   3. Discuss safety around the pool—jumping in too close to others, cramps, etc.

H. Vocabulary Builders—Spelling Words:
   1) **survival**   2) **buoyancy**   3) **breathing**
   4) **relaxation**   5) **technique**

I. Thought for Today:
   "When I see a child, he inspires me in two sentiments: tenderness for what he is, and respect for what he may become."—Louis Pasteur

Activity

A. Problem: *What Should I Do If I Become Lost in the Woods?*

B. Materials:
1. Watch
2. Matches
3. Rocks or pebbles
4. Miniature tent
5. Stick
6. Compass

C. Procedure:
1. Describe how people get lost in the city and in the country.
2. Tell the students that even the people who know the woods (hikers, foresters, scientists) get lost once in a while.
3. Have the students learn some basic rules:
   a. Since panic is the number one problem, sit down and give yourself time to calm down and think.
   b. If someone knows where you are going or roughly where you are, don't go anywhere—help will come to you.
   c. If you have matches or a lighter, make a fire and keep it going day and night. A smoke fire in the daytime can be seen from long distances and this can be made by using green or wet wood and brushes.
   d. Find an open clearing and make a large "HELP" sign out of rocks, limbs, or trenches in snow.
   e. Conserve your energy and strength.
   f. If nobody knows your whereabouts, then try to walk out in a straight line.
      1) Estimate direction of nearest help.
      2) If you have a compass use it, if not, then walk in straight line by lining up high landmarks.
   g. Many people have gone hungry in the woods with many kinds of edible plants surrounding them.
4. Demonstrate procedures with materials listed above.
5. If a person has a portable radio it can be used to determine direction of signal by turning radio until station comes in loudest. The sun will help in determining whether direction is coming from the front or the back of the radio.
6. If a person has a walkie-talkie, use it in short, half-hour periods to conserve batteries. It is a good idea if the person has one to make plans ahead of time to check in with buddy(ies) at designated intervals.

D. Result:
Students will learn a few basic safety rules about getting lost in the woods.

E. Supplemental Information:
1. If a stream is found, it should be noted that water will follow the deepest path down and consequently the shortest.
2. Noisemakers should be attempted by making reeds, blowing across cans or spent cartridges.
3. A wristwatch can be used as a compass. See Activity VII-B-2, "Finding Directions."
4. Hikers should never hike alone.
5. Bearings of mountain peaks, unusual physical features, can help determine placement.
6. People can go weeks without food, days without water, but only hours without heat, so keeping warm should be the primary concern.

F. Thought Questions:
1. What should a person take along when going into some large wooded areas where one is apt to get lost?
2. What is the buddy system?
3. Is it safe to explore alone?

G. Related Topics and Activities:
1. Talk to forest rangers about safety.
2. Discuss with sporting goods salesmen about safety in the woods.
3. See all Activities in this Section.

H. Vocabulary Builders—Spelling Words:
1) **lost**   2) **woods**   3) **help**   4) **hikers**
5) **panic**

I. Thought for Today:
"When I don't have anything to worry about, I begin to worry about that."

Activity

A. Problem: *How Can We Help Prevent Forest Fires?*

B. Materials:
1. Picture of Smokey the Bear
2. Matches
3. Dry grass
4. Metal tray
5. Pitcher of water
6. Quart jar

C. Procedure:
1. Explain the fire triangle:
   a. burnable material
   b. oxygen
   c. heat (kindling point)
2. Tell the pupils how the elimination of one of these will stop any fire.
3. Tell the pupils how if all three of these are present, fire will occur.
4. Place some dry grass on metal tray.
5. Light with a match carefully.
6. Cover with a quart jar. (eliminates oxygen)
7. Place some more dry grass on metal tray.
8. Light with a match carefully.
9. Place cold water on grass (reduces temperature or heat).
10. Light match on tray (nothing burns on the tray as there is nothing burnable).

D. Results:
1. Fire will be extinguished when oxygen is removed.
2. Fire will be extinguished when heat is removed.
3. Fire will not take place if no burnable material is present.

E. Supplemental Information:
1. Many fires are started without matches if the three major elements of the fire triangle are present.
2. For older students, heat can be applied to the tray and a wooden match on top can be ignited.

F. Thought Questions:
1. How are forest fires started?

2. What can be done to prevent forest fires? (Smokey says,
   a. "Break matches in two and put out carefully.
   b. Drown all campfire ashes and drown again.
   c. REMEMBER, ONLY YOU CAN PREVENT FOREST FIRES.")

G. Related Topics and Activities:
   1. See Activity V-G-4, "Safety in Homes."
   2. See Section II-B, "Fire and Heat."
   3. See all Activities in this Section.

H. Vocabulary Builders—Spelling Words:
   1) **Smokey**   2) **burnable**   3) **material**   4) **triangle**
   5) **oxygen**

I. Thought for Today:
   "One tree can make a million matches. One match can destroy a million trees."

Fun with Smokey the Bear

Where Did Smokey Come From?

State and U.S. Foresters appealed for help from the newly organized War Advertising Council, now called the Advertising Council, Inc. This public service agency agreed to sponsor a nationwide forest fire prevention campaign. The Foote, Cone and Belding Advertising Agency of Los Angeles contributed its facilities and talents to help conduct the campaign.

Copywriters and artists brandished pens and brushes, writing text and designing colorful campaign ads. Wartime slogans, such as "CARELESS MATCHES AID THE AXIS," and "OUR CARELESSNESS, THEIR SECRET WEAPON," were used in the 1942 and 1943 campaigns.

Walt Disney's Bambi proved a popular exponent of forest fire prevention on the 1944 posters.

In 1945 the advertisers experimented with still another idea. They portrayed a bear in a ranger's hat and firefighter's dungarees . . . a natural peacetime symbol which melded the emotional appeal of an animal with the ruggedness of a firefighter.

The bear was named Smokey. This friendly character and his slogans slipped into the hearts and homes of millions of Americans; the result—a decrease in forest fires.

Smokey made his public service debut on posters and car cards in 1945. Magazine and newspaper forest fire prevention advertisements soon followed, always showing Smokey in ranger's gear.

Forests are a wonderful place to camp, hike, swim, and play. Forests supply more than 5,000 valuable products and many jobs. The forests provide a home for many of our animal friends.

In the 1980's Smokey was still going strong and he is still needed as forest fires continue to plague all parts of the country. Let's make the 1990's the safest decade on record.

If not you, who?

78-CFFP-4 U.S. Department of Agriculture Forest Service and Your State Forester

Coloring Fun

Protect Little Trees from Fire!

Wouldn't this be a sad world without trees?

Trees are wonderful:

a. They give us shade.

b. They give us a nice place to play.

c. They give us wood.

d. They give us a nice place to live.

Fire kills trees:

a. Trees can't run away from fire like you can.

b. Even if fire doesn't kill trees, it may damage them.

c. Where fire has been, trees can't give us the things we need from them.

SOME THINGS TO DO

1. Make a list of other things trees give us.

2. Write down how trees help birds and animals.

3. Write down why you like to walk in the woods.

SOME THINGS TO REMEMBER

1. Don't play with matches.

2. Keep fire out of the woods.

3. Tell people who smoke to use an ashtray.

4. Put out your campfire with water.

5. Never burn trash when it is windy.

PLEASE, ONLY YOU CAN PREVENT
FOREST FIRES!

How to Build a Safe Campfire:

1. Check the weather—Never build a fire on a dry, windy day.

2. Select an open, level spot. Away from trees, logs, stumps, over-hanging branches, dense dry grass, and forest litter.

3. Clear a 10-foot fire circle to bare soil.

4. Dig a shallow fire pit in the center.

5. Circle fire pit with rocks.

6. Pile wood upwind from the fire.

7. Never leave the fire unattended, even for a moment.

8. Put out the campfire.

9. Be sure it's out-cold! Carefully feel all the ashes with your bare hands. Be sure.

10. Before you leave, check around your campsite for sparks.

Can you find Smokey's friends?

They don't play with matches.
And neither should you.

Part VI

Ecology

Section A: Biological Communities

Activity VIA1

A. Problem: *What Is the Balance of Nature?*

B. Materials:

On ecology:
1. Books
2. Magazines
3. Newspaper accounts
4. Pictures
5. Animal cut-outs

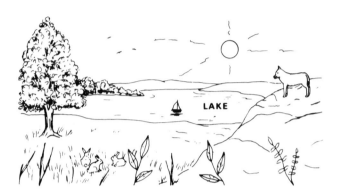

C. Procedure:
1. Discuss ecosystems. (Biotic communities and their environments)
2. Describe several biotic communities. (The interrelationships of all living things)
3. Discuss some of the ecosystems that include humans.
4. Describe some of the limitations of environments:
   a. temperature
   b. food supplies
   c. oxygen
   d. water
   e. land types, soil
5. Discuss the problems of doubling all existing animals (including humans).
6. Discuss the terms food chain and food web.
   a. Food chain—consists of a direct line of energy transfer from the:
      1) sun to plant (producer) to
      2) herbivore to
      3) primary consumer to
      4) secondary consumer to
      5) tertiary or final consumer.
   b. Food web—consists of all the possibilities of food sources and their interrelationships.
7. Students should draw charts of food chains and food webs that they have studied either at school or at home.

D. Results:
1. Students will learn about biotic communities and ecosystems.
2. The pupils will discover as animal populations expand, plant foods decrease.

E. Supplemental Information:
1. The two terms, biotic community and ecosystem, are going to become increasingly important in the language of all peoples especially with the pressure of growing populations and limitations in our food supplies.
2. Many species of animals have become extinct because their ecosystem was drastically changed in one way or another.
3. Many more species are in danger of becoming extinct.

F. Thought Questions:
1. Do we change ecosystems when we spray with strong insecticides?
2. Are there any animals that are 100% bad?
3. If human population doubles what will be the changes in the food web?

G. Related Topics and Activities:
1. See Part III, "Plants."
2. See Part IV, "Animals."
3. See all Activities in this Section.

H. Vocabulary Builders—Spelling Words:
1) **biological**   2) **balance**   3) **nature**
4) **ecosystem**   5) **herbivores**   6) **consumers**
7) **chain**   8) **web**

I. Thought for Today:
"When we were in school the hard stuff meant algebra."

Activity

A. Problem: *How Do We Make a Simple Biotic Community?*

B. Materials:
1. Five-gallon water container (glass)
2. Large cork
3. Sealing wax or paraffin
4. Gravel (small pebbles), sand
5. Freshwater plants (aquarium types)
6. Water
7. One small aquarium-type fish (goldfish is best)
8. Water snails
9. Stick or dowel about 20″ long to affix water plants

C. Procedure to Construct:
1. Fill container with water to about 3 inches from the top.
2. Add sand and gravel.
3. With stick, place plants in gravel and sand bottom. (Plants might have to be weighted.)
4. Have some floating plants as well.
5. Let stand for 24 hours.
6. Place snails and fish in container.
7. Place cork on top and seal with wax or paraffin.
8. Place container near window.

D. Procedure to Teach:
1. Explain to class the fundamentals of a biotic community (plants, animals, environment in balance).
2. Explain the oxygen and carbon dioxide cycle. (Plants in daytime give off oxygen and take in carbon dioxide; animals give off carbon dioxide and take in oxygen.)
3. Explain to class that you are going to make a biotic community with the fish and snails as the animals, the plants as the plants, and the air and the water in the container as the environment.
4. Ask the class how long they think the fish will live.

E. Results:
1. The students will learn more about biotic communities.
2. The fish should live for the entire semester.

F. Supplemental Information:
1. If the fish becomes too large or too sluggish, you may open the container and place the fish in a regular aquarium.
2. The students may keep a record of their observations noting any changes in any of the plants, snails, or fish.
3. A complete biotic community consists of:
   a. producers
   b. consumers
   c. decomposers (recyclers)
   d. materials

G. Thought Questions:
1. What would happen if there were no plants placed in the container?
2. What would happen if several large fish were placed in the container?
3. Does this prove that plants give off oxygen?

H. Related Topics and Activities:
1. See Part III, "Plants."
2. See Part IV, "Animals."
3. See all Activities in this Section.

I. Vocabulary Builders—Spelling Words:
1) **biotic**   2) **community**   3) **wax**
4) **paraffin**   5) **gravel**   6) **gallon**

J. Thought for Today:
"Many a child who watches television for hours will go down in history—not to mention arithmetic, English, and science."

Activity

A. Problem: *What Controls Animal Populations?*

B. Materials:

Pictures of animals:
1. Fish
2. Deer
3. Cattle
4. Sheep
5. Birds

C. Procedure:
1. Discuss food chains.
   See Activity VI-A-2, "Biotic Communities."
2. Discuss ways that animals lose their lives.
3. Students may want to read stories or do research about unusual food chains or animals. This might include:
   a. salmon
   b. wolves
   c. lemmings
   d. tuna
4. Discuss how people kill animals for food and sport.

D. Results:
1. Students will learn about food chains and food webs.
2. Pupils will learn that animal populations are controlled by:
   a. predators
   b. environment
   c. disease
   d. humans
      1) hunting
      2) poisoning
      3) changing environment
   e. animals themselves

E. Supplemental Information:
1. Humans have wiped out some animal species and have endangered many more.
2. Animals tend to balance themselves naturally if left alone.

F. Thought Questions:
1. Do endangered species ever make a comeback?
2. Do humans overhunt and overfish?

3. Who should control sport hunting and fishing?
4. Who should control hunting and fishing of endangered species?

G. Related Topics and Activities:
1. See Part III, "Plants."
2. See Part IV, "Animals."
3. See all Activities in this Section.

H. Vocabulary Builders—Spelling Words:
1) **control**   2) **animal**   3) **population**
4) **wolves**   5) **predators**   6) **disease**

I. Thought for Today:
"An ecologist wants to clean up the world: an environmentalist wants you to clean up your yard."

Activity

A. Problem: *How Do Animal Populations Control Their Numbers?*

B. Materials:
   1. Books or stories about salmon, lemmings, mice, etc.
   2. Large wire cage and accessories
   3. Pet mice

C. Procedure:
   1. Discuss the population problems of all animals.
   2. Discuss how food supplies are limited.
   3. Discuss all factors that are required for growing numbers of any animal population.
   4. Set up mice cage with accessories (nesting area, exercise devices, water source, food supply) (all the comforts of home).
   5. Plan with students to increase the mice population as much as possible.
   6. Keep a record of the number of mice and their physical activity during the course of the unit.
   7. Have one group of students study the life cycle of lemmings.

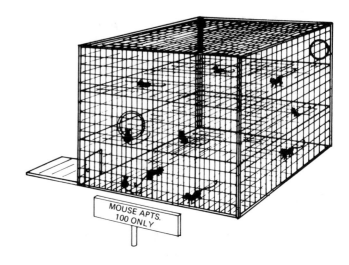

MOUSE APTS. 100 ONLY

D. Results:
   1. Students learn that animal populations control their numbers by adapting only to the limited life space available to them.
   2. In most cases the numbers will grow until they reach a certain number. At that time the students will find that the mice are physically mature but:
      a. mentally immature (act differently)
      b. emotionally immature (act differently)
      c. lazy
      d. refuse to mate

E. Supplemental Information:
   1. Animals, when they become too prolific, limit their populations.
   2. They refuse to reproduce.
   3. Lemmings swim out to sea and drown.

F. Thought Questions:
   1. Why do animals limit their population numbers?
   2. What limits animal populations in the wild?
   3. Many lemmings swim out to sea and drown. If survival of the fittest is the rule of nature why do the strongest lemmings swim out to sea and drown while the weakest ones stay on shore and survive?

G. Related Topics and Activities:
   1. See Part III, "Plants."
   2. See Part IV, "Animals."
   3. See all Activities in this Section.

H. Vocabulary Builders—Spelling Words:
   1) **populations**   2) **exercise**   3) **devices**
   4) **lemmings**   5) **immature**

I. Thought for Today:
   "Adult education will continue as long as children have homework."

Activity

A. Problem: *Are Any Animals Threatened with Extinction?*

B. Materials:

Pictures and accounts of as many of the following as possible:

1. Eastern Elk
2. Passenger Pigeon
3. American Alligator
4. Southern Bald Eagle
5. Columbian White-tailed Deer
6. Utah Prairie Dog
7. Ivory-billed Woodpecker
8. Whooping Crane
9. Wolves
10. Sea Otter
11. Giant Panda
12. Hawk
13. Pine Martin
14. Polar Bears
15. Leopards (five species)
16. Black-footed Ferret
17. Sea Turtles
18. Whales
19. Condors
20. Peregrine Falcon
21. Masked Bobwhite
22. Kirtland's Warbler
23. Eskimo Curlew

C. Procedure:

1. Have students study the general characteristics of each of the major categories in which these animals are found (elk, pigeons, eagles, etc.).
2. Emphasize the interrelationships of these animals to other animals.
3. Describe how these animals are interrelated with various plants.
4. Ask what these animals have in common?

D. Results:

1. The students will learn that the first two animals listed are now extinct.
2. The rest of the creatures are being threatened with extinction.

E. Supplemental Information:

1. Species survive because they have adapted and adjusted.
2. Hawaii, thought to be isolated, is an example of what has happened:
   a. Outside predators have been introduced.
   b. Humans have entered the scene.
   c. Both have reduced freshwater fish, land mullusks, and birds by over 36%.
3. Some ecologists are helping in selected instances.
   a. Sanctuaries in Texas have helped the whooping crane increase its numbers from 15 to nearly 80.

Alligator

Passenger pigeon

   b. Other conservationists have helped with the grizzly bear, bison, and African cheetah.
   c. Turtle farms provide safety to allow this animal to keep from being reduced in large numbers.
4. Defenders of wildlife claim that there are nineteen hundred (1,900) animal species nearing extinction.

F. Thought Questions:

1. Should people be encouraged to wear animal furs of endangered species?
2. What happens when the balance of nature is disturbed?
3. If an animal becomes extinct, can it ever be restored?
4. What can you do to keep nature's beautiful plants and animals from being destroyed?
5. What would happen to us if all the animals were to disappear?
6. What would happen to us if all the plants were to disappear?

G. Related Topics and Activities:

1. Visit a zoo.
2. Visit a fish hatchery.
3. Visit a game refuge.
4. Study how the government protects some animal species.
5. See Part IV, "Animals."
6. See all Activities in this Section.

H. Vocabulary Builders—Spelling Words:

1) **pigeon** 2) **alligator** 3) **eagle**
4) **woodpecker** 5) **wolves**

I. Thought for Today:

"The dictionary is the only place that success comes before work."

Activity

A. Problem: *Is There a Population Explosion? Is the World's Population Growing Too Fast?*

B. Materials:

About population statistics:
1. Magazines
2. Newspapers
3. Chart paper
4. Pencils

C. Procedure:
1. Have students look at all the evidence, statistics, etc. they can collect in regard to the population explosion.
2. Chart these findings for the world.
3. Chart these findings for the United States.
4. Discuss what these findings mean in the way of buildings, doctors, food, water, power, smog, schools, etc.

D. Results:
1. Students will see that there has been a real rise in population.
2. Added growth will create many new problems.

E. Supplemental Information:
1. The world's population in 1970 was 3.5 billion.
2. The expected world's population in 2005 will be about 7 billion (double 1970).
3. In 1987, the world's population rose to 5 billion (5,000,000,000) so we're running just about on schedule.
4. People in hungry countries are doubling twice as fast as individuals in well-fed areas.
5. Vital statistics:

Year	Population	Time to Double
6,000 B.C.	5,000,000	Doubled @
1650 A.D.	500,000,000	1200 yrs.
1850	1 billion	200 yrs.
1930	2 billion	80 yrs.
1975	4 billion	45 yrs.
2010	8 billion	35 yrs.
2900	100 people/sq. yd.	(estimated)

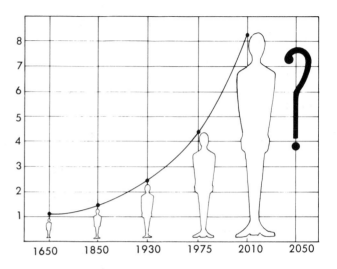

6. Even though the U.S. birthrate has dropped, there are still more women of childbearing age than old people, consequently we are recording more births than deaths.

F. Thought Questions:
1. Will there be enough food, water, air, beautiful rivers, forests, and wildlife in 2005?
2. Do you think there is enough space for all of us?
3. Do we act the same in crowded places as we do otherwise?
4. Do you think it is fair for the U.S., which has 5% of the world's population, to consume 35% of the world's resources?

G. Related Topics and Activities:
1. See Part V, "Health."
2. See Section IV-G, "Mammals."
3. See all Activities in this Section.

H. Vocabulary Builders—Spelling Words:
1) **population** 2) **explosion** 3) **evidence**
4) **statistics** 5) **graph**

I. Thought for Today:
"The glory of young people is their strength; of old people, their experience."

Activity

A. Problem: *Is There Enough Food to Feed All the People of the World?*

B. Materials:
1. Loaf of bread
2. Can of vegetables
3. Carton of milk
4. 10 dolls (paper, clay, flannel board, or real)

C. Procedure:
1. Set the food on the desk or table.
2. Set the ten dolls in a row in front of the food.
3. Ask the class if they think there is enough food to feed the peoples of the world.
4. Discuss some of the problems of producing, transporting, and distributing food to all peoples of the world.
5. Point out that the world is suffering from a food shortage problem and that two out of every ten individuals will die of starvation. (Take away two dolls.)
6. Discuss the problems of being underfed and/or undernourished.
7. Point out that half of the remaining people of the world do not get enough food or food of the right kind. (Many lack adequate protein.) (Take away five of the remaining dolls.)

D. Results:
1. Students will visualize dramatically that many people in the world are starving.
2. Many more people in the world are underfed and undernourished.
3. Students will begin to realize how lucky they are to be living in a country with no major food problems.

E. Supplemental Information:
1. About 18 million people starve to death every year. If the average life expectancy is 50 (which is too high) this means that the average person will have about two chances out of ten of starving to death. Consequently, the removing of two more dolls.
2. About two-thirds of the people of the world are barely existing as far as food is concerned.
3. The main problem now is not the production of food but its distribution. In the future, both will become vital concerns.

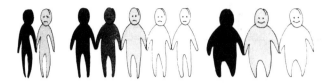

4. While some teachers may feel this is too sensitive an activity to discuss, these are cold facts and the food problems are going to get worse. Hiding from facts is like the proverbial ostrich that buried its head in the sand. The maturity of the students should be the major criterion for the teacher in utilizing this activity.
5. At the present time there is enough food to feed the people of the world, but we are unable to provide adequate means for its distribution, consequently many people are now starving to death.
6. In the future, the food shortage problem will be increased because production of food will not increase as fast as the need of the world's increasing population.

F. Thought Questions:
1. What is going to happen 35 years from now when the present world's population is supposed to be doubled?
2. Do you think the people in poor countries should be allowed to starve to death? or go hungry?
3. Should the United States be concerned about food problems in other countries?
4. Is it the business of the United States to help feed the poor countries of the world?

G. Related Topics and Activities:
1. See Section V-C, "Nutrition."
2. See Section VI-A, "Biological Communities."
3. See all other Activities in this Section.

H. Vocabulary Builders—Spelling Words:
1) **food**   2) **dolls**   3) **producing**
4) **transporting**   5) **distributing**

I. Thought for Today:
"Good manners are made up of petty sacrifices."

Section B: Conservation

Activity VI B 1

A. Problem: *How Does Running Water Affect Our Soil?*

B. Materials:
1. Pictures of rain, snow, floods
2. Containers to collect water from rivers, streams
3. Plaster of Paris
4. Water
5. Freezing compartment in freezer or refrigerator

C. Procedure:
1. Have students describe what they have seen when water comes in contact with land and soil:
   a. rain
   b. floods
   c. ocean tidal waves
   d. waterfalls
2. Test the effect of freezing water on rocks.
   a. Make a plaster of Paris mold with a hole in the center.
   b. Fill with water.
   c. Place in freezer.
3. Have a student make a report on the Mississippi River or the Amazon River and find out how much soil is lost to the ocean in a given period of time.
4. If there are rivers or streams nearby have the students collect samples of water of fast moving streams and slow moving streams.
5. Let these samples settle and check sediment.

D. Results:
1. Students will learn that topsoil can be washed away.
2. Pupils will learn that gullying occurs when there is no vegetation or dams.

E. Supplemental Information:
1. The age of a river can be told by its swiftness. The older rivers have carried the topsoil and rocks down so that the river becomes more level and slows down.

2. The illustration shows the results of too much rain. A large portion of topsoil has become water-soaked and, with the house and its foundation, has slipped down the embankment.

F. Thought Questions:
1. Does gullying hurt farming?
2. What ways can the farmer stop the topsoil from being washed away?
3. What methods can we use to conserve our soil?

G. Related Topics and Activities:
1. See Section I-C, "Water."
2. See Section VII-C, "Earth's Crust."
3. See all Activities in this Section.

H. Vocabulary Builders—Spelling Words:
1) **running**   2) **freezing**   3) **rain**   4) **tides**
5) **rivers**   6) **streams**   7) **ocean**

I. Thought for Today:
"Reading without reflection is like eating without digesting."—Edmund Burke

Activity

A. Problem: *How Does Moving Air Affect Our Soil?*

B. Materials:
   1. Electric fan
   2. Small flats, approximately 2′ × 2′ of:
      a. Grass-covered soil
      b. Scattered plants
      c. Rocks
      d. Gravel
      e. Sand
      f. Clay soil
      g. Humus soil, etc.

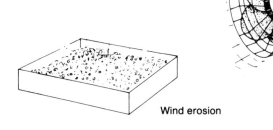

Wind erosion

C. Procedure:
   1. Have the class describe what they have seen the wind do to different types of soil.
   2. Test each soil by placing the electric fan close by, turning it on, and studying the effects of strong moving air on the soil.

D. Results:
   1. The wind will blow away loose soil.
   2. The wind will blow away fine soil or sand.
   3. The wind will have little effect on planted areas, rocks, or gravel.

E. Supplemental Information:
   1. Severe winds cause a lot of damage to physical property.
   2. Strong winds blow away valuable topsoil.
   3. Powerful winds may form gullies.

F. Thought Questions:
   1. What can a farmer do to keep topsoil from being blown away?
   2. Could we live without our topsoil?
   3. What are some other causes of soil erosion?

G. Related Topics and Activities:
   1. See Section III-D, "Soils and Germination."
   2. See Section I-B, "Air."
   3. See all Activities in this Section.

H. Vocabulary Builders—Spelling Words:
   1) **moving**   2) **affect**   3) **electric**   4) **plants**
   5) **rocks**   6) **gravel**   7) **humus**

I. Thought for Today:
   "If you are looking for a helping hand, look at the bottom of your shirt sleeve."

Activity

A. Problem: *How Can We Conserve Our Soil?*

B. Materials:

Pictures, models, or sketches of:
1. Terracing
2. Contour farming
3. Wattling process
4. Windbreaks
5. Crop rotation practices

C. Procedure:
1. Ask class why our soil is important.
2. Inquire of class members if any of them know how farmers keep their soil from being blown away, washed away, or used up.
3. Discuss the major soil conservation practices cited in Results.
4. Compare our soil conservation practices with those of other countries.

D. Results:
1. Pupils will learn that terracing means leveling and staircasing, and this prevents soil from being washed away.
2. Pupils will learn that contour farming is a technique to plow level around slopes to hold water, soil, and plants.
3. Students will learn that the wattling process is a method of building small dams with branches, twigs, rocks, etc., in gullies so that washed soil will build up behind them and hence prevent further gullying.
4. Windbreaks are usually planted trees that grow tall and slow down strong winds, hence preventing soil from being blown away.
5. Crop rotation practices are methods which farmers use to balance material in the soil. When one crop depletes one material, another crop is planted that will restore it.

E. Supplemental Information:
1. Write to the United States Soil Conservation Service or contact a local office for additional ideas and activities.
2. Someone once said that a nation could lose its freedom and survive but that if it lost its topsoil it could not exist.
3. The soil is one of our most vital possessions. It is eroding faster than we are reclaiming it. It's lost by:
   a. overcropping
   b. winds
   c. floods
   d. rains

F. Thought Questions:
1. What is soil?
2. Do all plants need the same basic nutrients?
3. How does water help the soil?
4. What animals help the soil?

G. Related Topics and Activities:
1. Study the problem of over-grazing.
2. Study the effectiveness of fertilizers.
3. Study how floods can be prevented.
4. See Section VII-C, "Earth's Crust."
5. See all Activities in this Section.

H. Vocabulary Builders—Spelling Words:
1) **conserve**   2) **soil**   3) **terracing**
4) **contour**   5) **wattling**   6) **gullying**

I. Thought for Today:

"Education is a ladder to gather fruit from the tree of knowledge, not the fruit itself."

Activity

A. Problem: *Can We Survive Strip Mining?*

B. Materials:
   1. Models of tractors, excavators
   2. Dioramas of land before and after strip mining

C. Procedure:
   1. Describe the problems of energy needs.
   2. Cite the dilemmas we are having and will have over land use. As our population increases shall our priorities for land use be with residences, non-resident urban uses, farming, or mining? Some of the arguments for farming and mining are cited below:
      a. Farming:
         1) Soil, sun, and rain produce food, fiber, and wood to feed, clothe, and shelter us.
         2) The topsoil must produce more grains, vegetables, and fruits to feed an evergrowing population here and abroad.
         3) Our lands produce the hay and greens for our pasture animals.
         4) Our farmlands must produce millions of bales of cotton to help clothe us.
         5) Our water must be kept clean and flowing to protect the animal life forms that help feed us and to quench our thirst.
         6) Our lands must provide an adequate supply of trees for housing and industry.
      b. Mining:
         1) More and more people are demanding energy.
         2) More and more people are demanding earthly goods.
         3) More and more people are demanding manufactured products.
         4) Most minerals lie close to the earth's surface.
         5) Coal, our last natural source of energy, also lies close to the earth's surface.
         6) We have built bigger and bigger machines to strip the earth of its precious resources and in so doing have destroyed the trees, flowers, and grasses.
      c. Problem: The lands we use for gathering needed minerals are the same lands that feed, clothe, and shelter us. There is no land to spare.
         d. One of our strip mining diggers stands nearly 200 feet high, has a boom of 310 feet long and scoops up 325 tons of earth with each scoop.
         e. We are losing almost 5,000 acres to strip miners every week!
   3. Show with the models and dioramas what strip mining does to the earth.

D. Result:
This lesson certainly should stimulate thinking as to what we should do about our natural resources.

E. Supplemental Information:
   1. As of 1986 we have lost over two million acres of potential agricultural lands to strip miners.
   2. Already 20% of our best agricultural lands have been lost to cities and highways.

F. Thought Questions:
   1. Is strip mining worth the price we are paying? we will have to pay?
   2. How long does it take to produce an inch of topsoil? (1,000 years)
   3. Should we insist on costlier, more dangerous types of mining, namely underground?

G. Related Topics and Activities:
   1. See Section III-D, "Soils and Germination."
   2. See Section VI-C, "Earth's Crust."
   3. See all Activities in this Section.

H. Vocabulary Builders—Spelling Words:
   1) **strip mining**   2) **survive**   3) **tractors**
   4) **excavating**   5) **diorama**   6) **farming**
   7) **mining**

I. Thought for Today:
"Some get lost in thought because it is such unfamiliar territory."

Activity

A. Problem: *How Can We Conserve Our Food Sources?*

B. Materials:
1. Cans of food
2. Packages of food
3. Pictures of food that have short shelf lives
4. Multi-sensory aids on food shortages
5. Newspaper clippings on food shortages in geographic areas

C. Procedure:
1. Discuss the problems of producing foods:
   a. agricultural supplies
   b. weather:
      1) climate
      2) winds
      3) rains
   c. human resources
   d. condition of land:
      1) soil type(s)
      2) pH (acid, neutral, or alkaline)
      3) flat or sloping
      4) erosion prevention losses:
         (a) contour farming
         (b) strip planting
         (c) windbreaks
         (d) crop rotation
   e. water adequacy:
      1) amounts
      2) condition
      3) water table
   f. fertilizers needed (nutrients needed)
   g. pest control:
      1) chemical
      2) biological
      3) physical (vacuuming)
   h. farming aids:
      1) animals
      2) tractors
      3) other equipment
      4) tools
2. Discuss the problems of transporting food from the grower to the consumer:
   a. means of transportation
   b. laws and regulations
   c. human resources available
   d. refrigeration

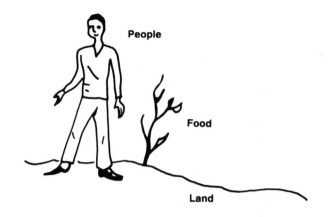

3. Discuss the amounts of food needed for various localities (areas).
4. Discuss ways we can conserve our present food sources:
   a. Conserve our soils
   b. Save our water supplies
   c. Prevent contamination/pollution
   d. Establish local laws to save our agricultural lands.

D. Results:
1. Class will learn that there are many considerations in growing food.
2. Students will learn that all areas have expanding populations.

E. Supplemental Information:
1. The most immediate problem is transportation of foods, not growing foods; that is, getting food to the areas where needed.
2. The next problem that must be faced is to prevent farming area loss. As our population increases, the farming areas are the first lost to residential developers.
3. Even though science will be able to help us produce more food per acre and be able to develop new foods, we still face a drastic food shortage situation.
4. Two-thirds of the world's people are now underfed or undernourished (not provided with adequate vitamins and minerals).
5. Food production and distribution are world problems.

F. Thought Questions:
   1. What will happen if our population doubles and our food supplies remain the same?
   2. How long does it take to make topsoil? (thousands of years)
   3. Do you think starving people would go to war to obtain food?

G. Related Topics and Activities:
   1. See Activity VI-A-6, "Population Statistics."
   2. See Activity VI-A-7, "World Food Needs."
   3. See all Activities in this Section.

H. Vocabulary Builders—Spelling Words:
   1) **soils**   2) **underfed**   3) **undernourished**
   4) **agriculture**   5) **farming**

I. Thought for Today:
   "And then there was the professor who was dieting—he wanted to win the nobelly prize."

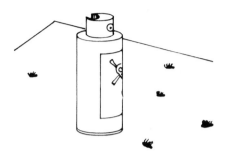

A. Problem: *Are Pesticides Helpful or Harmful?*

B. Materials:
1. Samples of various pesticides:
   a. Roach killers
   b. Flying insect killers
   c. Slug and snail killers
   d. Gopher killers, etc.
   e. Samples or specimens of agricultural pesticides
2. Specimens of various bugs, spiders, ants, etc.

C. Procedure:
1. Demonstrate how the commercial pesticides kill the various insects, spiders, etc.
2. Discuss the reasons why people kill these creatures:
   a. protect food supplies
   b. keep home clean
   c. keep the air pure
   d. protect furniture, clothing, etc.
   e. protect plants in the garden
   f. people dislike some insects
3. Discuss the reasons why we shouldn't use pesticides:
   a. disturb the natural environmental balances
   b. kill other living creatures, not known, i.e., indirectly
   c. unhealthy for humans, especially children
   d. unhealthy for household pets: dogs, cats, etc.
4. Discuss the reasons why we should use pesticides:
   a. need to produce more food
   b. make more money
   c. stop disease
5. Students should study the life cycles of some of these insects, bugs, small animals, etc.

D. Results:
1. Students will learn about the life cycles of specific animals.
2. Students will discover that most interference with the balance of nature causes more damage than good.
3. Hopefully, students will become a little more ecologically minded.

E. Supplemental Information:

Over 700 million pounds of pesticides are used in the United States every year. Because of insecticides, herbicides, fungicides, rodenticides, and other fumigants there is a danger that many animals will become extinct, and irreparable harm done to the balance of nature.

One example: Dr. Cole of Cornell University reported that:
   a. World Health Organization sent pesticides to Borneo to kill mosquitoes and roaches.
   b. It killed the mosquitoes but did not kill all the roaches.
   c. The roaches accumulated the pesticide in their bodies.
   d. Lizards ate the roaches, and became lethargic.
   e. Cats ate the lizards and died. Rats moved in. Plague threatened.
   f. Pesticide also killed a parasite that feeds on caterpillars.
   g. Caterpillars feed, in part, on thatched roofs.
   h. Roofs started falling down.

F. Thought Questions:
1. How has the pelican suffered from the use of pesticides?
2. Would people be better off without pesticides?
3. What are biological controls?
4. Are pesticides a form of air pollution?
5. What would the world be like without pesticides?
6. Are biological controls better than chemical controls of pests?

G. Related Topics and Activities:
1. See Part IV, "Animals."
2. See Sections III-D, "Germination" and III-E, "Plant Growth."
3. See all Activities in this Section.

H. Vocabulary Builders—Spelling Words:
1) **pesticide**   2) **herbicide**   3) **insecticide**
4) **specimens**   5) **unhealthy**

I. Thought for Today:
"Work is the greatest thing in the world, so we should save some of it for tomorrow."

Activity

A. Problem: *How Can We Conserve Our Water?*

B. Materials:
1. Class-constructed survey form
2. Writing implement

C. Procedure:
1. Have class list all the ways in which water is used around their homes. Such a list should include the following items. (It has been estimated the average amount of water used for each of the items in gallons or gallons per unit of time.)
   The list included:
   a. watering garden (60/hr)
   b. bathtub (25)
   c. showers(s) (5/min)
   d. washing machine (40)
   e. dishwater (25)
   f. toilet (6)
   g. drinking, cooking (5)
   h. refilling aquaria (if any); watering houseplants (2/week)
2. Have the students make a home survey of the amount of water that was used during a one-week period.
3. Discuss and describe the sources of water for your community.
4. Study the home survey sheets for ways that water can be conserved.
5. If a water bill can be obtained determine approximately how much money could be saved by conserving water.

D. Results:
1. Pupils will learn that conservation pays.
2. Parents, too, will become more conservation-minded.

E. Supplemental Information:
1. As our population grows, more water will be needed.
2. As business and industry grow, more water will be needed.
3. There is no other source of freshwater than what we already have.
4. We can get freshwater from the ocean but it is at present very costly.

F. Thought Questions:
1. Will increasing the price of water solve our water shortage problem?
2. Will cloud seeding increase our water supply?
3. Do you think we will ever have to ration water for everybody?

G. Related Topics and Activities:
1. If your community had its water supply cut in half, how would you budget your supply?
2. See Section I-C, "Water."
3. See Section VII-C, "Earth's Crust."
4. See all Activities in this Section.

H. Vocabulary Builders—Spelling Words:
1) **conserve**   2) **water**   3) **garden**
4) **bathtub**   5) **dishwasher**

I. Thought for Today:
"Teachers affect eternity; they can never tell where their influence stops."

Activity

A. Problem: *How Can We Conserve Our Fresh Air?*

B. Materials:
1. Pictures or models of autos
2. Pictures or models of businesses and industries
3. Empty cigarette package
4. Model of airplane
5. Model of motorcycle
6. Several electrical appliances
7. Picture of gas stove
8. Spray can
9. Science table

C. Procedure:
1. Place these objects and pictures on the science table and ask the question, (preferably on a large sign) "What do these have in common?"
2. Having built up their curiosity and if they have not guessed, tell the class that everyone of these items is ruining our fresh air.
3. Describe and discuss the effects of each of these:
   a. autos—exhausts
   b. industries—fumes
   c. cigarettes—smoke
   d. airplane—exhaust
   e. motorcycle—exhaust
   f. appliances—burn fossil fuels to get electricity
   g. gas stove—burns gas
   h. spray cans—propellants
4. Discuss ways that these and others can be reduced or eliminated.

D. Result:
Students will learn that there are many activities that contribute to polluting our fresh air from turning on lights to riding in automobiles.

E. Supplemental Information:
1. There is a limited amount of fresh air available to us. There is no new source. (Phytoplankton and trees do produce oxygen but we are gradually destroying phytoplankton and cutting down too many of our trees.)
2. We live in an ocean of air.
3. Air is composed of many gases.
4. Oxygen is the vital component of air for all of us.
5. Many products we put in the air are very harmful—even deadly. One scientist says that

living in our polluted air is like smoking two packs of cigarettes every day.

F. Thought Questions:
1. What would happen if our oxygen supply were cut in half?
2. What is the best source of oxygen production on earth?
3. Do trees produce much oxygen?

G. Related Topics and Activities:
1. See especially Activity VI-C-3, "Smog."
2. See Activity VI-C-2, "Air Pollution."
3. See all Activities in this Section.

H. Vocabulary Builders—Spelling Words:
1) **business**   2) **industry**   3) **appliance**
4) **exhausts**   5) **fumes**   6) **smoke**
7) **fossil**

I. Thought for Today:
"By the time a person realizes that maybe his father was right he usually has a child who thinks he is wrong."

Activity

A. Problem: *How Can We Conserve Electricity in Our Homes?*

B. Materials:

Pictures or actual articles that use electricity in our homes:
1. can opener
2. toothbrush
3. frypan
4. toaster
5. fan
6. light, etc.

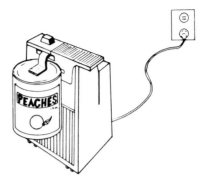

C. Procedure:
1. Discuss how great-grandmother and great-grandfather lived around 1900.
2. Describe how with no electricity in the home they had no electric items such as electric lights, electric irons, electric coffeepots, television, microwave ovens, etc.
3. Have students list all the electrical appliances they have in their homes.
4. Have them go over the list and classify them as:
   a. Absolutely essential
   b. Desirable, but not essential
   c. Could do without
5. Have students go over the list one more time and check to see if each item is used for:
   a. Convenience—comfort
   b. Health—cleanliness
   c. Entertainment
6. Have students go over the list and cite ways that use of appliances could be reduced.
7. Discuss our sources of power and how every time we use an electrical device we are adding to air polllution through our coal or fuel oil burning power plants or to water and land pollution if we use atomic power plants.

D. Results:
1. Students will learn that our grandparents lived without electricity and had clean air.
2. Pupils will realize that we have many, many electrical appliances and a lot of pollution.
3. The class will learn that some possible means of reducing our power needs are by:
   a. eliminating night advertising
   b. reducing our home lights
   c. having all sporting events in the daytime
   d. encouraging thrift
   e. increasing electric rates on a sliding scale
   f. free advertising of the problem
   g. reducing our population growth

h. avoiding electrical gadgets (toothbrushes, can openers, knife sharpeners, mixers, etc.)

E. Supplemental Information:

Electricity in the homes can be reduced by cutting down on the use of essential items and eliminating the non-essential items. (Different people will hold different views on what is essential and what is non-essential.)

F. Thought Questions:
1. Which is more valuable: electric gadgets or clean air?
2. Should power be rationed? or taxed for heavy use?
3. Do you think most people would like to go back to the days of our grandparents for clean air?
4. Would it be possible?

G. Related Topics and Activities:
1. Have students make specific recommendations on how electricity could be saved in the home such as:
   a. keep thermostat higher in summer, lower in winter
   b. close chimney vents when appropriate
   c. wash clothes in warm water
   d. proper ventilation
   e. close drapes in summer
   f. installing or improving insulation
   g. turn out lights when not in use.
2. See Section II-B, "Heat and Fire."
3. See all Activities in this Section.

H. Vocabulary Builders—Spelling Words:

1) **electricity**   2) **essential**   3) **desirable**
4) **thermostat**   5) **appliances**

I. Thought for Today:

"Teaching children to count is not as important as teaching children what counts."

Section C: Pollution

Activity VIC1

A. Problem: *What Are the Different Kinds of Pollution?*

B. Materials:
   1. Clippings from magazines and newspapers about pollution
   2. Models, specimens, pictures of pollution

C. Procedure:
   1. Have students collect pictures, stories, and information about pollution.
   2. Discuss each kind of pollution as to its description, cause, and possible ways to eliminate.

D. Results:
   1. Students will learn that there are many kinds of pollution including:
      a. air
      b. water (oceans, rivers, lakes, etc.)
      c. heat
      d. noise
      e. people
   2. Students will learn that there are many causes of pollution including:
      a. gases (automobile exhausts, factory emissions)
      b. mine acids
      c. pesticides
      d. herbicides
      e. oil slicks
      f. detergents
      g. raw sewage
      h. thermal materials

E. Supplemental Information:
   1. The pollution we allow depends on our values:
      a. Eliminating our wastes is a major concern about pollution.
      b. Manufacturing procedures cause a lot of pollution.
   2. Raising the temperature of river water by only 5° F. can cause disaster to fish. (Chinook salmon in Washington is a good example.) Many become sluggish and cannot obtain food.

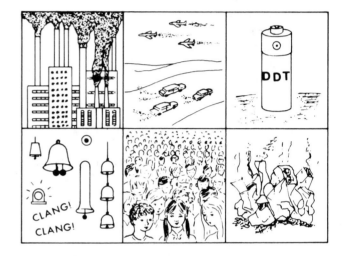

   3. DDT has proved far more deadly than anticipated even though it has been outlawed.

F. Thought Questions:
   1. Should Americans stop driving gasoline powered vehicles?
   2. Can insects that infest crops be destroyed by biological means?
   3. What should we do with our wastes from our homes, factories?
   4. Which pollutants are the most harmful?
   5. Which would be your first choice of pollution to control or eliminate?

G. Related Topics and Activities:
   1. See Section I-B, "Air."
   2. See Section on I-C, "Water."
   3. See all Activities in this Section.

H. Vocabulary Builders—Spelling Words:
   1) **gases**   2) **pesticides**   3) **herbicides**
   4) **sewage**   5) **detergents**

I. Thought for Today:
   "Ignorance is a form of environmental pollution."

Activity

A. Problem: *What Pollutants Are in the Air?*

B. Materials:

1. Pictures of air pollution (smog, industrial smoke, etc.)
2. Glass filled with clean air
3. Glass filled with smoke
4. Wooden matches
5. Two pint jars with caps

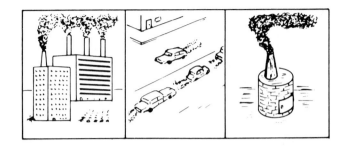

C. Procedure:

1. Take a pint jar like a mayonnaise jar and cap it. (This jar represents clean air.)
2. Take a similar jar and hold it upside down and burn three wooden matches in it. Cap quickly. (This jar represents dirty air.)
3. Pass the two jars around the class.
4. Ask the class which air they would like to breathe? Why?
5. Discuss what causes the air to become dirty.
6. Have students read, talk to adults about causes of air pollution.
7. Discuss how cities monitor air pollutants.

D. Results:

1. Students will learn that people contaminate the air.
2. Some of the contaminants are:
   a. oxides of nitrogen
   b. carbon monoxide (results from incomplete burning)
   c. hydrocarbons (burned fuels, industrial wastes)
   d. oxides of sulphur

E. Supplemental Information:

1. The facts are clear—the air is not.
2. Smog can do irreparable physical and psychological damage.
3. Smog robs air of vital oxygen and children need more oxygen than adults, especially when they play.

4. Smog has been linked to lung cancer, heart disease, brain damage, emphysema, pulmonary misfunctioning, respiratory diseases, tissue damage, and even death.
5. Carbon monoxide is the product of incomplete combustion (including smoking) and can cause death. It robs the body of needed oxygen.

F. Thought Questions:

1. What will happen if we continue to pollute our air?
2. Could plants reproduce if there was no air?
3. What can we do to get rid of some of our air pollutants?
4. Which do we need more, electricity or clean air?
5. Why do some areas have more air pollutants than others even though their population and industry are about the same?

G. Related Topics and Activities:

1. See especially Activity V-D-7, "Smoking."
2. See Section I-B, "Air."
3. See all Activities in this Section.

H. Vocabulary Builders—Spelling Words:

1) **pollutants**   2) **smog**   3) **industry**
4) **carbon monoxide**   5) **nitrogen**
6) **sulfur/sulphur** (both are correct spellings)

I. Thought for Today:

"A great many open minds should be closed for repairs."—Allen McReady

Activity

A. Problem: *What Is Smog?*

B. Materials:
 1. Gallon jug with cap or cover
 2. Matches
 3. Sulphur
 4. Paper

C. Procedure:
 1. Burn some matches and drop in jug and cover.
 2. Burn a little sulphur and drop in same jug and cover.
 3. Burn a little paper and drop in same jug and cover.
 4. Explain inversion (cold air over hot air to keep lid on and pollutants from rising). Warm air normally rises.
 5. Ask class how they would like to breathe this continuously in these large quantities? smaller quantities? at all?
 6. If possible have someone who is an expert in smog or smog control cite what steps have been taken to reduce smog. If not possible, gather information from newspapers and magazines.

D. Results:
 1. The jug will become full of dark, dirty, noxious air.
 2. Many of the air pollutants come from burning fossil fuels.
 3. Students will learn about smog and smog control.

E. Supplemental Information:
 1. Smog contains:
    a. sulphur dioxide
    b. oxides of nitrogen
    c. hydrocarbons
    d. industrial gases (fumes)
    e. particulates
 2. By reducing automobile and industrial combustion we could reduce smog.
 3. Smog is caused by the action of *sunlight* on *hydrocarbons* and the *oxides of nitrogen*.
 4. Hydrocarbons come mainly from unburned gasoline; oxides of nitrogen are present whenever burning takes place.

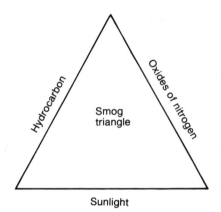

 5. There are three factors that need to be present for smog:
    a. hydrocarbons
    b. oxides of nitrogen
    c. sunlight
 6. The three items above are called the "Smog Triangle."
 7. Most cities that have smog problems have governmental agencies that control emissions that cause smog and air pollution.

F. Thought Questions:
 1. How much of these pollutants do you think need be in the air before people are poisoned?
 2. Have we ever had any deaths from smog?
 3. Do you think people will voluntarily reduce their automobile driving?

G. Related Topics and Activities:
   1. See Section I-B, "Air."
   2. See Section VII-E, "Weather."
   3. Interview a weather forecaster, reporter, or meteorologist about smog.
   4. See all Activities in this Section.

H. Vocabulary Builders—Spelling Words:
   1) **smog**   2) **nitrogen**   3) **hydrocarbons**
   4) **sunlight**   5) **triangle**   6) **inversion**

I. Thought for Today:
   "The smog was so bad this morning that most of the birds woke up coughing."

Activity   vi **C** 4

A. Problem: *How Do Automobiles Pollute the Air?*

B. Materials:
   1. Model cars
   2. Pictures of suburbia
   3. Pictures of gravestones

C. Procedure:
   1. Discuss the ways automobiles destroy our ecology. (exhausts, highways, automobile travel, abandoned cars, etc.)
   2. Make a list of these on chart paper or a chalkboard.
   3. Discuss what life would be like without automobiles.

D. Results:
   1. Students will learn that automobiles pollute the ecology in many ways.
   2. Students will learn that automobiles have advantages and disadvantages.

E. Supplemental Information:
   1. About 75% of all noise is made by automobiles.
   2. About 80% of the air pollution comes from automobiles using gasoline and oil.
   3. Highways and streets destroy natural land.
   4. Cars uproot residents by contributing to urban sprawl.
   5. Heavy automobile traffic clogs streets, highways, and freeways.
   6. Automobiles in the U.S. kill thousands of people (about 50,000 per year).
   7. They injure millions every year (about 2–3 million).

F. Thought Questions:
   1. Is the automobile worth the problems it has caused?
   2. Have you ever seen an abandoned car? What should be done about these?
   3. How effective have smog control devices been on automobiles?

G. Related Topics and Activities:
   1. See Section II-E, "Simple Machines."
   2. See Section V-D, "Personal Health."
   3. See all Activities in this Section.
   4. Study booklets and handouts from the state automobile agency.

H. Vocabulary Builders—Spelling Words:
   1) **automobiles** 2) **pollute** 3) **ecology**
   4) **highways** 5) **urban**

I. Thought for Today:
   "Automobiles continue to be driven at two speeds—lawful and awful."

Activity

A. Problem: *How Do Business and Industry Pollute the Air?*

B. Materials:
1. Paper
2. Matches
3. Sulphur
4. Gasoline
5. Fuel oil
6. Wood

C. Procedure:
1. Describe some manufactured products and explain that in the manufacturing process some form of burning or heating takes place that emits gases into the air. Some of these might be:
   a. manufacturing companies/industries that incinerate their paper, cardboard, and plastic packaging
   b. companies that manufacture chemicals
   c. power plants that burn coal or fuel oil
   d. gasoline refineries
   e. service stations that spill gasoline
   f. smelting plants
2. Have the class find out how many different pollutants are emitted into the air.
3. Burn each item listed under Materials. (This should be done by the teacher, or by students under close supervision.)
4. Make a collection of news items showing how business and industry are striving to curb pollution.

D. Results:
1. Students will learn that many industrial plants and businesses emit deadly fumes into the atmosphere.
2. These fumes are dirty, smelly, and reduce the oxygen content.
3. Students will learn that many businesses and industries are trying to reduce air pollutants but it is a very expensive proposition.

E. Supplemental Information:
1. We need more power for electricity. To create electricity we usually burn coal or fuel oils. Burning these adds to air pollution.
2. The more we demand of business and industry, the more air pollution they are going to cause.

F. Thought Questions:
1. Is it better to have a lot of convenience items, (e.g., air conditioners, electric appliances) or clean air?
2. Would your family give up unnecessary driving in exchange for clean air?
3. Do you think business and industry should be taxed according to the amount of pollutants they add to the atmosphere?

G. Related Topics and Activities:
1. See Section I-B, "Air."
2. See Section V-D, "Personal Health."
3. See all Activities in this Section.

H. Vocabulary Builders—Spelling Words:
1) **sulfur (or sulphur)**   2) **gasoline**
3) **fuel**   4) **incinerate**   5) **chemical**

I. Thought for Today:
"After all is said and done more is said than done."

Activity

A. Problem: *How Are Our Homes Adding to the Pollution Problem?*

B. Materials:

Pictures of:
1. Stereo
2. TV and VCRs
3. Gas or electric stove
4. Gas, electric, or oil furnace
5. Uncovered garbage can
6. Electric appliances
7. Fireplace
8. Leaf blower

C. Procedure:
1. Discuss the different kinds of pollution found in and around the home:
   a. noise
   b. garbage
   c. gas
   d. oil
   e. gasoline
   f. sewage
2. Discuss some means of reducing wastes and pollution:
   a. recycling
   b. reusing
   c. conserve fuels where possible
   d. keep home, yard, and garage clean
3. Have students develop a specific list of home practices they might do in order to reduce home pollution. See "Supplemental Information" for possible items.

D. Results:
1. Students will learn about wastes, pollution, and conservation.
2. Students will learn some means of reducing wastes.
3. Students will realize that pollution made in one home spreads to other areas directly and indirectly. (Electrical conveniences in homes cause air pollution everywhere. Sewage affects others in cost of treatment or pollution of waters and land.)

E. Supplemental Information:

Things to help ecology at home:
1. Do not use colored paper tissue, towels. (Dyes pollute.)
2. Use cloth napkins instead of paper.
3. Use a lunch box instead of a paper bag.
4. Reduce use of electricity during peak hours.
5. Do not waste water.
6. Take newspapers and aluminum cans to a recycling center.
7. Compost or bury garbage.

F. Thought Questions:
1. Can you think of any other things to do at home that will help our environment and help avoid pollution?
2. Do you think any of the damage done by pollution can be corrected? What and how?
3. Do you think it is time that we started a major program to reduce pollution everywhere?

G. Related Topics and Activities:
1. See Section VI-D, "Pollution Solutions."
2. See Section II-G, "Current Electricity."
3. See Section VI-B, "Conservation."
4. Make a home survey of "Pollution" activities.
5. See all Activities in this Section.

H. Vocabulary Builders—Spelling Words:
1) **home**   2) **furnace**   3) **garbage**   4) **electric**
5) **noise**   6) **wastes**   7) **sewage**

I. Thought for Today:
"To have lost your reputation is to be dead among the living."

Activity

A. Problem: *Are Our Lakes and Rivers Becoming Polluted?*

B. Materials:

On water pollution:
1. Pictures of lakes
2. Pictures of rivers
3. Magazines
4. Newspapers
5. Library books

C. Procedure:

1. Discuss the beauty of our lakes and rivers.
2. Ask students if they know of any lakes or rivers in the area.
3. If so, inquire as to what condition they are in. clean? polluted?
4. If there are some nearby water areas, have some students visit them and report to the class what they have found.

D. Results:

Students will learn that our lakes and rivers are being polluted by:
1. sewage
2. garbage
3. paper
4. plastics
5. cans
6. oil and gasoline
7. old automobile parts, etc.
8. odd junk

E. Supplemental Information:

1. The larger the lake the more the pollution.
2. Four out of five of our Great Lakes are greatly polluted. Some headway is being made by the strict enforcement of laws by the United States and Canada reducing the amounts of pollutants dumped into the Great Lakes by private industries and local city governments.
3. Our inland waters are still being polluted by sewage, phosphates, pesticides, soils, etc.
4. The Environmental Protection Agency ranks the following waterways that have shorelines that exceed government standards of pollution in terms of mileage by the following percentages:

Tampa Bay	66%
Cuyahoga River (Ohio)	58%
Monongahela River (Pa., W.Va.)	55%
Savannah River	49%
Ohio River	46%
Lake Ontario	46%
Lake Erie, western shore	45%
Mobile Bay	43%
Niagara River	40%
Lower Hudson River	36%
Green River (Wyo.)	33%
Lower Colorado River	31%
Mohawk River (N.Y.)	30%
Cumberland River (Tenn., Ky.)	27%
Lower Missouri River	27%
Narragansett Bay	26%
Tennessee River	23%
Upper Mississippi River (Rock Island to Cairo, Ill.)	23%
Illinois River	21%
Lake Michigan, western shore	19%
Susquehanna River (Pa., Md.)	19%
Middle Colorado River	18%
North Canadian River (Okla.)	17%
Housatonic River (Conn., Mass.)	16%
St. Lawrence River	14%
Potomac River	13%
Lake Huron, western shore	13%
Connecticut River	12%

Source: U.S. News and World Report

F. Thought Questions:

1. What would happen if we could not use our freshwaters?
2. If you had the authority, what would you do to clean up the freshwaters?
3. Whose responsibility is it to clean up our freshwaters?
4. Estuaries are also in deep trouble because these areas are where rivers and streams meet the oceans.

5. The longer the river the more pollution it picks up.

G. Related Topics and Activities:
   1. See Section I-C, "Water."
   2. See Section VII-C, "Earth's Crust."
   3. See all Activities in this Part.

H. Vocabulary Builders—Spelling Words:
   1) **lakes**   2) **rivers**   3) **estuary**   4) **sewage**
   5) **chemicals**

I. Thought for Today:
   "The politician's promises of yesterday are the taxes of today."

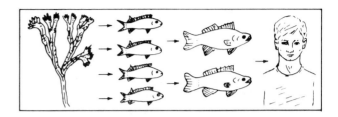

A. Problem: *How Does Pollution Affect the Food Chain?*

B. Materials:
Pictures or models of:
1. Plants
2. Herbivores (plant-eating animals)
3. First-level carnivore (meat-eating animals)
4. Second-level carnivore (larger carnivores that eat first-level carnivores)
5. Flannel board and flannel cut-outs (optional)

C. Procedure:
1. Describe several food chains:
   a. carrot, rabbit, people
   b. kelp, fish, tuna, people
   c. grass, cow, people
   d. kelp, small fish, large fish, people
2. Discuss ways pollution affects each of these:
   a. grass—harmed by air pollutants
   b. animals—harmed by insecticides
   c. people—harmed by increased poisons from all sources
3. If desired, these processes can be effectively shown on a flannel board adding one step in the food chain at a time.

D. Results:
1. Students will learn that pollution anywhere affects our food supply.
2. Students will learn that some poisons multiply as they move up the food chain.

E. Supplemental Information:
1. Poisons multiply as they go up the food chain. For example if plankton picks up mercury:
   a. Plankton picks up mercury (a poison) one part per million.
   b. Small fish eat plankton; they have one part per thousand.
   c. Large fish eat smaller fish, they have ten parts per thousand.
   d. People eat large fish, tuna, for example, and get very sick because of mercury poisoning.
2. Poisons become more concentrated as food moves up the food chain or food web.

F. Thought Questions:
1. How can people avoid being poisoned by themselves?
2. Do you think we should go back to living like we did hundreds of years ago? What would be the advantages? disadvantages?
3. What is the difference between a food chain and a food web?

G. Related Topics and Activities:
1. See Section IV-E, "Fish."
2. See Section IV-G, "Mammals."
3. See all Activities in this Part.

H. Vocabulary Builders—Spelling Words:
1) **plants**   2) **herbivores**   3) **carnivores**
4) **insecticides**   5) **mercury**

I. Thought for Today:
"A little learning is a dangerous thing—just ask any kid who comes home with a bad report card."

Activity

A. Problem: *Do Nuclear Power Plants Pollute the Air?*

B. Materials:
  1. Pictures of regular steam generating plants and atomic power plants
  2. Sketches of generating systems of both

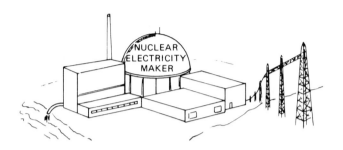

C. Procedure:
  1. Discuss the need for power and electricity:
     a. more people
     b. more labor-saving devices
  2. Briefly describe the steps in developing electricity from steam plant:
     a. coal is burned
     b. heat changes water into steam
     c. steam turns generators
     d. generators create electricity
     e. electricity sent to home, schools, and factories
  3. Briefly describe the steps in developing electricity from an atomic power plant:
     a. atoms are split creating heat
     b. heat changes water into steam
     c. rest of the steps are identical to those above
  4. Discuss the waste products of each:
     a. coal adds pollutants to the air
     b. atomic power residues make water warmer and slightly radioactive
     c. atomic furnaces produce wastes which stay radioactive for tens of thousands of years. The problem is where to put these wastes. We already have had many leaks.
  5. Discuss the pros and cons of coal-burning power plants and nuclear power plants.

D. Result:
Students will be better able to make comparisons between nuclear and non-nuclear power plants.

E. Supplemental Information:
  1. Most people come to the conclusion that atomic power plants are far more ecologically sound than coal-burning plants.
  2. One argument for nuclear power plants is that it stops strip mining of our lands.
  3. Many people are concerned about the possibility of nuclear accidents. The Three Mile Nuclear Plant in Pennsylvania has been our worst accident to date. The accident spewed radioactive gas and steam into the atmosphere and there was great concern that a nuclear meltdown would occur. If this had happened, lethal radioactive gases would have been released into the air. Fortunately this did not take place and the most serious problem was the contamination of 250,000 gallons of water which was contained in the plant.
  4. The Soviet Union had a nuclear power plant mishap in Chernobyl in 1986 which sent radiation across Europe and they reported only 31 deaths. There have been many other effects from this such as large increases in cancer rates in the area.
  5. It should also be noted that the chance for a nuclear explosion to take place is very, very remote as the amount of materials needed for a nuclear explosion approximates about 95% of fissionable materials and the nuclear power plants are working at about a 5% level.
  6. There are now about 250 nuclear power plants scattered throughout the world. At last count 66 were in the United States, 40 in Russia, 20 in Japan, 20 in the United Kingdom, 15 in France, and 14 in West Germany. There are now 26 countries using nuclear energy.

F. Thought Questions:
  1. If you had to develop more power for your country, which method would you employ?
  2. Are there other ways to create electricity other than fossil fuels or nuclear energy?
  3. Should we stop producing nuclear power until we can safely dispose of it's wastes?

G. Related Topics and Activities:
  1. See Activity I-A-6, "Atoms and Molecules."
  2. See Section II-G, "Current Electricity."
  3. See all Activities in this Section.

H. Vocabulary Builders—Spelling Words:
 1) **nuclear**   2) **power**   3) **generating**
 4) **atomic**   5) **labor-saving**

I. Thought for Today:
 "If you started counting in the year one and counted until this moment, you could not have counted enough atoms to cover a pinhead."

Section D: Pollution Solutions

Activity

A. Problem: *What Is the Best Way to Get Rid of Our Nontoxic Wastes?*

B. Materials:
1. Old tin cans
2. Newspapers
3. Glass containers (nonreturnable)
4. Plastic bags
5. Pictures of garbage
6. Pesticide

C. Procedure:
1. Discuss some of the ways that we presently get rid of wastes:
   a. burn
   b. bury
   c. dump in the ocean
   d. litter
2. Discuss whether these are good or bad practices.
3. Have class determine which solid materials should be recycled.
4. Have students make a survey of items in a grocery store that are packed in throw-away containers.
5. Discuss the attitude of many people who would rather throw something away than try to save it, recycle it, or return it.

D. Results:
1. Students will learn that the problem of wastes is a big problem and one that is getting bigger all the time as more and more people use more and more materials that must be disposed of.
2. Pupils will realize that some scarce materials can be reclaimed or recycled.

E. Supplemental Information:
1. Many materials can be reclaimed or recycled. Glass can be broken into many small parts and used as a base for roadbeds.
2. Meltable products can be reclaimed.
3. Some materials can be burned with a minimum of air pollution while others produce highly toxic pollutants.
4. Newspapers can be recycled.
5. In the last year alone, people threw out more than 100 million tires, 30 billion bottles, 60

billion cans, 9 million automobiles, 4 million tons of plastics, 1 million television sets, and uncounted millions of other appliances, large and small.

F. Thought Questions:
1. Can you think of any novel ways to get rid of our waste products?
2. Do you think we should levy a tax on disposable items?
3. Should we pass laws to prevent throw-away packaging for one-way containers?

G. Related Topics and Activities:
1. See Section VII-C, "Earth's Crust."
2. See Section VI-C, "Pollution."
3. See also other Activities in this Section.

H. Vocabulary Builders—Spelling Words:
1) **solids**   2) **wastes**   3) **litter**   4) **recycle**
5) **throw-aways**   6) **reuse**

I. Thought for Today:
"The mind is a wonderful thing. It starts working the minute you're born and never stops until you get up to speak in public."

Activity

A. Problem: *What Is Recycling? Salvaging?*

B. Materials:
1. Florence flask
2. Single-hole stopper
3. Stand and clamps
4. Heating device
5. Pyrex jar
6. Pyrex tubing
7. Piece of toweling
8. Dirt
9. Leaves
10. Salt
11. Colored ink
12. Gloves

C. Procedure:
1. Discuss with class the necessity of recycling and salvaging. (If we used only one thing once we would soon run out of things.)
2. Discuss biodegradable (naturally decompose) items.
3. Discuss how we now recycle and salvage some materials that we use.
4. Place some dirt, leaves, salt, and colored water in a Florence flask.
5. Place glass tubing connections in rubber stopper and fit on flask. (Tubing can be bent by gently warming over heating device and carefully rotating and bending as tubing gets hotter. Use gloves as a safety precaution against burns.)
6. Heat contents with Bunsen burner, hot plate, or Sterno.
7. Place wet rag around tubing to cool liquid.
8. Clear water will come out the condensed side.
9. Have class name other items that have been recycled or salvaged; paper, cars for metal, glass for roads, etc.

D. Results:
1. The water has been recycled.
2. Pure water has been salvaged.
3. Students will learn about using materials over and over again.

E. Supplemental Information:
1. Many discarded items made of paper, glass, plastic, cloth, etc. can be returned to industry for new products or energy. Recycling of this sort requires a major focus involving careful planning.

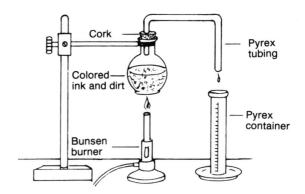

2. Even nonusable garbage can be used for land fills.
3. Some items can be burned, and if complete burning takes place the only products will be water and carbon dioxide. Incomplete burning will produce carbon monoxide, smoke, sulphur dioxide, nitrous oxides, etc.

F. Thought Questions:
1. Should we worry about salvaging and recycling, or should we let the next generation worry about itself?
2. Are some solid items biodegradable? (Glass about 100 years, aluminum about 1,000 years, plastics many thousands of years.)
3. Should we separate our garbage into salvageable and nonsalvageable items?

G. Related Topics and Activities:
1. Make a collection of items that could be recycled.
2. Make two lists of disposable items: one that is recyclable and one that is biodegradable.
3. List items that would make good compost (plant enrichment).
4. Students might want to develop a compost site for a school garden. The school gardener can make some good suggestions.
5. See all Activities in this Section.

H. Vocabulary Builders—Spelling Words:
1) **recycle**   2) **salvage**   3) **compost**
4) **reusable**   5) **biodegradable**

I. Thought for Today:
"Nothing is more confusing than people who give good advice but set bad examples."

Activity

A. Problem: *What Better Ecological Means of Land Transportation Do We Have Than Automobiles?*

B. Materials:
1. Toys or pictures of:
   a. Cars (large and small)
   b. Bicycles
   c. Buses
   d. Streetcars
   e. Trains
   f. People
   g. Motorcycles
   h. Monorail system
2. Resource person in charge of automobile emission test.

C. Procedure:
1. Discuss the problem of the automobile pollution.
2. Have students watch the number of cars that go past the school with only one or two people in them.
3. Have the students list the other kinds of transportation available that could be used instead of automobiles.
4. If toys are not available, then students could draw pictures, make mobiles of different kinds of land transportation, or make a transportation collage.
5. Have resource person discuss with class emission and state control laws.

D. Results:
1. Students will learn about automobiles and pollution.
2. Students will learn that there are many ways to help cut down automobile exhausts, e.g.:
   a. walk
   b. bicycle
   c. motorcycle
   d. public transportation
   e. car pools
   f. use smaller horsepower cars
   g. keep motors clean and in good repair
   h. use smog devices in cars

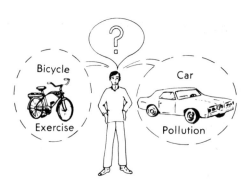

E. Supplemental Information:
1. The time is fast arriving when more catastrophes are going to demand the reduction of fossil fuel burning in cars and power plants.
2. Walking and bicycling are more healthy than riding in cars.

F. Thought Questions:
1. What public means of tranportation carries more people than any other each day in the United States? (Be careful—answer at end of next question.)
2. Do you think car pools should be made mandatory? Why or why not? (elevators)
3. As far as transportation is concerned, do you think there were more problems in the "horse and buggy days" than there are now?
4. What harm is done to our body from automobile exhaust?

G. Related Topics and Activities:
1. Make a transportation collage.
2. See previous Section VI-C, "Pollution."
3. See Section I-B, "Air."
4. See all Activities in this Section.

H. Vocabulary Builders—Spelling Words:
1) **ecology**   2) **transportation**   3) **bicycles**
4) **motorcycles**   5) **catastrophe**

I. Thought for Today:
"The greatest lesson in life is to realize that even fools are right sometimes."—Winston Churchill

Activity

A. Problem: *How Can We Help Solve the Pollution Problems?*

B. Materials:
1. Colored paper towels or tissue
2. Wire clothes hanger
3. Glass bottle
4. Newspaper
5. Lunch box, etc.

C. Procedure:
1. Discuss the problems of pollution.
2. Students can do research on or class can discuss ways in which each can personally help with the pollution solutions.

D. Results:

Students will learn that they can:
1. Avoid using colored paper or tissue. (Dyes pollute water.)
2. Use cloth towels instead of paper towels.
3. Use a lunch box rather than paper bags.
4. Reduce the amount of electricity consumed in the home. (Electricity requires generating plants which produce pollution.)
5. Save newspapers and magazines. (One ton of recycled paper saves 17 trees.)
6. Use both sides of writing paper at home and at school.
7. Walk and bicycle rather than asking parents to drive automobiles.
8. Compost or bury garbage (especially vegetable trimmings).
9. Return wire coat hanger to the cleaners.
10. Use containers that disintegrate easily (paper or cardboard).
11. Plant trees and vegetable gardens.
12. Stop littering.
13. Avoid wasting water.
14. Avoid buying products or clothes made from endangered species.
15. Use re-usable shopping bags (cloth and net types).
16. Avoid suntan lotions when swimming in a lake, river, or ocean.
17. Use biodegradable soap and cleaning products.
18. Refuse to buy overpackaged items.
19. Initiate rummage sales.
20. Talk and practice ecology.

E. Supplemental Information:

There are many adult practices that can also help in reducing pollution.

1. Avoid DDT and other pesticides.
2. Fertilize only during growing seasons.
3. Reduce automobile usage (bicycle or use public transportation).
4. Recycle glass, aluminum, and paper.
5. Avoid soft plastic containers.

F. Thought Questions:
1. Have students make lists of other items that can be added to those above.
2. What will happen if we don't think ecologically?
3. Is pollution everybody's responsibility or just the government's?

G. Related Topics and Activities:
1. See Part VI-C, "Pollution."
2. Make a collection of items and describe how they are involved in "Pollution Solutions."
3. Check how homes can be made more safe.
4. See all Activities in this Section.

H. Vocabulary Builders—Spelling Words:
1) **pollution**   2) **solution**   3) **colored**
4) **newspaper**   5) **problem**

I. Thought for Today:
"Thanks to the miles of superhighways under construction, America will soon be a wonderful place to drive—if you don't have to stop."

A. *How Can We Help Woodsy Owl Spread the Word?*

Whooo Is Woodsy Owl?

Woodsy Owl is America's official anti-pollution symbol—sponsored by the Forest Service, U.S. Department of Agriculture. He is a fantasy character, wise in the ways of the outdoor world. Woodsy knows a great deal about the environment, and he knows we can work together to make our earth a better place to live.

With his home on the edge of the forest, Woodsy perches on a high branch where he sees evidence of the pollution problems that threaten the forest and the city. He sees that these problems are interrelated: the smog from the cities' factories and cars is killing some of the trees in the forest, and the improper use of the land causes erosion that pollutes water used by the city people.

Investigate—Discover

Woodsy wants us all to learn about the environment and ways to improve it. He knows that environmental awareness and understanding must be a part of our educational system.

Discovering the way nature looks, sounds, and feels is how Woodsy thinks kids can enjoy environmental studies. Later, they can tackle environmental projects, and feel accomplishment by creating a better place to live.

Enjoy—Protect

Woodsy likes to have people go to the forest for recreation. He wants them to enjoy the forest and to protect it so those who come later can enjoy it too. That is why he is helping them to learn to stop littering, vandalism, noise, and water pollution. Here are some tips from Woodsy:
—When hiking, fishing or camping, carry out everything you carried in.
—Dispose of dishwater and human waste away from streams, lakes, or ponds.
—Protect soil and vegetation, particularly along stream banks.

Do Something

Woodsy wants everyone to help improve and protect the environment right in their own community. Here are some

Give a Hoot! Don't Pollute

projects for making things more attractive right around home:
—Plant a tree, shrub, or flowers.
—Clean up a vacant lot, sidewalk, trail, or stream.
—Clean up an old, unattended cemetery.
—Collect used clothing, furniture, and other items and give them to an organization that can use them.
—Make and install birdhouses, bird feeders, or birdbaths.
—Fix up and paint an old building, fence, park bench, or picnic table.
—Write a newspaper story about things people can do to help Woodsy improve our environment, and ask your editor to print it.

Give a Hoot! Don't Pollute

Help Woodsy spread the word!

GIVE A HOOT! DON'T POLLUTE!

Activity

A. Problem: *How Can We Keep Our Forests, Parks, and Beaches Attractive?*

B. Materials:
   1. Litterbag
   2. Spray paint can
   3. Shovel
   4. Pick
   5. Trash can, bucket
   6. Newspaper accounts of forest fires, vandalism, etc.

C. Procedure:
   1. Discuss where students take their vacations.
   2. Ask how many have been to our forests? parks? beaches?
   3. Discuss what they have seen that people have done to harm the attractiveness or usefulness of these resources.
   4. Discuss what they could have done to keep these resources beautiful.
   5. Show some of the materials that could be used to keep our public resources clean and beautiful and discuss some of the procedures that could help save our natural resources. These might include:
      a. Carry a litterbag in your car or boat and always use it.
      b. Don't paint on rocks, trees, or fences. Let the natural beauty show.
      c. Clean up a trail, stream, or camp spot.
      d. Put trash in your litterbag—not in streams, lakes, or oceans, or streets, freeways or highways.
      e. Picnic areas, beaches, parks, and roadsides do not provide maid service. Help keep these areas clean.
      f. Keep volume on your radio or tape deck set at moderate level.
      g. Have an effective muffler on your car, truck, motor bike, or boat.
      h. Sound your horn only when safety dictates.
      i. Help fight vandalism and graffiti that detract from the outdoor environment.
      j. Start an Ecology Club or environmental improvement committee in school or community.
      k. Be sure your community participates in beautification programs.

D. Result:
Students will realize that the beauty of natural resources is everybody's responsibility.

E. Supplemental Information:
   1. Our natural resources are things of natural beauty—let's keep them that way.
   2. Our forests and beaches are not only important to use but also to many species of animal life.

F. Thought Questions:
   1. Why should we take care of our forests and public parks?
   2. Who should have prime responsibility for their upkeep?
   3. What should we do about the vandalism in our public areas?
   4. Who owns the public forests and parks?

G. Related Topics and Activities:
   1. See Section VII-C, "Earth's Crust."
   2. See Section II-B, "Fire and Heat."
   3. See Section VI-C, "Pollution."
   4. See Part IV, "Animals."
   5. See all Activities in this Section.

H. Vocabulary Builders—Spelling Words:
   1) **litter**   2) **litterbag**   3) **ecology**
   4) **responsibility**   5) **resources**   6) **picnic**

I. Thought for Today:
   "Personal liberty ends where public safety begins."

Activity

A. Problem: *How Can We Keep America Beautiful?*

B. Materials:

Pictures of:
1. Litter
2. Strip-mined lands
3. Hovels
4. Auto junkyards

C. Procedure:

1. Discuss how America is made up of states: states have counties, counties have cities, cities have schools, and schools have classrooms.
2. To make America beautiful, the class should start with its own room.
3. After the room is made beautiful, initiate a clean campus campaign.
4. After the campus is cleaned up, the class or school might make a list of ways in which America is becoming dirty or littered and the ways that can be used to keep it clean.
5. Discuss ways that we can keep our forests and public parks attractive. This should include the items mentioned in the previous Activity plus:
   a. Recycling waste products
   b. Saving our forests
   c. Planting trees
   d. Car-pooling
   e. Reducing off-road vehicular traffic
   f. Rotating crops
   g. Planning new residential growth
   h. Saving water
   i. Reducing industrial wastes
   j. Eliminating dumping
   k. Cleaning up our landfills
   l. Reducing plastic packaging
   m. Preventing gullying
   n. Fighting erosion
   o. Reducing gasoline leaf blowers
   p. Saving wildlife
   q. Reducing phosphate detergents
   r. Using water-based paints
   s. Recycling glass products
   t. Protecting our ground water
   u. Using non-disposable materials
   v. Remembering the environmental 3 R's:
      1) Reduce
      2) Reuse
      3) Recycle

Don't be a LITTER-BUG!

KEEP AMERICA CLEAN

D. Results:
1. Class will learn that cleanliness is everybody's job.
2. By all helping a little, a great deal can be accomplished.

E. Supplemental Information:
1. Students can attack the problem of litter with appropriate posters, such as "Every litter bit hurts!"
2. Cleanliness in the city, in the country, and in our waters is everybody's job.

F. Thought Questions:
1. Why should we keep America clean?
2. Who should be responsible for keeping America clean?
3. How can vandalism be stopped?
4. Who owns the forests, parks, highway roadsides, beaches, etc.?

G. Related Topics and Activities:
   1. See Part I-C, "Water."
   2. See Part I-B, "Air."
   3. See all Activities in this Section.

H. Vocabulary Builders—Spelling Words:
   1) **beautiful**   2) **America**   3) **litter**
   4) **hovel**   5) **junkyard**

I. Thought for Today:
"In some of the smoggiest cities they are now printing stop signs in Braille."

Part VII

Earth and Space

Section A: Universe

Activity VII A 1

A. Problem: *What Kinds of Heavenly Bodies Are There?*

B. Materials:
1. Astronomy charts
2. Model spaceships
3. Books and pictures on space

C. Procedure:
1. Discuss travel by planes.
2. Discuss the difference between plane travel and space travel (leaving earth's atmosphere).
3. Ask the class to list all the different kinds of heavenly bodies that they know about outside the earth's atmosphere.
4. Have them read books and pamphlets about space and space travel.
5. Have them add to their list of heavenly bodies.

D. Results:
1. Students will learn that there are many kinds of heavenly bodies.
2. They will learn that the most common are:
   a. moons or satellites (many kinds)
   b. stars or suns
   c. planets
   d. meteors (shooting stars)
   e. comets (small bodies of ice)
   f. asteroids (minor planets, about 1,500 now known; majority are between Mars and Jupiter) (also called meteorites)
   g. constellations (groups of stars)
   h. galaxies (ours is the Milky Way) (groups of constellations) (billions of stars held together)
   i. novas (exploding stars)
   j. supernovas
   k. black holes (end product of a collapsed star; no light or matter can escape from it)
   l. clusters (dense groups of stars, up to millions)
   m. superclusters
   n. nebulae (swirling gases and dust)
   o. quasars (points of light or cores of galaxies; very small, very bright)

   p. rays (gamma, X-rays, ultraviolet light, infrared light)
   q. interstellar dust (small grains or matter between celestial objects)
   r. interstellar gas (mostly hydrogen and helium)
   s. atomic particles

E. Supplemental Information:
1. All heavenly bodies are contained in the universe.
2. No one knows whether our universe is finite or infinite.
3. No one knows how old the universe is or how it got started.

F. Thought Questions:
1. Would you like to take a space trip to another galaxy? (Even if it took 25–50 years?)
2. What would be some of the problems of such a trip?
3. Do you think there could be other planets like the earth where conditions would be similar and life could exist? (Scientists estimate that there should be about 10,000,000 planets like the earth in our universe.)

G. Related Topics and Activities:
   1. See Section I-A, "Matter."
   2. See Part II, "Energy."
   3. Visit an observatory.
   4. See all Activities in this Section.

H. Vocabulary Builders—Spelling Words:
Use the words listed in "Results" for the types of heavenly bodies.

I. Thought for Today:
   "An eminent scientist has announced that, in his opinion, intelligent life is possible on several planets—including the earth!"

Activity

A. Problem: *What Are Constellations?*

B. Materials:
1. Astronomy books
2. Astronomy pamphlets
3. Star charts
4. Constellation cardboards (punched holes in cardboard or heavy tagboard showing constellations). These are best viewed by placing in windows.

C. Procedure:
1. Ask the students if they have ever studied the stars at night.
2. Ask them if they have ever tried to make pictures or designs from groups of stars.
3. Tell them that constellations are groups of stars that astronomers and ancient observers have created pictures of for reference.
4. Have the students see if they can locate the following constellations in printed materials or night skies:
   a. Big Dipper (Ursa Major) (Big Bear)
   b. Little Dipper (Ursa Minor) (Small Bear)
   c. Cassiopeia
   d. Orion
   e. Southern Cross
   f. Hydra
   g. Boötes
   h. Corona Borealis
   i. Hercules
   j. Cepheus
   k. Lyra
   l. Pegasus
   m. Pisces
   n. Pleiades
   o. Taurus
   p. Gemini
   q. Cancer
   r. Leo
   s. Virgo
   t. Libra
   u. Andromeda
   v. Perseus
   w. Draco
   x. Ophiuchus
   y. Auriga
   z. Aquarius

D. Result:
Students will have fun learning the constellations.

E. Supplemental Information:
1. Ancients grouped stars together and named them after mythological persons, animals, or inanimate objects.
2. Although the stars in a constellation look close together, they are actually billions of miles apart.
3. Another star chart can be made by punching holes in the bottom of a tin can, with each hole representing a star. Use a flashlight or hold the can up to a window for viewing.

F. Thought Questions:
1. Can you create other pictures with the stars?
2. Are the brightest stars closest to us?
3. How can you tell the difference between a planet and a star when viewing the sky at night?

G. Related Topics and Activities:
1. See Part VII, "Earth and Space."
2. See Activity VII-B-4, "Day and Night."
3. See Activity VII-B-5, "Seasons."
4. See all Activities in this Section.

H. Vocabulary Builders—Spelling Words:
Use the names of the constellations in "Procedure."

I. Thought for Today:
"Superior to kind thought is a kind word. Superior to a kind word is a kind deed."

Section B: Solar System

Activity VII B 1

A. Problem: *What Are Planets?*

B. Materials:
 1. Construction paper
 2. Colored yarn
 3. Bulletin board, large
 4. Pins

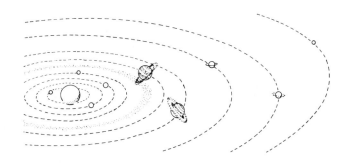

C. Procedure:
 1. From chart construct a scale that would represent various diameters and distances from the sun for each planet. (The following may be used.)
 2. Using scale 1″ = 16,000 miles the sun could be depicted by making a curved arc 62 ½″ in diameter at one side of bulletin board.
 3. Using a different scale of 1″ = 36 million miles place Mercury cut-out of construction paper one inch from arc of sun.
 4. Have students figure out how far the other planets should be placed from the sun. Place them where they belong.
 5. Cut out planets from different colors of construction paper and size indicated in chart on next page.
 6. With colored yarn make orbits for each planet going around sun. (Only parts of the orbits can be depicted.)

D. Results:
 1. Students will learn about the planets' relative sizes, distances from sun, and orbits.
 2. An understanding of the earth's position will be learned in relation to our solar system.

E. Supplemental Information:
 1. Most students will have to learn about relative sizes and distances. This can be developed by such things as comparing a model truck with a real truck or a model airplane with a real airplane. It is better to have the students select their own scale if possible. A larger and more accurate scale can be developed out in the school yard.

 2. Planets are celestial bodies like the earth, and including the earth, revolve around the sun.
 3. Five planets: Mercury, Venus, Mars, Jupiter, and Saturn can be seen at night with the unaided eye if conditions are right (clear sky, observable position).
 4. Planets with rings have many, not just one, ring.
 5. Pluto's orbit is more elliptical than the others.
 6. Most orbits of planets lie close to, but not exactly, on a single plane.

F. Thought Questions:
 1. How did we find out that all planets beyond Mars have rings around them? (Pluto is probable.)
 2. Why doesn't the earth shoot off into space or fall into the sun?
 3. Do you think life could exist on other planets?

G. Related Topics and Activities:
 1. Study our space shots—manned and unmanned.
 2. Visit an observatory.
 3. Look for planets at night in the sky. (They shine with a steady light while stars twinkle.)

H. Vocabulary Builders—Spelling Words:
See list of planets on next page.

I. Thought for Today:
 "For every person with a spark of genius, there are a dozen more with ignition troubles."

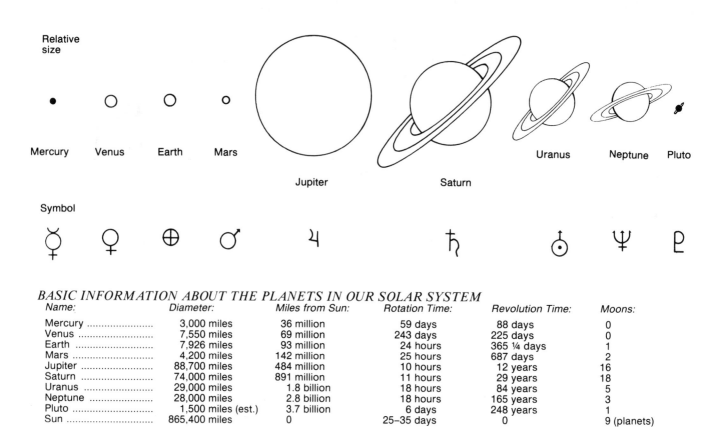

Relative size

Mercury Venus Earth Mars

Jupiter Saturn

Uranus Neptune Pluto

Symbol

BASIC INFORMATION ABOUT THE PLANETS IN OUR SOLAR SYSTEM

Name:	Diameter:	Miles from Sun:	Rotation Time:	Revolution Time:	Moons:
Mercury	3,000 miles	36 million	59 days	88 days	0
Venus	7,550 miles	69 million	243 days	225 days	0
Earth	7,926 miles	93 million	24 hours	365 ¼ days	1
Mars	4,200 miles	142 million	25 hours	687 days	2
Jupiter	88,700 miles	484 million	10 hours	12 years	16
Saturn	74,000 miles	891 million	11 hours	29 years	18
Uranus	29,000 miles	1.8 billion	18 hours	84 years	5
Neptune	28,000 miles	2.8 billion	18 hours	165 years	3
Pluto	1,500 miles (est.)	3.7 billion	6 days	248 years	1
Sun	865,400 miles	0	25–35 days	0	9 (planets)

Activity

A. Problem: *How Can We Find Directions by Using the Sun and a Watch?*

CAUTION: Never look directly at the sun. You can damage your eyes permanently.

B. Materials:
1. Compass
2. Wristwatch
3. Sun

C. Procedure:
1. Remove watch from wrist.
2. On the hour: six o'clock, seven o'clock, eight o'clock, etc., point the hour hand toward the sun.
3. Calculate which direction is south by looking at the point on the watch halfway between the hour hand and the minute hand.
4. Confirm the direction by using the compass.

D. Results:
1. When the hour hand points toward the sun, south is in a direction halfway between the hour hand and the minute hand.
2. We can find directions by using a watch and the sun.

E. Supplemental Information:
1. North can be calculated by the direction opposite south; for example, if south is indicated by 2 o'clock, north would be at 8 o'clock.
2. Facing north with outstretched arms, west would be in the direction the left arm is pointing, and east in the direction the right arm is pointing.

9:00 A.M.

F. Thought Questions:
1. Could you estimate direction if you had no watch?
2. How could you find northeast or southwest?
3. Does it make any difference whether you are on standard time or daylight saving time?

G. Related Topics and Activities:
1. Build a simple sundial and use it to tell time. (Shortest shadow would point to true south.)
2. Discuss the problem of making flat maps of the earth's curved surface.
3. See all Activities in this Section.

H. Vocabulary Builders—Spelling Words:
1) **direction** 2) **sun** 3) **watch** 4) **north**
5) **east** 6) **south** 7) **west**

I. Thought for Today:
"Time spent getting even would be better spent getting ahead."

Activity

A. Problem: *How Can We Tell Time by Using the Sun?*

CAUTION: Never look directly at the sun. You can damage your eyes permanently.

B. Materials:
1. Sunshine
2. Broom handle
3. Compass
4. Piece of cardboard, or heavy tagboard, about a foot square, for each student
5. Tall nail, or dowel, for each student
6. Tacks

C. Procedure:
1. Ask class if they can tell time by the sun.
2. Ask them if they have ever seen a sundial.
3. If so, have them relate their experiences.
4. Draw a circle about four or five feet in diameter in the open sunlight. By using compass for directions, number clock hours as shown on sundial beginning with the 6 to the west, 12 to the north, and 6 to the east (2 hours of each sundial equals one hour of watch time).
5. Place broom handle in center of circle.
6. Note shadow cast by sun and approximate time.
7. Have each student draw a dial with hour markings as shown in sketch.
8. Have students tack their dowels to the clockface.
9. Take the students outside to check their new dial clock.
10. The "12" on the clock should be pointed north.

D. Result:

The sun will cast a shadow which can be interpreted as the time on the sundial.

E. Supplemental Information:

We can tell time by a compass and shadows by drawing a dial. We do not need a watch; however, a watch is more accurate.

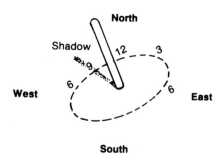

F. Thought Questions:
1. Will daylight saving time affect your readings?
2. Will the sundial work at any season of the year?
3. Why is the shadow longer at some seasons than others?
4. If your stick is pointed directly to the sun at twelve o'clock noon, so no shadow is cast, what would the angle of the dowel or nail to the ground represent in terms of your location on the earth?
5. How do sailors find the exact time by the sun?

G. Related Topics and Activities:
1. A more elaborate and permanent sundial can be made by nailing a wooden dowel to a wooden base.
2. See Section VII-A, "Universe."
3. See Section VII-E, "Weather."
4. See Activity VII-B-4, "Day and Night."

H. Vocabulary Builders—Spelling Words:
1) **time**   2) **direction**   3) **hours**
4) **compass**   5) **sunshine**

I. Thought for Today:

"Thanks to digital watches, students won't have to learn how to tell time."

Activity

A. Problem: *What Makes Day and Night?*

B. Materials:
   1. Globe (earth)
   2. Flashlight or slide projector
   3. Cellophane tape
   4. Paper

C. Procedure:
   1. Darken the room.
   2. Have one student shine the flashlight or slide projector on the globe. This represents the sun's rays; the globe represents the earth.
   3. Ask the students what causes night; what causes day.
   4. Cut a piece of paper and tape it on the globe to represent your city so the children can see where they live.
   5. Rotate the globe and show what happens to their city as the earth rotates.
   6. Ask the students how long it takes for the earth to rotate once. If you make it clear to them where the sun is shining to start with, they may be able to figure out for themselves that the earth rotates once a day. Have them work with the globe and light source to gain additional understanding.

D. Result:

The students will learn that the earth rotates once each day. This causes darkness (night) in part of the world while it is light (day) in the opposite part.

E. Supplemental Information:
   1. The rotation of the earth, not the movement of the sun, causes day and night.
   2. The earth is divided into time zones, otherwise it would be the same time for everybody all over the earth.
   3. We have 4 time zones in the United States:
      a. Pacific
      b. Mountain
      c. Central
      d. Eastern

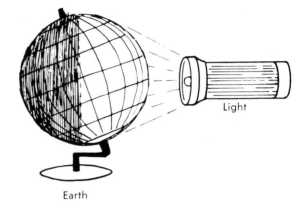

Light

Earth

F. Thought Questions:
   1. Can you figure out if the earth rotates from east to west or west to east?
   2. Why during some times of year are days longer than nights and at other times nights longer than days?
   3. How do we know the axis of the earth tilts in relation to the sun?
   4. If it is 1:00 P.M. in New York, what time is it in California? *in the sky during*
   5. Can you see farther in the daytime or nighttime? (Be careful—hint: stars?)

G. Related Topics and Activities:
   1. Discuss time zones in relation to friends or relatives who live in other parts of the country.
   2. Discuss rotation and revolution.
   3. See all Activities in this Section.

H. Vocabulary Builders—Spelling Words:
   1) **day**   2) **night**   3) **rotation**   4) **earth**
   5) **globe**

I. Thought for Today:
   "Daylight saving time just makes some people tired an hour earlier."

Activity

A. Problem: *How Does the Length of Day and Night Change from Season to Season?*

B. Materials:
1. Desk, table, or stand
2. Globe of the earth on stand
3. Filmstrip projector (Flashlight may be substituted.)
4. Compass
5. Chalkboard pointer or yardstick

C. Procedure:
1. Place globe on desk or table.
2. Place filmstrip projector about fifteen feet from the globe.
3. Darken the room.
4. Turn the projector on.
5. Shine the light from the projector to the globe. (The light side represents daytime; the dark side, nighttime.)
6. Using compass, tilt the globe northward until the elevation of the axis above the horizontal is the same as the latitude of the school. (If your community is located at 38° North Latitude, then the globe should be tilted 38° from the horizontal position. You can estimate tilt, it doesn't have to be exact.)
7. Slowly rotate the globe on its axis noting the amount of light on the North Pole and South Pole.
8. Select another point on the globe, and as the globe rotates, determine if it receives no light, all light, more than half or less than half of the light during one rotation.
9. Move the projector to the floor and repeat rotation.
10. Move the projector to a high level and repeat rotation.

D. Results:
1. Students will visualize that the North Pole is opposite the South Pole as to lightness and darkness.
2. Pupils will learn that lightness and darkness change as the seasons change. (Moving the projector up and down.)

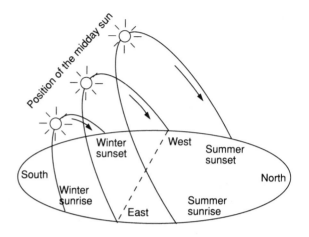

E. Supplemental Information:
1. In the spring and autumn the axis of the earth is neither tilted toward nor away from the sun, thus providing equal amounts of night and day.
2. In the northern hemisphere during the summer, the axis of the earth is tilted toward the sun. The daylight arc is longer than the nighttime arc, therefore, the days are longer than the nights.
3. In the northern hemisphere during winter, the axis of the earth is tilted away from the sun. The daylight arc is shorter than the nighttime arc, therefore, the days are shorter than the nights.

F. Thought Questions:
1. If you were rich and wanted to live where the daylight was the longest, where would you live in the summer? winter? autumn? spring?
2. Check with the weather bureau and find the average temperature of your locality for a winter month and a summer month. Is there much difference?
3. If you could redesign the axis of the earth, would you place it where it now is or change it? Why?
4. What is the international date line? Why is it necessary?

G. Related Topics and Activities:
   1. Design a test to prove that our earth tilts at 23½ degrees from its orbital plane.
   2. Discuss how plants, animals, and people adjust to each season.
   3. See Section VII-E, "Weather."
   4. See all Activities in this Section.

H. Vocabulary Builders—Spelling Words:
   1) **length** 2) **day** 3) **night** 4) **season**
   5) **orbit** 6) **tilt**

I. Thought for Today:
   "Winter is the season in which people try to keep the house as warm as it was in the summer when they complained about the heat."

Activity

A. Problem: *What Causes an Eclipse?*

B. Materials:
1. Globe to represent the earth
2. Table or desk
3. Tennis ball (to represent the moon)
4. Ice pick
5. Film projector
6. Wire

C. Procedure:
1. With ice pick, *carefully* punch two holes on opposite sides of tennis ball.
2. Attach wire through holes. (Makes demonstration more realistic by keeping your hand shadow off the globe.)
3. Set globe on desk or table.
4. Set up slide projector 10 to 15 feet away from globe.
5. Darken room.
6. Turn on projector.
7. Revolve tennis ball around the globe with globe situated so light from projector will cast shadows.
8. Revolve moon until it falls within the shadow cast by the earth. (Lunar eclipse)
9. Revolve the tennis ball close to earth until it comes between the earth and the sun, throwing its own shadow over the earth. This will produce a partial or total eclipse, depending on the observer's position on globe. (Solar eclipse)

D. Result:
Students learn that the shadows of the earth and moon are what causes eclipses of the moon and sun. When the moon has light from the sun cut off by the earth, it is a lunar eclipse (eclipse of the moon). When the earth has light cut off by the moon, it is a solar eclipse (eclipse of the sun).

E. Supplemental Information:
Solar eclipses are visible on limited sections of the earth because of the relatively small shadow cast by the moon. Lunar eclipses are visible over large areas of the earth's surface because they are caused by the earth casting a shadow on the moon. (The earth is much bigger than the moon.)

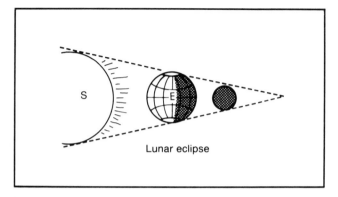

Lunar eclipse

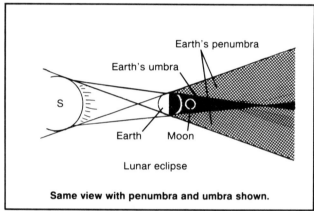

Lunar eclipse

Same view with penumbra and umbra shown.

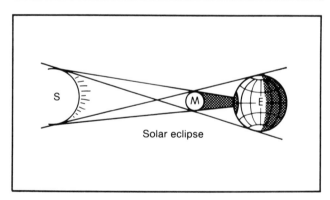

Solar eclipse

F. Thought Questions:
1. Do we have lunar eclipses every month?
2. Do other planets have moons?
3. Can we see both sides of the moon during one day, one week, or one month? Why or why not? (Hint: It rotates once for every revolution it makes around the earth.)

G. Related Topics and Activities:
   1. Discuss what causes the earth's umbra and penumbra.
   2. Discuss what we can learn during an eclipse.
   3. See Section VII-A, "Universe."
   4. See all Activities in this Section.

H. Vocabulary Builders—Spelling Words:
   1) **eclipse**   2) **sun**   3) **moon**   4) **shadow**
   5) **globe**
   For older students add:
   6) **umbra**   7) **penumbra**

I. Thought for Today:
   "Science can predict an eclipse of the sun many years in advance, but cannot accurately predict the weather over the weekend."

Activity

A. Problem: *Is the Earth Round?*

B. Materials:
    1. World globe
    2. Toy ship

C. Procedure:
    1. Ask class if any of them have been at the beach and seen ships disappear over the horizon.
    2. Have these students recount their experiences.
    3. Place globe where students can see that it is round.
    4. Hold the globe steady with one hand.
    5. Take the toy ship with the other hand and move it on the globe away from the students until it moves out of sight.

D. Result:
The toy ship disappears from the student's view. (The top of the ship disappears last.)

E. Supplemental Information:
Explain that when objects disappear over the horizon as did the toy ship it is an indication that the earth is curved.

F. Thought Questions:
    1. What other clues do we have that our world might be round?
    2. What are some problems that we have in launching a missile from the United States to the moon because our earth is round?

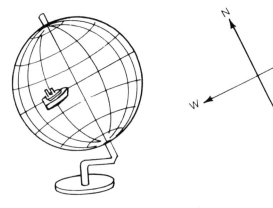

3. What are some possible reasons for our earth being round (spherical) rather than square (cubical) or even football-shaped?

G. Related Topics and Activities:
    1. See Activity VII-B-6, "Lunar Eclipse."
    2. See Section VII-A, "Universe."
    3. See Section VII-C, "Earth's Crust."
    4. See all Activities in this Section.

H. Vocabulary Builders—Spelling Words:
1) **earth**   2) **round**   3) **globe**
4) **ship**   3) **disappear**

I. Thought for Today:
"It would be nice if the poor were to get half of the money that is spent on studying them."

Activity VII**B**8

A. Problem: *How Fast Is the Earth Moving?*

B. Materials:

Pictures, charts, or models of:
1. Earth
2. Solar system
3. Milky Way
4. Supercluster
5. Observable universe

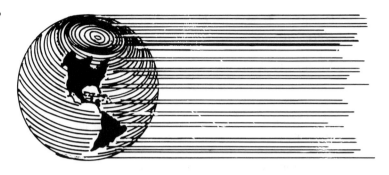

C. Procedure:
1. Have students discuss the various celestial bodies.
2. Have students discuss movement of people on earth in relation to fixed positions; relative to moving objects such as a student's speed on a bicycle in relation to the wind blowing on her back or toward her face.
3. Discuss the way the earth moves in relation to the:
   a. moon
   b. sun
   c. our solar system
   d. our galaxy (Milky Way)
   e. supercluster
   f. observable universe
4. Students can further study the relative movements of the earth by independent research.

D. Results:

Students will learn that:
1. Earth moves approximately 1,300 miles per hour in relation to the moon.
2. Earth moves approximately 66,500 miles per hour around the sun.
3. Earth moves approximately 481,000 miles per hour around its galaxy.
4. Earth moves around the center of the supercluster at approximately 1,350,000 miles per hour.
5. Earth moves with the supercluster at about 360,000 m.p.h.

E. Supplemental Information:
1. This study is part of the theory of relativity.
2. The fourth dimension of Einstein is time-space.

3. There are several other movements of the earth; for example, the earth also wobbles on its axis and thus our North Star has not always been the star closest to the direction in which the earth's axis points.
4. It takes the solar system, traveling at 418,000 m.p.h., 200 million years to make a single revolution around the axis of the Milky Way.

F. Thought Questions:
1. Can speed be measured by any one instrument?
2. Can anything travel faster than the speed of light?
3. If the earth is traveling so fast in so many directions, relatively, why doesn't our atmosphere dissipate or blow away?

G. Related Topics and Activities:
1. See Section II-F, "Movement and Resistance."
2. Devise some relative problems for the students to consider such as:
   "If you were on a train traveling 60 m.p.h. and you used a skateboard to skate 10 m.p.h. from the back of your railroad car to the front of it, how fast would you be traveling in relation to the ground?"
3. See all Activities in this section.

H. Vocabulary Builders—Spelling Words:
   1) **earth**   2) **solar system**   3) **supercluster**
   4) **universe**   5) **Milky Way**

I. Thought for Today:
"If you ask enough people, you can usually find someone who'll advise you to do what you were going to do anyway."

Activity

A. Problem: *How Can Our Latitude Be Determined?*

B. Materials:
   1. Sheet of paper or piece of thin pipe
   2. Protractor
   3. Thread
   4. Weight
   5. Cellophane tape
   6. Magnetic compass

C. Procedure:
   1. If you are using paper, roll it up in the shape of a pipe, about ¼" in diameter.
   2. Tape the protractor to the long part of the pipe or roll. (See sketch.)
   3. Fasten the thread to the center of the protractor at its base.
   4. Add a weight to the other end of the thread.
   5. At night, with magnetic compass, locate the general northerly direction.
   6. Look for the constellation of the Big Dipper in that general direction. (Pointers point to North Star.)
   7. Point the roll or pipe at the North Star.
   8. When the North Star is centered, hold the thread against the protractor and read the degrees.
   9. Repeat several times to be sure that results are accurate.
   10. Convert readings to scale shown in illustration.

D. Results:
   1. The North Star will be located.
   2. The angle of the North Star will be determined.
   3. The latitude of the observer is equal to the elevation of the North Star at that point.

E. Supplemental Information:
   1. The latitude of the North Star at the North Pole is 90° and would be directly overhead.
   2. The latitude of the North Star at the equator is 0° and would be directly horizontal if you could see it. The chances are that mountains, trees, houses, etc. would block it from your view.

F. Thought Questions:
   1. Could you make a protractor if you didn't have one?

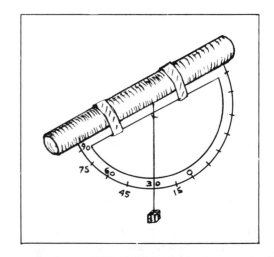

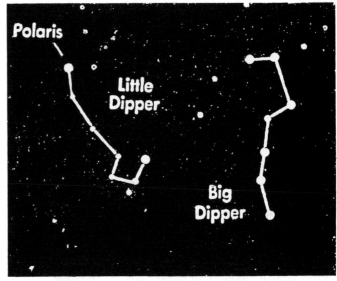

   2. Does the North Star appear to move?
   3. Does the Big Dipper appear to move?

G. Related Topics and Activities:
   1. Check the angle of buildings, trees, etc.
   2. Show older students math tables to convert angles to heights (study right angles).
   3. See all Activities in this Section.

H. Vocabulary Builders—Spelling Words:
   1) **latitude**   2) **protractor**   3) **compass**
   4) **angles**   5) **direction**

I. Thought for Today:
   "Wherever we look upon this earth, the opportunities take shape within the problems."

Activity

A. Problem: *How Does the Moon Travel?*

B. Materials:
   1. Globe
   2. Flashlight or slide projector
   3. Chalkboard
   4. Three cards labeled: "Earth," "Moon," and "Sun"
   5. Flannel board and cut-outs (optional)

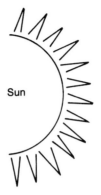

C. Procedure:
   1. Discuss with the class the concepts of rotation (spinning on its axis) and revolution (moving around another body).
   2. Discuss the causes of day and night, and lengths of a day, month, and a year.
   3. Use the flashlight or slide projector to explain day and night. (See Activity VII-B-4.)
   4. Have three students come to the front of the room and explain the relative movements of the earth, moon, and sun. Let one student be the sun; another student, the moon; and the third student, the earth. Have each student go through the motions of his celestial body, holding up his/her labeled card. Have all three students move as their celestial bodies move in relation to the others.

D. Result:
Students will become more aware of the effect the sun and moon have on the earth, and the relative movements of each.

E. Supplemental Information:
   1. This activity could be conducted on the school campus, with the orbit of the earth around the sun chalked on the surface of the school yard to more accurately show the relative distance between all three celestial bodies.
   2. The moon travels from west to east around the earth. The moon rises about 50 minutes later each night. It travels completely around the earth from one full moon to another. This takes approximately 27.3 days.

   3. The moon is approximately 240,000 miles from the earth.
      a. Its diameter is 2,160 miles.
      b. While the moon is rotating on its axis and revolving around the earth, its apparent motion of rising later each day is due to the rotation of the earth.

F. Thought Questions:
   1. What are some problems astronauts have in trying to land on the moon with a spaceship?
   2. Why is it that we can't see the moon on some nights?
   3. What causes the moon to change apparent shapes?
   4. Why does the moon look larger when it first rises (near the horizon) than it does when it is higher (closer to overhead)?

G. Related Topics and Activities:
   1. See Section VIII-B, "Satellites"
   2. See Activity VII-B-11, "Moonshapes."
   3. See Activity VII-B-4, "Day and Night."
   4. See all Activities in this Section.

H. Vocabulary Builders—Spelling Words:
1) **moon**   2) **travel**   3) **earth**   4) **rotation**
5) **revolution**   6) **celestial**

I. Thought for Today:
"Time is what we want the most, and what we use the worst."

Activity

A. Problem: *Why Does the Moon Appear to Change Shape?*

NOTE: This is a very difficult concept and should be undertaken over a period of time, depending on the maturity of the students.

B. Materials:

1. Globe or large ball
2. Electric lamp
3. Slide projector
4. Bulletin board (covered with light blue construction paper, preferably)
5. Flannel board, approximately 24″ × 36″ (light blue color, preferably)
6. Colored contruction paper cut into pieces to represent the following:
   a. the sun and its rays (yellow or orange, approximately 12″ in diameter)
   b. the earth (green—dark green, on half away from the sun, and light green on half toward the sun, approximately 4″ in diameter)
   c. eight moons (black and white, to represent eight phases of the moon, approximately 2″ each in diameter).

C. Procedures:

Procedure One:

1. Move chairs to sides of room.
2. Set the lamp in the middle of the room.
3. Turn lamp on.
4. Darken the room, except for the lamp.
5. Demonstrate the term rotation by having one student turn around slowly while staying in one spot. This student represents the earth or the moon. See sketch two, next page.
6. Explain the term revolution by having another student, Earth, walk very slowly around the lamp, Sun. See sketch two, next page.
7. Have two students perform:
   One representing the Earth should walk very, very slowly around the lamp Sun in a large circle while the second student is walking around the first student.

Result One:

This shows the movements of the earth and the moon in relation to the sun.

Procedure Two:

1. In a darkened room, turn on the slide projector and direct the beam toward a globe or ball about 6 feet away.
2. Have class notice light and dark areas on the globe or ball.
3. Have a few students at a time get up and observe light and dark areas on the globe or ball.

Result Two:

This shows how a round object receives light on one side, while the other side (or half) receives no light (is in darkness).

Procedure Three:

1. Turn on class light. Turn off lamp.
2. Place the construction paper "Sun" on one side of the flannel board, explaining that the sun gives off light in all directions.
3. Place the construction paper "Earth" about half way to the side of the flannel board, with the light half facing the "Sun."
4. Place 4 of the 8 moons representing each quarter around the "Earth." (See Sketch One.)

Result Three:

The students will see how the side facing the "Sun" is light while the side (half of hemisphere) facing away from the "Sun" is dark.

Procedure Four:

1. Draw an arc on the floor with a piece of chalk to represent ¹⁄₁₂ of the earth's path around the sun. The arc should be part of a circle about 12 feet in diameter.
2. Divide the arc into 4 equal parts and mark them as shown in Sketch Three.
3. Place a lighted lamp near the center of the arc.
4. Darken the room.
5. Have a student hold the globe or ball in front of him/her.
6. Have him/her make one slow rotation in his walk along the arc noting the change of the shape of the light on the globe or ball. (See Sketch Three.)

Result Four:

Students will see the different phases of the moon (globe or ball).

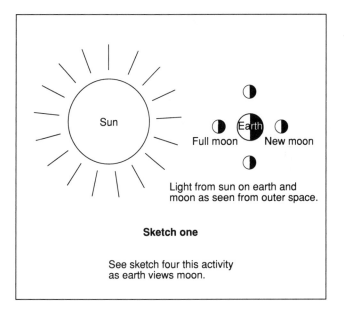

Sketch one

See sketch four this activity
as earth views moon.

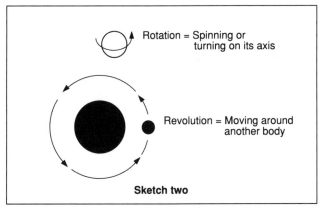

Rotation = Spinning or
turning on its axis

Revolution = Moving around
another body

Sketch two

Ball or globe represents moon.

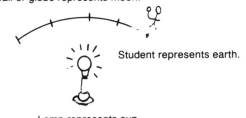

Student represents earth.

Lamp represents sun.

Sketch three

Procedure Five:

1. Put the eight "Moons" on the bulletin board in the sequence shown in Sketch Four.
2. Place the moons on the board as follows:
   a. new moon (no light from sun; back side)
   b. second phase or crescent-shaped moon (waxing; increasing in the amount of light seen)
   c. first quarter of the moon, appearing about one week after the new moon
   d. fourth phase
   e. full moon, appearing at the end of second week, and on side of earth away from the sun
   f. sixth phase
   g. third quarter of the moon, appearing third week of the cycle
   h. last phase; old moon, crescent-shaped

NOTE: If the moon is increasing in the amount of light seen from the earth each day, it is waxing; if decreasing, it is waning.

3. Explain that these are the views of the moon that people on earth see that are similar to the views of the students in Procedure Four.

D. Result:

The demonstrations should acquaint the students with facts about the moon and its change in shape.

E. Supplemental Information:

1. If an orrery is available, be sure to use it to supplement the activities cited here.
2. Important facts about the moon:
   a. The moon is a satellite revolving around the earth.
   b. It is about ⅓ the size of the earth; its diameter is about 2,160 miles.
   c. The moon is approximately 240,000 miles from the earth.
   d. The moon rotates every 27.3 days.
   e. The moon revolves around the earth every 27.3 days.
   f. Since the moon rotates once for every revolution, we see only one side of the moon.
3. The demonstrations should be preceded by discussion as well as reading of introductory materials about the universe. A thorough study of the material should be made before the demonstration is attempted.

Phases of the moon

New Moon	Waxing Crescent	First Quarter	Waxing (Gibbous)
Full Moon	Waning (Gibbous)	Last Quarter	Waning Crescent

The crescent shape appearances of the moon are due to the light from the sun shining on a *ball-shaped* moon.

as seen from the earth

Sketch four

F. Thought Questions:

1. How would the earth appear to change in shape if we were on the moon?
2. If it were possible to view the earth and moon from the sun, how would they appear to change in shape?
3. What causes an eclipse of the moon? of the sun?

G. Related Topics and Activities:

1. See Activity II-C-2, "How Light Travels."
2. Visit an observatory.
3. See all Activities in this Section.

H. Vocabulary Builders—Spelling Words:

1) **moon**   2) **phase**   3) **quarter**   4) **waxing**
5) **waning**   6) **gibbous**

I. Thought for Today:

"What we learn with pleasure, we never forget."

Section C: Earth's Crust

Activity VII C 1

A. Problem: *What Causes Tides?*

B. Materials:
1. Large globe or ball depicting sun
2. Small globe or ball depicting earth
3. Smaller globe or ball depicting moon (plastic balls work well)
4. Wide rubber band
5. Four cup hooks
6. Two supports, one for the sun and one for the moon (Sun's support may be fixed. The moon's support should be movable.)
7. Attach cup hooks and balls to rubber band as shown in sketch

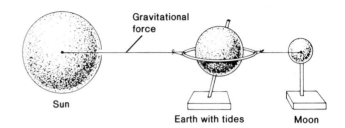

C. Procedure:
1. Explain that heavenly bodies attract each other. The sun attracts the earth and the earth attracts the sun. The earth attracts the moon and the moon attracts the earth.
2. Discuss how the moon attracts the earth and moves the oceans toward the moon.
3. Discuss how the sun attracts the earth and moves the oceans toward the sun.
4. Explain how the moon exerts a greater pull because it is so much closer to the earth.
5. By use of the apparatus the direction of pull can be demonstrated by the direction of the rubber band. (See drawing.)
6. Move the moon to various positions around the earth.
7. Explain when the sun, moon, and earth are in a straight line, the pull is greatest. These tides are called spring tides and occur twice a month. When the moon, earth, and sun form a right triangle (one week later) the tides are smallest and are called neap tides.
8. Discuss the causes of high and low tides each day. (The earth's rotation and its relation to the position of the moon.)

D. Results:
1. Students will learn that the sun and moon cause the tides.
2. Pupils will learn that the moon has a greater effect on tides than the sun.

E. Supplemental Information:
The daily newspapers usually report the time of high tides and low tides each day. Students can check the location of the moon at high tide and at low tide.

F. Thought Questions:
1. In some parts of the world the daily tides are less than 2 feet high, while in other parts of the world they are as great as 70 feet high. Why?
2. How can tides be used to help us?
3. Do you think tides could be used to generate electricity?

G. Related Topics and Activities:
1. See Section VII-B, "Solar System."
2. See Activities VII-B-10 and VII-B-11, "Moon."
3. See all Activities in this section.

H. Vocabulary Builders—Spelling Words:
1) **tide**   2) **gravity**   3) **attract**   4) **spring**
5) **neap**   6) **rotation**   7) **heavenly**

I. Thought for Today:
"Patience is bitter but its fruit is sweet."

Activity

A. Problem: *What Causes a Volcano to Erupt?*

B. Materials:
   1. Pie tin
   2. Length of plastic tubing, about 15″ long
   3. Salt and flour paste
   4. Puffed rice (cereal)
   5. Dry, ground cereal
   6. Tempera paint (brown)
   7. Any size soft drink bottle

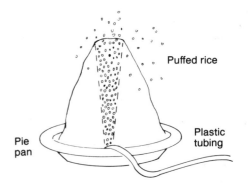

C. Procedure:
   1. Have a class committee do the research on the shape, general appearance, and structure of a volcano.
   2. They can make a paste of flour, salt, and water.
   3. From this paste students can make a model of a volcano. A vertical cone-shaped hole should be left in the center. A plastic tube should be connected with the bottom of this hole.
   4. When paste has hardened, paint volcano brown with tempera.
   5. Place some puffed rice cereal in the cavity.
   6. Have a student blow, with great force, into the end of the plastic tube.
   7. Open the soda bottle and notice the bubbles and some liquid droplets escaping.

D. Results:
   1. Gas pressure forces the bubbles to spray out of the bottle.
   2. The pressure from blowing forces the light cereal out of the vent and down the sides of the volcano, simulating an eruption.

E. Supplemental Information:
   1. Volcanic eruptions are due to gas pressures that build up from the molten material from the earth's core and reach the mantle and crust of the earth.
   2. This demonstration could lead to a discussion on the formation of mountains by pressure from the Earth's core.

F. Thought Questions:
   1. In what way is the model volcano similar to a real volcano erupting on earth?
   2. How does the model volcano differ from a real volcano?
   3. What causes the internal pressures within the earth?

G. Related Topics and Activities:
   1. See Section VII-C, "Earth's Crust."
   2. See Activity II-A-1, "Sources of Power."
   3. See Section II-F, "Movement and Resistance."
   4. Combine this activity with art work.
   5. See all Activities in this Section.

H. Vocabulary Builders—Spelling Words:
   1) **volcano**   2) **erupt**   3) **cone**
   4) **pressure**   5) **simulate**

I. Thought for Today:
   "If you think you have somebody eating out of your hand, it's a good idea to count your fingers."

Activity

A. Problem: What is erosion? What causes a loss in our topsoil?

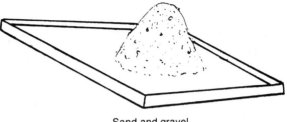
Sand and gravel

B. Materials:
1. Cookie sheet
2. Sand
3. Grass, square, 6″ × 6″
4. Gravel
5. Water
6. Small-necked, pint bottle
7. Newspapers
8. Table top or desk
9. Bucket

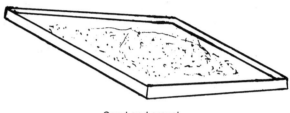
Sand and gravel

C. Procedure:
1. Lay the newspapers on the table or desk top.
2. Place the cookie sheet on the newspapers.
3. Using a mixture of two-thirds sand and one-third gravel, make a mound on the cookie sheet about six inches high.
4. Fill the bottle with water.
5. Slowly pour about half the water on top of the sand and gravel mound.
6. Notice the results.
7. Pour the excess water from the cookie sheet into the bucket.
8. Flatten the sand and gravel.
9. Carefully sprinkle some more water from the bottle over the whole area of sand and gravel.
10. Notice the results.
11. Pour the excess water from the cookie sheet into the bucket.
12. Shape the sand and gravel into a circular shape with a high ridge and a large depression in the center.
13. Fill the bottle with water again.
14. Pour about half of the contents into the middle of the depression.
15. Notice the results.
16. Remove all sand and gravel from the cookie sheet.
17. Place the grass square in the middle of the cookie sheet.
18. Pour the remaining half of water equally over the grass area.
19. Notice the results.

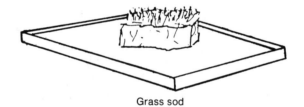
Grass sod

D. Results:
1. In the first trial, some sand and gravel will wash down the sides forming gullies.

2. In the second trial, there is little or no washing of sand and gravel.
3. In the third trial, the water will collect in the valley (middle of the depression).
4. In the last trial, the water will have little run-off because of the holding power of the grass sod.

E. Supplemental Information:

1. Moving water changes the surface of the earth.
2. Streams and rivers form from rains and snow run-offs.
3. Rains and melting snows develop streams and rivers.
4. All running waters from little streams to large rivers produce gulleys which wash away our topsoils by eroding our lands.
5. Our topsoils which produce our foods are becoming thinner and thinner due to gulleying, erosion, and poor farming techniques.
6. Many procedures are available to reduce gulleying, erosion, and loss of our precious topsoil. The most frequently used ones are:
   a. crop rotation
   b. terracing
   c. contour farming
   d. "wattling process" (constructing artificial fences across gulleys with limbs, branches, stones, etc. so that topsoil washed down the gulleys will collect in back of the fences forming a series of small terraces).
   e. planting trees to make windbreaks by reducing soil loss because of strong winds.
7. The first attempt to quantify global erosion rates estimated that cropland losses exceed new soil formation by 25.4 billion tons per year.
8. Another recent study claims that the average depth of our topsoil has been reduced from nine inches to six inches.
9. The "bottom line" is that we are losing our topsoil at a time when our population is increasing and we need more topsoil to produce more food crops.
10. We can add some chemical to the soil to enrich it but we cannot replace all the natural ingredients needed for most crops.
11. Scientists estimate that it takes nature 500 to 1,000 years to produce an inch of topsoil.

F. Thought Questions:

1. Do you think running water is a powerful force?
2. If you were a farmer, what kind of land surface would you prefer?
3. What techniques could be used to retain topsoil?

4. Can you think of any other ways that could be used to save our topsoil?

G. Related Topics and Activities:

1. Study how farmers in your area conserve their topsoil.
2. Study the different kinds of soil in your area.
3. See all Activities in Section VII-C, "Earth's Crust."
4. See all Activities in Section III-D, "Soils and Germination."

H. Vocabulary Builders—Spelling Words:

1) **erosion**   2) **gulleys**   3) **conservation**   4) **topsoil**
5) **sprinkle**   6) **valleys**

I. Thought for Today:

"A country can lose its freedom and regain it, but if it loses its topsoil the country is doomed forever."

Activity

A. Problem: *How Can the Bottom of the Ocean Be Explored?*

B. Materials:
1. Toy ships
2. Toy submarines
3. Toy diver
4. Picture of ocean salvage ship
5. Large dishpan
6. Glass bottle with two-hole stopper
7. Glass tubing
8. Plastic hose

C. Procedure:
1. Describe the importance of the oceans:
   a. Cover three-fourths of the surface of the earth
   b. Rich in plants and animals
   c. Hold minerals, gas, and oil
2. Discuss the problems of exploring the oceans:
   a. Tremendous weight or pressure on ship or diver:
      1) On land, this pressure is equal to 14.7 pounds per square inch.
      2) Under the ocean's surface, this pressure increases 14.7 pounds with each 33 feet of depth.
   b. Divers breathe a special mixture of gases.
   c. They have specially heated suits.
   d. They use specially designed tools.
   e. They are equipped with special communication system(s).
3. Discuss buoyancy, submarines, and what makes objects float or sink.
4. Compare the problems of underwater exploration with space exploration.
5. Fill the dishpan with water.
6. Insert glass tubing and hose as shown in sketch.
7. Place hose over one of the ends of glass tubing.
8. Close hose by pinching and place bottle in dishpan.
9. Periodically open and close hose under water.
10. After the bottle has sunk, blow air into the bottle through hose.

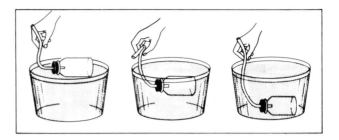

D. Results:
1. Water will enter the bottle through the second piece of tubing.
2. When sufficient water has entered the bottle it will sink.
3. When air is pumped back in, bottle will rise.

E. Supplemental Information:
1. Submarines operate in this fashion by taking in water and then pumping it out.
2. The density of any object is the volume divided by its weight.
3. When the density of any object is less than water, the object floats, when it is more, the object sinks.

F. Thought Questions:
1. Who should control the oceans?
2. Who should regulate ocean fishing, navigation, mining, etc.?
3. Who should control off-shore oil well drilling?
4. Should we use our oceans as dumping grounds for sewage and wastes?
5. If you were given the job of mining the oceans, what method(s) would you use?

G. Related Topics and Activities:
1. See Section I-C, "Water."
2. Have a scuba diver talk to class.
3. Study the cause of ocean waves.
4. See all Activities in this Section.

H. Vocabulary Builders—Spelling Words:
1) **bottom**   2) **ocean**   3) **exploration**
4) **submarine**   5) **surface**

I. Thought for Today:
"Science is proving that people can live in outer space and at the bottom of the sea. It's the area in between that's causing the trouble."

Activity

A. Problem: *How Are Crystals Formed?*

B. Materials:
1. Stove or hot plate
2. Quart mason jar
3. Three ounces powdered alum (obtain at pharmacy)
4. ¼ teaspoon vegetable dye
5. Circle of blotting paper, filter paper, or cheesecloth
6. Water
7. Cooking pot

C. Procedure:
1. Fill mason jar with water.
2. Pour into pot.
3. Heat to a rolling boil.
4. Add vegetable dye and stir.
5. Boil for a few minutes.
6. Turn off heat.
7. Add pinch of color and stir.
8. Remove from heat source.
9. Pour into jar through filter.
10. Allow to stand twenty-four hours. Tap jar occasionally while mixture is cooling to help formation of crystals.

D. Result:
Crystals form in the bottom of the jar.

E. Supplemental Information:
Crystals have different shapes and are formed in many different materials. To study different formations of crystals put both alum and salt crystals on slide under microscope (low magnification). The alum crystals are diamond-shaped, the salt cube-shaped.

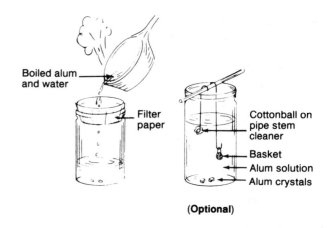

Boiled alum and water
Filter paper
Cottonball on pipe stem cleaner
Basket
Alum solution
Alum crystals

(Optional)

F. Thought Questions:
1. Can the same process be done with a saturated salt solution?
2. If an object were immersed in the Great Salt Lake for a few months, would it be covered with salt crystals?
3. Why do the alum crystals form when the saturated liquid is cooled?
4. Can you name any other crystals?

G. Related Topics and Activities:
1. See Activity VII-C-7, "Rocks."
2. See Activity VII-C-8, "Minerals."
3. See all Activities in this Section.
4. (Optional Procedure) If you suspend a small basket made of pipe cleaners or a ball of cotton in the solution, the crystals will adhere to it and make a decorative object.

H. Vocabulary Builders—Spelling Words:
1) **crystal**   2) **solution**   3) **filter**   4) **ounces**
5) **boiled**

I. Thought for Today:
"Interoffice memos increase our work by heaps and mounds."

Activity

A. Problem: *What Are Stalagmites? Stalactites?*

B. Materials:

1. Two one-quart glass jars
2. Yarn, soft, 24" long
3. Hot plate
4. Powdered alum, 8 oz. (obtain at pharmacy)
5. Water
6. Two small rocks

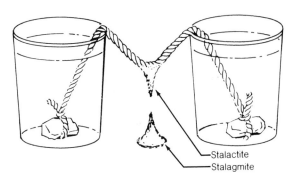

Stalactite
Stalagmite

C. Procedure:

1. Heat water and fill the two glass jars with water.
2. Stir in the powdered alum in both jars.
3. Tie one rock at each end of the yarn.
4. Place one rock in each of the jars.
5. Form a loop between the jars as shown in sketch.
6. Place apparatus in a corner where it can be watched.

D. Result:

After several days, a small salt-icicle will begin to form on the bottom of the loop of yarn and as the salt water drops on the surface from the loop, a small salt-icicle will begin to rise from the surface.

E. Supplemental Information:

1. The salt-icicle forming on the loop is called a stalactite. The salt-icicle forming on the surface and rising is called a stalagmite.
2. In many caves, stalactites and stalagmites are formed by water absorbing salts and then evaporating, leaving the salt deposited in icicle shapes.
3. Stalagmites grow from the ground; stalactites from the ceiling. A good way to remember this is that stalagmites have the letter "g" in it for ground and stalactites have the letter "c" in it for ceiling.

F. Thought Questions:

1. Where does the water get its salt?
2. How are water icicles formed similarly to salt icicles?
3. How are icicles formed in the refrigerator?

G. Related Topics and Activities:

1. See Section I-C, "Water."
2. If students have visited caves and seen stalagmites or stalactites, have them relate their experiences to the class.
3. See all Activities in this Section.

H. Vocabulary Builders—Spelling Words:

1) **stalagmites**   2) **stalactites**   3) **yarn**
4) **caves**   5) **evaporation**

I. Thought for Today:

"Modern science is simply wonderful. It would take fifty people twenty years to make the same mistake that a computer can make in two seconds."

Activity

A. Problem: *What Kinds of Rocks Are There?*

B. Materials:
1. Reference books on rocks
2. Tables of rock characteristics
3. Pictures of rocks
4. Rock collections (some should be brought in by pupils)
5. Hammer
6. Vinegar or dilute hydrochloric acid
7. Eyedropper
8. Multisensory aids

C. Procedure:
1. Discuss rocks using multisensory aids to motivate and stimulate pupil questions.
2. Ask students to collect as many different kinds of rocks as they can.
3. Make a display of the rocks.
4. With reference books, have pupils identify as many as possible.
   a. Being careful of fingers, tap the rock sample with the hammer to determine its relative hardness.
   b. Using vinegar or dilute hydrochloric acid, place 6 to 8 drops on the rock sample.
5. Have students label rocks and give characteristics and examples of each type.
6. Plan a field trip to increase the classroom collection.

D. Results:
1. Some rocks when hit will break into small pieces; some will chip and some will remain in one piece.
2. Some rocks will bubble when vinegar or dilute acid is placed on them showing the presence of carbonates. Rocks are carbonates or silicates.
3. Students will learn to identify the main types of rock formations.

E. Supplemental Information:
1. This activity is always motivating for students.
2. Students are natural collectors, and this activity makes use of this natural curiosity.
3. Many students will start rock collections of their own with a little persuasion from the teacher.
4. Rocks are classified by their color, hardness, cleavage, size, etc.

5. Rocks usually contain a mixture of minerals.
6. It's fun to collect minerals.
7. Minerals are building blocks of rocks.
8. There are over 2,000 known minerals.
9. Twenty of them make up 95% of the earth's crust.
10. Minerals contain no living or once living material. Silver, gold, and diamonds are minerals (and also elements). Diamonds are pure crystalline carbon.
11. Semi-precious stones such as sapphires, rubies, and emeralds are also minerals.
12. Minerals have definite physical characteristics; rocks do not.
13. Characteristics of minerals to look for:
    a. luster (glossy or dull)
    b. crystalline
    c. appearance when split
    d. color
    e. hardness (See Moh's Scale—next page)
    f. acid test (White vinegar is best for elementary students to use. Many minerals contain calcium carbonate ($CaCO_3$) and will bubble when acid is placed on them.)
    g. Older students may want to test specimens with a smelting or heat test to determine if sulphur or metals are present.
    h. Older students may want to use a flame test. A small sample is heated in a flame. Different substances have different colors when heated.
    i. magnetic or not

14. Rocks are of three major types:
   a. Sedimentary—formed by mineral deposits from oceans.
   b. Igneous—formed by cooling of hot lava.
   c. Metamorphic—formed by a combination of Igneous and Sedimentary rocks.

F. Thought Questions:
   1. Why do we need to know anything about rocks?
   2. How many ways can you name in which rocks are helpful or harmful to us?
   3. How do rocks differ?

G. Related Topics and Activities:
   1. See Activities I-A-9 and I-A-12, "Acids and Bases."
   2. See Section I-A, "Matter."
   3. See all Activities in this Section.

H. Vocabulary Builders—Spelling Words:
   1) **sapphire**   2) **diamond**   3) **silver**   4) **gold**
   5) **crystalline**   6) **carbon**   7) **luster**

I. Thought for Today:
   "Too little knowledge is the most dangerous thing."

COLOR TABLE

EXTERNAL COLOR	STREAK TEST	EXAMPLE
Blue or white	White	Calcite
Green, purple, white	White	Fluorite
Gray or green	White	Talc
Blue–green	White	Apatite
Gray	Gray	Galena
Pale yellow	Dark green	Pyrite
Orange–yellow	Green–black	Chalcopyrite
Gray; Red–brown	Red–brown	Hematite
Bright green	Pale green	Malachite
Brown	Ochre yellow	Limonite
Black	Black	Magnetite

HARDNESS TABLE (MOH'S SCALE)

HARDNESS NUMBER	HARDNESS TEST	EXAMPLE
1	Scratches easily with a fingernail	Talc
2	Scratches with a fingernail	Gypsum
3	Scratches with a pin or penny	Calcite
4	Scratches easily with a knife	Fluorite
5	Scratches with a knife	Apatite
6	Knife will not scratch rock; rock will not scratch glass	Feldspar
7	Scratches glass easily	Quartz
8	Scratches quartz easily	Topaz
9	Scratches topaz easily	Corundum
10	Scratches all other rocks	Diamond

SIZE TABLE

NAME	SIZE IN INCHES	(METRICS)
Boulder	More than 10 inches across	(25 cm)
Cobble	2½ to 10 inches across	(6–25 cm)
Pebble	⅛ to 2½ inches across	(30 mm–6 cm)
Granules	$\frac{1}{16}$ to ⅛ inches across	(15–30 mm)
Sand	$\frac{1}{64}$ to $\frac{1}{16}$ inches across	(5–15 mm)
Silt	As fine as scouring powder	(—)
Clay	Particles can only be seen with microscope	(—)

Activity

A. Problem: *What Are Some Common Uses of Minerals?*

B. Materials:
1. Talcum powder
2. Sandpaper
3. Table salt
4. Rocks
5. Epsom salts
6. Milk of Magnesia
7. Baking soda
8. Baking powder
9. Rings (finger)

C. Procedure:
1. Have students bring in one mineral found in the home or community.
2. Discuss what the mineral is and how it is used.
3. Describe some of the minerals listed in Materials and show how they are used.

D. Results:
1. Many minerals will be brought in that have practical applications at home and at work.
2. Discuss the difference between minerals, rocks, elements, compounds, salts, etc. (Minerals are considered to be ores found in nature.)

E. Supplemental Information:
1. Students like to collect rocks and this interest should be capitalized on to learn about uses of minerals.
2. Field trips can be taken to nearby areas to look for rocks and minerals.
3. A mineral is a chemical compound that is found in nature.
4. Minerals have definite crystalline structures.
5. Minerals are classified in four main groups:
   a. Silicious (contains silicon): quartz, feldspar, mica, and talc
   b. Non-metallic: rock salt, graphite, sulphur, gypsum
   c. Metallic ores: gold, silver, lead, zinc, aluminum, tin, mercury, titanium, and uranium

   d. Gems: opal, jade, garnet, topaz, tourmaline, emerald, aquamarine, ruby, amethyst, sapphire, zircon, and diamond
6. Tests for minerals include:
   a. color (cold and heated)
   b. luster
   c. crystalline form
   d. hardness
   e. weight (specific gravity)
   f. magnetic
   g. fluorescence
   h. radioactive

F. Thought Questions:
1. Where does the steel come from to make automobiles, stoves, etc.?
2. Is coal a mineral?
3. How many other uses of minerals can you name?

G. Related Topics and Activities:
1. See Activity VII-C-5, "Crystals."
2. See Activity VII-C-7, "Rocks."
3. See other Activities in this Section.

H. Vocabulary Builders—Spelling Words:
Use the words in the mineral groups cited in "Supplementary Information."

I. Thought for Today:
"If a gem be not polished it will not shine—if a person study not, the person will have no wisdom."
—*Jitsu go Kiyo*

Section D: Gravity

Activity VII D 1

A. Problem: *Do Heavy Objects Fall Faster Than Light Ones?*

B. Materials:
1. Any solid articles of contrasting size and weight such as 2 old books of different sizes
2. Child's block
3. Yarn, tightly wound
4. Old battery, small
5. Chalkboard eraser
6. Two or three other objects of varying sizes

C. Procedure:
1. Plan to drop 2 articles at the same time from the same height, but have them vary in size and weight.
2. Have class predict beforehand which will reach the ground first.
3. Drop the test items.
4. Repeat with different objects, still varying in size and weight.

D. Result:

All solid objects will fall to earth with the same speed when wind resistance is neglected.

E. Supplemental Information:
1. A light and a heavy solid object fall to earth at equal times.
2. The size or weight of the object makes no difference in its falling speed.
3. Tightly wound yarn may fall a little slower due to wind resistance.
4. The first, accurate tests of gravity were done by Galileo who dropped 3 unequal weights from the Leaning Tower of Pisa in the 16th century. All 3 hit the ground at about the same time. (Wind resistance had a small effect.)

F. Thought Questions:
1. Why does a rock fall faster than a feather?
2. Will a rock and feather fall at the same speed if placed in a vacuum?
3. Do all objects fall at an even rate of speed or do they fall faster and faster?

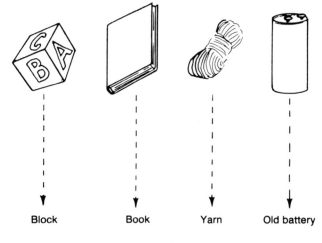

Block   Book   Yarn   Old battery

(Tightly packed)

G. Related Topics and Activities:
1. Place a feather on a book and drop them on a soft landing place that can't harm the book.
2. Drop a flat piece of paper to the floor and ask class where it will land. (Can't predict with any accuracy because of the zillions of air molecules that will affect it on its downward path.)
3. See Section I-A, "Matter."
4. See all Activities in this Section.

H. Vocabulary Builders—Spelling Words:
1) **gravity** 2) **heavier** 3) **size** 4) **weight**
5) **drop** 6) **predict**

I. Thought for Today:
"No one needs a smile so much as one who has none to give."

Activity

A Problem: *Which Falls Faster, a Dropped Object or a Horizontally Propelled Object?*

B. Materials:
1. Table
2. Plywood 2″ × 15″
3. Two coins
4. Ruler or dowel
5. Thin metal band 10″–15″ long
6. Two marbles or small balls

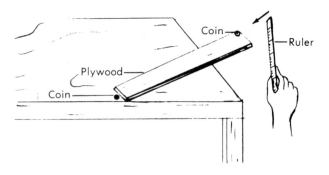

C. Procedure:
1. Place the plywood strip on the table with one end extending over the edge. (See sketch.)
2. Place the coins as shown in the illustration.
3. Tell the class to be extremely quiet and listen for sounds of the coins hitting the floor.
4. With the ruler or dowel, strike the end of the plywood that extends over the table with a sharp blow on the edge opposite the coin on the table.
5. Listen for the sounds of the coins hitting the floor.
6. Place two marbles or balls on the edge of the table.
7. Holding one edge of the metal band firmly, bend the other end back and release so that both balls or marbles will be hit at the same time but with different forces so that one will be propelled farther than the other. Several trials may be necessary to insure simultaneous striking of marbles or balls.
8. Listen for the sounds of the two objects hitting the floor.

D. Results:
1. The coins will strike the floor at the same time.
2. The marbles or balls will strike the floor at the same time.

E. Supplemental Information:
1. The only force acting *down* on the objects is gravity.
2. Since gravity is the same, the objects will fall at the same time, regardless of whether or not there is any propulsion to the side.

F. Thought Questions:
1. Does the size make any difference in falling objects?
2. Does weight make any difference?
3. Would a bullet fired horizontally hit the ground at the same time as one dropped from the same height?

G. Related Topics and Activities:
1. See Activity II-F-1, "Inertia."
2. Study the effects of "Momentum."
3. See all Activities in this Section.

H. Vocabulary Builders—Spelling Words:
1) **gravity** 2) **horizontal** 3) **propelled**
4) **simultaneous** 5) **dowel**

I. Thought for Today:
"Humanity's capacity for justice makes democracy possible; but humanity's inclination to injustice makes democracy necessary."

Activity

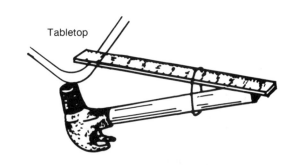

Tabletop

A. Problem: *How Can the Center of Gravity Cause Stability?*

B. Materials:
1. Ruler
2. Wire
3. Hammer
4. Tabletop or desktop

C. Procedure:
1. Make a loop of wire and place it in the position as shown in the illustration.
2. Place the edge of the ruler on the tabletop making sure that the head of the hammer is under the table or desktop.

D. Result:
The hammer and ruler will balance and not fall.

E. Supplemental Information:
1. Each object has a center of gravity.
2. If the center of gravity of the hammer is below the tabletop the device will balance.
3. If the center of gravity is beyond the tabletop, the apparatus will fall.

F. Thought Questions:
1. Is gravity the same everywhere?
2. Does the moon have gravity?
3. How did our astronauts make use of and work in the moon's gravity?

G. Related Topics and Activities:
1. The center of gravity of an irregular flat object can be determined by punching four holes along the edges and marking each with a line from the hole to a suspended weight on a string. The lines will intersect at the center of gravity. Put a pin at this point and move the object around. It will be perfectly balanced.
2. See Activity VII-B-1, "Planets."
3. See Activity II-F-1, "Inertia" and "Momentum."
4. See all Activities in this Section.

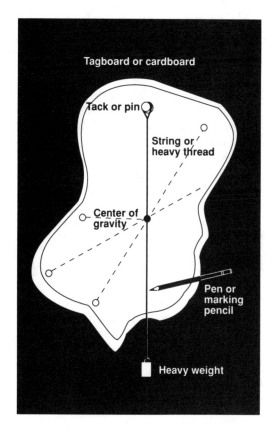

Tagboard or cardboard

Tack or pin

String or heavy thread

Center of gravity

Pen or marking pencil

Heavy weight

H. Vocabulary Builders—Spelling Words:
1) **hammer** 2) **ruler** 3) **table** 4) **center**
5) **gravity** 6) **stability**

I. Thought for Today:
"Neighbor to friend: 'My economic philosophy is middle of the road; I spend money left and right.'"

Activity

A. Problem: *How Can We Make a Simple Scale?*

B. Materials:
1. Heavy tagboard or cardboard
2. Four paper clips
3. Wide rubber band
4. Tape
5. String
6. Weights
7. Marking pen
8. Scissors

C. Procedure:
1. Cut tagboard to make a rectangle shape about 12″ × 4″.
2. Attach paper clip to the top of tagboard after bending the bottom part out slightly.
3. Attach the wide rubber band to the bottom of this paper clip.
4. With second paper clip bend it so that it looks like the one in sketch. This is the pointer.
5. Attach this to the bottom of the rubber band.
6. Tape string to the bottom of the pointer or you may attach string directly to pointer.
7. Slip the string through the paper clip at the bottom of the tagboard.
8. Bend the bottom loop of the paper clip so that the string is free to move.
9. Attach bottom paper clip to the string. Bend so that it will support whatever you wish to weigh.
10. Using known weights calibrate and mark the scale with the marking pen.

D. Result:
A simple measuring device for weighing small objects will be made.

E. Supplemental Information:
1. A rubber band will stretch equally with added weights up to a point and then its original elasticity will be destroyed. This can be determined by the pointer not returning to zero on the scale.
2. This weighing device can be hung on a wall or supported over the edge of a desk or chair.

F. Thought Questions:
1. Do all rubber bands of the same size and shape possess the same elasticity?
2. What is the main difference between a spring scale and a balance scale?
3. Where have you seen spring scales used?

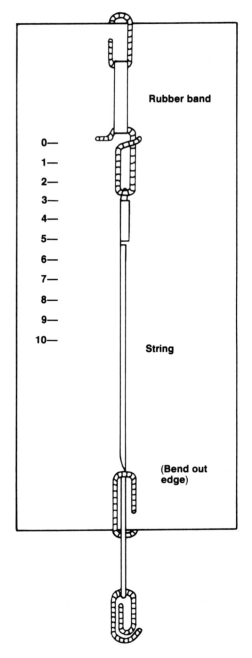

Rubber band

0—
1—
2—
3—
4—
5—
6—
7—
8—
9—
10—

String

(Bend out edge)

G. Related Topics and Activities:
1. Weigh various objects to compare weights (rocks, etc.).
2. See Activity II-E-4, "Pulleys."
3. See all Activities in this Section.

H. Vocabulary Builders—Spelling Words:
1) **scale**   2) **simple**   3) **elastic**
4) **calibrate**   5) **rubber**

I. Thought for Today:
"Life has become a struggle to keep our weight down and our spirits up."

Activity

A. Problem: *Can You Balance a Pencil on the Tip of Your Finger?*

B. Materials:
1. Two ice picks
2. One pencil

C. Procedure:
1. CAREFULLY push the points of the two ice picks into opposite sides of the pencil as shown in the photograph. Be sure that the handles of the ice picks extend outward at an angle and beyond the pencil point.
2. Place the pencil with the ice picks on the tip of your finger and balance as shown in the picture.

D. Result:
The pencil will remain upright as long as the ice picks are attached.

E. Supplemental Information:
This seemingly magic balancing is due to the fact that the center of gravity of the pencil is below the point where the pencil sets on the finger. Because of this, the center of gravity must be raised when the pencil changes position. In this set-up the pencil will balance perfectly regardless of its position on the finger. By changing the points of attachment, the pencil can be made to balance at some very odd angles.

F. Thought Questions:
1. What is the center of gravity?
2. Why do the ice pick handles need to fall below the point of attachment?
3. If three ice picks were attached, would it still be possible to balance the pencil on your finger?

G. Related Topics and Activities:
1. See Section I-A, "Matter."
2. See Activity VII-D-3, "Center of Gravity."
3. See all Activities in this Section.

H. Vocabulary Builders—Spelling Words
1) **balance**   2) **center**   3) **gravity**
4) **pencil**   5) **ice pick**

I. Thought for Today:
"You could get rich manufacturing crutches for lame excuses."

Activity VII E 1

A. Problem: *Why Are Summers Hotter Than Winters?*

B. Materials:
1. Flashlight
2. Chalk
3. Student helpers
4. Yardstick

C. Procedure:
1. Make a chalk mark on the floor.
2. Darken the room.
3. Have a student hold a flashlight about one yard above the mark and vertically shine the flashlight on the mark.
4. Have a second student draw a circle with chalk around the spot of light.
5. Moving the flashlight horizontally about one yard from the original spot, shine the light at the same mark on the floor. (The beam will be slightly slanted.)
6. Draw a line on the floor around the beam of light.
7. Compare the areas of light projection.

D. Result:
The second drawing will be much larger than the first.

E. Supplemental Information:
1. The sun is hotter when directly above us than when it is setting. The same amount of sunlight is given off by the sun in winter as in summer, but the light (heat) is distributed over a wider area and therefore, each small area receives less light (heat). In other words the slanting rays cover a wider area thus the same amount of energy is not received in winter.
2. The second most important factor in determining the earth's temperature is the length of time the sun shines each day. Because of the tilt of the earth the length of each day is much longer in the summertime than during the wintertime (about two hours longer in the mid-line of the United States).

A.

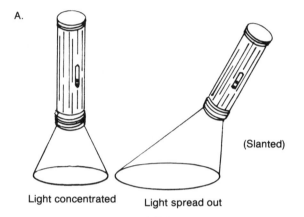

Light concentrated   Light spread out   (Slanted)

3. A slide projector could be used instead of a flashlight and the beam could be focused on a wall.

F. Thought Questions:
1. What causes the sun's rays to hit any spot on earth at 90°? slanting (less than 90°)?
2. Is there any difference in seasons between the northern and southern hemisphere? Why or why not?
3. How do scientists measure light intensity?
4. Is the sun ever directly overhead in your community?

G. Related Topics and Activities:
1. See Section VII-B, "Solar System."
2. See Part II, "Energy."
3. See Section II-C, "Light and Color."
4. See all Activities in this Section.

H. Vocabulary Builders—Spelling Words:
1) **summer**   2) **winter**   3) **direct**
4) **slanting**   5) **area**

I. Thought for Today:
"There's one thing to be said for inviting trouble, it usually accepts."

Activity

A. Problem: *What Makes the Wind Blow?*

B. Materials:
1. Weather maps (if possible) (from local newspaper)
2. Map of the United States or chalkboard drawing of the United States
3. Chalk

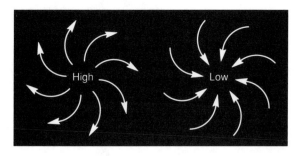

C. Procedure:
1. Locate highs (high pressure) areas and lows (low pressure) areas on weather map or sketch them as shown in the illustration.
2. Explain causes of air pressure changes: heating, cooling, movements, etc.
3. Explain how gases move from high concentration areas to low concentration areas. (Air is a mixture of gases.)
4. Review Activities in Section I-B, "Air."

D. Result:
Pupils will learn that winds are masses of air in motion.

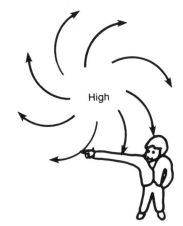

E. Supplemental Information:
1. Highs and rising pressures usually indicate fair weather.
2. Lows and falling pressures usually indicate poor weather.
3. High pressure areas normally rotate clockwise in the northern hemisphere and counterclockwise in the southern hemisphere.
4. Low pressure areas normally rotate counterclockwise in the northern hemisphere and clockwise in the southern hemisphere.
5. To locate the center of a high pressure area stand with your back to the wind then turn about 45° to your right. Extend your arms. Your right arm will point to the high pressure area, the left to the center of the low pressure area. Since winds usually move in an easterly direction you can tell whether fair weather or poor weather is approaching. Local conditions and weak masses and fronts may vary the conditions.
6. In coastal areas, during the day, the land heats up faster than the oceans so a land breeze develops. During the night, the oceans are warmer than the land so a sea breeze develops.
7. Pressure and temperature are the two main factors in producing wind.

F. Thought Questions:
1. Are winds affected by the earth's rotation?
2. Are winds affected by friction of the earth?
3. Do winds at high altitudes behave similarly to winds close to the earth's surface?

G. Related Topics and Activities:
1. See Section II-B, "Fire and Heat."
2. See Activities in Section I-B, "Air."
3. See all Activities in this Section.

H. Vocabulary Builders—Spelling Words:
1) **wind**   2) **weather**   3) **pressure**   4) **temperature**
5) **hemisphere**   6) **northern**   7) **southern**

I. Thought for Today:
"Philosophy is common sense in a dress suit."

Activity

A. Problem: *How Can We Make a Wind Vane?*

B. Materials:
1. Drinking straw
2. Straight pin
3. Pencil with eraser
4. Feather or strip of paper (See sketch.)
5. Fan (optional)

C. Procedure:
1. Place a feather or strip of paper on end of the drinking straw.
2. Put a pin half way between ends of apparatus.
3. Push pin into eraser of pencil.
4. Turn straw around a few times to make sure it turns easily.
5. Check vane with wind sources:
   a. outside
   b. in front of fan if available

D. Results:
1. The wind vane will point in the direction from which the wind is coming.
2. Students will learn that winds move weather vanes.
3. As they study winds more, they will learn that North winds blow *from* the *North*.

E. Supplemental Information:
1. Wind vanes and wind socks can be studied.
2. If any student has ever been sailing he/she might describe how wind conditions affected the boat.
3. You might want to have the class try to fly kites to show the effects of the wind.

F. Thought Questions:
1. Does wind help to dry laundry hung outside?
2. What makes the wind change directions?
3. What are some bad effects of wind? good effects?
4. Do pilots consider wind conditions when flying?
5. How do wind socks help pilots?

G. Related Topics and Activities:
1. Study sailing boats.
2. Study weather maps.

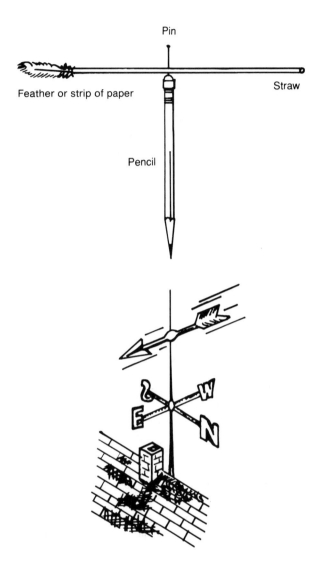

3. Study the classification of winds.
4. Make a permanent weather vane out of plywood shaped like an arrow using a dowel for support and a nail as pivot.
5. See all Activities in this Section.

H. Vocabulary Builders—Spelling Words:
1) **vane**   2) **weather**   3) **north**   4) **south**
5) **feather**   6) **dowel**

I. Thought for Today:
"Being grown up means that we can have our own way — at our own expense." — Hal Rogers

Activity

A. Problem: *How Can We Measure Wind Speed?*

B. Materials:
1. Four paper cups or paper cones
2. Wire coat hanger
3. Medicine dropper (glass part)
4. Two thin wooden slats, approx. 1″ × 18″
5. Wooden support (See sketch.)
6. Scissors or razor blade
7. Small nails or brads
8. Wire cutter (cutting pliers)
9. Red paint
10. Small paint brush
11. Knife or drill

C. Procedure:
1. Construct anemometer as shown in sketch.
   a. Nail slats together.
   b. Cut hole for eyedropper (glass part).
   c. Cut and shape coat hanger as shown in drawing.
   d. Cut slits in cups or cones for thin wooden boards (slats).
   e. Mark one cup so it is easily seen.
   f. Mount coat hanger on support.
   g. Paint one cup red.
   h. Place cups or cones on slats.
   i. Place eyedropper glass on end of coat hanger.
   j. Mount slats with cups on eyedropper glass.
2. Place anemometer outside where winds can hit it.
3. Count the revolutions per minute by the painted or marked cup.
4. Divide this number by ten and that is approximately the speed of the wind in miles per hour.

D. Results:
1. Students will learn how to construct an anemometer.
2. Pupils will learn that wind speed can be measured.
3. Students will learn that wind speeds vary.

E. Supplemental Information:
1. Tennis balls cut in half can be substituted for paper cups.

(Eyedropper)

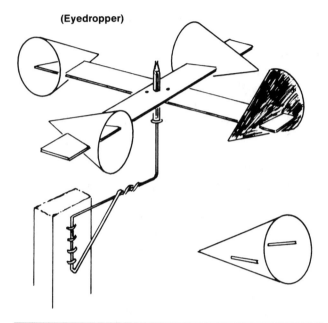

BEAUFORT WIND SCALE			
Number	Map Symbol	Descriptive Word(s)	Velocity (Miles/Hour)
1		Calm	1–3
2		Light breeze	4–7
3		Gentle breeze	8–12
4		Moderate breeze	13–18
5		Fresh breeze	19–24
6		Strong breeze	25–31
7		Moderate gale	32–38
8		Fresh gale	39–46
9		Strong gale	47–54
10		Full gale	55–63
11		Whole gale	64–75
12		Hurricane or violent storm	above 75

2. Winds are caused by rotation of the earth, differences in temperature of air masses, and differences in air pressures of air masses.

F. Thought Questions:
1. Does it make any difference which way the wind is blowing in determining wind speed with this anemometer?
2. What people in what occupations would be most interested in wind speeds?
3. Why is wind speed important to weather forecasters?

G. Related Topics and Activities:
   1. See Section I-B, "Air."
   2. See Section I-A, "Matter."
   3. See all Activities in this Section.

H. Vocabulary Builders—Spelling Words:
   1) **speed**   2) **Beaufort Scale**   3) **gale**
   4) **hurricane**   5) **modest**

I. Thought for Today:
   "If you know all the answers, you haven't asked all the questions."

A. Problem: *What Causes Changes in Air Pressure?*

B. Materials:

1. Shoe box
2. Cellophane, clear
3. Candle
4. Paper towel
5. Tape, cellophane or filament
6. Matches
7. Asbestos pad or metal tray

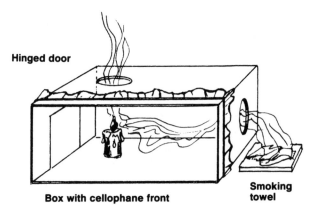

Hinged door

Box with cellophane front

Smoking towel

C. Procedure:

1. Remove the cover of the shoe box.
2. Cover the top with cellophane, securing it in place with Scotch or filament tape.
3. Cut out one end of the box to make a hinged door. (to insert candle)
4. Set the box on its side and place a short candle inside near one end.
5. Cut a hole the size of a quarter directly over the candle and another one the same size in the middle of the far end. (See sketch.)
6. Affix a candle to the base of the box as shown.
7. Light the candle and close the door.
8. Dampen a paper towel slightly and set in on fire for a moment. Blow out the dampened paper and it will give off smoke.
9. Place on pad or tray near the hole in the door.

D. Result:

As the warm air rises and leaves the box, the cooler, heavier air will rush in and fill the space that was occupied by the lighter, warmer air.

E. Supplemental Information:

The smoke moving through the box will trace the current of air. Wind is air in motion caused by differences in air pressure. This difference sometimes is the result of varying air temperatures. Air currents generally move from high pressures toward low pressures. The rotation of the earth also has a great effect on causes of winds and the directions they take.

F. Thought Questions:

1. How is the air on the earth's surface heated? cooled?
2. Does hot air always rise?
3. Will the winds blow toward the direction of the rising air?
4. What are some other causes of variation in air pressure on the surface of the earth?

G. Related Topics and Activities:

1. See Activity VII-E-2, "Why Winds Blow."
2. See Activity VII-E-4, "Wind Speed."
3. See other Activities in this Section.

H. Vocabulary Builders—Spelling Words:

1) **pressure**   2) **cellophane**   3) **candle**
4) **hinged**   5) **dampen**

I. Thought for Today:

"Sign in Iowa munitions factory: 'If you insist on smoking in this building be prepared to leave this world through a hole in the ceiling.'"

Activity

A. Problem: *How Can We Make a Simple Barometer?*

Rubber-capped bottle

B. Materials:

1. Wide-mouthed bottle, jar, or glass
2. Piece of balloon
3. Rubber band
4. Drinking straw
5. Glue or rubber cement
6. Chart material
7. Marking instrument
8. Light wax

C. Procedure:

1. Seal container with a piece of balloon and rubber band.
2. Affix drinking straw to this as shown in sketch.
3. Make a simple scale on chart material to which the drinking straw can point.
4. Mount this as shown.

D. Result:

Students will learn that air pressure varies.

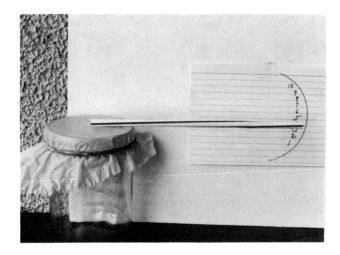

E. Supplemental Information:

The straw moves up and down chart to record the changes in air pressure. If the pointer goes up the scale, the pressure is high; if it goes down the scale, the pressure is low. This up and down movement is caused by the contraction or expansion of the air in the jar as a result in variances of atmospheric air pressures. A coating of light wax around the lip of the glass will help make an airtight seal. The rubber balloon should not be stretched too tight. If it is stretched too tight, it will not respond as readily to changes in air pressure. Changes in temperature will also affect the readings, so room temperatures should be kept as constant as possible. If the air pressure increases, the numbers on the scale shown will get larger; this portends good weather. If the air pressure decreases, the numbers on the scale shown will get smaller; this indicates poor weather coming.

OUR BAROMETER READINGS:			
Week of _____	Morning:	Afternoon:	Weather:
Monday			
Tuesday			
Wednesday			
Thursday			
Friday			

F. Thought Questions:

1. Is this same principle used in regular barometers?
2. How do regular barometers differ from this one?
3. How are pressure changes related to weather?

G. Related Topics and Activities:
1. See Section VII-B, "Solar System."
2. See Section I-B, "Air."
3. See all Activities in this Section.
4. Compare this barometer to a commercially produced one.
5. Keep a record of air pressure for a week as shown on previous page.

H. Vocabulary Builders—Spelling Words:
1) **barometer**   2) **balloon**   3) **scale**   4) **pressure**
5) **varies**   6) **contraction**   7) **expansion**   8) **rising**
9) **falling**

I. Thought for Today:
"Rain is something that, when you carry an umbrella, it doesn't."

A. Problem: *Is There Water in the Air? What Causes Dew?*

B. Materials:
  1. Two glasses
  2. Water
  3. Ice

C. Procedure:
  1. Fill one glass about ⅔ full of water.
  2. Fill the second glass about ½ full of water and add ice until the levels of water in the two glasses are the same.
  3. Set aside until droplets form on the outside of second glass.
  4. Ask the class where the droplets came from. (Some answers will surprise you, such as "the glass leaks," "spilled over," etc.)

D. Results:
  1. Water droplets will form on the outside of the glass which has ice in it.
  2. No droplets will form around the glass that has no ice in it.

E. Supplemental Information:
  1. There is always water in the air.
  2. Water vapor which condenses upon cooling is called dew. Clouds and fog are tiny condensed droplets of water on small particles of matter: sand, dust, etc.
  3. Fog is in contact with water or land; clouds are in the air.
  4. When dew freezes it is called frost.

No ice

With ice

F. Thought Questions:
  1. What causes fog?
  2. How is dew beneficial? harmful?
  3. What is humidity?
  4. What is relative humidity?
  5. What is hail? snow? sleet?

G. Related Topics and Activities:
  1. See Section I-C, "Water."
  2. See Activity I-A-3, "Change of State of Matter."
  3. See other Activities in this Section.

H. Vocabulary Builders—Spelling Words:
  1) **fog**   2) **clouds**   3) **condense**   4) **dew**   5) **frost**

I. Thought for Today:
  "Acupuncture makes us wonder whether it was penicillin that cured us or just the needle."

A. Problem: *How Is Fog Formed?*

B. Materials:
1. Clean, dry, empty, quart glass bottle or jar
2. Two ice cubes, frozen together
3. Glass
4. Water
5. Gooseneck desk lamp with 100-watt bulb (or substitute)
6. Electric hot plate
7. Teakettle or pan

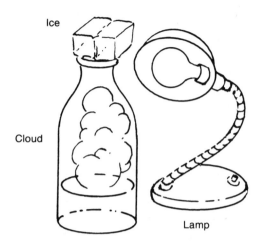

Ice

Cloud

Lamp

C. Procedure:
1. Boil water in teakettle or pan.
2. Preheat glass bottle (or jar) with boiling water to prevent cracking.
3. Discuss with students the problems of driving an automobile in a fog.
4. Discuss with class the problems of an airplane flying in a fog.
5. Set lamp to one side.
6. Turn lamp on.
7. Set bottle (or jar) next to lamp.
8. Add a small amount of boiling water to the glass bottle.
9. Quickly place ice cubes over mouth of bottle.
10. Hold bottle in front of lighted lamp.
11. Keep the ice cubes over mouth of the bottle to prevent escape of steam.

D. Results:
1. The warm moist air will rise from the hot water and meet the cool air under the ice cubes.
2. The moisture in the warm, moist air will be cooled forming tiny drops of water as fog.
3. When held in front of light, the fog will be seen swirling around in the bottle.

E. Supplemental Information:
The air of our atmosphere (represented by the cool air from the ice cubes) cools faster than the water in bodies of water on the earth (represented by hot water in bottle). The moist warm air rising from these bodies of water comes in contact with the cooled air and condenses, thereby forming fog. This demonstration can be used effectively for class presentation by pupils as an introduction to the study of weather.

F. Thought Questions:
1. How is fog dangerous to people?
2. What is the difference between fog and clouds?
3. Is fog basically water that is in a gaseous, liquid, or solid state?

G. Related Topics and Activities:
1. See specifically next two activities on "Clouds."
2. See Section I-C, "Water."
3. Discuss with class the problems of safety of all people in foggy conditions.
4. See all Activities in this Section.

H. Vocabulary Builders—Spelling Words:
1) **fog**   2) **condense**   3) **droplets**
4) **preheat**   5) **frozen**

I. Thought for Today:
"Science is nothing but trained and organized common sense."

Activity

A. **Problem:** *Where Do Clouds Come From?*

B. **Materials:**
1. Clean, dry, empty gallon glass jug
2. Rubber stopper (with a small hole through the center) that fits the mouth of the jug tightly
3. Tire pump
4. Rubbing alcohol, pint

C. **Procedure:**
1. Discuss with class their experiences with clouds: sizes, colors, weather conditions, etc.
2. Discuss any clouds in the sky today and then pose the question, "Where do clouds come from?"
3. Pour enough alcohol into the jug to cover the bottom.
4. Place stopper tightly into the mouth of the jug.
5. Place end of hose of the tire pump over the hole in the stopper as tightly as possible, and pump air into the jug.
6. After a few strokes on the pump handle, quickly and simultaneously remove the stopper and air hose.

D. **Result:**
When the stopper and hose are removed a loud pop will be heard and a cloud will form in the jug.

E. **Supplemental Information:**
As a result of the pumping, the air in the jug was compressed and its temperature raised, making it possible for it to hold more moisture which it picks up from the alcohol. When the stopper was removed the air immediately expanded and cooled, at which time it could no longer hold as much moisture. Consequently tiny droplets of moisture collected and formed a cloud inside the jug. Alcohol is used because it condenses at a lower temperature than water.

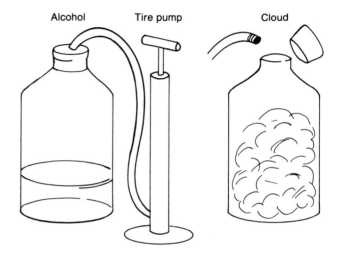

Alcohol   Tire pump   Cloud

F. **Thought Questions:**
1. What caused the loud noise when the stopper was removed?
2. How do these clouds differ from regular clouds?
3. How do clouds help us?
4. How are clouds dangerous to us?

G. **Related Topics and Activities:**
1. See previous Activity on "Fog."
2. See following Activity on "Clouds."
3. See Section I-C, "Water."
4. See all Activities in this Section.

H. **Vocabulary Builders—Spelling Words:**
1) **alcohol**   2) **pump**   3) **gallon**   4) **stroke**
5) **compress**   6) **moisture**   7) **temperature**
8) **droplets**   9) **cloud**

I. **Thought for Today:**
"A dog has so many friends because he wags his tail instead of his tongue."

A. Problem: *What Kinds of Clouds Are There?*

B. Materials:
1. Reference book on clouds
2. Tagboard, or other suitable material for mounting pictures
3. Pictures of clouds

C. Procedure:
1. Mount pictures of clouds on tagboard.
2. Identify them by types.
3. Explain the common cloud formations, and describe the type of weather that is usually associated with each type.

D. Result:
Students will become familiar with the various types of cloud formations, and will associate the chart pictures with the actual formations.

E. Supplemental Information:
Weather is predictable, and observing clouds is one of the means of predicting future weather conditions. There are ten major cloud formations. Four of the most easily identified and the type of weather they portend are:
1. Nimbostratus—Generally indicates turbulent weather conditions. The fast rising updrafts normally cause rain and hail.
2. Stratus—Associated most often with outside edges of cyclone (low pressure area) and hence good weather usually follows (little vertical movement of air to cause rain). (A high pressure area is called an anticyclone.)
3. Cirrus—Usually precede low pressure areas (cyclones). These are often the first warnings of an approaching hurricane (tropical cyclone). They may be associated with fair weather. If they move fast and change into sheets, they forecast bad weather. If they dissipate, fair weather will follow.
4. Cumulus—Generally are signs of good weather, unless they continue into the night. If so, rain is probable.
5. Other cloud types are:
   a. Cirrostratus—usually bring rain within twelve (12) hours
   b. Altostratus—could develop into rain clouds

Nimbostratus

Stratus

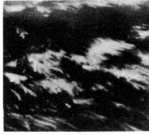
Cirrus

Cumulus

   c. Stratocumulus—dry weather
   d. Altocumulus—temporary, good weather coming
   e. Cumulonimbus—showers and thunderstorms

F. Thought Questions:
1. Do the clouds you see in the sky help to predict what the weather will be for the next day?
2. By looking at clouds, can you tell whether or not they are rain clouds?
3. What makes clouds change in size, shape, and color?

G. Related Topics and Activities:
1. See Activity VII-E-8, "Fog."
2. See previous Activity on "Cloud Formation."
3. See Section I-C, "Water."
4. See all Activities in this Section.

H. Vocabulary Builders—Spelling Words:
1) **predict**   2) **weather**   3) **forecasting**
4) **formation**   5) **specific cloud types mentioned in Supplemental Information.**

I. Thought for Today:
"The value of a book is not the book but in the subsequent behavior of its readers."

Activity

A. Problem: *Where Does Rain Come From?*

B. Materials:
1. Teakettle
2. Small saucepan
3. Candle, electric plate, or heating apparatus
4. Water
5. Ice cubes

C. Procedure:
1. Add water to pot.
2. Add ice to water in pot.
3. Add water to teakettle.
4. Bring water in teakettle to boiling point so steam is rising from spout.
5. When steam is rising from kettle, hold pot of ice over spout so steam from spout will strike bottom and sides of pan.

Pot of ice water

D. Result:

The steam from the kettle, upon striking the cold pan, is cooled and condenses to form droplets of water on the outside of the pan. These droplets collect and fall from the pan like rain falling from a cloud.

E. Supplemental Information:

Water, when heated, rises in the form of vapor (gas) into the air. Upon striking cool air, the vapor condenses into tiny droplets of water or moisture. These droplets collect upon particles of dirt in the air to form clouds. When condensed further, this moisture falls from the clouds in the form of rain. This demonstration can be used effectively by the pupils in the classroom to further their understanding of how rain is formed. Used in conjunction with demonstrations of how fog and clouds are formed, the combined demonstrations can be very effective. The visible part of what we call steam is actually small droplets of liquid water. Water vapor (gas) is invisible. A simple rain gauge can be made by collecting rain water in a coffee can with a ruler affixed inside.

F. Thought Questions:
1. How does rain help us?
2. Is rain ever harmful to us?
3. What would happen if it never rained?
4. Can you see steam (gaseous water)?

G. Related Topics and Activities:
1. See Activity VII-E-8, "Fog."
2. See Activities VII-E-9 and VII-E-10, "Clouds."
3. See next Activity VII-E-12, "Measuring Rainfall."
4. See all Activities in this Section.

H. Vocabulary Builders—Spelling Words:
1) **rain**   2) **steam**   3) **vapor**   4) **boiling**
5) **teakettle**   6) **spout**

I. Thought for Today:
"American youngsters tend to live as if adolescence were a last fling at life, rather than a preparation for it."

A. Problem: *How Can We Measure Rainfall?*

B. Materials:
   1. Baseboard (approximately 6″ × 8″)
   2. Piece of lumber (1″ × 1″ × 6″)
   3. Nails
   4. Hammer
   5. Ruler (or piece of yardstick)
   6. Wide, straight edged, glass container
   7. Wire

Glass container

C. Procedure:
   1. Nail piece of lumber to baseboard as shown in sketch.
   2. Nail ruler or piece of yardstick with zero edge at baseboard to upright piece of lumber.
   3. Wire the glass container to the measuring device.
   4. When it rains, place apparatus out in an open area.
   5. Record reading(s) when desired. Reading should be the nearest tenth of an inch.

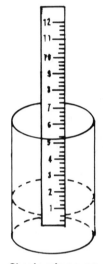

Simple rain gauge

D. Results:
   1. Students will construct a rain gauge.
   2. Students will learn how to read a rain gauge.

E. Supplemental Information:
   1. The students may want to use a magnifying glass for more accurate reading.
   2. Charts and graphs of rainfall can be made.
   3. Simpler rain gauges can be made with only a ruler and a glass container. Fingernail polish can be used for marking.

Rain gauge

F. Thought Questions:
   1. Would the readings be inaccurate if the rain seemed to be falling diagonally?
   2. What is the average annual rainfall in your community?
   3. About how much rain does an average rainfall bring to your community?
   4. Would a wide container collect a higher level of water than a narrow one?

   3. See Activities VII-E-9 and VII-E-10, "Clouds."
   4. See all Activities in this Section.

H. Vocabulary Builders—Spelling Words:
   1) **measure** 2) **rainfall** 3) **calibrate**
   4) **fingernail** 5) **polish** 6) **indicator**

G. Related Topics and Activities:
   1. See Section I-C, "Water."
   2. See Activity VII-E-8, "Fog."

I. Thought for Today:
   "Don't pray for rain if you're going to complain about the mud."

A. Problem: *How Can We Measure Humidity in the Air?*

B. Materials:
 1. Quart milk carton
 2. Single-edged razor blade (or knife)
 3. Long straight hair
 4. Broom straw
 5. Needle
 6. Nail polish
 7. Paper clip
 8. Soapy water
 9. Cello tape
 10. Penny
 11. Basin
 12. Sponge
 13. Towel
 14. Water

C. Procedure:
 1. Cut an "H" along one side of the milk carton as shown in sketch.
 2. Bend the two tabs up.
 3. Wash hair in soapy water and let dry.
 4. Make a hole in each tab with needle so that needle can turn freely.
 5. Cut broom straw to 3″ and place in eye of needle.
 6. Secure straw to needle with drop of nail polish. (This is the pointer.)
 7. Make a scale similar to the one on the front of the carton as shown in sketch.
 8. Cello tape this to front of milk carton with midpoint of 5 and 6 perpendicular to vertical pointer (down position).
 9. Cello tape paper clip to top of milk carton so that the clip is half exposed. (See sketch.)
 10. Affix one end of hair to penny with nail polish.
 11. Letting the penny hang half-way down in the carton, wrap the hair around the needle so that it goes under the needle and around and then secure it to paper clip.
 12. To set hygrometer, place it in a basin with wet sponge close by, but not touching, and cover with a wet towel. Let stand for 15 minutes. Take off towel and adjust pointer to point at "10."
 13. Place hygrometer in a sheltered place outdoors being careful not to shake.
 14. Take daily readings. Note changes.

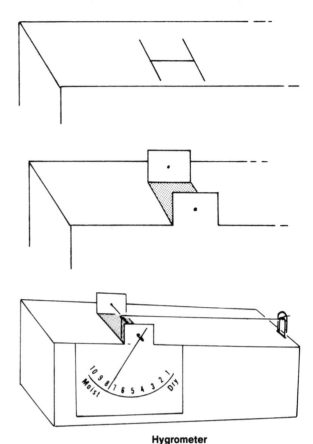

Hygrometer

D. Results:
 1. Students will learn how to construct a hygrometer.
 2. Pupils will learn that moisture in the air varies from day-to-day, season-to-season.

E. Supplemental Information:
 1. In damp (moist) air the hair becomes a little longer. In this case the pointer will move towards the larger numbers.
 2. In dry air the hair becomes a little shorter. In this case the pointer will move towards the smaller numbers.

F. Thought Questions:
 1. How does the weather forecaster use the hygrometer in weather forecasting?
 2. What happens to your hair when the weather is damp and rainy?
 3. Can you think of any other ways that moisture in the air effects people?

G. Related Topics and Activities:
   1. See Section I-C, "Water."
   2. See Activity VII-E-8, "Fog."
   3. See Activities VII-E-9 and VII-E-10, "Clouds."
   4. See Activity VII-E-14, "Determining Relative Humidity."
   5. See all Activities in this Section.

H. Vocabulary Builders—Spelling Words:
   1) **hygrometer**   2) **needle**   3) **penny**
   4) **sponge**   5) **towel**   6) **pointer**
   7) **perpendicular**

I. Thought for Today:
   "Sign in metropolitan high school, 'Free every Monday through Friday—knowledge. Bring your own containers.'"

A. Problem: *What Is a Simple Method for Determining Relative Humidity?*

B. Materials:
1. Two thermometers
2. Two square inches of cheesecloth
3. Rubber band
4. Water

C. Procedure:
1. Fold the piece of cheesecloth and wrap it around the bulb of one of the thermometers.
2. Secure it in place with the rubber band.
3. Dip the wrapped bulb in water.
4. Fan or shake the wet-bulb thermometer.
5. After fanning for a few moments, compare the reading of the wet-bulb thermometer with the reading on the dry-bulb thermometer.
6. Record the difference in two readings.
7. By checking the reading on the dry-bulb thermometer and the difference in temperatures recorded by the two thermometers, the relative humidity can be determined from the table on the next page.

D. Results:
1. Students will learn how to read thermometers.
2. Pupils will learn about relative humidity.

E. Supplemental Information:
1. Humidity is a term which is used to refer to the moisture in the air.
2. Relative humidity is the amount of water that is in the air compared to the maximum amount of water it could hold for each temperature reading. It is reported in percentages. When the air is dry, evaporation takes place much more rapidly. This causes the thermometer bulb to cool. Therefore, the table will give an indication of the relative humidity in the atmosphere.
3. An instrument that contains both a dry-bulb and a wet-bulb thermometer is called a sling psychrometer.

F. Thought Questions:
1. Why is it necessary to have a wet cloth around the thermometer in order to determine the wet-bulb reading?
2. Do you feel better when the humidity is very high, very low, or somewhere in between?
3. How is humidity related to weather conditions?

G. Related Topics and Activities:
1. See Activity VII-E-8, "Fog."
2. See Activities VII-E-9 and VII-E-10, "Clouds."
3. See Section I-C, "Water."
4. See all Activities in this Section.

H. Vocabulary Builders—Spelling Words:
1) **relative**   2) **humidity**   3) **bulb**   4) **thermometer**
5) **temperature**   6) **percentage**

I. Thought for Today:
"Modern people have the genius to make rain, but often lack enough common sense to come in out of it."

RELATIVE HUMIDITY IN PERCENTAGES

Readings of dry-bulb thermometer	Difference in degrees Fahrenheit between wet- and dry-bulb thermometers															
	0	1	2	3	4	5	6	7	8	9	10	11	12	13	14	15
60	100%	94%	89%	84%	78%	73%	68%	63%	58%	53%	49%	44%	40%	35%	31%	27%
61	100	94	89	84	79	74	68	64	59	54	50	45	40	36	32	28
62	100	94	89	84	79	74	69	64	60	55	50	46	41	37	33	29
63	100	95	90	84	79	74	70	65	60	56	51	47	42	38	34	30
64	100	95	90	85	79	75	70	66	61	56	52	48	43	39	35	31
65	100	95	90	85	80	75	70	66	62	57	53	48	44	40	36	32
66	100	95	90	85	80	76	71	66	62	58	53	49	45	41	37	33
67	100	95	90	85	80	76	71	67	62	58	54	50	46	42	38	34
68	100	95	90	85	81	76	72	67	63	59	55	51	47	43	39	35
69	100	95	90	86	81	77	72	68	64	59	55	51	47	44	40	36
70	100	95	90	86	81	77	72	68	64	60	56	52	48	44	40	37
71	100	95	90	86	82	77	73	69	64	60	56	53	49	45	41	38
72	100	95	91	86	82	78	73	69	65	61	57	53	49	46	42	39
73	100	95	91	86	82	78	73	69	65	61	58	54	50	46	43	40
74	100	95	91	86	82	78	74	70	66	62	58	54	51	47	44	40
75	100	96	91	87	82	78	74	70	66	63	59	55	51	48	44	41
76	100	96	91	87	83	78	74	70	67	63	59	55	52	48	45	42
77	100	96	91	87	83	79	75	71	67	63	60	56	52	49	46	42
78	100	96	91	87	83	79	75	71	67	64	60	57	53	50	46	43
79	100	96	91	87	83	79	75	71	68	64	60	57	54	50	47	44
80	100	96	91	87	83	79	76	72	68	64	61	57	54	51	47	44

Activity

A. Problem: *What Is Lightning?*

B. Materials:

1. Pieces of fur
2. Piece of flannel
3. Piece of silk
4. Glass rod
5. Stick of sealing wax

C. Procedure:

1. Rub the glass rod briskly with the three pieces of material, one at a time.
2. Note any differences.
3. Rub the three pieces of material on the sealing wax, one at a time.
4. Place the sealing wax near your finger.
5. Note any differences.
6. Ask class if anyone has ever had a shock when walking on a carpet and touching a metal object such as a doorknob.

D. Result:

When the glass rod is rubbed with the flannel a cracking sensation should be experienced, but not with the silk and the fur. A spark should occur when the wax is rubbed with the flannel, but not with the silk or the fur.

E. Supplemental Information:

1. Lightning is a huge electrical spark produced during severe weather.
2. Fast-rising air rubs against the water droplets in the cloud and charges them electrically.
3. One side of the cloud becomes positively charged while the other side becomes negatively charged.
4. Sometimes the force of the fast-rising air is strong enough to rip the cloud in two so that each half has a different electrical charge.
5. When the force of attraction between the positive and negative charged parts of a cloud, or between two clouds, becomes great enough, a huge spark of electricity, called lightning, flows from the negatively charged part to the positively charged part.
6. Lightning can jump between two sides of the same cloud, between two clouds of different charges, from a cloud to the earth, and sometimes even from the earth to a cloud.

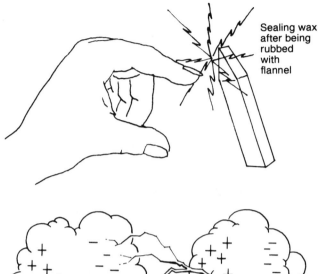

Sealing wax after being rubbed with flannel

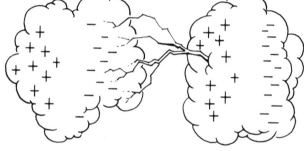

7. During thunderstorms people should avoid open areas especially those that contain good conductors of electricity.
8. Lightning is very hot; 27,000° F. or hotter.

F. Thought Questions:

1. What is a lightning rod?
2. What should you do if you are caught in a lightning storm?
3. Is lightning related to static electricity?
4. Is it a good idea to go swimming during an electrical storm?

G. Related Topics and Activities:

1. See Section I-E, "Static Electricity."
2. See Activity I-A-6, "Atoms."
3. See all Activities in this Section.

H. Vocabulary Builders—Spelling Words:

1) **lightning** 2) **thunderstorm** 3) **charged**
4) **negative** 5) **positive**

I. Thought for Today:

"Greatness lies not in being strong but in the right use of strength."

Activity

A. Problem: *What Makes Thunder?*

B. Materials:

Paper bags

C. Procedure:
1. Discuss with class their experiences and ideas about thunder.
2. Bring out the following points:
   a. Lightning flashes are big sparks of electricity.
   b. Lightning is very hot.
   c. Air is suddenly made hot and expands.
   d. Sudden movement of expanded air makes thunder.
3. Give several students paper bags and have them inflate them by blowing them up.
4. Let each student pop his inflated bag.

D. Results:
1. A loud noise will result.
2. Students will learn something about sound and the cause of thunder.

E. Supplemental Information:
1. The loud noise results from the sudden movement of air out of the bag. Lightning heats the air causing it to expand suddenly and this makes the loud noise that we call thunder. This is the sound produced by the rapid heating and expansion of the air through which lightning passes. The rumbling that thunder makes is really a series of echoes that are bounced off by the clouds. This is similar to air compression and its rapid expansion in the firing of a cannon. It is also similar to the rapid movement of air which is caused when an airplane goes faster than sound. This is what we call a sonic boom.
2. If you count the number of seconds between the time you see the lightning and the time you hear the thunder and multiply this number by 5 you will get a good approximation of the distance in miles to the storm cloud. Sound

Bang!

travels about 5 miles per second. Light travels at 186,000 miles per second. Because light travels so fast, we just assume it to be instantaneous when doing this fast approximation.

F. Thought Questions:
1. Why does a loud noise result when you stick a pin in an inflated balloon?
2. What are some other ways in which you might cause air to move rapidly enough to make noise?
3. Does the bang of a flat tire represent the same principle?

G. Related Topics and Activities:
1. See previous Activity VII-E-15, "Lightning."
2. See Section II-D, "Sound."
3. See Activities V-B-10 and V-B-11, "Ears and Hearing."
4. See all Activities in this Section.

H. Vocabulary Builders—Spelling Words:
1) **thunder**   2) **expansion**   3) **lightning**   4) **electrical**
5) **heating**   6) **sonic boom**

I. Thought for Today:

"Glass blowers will never produce anything as fragile as the human ego."

Part VIII

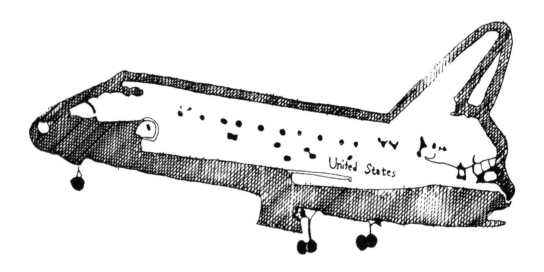

Aviation, Satellites, and Space Travel

Activity

VIII A 1

A. Problem: *How Does an Airplane Get Lift From Its Wings?*

B. Materials A:
1. Sheet of paper 10″ × 4″
2. Pencil
3. Paste or cellophane tape

Materials B:
1. Strip of writing paper 3″ × 6″
2. Book

C. Procedure A:
1. Paste or tape ends of paper together.
2. Curve surfaces until it takes the shape of a cross section of an airplane wing.
3. Slip pencil through loop, hold up pasted end for moment, and blow across *upper* surface of the paper wing until the wing moves.

Procedure B:
1. Place one end of the paper in the book (which is standing up) so that the weight of the paper causes it to bend over, away from you. (See sketch.)
2. Blow gently across the surface of the curved paper.

D. Result:
In each case the lowered end of the paper will rise.

E. Supplemental Information:
1. Air flowing over the surface of the wing or blown over the top of the paper causes a lower pressure above the surface results in an upward force or lift.
2. In an actual plane in flight, more than ¾ of the entire weight of the plane is held up by the reduced air flow on top of the wing(s), and only ¼ by the force of the air on the bottom of the wing(s).
3. There are 4 major forces acting on a plane: 1) lift, 2) gravity, 3) thrust, and 4) drag.

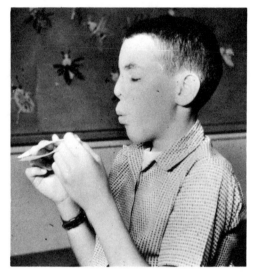

Procedure A

Procedure B

Slightly curved top

Round leading edge

Flat bottom surface

Cross section of an airplane wing

F. Thought Questions:
1. What is Bernoulli's Principle?
2. Is lift a problem in rockets to the moon?
3. Is the turning of an airplane accomplished by lift?
4. How does gravity affect lift?

G. Related Topics and Activities:
1. See Section I-B, "Air."
2. See Section VII-E, "Weather."
3. If any student has a model airplane, have him/her bring it to class and explain how it works.
4. See all Activities in this Section.

H. Vocabulary Builders—Spelling Words:
1) **lift**   2) **curved**   3) **surface**
4) **pressure**   5) **underneath**

I. Thought for Today:
"Air travel is wonderful. It allows you to pass motorists at a safe distance."

Activity

A. Problem: *How Does an Airplane Propeller Work?*

B. Materials:

1. Top of large tin can or metal disc
2. Wooden rod
3. Large spike or nail
4. Metal file
5. Two small nails
6. Spool (from thread)
7. Cord or heavy string
8. Ruler
9. Tin snips
10. Cutting pliers
11. Hammer
12. Awl

C. Procedure:

1. For construction of propeller use top of large tin can or lightweight metal disc about 6 inches in diameter. (Lightweight metal is important because it gives a better flight.)
2. Find center of disc. Draw diameter lines to determine this point.
3. Mark disc as shown in Fig. 1.
4. Cut out propeller with tin snips and smooth with file. (Twist ends slightly in opposite directions.)
5. To make a rotary: (a) Pound a nail part way into a wooden rod. The wooden rod is the handle. (b) Place the spool on the nail so that it can spin freely.
6. Remove the heads from the two small nails with cutting pliers and nail them into the top of the spool. Make sure they are directly opposite each other.
7. Punch two small holes in the center of the propeller with awl so that it will fit loosely over the two nails and rest on top of the spool.
8. Give each blade of the propeller a twist in the same direction, similar to the vanes of a windmill. Make them of equal pitch.
9. Wind a few feet of strong cord around the spool. Be sure the cord is wound evenly around the spool to avoid tangles and to make a smoother, more successful flight.
10. Hold wooden rod vertically and pull out briskly on cord.

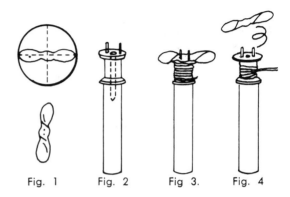

Fig. 1   Fig. 2   Fig 3.   Fig. 4

D. Result:

Propeller will spin rapidly and rise into the air.

E. Supplemental Information:

The pitch or bend in the tin makes the propeller exert change of pressure in the air as it spins. This air pressure causes the propeller to rise. There are many games and contests that can be played adding zest to the use of this propeller.

F. Thought Questions:

1. How does a propeller on a plane compare to one on a boat?
2. How many ways can people lift objects into the air?
3. Would a four-bladed propeller of equal diameter have more lifting power than a two-bladed propeller?

G. Related Topics and Activities:

1. See Section VII-E, "Weather."
2. See Section I-B, "Air."
3. Students can make paper windmills. (See Activity II-A-4.)
4. See all Activities in this Section.

H. Vocabulary Builders—Spelling Words:

1) **propeller**   2) **airplane**   3) **rotary**
4) **vertical**   5) **pitch**

I. Thought for Today:

"Airplane fares have been increasing considerably; even the cost of going up is going up."

Activity VIII A 3

A. Problem: *How Does a Pilot Control an Airplane?*

B. Materials:
1. Plyboard frame
2. Apple crate
3. Scrap lumber
4. Eye screws
5. Flexible wire
6. Leather for hinges
7. Ball-and-socket device

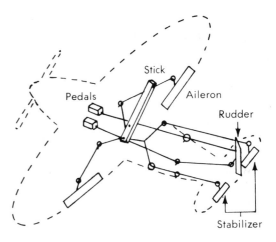

C. Procedure:
1. Have students study the main parts of a plane's control system.
2. Define control terms: pedals, stick, ailerons, rudder, and stabilizers.
3. Outline airplane on plyboard frame.
4. Using apple crates and scrap lumber, build wings so that controls can be attached.
5. Construct pedals and stick and attach to ailerons, rudder, and stabilizers as shown in sketch.
6. Pedals should be hinged to base with wires going to rudder.
7. Stick should be a ball-and-socket joint or near facsimile at the base so that when the stick is moved from side to side, the aileron on the side toward which the stick is moved rises and the opposite aileron depresses.
8. The stick should also have wires running to the horizontal stabilizers so that when the stick is moved forward the stabilizers depress and when the stick is pulled back the stabilizers elevate.
9. One apple crate can be used as a pilot's seat.

D. Result:

An understanding of an airplane's control system will be learned as the students see and move the pedals and stick. They will begin to realize the effects of air pressure against the various movable parts of the airplane.

E. Supplemental Information:
1. Students can make the model, thereby gaining experience and knowledge.
2. Aileron, rudder, and stabilizers are movable parts controlling the plane and are operated by the pedals and stick.

3. These controls operate like ships' rudders by extending part of air stream which pushes that part of plane, thus changing directions.
4. Stabilizers for up or down; stick back points plane up; etc.
5. Rudder for turning; extended to right—plane turns right, etc.
6. Aileron for banking plane is needed for balance. Ailerons work together: If one goes up, the other goes down. The up aileron forces that side of the plane to go down.

F. Thought Questions:
1. What are trim tabs?
2. How else does a pilot control a plane in flight?
3. What is the function of the propeller?
4. What is drag?

G. Related Topics and Activities:
1. See Section I-B, "Air."
2. See Section VII-E, "Weather."
3. See all Activities in this Section.
4. If any students have model planes, have them bring them to class for study.

H. Vocabulary Builders—Spelling Words:

1) **pedal** 2) **stick** 3) **rudder**
4) **aileron** 5) **stabilizer**

I. Thought for Today:

"There would be fewer arguments if we tried to determine what is right instead of who is right."

Activity

A. Problem: *How Can Pilots Tell How High They Are? How Can We Make an Altimeter?*

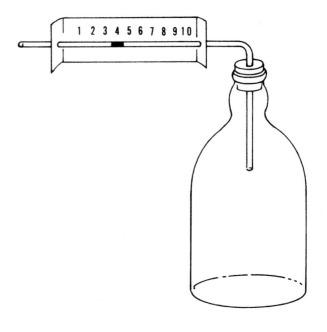

B. Materials:
1. Large bottle
2. One-hole rubber stopper to fit
3. Glass tubing, 8 inches long, bent into an "L" shape
4. White card, 2" × 4" scaled as shown in sketch
5. Water, colored red
6. Water, uncolored
7. Hot plate
8. Ice

C. Procedure:
1. Wet rubber stopper and insert glass tubing as shown in sketch.
2. A drop of red water can be placed in tube by inserting tubing in red water holding one end then shaking some out. By sucking the other end, indicator drop can be positioned as required.
3. Carefully insert tubing into jar. Several trials may be necessary to get indicator drop in correct position, as drop will move out because of increased pressure in jar.
4. Attach card to glass tubing.
5. To simulate flying conditions, warm bottle over hot plate or place in hot water to have bottle pressure greater than outside pressure, which would be true, if plane were climbing (ascending).
6. At room temperature, place bottle in ice water to simulate plane descending.

D. Result:
A simple altimeter will be created.

E. Supplemental Information:
1. An altimeter works like a barometer measuring differences in air pressure.
2. As an airplane climbs to higher altitudes the air pressure is less, therefore, the air in the jar (altimeter) pushes the red drop (indicator) out toward the open end. As an airplane descends the air pressure outside increases and the red drop (indicator) moves in away from the open end.

3. If there are tall buildings or hills nearby, the altimeter can be used and differences in air pressure can be noted.

F. Thought Questions:
1. Why does it take vegetables longer to cook at high altitudes?
2. Is it easier to run at high altitudes or low altitudes? Why?
3. Is it possible to have planes reach a point where there is not enough air to have them fly any higher?

G. Related Topics and Activities:
1. See Section I-B, "Air."
2. See Section VII-E, "Weather."
3. See especially Activity VIII-A-3, on "Airplane Controls."
4. See all Activities in this Section.

H. Vocabulary Builders—Spelling Words:
1) **altimeter**   2) **tubing**   3) **ascending**
4) **descending**   5) **indicator**

I. Thought for Today:
"Discussion is the exchange of knowledge; argument is the exchange of ignorance."

Activity

A. Problem: *How Does a Parachute Work?*

B. Materials:
1. Handkerchief
2. Four pieces of string
3. Metal ring or other weight

C. Procedure:
1. Tie a string to each corner of the handkerchief.
2. Tie the other ends of the strings together.
3. Tie the weight to the place where the strings are joined.
4. Fold the weight in the middle of the handkerchief.
5. Throw the parachute as high as possible.

D. Result:

Parachute will open and descend slowly.

E. Supplemental Information:
1. As the parachute falls, it cups the air and this added air pushes up against the cloth, causing an upward pressure. This causes the parachute to descend slowly because any force going in one direction impedes the progress of a force going in the other direction.
2. While this might seem like a toy, this is a very important scientific method of rescuing pilots whose planes had to be abandoned in flight.

F. Thought Questions:
1. What will happen to the parachute if only two corners are tied instead of four?
2. By changing the weight position on the string, can we influence the direction in which the parachute will fall?

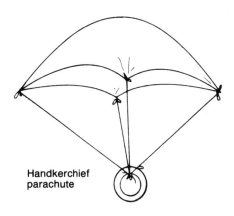

Handkerchief parachute

3. How does this toy parachute differ from a real one?

G. Related Topics and Activities:
1. See Section I-B, "Air."
2. See Section VII-E, "Weather."
3. See all Activities in this Section.

H. Vocabulary Builders—Spelling Words:
1) **parachute**   2) **handkerchief**   3) **weight**
4) **upward**   5) **pressure**

I. Thought for Today:
"The person who said: 'What goes up must come down' must have lived before they invented taxes and postal rates."

Section B: Satellites

Activity   VIII B 1

A. Problem: *What Direction Will a Circular Moving Ball Go if All External Forces Are Removed?*

B. Materials:
  1. Pie tin
  2. Marble
  3. Tin snips
  4. Metal file

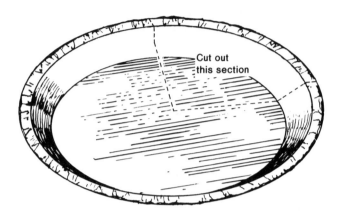

C. Procedure:
  1. Cut one quarter of the pie tin out as shown in sketch. File edges to make smooth.
  2. Place marble near the edge of the remaining ¾ portion.
  3. Ask students to guess which direction the marble will go if it is pushed quickly along the flat edge and then released.
  4. Discuss reasons for guesses.
  5. Push marble as mentioned.

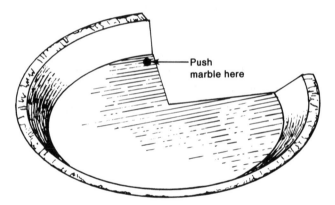

D. Result:
The marble will exit in a straight line along a tangent to the radius.

E. Supplemental Information:
  1. Part of Newton's first law of motion states that a body in motion will continue to move in a straight line unless acted on by some external force.
  2. When the edge in the pie tin no longer acted on the marble it continued to move in the direction it was going when the force was removed. This was a straight line.
  3. As it exited there were no forces pushing it to either side.
  4. Inertia is the term we use to show the condition of the body. We say that a body at rest tends to stay at rest unless acted on by some external force and/or a body in motion tends to stay in motion unless acted on by some external force (Newton's first law of motion). Inertia is the condition of the body at rest or in motion. It requires a force to overcome inertia either in moving it if it is at rest or slowing or stopping it if it is in motion.

F. Thought Questions:
  1. What forces are acting on satellites? our moon? on the earth itself?
  2. Does inertia play a role in stopping an automobile or a bicycle?
  3. Which helps us more, inertia or gravity?

G. Related Topics and Activities:
  1. See Section II-E, "Simple Machines."
  2. See Activity II-F-1, "Inertia and Momentum."
  3. See Activity II-F-6, "Overcoming Friction."
  4. See all Activities in this Section.

H. Vocabulary Builders—Spelling Words:
  1) **force**   2) **direction**   3) **marble**
  4) **Newton**   5) **motion**

I. Thought for Today:
"It's unfortunate that ignorance isn't painful."

A. Problem: *Why Does Water Stay in a Fast-swinging Bucket?*

B. Materials:

1. Bucket with a handle on the top
2. Supply of water
3. Sink (if inside) or planted area (if outside)

C. Procedure:

1. Fill a bucket about three-fourths full of water.
2. Have a student hold it to one side over a sink or planted area and invert it quickly.
3. Fill the bucket about three-fourths full again.
4. Have the student hold the bucket to his/her side and gently swing the bucket back and forth as a pendulum swings.
5. Keep increasing the height of the swing until it is about six inches below the horizontal plane.
6. When the swing reaches this height quickly accelerate the swing very rapidly so that it goes all the way around.
7. Swing it around in a circle several times, then gradually decelerate the swing until the bucket can be set down.

D. Results:

1. When the bucket is held to one side and inverted, the water falls out.
2. When the water in the bucket is swung quickly around, the water stays in the bucket.

E. Supplemental Information:

1. When the bucket is held to one side and inverted, the force of gravity makes the water fall out.
2. When the bucket is swung around the hand, (actually the shoulder), the only additional force applied is *centripetal force*. This force is generated by the pupil and is directed toward the center of the circle. The student can actually feel that she/he is pulling the bucket towards him/her. In order to fully understand this phenomenon one must study Newton's Laws of Motion. His laws applicable to this activity are:
   First Law: An object in motion continues in motion along a straight line unless acted upon by some external force.
   Second Law: The mass of a body accelerates in direct proportion to the force applied to it.

Third Law: For every action there is an equal and opposite reaction.
3. In this activity with the bucket swinging in a full circle Newton's Laws apply as follows: The bucket has a tendency to move in a straight line but this is changed by:
   a. *gravity*—a force pulling the bucket of water down toward the center of the earth and
   b. *centripetal force* which is applied by the student and directed toward the center of the swing.
4. IN THIS ACTIVITY, NO OTHER FORCES AFFECT THE RESULTS.
5. As the student increases his/her muscle strength he/she creates an unbalanced force on the bucket and it speeds up and changes direction. (An unbalanced force causes an object to:
   a. speed up
   b. slow down and/or
   c. change directions.)
6. Centripetal force holds the bucket and water in a circular path and prevents the water from falling out of the bucket.

F. Thought Questions:

1. What would happen to the bucket of water if it were released at the side of the swinger's outstretched arm?
2. Would it make any difference in the forces exerted if a block of ice were swung rather than a bucket of water?
3. What do you think would happen if the swing became slower and slower?

4. Can this principle be used to train astronauts for their weightlessness in space?
5. Why do you think our space vehicles bend their flight paths soon after their initial vertical takeoffs?
6. Can you name some rides at amusement parks that use centripetal force to hold riders in position?

G. Related Topics and Activities:

1. See Section I-B, "Air."
2. See Section I-C, "Water."
3. See Activity II-F-1, "Inertia and Momentum."
4. See all Activities in this Section.

H. Vocabulary Builders—Spelling Words:

1) **bucket**   2) **water**   3) **centripetal**
4) **gravity**   5) **pendulum**

I. Thought for Today:

"Don't kill your ideas, execute them!!!"

Activity

A. Problem: *What Keeps a Satellite in Orbit?*

B. Materials:
1. Ping-pong balls
2. Filament tape
3. Four or five rubber bands (May use a rubber ball and long rubber line from a paddle ball.)

C. Procedure:
1. Drop the ping-pong ball on a table.
2. Interlock the rubber bands.
3. Tape the rubber bands to another ping-pong ball.
4. Slowly swing rubber bands, with ball attached, in a circular motion. Note the distance from your hand.
5. Increase the speed of circular swing. Note the distance in this case.
6. Discuss why the ping-pong ball falls to the tabletop, and why the distance from the hand increases as the ball revolves at a greater speed.

D. Results:
1. The ping-pong ball will fall to the tabletop.
2. In step four above as the ball moves slowly it revolves at a certain distance from the hand.
3. In step five above as the speed is increased the ball moves farther from the hand.

E. Supplemental Information:

In the first experiment there was one major force acting on the ball and that was gravity, causing the ball to fall. In the second experiment there were two forces acting on the ball. One was gravity and the second was centripetal force generated by the muscles of the hand and wrist. Gravity tends to pull the ball to the center of the earth. The momentum of the ball tends to move it in a straight line perpendicular to the rubber bands but the centripetal force tends to move the ball to the hand and wrist. The balancing of gravity and the centripetal force cause the ball to revolve around the hand and wrist. This adds momentum to the ball. As more centripetal force is applied the ball will move farther away. As centripetal force is decreased the ball will move closer to the hand. Earth satellites have only two forces acting on them, gravity and centripetal force. Earth satellites are sent high into space and given an initial thrust to start them revolving. Since a body in motion continues to stay in motion, the satellites continue to revolve. Because there is a very light density

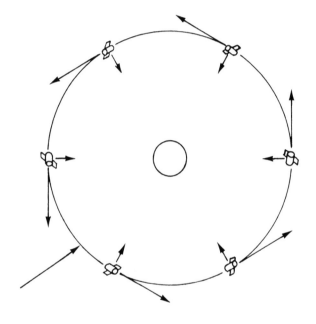

of air even at high altitudes, these satellites will slow down, come closer to earth, meet denser air and slow down still more. This continues until the satellites finally fall to earth or burn up as they meet denser and denser air. This may take several hundred years in smaller satellites in high orbits or may take a few days as in our heavier satellites in low orbits.

F. Thought Questions:
1. What happens to our satellites that maintain an orbit of about 22,300 miles from earth?
2. Could satellites move in any general direction around the earth as east to west, north to south, southeast to northwest?
3. What are some potential dangers to our satellites in orbit around the earth?

4. Are there dangers from falling space junk?
5. Have you seen pieces of tires from trucks lying on highways? What causes the pieces to fly?

G. Related Topics and Activities:
1. See Activity II-F-1, "Inertia and Momentum."
2. See Activity VIII-A, "Aviation."
3. See all Activities in this Section.

H. Vocabulary Builders—Spelling Words:
1) **satellite**   2) **orbit**   3) **circular**
4) **momentum**   5) **distance**

I. Thought for Today:
"You can't get through this world without making mistakes. The person who makes no mistakes does nothing, and that is a mistake."

Activity

A. Problem: *What Good Are Manufactured Satellites?*

B. Materials:
1. Models or pictures of satellites
2. Camera
3. Pictures of vocations described in "Results" (D., c) below
4. Weather maps
5. Rocks, mineral specimens

C. Procedure:
1. Discuss the development of manufactured satellites.
2. Have students find out about the different kinds of satellites.
3. Discuss the purposes of satellites.
4. Discuss the costs of satellites and the results that might be achieved.

D. Results:

Students will learn that:
a. Up to now there have been over a thousand manufactured satellites.
b. Most of them have been used for bouncing television pictures and sending messages over long distances, even between continents.
c. Satellites are helping:
   1) farmers—better farmlands and resources
   2) fishermen—locate water depths, temperatures
   3) foresters—locate best woods (soft, hard, etc.)
   4) industrialists—best location for factories
   5) geologists—locate "faults," shifting glaciers, etc.
   6) hydrologists—water movement, pollution, better use
   7) mineralogists—locate deep sources of minerals
   8) mapmakers—better, up-to-date, more detailed
   9) ecologists—detect water, air pollution
   10) conservationists—locate forest fires early
   11) sailors—report best course for sailing
   12) city planners—up-to-date maps, locate pollution

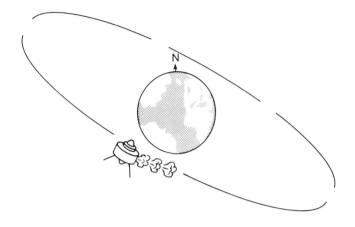

   13) military—monitoring military installations of other nations
   14) teachers—to relay school lessons

E. Supplemental Information:
1. Many modern instruments on satellites can see or "feel." These instruments are cameras and remote sensors.
2. Different objects can be detected by the energy patterns that are emitted and/or reflected.
3. We now use cameras with folded optics which increase the seeing power by a series of mirrors within the camera.
4. We also have multiband cameras which can take pictures simultaneously of the visible and infrared portions of the spectrum.
5. Microwave devices, radar, can detect cloud formations and changes of foliage.
6. Magnetometers can locate buried minerals by their magnetic anomalies.

F. Thought Questions:
1. Can you think up any other uses of earth satellites?
2. Do you think we should develop a space station where people could work and we could develop better instruments?
3. What would be some problems of people living on a space station? (It is in the planning stages now.) (The Soviet Union already has one in space.)

G. Related Topics and Activities:
1. See Section I-B, "Air."
2. See Section VII-A, "Universe."
3. See Activity II-F-1, "Inertia and Momentum."
4. See all Activities in this Section.

H. Vocabulary Builders—Spelling Words:
Use the occupations cited in "Results."

I. Thought for Today:
"One who thinks only of oneself is hopelessly uneducated."

Section C: Space Travel

Activity   VIII C 1

A. Problem: *What Makes a Rocket Plane Fly?*

B. Materials:
1. Elongated balloon
2. Monofilament fishline
3. Paper clips
4. Rubber bands
5. Screw eye to fasten line to wall

C. Procedure:
1. Fasten screw eyes to opposite walls.
2. Put fish line through screw eyes; tighten line and knot tautly.
3. Bend several paper clips so that they form an eye at one end that goes around the fish line.
4. Curve the middle part of the paper clip so that it roughly takes the shape of the balloon.
5. Attach a rubber band to each paper clip making a loop at the other end of the paper clip.
6. Slide the apparatus to one end of the line.
7. Insert balloon between curved part of paper clips and rubber bands. (They make a harness.)
8. Explain Newton's Third Law of Motion. This simply stated is " . . . for every action there is an equal and opposite reaction."
9. Blow up balloon; tightly close open end.
10. Release the balloon.
11. If this procedure is impractical, the same results can be achieved by blowing up an elongated balloon and releasing it before closing the open end.

D. Result:
The air in the balloon, upon being released, will push against the air that was outside the balloon and will cause the balloon to move forward. The faster the air is expelled the faster the balloon will move forward.

E. Supplemental Information:
The action of the air being released from the balloon causes an equal and opposite reaction so the balloon moves forward.

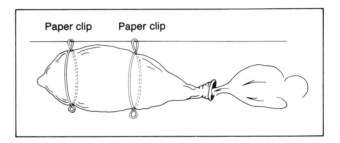

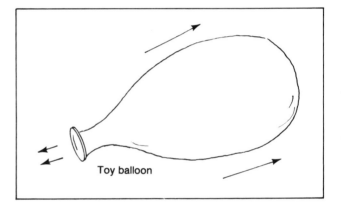

F. Thought Questions:
1. How many examples of Newton's Third Law of Motion can you name?
2. Does this principle apply to a ball being kicked or hit?
3. What were Newton's First and Second Laws of Motion?
4. How is the movement of the balloon similar to the motion of a jet plane?
5. What makes the balloon stop moving?
6. Would the balloon stop moving if released in outer space?
7. If a student is on roller skates and pushes against a wall, what would happen? Why?

G. Related Topics and Activities:
1. See Section I-B, "Air."
2. See Section VII-B, "Solar System."
3. See Section VIII-B, "Satellites."
4. See Section VIII-A, "Aviation."

5. Another method of demonstrating this activity is to have the balloon and a drinking straw secured with filament tape and passing the wire through the drinking straw.
6. See all Activities in this Section.

H. Vocabulary Builders—Spelling Words:
1) **rocket**   2) **elongated**   3) **fishline**
4) **Newton**   5) **action**   6) **reaction**

I. Thought for Today:
"A smile is an inexpensive way to improve your looks."

Activity

A. Problem: *What Is a Space Shuttle?*

B. Materials:
  1. Models of space shuttles
  2. Drawings of space shuttles
  3. Newspaper and magazine accounts of recent space shuttle flights.

C. Procedure:
  1. Students can design and build space shuttles or obtain models, pictures, or drawings of them.
  2. Discuss the unique problems of space shuttles. See Activity VIII-C-3.
  3. Discuss the differences between manned earth satellites and space shuttles.
  4. Plan a space shuttle mission to the moon and back.

D. Result:
Students will learn that space shuttles are controlled, maneuverable flights from take-off to landing.

E. Supplemental Information:
  1. Space shuttles save a lot of money because the crafts are reusable.
  2. Civilians will be able to take flights into space on space shuttles.
  3. We lost one space shuttle crew on January 28, 1986.
  4. There is always a risk in space flights.
  5. A space shuttle coasting in space is in free flight. There are no forces acting on it such as thrust, friction, pressure—only the gravitational pull of the earth, moon, sun, planets, etc., and its own inertia. The gravitational pull and its own inertia keep it in orbit.

F. Thought Questions:
  1. What are the dangers in a space shuttle flight?
  2. How would the earth look from up in space?
  3. How can space shuttles benefit us?

G. Related Topics and Activities:
  1. See Section I-B, "Air."
  2. See Section VII-B, "Solar System."
  3. See Section V-D, "Personal Health."
  4. See Section VIII-A, "Aviation."
  5. See Section VIII-B, "Satellites."
  6. See all Activities in this Section.

H. Vocabulary Builders—Spelling Words:
  1) **shuttle** 2) **space** 3) **manned**
  4) **free flight** 5) **friction** 6) **gravitational**

I. Thought for Today:
"Science is only a tool. The harm or good it does depends on how people use it."

A. Problem: *What Are Some of the Problems of Space Travel?*

B. Materials:
1. Jumpsuits or substitute clothing
2. Large paper bag with cellophane front
3. Mock spaceship of cardboard boxes with controls

C. Procedure:
1. Build a mock spaceship.
2. Plan on the crew members.
3. Determine destination.
4. Plan needs of voyagers:
   a. oxygen
   b. food and water
   c. sleeping quarters
   d. exercise area
   e. heating apparatus or equipment (Sun will be on one side only.)
   f. propellants for escape velocity
   g. means of controlling spacecraft from: roll, pitch, swaying (yawing), etc.
   h. live in weightlessness
   i. means of controlling speed
   j. games or recreation
   k. communication system with earth
   l. design your instrument panel
   m. re-entry equipment and/or landing equipment
5. Take your simulated trip.

D. Result:
Students will realize that space travel is not just fun, but a lot of hard work with many discomforts.

E. Supplemental Information:
1. An impossible concept to teach is the element of time aboard a spacecraft because time on a spacecraft is far different from time on earth. The longer the earth time, the greater speed-up time on a spaceship. It will be possible for astronauts to visit stars and even other galaxies because of the time factor.
2. Space begins where the earth's atmosphere has so little density that it no longer affects objects passing through it. The atmosphere becomes thinner and thinner above the earth; 99% of the atmosphere lies below 20 miles. There is enough air at 75 miles to make meteors glow from friction against it. At 100 miles up there is still enough air that satellites are slowed up

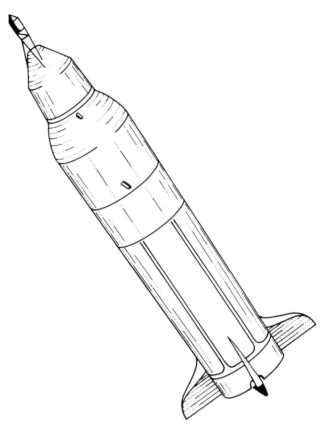

and dropped to lower levels. For all practical purposes we can say that space begins at 100 miles up.

F. Thought Questions:
1. What other problems might arise in a long space journey?
2. What problems might be encountered from outside sources?
3. What safety precautions should be taken into account?

G. Related Topics and Activities:
1. See Section I-B, "Air."
2. See Section VII-B, "Solar System."
3. See Section V-C, "Nutrition."
4. See Section V-D, "Personal Health."
5. See Section V-G, "Safety."
6. See all Activities in this Section.

H. Vocabulary Builders—Spelling Words:
1) **space** 2) **travel** 3) **oxygen**
4) **water** 5) **weightlessness**

I. Thought for Today:
"Money can build a house, but it takes love to make it a home."

Activity

A. Problem: *What Are the Timing Problems of Landing on the Moon?*

B. Materials:
1. Playground large enough to have a 200-foot diameter track or surface in which a circular track can be drawn
2. Tape measure
3. Watch or clock which measures seconds

C. Procedure:
1. Lay out a distance of 200 feet (in the playground) and mark the center point.
2. Roughly outline a circle using a 100-foot radius as a guide.
3. Measure a 12-foot diameter circle around the center point.
4. Roughly outline a typical path from the circumference of a small circle to intersect with the large circle as shown in the drawing.
5. Have a student start jogging around the large track (outside circle) and record time of how long it takes her to go around the path.
6. Have another student jog very slowly around the small track, inside of the large track. Record the time to see how long it takes her to follow the satellite's path.
7. Estimate point where the paths (joggers) will meet.
8. Estimate the position where the outside jogger must start in order to have the time of intersection perfect.
9. Set up the starting time of both joggers to see how close they can come at the intersection time.

D. Result:
It will take several experimental joggings and quite accurate timing in order to have the person who is on the inside track intersect the one on the outside track at any exact position. Use the accompanying diagram to help in working out this experiment.

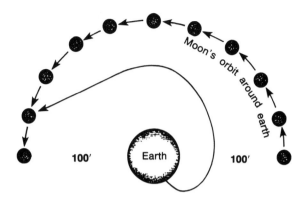

E. Supplemental Information:
When a spaceship is leaving the earth's gravity, exact calculations must be made so that the spaceship will leave the earth's force of gravity at an exact time in order to give it the correct direction and time for intersecting the orbit of the moon.

F. Thought Questions:
1. What is the speed of the moon?
2. What is the speed of our space rockets?
3. If a space crew was off its target course, could they correct their course to reach the moon? How?

G. Related Topics and Activities:
1. See Section I-B, "Air."
2. See Section VIII-B, "Satellites."
3. See all Activities on "Time."
4. Integrate this Activity with math problems.
5. See all Activities in this Section.

H. Vocabulary Builders—Spelling Words:
1) **timing**   2) **diameter**   3) **path**
4) **measure**   5) **playground**

I. Thought for Today:
"What was most significant about the lunar voyage, was not that people set foot on the moon but they set eye on earth."—Norman Cousins

Glossary

Science words and expressions as well as other words needing explanation, are included in this Glossary. Words are broken down into their basic syllables.

ab a lo ne: large, univalve shellfish.

ab sorb: to take in, or suck up, liquids.

ac id: a substance, sour to taste, which dissolves in water. In chemical tests acids turn blue litmus red.

ac id rain: rain from the burning of fossil fuels, particularly sulphur dioxide and nitrogen dioxide.

a corn: the nut, or fruit, of an oak tree.

ad ap ta tion: a change in structure, form, or habits to fit different conditions.

ad e noids: growth of lymphoid tissue in the throat behind the nose.

AIDS: disease affecting the immune system, usually fatal

air craft: machine for flying in the air; either lighter or heavier than air.

al co hol: usually means *ethyl,* or *grain,* alcohol, a colorless liquid with a strong odor formed by the action of organisms on sugar. Alcohol has many uses in science and industry.

al gae: group of plants that have chlorophyll but do not have true roots, stems, or leaves.

al li ga tor: a large reptile with a long body, four short legs, a thick skin, and a long tail. Alligators live in rivers and marshes of warm parts of America.

al ni co mag net: a very strong permanent magnet made of aluminum, nickel, cobalt, and iron.

al tim e ter: instrument for measuring heights; most frequently used in planes for determining altitude.

a lu mi num: a silvery, metallic metal, used for its lightness.

am mo nia: a solution in water of a gas obtained by distilling organic bodies containing nitrogen.

am phet a mine: drug to overcome fatigue, mental depression; also used in diets.

am phib i an: usually refers to members of the class Amphibia, which includes frogs, toads, and salamanders. The young of these animals are hatched and develop in water, but the adults of many species emerge from the water to live on land.

a nem i a: reduction in red blood cells or hemoglobin in the blood.

an e mom e ter: instrument that measures wind speed.

an i mal: any living organism that has senses and can move.

an ode: positive pole on a battery.

an ten nae: feelers on the head of an insect.

an thrax: a contagious disease, attended by fever, of human beings and animals.

an ther: top of the stamen in plants

an thra cite: hard coal which gives much heat and little smoke.

an ti dote: something that hinders or removes the effects of poison or disease.

an ti sep tic: a solution which will check or prevent the growth of bacteria; a disinfectant.

an ti tox in: a substance produced in living tissues of plant or animal to check or hinder or make neutral a bacterial poison that produced it.

ap o gee: point that is the greatest distance from the earth.

ap pa ra tus: the equipment, tools, device, or appliance by which a process of work or play is carried on.

a quar i um: tank or bowl in which water plants and water animals are kept.

a rach nid: any of a large group of small arthropods including spiders, scorpions, mites, etc. An arachnid is air-breathing, has four pairs of walking legs, and no antennae; the body is usually divided into two regions.

Ar chi me des: early Greek who invented the screw to raise water.

ar ter y: any of the blood vessels that carry blood away from the heart.

ar thro pod: one of a large group of invertebrate animals having segmented (jointed) bodies and legs. Insects, arachnids, and crustaceans are arthropods.

ar ti fi cial: made or contrived by human labor; not natural.

a scor bic ac id: vitamin C.

as ter oid: any one of the very small bodies revolving around the sun between the orbit of Mars and the orbit of Jupiter.

a stig ma tism: defect of the eye, or lens of the eye, that makes objects look indistinct or gives imperfect images.

as tro naut: person trained to fly in space.

as tron o mer: a scientist who studies the earth's relation to the sun, moon, stars, and other heavenly bodies.

at mos phere: 1. the gaseous envelope of a planet. 2. the air that surrounds the earth.

at om: the smallest particle of an element that can exist. Atoms are the very small particles that make up molecules.

a tom ic: pertaining to an atom or atoms; energy from the nucleus of an atom.

a tom ic en er gy: energy from the nucleus of the atom.

at tract: to draw to oneself as a magnet draws iron filings toward itself.

au to mat ic: able to move or act without help from another source.

au to mat i cal ly: in an automatic manner.

back bone: the bony column that extends along the middle of the back in man, mammals, birds, reptiles, and fishes; the spine. The backbone consists of many separate bones, called vertebrae, held together by muscles and tendons and separated by pads of cartilage. The backbone protects the spinal cord, which it encloses.

bac te ria: a group of plant organisms, too small to be seen without a microscope.

bak ing so da: sodium carbonate; used in baking as leavening agent.

ball-and-sock et joint: a flexible skeletal joint formed by a ball or knob of one bone fitted into the cupped end of another bone. The shoulder and hip are ball-and-socket joints. As such they permit some motion in every direction.

bar bi tu rate: drug used as a sedative or pain deadener.

bas es: chemicals that react opposite to acids; contain hydroxyl ions.

beak: bill or nib of a bird.

bea ver: amphibious animal, found in lakes and ponds; builds underwater homes.

Ben e dicts So lu tion: a chemical solution used to test for sugar(s).

bi cus pid: a double-pointed tooth; human adults have eight such teeth.

bind ing post: one of two small metal knobs at the top of a dry cell. One post is attached to a zinc outer shell and the other post extends from the central carbon rod.

bi o de grad a ble: easily decomposable, especially biologically.

bi o tic com mun i ty: area where living things are mutually dependent.

bite: seizing by teeth or mouth.

blind spot: a round spot on the retina of the eye not sensitive to light.

blood ves sel: any of many tubes in the body through which blood flows. The three types of blood vessels are arteries, veins, and capillaries.

blow hole: hole for breathing located in the top of the head of whales and some other air-breathing animals. The blowhole usually has a flap of skin that keeps water out of the animal's lungs.

boil er: 1. a container for heating liquids. 2. a tank for making steam to heat buildings or to drive engines. 3. a tank for holding hot water.

boil ing point: point where a liquid changes to a gas.

brain: the part of the nervous system enclosed in the skull.

burns: injury due to excessive heat.

buoy an cy: quality of floating on the surface of a liquid such as water.

caf feine: the stimulant found in coffee and tea.

cal ci um: silver-white chemical element found in limestone.

cal o rie: unit of heat. Heat required to raise one gram of water one degree centigrade.

cam ou flage: disguise, change appearance.

cap il lar y: a small blood vessel with very thin walls. A network of capillaries joins the arteries and veins.

car bo hy drates: sugars and starches.

car bon: chemical element found in diamonds, graphite, and organic compounds.

car bon cy cle: sequence of states that the element passes through.

car bon di ox ide: a heavy, colorless, odorless gas present in the air. Green plants use carbon dioxide to make food.

car bon mon ox ide: a deadly gas, usually the product of incomplete combustion.

car di o pul mon a ry re sus ci ta tion: a method of restoring breathing and/or heartbeat to a victim.

car ni vore: flesh-eating animal.

car ti lage: the firm, tough, flexible substance that forms parts of the skeleton of vertebrates; gristle.

Cas si o pe ia: a northern constellation between Andromeda and Cepheus.

cath ode: negative pole on a battery.

cell: the unit of living matter, usually microscopic, of which all plants and animals are made. Cells vary in form according to their use.

Cel si us: scale for measuring heat with water freezing at zero degrees and water boiling at one hundred degrees.

cen ti grade: same as Celsius.

cen trif u gal: moving away from center.

cen trip e tal: moving toward the center.

chain re ac tion: chemical reactions where each step is initiated by former step.

char ac ter is tic: a special quality or feature.

chem i cal: a substance obtained when two or more substances act upon one another to cause permanent change.

chis el: 1. a cutting tool with a sharp edge at the end of a strong blade, used to cut or shape wood, stone, or metal. 2. to cut or shape with a chisel.

chlam y di a: most common, severe venereal disease.

chlo rine: a heavy poisonous gas used in liquid form as a disinfectant.

chlo ro flour o car bons: chemicals used in sprays destroying ozone.

chlo ro phyll: the green-colored material in the cells of green plants.

chok ing: severe gasping, suffocating.

chol er a: an acute disease of the stomach and intestines.

cho les ter ol: a substance contained in all animal fats.

chrys a lis: a form of an insect when it is encased in a pupa, cocoon.

cir cuit: a complete path made of conductors through which an electric current can flow from the source of electrical energy and back again.

cir cu late: 1. move around 2. move through a closed system as the blood moves through the blood vessels, or as air moves through a hot-air heating system.

cir cum fer ence: 1. boundary line of a circle. Every point in the circumference of a circle is at the same distance from the center. 2. the distance around a round object.

cit rus: relating to fruits such as the orange, lemon, lime, and grapefruit.

clas si fy: to arrange in groups, usually according to certain structures or functions.

clay: fine-grained earth, usually silicates.

coal: combustible mineral solid used for burning and heating.

co caine: drug, narcotic, local anesthetic, addictive.

cold-blood ed: having blood that is about the same temperature as the air or water around the animal; having blood that changes its temperature as the temperature of the surroundings changes.

com bus tion: the act of burning.

com et: a bright heavenly body with a starlike center and often with a cloudy tail of light.

com mu ni ca ble: that which can be spread or communicated from person to person or place to place, as a disease.

com mu ni ca tion: imparting knowledge, opinions, or facts.

com pare: to find out or point out how things are alike and how they differ.

com pass: 1. an instrument for showing directions; it consists of a free-turning magnetic needle mounted on a card showing directions. 2. an instrument for drawing a circle.

com pound: to put together.

com press: a pad of folded cloth.

con cave: lens shallower in the center.

con clu sion: final decision.

con dense: to change from a gas to a liquid.

con di tion: the state in which a person or thing is; a runner may be in good condition for a race or a book may be in poor condition after falling to the floor.

con duc tion: the passing of heat from one particle to another. The particles vibrate but do not move from one place to another.

cones: the seed-bearing part of pine, cedar, fir, and other evergreen trees.

con ser va tion: preservation; avoidance of waste.

con stel la tion: a group of stars that seems to form a picture in the sky.

con ta gious: that which is communicable, catching, as a disease; can be spread from person to person.

con tam i nate: to spoil or make impure by contact with waste matter or impurities.

con test ing: 1. competing with others for something. 2. fighting; struggling.

con ti nen tal code: scheme of dots and dashes used in telegraphy.

con tour far ming: following natural ridges and furrows to avoid soil erosion.

con tract: to draw together or to make shorter; to shrink or become smaller.

con vection: the movement of particles of a liquid or a gas from a cold place to a warmer one. The movement is somewhat circular, the colder material pushing the warmer material sideways and upward.

con vec tion cur rent: a current set up within a mass of gas or of liquid when it is heated. Convection currents are set up whenever a heated gas or liquid expands and a colder gas or liquid pushes against the lighter heated material, forcing it upward.

con vex: lens thicker in the center.

con vey: to carry.

core: inner part as the earth's core.

cor ne a: the transparent part of the outer coat of the eyeball. It covers the iris and the pupil.

CPR: —See cardiac pulmonary resuscitation.

cray fish: a freshwater animal of the class Crustacea that looks like a small lobster; a similar but larger saltwater shellfish.

croc o dile: large, amphibious lizard, rounded nose.

crus ta cean: any of a group of water animals having tough shells, jointed bodies and legs, and gills for breathing. Crabs, lobsters, and shrimps are crustaceans.

cu ta ne ous: pertaining to the skin.

dam: a framework to obstruct water.

DDT: potent, persistent, pesticide; contaminates food, causes many birds to lay eggs with too thin shells.

de cay: to rot; also, material that has rotted, as tooth decay.

dec i bel: a unit for measuring the volume of sound.

def i nite: 1. clear; precise. 2. having set limits.

de ger mi nat ed: that grain from which the germ has been removed.

de gree: 1. a step in the scale; a stage in a process. 2. a unit for measuring temperature.

de hy dra tion: the process of removing water from food and other substances; drying.

del ta: the deposit of earth and sand that collects at the mouth of some rivers. A delta is usually three-sided.

den tin: the hard material of which the main part of the tooth is composed.

de ter gent: a cleansing substance.

dew: condensed water from the air.

di a phragm: the partitions or walls of tissues, sinew, or muscle, for the purpose of separating and protecting adjoining parts in the body or in instruments.

di et: the kind and amount of food and drink that a person or animal usually eats.

dif fer ence: 1. being different. 2. the amount or manner of being different; the way in which people or things are different.

di gest: to change (food) within the stomach and intestines so that it can be absorbed by the body.

di ges tive juice: a juice produced by the body for use in the digestion of food.

dis ease: an illness or weakened condition of health.

dis in fec tant: something that destroys bacteria and/or viruses.

dis solve: to make liquid; to become liquid, especially by putting or being put into a liquid. When a solid has dissolved completely, it cannot be separated from the liquid by filtering.

downers: slang term for drugs that are depressing.

drug: prescribed medicine, narcotic, habit-forming.

dry ice: solid carbon dioxide, refrigerant.

dys en ter y: a painful disease of the intestines.

earth quake: undulating movement of the earth's crust.

e clipse: a darkening of the sun or the moon.

e col o gist: a scientist who studies the relation of living things to their community and to each other.

ec o sys tem: area where living things are mutually dependent.

egg: oval bodies laid by birds, fish, and reptiles; reproductive cell.

e lec trode: either of the two pieces of material used with an electrolyte to make an electric cell.

e lec tro mag net: a piece of iron that becomes a temporary magnet when an electric current passes through wire coiled around it.

e lec tron: a kind of particle that moves rapidly around the nucleus of an atom. Every electron has a negative charge.

e lec tro scope: a device for detecting small changes in electricity.

el e ment: a part; that which cannot be detected or separated without chemical or metal analysis.

e lim i na tion: the act of getting rid of, removing.

e lo de a: an aquatic plant often used in aquariums. It floats beneath the surface, but its roots can take hold in the soil under low-water conditions.

em phy se ma: an abnormal swelling of body tissue, often found in the air sacs in the lungs.

en dan gered species: an organism threatened with extinction.

en er gy: ability to do work or to act; capacity for work.

en vir on ment: surroundings of an organism.

en zyme: a catalyst that helps bring about chemical changes in the body.

e ro sion: process of eating away or of being worn away gradually. In nature, wind and water cause most erosion of rock and soil.

es cape ve loc i ty: the speed of spaceship to overcome earth's gravity.

Eu sta chian tube: slender canal between the pharynx and the middle ear.

eu troph i ca tion: process(es) of aiding nutrition.

e vap o rate: to change from a liquid to a gas. Molecules of the liquid escape from its surface into the air in the form of vapor.

e vap o ra tion: the process of evaporating.

ev er green: having green leaves throughout the year.

ex er cise: movement, put into action, train.

ex ert: to use; put into use; use fully.

ex hale: breathe out.

ex pand: to grow larger or cause to grow larger.

ex pec to rate: to spit.

ex per i ment: 1. to test; 2. a test that is made to find out something.

ex tinc tion: no longer existing.

Fahr en heit: a kind of thermometer on which the boiling point of water is at 212° and the freezing point is at 32°.

fam ine: scarcity of food, destroy with hunger.

fa tigue: tiredness or weariness.

fats: greasy or oily substances of the body. Also oils and parts of meat or other foods that yield oils and grease.

fault: a break in a mass of rock in which one part slides past another part.

fer men ta tion: the chemical change which causes milk to sour, apple juice to turn to vinegar, and starches to turn to sugars.

ferns: any of a group of plants having roots, stems, and leaves, but no flowers, and reproducing by spores instead of seeds.

fer tile: capable of growing, producing fruit or vegetation.

fer ti li zer: any material to improve the quality of the soil.

fil a ment: thread-like; part of the stamen bearing the anther.

fil ter: 1. a device for passing liquids or gases through some substance in order to remove certain particles. 2. the material (often paper) through which a liquid or gas passes so that certain things can be removed. 3. to put a material through a filter.

fire: active burning, combustion.

fire box: the place in which fuel is burned in a furnace or boiler.

fire ex tin guish er: device for putting out fires.

fire tri an gle: the three elements needed for fires: heat, material, and oxygen.

fish: vertebrate animals living in water and breathing with gills.

fis sion: 1. a method of reproduction in which a one-celled living thing divides, forming two new individuals. 2. the splitting of large atoms such as uranium atoms into smaller atoms, releasing atomic energy.

flesh: 1. the soft part of the body that covers the bones and is covered by skin. Flesh consists mostly of muscles and fat. 2. the soft part of fruits and vegetables.

flood: an overflowing of water on land.

flow er: part of the plant that contains the reproductive organs.

force: any cause that produces changes in, starts, or stops motion of, an object.

fore cas ting: predicting, estimating.

form: 1. a shape. 2. to shape or make. 3. a condition or state.

fos sil: preserved remains of a living thing.

fos sil fu els: materials from the past that are used for energy.

frac tion al dis til la tion: removing each material separately by continuing to increase temperature.

frame work: a support or skeleton; the stiff parts that give shape to something.

freez ing point: the temperature at which a liquid freezes or changes to a solid. The freezing point of water at sea level is 32 degrees Fahrenheit or 0 degrees Centigrade.

fre quen cy: the number of times any action occurs.

fric tion: the rubbing of one body against another.

fu el: a substance, or mixture of substances, that can be burned to produce heat or some other form of energy.

ful crum: balance point on a lever.

fun gi: any of a group of plants without flowers, leaves, or green coloring matter.

fu sion: the combining of small atoms, such as hydrogen, forming larger atoms and releasing atomic energy.

gal ax y: a huge group of stars.

gar ter snake: a common, harmless snake that is brown or green with long yellow stripes.

gas: a material, like air, that is neither a solid nor a liquid. The molecules of a gas do not attract each other strongly. They move about freely, spreading apart until they fill all the available space.

gas, nat u ral: gas that is extracted from the earth.

gas oline: a fuel from petroleum used in internal combustion engines.

gen er a tor: a device for transforming mechanical energy into electric energy.

ge o graph ic North Pole: one end of the axis about which the earth rotates. The axis is an imaginary line through the center of the earth. The geographic North Pole marks the most northerly point on the earth.

geo graph ic South Pole: one end of the earth's axis. The geographic South Pole is the most southerly point on the earth.

ge ol o gist: scientist who studies the earth.

ge o therm al: relating to the internal heat of the earth.

ger mi na tion: starting to grow or develop, sprouting.

germs: microscopic animals or plants that cause disease.

gey ser: a spring of hot water that gushes into the air.

gill: in certain water animals, a body structure used for breathing. The gill takes in oxygen from the water habitat and sends out carbon dioxide.

gla cier: a large mass of ice, formed from snow, that moves slowly down a mountainside or sloping valley, or outward from a center as in a continental glacier. The movement of glaciers causes erosion and piling up of soil and rocks.

glands: small organs in the body which produce different substances to be used by or discharged from the body.

gold: heavy, yellow, metallic element that is a precious metal.

gon or rhe a: a serious venereal disease that affects mucous membranes.

gourd: a climbing plant like a squash; hollowed, dry shell of same.

grass es: plants with blade-like leaves, single seed and includes barley, oats, rye, and wheat.

grav i ty: natural force that tends to move objects toward the center of the earth.

Green house Ef fect: rising of the atmosphere's temperature due to pollutants that reflect earth's radiant heating back toward earth.

guin ea pig: a small, fat mammal in the rat family with short ears and short tail.

gul ly: a small valley or a ditch cut by running water.

gup py: a very small, usually brightly colored fish that lives in tropical freshwater.

hab i tat: the place where an animal or plant lives and grows.

half life: time of a radioactive material to lose half of its original substance.

hal lu ci na tion: apparent perception by senses that are not actually present.

ham ster: small, short-tailed rodent with large cheek pouches.

hear ing graph: a graph that shows a person's hearing range or ability.

heart: a small muscle that pumps the blood to all parts of the body and back again.

heat: quality of being hot from molecular action.

Heim lich Ma neu ver: a first aid procedure to help a choking person.

he mo phil i a: a condition in which the blood fails to clot quickly enough.

herb i cides: chemicals used to destroy unwanted plants.

her bi vore: any animal that feeds on plants.

her pes: a viral infection of the skin or mucous membrane(s).

hi ber nate: to spend the winter in a sleep or in an inactive condition. In true hibernation, body processes are slowed.

highs: high pressure air masses identified with good weather.

ho mog e nized: blended or mixed by force into one part, as homogenized milk in which the butterfat and whey are blended to the point at which they will not separate.

Ho mo Sa pi ens: only living species of the genus Homo is the human being.

hu mid i ty: dampness and moisture of the air.

hu mus: soil made from decaying leaves and other vegetable matter.

hur ri cane: a violent storm with winds from 70 to 100 m.p.h. usually with rain and thunder.

hy dro car bons: chemical compounds that contain only hydrogen and carbon. Four groups of hydrocarbons are found in automobile exhausts.

hy dro e lec tric: having to do with the production of electricity by water power.

hy drol o gist: an expert in the study of water.

hy drom e ter: a device to determine the specific gravity of liquids (thickness and weight).

ice: solid form of water

Ice house Ef fect: lowering of the atmosphere's temperature due to pollutants that prevent the sun's radiation from striking the earth by reflecting back the sun's rays before they strike the earth.

ig ne ous: 1. of or having to do with fire. 2. produced by fire, great heat, or the action of a volcano.

im age: the view seen by the reflection of light rays.

im mu ni za tion: the state of being immune or protected from a disease.

in can des cent: to glow with heat.

in ci sion: a cut or gash.

in ci sor: tooth having a sharp edge for cutting.

in cu ba tor: an apparatus for hatching eggs artificially.

in er ti a: tendency to remain in the state one is in whether stationary or in motion.

in fec tion: a condition or disease caused by contact with certain harmful organisms.

in hale: to breathe in, to draw into the lungs.

in ner ear: the innermost part of the ear. The inner ear is made up of several canals that are filled with fluid. This part of the ear is connected to the brain by a nerve. When the fluid vibrates, it sets up impulses in this nerve which are received in the brain as sound.

in sect: any member of a group of small invertebrate animals having a body that has three parts, three pairs of legs, two feelers, and usually two pairs of wings.

in sec ti cides: chemicals used to kill insects.

in stru ment: a tool, mechanical device.

in su la tion: a material or materials that covers another to prevent loss of heat or electricity.

in ten si ty: amount of heat, light, or sound per unit.

in tes tine: the part of the digestive system that extends from the lower end of the stomach. It receives food from the stomach, digests it further, and absorbs it. The intestine consists of two parts: the small intestine, a coiled tube that is about 22 ft. long in the adult; and the large intestine, a thicker tube about 5 feet long.

in ver sion: act of being inverted or reverse.

in ver te brate: 1. without a backbone. 2. an animal without a backbone. All animals except fishes, amphibians, reptiles, birds, and mammals are invertebrates.

i o dized: having had iodine added.

i ris: the colored area that surrounds the pupil of the eye.

i ron: a metal that rusts easily and is strongly attracted by magnets; a mineral important to the body.

ir ra di a tion: emitting atomic or subatomic rays or particles.

joint: in an animal, a place where two bones are joined together by ligaments. The movable joints are kept moist by a liquid. Some joints are not movable.

Kel vin: a temperature scale measured in Celsius degrees with absolute zero equal to −273° C.

ki net ic en er gy: the energy of a body that is in motion which includes its mass and its velocity.

king dom: one of the main sub-divisions of all living things.

Kra ka to a: the volcano that produced the greatest noise known.

lac er a tion: a jagged tear or cut.

lar va: the form in which most insects hatch from the egg, wingless and sometimes wormlike.

Lat in: language of the ancient Romans. It is still used in science and religion.

lat i tude: a distance north or south of the equator, measured in degrees.

la va: 1. molten rock flowing from a volcano. Before emerging at the surface, it is called magma. 2. rock formed by the cooling of this molten rock. Some lavas are hard and glassy; others are light and full of air spaces.

lay er: one thickness or fold.

leaf: flat usually green plant part growing from stem.

leg umes: vegetables that have pods, such as peas and beans.

length en: to become longer.

lens: the part of the eye, glasses, or camera, that focuses light to form clear images.

leu ke mi a: a disease in which there is an extra large number of white blood cells.

lift: upward force on an airplane wing caused by upper curved surface of the wing which thins the air over the wing causing greater pressure below the wing.

lig ament: a band of strong tissue that connects bones or holds parts of t he body in place.

light ning: discharge or flash of electricity in the sky.

like ness: a way in which two or more things resemble each other.

lime: calcium oxide, used in neutralizing soil acids.

lime stone: a sedimentary rock formed under water, usually from the remains of sea animals.

lines of force: 1. invisible lines from one pole of a magnet to the other pole that indicate the direction in which the force of the magnet is acting. 2. the magnetic field of a magnet.

liq uid: 1. a material that is not a solid or a gas and that can flow freely like water and take the shape of its container. 2. in the form of a liquid; melted.

lit ter: that which is scattered about needlessly.

liv er wort: a plant that is somewhat amorphous like a moss.

liz ard: large groups of reptiles with thin bodies and four legs, live in hot, dry areas.

loam: vegetable matter with clay and sand.

lode stone: a kind of iron ore, called magnetite, that attracts iron and some kinds of steel just as a magnet does.

lows: low pressure air masses identified with poor weather.

lu mi nous: giving off light.

lungs: the breathing organs found in the chest of man and of many other animals with backbones.

ma chine: a mechanical vehicle.

mag gots: wormlike larvae of an insect.

mag net ic: 1. having the properties of a magnet. 2. able to be attracted by a magnet.

mag net ic pole: each end of a magnet.

mag ne tize: to give something the properties or qualities of a magnet.

mag ni fy ing glass: a lens which enlarges the viewing material.

mam mal: any member of a group of warm-blooded vertebrates that have fur or hair and that produce milk to feed their young.

man u fac tured: having been made by people, and not the result of a natural cause.

mar ble: the metamorphic crystallized form of limestone, white or colored; it is capable of taking a high polish.

mar i jua na: poisonous drug made from hemp leaves and flowers.

mass: volume

meat: the flesh of an animal, the muscles of an animal.

melt ing point: the temperature at which a solid substance begins to melt or become liquid.

mem brane: a thin, soft layer of tissue in the body of an animal or plant.

met a mor phic: characterized by change of form; having to do with change of form. A metamorphic rock is one that has been changed to a different form by heat, pressure, or both.

met a mor pho sis: change of form, example—tadpoles to frogs.

me te or ite: a large meteor that falls to the earth before it is completely burned up.

mi cro scope: a magnifying instrument that has a lens or combination of lenses for making objects clearly visible with the aid of light.

mid dle ear: in humans, the cavity of the ear that is separated from the other ear by the eardrum, and which contains the three small bones called the hammer, the stirrup, and the anvil. The cavity of the middle ear is filled with air and is connected to the throat by a tube.

mi gra tion: 1. a moving from one place to another with a change in the seasons, as birds moving south in autumn and north in spring. 2. a move from one place to settle in another.

milk: fluid secreted by female mammals to feed their young.

Milky Way: our galaxy.

mil lion: one thousand thousand; 1,000,000.

min er als: inorganic substances, that is, substances that are neither vegetable nor animal in nature.

mix ture: two or more substances mixed together but not chemically combined. Each of the substances has its own properties and doesn't change when in contact with the other substance or substances present.

moist: slightly wet or damp.

mol e cule: the smallest particle into which a substance can be divided without changing the chemical nature of that substance.

mol lusk: invertebrates that live in water which includes oysters, clams, mussels, snails, squids, and octopi.

mo men tum: force with which a body moves. It is equal to its mass times its velocity.

Mo ne ra: one-celled animals without any definite structure; recently named a kingdom.

moss: any of various very small, soft, green or brown plants that grow close together like a carpet on the ground, on rocks, on trees, etc.

moth ball: naphthalene or camphor which repels moths.

moun tain: large mass of earth and rock above ground level.

mus cle: a bundle of fibers, made up of cells, that contracts or extends to move a part of the body.

muskrats: a North American water rodent, somewhat like a rat but larger.

nar cot ic: a substance that eases pain and may cause sleep.

na sal pas sage: air pathway inside the head extending from the nostrils to the throat.

nat u ral: found in nature, not artificial.

nerv ous sys tem: a network of nerves and nerve centers in a person or animal. In man, the central nervous system is made up of the brain and spinal cord.

neu trons: neutral charge masses that lie with the nucleus of atoms.

ni a cine: nicotinic acid, a vitamin, the lack of produces pellagra, (red, dry, skin, and a sore mouth).

niche: area in which an organism usually lives.

nic o tine: the drug contained in tobacco.

ni trates: soluble salts needed by plants and animals for growth; used to fertilize the soil.

non magnet ic: 1. lacking the properties of a magnet. 2. not attracted by a magnet.

nu cle ar: having to do with the nucleus (center) of the atom.

nu cle us, plural nu cle i: 1. the part of a cell that controls much of what happens in the cell. 2. the central part of an atom.

nu tri ent: a food substance that gives nourishment to the body.

nu tri tion: nourishment; food; the act or process of absorbing food or nourishment.

oat: edible seed, small grain, thought to reduce cholesterol.

ob ser va tion: 1. the act of seeing and noting. 2. something seen and noted.

oc cu py: to take up; to fill.

o cean: a great body of salt water, there are five main oceans.

o cean og ra pher: scientist who studies the oceans.

Old Faith ful: a natural, large geyser in Yellowstone National Park.

om nivore: animal that eats both plants and other animals.

or bit : the curved path that a planet follows around the sun.

or gan: a main part of an animal or plant, made up of several kinds of tissues.

or gan ic: having characteristics of living organisms.

or gan isms: any living beings.

out er ear: in humans, the visible part of the ear and the passageway leading to the middle ear. The eardrum separates the outer ear from the middle ear.

ox i da tion: the combination of an element with oxygen.

ox ide: compound of oxygen with another element or radical.

ox y gen: a colorless, odorless gas that makes up part (about one fifth) of the air. It supports burning and is necessary to animal life. Oxygen is a chemical element; combined with other elements it is present in many substances.

ox y gen cy cle: sequence of states that the element passes through.

oys ter: a kind of shellfish or mollusk that has a rough, irregular shell. It is an important food.

o zone: form of oxygen produced by electricity and thunderstorms.

pan da: a white and black bearlike animal found in Asia.

par al lel: at or being the same distance apart like railroad tracks.

par a site: a living thing that must live in or on another living thing in order to get food, shelter, or something else that it needs. A parasite gives nothing in return to the animal or plant it lives on.

par ti cle: a very small bit of material.

pas teur i za tion: a process which is used to destroy harmful bacteria in milk and other liquids. The liquid is kept at a temperature of between 140° and 150° Fahrenheit for a certain period of time, then chilled.

per i gee: the elliptical point which is closest to the earth.

per ma nent: lasting; intended to last; not for a short time only.

per son al i ty: the quality of being a person, habitual patterns of a person.

per spi ra tion: sweat.

pes ti cides: chemicals used to kill unwanted animals.

pet al: leaf of a corolla.

Pe tri dish: small transparent container (dish and lid) used in scientific research particularly in studying bacterial growth.

phar ynx: tube that connects the mouth with the esophagus.

phos phates: salts of phosphorus that stimulate growth, many times excessive such as in ponds and lakes.

phos pho rus: one of the minerals found in and necessary to the health of teeth and bones.

pho to syn the sis: process by which plant cells make sugar from carbon dioxide and water in the presence of chlorophyll and light.

pho to tro pism: attracted toward or away from light.

phy to plank ton: microscopic, aquatic plants that produce most of the world's oxygen supply.

pis til: the seed-bearing part of a flower, contains the ovary, stigma, and often the style.

pitch: tone level.

plague: a contagious, epidemic disease.

plan et: 1. an object or body that travels about the sun in an orbit. 2. commonly, the nine major heavenly bodies that orbit the sun and reflect its light. The sun's planets are Mercury, Venus, Earth, Mars, Jupiter, Saturn, Uranus, Neptune, and Pluto.

plants: a tree, shrub, or herb; non-mobile organism.

plaque: scum-like substance that covers teeth; main cause of tooth decay.

plas tics: chemicals that can be molded.

poi son: a substance, usually a drug that causes severe sickness or death.

Po la ris: the North Star.

pole: 1. place where the force of a magnet is strongest. 2. either end of the earth's axis.

pol lu tion: state of being unclean or impure.

pop corn: a variety of Indian Corn with small kernels that pop open when heated.

pore: a very small opening in the skin or in a covering of a plant.

po tas si um: one of the minerals necessary to maintain good health.

po ten tial en er gy: the energy of a body that is obtained by its position in space.

pre da tor: any animal that preys on other animals.

pres er va tion: to keep from injury or destruction.

pri mate: the most highly developed order of animals including humans, apes, lemurs, and monkeys.

pro tec tive ad ap ta tion: a special kind of structure or way of behaving that helps a living thing survive in its habitat.

pro tein: a nourishing food element, important to all living cells, animal or plant.

pro tist: one of the three main classification kingdoms consisting of small organisms that usually have both animal and plant characteristics.

pro tons: positive charge masses that lie within the nucleus of atoms.

pro to zo a: a group of one-celled, microscopic animals.

pulse: the regular beating of blood against the wall of an artery caused by the pumping of the heart. The pulse is best felt on the wrist near the base of the thumb or at the side of the neck.

pump: a device that moves liquid or gas from one area to another.

pu pa: the cocoon or case stage in the development of an insect; the stage which follows the larva.

pu pil: the opening at the center of the iris of the eye. The pupil regulates the amount of light that enters the eye and usually expands in dim light and contracts in bright light.

pur pu ra: a disease that colors skin purple from escaping blood from its vessels.

rad: a measurement of radiation.

ra di ant en er gy: energy that is given off as rays by a hot object. The sun is a source of radiant energy.

ra di a tion: 1. act or process of giving off light or other kinds of radiant energy. 2. the energy radiated.

ra di a tion de tect or: a device that senses small amounts of radiation.

ra di a tor: 1. a heating device consisting of a set of pipes through which steam or hot water passes. 2. a device for cooling circulating water, i.e., the radiator of an automobile.

rain bow: an arc consisting of all colors of the spectrum due to water vapor acting like a prism.

rain for est: tropical woodlands that provide much of the oxygen and mild climates.

re claim: to bring back, to keep from being lost or destroyed.

re cycle: to reclaim and reuse needed materials.

ref use: waste material; garbage; rubbish.

rel a tive: having a relationship or connection to one another.

rem: a measure of radiation about one roentgen of an X-ray (*R*adiation *E*quivalent in *M*an.).

re pel: to push away, or to drive back. Magnetic poles that are alike repel each other.

re pro duce: to produce its own kind, as an animal produces young or a plant produces seeds.

rep tile: a cold-blooded vertebrate that creeps or crawls and that is covered with scales or bony plates. Snakes, lizards, turtles, alligators, and crocodiles are reptiles.

re sis tance: opposing, power to resist as force, disease, or electricity.

re spi ra tory: the system of organs used for breathing.

re sus ci ta tion: bring back or come back to consciousness.

ret i na: the membrane lining of the back part of the eyeball; the part of the eye that receives images of vision.

re use: use needed materials over again.

rev o lu tion: a movement of one body around another such as the moon around the earth or earth around the sun.

ri bo fla vin: Vitamin B-2.

Ri ker box: container or mount for the collection of insects.

riv er: a large stream of water emptying into a larger body of water.

rock: a piece of mineral material.

roc ket: a self-propelling device operated by means of gas escaping from a nozzle or jet at the rear of a combustion chamber.

ro dent: any of a group of mammals having teeth especially adapted for gnawing wood and similar material. Rats, mice, squirrels, hares, and rabbits are rodents.

roent gen: a unit of X-ray radiation.

roll: to move around an object's horizontal axis.

roots: part of plant below surface that provides food, water, and stability to the plant.

ro ta tion: any object that turns around on its own axis.

rye: a cereal plant, a grass.

sal a man der: an amphibian shaped somewhat like a lizard, closely related to the frogs and toads.

sa li va: a digestive juice produced by glands in the mouth. Saliva keeps the mouth moist and aids in the digestion of food.

sal vage: act of saving reusable materials.

sand dune: a mound or ridge of loose sand heaped up by the wind.

sand stone: a sedimentary rock formed mostly of grains of sand that have been pressed together over a long period of time.

sat el lite: any object that revolves around another object.

scald: to burn or injure with a hot liquid or gas.

scale: 1. one of the thin, flat, hard plates forming the outer covering of snakes, lizards, and some fishes. 2. a series of spaces marked by lines and used in measuring distances. 3. an instrument for weighing materials.

scale of dis tance: a scale found on a map or globe for measuring distances between places.

scav en ger: one who, or that which, cleans up dirt and filth.

sci ence prin ci ples: rules or laws of science.

scor pi on: gray lizard with a curved tail, and poisonous sting.

sea shell: shell of a salt water mollusk, whole or part.

sea son: one of the four periods of the year: spring, summer, autumn, winter.

se cre tions: substances prepared by parts of the body.

sec tion: a part cut off; part; division; slice.

sed i ment: material that settles to the bottom of a liquid.

sed i men tary: 1. of sediment; having something to do with sediment. 2. formed from sediment as sedimentary rocks.

seed: the part of a flowering plant that will develop into a full plant.

sen sa tion: the feeling or experience caused by action on the sense organs.

sense or gan: the eye, ear, or other part of the body by which a person or an animal receives information about the surroundings. The messages from such organs are interpreted in the brain as sensations of heat, color, sound, smell, etc.

sen si tive: easily affected or influenced.

se pal: a leafy division of the calyx.

ser ies: objects placed one after the other.

shale: a sedimentary rock formed from hardened clay or mud. Shale splits easily into thin layers.

shoul der: a body joint to which an arm, foreleg, or wing is attached.

silt: fine particles of sand and/or soil.

si phon: a tube-shaped organ that draws in and sends out water. It is found in some shellfish.

skel e ton: the bony structure of a body. The skeleton is a frame to which muscles and tendons are attached.

skull: the bony framework of the head.

slate: a bluish-gray metamorphic rock, made from shale, that splits easily into thin smooth layers.

smog: air pollution of smoke and fog, also other air pollutants.

smoke: the vaporous and solid materials arising from something burning.

smoke-mak er: a piece of rope or other material that will produce much smoke while burning slowly.

snail: a creepy animal that has curved, protective shell.

snake: legless reptile with an elongated body and tapering tail.

Snel len Chart: eye chart to determine visual acuity.

soil wa ter: water that occurs in the soil. It is absorbed by the roots of plants and provides the minerals they need.

so lar sys tem: the sun and the other heavenly bodies that move around it.

sol id: 1. a kind of material that has shape and size; it is not a liquid or a gas. 2. not hollow. 3. hard; firm; strongly put together.

so lu tion: 1. a combination of substances, especially a liquid formed by dissolving one substance in another. 2. answer to a problem.

sound ing board: a board with upright nails to test materials for sound.

space: 1. unlimited room or place extending in all directions. 2. a part or place marked off in some way.

space ship: a rocket-propelled vehicle for travelling in outer space.

space shut tle: a self-contained vehicle that can enter space and return.

space sta tion: a structure designed to orbit above the earth.

spe cies: a group of animals or plants that have certain permanent characteristics in common.

spec trum: series of colored light bands from the division of a prism.

spi der: a small animal with eight legs, no wings, and a body with two main divisions. It belongs to the arachnid group.

spi nal col umn: the backbone.

spi nal cord: the thick, whitish bundle of nerves enclosed by the spinal column.

spi ra cle: in animals, a breathing hole.

spore: a single cell capable of growing into a new plant or animal. Ferns produce spores.

sprout: 1. to begin to grow; shoot forth. 2. a shoot of a plant.

stag nant: having become dirty and impure from standing still, as of air and water.

sta lac tite: formation of lime, shaped like an icicle hanging from the roof of caves.

sta lag mite: formation of lime, shaped like a cone that is built up from the floor of caves.

sta men: male reproductive organ in flowers, within the petals.

state: 1. the condition of a person or thing. 2. the structure or form of a material; the three states that materials take are solid, liquid, and gaseous.

stat ic e lec tric i ty: electrical discharges that result from moving objects.

steam heat ing sys tem: a heating unit that produces steam and sends it through an arrangement of steel pipes or radiators, or both, to all parts of large buildings.

stem: stalk of a plant.

ster ile: free from living germs.

steth o scope: an instrument used in examination of a person's chest to convey sounds.

stim u lus: whatever makes a living thing act in response to it.

sting: a prick or wound from a plant or animal.

stoma: a small opening such as a pore.

sto ma ta: more than one stoma. The stomata of green leaves regulate the passage of water vapor out of the plant. The carbon dioxide that green leaves use for food making enters through the stomata.

stran ger: a person who is not familiar, a foreigner.

stream: a small river.

strip min ing: surface mining; many times leaving earth scarred.

stron ti um: a pale yellow, metallic element; a by-product of atomic bombs.

struc tural ad ap ta tions: body parts that have developed in special ways to fit an animal or plant for survival in its habitat.

struc ture: 1. arrangement of parts. 2. a building or something built.

sub ma rine: a warship that can operate under water and carries torpedos.

suck ing coil: electrical device that moves a central core.

sug ar: sweet substance from sugar cane or sugar beets, a carbohydrate.

sul phur: a pale yellow nonmetallic element.

sul phur di ox ide: an air pollutant that is a nonflammable, non-explosive, colorless gas: found in acid rain.

sun spot: a dark, cooler area on the surface of the sun.

su per sti tion: a belief or practice based on ignorant fear or mistaken reverence.

sur viv al: remaining alive.

sur viv al ad ap ta tion: any special means that a species has developed to promote the survival of its kind.

swamp: spongy, low ground filled with water, a marsh or bog.

sweat: moisture given out by glands in the skin of some vertebrates. As sweat evaporates, it lowers the body temperature.

symp toms: signs or indications of a disease or illness.

syn thet ic: not of natural growth or development; made artificially; made of artificial products.

tad pole: an undeveloped frog or toad. At this stage of development, the animal has gills and a tail and must live in water.

taste bud: any of certain small groups of cells on the tongue or lining of the mouth that serve as organs of taste.

tel e scope: an instrument for making distant objects appear closer.

tem per a ture: the extent to which anything is hot or cold, given as degrees. The temperature of freezing water is 32° Fahrenheit; the temperature of boiling water is 212° Fahrenheit.

tem po rary: lasting for a short time only.

ter ra cing: flattening land from sloped areas to prevent soil erosion.

ter rar i um: an enclosure in which small land plants and/or small animals are kept, contains soil only.

ther mal pol lu tion: pollution of the atmosphere due to abnormal heating.

ther mom e ter: an instrument for measuring temperature.

tho ri um: a heavy, gray radioactive element.

thy roid: pertaining to the large gland which lies near the throat in human beings.

tide: the rise and fall of the ocean; occurs about once every twelve hours.

tis sue: the cells and substance around them which form the bodies of plants and animals.

toad: a small animal somewhat like a frog, which starts life in water but usually leaves it to live on land. The toad returns to the water to deposit its eggs.

top soil: the upper part of the soil; surface soil.

tor na do: violent wind with a funnel-shape cloud that destroys much in its path.

tour ni quet: device for stopping severe bleeding by compressing blood vessel with bandage by twisting with stick.

tox ins: poisons produced by chemical changes in animal and plant tissue.

trans lu cent: letting light pass through without being transparent.

trans par ent: easily seen through.

tran spi ra tion: passing off vapor from the surface as from leaves of plants or skins of animals.

tree: a tall, woody, perennial plant with many branches.

tsu na mi: giant waves caused by underground earthquakes.

tu bers: thickened, underground stems of plants, such as in potatoes or dahlias.

tung sten: one of the chemical elements. It is a rare metal used in making steel and for electric-lamp filaments.

tur tle: fresh and salt water reptiles with soft body in a hard shell.

ty phoon: a violent, cyclonic windstorm, usually near the China Sea, a hurricane.

un du lat ing: moving back and forth in waves.

u ni verse: all of the cosmos, totality of space.

up pers: slang term for drugs that are stimulators.

vac ci na tion: the act of injecting killed or weakened organisms into the blood of people to make them immune to a particular disease, such as smallpox or polio.

vac u um: an enclosed empty space from which all of the air has been removed.

vein: one of the three kinds of blood vessels. The veins carry the blood that is returning to the heart from all parts of the body.

ve ne re al dis ease: a disease transmitted by sexual intercourse.

ven ti late: to change or purify air in a room by circulating fresh air.

ven tri cle: either of the two lower chambers of the heart that receive blood.

ver te bra: any of the bones of the backbone.

ver te brate: any animal that has a backbone. Fishes, amphibians, reptiles, birds, and mammals are vertebrates.

vi brate: to move rapidly back and forth or up and down.

vi rus: group of disease producing agents, very small, and dependent upon their host for reproduction and growth.

vi su al per sis ten cy: the ability to see an object after it is gone from view.

vi tal: essential or very important to life; having the qualities of living bodies.

vi ta mins: elements found in many foods that are important and necessary to the physical development of man, animals, and plants.

vi var i um: an enclosure in which small plants and/or animals are kept; contains soil(s) and water.

vol ca no: 1. mountain having an opening through which ashes and lava are expelled. 2. an opening in the earth's surface out of which lava, steam, etc., pour.

volt: a unit used to measure electromotive force.

vol ume: the amount of space that a material takes up.

warm-blood ed: having warm blood. The body temperature of different warm-blooded animals is from 98° to 112° Fahrenheit. It is relatively constant for each animal.

wasp: winged insect with a slender body and biting mouth parts; has a vicious sting.

wastes: unwanted, formerly used products.

wa ter cy cle: sequence of states that water passes through.

wa ter jack et: a casing with water in it. It may be put around an engine to cool it or around a heating unit as part of a hot-water heating system.

wa ter lev el: the height of the surface of still water.

wa ter shed: area drained by a river or rain.

wa ter ta ble: the level below which the ground is saturated with water.

wa ter va por: water in a gaseous state. The term is used for vapor formed below the boiling point of water. At boiling point and higher it is called steam.

Wat tling Proc ess: method of conserving land by building fences in gullies to prevent excessive soil erosion.

waves: the up and down movement of water or sound.

wax: dull yellow substance secreted by bees for building cells.

weath er: the state of the atmosphere which includes temperature, pressure, humidity, and winds.

weath er ing: the physical and chemical changes that take place in rocks when they are exposed to conditions at the earth's surface.

weath er vane: instrument that indicates wind direction.

weight: the amount of force with which gravity pulls down on any object.

wind: motion of the air.

wind break: a shelter from the wind to prevent soil erosion.

wind pipe: the hollow tube that extends from the throat to the lungs.

wood chuck: a North American marmot; the groundhog.

worm: long, slender, creeping animal with a soft belly living underground.

wreath: a twisted, circular band of flowers or leaves.

X-rays: electro-magnetic radiation; can't be seen; used in medicine and dentistry for examinations.

yaw: to move back and forth sideways from intended course.

zoo: place where wild animals are kept.

Index

CAPITAL LETTERS = MAIN PARTS OR SECTIONS
Small Letters = Topics
Numbers in parentheses ( ) include all pages in Parts or Sections.